The Law of Commercial Surety and Miscellaneous Bonds

Third Edition

SAMUEL J. ARENA, JR., KATHRYN M. TRUMAN,
JULIE S. ALLEYNE, AND JUSTIN D. WEAR,
EDITORS

JEFFREY S. PRICE
CHAIR, TIPS FIDELITY AND
SURETY LAW COMMITTEE

AMERICAN BAR ASSOCIATION
Tort Trial and Insurance
Practice Section

Cover design by ABA Design

Printed in the United States of America.

26 25 24 23 22   5 4 3 2

A catalog record for this book is on file with the Library of Congress.

PREFACE TO THIRD EDITION

This publication has been prepared for use in conjunction with the 2022 Spring Surety Program on The Law of Commercial Surety and Miscellaneous Bonds sponsored by the Fidelity and Surety Law Committee of the Tort Trial and Insurance Practice Section of the American Bar Association. This is the third national program involving commercial surety and miscellaneous bonds sponsored by the American Bar Association. The first program took place in January 2001 in New York City and was co-chaired by Todd Kazlow and Bruce King. The second program was presented in Hilton Head, South Carolina, in April 2012, and was co-chaired by Bruce King, Rich Towle, and Sam Arena. These prior programs, and the earlier editions of this publication, have been the most comprehensive and authoritative treatment of these bonds available to practitioners in the field.

The chapters in this book build on the contributions of the prior authors. This book updates and expands upon the materials from the 2001 and 2012 editions and should prove to be an indispensable reference for commercial surety and miscellaneous bond practitioners, underwriters, and claim professionals. These and other publications of the Fidelity and Surety Law Committee of the Tort Trial and Insurance Practice Section of the American Bar Association are available for purchase from ABA Publications, 321 N. Clark Street, Chicago, Illinois 60654 (online https://www.americanbar.org/products/).

The Fidelity and Surety Law Committee thanks each of the authors for their contributions to these materials and the 2022 Spring Surety Program on The Law of Commercial Suretyship and Miscellaneous Bonds.

Julie S. Alleyne
Samuel J. Arena, Jr.
Kathryn M. Truman
Justin D. Wear
Editors

CONTRIBUTORS

EDITORS

JULIE S. ALLEYNE • Vice President of Policy and General Counsel, Secretary, and Treasurer of The Surety & Fidelity Association of America. Mrs. Alleyne graduated from Drew University (B.A. 1992) and from Syracuse University College of Law (J.D. 1995). She began her career in private practice with a focus on construction and bankruptcy litigation and has spent much of her career in various claims and legal positions with Travelers Bond and The Hartford Bond Department.

SAMUEL J. ARENA, JR. • Senior Counsel with the law firm of Stradley Ronon Stevens & Young, LLP in Philadelphia, Pennsylvania. Mr. Arena graduated, *magna cum laude*, from Ursinus College (B.A. 1979) and, *cum laude*, from Villanova University School of Law (J.D. 1983). He is Past Chair of the Fidelity and Surety Law Committee, Tort Trial and Insurance Practice Section, of the American Bar Association, and received that committee's Martin J. Andrew Award for Lifetime Achievement in Fidelity and Surety Law in 2019. Mr. Arena serves as an Advisor to The Surety & Fidelity Association of America.

KATHRYN M. TRUMAN • Commercial Surety Leader with Westfield in Northeast Ohio. Mrs. Truman is a graduate of the University of Akron (B.S. 1992) and the University of Akron School of Law (J.D. 1996). She started her surety career as surety claims counsel and has been a frequent author and presenter of surety topics.

JUSTIN D. WEAR • Partner with the law firm of Manier & Herod, P.C. in Nashville, Tennessee. Mr. Wear graduated, *magna cum laude*, from the University of the South in Sewanee, Tennessee (B.A. 2001) and, *summa cum laude*, from the University of Tennessee College of Law (J.D. 2004). He currently serves as the Chair of his firm's Surety & Fidelity Practice Group.

AUTHORS

GEORGE J. BACHRACH • Partner with the law firm of Wright, Constable & Skeen, LLP, in Baltimore, Maryland. Mr. Bachrach graduated, *cum laude*, from Harvard University (B.A. 1971) and from the Georgetown University Law Center (J.D. 1974). He is a Past Chair of the Fidelity and Surety Law Committee, Tort Trial and Insurance Practice Section, of the American Bar Association, and received that committee's Martin J. Andrew Award for Lifetime Achievement in Fidelity and Surety Law in 2009.

CONNOR L. CANTRELL • Shareholder and Vice President of the Hustead Law Firm in Denver, Colorado. Mr. Cantrell graduated *summa cum laude* from Murray State University (B.A. 2004) and from the University of Denver Sturm College of Law (J.D. 2007).

GERALD N. CAROZZA, JR. • Assistant Vice President at Selective Insurance Company of America, responsible for surety and fidelity bond claims. Mr. Carozza graduated from Boston University (B.A. 1982) and from Villanova University (J.D. 1985). He is a Past Vice Chair of the Fidelity and Surety Law Committee of the Tort Trial and Insurance Practice Section of the American Bar Association and a Past Chair of that committee's International Subcommittee. Mr. Carozza is a retired Army Colonel and Afghan War Veteran.

GARY M. CASE • Vice President and General Counsel of ACSTAR Insurance Company in Farmington, Connecticut. Mr. Case received his B.S. from Fairfield University and his J.D. and LLM (Insurance Law) from the University of Connecticut School of Law. He manages surety claims, litigation, and corporate compliance for ACSTAR.

JOSEPH W. CATUZZI • Associate with the Philadelphia law firm of Stradley Ronon Stevens & Young, LLP in Philadelphia, Pennsylvania. Mr. Catuzzi graduated *cum laude* from Villanova University (B.S. 2011) and *magna cum laude* from Villanova University School of Law (J.D. 2014). Mr. Catuzzi is a member of his firm's Fidelity and Surety Practice Group.

ELLEN M. CAVALLARO • Assistant Vice President of Berkley Surety, Morristown, New Jersey. Ms. Cavallaro is a graduate of Fordham University (B.A. 1979), Columbia University (M.A. 1981), and Fordham University School of Law (J.D. 1988). She is a Vice Chair of the Fidelity and Surety Law Committee, Tort Trial and Insurance Practice Section, of the American Bar Association and a member of the Board of Directors of the Surety Claims Institute.

JEFFREY J. CLAYTON • Executive Director at American Bail Coalition. Mr. Clayton is a graduate of Baylor University Hankamer School of Business (B.B.A. 1997), the University of Rochester (M.S. 1999), and the University of Denver (J.D. 2003).

CHARCRETIA V. DI BARTOLO • Partner with the law firm of Watt, Tieder, Hoffar & Fitzgerald, LLP, in its Boston and Providence offices. Ms. Di Bartolo is a graduate of Washington University in St. Louis (B.A. 1988) and Washington University School of Law (J.D. 1991). She currently serves as a Vice Chair of the Fidelity and Surety Law Committee, Tort Trial and Insurance Practice Section, of the American Bar Association and is an Advisor Emeritus to the Fidelity Law Association.

MICHAEL J. DUDEK • Surety Claim Director for RLI Insurance Company. Mr. Dudek graduated from the Illinois State University (B.S. 2002) and, *cum laude*, from the John Marshall Law School (J.D. 2007).

ROBERT J. DUKE • Vice President and Legal Counsel for Markel Surety. Previously, Mr. Duke was Surety Legal Counsel for Euler Hermes North America and General Counsel for the Surety & Fidelity Association of America. He graduated, *summa cum laude*, from Columbus School of Law, Catholic University (J.D. 2005), *summa cum laude* from Loyola University, Maryland (B.A. 1988), and from Loyola University, Maryland (M.B.A. 1992).

JONATHAN J. DUNN • Partner with the law firm of SMTD Law LLP in Irvine, California. Mr. Dunn is a graduate of Seattle University School of Law (J.D. 1992), and the University of California, Los Angeles (B.A. 1989). He is a Chambers recognized lawyer, and Past Chair of the Legal Advisory Committee to the Associated General Contractors, California. Mr. Dunn is a Past Vice Chair of the Fidelity and Surety Law Committee, Tort Trial and Insurance Practice Section, of the American Bar Association.

NINA M. DURANTE • Senior Surety Claims Counsel with Liberty Mutual Insurance Company in its Commercial Claims Department. Ms. Durante received her B.A. in Political Science from Seattle University and her J.D. from the University of Puget Sound School of Law (now Seattle University School of Law). She is an active member of the Washington State Bar Association and the Tort Trial and Insurance Practice Section of the American Bar Association.

W. BLAINE EARLY III • Member of the law firm of Stites & Harbison, PLLC, based in its Lexington, Kentucky, office. He obtained his B.A. degree from Depauw University, his Ph.D. from the University of Louisville, and his law degree, *with distinction*, from the University of Kentucky.

T. RANDOLPH FERGUSON • Member of the law firm of Sandler, Travis & Rosenberg, P.A. Mr. Ferguson is a graduate of Stanford University (B.A. 1967), the University of California at Berkeley (M.B.A. 1969), and the University of San Francisco (J.D. 1973).

PATRICIA A. FRAMKE • Senior Claim Specialist with CapSpecialty Insurance Company in Middleton, Wisconsin. She is a graduate of St. Ambrose University and has earned her AFSB (Associate in Fidelity and Surety Bonding) and AINS (Associate in General Insurance) designations from The Institutes. Ms. Framke has more than 20 years of experience handing commercial surety claims.

WILLIAM T. GORTON III • Member of the law firm of Stites & Harbison, PLLC, based in its Lexington, Kentucky, office. Mr. Gorton graduated from Pennsylvania State University (B.S. 1976) and, *with distinction and Order of the Coif*, from the University of Kentucky College of Law (J.D. 1988). Prior to law school, Mr. Gorton was manager of the Kentucky office of Skelly and Loy Engineers-Consultants and managed mining and reclamation projects throughout the United States.

DARREN GRZYB • Partner with the law firm of Chiesa Shahinian & Giantomasi PC in West Orange, New Jersey, and New York, New York, where he practices in the firm's Fidelity & Surety Group. Mr. Grzyb graduated from Rutgers University (B.A. 2002) and, *with high honors*, from Rutgers University School of Law (J.D. 2005).

OMAR J. HARB • Partner with the law firm of Lipson Neilson, P.C. in Bloomfield Hills, Michigan. Mr. Harb graduated from Cornell University (B.A. 1991) and, *cum laude*, from the University of Michigan Law School (J.D. 2004). He is a Past Co-Chair of the Young Professional's Committee and a Past Chair of the Technology Committee of the Fidelity and Surety Law Committee, Tort Trial and Insurance Practice Section, of the American Bar Association. Mr. Harb currently serves as an Editor-in-Chief of the Fidelity and Surety Law Committee Newsletter.

MARK T. HOLTSCHNEIDER • Executive Vice President and General Counsel, Lexington National Insurance Corporation. Mr. Holtschneider graduated, *summa cum laude*, from Towson University (B.S. 1982) and, *summa cum laude*, from the University of Baltimore School of Law (J.D. 1986). Before joining Lexington National in 2004, he practiced civil litigation for several years and then moved in-house to U.S. Fidelity and Guaranty Company and then to St. Paul Fire and Marine Insurance Company.

JANE A. HORNE • Partner with the law firm of Peabody & Arnold LLP in Boston, Massachusetts. Ms. Horne graduated, *cum laude*, from the George Washington University (B.A. 2004) and, *Dean's List*, from St. John's University School of Law (J.D. 2008).

MATTHEW M. HOROWITZ • Counsel to Neubert, Pepe & Monteith PC with offices in Hartford and New Haven, Connecticut. Mr. Horowitz graduated, *summa cum laude*, from Tufts University (B.A. 1973) and, *Order of the Coif*, from New York University School of Law (J.D. 1976).

JAMES D. HOUSTON • Partner with the law firm of Strauss Troy in Cincinnati, Ohio. Mr. Houston graduated from the Miami University (B.A. 1994) and, *cum laude*, from the University of Dayton School of Law (J.D. 2000).

PATRICK Q. HUSTEAD • Founder of the Hustead Law Firm, *A Professional Corporation*, in Denver, Colorado. Mr. Hustead is a graduate of the University of Colorado (B.S. 1981) and, *cum laude*, the Boston College Law School (J.D. 1987). He is a Past Co-Chair of the Extra-Contractual Liability Committee of the Fidelity and Surety Law Committee, Tort Trial and Insurance Practice Section, of the American Bar Association.

CHRIS INDELICATO • Manager, U.S. Surety Legal for Liberty Mutual Surety. Mr. Indelicato is a graduate, *cum laude*, of Temple University School of Law (J.D. 1999).

SUSAN B. JORDAN • Regional Surety Leader at Westfield in Charlotte, North Carolina. Ms. Jordan is a graduate from the Bryan School of Business and Economics at the University of North Carolina at Greensboro (B.S. 1981) and has been in the surety industry for more than 30 years.

STEVEN S. KATZ • Counsel with Chiesa, Shahinian & Giantomasi PC in West Orange, New Jersey, where he practices in the firm's Fidelity & Surety Practice Group. Mr. Katz graduated from Brandeis University (B.A. 1983) and the State University of New York at Buffalo Law School (J.D. 1987).

PATRICK R. KINGSLEY • Partner with the firm of Stradley Ronon Stevens & Young, LLP in Philadelphia, Pennsylvania. Mr. Kingsley graduated, *magna cum laude*, from the University of Pittsburgh (B.A.) and, *magna cum laude*, from the University of Pittsburgh School of Law (J.D.). Mr. Kingsley is a member of his firm's Fidelity and Surety Practice Group.

RALPH J. KOOY • Partner with the Law Offices of T. Scott Leo, P.C., in Chicago, Illinois. Mr. Kooy is a graduate of the University of Illinois (B.A. 1989) and the University of Illinois College of Law (J.D. 1992).

ROBERT G. LAVITT • Vice President, Director of Surety Claims, and Counsel with Argonaut Surety. Mr. Lavitt is a graduate of the University of Chicago (B.A. 1984) and Boston University School of Law (J.D. 1987).

BRIAN LEBRUN • Lead Bond Claims Representative with the Hanover Insurance Company. Mr. Lebrun is a graduate of Northeastern University (B.S. 2004).

T. SCOTT LEO • Shareholder of the Law Offices of T. Scott Leo, P.C. Mr. Leo served as an Adviser to the Restatement (Third) of Suretyship and Guaranty (1996) and is a Past Chair of the Fidelity and Surety Law Committee, Tort Trial and Insurance Practice Section, of the American Bar Association.

SCOTT W. LICHTENSTEIN • Counsel with the law firm of Chiesa Shahinian & Giantomasi PC in West Orange, New Jersey, and New York, New York, where he practices in the firm's Fidelity & Surety Practice Group. Mr. Lichtenstein graduated, *magna cum laude*, from Rutgers College (B.A. 2006) and from Rutgers Law School (J.D. 2009).

GINA D. LOCKWOOD • Director of Claims at Merchants Bonding Company. Ms. Lockwood graduated from the University of Texas at Dallas (B.A. 2007) and the Southern Methodist University in Dallas, Texas (J.D. 2010). Prior to joining Merchants, Ms. Lockwood spent nearly a decade in private practice where she focused her practice on construction and surety matters.

LAURA J. MAURER • Bond Claim Manager with Navigators, a brand of The Hartford. Ms. Maurer obtained her Customs House Broker License in 2002 and graduated from William Rainey Harper College (A.A.S.). She has 37 years of experience handling U.S. Customs claims.

LAURA M. MURPHY • Senior Claims Counsel with Travelers Bond & Specialty Insurance. Ms. Murphy graduated from Trinity College (B.A.) and Western New England School of Law (J.D.). She joined Travelers in 2008.

LAURA P. NASH • Counsel with Robins Kaplan LLP. Ms. Nash graduated, *cum laude*, from Loyola Marymount University (B.A. 1985) and from the University of California, Los Angeles (J.D. 1988).

DAVID C. OLSON • Owner of NewEnglandSuretyLaw.com. Mr. Olson graduated, *cum laude*, from Williams College (B.A. 1971) and from The Ohio State College of Law (J.D. 1978). Mr. Olson is a Past Chair of the Fidelity and Surety Law Committee, Tort Trial and Insurance Practice Section, of the American Bar Association.

MAURA Z. PELLETERI • Special Partner with the law firm of Pugh Accardo, LLC in New Orleans, Louisiana. Ms. Pelleteri is a graduate of the University of Maryland (B.S. 1977) and Loyola University New Orleans College of Law (J.D. 1983).

DEREK POPEIL • Vice President and Surety Claims Manager for Chubb. Mr. Popeil graduated from Muhlenberg College (B.A. 1988) and from Widener University School of Law (J.D. 1991). He is a Vice Chair of the Fidelity and Surety Law Committee, Tort Trial and Insurance Practice Section, of the American Bar Association and serves on that committee's Performance Bond Committee.

JAMES D. PORTMAN • Chief Legal Officer of AIA Surety, a managing general agent for bail in Westlake Village, California. Mr. Portman also is Vice President, Senior Bond Counsel of Allegheny Casualty Company, a licensed surety domiciled in New Jersey. Mr. Portman is a graduate of the University of California at Davis (B.A. 1982) and California Western School of Law (J.D. 1986). He is a Board Member of the American Bail Coalition.

MICHELLE RANDALL • Vice President, Surety Risk Solutions, Zurich North America. Ms. Randall graduated from the University of

Massachusetts Amherst (B.A. 1993) and from Western New England University School of Law (J.D. 2005).

MICHAEL A. SAFRIS • Senior Consultant at Nationwide Mutual Insurance Company in Des Moines, Iowa. Mr. Safris graduated from the Buena Vista University (B.A. 1997) and, *with honors*, from Drake University School of Law (J.D. 2001). Prior to joining Nationwide, he was an Assistant Vice President of Surety Claims at Merchants Bonding Company (Mutual) and operated Sure-T-Con Solutions, a surety and construction claims consulting firm. He is a Past Chair of the Young Professionals Subcommittee of the Fidelity and Surety Law Committee, Tort Trial and Insurance Practice Section, of the American Bar Association.

ROBERT SCANLON • AVP and Counsel with Travelers where he leads the Commercial Surety claim team. Mr. Scanlon is a graduate of the University of Connecticut Law School (J.D. 1999). Prior to joining Travelers in 2004, he practiced law in the Corporate Department of Murtha Cullina LLP in Hartford, Connecticut.

ELLIOT SCHARFENBERG • Partner with the law firm of Krebs, Farley & Dry, PLLC in the firm's New Orleans office. Mr. Scharfenberg graduated from Baylor University (B.A. 2007) and, *magna cum laude*, from Tulane University Law School (J.D. 2013).

CHAD L. SCHEXNAYDER • Partner with the law firm of Jennings Haug Keleher McLeod in Phoenix, Arizona. Mr. Schexnayder graduated, *cum laude*, from Washington University at St. Louis (A.B. 1981) and, *cum laude*, from the Sandra Day O'Connor School of Law at Arizona State University (J.D. 1984). He is a Past Chair of the Fidelity and Surety Law Committee, Tort Trial and Insurance Practice Section, of the American Bar Association.

JONATHAN SCHNEIDER • Senior Vice President of Court Bond Underwriting with Tokio Marine HCC since 2012. Mr. Schneider has more than 30 years of experience in various underwriting, financial, and auditing capacities all within the broader insurance industry. Mr. Schneider is a graduate of San Diego State University (B.A. 1990).

LEAH S. SCHOEN • Associate General Counsel of AIA Surety, a managing general agent for bail in Westlake Village, California. Mrs. Schoen is also Bond Counsel of Allegheny Casualty Company, a licensed surety domiciled in New Jersey. She is a graduate of the University of California at Los Angeles (B.A. 2009), California State University of Northridge (M.P.A. 2013), and University of West Los Angeles (J.D. 2020).

CHRIS SIMMELINK • Manager, Contract Surety (Claims) at Hudson Insurance Group. Mr. Simmelink previously served as the Claims Director at RLI and Contractors Bonding and Insurance Company. He has more than 20 years of experience managing complex payment and performance bond claims throughout the United States and has handled claims in Canada and Puerto Rico. Mr. Simmelink has experience in a broad portfolio of claims in the contract, commercial, miscellaneous, and energy bond spaces.

MATTHEW H. SLOAN • Partner with the law firm of Jennings Haug Keleher McLeod in Phoenix, Arizona. Mr. Sloan graduated from the University of Arizona (B.A. 1993) and from Arizona State University (J.D. 1997).

MICHAEL A. STOVER • Partner at the law firm of Wright, Constable & Skeen, LLP in Baltimore, Maryland. Mr. Stover graduated from the University of Maryland (B.S. 1987) and, *with honors*, from the University of Maryland School of Law (J.D. 1991). He is a Vice Chair of the Fidelity and Surety Law Committee, Tort Trial and Insurance Practice Section, of the American Bar Association and the creator and host of the Surety Today podcast.

FRANK J. TANZOLA • Chief Legal Officer for IAT Surety, a member of IAT Insurance Group. Mr. Tanzola graduated, Phi Beta Kappa, from Lehigh University (B.A. 1983) and from the Georgetown University Law Center (J.D. 1986). Prior to joining IAT, Mr. Tanzola practiced law in the areas of commercial litigation, surety, and construction law.

MEEGHAN H. TIRTASAPUTRA • Litigation and Appellate Associate with the law firm of Fox Rothschild in Los Angeles, California. Ms. Tirtasaputra graduated from the University of Southern California Gould School of Law (J.D. 2018) and from the University of La Verne (B.A. 2015). She was an Associate at Robins Kaplan LLP at the time she assisted in writing this publication.

DAVID C. VEIS • Partner with the law firm of Robins Kaplan LLP in Los Angeles, California. Mr. Veis graduated from the University of

California, Los Angeles (B.A. 1974), *with honors* from the University of Southern California (M.A. 1975), and from Southwestern University School of Law (J.D. 1978).

SCOTT C. WILLIAMS • Principal with Manier & Herod, P.C. in Nashville, Tennessee, where he practices in the firm's Surety & Fidelity Practice Group. Mr. Williams graduated from Rhodes College (B.A. 1995) and, *magna cum laude*, from the Cumberland School of Law, Samford University (J.D. 2001).

DOUGLASS F. WYNNE, JR. • Partner with the law firm of Simon, Peragine, Smith & Redfearn, LLPP in New Orleans, Louisiana. Mr. Wynne graduated from Tulane University (B.S. 2005) and from Loyola University New Orleans School of Law (J.D. 2008).

CONTENTS

Preface to Third Edition iii
Contributors v

CHAPTER 1
MEDICARE AND MEDICAID SURETY BONDS 1

Robert J. Duke and Omar J. Harb

Introduction 1
I. Brief Primer of Medicare and Medicaid 2
A. Medicare 2
B. Medicaid 5
II. Federal Medicare Bonds 6
A. Statutory and Regulatory Background 6
B. The HHA Bond Requirement 7
C. The DME Bond Requirement 8
D. The Claims Process per CMS Guidance 14
E. Review of Past Ten Years of Experience 17
F. Underwriting and Claims Considerations 20
III. State Bond Requirements 26
A. Florida 26
B. Alabama 30
C. District of Columbia 31
D. Iowa 32
E. Indiana 33
F. Minnesota 34
G. Texas 36
Conclusion 37
Appendix A 39

CHAPTER 2
DEVELOPERS OR SUBDIVISION BONDS 45

Michael J. Dudek, Ralph J. Kooy, and T. Scott Leo

I. The Unique Nature of Subdivision Bonds 45
II. Legislative Origin of Subdivision Bonds 47
A. Statutes and Ordinances 47
B. The Subdivision Agreement 48

III. Common Terms of Subdivision Bonds 49
A. The Subdivision Bond Amount 50
B. Reducing the Subdivision Bond Amount 51
C. Estimated Costs of Completion 51
IV. Collateral for Subdivision Bonds 52
A. The Set Aside Letter 52
B. Disputes Relating to Bank Set Aside Letters 52
V. Subdivision Bonds Are Not Public Works Bonds 55
A. Under Illinois Law, Subdivision Bonds Are Payment and Performance Bonds for Public Works: *Lake County Grading Co., LLC v. Village of Antioch* 55
B. Scope and Limits of Subdivision Bond Coverage 61
C. Expanding the Scope of Coverage Beyond the Statute or Ordinance 61
D. Time Limitations for Bringing Suit 63
VI. Considerations in Handling Claims 64
A. Obtain Project Schedule and Monitor Work Progress 64
B. Monitor Financial Status 64
C. Assess Defenses to Subdivision Bond Claims 65
D. Standing of the Claimant 65
E. The Sweetheart Deal 67
F. Third-Party Beneficiaries 71
G. Has the Claim Been Timely Presented? 73
H. Has the Municipality Complied with the Applicable Enabling Statute and Its Own Ordinances? 75
I. The Status of the Work: Has the Developer Started the Improvement Work? 77
J. No Liability Until Commencement of Development 79
K. Damages Resulting from the Developer's Failure to Complete the Improvements 82
VII. Successor Liability for Subdivision Improvements 86
VIII. Bankruptcy Issues and the Subdivision Bond Surety 89
Conclusion 94

CHAPTER 3
FINANCIAL GUARANTY INSURANCE AND SURETY BONDS **95**

Darren Grzyb, Scott W. Lichtenstein, Steven S. Katz, and Christopher Indelicato

Introduction 95
I. Financial Guaranty Insurance Model Act 97
A. Perceived Need for Separate Regulation 97
B. The Model Act 100
II. Financial Guaranty Insurance Legislation 103
A. New York 103
B. Florida 142
C. California 150
D. Connecticut 155
E. Other States 160
F. Surety Bonds Guaranteeing Payments of Premiums, Deductibles, and Self-Insured Retentions 161
III. Extraterritoriality: New York's "Appleton Rule" 163
A. New York Domestic Insurers 163
B. Foreign and Alien Insurers—Application of the "Appleton Rule" 166
C. Exception to the "Appleton Rule": Insurers Expressly Licensed to Insure Risks of Every Kind or Description Outside of the United States 169
D. Penalties for Violating the "Appleton Rule" 174
Conclusion 175

CHAPTER 4
PROBATE BONDS **177**

Matthew M. Horowitz, Michelle Randall, and Brian Lebrun

Introduction 177
I. The Fiduciary 178
A. Types of Fiduciaries 178
B. Scope of the Fiduciary Duty 180
II. The Probate Bond 188
A. Terms and Conditions 188
B. Construction 191
C. Scope of Coverage and Defenses to Coverage 192
D. Procedural Issues and Defenses 214

E. Damages 224
F. The Surety's Rights to Recovery of Claims Payments and Other Expenses 229
Conclusion 233

CHAPTER 5
BANKRUPTCY TRUSTEE/RECEIVER BONDS 235

Chad L. Schexnayder, Susan B. Jordan, and Matthew H. Sloan

Introduction 235
I. Bankruptcy Trustee Bond 235
A. The Bond 235
B. The Role of the Bankruptcy Trustee 238
C. Liability of the Bankruptcy Trustee and the Bond 242
D. Limitation Period for Claims on the Bond 245
II. Receivership Bonds 246
A. State Court 247
B. Federal Court 247
C. When and Where a Receiver Can Be Sued 248
III. Special Rights of Subrogation Available to a Surety of a Fiduciary 250
Conclusion 251

CHAPTER 6
PUBLIC OFFICIAL BONDS 253

Patrick R. Kingsley, Gerald N. Carozza, Jr., and Joseph W. Catuzzi

Introduction 253
I. Who Has Standing as an Obligee? 255
A. The Narrow View 255
B. The Expansive View 256
II. The Scope of Public Official Bond Coverage 257
A. Faithful Performance 257
B. Statutory Duties 260
C. Specific Claims 262
III. The Principal's Underlying Liability 269
A. The Requirement That the Principal Be Independently Liable 269
B. Color of Office 271
C. A Principal Holding Multiple Offices 274

D. Vicarious Liability 275
E. Immunity 277
IV. Damages 281
A. Actual Damages 281
B. The Penal Sum as a Cap on Damages 282
C. Interest 284
D. Fines and Punitive Damages 284
E. Attorney and Audit Fees 285
F. Stacking and the Cumulation of Liability 286
V. Defenses 290
A. Defaults Before and After the Bonded Term 290
B. Statutes of Limitations 291
C. Rescission 292
D. Traditional Suretyship Defenses 293
VI. Subrogation and Indemnity 293
Conclusion 294

CHAPTER 7
RECLAMATION BONDS **295**

Walter Blaine Early, III, William T. Gorton III,
Robert L. Scanlon, and Laura M. Murphy

I. Introduction to Reclamation Bonds 295
A. The Nature of the Industries 295
B. Underwriting Reclamation Bonds 301
II. Mining Program Financial Assurances Requirements 303
A. Coal Industry: The Surface Mining Control and Reclamation Act 304
B. Hardrock Industry (Federal Land): Federal Land Policy and Management Act 308
C. Other Lands 310
III. Suretyship in an Environmental and Administrative Law Framework 312
A. Suretyship Is a Three-Party Relationship 313
B. Parties to the Relationship 314
IV. Bond Releases 315
A. Release of Coal Mining Reclamation Bonds 316
B. Release of Hardrock Mining Reclamation Bonds 316
V. Principal Default: Bond Forfeiture 317
VI. Appeals of Administrative Actions 320
VII. Surety Performance 321

VIII. Unexpected Obligations 323
A. Water Quality 323
B. Other Potential Liabilities 326
Conclusion 327

CHAPTER 8
COMMERCIAL BAIL BONDS **329**

Jeffrey Clayton, Mark Holtschneider, James Portman, and Leah Schoen

Introduction 329
I. Background 331
A. Bail's Purpose 332
B. How Bail Works 333
II. Agreements Critical to the Process 334
A. The Bail Bond 334
B. The Power of Attorney 334
C. General Qualifying Power of Attorney 335
D. The Bail Bond Application 335
E. The Indemnity Agreement 336
F. The Surety and Bail Bond Producer Agreement 336
III. The Regulatory Framework 337
A. The Nuts and Bolts 339
IV. The Administration of Justice and Economic Benefits of Commercial Bail 359
A. The Impact of Secured Release on the Administration of Justice 359
B. Positive Economic Impact 360
Conclusion 361
Appendix A 363

CHAPTER 9
LICENSE AND PERMIT BONDS **367**

Patrick Q. Hustead, Connor L. Cantrell, and Patricia Framke

I. Dispensaries, Motor Vehicle Dealers, Slaughterhouses, and Shooting Gallery Operators 367
II. Bond Coverage 369
III. Not as Simple as They Seem 370
A. The Extent of Recovery on a Bond 370
B. Liability Periods: Cumulative Versus Continuous 374

C. The "Loss Suffered" May Know No Bounds 376
D. Extraterritorial Application of License and Permit Bonds 380
Conclusion 383

CHAPTER 10
MECHANIC'S LIEN DISCHARGE BONDS 385

Jonathan J. Dunn and Derek Popeil

Introduction 385
I. Nature and Purpose of Mechanic's Lien Discharge Bonds 386
A. Bond Serves as Substitute Security for Property 391
B. Any Interested Person May Provide the Lien Discharge Bond 392
C. Unless Owner Is Principal on Bond or Privity Exists, Owner Is to Be Dismissed 393
D. Effect of Posting Bond Prior to or Post Litigation 394
E. Scope of the Surety's Liability 395
II. The Surety's Defenses 396
A. Defects in Lien Claim 396
B. Substantive Defenses 403
C. Suretyship Defenses 407
III. Subrogation, Contribution, Subsuretyship, and the Competing Obligations of Lien Discharge and Payment Bond Sureties 410
A. Subrogation 410
B. Contribution and Subsuretyship 411
C. Lien Discharge Bond Versus Payment Bond 412
Conclusion 415

CHAPTER 11
FRINGE BENEFIT BONDS 417

David C. Olson, James D. Houston, and Ellen M. Cavallaro

Introduction 417
I. Fringe Benefit Bonds—Generally 417
A. Overview 417
B. Typical Provisions 420
II. Payment Bonds as Fringe Benefit Bonds 421
A. Federal Public Works Projects—Miller Act Payment Bonds 422

B. State Public Works Projects—"Little Miller Act" Payment Bonds 424
C. Private Payment Bonds 429
III. Issues Affecting the Surety's Liability 432
A. The Bond Claimant's Standing 432
B. Scope of Bond Coverage 436
C. Cancellation and Expiration of the Bond 439
D. Notice to the Surety 441
E. Traceability Requirement 444
IV. When Both a Fringe Benefit Bond and a General Payment Bond May Provide Coverage 446
A. Cosuretyship 447
B. Subsuretyship 449
C. Which Doctrine (Cosuretyship or Subsuretyship) Applies to the Coexisting Fringe Benefit Bond-Payment Bond Situation? 450
V. The ERISA Preemption Defense 453
Conclusion 461

CHAPTER 12
CUSTOMS BONDS, CLAIMS, AND LITIGATION 463

T. Randolph Ferguson and Laura Maurer

Introduction 463
I. Customs Bonds 463
II. Liquidated Damages Claims 466
A. Failure to File Entry Documents or Deposit Estimated Duties 467
B. Failure to Evidence Admissibility of Merchandise or Failure to Comply with Notice to Redeliver 468
III. Increased Duty Claims 470
A. Liquidation of Entries 470
B. Entries Deemed Liquidated by Operation of Law 471
IV. Collection of Lost Revenue Resulting from an Importer's Negligence or Fraud in Making the Entry 473
V. Surety Remedies and Defenses 473
A. Petition to Remit or Mitigate the Assessment of Liquidated Damages Claimed on CF 5955A 474
B. Protest to Challenge the Assessment of Increased Duties 476
C. Subrogation 481

VI. Delinquent Sureties: Billing, Show Cause, and Sanctions 481
A. Billing Delinquent Debts 482
B. Show Cause Letters 484
C. Sanctions 485
VII. Waiver of the Statute of Limitations 485
VIII. The Court of International Trade 486
A. Denied Protests 487
B. Enforcement Actions 488
C. Third-Party Claims for Indemnity and Reimbursement 488
IX. Indemnity, Collateral, and Collateral Return 489
A. The Six-Year Statute of Limitations: Duty and Liquidated Damages 497
B. The Five-Year Statute of Limitations: Claims for "Lost Revenue" 499
Conclusion 501

CHAPTER 13
FEDERAL EXCISE BONDS PAST, PRESENT, AND FUTURE IN A POST-PANDEMIC WORLD **503**

Jane A. Horne and Frank J. Tanzola

Introduction 503
I. TTB Bonds—General Overview 504
A. New Federal Bond Exemptions for Breweries, Distilleries, and Wineries 505
B. Taxable Goods and Types of Excise Bonds 507
C. Features of Internal Revenue Excise Bonds 509
Conclusion 513
Appendix A 515

CHAPTER 14
WORKERS' COMPENSATION BONDS **519**

CharCretia V. Di Bartolo and Gary Case

Introduction 519
I. Self-Insurance Generally 519
II. Self-Insurance Surety Bonds 521
A. Parties 521
B. Penal Sum of the Bond 523
C. Tail Exposure Under the Bond 524
D. Claims Administration Under the Bond 526
E. Discharge or Termination of Liability Under the Bond 528
F. Effect of Multiple Sureties 529

G. Effect of Other Forms of Replacement Security 530
H. Liability for Multiple Claims That Exceed the Penal Sum of the Bond 531
I. Potential Cumulative or Stacking Liability 531
J. Potential Liability for Attorneys' Fees 532
K. The Surety's Subrogation Rights 532
L. Bankruptcy Issues 534
Conclusion 536
Appendix A 537

CHAPTER 15
JUDICIAL BONDS **559**

Gina D. Lockwood and Scott Williams

Introduction 559
I. Types of Judicial Bonds and the Federal Rules That Govern Them 560
A. Appeal Bonds 560
B. Injunction Bond 575
C. Bonds for Remedies Provided by Federal Rule of Civil Procedure 64 581
II. Enforcement of Judicial Bonds 585
A. Enforcement by Motion in the Underlying Proceeding 587
B. Enforcement by an Independent Action 587
III. Scope of Liability 588
A. Terms of the Bond 588
B. Damages 589
IV. Discharge of Judicial Bonds 595
A. Injunction, Attachment, and Replevin Bonds 595
B. Supersedeas Bonds 595
V. Quick Reference Practice Tips 601
A. Judicial Bonds' Relevance in Practice 601
B. Enforcement of Judicial Bonds in Practice 604
Conclusion 605

CHAPTER 16
SEAS, SHIPS, AND SURETYSHIP **607**

Maura Z. Pelleteri and Robert G. Lavitt

Introduction 607
I. Admiralty Jurisdiction 607
A. Vessels and Navigable Waters 609
B. Maritime Contracts and Torts 610

C. Maritime Liens 614
D. Enforcing Maritime Liens—In Rem Actions 616
E. Quasi In Rem Attachment 617
F. Amount of Security 618
G. Priority of Maritime Liens 619
II. Suretyship in Admiralty 621
A. Special Admiralty Procedures 622
III. Conventional Performance Guarantees in Maritime Setting 629
A. Statutory Passenger-Related Protections 629
B. Security for Maritime Safety and Environmental Disasters 630
Conclusion 631

CHAPTER 17
LOST INSTRUMENT BONDS **633**

David C. Veis, Laura P. Nash, Meeghan H. Tirtasaputra, and Jonathan Schneider

Introduction 633
I. The Relationships Formed upon the Issuance of a Lost Instrument Bond 634
II. The Bond Penalty Amount—Fixed Versus Open Penalty 635
A. Fixed Penalty Bonds 635
B. Open Penalty Bonds 636
III. The Scope of the Surety's Liability in the Event of a Claim on a Lost Instrument Bond 638
A. Third-Party Forgery or Fraud Does Not Relieve the Surety of Liability 638
B. The Obligee's Mistake or Neglect May Not Release the Surety of Liability 639
C. The Surety Is Not Liable to Third Parties 643
IV. Courts' Strict Enforcement of the Bond Requirements Imposed by the Uniform Commercial Code and Comparable State Statutes 646
V. Notable Aspects of Lost Instrument Bond Underwriting 648
A. The Principal's Integrity and Financial Responsibility 648
B. The Nature and Negotiability of the Instrument 650
C. The Circumstances Surrounding the Lost Instrument 650
D. The Duration of the Surety's Exposure Under the Bond 650
Conclusion 652
Appendix A 653
Appendix B 655

CHAPTER 18
NOTARY BONDS **657**

Michael Safris and Douglass F. Wynne, Jr.

I. What Is a Notary Bond? 657
II. What Bond Is Required? 657
III. How Are the Notary's Powers and Duties Known? 658
IV. What Is the Liability of the Notary and Surety? 660
V. Negligent Misconduct 661
VI. Willful Misconduct 666
VII. What Are the Surety's Defenses? 669
VIII. What Damages Are Recoverable? 672
IX. The Rise of Online Notarization 673
Conclusion 675

CHAPTER 19
WAREHOUSE AND CUSTOMS BONDS **677**

Elliot Scharfenberg and Chris Simmelink

Introduction 677
I. United States Warehouse Act 678
A. Bond Requirements Under the United States Warehouse Act 679
B. Obligations of the Federally Licensed Warehouse Operator 680
C. Federal Question Jurisdiction and Preemption 682
D. The Liability of the Warehouse Bond Surety 685
II. State Warehouse Statutes 689
A. State-by-State Bonding Requirements 690
B. Damage or Loss During Bond Period and Failure to Deliver 695
C. Faithful Performance of the Principal's Obligations 697
III. U.S. Customs Bonded Warehouses 699
A. Classes of Customs Bonded Warehouses 700
B. Bond Requirements for Customs Bonded Warehouses 702
C. The Liability of the Customs Bond Surety 704

CHAPTER 20
THE COMMERCIAL SURETY'S COLLATERAL IN THE PRINCIPAL'S BANKRUPTCY CASE **707**

George J. Bachrach, Michael A. Stover, and Nina M. Durante

Introduction 707
I. Underwriting the Principal and Obtaining the Collateral 708
A. The Surety's Indemnity Agreement with the Principal 710
B. Acquiring the Collateral and the Collateral Agreement 713
II. The Effect of the Principal's Bankruptcy Case on the Surety's Collateral 721
A. The Property of the Principal's (the Debtor's) Estate (11 U.S.C. § 541) 722
B. The Automatic Stay (11 U.S.C. § 362) 723
C. The Surety's Secured Claim (11 U.S.C. § 506) 725
D. The Principal's (the Debtor's) Use of the Collateral (11 U.S.C. § 363) 727
E. The Principal's (the Debtor's) Plan of Reorganization 729
III. The Surety's Right and Ability to Use the Surety's Collateral After the Principal Files for Bankruptcy 735
A. Letters of Credit as the Surety's Collateral in Bankruptcy 735
B. The Principal's Property as the Surety's Collateral in Bankruptcy 743
C. The Surety's Use of the Surety's Collateral 744
IV. Obligee and Third-Party Claims Against Commercial Surety Bonds as They Affect the Surety's Use of the Collateral 746
A. The Nature of the Claimants and the Types of Bonds 747
B. The Surety's Claims Handling 749
C. The Principal's Attempts to Set a Surety Claims Bar Date Against the Commercial Surety's Bonds to Obtain a Release and Return of the Collateral 752
V. Maintaining and Preserving the Surety's Collateral for Future Claims 757
A. The Surety's Actions to Avoid Future Claims and/or to Preserve the Surety's Rights Against the Surety's Collateral 758
B. The Principal's/Trustee's Actions Under the Bankruptcy Code to Obtain a Release and Return of the Surety's Collateral to the Bankruptcy Estate 762

C. What Else May Happen to the Surety's Collateral in the Principal's Bankruptcy Case? 777
D. Litigation Issues to Consider 795
Conclusion 813

CHAPTER 1

MEDICARE AND MEDICAID SURETY BONDS

Robert J. Duke
Omar J. Harb

Introduction

Although certain bonds can be categorized under a common category of "Medicare and Medicaid Bonds," bonds that secure obligations under Medicare and Medicaid are quite diverse in terms of the scope of the obligations under the bond, the underlying obligations of the bond principal, and the relevant statutes and regulations. Such bonds are found at the federal and state levels. This chapter will examine bonds required by the federal government in connection with Medicare and bonds required by states in connection with Medicaid, particularly with respect to the supply of medical equipment and the provision of home health services. The discussion will provide a statutory and regulatory context, as well as underwriting and risk considerations.

By way of brief background, there is a consensus among policymakers at all levels of government—and regardless of political affiliation—that waste, billing errors, and abuse, as well as outright fraud, are endemic to our health care system, costing the public billions of dollars a year. According to a Thomson Financial News story by Tom Brown entitled "Cancer of Fraud Permeates U.S. Healthcare System" dated November 25, 2009, John Gillies of the Federal Bureau of Investigation "estimates that fraud accounts for 3% to 10% of U.S. healthcare expenditures per year, and . . . easily cost about $200 billion annually."

In testimony before the U.S. Senate Judiciary Committee on Health Care Fraud on October 28, 2009, William Corr, Deputy Secretary of the U.S. Department of Health and Human Services (HHS), stated:

> DME [durable medical equipment] fraud appears to be the most prevalent type of criminal activity in Medicare and Medicaid . . . Using authorities provided by Congress, we are requiring DME providers to post surety bonds, be certified by nationally recognized accreditation organizations, which includes onsite

review of the supplier, and submit to new rigorous competitive bidding processes . . . .[1]

In a November 23, 2009, article written by Gregg Blesch in *Modern Healthcare*, "To Err Is Expensive; CMS Erroneously Paid $54 Billion in Fiscal 2009 . . .,"[2] White House Budget Chief Peter Orzig stated that $54 billion of what the *Medicare* program paid in fiscal year 2008 was paid in error—an unofficial error rate of more than 12 percent. Other estimates put the dollar figure much higher.

This type of fraud and abuse paved the way for Medicare and Medicaid bonds. However, more than a decade later, the problem remains significant. The COVID-19 pandemic brought with it a host of additional opportunities for fraud and abuse, causing the U.S. Department of Justice (DOJ) to form the COVID-19 Fraud Enforcement Task Force. In May 2021, DOJ announced criminal charges against 14 defendants for various health care fraud schemes resulting in more than $143 million in false billings.[3]

Health care fraud and overbilling are clearly not going away any time soon, placing an even greater emphasis on the need for Medicare and Medicaid bonds.

I. Brief Primer of Medicare and Medicaid

A. *Medicare*

Medicare was created in 1965 as title XVIII of the Social Security Act. It was entitled "Health Insurance for the Aged and Disabled."[4] Initially, Medicare consisted of two parts: Hospital Insurance (HI), also known as

---

1. *Effective Strategies for Preventing Health Care Fraud Before the S. Judiciary Comm.*, 111th Cong. 1–14 (2009) (statement of William Corr, Dep'y Sec'y of the U.S. Dep't of Health & Human Servs.).
2. https://www.modernhealthcare.com/article/20091123/NEWS/911209981/to-err-is-expensive
3. Brian Rafferty & William D. Ezzell, *Two Week Old DOJ COVID-19 Fraud Task Force Announces First Wave of Prosecutions—Many More Are Likely on the Horizon*, Nat'l L. Rev. (May 28, 2021), https://www.natlawreview.com/article/two-week-old-doj-covid-19-fraud-task-force-announces-first-wave-prosecutions-many.
4. 42 U.S.C. §§ 1395–1395lll.

Part A, and Supplementary Medical Insurance (SMI), known as Part B.[5] Since its inception, Parts C and D have been added. Part C, known also as Medicare Advantage, is an alternative to Parts A and B and provides benefits through private insurers. Part D is a voluntary prescription drug plan. In 2019, Medicare covered 61.2 million persons with about 85 percent aged 65 and older.[6] Medicare expenditures in 2019 totaled $796.2 billion and total income was $794.8 billion.[7] Medicare is administered by the Centers for Medicare and Medicaid Services (CMS).

Part A covers inpatient hospital care, home health care, skilled nursing facilities, and hospice care.[8] As noted in 42 U.S.C. § 1395c, Part A, which is typically premium free, "provides basic protection against the costs of hospital, related post-hospital, home health services, and hospice care" for

- individuals who are age 65 or over and are eligible for Social Security retirement benefits;
- individuals under age 65 who have been entitled to Social Security or Railroad Retirement Board disability benefits for at least 24 months;
- certain individuals determined to have end-stage renal disease; and
- certain persons over 65, not otherwise eligible for Social Security benefits who elect to pay a premium for Medicare coverage.[9]

Part A's income primarily comes from the payroll tax.[10] Part A beneficiaries are subject to a deductible and coinsurance for hospital stays

---

5. BARBARA S. KLEES ET AL., HHS, BRIEF SUMMARIES OF MEDICARE & MEDICAID, TITLE XVII AND TITLE XIX OF THE SOCIAL SECURITY ACT 6 (2009) [hereinafter CMS MEDICARE SUMMARY], https://www.cms.gov/research-statistics-data-and-systems/statistics-trends-and-reports/medicareprogramratesstats/downloads/medicaremedicaidsummaries2009.pdf.
6. 2020 ANNUAL REPORT OF THE BOARDS OF TRUSTEES OF THE FEDERAL HOSPITAL INSURANCE AND FEDERAL SUPPLEMENTARY MEDICAL INSURANCE TRUST FUNDS 6 (2020) [hereinafter TRUSTEES' REPORT], https://www.cms.gov/files/document/2020-medicare-trustees-report.pdf.
7. *Id.*
8. CMS MEDICARE SUMMARY, *supra* note 5, at 6.
9. 42 U.S.C. § 1395c.
10. CMS MEDICARE SUMMARY, *supra* note 5, at 11.

and daily coinsurance payments for stays at skilled nursing facilities.[11] After the applicable deductible and coinsurance, providers of services under Part A are paid under a prospective payment system by which the provider is paid a fixed fee based on the classification of the service provided, rather than actual cost incurred.[12]

Total Plan A expenditures in 2019 were $328.3 billion with 60.9 million persons participating.[13]

Part B covers physician, outpatient hospital, home health, and other services, such as durable medical equipment (DME).[14] Persons age 65 or over, and all disabled persons, are entitled to coverage under Part B and may enroll thereunder on a voluntary basis.[15] The trust fund related to Part B (Supplementary Medical Insurance Trust Fund) is funded by beneficiary premiums (which generally cover 25 percent of program costs) and the general fund of the U.S. Treasury.[16] Beneficiaries are generally subject to a deductible and a 20 percent coinsurance requirement. Physician charges are generally reimbursed the lesser of (1) the submitted charges, or (2) the amount determined by a fee schedule. Payments for DME and clinical laboratory services are also based on a fee schedule. Most hospital outpatient services and home health services are reimbursed on a prospective payment system.[17] Total 2019 expenditures for Plan B were $370.3 billion, with 56.1 million persons participating.[18]

Of note with respect to DME, a provider must "win" the right to provide Medicaid-eligible DME through a competitive bidding system. The Competitive Bidding Program was established through the Medicare Prescription Drug, Improvement, and Modernization Act of 2003 (section 302 of Public Law No. 108-173). Under competitive bidding, CMS replaced the fee schedule payment methodology for certain Durable Medical Equipment, Prosthetics, Orthotics, and Supplies (DMEPOS) items with a competitive bid process. CMS awards contracts to a supplier based on the best price and applicable quality and financial standards.

---

11. MEDICARE PRIMER, NAT'L ACAD. OF SOC. INS. 5 (Mar. 2020), https://www.nasi.org/wp-content/uploads/2009/06/Medicare-Primer.pdf.
12. CMS MEDICARE SUMMARY, *supra* note 5, at 14.
13. TRUSTEES' REPORT, *supra* note 6, at 10.
14. 42 U.S.C. § 1395k.
15. CMS MEDICARE SUMMARY, *supra* note 5, at 8.
16. *Id.* at 11.
17. *Id.* at 14.
18. TRUSTEES' REPORT, *supra* note 6, at 10.

The price at which the suppliers are reimbursed is the bid price. Bidders must provide a bid bond, providing assurance the winning bidder will enter into an agreement with CMS.

B. Medicaid

Medicaid was created in 1965 as title XIX of the Social Security Act.[19] The program is jointly funded by the federal government and state governments to assist states in providing medical assistance to eligible low-income persons and families. Each state administers its own program in accordance with federal guidelines and subject to the oversight of CMS. State participation in Medicaid is voluntary but all states participate. Federal law establishes basic requirements as a condition of federal funding. However, states have flexibility beyond that regarding issues such as coverage, eligibility, and how providers are paid. Thus, a Medicaid program in one state may vary significantly from that in another state. The state programs are similar only to the extent of adhering to the basic federal requirements.

Federal regulations require that a state program must offer certain mandatory services: (1) inpatient hospital care, not including care in hospitals for mental illness or tuberculosis; (2) outpatient hospital care; (3) laboratory and X-ray services; (4) skilled nursing home services for those over age 21; and (5) physicians' services.[20] States may offer services beyond these core requirements.

The Medicaid program is funded with both state funds and federal funds. The federal government matches state Medicaid spending based on a formula. The federal match must be at least 50 percent. However, the match can be higher for states with low per capita income.[21] In 2019, Medicaid expenditures totaled $627 billion, with the federal government paying $405 billion.[22]

---

19. 42 U.S.C. §§ 1396–1396w-5.
20. Judith D. Moore & Donald G. Smith, *Legislating Medicaid: Considering Medicaid and Its Origins*, HEALTH CARE FINANCING REV., Winter 2005/2006, at 45, 50.
21. KAISER COMMISSION ON MEDICAID AND THE UNINSURED, MEDICAID: A PRIMER 5 (2013), https://www.kff.org/wp-content/uploads/2010/06/7334-05.pdf.
22. CONGRESSIONAL RESEARCH SERVICE, MEDICAID FINANCING AND EXPENDITURES 2 (2020), https://fas.org/sgp/crs/misc/R42640.pdf.

II. Federal Medicare Bonds

A. Statutory and Regulatory Background

Section 4312(a) of the Balanced Budget Act of 1997[23] (BBA) amended section 1834(a) of the Social Security Act by adding a new paragraph 16 in the payment rules for particular items that would condition the certification of a supplier of DME to the furnishing of "a surety bond in a form specified by the Secretary and in an amount that is not less than $50,000."[24] Section 4312(b)(1) of the BBA amended section 1861(o) of the Social Security Act by adding a new paragraph 7 in the definition of "Home Health Agency" (HHA) participating in the Medicare program as an entity that provided the secretary of HHS "a surety bond in a form specified by the Secretary and in an amount that is not less than $50,000."[25] The bonding requirements would take effect on January 1, 1998.[26] In 2015, the Medicare Access and CHIP Reauthorization Act was enacted.[27] Section 513 amended 42 U.S.C. § 1395x, such that the bond amount is no less than $50,000 or an amount that the secretary of HHS determines is commensurate with the volume of payments CMS makes to the HHA. As discussed below, no regulations with a definitive compliance date have been established.

The apparent purpose of the new bond requirements was to provide security to the Health Care Financing Administration[28] (the agency tasked with oversight of Medicare) to facilitate the collection of overpayments of benefits to a participating HHA or DME due to billing errors, abuse, or fraud.

---

23. Pub. L. No. 105-33, 111 Stat. 251.
24. 42 U.S.C. § 1395m(a)(16).
25. *Id.* § 1395x(o)(7).
26. BBA § 4312(f). Section 4724(b) of the BBA also amended section 1903(i) of the Social Security Act to prohibit federal financial participation in payments under Medicaid programs for home health services unless the HHA provided the state Medicaid agency a surety bond in an amount not less than $50,000. Because the bond that ultimately was implemented at the federal level involved the Medicare program, this section will address only the Medicare requirements.
27. Pub. L. No. 114-10, 129 Stat. 87.
28. Since enactment of the BBA, the name of the agency has been changed to the Centers for Medicare and Medicaid Services (CMS). This chapter will refer to the agency as CMS.

Despite the apparent purpose of the bond—to provide security for overpayments due to billing errors, abuse, or fraud—the statute did not provide guidance or clarity as to the nature and scope of the surety bond's coverage. These details would be left to the regulations.

B. The HHA Bond Requirement

On January 5, 1998, CMS issued regulations to implement the HHA bond requirement at 42 C.F.R. § 441.16.[29] The regulation required a bond in the amount of 15 percent of the HHA's prior year's revenues, but not less than $50,000.[30] The bond guaranteed the repayment of overpayments made during the term of the bond and any civil penalties or assessments.[31] The BBA provided CMS the authority to waive the bond requirement for entities that provide a comparable bond under state law. CMS elected not to exercise its waiver authority under the regulations.[32] On June 1, 1998, CMS issued revised regulations that addressed some concerns stemming from the initial regulations.[33] The regulations placed a time limit within which a claim could be made. In addition, the regulations permitted a single continuous bond, rather than successive annual bonds. Further, the revised regulations gave HHAs until July 31, 1998, to file the bonds (with an effective date of January 1, 1998).[34]

Although 40 percent of HHAs had secured the required bonds under the regulations, there was a great deal of political pressure to amend or even get rid of the bond requirement due to the "onerous" burden placed on HHAs.[35] Congress introduced joint resolutions to disapprove the June 1 regulations.[36] Under pressure of disapproval, CMS agreed with Congress to further delay implementation of the bond requirement until the General Accounting Office (GAO) conducted a review of the requirement.[37]

---

29. Edward G. Gallagher, *Medicare and Medicaid Bonds*, *in* THE LAW OF MISCELLANEOUS AND COMMERCIAL SURETY BONDS 1 (Todd C. Kazlow & Bruce C. King eds., 2001) (citing 63 Fed. Reg. 292 (Jan. 5, 1998)).
30. *Id.*
31. *Id.*
32. 63 Fed. Reg. 292, 293 (Jan. 5, 1998).
33. Gallagher, *supra* note 29, at 2 (citing 63 Fed. Reg. 29,648 (June 1, 1998)).
34. *Id.*
35. *Id.*
36. S.J. Res. 50, 105th Cong. (1998).
37. Gallagher, *supra* note 29, at 2.

By removing from the regulations (42 C.F.R. § 441.16(i)) the date by which HHAs must submit the bond, CMS effectively suspended enforcement of the bond requirement until CMS reviewed the GAO report and published a new final rule.[38] On January 29, 1999, GAO completed its review and released a report. The GAO concluded that CMS "made a prudent choice in specifying the surety bond as a financial guarantee."[39] However, the GAO recommended that CMS reconsider the bond amount, as a bond in the amount of 15 percent of revenues may be too burdensome.[40] In addition, CMS should consider exempting HHAs that had a demonstrated track record of fiscal responsibility.[41] Despite the release of the report, CMS to date has not published final regulations implementing the HHA bond requirement, despite a statute requiring bonds by January 1, 1998. Nevertheless, as noted below, several states have effectively implemented the requirement and require HHAs furnish a surety bond as a condition to participating in Medicaid.

C. The DME Bond Requirement

The road from the BBA to implementation of a bond requirement for DMEs was just as long and tortuous as the implementation process for the HHA bond requirement, perhaps even more so. However, for the DME bond requirement, the road from statute to implementation ultimately resulted in a bond to CMS actually being written.

As noted, section 4312(a) of the BBA amended section 1834(a) of the Social Security Act to condition the certification of a supplier of DME to the furnishing of a surety bond of not less than $50,000.

CMS's first attempt to implement the DME bond requirement was the proposed rule published on January 20, 1998.[42] The proposed rule sought to implement regulations affecting various areas of DME oversight, including the bond requirement. Under proposed 42 C.F.R. § 424.57(e), a supplier would have been required to furnish a surety bond for each tax identification number for which it had a billing number issued by

---

38. 63 Fed. Reg. 41,170 (July 31, 1998).
39. GAO, Medicare Home Health Agencies, Role of Surety Bonds in Increasing Scrutiny and Reducing Overpayments (1999) (GAO/HEHS-99-23).
40. *Id.*
41. *Id.*
42. 63 Fed. Reg. 2,926 (Jan. 20, 1998).

Medicare.[43] The bond would be for a term of 12 months and renewed annually.[44] The amount would be 15 percent of the prior year's claims, but not less than $50,000 nor more than $3 million.[45] The bond's coverage extended to overpayments, interest, civil penalties, and assessments.[46]

However, delay in implementation was caused by three factors: (1) the slow pace at CMS; (2) resistance to the bond requirement by suppliers of DMEs; and (3) a statutory roadblock. Other regulatory provisions affecting DME oversight were finalized in an October 11, 2000, final rule.[47] However, due to a significant number of comments that CMS received opposing the requirement, CMS decided to "make extensive changes to this requirement and build on our experience with surety bond requirements for home health agencies, as well as a General Accounting Office study of Medicare surety bonds" and not incorporate the bond provision in the October 11, 2000, final rule.[48] The regulations regarding the DME bond requirement would be promulgated at a later date. Delay in implementation continued because CMS was slow in finalizing the regulations and section 902 of the Medicare Prescription Drug, Improvement, and Modernization Act of 2003 prohibited finalization of any proposed rule that was published more than three years earlier.[49] Because the bond requirement was proposed in 1998, CMS could not finalize the regulations and had to start from the beginning.

Bond regulations were again proposed on August 1, 2007.[50] As proposed, a DME would be required to furnish a $65,000 bond for each National Provider Identifier (NPI).[51] CMS finalized the regulations

---

43. *Id.* at 2,939.
44. *Id.*
45. *Id.*
46. *Id.*
47. 65 Fed. Reg. 60,366 (Oct. 11, 2000).
48. *Id.* at 60,372.
49. 72 Fed. Reg. 42,001, 42,002 (Aug. 1, 2007), Pub. L. No. 108-172, 111 Stat. 2066. Section 902 sets a timeline for the publication of final HHS regulations, stating, "Such timeline may vary among different regulations based on differences in the complexity of the regulation, the number and scope of comments received, and other relevant factors, but shall not be longer than 3 years except under exceptional circumstances." 42 U.S.C. § 1395hh(a)(3)(B).
50. 72 Fed. Reg. 42,001 (Aug. 1, 2007).
51. An NPI is a unique identification number for covered health care providers that must be used by providers in its administrative and financial

on January 2, 2009, 17 months after the publication of the proposed regulation and 11 years after the authorizing statute was enacted with a $50,000 bond requirement.[52]

1. The Parameters of the Bond Requirement

Under 42 C.F.R. § 424.57(d), DMEs enrolled or enrolling in the Medicare program are required to furnish a separate surety bond in the amount of $50,000 for each NPI number to which Medicare has granted billing privileges.[53] Any given DME may have more than one NPI number. Typically, NPI numbers are location driven. If a DME has more than one NPI number, it must post a bond in the penal sum of $50,000 (or more as described below) for each such NPI. A single "master bond" scheduling all locations may be furnished. However, the bond liability is noncumulative in that the bond penal sum under one bond for a particular NPI of a given DME cannot be applied to infractions committed under a different NPI number of the same DME.

Under the regulations, a DME supplier is a person or entity "which sells or rents Part B covered items to Medicare beneficiaries."[54] Items are varied and include wheelchairs, walkers, oxygen tanks, braces, home dialysis supplies, diabetes test strips, hospital beds, and prosthetics.

The following events can trigger the bond requirement:

- A new DME enrolling in the Medicare program
- An existing DME that is making a change in ownership or responding to a revalidation or reenrollment request
- An existing DME with a new location (and new NPI)

For "high-risk" suppliers, those that have a history of adverse legal action, a larger bond is required. The increase is $50,000 for each adverse legal action within the ten years preceding enrollment with Medicare, plus the base amount of $50,000.[55] The regulations define "final adverse

---

transactions. The NPI numbering system was established in 2004. 69 Fed. Reg. 3,434 (Jan. 23, 2004).

52. 74 Fed. Reg. 166 (Jan. 2, 2009).

53. 42 C.F.R. § 424.57(d) (2020). It is quite common that a single DME could have several NPIs. A DME with hundreds of branch locations, such as a chain pharmacy, could have hundreds of NPIs.

54. *id.* § 424.57(a).

55. *Id.* § 424.57(d)(3)(ii).

action" as (1) a revocation of Medicare billing privileges; (2) a suspension or revocation of a license to provide health care; (3) revocation or suspension by an accreditation organization; (4) a conviction of a federal or state felony offense within the ten years preceding enrollment, revalidation, or reenrollment; or (5) an exclusion or debarment from participation in a federal or state health care program.[56]

Under the bond, the surety is required to pay CMS within 30 days of receiving "sufficient evidence" establishing liability for unpaid claims for overpayments, civil money penalties (CMPs), or assessments. The amount required to be paid by the surety is (1) the amount of any unpaid claim for which the supplier is responsible (plus accrued interest), and (2) the amount of any CMP or assessment imposed by CMS or the Office of Inspector General (OIG).[57] If the bond is terminated and the suppler fails to furnish a replacement bond, the last bond provided has a two-year tail for claims, penalties, and assessments based on "overpayments or other events" that took place during the bond term and were assessed within the two-year period. The two-year period commences from the later of either (1) the failure to provide a replacement bond or (2) the termination of billing privileges.[58] Under the final rule, it is important for a DME to maintain a bond in place. Failure to maintain a bond in place for each NPI will result in the supplier irreversibly forfeiting any receivables due from CMS during the time period for which a DME bond was not in place.

The regulation exempts the following groups from the bond requirement: (1) government-operated DMEs if the supplier has provided CMS with a comparable surety bond under state law; (2) state-licensed orthotic and prosthetic personnel in private practice making custom-made orthotics and prosthetics if the business is solely owned and operated by the orthotic and prosthetic personnel, and the business is only billing for orthotic, prosthetics, and supplies; (3) physicians and nonphysician practitioners as defined in section 1842(b)(18) of the Social Security Act when items are furnished only to the physician or nonphysician practitioner's own patients as part of his or her physician service; and (4) physical and occupational therapists in private practice if the business

56. *Id.* § 424.57(a). The term in the regulation's definitions is "final adverse action" but the term used in the "elevated surety bond amount" provision is "adverse legal action."

57. *Id.* § 424.57(d)(5)(i).

58. *Id.* § 424.57(d)(5)(iii).

is solely owned and operated by the physical or occupational therapist, the items are furnished only to the physical or occupational therapist's own patients as part of his or her professional service, and the business is only billing for orthotics, prosthetics, and supplies.[59]

2. Bond Coverage—Occurrence or Claims Made?

The regulation is not a model of clarity with respect to the scope of the bond's coverage. It is not entirely clear whether the bond's liability is on a claims-made or occurrence basis. For example, 42 C.F.R. § 424.57(d)(5)(ii) states the bond must state the surety is liable for unpaid claims, CMPs, or assessments "that occur during the term of the bond." In addition, § 424.57(d)(9) addresses replacement sureties and requires the surety that is replaced "is responsible for any overpayments, CMPs, or assessments that occurred up to the date of the change of surety." These provisions seem to suggest that coverage is on an occurrence basis.

On the other hand, in its discussion regarding the replacement of a surety, CMS agreed with the position that "the replaced bond and its surety should have no further liability other than for claims already made."[60] This discussion suggests claims-made coverage. Furthermore, the regulations require the supplier have a bond in place at all times. Otherwise, its billing privileges are revoked. However, under 42 C.F.R. § 424.57(d)(5)(iii), if a supplier no longer maintains a bond, the last bond must provide coverage until the end of the bond term and "the surety remains liable for unpaid claims, CMPs, or assessments that . . . (B) Were imposed or assessed by CMS or the OIG during the 2 years following the date that the DMEPOS supplier failed to submit a bond." It seems if the bond were on an occurrence basis that covered all liabilities accruing during the bond term, a two-year tail would not be necessary. Adding to the confusion is the comment made by CMS in the final rule. It stated, in response to public comment, it was deleting the final two sentences in § 424.57(d)(9) that suggested occurrence coverage (implying that claims-made coverage was intended).[61] However, the regulations do not reflect such a deletion.

---

59. *Id.* § 424.57(d)(15).
60. 74 Fed. Reg. 166, 176 (Jan. 2, 2009).
61. *Id.* ("The commenter stated that if the DMEPOS supplier provides an acceptable bond from a different surety, then the new bond should be liable for any claims made after its effective date 'regardless of when the

Ancillary materials released by CMS after the implementation of the regulation suggest a bond on an occurrence basis. CMS issues bulletins through the Medicare Learning Network (MLN) to educate providers and suppliers. MLN Matter Number MM7167 stated: "A surety is liable for any overpayments incurred during the term of the surety bond. This includes overpayment determinations made on or after the surety bond effective date."[62] A 2013 CMS OIG report described the surety bond as guaranteeing "that the surety will pay CMS the amount (including accrued interest) of any overpayments, civil monetary penalties, or assessments incurred during the term of the bond and for which the supplier is responsible, up to the surety's maximum obligation."[63] Lastly, a private company that manages the supplier enrollment process for CMS (Palmetto GBA) has available "Frequently Asked Questions" (FAQs) regarding the surety bond requirement that were drafted by CMS. An FAQ reiterates the requirement that the "surety is liable for unpaid claims, civil monetary penalties, or assessments that occur during the term of the bond."[64]

Nevertheless, the ambiguity persists. The Surety & Fidelity Association of America (SFAA) created a sample form that is available to its member surety companies. The form is on a claims-made basis and responds to claims made against the bond during the bond term. Palmetto GBA has been accepting the form since implementation in 2009. The SFAA form and related endorsements are attached as Appendix A to

---

payment, overpayment or other event giving rise to the claim' occurred, and the replaced bond and its surety should have no further liability other than for claims already made. Therefore, the commenter suggested striking the last two sentences of proposed § 424.57(c)(26)(x). Response: We agree and have revised § 424.57(d)(9) (proposed § 424.57(c)(26)(x)) by removing the last two sentences.").

62. CMS, MLN Matter Number MM7167, Claims against Surety Bonds for Suppliers of Durable Medical Equipment (DME), Prosthetics, Orthotics, and Supplies (DMEPOS) (Feb. 21, 2012).

63. Daniel R. Levinson, HHS OIG, Surety Bonds Remain an Underutilized Tool to Protect Medicare from Supplier Overpayments 2 (2013) (OEI-3-11-00350).

64. Centers for Medicare and Medicaid Services, *Surety Bond Requirement for Suppliers of Durable Medical Equipment, Prosthetics, Orthotics and Supplies (DMEPOS)* 3 (Sept. 10, 2009), https://www.palmettogba.com/palmetto/providers.nsf/files/suretybondfaqs.pdf/$FILE/suretybondfaqs.pdf.

this chapter. These forms address claims on a claims-made basis. Under paragraph 1 of the SFAA form, the bond responds to claims for which CMS demanded payment from the surety during the term of the bond, subject to the two-year tail. Contemplating the possibility that penalties and assessments could relate to conduct in the past before the oversight established by these regulations was put in place, the bond form requires the claim to relate to overpayment or other events that occurred on or after March 3, 2009, the effective date of the regulations (a proxy for when DME oversight began). CMS has indicated that, for an entity with multiple NPIs, it will accept a single bond scheduling all NPIs. (The SFAA has also developed a schedule bond.) Other industry forms have followed suit.

To date, there have not been any reported cases in which this ambiguity is an issue regarding whether a claim is paid. However, it is likely a matter of "when" and not "if." When the dispute arises, it can be reasonably expected that CMS will draw from the bond form (claims made) or the regulation and ancillary materials (occurrence) to support its claim.

D. The Claims Process per CMS Guidance

The *Code of Federal Regulations* set forth the claims process for DMEPOS supplier bonds at 42 C.F.R. § 424.57.

1. Steps Required Before a Bond Claim Can Be Made

There are no specific conditions precedent to be followed by CMS (or a CMS contractor) prior to the time a claim may be made on the bond. However, as noted above, there must be "sufficient evidence" to establish the surety's liability, so CMS or the CMS contractor need only have obtained documentation indicating that an overpayment has been made to a DMEPOS supplier prior to seeking payment under the bond.

Further, the surety's liability is for "unpaid claims, CMPs, and assessments."[65] This implies that, before a surety can be liable, the claimant must make a claim or assessment (or establish a CMP) against the principal that remains unpaid.

---

65. 42 C.F.R. § 424.57(d)(5)(i) (2020).

2. Who Can Make Claims on the Bond?

Under the regulations, "actions under the bond may be brought by CMS or by CMS contractors."[66] CMS contractors include carriers, fiscal intermediaries, or Medicare administrative contractors.[67]

3. When Must a Claim Be Made on the Bond?

There is no specific time limit regarding when CMS or the CMS contractor must make a claim on the bond. Further, as discussed earlier, a surety's liability can be extended past the date the surety terminates its bond, if the DMEPOS supplier fails to obtain a new bond. Specifically, a surety is liable for "unpaid claims, CMPs, or assessments" that took place "during the term of the bond," and "were imposed or assessed . . . during the 2 years following the date that the DMEPOS supplier failed to submit a bond or required rider, or the date the DMEPOS supplier's billing privileges were terminated, whichever is later."[68]

This provision effectively extends the claim period against a surety, and only requires that (1) the overpayment took place during the term of the bond and (2) the claim was assessed against the principal within two years after a new bond should have been provided or the DMEPOS supplier lost its ability to bill.

4. What Must the Claimant Show?

As noted, a surety is responsible if there is "sufficient evidence" of the surety's liability for unpaid claims, CMPs, and assessments.[69] "Sufficient evidence" is defined in 42 C.F.R. § 424.57(a) to mean: "documents CMS may supply to the surety in order to establish that a DMEPOS supplier had received Medicare funds in excess of the amount due and payable under the statute and regulations, the amount of a CMP, or the amount of some other assessment against the DMEPOS supplier."

The regulations do not provide guidance as to what documents must be provided to establish such overpayments or penalties. At a minimum, presumably, CMS must show there is an unpaid claim, CMP, or assessment. To establish the surety's liability, the claimant must be able

---

66. *Id.* § 424.57(d)(7).
67. *Id.* § 405.800.
68. *Id.* § 424.57(d)(5)(B)(iii).
69. *Id.* § 424.57(d)(5)(i).

to point to relevant Medicare guidelines and establish that the principal's billings reflected overpayments under such guidelines. This is a fact- and document-intensive procedure that would likely include a review of any audits conducted, as well as documentation of billing and payments.

5. The Surety's Obligation After Receiving a Claim

When provided with a claim, the surety must evaluate the documentation provided and determine its liability. To the extent CMS or the CMS contractor provides "sufficient evidence" of the surety's liability, the surety is then obligated to pay CMS "within 30 days" of receiving notice from the claimant.[70] While 30 days is obviously very little time to complete an investigation, the surety could argue the 30-day period does not begin until the claimant provides "sufficient evidence." This could indefinitely extend the surety's response date while the claimant obtains and produces supporting documentation, including Medicare guidelines, audits, and billing and payment information for the DMEPOS supplier.

6. Limitations Period

Because the regulations do not contain a separate limitations period for actions under the bond, one must look to general federal statute for guidance. Under 28 U.S.C. § 2415,

> every action for money damages brought by the United States or an officer or agency thereof which is founded upon any contract express or implied in law or fact, shall be barred unless the complaint is filed within six years after the right of action accrues or within one year after final decisions have been rendered in applicable administrative proceedings required by contract or law, whichever is later.

Because CMS is a federal agency (under HHS), this statute would be applicable to actions against the surety on Medicare bonds. Under that statute the "accrual" date is likely the date that the principal fails to pay any claim, assessment, or CMP.

---

70. *Id.*

E. Review of Past Ten Years of Experience

1. Claim Statistics

According to available statistics from the SFAA, the bulk of the premium and loss activity is with respect to federal DME Medicare bonds. The total written premium of these bonds generally decreased between 2014 and 2018, from $15.4 million to $12.6 million. However, the written premium increased to $15.1 million in 2019. Loss ratios have generally been low. However, in 2019, this class of bonds had $3.2 million in direct incurred losses, a 23.8 percent loss ratio (the highest in the past six years). Nevertheless, the loss experience for all classes of Medicare and Medicaid bonds is quite low.[71] This could reflect more careful and comprehensive underwriting as sureties adjusted to this relatively new type of bond. It could also reflect a "weeding out" of less scrupulous (or careful) DMEPOS suppliers, which could have had their right to bill Medicare suspended or revoked following overpayment issues.

2. Court and Regulatory Decisions

Given Medicare bonds have only recently been required, there have been few opinions relating to such bonds. Some of these are administrative decisions issued by the Departmental Appeals Board (DAB) of HHS.

In an administrative proceeding, the HHS DAB upheld a CMS revocation of a provider's supplier number for failure to maintain a surety bond.[72] The DAB reviewed 42 U.S.C. § 1395m(a)(16)(B) and the related regulations, and held that "a supplier must meet the surety bond requirements . . . on a continuing basis."[73] The DAB further stated that "a belated surety bond cannot therefore satisfy the statutory and regulatory purpose of providing continuous protection to the Medicare program from the risk of loss due to a supplier's fraud or abuse."[74] The DAB

---

71. In 2019, the direct written premium for the other classes of bonds were: federal HHA bonds—$180,262; state HHA bonds—$1.8 million; state DME bonds—$1.3 million; federal (all other)—$1.6 million; and state (all other)—$5.5 million.
72. A Brighter Future Healthcare Servs., Inc. v. Ctrs. for Medicare & Medicaid Servs., Docket No. C-10-663, Decision No. CR2267, 2010 HHSDAB LEXIS 77 (HHS DAB Oct. 15, 2010).
73. *Id.* at *10.
74. *Id.* at *12.

therefore declined to waive the compliance requirement or provide a time extension, or otherwise grant any relief.[75]

Another DAB decision rejected a supplier's argument it did not receive notice of the new surety bond requirements.[76] The DAB noted "participants in the Medicare program have a 'duty to familiarize [themselves] with the legal requirements for cost reimbursement.'"[77] Citing the regulations, the DAB held:

> The law expressly holds Medicare suppliers responsible for knowing the regulatory requirements . . . published in the *Federal Register* and treats such publication as constructive notice whether or not the supplier actually was aware of the requirements.[78] CMS was therefore within its rights to revoke the petitioner's supplier number for failing to timely have in place a surety bond as required.[79]

Court opinions relating to Medicare bonds have thus far been restricted to indemnity matters. However, at least one decision in an indemnity case touched on matters of surety liability under a Medicare bond. In a federal court action, a surety sought indemnification from its principal after paying a claim on a Medicare bond.[80] The indemnitor argued the surety paid the claim in bad faith, alleging the surety failed to obtain patient medical records and corresponding payment records to verify that the CMS's audit was accurate. However, the court stated that "patient information is protected by [the Health Insurance Portability and Accountability Act (HIPAA)] and [surety] had no legal basis upon which

---

75. *Id.* at *13.
76. Clairmont Nichols Opticians v. Ctrs. for Medicare & Medicaid Servs., Docket No. C-10-715, Decision No. CR2265, 2010 HHSDAB LEXIS 75 (HHS DAB Oct. 8, 2010).
77. *Id.* at *13 (quoting Heckler v. Cmty. Health Servs. of Crawford County, Inc., 467 U.S. 51, 64 (1984)).
78. *Id.* at *13–14 (citing 42 C.F.R. § 411.406(e)(2) (2020)).
79. *Id.* at *17. *See also* Pepper Hill Nursing & Rehab. Ctr., LLC v. Ctrs. for Medicare & Medicaid Servs., Docket No. C-10-795, Decision No. CR2293, 2010 HHSDAB LEXIS 85 (HHS DAB Dec. 14, 2010) (holding that even the furnishing of a retroactive surety bond—covering earlier claims—was not sufficient to avoid revocation).
80. Lexon Ins. Co. v. Naser, Case No. 4:12-CV-13218, 2014 U.S. Dist. LEXIS 52490 (E.D. Mich. Apr. 16 2014), *aff'd*, 781 F.3d 335 (6th Cir. 2015).

to obtain such information during the 30 day period in which [surety] had to pay CMS' claims."[81] There was no discussion in the opinion of the fact that the 30-day period should not begin until there is "sufficient evidence" of the overpayments to the principal.

3. *Trends in Medicare Fraud*

a. License Revocations. In a 2013 statement to the U.S. Senate Committee on Homeland Security and Governmental Affairs, CMS leadership noted a decrease in the number of DMEPOS suppliers enrolled in Medicare of 14 percent over the previous six years, and attributed that decline to the requirement that such suppliers obtain a surety bond.[82] Further, more than 10,500 DMEPOS suppliers' licenses were revoked between October and December 2009 (the first three months that previously enrolled suppliers were required to obtain a bond).[83]

b. OIG Recommendations for Expanded Bond Program and Enforcement. In order to determine whether CMS was taking full advantage of the Medicare bond program, the OIG of HHS conducted an analysis of overpayments from October 2, 2009, to April 1, 2011.[84] The study resulted in a 2013 report concluding CMS lacked accurate surety bond information for "thousands of bonded suppliers," and that there were "tens of millions in uncollected overpayments."[85]

The OIG provided several recommendations: (1) improve oversight of supplier and bond data; (2) ensure CMS is making claims against sureties for all bonded suppliers with outstanding debts; (3) take advantage of the legislative authority under the Affordable Care Act of 2010 to require increased surety bond amounts for certain high-billing suppliers; and (4) revise collection guidelines to provide that a surety is liable for payments made for claims with dates of service after March 3, 2009

---

81. *Id.* at *21–22.
82. *Oversight and Business Practices of Durable Medical Equipment Companies, Statement before the Subcomm. on Fin. & Contracting Oversight of the S. Comm. on Homeland Sec. & Governmental Affs.*, 113th Cong. 8 (2013) (statement of Peter Budetti, Deputy Administrator and Director, Center for Program Integrity, CMS, and Laurence D. Wilson, Director, Chronic Care Policy Group, Center for Medicare, CMS).
83. *Id.* at 9.
84. LEVINSON, *supra* note 63.
85. *Id.* Executive Summary.

(rather than simply payments made after that date, as the prior guidelines provided).[86]

However, it appears the situation did not improve in the ensuing years. A follow-up report in September 2017 noted the data "continue to raise questions regarding the effectiveness of the procedures currently in place to track overpayments. These discrepancies raise concerns that overpayment dollars may be left unaccounted for and uncollected."[87]

Among the recommendations of the OIG in 2017 was to implement a surety bond requirement for home health providers and other providers. The report stated:

> Federal law requires surety bonds specifically for DME and home health providers. CMS has implemented this requirement for DME providers but not for home health providers. Therefore, we recommend that CMS implement the statutory requirement for home health providers to have surety bonds. Furthermore, in addition to requiring surety bonds for DME and home health providers, the Secretary of HHS has the authority to require surety bonds for other providers based on their level of risk. CMS should consider implementing a surety bond requirement for other types of Medicare providers determined to be a high financial risk to the program. Previous OIG reports found that the use of surety bonds could result in substantial recoveries for the Medicare program.[88]

As of the date of publication of this chapter, CMS has not yet implemented a surety bond requirement for home health providers, despite statutory support for doing so.

F. Underwriting and Claims Considerations

As discussed above, the primary purpose of the bond is financial protection against overpayments that are not repaid. Therefore, a brief description and understanding of the Medicare billing process and

---

86. *Id.* at 16–17.
87. DANIEL R. LEVINSON, HHS OIG, ENHANCEMENTS NEEDED IN THE TRACKING AND COLLECTION OF MEDICARE OVERPAYMENTS IDENTIFIED BY ZPICS AND PSCS 18 (2017) (OEI-03-13-00630).
88. *Id.* at 19–20.

regulatory structure is in order. Supplies provided by DMEs are covered under Medicare Part B and include items such as oxygen, wheelchairs, and prosthetic limbs. Beneficiaries typically obtain the supplies from the supplier and the supplier submits a claim to Medicare.

The applicable CMS regulations and policies set forth certain timelines for submitting a bill to CMS and timelines for reviewing the propriety of a payment. These timelines are important from an underwriting perspective as they assist the surety in its exposure assessment. Under the Patient Protection and Affordable Care Act, a DME has 12 months from the date of service to submit a claim. The processing and paying of claims are handled through regional contractors of CMS. In paying the DME, it may be discovered there was an overpayment. An overpayment is a Medicare payment the supplier received that exceeds the amounts that are due and payable. An overpayment can occur for several reasons:

- Payment for suppler services after benefits have been exhausted
- Incorrect application of deductible or coinsurance
- Payment for non-covered items
- Payment based on a charge that exceeds a reasonable charge
- Duplicate processing of claims
- Payment for items during a period of non-entitlement[89]

Overpayments are discovered or determined in several ways. There are a variety of audit schemes within CMS. The CMS contractor that administers claims and payments can conduct post-payment audits. There is also the Recovery Audit Contractor (RAC) program, which was made permanent by the Tax Relief and Health Care Act of 2006 (Public Law No. 109-432). RACs were established "for the purpose of identifying underpayments and overpayments and recouping overpayments."[90] CMS contractors or RAC contractors may reopen the consideration of a claim, subject to certain time limits.

Pursuant to 42 C.F.R. § 405.980(b), a contractor may reopen and revise its initial determination or redetermination:

(1) Within 1 year from the date of the initial determination or redetermination for any reason.

---

89. CMS, MEDICARE FINANCIAL MANAGEMENT MANUAL ch. 3 § 10.2 (rev. Jan. 2020), https://www.cms.gov/manuals/downloads/fin106c03.pdf.

90. 42 U.S.C. § 1395ddd(h).

(2) Within 4 years from the date of the initial determination or redetermination for good cause as defined in § 405.986.
(3) At any time if there exists reliable evidence as defined in § 405.902 that the initial determination was procured by fraud or similar fault as defined in § 405.902.
(4) At anytime if the initial determination is unfavorable, in whole or in part, to the party thereto, but only for the purpose of correcting a clerical error on which that determination was based.
(5) At any time to effectuate a decision issued under the coverage appeals process.

Pursuant to 42 C.F.R. § 405.986(a), "good cause" may be established when:

(1) There is new and material evidence that—
    (i) Was not available or known at the time of the determination or decision; and
    (ii) May result in a different conclusion; or
(2) The evidence that was considered in making the determination or decision clearly shows on its face that an obvious error was made at the time of the determination or decision.

Thus, claims that were submitted to CMS and were found to be proper (with no overpayment owing) may later (sometimes much later) be reopened and result in an overpayment.

Another audit scheme is the Zoned Program Integrity Contractor (ZPIC) program, the goal of which is to prevent and detect Medicare fraud. Examples of fraudulent activity include:

- Billing for supplies not provided
- Altering claim forms to obtain a higher payment amount
- Seeking duplicate payments
- Billing non-covered items
- Soliciting, offering, or receiving a kickback[91]

---

91. Holly Stockdale, Congressional Research Service, Medicare Program Integrity: Activities to Protect Medicare from Payment Errors, Fraud, and Abuse 4 (2010).

To detect fraudulent DMEs, a ZPIC would conduct billing analyses to identify improper billing patterns, perform provider audits, investigate fraud leads, and refer cases to the OIG.[92]

Although CMS employs a series of payment integrity programs meant to *prevent* overpayments, much of the payment integrity efforts occur post payment. Thus, oversight and regulation come, in large part, in the form of detecting and recouping overpayment. In other words, overpayments—from billing errors to conspiratorial fraud—are systemic. According to the GAO, $700 million in improper overpayments for DME and supplies were made from April 1, 2005, through March 31, 2006 (about 7.5 percent of total payments), skyrocketing to $2.6 billion in 2018, largely attributable to insufficient documentation.[93] And bonds are part of the remedies available to CMS for unpaid overpayments. Ironically, in the case of major billing fraud, the penal sum available to CMS under the DME bond does not seem to correlate to this exposure. According to a press release from the U.S. Attorney General for the Central District of California, a joint strike force composed of the U.S. Justice Department and the OIG of HHS charged 20 defendants in the Los Angeles area of fraudulently billing Medicare $26 million for wheelchairs, orthotic devices, and other medical equipment that was either unnecessary or never delivered.[94] Similarly, the HHS OIG found in its 2013 report that, because the bonds were limited to $50,000, "CMS cannot recover all of the overpayments owed by bonded suppliers" and $42 million of the $50 million owed by bonded suppliers will "likely remain uncollected."[95]

As noted, the bond also responds to penalties and assessments. These penalties and assessments go to the conduct of the provider. "Civil money penalty" and "Assessment" are defined in 42 C.F.R. § 424.57(a). "Civil money penalty" is defined as a sum that CMS has the authority to impose

---

92. *Id.* at 9.
93. GAO, MEDICARE: IMPROVEMENTS NEEDED TO ADDRESS IMPROPER PAYMENTS FOR MEDICAL EQUIPMENT AND SUPPLIES 1 (2007) (GAO-07-59); GAO, MEDICARE AND MEDICAID: CMS SHOULD ASSESS DOCUMENTATION NECESSARY TO IDENTIFY IMPROPER PAYMENTS 43 (2019) (GAO 19-277).
94. Press Release 09-124, U.S. Att'y Gen. for the Cent. Dist. of Cal., L.A. Medicare Fraud Strike Force Charges 20 in Health Care Fraud Cases Involving Durable Medical Equipment (Oct. 21, 2009), https://www.justice.gov/archive/usao/cac/Pressroom/pr2009/124.html.
95. LEVINSON, *supra* note 63.

under 42 C.F.R. § 402.1. This provision lists 33 instances in which a penalty may be imposed, some applicable to a supplier, including:

- Knowingly and willfully distributing a certificate of medical necessity in violation of applicable law
- Knowingly or willfully failing to make refunds to beneficiaries
- Knowingly or willfully imposing a charge for completing and submitting the standard claim form
- Engaging in prohibited contact with beneficiaries

A CMP also includes amounts the OIG can impose under section 1124A of the Social Security Act or 42 C.F.R. part 1003. Section 1003.102 sets forth the basis for a penalty and includes an extensive list of violative conduct involving the presentation of false claims, failure to disclose certain information, and failure to report certain conduct.

"Assessment" is defined as "a sum certain that CMS or the Office of Inspector General (OIG) may assess against a DMEPOS supplier under Titles XI, XVIII, or XXI of the Social Security Act or as specified in this chapter." Title XI includes penalties for knowingly filing improper claims. Title XVIII includes the various insurance programs for the aged and disabled and includes the provisions addressing payment integrity. Title XXI addresses the State Health Insurance Assistance Program.

Considering the broad range of obligations brought into the bond through the reference to "assessments" and "civil money penalty," the obligations being secured by the bond are more than the financial obligation to repay overpayments. The responsibility for assessments and CMPs implicates the conduct of the DME supplier. Fulfillment of the obligations secured by the bond requires that the DME has the financial wherewithal to repay overpayment or to pay the assessment or penalty, and (just as importantly) has an operation with the necessary experience, controls, and integrity to *avoid* overpayments, penalties, and assessments.

In this regard, the underwriting of the DME bond should focus on the following issues and information:

- **Enrollment application form CMS-855S**. This is the form the supplier submits to enroll in the Medicare program and receive an NPI. It gives a very good snapshot of the DME—the type of supplier, products to be furnished, accreditation information, whether there are any final adverse actions, medical record storage practices, and whether it uses a billing agency to submit claims.

- **A copy of the last Medicare audit.** The underwriter should ask for audits by the contractor, RAC contractor audits, ZPIC audits, and audits under the Comprehensive Error Rate Testing (CERT) program.[96]
- **Accreditation.** Most DMEs (except certain pharmacies) are required to be accredited as meeting quality standards under Medicare Part B. If the DME must be accredited, the accreditation information will shed light on the DME's standards of operation.
- **The results of the latest internal audit.**
- **The supplier compliance plan.** In particular, the plan should address the operational aspects and supplier standards contained in 42 C.F.R. § 424.57(c). This provision contains 30 operational standards, including:
    - Operates its business and furnishes Medicare-covered items in compliance with the applicable laws
    - Has not made, or caused to be made, any false statement or misrepresentation of a material fact on its application for billing privileges
    - Must have the application for billing privileges signed by an individual whose signature binds a supplier
    - Fills orders, fabricates, or fits items from its own inventory or by contracting with other companies for the purchase of items necessary to fill the order
    - Advises beneficiaries that they may either rent or purchase inexpensive or routinely purchased DME
    - Honors all warranties expressed and implied under applicable state law
    - Maintains a physical facility on an appropriate site
    - Permits CMS to conduct on-site inspections to ascertain supplier compliance with the supplier standards
    - Agrees not to make a direct solicitation of a Medicare beneficiary

---

96. Under the CERT program, the CERT contractor selects random samples of claims from each Medicare claims processing contractor for medical review. For each claim selected, the CERT contractor verifies that the services were billed correctly, and that the decisions regarding the payment were proper.

- Must comply with the ownership/financial control disclosure provisions in 42 C.F.R. § 420.206
- Must have a complaint resolution protocol to address beneficiary complaints

A sound assessment of the quality of the DME's organization is crucial to avoid a bond loss. As required in the regulations and as noted earlier, the surety agrees to pay a claim within 30 days of receiving notice of the claim and "sufficient evidence" to establish the surety's liability. As noted above, "Sufficient evidence" is defined in 42 C.F.R. § 424.57(a) to mean: "documents CMS may supply to the surety in order to establish that a DMEPOS supplier had received Medicare funds in excess of the amount due and payable under the statute and regulations, the amount of a CMP, or the amount of some other assessment against the DMEPOS supplier."

The definition indicates, with regard to penalties and assessments, the documentation needs to establish the amount of the overpayment and also show such amount was "in excess" of the amount payable. This certainly implies the surety would have the ability to contest the propriety of the assessment or penalty. However, given the 30-day payment requirement, the ability of a surety to conduct a thorough analysis is significantly curtailed. As discussed above, the surety could argue the notice or claim from CMS did not contain "sufficient evidence" to show the surety's liability (and therefore did not trigger the 30-day period). However, it is possible the surety will not be able to thoroughly analyze the documents (and compare them to the Medicare guidelines to determine appropriateness) within the 30-day window, even if the documents did contain "sufficient evidence." In any event, the difficulty in analyzing and defending claims puts an even greater importance on thoroughly underwriting DMEPOS suppliers, to avoid future claims.

III. State Bond Requirements

In addition to the federal requirements, a handful of states require providers of health services or supplies furnish a bond as a condition for participation in the state Medicaid program. This discussion sets forth these state bond requirements.

A. *Florida*

Certain Medicaid providers in Florida may be required to furnish a $50,000 surety bond. Before entering into the provider agreement, or as a condition of continuing participation in the Medicaid program, the agency may also require Medicaid providers reimbursed on a fee-for-services basis or fee-schedule basis that is not cost based, to post a surety bond not to exceed $50,000 or the total amount billed by the provider to the program during the current or most recent calendar year, whichever is greater.[97] Of the different types of providers, only the bond for DME providers is universally applicable.[98]

DMEs must provide a surety bond of $50,000 for each provider location up to a maximum of five bonds statewide or an aggregate bond of $250,000 statewide per federal Employer Identification Number.[99] DMEs owned by a government entity or operating within a pharmacy currently enrolled as a Medicaid pharmacy provider are exempt from the bond requirement. Certain physician groups and orthotists/prosthetists are also exempt.[100]

As for HHAs, only those that are "bad actors" are required to furnish a surety bond in the amount of $50,000 or the total amount billed to Medicaid during the most recent calendar year, whichever is greater. Specifically, a surety bond is required only for HHAs that have been sanctioned or terminated by Florida's Medicaid program within the past five years. Further, HHAs that must furnish a bond need only do so for three years. If, at the end of three years, there has been no other adverse action against the HHA, the HHA is exempt from the bond requirement. Thus, with respect to the HHA bond requirement, there is adverse selection against the surety. The bond's obligations relate to the provider's conduct and the HHA already has a history of bad conduct.[101]

Physician groups that are more than 50 percent owned by nonphysicians and transportation services that are not ambulance, air ambulance, government and municipal transport, private transportation, and nonprofit transportation must furnish a surety bond.[102] Laboratories must provide a bond for their first year of enrollment in the Medicaid program.[103]

---

97. Fla. Stat. Ann. § 409.907.
98. Agency for Health Care Administration, Florida Medicaid: Provider General Handbook 2-30 (2012) [hereinafter AHCA Handbook].
99. Fla. Stat. Ann. § 409.912(45)(b)(7).
100. AHCA Handbook, *supra* note 98, at 2-30.
101. *Id.* at 2-31.
102. *Id.* at 2-33.
103. *Id.*

The scope of the surety's obligation is described in the bond form (AHCA Form 5000-1064 (June 2019)). The bond is provided to "insure compliance with the attached provider agreement." The condition of the bond is fairly broad—the provider will "conform to and abide by the provisions of the above statute, implementing regulations and bulletins . . . and . . . honestly and faithfully appl[y] funds received, and faithfully and honestly perform[] all obligations and undertakings made pursuant to the provisions of such statute . . . ."

Thus, what is being secured is informed by the provider agreement, the underlying statute, regulation, and other documents. First, the controlling agency, the Agency for Health Care Administration (AHCA), makes payments to a provider in accordance with the provider agreement with that provider.[104] The provider agreement sets forth details regarding the provider's obligations. Florida Statutes Annotated section 409.907(1) states:

> Each provider agreement shall require the provider to comply fully with all state and federal laws pertaining to the Medicaid program, as well as all federal, state, and local laws pertaining to licensure, if required, and the practice of any of the healing arts, and shall require the provider to provide services or goods of not less than the scope and quality it provides to the general public.

Second, the applicable statutes regarding the Florida Medicaid program are Florida Statutes Annotated sections 409.901 through 409.9205 and establish the provider's obligations. For example, section 409.920(2)(a) prohibits a provider from engaging in certain conduct:

> A person may not:
>
> 1. Knowingly make, cause to be made, or aid and abet in the making of any false statement or false representation of a material fact, by commission or omission, in any claim submitted to the agency or its fiscal agent or a managed care plan for payment.
>
> 2. Knowingly make, cause to be made, or aid and abet in the making of a claim for items or services that are not authorized to be reimbursed by the Medicaid program.
>
> 3. Knowingly charge, solicit, accept, or receive anything of value, other than an authorized copayment from a Medicaid

---

104. Fla. Stat. Ann. § 409.907.

recipient, from any source in addition to the amount legally payable for an item or service provided to a Medicaid recipient under the Medicaid program or knowingly fail to credit the agency or its fiscal agent for any payment received from a third-party source.

4. Knowingly make or in any way cause to be made any false statement or false representation of a material fact, by commission or omission, in any document containing items of income and expense that is or may be used by the agency to determine a general or specific rate of payment for an item or service provided by a provider.

5. Knowingly solicit, offer, pay, or receive any remuneration, including any kickback, bribe, or rebate, directly or indirectly, overtly or covertly, in cash or in kind, in return for referring an individual to a person for the furnishing or arranging for the furnishing of any item or service for which payment may be made, in whole or in part, under the Medicaid program, or in return for obtaining, purchasing, leasing, ordering, or arranging for or recommending, obtaining, purchasing, leasing, or ordering any goods, facility, item, or service, for which payment may be made, in whole or in part, under the Medicaid program.

6. Knowingly submit false or misleading information or statements to the Medicaid program for the purpose of being accepted as a Medicaid provider.

7. Knowingly use or endeavor to use a Medicaid provider's identification number or a Medicaid recipient's identification number to make, cause to be made, or aid and abet in the making of a claim for items or services that are not authorized to be reimbursed by the Medicaid program.[105]

Third, the applicable regulations, Rule 59G-1.001, Florida Administrative Code *et seq.*, further define these statutory requirements.

All these sources (statutes, provider agreement, handbooks, and regulations) are needed to define the provider's obligation. Then, information from the provider is necessary to assess the provider's qualifications in the context of those obligations. The provider should furnish information similar to the information suggested to underwrite

---

105. *Id.* § 409.920.

the federal DME bond: enrollment applications, audit information, and financial information.

B. Alabama

Pursuant to Alabama Administrative Code 560-X-13-.02(5), DMEs participating in the Alabama Medicaid program are required to provide a $50,000 bond for each NPI. However, several DMEs are exempt from the requirement, subjecting the surety to adverse selection. Some of the exemptions are similar to the federal regulations (e.g., a government operated DME, physicians and DMEs in private practice making custom-made orthotics and prosthetics). However, the Alabama regulations also exempt pharmacies, small DMEs (receiving less than $100,000 in Medicaid payments in the past two years), and DMEs that have been a Medicaid provider for five years or longer with no record of impropriety.

The applicable regulations do not provide details regarding what obligations are secured by the bond and the Alabama Medicaid Agency does not have a standard form. Forms used in the market secure the DME's compliance with applicable statutes and regulations. The Provider Manual sets forth certain required conduct, including record retention, confidentiality of patient records, compliance with federal requirements, and verification of patient eligibility to receive Medicaid assistance.[106]

Underwriting should begin with an awareness that the pool of applicants consists of larger DMEs that have had some history of impropriety. Then, there should be a review of the DME's operations, finances, and controls. Again, much of the information furnished for the federal DME bond would be helpful in this case.

---

106. Alabama Medicaid Management Information System Provider Manual (Jan. 2021), https://medicaid.alabama.gov/content/Gated/7.6.1G_Archived_Manuals/7.6.1.G_PM_January_2021_Bookmarked.pdf. Section 7-1 states, "This section describes provider responsibilities such as maintenance of provider information, retention of records, release of confidential information, compliance with federal legislation, billing recipients, and agreement to the certification statement described in the Alabama Medicaid Agency Administrative Code."

C. District of Columbia

The District of Columbia Department of Health Care Finance requires certain providers furnish surety bonds as a condition to participate in the Medicaid program.

A provider of DME participating in the District of Columbia Medicaid program is required to provide a $50,000 bond for each NPI.[107] The bond responds to financial liability for "claims, suits, judgments, or damages including court costs and attorneys' fees arising out of the negligence or omissions of the provider in the course of providing services to a Medicaid beneficiary or a person believed to be a Medicaid beneficiary."[108] The scope of the obligation appears to go well beyond the obligation established in Florida and Alabama, which were tied to compliance with statutes and regulations. In the case of the District of Columbia bond requirement, the bond secures the DME's obligation to pay judgments and damages arising from the DME's negligence. The surety must ensure the DME follows not only the applicable statutes and regulations, but the general standard of care for a DME. (Notably, the regulations specifically require the DME maintain at least $300,000 in liability insurance.) The bond is a continuous bond, and a single bond penalty applies to all license periods.

Under D.C. Municipal Regulation title 29, section 947.15(e), private-duty nursing services[109] must provide a $50,000 surety bond in accordance with the federal requirement for HHAs participating in Medicaid. Therefore, although the federal requirement for HHAs is effectively not enforced (i.e., all Medicaid agencies are not required to establish the bond requirement) (see discussion above), the District of Columbia uses the requirement as the basis for the bond requirement for private-duty nursing services. The bond requirement is set forth in 42 C.F.R. § 441.16 and states:

> Except as provided in paragraph (d) of this section, each HHA that is a Medicaid participating HHA or that seeks to become a Medicaid participating HHA must—

---

107. D.C. Mun. Regs. tit. 29, § 996.4.
108. *Id.*
109. Private-duty nursing services provide care to Medicaid beneficiaries who are dependent on ventilator equipment or other life-sustaining technology and require constant nursing supervision. 65 D.C. Reg. 000408.

> (1) Obtain a surety bond that meets the requirements of this section and instructions issued by the Medicaid agency; and
> (2) Furnish a copy of the surety bond to the Medicaid agency.

The District of Columbia Department of Health Care Finance does not appear to have a standard bond form. Under 42 C.F.R. § 441.16, the bond must cover uncollected overpayments, "provided such uncollected overpayments are determined during the term of the bond and regardless of when the overpayments took place."[110] Under § 441.16(h)(3)(i), a surety's liability "may be extinguished" upon providing the Medicaid agency 60 days prior notice. However, if the surety bond is not replaced, the surety remains on the risk for an additional two-year period.[111]

Similarly, skilled duty nursing services must furnish a $50,000 bond under D.C. Municipal Regulation title 29, section 9901 in accordance with federal requirements.

A personal care aid must provide a surety bond under D.C. Municipal Regulation title 29, section 5011.2. The bond must meet the following requirements:

> A continuous surety bond in the amount of fifty thousand dollars ($50,000) against all PCA [personal care aid] services claims, suits, judgments, or damages including court costs and attorney's fees arising out of the negligence or omissions of the Provider in the course of providing services to a Medicaid beneficiary or a person believed to be a Medicaid beneficiary.

This is similar to that of the bond required of providers of DME.

D. Iowa

In Iowa, HHAs participating in the Medicaid program must furnish a $50,000 surety bond.[112] The bond guarantees the payment of any uncollected overpayment made by the Iowa Department of Human Services to the HHA during the term of the bond. "The bond shall provide that payment may be demanded from the surety after available administrative collection methods for collecting from the home health

---

110. 42 C.F.R. § 441.16(h)(2) (2020).
111. *Id.*
112. IOWA ADMIN. CODE r. 441-77.9(249A).

agency have been exhausted."[113] The regulations require the surety to make payment within 60 days of demand. The surety may cancel the bond with 60 days prior notice.

E. Indiana

Starting in 2013, Indiana has required transportation providers to obtain a surety bond to enroll in the Indiana Medicaid program. The bond must meet the following requirements:

- The bond must be continuously in effect for at least three years after the application is made.
- The bond must provide liability coverage of at least $50,000.
- The bond must name the transportation provider as the principal and the Indiana Office of Medicaid Policy and Planning as the obligee, and the person issuing the bond (and that person's heirs, successors, etc.) as surety.[114]

The bond must provide that the surety will pay within 30 days after receiving "sufficient evidence to establish surety's liability" of any "duplicate, erroneous, or false claim that was previously paid" to the transportation provider, plus interest, along with additional sanctions available under Burns Indiana Code section 12-15-22.[115]

Additionally, the surety's liability remains until the last day of the bond coverage period, even if the provider agreement is terminated.[116] In other words, the bond remains in effect for its full term despite any termination of the transportation provider's underlying agreement, and the surety would remain liable for any overpayments made to the provider during such bond term. Finally, actions on such bond may be brought by the Indiana Office of Medicaid Policy and Planning or by the Indiana Attorney General.[117]

---

113. *Id.*
114. IND. CODE § 12-15-11-2.5(d).
115. *Id.* § 12-15-11-2.5(d)(7).
116. *Id.* § 12-15-11-2.5(d)(8).
117. *Id.* § 12-15-11-2.5(d)(9).

F. Minnesota

Minnesota requires a variety of entities to obtain bonds related to Medicaid, specifically DMEPOS suppliers, personal care assistance providers, community-based personal assistance providers, and other providers. Each type of entity and the requirements are discussed below in more detail.

1. DMEPOS Suppliers

Minnesota requires a Medicaid bond to be obtained by "all durable medical equipment, prosthetics, orthotics, and supplies (DMEPOS) medical suppliers" to the extent they "can purchase medical equipment or supplies for sale or rental to the general public and [are] able to perform or arrange for necessary repairs to and maintenance of equipment offered for sale or rental."[118]

If an enrolling or reenrolling DMEPOS supplier's Medicaid revenue is $300,000 or less, then the bond amount is $50,000. If its Medicaid revenue is more than $300,000, then the supplier must purchase a $100,000 bond.[119] The bond "must allow for recovery of costs and fees in pursuing a claim on the bond."[120]

Per the statute, the bond must be annually renewed and designate the Minnesota Department of Human Services as obligee, and in a form approved by the commissioner of Human Services.[121]

There are some medical suppliers exempt from the statutory requirement of obtaining a Medicaid bond, including federally qualified health centers, HHAs, pharmacies, and rural health clinics.[122]

2. Personal Care Assistance Providers

Minnesota also requires "personal care assistance providers" to obtain a $50,000 surety bond if the provider's Medicaid revenue in the prior calendar year is $300,000 or less.[123] Those providers with Medicaid

---

118. MINN. STAT. § 256B.04, subdiv. 21(l)(1) and (3).
119. *Id.* § 256B.04, subdiv. 21(l)(2).
120. *Id.*
121. *Id.* § 256B.04, subdiv. 21(l)(1).
122. *Id.* Note that the statute and amendment notes do not set forth any particular rationale for such exemptions.
123. *Id.* § 256B.0659, subdiv. 21(a)(2).

revenue exceeding $300,000 must obtain a $100,000 bond.[124] The bond must "be in a form approved by the commissioner, must be renewed annually, and must allow for recovery of costs and fees in pursuing a claim on the bond."[125]

A court addressed this type of bond in *Washington International Insurance Co. v. Hannaya Health Care*.[126] In that matter, the state brought a criminal complaint against the principal, a personal care agency, based on fraudulent billings. Following a guilty plea, there was an agreed-upon restitution order in the amount of approximately $32,000. Thereafter, the Department of Human Services submitted a claim in the amount of approximately $42,000 under the principal's $50,000 surety bond, and the surety paid the full claim amount, plus interest. The surety subsequently brought an indemnification suit against the principal and indemnitor.[127]

The principal and indemnitor brought a third-party claim against the state of Minnesota under theories of "breach of contract" and "unjust enrichment," arguing the state breached the plea agreement by collecting additional civil damages on the bond (in excess of the restitution amount).[128] The court of appeals found there was no release from civil claims contained in the plea agreement. Further, the court held that the bond itself allowed the commissioner recovery on the bond "in addition to all other legal remedies" and therefore held that the state was not restricted to the restitution amount with respect to its bond claim.[129] The court therefore affirmed the trial court's dismissal of the third-party claim.[130]

3. *Community-Based Personal Assistance Providers*

Minnesota similarly requires a $50,000 or $100,000 bond (using the same scale as for personal care assistance providers discussed above) for "community first services and supports" or "CFSS" providers.[131] Such

---

124. *Id.*
125. *Id.*
126. Case No. A19-1174, 2020 Minn. App. Unpub. LEXIS 214 (Minn. Ct. App. Mar. 16, 2020).
127. *Id.* at *2–3.
128. *Id.* at *3.
129. *Id.* at *5–6.
130. *Id.* at *7.
131. Minn. Stat. § 256B.85, subdiv. 12(a)(2).

bonds must be renewed annually and allow for recovery of costs and fees in pursuing a bond claim.[132]

4. Other Providers

In addition to the preceding bond requirements, the Minnesota Department of Human Services "may" require a "provider" to obtain a surety bond as a condition of enrollment or reenrollment under certain circumstances, including (1) a failure to demonstrate financial viability; (2) a determination by the department that there is "significant evidence of or potential for fraud and abuse by the provider"; or (3) the provider is considered "high-risk" per 42 C.F.R. § 455.450.[133]

The bond is in the amount of $100,000 or 10 percent of the provider's Medicaid payment for the previous 12 months (whichever is greater).[134] The bond must name the Department of Human Services as obligee and allow for the recovery of "costs and fees in pursuing a claim on the bond."[135]

G. Texas

Texas's rules requiring Medicaid providers to obtain a surety bond were adopted effective December 31, 2012. The requirements are embodied in the Texas Administrative Code.[136] Providers are only required to obtain a bond if (1) the provider has been identified by a federal or state agency as having a history of (or potential for) fraud, waste, or abuse, or (2) the Texas Health and Human Services Commission (HHSC), in its sole discretion, determines that a provider—based on its conduct—should be required to obtain a bond.[137] Such conduct can include "falsifying information or any material misrepresentation."[138]

If a Medicaid bond is required, the provider must maintain a current bond to continue participation in Medicaid.[139] The bond must be in an

---

132. *Id.*
133. *Id.* § 256B.04, subdiv. 21(m).
134. *Id.*
135. *Id.*
136. 1 TEX. ADMIN. CODE § 352.15.
137. *Id.* § 352.15(a).
138. *Id.* § 352.15(a)(2).
139. *Id.* § 352.15(b).

amount of at least $50,000 and must list the provider as principal and the HHSC as obligee.[140]

The bond must provide that the surety is liable for "uncollected overpayments determined to have occurred during the term of the bond, regardless of when the overpayments are discovered."[141] Furthermore, the surety remains liable on the bond for two years after its expiration (for overpayments that occurred during the term of the bond) unless the provider furnishes a new bond.[142] Additionally, the surety remains liable (as to services during the bond period) for two years after the HHSC terminates the provider agreement.[143]

The bond must also provide that the surety's liability to the HHSC is not affected by any action of the provider or surety to terminate or limit the scope of the bond, or the provider's ceasing operation, transferring ownership interest, or filing for bankruptcy protection.[144] The surety may only terminate its liability by providing the HHSC written notice of its intent to terminate the bond no later than 30 days before the effective date of such termination.[145] The surety's liability will also be terminated when the provider furnishes a new bond.[146]

The regulations do not provide the surety with any means to avoid liability after receiving a claim. They state "the Surety guarantees that upon receipt of written request for payment by HHSC or its designee, the Surety will reimburse Medicaid . . . the amount in the request up to the stated amount of the bond."[147]

Given the obligation to pay any claim received, and the fact that bonds are only required for high-risk providers, thorough underwriting would seem to be of prime importance for Texas Medicaid bonds.

Conclusion

Under the statutory and regulatory framework of Medicaid and Medicare, there are a variety of surety bonds. At the federal level, the

---

140. *Id.* § 352.15(e)(2) and (f).
141. *Id.* § 352.15(g)(1).
142. *Id.* § 352.15(g)(2)(A).
143. *Id.* § 352.15(g)(2)(B).
144. *Id.* § 352.15(g)(3).
145. *Id.* § 352.15(g)(4)(A).
146. *Id.* § 352.15(g)(4)(B).
147. *Id.* § 352.15(g)(5).

primary bond is the bond that must be furnished by suppliers of DME. Improper payments remain as big a problem today, even 12 years after the bond's implementation, and yet loss experience remains low. The obligation is largely a financial one, as the bond secures the repayment of overpayments. Given the striking data regarding the current amount of improper payments and the robust audit schemes in place, it is not a matter of *if* an overpayment will be discovered, but *when* it will be discovered. Thus, the focus of the underwriting should be on the bond principal's demonstrated history and financial wherewithal to repay the government. Unfortunately (or perhaps fortunately), despite the existence of the bond for more than a decade, there is very little in terms of case law to test the contours of the bond obligation to guide further the claims handling and underwriting. CMS regulations and administrative materials remain the primary guides.

At the state level, six states and the District of Columbia require bonds to secure providers' obligations under their Medicaid programs (District of Columbia, Alabama, Florida, Iowa, Indiana, Minnesota, and Texas). The type of provider that must provide the bond varies, including equipment suppliers, care providers, and HHAs. The nature of the obligations varies, ranging from compliance with statutes to repayment of overpayments. As with the federal bond, the regulations provide the guideposts. In addition to the bond form, underwriters and claim professionals should pay special attention to the underlying regulations and administrative materials.

APPENDIX A

DME Bond Form—Single

Surety Bond

Suppliers of Durable Medical Equipment, Prosthetics, Orthotics and Supplies

Medicare Program

KNOW ALL PERSONS BY THESE PRESENTS, that subject to the terms, conditions and limitations of this bond, ________________, as Principal, and __[SURETY NAME] AND [MAILING ADDRESS] ____________________, a corporation organized and existing under the laws of ____________________, as Surety, are held and firmly bound unto the Centers for Medicare & Medicaid Services, an agency of the United States Department of Health and Human Services, ("CMS"), as Obligee, in the Penal Sum of ____________________ Dollars ($__________) for the payment of which Principal and Surety bind themselves, their heirs, executors, administrators and assigns, jointly and severally, by these presents.

WHEREAS, Principal is enrolled in or is seeking to be enrolled in the Medicare program as a supplier of durable medical equipment, prosthetics, orthotics and supplies ("DMEPOS"); and

WHEREAS, pursuant to Section 4312(a) of the Balanced Budget Act of 1997 (Pub. L. 105-33) and 42 CFR § 424.57, the Principal is required to provide a surety bond as a condition of participation in the Medicare program, and this bond is provided in compliance with the supplier's obligations as set forth in those authorities.

NOW THEREFORE, the condition of this Bond is that if the Principal shall pay the Obligee any unpaid claims, civil money penalties and assessments (as such terms are defined by 42 CFR § 424.57(a)) then this Bond shall be null and void, otherwise to remain in full force and effect, subject, however, to the following:

1. Principal and Surety are liable under this Bond for only the amount of any unpaid claim, civil money penalty or assessment (as such terms are defined by 42 CFR § 424.57(a)) imposed by CMS or the Office of Inspector General, plus accrued interest,

for which the Principal is responsible and for which, subject to Paragraph 7, the Obligee first demands payment from the Surety during the term of this Bond; provided, however, that any claim under this Bond must be related to overpayments or other events that occurred on or after March 3, 2009.

2. Surety agrees to pay a claim within 30 days of receiving written notice of the claim and sufficient evidence (as such term is defined by 42 CFR § 424.57(a)) to establish Surety's liability under this Bond.
3. CMS is the sole Obligee of this Bond, and no action may be brought on it by, or for the use or benefit of, any person or entity other than CMS or its contractors.
4. Regardless of the number of years this Bond is in effect, the number of premiums paid, or the number of claims made, the Surety's aggregate liability shall not be more than the penal sum of this Bond.
5. Subject to Paragraph 7, the Surety's liability under this Bond shall terminate and the Surety shall have no further liability upon the effective date of cancellation or expiration of this Bond by the Surety or Principal in accordance with Paragraph 6 of this Bond.
6. The Surety or Principal may cancel this Bond by providing written notice of such cancellation to the Obligee. Cancellation or expiration shall be effective 30 days after notice of cancellation or expiration is sent to the Obligee's contractor, the National Supplier Clearinghouse, provided such notice is actually received.
7. In the event this Bond is cancelled or expires, and the Principal fails to submit a new bond to the Obligee, the Surety remains liable for unpaid claims, civil money penalties or assessments that were imposed or assessed by CMS or the Office of Inspector General during the 2 years following the effective date of cancellation or expiration of this Bond.

In witness whereof, the undersigned Principal and Surety have set their hands and seals on this ____ day of __________, 20__.

Principal

____

Surety

____

DME Bond Form—Schedule

Surety Bond

Suppliers of Durable Medical Equipment, Prosthetics, Orthotics and Supplies

Medicare Program

Schedule Bond

KNOW ALL PERSONS BY THESE PRESENTS, that subject to the terms, conditions and limitations of this bond, _______________, as Principal, and __ [SURETY NAME] AND [MAILING ADDRESS] ______________________________, a corporation organized and existing under the laws of ____________________, as Surety, are held and firmly bound unto the Centers for Medicare & Medicaid Services, an agency of the United States Department of Health and Human Services, ("CMS"), as Obligee, in the Penal Sum not exceeding the Limit of Liability specified for each National Provider Identifier ("NPI") in the attached schedule for the payment of which Principals and Surety bind themselves, their heirs, executors, administrators and assigns, jointly and severally, by these presents.

WHEREAS, Principal is enrolled in or is seeking to be enrolled in the Medicare program as a supplier of durable medical equipment, prosthetics, orthotics and supplies ("DMEPOS") under the NPIs set forth in the attached schedule; and

WHEREAS, pursuant to Section 4312(a) of the Balanced Budget Act of 1997 (Pub. L. 105-33) and 42 CFR § 424.57, the Principal is required to provide a surety bond as a condition of participation in the Medicare program, and this bond is provided in compliance with the supplier's obligations as set forth in those authorities.

NOW THEREFORE, the condition of this Bond is that if the Principals shall pay the Obligee any unpaid claims, civil money penalties and assessments (as such terms are defined by 42 CFR § 424.57(a)) then this Bond shall be null and void, otherwise to remain in full force and effect, subject, however, to the following:

8. Principal and Surety are liable under this Bond for only the amount of any unpaid claim, civil money penalty or assessment imposed by CMS or the Office of Inspector General, plus accrued interest, for which the Principal is responsible and for which,

subject to Paragraph 7, the Obligee first demands payment from the Surety during the term of this Bond; provided, however, that any claim under this Bond must be related to overpayments or other events that occurred on or after March 3, 2009.

9. Surety agrees to pay a claim within 30 days of receiving written notice of the claim and sufficient evidence (as such term is defined by 42 CFR § 424.57(a)) to establish Surety's liability under this Bond.
10. CMS is the sole Obligee of this Bond, and no action may be brought on it by, or for the use or benefit of, any person or entity other than CMS or its contractors.
11. Regardless of the number of years this Bond is in effect, the number of premiums paid, or the number of claims made, the Surety's aggregate liability for any one NPI shall not be more than the Limit of Liability specified in the attached schedule for that NPI.
12. Subject to Paragraph 7, the Surety's liability under this Bond shall terminate and the Surety shall have no further liability upon the effective date of cancellation or expiration of this Bond by the Surety or Principal in accordance with Paragraph 6 of this Bond.
13. The Surety or Principal may cancel this Bond by providing written notice of such cancellation to the Obligee. Cancellation or expiration shall be effective 30 days after notice of cancellation or expiration is sent to the Obligee's contractor, the National Supplier Clearinghouse, provided such notice is actually received. The Surety may cancel this Bond as to specified NPIs or in its entirety.
14. In the event this Bond is cancelled or expires, and the Principal fails to submit a new bond to the Obligee, the Surety remains liable for unpaid claims, civil money penalties or assessments that were imposed or assessed by CMS or the Office of Inspector General during the 2 years following the effective date of cancellation or expiration of this Bond.

In witness whereof, the undersigned Principal and Surety have set their hands and seals on this ____ day of __________, 20__.

Principal

____

Surety

____

Schedule

This Schedule amends and becomes a part of Surety Bond No. ______________________________. The Surety's liability for bond claims involving a particular National Provider Identifier ("NPI") shall not exceed the applicable Limit of Liability set forth in the Schedule below. All other provisions of the Bond remain unchanged.

Principal (Legal Business Name)/Address/NPI/Tax Identification Number/NSC—PTAN/Limit of Liability

Change Rider for Schedule Bond

Schedule Change Rider (Rider)

This Rider amends the Schedule attached to Surety Bond No. ______________________________ written by _____________ as Surety and __________ as Principal (Bond). This Rider is effective as of ____________________________ (Effective Date).

Principal (Legal Business Name)	**Address**	**NPI**	**Tax Identification Number**	**NSC/PTAN**	**Limit of Liability**
ADD					
DELETE					

The NPIs shown in this Rider are (in addition to) (and/or) (deleted) from the NPIs appearing in the Schedule attached to Bond No.

________________________. As to each of the added NPIs set forth in this Rider, the Principal and Surety are liable under this Bond for only the amount of any unpaid claim, civil money penalty or assessment imposed by CMS or the Office of Inspector General, plus accrued interest, for which the Principal is responsible and for which the Obligee first demands payment from the Surety on or after the Effective Date of the Rider and during the term of this Bond, up to the Limit of Liability set forth in this Rider. As to each of the deleted NPIs set forth in this Schedule, the Surety's liability under this Bond shall terminate and the Surety shall have no further liability as of the Effective Date of this Rider. However, if the Principal fails to submit a new bond to the Obligee for an NPI deleted by this Rider, the Surety remains liable for unpaid claims, civil money penalties or assessments that were imposed or assessed by CMS or the Office of Inspector General during the 2 years following the Effective Date of this Rider, for that NPI.

All other terms and conditions of this Bond remain in effect.

Surety:
By ____

Principal:
By ____

CHAPTER 2

DEVELOPERS OR SUBDIVISION BONDS

Michael J. Dudek
Ralph J. Kooy
T. Scott Leo

I. The Unique Nature of Subdivision Bonds[1]

Subdivision bonds secure the performance of public improvements required by ordinance or regulation of municipal governments and other government entities on privately developed properties. These bonds often refer to a subdivision improvement agreement, an infrastructure improvement agreement, an annexation agreement, or a planned development agreement between the municipality and the principal that defines the scope of the improvements required by the municipality for subdivision. The principal usually is the owner of the property upon which the bonded subdivision improvements are to be performed.[2] There are no other types of bonds, contract or commercial, that involve improvements to property owned by the principal.

---

1. The original version of this chapter appeared in the 2001 edition of THE LAW OF MISCELLANEOUS AND COMMERCIAL SURETY BONDS (Todd C. Kazlow & Bruce C. King eds., 2001) and a subsequent version of this chapter appears in THE LAW OF COMMERCIAL SURETY AND MISCELLANEOUS BONDS (Bruce C. King et al. eds., 2d ed. 2012). Portions of this chapter are borrowed liberally from these earlier works. The authors of this chapter focused more on recent developments of the law of subdivision bonds than on providing a history or survey of the law. The earlier chapters address the history of these bonds in greater detail than presented here and should be referred to for that information. The authors thank their predecessor authors for their thorough and insightful work, which helped considerably in the preparation of this chapter.
2. There are instances where the principal may lease property for which the principal may need to obtain an improvement or restoration bond. But most subdivision bonds are issued on behalf of principals that own and develop private property.

Because the subdivision bond obligations are derived from statutes and ordinances that prescribe the use and development of the properties, they often are described as securing obligations that "run with the land." A successor developer, therefore, acquiring the properties may also acquire the obligation to install the subdivision improvements. As described below, sureties have asserted this principle with some success to argue that successor developers have liability for the subdivision improvements.

In a bankruptcy proceeding of the principal, the fact that the principal owns the property means that any improvement or act to secure or lien the property requires relief from the automatic stay. Ordinarily, a surety, as a joint and several obligor with the principal, would not have the benefit of the principal's automatic stay when an obligee asserts a claim against the bond. Additionally, a creditor asserting a lien against a non-debtor obligee's property may not need to lift the stay where the lien relates back to the date of the work or contract. The sale of the principal's property in bankruptcy has given rise to disputes over the ability of the bankruptcy court to strip away obligations that "run with the land" or to bar successor liability suits through the release and exculpation clauses of chapter 11 plans.

Subdivision bonds involve the construction of improvements on real property, like contract bonds, but are classed as commercial bonds. For that reason, they can be viewed as the platypuses of commercial surety—the egg-laying mammals of commercial bonds. Subdivision bond claims tasks and transactional documents are akin to the procedures and documents adopted in contract bond claims. The claims representatives may need to review bids for the work, evaluate the quality of construction work, deal with construction lien claims, and even deal with payment bond claims.

The platypus-like nature of subdivision bonds may explain why claimants and courts are tempted to treat these bonds as contract bonds for public works. Notwithstanding the unambiguous language of the bonds, and the unsound policy in expanding the scope of these bonds to cover payment and performance obligations, at least one court since the last edition of this book held that subdivision bonds are effectively bonds for performance and payment of public improvements.[3]

---

3. Lake Cnty. Grading Co., LLC v. Vill. of Antioch, 19 N.E.3d 615 (Ill. 2014).

This chapter offers an overview of subdivision bond law and practice as did the chapter in the second edition of *The Law of Commercial Surety and Miscellaneous Bonds*. But it also addresses in greater depth specific issues arising in the cases decided since the second edition. Those issues include the obligation of successor developers to the surety; the blurring of the distinction between subdivision bonds and bonds for public works; the treatment of subdivision bonds in bankruptcy; and collusive deals between the obligee and successor developer to impose the cost of improvements on the original developer's surety. The treatment of these issues by the courts is not entirely favorable for the surety industry. The impact of these cases underscores the need for surety lawyers and surety professionals to understand the law and to diligently handle claims.

II. Legislative Origin of Subdivision Bonds

A. *Statutes and Ordinances*

The law relating to subdivision of land is entirely a creature of legislation.[4] The general purpose and intent is to regulate and control the design and improvement of a subdivision. This legislation therefore facilitates the coordination of subdivision planning (lot size, configuration, street patterns, and utility easements), as well as overall community planning.[5]

Statutes and ordinances aim to ensure that the developer properly installs streets, sewers, lighting, sidewalks, and drains prior to their dedication to the public body and its taking over their maintenance.[6] The

4. *See, e.g.*, Pennington Homes, Inc. v. Stanhope, 197 A.2d 870 (N.J. 1964).
5. The basic purpose of a subdivision performance bond is to "assure those who purchase homes in a new subdivision that they will receive the public improvements that were a large part of the inducement to purchase lots and/or homes in that development." Town of Southington v. Commercial Union Ins. Co., 735 A.2d 835, 839 (Conn. App. Ct. 1999), *rev'd*, 738 A.2d 1093 (Conn. 1999); Town of Southington v. Commercial Union Ins. Co., 757 A.2d 549 (Conn. 2000); H.N. & Frances C. Berger Found. v. Perez, 159 Cal. Rptr. 3d 434 (Cal. Ct. App. 2013).
6. *See, e.g.*, Evola v. Wendt Constr. Co., 338 P.2d 498 (Cal. Dist. Ct. App. 1959) (the Subdivision Map Act discussed in this case has since been amended).

goal is to prevent the subdivision from becoming an undue burden on the community and local taxpayers.[7]

B. The Subdivision Agreement

Surety bonds usually secure an underlying obligation or contract.[8] If there is any document that might fulfill the role of the underlying obligation in the subdivision bond context (in addition to the ordinance prescribing the development of the property), it is the subdivision agreement or other agreement that the developer enters into with the public body. This agreement can be called a subdivision agreement, an annexation agreement, or a development agreement.

These agreements may include requirements for developing the properties in some detail, such as streets, grading, pavement, gutters, curbs, sidewalks, street lighting, shade trees, surveyor's monuments, water mains, culverts, storm sewers, sanitary sewers or other means of sewerage disposal, drainage structures, erosion control, sediment control, landscaping, and public improvements of open space. The agreements often include a warranty of the public development work for a period of one year or more,[9] and may require the developer to furnish a maintenance bond.[10]

---

7. "The reason for requiring the subdivider to install street improvements is directly related to the public health, safety and welfare. Such a requirement assures suitable access routes, advances the objectives of the community plan, and protects the municipality and its taxpayers from the burden of constructing additional streets to accommodate new developments." Gen. Ins. Co. of Am. v. City of Colorado Springs, 638 P.2d 752, 757 (Colo. 1982); *see also* Fleck v. Nat'l Prop. Mgmt., Inc., 590 P.2d 1254, 1257 (Utah 1979).
8. RESTATEMENT (THIRD) OF SURETYSHIP AND GUARANTY § 1 (1996).
9. *See, e.g.*, CAL. GOV'T CODE § 66499.9(c) (West 2021).
10. Maintenance bonds may present their own unique challenges for sureties, including the extension of the surety's exposure to claims for a substantial period of time after the completion of the public improvements. Moreover, the penal sum of the maintenance bond, in the experience of some of the authors, may range from as little as 10 percent to as much as 50 percent or more of the total cost of the improvements. These issues, however, and others that may arise as a result of the surety issuing maintenance bonds, are beyond the scope of this chapter due to the breadth of significant case law discussing these types of bonds. Such case law is widely available

III. Common Terms of Subdivision Bonds

The key purpose of the provisions of subdivision bonds is to secure the performance of the subdivision improvements by the developer in accordance with the plans and ordinances of the public body.[11] Subdivision bonds are financial assurances that a developer of either residential or commercial land will complete the requisite improvements.[12]

---

should the reader be so inclined to investigate further. *See generally* Lower Salford Twp. v. Int'l Fid. Ins. Co., No. 09-cv-5081, 2010 WL 1741356, at *3–4 (E.D. Pa. Apr. 27, 2010) (surety not responsible under maintenance bond for improvements developer failed to construct, only for "defective materials and workmanship" in already constructed improvements); Legion Manor, Inc. v. Mun. Counsel, 231 A.2d 201 (N.J. 1967) (discussing the differences between performance bonds and maintenance bonds); Itzen & Robertson, Inc. v. Bd. of Health, 222 A.2d 769 (N.J. Super. Ct. App. Div. 1966) (municipal ordinance that compelled installer of sewage disposal system to furnish maintenance bond was beyond scope of statute defining powers of local boards of health); Wright v. Town of La Grange, 694 N.Y.S.2d 862 (N.Y. Sup. Ct. 1999) (holding that town acted in arbitrary manner by refusing to return security for maintenance bond upon expiration of bond when town had not provided notice to developer prior to expiration of bond of any corrective measures needed and it was questionable whether the public improvements in need of remediation were even covered by the bond); S.C. Pub. Serv. Comm'n v. Colonial Constr. Co., 266 S.E.2d 76 (S.C. 1980) (maintenance bond only covered costs of maintenance and repairs for existing sewer facility, but did not cover cost of improvements mandated by administrative regulations enacted after the execution of the bond).

11. *See, e.g.*, CAL. GOV'T CODE § 66499 (West 2021); CONN. GEN. STAT. § 8-25 (West 2011); N.J. STAT. ANN. § 40:55D-53(a) (West 2021); OKLA. STAT. tit. 11, § 47-114 (West 2020); WASH. REV. CODE § 58.17.130 (West 2021).

12. The basic purpose of a subdivision performance bond is to "assure those who purchase homes in a new subdivision that they will receive the public improvements that were a large part of the inducement to purchase lots and/or homes in that development." Town of Southington v. Commercial Union Ins. Co., 735 A.2d 835, 839 (Conn. App. Ct. 1999), *rev'd*, 738 A.2d 1093 (Conn. 1999); Town of Southington v. Commercial Union Ins. Co., 757 A.2d 549 (Conn. 2000); H.N. & Frances C. Berger Found. v. Perez, 159 Cal. Rptr. 3d 434 (Cal. Ct. App. 2013).

Subdivision bonds come in different forms and may have different terms. Typically, they are indemnity bonds requiring performance or payment up to the penal sum of the bond from a surety if a developer defaults on its obligations under the subdivision agreement. In some jurisdictions, they are treated as either pure forfeiture bonds or financial guarantee bonds. Some jurisdictions also require a payment bond, guaranteeing payment to laborers, subcontractors, and material suppliers. The statute or ordinance requiring the bond may prescribe the terms of the bonds.[13] Statutes and ordinances may permit other types of security, such as letters of credit, certificates of deposit, or other financial instruments.[14]

A. *The Subdivision Bond Amount*

The amount of the subdivision bond is determined by the public body usually within a legislatively prescribed range. For a subdivision agreement, the security required for completion of the public improvements generally is calculated as a percentage of the total estimated cost of the improvements to be installed; such costs are frequently determined by an engineer on staff or retained by the public body. In some instances, however, the developer may prepare the estimate of costs to construct the public improvements. The amount of the subdivision bond required in some states is set at no less than 50 percent, and no greater than 100 percent, of the total estimated cost of the improvements.[15] In addition to the base cost of the improvements, the security often covers costs and reasonable expenses, including attorneys' fees, of the public body incurred in enforcing the secured obligation.[16]

---

13. *See, e.g.*, CAL. GOV'T CODE §§ 66499.1–.2 (West 2021); N.J. STAT. ANN. § 40:55D-84 (West 2021); N.Y. TOWN LAW § 277(1) (McKinney 2011).
14. *See* Huntley Constr. Co. v. Wells Fargo Bank (*In re* Versant Props., LLC), No. 08-10930, 2011 WL 1131057 (W.D.N.C. Mar. 25, 2011) (public body accepted letter of credit); Vale Dean Canyon Homeowners Ass'n v. Dean, 785 P.2d 772 (Or. Ct. App. 1990) (public body required a certificate of deposit).
15. *See* N.J. STAT. ANN. § 40:55D-53(a) (West 2021) (authorizing a performance subdivision bond "not to exceed 120% of the cost of installation of improvements").
16. *See, e.g.*, CAL. GOV'T CODE § 66499 (West 2021).

B. Reducing the Subdivision Bond Amount

Several jurisdictions provide a statutory mechanism to obtain a reduction of the penal sum of the subdivision bond as construction of the required improvements is completed.[17] Such reductions in the penal sum act as a partial release of the surety and, therefore, limit the surety's potential liability should the developer be declared in default or otherwise fail to complete the remaining improvements.[18] The developer must comply with statutory requirements for obtaining approval of completed work and a reduction of the bond.[19]

C. Estimated Costs of Completion

Often attached to the subdivision bond or identified in the agreement governing the subdivision improvements there is an estimated cost of completion. This document may be prepared by the public body or prepared by the developer and submitted for approval to the public body. The surety underwriter should attempt to ascertain the accuracy of the engineer's estimates and whether there are any major deviations between the engineer's estimates and the amount the developer has budgeted for completion. In the event there is a claim, this estimate provides an initial basis for assessing the cost to complete.

---

17. *See, e.g.*, *id.* §§ 66499(b), 66499.5; N.J. STAT. ANN. § 40:55D-53(d)(1) (West 2021).
18. *See* Edgewater Park Twp. v. Silver Park W., LLC, No. Bur-3475-06 (N.J. Super. Ct. Law Div. Sept. 26, 2008) (order granting partial summary judgment reducing liability of Greenwich Insurance Company due to Edgewater Park Township's acceptance of improvements and reduction of subdivision bond line item; holding, inter alia, that pursuant to New Jersey Statutes Annotated section 40:55D-53(e)(1), a municipality's reduction of a subdivision bond line item constitutes a determination by the municipality that the improvement has been completed in a satisfactory manner); *see also* RESTATEMENT (THIRD) OF SURETYSHIP AND GUARANTY § 39, cmt. e (1996) ("Partial performance by the principal obligor discharges the secondary obligor [the surety] to the extent of that performance.").
19. *See* Kern Cnty. v. Edgemont Dev. Corp., 35 Cal. Rptr. 629 (Cal. Dist. Ct. App. 1963) (court refused to declare a portion of work complete, or that the developer otherwise had an absolute right to have the work accepted, where the developer failed to file the required application for acceptance).

IV. Collateral for Subdivision Bonds[20]

A. The Set Aside Letter

A form of collateral that is unique to subdivision bonds known as a "set aside letter" or agreement is intended to assure that the bank funding for the development is applied to the public improvements. The demise of a developer sometimes is followed by litigation between the developer's bank and its surety over the obligation of the bank to pay for improvements under the terms of a set aside letter.

If a project is funded by the developer, the surety must be assured that the developer has committed sufficient funds to complete the required improvements. The surety can take traditional forms of collateral from the developer in the form of cash deposits or letters of credit. If a project is to be financed through a bank, the surety often obtains a set aside letter or other financial arrangement from the principal's bank, which provides that as part of the bank's commitment to fund the entire project, the bank has segregated sufficient funds to be used solely for the completion of the subdivision improvements.[21] Ascertaining the precise source of payment and procedure to be followed in funding the subdivision improvements is an essential underwriting consideration.[22]

B. Disputes Relating to Bank Set Aside Letters

Disputes sometimes arise between the surety and the bank with respect to the funds the bank is holding for completion of the project. In *Gulf Insurance Co. v. First Bank*,[23] the court refused to reconsider its prior order granting summary judgment in favor of a surety against the defendant bank that had issued a set aside letter making an irrevocable promise to advance certain funds for use in performing the bonded subdivision

---

20. The authors limited the discussion of collateral to set aside letters as this is a type of collateral unique to subdivision or development bonds.
21. *See, e.g.*, City of Los Angeles v. Anchor Cas. Co., 22 Cal. Rptr. 278 (Cal. Dist. Ct. App. 1962).
22. For additional information regarding the form and issues that may arise in negotiating set aside agreements, see Patricia J. Frobes, *Selected Issues in Secured Construction Lending*, *in* REAL ESTATE FINANCING DOCUMENTATION STRATEGIES FOR CHANGING TIMES 155, 157 (2007).
23. No. CIV-S-08-209(LKK/JFM), 2009 WL 1953444 (E.D. Cal. July 7, 2009), *aff'd*, 400 Fed. App'x 188 (9th Cir. 2010).

work. Following the developer's default, the surety sought to compel the bank to advance the balance of its committed funds to the surety, which was called upon to complete the improvements. The bank argued that the developer had refinanced its loan and obtained funds in excess of the set aside amount from other lenders. The court nonetheless ruled in favor of the surety, finding that the bank had breached its unambiguous, and irrevocable, agreement with the surety to advance the set aside funds for completion of the project.

In *Lincoln General Insurance Co. v. Tri Counties Bank*,[24] the court rejected the arguments by a bank that it was not required to pay the surety under the terms of a set aside letter. In *Lincoln*, Sanderson Company Inc. planned to develop a subdivision in Anderson, California. To fund the development, Sanderson secured a revolving credit line of $6 million from defendant Tri Counties Bank, although the total estimated construction cost was almost $8 million. Lincoln General Insurance provided Sanderson with a subdivision bond on which the city of Anderson was the obligee.[25]

Before Lincoln issued the bond, Lincoln received a set aside letter from the bank in which the bank agreed to set aside from the construction funds an amount equal to the amount of the subdivision bond, $444,287 (set aside funds) to be used for payment of the improvements. The set aside letter also provided that the bank would create a separate account to contain the set aside funds and that the funds would be immediately available to Lincoln if Sanderson failed to complete and pay for the improvements. The set aside letter specifically provided that the funds "are for the benefit of the Surety Company in connection with the Surety's liability under the . . . bonds."[26]

Sanderson failed to complete the improvements and Anderson made a demand on Lincoln's subdivision bond. Lincoln requested that the bank produce the remaining set aside funds, but the bank refused. Anderson filed suit against Lincoln. Lincoln settled the suit with Anderson, and then filed suit against the bank for breach of contract and conversion,

---

24. No. 2:10-CV-01442(FCD/EFB), 2010 WL 3069874 (E.D. Cal. Aug. 5, 2010). After a year of litigation, this case settled in mediation for an undisclosed amount. *See* Order for Dismissal with Prejudice, No. 2:10-CV-01442(FCD/EFB), 2010 WL 3069874 (E.D. Cal. June 9, 2011), *available at* http://ecf.caed.uscourts.gov.

25. *Lincoln Gen. Ins. Co.*, 2010 WL 3069874, at *1.

26. *Id.*

among other claims.[27] The bank moved to dismiss all causes of action on the basis that the set aside agreement had not been fully executed and was thus not valid and enforceable. The bank claimed that although it had executed the set aside letter, neither Lincoln nor Sanderson had signed it. The court held that although the set aside letter was not signed by Lincoln or Sanderson, the required manifestations of consent to the terms of the agreement were evident. The set aside letter was a precondition to Lincoln issuing the subdivision bond, and because Lincoln did, in fact, issue the subdivision bond, it had evidenced its consent in this manner.[28] Sanderson evidenced its consent by purchasing the subdivision bond from Lincoln, while knowing that Lincoln required all parties to enter the set aside letter.[29]

A bank also offered some creative reasons why it was excused of its obligation to pay for the improvements in *Developers Surety & Indemnity Co. v. American National Bank*.[30] In that case, the court granted summary judgment against the bank and in favor of the surety and rejected the bank's argument that the set aside letter did not require the bank to segregate loan proceeds, that the bank paid the full amount of the loan to the developer for improvements that fell within the definition of "improvements" under the ordinance but were not bonded improvements. The bank's argument that payment for "any" improvements was a payment that qualified under the set aside letter was belied by the evidence of an engineer's estimate of costs specifying the improvements required by the municipality.

Sureties might avoid disputes over the execution and scope of set aside letters by making sure they are fully executed and reference or append the actual engineer's estimate of costs to the letter to define the scope of the improvements for which loan proceeds are being set aside. Many banks are aware of the status of the developments and the

---

27. *Id.*

28. *Id.* at *3.

29. *Id.* at *4. The court also denied the bank's motion to dismiss with respect to Lincoln's conversion claim, noting that although "a generalized claim for money is not actionable as conversion . . . [t]his court has repeatedly held that funds identified in a set aside agreement may constitute such a specific and identifiable sum." *Id.* The court further noted that while ownership or right to possession of the subject property is an element of a conversion claim, "even where the ownership interest in the property is conditioned on default, once the condition has been met, there is sufficient possessory interest to support a cause of action for conversion." *Id.* at *5.

30. No. 10 C 50195, 2012 WL 2906244 (N.D. Ill. July 16, 2012).

construction of improvements by their borrowers. Bear in mind, bank loan officers often obtain pay requests and schedules of values to monitor their borrowers' progress on major developments, and the requirements for set aside funds may be part of the loan file. Complete and thorough documentation might avoid creative arguments that lead to lawsuits.

V. Subdivision Bonds Are Not Public Works Bonds

Public works bonds and subdivision bonds serve different purposes and secure different obligations.[31] Subdivision bonds assure that a private developer will perform the improvements within a private development that may eventually become dedicated to the public body. Public works bonds require completion of work being performed for the public body and payment of parties supplying labor and materials for that work. They protect public funds and provide a remedy to parties who cannot perfect liens in property owned by a governmental entity.

A. *Under Illinois Law, Subdivision Bonds Are Payment and Performance Bonds for Public Works: Lake County Grading Co., LLC v. Village of Antioch*[32]

The Illinois Supreme Court obliterated any distinction between a public works bond and a subdivision bond. Now, under Illinois law, a surety issuing a subdivision bond must assume that bond is also, in effect, a payment and performance bond for a public project. In 2014, the Illinois Supreme Court held in *Lake County Grading Co., LLC v. Village of Antioch* that a subdivision bond naming a municipality as the obligee will be deemed to include the language in the Illinois Public Construction Bond Act.[33] This means that a subdivision bond also stands as security to pay parties supplying labor and materials for the improvements to the property.

The ruling is contrary to prior Illinois cases that found payment bond claimants have no standing to assert claims under subdivision bonds and expands the scope of the risk of subdivision bonds far beyond the

---

31. Public works bonds refer generally to those bonds securing performance and payment for labor and materials required for projects administered and owned by a public entity, as distinguished from a private developer.
32. 19 N.E.3d 615 (Ill. 2014).
33. 30 Ill. Comp. Stat. 550/1, 550/2 (2020).

surety's expectations in writing these bonds. What is perplexing in both the majority opinion and dissent in *Lake County Grading* is that both opinions assume that the subdivision improvements should be deemed a public work and neither opinion mentions a separate provision of the Illinois Compiled Statutes that applies to subdivision bonds.[34] This case stands as an exemplar of how surety obligations can be construed to cover more than intended through confusion of the issues and misunderstanding of surety law generally.

The misunderstanding begins with a claimant, Lake County Grading, pursuing an invalid theory of recovery; the defendant, the Village of Antioch, asserting an improper defense; and ends with the courts failing to understand the nature of the bonds as developed in Illinois case law and in the statutes—a perfect storm of faulty reasoning and flawed advocacy resulting in a completely wrong decision that will stand as law until the legislature corrects it. And, unfortunately, correcting somewhat obscure issues of surety law is not the most urgent priority of most legislative bodies. This was the first decision in 50 years by the Illinois Supreme Court addressing an issue of surety law. What is yet more interesting about the case, the surety was neither sued nor a party to the appeals!

Neumann Homes, Inc. was the developer of two subdivisions within the Village of Antioch, a far north suburb of Chicago. Like many developers at the time, Neumann Homes sought bankruptcy relief and eventually liquidated. Four subdivision bonds were issued in favor of the village, the underlying obligation of these bonds being two infrastructure agreements between the village and Neumann. Like many subdivision bonds, the condition of the bonds merely required completion of the improvements identified in the engineer's estimates.[35]

Lake County Grading performed grading work for which Neumann did not pay. The record showed that Lake County Grading finished work on one subdivision on December 23, 2006, and on a second subdivision

---

34. *Id.* 550/3.

35. The bonds provided in part:

> The Principal [Neumann] shall perform and complete . . . improvements to . . . development in accordance with either the plan(s)/specification(s)/agreement [prepared by Pearson Brown & Associates, Inc. or Manhard Consulting] then this obligation shall be void . . . . This bond will terminate upon written acceptance of the improvements by the obligee [Village] to the principal [Neumann] and/or surety [Fidelity].

on April 16, 2007, and that Neumann sought bankruptcy relief on November 1, 2007. Nearly ten months after completing the work on the last subdivision, Lake County Grading served notices of lien claims on the village and Neumann.

Lake County Grading never asserted a claim against the subdivision bonds, possibly because it understood it did not have standing to make a claim against a subdivision bond, but brought lien claims against funds held by the village asserting that set aside funds for the improvements were subject to a lien, probably because it misunderstood that the subdivision developments were not public projects. The first mistake was this assumption that a subdivision development is a public project.

In defense of the claim, the village made the second mistake, incorrectly arguing it met the requirement to obtain public bonds because the subdivision bonds were bonds that included the language of the Illinois Public Construction Bond Act, 30 Illinois Compiled Statutes 550/1 and 550/2, which provides that all bonds provided for public works in Illinois are deemed to require payments to parties supplying labor and materials.[36] The village consequently argued that Lake County Grading's claim was untimely because the payment provision of the Bond Act, 550/2, requires notice of the claim within 180 days of the date of the last work.

Lake County Grading prevailed at the trial court and the appellate court on its claim that the village was liable in failing to require Neumann

---

36. 19 N.E.3d at 617. 30 Illinois Compiled Statutes 550/1 provides in part:

> Each such bond is deemed to contain the following provisions whether such provisions are inserted in such bond or not:
>
> > The principal and sureties on this bond agree that all the undertakings, covenants, terms, conditions and agreements of the contract or contracts entered into between the principal and the State or any political subdivision thereof will be performed and fulfilled and to pay all persons, firms and corporations having contracts with the principal or with subcontractors, all just claims due them under the provisions of such contracts for labor performed or materials furnished in the performance of the contract on account of which this bond is given, when such claims are not satisfied out of the contract price of the contract on account of which this bond is given, after final settlement between the officer, board, commission or agent of the State or of any political subdivision thereof and the principal has been made.

to provide the performance and payment bonds for public work under Illinois law, the 550/1 and 550/2 bonds.[37] Illinois law recognizes a party supplying labor and materials to a public project requiring such bonds has a right of action against the official or public body for a failure to require the contractor to post the bonds.[38] Assuming the subdivision infrastructure agreements related to public projects, the appellate court held that public bonds were required and that the terms of subdivision bonds are not the required public bonds.

The third and culminating mistake that led to the Illinois Supreme Court decision was the argument by the village that because of the language in section 550/1 that payment terms are to be deemed to be included in any bonds posted for public improvements, those terms were included in the subdivision bonds and the village accordingly met its obligation to require payment bonds.[39] The Supreme Court adopted

---

37. *Id.* 550/1 & 550/2.

38. *See* Ardon Elec. Co. v. Winterset Constr., Inc., 820 N.E. 2d 21 (Ill. App. Ct. 2004).

39. On this point, in the second edition of this book, the authors of this chapter stated the following at note 74:

> There is some dispute among practitioners in Illinois as to the extent the Illinois Bond Act applies to a Subdivision bond and thus confers third-party beneficiary status on subcontractors under the terms of the Subdivision bond. The Illinois Bond Act provides that the amount of a performance bond on a public project "shall be conditioned for the completion of the contract, for the payment of material used in the work and for all labor performed in the work, whether by subcontractor or otherwise." *Id.* As the court in *Ardon Elec. Co. v. Winterset Constr., Inc.*, 820 N.E.2d 21, 27 (Ill. App. Ct. 2004) noted, "the provisions of the Bond Act are read into all public works contracts between a public entity and a general contractor." *See also* A.E.I. Music Network, Inc. v. Bus. Computers, Inc., 290 F.3d 952, 955 (7th Cir. 2002) (finding that where the public entity failed to obtain a bond, the subcontractor could bring suit for breach of contract against the public entity as a third-party beneficiary because "[t]he requirement of posting a bond found in section 1 of the Bond Act is read into every construction contract of a public entity precisely to give the subcontractor a remedy") (internal citations omitted). Thus, some have asserted that it is conceivable that at some time in the future, the Illinois courts may apply Section 1 of the Illinois Bond Act to Subdivision bonds and find that subcontractors in Illinois are third-party beneficiaries of

this reasoning and held the subdivision bonds contain the public bond payment terms.

The surety's perspective on the issues did not find a way into the case until the briefing of the appeal to the Illinois Supreme Court. The Surety & Fidelity Association of America (SFAA) sought leave to file an amicus brief that argued (1) a subdivision bond is not a public works bond, and (2) the village would not be liable because a subdivision improvement does not require a public bond. The village objected to the motion for leave to file and asked the court to strike the brief, notwithstanding that the brief argued an alternative theory that the village was not liable for a failure to require bonds. The Illinois Supreme Court struck the SFAA amicus brief.

The Illinois Supreme Court ultimately reached the right result—that the village was not liable to Lake County Grading—for the wrong reason. The reason the village was not liable to Lake County Grading was that a public bond is not required for subdivision improvements in Illinois, and not as the court held, because subdivision bonds qualify as public work bonds.[40] How blind advocacy led to faulty judicial reasoning is starkly apparent in the failure of both the dissent and the majority opinion to note that there is a separate section of the Illinois statutes relating to subdivision bonds.[41] The dissent appears to assume that subdivision public improvements qualify as public works but disagrees with the majority that a bond securing public works cannot limit by its terms the scope of the obligations.

---

the terms of the Subdivision bond. Arguably, this position may be difficult to sustain in as much as the subdivision of private land is not a public project.

The Illinois Supreme Court eliminated the conjecture in this footnote in holding that subdivision bonds incorporate the payment terms of the Illinois Public Construction Bond Act. As set forth in this section of the chapter, the authors believe the *Lake County Grading* decision was wrong because a subdivision bond relates to private property, against which parties supplying labor and materials can assert liens, and the subdivision bond is separately dealt with in a separate section of the Illinois Compiled Statutes. The scope of the obligation of the bond is different because it serves a different purpose.

40. 30 Ill. Comp. Stat. 550/3 (2020).

41. Lake Cnty. Grading Co., LLC v. Vill. of Antioch, 19 N.E.3d 615, 624 (Ill. 2014).

The court failed to understand that the subdivision bond is not needed to meet any of the purposes for which a public bond is required (i.e., to protect public funds and to protect parties furnishing labor and materials who have no lien rights). The village's public funds were not at risk and the claimant could have perfected mechanic's lien rights against the property of Neumann. Moreover, repurposing surety bonds for obligations for which they are not intended can lead to unintended and inequitable consequences. In the case of a subdivision surety facing payment bond claims after the default and insolvency of the principal developer, if the penal sum of the bond is consumed paying claimants, there will be no security for installing the improvements, a primary purpose of the bond under Illinois law as recognized in the section of the statutes that properly applies to these bonds, 550/3.[42]

This ruling by the Illinois Supreme Court cannot be squared with the purposes of subdivision bonds and the statute providing for these bonds. The claimant lost its rights when it did not pursue a mechanic's lien against the properties. It did not need a remedy against a public bond.

The lesson for the surety practitioner and claims representative from the *Lake County Grading* case is that it is important to make sure that courts understand the underlying purpose the subdivision bond serves and the potential economic consequences of expanding the scope of the subdivision bond beyond its terms. Had the SFAA been permitted to explain to the Illinois Supreme Court the general impact of its ruling on sureties and municipalities, the court may have arrived at the right result for the right reason. But there was no such advocate in the room.

---

42. The Illinois statute describes the subdivision bond as a bond posted in lieu of cash from the developer and states it is for completion of the improvements. Some jurisdictions like California, in recognition of the public interest that parties supplying labor and materials ought to be paid, require a separate payment bond in addition to the subdivision bond. But the obligations and purposes of each bond are described in the terms of each bond. California statute authorizes municipalities to require payment bonds to secure payments to parties furnishing labor and materials for subdivision improvements. CAL. CIV. CODE §§ 8600–8914 (2010). The bond form terms are prescribed by statute. *Id.* § 66499.2 (1974). Lenders also may require payment bonds for subdivision improvements to satisfy claims that might be liens against the properties.

B. Scope and Limits of Subdivision Bond Coverage

Subdivision bonds offer financial assurance to the public body and are typically indemnity bonds. The scope of the security of these bonds is limited, and some public bodies may additionally require maintenance or warranty bonds. Subdivision bonds generally do not include coverage for delay, or consequential or liquidated damages.[43] The key to coverage is whether there is a public improvement. One court, for example, concluded that the cost of electricity was not an improvement and therefore not a proper claim against the subdivision bond.[44]

C. Expanding the Scope of Coverage Beyond the Statute or Ordinance

The statute or other legislation authorizing bonds may also determine the coverage and standing. In Eastern Planned Communities at Lincroft, Inc. v. Middletown Township, a public body refused to release a bond because the developer "failed to form a homeowner's association as required by the planning board resolution."[45] Faced with that position, the court held that the public body lacked statutory authority to retain the subdivision bonds.

Other states follow the general proposition that a government entity may not impose upon a developer a bonding requirement of broader scope than that set forth within the legislation.[46] This principle has been

---

43. *See, e.g.*, Bd. of Supervisors v. Safeco Ins. Co. of Am., 310 S.E.2d 445, 450–51 (Va. 1983) (rejecting county's claim for consequential damages, other than interest, limiting recovery to the principal amount of the subdivision bond).
44. N.J. Shore Builders Ass'n v. Twp. of Marlboro, 591 A.2d 950, 953–54 (N.J. Super. Ct. App. Div. 1999).
45. 563 A.2d 81, 82 (N.J. Super. Ct. Law Div. 1989).
46. *See, e.g.*, Arrowhead Dev. Co. v. Livingston Cnty. Rd. Comm'n, 322 N.W.2d 702 (Mich. 1982) (state constitution and statutes did not permit commission to condition plat approval for subdivision on agreement by developer to pay for county road improvements outside the subdivision); *cf.* Somers v. Town of Oxford, No. CV020080319S, 2004 WL 202885 (Conn. Super. Ct. Jan. 13, 2004) (plaintiff could not bring mandamus action to force town to call subdivision bond under Connecticut General Statutes § 8-26c when statute only provided for improvements in the subdivision, not property outside the subdivision).

applied to defeat claims of contractors that allege that they are third-party beneficiaries of the subdivision bonds.[47]

A surety, however, can voluntarily undertake obligations that are more burdensome than the requirements of a statute or other regulation.[48] A surety can agree its bond imposes broader obligations than the statute.[49] In *Rexroth & Rexroth v. General Casualty Co. of America*, a surety was held bound to an express material and labor bond that was printed and executed on the reverse side of a subdivision performance bond.[50]

---

47. Evola v. Wendt Constr. Co., 338 P.2d 498, 501 (Cal. Dist. Ct. App. 1959) ("No authority is given by the section which would authorize the governing body to enact an ordinance on the subject; none that would permit the county to expand the agreement to protect labor or material claimants."); Hewson Constr., Inc. v. Reintree Corp., 685 P.2d 1062, 1065 (Wash. 1984) ("The Washington statute gives only the municipality power to enforce plat obligation bonds [sic]; thus contractors such as Hewson have no right of action to enforce these bonds."); *see also* W.S. Dickey Clay Mfg. Co. v. Ferguson Inv. Co., 388 P.2d 300, 303 (Okla. 1963) ("The construction of the bond should be consonant with the effectuation of the apparent purposes of the Legislature and the City Council.").
48. RESTATEMENT (THIRD) of SURETYSHIP and GUARANTY § 72(2) (1996).
49. *See, e.g.*, Mount Florence Grp. v. City of Peekskill, 652 N.Y.S.2d 814 (N.Y. App. Div. 1997) (holding that where a subdivision bond provided for a longer limitations period than the relevant statute, the surety was bound by the more liberal language of the subdivision bond). In *Board of County Supervisors v. Sie-Gray Developers, Inc.*, 334 S.E.2d 542, 546 (Va. 1985) (quoting 10 Eugene MCQUILLIN, THE LAW OF MUNICIPAL CORPORATIONS § 29.133 (3d ed. 1981)) (citations omitted), the court held as follows:

   > To allow appellees to assert a defense of ultra vires would contravene the general principle that "one who makes a contract with a municipality is estopped to assert that it was ultra vires, when it is sought to be enforced against him." A defense unavailable to Sie-Gray would likewise be unavailable to Republic, as surety.

50. 51 Cal. Rptr. 505 (Cal. Dist. Ct. App. 1966). Although the text of the performance bond is not recited in the opinion, one might infer from the context of the opinion that the bonding agent erroneously selected a bond form intended for construction projects, with performance and payment bond language on alternate sides of the form. *See generally Sie-Gray Developers*, 334 S.E.2d 542 (agreement between developer and town to complete improvements to county road outside subdivision enforceable where court found developer voluntarily agreed to complete

Under the circumstances, the court held, "We conclude that since there is nothing in the record indicating that the material and labor bond was written under the compulsion of the county, there is no reason why it is not a valid common-law bond."[51]

D. Time Limitations for Bringing Suit

In contrast to most public works bond statutes that set forth limited time frames to bring suit, the time for bringing suit on a subdivision bond can be much longer.[52] The limitations period may not start to run until the improvements are completed and dedicated. Delays in development due to market and other conditions may result in extensions of time for completion of the improvements.

The suit limitation is often a key provision for limiting the surety's exposure, but a surety may not be entitled to notice of any extensions of time for the completion of the subdivision improvements.[53] To properly evaluate its exposure, the surety should periodically monitor the financial status of the developer and the progress of the required improvements.[54] Booms and busts in the housing market are not unusual.[55]

If a project is extended, it is incumbent upon the developer and the surety to assure themselves that the set aside letter does not contain an

---

such improvements, even though county exceeded bounds of its statutory authority in requiring such improvements for approval of subdivision).

51. *Rexroth*, 51 Cal. Rptr. at 509.

52. *See* Commercial Standard Ins. Co. v. Tab Constr., Inc., 583 P.2d 449 (Nev. 1978) (subdivision payment bond contained six-month limitations period from the date of completion of improvements). *But see Sherwood Forest No. 2 Corp. v. City of Norman*, 632 P.2d 368 (Okla. 1980) (citing City of Norman v. Liddell, 596 P.2d 879 (Okla. 1979)), where the Supreme Court of Oklahoma rejected a limitations period set forth in the subdivision bond as void by a local statute, and further held a two-year limitations period set forth in a sidewalk ordinance to be void as a violation of the state's constitution. Instead, the court applied a five-year limitations period for breach of contract.

53. *See, e.g.*, City of Sacramento v. Trans Pac. Indus., 159 Cal. Rptr. 514, 520 (Cal. Ct. App. 1979).

54. For further discussion of steps the surety should take to protect itself when the developer's financial situation worsens, see *infra* Part VIII.

55. On December 30, 2008, the Case-Shiller Home Price Index reported the largest price drop in its history.

expiration date or is likewise extended. Financing and funding the work often is a primary concern of a subdivision bond surety when development completion time is extended. If the need for the extension is the product of market conditions, there is an increasing risk the necessary financing may not be available for the developer to start and complete the work.

Subdivision bond statutes and legislation, and the bonds themselves, likely do not include a specific suit limitation. The limitation that applies will generally be determined by what state statutes provide for this type of contract. An Illinois case noted that the suit limitation that applied to subdivision bonds was the four-year suit limitation that applied in that state to construction projects.[56]

VI. Considerations in Handling Claims

A. *Obtain Project Schedule and Monitor Work Progress*

The surety may obtain a projected schedule of completion of the subdivision improvements and periodic status reports from the developer to compare the actual completion of the work with the developer's projected schedule. The surety should watch for market conditions and whether the developer is straggling in performance of the work—signs the project is underfunded or not marketable.

B. *Monitor Financial Status*

The surety may communicate with the developer and the bank that issued the set aside letter or provided other financing to ensure that if the bank forecloses on the property, it will require any third-party purchaser to assume or take title to the property subject to the developer's subdivision improvement obligations. These negotiations should also deal with the bank's obligations under the set aside letter or other financial arrangement. Although a bank may not have a legal obligation to work with the surety, if properly presented as an option, a bank will often work with the parties to deal fairly with the property.

---

56. 735 Ill. Comp. Stat. 5/13-214(a) (2020); United City of Yorkville v. Ocean Atl. Serv. Corp., No. 11 CV 1984, 2013 WL 5433429 (N.D. Ill. Sept. 30, 2013).

C. Assess Defenses to Subdivision Bond Claims

If a principal is declared in default on a subdivision bond, the initial investigation relative to the default is rather straightforward. If the time frame for completing the subdivision improvements has expired and it is within the limitations period for making a claim, generally the principal will have no defense to a demand. The surety will face completing the work using a completion contractor or paying the obligee an amount necessary for the construction and installation of the required improvements.[57]

Claims, however, do not always come from the obligees or are not brought by the obligees immediately upon default. Claims can come from parties supplying labor and materials to the developer. They may be asserted years later for developments that were mothballed because of market conditions. At the time of a demand, constructing the improvements might not be feasible because of the market and the status of the development. Putting in public improvements on undeveloped property will lead to additional expense to the public body to maintain improvements to property where no taxpayers live, and lead to the eventual deterioration of the improvements to the properties. Moreover, work may require delaying installation of improvements until other work is completed to avoid damage to the improvements.

D. Standing of the Claimant

Most subdivision performance bonds identify the public body as the sole obligee. A number of decisions find that standing to assert a claim is limited to the obligee.[58] A key issue that arises in claims under subdivision

---

57. In *General Insurance Co. of America v. City of Colorado Springs*, 638 P.2d 752, 757 (Colo. 1981), the Supreme Court of Colorado rejected the City's contention that the subdivision bond was a "penalty bond," liable in the full amount for the principal's failure to perform, but rather deemed the bond an "indemnity bond," liable only for the actual cost of completing the required improvements.

58. In *Hewson Construction, Inc. v. Reintree Corp.*, 685 P.2d 1062 (Wash. 1984) (en banc), the court denied the subcontractor who installed the sidewalks on a subdivision improvement a right of action to enforce a subdivision performance bond. The court rejected the subcontractor's argument that it was a third-party beneficiary of the subdivision performance bond, holding that the subdivision bond runs solely to the

bonds is whether the successor owner is liable to the surety for the cost of improvements or is a beneficiary of the subdivision bond.[59]

---

public body, as obligee. Similarly, in *W.S. Dickey Clay Manufacturing Co. v. Ferguson Investment Co.*, 388 P.2d 300 (Okla. 1963), the court denied a material supplier a right of action against a subdivision bond despite the fact that the subdivision bond included language binding the surety to laborers and materialmen. Finding that the subdivision law did not require the developer to guarantee payment for labor and materials, the court held that the material supplier was confined to the measure of liability as contemplated by the law requiring the subdivision bond. *See also* Norton v. First Fed. Sav., 624 P.2d 854 (Ariz. 1981); Evola v. Wendt Constr. Co., 338 P.2d 498 (Cal. Dist. Ct. App. 1959). In *Vale Dean Canyon Homeowners Association v. Dean*, 785 P.2d 772 (Or. Ct. App. 1990), however, the court did allow lot owners, as third-party beneficiaries of the subdivision agreement, to enforce the terms of the subdivision agreement. In part, the court found that in entering into the subdivision agreement, the public body intended to benefit the lot owners. Interestingly, the court refused to give much credence to testimony by the public body that its intent was to assure that the improvements would be placed at no cost to itself. This case may however be limited to its particular circumstances and the language of the particular subdivision agreement.

59. In the discussion of the "sweetheart deal" in the next section, the successor owner arranges through a deal with the municipality to obtain the benefit of the bonds to pay the costs of the improvements. Absent the role of the municipal body in that arrangement it is doubtful a successor owner has standing to assert claim against a subdivision bond. *See* H.N. & Frances C. Berger Found. v. Perez, 159 Cal. Rptr. 3d 434 (Cal. Ct. App. 2013) (holding a successor owner through foreclosure has no standing to assert a subdivision bond claim). The decision strongly rejects the notion a successor owner should have the benefit of the bond in stating:

> Moreover, plaintiff has not established that its claims is a consequence that was contemplated by the statutory enactments requiring surety bonds. (citation omitted). The statutory enactments requiring the Bonds were not intended to protect the plaintiff as a property owner . . . . Instead, the purpose of requiring the Bonds was to protect Riverside [the public body] and the public. (County of Yuba v. Central Valley Nat. Bank (1971 20 Cal. App. 3d 109, 112 [97 Cal. Rptr. 369] ["purpose for requiring security for street improvement work is to insure faithful performance of the subdivider's obligation to place streets in a proper condition for use by the public"].)

H.N. & Frances C. Berger Found., 159 Cal. Rptr. 3d at 443–44.

E. The Sweetheart Deal

Successor owners of property developments have used so-called "sweetheart deals" to evade standing arguments and to make the surety pay for improvements. In the "sweetheart deal" scenario, an obligee making a claim may be doing so for the benefit of a third-party successor developer who has agreed to complete the improvements and/or develop the property. In the end, the successor developer and the public entity get the public improvements at the surety's expense and the surety's only recourse is to pursue the original developer who may, by this time, be out of business or judgment-proof.[60] As underhanded as such a deal may seem, courts may not find that such a deal is an unlawful assignment of the subdivision bond.[61]

In *City of Merced v. American Motorists Insurance Co.*,[62] the City of Merced, the obligee, adopted the Campus North Specific Plan, which involved subdividing several tracts to have hundreds of residential units built by various developers. Grant Homes, Inc. entered into a subdivision agreement with Merced to develop a portion of the Campus North

---

60. *See* David C. Veis & David L. Lynch, *Watching Out for Sweetheart Deals*, BRIEF, Summer 2009, at 52 (discussing, inter alia, how the economic downturn in the housing market impacts claims brought against sureties on subdivision bonds and offers some insights to protect against, and potentially minimize, losses); *see also* Westchester Fire Ins. Co. v. City of Brooksville, 731 F. Supp. 2d 1298 (M.D. Fla. 2010) (successor developer would only agree to complete subdivision if city sued surety, and prevailed, on claim to complete public improvements).

61. *See, e.g.*, City of Sacramento v. Trans Pac. Indus., 159 Cal. Rptr. 514, 520 (Cal. Ct. App. 1979) ("Fireman's [the surety's] argument that the City-[successor developer] reimbursement contract constituted an unlawful attempt to assign a public subdivision bond is without merit. City did not assign its chose-in-action against TPI [the original developer] or Fireman's; it merely promised to pay [successor developer] for his work [i]f it was successful in the lawsuit."). Although sureties have had little luck to date in recovering any losses against successor developers, certain scholars believe that there may still be avenues available to do so as the law in this area develops. *See* Marilyn Klinger & Kenneth C. Ryken, *Successor Developers: Untapped Opportunities for Subdivision Bond Sureties*, 62 DEF. COUNS. J. 577 (1995).

62. 24 Cal. Rptr. 3d 788 (Cal. Ct. App. 2005).

project.[63] The subdivision agreement required Grant to agree to construct certain improvements within one year of commencing construction, and additional improvements, known as the "deferred work," at a later time during other phases of development of the land.[64] American Motorists Insurance Company (AMIC) issued a subdivision bond on Grant's behalf to Merced, as obligee, in the amount of $45,000, which was Grant's pro-rata share of the "deferred work." Two years later Grant entered into a second subdivision agreement and AMIC provided a second subdivision bond in the amount of $90,400.[65]

After Grant completed construction of the homes in the second development, Merced learned that Grant was insolvent and would be unable to perform the work. Union Bank took title to Grant's property and conveyed the remaining undeveloped property to another developer, Joe Wu. Prior to purchasing the property, Wu learned from Merced's senior civil engineer that Grant was obligated to perform the deferred work and was bonded for such work. [66] Merced's director of planning told Wu that if he purchased the property, Wu would then be responsible for completing Grant's deferred work. Wu was also told by these city officials that if Wu agreed to perform the work, Merced would make demand on the subdivision bonds and use its "best efforts" to obtain the subdivision bond proceeds, which it would pay to Wu to defray the costs of constructing the improvements. In light of this, Wu agreed to purchase the property from the bank.[67]

After Wu bought the property, Merced demanded that Grant perform the work. When Grant advised that it had ceased operations and could not perform, Merced made demand to AMIC for payment on Grant's subdivision bond. Merced then authorized Wu's attorney to file on its behalf a lawsuit against the surety to enforce the subdivision bond.[68] The trial court entered judgment against the surety and in favor of Merced for the full amount of the subdivision bond, plus interest, and provided that the judgment could be amended to award costs and attorneys' fees.[69]

---

63. *Id.* at 789.
64. *Id.* at 790.
65. *Id.*
66. *Id.*
67. *Id.* at 791.
68. *Id.*
69. *Id.* at 792.

The surety appealed and raised two issues: (1) that Merced had not suffered damages; and (2) that the agreement between Wu and Merced constituted an illegal assignment.[70] The appellate court rejected the surety's arguments and affirmed the lower court's ruling. The appellate court found that even though Wu agreed to perform Grant's share of the deferred work before Grant had to perform, Merced continued to have a contractual right to look to Grant to perform the work. Once Grant failed to perform, Merced had the right to look to Wu for performance. Merced, however, still may have suffered damages because Wu only agreed to perform if Merced repaid him; this was contingent upon Merced prevailing in the action against the surety on the surety's subdivision bonds.[71] The

---

70. *Id.*

71. *Id.* at 794 (citing City of Sacramento v. Trans Pac. Indus., 159 Cal. Rptr. 514 (Cal. Ct. App. 1979)); *see also* Town of Carolina Shores v. Cont'l Ins. Co., No. 7:10-CV-13-D, 2010 WL 4338437 (E.D.N.C. Oct. 26, 2010). In *Carolina Shores*, the developer obtained a loan from Wells Fargo Bank, N.A., secured by the development. Continental Insurance Co. provided the subdivision bond on behalf of the developer to the town of Carolina Shores as obligee. The developer defaulted on the loan, Wells Fargo foreclosed on the development, and purchased the property itself. *Id.* at *1. Carolina Shores sued the surety to complete the improvements and the surety filed a third-party complaint against Wells Fargo. The court held that Wells Fargo was not a successor-in-interest on the subdivision bond, and thus while Wells Fargo acquired the rights and responsibilities of a successor in title, it had not acquired the obligations under the subdivision bond because Wells Fargo was not a party to the subdivision bond. Although the subdivision bond in *Carolina Shores* provided that the subdivision bond would apply to any "successors," the court held that this term applied to "successor-developers." However, the court found that Wells Fargo was not a "successor-developer" because Wells Fargo was not a developer and had not agreed to finish developing the subdivision. *Id.* at *2. Thus, Wells Fargo was not bound by the terms of the subdivision bond. The court dismissed the surety's unjust enrichment claim against Wells Fargo on the basis that it was premature because Continental had not completed the improvements but noted that such claim would fail in any event because the benefit conferred "must be conferred directly from plaintiff to defendant, not through a third party." *Id.* at *5. The court noted that "[w]here a third person benefits from a contract entered into between two other persons[,] the mere failure of performance by one of the contracting parties does not give rise to a right of restitution against the third person." *Id.*

court concluded the city was damaged when Grant refused to perform after Merced demanded it do so, and that the amount of damages was equal to the cost of completing Grant's share of the deferred work.[72] The California Court of Appeals also found that Merced had not assigned its right to sue on the subdivision bond to Wu, but "merely promised to pay Wu for his work if Merced was successful in this lawsuit, and authorized his attorney to file suit in the city's name."[73] The court of appeals further noted that there was nothing in the record that demonstrated that Merced had relinquished control of the litigation to Wu or that Wu's attorney was acting on behalf of, and at the direction of, Wu, and not Merced. Thus, there was nothing demonstrating that Merced had attempted "to alienate its right to bring the action."

More recently, the Kentucky Supreme Court affirmed a decision permitting recovery by a bank from a subdivision bond surety through a sweetheart deal with a county.[74] The court distinguished the *Brooksville* case, discussed ahead, holding that there was nothing in the bonds or ordinance that made construction of homes a condition precedent to recovery, and that the developer had started constructing the improvements.[75] The court also cited the *Merced* decision in support of the arrangement between the county and the bank to recover on the bonds.[76]

---

72. *City of Merced*, 24 Cal. Rptr. 3d at 794. To overcome the sweetheart deal dilemma, municipalities could require the successor developer to post replacement subdivision bonds, thereby releasing the surety of the predecessor developer from its obligations on its subdivision bonds. Unfortunately, especially in these turbulent economic times, while the municipality often is eager for a sale of the development, many potential purchasers do not want to be saddled with the cost of completing the improvements, especially if there is a subdivision bond already in place. As creatures of statute, in some jurisdictions, the only way to remedy this inequity for the sureties may be through changes to the state statutory schemes, mandating by law that successor developers post replacement subdivision bonds.
73. *Id.* at 797.
74. Furlong Dev. Co., LLC v. Georgetown-Scott Cnty. Plan. & Zoning Comm'n, 504 S.W.3d 34 (Ky. 2016).
75. *Id.* at 39. Westchester Fire Ins. Co. v. City of Brooksville, 731 F. Supp. 2d 1298 (M.D. Fla. 2010).
76. *Furlong Dev. Co.*, 504 S.W.3d at 40.

F. Third-Party Beneficiaries

Most courts will strictly construe the subdivision bond to be only for the benefit of the named obligee. In *City of Yorkville v. Ocean Atlantic Service Corp.*,[77] three subcontractors, Pirtano Construction Company, Aurora Blacktop, Inc., and Ryan Incorporated Central, Inc., claimed that they were bringing an action, collectively as plaintiffs, in the name of the City of Yorkville, which was the only beneficiary named in the subdivision bond, to obtain payment for work performed on the subdivision.[78] Each subcontractor was hired by Ocean Atlantic Service Corporation, the developer, to perform work on the subdivision. Each subcontractor recorded a mechanic's lien on the property for the amount allegedly owed to it by Ocean Atlantic for the work it performed.[79]

Ocean Atlantic obtained several subdivision bonds that were identical except for the amount of the subdivision bond and the specific improvements covered by the subdivision bond. Each subdivision bond included a list of events or conditions, the occurrence of which provided the City of Yorkville with the right to declare Ocean Atlantic in default and call upon the subdivision bond. These events included if the improvements became, or were likely to become, the subject of liens or claims by the subcontractors.[80]

On June 17, 2009, Ocean Atlantic wrote a letter to the city clerk of Yorkville, recommending that the City assert a claim under some of the subdivision bonds and arrange for payment of the subcontractors in order to produce releases of the mechanic's liens. At that time, Ocean Atlantic admitted that it was unable to complete the improvements and that there were three foreclosures pending on the project.[81] On August 31, 2009, the Yorkville city clerk sent a "Certificate of the City Clerk Regarding Demand on Bond" making demand on seven of the subdivision bonds. Plaintiffs brought suit alleging that due demand had been made on the subdivision bonds and the surety failed to pay.[82]

---

77. Nos. 10-cv-1261, 10-cv-1473, 10-cv-2252, 2010 WL 3385461 (N.D. Ill. Aug. 24, 2010), *aff'd*, 654 F.3d 713 (7th Cir. 2011).
78. *Id.* at *1.
79. *Id.*
80. *Id.*
81. *Id.* at *2.
82. *Id.*

Ultimately, the court held that the plaintiffs were not entitled to recover under the subdivision bonds as third-party beneficiaries.[83] Under Illinois law, the contract has to be "clear and direct" that a third-party beneficiary is intended by the language of the contract; there was no such intention present in the language of the subdivision bonds.[84] Thus, the City of Yorkville was the only party that had standing to bring suit or make a claim on the subdivision bonds.[85] Moreover, the court held that the subdivision bonds guaranteed the *performance* of Ocean Atlantic, but not its *payment* obligations to third parties.[86]

Similarly, in *Shaw v. County of San Diego*,[87] the Court of Appeal for the Fourth District of California held that a subdivision developer who entered into an agreement with another developer to construct a sewer and storm drain over the property of one development could not force the county to call the subdivision bond posted by the other developer when that developer failed to complete the improvements. Plaintiff, Walter M. Shaw, purchased land for commercial and industrial development. At about the same time, an adjacent landowner-developer, Cal West Alpine Associate, was seeking to develop a 300-home subdivision. Both applied to the county of San Diego for approvals to develop their respective properties.

San Diego required Shaw to grant a sewer easement to the Alpine Sanitation District and a drainage easement to the County of San Diego Flood Control District and various other improvements. Shaw agreed to construct the improvements and posted subdivision bonds. Cal West wanted to connect its subdivision sewer line to the trunk line by constructing a sewer line over property owned by Shaw and another landowner, Thomas Dyke.

---

83. *Id.*

84. *Id.* at *4–5.

85. *Id.* at *8; *see also* Rutherford Cnty. v. Bond Safeguard Ins. Co., No. 1:09-cv-292, 2011 WL 809821, at *6 (W.D.N.C. Mar. 2, 2011) (community association did not have standing to bring claim against subdivision bond as it was not a named third-party beneficiary under the subdivision bond).

86. *City of Yorkville*, 2010 WL 3385461, at *6, *8. *But see* 30 ILL. COMP. STAT. 550/1 (2010). The holding in the *City of Yorkville* case is effectively overturned by the Illinois Supreme Court decision in *Lake County Grading*, discussed in Part V.A. A subdivision bond under Illinois law is a payment bond for public works and a payment bond claimant has standing. *See supra* note 31.

87. No. D043509, 2005 WL 1654996 (Cal. Ct. App. July 15, 2005).

Cal West and Shaw entered into a joint venture agreement that provided that the parties desired to construct a sewer and storm drain over Shaw's property for their mutual benefit. Cal West, Shaw, and Dyke entered into a development and easement agreement for grading and construction of the sewer line on Shaw's and Dyke's properties. Under that agreement, Dyke was to grade the land and Shaw would pay for the grading. Cal West would install and pay for all improvements Shaw had promised San Diego, including the drainage system and sewer main. Cal West also posted subdivision bonds, with itself as principal, and the county of San Diego as obligee.[88]

Dyke and Cal West constructed the improvements on Shaw's property but failed to satisfactorily complete them. San Diego refused to approve the work and accept dedication of the improvements.[89] Shaw requested that San Diego complete the drainage and grading improvements on Shaw's land, either by enforcing the subdivision bonds against Cal West or by dedicating the storm drain and sewer line to public use. San Diego took neither of these requested actions.

Shaw attempted to sell the property, but he found that without correcting the storm drain issue, he could not sell the property for its full commercial value. Shaw filed suit against San Diego, seeking damages due to breach of mandatory duty, negligence, and inverse condemnation. The trial court granted San Diego's summary judgment motion, and the court of appeal affirmed. Both courts held that Shaw's claims were time barred and that Shaw was not a third-party beneficiary of the bonding agreement between Cal West and San Diego. Thus, Shaw had no right to enforce the subdivision bonds.[90]

G. Has the Claim Been Timely Presented?

A surety always will consider whether any claim is timely. As noted earlier, the subdivision agreement alone will not determine the completion date.

---

88. *Id.* at *1.

89. *Id.* at *2. Shaw sued Dyke for the improper construction and Dyke counterclaimed for payment. Dyke was awarded more than $2 million for payment, and Shaw declared bankruptcy when Dyke attempted to collect on the judgment. The bankruptcy proceeding was dismissed, and Shaw agreed to pay Dyke $2 million or forfeit the property. When Shaw could not sell the property to pay Dyke's judgment, he turned the property over to Dyke. *Id.*

90. *Id.*

Extensions of time are commonly allowed to which the surety may not receive notice. The state statute of limitations that applies for contracts will likely apply to a claim against a subdivision bond, absent some specific limitation in the bond or ordinance.

An interesting decision from the Northern District of Illinois granted summary judgment in favor of a surety, finding the municipality's claim was barred by laches.[91] The case is a prime example of how diligent claims handling can pay off.[92] Although the bond defined a default to include knowledge on the part of the obligee, the City of Yorkville, that the property for development is subject to claims for liens, the bond itself required performance of the subdivision improvements by the surety. The City became aware that three of the subcontractors for the developer were not paid in 2007. The City made demand to the surety, American Southern, to pay the claimants in 2009. American Southern, through a claim consultant, advised the City that the bonds covered performance and not payment of the claimants, and also did so in a subsequent letter in September 2009 to the City saying the bond covered performance, essentially soliciting a performance claim from the City. The City waited to file suit until March 21, 2011, and, in June 2012, ultimately amended the complaint to state a claim for performance of the subdivision improvements.

Current Illinois law after the *Lake County Grading* decision would allow the City to demand the surety remove the liens because the subdivision bond would likely be treated as a public works bond.[93] The court would never need to consider whether laches applied.[94] The discussion by the court on the issue of laches may nevertheless be instructive about the factors that give rise to a laches defense. In discussing laches, the court noted the surety's argument and evidence that in the six years since the City was aware of a right to assert a claim,

---

91. United City of Yorkville v. Ocean Atl. Serv. Corp., No. 11 CV 1984, 2013 WL 5433429 (N.D. Ill. Sept. 30, 2013).

92. This case is also cited above for its finding that the limitations that applied to subdivision bonds is the Illinois statute that applies to construction improvements. *See supra* note 56.

93. Lake Cnty. Grading Co., LLC v. Vill. of Antioch, 19 N.E.3d 615, 624 (Ill. 2014).

94. If a subdivision bond is an Illinois bond for public work, the payment claimants' claims should be subject to the one-year suit limitation found in 30 Illinois Compiled Statutes 550/2.

the property deteriorated. The surety asserted the City's failure to act increased the cost of performance. The court noted the surety continually advised the City of its rights and what the bonds covered. The court noted the evidence that the cost of performance increased the surety's liability anywhere from $968,073.02 to $1,098,073.02. The court held:

> American Southern has shown by a preponderance of the evidence that Yorkville neglected to assert its performance claim in a timely manner. American has shown, further, that the delay caused prejudice: Defendant was denied the opportunity to remedy the construction problems in a cost-effective way, and the cost of performance on the contract increased significantly. Yorkville's claim for performance asserted in Count IV is barred by the laches defense. Therefore, American Southern's motion for summary judgment is granted and Yorkville's motion is denied.[95]

Given the time frame from when a problem on a development might appear and when the actual development is feasible and the surety is called upon to perform the construction of subdivision improvements, whether the delay is the product of some neglect on the part of the obligee can potentially be a defense for the surety.

H. Has the Municipality Complied with the Applicable Enabling Statute and Its Own Ordinances?

A municipality may include within its claim the installation or provision of items beyond those for which the applicable enabling statute authorized the municipality to require a performance guaranty. In such cases, the municipality's demands upon the developer and surety are ultra vires and

---

95. The court's language describing the impact of the City's conduct on the surety mirrors the language of the Restatement of Suretyship and Guaranty describing impairment of suretyship status: "(1) if the obligee acts to increase the secondary obligor's risk of loss by increasing its potential cost of performance or by decreasing its potential ability to cause the principal obligor to bear the cost of performance, the secondary obligor is discharged . . ." RESTATEMENT (THIRD) OF SURETYSHIP AND GUARANTY § 37(1) (1996).

should create no liability.[96] But a developer that voluntarily undertakes work beyond the scope of the statute or ordinance may be estopped from defending a claim for that work because it was ultra vires.[97]

In *Bama, Inc. v. Anne Arundel County*,[98] for example, the bond secured the obligation of the developer to improve a road adjoining its development and to donate 15 feet of land to widen it. At the time of the agreement, the county had not yet passed an ordinance that authorized it to make such a requirement a condition of subdivision approval. On appeal, the court held the requirement was ultra vires and not binding as a matter of law, but nevertheless, remanded the case to the trial judge for a determination of whether the developer was estopped from raising a plea of ultra vires. The instructions on remand directed the trial court to focus on the extent to which the developer questioned the county's authority prior to agreeing to the county's conditions for subdivision approval.

---

96. *See* N.J. Shore Builders Ass'n v. Twp. of Marlboro, 591 A.2d 950 (N.J. Super. Ct. App. Div. 1999) (the cost of electricity for street lighting held not an improvement for which a municipality was authorized to require a bond from developers); E. Planned Cmtys. at Lincroft, Inc. v. Middletown Twp., 563 A.2d 81 (N.J. Super. Ct. Law Div. 1989) (municipality is without statutory authority to require a developer to form a homeowners' association as a condition for releasing performance security). See also *Hilton Acres v. Klein*, 35 N.J. 570, 581 (1961), observing as follows:

    > The Appellate Division held that, since the extension provision was void for lack of municipal power and in contravention of the enabling statute, plaintiffs were not entitled to the benefit of it.
    >
    > This conclusion rests on established and eminently sound law. Our cases have consistently held that municipal action in the land use control field taken in direct violation of law or without legal authority is void ab initio and has no legal efficacy. So a building permit issued contrary to a zoning ordinance or building code cannot ground any rights in the applicant.

97. Bd. of Cnty. Supervisors v. Sie-Gray Developers, Inc., 334 S.E.2d 542 (Va. 1985).
98. 451 A.2d 1261 (Md. Ct. Spec. App. 1982).

I. The Status of the Work: Has the Developer Started the Improvement Work?

The commencement of the improvement work in some jurisdictions may impose on the surety the obligation to complete that work.[99] The developer and its surety also may be obligated to maintain and repair any completed improvements until all subdivision improvements are completed and accepted.[100]

In other jurisdictions, the surety's liability has been limited to the cost of those specified improvements required to service the homes on which construction has actually commenced. In *Town of Shawangunk v. Goldwil Properties Corp.*, the court found the obligation of the subdivision bond surety was limited to that portion of the improvements required for the structures actually constructed.[101] The court ordered the payment of the penal sum of the bond to the town so that it could complete improvements reasonably justified by that part of the subdivision that had been developed and ordered the town refund of any amount not needed to complete that portion of the work.[102]

Whether the property is entirely abandoned may impact the surety's obligation to construct improvements. The Office of the State Comptroller of New York[103] ruled that a town planning board may not require a

---

99. *See, e.g.*, City of Palmdale v. Bond Safeguard Ins. Co., No. CV 13-1662, LEXIS 193870 (C.D. Cal. Nov. 12, 2013); City of Sacramento v. Trans Pac. Indus., 159 Cal. Rptr. 514 (Cal. Ct. App. 1979); Kern Cnty. v. Edgemont Dev. Corp., 35 Cal. Rptr. 629 (Cal. Dist. Ct. App. 1963); Mount Florence Grp. v. City of Peekskill, 652 N.Y.S.2d 814 (N.Y. App. Div. 1997); *cf.* Town of Southington v. Commercial Union Ins. Co., 757 A.2d 549 (Conn. 2000) (interpreting a Connecticut statute to grant a municipality discretion to call subdivision bond whether or not any lots have been conveyed).

100. *Kern Cnty.*, 35 Cal. Rptr. 629; *Mount Florence Grp.*, 652 N.Y.S.2d 814.

101. 403 N.Y.S.2d 784 (N.Y. App. Div. 1978) (relying, in part, on New York Town Law section 277, subdivision 1); *see also* Town of Southeast v. Seaboard Sur. Co., 616 N.Y.S.2d 812 (N.Y. App. Div. 1994); Westchester Fire Ins. Co. v. City of Brooksville, 731 F. Supp. 2d 1298 (M.D. Fla. 2010).

102. *See* City of Peekskill v. Cont'l Ins. Co., 999 F. Supp. 584 (S.D.N.Y. 1998), *aff'd*, 166 F.3d 1199 (2d Cir. 1998); Vill. of Warwick v. Republic Ins. Co., 428 N.Y.S.2d 589 (N.Y. Sup. Ct. 1980).

103. Op. State Comptroller of N.Y. 81-158 (1981).

developer or its surety to construct streets and other improvements that would lie entirely within an area abandoned by the developer, and that would service only the abandoned lots. A developer who elects to phase a subdivision development can build and sell homes in only one phase and complete the public improvements for that phase alone. The developer will not be required to complete public improvements in the remaining phases if the developer decides not to start work on the additional phases.

In contrast, a Virginia court required the surety to pay the public body the amount of its bond that secured improvements to an abandoned development. Moreover, there was no direct evidence that the county actually intended to complete the bonded improvements. In that case, the court held it must presume the county would properly use the bond proceeds.[104]

More recently, in *Town of Groton v. Mardie Lane Homes, LLC*,[105] East Haven Builders Supply, Inc., which held a mortgage on certain lots in the subdivision, brought suit against the town of Groton and the surety to complete the public improvements in the subdivision pursuant to Connecticut General Statutes Annotated section 8-26c(c).[106] This statute sets a five-year deadline for the developer to complete all work, including the public improvements, starting from the date of the approval of the subdivision plan.[107] If the developer fails to complete the improvements within the five-year period, the subdivision plan of approval is deemed expired. However, if during the five-year period, "lots have been conveyed," the town "shall call the subdivision bond . . . to the extent necessary to complete the bonded improvements and utilities required to serve those lots."[108]

---

104. Bd. of Supervisors v. Safeco Ins. Co. of Am., 310 S.E.2d 445 (Va. 1983) (citing *City of Sacramento*, 159 Cal. Rptr. 514, and declining to follow Cnty. of Yuba v. Cent. Valley Nat'l Bank, Inc., 97 Cal. Rptr. 369 (Cal. Ct. App. 1971)). It should be noted, however, that two justices dissented, stating that where there is no likelihood the development will be constructed, the court's ruling amounts to a forfeiture, penalizing the surety under the guise of enforcing the terms of an indemnity bond. *Id.* at 449–50; *see also* Furlong Dev. Co., LLC v. Georgetown-Scott Cnty. Plan. & Zoning Comm'n, 504 S.W.3d 34 (Ky. 2016).

105. 943 A.2d 449 (Conn. 2008).

106. *Id.* at 451.

107. *Id.* at 452.

108. *Id.*; *see also* CONN. GEN. STAT. § 8-26c(c) (West 2011).

By the end of the five-year period, the public improvements had not been completed in the subdivision. The town commission determined that the subdivision plan had expired and recorded a formal notice of subdivision expiration in the town land records. Several of the parties that had acquired interests in certain lots in the subdivision demanded that the town retract the expiration notice and call the subdivision bond to complete the improvements servicing those lots in which they held an interest.[109]

In response, the town of Groton and the surety filed a declaratory judgment action against all parties with an interest in the lots, seeking a judgment that the town had no obligation to call the subdivision bond as a result of the transfers of interests in the subdivision lots. The town and the surety asserted that the transfer of such interests, such as the mortgage held by defendant Mardie Homes, was not the type of "conveyance" referred to in the statute and no obligation on the part of the town arose.[110]

The Supreme Court of Connecticut reviewed the statute and concluded that based upon the language of the statute, the statute did not refer to "conveyances" in the general sense of the word, but specifically to the conveyance of lots.[111] Ultimately, the court held that the transfer of a mortgage interest was not the same as the conveyance of a lot because the conveyance of a lot specifically meant that "the interest conveyed is ownership of a parcel of land."[112] Because no conveyance of a lot had occurred, the town did not have an obligation to call the subdivision bond to complete the public improvements.

J. No Liability Until Commencement of Development

One California court has held that the subdivision bond surety's obligation arises after the principal begins construction of the improvements.[113]

---

109. *Town of Groton*, 943 A.2d at 452.
110. *Id.* at 452–53.
111. *Id.* at 453–54.
112. *Id.* at 454.
113. Cnty. of Yuba v. Cent. Valley Nat'l Bank, Inc., 97 Cal. Rptr. 369 (Cal. Ct. App. 1971). The holding in *County of Yuba* was limited by *City of Sacramento v. Trans Pacific Industries, Inc.*, 159 Cal. Rptr. 514 (Cal. Ct. App. 1979), and further limited by *City of Los Angeles v. Amwest Surety Insurance Co.*, 73 Cal. Rptr. 2d 729 (Cal. Ct. App. 1998). In these decisions that followed *Yuba*, the California courts have held that where at least some development has occurred, and where it appears that the

The court in *County of Yuba v. Central Valley National Bank, Inc.* stated, "The language of the instrument of credit executed by [the bank] indicates that the parties intended to provide security for full completion of improvements whose construction had already begun."[114] Due to a shift in the local population base, the developer found it impossible to sell homes. As a result, no development was ever commenced on the tract for which the instrument of credit was issued. The court denied recovery noting that "construction of streets would serve no useful purpose in the absence of such a subdivision and that none of the parties intended streets to be constructed except as part of construction of such a subdivision."[115] The court based its ruling on the doctrine of "frustration of purpose" and stated that to require the bank to pay the county "would be to uphold an illegal forfeiture."[116]

Similarly, in *River Vale Planning Board v. E&R Office Interiors, Inc.*, a New Jersey appellate court rejected a public body's attempt to enforce a variance, site plan conditions, and a subdivision agreement for a project that had been abandoned *prior* to the commencement of any construction.[117] The developer argued that its obligation to perform was contingent upon commencing construction of the project itself. Both the trial court and the appellate court agreed, finding that once the site plan application had been abandoned, there was no need to proceed with the improvements.[118]

Yuba and *River Vale* laid the groundwork for other decisions that also found a surety will not be held liable on claims against the subdivision bond when the developer abandons construction of the subdivision before construction of homes has even begun. In *Westchester Fire*

---

municipality intends to complete the improvements, the municipality has a valid claim under a subdivision bond. *See also* Bd. of Supervisors v. Safeco Ins. Co. of Am., 310 S.E.2d 445 (Va. 1983), and the dissent thereto.

114. 97 Cal. Rptr. at 371.

115. *Id.*

116. *Id.* at 372.

117. 575 A.2d 55 (N.J. Super. Ct. App. Div. 1990).

118. *Id.* at 59–60 (citing, inter alia, New Windsor v. Inbro Dev., 448 N.Y.S.2d 99 (N.Y. Sup. Ct. 1982) (condition of subdivision bond not actuated where developer fails to commence work)). While not brought in the context of a subdivision bond claim against a surety, it can be fairly argued that the citation was an endorsement, albeit in dicta, by the appellate division of the result of the case cited.

Insurance Co. v. City of Brooksville,[119] the developer, Levitt and Sons of Hernando County, purchased property and planned to construct a five-phase residential housing project in the City of Brooksville. Brooksville approved the final plat for Phase Two, which required the developer to construct several improvements, including roadways, storm lines, potable water lines, and sanitary sewer lines.[120] These improvements would only benefit the lots in Phase Two. To ensure the construction of the improvements so "that future owners will be able to connect their lots to [Brooksville's] utility services," the developer was required to obtain a bond.[121] Westchester Fire Insurance Co. issued two subdivision bonds on behalf of the developer, Levitt, as principal, and in favor of Brooksville, as obligee, in a total sum of more than $4 million.[122]

Less than one year later, before beginning construction of Phase Two, Levitt filed for bankruptcy.[123] Levitt had removed trees and cleared some land but had not begun constructing any homes in Phase Two. Levitt also had not marketed or sold any parcels in Phase Two.[124] Brooksville demanded payment on the bonds and sued Westchester. In the meantime, Key Bank purchased the property at a foreclosure sale and assigned the property to Oreo Corp. of Ohio. Oreo sold the property to the Kolter Group, LLC.[125] The City attempted to negotiate modifications with Kolter to the City's Utility Services Agreement on the condition that Kolter purchase the property in its present condition and post new performance and payment bonds. Kolter refused to execute new bonds and told the City that it would need to pursue its rights against the surety under the existing bonds. Kolter also stated that it most likely would not commence construction for another three years.[126]

The surety prevailed on two defenses to Brooksville's claims. First, citing *River Vale*, the court held that there was an implied condition that the developer had to begin construction of Phase Two before Brooksville could collect against the subdivision bond.[127] Brooksville's ordinance

---

119. 731 F. Supp. 2d 1298 (M.D. Fla. 2010).
120. *Id.* at 1300.
121. *Id.*
122. *Id.*
123. *Id.* at 1301.
124. *Id.*
125. *Id.*
126. *Id.* at 1302–03.
127. *Id.* at 1305–06.

requires the subdivision bonds to ensure that the residents who purchase the homes in the development have access to Brooksville's utility services. Because there were no homes built that required such access, and no homes would be built for several years, the surety was not liable for the cost of the improvements. The court held that requiring the surety to pay would cause an unreasonable windfall to Brooksville and an unreasonable forfeiture to the surety.[128]

The court also held that Brooksville suffered no damages.[129] Brooksville sought payment of the full penal sum of the subdivision bonds, but under Florida law, as the court discussed, the surety will only be required to pay the full penal sum of the subdivision bond if the obligee's damages are not "capable of being liquidated in money."[130] Here, Brooksville's damages could have been liquidated, but Brooksville did not attempt to construct the improvements or solicit bids to determine the expected cost of construction.[131] In addition, Brooksville had no obligation to construct the improvements, and, as alluded to in the opinion, the court did not want to award Brooksville the full amount of the subdivision bonds, especially when Brooksville had no obligation to actually use that money for the improvements.[132]

K. Damages Resulting from the Developer's Failure to Complete the Improvements

Claims evaluation includes an assessment of damages. The terms of the bond may bear on the surety's obligation to perform or pay. Some subdivision bonds are penalty bonds. A penalty bond may be a liquidated damage in the event the developer fails to complete the improvements. Upon the default of the principal and timely notice of claim, the surety will be required to pay the full penal sum of the subdivision bond, regardless of whether the public body incurred damages or intends to complete the improvements.[133]

A more typical subdivision bond provides for indemnity and the surety will be liable only for the actual cost of completing the required

---

128. *Id.* at 1307.
129. *Id.* at 1307–09.
130. *Id.* at 1308.
131. *Id.* at 1309.
132. *Id.* at 1307 n.2.
133. *See, e.g.*, Clark v. Barnard, 108 U.S. 436 (1883).

improvements.[134] The purpose of such a bond is to provide funds necessary to cover the costs of completing the improvements. Recovery is limited to the reasonable completion costs and may not exceed the face amount of the bond.[135] Contrary to this general rule and the ordinary understanding of what indemnity means, some courts allow recovery in the absence of an actual loss or an intent of the public body to complete the development.[136] Such results arguably foster penalties that are contrary to public policy.[137]

In assessing the amount of damages, the surety may obtain an initial evaluation of the state of completion of the improvements by an experienced engineer or builder. Such evaluation should be compiled after a walk-through of the site either with or without a representative of the obligee. Aerial photographs of the site may be helpful in assessing the improvements remaining to be installed. Aerial or inspection photographs

---

134. In *General Insurance Co. of America v. City of Colorado Springs*, 638 P.2d 752, 757 (Colo. 1981), relying upon *United States v. Zerbey*, 271 U.S. 332 (1926), the court rejected the City's contention that the subdivision bond was a "penalty bond," but rather deemed the bond an "indemnity bond," liable only for the actual cost of completing the required improvements. *See also* Morro Palisade Co. v. Hartford Accident & Indem. Co., 340 P.2d 628 (Cal. 1959); Cnty. of Los Angeles v. Margulis, 44 P.2d 608 (Cal. Dist. Ct. App. 1935).
135. *See* Town of Poughkeepsie v. Holden Constr. Co., Inc., 419 N.Y.S.2d 531 (N.Y. App. Div. 1979) (case remanded to assess public body's damages resulting from developer's breach); Bd. of Cnty. Supervisors v. Sie-Gray Developers, Inc., 334 S.E.2d 542 (Va. 1985); Bd. of Supervisors v. Safeco Ins. Co. of Am., 310 S.E.2d 445, 448 (Va. 1983).
136. *Bd. of Supervisors*, 310 S.E.2d at 448 (a surety stands in the shoes of its principal and may not assert defenses that are not available to the principal). But the result in *Board of Supervisors v. Safeco Insurance Co. of America* appears to be anomalous, as the surety had conceded that the county's lack of intent to complete the improvements was not a viable defense to the principal's failure to complete the improvements. *See id.* (citing Cohen v. Mayflower Corp., 86 S.E.2d 860, 866 (Va. 1955)); *see also* Furlong Dev. Co., LLC v. Georgetown-Scott Cnty. Plan. & Zoning Comm'n, 504 S.W.3d 34 (Ky. 2016).
137. Ogden Dev. Corp. v. Fed. Ins. Co., 508 F.2d 583, 584 (2d Cir. 1974) (complete legal defense to surety where subdivision bond prescribed a penalty rather than a legally enforceable provision for liquidated damages).

may also be used as an exhibit in the event the surety asserts defenses to the claim and the matter proceeds to a trial.

The claims professional should make sure the list of uncompleted work provided by the public body does not include improvements beyond the scope of the subdivision bonds or subdivision agreement. Both the language of the bonds and the agreement should be reviewed to determine the scope of the improvements. At least one court, however, has held that where the agreement and the subdivision bonds are inconsistent about the scope of the improvements, the terms of the bond define the scope.[138] In *Construction 70, Inc. v. Bond Safeguard Insurance Co.*, the developer, Engle Homes Residential Construction, LLC, entered into a contract with ApexCapital Fund 2, LLC to serve as the general contractor for constructing improvements in a subdivision project. A year later, the construction agreement was amended, in part, to require Engle Homes to obtain a "performance and completion bond."[139] The amendment also provided that the "issuer of the bond shall be committed to complete all improvements to Sossaman Road which [Engle Homes] is obligated to complete."[140] The bond also was to be issued in an amount of not less than 100 percent of the costs "to complete construction of all improvements to Sossaman Road."[141]

On the same date of the amendment, Bond Safeguard Insurance Company issued a subdivision bond that provided in relevant part that "if said Principal and/or contractor or subcontractor fails to pay for any materials, provisions, or rented equipment used in, upon, or for or about the construction of the public improvements . . . said surety will pay the same."[142]

Engle Homes retained Construction 70 to perform the paving and concrete work for the subdivision. Construction 70 completed the work and submitted payment requests to Engle Homes. Engle Homes paid a small amount of the money owed and then filed for bankruptcy. Construction 70 demanded payment from Bond Safeguard and filed two lien actions against Apex, which it voluntarily dismissed.[143] Construction

138. *See* Constr. 70, Inc. v. Bond Safeguard Ins. Co., No. 1 CA-CV 10-0137, 2011 WL 553239 (Ariz. Ct. App. Feb. 17, 2011).
139. *Id.* at *1.
140. *Id.*
141. *Id.*
142. *Id.*
143. *Id.*

70 filed a third lien foreclosure action, this time naming the surety as a defendant, and then moved for summary judgment. The court granted summary judgment in favor of Construction 70.[144] The surety filed a motion for reconsideration, which was denied, and then appealed.

On appeal, the Arizona Court of Appeals affirmed the trial court's decision. The surety had argued that in light of the extrinsic evidence, such as the amendment, which should be used to interpret the subdivision bond, there were factual issues not ripe for summary judgment. The court held the language of the bond was the language of a payment bond, even though the agreement called for a performance bond. Moreover, while the language of the amendment to the construction agreement appeared to limit the scope of the surety's liability to public improvements on Sossaman Road, the court held that the subdivision bond specifically provided for payment for the "construction of public improvements" throughout the subdivision, including the paving and concrete work performed by Construction 70.[145] This case points out the importance of the surety's review of the subdivision agreements prior to issuing the subdivision bond to make sure the language is consistent and the scope of the developer's and surety's responsibilities with respect to public improvements is clearly defined.[146]

The surety is not ordinarily obligated to pay for the cost of operating or maintaining the subdivision improvements.[147] Other damages that

---

144. *Id.* at *2.
145. *Id.* at *3.
146. The surety belatedly tried to introduce evidence on a motion for reconsideration of the engineer's estimate that purportedly would have demonstrated that the subdivision bond was intended to cover the work for Sossaman Road only. The trial court granted Construction 70's motion to strike the estimate and the appellate court refused to consider an argument raised for the first time in a motion for reconsideration. *Id.* at *4; *see also* City of Summit v. Horton Corp., 407 A.2d 371 (N.J. Super. Ct. App. Div. 1961) (holding that city could not condition release of subdivision bonds upon performance of work by the developer that was not part of the original subdivision agreement and directing the city to accept the improvements).
147. N.J. Shore Builders Ass'n v. Twp. of Marlton, 591 A.2d 950 (N.J. Super. Ct. App. Div. 1991); *see also* E. Planned Cmtys. at Lincroft, Inc. v. Middletown Twp., 563 A.2d 81 (N.J. Super. Ct. Law Div. 1989) (holding that an obligation on the part of the developer to form a homeowners' association pursuant to the planning board approvals was not a bondable

may not be covered by the subdivision bond include cracked sidewalks, chipped curbing, and dead or dying plants that appear after the improvements were completed by the developer and dedicated to the public body. The public body may overreach in making a claim and seek recovery for problems resulting from its failure to properly maintain properly dedicated improvements. Noting the foregoing potential limits of damage claims, one should review the subdivision bonds and subdivision agreement to determine whether specific claims asserted by the public body fall within the subdivision bond's coverage.[148]

VII. Successor Liability for Subdivision Improvements

Several recent Illinois decisions further support the principle that a successor developer can be liable to the surety for the cost of improvements.[149] These cases arise out of the Kimball Hill, Inc. bankruptcy,[150] and support the proposition that the successor developer is a substituted principal and accordingly must reimburse the surety. The *Kimball Hill* opinions reverse the trial courts' orders granting motions to dismiss the claims of the surety against the successor developer and they are not adjudications on the merits.

---

item and release of the subdivision bond could not be withheld pending this event).

148. This review may require evaluating how courts treat incorporation by reference and how specific terms of the bond limit the scope of work. *Compare* Developers Sur. & Indem. Co. v. City of Durham, No. 1:11CV515, 2014 WL 4677181 (M.D.N.C. Sept. 18, 2014) (limiting surety's obligation to construct sidewalks to work described in the bond and rejecting the city claim the developer agreement required everything needed for the street to be accepted by the city), *with* O'Fallon v. Bank of Belleville, 525 N.E.2d 1162 (Ill. App. Ct. 1988) (noting the developer agreement and city ordinances are incorporated in the bond and finding the adjacent culvert was included in the obligation to install streets and sidewalks).

149. Until these Illinois decisions, there was very little case authority on the liability of successor developers for the cost of the public improvements. Logically, the liability for obligations that run with the land ought to be borne by the owner. *See* Klinger & Ryken, *supra* note 61.

150. *In re* Kimball Hill, Inc., No. 08-bk-10095 (Bankr. N.D. Ill. filed Apr. 23, 2008).

These rulings examined closely the underlying annexation agreements that relate to the bonds. These decisions plainly articulate why a successor developer remains liable for the public improvements:

> The trial court held, when Kimball Hill's bankruptcy trustee sold all of the remaining property in the development to TRG [the successor developer], the sale discharged Kimball Hill's obligation to complete the public improvements. However, that underlying obligation was a covenant that ran with the land and thus bound TRG. Although TRG has reserved its right to contest this holding in the context of the City's claim against TRG, we accept it for the purposes of analyzing the sufficiency of Fidelity's [the surety's] counterclaim. The Annexation Agreement, which was recorded shortly after it was entered into, clearly provides that any subsequent development must comply with the terms therein. The agreement provides that it is binding upon successors and assigns and that its terms constitute a covenant running with the land. Moreover, state law likewise provides that annexation agreements "shall be binding upon the successor owners of record of the land which is the subject of the agreement." 65 ILCS 5/11-15.1-4 (West 2012). On the record before us, TRG's successor liability would appear to be a matter of public record and statutory law, which is incorporated into every contract unless the contract provides to the contrary.[151]

The Appellate Court of Illinois Second District issued another opinion reversing the trial court's dismissals of the surety's third-party complaints against TRG.[152] It held that the development agreements at issue run with the land, and as such bind successor owners even though they are not signatories.[153] The court painstakingly reviewed the terms and provisions of the development agreement and case authority involving the same parties on a different development and found that the surety had sufficiently stated a claim that TRG and another developer were successor developers bound by the terms of the development agreement.[154] Citing a

151. City of Elgin v. Arch Ins. Co., 53 N.E.3d 31, 40 (Ill. App. Ct. 2015).
152. United City of Yorkville v. Fid. & Deposit Co. of Md., 143 N.E.3d 69 (Ill. App. Ct. 2019).
153. *Id.*
154. *Id.*

prior case among the parties, the appellate court also stated that TRG had obtained lots by warranty deed in that case but the municipality had not received a substitute letter of credit or performance bonds from Kimball Hill.[155] After a review of the development agreements and the statutes, the court determined:

> First, a party's duties under the [development agreement] transfer necessarily to successors in interest. Second, [the applicable statute's] exception for purchases of lots "for residential occupation" applies alike to purchase of single and multiple lots, whether emptied or improved. Third, acquisition of lots for development purposes, *i.e.*, for construction or renovation of residences for sale to third parties, is not acquisition "for residential occupation." Fourth, [the development agreement] permits joint liability among the original developer and a successor developer or developers. Finally, [the applicable statute] permits a residential purchaser to assume development duties but has no language permitting a successor developer to avoid development duties.[156]

Any optimism these cases offer to a subdivision bond surety that the cost of developments can be recovered by a subdivision bond surety from a successor purchaser is dimmed by the strategies available to purchasers to avoid successor obligations. As noted above, a purchaser or foreclosing bank can enter into a "sweetheart deal" with the public body. And, as discussed next, a bankruptcy sale order or plan release might be used to protect the purchaser of a development from obligations that normally run with the land.[157]

---

155. *Id.*
156. *Id.* at 90.
157. 11 U.S.C. § 363(f) enables a court to sell property free and clear of all liens. Provisions of plans of reorganization often contain release provisions. An Illinois bankruptcy court interpreted a plan release provision to release the liability of a successor developer for the costs of improvements required by ordinance. *In re* Kimball Hill, Inc., 565 B.R. 878 (Bankr. N.D. Ill. 2017).

VIII. Bankruptcy Issues and the Subdivision Bond Surety

The filing by the principal of a bankruptcy petition is never a good day in the life of its surety. Subdivision developer bankruptcies appear in waves or phases. In 2008, after the housing bubble burst, there were websites devoted solely to reporting on subdivision developer bankruptcies. This was a busy time for their sureties. Some lessons emerged from the bankruptcy cases during this phase.

There usually is no contract balance to which a subdivision surety can look to apply to the cost of performance as would a performance bond surety. There may be set aside funds that a municipality has set aside for subdivision improvements, but these are not funds payable to the principal and may not be available to the surety for installation of the improvements. The surety may have recourse against set aside funds held by a financing bank for subdivision improvements, as discussed earlier.[158]

The subdivision property likely belongs to the debtor principal, which means that to proceed with improvements to the property and to make a claim against the bond, the obligee (municipality) needs to lift the automatic stay imposed by the Bankruptcy Code.[159] Ordinarily, an obligee would not be required to lift the stay to sue or make a demand on the surety because as a jointly liable co-obligor with the principal, the stay does not apply to the surety.[160]

That surety bonds are financial accommodations that cannot be assumed by a debtor in bankruptcy will be addressed elsewhere in this book.[161] With respect to subdivision agreements, one bankruptcy court found an annexation or subdivision agreement is not an executory

---

158. *See* Developers Sur. & Indem. Co. v. Am. Nat'l Bank, No. 10 C 50195, 2012 WL 2906244 (N.D. Ill. July 16, 2012).
159. 11 U.S.C. § 362(a).
160. *See* Fisher Sand & Gravel Co. v. W. Sur. Co., No. CV 09–727, 2009 WL 4099768 (D.N.M. Oct. 20, 2009) (dismissing a subcontractor's tolling argument concluding that the automatic stay did not apply to actions against codebtors of the debtor and the bankruptcy court had not been requested to extend the stay to the surety); United States *ex rel.* Cent. Bldg. Supply, Inc. v. William F. Wilke, Inc., 685 F. Supp. 936 (D. Md. 1988) (Miller Act surety not protected by the automatic stay that applies to its principal); *In re* Duplitronics, Inc., 183 B.R. 1010 (Bankr. N.D. Ill. 1995) (bonds are not property of the estate and are not subject to the automatic stay).
161. *See also* 11 U.S.C. § 365(c).

contract within the meaning of § 365 of the Bankruptcy Code.[162] The requirements of the municipal ordinances, or the annexation/development agreements, are not executory contracts the debtor can reject, nor are they liens or interests in property that can be stripped away and compensated by paying cash.[163]

Notwithstanding the better reasoned view that development obligations are not executory contracts and cannot be assumed by the debtor nor stripped away from the underlying properties, bankruptcy courts have stripped these obligations from development properties, leaving the purchaser free to obtain the cost of improvements from the surety, and leaving the surety without recourse against the purchaser to recover these costs.[164] The courts find the power to eliminate these obligations in § 363 sale orders or plan releases and injunctions in chapter 11 plans. Bankruptcy courts tend to view their powers to strip liens from properties expansively. The courts eliminate the successor or purchaser obligations to enhance the value of the debtors' estates by increasing the sale value of the properties.

The failure of a subdivision improvement bond surety to object to a sale order apparently doomed its claim to recover the cost of improvements from a successor developer in *Travelers Casualty & Surety Co. of America v. Morgan Acquisitions, LLC*.[165] This case involved a district court recovery/subrogation action brought by a subdivision bond surety

---

162. *Id.* § 365.

163. *In re* Banning Lewis Ranch Co., LLC, 532 B.R. 335 (Bankr. D. Colo. 2015) (a development agreement is not a contract, and if it is a contract, it is not an executory contract, and further stating that even if it is an executory contract capable of rejection, rejection does not terminate the contract). The *Banning* case also stated that restrictions that run with the land, such as development or annexation agreements, are not "interests" that fall within 11 U.S.C. § 363(f)'s provision allowing sales of property free and clear of interests.

164. Among the reasons obligations that run with the land should not be stripped away is that the bankruptcy court should not interfere with the state's exercise of police power. *See In re* Union Golf of Fla., Inc., 242 B.R. 51 (Bankr. M.D. Fla. 1998) (chapter 11 plan could not strip away zoning regulation requiring a private golf course); Skyline Woods Homeowners Ass'n v. Broekemeier, 758 N.W.2d 376 (Neb. 2008) (action brought to enforce a restrictive covenant was not a collateral attack on a bankruptcy sale order).

165. No. 10-10965, 2010 WL 2474631 (E.D. Mich. June 14, 2010).

against a successor owner of property that acquired the property through a bankruptcy § 363 sale, which provided the sale of property was free and clear of all liens. The obligee demanded that the surety complete the improvements covered by the bond, and the surety demanded that the purchaser of the property do so. The purchaser refused, and the surety paid to complete the bonded work. The surety then sued the purchaser as subrogee of the obligee. The purchaser moved to dismiss the suit as an impermissible collateral attack on the bankruptcy court's order approving the sale barred by res judicata. The court agreed and dismissed the suit for failure to state a claim. The court reasoned that the surety entered its appearance in the bankruptcy proceeding and could have objected to the sale order.

The surety argued that the order did not bar its current claim because the order exempted enforcement of liability to a governmental unit under police and regulatory statutes or regulations. The court held that the underlying permit was a contractual obligation of the principal to the obligee, and the surety bond merely guaranteed that contractual obligation. The order approved the sale free and clear of the obligation; therefore, the purchaser did not have to reimburse the surety for the cost to complete the work. The court also held that the surety could have made its objections in the bankruptcy proceeding and the order approving the sale was a final order that barred the surety's claim.

A bankruptcy court recently found that a subdivision bond surety's suit against a successor developer violated a chapter 11 plan injunction. Unfortunately, this ruling related to the Kimball Hill subdivision bond decisions that held a successor developer could be a substituted principal, as discussed above.

In the Kimball Hill plan, neither the release nor plan injunction language on their face suggest that a suit by a surety against a successor developer that acquired the property from a plan trust would violate the terms of the plan.[166] But in ruling that the surety violated the plan and ordering sanctions of $9.5 million against the surety, the bankruptcy

166. The discussion of the terms of the release and injunction in the Kimball Hill plan are fairly typical. The court found the successor developer TRG was released from any claim by the surety as a successor to the debtor under the plan. The discussion is found at *In re* Kimball Hill, Inc., 565 B.R. 878, 884–86 (Bankr. N.D. Ill. 2017).

court noted the surety voted for the plan and did not object to the terms of the plan.[167]

After the surety won the appeals in state court recognizing the right of a surety to proceed with a suit against a successor developer and many years after the surety filed suit against TRG as a successor developer, TRG moved in the bankruptcy court to enjoin the surety from asserting claims against TRG arising in connection with its acquisition from a non-debtor of real property that was the subject of certain development agreements between chapter 11 debtor Kimball Hill, Inc. and various municipalities in Illinois.[168] Kimball Hill sold the development post-plan confirmation to a non-debtor entity, JNI, LLC, who subsequently sold the development to TRG.[169]

In its motion to enjoin the surety's assertion of its claim against TRG, TRG argued that the surety was enjoined from asserting claims against TRG, which benefitted from the broad third-party release and injunction provisions under the plan.[170] TRG also asked the bankruptcy court to direct the dismissal of the surety's state court lawsuits, and to award damages for violating the release and injunction provisions of the plan.[171] The surety had filed numerous proofs of claim in Kimball Hill's chapter 11 case, and voted in favor of the plan.[172] The plan specifically provided that all holders of claims "voting to accept the Plan . . . shall be deemed to have conclusively, absolutely, unconditionally, irrevocably and forever, released and discharged the debtors . . . the Liquidating Trust . . . and the Released Parties."[173] The released parties expressly included successors.[174] The bankruptcy court found the surety was bound by the release.[175] The issue was whether the release and injunction provisions extended to TRG and, in effect, precluded a suit by a non-debtor surety against a non-debtor seeking recovery in state court on a cognizable state law claim.[176]

---

167. The bankruptcy court noted: "Further, F&D [the surety] voluntarily subjected itself to the Release and Plan Injunction by voting in favor of the Plan." *Id.* at 898.
168. *Kimball Hill*, 565 B.R. 878.
169. *Id.* at 886.
170. *Id.*
171. *Id.*
172. *Id.* at 884–85.
173. *Id.*
174. *Id.* at 899–90.
175. *Id.* at 884–85.
176. *Id.*

The court found that the scope of the release included the surety's claim against TRG.[177] The bankruptcy court then ordered (1) that the surety dismiss its claims against TRG in the state court lawsuits, and (2) that it would conduct a separate hearing on contempt damages.[178] The bankruptcy court subsequently denied the surety's motion to reconsider.[179] The court awarded $9.5 million against the surety and in favor of TRG comprising (1) approximately $1.2 million in legal fees; (2) approximately $194,000 in consultant fees; (3) approximately $362,000 in project management fees; and (4) approximately $7.7 million in lost property value.[180] At the time of the writing of this chapter, the bankruptcy court ruling is on appeal.[181]

There are lessons in these cases for the subdivision bond surety in bankruptcy. First, the surety should participate in the bankruptcy case and take steps to prevent a sale order or plan from cutting off rights and obligations, and make objections. Second, the surety might consider getting a finding from the bankruptcy court that the bonds or the development agreements are not executory contracts and can neither be assumed nor rejected by the debtor. Third, the surety should not vote for or give assent to a chapter 11 plan that might improperly cut off rights and eliminate obligations. Fourth, when in doubt about whether an action or legal proceeding might violate the automatic stay or plan injunction, before taking such an action, the surety should move to lift the stay or to modify the plan injunction to permit that action.

The surety can no longer be sanguine about what occurs in the bankruptcy of its principal and assume that a plan sale or § 363 sale will not affect obligations of a purchaser that presumably run with the land. Bankruptcy courts are tempted to overreach and exceed their jurisdiction in pursuing the goal of enhancing the value of the estate by approving

---

177. *Id.* at 889–90. These cases were wrongly decided for several reasons. Among them is the language of the release in the plan cannot conceivably be construed to release obligations of the subdivision bond surety and successor developer that "run with the land." A second reason is the bankruptcy court lacked jurisdiction to enjoin an action between non-debtor parties relating to payment of obligations that run with the land.

178. *Id.* at 903.

179. *In re* Kimball Hill, Inc., Case No. 08-10095, Docket Entry No. 4187.

180. *Id.* Docket Entry No. 4292.

181. Fid. & Deposit Co. of Md. v. TRG Venture Two LLC, No. 1:20-cv-06105 (N.D. Ill. filed Oct. 14, 2020).

expansive releases in plans or by stripping obligations that should not be stripped in bankruptcy sales.

Conclusion

Some of the decisions since the last edition of this book are game-changing for the surety claims professional and underwriter. Several of these cases recognized the surety's ability to assert claims against successor developers for the cost of improvements. This positive development was dampened by bankruptcy decisions finding a successor developer claim can either be stripped like a lien in a bankruptcy sale or can be released and enjoined through the provisions of a chapter 11 plan, and a surety now faces a $9.5 million sanction for violating a plan injunction when it sued a successor developer.

Through the so-called "sweetheart deal," successor developers and municipalities have been able to impose the costs of improvements on the surety and eliminate any recourse against the subsequent developer, resulting in unjust enrichment in favor of the successor and to the detriment of the surety. And since the last edition of this book, the Illinois Supreme Court obliterated the distinction between public works bonds and subdivision bonds in that state in the *Lake County Grading* decision.

The problem posed by the Lake County Grading decision might only be cured through legislation. The adverse consequences of the other recent decisions, however, may be overcome by more ardent claims advocacy. More assertive handling of bankruptcy cases may enable the surety to preserve its rights of recourse against successor developers. Active engagement in the settlement of claims can help the surety avoid the sweetheart deal. Objecting to orders that impact the surety's rights or taking a more assertive hand in settlements may cost more money in the short term but may ultimately lead to a better outcome for the surety facing claims on subdivision bonds.

CHAPTER 3

FINANCIAL GUARANTY INSURANCE AND SURETY BONDS

*Darren Grzyb**
Scott W. Lichtenstein
Steven S. Katz
Christopher Indelicato

Introduction

Financial guaranty insurance (FGI)[1] guarantees the insured against the nonpayment of principal and interest when due by the obligor on an insured debt obligation. It is, in essence, a highly refined kind of surety bond. Like surety insurance, FGI expects no underwriting losses. Both products protect against the nonpayment of monetary obligations. Unlike suretyship, however, FGI has primarily been used by financial markets to improve the investment grade of an underlying obligation to pay principal and interest on a fixed schedule.[2] By lending its claim-paying ability to its

---

* The authors wish to acknowledge the contributions to the scholarship on this subject of Martha L. Perkins, Rosemary Quinn, and James D. Ferrucci. Ms. Perkins and Ms. Quinn co-authored the version of this chapter appearing in the first edition of *The Law of Miscellaneous and Commercial Surety Bonds*. Mr. Ferrucci and Ms. Quinn subsequently co-authored a prior version of this chapter, which appeared in the second edition of *The Law of Commercial Surety and Miscellaneous Bonds*. The authors also wish to thank Andrew Kent for his insights regarding and contribution to the discussion of "international FGI" in Part III.C of this chapter.

1. For conciseness, the acronym FGI will be used unless doing otherwise is warranted (e.g., when quoting or referring to a statutory definition of "financial guaranty insurance").

2. In 2000–2002, some credit rating agencies announced the establishment of a financial enhancement rating system for multiline insurers that provided bonds for structural financed transactions. *See* Martha L. Perkins & Rosemary Quinn, *Financial Guaranty Insurance and Surety Bonds*, *in* THE LAW OF MISCELLANEOUS AND COMMERCIAL SURETY BONDS 25, 48–49 (Todd C. Kazlow & Bruce C. King eds., 2001); James S. Gkonos

customers, such as municipal bond insurers, a financial guaranty insurer lowers the costs of the bond issuance.[3]

Although generally regulated as a type of surety insurance, FGI became subject to strict regulation as a separate and distinct line of insurance in New York, Florida, California, and Connecticut when those four states enacted comprehensive FGI laws in the late 1980s and early 1990s. Those enactments were based on a model statute promulgated by the National Association of Insurance Commissioners (NAIC) in 1986. Part II of this chapter outlines the events that created the perceived need for the separate regulation of FGI and addresses the model act that emanated from that perception.

Generally, these financial guaranty laws provide that only financial guaranty insurers may write FGI. They are termed "monoline" insurers because they are only permitted to write (with limited, specific exceptions) one line of insurance: FGI. "Multiline" insurers, such as the property/casualty companies that typically issue surety bonds, are prohibited from writing FGI.[4] Thus, whether a specific product is deemed to be "financial guaranty insurance" or "surety insurance" pursuant to the financial guaranty law of a specific state is a critical question for multiline insurers because they are forbidden to issue the former but may issue the latter. That question may be a difficult one, as financial guaranty laws can be both complex and confusing. Part II of this chapter details the financial guaranty laws of New York, Florida, California, and Connecticut, and discusses the difficulties in statutory construction created by an overlap between the definitions of "financial guaranty insurance" and "surety insurance."

Special attention is paid to New York's laws because of their significant extraterritorial reach, an effect of which is known as New

---

& James D. Ferrucci, Financial Guaranty Bonds and the Appleton Rule 25–26 (2000) (unpublished paper submitted at the 11th Annual Northeast Surety and Fidelity Claims Conference (Sept. 21–22, 2000)). At that time, there was concern that such a list could implicate the prohibitions upon FGI imposed by New York and other states. To the best of the authors' knowledge, such a list for domestic multiline insurers does not currently exist.

3. There is some anecdotal evidence that the use of FGI as a credit enhancement in current financial markets seems to have diminished.

4. The exception is Florida, where a property/casualty insurer that meets certain statutory requirements could qualify for a license to write FGI. *See infra* text accompanying notes 172–176.

York's "Appleton Rule." That is to say, if a multiline insurer licensed in New York proceeds to issue a product *outside* of New York that is ultimately deemed to be "financial guaranty insurance" (as that term is defined in New York's insurance statutes), the insurer will have violated New York law and could be subject to fines and/or the revocation of its New York license. This extraterritorial effect is unique to New York's insurance laws. It makes New York's prohibition on the issuance of FGI by multiline companies relevant even if the insured risk is located outside of New York. Therefore, multiline insurers must understand and comply with New York's financial guaranty laws, even when considering FGI in one of the many states that do not regulate FGI. Part III of this chapter addresses the application of, and certain exceptions to, New York's "Appleton Rule."

I. Financial Guaranty Insurance Model Act

A. Perceived Need for Separate Regulation

The modern FGI industry emerged in the early 1970s when insurance policies were written to guarantee municipal bond obligations primarily by monoline companies.[5] A principal purpose and primary attraction of FGI was the "credit enhancement" that occurs when the higher credit rating of the insurer adheres to the lower rated obligation by reason of the guaranty. This is financially advantageous to the governmental or corporate borrower because the premium charged by the insurer for the guaranty has historically been substantially less than the savings generated by the lower interest rate that accompanies the higher rating.[6]

In the 1980s, the market for FGI expanded rapidly and evolved from guaranties of municipal bonds to include a diversity of far more complex

---

5. Conning & Co., Financial Guaranty Insurance: From an Acorn to an Oak Tree 57 (1998). In 1971, a single policy was written to guarantee a general obligation issued for the city of Juneau, Alaska. *Id.* Municipal bond insurers lend their credit rating to bonds, notes, and other evidences of indebtedness issued by states and their political subdivisions, utility districts, public universities and hospitals, and other public entities.
6. NAIC, *Statement in Support of Model Act*, 1986 Proc. Nat'l Ass'n Ins. Comm'rs II attach. two-c (1986) [hereinafter *NAIC Model Act Statement*]; *Memorandum of the State Executive Department*, *in* 2 McKinney's 1989 Sess. Laws of N.Y. 2045, 2054 (McKinney 2009) [hereinafter *N.Y. Executive Department Memorandum*].

products,[7] particularly asset-backed securities[8] and the obligations of other countries.[9] The demand for FGI was fueled by the highly publicized failures of several issuers.[10] Those defaults motivated investors to look for ways to protect their investments through financial guaranties. Responding to the demand, multiline property/casualty insurers entered the market. As a result of then-permitted federal tax shelters, a popular product was the limited partnership financial guaranty bond, which secured the limited partners' installment payments under their promissory notes. Surety companies began to issue such bonds in order to expand their opportunities in the financial services arena.[11]

The issue of regulating this line of business became critical in the mid-1980s, with regulators concerned that regulating FGI as property/casualty insurance or as surety insurance was inadequate. The rapid expansion of the FGI market contributed to a series of defaults, as a result of which both monoline and multiline companies sustained large losses in their financial guaranty lines. Indeed, the significant amount of outstanding exposures ultimately led to a number of insolvencies, as a financial guaranty insurer could suffer a single catastrophic loss

---

7. Robert D. Hogue, *Financial Perspectives and Overviews: The Changing Financial Guaranty Insurance Market*, INS. ADVOC., June 12, 1999, at 39.
8. An asset-backed transaction or securitization is a form of structured financing that is secured by a specific pool of assets held by the issuing entity. These asset pools are typically composed of mortgage-backed securities, home equity loans, credit card and auto loan receivables, or other assets. *Id.*
9. *Id.* at 38. CONNING & CO., *supra* note 5, at 27. In 1986, it was estimated that insurers' aggregate exposure to loss under various types of financial guaranties exceeded $500 billion. *NAIC Model Act Statement*, *supra* note 6.
10. A well-known default occurred in 1983, when the Washington Public Power Supply System defaulted on more than $2 billion of revenue bonds. *See N.Y. Executive Department Memorandum*, *supra* note 6, at 2055; *NAIC Model Act Statement*, *supra* note 6.
11. *See* H. Bruce Shreves, *Financial Guaranty Bonds*, *in* THE LAW OF SURETYSHIP 18-1 (Edward G. Gallagher ed., 1993) (discussing limited partnership financial guaranty bonds in detail and analyzing the legal issues faced by the issuing bonding company upon the failure of a limited partnership). *See also* Martha L. Perkins, *Financial Guaranty*, *in* THE LAW OF SURETYSHIP 303, 304 (Edward G. Gallagher ed., 2d ed. 2000).

due to just one bond issuer failing to meet its obligation.[12] In addition, numerous failures in connection with just one financial guaranty product could provide inordinate risk to the insurance companies that issued such products. For example, the limited partnership financial guarantee bond flourished until the confluence of federal tax reform legislation in 1986 and the financial market crisis in October 1987, by virtue of which many limited partnerships failed, and their financial guaranty insurers became entrapped.[13]

FGI originally consisted of guaranties of municipal bond debt,[14] and a few states undertook to regulate municipal bond insurance as a separate line.[15] New York did so in 1970,[16] Wisconsin in 1984,[17] California in 1985,[18]

---

12. Insurance regulators in the 1980s cited "the catastrophic losses on financial guaranties" sustained by Fireman's Fund Insurance Company, Industrial Indemnity Insurance Company, Cal-Farm Insurance Company, and Glacier General Assurance Company, which resulted in the insolvency of the latter two insurers. *N.Y. Executive Department Memorandum, supra* note 6, at 2055; *see also NAIC Model Act Statement, supra* note 6. Regulators also noted the very large losses to which American Municipal Bond Assurance Corp. (AMBAC), a monoline company, was exposed when Washington Public Power Supply System and other issuers defaulted on bonds guaranteed by AMBAC. *N.Y. Executive Department Memorandum, supra* note 6, at 2055; *NAIC Model Act Statement, supra* note 6.
13. *See N.Y. Executive Department Memorandum, supra* note 6, at 2055; *NAIC Model Act Statement, supra* note 6; *Perkins, supra* note 11, at 304; Shreves, *supra* note 11, at 18-1. The insurance regulators specifically noted that Mutual Fire, Marine, and Inland Insurance Company defaulted on claims under guaranties of limited partnerships involving tax-sheltered oil and gas and real estate ventures. *N.Y. Executive Department Memorandum, supra* note 6, at 2055; *NAIC Model Act Statement, supra* note 6.
14. *N.Y. Executive Department Memorandum, supra* note 6, at 2053; *NAIC Model Act Statement, supra* note 6.
15. *N.Y. Executive Department Memorandum, supra* note 6, at 2053; *NAIC Model Act Statement, supra* note 6.
16. *See N.Y. Executive Department Memorandum, supra* note 6, at 2053.
17. *See* Wis. Admin. Code Ins. § 3.08 (West, Westlaw through Wisconsin Register 784B, published Apr. 26, 2021).
18. In 1985, California adopted a Municipal Bond Insurance Act (Cal. Ins. Code §§ 12100–12109 (West 1985)), which was repealed in 1990 when

and Illinois[19] and New Jersey in 1987.[20] However, those regulations were limited to municipal bond insurance, which was principally issued by monoline companies. As multiline property/casualty companies began to issue other, nontraditional types of financial guaranty bonds, some insurance regulators became concerned that the rules that applied to property/casualty insurance generally were not adequate for "the much riskier non-municipal bond guaranties."[21] The Statement in Support of the NAIC's Financial Guaranty Insurance Model Act described a fundamental difference between FGI and property/casualty insurance:

> Property/casualty insurance is based on the law of large numbers—a large group of homogeneous risks joined together to create a pool of money to pay for the losses of a few. The number of losses incurred is generally frequent, and severity in relation to surplus is relatively low. In contrast, under financial guaranty insurance a single loss, e.g., the failure of a bond issuer to meet its obligations, could result in a potentially catastrophic financial loss affecting large numbers of insured bondholders.[22]

The NAIC also noted that while the premium for property/casualty coverages can be adjusted upon annual renewal "to reflect changing risk factors, the upfront premium charged for financial guaranty insurance covers the life of the obligation, which could be as long as 30 years."[23]

B. The Model Act

By the mid-1980s, insurance regulators came to view FGI as a new and "unique type of coverage requiring specialized treatment."[24] In

---

California enacted its FGI statute. *See infra* Part II.C (discussing in detail California's FGI statute).

19. *See* ILL. ADMIN. CODE tit. 50, §§ 205.10–.90 (West through rules published in the Illinois Register vol. 45, issue 25, June 18, 2021).

20. *See* N.J. ADMIN. CODE §§ 11:17-1.1–.5 (2011).

21. *NAIC Model Act Statement*, *supra* note 6; *accord N.Y. Executive Department Memorandum*, *supra* note 6, at 2055.

22. *NAIC Model Act Statement*, *supra* note 6; *accord* N.Y. *Executive Department Memorandum*, *supra* note 6, at 2053.

23. *NAIC Model Act Statement*, *supra* note 6; *accord N.Y. Executive Department Memorandum*, *supra* note 6, at 2055.

24. *NAIC Model Act Statement*, *supra* note 6.

1985, the NAIC appointed the Financial Guaranty Insurance Study Group (the Study Group) to develop a regulatory response to that then rapidly growing line of business. The Study Group was composed of the states of California, Illinois, Nebraska, New York, Texas, Virginia, and Wisconsin, and was chaired by James P. Corcoran, who was then the superintendent of the New York Insurance Department.[25] The first draft was released in December 1985, and the NAIC adopted the Financial Guaranty Insurance Model Act (the Model Act)[26] in June 1986,[27] with several amendments made to it in 1987.[28]

The purposes for the Model Act, as enumerated by the Study Group, included (1) defining FGI as a separate line of insurance; (2) authorizing the formation and licensing of monoline FGI that would guarantee payment of municipal and corporate bonds and other specified transactions; (3) redefining surety insurance by eliminating those transactions that are a type of FGI; and (4) proscribing multiline insurers from writing FGI after a phase-out period.[29] The Study Group also observed that the monoline structure would enable regulators to more easily identify the risks incurred in underwriting financial guaranty coverage and the capital supporting that business. This was necessary "because of the unique nature of financial guaranties, which are a hybrid of insurance and investment banking."[30]

Section 1.A of the Model Act defined "financial guaranty insurance" as a separate and distinct line of insurance:

> (1) "Financial guaranty insurance" means a surety bond, insurance policy or, when issued by an insurer, an indemnity contract and any guaranty similar to the foregoing types, under

---

25. *N.Y. Executive Department Memorandum*, *supra* note 6, at 2053.
26. Fin. Guar. Ins. Model Act (Nat'l Ass'n of Ins. Comm'rs 1986) [hereinafter Model Act]. In 2007, the NAIC renamed the Model Act the "Financial Guaranty Insurance Guideline." Fin. Guar. Ins. Guideline (Nat'l Ass'n of Ins. Comm'rs 2011) (West, Westlaw through November 2019 update).
27. 1986 Proc. Nat'l Ass'n Ins. Comm'rs II, at 12, 17, 206–07 (Report of Financial Guaranty Insurance Study Group), 216–19, 219–27.
28. 1987 Proc. Nat'l Ass'n Ins. Comm'rs I, at 11, 18, 161 (Report of Financial Guaranty Insurance Study Group), 163–74.
29. NAIC, *Model Bill Memorandum*, 1986 Proc. Nat'l Ass'n Ins. Comm'rs II attach. two-c (1986) [hereinafter *NAIC Model Bill Memorandum*].
30. *NAIC Model Act Statement*, *supra* note 6.

which loss is payable upon proof of occurrence of financial loss to an insured claimant, obligee or indemnitee as a result of any of the following events:

(a) failure of any obligor on any debt instrument or other monetary obligation (including common or preferred stock guaranteed under a surety bond, insurance policy or indemnity contract) to pay when due principal, interest, premium, dividend or purchase price of or on such instrument or obligation, when such failure is the result of a financial default or insolvency, regardless of whether such obligation is incurred directly or as guarantor by or on behalf of another obligor that has also defaulted;
(b) changes in the levels of interest rates, whether short or long term, or the differential in interest rates between various markets or products;
(c) changes in the rate of exchange of currency;
(d) inconvertibility of one currency into another for any reason, or inability to withdraw funds held in a foreign country resulting from restrictions imposed by a governmental authority;
(e) changes in the value of specific assets or commodities, financial or commodity indices, or price levels in general; or
(f) other events which the commissioner determines are substantially similar to any of the foregoing.[31]

The Model Act specifically excluded certain types of insurance from the definition of "financial guaranty insurance" including, among others, public official bonds; contract bonds;[32] court bonds; license and permit bonds; lease, purchase, and sale, or concessionaire surety bonds; credit insurance; and mortgage guaranty insurance.[33]

The Model Act set forth its linchpin precept—the monoline company requirement—in section 3.A: "[f]inancial guaranty insurance may be

---

31. MODEL ACT, *supra* note 26, § 1.A(1)(a)–(f).
32. The specific language excluding "contract bonds" from the definition of "financial guaranty insurance" was: "any contract bond, including bid, payment or maintenance bond, or a performance bond where the bond is guarantying the execution of any contract other than a contract of indebtedness or other monetary obligation . . ." *Id.* § 1.A(2)(c).
33. *Id.* § 1.A(2)(a)–(n).

transacted in this state only by a corporation licensed for such purpose."[34] In addition to FGI, the act permitted such corporations to write only residual value insurance, surety insurance, and credit insurance.[35] The act also required such monoline companies to have paid-in capital of at least $10 million and paid-in surplus of at least $40 million[36] and to meet specifically defined reserves.[37] The NAIC also began requiring insurance companies to report their FGI and surety businesses separately.[38]

II. Financial Guaranty Insurance Legislation

A. *New York*

1. *Purpose of the New York Financial Guaranty Law*

The New York Insurance Department spearheaded the effort by the NAIC to secure the adoption of the Model Act. In 1989, the New York State Legislature enacted chapter 48 of the Laws of 1989, which added Article 69 (entitled "Financial Guaranty Insurance Corporations")[39] to the New York Insurance Law and amended section 1113(a) thereof.[40] Article 69 was based directly on the Model Act[41] and implemented the Model Act's key purpose of limiting the authority to write FGI to monoline insurers.[42]

---

34. *Id.* § 3.A
35. *Id.* § 2.A(1).
36. *Id.* § 2.B(1).
37. *Id.* § 2.B(2)–(4).
38. CONNING & CO, *supra* note 5, at 46–47.
39. N.Y. INS. LAW §§ 6901–6909 (McKinney, Westlaw through L.2021).
40. *Id.* § 1113. The legislation also amended section 1115(b) of the Insurance Law, *id.* § 1115(b), to add FGI to the types of insurance to which the prohibition on an insurer's exposing itself "to any loss on any one risk in an amount exceeding ten percent of its surplus to policyholders," applies. *Id.* § 1115(a).
41. *N.Y. Executive Department Memorandum*, *supra* note 6, at 2053.
42. N.Y. INS. LAW § 6904 (current through L.2021, chapters 1 to 833, and L.2022, chapters 1 to 12); *see also* discussion *infra* Part II.A.2. The Model Act also served as the prototype for FGI legislation enacted in Florida, California, and Connecticut. *See* FLA. STAT. ANN. §§ 627.971–.975 (West, Westlaw through laws of the 2021 1st Reg. Sess. of the 27th Leg. in effect through June 22, 2021); CAL. INS. CODE §§ 12100–12123 (West, Westlaw through urgency legislation through ch. 19 of 2021 Reg. Sess.); CONN. GEN. STAT. ANN. §§ 38a-92a–38a-92n (West, Westlaw

The New York legislation is particularly important because many of the business opportunities to which the law may apply emanate from New York. Moreover, New York's extraterritorial "Appleton Rule," discussed further in Part III, can impact insurers licensed in New York irrespective of the location of the risk that is underwritten.[43]

The bill, which became Article 69, was accompanied by a memorandum promulgated by the New York State Executive Department.[44] That memorandum closely tracked the Model Bill Memorandum and Statement in Support, which was issued with the Model Act by the Study Group.[45] As stated in the New York memorandum, the purpose of the new legislation was, in part:

- To define "financial guaranty insurance" as a separate kind of insurance.
- To authorize the formation and licensing of financial guaranty insurance corporations which would essentially be monoline insurers but would also be permitted to write surety, residual value and credit insurance.
- To provide a transition period for multiline property/casualty insurers to convert to monoline insurers.
- To specify the types of obligations for which financial guaranties may be written by a financial guaranty insurance corporation which would include municipal and corporate bonds.
- To prohibit the writing of guaranties for other types of obligations (unless substantially similar) without further enabling legislation.
- To establish a regulatory framework, including realistic capital and reserve requirements, prudent aggregate and

---

through all enactments of 2021 Reg. Sess. enrolled and approved by the governor on or before June 16, 2021, and effective on or before June 16, 2021). *See infra* Parts II.B, II.C, and II.D (discussing in detail the Florida, California, and Connecticut statutes, respectively).

43. *See infra* Part III (discussing in detail New York's "Appleton Rule" and its extraterritorial effect).
44. *N.Y. Executive Department Memorandum*, *supra* note 6.
45. *Compare* N.Y. *Executive Department Memorandum*, *supra* note 6, *with NAIC Model Bill Memorandum*, *supra* note 29, *and NAIC Model Act Statement*, *supra* note 6.

single risk limitations and appropriate reinsurance requirements.

- To unlink fidelity insurance and surety insurance and treat them as separate kinds of insurance so as to permit a financial guaranty insurance corporation to write surety coverage but not fidelity, and *to redefine surety insurance by eliminating the kinds of transactions which become financial guaranty insurance subject to the provisions of new Article 69 (Financial Guaranty Insurance Corporations).*[46]

The legislative intent animating that purpose can be discerned from the problems that the drafters of the 1989 amendments perceived to arise from allowing multiline insurers to continue writing FGI (which problems the amendments were intended to avoid). According to the New York State Executive Department, the drafters recognized the following problems with the multiline format:

> 1. Potential to bankrupt company. When written as a sideline by a multiline insurer, financial guaranty insurance has the potential to bankrupt a company or to so limit its capacity as to prevent it from maintaining its market capacity to underwrite traditional and more essential lines of business. [A]t least three multiline companies have been rendered insolvent by their financial guaranty writings. The monoline approach protects property/casualty insurance policyholders from the negative impact of adverse experience in financial guaranty business. Multiline insurers would not be tempted to divert currently insufficient resources to financial guaranty business for the enhancement of cash flow.
>
> 2. Burdening the Security Fund. Even if not covered by the Property/Casualty Insurance Security fund, an insolvency

---

46. *N.Y. Executive Department Memorandum*, *supra* note 6, at 2045–46 (emphasis added) (footnote omitted). The NAIC Model Bill Memorandum's delineation of the purposes of the model bill differs from that in the New York Executive Department Memorandum, but both include defining FGI as a separate line, limiting the authority to issue FGI to monoline insurers, prohibiting multiline companies from writing FGI, and redefining surety insurance. *See NAIC Model Bill Memorandum*, *supra* note 29 and accompanying text.

of a multiline insurer resulting from financial guaranty losses would expose the Security Fund to claims for all the property/casualty lines written by the insurer. Insurers which did not write financial guaranties and the vast majority of the public who never benefit from the guaranties would be burdened with cost of losses covered by the Security Fund.

3. Lack of accountability. In a multiline operation, capital supports many lines of business. A monoline structure would enable the regulator to readily identify the risks insured and the capital supporting the business. This identification is necessary because of the unique nature of financial guaranties, which are a hybrid of insurance and investment banking.

4. Lack of expertise. Few multiline insurers will have the necessary expertise to write financial guaranties, especially of the new and more exotic products. The expertise required to underwrite financial guaranties bears no relationship to traditional property/casualty underwriting, which utilizes actuarial and loss experience to evaluate and price a risk. Financial guaranty business requires in-depth expertise of investment bankers and economists, as is the case with existing monoline financial guaranty insurers.

5. Regulatory constraints. Because of its nature underwriting financial guaranty insurance in a multiline environment adds undue complexity to the analysis and monitoring of an insurer's financial condition with no discernable benefit. It causes unwarranted diversion from the pressing regulatory responsibilities of the Insurance Department in expending finite resources to monitor this line of business in a multiline environment.[47]

2. The Statutory Scheme

The first problem that the drafters identified with multiline companies issuing FGI was the "[p]otential to bankrupt [the multiline] company."[48]

---

47. *N.Y. Executive Department Memorandum*, *supra* note 6, at 2056. The Statement in Support of the Model Act identifies the same problems, utilizing similar language. *NAIC Model Act Statement*, *supra* note 6.

48. *N.Y. Executive Department Memorandum*, *supra* note 6, at 2056. The Statement in Support of the Model Act lists the potential to bankrupt the

Like the Model Act, the lynchpin of the New York statute is the monoline company requirement, which is set out in section 6904 of Article 69 of the Insurance Law:

> § 6904. Limitations
>
> (a) Financial guaranty insurance may be transacted in this state *only* by a corporation licensed for such purpose pursuant to section 6902 of this article.[49]

Section 6901(a)(1)[50] defines the types of transactions that constitute "financial guaranty insurance" as follows:

> § 6901. Definitions
>
> "Financial guaranty insurance" means a surety bond, an insurance policy or, when issued by an insurer or any person doing an insurance business as defined in paragraph one of subsection (b) of section one thousand one hundred one of this chapter, an indemnity contract, and any guaranty similar to the foregoing types, under which loss is payable, upon proof of

---

multiline company as the sixth out of seven problems. *NAIC Model Act Statement*, *supra* note 6, at 2056.

49. N.Y. Ins. Law § 6904(a) (McKinney, Westlaw through L.2021) (emphasis added). Because certain kinds of "surety insurance" are excluded from the definition of "financial guaranty insurance," multiline insurers may issue some types of surety bonds that might otherwise constitute FGI and be forbidden to them. Whether a particular risk falls within that definitional exclusion can involve a complex statutory analysis, which is typically the critical issue in this area. *See* discussion *infra* Parts II.A.3 and II.A.4. Section 6904(a) constitutes an adoption, almost verbatim, of section 3.A of the Model Act. *See* Model Act, *supra* note 26, § 3.A. In 2005, New York adopted an amendment permitting multiline insurers to write FGI when the aggregate amount of the insured indebtedness of one obligor does not exceed $10 million. *See infra* Part II.A.4 (discussing the 2005 amendment). The current NAIC Financial Guaranty Insurance Guideline contains a similar provision, which was presumably added after the 2005 New York amendment. *See* Fin. Guar. Ins. Guideline § 1.A(2)(h) (Nat'l Ass'n of Ins. Comm'rs 2019) (West, Westlaw through November 2019 update).

50. N.Y. Ins. Law § 6901(a)(1) (McKinney, Westlaw through L.2021).

occurrence of financial loss, to an insured claimant, obligee or indemnitee as a result of any of the following events:

(A) failure of any obligor on or issuer of any debt instrument or other monetary obligation (including equity securities guarantied under a surety bond, insurance policy or indemnity contract) to pay when due to be paid by the obligor or scheduled at the time insured to be received by the holder of the obligation, principal, interest, premium, dividend or purchase price of or on, or other amounts due or payable with respect to, such instrument or obligation, when such failure is the result of a financial default or insolvency or, provided that such payment source is investment grade, any other failure to make payment, regardless of whether such obligation is incurred directly or as guarantor by or on behalf of another obligor that has also defaulted;

(B) changes in the levels of interest rates, whether short or long term or the differential in interest rates between various markets or products;

(C) changes in the rate of exchange of currency;

(D) changes in the value of specific assets or commodities, financial or commodity indices, or price levels in general; or

(E) other events which the superintendent determines are substantially similar to any of the foregoing.[51]

Thus, the five types of transactions included in section 6901(a)(1)'s definition of "financial guaranty insurance" are (1) "guaranties of indebtedness"; (2) "interest rate guaranties"; (3) "currency rate guaranties"; (4) "guaranties of financial or commodity indices"; and (5) "guaranties of other events determined by the Superintendent to be substantially similar to the foregoing."[52] Section 6902(a) authorizes the organization and licensing of New York and foreign FGI corporations,[53] and section

---

51. *Id.* Section 6901(a)(1) tracks the 1986 version of the Model Act almost verbatim. *See* MODEL ACT, *supra*, note 26, § 1.A(1). *See also supra* text accompanying note 50 (quoting § 1.A(1)). There are some minor and immaterial differences between the wording of subparagraph (A) of section 6901(a)(1) and that of subsection 1.A(1)(a) of the Model Act. Moreover, subsection 1.A(1)(d) of the Model Act is not included in section 6901(a)(1) at all.
52. *N.Y. Executive Department Memorandum*, *supra* note 6, at 2046.
53. N.Y. INS. LAW § 6902(a) (McKinney, Westlaw through L.2021).

6901(b) defines a "'[f]inancial guaranty insurance corporation'" as "an insurer licensed to transact the business of financial guaranty insurance in this state."[54] And, as noted, section 6904(a) limits the authorization to write FGI to licensed monoline companies, which effectively prohibits multiline insurers from doing so.[55]

While all five types of transactions listed in section 6901(a)(1) constitute FGI, which multiline insurers are prohibited from issuing, section 6904(b)(1)[56] provides that the only type of FGI that may be written by a financial guaranty corporation is the type defined in subparagraph (A) of section 6901(a)(1)—the so-called "guarant[y] of indebtedness."[57] Thus, even a monoline financial guaranty corporation is prohibited by the statute from writing interest rate guaranties, currency rate guaranties, guaranties of financial or commodity indices, or substantially similar guaranties. These are the financial guaranties listed in subparagraphs (B) through (E) of section 6901(a)(1), which the New York Insurance Department has described as "a crap shoot."[58]

In addition to limiting permissible FGI to the guaranties of indebtedness described in section 6901(a)(1)(A), section 6904(b)(1) specifically limits the types of indebtedness that may be guaranteed:

---

54. *Id.* § 6901(b).

55. N.Y. Ins. Law § 6904(a) (current through L.2021, chapters 1 to 833, and L.2022, chapters 1 to 12).

56. *Id.* § 6904(b)(1) (providing that "[t]he superintendent shall not permit the writing of financial guaranty insurance except as defined in subparagraph (A) of section 6901(a)(1)(A) of this article . . .").

57. *N.Y. Executive Department Memorandum*, *supra* note 6, at 2046. "The plain import of §§ 6901 and 6904, read together, is that only coverage coming within the definition set out in § 6901(a)(1)(A) is authorized to be written in New York." Gen. Couns. Op. No. 11-21-91, 1991 WL 11630471, at *2 (N.Y. Ins. Dep't Nov. 21, 1991). *See infra* note 73 and text accompanying notes 87–90 (discussing the nature and role of the opinions of the General Counsel's Office of the former New York State Insurance Department and current New York State Department of Financial Services).

58. *N.Y. Executive Department Memorandum*, *supra* note 6, at 2057; *accord NAIC Model Act Statement*, *supra* note 6 ("These guaranties are at best speculative and should be viewed as gambling contracts.").

> [A] corporation may insure the timely payment of United States dollar debt instruments, or other monetary obligations, only in the following categories:
>
> (A) municipal obligation bonds;
> (B) special revenue bonds;
> (C) industrial development bonds;
> (D) obligations of corporations, trusts or other similar entities established under applicable law;
> (E) partnership obligations;
> (F) asset-backed securities, trust certificates and trust obligations other than [certain] mortgage-backed securities . . . ;
> (G) installment purchase agreements executed as a condition of sale;
> (H) consumer debt obligations;
> (I) utility first mortgage obligations; and
> (J) any other debt instrument or financial obligation that the superintendent determines to be substantially similar to any of the foregoing or shall otherwise be approved by the superintendent.[59]

Still other restrictions set forth in section 6904 include the following:

- Only investment-grade municipal obligation bonds, special revenue bonds, and industrial development bonds may be insured, unless at least 95 percent of the insurer's aggregate net liability on such obligations is investment grade.[60]
- Non-United States dollar debt instruments or other monetary obligations may be insured, unless the obligation's currency is that of an Organization for Economic Cooperation and Development country, or another country with an investment-grade rating.[61]
- The reserve and risk limitation requirements for non-investment grade or non-United States dollar debt instruments are more onerous than the requirements imposed as to municipal,

---

59. N.Y. INS. LAW § 6904(b)(1) (current through L.2021, chapters 1 to 833, and L.2022, chapters 1 to 12).
60. *Id.* § 6904(b)(2).
61. *Id.* § 6904(b)(4).

special revenue, and industrial development obligations that are investment grade, or as to obligations that are United States dollar debt instruments.[62]

Moreover, even though Article 69 was intended to isolate FGI and its dangers to companies writing only that kind of insurance, section 6902(a)(1) allows financial guaranty companies to write a limited number of other kinds of products. Those include specifically defined types of surety insurance (which are excluded from the definition of "financial guaranty insurance," and are therefore permissible for multiline insurers to write as well).[63]

3. *Statutory Ping-Pong: "Financial Guaranty Insurance" or "Surety Insurance"?*

Notwithstanding the definition of "financial guaranty insurance" set out in section 6901(a)(1), section 6901(a)(2) provides that certain enumerated transactions will *not* be considered FGI.[64] Among the transactions excluded from the definition of "financial guaranty insurance" are "fidelity and surety insurance as defined in [section 1113(a)(16)]."[65] As

---

62. *Id.*
63. *Id.* § 6902(a)(1)(B). Under that provision, financial guaranty companies are permitted to write surety insurance within the definitions of subparagraphs (C) through (I) of section 1113(a)(16), while subparagraphs (C) through (G) of section 1113(a)(16) are excluded under section 6901(a)(2) from the definition of "financial guaranty insurance." *Id.* § 1113(a)(16)(C)–(G). The other types of "additional kinds of insurance" that a financial guaranty insurer may write are designated types of "residual insurance," *id.* § 6902(a)(1)(A), and designated types of "credit insurance," *id.* § 6902(a)(1)(C). For opinions touching on and/or addressing the difference between FGI and "credit insurance," see Gen. Couns. Op. No. 1-10-2002, 2002 WL 34245389 (N.Y. Ins. Dep't Jan. 10, 1994); Gen. Couns. Op. No. 6-16-2000, 2000 WL 346 (N.Y. Ins. Dep't June 16, 2000).
64. N.Y. Ins. Law § 6901(a)(2) (McKinney, Westlaw through L.2021); *see also N.Y. Executive Department Memorandum*, *supra* note 6, at 2046 ("Subsection (a)(2) provides that, notwithstanding their falling within the literal definitions of (a)(1), certain enumerated transactions shall not be considered financial guaranty insurance.").
65. N.Y. Ins. Law § 6901(a)(2)(B) (current through L.2021, chapters 1 to 833, and L.2022, chapters 1 to 12).

a result, multiline insurers are not prohibited from writing bonds that fall within the definition of "fidelity and surety insurance," even if those bonds would otherwise also fall within the definition of "financial guaranty insurance."

Accordingly, section 1113(a)(16) must be examined in order to determine whether a proposed bond is surety insurance, which may be written by a multiline insurer, or FGI, which is forbidden to it. Section 1113 is part of Article 11 of the New York Insurance Law,[66] which identifies and defines "[t]he kinds of insurance which may be authorized in this state"[67] including "'[f]idelity and surety insurance,'" which is defined in section 1113(a)(16).[68] Subparagraphs (C) through (J) of subsection 1113(a)(16) identify the kinds of "traditional types of surety contracts"[69] that are excluded from the definition of "financial guaranty insurance" under section 6901(a)(1) and therefore may be written by a multiline insurer pursuant to section 6901(a)(2)(B) and, except for subparagraph (J), by a monoline financial guaranty company under section 6902(a)(1)(B).[70] Those subparagraphs of section 1113(a)(16) set forth the definition of surety insurance as follows:

---

66. *Id.* §§ 1101–1121.
67. *Id.* § 1113(a).
68. *Id.* § 1113(a)(16). Subsection 1113(a)(25) also defines "'[f]inancial guaranty insurance'" as "the kind of insurance defined in [section 6901(a)(1)]."
69. *N.Y. Executive Department Memorandum*, *supra* note 6, at 2046. As the New York State Executive Memorandum was written in connection with original Article 69, its statement regarding "traditional types of surety contracts" referred to subparagraphs (C) through (F) and what is now subparagraph (J) of section 1113(a)(16). It did not refer to subparagraphs (G), (H), and (I), which were added by the 2005 amendment to section 1113(a)(16). *See* discussion *infra* Part II.A.4.
70. Subparagraphs (A) and (B) of section 1113(a)(16) define the types of fidelity insurance that a multiline insurer may issue. N.Y. INS. LAW § 1113(a)(16)(A)–(B) (McKinney, Westlaw through L.2021). Those subparagraphs are straightforward and do not contain the exception for FGI, which is found with respect to surety insurance in subparagraph (E). The types of guaranties identified in subparagraph (J), which monoline companies may not write, relate to the payment of premium, deductible, or self-insured retention to insurers issuing workers' compensation or liability policies.

(C) Any contract bond; including a bid, payment or maintenance bond or a performance bond where the bond is guaranteeing the execution of any contract other than a contract of indebtedness or other monetary obligation;

(D) An indemnity bond for the benefit of a public body, railroad or charitable organization; a lost security or utility payment bond;

(E) Becoming surety on, or guaranteeing the performance of, any lawful contract, not specifically provided for in this paragraph, *but does not include* becoming surety on, or guaranteeing the performance of:

(i) any insurance contract except as authorized pursuant to section [1114] of this article; or

(ii) any contract, if becoming a surety on, or guaranteeing the performance of that contract, would constitute:

a. mortgage guaranty insurance as defined in [section 6501(a)] of this chapter;

b. *financial guaranty insurance as defined in [section 6901(a)] of this chapter*;

c. service contract reimbursement insurance as defined in paragraph twenty-eight of this subsection;

(F) Becoming surety on, or guaranteeing the performance of, bonds and undertakings required or permitted in all judicial proceedings or otherwise by law allowed, including surety bonds accepted by states and municipal authorities in lieu of deposits as security for the performance of insurance contracts; and

(G) Becoming surety on, or guaranteeing the performance of, any agreement for the lease or rental of non-residential real property or tangible personal property, provided that the obligation of the insurer shall not exceed a period of five years, and the bond is not issued directly or indirectly in connection with the sale of securities, a pooling of financial assets or a credit default swap as defined by article sixty-nine of this chapter;

(H) Becoming surety on, or guaranteeing the performance of, a contract of indebtedness or other monetary obligation where: (i) the aggregate gross principal, interest, and other amounts of indebtedness or other monetary obligations of any obligor whose obligations are guaranteed by the insurer under all bonds issued to that obligor pursuant to this subparagraph by the insurer does not exceed ten million dollars; and (ii) the bond is not issued directly or indirectly in connection with the

> sale of securities, a pooling of financial assets, or a credit default swap as defined by article sixty-nine of this chapter; and (iii) the bond by its terms terminates upon any sale or other transfer of the insured obligation in connection with the sale of securities, pooling of financial assets, or a credit default swap as defined by article sixty-nine of this chapter;
>
> (I) A depository bond that insures deposits in financial institutions to the extent of the excess over the amount insured by the Federal Deposit Insurance Corporation; and
>
> (J) Becoming surety on, or guaranteeing the performance of, a bond, which shall not exceed a period greater than five years, that guarantees the payment of a premium, deductible, or self-insured retention to an insurer issuing a workers' compensation or liability policy.[71]

As the statutes are written, the permission to issue surety bonds, which was vouchsafed to multiline insurers in section 6901, was annulled by section 1113(a)(16). While section 6901(a)(2)(B) excludes from the definition of "financial guaranty insurance" "fidelity and surety insurance as defined in [section 1113(a)(16)],"[72] subparagraph (E)(ii)(b) of section 1113(a)(16) excludes from the types of permissible "surety insurance" any "contract that would constitute FGI as defined in [section 6901(a)(1)]." A reader trying to determine whether a proposed bond constitutes surety insurance or FGI would be perpetually bounced back and forth between those two provisions. That ping-pong effect has caused even the Office of the General Counsel of the New York Superintendent of Insurance (OGC)[73] to waffle as to the treatment of coverages that fall

---

71. *Id.* § 1113(a)(16)(C)–(J) (emphasis added).
72. *Id.* § 6901(a)(2)(B).
73. The OGC of the New York State Insurance Department, or of the New York State Department of Financial Services after its creation as of October 3, 2011, *see infra* note 88, issues written opinions that constitute the Department's response to inquiries concerning the Department's interpretation and intended application of the Insurance Law. *See infra* notes 88–90 and accompanying text (discussing in detail the nature and role of the opinions of the OGC). The same ping-pong effect should also result from the interplay between section 6901(a)(2)(B) and section 1113(a)(16)(C). The latter section applies to contract bonds generally and provides that such a bond constitutes surety insurance unless it guarantees "a contract of indebtedness or other monetary obligation." N.Y. INS.

under the broad definition of "financial guaranty insurance" and yet also meet the definition of one of the permissible types of surety insurance.[74] The extent to which OGC opinions have clarified the interplay of sections 6901(a)(2)(B) and 1113(a)(16)(E)(ii) will be considered[75] after the following discussion of the significant revisions made to section 1113(a)(16) in 2005.

4. The 2005 Amendment to Section 1113(a)(16)

When Article 69 was enacted in 1989, subparagraphs (A) through (G) of section 1113(a)(16) identified seven types of transactions that were defined as "fidelity and surety insurance." In September 2005, an amendment to section 1113(a)(16) was enacted.[76] The 2005 amendment added three more types of transactions to the definition, which were designated as subparagraphs (G), (H), and (I). What was originally subparagraph (G) was relettered as subparagraph (J).

LAW § 1113(a)(16)(C) (current through L.2021, chapters 1 to 833, and L.2022, chapters 1 to 12). A bond securing a contract of indebtedness, however, would fall squarely within the definition of "financial guaranty insurance" under section 6901(a)(1)(A), with the result that while section 6901(a)(2)(B) excludes surety insurance from the definition of "financial guaranty insurance" by reference to section 1113(a)(16), the latter section cancels that exception by excluding from the definition of permissible "surety insurance" those contract bonds that guarantee a contract of indebtedness or other monetary obligation. Section 1113(a)(16)(C) sends the reader right back into the definition of "financial guaranty insurance" in section 6901(a)(1)(A). The OGC, however, seems to not regard subparagraph (C) of section 1113(a)(16) as referring the reader to section 6901(a)(1)(A). *See* Gen. Couns. Op. No. 8-11-94 (#3), 1194 WL 16305901, at *1 (N.Y. Ins. Dep't Aug. 11, 1994), discussed in detail *infra* text accompanying notes 118–128. On the other hand, that opinion did consider, as a first level analysis, that the exclusion in subparagraph (E)(ii) of section 1113(a)(16) might apply to the other subparagraphs, but ultimately concluded that the exclusion was limited to subparagraph (E), which covers lawful contracts that are not otherwise specifically provided for in section 1113(a)(16). *Id.*

74. *See infra* Part II.A.5.b.

75. *See id.*

76. Act of September 16, 2005, ch. 672, § 1113(a)(16), 2005 N.Y. SESS. LAWS (McKinney).

Thus, in summary:

- Subparagraph (G) added to the definition of "fidelity and surety insurance" bonds guaranteeing performance under an agreement for the lease or rental of nonresidential real property, provided that the bond does not exceed five years and is not issued directly or indirectly in connection with a capital market transaction.
- Subparagraph (H) added bonds guaranteeing the repayment of indebtedness where (1) the aggregate amount of the bonded indebtedness of any one obligor does not exceed $10 million; (2) the bond is not issued directly or indirectly in connection with a capital market transaction; and (3) the bond terminates by its terms upon the sale or transfer of the underlying obligation in connection with a capital market transaction.
- Subparagraph (I) added depository bonds insuring bank deposits to the extent that the deposits exceed the amount insured by the Federal Deposit Insurance Corporation (FDIC).[77]

The sponsor of Senate Bill 4061, which provided for this amendment, traced its need to two particular 2004 opinions of the OGC. In both opinions, the OGC concluded that a lease bond, which secured a tenant's obligation to pay rent to the landlord, would constitute FGI, with the result that multiline insurers would be prohibited from issuing lease bonds.[78] According to the sponsor, under the reasoning of those opinions, "many of the bonds understood to be surety bonds would have to be reclassified as financial guaranty instruments."[79] Such a result would present the following problem:

---

77. N.Y. INS. LAW § 1113(a)(16)(G), (H) & (I) (McKinney, Westlaw through L.2021). *See supra* text accompanying notes 71–74 (discussing and quoting subparagraphs (C)–(J) of section 1113(a)(16)). The 2005 amendment is also discussed in James D. Ferrucci, *A Closer Look at the Partial Repeal of New York's Ban on Financial Guaranty Bonds*, SUR. & FID. CLAIMS INST. NEWSL., Oct. 2006, at 5; Kimberly Rennie More, *NY S.B. 4061-B Permits Surety to Write Lease Bonds (Along with Other Additions) Effective upon Passing*, SUR. & FID. CLAIMS INST. NEWSL., Oct. 2005, at 17.
78. Gen Couns. Op. No. 5-4-2004 (#2), 2004 WL 3774624, at *1 (N.Y. Ins. Dep't May 4, 2004); Gen. Couns. Op. No. 4-27-2004 (#2), 2004 WL 3774618, at *1 (N.Y. Ins. Dep't Apr. 27, 2004).
79. James L. Seward, Introducer's Mem. in Supp. of Legis. S. 4061 (June 7, 2005), N.Y. Bill Jacket, 2005 S.B. 4061, ch. 672, at *3 (Westlaw).

> [T]he financial guaranty insurers have no interest in writing these bonds, as these insurers focus on capital market transactions. This leads to a situation where bonds that were thought to be surety bonds are reclassified in such a way that no entities that want to offer these products will be able to do so legally in the marketplace.
>
> The bonds in question, such as lease bonds, provide important financial backing for many transactions. Sureties have written these bonds in the past and would like to continue to do so. Financial guaranty insurers have no interest in this segment of the market. This legislation would simply allow willing providers to provide a financial service to their clients.[80]

New subparagraph (G), which defines as surety insurance a guaranty of "any agreement for the lease or rental of non-residential real property or tangible personal property," clearly solves the problem created by the two OGC opinions, without the need for more.

> The amending legislation, however, also added subparagraph (H), which includes in the definition of "surety insurance" a guaranty of "a contract of indebtedness or other monetary obligation" so long as the indebtedness under all bonds issued on behalf of a single obligor does not exceed $10 million. Thus, up to the $10 million limit, subparagraph (H) effectively repeals the heart of Article 69's ban on the issuance of FGI by multiline insurers.[81] Indeed, the sponsor said as much explicitly: "Subparagraph (H) permits sureties to write bonds that would otherwise be defined as financial guaranty insurance if the total exposure to such bonds is $10 million or less and the bonds are not used in connection with a capital markets transaction."[82]

---

80. *Id.*
81. N.Y. Ins. Law §§ 6904(a) (McKinney, Westlaw through L.2021) ("Financial guaranty insurance may be transacted in this state only by a corporation licensed for such purpose . . . ."); 6901(a)(1)(A) (McKinney, Westlaw through L.2021) (defining "financial guaranty insurance" to include guaranties of financial loss resulting from the "failure of any obligor on or issuer of any debt instrument or other monetary obligation . . . to pay when due to be paid . . . principal, interest, premium, dividend or purchase prices . . . .").
82. Seward, *supra* note 79, at *2.

The legislative history includes comments on Senate Bill 4061 from the superintendent of the Insurance Department to the governor's office.[83] The superintendent's commentary did not tie the amendment to the OGC opinions on lease bonds or even refer to them. Instead, the superintendent applied his reasoning to all three of the new subparagraphs of 1113(a)(16), saying of them:

> While these debt obligations [contained in the amendment] fall under the definition of financial guaranty insurance, financial guaranty insurers have chosen not to write these coverages because of their relatively small size. The time, effort and expense of underwriting these kinds of coverages did not justify financial guaranty insurers writing this business. Surety insurers, on the other hand, have expressed an interest in writing these kinds of coverages and this bill explicitly includes these debt obligations as "fidelity and surety insurance" enabling surety insurers to write them . . . . The Department worked with the industry in crafting this legislation. It is our position that these debt obligations are an appropriate type of risk for surety insurers to write and are not the kinds of large risks that ought to be serviced by financial guaranty insurers.[84]

Article 69 was enacted in 1989, in light of a concern that "[w]hen written as a sideline by a multiline insurer, financial guaranty insurance has the potential to bankrupt a company or to so limit its capacity as to prevent it from maintaining its market capacity to underwrite traditional and more essential lines of business."[85] The legislative history of Senate Bill 4061 contains no finding that these dangers presented by FGI had declined since 1989. The $10 million restriction in subparagraph (H) was apparently intended to limit those dangers. While guaranties of the indebtedness of one obligor may not exceed that amount, there is no limitation on the number of obligors on whose behalf a multiline company may issue such guaranties. Presumably, the superintendent reasoned that the default of one obligor would expose a surety to a loss

---

83. Letter from Howard Mills, Superintendent, New York State Insurance Department, to Richard Platkin, Counsel to the Governor (Aug. 15, 2005), N.Y. Bill Jacket, 2005 S.B. 4061, ch. 672, at *5 (Westlaw).

84. *Id.* at *6.

85. *N.Y. Executive Department Memorandum*, *supra* note 6, at 2056.

of no more than $10 million, and that it would be sufficiently unlikely for multiple obligors to default and cause the surety to incur a substantially greater loss.[86]

Subparagraph (H) raises but does not answer certain questions. For instance, what constitutes an "obligor" for the purposes of the $10 million restriction? For example, would bonding the obligations of two subsidiaries owned by the same corporation be subject to a $10 million or a $20 million limit? In the years since the enactment of subparagraph (H), the OGC has not issued an opinion addressing subparagraph (H). The Department's interpretation of the statutory language is not known.

In any event, subparagraph (H) appears to give the surety industry some leeway to accommodate traditional clients who may occasionally require a financial guaranty bond.

5. *Interpretation of Statutory Provisions*

The basic proscriptions and prescriptions of Article 69 are simple in concept. For example, the command that only monoline companies may issue FGI is easily understood in the abstract. The difficulty lies in the statutory definitions. Such issues are generally raised by way of requests for an advisory opinion from the Insurance Department and are usually resolved by a close reading and interpretation of the pertinent statutory definitions by attorneys in the OGC.[87] As a consequence, aside from the

---

86. NAIC's current Financial Guaranty Insurance Guideline also permits a multiline company to write FGI when the aggregate amount of the insured indebtedness of one obligor does not exceed $10 million. FIN. GUAR. INS. GUIDELINE § 1.A(2)(h) (NAT'L ASS'N OF INS. COMM'RS 2019) (West, Westlaw through November 2019 update). Presumably, the guideline was revised in response to New York's addition of subparagraph (H) to section 1113(a)(16) by the 2005 amendment.

87. Effective October 3, 2011, the New York State Insurance Department was consolidated by statute with the New York State Banking Department to create the new New York State Department of Financial Services. *See* N.Y. FIN. SERVS. LAW §§ 101–501 (West, Westlaw through L.2021, chs. 1 to 156). The former Insurance Department became the Insurance Division of the new Department of Financial Services, and the OGC of the former Insurance Department became part of the OGC of the new Department of Financial Services. *Id.* § 205. References herein to the "Insurance Department" or the "Department" refer to the New York State Insurance Department for the period before October 3, 2011, and to the

statutory language itself and the legislative history, the primary source of information about the Department's construction of the statutes and their application to complex transactions is to be found in opinions of that office.[88] The opinions are advisory in nature and are not binding on courts or hearing officers. Moreover, as stated by the OGC, the opinions are "limited to the facts disclosed in the materials submitted . . . [and] have been published solely to demonstrate the thinking and evaluation of the Insurance Department attorneys on the date the opinions are issued."[89] Nevertheless, the opinions do represent the Insurance Department's interpretation of the applicable statutory definitions.[90] It should be noted, however, that the OGC ceased issuing formal public opinions in 2011 (but has since then on occasion issued informal opinions via email).

It is important for multiline insurers to understand and carefully consider the interplay of the statutory definitions as interpreted by the OGC when evaluating new and creative obligations. The Insurance Department enforces Article 69, and in 1997 fined a U.S. branch of a property/casualty insurer $1 million for writing business that the Department determined was FGI.[91] In addition, business that is classified

---

New York State Department of Financial Services for the period from and after October 3, 2011. *See* N.Y. Ins. Law § 107(17) (McKinney through L.2021, chs. 1 to 156). References herein to the "superintendent" refer to the superintendent of the New York State Insurance Department for the period before October 3, 2011, and to the superintendent of the New York State Department of Financial Services for the period from and after October 3, 2011. *See id.* § 107(41).

88. Before the creation of the New York State Department of Financial Services on October 3, 2011, *see supra* note 73, the opinions were rendered by the OGC of the New York State Insurance Department, and on and after that date by the OGC of the New York State Department of Financial Services.

89. Opinions of the General Counsel iii (NILS Pub. Co.).

90. The opinions sometimes state explicitly that the OGC is speaking for the Insurance Department. *See, e.g.*, Gen. Couns. Op. No. 4-20-2004 (#2), 2004 WL 3774608, at *2, (N.Y. Ins. Dep't Apr. 20, 2004); Gen. Couns. Op. No. 9-22-2000, 2000 WL 34630133, at *3 (N.Y. Ins. Dep't Sept. 22, 2000); Gen. Couns. Op. No. 1-19-99 (#1), 1999 WL 34011967, at *2 (N.Y. Ins. Dep't Jan. 19, 1999).

91. The multiline insurer considered the subject policies to be credit insurance. It contended that it had been defrauded by its own insured, cooperated fully with the Department's investigation, and paid the $1 million fine.

as FGI may be subject to exclusions or limitations under a multiline insurer's reinsurance treaties. Thus, the financial risks to an insurer can extend beyond sanctions or fines.

a. Permissible FGI. Subparagraphs (A) through (E) of section 6901(a)(1) define the five types of transactions that are identified as FGI.[92] Even a monoline financial guaranty corporation may write *only* the one type of FGI specified in subparagraph (A): the so-called "guaranty of indebtedness."[93] Subparagraph (A) defines, in general terms, this permissible kind of FGI as

> a surety bond, an insurance policy or, when issued by an insurer or any person doing an insurance business as defined in paragraph one of subsection (b) of section [1101] of this chapter, an indemnity contract . . . under which loss is payable, upon proof of financial loss, . . . as a result of . . . : (A) failure of any obligor on or issuer of *any debt instrument or other monetary obligation* (including equity securities guarantied under a surety bond, insurance policy or indemnity contract) to pay when due . . . principal, interest, premium, dividend or purchase price of or on, or other amounts due or payable with respect to, such instrument or obligation . . . .[94]

The key phrase "any debt instrument or other monetary obligation" was construed by the Department in a September 14, 1992, OGC opinion regarding whether an authorized financial guaranty insurer may insure the monetary obligations of life insurers under guaranteed

---

See Stipulation, *In re* Generali U.S. Branch (N.Y. Dep't of Ins. Apr. 17, 1997). The superintendent can impose a penalty of up to $1,000 for each violation of a provision of the New York Insurance Law. N.Y. INS. LAW § 109 (McKinney, Westlaw through L.2021). *See also* Gen. Couns. Op. No. 8-31-2004, 2004 WL 3774702, at *1 (N.Y. Ins. Dep't Aug. 31, 2004); *infra* Part III.D (discussing the penalties for violating the "Appleton Rule").

92. N.Y. INS. LAW § 6901(a)(1)(A)–(E) (McKinney, Westlaw through L.2021). *See supra* text accompanying notes 50–52 (discussing in detail and quoting subparagraphs (A) through (E)).

93. *Id.* § 6904(b)(1). *See supra* text accompanying notes 56–58 (discussing in detail that limitation on permissible FGI).

94. *Id.* § 6901(a)(1)(A) (emphasis added).

investment contracts.[95] The Department concluded that although Article 69 authorizes monoline insurers to write certain kinds of FGI, it was not intended to constitute an exemption from the preexisting prohibition against guaranteeing insurance contracts. In reaching that conclusion, the Department discussed section 6901(a)(1)(A)'s use of the term "obligation," and stated: "While some may argue that 'obligation' is limited to stocks, securities or other similar instruments, we think that 'obligation' has its common dictionary meaning; that is, the contract, promise, etc., that compels one to follow a certain course of action."[96]

On several occasions, the Department ruled that certain products constituted FGI (and therefore could not be written by a multiline insurer), but at the time did not constitute a guaranty of indebtedness per subparagraph (A) of section 6901(a)(1) (and therefore could not be written by a monoline insurer, either). For example, the Department concluded that a synthetic guaranteed interest contract, also known as a "wrap contract," constituted an unauthorized type of FGI.[97] Under such a contract, the insurer would pay the book value of assets held by a pension plan regardless of the actual market value of the supporting assets. The Department concluded that a "wrap contract" therefore insured against changes in the levels of

---

95. Gen. Couns. Op. No. 9-14-92, 1992 WL 12495411, at *1 (N.Y. Ins. Dep't Sept. 14, 1992).

96. *Id.* at *2. The opinion posited that if section 6901(a)(1)(A) were construed literally, an insurance company's contractual obligation under its insurance contract to pay money constituted a "monetary obligation" and that therefore a guaranty of payment under an insurance contract would fall within the scope of FGI that the statute permits a monoline insurer to issue. The fact that the opinion declined to adopt a literal reading of the statute and approve the proposed coverage was not based on a conclusion that a contractual obligation to pay was not a monetary obligation; it was the result of the opinion's construction of other provisions specific to the issue of guaranteeing obligations under an insurance contract. *Id.* In August 1995, the Insurance Department reconsidered its general ban on guaranties of insurance contracts and announced that the superintendent had determined that there was no statutory prohibition against guaranteeing certain guaranteed interest insurance contracts and guaranties of certain reinsurance recoveries. Circular Letter No. 1995-13, 1995 WL 17237023 (N.Y. Ins. Dep't Aug. 17, 1995).

97. Gen. Couns. Op. No. 6-13-94 (N.Y. Ins. Dep't June 13, 1994) (on file with the New York Department of Financial Services, Office of the General Counsel).

interest rates (thus falling within subparagraph (D) of section 6901(a)(1)) or changes in the value of specific assets or commodities (thus falling within subparagraph (B)). As section 6904(b)(1) limits authorized FGI to that defined in subparagraph (A), a "wrap contract" was not permitted in New York at all.[98] Similarly, the Department twice ruled that a proposal aimed at guaranteeing the performance of mutual funds constituted a guaranty of changes in the value of specific assets or commodities (within the meaning of subparagraph (D) of section 6901(a)(1)), and hence was not permitted in New York, either.[99]

Another component of the definition of FGI is illustrated by an October 1996 OGC opinion[100] that evaluated a proposal to insure a motor vehicle lender (such as a bank) against the possibility that, in the event of a borrower defaulting on a loan, the outstanding loan balance would exceed the value of the repossessed vehicle. The Department concluded that the proposed coverage did not constitute FGI, reasoning:

> A key element of financial guaranty insurance is not present . . . since coverage is not conditioned upon the default of the lender. While the vehicle will be repossessed typically only after a default, it is the deficiency amount upon the sale of the vehicle which triggers the coverage. If the vehicle is not sold, there is no coverage. Nor do we think that the policy covers changes in the value of specific assets.[101]

---

98. *Id.*
99. Gen. Couns. Op. No. 2-29-96, 1996 WL 33693828, at *2–3 (N.Y. Ins. Dep't Feb. 29, 1996); Gen. Couns. Op. No. 5-31-95, 1995 WL 17236540, at *2–3 (N.Y. Ins. Dep't May 31, 1995).
100. Gen. Couns. Op. No. 10-24-96, 1996 WL 33693906, at *1 (N.Y. Ins. Dep't Oct. 24, 1996).
101. *Id.* at *2. The Department also ruled that the coverage could be written as residual value insurance, which is an authorized form of insurance in New York (*see* N.Y. INS. LAW § 1113(a)(22) (McKinney, Westlaw through L.2021)), and is not subject to Article 69's limitations upon FGI. *Accord* Gen. Couns. Op. No. 1-8-2003, 2003 WL 24312610, at *2 (N.Y. Ins. Dep't Jan. 8, 2003) (ruling that the proposed policy was residual value insurance, and not FGI, because coverage was not conditioned upon a borrower default); Gen. Couns. Op. No. 10-26-94 (#2), 1994 WL 16305929, at *1 (N.Y. Ins. Dep't Oct. 26, 1994) (ruling that the proposed stop-loss unemployment insurance was not triggered by a financial default or insolvency, and therefore was not permissible FGI). Conversely, when

Section 6904(b)(1) imposes a second layer of restriction upon the kinds of permitted FGI. Not only are authorized guaranties limited to those insuring payment under "any debt instrument or other monetary obligation" within the meaning of section 6901(a)(1)(A), but they are further confined to indebtedness arising from the ten categories of obligation defined in section 6904(b)(1).[102]

In a December 1992 OGC opinion,[103] the Department considered four of those categories: consumer debt obligations,[104] installment purchase agreements executed as a condition of sale,[105] corporate obligations,[106] and partnership obligations.[107] The OGC considered whether an insurer could issue to a lender or lessor a bond guaranteeing the performance of a customer's continuing obligation under a lease or finance contract (presumably, the obligation to make payments). The Department concluded that such a bond would constitute FGI and would, therefore, be permissible only if it satisfied both criteria of section 6904(b)(1): (1) that the coverage constitute a guaranty of indebtedness

---

coverage is triggered by a borrower default, the Department has ruled that the policy constitutes FGI, not residual value insurance, and therefore may not be issued by a multiline insurer. *See* Gen. Couns. Op. No. 9-22-2000, 2000 WL 34630133, at *3–4 (N.Y. Ins. Dep't Sept. 22, 2000) (proposed "repossession insurance," which would cover the lender on a vehicle purchase balloon loan, upon a borrower default, for the amount by which the outstanding balance at the time of default exceeded the amount that the balance would have been on a conventional loan).

102. N.Y. INS. LAW § 6904(b)(1)(A)–(J) (McKinney, Westlaw through L.2021). *See supra* text accompanying notes 59–62 (discussing in detail and quoting the ten categories of permissible obligations).

103. Gen. Couns. Op. No. 12-1-92, 1992 WL 12495649, at *1 (N.Y. Ins. Dep't Dec. 1, 1992).

104. *See* N.Y. INS. LAW § 6904(b)(1)(H) (current through L.2021, chapters 1 to 833, and L.2022, chapters 1 to 12).

105. *See id.* § 6904(b)(1)(G).

106. *See id.* § 6904(b)(1)(D).

107. *See id.* § 6904(b)(1)(E). The remaining six categories of obligations under section 6904(b)(1) are municipal bond obligations, subparagraph (A); special revenue bonds, subparagraph (B); industrial development bonds, subparagraph (C); certain asset-backed securities, trust certificates, and trust obligations, subparagraph (F); utility first mortgage obligations, subparagraph (I); and substantially similar debt instruments or financial obligations approved by the superintendent of the Insurance Department, subparagraph (J).

within subparagraph (A) of section 6901(a)(1) (rather than one of the types of guaranty defined in subparagraphs (B) through (E)), and (2) that the insured indebtedness arise from one of the categories of obligations designated in subparagraphs (A) through (J) of section 6904(b)(1).[108] The Department pointed out that a consumer debt obligation arising from a loan made in connection with the extension of credit to an individual for nonbusiness purposes would constitute a consumer debt obligation under subparagraph (H) of section 6904(b)(1) and, hence, would constitute permissible FGI. Subparagraph (H) is limited by its terms to "consumer debt obligations," and, therefore, "[f]inancial guaranty insurance for a business loan or lease could not be written unless the bond came within one of the other permissible types [designated in section 6904(b)(2)], for example, where the obligor is a corporation or a partnership that defaults on its obligation (either a loan or a lease)."[109] Under subparagraphs (D) and (E) of section 6904(b)(1), corporate and partnership obligations are two of the categories of transactions as to which a financial guaranty insurer may issue a guaranty if the obligations arose from a debt instrument or otherwise constituted a monetary obligation within the definition of section 6901(a)(1)(A). It appears clear from the quoted sentence that the Department holds the opinion that where an obligor on a business lease is a corporation or partnership, guaranteeing its obligations under the lease would constitute FGI, which a monoline financial guaranty insurer is permitted to write.[110]

b. Which "Exclusion" Governs Surety Bonds (Bank Depository Bonds)? The definition of FGI in section 6901(a) excludes "surety insurance" as defined in section 1113(a)(16),[111] and section 1113(a)(16) excludes from the definition of surety insurance any coverage that falls within the definition of FGI under section 6901(a)(1).[112] Thus, as discussed above, the statutory definitions perpetually bounce the reader back and forth between the two exclusions.[113]

---

108. Op. No. 12-1-92, 1992 WL 12495649, at *2.
109. *Id.* at *3.
110. An earlier 1992 opinion employed the same reasoning and almost identical language regarding business leases. Gen. Couns. Op. No. 10-1-92, 1992 WL 12495414, at *2–3 (N.Y. Ins. Dep't Oct. 1, 1992).
111. N.Y. INS. LAW § 6901(a)(2)(B) (McKinney, Westlaw through L.2021).
112. *Id.* § 1113(a)(16)(E)(ii).
113. *See supra* Part II.A.3 (quoting the statutory definitions and discussing their "ping-pong" effect).

The short and fascinating history of the complexities and confusion generated by the intertwining of sections 6901(a)(1) and 1113(a)(16) is neatly illustrated in three OGC opinions, each of which addressed whether a multiline insurer can issue a bank depository bond. Bank depository bonds typically guarantee the repayment of funds that a public entity deposits in a bank, in excess of the amount insured by the FDIC. In each case, this issue begged the question of whether a bank depository bond constitutes FGI within the definition of section 6901(a)(1), and is therefore forbidden to a multiline insurer, or whether it constitutes permissible surety insurance under section 1113(a)(16).

In the first opinion, which was rendered in 1990,[114] the Department concluded that a bank depository bond fit squarely within the definition of "financial guaranty insurance" set forth in section 6901(a)(1) because

> [l]oss is payable, upon proof of financial loss, to an insured obligee (the public entity) as a result of the failure of the obligor (the depository bank) to pay amounts due with respect to such obligation (the obligation being the duty pursuant to the contract between the public entity as depositor of funds and the bank as depository to make available the depositor's funds upon proper request) when such failure is the result of insolvency (which must have occurred since the depository bond only provides excess coverage after exhaustion of the Federal Deposit Insurance Corporation coverage).[115]

The Department conceded that section 6901(a)(2)(B) carves out an exception for fidelity and surety insurance as defined in section 1113(a)(16). Nevertheless, it concluded that this exception was unavailing because subparagraph (E)(ii) of section 1113(a)(16) excluded from permissible surety insurance any coverage that fell within the definition of "financial guaranty insurance" under section 6901(a)(1)—which could

---

114. Gen. Couns. Op. No. 6-1-90 (#2), 1990 WL 10496483, at *1 (N.Y. Ins. Dep't June 1, 1990). In that opinion, the Department reaffirmed an earlier ruling that the same proposed bond constituted FGI, which could not be issued by a multiline insurer. *Id.* at *3. *See* Gen. Couns. Op. No. 2-15-90 (#2), 1990 WL 10496697, at *1 (N.Y. Ins. Dep't Feb. 15, 1990).

115. Op. No. 6-1-90 (#2), 1990 WL 10496483, at *2.

only be issued by an authorized monoline insurer.[116] The Department observed:

> The bank depository bond, which prior to passage of the financial guaranty legislation would have been authorized as fidelity and surety insurance, was one of those coverages which was reclassified, consistent with [Insurance] Department intent and legislative purpose, as financial guaranty insurance based upon critical characteristics of the bond discussed herein.[117]

In 1994, another multiline insurer proposed to write a bank depository bond, giving rise to a second OGC opinion on the issue.[118] The proposed bond would be issued pursuant to an Ohio statute that requires security for the repayment of public deposits made with a bank in excess of amounts insured by the FDIC.[119] In the 1994 opinion, however, the Department concluded that the multiline insurer *could* issue the proposed bank depository bond because the bond met the definition of "surety insurance" authorized under subparagraph (F) of section 1113(a)(16) ("bonds and undertakings required or permitted in all judicial

---

116. *Id.* at *3. The proponent of the depository bond argued that the bond should be exempted from the FGI prohibition via section 1113(a)(16)(D) as "'[a]n indemnity bond for the benefit of a public body,' or, alternatively, via section 6901(a)(2)(J) as being 'any other form of insurance covering risks which the superintendent determines to be substantially similar to any of the foregoing [exceptions listed under subparagraphs (A) through (I) of section 6901(a)(2)].'" *Id.* at *2 (internal quotation marks omitted). The Department rejected both arguments.

117. *Id.* at *3. That conclusion was consistent with the Department's later rulings that when a bond falls within the definition of both "fidelity and surety insurance" and "financial guaranty insurance," the presumption should be in favor of FGI because "the intent of the legislation was to remove certain types of contracts of surety and guaranty from fidelity and surety insurance, and to treat them as financial guaranty insurance." Gen. Couns. Op. No. 12-1-92, 1992 WL 12495649, at *2 (N.Y. Ins. Dep't Dec. 1, 1992) (addressing bonds guaranteeing consumer debt obligations); Gen. Couns. Op. No. 10-1-92, 1992 WL 12495414, at *2 (N.Y. Ins. Dep't Oct. 1, 1992) (same).

118. *See* Gen. Couns. Op. No. 8-11-94 (#3), 1994 WL 16305901, at *1 (N.Y. Ins. Dep't Aug. 11, 1994).

119. *See* OHIO REV. CODE ANN. § 135.18 (West, Westlaw through file 27 of the 134th Gen. Assemb. (2021–2022)).

proceedings or otherwise by law allowed"), and was therefore excluded from the general prohibition against the issuance of FGI by multiline companies.[120] In so ruling, the Department retreated from its earlier opinion and stated a more refined analysis of the interplay between the "surety insurance" and "financial guaranty insurance" provisions of sections 1113(a)(16) and 6901(a)(1). The Department conceded that

> we have in the past opined that to the extent that a product comes within the definitions of both surety and financial guaranty insurance, it was the intent of the legislation to require that the product be considered financial guaranty insurance. *However, we now conclude that such a reading of the exclusion in* [section 1113(a)(16)(E)[121]] *is overbroad.* Since the exclusion for financial guaranty insurance is contained only in subparagraph (E) [of section 1113(a)(16)], it ought not be interpreted to apply to products written under subparagraphs (C), (D), or (F) [of section 1113(a)(16)]. When viewed in this light, the two exclusions no longer appear to be contrary. To the extent that a product overlaps subparagraph (E) and Section 6901(a)(1), it must be treated as financial guaranty insurance. *However, if the product comes within one of the other subparagraphs of paragraph (16), then the Section 6901(a)(2)(B) exclusion takes it out of financial guaranty insurance and places it squarely under surety insurance, even though it would otherwise come within the meaning of Section 6901(a)(1).*[122]

Thus, the Department concluded that while it might initially appear that the multiline insurer would be prohibited from issuing a bond that fits within section 6901(a)(1)'s definition of "financial guaranty

120. Op. No. 8-11-94 (#3), 1994 WL 16305901, at *2.
121. N.Y. Ins. Law § 1113(a)(16)(E) (McKinney, Westlaw through L.2021). That provision authorizes becoming a surety on "any lawful contract" not specifically provided for in the other subparagraphs of section 1113(a)(16), with the exception of "any contract . . . [that] would constitute . . . financial guaranty insurance as defined in [section 6901(a)(1)]," *id.* § 1113(a)(16)(E)(ii)b, as well as other specified transactions that do not implicate the definition of "financial guaranty insurance." *See supra* text accompanying notes 69–71 (discussing and quoting subparagraphs (C)–(J) of section 1113(a)(16)).
122. Op. No. 8-11-94 (#3), 1994 WL 16305901, at *3 (emphasis added).

insurance," the multiline company is permitted to issue such a bond if the particular type of bond qualifies as "surety insurance" by virtue of fitting within subparagraphs (C), (D), or (F) of section 1113(a)(16). Although the August 1994 opinion predated the 2005 amendment of section 1113, there is no reason to suppose that its reasoning would not also be applied to new subparagraphs (G), (H), and (I) of section 1113(a)(16), which were added by the 2005 amendment, and to current subparagraph (J), which was relettered by that amendment.[123] It is true that new subparagraph (I),[124] which specifically included bank depository bonds within section 1113(a)(16)'s definition of "surety insurance," may have mooted the August 1990 opinion. However, the ruling in that opinion should still apply to the other subparagraphs of section 1113(a)(16), which specify transactions that constitute surety insurance.

In the 1994 opinion, in order to determine whether the bond at issue fell within subparagraph (F) of section 1113(a)(16), the Department considered the fact that the Ohio statute at issue did not actually *require* a bond. Posting a bond was one alternative for satisfying the security requirement. Under subparagraph (F), surety insurance includes "bonds and undertakings required or permitted in all judicial proceedings or otherwise by law allowed."[125] That phrase originally read "or by law required," but had been amended by replacing "required" with "allowed." Based on this legislative history, the Department concluded that subparagraph (F) included "bonds which are acceptable as security, but where the law permits other methods of satisfying the security"

---

123. N.Y. INS. LAW § 1113(a)(16)(G)–(J) (current through L.2021, chapters 1 to 833, and L.2022, chapters 1 to 12). *See also supra* Part II.A.4 (discussing the 2005 amendment in detail). Before the 2005 amendment, subparagraph (J) was designated subparagraph (G), which had been added to section 1113(a)(16) by an amendment in 1996. Subparagraph (G), now subparagraph (J), expanded the definition of "surety insurance" to include guaranteeing, for a period of not more than five years, "the payment of a premium, deductible, or self-insured retention to an insurer issuing a workers' compensation or liability policy." N.Y. INS. LAW § 1113(a)(16)(J). *See infra* Part II.F.1 (discussing such guaranties).

124. N.Y. INS. LAW § 1113(a)(16)(I) (current through L.2021, chapters 1 to 833, and L.2022, chapters 1 to 12). *See also supra* text accompanying notes 70–71 (quoting subparagraph (I)) & *infra* note 133.

125. N.Y. INS. LAW § 1113(a)(16)(F) (current through L.2021, chapters 1 to 833, and L.2022, chapters 1 to 12).

requirement, as was the case under the Ohio statute.[126] The Department then stated the fundamental criteria for inclusion in subparagraph (F): "Essentially, . . . the bond must provide a benefit to the public that has been identified by an appropriate legislative body as being necessary for the public good."[127]

The Department noted that in the absence of Ohio's statutory security requirement, the bank depository bond would have fallen under subparagraph (E) of section 1113(a)(16) ("[b]ecoming surety on, or guaranteeing the performance of, any lawful contract, not specifically provided for in this paragraph"). And due to the exclusion in sub-subparagraph (ii)b of subparagraph (E) (except for contracts that "would constitute . . . financial guaranty insurance as defined in [section 6901(a)(1)]"), the bond would have been classified as a type of FGI forbidden to multiline insurers. Thus, Ohio's statutory security obligation placed the proposed bond under subparagraph (F) of section 1113(a)(16). And in light of section 6901(a)(2)(B)'s exclusion for "fidelity and surety insurance as defined in [section 1113(a)(16)]," the bond fell within the kinds of surety insurance that both multiline and monoline insurers can write.

Although it conceded that the product at issue was surety insurance, the Department warned regarding the construction of its opinion:

> We wish to underscore the strict delimitations of this opinion. It assumes, as we believe is the case, that laws requiring or expressly permitting bonds for security are usually enacted only for the purposes of the common good, and not to protect or promote private interests. We do not address at this time a law that expressly permits a bond as security for a purely private obligation, not affecting the public interest.[128]

The clear inference, however, is that, to the extent a bond promotes a private interest rather than the public good, the Department may not deem such a product to fall under the section 1113(a)(16)(F) definition of "surety insurance."

In 1998, the OGC issued a third opinion on whether a bank depository bond constitutes "fidelity and surety insurance" pursuant to section 1113(a)(16), or "financial guaranty insurance" pursuant to section

---

126. Op. No. 8-11-94 (#3), 1994 WL 16305901, at *2.
127. *Id.*
128. *Id.* at *3.

6901(a).[129] The opinion was occasioned by the request of a monoline financial guaranty insurer that the Department reconsider its August 11, 1994, opinion (which the financial guaranty insurer described as "tortured"). The Department expressly reaffirmed its earlier opinion, but also restated its limitations:

> The letter [dated August 11, 1994] applies ONLY TO bonds issued in satisfaction of a statutory security obligation in regard to municipalities or other public entities where a bond is either required or permitted to satisfy such an obligation. The opinions expressed in the earlier letters continue to represent the Department's position in the absence of such obligation.[130]

The Department also emphasized that the 1994 opinion, and hence the scope of subparagraph (F) of section 1113(a)(16), "applied only to those bonds intended as security for the public interest, and not to protect or promote private interests."[131]

A multiline insurer would ignore this lesson regarding non-statutory FGI at its peril. For example, in two opinions rendered in November 2002,[132] the Department ruled that a bond providing "excess FDIC insurance" constituted FGI that may be written only by a monoline company. Apparently, the proposed bonds had not been "identif[ied] by an appropriate legislative body as being necessary for the public good."[133]

---

129. Gen. Couns. Op. No. 12-7-98, 1998 WL 34383103, at *1 (N.Y. Ins. Dep't Dec. 7, 1998).
130. *Id.*
131. *Id.* at *2.
132. Gen. Couns. Op. No. 11-12-2002 (#3), 2002 WL 33011213, at *1 (N.Y. Ins. Dep't Nov. 12, 2002); Gen. Couns. Op. No. 11-13-2002 (#1), 2002 WL 33011176, at *1 (N.Y. Ins. Dep't Nov. 13, 2002).
133. Gen. Couns. Op. No. 8-11-94 (#3), 1994 WL 16305901, at *2 (N.Y. Ins. Dep't Aug. 11, 1994). Both OGC Opinion No. 11-12-2002 and OGC Opinion No. 11-13-2002 concluded that the proposed bonds fall within the definition of "financial guaranty insurance" under section 6091(a)(1). *See* Op. No. 11-12-2002(#3), 2002 WL 33011213, at *3; Op. No. 11-13-2002 (#1), 2002 WL 33011176, at *2. However, in neither opinion did the OGC provide a reason for that conclusion. Nor did it address any of the section 1113(a)(16) exclusions from that definition. As described in those opinions, the "excess FDIC insurance" appeared to be the equivalent of a bank depository bond. Both opinions cited the earlier

In later opinions, the Department would continue to cite to its August 11, 1994, opinion as setting forth its position regarding the reach of section 1113(a)(16)(F).[134]

c. Agreements with Mixed Obligations: FGI or Surety Insurance? One of the two 2004 OGC opinions discussed earlier (which ruled that lease bonds constituted FGI, not surety insurance, thus prompting the addition of subparagraph (G) to section 1113(a)(16) via the 2005

1990 opinion (Gen. Couns. Op. No. 2-15-90 (#2), 1990 WL 10496697, at *1 (N.Y. Ins. Dep't Feb. 15, 1990)), which ruled that bank depository bonds constituted FGI. Op. No. 11-12-2002(#3), 2002 WL 33011213, at *4; Op. No. 11-13-2002, 2002 WL 33011176, at *3. However, neither opinion contains a mention of the 1994 and 1998 opinions, in which the OGC came to the opposite conclusion. *See* Op. No. 8-11-94 (#3), 1994 WL 16305901, at *3; Op. No. 12-7-98, 1998 WL 34383103, at *2–3. The ruling in the November 2002 opinions was effectively reversed by the 2005 amendment to section 1113, which added subparagraph (I) to subsection 1113(a)(16). *See supra* Part II.A.4 (discussing the 2005 amendment). Subparagraph (I) provides that "[a] depository bond that insures deposits in financial institutions to the extent of the excess over the amount insured by the Federal Deposit Insurance Corporation" is included in the definition of "fidelity and surety insurance" under section 1113(a)(16) and therefore may be issued by a multiline insurer even though it may not be "allowed" by any other subparagraph under section 1113(a)(16)(E). N.Y. INS. LAW § 1113(a)(16)(I) (McKinney, Westlaw through L.2021). There is nothing, however, in the legislative history to suggest that the addition of subparagraph (I) was intended as a rejection of the reasoning in the two November 2002 opinions. *See also supra* text accompanying notes 123–124.

134. *See* Gen. Couns. Op. No. 8-23-2004 (#3), 2004 WL 3774694, at *3 (N.Y. Ins. Dep't Aug. 23, 2004) (citing Gen. Couns. Op. No. 8-11-94 (#3), 1994 WL 16305901, at *1 (N.Y. Ins. Dep't Aug. 11, 1994), and opining that a New York City debt collector's license bond is surety insurance under section 1113(a)(16)(F)); Gen. Couns. Op. No. 8-1-08, 2008 WL 4455542, at *6 (N.Y. Ins. Dep't Aug. 1, 2008) (applying same rationale to declare that a U.S. Customs bond would constitute surety insurance under subparagraph (F)); Gen. Couns. Op. No. 3-22-2005 (#7), 2005 WL 3980746, at *2 (N.Y. Ins. Dep't Mar. 22, 2005) (concluding that a "payment bond for liability" described in the Texas Administrative Code is surety insurance under either subparagraph (C) or subparagraph (F)). However, in none of those three opinions was the issue of FGI expressly discussed.

amendment)[135] addressed a proposed bond guaranteeing a contract containing both a financial guaranty obligation and a surety obligation. The proposed bond would guarantee to the landlord the tenant's obligations under the lease to pay rent *and* to pay for damage to the leased premises. The Department concluded that a failure to pay rent was clearly a failure to pay a monetary obligation as a result of a financial default—and thus fell within section 6901(a)'s definition of "financial guaranty insurance," and not within any of the specific kinds of surety insurance excluded from the definition of "financial guaranty insurance," pursuant to subparagraphs (C), (D), and (F) through (J) of section 1113(a)(16). It also concluded that, by reason of the exclusionary language of section 1113(a)(16)(E)(ii)b, the failure to pay rent could not come within subparagraph (E), either. At the same time, the proposed bond would also "guarantee[] non-monetary lease obligations . . . such as maintaining the premises in an undamaged condition, [and if that were the sole coverage, the bond] would constitute surety insurance."[136] Addressing the treatment of a bond guaranteeing a

---

135. Gen. Couns. Op. No. 4-27-2004 (#2), 2004 WL 3774618, at *1 (N.Y. Ins. Dep't Apr. 27, 2004). The other was General Counsel Opinion No. 5-4-2004 (#2), 2004 WL 3774624, at *1 (N.Y. Ins. Dep't May 4, 2004). *See supra* Part II.A.4 (discussing in detail those opinions and their relation to the 2005 amendment). Subparagraph (G) provides that the definition of "fidelity and surety insurance" under section 1113(a)(16) includes "[b]ecoming surety on, or guaranteeing the performance of, any agreement for the lease or rental of non-residential real property or tangible personal property, provided that the obligation of the insurer shall not exceed a period of five years and the bond is not issued directly or indirectly in connection with" a capital market transaction. N.Y. INS. LAW § 1113(a)(16)(G) (current through L.2021, chapters 1 to 833, and L.2022, chapters 1 to 12). Although the 2005 amendment was adopted in reaction to the two lease bond opinions, the fact that the legislature expressly placed a five-year limit on lease bonds when making the amendment suggests that the legislature agreed with the reasoning set forth in the opinions. Otherwise, the legislature would have adopted an amendment, effective retroactively, to "clarify" what the legislature regarded as the intended meaning of the original statute. As such, although specified types of lease bonds are now considered to be authorized surety bonds by virtue of the 2005 amendment, the *rationale* of the opinions on that subject appears to carry the imprimatur of the legislature.

136. Op. No. 4-27-2004 (#2), 2004 WL 3774618, at *3.

mix of monetary and nonmonetary obligations, the Department began its analysis with the following general rule:

> The Department's opinions have generally considered as financial guaranty insurance any bond where the principal performance guaranteed is the payment of a debt obligation and as surety insurance any bond where the debt obligation is not the principal obligation, but may be incidental, except where the statute defines the debt obligation explicitly as surety insurance or contains an exclusion.[137]

The Department then went on to conclude that only a monoline financial guaranty insurer could issue the mixed obligation guaranty, reasoning that

> the proposed bond would not be so limited [to solely nonmonetary obligations] since it would also be a guaranty of the payment of rent. The rental guaranty is not incidental to the non-monetary performance guaranty; rather, the bond would be guarantying separate and distinct obligations. An insurer's writing authority is limited by the definitions of the kinds of insurance contained in § 1113 and other sections of the Insurance Law, including, in particular, § 6901(a). *An insurer may not combine kinds of insurance that it is not licensed to write within a policy or contract covering insurance of the kinds that it is authorized to write.*[138]

The rule stated in the italicized sentence is a zero-sum game and categorically precludes a multiline insurer from issuing a bond that guarantees, in *any* part, a monetary obligation. The "principal performance" test set forth in the first quotation from the opinion, however, is not an all-or-nothing proposition. It contemplates that a multiline company can guarantee mixed obligations, so long as the nonmonetary

---

137. *Id.*

138. *Id.* (emphasis added). In the second lease bond opinion that led to the 2005 amendment, the proposed bond was described as guaranteeing only the obligation to pay rent, and not any nonmonetary obligation. Op. No. 542004 (#2), 2004 WL 3774624, at *3 (concluding that the proposed lease bond constituted FGI).

obligation is the principal performance guaranteed (and, conversely, the monetary obligation is incidental). The two propositions seem to conflict. However, the Department appears to have separately applied each of the two propositions to different types of cases. It has employed the categorical, all-or-nothing rule when evaluating a bond guaranteeing a mix of monetary and nonmonetary obligations, thereby avoiding the possibility of permitting a multiline insurer to include "incidental" FGI in its coverage, when prohibiting multiline insurers from issuing FGI was a primary objective of Article 69. On the other hand, when the proposed guaranty could be classified as *either* FGI or surety insurance, but not a *combination* of the two, the possibility of a multiline insurer issuing "incidental" FGI would not exist as a practical matter (even though the principal performance test, when read literally, allows for the possibility of permitting a multiline company to write FGI). Therefore, in a case of a bond that is either FGI or surety insurance, the principal performance test can be applied. It was confusing, however, for the Department to invoke both the "principal performance" and "all-or-nothing" test in support of its conclusion, in Opinion No. 4-27-2004 (#2), that the multiline insurer could not issue the proposed coverage.

The 2010 request for an opinion in connection with another lease bond illustrates the Department's application of the categorical rule when faced with proposed coverage for mixed obligations. The bond was intended to take the place of the traditional cash security deposit and would indemnify the landlord for physical damage to the leased premises as well as lost rent in the event that the tenant vacated the premises before the lease ended. In the responding OGC opinion,[139] the Department found, as it had with prior lease bonds, that the proposed bond guaranteed a contract with a mix of monetary and nonmonetary obligations.[140] The guaranty of the security deposit constituted surety insurance under subparagraphs (C) or (E) of section 1113(a)(16) because it guaranteed performance of "a contract other

---

139. Gen. Couns. Op. No. 9-13-2010, 2010 WL 3855324, at *1 (N.Y. Ins. Dep't Sept. 13, 2010).

140. *Id.* The opinion noted that the proposed bond form was not statutorily excluded from the definition of "financial guaranty insurance" set forth in section 6901 by virtue of the new subparagraph (G) added to section 1113(a)(16) by the 2005 amendment. This was because the new subparagraph (G) was limited by its terms to nonresidential leases. The proposed bond form, on the other hand, applied to residential leases. *Id.* at *2.

than a contract of indebtedness[;] [s]pecifically, . . . the tenant's promise to return the leased premises to the landlord free of physical damage."[141] The coverage for rent lost when the tenant vacated the premises before the end of the lease, however, guaranteed a monetary obligation. As a result, the Department concluded that the proposed bond constituted FGI and that, because only an authorized financial guaranty insurer could write FGI, a multiline company could not issue the proposed bond.[142] There was no discussion as to whether the monetary or nonmonetary obligation was the principal obligation guaranteed, or whether the coverage for lost rent was incidental to the coverage for losses due to physical damage. And no reference was made to the Department's use of the principal performance test as the basis for distinguishing between surety insurance and FGI. The fact that part of the coverage guaranteed a monetary obligation trumped everything else.

By contrast, the Department based a 2002 opinion that a proposed bond constituted FGI, and not surety insurance, entirely on the principal performance test.[143] There, a finance company wished to direct individuals seeking a loan to a bank that would make the loan, while the finance company would, for a fee, issue a bond guaranteeing the repayment of the loan. The finance company asked whether this constituted engaging in an insurance business for which licensing would be required. The Department ruled that because the finance company would be guaranteeing the loans as a "vocation," it would be operating as an insurance business.[144] As to the question whether the bond would

---

141. *Id.* at *2–3.
142. *Id.* at *3–4.
143. Gen. Couns. Op. No. 6-18-2002 (#1), 2002 WL 33011071, at *1 (N.Y. Ins. Dep't June 18, 2002).
144. *Id.* at *2. The New York Insurance Law defines "doing an insurance business," in pertinent part, as "making, . . . as warrantor, guarantor or surety, any contract of warranty, guaranty or suretyship as a vocation and not as merely incidental to any other legitimate business or activity of the warrantor, guarantor or surety; . . . ." N.Y. INS. LAW § 1101(b)(1)(B) (McKinney, Westlaw through L.2021). It is that provision that allows a parent corporation to guarantee the monetary obligations of a subsidiary without running afoul of the statute limiting authorization to issue FGI to financial guaranty insurance corporations. *See* Gen. Couns. Op. No. 10-10-2002 (#1), 2002 WL 33011241, at *2 (N.Y. Ins. Dep't Oct. 10, 2002) ("[W]here a parent corporation is acting as surety for the obligations of its subsidiary, the [parent] corporation would not be making contracts of

constitute FGI or surety insurance, the Department, citing only the principal performance test, concluded that the bond would constitute FGI, because the finance company would be guaranteeing the borrower's obligation to repay the loan. As the guaranteed obligation was based on a debt instrument, the proposed bond fell squarely within the definition of "financial guaranty insurance" under section 6901(a)(1)(A)[145] and not within any of the "fidelity and surety" exceptions set forth in section 1113(a)(16).[146] More importantly, repayment of the loan was the only obligation that would be guaranteed; it was not combined with any other coverage.[147]

In another 2002 opinion, the Department approved as surety insurance a guaranty of a monetary obligation that was triggered solely by an underlying failure of physical performance, and limited to the consequences of that failure.[148] The opinion responded to the inquiry of a bank that regularly issued "performance letters of credit" to municipalities on behalf of the bank's developer clients. These "performance letters of credit" guaranteed the developer's performance of specific items of work identified in the developer's contract with the municipality.[149] If the developer failed to perform those items, the municipality would be entitled to draw on the letter of credit. An indemnity agreement between the bank and the developer obligated the developer to reimburse the bank for all payments made by the bank on the letter of credit. The bank wished to purchase insurance coverage for losses caused by the

---

surety as a vocation[;] [t]hese contracts would be made merely incidental to any other legitimate business activities that the corporation would be engaged in."). *See also* Gen. Couns. Op. No. 1-23-2003 (#2), 2003 WL 24312366, at *1 (N.Y. Ins. Dep't Jan. 23, 2003); Gen. Couns. Op. No. 3-15-90 (#1), 1990 WL 10496590, at *1 (N.Y. Ins. Dep't Mar. 15, 1990).

145. Op. No. 6-18-2002 (#1), 2002 WL 33011071, at *3.
146. N.Y. INS. LAW § 1113(a)(16)(A) (McKinney, Westlaw through L.2021).
147. *See also* Gen. Couns. Op. No. 11-16-2001 (#2), 2001 WL 34906782, at *1 (N.Y. Ins. Dep't Nov. 16, 2001) (invoking only the principal performance test to rule that a bond guaranteeing the real estate purchaser's obligation to pay a deposit was FGI and not surety insurance).
148. Gen. Couns. Op. No. 5-29-2002 (#1), 2002 WL 33011050, at *1 (N.Y. Ins. Dep't May 29, 2002).
149. *Id.* at *1–2. From the description in the opinion, the performance security provided by the "performance letters of credit" was similar to that afforded by traditional developers or subdivision bonds. Such bonds are discussed in detail in Chapter 2 of this volume.

developer's failure to perform the work required by its contract with the municipality. It appears from the opinion that the coverage guaranteed the developer's obligations to the municipality but did not directly guaranty the developer's obligations of indemnity to the bank. Nevertheless, the bank's losses would presumably arise from the developer's failure to reimburse the bank, and insurance against that possibility would arguably fall within the definition of "financial guaranty insurance" under section 6901(a)(1).[150] However, the Department, citing only the "contract" surety provisions of section 1113(a)(16),[151] concluded that the coverage was permissible surety insurance and not FGI, and therefore could be written by a multiline company, reasoning as follows:

> Based upon the facts as provided, the proposed contract would be a type of surety insurance, if it guarantees to the bank the performance of the developer and it is limited to the developer's failure to perform. The letters of credit may be drawn upon only if the developer fails to complete specific tasks pursuant to the tasks filed with the municipality, and not based upon the *financial* default of the developer. The proposed contract does not guarantee the bank's performance under the letters of credit nor does it guarantee a financial default, which would be financial guarantee insurance.[152]

The Department distinguished the developer's obligation to repay the bank from FGI because the obligation to repay "does not take the form of a loan. Rather, the bank's right to recovery against the developer is based on an indemnification agreement entered into between the bank and the developer."[153]

6. Reinsurance—Multiline Insurers and FGI

Article 69 of the New York Insurance Law generally provides for the establishment of monoline financial guaranty insurers and limits the

---

150. N.Y. Ins. Law § 6901(a)(1) (current through L.2021, chapters 1 to 833, and L.2022, chapters 1 to 12).
151. *Id.* § 1113(a)(16)(C) & (E).
152. Op. No. 5-29-2002 (#1), 2002 WL 33011050, at *2 (emphasis added).
153. *Id.* at *1.

authority to write FGI to those insurers.[154] Section 6906 of Article 69, however, permits monoline financial guaranty insurers to cede FGI risks to another financial guaranty insurer or to a "property/casualty insurer or an accredited reinsurer licensed or accredited to reinsure risks of every kind or description . . . as set forth in subsection (c) of [section 4102[155]] of this chapter"[156] and "to receive credit for [the] reinsurance . . . as an asset or as a reduction from liabilities . . . ."[157] Thus, under section 6906, if a multiline property/casualty insurer is licensed to reinsure risks pursuant to section 4102(c), then it is authorized to assume risks on financial guaranties written by monoline insurance companies, even though Article 69 would otherwise prohibit the multiline company from writing such risks.[158]

---

154. *See* N.Y. INS. LAW §§ 6901(b), 6902(a) & 6904(a) (McKinney, Westlaw through L.2021); *see also supra* Part II.A.1 (discussing in detail the statutory limitation on the issuance of FGI by monoline insurers).

155. N.Y. INS. LAW § 4102(c) (McKinney, Westlaw through L.2021). Section 4102 is part of Article 41 (Property/Casualty Insurance Companies) of the New York Insurance Law. Although section 1114(a) of the New York Insurance Law generally permits a New York domestic stock or mutual insurance company to reinsure only those kinds of insurance businesses that it is licensed to issue directly, section 4102(c) authorizes a property/casualty insurer licensed to write any basic kind of insurance to "reinsure risks of every kind and description." *Id. See also* Gen. Couns. Op. No. 3-4-97, 1997 WL 33841442, at *1 (N.Y. Ins. Dep't Mar. 4, 1997).

156. N.Y. INS. LAW § 6906(a)(2) (McKinney, Westlaw through L.2021).

157. *Id.* § 6906(a). *See* Gen. Couns. Op. No. 11-12-2002 (#3), 2002 WL 33011213, at *4 (N.Y. Ins. Dep't Nov. 12, 2002) ("[T]he New York Insurance Law permits property/casualty insurers that meet certain thresholds to reinsure financial guaranty risks."); Op. No. 3-4-97, 1997 WL 33841442, at *1 (concluding that under section 4102(c), a New York property/casualty insurance company may reinsure an FGI risk issued outside of New York by a non-New York insurer, even though the reinsurance contract contained a "cut-through" provision).

158. N.Y. INS. LAW § 6904(a) (current through L.2021, chapters 1 to 833, and L.2022, chapters 1 to 12) (limiting the issuance of FGI to monoline financial guaranty insurers). *See* Op. No. 11-12-2002 (#3), 2002 WL 33011213, at *4 ("[A]lthough the insurers in question [property/casualty carriers] may not write financial guaranty insurance directly, the New York Insurance Law permits [such carriers] that meet certain thresholds to reinsure financial guaranty risks") (citing section 6906(a)). Section 6906 is derived from section 5 of the Model Act. The Model Act does not

Whether FGI risks are ceded to another monoline financial guaranty insurer or to a property/casualty company, the reinsurance agreement must provide that it may be amended or terminated

> (i) at the option of the reinsurer or the ceding insurer, if the reinsurance agreement provides that the liability of the reinsurer with respect to policies in effect at the date of termination shall continue until the expiration or cancellation of each such policy, or (ii) with the consent of the ceding company, if the reinsurance agreement provides for a cutoff of the reinsurance in force at the date of termination, or (iii) at the discretion of the superintendent acting as rehabilitator, liquidator or receiver of the ceding or assuming insurer.[159]

If the financial guaranty insurer obtains reinsurance from a property/casualty company, section 6906(a)(2) also provides that the reinsurance agreement must require that the reinsurer:

> (A) have and maintain a surplus to policyholders of at least thirty-five million dollars;
>
> (B) establish and maintain the reserves required in [section 6903] of this article, except that if the reinsurance agreement is not pro rata the contribution to the contingency reserve shall be equal to fifty percent of the quarterly earned reinsurance premium. However, the assuming insurer need not establish and maintain such reserve to the extent that the ceding insurer has established and continues to maintain such reserve;
>
> (C) comply with the provisions of [section 6904(c)] of this article, except that the maximum total exposures reinsured net of retrocessions and collateral shall be one-half of that permitted for a financial guaranty insurance corporation;

---

authorize the ceding of FGI risks to property/casualty insurers expressly but to "another type of insurer licensed to write surety insurance." MODEL ACT, *supra* note 26, § 5.A(2). As property/casualty insurers can generally be licensed to write surety insurance, the Model Act contemplated reinsurance with multiline property/casualty carriers.

159. N.Y. INS. LAW § 6906(a) (current through L.2021, chapters 1 to 833, and L.2022, chapters 1 to 12).

(D) if a parent of the insurer, another subsidiary of the parent of the insurer, or a subsidiary of the insurer, then the aggregate of all risks assumed by such reinsurers shall not exceed ten percent of the insurer's exposures, net of retrocessions and collateral. Direct or indirect ownership interests of fifty percent or more shall be deemed a parent/subsidiary relationship;[160]

(E) if an affiliate of the insurer, such affiliate shall not assume a percentage of the insurer's total exposures insured net of retrocessions and collateral in excess of its percentage of equity interest in the insurer; and

(F) assumes from the financial guaranty insurer [and related financial guaranty insurers or those writing only FGI] less than fifty percent of the total exposures insured by the financial guaranty insurer . . . .[161]

It is important to note that the contingency reserve requirements set forth in subparagraph (B) of section 6906(a)(2) are only required if the reinsurance agreement requires the reinsurer to maintain such reserves, or the ceding insurer is not maintaining such reserves: "the assuming insurer need not establish and maintain such reserve to the extent that the ceding insurer has established and continues to maintain such reserve."[162]

The specific reserve requirements are set out in section 6903 of Article 69,[163] and the surplus requirements and limitations on risk in section 6904.[164] The restrictions on the amount of reinsurance taken by a multiline reinsurer are enforced not against the reinsurer but against the ceding company. Accordingly, the ceding company loses credit for reinsurance from a multiline company if it cedes more of a given financial guaranty risk to a reinsurer than the law permits, or if it fails

---

160. Subparagraph (D) imports, in substance, the so-called "single risk rule," which is found generally in section 1115. *Id.* § 1115(a) ("[N]o insurer doing business in this state shall expose itself to any loss on any one risk in an amount exceeding ten percent of its surplus to policyholders.").

161. *Id.* § 6906(a)(2)(A)–(F). The requirements of subparagraphs (A) through (F) of section 6906(a)(2) track the Model Act with only minor variations. *See* Model Act, *supra* note 26, § 5.A(2)(a)–(g).

162. N.Y. Ins. Law § 6906(a)(2)(B) (current through L.2021, chapters 1 to 833, and L.2022, chapters 1 to 12).

163. *Id.* § 6903.

164. *Id.* § 6904. *See also* Gkonos & Ferrucci, *supra* note 2, at 21–22 (discussing in detail the requirements of both section 6903 and section 6904).

to ensure that the reduction in its reserves are offset by an increase in the multiline reinsurer's reserves. Whether a multiline insurer might be subject to regulatory punishment for failing to abide the requirements of section 6906 is still an open issue.[165]

B. Florida

1. The Statutory Scheme

In 1988, the state of Florida enacted part XX ("Financial Guaranty Insurance") of chapter 627 of the Florida Insurance Code,[166] thereby becoming the first state to adopt a law governing FGI. Like New York, Florida's law is based upon the Model Act. Unlike New York, however, Florida has not published any advisory opinions or circular letters concerning its construction or application of the statutory provisions.

Florida's definition of "financial guaranty insurance" is set forth in section 627.971 of its FGI law, and closely tracks both section 1.A(1) of the Model Act and section 6901(a)(1) of the New York Insurance Law. The Florida definition states:

> As used in this part:
>
> (1)(a) "Financial guaranty insurance" means a surety bond, insurance policy, an indemnity contract issued by an insurer, or any similar guaranty, under which loss is payable upon proof of occurrence of financial loss to an insured claimant, obligee, or indemnitee as a result of:
>
> 1. The failure of an obligor on a debt instrument or other monetary obligation, including common or preferred stock guaranteed under a surety bond, insurance policy, or indemnity contract, to make principal, interest, premium, dividend, or purchase price payments when due, if the failure is the result of a financial default or insolvency, whether such obligation is incurred directly or as guarantor by or on behalf of another obligor who also defaulted;

---

165. Gkonos & Ferrucci, *supra* note 2, at 24–25.

166. FLA. STAT. ANN. §§ 627.971–.975 (West, Westlaw through laws of the 2021 1st Reg. Sess. of the 27th Leg. in effect through June 22, 2021). *See generally* 30 FLA. JUR. 2D *Insurance* §§ 785–794 (West, Westlaw through June 2021 update) (addressing Florida's financial guaranty law).

2. Changes in the levels of interest rates or the differential in interest rates between various markets or products;
3. Changes in the rate of exchange of currency;
4. Changes in the value of specific assets or commodities, financial or commodity indices, or price levels in general; or
5. Other events which the office determines are substantially similar to any of the foregoing.[167]

Like the Model Act and the New York statute, the Florida definition lists those types of coverages that do not constitute FGI. And like New York's statute, Florida's statute excludes surety insurance by reference to another statutory section:

> (b) However, "financial guaranty insurance" does not include:
>
> . . .
>
> 12. Any form of surety insurance as defined in s. 624.606; . . . .[168]

---

167. FLA. STAT. ANN. § 627.971(1)(a) (West, Westlaw through laws of the 2021 1st Reg. Sess. of the 27th Leg. in effect through June 22, 2021). Like New York, Florida's definition of "financial guaranty insurance" does not include section 1.A(1)(d) of the Model Act. MODEL ACT, *supra* note 26, § 1.A(1)(d) ("inconvertibility of one currency into another . . . or inability to withdraw funds held in a foreign country resulting from restrictions imposed by a governmental authority"). *See also supra* note 51 (discussing the noninclusion of section 1.A(1)(d) in the New York definition of "financial guaranty insurance"). In addition, there are minor substantive differences between the Florida provision and those of both the Model Act and the New York law.

168. FLA. STAT. ANN. § 627.971(1)(b)(12) (citing FLA. STAT. ANN. § 624.606 (West, Westlaw through laws of the 2021 1st Reg. Sess. of the 27th Leg. in effect through June 22, 2021) (defining "surety insurance"). Section 6901(a)(2)(B) of the New York FGI law (N.Y. INS. LAW § 6901(a)(2)(B) (McKinney, Westlaw through L.2021)), refers to "fidelity and surety insurance as defined in" section 1113(a)(16). N.Y. INS. LAW § 1113(a)(16) (McKinney, Westlaw through L.2021). *See supra* Parts II.A.2 and II.A.3 (discussing the New York definition of "financial guaranty insurance" and the exception therefrom of fidelity and surety insurance). The exclusion of surety insurance from the definition of "financial guaranty insurance" under Florida's financial guaranty law is discussed in detail *infra* Part II.B.2.

Also like the Model Act and the New York Insurance Law, Florida's FGI law provides: "Financial guaranty insurance shall be transacted in this state only by a corporation licensed for such purpose . . . ."[169] In addition to the transaction of FGI, a financial guaranty corporation in Florida may write only residual value insurance, surety insurance, credit insurance, and mortgage guaranty insurance.[170]

Unlike the Model Act and New York, however, Florida carves out a significant exception to the requirement that FGI may be written by only a monoline financial guaranty corporation:

> (1) Financial guaranty insurance shall be transacted in this state only by a corporation licensed for such purpose, except that a property and casualty insurer transacting business pursuant to the provisions of this code may transact financial guaranty insurance in this state if the following conditions are met:
>
> (a) Total policyholders' surplus exceeds $100 million;
>
> (b) Not more than 20 percent of total net premiums written are applicable to or for financial guaranty insurance;
>
> (c) The provisions of this part [the FGI law] are applied to the insurer's financial guaranty insurance business;
>
> (d) Not more than 20 percent of the insurer's total policyholder's [sic] surplus is applied toward meeting the provisions of this part;

---

169. Fla. Stat. Ann. § 627.973(1) (West, Westlaw through laws of the 2021 1st Reg. Sess. of the 27th Leg. in effect through June 22, 2021).

170. *Id.* § 627.972(1)(a). In contrast, the Model Act and the New York Insurance Law permit a financial guaranty corporation to also write residual value, surety, and credit insurance, but not mortgage guaranty insurance. *See* Model Act, *supra* note 26, § 2.A.(1); N.Y. Ins. Law § 6902(a)(1) (McKinney, Westlaw through L.2021). California permits the financial guaranty corporation to also write surety insurance, but not other types of coverages. *See* Cal. Ins. Code § 12102(b) (West, Westlaw through urgency legislation through ch. 19 of 2021 Reg. Sess.). Connecticut does not permit a financial guaranty corporation to write any other products at all. *See* Conn. Gen. Stat. Ann. § 38a-92g(b) (West, Westlaw through all enactments of 2021 Reg. Sess. enrolled and approved by the governor on or before June 16, 2021, and effective on or before June 16, 2021). *See also infra* Part II.C (discussing the California Financial Guaranty Insurance Law) & Part II.D (discussing the Connecticut Financial Guaranty Insurance Act).

(e) The policyholders' surplus once utilized to meet the requirements of this part shall not be available for meeting any policyholders' surplus requirements for any other type of insurance;
(f) The insurer is licensed to write financial guaranty insurance; and
(g) Unless the insurer is transacting financial guaranty insurance prior to July 1, 1988, and otherwise meets the requirements of this section, prior to the issuance of a license, the insurer must submit to the office for approval, a plan of operation complying with s. 627.972(1)(b).[171]

The original Model Act and the New York law prohibited a multiline company from writing FGI at all. Even after the 2005 amendment,[172] the current NAIC Financial Guaranty Insurance Guideline and New York forbid a multiline company from issuing FGI when the aggregate amount of the bonded indebtedness of one obligor exceeds $10 million.[173] In Florida, however, a multiline property/casualty insurer may issue FGI without any other limitation if it (1) transacts business pursuant to the Florida Insurance Code and (2) satisfies the requisite statutory requirements. One of the aforementioned requirements is that the

---

171. FLA. STAT. ANN. § 627.973(1) (West, Westlaw through laws of the 2021 1st Reg. Sess. of the 27th Leg. in effect through June 22, 2021).
172. *See* discussion *supra* Part II.A.4.
173. *See* FIN. GUAR. INS. GUIDELINE § 1.A(2)(h) (NAT'L ASS'N OF INS. COMM'RS 2011) (West, Westlaw through November 2019 update) (excluding from the definition of "financial guaranty insurance," and thereby from the prohibition on the issuance of FGI by a multiline insurer, FGI for which the aggregate amount of the bonded indebtedness of one obligor does not exceed $10 million); N.Y. INS. LAW § 1113(a)(16)(H) (McKinney, Westlaw through L.2021) (including within the definition of "surety insurance," which is excluded from the definition of "financial guaranty insurance," and thereby from the prohibition on the issuance of FGI by a multiline insurer, FGI for which the aggregate amount of the bonded indebtedness of one obligor does not exceed $10 million). Presumably, the NAIC revised its Financial Guaranty Insurance Guideline after New York adopted the 2005 amendment.

multiline insurer be licensed to issue FGI.[174] Thus, while the Model Act and New York limit the issuance of FGI, in an amount in excess of $10 million for any one obligor, to monoline financial guaranty insurers, Florida appears to allow multiline companies to issue FGI, so long as the companies satisfy certain licensing criteria. Presumably, Florida believes that the perceived risks of FGI, which are reflected in the Model Act and the New York statutes, will be sufficiently ameliorated if the multiline insurer meets the statutory requirements.

> Florida is also more flexible with respect to the types of FGI that a financial guaranty corporation can insure. Florida defines as "financial guaranty insurance" substantially the same five types of transactions that constitute the definition of "financial guaranty insurance" in both the Model Act and the New York Insurance Law.[175] Of those five, the Model Act and the New York statute provide that *only* the guaranty of obligations arising out of a "debt instrument or other monetary obligation" (the so called guaranty of indebtedness[176]) constitutes permissible FGI. Even a monoline financial guaranty insurer may not issue the other four types of coverage included in the definition.[177] Section 627.973[178] of the Florida statute also limits permissible FGI to guaranties of indebtedness[179] with, however, the added proviso that "obligations defined in s. 627.971(1)(a)2., 3., 4., and 5. [the other four types of FGI] may be written with the prior written approval of the office pursuant to limitations and restrictions

---

174. *See* FLA. STAT. ANN. § 627.972 (West, Westlaw through laws of the 2021 1st Reg. Sess. of the 27th Leg. in effect through June 22, 2021) (setting forth the requirements for a license to write FGI).
175. *Compare id.* § 627.971(1)(a)1–5, *quoted supra* text accompanying note 167, *with* MODEL ACT, *supra* note 26, § 1.A(1)(a)–(e), *quoted supra* text accompanying note 31, *and* N.Y. INS. LAW § 6901(a)(1)(A)–(E) (McKinney, Westlaw through L.2021) (*quoted supra* text accompanying note 51).
176. MODEL ACT, *supra* note 26, § 1.A(1)(a); N.Y. INS. LAW § 6901(a)(1)(A) (current through L.2021, chapters 1 to 833, and L.2022, chapters 1 to 12).
177. MODEL ACT, *supra* note 26, § 4.B(1); N.Y. INS. LAW § 6904(b) (McKinney, Westlaw through L.2021).
178. FLA. STAT. ANN. § 627.973(2) (West, Westlaw through laws of the 2021 1st Reg. Sess. of the 27th Leg. in effect through June 22, 2021).
179. *Id.*

promulgated by rule that the commission deems appropriate and necessary to protect the policyholders of the insurer."[180]

It is unlikely that such approval has ever been requested or provided because no such rule appears to have been published.

2. Interpretation of Statutory Provisions

As in New York, the statutory definition of "financial guaranty insurance" in Florida overlaps with the statutory definition of "surety insurance." The Florida definition of "financial guaranty insurance," in section 627.971, excludes "surety insurance as defined in § 624.606,"[181] which provides as follows:

> (1) "Surety insurance" includes:
> (a) A contract bond, including a bid, payment, or maintenance bond, or a performance bond, which guarantees the execution of a contract other than a contract of indebtedness or other monetary obligation;
> (b) An indemnity bond for the benefit of a public body, railroad, or charitable organization or a lost security or utility payment bond;
> (c) Becoming surety on, or guaranteeing the performance of, any lawful contract where the bond is guaranteeing the execution of a contract other than a contract of indebtedness or other monetary obligation;

---

180. *Id.* Unlike the New York statute and the Model Act, the Florida statute does not expressly limit the types of indebtedness that may be guaranteed to specified categories such as municipal bond obligations, special revenue bonds, industrial development bonds, corporate obligations, partnership obligations, certain asset-backed securities, installment purchase agreements, and consumer debt obligations. *See* MODEL ACT, *supra* note 26, § 3.B; N.Y. INS. LAW § 6904(b)(1) (current through L.2021, chapters 1 to 833, and L.2022, chapters 1 to 12). *See also supra* text accompanying notes 60–63 (discussing the second layer of restrictions on the kinds of permissible FGI under the New York statute).

181. FLA. STAT. ANN. § 627.971(1)(b)12 (current with laws and joint resolutions in effect from the 2021 First Regular Session and Special "A" and "B" Sessions of the Twenty-Seventh Legislature).

(d) Becoming surety on, or guaranteeing the performance of bonds and undertakings required or permitted in a judicial proceeding or otherwise allowed by law, including surety bonds accepted by states and municipal authorities in lieu of deposits as security for the performance of insurance contracts;
(e) Fidelity insurance as defined in s. 624.6065 for the purposes of the Florida Insurance Code other than part XX of chapter 627; or
(f) Residual value insurance as defined in s. 624.6081.

(2) "Surety insurance" does not include:

. . .

(b) *Financial guaranty insurance, as defined in s. 627.971*; . . . .[182]

Thus, in Florida, as in New York, the definition "financial guaranty insurance" excludes "surety insurance," and the definition of "surety insurance" excludes "financial guaranty insurance." That overlap creates in Florida the same potential for a ping-pong effect between the two definitions as existed in New York.[183] Unlike New York, however, Florida has published no advisory or interpretive opinions to provide guidance as to whether a product that falls within both definitions should be treated as FGI or surety insurance. In New York the exclusion of FGI from the definition of "surety insurance" appears only in subparagraph (E) of section 1113(a)(16), which includes in the definition of "surety insurance": "guaranteeing the performance of [] any lawful contract, not specifically provided for in this paragraph."[184] Accordingly, New York was able to largely solve the definitional overlap problem by applying the exclusion of FGI from surety insurance only when a product meeting the definition of "financial guaranty insurance" also fell within the definition of "surety insurance" under only subparagraph (E) of section

182. *Id.* § 624.606 (emphasis added). The definition of "surety insurance" also expressly excludes "[m]ortgage guaranty insurance as defined in § 635.011," *id.* § 624.606(2)(a), and "[a]ny reinsurance contract authorized pursuant to § 624.610," *id.* § 624.606(2)(c).
183. *See supra* Parts II.A.3 and II.A.5.b (discussing in detail the ping-pong effect created by New York's cognate statutes).
184. N.Y. Ins. Law § 1113(a)(16)(E) (McKinney, Westlaw through L.2021).

1113(a)(16), but not when such a product fell within the definition of the other subparagraphs of that section.[185] The difficulty with employing that approach in Florida is that the Florida definition of "surety insurance" contains a separate, general exclusion for FGI,[186] which by the structure of the statute applies to the entire definition of "surety insurance" and not to just one subsection. Thus, under the language of the Florida statute, a product that falls within the definition of "financial guaranty insurance" and the definition of *any* of the coverages designated as "surety insurance" would likely be treated as FGI, and not surety insurance.

For example, subparagraph (F) of New York's section 1113(a)(16) and subsection (d) of Florida's section 624.606(1) use virtually identical language to include within the definition of "surety insurance" those bonds that are required or permitted in judicial proceedings or otherwise allowed by law.[187] The New York Department of Insurance found that bank depository bonds fell within both the definition of "surety insurance" under subparagraph (F) and the definition of "financial guaranty insurance." Nevertheless, the Department concluded (after some waffling) that a multiline insurer could issue a bank depository bond because the exclusion of FGI from surety insurance was contained in subparagraph (E), and did not appear in subparagraph (F).[188] The Florida definition of "surety insurance," however, contains an exclusion of FGI that applies to that definition as a whole, including subsection (d) of section 624.606(1), and therefore the reasoning of the New York Insurance Department would not apply to the Florida statute. On the other hand, because Florida permits a property/casualty company to become

---

185. *See supra* Part II.A.5.b (discussing the OGC opinions interpreting subparagraph (E)).

186. FLA. STAT. ANN. § 624.606(2)(b) (current with laws and joint resolutions in effect from the 2021 First Regular Session and Special "A" and "B" Sessions of the Twenty-Seventh Legislature).

187. *Compare* N.Y. INS. LAW § 1113(a)(16)(F) (current through L.2021, chapters 1 to 833, and L.2022, chapters 1 to 12) (bonds that are "required or permitted in all judicial proceedings or otherwise by law allowed"), *with* FLA. STAT. ANN. § 624.606(1)(d) (current with laws and joint resolutions in effect from the 2021 First Regular Session and Special "A" and "B" Sessions of the Twenty-Seventh Legislature) (bonds that are "required or permitted in a judicial proceeding or otherwise allowed by law").

188. *See supra* Part II.A.5.b (discussing the OGC opinions that addressed bank depository bonds).

licensed to write FGI,[189] a multiline company that meets the statutory requirements could issue a bank depository bond even though such a bond would be regarded as FGI. So, the net result could be the same in both Florida and New York.

3. Reinsurance

Florida permits an insurer writing FGI to receive credit for reinsuring such risks with an insurer licensed to write either FGI or surety insurance, provided that the reinsurance agreement includes limitations on the reinsurer's ability to amend or terminate the reinsurance.[190] If the reinsurance is placed with an insurer licensed to issue surety insurance, that insurer must satisfy certain surplus, reserve, and risk limitation requirements.[191]

C. California

1. The Statutory Scheme

In 1990, the state of California enacted its Financial Guaranty Insurance Law (FGIL),[192] which, like the New York and Florida statutes, was derived from the Model Act. Thus, California's statutory definition of "financial guaranty insurance" closely follows section 1.A(1) of the Model Act.[193] The California definition states:

> (a)(1) "Financial guaranty insurance" means a surety bond, an insurance policy or, when issued by an insurer, an indemnity contract and any guarantee similar to the foregoing types, under which loss is payable upon proof of occurrence of financial loss

---

189. *See* discussion *supra* text accompanying notes 172–175.
190. FLA. STAT. ANN. § 627.975 (West, Westlaw through laws of the 2021 1st Reg. Sess. of the 27th Leg. in effect through June 22, 2021). Florida's section 627.975 follows the reinsurance provision of the Model Act. *See* MODEL ACT, *supra* note 26, § 5.
191. FLA. STAT. ANN. § 627.975 (West, Westlaw through laws of the 2021 1st Reg. Sess. of the 27th Leg. in effect through June 22, 2021).
192. CAL. INS. CODE §§ 12100–12123 (West, Westlaw through urgency legislation through ch. 19 of 2021 Reg. Sess.).
193. MODEL ACT, *supra* note 26, § 1.A(1).

to an insured claimant, obligee, or indemnitee as a result of any of the following events:

(A) Failure of any obligor on or issuer of any debt instrument or other monetary obligation (including equity securities guaranteed under a surety bond, insurance policy, or indemnity contract) to pay, when due to be paid by the obligor or scheduled at the time insured to be received by the holder of the obligation, principal, interest, premium, dividend, purchase price of or on the instrument or obligation, or other monetary payment when the failure is the result of financial default or insolvency, or, provided that the payment source is investment grade, any other failure of that payment source to make payment, regardless of whether the obligation is incurred directly or as guarantor by or on behalf of another obligor that has also defaulted.

(B) Changes in the levels of interest rates, whether short or long term, or the differential in interest rates between various markets or products.

(C) Changes in the rate of exchange of currency.

(D) Changes in the value of financial or commodity indices, or price levels in general.

(E) Other events that the commissioner determines by order, regulation, or written consent are substantially similar to any of the foregoing.[194]

Like the Model Act and the New York and Florida statutes, the California definition lists those types of coverages that do not constitute FGI. Surety insurance is excluded by reference to another section of the insurance code, thus:

(2) Notwithstanding paragraph (1) [of section 12100(a)], "financial guaranty insurance" shall not include any of the following:

---

194. Cal. Ins. Code § 12100 (West, Westlaw through urgency legislation through ch. 19 of 2021 Reg. Sess.). Like New York and Florida, California did not include in its definition of "financial guaranty insurance" section 1.A(1)(d) of the Model Act. Model act, *supra* note 26, § 1.A(1)(d). *See also supra* notes 51 & 168 (discussing the noninclusion of said section in the New York and Florida statutes).

. . . .

(C) Surety insurance as authorized by Section 105.[195]

And like the Model Act and the New York and Florida statutes, the California law provides that "financial guaranty insurance may be transacted in this state only by an insurer admitted to transact financial guaranty insurance."[196] California also provides for the organization of insurers to transact FGI[197] and prohibits such insurers from "transact[ing] any other classes of insurance in this state except surety insurance."[198] However, if an insurer is licensed to write any business other than FGI, surety insurance, and credit insurance in California or any other state, that insurer will not be permitted to obtain a license to write FGI in California.[199] Unlike the Model Act or the New York and Florida statutes, California's FGIL does not permit financial guaranty insurers to write any lines of insurance other than FGI and surety insurance.[200]

---

195. CAL. INS. CODE § 12100(a)(2)(C) (West, Westlaw through urgency legislation through ch. 19 of 2021 Reg. Sess.) (citing the definition of "surety insurance" in CAL. INS. CODE § 105). *See also supra* note 168 (discussing a similar provision in Florida's statute).
196. CAL. INS. CODE § 12112(a) (West, Westlaw through urgency legislation through ch. 19 of 2021 Reg. Sess.).
197. *Id.* § 12101.
198. *Id.* § 12102(b). *See also id.* § 12102(a) ("[a]n insurer with a certificate of authority to transact the business of financial guaranty insurance . . . may also transact the business of surety insurance . . . ."). The Model Act and the New York and Florida laws also permit financial guaranty insurers to write at least certain kinds of surety insurance. *See* MODEL ACT, *supra* note 26, § 2.A(1)(b); N.Y. INS. LAW § 6902(a)(1)(B) (McKinney, Westlaw through L.2021); FLA. STAT. ANN. § 627.972(1)(a)(2) (West, Westlaw through laws of the 2021 1st Reg. Sess. of the 27th Leg. in effect through June 22, 2021).
199. CAL. INS. CODE § 12102(c) (current with urgency legislation through Ch. 1 of 2022 Reg. Sess.). Thus, the California FGIL could have an extraterritorial effect in very limited circumstances. *But see infra* Part III (discussing in detail the far greater extraterritorial effect of New York's "Appleton Rule").
200. *Compare* MODEL ACT, *supra* note 26, § 2.A(1), *and* N.Y. INS. LAW § 6902(a)(1) (current through L.2021, chapters 1 to 833, and L.2022, chapters 1 to 12) (permitting the financial guaranty insurer to write residual value insurance and credit insurance as well as surety insurance), *and* FLA. STAT. ANN. § 627.972(1)(a) (current with laws and joint resolutions

Following the approach taken by the Model Act and New York (but not by Florida[201]), California limits the types of indebtedness that may be guaranteed by the financial guaranty insurer. Permissible FGI is limited to the payment of contractual obligations (including principal and interest, purchase obligations, dividends, or other payment obligations) if characterized as one of the following:

> (A) Municipal obligation bonds.
> (B) Special revenue bonds.
> (C) Industrial development bonds.
> (D) Obligations of corporations, trusts, or similar entities established under applicable law.
> (E) Partnership obligations.
> (F) Asset-backed securities, trust certificates and trust obligations other than [certain] mortgage-backed securities. . . .
>
> . . .
>
> (G) Installment purchase agreements executed as a condition of sale.
> (H) Consumer debt obligations.
> (I) Utility first mortgage obligations.

---

in effect from the 2021 First Regular Session and Special "A" and "B" Sessions of the Twenty-Seventh Legislature) (permitting the financial guaranty insurer to write residual value insurance, credit insurance, and mortgage guaranty insurance as well as surety insurance), *with* CAL. INS. CODE § 12102(b) (current with urgency legislation through Ch. 1 of 2022 Reg. Sess.) (limiting to surety insurance the other classes of insurance that the financial guaranty insurer may transact). The Connecticut act does not contain a provision that permits the financial guaranty insurer to write any products other than FGI. CONN. GEN. STAT. ANN. § 38a-92g(b) (West, Westlaw through all enactments of 2021 Reg. Sess. enrolled and approved by the governor on or before June 16, 2021, and effective on or before June 16, 2021). *See also infra* Part II.D (discussing the Connecticut Financial Guaranty Insurance Act).

201. *See supra* note 180 (discussing section 627.973(2) of the Florida Insurance Code (FLA. STAT. ANN. § 627.973(2) (West, Westlaw through laws of the 2021 1st Reg. Sess. of the 27th Leg. in effect through June 22, 2021)), which does not limit to specified categories the types of indebtedness that the financial guaranty insurer may guarantee).

(J) Any other debt instrument or monetary obligation that the commissioner determines by order, regulation, or written consent to be substantially similar to any of the foregoing.[202]

2. Overlap of Statutory Definitions

Unlike New York and Florida, California does not define "surety insurance" by listing the particular obligations that are deemed to constitute that product. Rather, the California statute sets out a broad, functional definition:

> Surety insurance includes:
>
> (a) The guaranteeing of behavior of persons and the guaranteeing of performance of contracts (including executing or guaranteeing bonds and undertakings required or permitted in all actions or proceedings or by law allowed), other than insurance policies and other than for payments secured by a mortgage, deed of trust, or other instrument constituting a lien or charge on real estate.[203]

Like Florida, however, the California definition of "surety insurance" contains a general exclusion of FGI:

> (d) No insurance may be written as surety insurance if it falls within the definition of financial guaranty insurance as set forth in Section 12100.[204]

Because the California definition of "surety insurance" excludes FGI and the definition of "financial guaranty insurance" excludes surety insurance,[205] the California law shares the same potential definitional

---

202. CAL. INS. CODE § 12112(b)(1) (West, Westlaw through urgency legislation through ch. 19 of 2021 Reg. Sess.).

203. *Id.* § 105(a).

204. *Id.* § 105(d). *See* FLA. STAT. ANN. § 624.606(2)(b) (West, Westlaw through laws of the 2021 1st Reg. Sess. of the 27th Leg. in effect through June 22, 2021).

205. CAL. INS. CODE § 12100(a)(2)(C) (West, Westlaw through urgency legislation through ch. 19 of 2021 Reg. Sess.).

"ping-pong" effect as the New York and Florida statutes.[206] The exclusion of FGI from the California definition of "surety insurance" applies generally to that definition, and is not limited to only a part of the definition, as is the case in New York. Therefore, California's "ping-pong" effect cannot be resolved by the New York solution of limiting the exclusion of FGI to the particular subpart of the definition in which it appears. Rather, in California, a product that falls within the definitions of both "financial guaranty insurance" and "surety insurance" would likely be treated as FGI, and not surety insurance.[207]

3. Reinsurance

California allows financial guaranty insurers to take credit for insurance placed with either other financial guaranty insurers or with insurers that are authorized to write surety insurance.[208] Because a property/casualty company may be licensed to write surety insurance, California, like New York, permits a multiline insurer to reinsure FGI even though the multiline insurer could not itself issue such coverage. If reinsurance is obtained from such a multiline company, it must meet various statutory surplus, reserve, and risk limitation requirements.[209]

D. Connecticut

1. The Statutory Scheme

The state of Connecticut adopted its Financial Guaranty Insurance Act (FGIA)[210] in 1993. Connecticut's definition of "financial guaranty

---

206. *See supra* text accompanying notes 64–75, 113–134 & 182–189.
207. Because, like California, the Florida definition of "surety insurance" contains a general as well as a specific exclusion for FGI, there is a similar difficulty in applying the New York solution to the "ping-pong" effect of the Florida statutes. *See supra* text accompanying notes 184–188.
208. Cal. Ins. Code § 12121 (West, Westlaw through urgency legislation through ch. 19 of 2021 Reg. Sess.). Section 12121 is derived from section 5 of the Model Act. *See* Model Act, *supra* note 26, § 5.
209. Cal. Ins. Code § 12121(b)(3) (current with urgency legislation through Ch. 1 of 2022 Reg. Sess.).
210. Conn. Gen. Stat. Ann. § 38a-92a *et seq.* (West, Westlaw through all enactments of 2021 Reg. Sess. enrolled and approved by the governor on or before June 16, 2021, and effective on or before June 16, 2021).

insurance," like that of New York, Florida, and California, closely follows section 1.A.(1) of the Model Act:

> (1)(A) "Financial guaranty insurance" means a surety bond, an insurance policy or, when issued by an insurer, an indemnity contract and any guaranty similar to the foregoing types, under which loss is payable upon proof of occurrence of financial loss to an insured claimant, obligee or indemnitee as a result of any of the following events: Failure of any obligor on any debt instrument or other monetary obligation, including common or preferred stock guaranteed under a surety bond, insurance policy or indemnity contract, to pay when due principal, interest, premium, dividend, purchase price of or on the instrument or obligation or other monetary payment when due when the failure is the result of a financial default or insolvency, regardless of whether the obligation is incurred directly or as guarantor by or on behalf of another obligor that has also defaulted, or any other failure to make payment, provided the payment obligation or risk which is insured is investment grade; changes in the levels of interest rates, whether short or long-term, or the differential in interest rates between various markets or products; changes in the rate of exchange currency; changes in the value of financial or commodity indices or price levels in general; or other events as determined by the commissioner.[211]

The Connecticut definition of "financial guaranty insurance" also excludes surety insurance, which is defined in the FGIA itself as

> [g]uaranteeing the fidelity of persons holding positions of public or private trusts; indemnifying financial institutions against loss of moneys, securities, negotiable instruments and other tangible items of personal property caused by larceny, misplacement, destruction or other stated perils; insuring against loss caused by forgery of signatures on, or alterations of specified documents, instruments and papers; becoming surety on or guaranteeing the performance of a bond which shall not exceed a period greater than five years, that guarantees the payment of a premium deductible, or self-insured retention to an insurer issuing a

---

211. *Id.* § 38a-92a(1)(A). *See* MODEL ACT, *supra* note 26, § 1.A(1).

> workers' compensation or liability policy; guaranteeing the performance of contracts for services, including a bid, payment or performance bond where the bond is guaranteeing the execution of any contract other than a contract of indebtedness or other monetary obligation; and guaranteeing or otherwise becoming surety for the performance of any lawful contract, not specifically provided for in this subdivision, except any insurance contract which constitutes either mortgage guaranty insurance or financial guaranty insurance, as defined in subparagraph (A) of this subdivision . . . .[212]

Like New York, California, and the Model Act, Connecticut restricts the writing of FGI to monoline financial guaranty insurers: "financial guaranty insurance may be transacted in this state only by an insurer licensed to transact financial guaranty insurance."[213] Unlike all of the other financial guaranty laws, including the Model Act, Connecticut's FGIA contains no language expressly allowing the financial guaranty insurer to write other products, such as residual value insurance, surety insurance, or credit insurance.[214]

---

212. CONN. GEN. STAT. ANN. § 38a-92a(1)(B)(ii) (West, Westlaw through all enactments of 2021 Reg. Sess. enrolled and approved by the governor on or before June 16, 2021, and effective on or before June 16, 2021) (emphasis added).

213. *Id.* § 38a-92g(a). Florida's statute permits multiline property/casualty insurers that meet certain statutory requirements to issue FGI. *See* FLA. STAT. ANN. § 627.973(1) (West, Westlaw through laws of the 2021 1st Reg. Sess. of the 27th Leg. in effect through June 22, 2021). *See also supra* text accompanying notes 171–174.

214. *Compare* CONN. GEN. STAT. ANN. § 38a-92g(b) (statutes and constitution current with all enactments of the 2021 Regular Session and the 2021 June Special Session), *with* FLA. STAT. ANN. § 627.972(1)(a) (West, Westlaw through laws of the 2021 1st Reg. Sess. of the 27th Leg. in effect through June 22, 2021) (allowing the financial guaranty insurer to also write residual value, surety, credit, and mortgage guaranty insurance), *and* MODEL ACT, *supra* note 26, § 2.A(1) (allowing the financial guaranty insurer to also write residual value, surety, and credit insurance), *and* N.Y. INS. LAW § 6902(a)(1) (McKinney, Westlaw through L.2021) (same), *and* CAL. INS. CODE § 12102(b) (West, Westlaw through urgency legislation through ch. 19 of 2021 Reg. Sess.) (allowing the financial guaranty insurer to also write surety insurance).

Like the Model Act, New York, and California, but unlike Florida,[215] Connecticut expressly limits the types of indebtedness that the FGI corporation is permitted to guaranty to

> timely payment of contractual obligations, including principal and interest, purchase obligations, dividends or any other payment obligations such as: (1) Municipal obligation bonds; (2) special revenue bonds; (3) industrial development bonds; (4) corporate obligations; (5) partnership obligations; (6) asset-backed securities, trust certificates and trust obligations other than [certain] mortgage-backed securities . . . ; (7) installment purchase agreements executed as a condition of a sale; (8) consumer debt obligations; (9) utility first mortgage obligations; and (10) any other debt instrument or monetary obligation that the commissioner determines to be substantially similar.[216]

2. *Interpretation of Overlapping Definitions*

As is the case with all other financial guaranty laws, Connecticut's definition of "financial guaranty insurance" excludes surety insurance, and its definition of "surety insurance" excludes FGI.[217] Thus, the Connecticut act also creates the potential for definitional "ping-pong" when a product falls within the definitions of both "financial guaranty insurance" and "surety insurance." Like New York, the exclusion from the definition of "surety insurance" of FGI appears only as an exception to one of the types of obligations that are included in the definition of "surety insurance" (that is, guaranteeing "any lawful contract, not specifically provided for in this subdivision"), and not to the other types. Therefore, as is the case with the New York statute, the structure of the Connecticut statute would allow the exclusion to be applied only if a product meeting the definition of "financial guaranty insurance" also fell

---

215. *See supra* text accompanying notes 178–180 (discussing Florida's statute, which does not limit to specified categories the types of indebtedness that the financial guaranty insurer may guarantee).

216. CONN. GEN. STAT. ANN. § 38a-92g(b) (statutes and constitution current with all enactments of the 2021 Regular Session and the 2021 June Special Session). Because of the phrase "such as," this provision could be construed as not limiting permissible FGI to the enumerated types of obligations.

217. *Id.* § 38a-92a(1)(B)(ii) (*quoted supra* text accompanying notes 212–213).

within the type of obligation to which the exclusion is appended, but not if it came within the definition of one of the other types of obligations.[218] Even though the Connecticut Insurance Department does not promulgate advisory opinions, it could find the New York OGC opinions persuasive, and therefore similarly limit the application of the exclusion of FGI.

Like New York, but unlike Florida and California, Connecticut specifically includes within the definition of "surety insurance" guaranteeing the payment of premiums, deductibles, and self-insured retentions.[219] However, missing from the Connecticut definition is the phrase "otherwise by law allowed," which is included in the definition of "surety insurance" contained in the statutes of all of the other states that have so far been discussed.[220] The absence of such language should not lead to the conclusion that surety bonds that are written pursuant to a lawful statute or rule, or are otherwise allowed by law, cannot be classified as surety insurance whenever there is an overlap with the definition of "financial guaranty insurance." The intent of a legislature or a regulatory authority to allow certain public-related obligations to be guaranteed by a surety bond should not be trumped by ambiguous overlapping definitions. Doing so could lead to the nonsensical result that neither a surety insurer nor a financial guaranty insurer is allowed to write the obligation. Therefore, such obligations should be classified as a permissible surety obligation.

3. Reinsurance

Connecticut allows financial guaranty insurers to take a credit for insurance placed with either other financial guaranty insurers or with

---

218. *See supra* Part II.A.5.b (discussing the opinions of the OGC, which limit the effect of the exclusion from the definition of "surety insurance" of FGI under New York law).

219. CONN. GEN. STAT. ANN. § 38a-92a(1)(B) (statutes and constitution current with all enactments of the 2021 Regular Session and the 2021 June Special Session). Such guaranties were added to the New York and Connecticut definitions of "surety insurance" by amendment. *See* discussion *infra* Part II.F.

220. *See* N.Y. INS. LAW § 1113(a)(16)(F) (current through L.2021, chapters 1 to 833, and L.2022, chapters 1 to 12); FLA. STAT. ANN. § 624.606(1)(d) (West, Westlaw through laws of the 2021 1st Reg. Sess. of the 27th Leg. in effect through June 22, 2021); CAL. INS. CODE § 105(a) (West, Westlaw through urgency legislation through ch. 19 of 2021 Reg. Sess.).

insurers that are licensed to transact surety insurance or reinsurance.[221] As a property/casualty company may be licensed to write surety insurance, Connecticut, like New York and California, permits a multiline insurer to reinsure FGI, even though that multiline insurer could not itself issue such coverage. If reinsurance is obtained from such a multiline insurer, it must meet various statutory surplus, reserve, and risk limitation requirements.[222]

E. Other States

Only the states of New York, Florida, California, and Connecticut have heeded the NAIC's recommendation by enacting a comprehensive law governing FGI. Other states, however, regulate some aspects of that business to a lesser degree.[223]

For example, Alaska has adopted a rule that exempts FGI from filing and prior-approval requirements that are otherwise applicable to policy forms and rates.[224] Several states limit their regulatory oversight to guaranties of municipal bond obligations and focus on the capital, surplus, and reserve requirements if an insurer guarantees such obligations.[225] Iowa imposes capital surplus and reserve requirements on insurers approved to transact FGI-related business.[226] Even if the insurer is already complying with New York law, the contingency reserve requirements of the various states should be monitored in order to assure that the financial guaranty insurer is in compliance when conducting business in these other jurisdictions.

---

221. CONN. GEN. STAT. ANN. § 38a-92m (West, Westlaw through all enactments of 2021 Reg. Sess. enrolled and approved by the governor on or before June 16, 2021, and effective on or before June 16, 2021). Connecticut's section 38a-92m is derived from section 5 of the Model Act. *See* MODEL ACT, *supra* note 26, § 5.
222. CONN. GEN. STAT. ANN. § 38a-92m (West, Westlaw through all enactments of 2021 Reg. Sess. enrolled and approved by the governor on or before June 16, 2021, and effective on or before June 16, 2021).
223. Those states include Alaska, Illinois, Iowa, New Jersey, and Wisconsin.
224. Ala. Ins. Order No. R90-2, 1990 WL 10514701 (Ala. Dir. of Ins. Mar. 7, 1990).
225. *See* discussion accompanying *supra* notes 16–21.
226. IOWA ADMIN. CODE § 191-22.2(515) (West, Westlaw through the IAC supplement dated June 2, 2021).

F. Surety Bonds Guaranteeing Payments of Premiums, Deductibles, and Self-Insured Retentions

One area of overlap between the definitions of "financial guaranty insurance" and "surety insurance" that has raised some controversy over the years is the guaranty of premium, deductible, and self-insured retention payment obligations. The confusion was prompted primarily by the New York Insurance Department's responses to inquiries from multiline insurers concerning their authority to guarantee such obligations.

1. New York and Connecticut

In the mid-1990s, New York and Connecticut amended their respective definitions of "surety insurance" to specifically include the guaranty of premium, deductible, and self-insured retention payment obligations.[227] However, in order to qualify as a permissible surety product, the bond or guaranty must (1) not exceed five years; (2) concern the payment obligations under a liability or workers' compensation insurance policy; (3) concern only the payment of premiums, deductibles, and self-insured retentions; and (4) run to the benefit of the insurer that wrote the underlying liability or workers' compensation policy.

It is not unusual for such a guaranty to be required by a premium finance company, in which case the policy runs to an entity other than the insurer under the liability or workers' compensation policy. In that case, the guaranty would be classified as FGI, not surety insurance, in New York and Connecticut.

Similarly, such guaranties often are continuous and/or include unlimited or unspecified bond terms (rather than the maximum five-year term necessary for classification as "surety insurance"), in which case such guaranties might be classified as FGI. That being said, even if the guaranty *is* continuous, it might still qualify as "surety insurance" if (1) the bond includes a cancellation provision, and (2) the surety can unilaterally cancel the bond for any reason within five years of the bond's

---

227. *See* N.Y. Ins. Law § 1113(a)(16)(J) (McKinney, Westlaw through L.2021); Conn. Gen. Stat. Ann. § 38a-92a(1)(B)(ii) (West, Westlaw through all enactments of 2021 Reg. Sess. enrolled and approved by the governor on or before June 16, 2021, and effective on or before June 16, 2021).

effective date, and without triggering bond liability for obligations arising after the bond is effectively cancelled. Bonds of this nature often provide that, in the event of cancellation, the obligee may draw on the bond if an acceptable replacement is not delivered prior to the cancellation date. Such a trigger does not preclude the bond's treatment as a surety bond, so long as the draw may only be applied to obligations arising prior to the fifth anniversary of the bond's effective date (and, thus, truly limiting the term of the bond to five years).

2. *Florida and California*

Unlike the New York and Connecticut statutes, the Florida and California statutes do not specifically address bonds that guarantee premium, deductible, and self-insured retention obligations. However, this does not mean that such guaranties should necessarily be treated as FGI products.

That view is supported by the legislative history of the 1996 amendment that added to New York's definition of "surety insurance" what is now subparagraph (J) to section 1113(a)(16).[228] The sponsor of this amendment justified it on the grounds that (1) the FGI law is confusing; (2) the FGI law was intended to govern unorthodox surety products used to either enhance corporate or municipal debt issuance or to secure lenders in limited partnership arrangements; (3) cash flow premium payment retro bonds are limited in scope and carry little or no concentration of credit risk; and (4) those kinds of surety bonds are permitted to be written by surety companies in other states, including those with similar FGI laws.[229]

Florida and California have not issued any opinions, regulations, or advisory letters implying that the guaranty of such obligations is the business of financial guaranty insurers. In addition, liability under these bonds is generally the result of a loss covered by the underlying workers' compensation or liability policy, which is payable upon the occurrence of a fortuitous event. Combined, these considerations lead to the conclusion that the guaranty of premium payment, deductible, and self-insured

---

228. Subparagraph (J) had originally been designated as subparagraph (G) when it was added to section 1113(a)(16) in 1996. The 2005 amendment relettered that provision as subparagraph (J). *See supra* Part II.A.4 (discussing the 2005 amendment).

229. Guy J. Velella, Introducer's Mem. in Supp. of Legis. S. 3459-B (1996), N.Y. Bill Jacket, 1996 S.B. 3459, ch. 23, at *6–7 (Westlaw).

retention obligations should be regarded as a permissible business for multiline insurers licensed to write surety insurance.

III. Extraterritoriality: New York's "Appleton Rule"

As a general proposition, "[t]he New York Insurance Law does not govern a contract of insurance, including a contract of guaranty or surety, entered into outside the state."[230] Article 69 of the New York Insurance Law,[231] which regulates financial guaranty insurers, does not expressly prohibit either a New York or a non-New York multiline insurer from writing FGI in other states or countries. However, licensing provisions, including New York's so-called "Appleton Rule,"[232] which appear in Article 11 of the New York Insurance Law,[233] do restrict the kinds of insurance business in which an insurer licensed in New York may engage. Those provisions thereby effectively prohibit any multiline insurer licensed in New York from issuing, either in or outside of New York, those products that fall within the definition of "financial guaranty insurance" under section 6901(a)[234] of the New York Insurance Law. Put another way, a New York domestic multiline insurer may not write, outside of New York, the kinds of insurance that it is forbidden to write within New York.[235] The prohibition against the issuance of FGI by a multiline insurer also applies to non-New York multiline insurers that wish to remain, or to become, licensed in New York.[236] Thus, such non-New York insurers, which might otherwise be permitted to issue a bond that constitutes FGI under section 6901(a), are precluded from writing that product *anywhere* by virtue of becoming licensed to write insurance within the state of New York.

A. *New York Domestic Insurers*

The New York Insurance Law defines a "domestic insurer" as "any authorized insurer incorporated or organized under any law of this

---

230. Gen. Couns. Op. No. 3-15-90 (#1), 1990 WL 10496590, at *2 (N.Y. Ins. Dep't Mar. 15, 1990).
231. N.Y. Ins. Law §§ 6901–6909 (McKinney, Westlaw through L.2021).
232. *See* discussion *infra* Part III.B.
233. N.Y. Ins. Law §§ 1101–1121 (McKinney, Westlaw through L.2021).
234. *Id.* § 6901(a).
235. *Id.* § 1102(b) & (d). *See also* discussion *infra* Part III.A.
236. N.Y. Ins. Law § 1106(b)(1) (current through L.2021, chapters 1 to 833, and L.2022, chapters 1 to 12). *See* discussion *infra* Part III.B.

state."[237] Among the licensing provisions of Article 11, two subsections of section 1102 bear upon a New York domestic insurer doing business outside of the state:

> (b) No corporation organized under any law of this state shall do an insurance business outside this state unless so authorized pursuant to the provisions of this chapter . . . .[238]
>
> . . . .
>
> (d) Except as otherwise provided in subsection (h) hereof [insurers controlled by another state or foreign government], the superintendent may issue a license to any insurer to do in this state the kinds of insurance business for which such insurer is qualified under the provisions of this chapter and under its charter.[239]

Subsection (b) forbids a New York domestic insurer from conducting an insurance business outside of New York unless authorized to do so. Subsection (d) limits the scope of the insurance for which an insurer may be licensed to those kinds of insurance for which it is qualified under "this chapter," which is chapter 28 of the New York Insurance Law. Chapter 28 includes Article 69, which, as discussed earlier, prohibits a multiline insurer from writing FGI.[240] Thus, through section 1102(b) and (d), Article 69's prohibition against a New York domestic multiline insurer issuing FGI is given extraterritorial effect. That multiline company may not issue FGI in New York or *anywhere else*.

In a 2000 OGC letter,[241] the Insurance Department came to such a conclusion through a more elaborate analysis, which ignored section 1102(b). The matter involved a proposed merger between a New York domestic financial guaranty insurer and a property/casualty insurer licensed in almost all states to issue most kinds of property and casualty insurance. The surviving entity would be the property/casualty company,

---

237. N.Y. INS. LAW § 107(a)(19) (current through L.2021, chapters 1 to 833, and L.2022, chapters 1 to 12).
238. *Id.* § 1102(b).
239. *Id.* § 1102(d).
240. *See supra* Part II.A.2.
241. Letter from Joan Siegel, Associate Attorney, New York Insurance Department, to Robert J. Sullivan, Partner, Skadden, Arps, Slate, Meagher & Flom LLP (Apr. 4, 2000) (on file with the New York Department of Financial Services, Office of the General Counsel).

which proposed to adopt the charter of the financial guaranty insurer and to have its own foreign licenses restricted to the lines of business for which the financial guaranty insurer was authorized. The question was whether the Department could approve the merger before the surviving entity obtained the revisions to its foreign licenses and removed from its books all of its nonfinancial guaranty business. The Department answered in the negative. It noted that "[a]n insurer's powers under its charter must be consonant with its powers under its license."[242] Therefore, the charter's authorization of FGI is subject to the statutory limitations on the kinds of coverages for which a financial guaranty insurer may be licensed in New York. Although the opinion offers no authority for that proposition, the language of section 1102(d), as discussed earlier, does require that conclusion. Thus the merger as proposed could not be approved because it would result in the surviving entity's being in violation of its adopted charter and, accordingly, of the statutory provisions under which a financial guaranty insurer is restricted to writing FGI and only certain other coverages.[243] The Department summarized its reasoning as follows:

> The courts have stated that wherever a corporation goes for business, it carries its charter and the charter is the same abroad as it is at home. Consequently, if London [the surviving property and casualty insurer] were to adopt XLCA's [the New York-domiciled financial guaranty insurer] charter, it could only do those kinds of business enumerated therein. *It could not be licensed as a financial guaranty insurer in New York and then do business outside of New York that would be ultra vires of its charter, pursuant to its broader continuing foreign licenses.*[244]

There is no reason to suppose that the converse is not also true: that the statutory ban against a New York domestic multiline insurer's writing FGI in New York would follow that insurer out of state and prohibit it from issuing FGI elsewhere.

---

242. *Id.*
243. *See* N.Y. INS. LAW §§ 6901(b), 6902(a)(1) & 6904(b) (McKinney, Westlaw through L.2021).
244. Letter from Joan Siegel, *supra* note 241 (emphasis added) (footnote omitted) (citations omitted).

B. Foreign and Alien Insurers—Application of the "Appleton Rule"

The extraterritorial ban on the issuance of FGI by a multiline insurer applies to "foreign" and "alien" insurers, which are licensed in New York, as well as New York domestic insurers, though through different statutory provisions. Under the New York Insurance Law, a "foreign insurer" is defined as "any insurer incorporated or organized under the laws of any state [and the commonwealth of Puerto Rico and the District of Columbia], other than this state."[245] An "alien insurer" is defined as "any insurer incorporated or organized under the laws of any foreign nation, or of any province or territory not included in the definition of foreign insurer."[246] Section 1106 of Article 11 imposes additional requirements for a foreign or alien insurer's license,[247] which operate to prohibit those insurers from writing elsewhere the kinds of insurance that they may not issue in New York. That prohibition, known as the "Appleton Rule" (named after the deputy superintendent of the New York Insurance Department who created it), originated in the early 1900s as an administrative regulation and was enacted as part of the New York Insurance law in 1939.[248] When applied to FGI, the Appleton Rule

245. N.Y. Ins. Law § 107(a)(21) (McKinney, Westlaw through L.2021).
246. *Id.* § 107(a)(5).
247. *Id.* § 1106.
248. *See* Perkins, *supra* note 11, at 311–12. The Appleton Rule is now codified in Article 11. *See* N.Y. Ins. Law § 1106(f) (McKinney, Westlaw through L.2021). The Appleton Rule was not part of the Model Act, *see* Model Act, *supra* note 26, or of New York's Article 69 (which was based on the Model Act). Nor is it included in the financial guaranty laws of the other states that have adopted the Model Act. The Appleton Rule exists solely by virtue of Article 11 of the New York Insurance Law, which governs the licensing of insurers generally. Thus, the Appleton Rule is unique among states with financial guaranty laws. However, California's FGIL contains a provision that could have an extraterritorial effect in extremely limited circumstance. *See* Cal. Ins. Code § 12102(c) (West, Westlaw through all 2011 Reg. Sess. laws; all 2011–2012 1st Ex. Sess. laws; and Gov. Reorg. Plan No. 1 of 2011); *see also supra* note 199 and accompanying text. Although the term "Appleton Rule" has often been used as a shorthand reference to New York's prohibition on the issuance of FGI by a multiline insurer, that use is inaccurate. Despite its impact in the FGI area, the Appleton Rule applies to any kind of insurance.

prohibits a foreign or alien multiline insurer licensed in New York from writing *anywhere else* the kinds of insurance that it is prohibited from issuing in New York.

Subsection (c) of section 1106 limits the authority of foreign insurers to do business in New York as follows:

> (c) No foreign insurer shall be licensed to do in this state any kind of insurance business, or combination of kinds of insurance business, which are not permitted to be done by domestic insurers hereafter to be licensed under the provisions of this chapter . . . .[249]

Thus, a foreign insurer may write in New York only those kinds of insurance that a New York domestic insurer may write. Accordingly, foreign multiline insurers, as well as New York multiline insurers, are forbidden to issue FGI in New York. The same restriction is placed on the authority of alien insurers.[250]

Additionally, and importantly, the New York Insurance Law also limits the kinds of insurance that foreign and alien insurers may write *outside* of New York. It does so by utilizing its control over access to the New York insurance market. Section 1106(f), the current codification of the Appleton Rule,[251] provides:

> (f) No foreign insurer and no United States branch of an alien insurer which does outside of this state any kind or combination of kinds of insurance business not permitted to be done in this state by similar domestic insurers hereafter organized, shall be or continue to be authorized to do an insurance business in this state, unless in the judgment of the superintendent the doing of such kind or combination of

249. N.Y. Ins. Law § 1106(c) (current through L.2021, chapters 1 to 833, and L.2022, chapters 1 to 12).

250. *Id.* § 1106(d). *See* Gen. Couns. Op. No. 11-12-2002 (#3), 2002 WL 33011213, at *3 (N.Y. Ins. Dep't Nov. 12, 2002) ("As financial guaranty insurance is a monoline type of business, neither of the companies named in the inquiry, as [foreign] property/casualty insurers, would be permitted to write such business in New York.").

251. Perkins, *supra*, note 11, at 311.

> kinds of insurance business will not be prejudicial to the best interests of the people of this state.[252]

With certain limited exceptions, a New York domestic multiline insurer is prohibited from issuing FGI outside of, as well as within, New York.[253] Consequently, under section 1106(f), a non-New York multiline insurer risks losing its New York license if it writes FGI outside of New York,[254] unless the superintendent of insurance finds that doing so will not prejudice the people of New York.[255]

The prohibition against a foreign insurer's issuing outside of New York a product that was not permitted in New York was alluded to in connection with FGI in a 1995 OGC opinion.[256] In that matter, an automobile dealer association proposed to act as an administrator of a program whereby dealers undertook to provide a discount to purchasers whose vehicles were declared to be a total loss due to accident or unrecovered theft. The dealers were to pay fees to the administrating dealer association that intended to purchase insurance to cover risks from uncollectable fees. The contemplated insurance would not insure New York dealers or provide any benefit to them, and would be purchased outside of New York by a dealer association located outside of New York.

---

252. N.Y. INS. LAW § 1106(f) (current through L.2021, chapters 1 to 833, and L.2022, chapters 1 to 12). *See also id.* § 1106(e) (requiring foreign and alien insurers "to comply substantially with any requirement or limitation of this chapter, applicable to similar domestic insurers" upon pain of loss of license).
253. *Id.* § 1102(b) & (d). *See* discussion *supra* Part II.A.
254. Op. No. 11-12-2002 (#3), 2002 WL 33011213, at *3 ("Similarly, neither [of the foreign property/casualty insurers] would be able to write such business [FGI] outside of New York while maintaining a New York license.") (citing N.Y. INS. LAW § 1106(f)).
255. The Insurance Department's OGC has recommended that if a foreign insurer wishes to issue outside of New York that insurance that may not be written in New York, it seek in advance a determination that the issuance of such insurance will not be prejudicial to New York. *See* Gen. Couns. Op. No. 7-9-93, 1993 WL 13482412, at *1 (N.Y. Ins. Dep't July 7, 1993) (so advising a foreign insurer proposing to issue aircraft title insurance, which is not permitted in New York, because section 1106(f) would bar it from doing so without such a determination).
256. Gen. Couns. Op. No. 6-26-95, 1995 WL 17236551, at *1 (N.Y. Ins. Dep't June 26, 1995).

The Department noted that the proposed insurance appeared to constitute FGI under New York law, but that the proposal did not specify whether the insurer would be licensed in New York. As a result, the Department concluded: "If the insurer is authorized in New York, it would have to be licensed as a financial guaranty insurer. If the insurer was not authorized in New York, it would not be subject to New York Insurance Law."[257] Thus, even where FGI had virtually no connection to New York, the insurance could not be written by an insurer that was authorized to conduct insurance business in New York unless that insurer was licensed as an FGI corporation under New York law. Although neither section 1106(f) nor its moniker, the "Appleton Rule," were mentioned, the Department's analysis drew no distinction between domestic and foreign insurers. The operative issue was whether the proposed insurer was authorized in New York.

Thus, under section 1106(f), a foreign or alien multiline insurer licensed to do business in New York is prohibited from writing FGI in New York or anywhere else throughout the world; and it stands to lose (or not receive, as the case may be) its license to do business in New York if it issues a product that falls within the definition of "financial guaranty insurance" under New York law.[258] The amount of the potential premium volume in New York provides a strong incentive for foreign and alien multiline companies to accept the limitations of the New York financial guaranty insurance law.

C. Exception to the "Appleton Rule": Insurers Expressly Licensed to Insure Risks of Every Kind or Description Outside of the United States

Section 4102(c) of the New York Insurance Law provides:

> A property/casualty insurance company organized and licensed to write any basic kind of insurance, may be licensed, except with respect to the kinds of insurance defined respectively in the following paragraphs of subsection (a) of section one thousand

---

257. *Id.* at *3. Such an unauthorized insurer could not become licensed in New York if it issued outside of New York coverages that it could not issue within New York. N.Y. INS. LAW § 1106(f) (current through L.2021, chapters 1 to 833, and L.2022, chapters 1 to 12).

258. *See* discussion of penalties *infra* Part III.D.

> one hundred thirteen of this chapter: life insurance (1), annuities (2) and title insurance (18), to (i) reinsure risks of every kind or description and (ii) *insure property or risks of every kind or description located or resident outside of the United States, its territories and possessions.*[259]

The italicized language was added to the statute as part of chapter 517 of the Laws of 1989. The statute had previously authorized the licensing of a qualified property/casualty insurer to write "any kind of insurance on risks outside of the United States." That text was changed to "insure property or risks of every kind or description." The purpose of this amendment was to allow authorized and sufficiently capitalized insurers[260] to compete overseas on even terms with their competitors in overseas markets.

The current language of section 4102(c) and its legislative history appear to establish that a property/casualty insurer may become licensed to insure literally any kind of risk (except life insurance, annuities, and title insurance risks), provided that the risk is located outside of the United States. This appears to be the case even if the risk in question cannot be legally insured by any insurer within the state of New York. As explained in a statement of support from John P. Gemma, special counsel to the superintendent of insurance:

> The broad scope of the existing authority to reinsure risks of every kind or description and of the proposed language ("to insure property or risks of every kind or description located or resident outside of the United States, its territories or possessions") requires that its utilization be limited to insurers with sufficient financial strength. The issuance of such authorities to an insurer which is only required to maintain under the current law a surplus to policyholders of $3,000,000 (or $1,500,000 if licensed prior to July 1, 1982) only encourages companies to request them although

---

259. N.Y. INS. LAW § 4102(c) (McKinney, Westlaw through L.2021) (emphasis added).

260. *Cf.* CAL. INS. CODE § 12116.5 (West, Westlaw through urgency legislation through ch. 19 of 2021 Reg. Sess.) (enabling statute permitting the California insurance commissioner to safeguard insurer solvency by establishing reasonable conditions or limitations under which any or all admitted FGI corporations may issue policies of insurance).

> they may have no occasion or need to ever use them. This bill will increase the prerequisite financial and deposit requirements, thereby reducing the number of insurers who qualify for these special authorizations. At the same time the meaningfulness of the authorities will be increased by (i) clarifying and revising the authority to insure risks located outside the United States and (ii) permitting mortgage guaranty insurers to cede business to property/casualty or reciprocal insurers who possess the authority to reinsure risks of every kind or description.
>
> . . .
>
> In addition, the revised authority to insure risks of every kind or description located outside of the United States will enable larger American property/casualty and reciprocal insurers to compete on terms of equality with alien insurance companies when offering insurance protection to multi-national corporations.
>
> The provisions of this bill dealing with insurance outside the United States and reinsurance of all risks affect only kinds of insurance business not permitted in New York and, therefore, their enactment will only have a positive impact on New York property/casualty insurance capacity.[261]

It appears to follow from the broad language of section 4102(c) and its legislative history that a multiline insurer so authorized under that section, when operating outside of the United States, should be able to issue what would otherwise be regarded as FGI under Article 69 of New York's Insurance Law, even though that same insurer could not legally issue FGI within New York (nor, under the "Appleton Rule," in any other part of the United States). Such an insurer, if so licensed under section 4102(c), may also reinsure FGI, even within the United States. In Circular Letter No. 12, dated August 24, 1989, James P. Corcoran, superintendent of insurance, explained the statutory change as follows in relevant part:

> The authority to do "multiple reinsurance" permits a property/casualty insurer to reinsure kinds of insurance which it is not licensed to write in this State. For example, a property/casualty insurer which is licensed to write only glass insurance may by

---

261. John P. Gemma, Memorandum, N.Y. Assembly Bill Jacket, L. 1989, ch. 517, at *3–4.

> the terms of its license also reinsure only glass insurance. With the addition of "multiple reinsurance" authority in its New York license such an insurer would be empowered to reinsure all kinds of property/casualty insurance and, if it meets the requirements in Insurance Law Article 65 and/or 69, it could also reinsure financial guaranty and/or mortgage guaranty insurance. If such an insurer does not meet the new requirements for the "multiple reinsurance" authority it could amend its New York license to include only those types of property/casualty insurance which it intends to reinsure. For example, if a property/casualty insurer is licensed to do only glass insurance and wishes to reinsure credit insurance it could, upon meeting the applicable financial and statutory requirements, apply to add credit insurance to its New York license.
>
> Chapter 517 also amended the financial requirements which must be met to insure property or risks of every kind or description located or resident outside of the United States, as set forth in Insurance Law Section 4102(c). Under this authority a property/casualty insurer licensed to do only glass insurance could write a fire insurance policy on a risk located outside of the United States. The revised financial requirements are identical to those outlined above for "multiple reinsurance".[262]

In addition, in an OGC opinion dated March 4, 1997, Paul F. Altruda (who was then the acting attorney general) opined that a multiline insurer authorized to "reinsure risks of every kind or description" under section 4102(c) may reinsure FGI, even if the reinsurance contract includes a "cut-through provision" that "would give the insureds the right, in the case of the insolvency of the insurer, to look directly to the reinsurer for payment of claims."[263] Applying the same logic to an insurer authorized to directly insure against "risks of every kind or description" if located outside of the United States, such an insurer should be able to issue an FGI policy insuring against a financial risk located outside of the United States, without violating New York law. After all, the identical phrase "risks of every kind or description," appearing twice in the same statutory section,

---

262. James P. Corcoran, Superintendent of Insurance, New York State Insurance Department, Circular Letter No. 12 (Aug. 24, 1989).

263. Gen. Couns. Op. No. 3-4-97, 1997 WL 33841442 (N.Y. Ins. Dep't June Mar. 4, 1997).

has been interpreted to permit section 4102(c)-licensed companies to reinsure FGI, by no less of an authority than the superintendent of insurance and the acting attorney general of the state of New York.

The phrase "risks of every kind or description" would likely be construed by a court to unambiguously include FGI-style risks. Moreover, courts applying New York law recognize "that meaning and effect should be given to every word of a statute and that an interpretation that renders words or clauses superfluous should be rejected," and that "[w]hen the statutory language at issue is but one component in a larger statutory scheme, it must be analyzed in context and in a manner that harmonizes the related provisions and renders them compatible."[264] The Appleton Rule, codified in section 1106(f) of the New York Insurance Law, generally prohibits insurers licensed within the state of New York from issuing outside of New York any kind or combination of kinds of insurance business not permitted to be done in New York. However, section 1106(f) expressly does not apply when "in the judgment of the superintendent the doing of such kind or combination of kinds of insurance business will not be prejudicial to the best interests of the people of this state." And, the plain language of section 4102(c) unambiguously authorizes a particular class of qualified, expressly licensed insurers to directly insure "risks of every kind or description" (with three exceptions) if located outside of the United States. Sections 4102(c) and 1106(f) may therefore be read in harmony to permit a section 4102(c)-authorized insurer to issue FGI outside of the United States, despite the fact that the "combination" of FGI and multiline property/casualty business is ordinarily prohibited by New York law, because by issuing to that insurer a section 4102(c) license, the superintendent has in effect determined that it is not prejudicial to the best interests of the people of New York to permit that insurer to conduct its overseas business in a more flexible manner than would be permitted domestically. In contrast, if one were to interpret section 1106(f) to confine a section 4102(c)-licensed insurer to following New York's restrictions overseas, that would impermissibly render section 4102(c) meaningless.

It is important to note that the Appleton Rule is not enforced by courts in the first instance. It is enforced by New York's Department of Financial Services. And, given the very strong public policy behind the FGI statute of limiting large FGI-style risks to qualified monoline insurers, it remains possible that the Department could opine that the

---

264. Mestecky v. City of New York, 88 N.E.3d 365 (N.Y. 2017).

specific restrictions of the FGI statute control over the general (albeit broad) language of section 4102(c). And, as explained below, the potential consequences for an Appleton Rule violation (or perceived Appleton Rule violation) include the possible loss of an insurer's New York license.

Thus, as an option and a hedge against regulatory risk, prior to undertaking to insure overseas FGI risks (in excess of that authorized by section 1113(16)(H), such a section 4102(c)-licensed insurer may consider requesting an opinion from the Department as to the permissibility of that practice. On this point, it should be noted that the OGC ceased issuing formal, public opinions in 2011. However, informal emailed opinions from the OGC have on occasion been obtained.

D. Penalties for Violating the "Appleton Rule"

Section 1106(f) states that "[n]o foreign or alien insurer [that violates the "Appleton Rule"] shall be or continue to be authorized to do an insurance business in this state [unless exempted by the superintendent]."[265] Citing that language, the Insurance Department has concluded that "the penalty provided here [in section 1106(f)] is revocation of licenses or denial of license applications."[266] The Department also noted the presence of similar language in paragraphs (c), (d), and (e) of section 1106, clearly implying that those paragraphs also authorized license revocation or denial as a penalty.[267] Further, section 109 permits the imposition of a penalty of not more than $1,000[268] "that shall be in addition to any non-monetary penalty otherwise provided by law."[269] Lastly, the statute that created the New York State Department of Financial Services in October 2011 expressly provided that "penalties for regulated persons under the insurance law shall be as provided for in the insurance law."[270]

---

265. N.Y. INS. LAW § 1106(f) (McKinney, Westlaw through L.2021).
266. Gen. Couns. Op. No. 8-31-2004, 2004 WL 3774702, at *2 (N.Y. Ins. Dep't Aug. 31, 2004).
267. *Id.*
268. N.Y. INS. LAW § 109 (McKinney, Westlaw through L.2021) (providing penalties generally for the violation of any provision of chapter 28 of the New York Insurance Law).
269. Op. No. 8-31-2004, 2004 WL 3774702, at *2.
270. N.Y. FIN. SERVS. § 408(a)(3)(B) (McKinney, Westlaw through L.2021). *See also supra* notes 87–88 (discussing the consolidation of the former New York State Banking Department and Insurance Department to form the New York State Department of Financial Services).

Conclusion

The comprehensive FGI laws of New York, Florida, California, and Connecticut are based on the Model Act promulgated in 1986 by the NAIC. Though there are some significant variations, those laws all recognize the potentially catastrophic risks that financial guaranties pose for multiline insurers, and therefore seek to limit the issuance of such guaranties to monoline financial guaranty insurers. Even the Florida regulators seem not to have authorized multiline companies to issue FGI although the Florida statute theoretically permits such authorization under certain circumstances.[271]

Multiline insurers, however, are permitted to write surety insurance in those states, because the FGI laws were not intended to prohibit multiline companies from issuing traditional types of surety bonds. Thus, the critical question for the multiline company becomes whether a proposed product is properly classified as FGI, which it may not issue, or surety insurance, which it may issue. Answering that question can involve an intricate statutory analysis without the guidance of judicial decisions or even regulatory interpretations (with the exception of New York). Clearly, a thorough understanding of a specific jurisdiction's statutes, regulations, and any available advisory opinions is essential in order to make an informed determination on that issue. Moreover, because of the extraterritorial effect of the "Appleton Rule," a multiline insurer that is, or wishes to be, licensed in New York must also carefully assess whether it may guaranty a particular obligation under New York law, even if the risk is located in another state or outside of the United States.

---

271. *See* discussion *supra* text accompanying notes 171–174.

CHAPTER 4

PROBATE BONDS

*Matthew M. Horowitz**
Michelle Randall
Brian Lebrun

Introduction

Most jurisdictions have specialized courts tasked to determine the validity of wills, oversee the administration of decedent and intestate estates and trusts, determine the need for and oversee conservatorships or guardianships for persons with cognitive impairments or limitations, and determine the need for and oversee guardianships for minors who have been awarded financial recoveries through the judicial system.[1] Courts having these responsibilities are most commonly referred to as "probate courts," but some jurisdictions may refer to these courts as "surrogate's courts," "courts of ordinary," or "orphan's courts."[2]

A probate court's jurisdiction typically extends to cases involving parties who are unable to protect their own interests and require the appointment and supervision of fiduciaries to provide that protection. One common feature of probate courts and the legislation governing them is the requirement under many circumstances that fiduciaries appointed by the court or designated by estate planning documents must post a probate bond to secure against, and provide a remedy for, breaches of fiduciary duty.

This chapter will address the following probate bond issues:

- The types of fiduciaries who may be required to obtain a probate bond
- The scope of a fiduciary's obligations
- Standing requirements for asserting a claim under a probate bond

---

* The authors gratefully acknowledge Kevin Musco for his significant contributions to the editing and formatting of this chapter.

1. BLACK'S LAW DICTIONARY 449 (11th ed. 2019).
2. *Id.*

- The scope of the coverage that may be afforded under a probate bond
- Procedural issues common to many probate bond claims
- Common defenses available to a probate bond surety
- Damages typically available under a probate bond
- The probate bond surety's right to indemnification from its principal
- The scope of a probate bond surety's subrogation rights

I. The Fiduciary

A "fiduciary" is a person who is appointed by probate or contract documents, or by court order, to act for the benefit of another person.[3] There are multiple types of fiduciaries, depending on the characteristics of the protected person, including that person's age, cognitive capabilities, and the nature of that person's rights to property included within the probate estate. There is an extended body of case law and commentary regarding the duties common to all fiduciaries, as well as the unique application of these duties as applied to the various categories of fiduciaries and protected persons.[4]

A. *Types of Fiduciaries*

Probate bonds may be required by statute or testamentary documents for any of the following kinds of fiduciaries.

1. Executors and Administrators

Fiduciaries are generally designated to manage decedent estates. If the decedent executed a will, the will may designate an "executor" to manage the estate.[5] In the case of an intestacy, the court may appoint an "administrator."[6] The executor or administrator is typically obligated to collect and inventory the estate's assets, preserve and manage the assets

---

3. *Id.* at 770.
4. *See generally* RESTATEMENT (THIRD) OF TRUSTS (2007); GEORGE G. BOGERT, THE LAW OF TRUSTS AND TRUSTEES (rev. 3d ed. 2020).
5. RESTATEMENT (THIRD) OF TRUSTS (2007); BOGERT, *supra* note 4; 33 C.J.S. *Executors and Administrators* § 3 (2021); 31 AM. JUR. 2D *Executors and Administrators* § 4, at 63–64 (2021).
6. BLACK'S LAW DICTIONARY 56 (11th ed. 2019).

during the term of the estate, pay debts duly owing by the estate, account to the court for all transactions during the life of the estate, and release funds owing to heirs or beneficiaries.[7] In the case of an executor, these duties may be substantially directed by the terms of the will. In the case of an administrator, these duties are directed by statute.

2. Trustees

A trustee is designated by a trust document to hold legal title to the trust res and manage the affairs of the trust.[8] This typically includes collecting the property of the trust, managing the trust property, distributing income and principal, and accounting to the settler, beneficiaries, and a court.[9] The trustee's actions are often dictated in substantial part by the terms of the trust document.[10]

3. Conservators

A "conservator" may be appointed where a person is determined to be cognitively impaired and in need of support in managing his or her affairs.[11] A conservator's role may extend to the person, property, or both of the protected person.[12] A conservator for the protected person's estate is usually obligated to collect and inventory the estate's assets, invest the assets, manage the assets during the term of the estate, pay debts duly owing by the estate including for the living expenses of the protected person, file periodic accountings and reports, account to the court for all transactions during the life of the estate, and file a final accounting

---

7. UNIF. PROB. CODE § 3-715 (UNIF. L. COMM'N amended 2010). *See Matter of* Est. of Waller, 559 S.W.2d 312, 314 (Mo. Ct. App. 1977); *In re* Est. of Camarda, 425 N.Y.S.2d 1012, 1017 (Surr. Ct. 1980); Christie v. Dold, 524 N.W.2d 866, 871 (S.D. 1994); Guerra v. Guerra, No. 04-10-00271, 2011 WL 3715051, at *3 (Tex. App. Aug. 24, 2011); *Matter of* Est. of Erlien, 527 N.W.2d 389, 392 (Wis. Ct. App. 1994).
8. BLACK'S LAW DICTIONARY 1817 (11th ed. 2019); 90 C.J.S. *Trusts* § 2 (2021).
9. *See* RESTATEMENT (THIRD) OF TRUSTS § 76, at 68–73 (2007).
10. *Id.*
11. UNIF. PROB. CODE §§ 5-303, 5-431 (UNIF. L. COMM'N amended 2010). In some jurisdictions, this kind of fiduciary may be referred to as a "guardian."
12. *Id.*

upon the termination of the conservatorship by death or otherwise.[13] The protected persons in conservatorships are often cognitively disabled adults with complicated medical or psychiatric disabilities or elderly individuals experiencing dementia or similar impairments. The estates may not be time limited and may involve extraordinarily difficult decision-making on the part of the conservator.

4. Guardians for Minors

Many states require that sums recovered on behalf of a minor, including through litigation or settlements of litigation, be paid into a guardianship estate.[14] The guardian may be a parent or other relative or may have no relationship with the minor. The guardian is obligated to segregate the funds and apply them solely for the interests of the minor.[15] Typically, the funds may not be used as a substitute for a parent's support obligation to the extent that the parent has the capacity to discharge that obligation from his or her own income or assets.[16]

B. Scope of the Fiduciary Duty

A fiduciary relationship is characterized by a unique degree of trust between two parties, one of whom having superior knowledge, skill, or expertise and having a duty to represent the interests of the other.[17] The superior position of the fiduciary affords an opportunity for misconduct.[18] Where a party alleges a breach of fiduciary duty and presents some

---

13. *See id.* §§ 5-418 to -420.
14. *Id.* § 5-201 *et seq. See In re* Bingaman, 397 B.R. 444 (Bankr. C.D. Ill. 2008); *In re* Tato, 387 B.R. 833 (Bankr. D. Kan. 2008).
15. *Tato*, 387 B.R. at 839–44. *See* W. Sur. Co. v. Meek, 25 B.R. 58 (Bankr. D. Or. 1982) (surety incurs liability where fiduciary uses minor's funds for purposes unrelated to minor's interests).
16. *Tato*, 387 B.R. at 839–44; *In re* Guardianship of Thomas, No. 06MO7, 2008 WL 2081274, at *19 (Ohio Ct. App. May 12, 2008).
17. *See* Petra v. Living Centers-East, Inc., 935 F. Supp. 808, 812 (E.D. La. 1996); Cadle Co. v. D'Addario, 844 A.2d 836, 847–49 (Conn. 2004); Cochrane v. Alman, 257 P.3d 1219 (Haw. Ct. App. 2011); Emerson Elec. Co. v. Marsh & McLennan Co., No. ED 95942, 2011 WL 3890550, at * 3 (Mo. Ct. App. Sept. 6, 2011).
18. *See Petra*, 935 F. Supp. at 812; *Cadle Co.*, 844 A.2d at 847–49; *Cochrane*, 257 P.3d 1219; *Emerson Elec. Co.*, 2011 WL 3890550, at * 3.

evidence of suspicious circumstances, some jurisdictions shift a portion of the burden of proof or burden of production to the fiduciary to prove an absence of improper conduct.[19] However, a merely technical appearance of impropriety may not result in sanctions, absent a corresponding loss.[20]

The standards of conduct applicable to fiduciaries include the following.

1. Duty of Prudence

A fiduciary has a duty to exercise reasonable skill, effort, care, and caution in administering an estate.[21] If the fiduciary possesses greater skills than that of an ordinary person, the fiduciary has a duty to reasonably use those skills.[22] If certain tasks reasonably require consultation with individuals or firms having specialized skills, the fiduciary is obligated to engage in those consultations.[23] If a reasonable person would gather information in order to make a decision, the fiduciary is under an obligation to make reasonable efforts to collect and assess that information. The fiduciary is obligated to exercise the caution that would be exercised by a reasonable person acting under the circumstances confronting the fiduciary.[24]

The fiduciary's conduct is judged based on the circumstances that reasonably should have been known to the fiduciary at the time of his or her conduct.[25] The fiduciary is not an insurer of good results and the

---

19. *In re* Est. of Heyn, 47 P.3d 724, 726 (Colo. Ct. App. 2002); *Cadle Co.*, 844 A.2d at 847–49; Becker v. Knoll, 199 P.3d 786, 790 (Kan. Ct. App. 2008); United Founders Life Ins. Co. v. Carey, 347 S.W.2d 295, 307 (Tex. Civ. App. 1961), *rev'd on other grounds*, 363 S.W.2d 236 (Tex. 1962). *See* 37 AM. JUR. 2D *Fraud and Deceit* § 461 (2021).
20. *See* Laws. Sur. Corp. v. Whitehead, 719 So. 2d 833 (Ala. 1998).
21. UNIF. TRUST CODE § 804 (UNIF. L. COMM'N amended 2010); RESTATEMENT (THIRD) OF TRUSTS § 77 (2007). *See* Jewish Hosp. v. Boatmen's Nat'l Bank, 633 N.E.2d 1267, 1281 (Ill. App. Ct. 1994); Christie v. Dold, 524 N.W.2d 866, 871 (S.D. 1994).
22. UNIF. TRUST CODE §§ 804, 806 (UNIF. L. COMM'N amended 2010); RESTATEMENT (THIRD) OF TRUSTS § 77 cmt. b (2007). *See* Est. of Knipp, 414 A.2d 1007, 1008–09 (Pa. 1980).
23. *See* RESTATEMENT (THIRD) OF TRUSTS § 77 cmt. b (2007).
24. *Id.* § 77; UNIF. TRUST CODE §§ 804, 806 (UNIF. L. COMM'N amended 2010).
25. *See* RESTATEMENT (THIRD) OF TRUSTS § 77 cmt. a (2007).

fiduciary is not obligated to account for a bad outcome if the fiduciary's decisions were reasonable when made.[26]

2. Duty of Loyalty

A fiduciary is bound by a duty of loyalty to administer an estate solely in the interests of the protected person(s).[27] The fiduciary generally is prohibited from engaging in transactions involving self-dealing or that otherwise create a conflict between the fiduciary's personal interests and those of the protected person.[28] However, an otherwise prohibited transaction may be permissible if the fiduciary seeks prior permission from the probate court and the court determines that the transaction furthers the interests of the protected person (i.e., if it is in the protected person's interest to sell property of the estate and the fiduciary seeks to purchase the property for an amount in excess of the best price that could be obtained through a transaction with a disinterested person).[29] A fiduciary also may be able to engage in self-interested actions authorized by a controlling trust document, though the fiduciary still would remain obligated to discharge its duties of prudence and loyalty.[30]

The duty of loyalty is commonly implicated where a fiduciary seeks to purchase property from an estate, borrows funds from an estate for the fiduciary's personal needs, receives a fee from a third party for an act done by the fiduciary in furtherance of the fiduciary's duties to the estate, engages in transactions on behalf of the estate with parties with whom the fiduciary is closely related or associated, or appropriates a financial opportunity available to an estate.[31] The duty of loyalty does not strictly prohibit a fiduciary from providing compensated services to the

---

26. *Id. See In re* Conservatorship of J.R., 252 P.3d 163, 171 (Mont. 2011); *Knipp*, 414 A.2d at 1008. *See also* cases cited *infra* notes 85–88.
27. RESTATEMENT (THIRD) OF TRUSTS § 78 (2007). *See* Guerra v. Guerra, No. 04-10-00271, 2011 WL 3715051, at *3 (Tex. App. 2011).
28. RESTATEMENT (THIRD) OF TRUSTS § 78 (2007). *See* Phillips v. Moeller, 170 A.2d 897, 902 (Conn. 1961); *In re* Est. of Scholz, 859 N.E.2d 731, 736 (Ind. Ct. App. 2007); *In re* Will of McNair, 841 N.Y.S.2d 826 (Surr. Ct. 2007).
29. *See* RESTATEMENT (THIRD) OF TRUSTS § 78 cmt. c (2007).
30. *Id.*
31. *See* Ramsey v. Boatmen's First Nat'l Bank of Kan. City, 914 S.W.2d 384, 389–90 (Mo. 1996); Yeaton v. Skillings, 172 A.2d 354, 355 (N.H. 1961); *In re* Est. of Bartlett, 680 P.2d 369, 375–76 (Okla. 1984).

estate in addition to its fiduciary duties nor does it necessarily prohibit the fiduciary from making a loan to the estate, but any such transactions are subject to careful scrutiny under the duty of prudence and duty of loyalty.[32] In the case of a conservatorship, the fiduciary has an obligation solely to the protected person and his or her dependents.[33] A conservator may not take actions to further the interests of the heirs of the protected person unless those interests coincide with that of the protected person.[34] In the case of trusts having multiple beneficiaries, including income and principal beneficiaries, the fiduciary has a duty to comply with the terms of the trust document for distributions and otherwise has a duty not to favor one category of beneficiary over another.[35]

The fact that a fiduciary serves a protected person in two capacities, for instance as conservator and trustee, does not inherently create a conflict of interest.[36] However, a fiduciary's dual roles may create a breach of the duty of loyalty where those roles conflict; for instance, if a fiduciary serves as both trustee and conservator and the trust is legally obligated to bring suit against the conservatorship.[37]

A probate court has substantial discretion in evaluating a claim of alleged breach of the duty of loyalty by a fiduciary. Even if there is a technical breach of the duty of loyalty, a court may decide in its discretion not to impose liability on the fiduciary or its surety if the fiduciary acted in good faith and the interests of the estate were not prejudiced.[38]

---

32. *See* RESTATEMENT (THIRD) OF TRUSTS § 78 cmts. c–e (2007); UNIF. PROB. CODE § 5-421 (UNIF. L. COMM'N amended 2010).
33. *See* 39 AM. JUR. 2D *Guardian and Ward* § 99 (2021). *See* Est. of Berger, 520 N.E.2d 690, 698 (Ill. App. Ct. 1988).
34. *See* Jones v. Lambourn, 411 P.2d 11, 13–14 (Colo. 1966); *In re* MacEslin, No. CV 93-0064048S, 1994 WL 60098, at *2 (Conn. Super. Ct. Feb. 15, 1994).
35. *See* RESTATEMENT (THIRD) OF TRUSTS § 79 (2007).
36. *See* Ramsdell v. Union Tr. Co., 519 A.2d 1185, 1189–90 (Conn. 1987); Est. of Reinek, No. A-95-1195, 1997 WL 618740, at *21–22 (Neb. Ct. App. Sept. 30, 1977). *See also infra* text accompanying notes 126–128.
37. *See Ramsdell*, 519 A.2d at 1189–90; *Reinek*, 1997 WL 618740, at *21–22.
38. *See In re* Est. of Kennedy, 369 N.W.2d 63, 65 (Neb. 1985) (penalties need not be imposed where fiduciary acts in good faith and interests of the estate are not impaired). *But see In re* Beacons Assocs. Litig., Nos. 09 Civ. 777(LBS)(AJP), 10 Civ. 8000(LBS) (AJP), 2011 WL 3586129, at *2 (S.D.N.Y. Aug. 11, 2011); Ertel v. O'Brien, 852 S.W.2d 17, 22 (Tex. App.

3. *Duty to Keep Records and Furnish Information*

A fiduciary has a duty to maintain accurate and complete records and file periodic reports with the probate court.[39] Typically, the fiduciary will be obligated to collect the assets of the estate and file an inventory of those assets with the probate court within a limited time period after accepting the role of fiduciary.[40] The probate court may obligate the fiduciary to submit periodic partial accountings. The fiduciary will be obligated to submit a final accounting at the conclusion of activity involving the estate, tracking the disposition of all assets reflected on the initial inventory and all assets subsequently received, all income received by the estate, and payments issued by the fiduciary.[41] The fiduciary is obligated to maintain documentation supporting all transactions reported on the accountings.[42] The failure on the part of a fiduciary to maintain adequate records or file complete and accurate accountings may cause a probate court to find a breach of fiduciary duty.[43]

A fiduciary may also have a duty to disclose certain information to beneficiaries of a trust or other estates.[44] Where a fiduciary has accurately disclosed transactions to a probate court through an accounting and the court has approved the accounting, the fiduciary may be deemed to be discharged from further liability as to matters fairly disclosed.[45]

1993) (holding that "good faith" is not a defense to a claim of breach of fiduciary duty).

39. Rasmus v. Comm'r, No. 9802-79, 1984 WL 15422 (T.C. Jan. 4, 1984); Walling v. Hubbard, 389 S.W.2d 581, 589 (Tex. Civ. App. 1965); Est. of Johannes, 144 Wash. App. 1009, at *13 (2008); *See* RESTATEMENT (THIRD) OF TRUSTS § 83 (2007); UNIF. PROB. CODE §§ 5-417, 5-418 (UNIF. L. COMM'N amended 2010).
40. *See* UNIF. PROB. CODE § 5-419 (UNIF. L. COMM'N amended 2010).
41. *Id.* § 5-420.
42. *Id.* § 5-419; RESTATEMENT (THIRD) OF TRUSTS §§ 82–83 (2007).
43. *Rasmus*, 1984 WL 15422; *Johannes*, 144 Wash. App. at *13; Wood v. Tuohy, 854 N.E.2d 96, 101 (Mass. App. Ct. 2006).
44. *See* RESTATEMENT (THIRD) OF TRUSTS §§ 82–83 (2007).
45. *See* Patterson v. Travelers Cas. & Sur. Co., 936 A.2d 241, 243 (Conn. App. Ct. 2007).

4. Duty to Segregate Estate Property

A fiduciary is under a duty to earmark property of an estate and keep that property separate from his or her personal property or other property.[46] The fiduciary must maintain separate bank and other financial accounts in the name of the estate. Comingling of estate funds and personal funds are generally prohibited.[47]

5. Duties as to the Investment of the Estate's Assets

When a fiduciary is involved with the administration of conservatorships, trusts, and possibly other estates, the fiduciary may be obligated to manage financial and other assets over an extended period of time. The duties of loyalty and prudence are fully applicable to the role of the fiduciary as investor.[48] In addition, most all jurisdictions have enacted the Uniform Prudent Investor Act or like statutes.[49] These statutes typically impose upon a fiduciary the obligation to prudently implement modern investment theory, which includes the following rules:

- Fiduciaries have a duty to establish an individualized investment plan for an estate taking into consideration the unique needs of the protected person for income and capital preservation.[50]
- The fiduciary is ordinarily required to diversify assets unless there are valid reasons under the investment plan for not doing so.[51]

---

46. Restatement (Third) of Trusts § 84 (2007). *See* Hewitt v. Sanborn, 130 A. 472, 479 (Conn. 1925); *In re* Feder's Est., 275 N.E.2d 750, 753 (Ill. App. Ct. 1971).
47. *See* Forsyth v. Woods, 78 U.S. 484, 487 (1870); Fall v. Miller, 462 N.E.2d 1059, 1063 (Ind. Ct. App. 1984).
48. *See* Restatement (Third) of Trusts § 90 (2007); Uniform Prudent Investor Act §§ 5, 6 (1995).
49. Uniform Prudent Investor Act (1995).
50. *See* Restatement (Third) of Trusts § 90 (2007); Uniform Prudent Investor Act §§ 2, 3 (1995).
51. Restatement (Third) of Trusts § 90 (2007); Uniform Prudent Investor Act §§ 2, 3 (1995). *See In re* Janes, 630 N.Y.S.2d 472 (N.Y. App. Div.), *modified*, 643 N.Y.S.2d 972 (App. Div. 1996), *aff'd*, 681 N.E.2d 332 (N.Y. 1997); *In re* Wellington Trs., 18 N.Y.S.3d 582 (Surr. Ct. 2015); Est. of Knipp, 414 A.2d 1007, 1008–09 (Pa. 1980); cases cited *infra* note

- The levels of risk and return must be determined based on the profile of the overall portfolio and not per each specific investment.[52] The overall level of risk and return must conform to the investment plan for the estate. Investments that are too speculative for one estate may be appropriate for another estate. A fiduciary may breach his or her fiduciary duty by structuring an investment portfolio that is either too conservative or too speculative depending on the appropriate risk/reward profile for the particular portfolio.[53]
- The fiduciary may delegate investment decisions to a trained professional and may have an obligation to do so, taking into account the fiduciary's financial sophistication and the size and complexity of the estate, though the fiduciary always retains a duty to reasonably supervise any such professional.[54]
- The fiduciary has a duty to minimize fees, transaction costs, and other expenses except as reasonably necessary given the size of the estate and the estate's investment plan.[55]
- The fiduciary has a duty within a reasonable time after accepting an appointment to make and implement decisions regarding the retention or disposition of the preexisting investments.[56] The fiduciary may reasonably consider transaction costs and market conditions in determining the timing of selling assets that are not necessarily consistent with the estate's overall investment plan.[57]

---

183. *See also* Uniform Prudent Investor Act §§ 2, 3 (1995); RESTATEMENT (THIRD) OF TRUSTS § 90 cmt. g (2007).

52. *See* RESTATEMENT (THIRD) OF TRUSTS § 90 cmt. e (2007); Uniform Prudent Investor Act §§ 2, 3 (1995).

53. RESTATEMENT (THIRD) OF TRUSTS § 90 cmt. e (2007); Uniform Prudent Investor Act §§ 2, 3 (1995). *See infra* cases cited at notes 182–184.

54. RESTATEMENT (THIRD) OF TRUSTS § 90 cmt. d (2007); Uniform Prudent Investor Act § 9 (1995). *See* Shriners Hosps. v. Gardiner, 733 P.2d 1110, 1111–12 (Ariz. 1987) (noting that the trustee breached her fiduciary duty by delegating investment decision-making to co-trustee).

55. *See* RESTATEMENT (THIRD) OF TRUSTS § 90 cmts. f & h (2007); Uniform Prudent Investor Act § 7 (1995).

56. RESTATEMENT (THIRD) OF TRUSTS § 92 (2007); Uniform Prudent Investor Act § 4 (1995). *See infra* text accompanying notes 177–195.

57. RESTATEMENT (THIRD) OF TRUSTS § 92 (2007); Uniform Prudent Investor Act § 4 (1995). *See* RESTATEMENT (THIRD) OF TRUSTS § 90 cmts. f & h, § 92 cmt. b (2007).

> The fiduciary's decision to retain assets may be influenced by the protected person's special interest in certain property (either made explicit or inferred from the circumstances), such as a family business or a family-owned farm.[58] An estate may own and operate such a business over an extended period, with consent of court, but only to the extent that such ownership is consistent with the overall investment plan of the estate and does not prejudice the flow of income needed by the protected person.[59]

Though a fiduciary is obligated to exercise reasonable care regarding investment decisions, the fiduciary is not a guarantor of a profitable result.[60]

6. Duty to Comply with Statutory Directions

In most jurisdictions, a probate or like code will set out a broad range of actions that may be taken by a fiduciary in his or her reasonable discretion, consistent with the other standards of conduct discussed herein. As to those statutorily authorized actions, the probate court typically will not interfere with the reasonable discretion exercised by the fiduciary or require prior court approval and probate court involvement will be limited to investigating and remedying instances of abuse.[61] In contrast, most jurisdictions require prior judicial consent for certain actions that may be contemplated by a fiduciary. For instance, in many states, a fiduciary may not sell real property held in the name of the estate without probate court approval.[62] As noted above, a fiduciary may not

---

58. *See* Restatement (Third) of Trusts §§ 90, 92 cmt. c (2007).
59. *Id.* § 92 cmt. e. *See* State *ex rel.* Raskin v. Schachat, 180 A. 502 (Conn. 1935); Guerra v. Guerra, No. 04-10-00271, 2011 WL 3715051, at *3–4 (Tex. App. 2011*). See also infra* text accompanying notes 177–195.
60. *See* Restatement (Third) of Trusts § 90 cmt. b (2007); *infra* cases cited at notes 85–88.
61. Restatement (Third) of Trusts § 87 (2007). *See* Est. of Berger, 520 N.E.2d 690, 697 (Ill. App. Ct. 1988) (noting that a conservator need not obtain a court order to expend money for necessities for ward).
62. *Compare In re* Tetreault, 11 A.3d 635, 642–44 (R.I. 2011) (noting that a fiduciary needs prior court approval to sell real property), *and* Wachovia Bank v. Casey, No. CV096002803, 2010 WL 3787230, at *4 (Conn. Super. Ct. Aug. 27, 2010) (same), *with* Conservatorship of Kinney, 495

take actions that implicate a fiduciary's own personal financial interests and might therefore violate the duty of loyalty without first seeking and receiving probate court approval.[63]

If the fiduciary violates any of these duties, the probate court may under certain circumstances void the wrongful actions and the fiduciary may be personally liable to the estate or certain third parties for the resulting losses.[64] This may result in a claim on the probate bond by a successor fiduciary or certain third parties having the necessary standing. However, the failure of a fiduciary to secure prior approval from a probate court where required by statute is not a per se breach of duty if the actions taken by the fiduciary are otherwise deemed consistent with the applicable standard of care.[65]

II. The Probate Bond

A. *Terms and Conditions*

The probate bond sets forth the terms and conditions under which the surety may be held liable for the acts or omissions of the fiduciary and is an express contract among the parties to the bond.[66] A probate bond

---

N.W.2d 69, 71 (N.D. 1993) (fiduciary can sell real property without prior court approval). *See* Bruner v. Wolford's Est., 191 N.E. 70, 72 (Ill. 1934) (conservator can make a loan from assets of the estate to a third party without securing prior court approval but is exposed to personal liability if there is a breach of fiduciary duty). *See also* MASS. GEN. LAWS ANN. ch. 190B, §§ 5-421, 5-423(c) (West 2021); *id.* ch. 202, §§ 21–29.

63. *See* RESTATEMENT (THIRD) OF TRUSTS § 78 cmt. c (2007).

64. UNIF. PROB. CODE §§ 3-712, 3-713 (UNIF. L. COMM'N amended 2010). *See In re* Est. of West, 948 P.2d 351 (Utah 1997). *But see In re* Est. of Kennedy, 369 N.W.2d 63, 65 (Neb. 1985) (holding that sanctions need not be imposed where a fiduciary acts in good faith and interests of the estate are not impaired).

65. *In re* Conservatorship of Alessio, 803 N.W.2d 656 (Iowa 2011) (holding that a conservator was not strictly liable where he failed to secure prior probate court approval before investing ward's funds). *See Bruner*, 191 N.E. at 72; Winter v. Hope, 861 P.2d 1282, 1287 (Kan. 1993); U.S. Fid. & Guar. Co. v. Conservatorship of Melson, 809 So. 2d 647, 657–61 (Miss. 2002); Est. of Powell, 245 S.W.3d 280, 283–86 (Mo. Ct. App. 2008).

66. Laws. Sur. Corp. v. Whitehead, 719 So. 2d 833, 835 (Ala. 1998); Morgan v. Morgan, 784 N.Y.S.2d 921, at *3 (Sup. Ct. 2004); *In re* Est. of Camarda, 425 N.Y.S.2d 1012, 1015 (Surr. Ct. 1980).

typically affords coverage for breaches of fiduciary duty.[67] There are three parties to the probate bond: (1) the principal/fiduciary, whose obligations are being secured; (2) the obligee/beneficiary, to whom the obligation runs; and (3) the surety, who undertakes to perform the obligation or pay a sum if the principal defaults.[68] The obligee on a surety bond typically is the state or commonwealth, acting for the benefit of all persons with an interest in the estate.[69] The usual condition of the bond is that it will be released by the "faithful discharge by the fiduciary of all duties according to law."[70] The scope of the bonded obligation generally is commensurate with the scope of the administrator's fiduciary obligations to the estate.[71] The Uniform Probate Code permits a proceeding to be brought against the surety on the petition of the successor fiduciary, any other fiduciary of the same decedent or conserved person, or any interested person claiming a breach of the obligation of the bond.[72] The surety is jointly and severally liable for such breaches with the personal representative for whom the bond is given, to the extent of the penal sum, or penalty, of the bond.[73] The terms of the bond also generally provide that the bond may be proceeded against multiple times until the entire penal sum of the bond is exhausted.[74]

---

67. Lori-Kay Golf, Inc. v. Lassner, 460 N.E.2d 1097 (N.Y. 1984); Lawton v. Bank of Am. Corp., No. 07-239S, 2007 WL 4480222, at *3 (D.R.I. Dec. 17, 2007). *See* CONN. GEN. STAT. ANN. §§ 45a-139(a), 45a-499(A)(1) (West 2021); OHIO REV. CODE ANN. § 2109.04(A)(1) (West 2021); 33 R.I. GEN. LAWS ANN. § 33-17-2 (West 2021).
68. *Camarda*, 425 N.Y.S.2d at 1015.
69. UNIF. PROB. CODE § 3-606(a)(1) (UNIF. L. COMM'N amended 2010) ("Bonds shall name the [state] as obligee for the benefit of the persons interested in the estate . . . .").
70. *Id.*
71. *Lori-Kay Golf, Inc.*, 460 N.E.2d 1097; *Bank of Am. Corp.*, 2007 WL 4480222, at *3. *See* statutes cited *supra* note 67.
72. UNIF. PROB. CODE § 3-606(a)(4) (UNIF. L. COMM'N amended 2010). The issue of standing to assert a claim under a probate bond is addressed in greater detail in the text corresponding to notes 89–98, *infra*.
73. UNIF. PROB. CODE § 3-606(a)(2) (UNIF. L. COMM'N amended 2010). The coverage implications of a probate bond's penal sum are addressed *infra* at the text accompanying notes 137–151.
74. UNIF. PROB. CODE § 3-606(a)(5) (UNIF. L. COMM'N amended 2010).

A penal sum is the maximum limit of a surety's exposure for claims under a bond.[75] Put simply, the penal sum is the amount of the bond. It is the sum that fixes the ultimate liability of the surety and, in theory, the penal sum cannot be exceeded.[76] Probate bonds are creatures of statute and thus the question of what the penal sum on a personal representative or conservator's bond should be usually is answered by referring to the applicable state law. Most states require a fiduciary bond in an amount equal to the value of the personal property that will be controlled by the fiduciary, including sums the fiduciary is expected to receive during a specific accounting period or during the expected duration of the estate. A number of states have adopted the Uniform Probate Code, which provides for different calculations for the penal sum of the probate bonds for personal representatives and conservators.[77] Some jurisdictions do not offer any specific statutory guidance for the amount of the probate bond and allow the probate court to determine the amount sufficient to protect the state. For example, the Connecticut statutes regarding probate administration provide only that a probate bond "shall be in such amount and with such security as shall be required by the judge of probate having jurisdiction."[78] Some cases hold that even where the amount is not specifically identified by statute, the bond should be at least equal to

---

75. Travelers Indem. Co. v. Askew, 280 So. 2d 469, 471 (Fla. Dist. Ct. App. 1973); Great Am. Ins. Co. v. N. Austin Mun. Util. Dist. No. 1, 908 S.W.2d 415, 426 (Tex. 1995).
76. *See, e.g.*, *In re* Spinner, 717 A.2d 362, 366 (D.C. Ct. App. 1998) (ordering reduction of surcharge from $15,000 to $1,000 because penal sum of representative bond could not be exceeded); Moseley v. Johnson, 56 S.E. 922, 923 (N.C. 1907) (refusing to award prejudgment interest where the award of interest would yield a judgment in excess of the penal sum). *See also infra* text accompanying notes 137–149.
77. The following states have largely adopted the Uniform Probate Code, with some modifications: Alaska, Arizona, Colorado, Hawaii, Idaho, Maine, Massachusetts, Michigan, Minnesota, Montana, Nebraska, New Jersey, New Mexico, North Dakota, South Carolina, South Dakota, and Utah. A number of other states have adopted parts of the Uniform Code.
78. Conn. Gen. Stat. Ann. § 45a-139 (West 2021). *See also* 20 Pa. Cons. Stat. § 3171 (2021) (noting that "before letters shall be granted to any personal representative, he shall execute and file a bond which shall be in the name of the Commonwealth, with sufficient surety, in such amount as the register considers necessary, having regard to the value of the personal estate which will come into the control of the personal representative").

the value of the assets received by the fiduciary.[79] Most states allow for a petition by the fiduciary to reduce or increase the penal sum of the bond if there has been a significant change in the assets of the estate.[80]

B. Construction

The terms of a probate bond are given their ordinary meaning, but because probate bonds are generally derived from statute and are therefore statutory bonds, the applicable statute is read into the bond and controls over any conflicting terms in the bond itself.[81] This means that some terms of the bond may not be explicitly stated in the bond form itself but are found instead in the statute applicable to the bond. The fact that a probate bond is not executed and approved in the manner prescribed by statute may not be the basis for an argument by the surety that the statutes do not apply and are not therefore read into the bond.[82] Similarly, the invalidity of a fiduciary's appointment by a court having jurisdiction over the estate may not serve as a defense for the surety.[83] The surety also may not assert as a defense that it was fraudulently induced to issue a probate bond, unless the beneficiary or the party seeking to recover on the bond participated in the alleged fraud.[84]

When interpreting the duties and liabilities of a surety under a probate bond, and when determining whether a principal has breached the terms

---

79. *In re* Blanchfield's Est., 2 Pa. D. & C.3d 230, 234–35 (C.P. Orphans' Ct. 1975).
80. *See* GA. CODE ANN. § 29-5-42 (West 2021) ("If the value of the ward's bonded estate decreases, the court may permit a corresponding reduction in the value of the bond, but this reduction does not affect the liability of the surety for prior waste or misconduct of the conservator.").
81. Goldberg v. Hartford Fire Ins. Co., 849 A.2d 368, 373 (Conn. 2004); Massie v. De Shields, 62 S.W.2d 322, 324 (Tex. App. 1933). *See also, e.g.*, Alaska Nat'l Ins. Co. v. Nw. Cedar Structures, Inc., 153 P.3d 336, 338 n.4 (Alaska 2007) (general contractor bond); Chi. Hous. Auth. for Use of Gen. Bronze Corp. v. U.S. Fid. & Guar. Co., 199 N.E.2d 217, 219 (Ill. App. Ct. 1964) (public works performance and payment bonds).
82. *In re* Guardianship of Hampton, 374 N.W.2d 264, 267 (Minn. 1985).
83. *Massie*, 62 S.W.2d at 323; State *ex rel.* Stone v. U.S. Fid. & Guar. Co., 78 N.E.2d 881, 886 (Ind. Ct. App. 1948); Fid. & Deposit Co. of Md. v. Anderson, 150 S.E. 413, 418 (Va. 1929).
84. *In re* Est. of Polevski, 452 A.2d 469, 471 (N.J. Super. Ct. App. Div. 1982); Judge of Prob. v. Nudd, 199 A.2d 296, 297 (N.H. 1964).

of the bond, it must be remembered that neither the principal nor the surety is an insurer of the estate's financial health.[85] A surety is not liable unless its principal is liable and, therefore, a surety may assert any defense available to the principal with the exception of purely personal defenses such as infancy, incapacity, or bankruptcy.[86] Unless the principal violates some duty to the estate, there is no liability for the surety.[87] If the estate incurred a loss, for example from a decline in the value of certain mutual funds into which estate funds were invested, neither the principal nor the surety will be held liable for the loss provided the principal exercised reasonable care and breached no duty.[88]

C. Scope of Coverage and Defenses to Coverage

1. Parties with Standing to Assert Claims

Though the nominal obligee on the face of most probate bonds is the probate court or the state where the probate court is located, the party asserting a claim typically is a successor fiduciary who asserts the claim on behalf of the estate for losses caused to the estate as a result

---

85. Birmingham Tr. Nat'l Bank v. Henley, 371 So. 2d 883, 895–96 (Ala. 1979), *cert. denied*, 445 U.S. 915 (1980).

86. Cain v. Panitch, No. 16AP-758, 2018 WL 1953116, at *10 (Ohio Ct. App. Apr. 24, 2018); *In re* Est. of Bishop, No. 20102, 2004 WL 917693, at *2 (Ohio Ct. App. Apr. 30, 2004); Hopkins v. INA Underwriters Ins. Co., 542 N.E.2d 679, 683 (Ohio Ct. App. 1988).

87. *See* cases cited *supra* note 86.

88. *See Birmingham Tr. Nat'l Bank*, 371 So. 2d at 895 (no liability where fiduciary lawfully sold trust property that thereafter appreciated in value); Mann v. Rudder, 144 So. 13, 15 (Ala. 1932) (no breach of duty where an investment properly chosen by trustee depreciates in value); Citizens & S. Nat'l Bank v. Haskins, 327 S.E.2d 192 (Ga. 1985) (no liability where an investment properly chosen by a trustee depreciates in value); Springfield Safe Deposit & Tr. Co. v. First Unitarian Soc'y, 200 N.E. 541, 546 (Mass. 1936) (no liability where a trustee sells property and the property thereafter appreciates in value); *In re* Clark's Will, 177 N.E. 397, 398 (N.Y. 1931) (no liability where a properly chosen investment depreciates in value); *In re* Darlington's Est., 91 A. 486, 488 (Pa. 1914) ("A trustee is not an insurer of trust funds against the possibility of loss, and all that is required of him is good faith and reasonable diligence.").

of the prior bonded fiduciary's alleged breach of fiduciary duty.[89] Many probate statutes address the question of standing to assert a claim under a bond.[90] In some jurisdictions, standing is restricted to a limited universe of claimants.[91] In other jurisdictions, standing to assert a claim under a probate bond extends to a broad range of parties claiming a loss as a result of a breach of fiduciary duty on the part of the bonded fiduciary.[92] Depending on the jurisdiction, parties having standing may include:

- A judgment creditor of a decedent claiming that the decedent had failed to pay antemortem obligations[93]
- A nursing home or other medical provider claiming that its bills for care for the protected person were unpaid in whole or part because the conservator had been untimely in applying for coverage under the Medicaid program[94]
- A decedent's estate or a trust claiming that after the protected person in a conservatorship had passed away, the conservator

---

89. *See In re* Est. of Bartlett, 680 P.2d 369 (Okla. 1984); U.S. Fid. & Guar. Co. v. Decker, 171 N.E. 333, 335 (Ohio 1930).

90. *See* UNIF. PROB. CODE § 3-606(a)(4) (UNIF. L. COMM'N amended 2010).

91. *See* State *ex rel.* Scott v. State Farm Fire & Cas. Co., 947 S.W.2d 530, 534 (Mo. Ct. App. 1997) (noting that a ward's family does not have standing to assert a claim against the ward's conservator); *In re* Est. of Vitale, 414 N.Y.S.2d 370, 371 (App. Div. 1979) (denying standing to creditor of estate).

92. Jewish Home for the Elderly v. Cantore, 778 A.2d 93, 100–01 (Conn. 2001); Fed. Kemper Life Assurance Co. v. Old Republic Sur. Co., 561 N.E.2d 1208, 1210–11 (Ill. App. Ct. 1990). *See* UNIF. PROB. CODE § 3-606(a)(4) (UNIF. L. COMM'N amended 2010).

93. *See In re* Grant, 381 N.E.2d 1348, 1354 (Ohio Ct. App. 1978). *But see Vitale*, 414 N.Y.S.2d at 371 (denying standing to creditor of estate). *See also* Action Carting Env't Servs., Inc. v. Bohannon, No. CV 08-4024733S, 2008 WL 2502771, at *2–4 (Conn. Super. Ct. June 9, 2008) (creditor of an heir does not have standing to assert claim under probate bond); Jaser v. Fischer, No. CV 980418196S, 2000 WL 277313, at *5–8 (Conn. Super. Ct. Mar. 1, 2000), *aff'd*, 783 A.2d 28 (Conn. App. Ct. 2001) (same).

94. *See Cantore*, 778 A.2d at 100–01; Gardner Heights Health Care Ctr., Inc. v. Korolyshun, No. CV064024480, 2008 WL 907511 (Conn. Super. Ct. Mar. 17, 2008); *In re* Ewanicky, No. 81742, 2003 WL 21469181, at *2 (Ohio Ct. App. June 26, 2003).

had failed to pay over all funds from the conservatorship owing to the decedent's estate or trust[95]

- Parties claiming that the fiduciary had failed to release property belonging to them and not the estate[96]
- Beneficiaries of a will or intestacy claiming that the executor had failed to properly distribute bequests or inheritances[97]

In a decedent's estate, heirs at law or beneficiaries under a will typically do not have standing to assert a claim under the bond challenging the conduct of the fiduciary, except where there has been a finding that they did not receive funds from the estate to which they were entitled.[98]

2. *Coverage for Losses That Predate the Issuance of the Bond*

There is a split in the case law regarding whether a probate bond affords coverage for losses that predate the issuance of the bond.

In many jurisdictions, a probate bond surety is not liable for the wrongful acts of its principal that occurred prior to the effective date of the bond unless the terms of the bond specifically provide for retroactive coverage.[99] In these jurisdictions, a surety would be liable only for

---

95. *See* Am. Fid. Co. v. Barnard, 181 A.2d 628 (N.H. 1962).
96. *See* Shepherd v. Townsend, 162 So. 2d 878 (Miss. 1964); *Scott*, 947 S.W.2d 530; Gilliam v. Hopkins, 472 S.W.2d 436 (Mo. Ct. App. 1971).
97. *See Shepard*, 162 So. 2d 878; Stofft v. O'Shaughnessy, 107 N.E.2d 643 (Ohio 1952).
98. *See Scott*, 947 S.W.2d at 534–35.
99. *See* Nat'l Sur. Corp. v. Williams, 110 F.2d 873, 876 (8th Cir. 1940), *cert. denied*, 311 U.S. 674 (1940); Bolmer v. U.S. Fid. & Guar. Co., 11 F. Supp. 560, 563 (W.D. Ky. 1935); Howe v. White, 69 N.E. 684, 687 (Ind. 1904); State *ex rel.* Bird v. Hood, 7 Blackf. 127, 128–29 (Ind. 1844); Martin v. Hanschu, 738 P.2d 96, 97 (Kan. 1987); Slack v. Ohio Cas. Ins. Co., 509 N.W.2d 861, 862 (Mich. Ct. App. 1993); *In re* Van Bokkelen's Est., 20 N.Y.S.2d 735, 737–38 (App. Div. 1941); Thomson v. Am. Sur. Co., 67 N.Y.S. 564, 568–69 (App. Div. 1900); Thomson v. MacGregor, 81 N.Y. 592, 596 (1880); Cont'l Cas. Co. v. Ackerman, 152 N.E.2d 778, 781–82 (Ohio Ct. App. 1935); Gabriel v. Snell, 613 S.W.2d 810, 814 (Tex. Civ. App. 1981); Freedman v. Vallie, 75 S.W. 322, 324–25 (Tex. Civ. App. 1903); Peterson v. Schrieber, 238 N.W.2d 722, 724–25 (Wis. 1976). *See generally* Annotation, *Liability of Sureties on Bond of Guardian, Executor, Administrator, or Trustee for Defalcation or Deficit Occurring Before Bond Was Given*, 82 A.L.R. 585 (1933).

defalcations or losses incurred during the bond period and involving assets in the control of the principal during the bond period.[100] The surety would not be liable for a diminution in the value of an investment occurring before the bond was effective.[101] Nor would the surety be responsible for a conversion by the fiduciary occurring prior to his or her appointment and the execution of the bond.[102] While many of these decisions are resolved on common law principles, retroactive effect may also be denied based on the express terms of the bond.[103]

In other jurisdictions where a bond is issued after the effective date of the estate, the coverage afforded under the bond can relate back to the appointment of the principal as fiduciary even if the alleged breaches of fiduciary duty predate the effective date of the bond.[104] In still other jurisdictions, the coverage afforded under the bond can also relate back to actions of the principal that occurred prior to his or her appointment as fiduciary.[105] Some of the decisions affording retroactive coverage are predicated on the express terms of the particular bond or the particular

---

100. King v. Jones, 971 S.W.2d 916, 919–22 (Mo. Ct. App. 1998) (conservator's bond). *See* cases cited *supra* note 99.

101. *Slack*, 509 N.W.2d at 862.

102. *Martin*, 738 P.2d at 97–98.

103. *See* State v. Hunter, 47 A. 665, 667 (Conn. 1900); *Van Bokkelen's Est.*, 20 N.Y.S.2d at 737–38; *Thomson*, 81 N.Y. at 596.

104. *See In re* Pacheco, 199 P.3d 676, 680–82 (Ariz. Ct. App. 2008); State v. Howarth, 48 Conn. 207, 213 (1880); Merrells v. Phelps, 34 Conn. 109, 112 (1867); Hartford Fin. Servs. Grp., Inc. v. Hand, 30 A.2d 180, 185–86 nn.4–6 (D.C. Ct. App. 2011); Pinkstaff v. State, 59 Ill. 148 (1871); Hartford Fire Ins. Co. v. Est. of Sanders, 155 A.3d 915, 931–35 (Md. Ct. Spec. App. 2017); Brooke v. Am. Sav. Bank, 223 N.W. 500, 502–04 (Iowa 1929); Succession of Reilly v. Am. Bonding Co., 70 So. 237, 239–40 (La. Sup. Ct. 1915); State *ex rel.* Enyart v. Doud, 269 S.W. 923, 925 (Mo. Ct. App. 1925); Mitchell v. Columbia Cas. Co., 106 P.2d 344, 344–46 (Mont. 1940); Century Indem. Co. v. Md. Cas. Co., 193 A. 221 (N.H. 1937); *In re* Est. of Camarda, 425 N.Y.S.2d 1012, 1017 (Surr. Ct. 1980); Baird v. Patterson, 44 P.2d 90, 92 (Okla. 1935); Bellinger v. Thompson, 37 P. 714, 718–19 (Or. 1894); Manson v. Goss, No. M2000-03206-COA-R3-CV, 2003 WL 1876965, at *4–6 (Tenn. Ct. App. Apr. 15, 2003); Owens v. McMahan, 210 P. 200, 200–01 (Wash. 1922). *See also* Annotation, *supra* note 99.

105. *Succession of Reilly*, 70 So. at 239; Wood v. Tuohy, 854 N.E.2d 96, 101–02 (Mass. App. Ct. 2006); *Enyart*, 269 S.W. at 925; *In re* Est. & Guardianship of Wyman, 429 P.2d 629, 632 (Mont. 1967).

language of the statute requiring that a bond issue.[106] Many of these decisions have adopted a "continuing violation" analysis, holding that a principal who eviscerates assets prior to the effective date of the bond or prior to being appointed as a fiduciary commits a breach of the bond after its effective date by failing to disclose and remedy the prior breach.[107] Even where this theory has been adopted, some courts hold that the extent of the surety's liability for actions predating the bond is limited to the extent that the fiduciary has access to assets as of the effective date of the bond that could have been applied to remedy the loss of funds.[108] Other courts impose full liability for prior acts even if there were no funds available to remedy the wrongful conduct as of the bond's effective date.[109]

A related issue arises where the fiduciary owes an obligation to the ward or decedent that predates the fiduciary's appointment. In

---

106. *See* LaCoste v. Splivalo, 30 P. 571, 572–73 (Cal. 1883) (according retroactive effect to a statutory bond based on the terms of the statute); Bromen v. O'Connell, 241 N.W. 54, 55–56 (Minn. 1932) (same). *But see Hand*, 30 A.3d at 185 (holding that, where a bond rider increased the penal sum of the bond as to "losses occurring thereafter," the estate sustained a loss not when funds were initially misappropriated but rather when the guardian was no longer able to reimburse the estate from her personal assets).

107. *See Pinkstaff*, 59 Ill. 148; *Succession of Reilly*, 70 So. 237; *Wood*, 854 N.E.2d at 101–02; King v. Jones, 971 S.W.2d 916, 919–22 (Mo. Ct. App. 1998); Gilliam v. Hopkins, 472 S.W.2d 436, 447 (Mo. Ct. App. 1971); *Wyman*, 429 P.2d at 632; *Century Indem. Co.*, 193 A. 221.

108. *See* Buckel v. Smith's Admin., 82 S.W. 235 (Ky. 1904); State v. Gregory, 22 N.E. 1 (Ind. 1889); *King*, 971 S.W.2d at 919–22; Howell v. Anderson, 92 N.W. 760 (Neb. 1902); *Matter of* Piper's Est., 15 Pa. 533 (1850); Kader v. Yeargin, 3 S.W. 178 (Tenn. 1887); Am. Sur. Co. v. Norton, 238 S.W. 1111, 1112–13 (Tex. Comm'n App. 1922); Glens Falls Indem. Co. v. Wall, 177 S.E. 901, 902–04 (Va. 1934); West Virginia v. Citizens' Tr. & Guar. Co., 100 S.E. 685, 686–87 (W. Va. 1919).

109. *In re* Jones Est., 2 P.2d 483, 486 (Cal. Ct. App. 1931) (holding a probate bond surety liable to estate where executor had a debt to the deceased that predated the date of death but lacked the funds necessary to pay the debt as of the date of his appointment as executor and at all times going forward). *See* Wright v. Lang, 66 Ala. 389 (1880); *Brooke*, 223 N.W. at 582–84; *Wood*, 854 N.E.2d at 101–02; Prob. Judge v. Sulloway, 44 A. 720 (N.H. 1896); James v. West, 65 N.E. 156 (Ohio 1902); Greer v. McNeal, 69 P. 893 (Okla. 1902).

most jurisdictions, a fiduciary who is personally insolvent at the time of appointment and remains insolvent throughout the term of the estate does not breach a duty to the estate by failing to reimburse the estate for a "pre-appointment obligation."[110] A minority of courts have held that an insolvent fiduciary's failure to pay a preexisting obligation constitutes a breach of fiduciary duty, based on a fiction that all preexisting debts from the fiduciary to the estate are deemed to have been paid to the estate as of the date of the fiduciary's appointment.[111]

Based on the foregoing, a surety that issues a bond in the midst of its principal's performance as a fiduciary or to a fiduciary that owes obligations to the ward or decedent that predate the estate assumes a risk in many jurisdictions that coverage will extend to losses that occurred prior to the bond's effective date.

3. Coverage for Losses Occurring After the Bond Has Been Terminated or Discharged

When a probate court approves a final accounting, it generally enters an order discharging the fiduciary and his or her surety and closing the estate. The discharge of the bond generally is prospective only.[112] The surety typically remains liable for prior fiduciary breaches subsequently discovered, subject to applicable limitations periods and a laches defense.[113]

A surety bond can also be discharged in the course of the estate. This may occur where the fiduciary changes sureties in midstream and the court approves the discharge of the prior bond upon acceptance of the subsequent bond. In some jurisdictions, a surety can petition a probate court to be discharged in advance of its principal's discharge. In some jurisdictions this may be done as a matter of right,[114] while elsewhere it

---

110. *See Wall*, 177 S.E. at 902.

111. *See Wright*, 66 Ala. at 397; Commonwealth v. Gould, 118 Mass. 300, 307 (1875). *But see Wall*, 177 S.E. at 902.

112. *See* New Amsterdam Cas. Co. v. Bookhart, 235 N.W. 74, 77–78 (Iowa 1931); *In re* Pope's Est., 69 A. 616 (Me. 1908); Judge of Prob. v. Nudd, 219 A.2d 454, 456 (N.H. 1966).

113. *In re* Est. of DiAndrea, 847 P.2d 249, 250 (Colo. Ct. App. 1993); *Pope's Est.*, 69 A. 616; Eichelberger v. Gross, 42 Ohio St. 549 (1885).

114. *In re* Est. of Rowell, 156 So. 2d 812, 812–13 (Miss. 1963).

is at the discretion of the court.[115] A replacement bond or other security generally must be posted for the protection of the estate.[116] The surety need not show malfeasance by its principal.[117] In many, but not all, jurisdictions, the discharge only includes acts occurring subsequent to the discharge.[118] However, some courts have held that a surety whose bond has been discharged is not exposed to claims arising out of prior acts of misconduct so long as a substitute bond has been posted that assumes coverage for these prior acts.[119]

4. Cosuretyship

As previously noted, there may be circumstances where multiple bonds afford coverage for the same loss, including but not limited to where a bond has retroactive effect or where a bond has been discharged but continues to afford coverage for losses occurring prior to the discharge.[120] Where two or more sureties are liable for the defaults of the same principal, the legal relationship between the sureties generally is described as "cosuretyship."[121] Under circumstances where the common law creates a cosurety relationship, sureties generally are liable for their proportionate share of an obligation based on the penal sum amounts of the respective

---

115. Spradley v. St. Paul Fire & Marine Ins. Co., 134 S.E.2d 850, 852–53 (Ga. Ct. App. 1964).
116. Gabriel v. Snell, 613 S.W.2d 810, 813 (Tex. Civ. App. 1981).
117. *Spradley*, 134 S.E.2d at 852–53.
118. *See* Osborne Bonding & Sur. Co. v. Glaze, 497 S.E.2d 612, 613 (Ga. Ct. App. 1998) (holding that a discharged surety was liable for acts occurring prior to discharge); Century Indem. Co. v. Md. Cas. Co., 193 A. 221, 222 (N.H. 1937) (same). *Cf.* Judge of Prob. v. Nudd, 219 A.2d 454, 456 (N.H. 1966) (holding that a discharged surety was not liable for losses occurring subsequent to discharge).
119. *See* Brooke v. Am. Sav. Bank, 223 N.W. 500, 502–04 (Iowa 1929) (holding that an initial surety can be released from prior unknown exposures if the bond is properly discharged and a "substitute" bond has been posted that clearly provides coverage for prior acts).
120. *See supra* text accompanying notes 99–119.
121. RESTATEMENT (THIRD) OF SURETYSHIP AND GUARANTY § 53(1) (AM. L. INST. 1996). *See generally* United States v. Horvath Bros., Inc., 278 F. Supp 159, 161 (E.D. Wis. 1967), *aff'd on other grounds*, 453 F.2d 896 (10 Cir. 1972); Indem. Ins. Co. v. Am. Sur. Co., 268 N.Y.S. 203, 205 (App. Div. 1933).

bonds.[122] An equitable right of contribution exists between cosureties.[123] Thus, if one cosurety is required to pay more than its equitable share of the obligation, it is entitled to recover its overpayment from the other cosurety.[124] When sureties purposefully issue bonds for the same obligation, they often enter into a cosurety agreement, setting forth terms on matters such as percentage of loss, the lead surety for claims handling, one surety's insolvency, and the sharing of collateral.

In jurisdictions where a probate bond issued in the midst of an estate has retroactive application to losses occurring prior to its operative date, or in jurisdictions where a discharged bond continues to afford coverage for losses incurred prior to the discharge, the discharge of one probate bond and the substitution of a different bond may have the effect of creating a "cosuretyship" as to losses occurring prior to the discharge of the bond that is earlier in time.[125]

5. Coverage Issues Where a Principal Serves in Multiple Fiduciary Capacities

A bond principal may be a protected person's conservator and later may be designated as the executor or administrator of the decedent estate of the protected person.[126] Alternatively, a principal may serve simultaneously

---

122. Restatement (Third) of Suretyship and Guaranty § 53(1) (1996); 74 Am. Jur. 2d *Suretyship* § 153 (2021). *See* Schoenfeld v. Neher, 428 F.2d 152, 154 (10th Cir. 1970); *Horvath Bros.*, 278 F. Supp 159; Tindall v. Holder, 892 S.W.2d 314, 324 (Mo. Ct. App. 1994); *Indem. Ins. Co.*, 268 N.Y.S 203; Keystone Bank v. Flooring Specialists, Inc., 518 A.2d 1179, 1185–86 (Pa. 1986).
123. Restatement (Third) of Suretyship and Guaranty § 57(1) (Am. L. Inst. 1996); 74 Am. Jur. 2d *Suretyship* § 153 (2021). *See Schoenfeld*, 428 F.2d at 154; *Indem. Ins. Co.*, 268 N.Y.S 203; *Keystone Bank*, 518 A.2d at 1185–86.
124. Restatement (Third) of Suretyship and Guaranty § 57(1) (Am. L. Inst. 1996); 74 Am. Jur. 2d *Suretyship* § 153 (2021). *See Schoenfeld*, 428 F.2d at 154; *Indem. Ins. Co.*, 268 N.Y.S 203; *Keystone Bank*, 518 A.2d at 1185–86.
125. *See* New Amsterdam Cas. Co. v. Bookhart, 235 N.W. 74, 77–78 (Iowa 1931); Century Indem. Co. v. Md. Cas. Co., 193 A. 221 (N.H. 1937). *See also* Brooke v. Am. Sav. Bank, 223 N.W. 500, 502–04 (Iowa 1929).
126. *See* Am. Fid. Co. v. Barnard, 181 A.2d 628, 632–33 (N.H. 1962), *aff'd*, 182 A.2d 471 (1962).

as the protected person's conservator and as a trustee for a trust for which the protected person is the beneficiary. The principal may be required to post probate bonds for each of his or her distinct fiduciary roles. If the principal properly performs obligations under one such role and properly transfers any funds owing from that one estate to another, the probate bond issued for the initial estate should not be subject to surcharge if a fiduciary breach occurs in the course of the administration of the follow-on estate.[127] On the other hand, if the principal acting in the role of conservator breaches the duty as conservator by failing to transfer funds to accounts he or she maintains as trustee, there may also be a breach of fiduciary duty as trustee and a cause of action under the trustee bond if the trustee fails to exercise the duty to recover property owed to the trust.[128] It therefore is possible that where a fiduciary acts in multiple capacities there may be multiple breaches of duty and possible claims on multiple bonds for the same or related loss.

6. Coverage Where the Fiduciary's Actions Were Approved by the Probate Court

A surety should have no liability to the extent that a fiduciary secured prior approval from the probate court regarding actions challenged through a bond claim.[129] The probate court's after-the-fact approval of actions taken by the fiduciary should also be a defense to a bond claim.[130] However, the courts have also held that a probate court lacks the authority

---

127. *See* Schilt v. Duvall, 479 F.2d 1228, 1232 (D.C. Cir. 1973); *Matter of* Est. of Erlien, 527 N.W.2d 389, 392-93 (Wis. Ct. App. 1994).
128. *See Barnard*, 181 A.2d at 632–33; Sierad v. Barnett, 164 S.W.3d 471, 480 (Tex. App. 2005).
129. *See* Zanoni v. Hudon, 708 A.2d 222, 224–25 (Conn. App. Ct. 1998); Desjardins v. Fontanella, No. CV135006229S, 2014 WL 4494414 (Conn. Super. Ct. July 30, 2014). *Compare* Gross v. Rell, 40 A.3d 240, 253–54 (Conn. 2012) (noting that a conservator is entitled to qualified immunity from damages actions as to actions approved by the probate court), *with* Cok v. Cosentino, 876 F.2d 1, 3 (1st Cir. 1989) (affording absolute immunity to a conservator).
130. *See* Bruner v. Wolford's Est., 191 N.E. 70, 72 (Ill. 1934); *In re* Conservatorship of Alessio, 803 N.W.2d 656 (Iowa 2011); Winter v. Hope, 861 P.2d 1282, 1287 (Kan. 1993); Est. of Powell, 245 S.W.2d 280, 283–84 (Mo. Ct. App. 2008); U.S. Fid. & Guar. Co. v. Conservatorship of Melson, 809 So. 2d 647, 657–61 (Miss. 2002).

to authorize a fiduciary to personally borrow money from the estate or use the estate's assets as collateral and that prior approval of such actions by the probate court is void and does not preclude liability on the part of the fiduciary or its surety to account for the estate's losses resulting from such transactions.[131]

7. Liability of Co-Fiduciaries

Co-fiduciaries are generally liable for each other's wrongful acts committed in their fiduciary capacities.[132] If co-fiduciaries execute a joint probate bond, a breach of conduct by either fiduciary triggers liability under the bond.[133] Recourse to the bond is not dependent on wrongdoing by both principals.[134]

8. Non-Estate Property Obtained While Acting Under Color of Office

A fiduciary may engage in misconduct that causes damage to third parties and not to the estate. For instance, a fiduciary may steal property from another purportedly acting in his or her capacity as fiduciary (i.e., acting under "color of office") and add that property to the assets of the estate. While the fiduciary may be personally liable to any third-party victims, the surety should not be liable for property illicitly received unless the bond or a statute expressly so provides.[135] However, there is a minority

---

131. *See* Fid. & Cas. Co. v. State, 184 N.E. 916, 920–23 (Ind. Ct. App. 1933); Sowers v. Pollock, 212 P. 103, 104 (Kan. 1923); *In re* Bender's Est., 224 N.W. 381, 382 (Mich. 1929). *But see* Kirkbride v. Hickok, 89 N.E.2d 91, 94–95 (Ohio Prob. Ct. 1949) (noting that a fiduciary may borrow from the estate if such action is approved by a statute or a trust document and authorized by the probate court).
132. Douglas Reservoirs Water Users Ass'n v. Garst, 451 P.2d 451, 454 (Wyo. 1969). *See* Ames v. Armstrong, 106 Mass. 15 (1870); Newton v. Newton, 53 N.H. 537 (1873); Eckert v. Myers, 15 N.E. 862 (Ohio 1888). *See also* L.S. Tellier, Annotation, *Coexecutor's, Coadministrator's, or Cotrustee's Liability for Defaults or Wrongful Acts of Fiduciary in Handling Estate*, 65 A.L.R. 2d 1019, § 25 (1959). *But see* Abbott v. Fisher, 124 Mass. 414 (1878).
133. *See Douglas Reservoirs Water Users Ass'n*, 451 P.2d at 454; *Ames*, 106 Mass. 15.
134. *See* cases cited *supra* note 133.
135. *See* Fed. Kemper Life Assurance Co. v. Eichwedel, 639 N.E.2d 246, 252 (Ill. App. Ct. 1994) (surety not liable for fraudulently procured life

view under which the surety may be liable for property wrongly received by the estate.[136]

9. Coverage Limitations Arising from the Operative Effect of the Penal Sum

The penal sum, or penalty, of the bond fixes the upper limit of the surety's liability, regardless of whether the damages determined by the court or other fact finder exceed that amount.[137] In that regard, a probate bond only covers loss to the estate to the extent of the penal sum of the bond, which, as noted earlier, may not always reflect the entire amount of the estate.[138] There are some circumstances, however, where claimants and the courts have attempted—sometimes successfully—to hold the surety liable for amounts that exceed the penal sum.

Jurisdictions diverge on whether and in what circumstances interest may be collected from the surety in excess of the penal sum of the bond. Some jurisdictions hold that interest from the date of the loss to the estate cannot be recovered if it will result in an award exceeding the amount of the bond.[139] Other jurisdictions hold that a surety can be held liable for interest beyond the penal sum of the bond based upon a judicial

---

insurance proceeds); Greenwich Sav. Bank v. U.S. Fid. & Guar. Co., 345 N.E.2d 290, 292 (N.Y. 1976) (surety not liable for fraud committed by administrator against third party to estate). *See also* Globe Indem. Co. v. Bruce, 81 F.2d 143, 154 (10th Cir. 1935); Brockelman v. W. Sur. Co., No. CV950258, 2000 WL 1273438, at *8–9 (Mass. Super. Ct. June 6, 2000). *But see* Fed. Kemper Life Assurance Co. v. Old Republic Sur. Co., 561 N.E.2d 1208, 1211 (Ill. App. Ct. 1990) (surety may be liable for injuries inflicted on third party per terms of statute). *See generally* Herbert Chermside, Annotation, *What Funds, Not Part of the Estate, Are Received under Color of Office so as to Render Liable Surety on Executor's or Administrator's Bond*, 82 A.L.R. 3d 869 (1978).

136. *See* Gnekow v. U.S. Fid. & Guar. Co., 163 S.W.2d 86, 87–90 (Mo. 1942); Parker v. Potter, 168 S.E. 490 (N.C. 1933). *See generally* Chermside, *supra* note 135.
137. *See* Bill Curphy Co. v. Elliott, 207 F.2d 103, 106 (5th Cir. 1953); Mass. Bonding & Ins. Co. v. United States, 97 F.2d 879, 881 (9th Cir. 1938); Colonial Am. Cas. & Sur. Co. v. Scherer, 214 S.W.3d 725, 734 (Tex. App. 2007).
138. *See supra* text accompanying notes 75–80.
139. Polk v. Am. Cas. Co. of Reading, Pa., 816 S.W.2d 178, 179 (Ky. 1991); Moseley v. Johnson, 56 S.E. 922, 923 (N.C. 1907). *But see* Ohio Cas. Ins. Co. v. Wilson, 923 S.W.2d 904, 908–09 (Tex. App. 1996).

determination that the surety wrongfully delayed paying a claim.[140] Even in those jurisdictions where courts have granted claims for interest in excess of the penal sum, it would appear that the courts limit this remedy to amounts that are directly attributable to some action, or inaction, on the part of the surety.

It is generally held that a surety cannot be held liable for attorneys' fees in any circumstance where those fees, when added to other liabilities under the bond, exceed the bond's penal sum.[141] However, the limitation of attorneys' fees to the penal sum can be varied by the terms of the bond.[142] Attorneys' fees may also be awarded as a component of punitive damages as a result of bad faith or unfair handling of the bond claim.[143] Awards of attorneys' fees for adjudged bad faith claims administration may not be limited by the penal sum of the bond.[144]

A common argument made to extend the surety's liability beyond the penal sum of the bond is that the bond is cumulative and therefore the penalty should be "stacked" year after year. For example, a fiduciary is required to give a $200,000.00 bond representing one year of income for the estate. After five years, it is discovered that the fiduciary misappropriated over $350,000.00. The successor fiduciary may argue that the surety is liable up to $1,000,000.00, representing a stacking of the penal sum every year for five years. However, most courts reject this

---

140. Burns v. Mass. Bonding & Ins. Co., 146 P.2d 29, 30 (Cal. Ct. App. 1944); Borough of Totowa v. Am. Sur. Co., 188 A.2d 586, 595–96 (N.J. 1963); Lyerly v. Yeadon, 19 S.E.2d 648, 657 (S.C. 1942); Valdez v. Hollenback, No. 0441-00739, 2013 WL 1749397, at *21–23 (Tex. App. May 16, 2013), *rev'd on other grounds*, 465 S.W.3d 217 (Tex. 2015); *In re* Davison, 642 P.2d 1259, 1262 (Wash. Ct. App. 1982); Whereatt v. Ellis, 79 N.W. 416, 418 (Wis. 1899).

141. 74 AM. JUR. 2D *Suretyship* § 167 (2021); *Scherer*, 214 S.W.3d at 734; *Davison*, 642 P.2d at 1261. *See also* T&R Painting Constr., Inc. v. St. Paul Fire & Marine Ins. Co., 23 Cal. App. 4th 738, 746 (1994) (construction bond).

142. United Bonding Ins. Co. v. Banco Suizo-Panameno, S.A., 422 F.2d 1142, 1149 (5th Cir. 1970); *Davison*, 642 P.2d at 1261.

143. Old Republic Sur. Co. v. Reischmann, 713 So. 2d 434, 436 (Fla. Dist. Ct. App. 1998); Nichols v. Preferred Nat'l Ins. Co., 704 So. 2d 1371, 1374 (Fla. 1997); *Davison*, 642 P.2d at 1261.

144. For a general discussion of the availability of awards of attorneys' fees as part of the recovery under a probate bond claim, see *infra* text accompanying notes 258–262.

argument and decline to interpret an annual bond as cumulative unless the terms expressly state so.[145] One court's further reasoning is that since the operative probate statute required annual accountings, there was an opportunity to evaluate the estate every year and make a timely determination of defalcation, and therefore the surety's obligation was limited to the face amount of the bond.[146]

Aside from successor fiduciaries making claims on behalf of the estate, there may be other types of claimants on a probate bond, such as creditors of the estate or other third parties having claims against the estate. Some states define "proper claimants" as anyone who is "aggrieved" by the fiduciary's breach of duty, the meaning of which can be interpreted variously.[147] This could result in multiple claims whose total exceeds the penal sum of the bond. In that case, the penal sum may be used as a defense once it is exhausted.[148] A surety is generally entitled to pay bond claims on a pro rata basis up to the penal sum.[149] If it is clear that there are multiple claimants with valid claims exceeding the penal sum, in order to preserve its penal sum defense and take itself out of the position of deciding how to apportion limited funds, it may make sense for the surety to deposit the penalty of the bond with the court and file an interpleader action.[150]

A surety will not be held liable for punitive damages imposed on the fiduciary for actions such as embezzlement or statutory theft, which in many cases would result in damages far exceeding the amount of the bond. Courts have held that an innocent surety should not be held

---

145. U.S. Fid. & Guar. Co. v. Christoffel, 566 P.2d 308 (Ariz. 1977); May v. Cont'l Cas. Co., 936 A.2d 747 (D.C. 2007); North Carolina *ex rel.* Duckett v. Pettee, 273 S.E.2d 317 (N.C. Ct. App. 1980).
146. *May*, 936 A.2d at 750–51.
147. *See, e.g.*, CONN. GEN. STAT. ANN. § 45a-144 (West 2021); MASS. GEN. LAWS ANN. ch. 205, § 23 (West 2021); N.J. STAT. ANN. § 3B:15-24 (West 2021); N.Y. SURR. CT. PROC. ACT LAW § 809 (McKinney 2021).
148. UNIF. PROB. CODE § 5-415 (UNIF. L. COMM'N amended 2010).
149. Dugas v. Am. Sur. Co., 300 U.S. 414 (1937); Md. Cas. Co. v. Glasell-Taylor & Robinson, 156 F.2d 519 (5th Cir. 1946).
150. *Cf. Dugas*, 300 U.S. 414; Montgomery Ward & Co. v. Fid. & Deposit Co., 162 F.2d 264 (7th Cir. 1947); *Glasell-Taylor & Robinson*, 156 F.2d 519; Pa. Fire Ins. Co. v. Am. Airlines, Inc., 189 F. Supp. 239 (E.D.N.Y. 1960).

liable for the exemplary damages imposed for the misdeeds of the guilty fiduciary because they do not represent actual loss to the estate.[151]

10. Special Coverage Issues

a. Coverage for Unpaid Obligations to Creditors of the Estate. A fiduciary is not personally liable for a failure on the part of the estate to pay the debts of the protected person that preexisted the creation of the estate unless nonpayment results from negligence or other breach of fiduciary duty on the part of the fiduciary.[152] Similarly, neither a conservator nor its surety should be liable for unpaid debts incurred after the estate is established unless the inability to pay these debts arises as a result of a breach of fiduciary duty.[153] In jurisdictions that afford standing to an estate's unpaid creditors to assert a bond claim, the surety may be liable to an unpaid creditor to the extent that the fiduciary's failure to pay a debt arises out of its failure to properly marshal or manage the assets and potential assets of the estate.[154]

b. Coverage for Failure to Timely Secure Medicaid Eligibility. Due to their cognitive disabilities, a fair proportion of protected persons in conservatorships or guardianships may require institutional care, often in nursing homes or like facilities. Because custodial care costs are so substantial, the protected person's income may not be sufficient to pay the nursing home bills and the fiduciary in many circumstances may exhaust all of the estate's assets though the protected person continues to need custodial care. When these assets are exhausted, it may be necessary for the protected person to qualify for assistance under the

151. Mitchell v. McGuire, 12 So. 2d 180, 181 (Ala. 1943); Ames v. Comm'r of Motor Vehicles, 839 A.2d 1250, 1257–58 (Conn. 2004); *In re* Est. of Gladstone, 814 S.E.2d 1, 3–4 (Ga. 2018); Koch v. Merchants Mut. Bonding Co., 507 P.2d 189, 195 (Kan. 1973); C & I Steel, LLC v. Travelers Cas. & Sur. Co. of Am., 876 N.E.2d 442, 446–47 n.7 (Mass. App. Ct. 2007); N.H. Ins. Co. v. Gruhn, 670 P.2d 941, 943 (Nev. 1983).

152. *See* Brown v. Eggleston, 2 A. 321, 323 (Conn. 1885); Brockelman v. W. Sur. Co., No. CV950258, 2000 WL 1273438, at *7 (Mass. Sup. Ct. June 6, 2000); McIntire v. Cottrell, 69 N.E. 1091, 1092 (Mass. 1904); Potter v. Cummings, 18 Me. 55 (1841).

153. *In re* Ewanicky, No. 81742, 2003 WL 21469181, at *2 (Ohio Ct. App. June 26, 2003). *See* cases cited *supra* note 136.

154. *See* Jewish Home for the Elderly v. Cantore, 778 A.2d 93 (Conn. 2001); *Ewanicky*, 2003 WL 21469181, at *2.

government's Medicaid program in order to fund these costs. Where the protected person is subject to a conservatorship, the conservator may be the only party having the right to file a Medicaid application on the part of a protected person.[155]

The application process for Medicaid assistance is complicated, tedious, and confusing. Even persons who have extensive experience with the application process may find the process bewildering under certain circumstances. Where errors are made in the application process or the applicant makes a judgment as to how to proceed that later is deemed incorrect by the program, coverage under Medicaid may not be afforded for all of the unpaid bills owed to the custodial caregiver and the estate will be without assets to fund this obligation since spending down assets is a prerequisite to applying for coverage. In some circumstances, nursing homes have asserted claims under probate bonds claiming to be creditors of the estate with a right to recover for these unreimbursed charges.[156] Nursing home claimants can differentiate themselves from other creditors for purposes of a bond claim, noting that the administrator's failure to provide and pay a safe and appropriate living environment for the protected person constitutes a breach of the fiduciary duty owing to the protected person.[157]

In some jurisdictions, the courts have recognized that a nursing home can assert a cause of action under a probate bond where the protected person is not timely admitted into the Medicaid program with a resulting gap in payment to the nursing home.[158] Other jurisdictions have refused to recognize such a cause of action under a bond.[159] However, even where this cause of action is recognized, neither the fiduciary nor the surety is strictly liable for a gap in coverage for nursing home payments and liability under the bond only arises if the fiduciary acted negligently in either applying for benefits or failing to timely apply.[160]

---

155. *In re* Restaino, 950 N.Y.S.2d 687 (N.Y. Sup. Ct. 2012). *See* State v. Tarcha, 207 A.2d 72, 74 (Conn. Cir. Ct. 1964).
156. *See Cantore*, 778 A.2d 93; *Ewanicky*, 2003 WL 21469181, at *2.
157. *Cantore*, 778 A.2d 93; *Ewanicky*, 2003 WL 21469181, at *2.
158. *See* cases cited *supra* note 156.
159. *In re* Guardianship of Minnick, No. 64874 (Minn. Prob. Ct. July 16, 1981).
160. *See* Gardner Heights Health Care Ctr. v. Korolyshun, No. CV064024480, 2008 WL 907511, at *3–4 (Conn. Super. Ct. Mar. 17, 2008) (holding that, where the fiduciary made reasonable but unsuccessful efforts to collect the information necessary to complete a Medicaid application, a nursing

c. Coverage for Losses Arising as a Result of the Negligence of the Fiduciary's Counsel or Accountant. Courts readily acknowledge the need for fiduciaries to enlist the assistance of professionals to advise and execute any number of the duties that the fiduciary is required to perform.[161] A lay fiduciary may employ an attorney to help navigate the probate process or handle purchase and sale transactions,[162] or litigation involving the estate.[163] A fiduciary may retain an accountant to assist with tax returns or accountings.[164] A fiduciary may retain an accountant or lawyer to file and oversee a Medicaid application.[165] If the professional's work product for the estate falls below the standard of care and the estate or some other party sustains a resulting loss, a question may arise as to whether the fiduciary or the probate bond should be held liable for the professional's lack of care.[166]

The courts generally do not impose liability on a fiduciary or its surety for the negligence of the estate's professionals so long as the fiduciary exercised due care in selecting the professional, there was no misconduct on the part of the fiduciary in hiring the professional, the fiduciary properly supervised the professional and did not surrender control of the estate to the professional, and there was no collusion, negligence, or inattention on the part of the fiduciary.[167]

---

home had no claim under the bond for gap in coverage as a result of delays in the filing of the Medicaid application).

161. Est. of Barbikas, 341 P.2d 32, 37 (Cal. Ct. App. 1959); McClure v. Middletown Tr. Co., 110 A. 838, 840 (Conn. 1920). *See* RESTATEMENT (THIRD) OF TRUSTS § 80 (AM. L. INST. 2007).
162. *Barbikas*, 341 P.2d 32; *In re* Est. of Rosenthal, 189 So. 2d 507 (Fla. Dist. Ct. App. 1966).
163. Murdock v. Murdock, 370 So. 2d 290 (Ala. 1979); People *ex rel.* Rotchford v. Rotchford, 1 N.E.2d 249 (Ill. App. Ct. 1936).
164. Wohl v. Lewy, 505 So. 2d 525 (Fla. Dist. Ct. App. 1987); Jewish Hosp. v. Boatman's Nat'l Bank, 633 N.E.2d 1267 (Ill. App. Ct. 1994).
165. *Cf. supra* text accompanying notes 153–157.
166. *See generally* Howard J. Alperin, Annotation, *Liability of Executor or Administrator, or His Bond, for Loss Caused to Estate by Act or Default of His Agent or Attorney*, 28 A.L.R. 3d 1191 (1969).
167. *See Murdock*, 370 So. 2d at 292–93; *Barbikas*, 341 P.2d at 37; Laramore v. Laramore, 64 So. 2d 662, 666–68 (Fla. 1953); *Wohl*, 505 So. 2d 525; *Rosenthal*, 189 So. 2d 507; *In re* Est. of Heller, 401 N.W.2d 602, 609–10 (Iowa Ct. App. 1986); Christy v. McBride, 2 Ill. 75 (1832); *In re* Hartzell's Will, 192 N.E.2d 697, 707–08 (Ill. App. Ct. 1963); *Rotchford*,

d. Coverage for Losses Incurred by Third Parties as a Result of an Administrator's Contract Breaches or Tortious Conduct. An administrator of a decedent estate may incur financial obligations in the course of estate administration. These may include charges owed to professionals such as lawyers and accountants for services provided to the estate. Less commonly, charges may arise in the course of the administration of an estate out of alleged wrongful conduct on the part of the administrator, such as if a third party alleges that it sustained personal injuries at real property owned by the estate due to alleged negligence in maintaining the property or if debts arise as a result of the administrator continuing the decedent's business operations.

The traditional rule at common law was that a probate estate or trust was not liable for torts committed by its administrator.[168] An estate or trust also was not liable for breaches of contracts entered into by its administrator.[169] Obligations incurred in the course of estate

1 N.E.2d 249; Kaufman v. Kaufman's Admin., 166 S.W.2d 860, 863–64 (Ky. 1942); Donaldson v. Allen, 81 S.W. 1151 (Mo. 1904); Julian v. Abbott, 73 Mo. 580 (1881); *In re* Hazeltine's Est., 182 A. 357, 359–61 (N.J. Eq. 1936); *In re* Sharp's Est., 48 A. 327 (N.J. Eq. 1901); Dodge v. Stickney, 62 N.H. 330 (1882); Christie v. Dold, 524 N.W.2d 866, 871–72 (S.D. 1994). *Compare* Est. of Guiol, 105 Cal. Rptr. 35, 38–39 (Cal. Ct. App. 1972) (imposing liability on the fiduciary for losses perpetuated by counsel where the fiduciary breached its duty to supervise counsel).

168. Herbert Chermside, Annotation, *Liability of Estate for Tort of Executor, Administrator, or Trustee*, 82 A.L.R. 3d § 2, at 892, 897 (1978). *See* Vance v. Est. of Myers, 494 P.2d 816 (Alaska 1972); Main v. Norman, 36 A.2d 256 (Conn. 1944); Christensen v. Frankland, 58 N.E.2d 289 (Ill. App. Ct. 1944); Jamison v. United Cigar Whelan Stores, 68 Pa. D. & C. 121 (C.P. Phila. Cnty. 1949); Prager v. Gordon, 78 Pa. Super. 76 (1921); Belvin's Ex'rs v. French, 3 S.E. 891 (Va. 1887); Massey v. Paine, 155 S.E. 658 (W. Va. 1930).

169. Burke v. Terry, 28 Conn. 414, 415–16 (1859); Tayler v. Mygatt, 26 Conn. 184, 190–91 (1857); Brickell v. McCaskill, 106 So. 470, 472 (Fla. 1925); Harrington v. Lord, 704 A.2d 1211 (Me. 1997); Jones v. Silsby, 61 A.2d 117, 119 (Me. 1948); Baker v. Moor, 63 Me. 443, 445–46 (1874); Reid v. Porter, 54 Mo. 265, 266–67 (1873); Hailey v. Wheeler, 49 N.C. 159, 161 (1856); *Christie*, 524 N.W.2d at 870–71; Merchants Nat'l Bank v. Weeks, 53 Vt. 115, 118–19 (1880). *See* Loomis v. Lupoli, No. NNHCV116018843S, 2012 WL 6785544, at *2–4 (Conn. Super. Ct. Dec. 10, 2012); DiFrancesca v. Rousseau, 36 Conn. Supp. 34 (1979); *In re* Barnes' Est., 20 Conn. Supp. 179 (1956).

administration were deemed to be the personal debt of the administrator.[170] Parties who provided services to the estate or who were otherwise injured by the actions of the administrator could recover solely against the administrator in his or her personal capacity.[171] Although third-party creditors could not claim against the estate for alleged losses incurred in the course of estate administration, the administrator could petition the court for reimbursement to the administrator out of the estate's assets for costs and exposures incurred by the administrator in the course of estate administration (at least to the extent that the administrator had acted in good faith and to further the interests of the estate) and any such costs, once approved, would be credited against the estate on interim or final accountings.[172]

In jurisdictions that do not allow third-party creditors to claim against the estate for tortious conduct or contract breaches incurred during estate administration, the scope of coverage afforded under the probate bond may be limited to the obligations that existed prior to the creation of the estate.[173]

The more recent commentaries have advocated departures from the traditional common law rule in favor of allowing third parties to sue an estate for the conduct of its administrators, particularly where the third parties are aware that the administrator was acting in a fiduciary capacity

---

170. *Main*, 36 A.2d 256; *Burke*, 28 Conn. at 415–16; *Tayler*, 26 Conn. at 190–91; *Brickell*, 106 So. at 472; *Christensen*, 58 N.E.2d 289; *Harrington*, 704 A.2d 1211; *Jones*, 61 A.2d at 119; *Baker*, 63 Me. at 445–46; *Reid*, 54 Mo. at 266–67; *Hailey*, 49 N.C. at 161; *Prager*, 78 Pa. Super. 76; *Christie*, 524 N.W.2d at 870–71; *Weeks*, 53 Vt. at 118–19. *See Loomis*, 2012 WL 6785544, at *2–4; *DiFrancesca*, 36 Conn. Supp. 34; *Barnes' Est.*, 20 Conn. Supp. 179.
171. *Main*, 36 A.2d 256; *Burke*, 28 Conn. at 415–16; *Tayler*, 26 Conn. at 190–91; *Brickell*, 106 So. at 472; *Christensen*, 58 N.E.2d 289; *Harrington*, 704 A.2d 1211; *Jones*, 61 A.2d at 119; *Baker*, 63 Me. at 445–46; *Reid*, 54 Mo. at 266–67; *Hailey*, 49 N.C. at 161; *Prager*, 78 Pa. Super. 76; *Christie*, 524 N.W.2d at 870–71; *Weeks*, 53 Vt. at 118–19. *See Loomis*, 2012 WL 6785544, at *2–4; *DiFrancesca*, 36 Conn. Supp. 34; *Barnes' Est.*, 20 Conn. Supp. 179.
172. Chermside, *supra* note 168, § 8. *See Vance*, 494 P.2d 816; *Loomis*, 2012 WL 6785544, at *2–4; *DiFrancesca*, 36 Conn. Supp. 34; *Barnes' Est.*, 20 Conn. Supp. 179; *Brickell*, 106 So. at 472; Smith v. Rizzuto, 276 N.W. 406 (Neb. 1937); Leigh v. Lockwood, 15 N.C. 577 (1834).
173. *Tayler*, 26 Conn. at 190–91; *Baker*, 63 Me. at 445–46.

and the estate was the intended beneficiary of the original transaction.[174] Either by statute or common law, many but not all jurisdictions have narrowed or abandoned the traditional rule and now allow third parties to sue an estate for the acts of its administrator in some or all circumstances.[175]

Allowing direct claims against an estate by third-party tort plaintiffs and creditors whose claims arise in the course of estate administration poses the possibility of expanding the pool of potential claims that can be asserted under a probate bond. As previously noted, the universe of claims compensable under a probate bond are typically limited to those that allege losses due to the administrator's breach of its fiduciary duty.[176] Arguably, an administrator does not owe a duty that is "fiduciary" in character to third-party creditors and tort complainants for obligations arising after the inception of the estate. However, to the extent that third parties can recover damages directly against the estate, the estate may be able to assert a claim against the probate bond by alleging that the administrator had breached a fiduciary duty to the estate by causing the estate to incur a loss through its exposure to claims asserted by third parties.

e. Coverage for Losses Arising from Holding or Selling Investments Owned by an Estate. As noted above, a fiduciary may be obligated to manage financial and other assets over an extended period of time.[177] To the extent that the assets are liquid, the fiduciary will be obligated in most states to follow modern investment principles as incorporated into the Uniform Prudent Investor Act or like statutes as enacted in the jurisdiction.[178] This will require, in part, establishing an appropriate

---

174. UNIF. PROB. CODE § 3-808 (UNIF. L. COMM'N amended 2010); RESTATEMENT (THIRD) OF TRUSTS § 105 (AM. L. INST. 2007). *See* BOGERT, *supra* note 4, §§ 712–713.

175. *Vance*, 494 P.2d 816 (tort action); Schumann v. Weathers, 643 So. 2d 690, 692 (Fla. Dist. Ct. App. 1994) (tort action); Robinson v. Lindsey, 195 S.E. 917 (Ga. Ct. App. 1938) (contract action); Silvey v. Rosenauer, 814 S.W.2d 680, 681–82 (Mo. Ct. App. 1991) (tort action); Khan v. Regions Bank, 572 S.W. 3d 189 (Tenn. Ct. App. 2018) (contract/statutory tort action). For a list of statutes and cases that have modified the traditional common law rule in whole or in part, see BOGERT, *supra* note 4, § 712.

176. *See* cases cited *supra* note 67.

177. *See supra* text accompanying notes 48–60.

178. Uniform Prudent Investor Act (1995). The pertinent provisions of this act are summarized in the text accompanying notes 48–60. These provisions

investment plan based on a determination of the levels of risk and return appropriate for the estate's assets.[179] Under all circumstances, the fiduciary is not an insurer or guarantor of anticipated investment outcomes and its duty is limited to acting reasonably consistent with the operative standard of care.[180]

A determination of whether a fiduciary breached the Uniform Prudent Investor Act or its local variants must be based on the facts known to the fiduciary as of the time that the investment decisions under challenge were made and not based on hindsight or on how the investment performed.[181] Whether or not a fiduciary's investment decisions violate a duty depends on the unique facts and needs of the particular protected person and the nature of the investment plan that makes sense in light of those needs.[182] For example, the failure of a conservator to diversify the assets of the ward's portfolio does not in and of itself constitute a breach of fiduciary duty.[183] A fiduciary is also not absolutely precluded from holding, or even making, speculative investments, provided the circumstances surrounding the portfolio make it prudent to do so.[184]

---

include requirements that the fiduciary must generally implement an individualized investment plan for the estate and diversify the estate's assets. *Id.*

179. *Id.*

180. *See* cases cited *supra* notes 85–88.

181. *In re* Conservatorship of J.R., 252 P.3d 163, 171 (Mont. 2011); *Matter of* Tr. of Charlotte P. Hyde, 845 N.Y.S.2d 833, 835–36 (App. Div. 2007); Est. of Knipp, 414 A.2d 1007, 1009 (Pa. 1980); Baker v. Boyer Nat'l Bank, 719 P.2d 583, 587–88 (Wash. Ct. App. 1986).

182. *See In re* Conservatorship of Anderson, No. A-05-134, 2006 WL 327853, at *10–12 (Neb. Ct. App. Feb. 14, 2006).

183. *In re* Wellington Trs., 18 N.Y.S.3d 582 (Surr. Ct. 2015); *Tr. of Charlotte P. Hyde*, 845 N.Y.S.2d at 835–36; Brackett v. Tremaine (*In re* Tr. Created by Inman), 693 N.W.2d 514, 520–21 (Neb. 2005); Puhl v. U.S. Bank, N.A., 34 N.E.3d 530, 534–35 (Ohio Ct. App. 2015); *Knipp*, 414 A.2d at 1009; Glass v. Suntrust Bank, 523 S.W.3d 61, 68 (Tenn. Ct. App. 2016); *Baker*, 719 P.2d at 587–88. *See* cases cited *supra* note 51. *See also* Wood v. U.S. Bank, N.A., 828 N.E.2d 1072, 1079 (Ohio Ct. App. 2005) (noting that there is a mandatory duty to diversify in the absence of special circumstances regarding the beneficiaries or language in a trust or will explicitly authorizing a nondiverse portfolio).

184. *See* State v. Morgan Stanley & Co., 459 S.E.2d 906, 916–17 (W. Va. 1995) (whether investments are improper "speculation" is measured against what a prudent investor would do under the circumstances). *Compare*

f. Coverage for Losses Incurred by a Fiduciary in Operating a Business for the Estate. A decedent may own a business at the time of his or her death or a ward may own a business at the time that he or she is made subject to a conservatorship. As with all assets of the estate, the administrator's principal duty is generally to preserve the value of an estate's assets and not to invest those assets for further growth.[185] This poses the question of whether an estate can continue to operate the business and, if so, for what period of time.

In many jurisdictions, a fiduciary may not continue to operate a ward's or decedent's business without the consent of the court unless such authority is express on the face of a will or trust document.[186] Courts have permitted an estate to own and operate a business on an interim basis if ownership is consistent with the overall investment plan of the estate and does not prejudice the flow of income needed by the protected person.[187] In some jurisdictions, a fiduciary may be permitted to operate the business for a limited period of time after appointment without express judicial consent in order to wind the business down in an orderly fashion for the benefit of the estate.[188]

If a conservatorship or a decedent estate incurs a loss as a result of a fiduciary operating a business without authority from the court to do so, recovery for the loss may be available against the administrator to the

---

Appeal of Matthews, 57 A. 694, 697 (Conn. 1904) (administrator liable for losses on speculative investments that should have been settled at outset of estate).

185. Est. of Baldwin, 442 A.2d 529, 532–36 (Me. 1982).

186. *See* Pearce v. Pearce, 74 So. 952 (Ala. 1917); Graybar Elec. Co. v. McClave, 371 P.2d 350, 351–52 (Ariz. 1962); State *ex rel.* Raskin v. Schachat, 180 A. 502 (Conn. 1935); *In re* Blaszkiewicz' Est., 227 N.Y.S.2d 785, 788 (Surr. Ct. 1962); Sudnick v. Klein, No. 2001-G-2356, 2002 WL 31895117, at *5 (Ohio Ct. App. Dec. 31, 2002); Richland Cnty. Bar Ass'n v. Gibson, 654 N.E.2d 1247 (Ohio 1965); Lucht v. Behrens, 28 Ohio St. 231, 236–38 (1876); *In re* Kurkowski's Est., 409 A.2d 357, 360–61 (Pa. 1979).

187. *See Raskin*, 180 A. 502; Guerra v. Guerra, No. 04-10-00271, 2011 WL 3715051, at *3–4 (Tex. App. 2011). *But* see *Sudnick*, 2002 WL 31895117, at *5 (holding an executor who operated the deceased's business for six years liable for decrease in value of business that should have been wound up and sold within one month of opening of estate).

188. *McClave*, 371 P.2d at 351–52; *Raskin*, 180 A. 502; *Blaszkiewicz' Est.*, 227 N.Y.S.2d at 788; *Kurkowski's Est.*, 409 A.2d at 360–61.

extent that the estate's assets and the interests of heirs, beneficiaries, or the ward in these assets have been impaired by the fiduciary's ultra vires conduct.[189] An administrator may also be exposed to liability for losses incurred in operating a business to the extent that the administrator is an employee, officer, or investor in the business or otherwise personally benefits from the business or a concentration of the estate's assets in a single business entity violates the administrator's duties under the Uniform Prudent Investor Act or similar state statutes.[190]

Operation of a business by an administrator, even with the required court approval, may pose financial risks to the estate. There may be commercial obligations and disputes that generate claims and litigation.[191] Personal injury claims may arise in the course of business operations.[192] Disputes may be generated if an administrator rents real property to third-party tenants.[193] There should be no coverage for such third-party claims under a probate bond because whatever duty is owed to a personal injury plaintiff or a commercial party is not "fiduciary" in character.[194]

Moreover, there also should not be bond coverage in jurisdictions that subscribe to the traditional rule under which liability for these third-party exposures is imposed solely on the administrator in its personal capacity and not with the estate.[195] However, to the extent that a jurisdiction allows a third-party claimant to sue the estate directly and the estate incurs a loss, the estate may seek to recover the loss through

---

189. *Blaszkiewicz' Est.*, 227 N.Y.S.2d at 788; *Sudnick*, 2002 WL 31895117, at *5; *Kurkowski's Est.*, 409 A.2d at 360–61.

190. *In re* Guardianship of Styer, 536 P.2d 717, 721 (Ariz. Ct. App. 1975); *In re* Wedge Tr., No. 271244, 2018 WL 2439904, at *3, *5 (Mich. Ct. App. June 17, 2008).

191. *See supra* text accompanying notes 169–176.

192. *See* Vance v. Est. of Myers, 494 P.2d 816 (Alaska 1972); Belvin's Ex'rs v. French, 3 S.E. 891 (Va. 1887); Massey v. Payne, 155 S.E. 658 (W. Va. 1930).

193. Christensen v. Frankland, 58 N.E.2d 289 (Ill. App. Ct. 1944); Prager v. Gordon, 78 Pa. Super. 76 (1921).

194. Lori-Kay Golf, Inc. v. Lassner, 460 N.E.2d 1097 (N.Y. 1984);Lawton v. Bank of Am. Corp., No. 07-239S, 2007 WL 4480222, at *3 (D.R.I. Dec. 17, 2007). *See* CONN. GEN. STATS. ANN. §§ 45a-139(a), 499o(A)(1) (West 2021); OHIO. REV. CODE ANN. § 2109.04(A)(1) (West 2021); 33 R.I. GEN. LAWS ANN. § 33-17-2 (West 2021).

195. Tayler v. Mygatt, 26 Conn. 184, 190–91 (1857); Baker v. Moor, 63 Me. 443, 445–46 (1874).

a bond claim, arguing that the administrator's conduct in relation to the loss breached the administrator's fiduciary duty to the estate. The outcome of any such claim may depend on whether the administrator's conduct was in fact wrongful to the estate or whether the loss was of a kind that reasonably should have been anticipated to occur in the course of the ongoing business operations that presumably provided an overall financial benefit to the estate.

D. Procedural Issues and Defenses

1. Life of a Typical Probate Bond Claim

While different jurisdictions, and even individual probate courts, may have unique rules and procedures for handling probate bond claims, there tends to be a common general life cycle for probate bond claims. The process usually begins when someone with an interest in the estate—a beneficiary, a ward's family member, a creditor, or even the probate court itself—discovers or suspects that a breach of duty has occurred.[196] This interested person may take a number of different steps at this point, including making a demand for an accounting and applying to the probate court for removal of the fiduciary and appointment of a successor. Once there is evidence that a breach of duty has occurred and the estate has suffered a loss as a result, or there has been an actual determination that the estate sustained a loss because of a breach by the principal, an interested person may apply for recovery on the probate bond or for a surcharge against the bond.[197] Typically, the surety will receive notice of this application and be given an opportunity to appear at the hearing on the application and present a defense.[198] There also usually is a period in which an appeal can be taken from a decree by the court ordering payment from the surety.[199] As the bond principal could appeal the decree, the practice of many sureties who do not intend to appeal the probate court's decision is to wait until this appeal period has

---

196. *See supra* text accompanying notes 89–98.
197. *See supra* text accompanying notes 67–74.
198. *See infra* text accompanying notes 203–210, 219–220.
199. *See, e.g.*, CONN. GEN. STAT. § 45a-186 (2021) (allowing appeal to superior court); GA. CODE ANN. § 15-9-123 (West 2021) (allowing appeal to supreme or appellate court); MICH. COMP. LAWS ANN. § 600.308 (West 2021) (allowing appeal to circuit court).

passed before paying any amount to the estate in case another party files an appeal.

In some states, those with standing to make a probate bond claim may decide to bypass the probate court and bring a lawsuit against the surety on the bond.[200] In other states, the bringing of a lawsuit requires permission from the probate court.[201]

Sometimes it is in the best interests of all the parties to resolve the bond claim by settling the claim. Because the probate court has the ultimate responsibility for the estate, it is typical that the probate court must approve any compromise or settlement of a claim relating to the estate.[202]

If the bond claim exhausts the penal sum, the surety should seek a formal release of the bond from the probate court. If the claim does not exhaust the penal sum, the bond may need to stay in place until a final accounting is approved, and the surety may remain exposed to other claims up to the penal sum of the bond. When there is a settlement of a claim, the surety may be able to negotiate a full release of the bond, even if some of the penal sum remains and the estate is not yet closed.

2. Ripeness

In some jurisdictions, a judicial determination of the fiduciary's liability or a finding of a deficiency is a precondition to the assertion of a bond claim and to the attachment of liability under the bond.[203] In other states,

---

200. *See, e.g.*, CONN. GEN. STAT. § 45a-144 (2021) (allowing person aggrieved by breach of probate bond to bring action in superior court or apply to probate court for recovery).
201. *See, e.g.*, VT. STAT. ANN. tit. 14, § 2108 (West 2021) (requiring probate court for certain bond claim suits to be brought in court); WIS. STAT. ANN. § 878.07(2) (West 2021) (same).
202. Ark. Dep't of Hum. Servs. v. Est. of Hogan, 858 S.W.2d 105, 107 (Ark. 1993); McMann v. Gen. Accident Assurance Corp., 267 N.W. 601 (Mich. 1936); Est. of Merry, 436 N.W.2d 421, 424 (Mich. Ct. App. 1989); Est. of Alexander, 634 N.E.2d 670, 676 (Ohio Ct. App. 1993); Busch v. Farmington Ctr. Beaverton, 124 P.3d 1282, 1285 (Or. Ct. App. 2005).
203. United States v. Westchester Fire. Ins. Co., 478 F.2d 133, 136–38 (2d Cir. 1973); Alexandrou v. Alexander, 112 Cal. Rptr. 307, 309–10 (Cal. Ct. App. 1974); Est. of Dwyer, 335 P.2d 718, 721–22 (Cal. Ct. App. 1959); Weihe v. Statham, 7 P. 143, 143 (Cal. 1885); Tudhope v. Potts, 51 N.W. 1110, 1111 (Mich. 1892); Jones v. Irvine, 23 Miss. 361, 365 (1852); State

the claimant is permitted to sue the principal and the surety in one action to determine the liability of each.[204] If a statute requires that a claim be presented against an estate before the estate is terminated, the failure to do so may bar relief against the surety.[205]

Regardless of whether a beneficiary or creditor can be joined as a party in an action to determine the fiduciary's liability, the surety should have the right to intervene in such proceeding. This right is particularly critical in jurisdictions where the surety is bound by the fact finding and judgment entered in an action against its principal.[206]

3. The Extent to Which the Surety Is Bound by Decisions Rendered Against Its Principal

Given that many jurisdictions do not allow a bond claim to made until *after* it is concluded that the fiduciary breached duties, it is entirely possible that a claimant may secure a judgment against the principal in a proceeding in which the surety is not a participant. This raises the question of whether the surety is bound by the findings of fact in that proceeding when there is a subsequent action on the bond. The answer may be found in how the doctrine of collateral estoppel is interpreted with respect to sureties.

Generally, a party and those with whom it is in privity are collaterally estopped from challenging findings of fact that have been actually litigated and decided and that are necessary to a judgment in a prior

---

ex rel. Scott v. State Farm Fire & Cas. Co., 947 S.W.2d 530, 534 (Mo. Ct. App. 1997); Howard v. Jeffrey, 268 P.2d 897, 899 (Okla. 1953); Griffith v. W. Sur. Co., 432 P.2d 1019, 1020 (Or. 1967); Werner v. Am. Sur. Co. of N.Y., 423 P.2d 86, 87–88 (Wyo. 1967).

204. Vargas v. Superior Ct. of Apache Cnty., 138 P.2d 287, 288 (Ariz. 1943); *Matter of* Est. of Dyniewicz, 648 N.E.2d 1076, 1084 (Ill. App. Ct. 1995); *In re* Grant, 381 N.E.2d 1348, 1353 (Ohio Ct. App. 1978). *See also* Simmons v. Harleysville Ins. Co., No. 4:18-cv-00055, 2021 WL 1947868 (S.D. Ga. May 14, 2021) (holding under Georgia law that an individual may only recover damages from a surety under a probate bond if the individual obtains a prior or contemporaneous judgment against the fiduciary).

205. Cuda v. Safeco Ins. Co. of Am., 882 F. Supp. 967, 971 (D. Or. 1995).

206. Est. of Davis, 268 Cal. Rptr. 384, 388–89 (Cal. Ct. App. 1990).

proceeding.[207] Some jurisdictions hold that a probate bond surety is in privity with its principal and is bound by findings of fact determined in a prior proceeding, regardless of whether the surety had notice and an opportunity to participate in the prior proceeding.[208] In other jurisdictions, a probate bond surety is not conclusively bound by the findings reached in a prior proceeding in which it did not participate unless it had notice and opportunity to participate in the proceeding.[209]

Some courts have decided that the text of the probate bond is the lodestar for determining whether or not the surety is bound by findings against the principal in a prior proceeding.[210] If the text of the bond indicates that the bonded obligation is solely to ensure the faithful performance of the principal's fiduciary duties, without explicitly obligating the surety to pay the damages and costs that may be recovered against the principal, a judgment against the principal may be treated as only prima facie evidence against a surety that did not have notice and an opportunity to participate in the proceedings brought against the principal.[211] However, if the bonded obligation is fairly interpreted as

---

207. *See* Aetna Cas. & Sur. Co. v. Jones, 596 A.2d 414, 421–25 (Conn. 1991); Commonwealth v. Holder, 805 A.2d 499, 502–05 (Pa. 2002); Christian v. Sizemore, 407 S.E.2d 715, 718–19 (W. Va. 1991).
208. Stovall v. Banks, 77 U.S. 583, 588 (1871); Wisniewski v. Travelers Cas. & Sur. Co., 390 F. App'x 153, 156 (3d Cir. 2010); Mass. Bonding & Ins. Co. v. Winters Nat'l Bank & Tr. Co. of Dayton, Ohio, 130 F.2d 5, 8–9 (6th Cir. 1942); Nat'l Sur. Corp. v. Ellison, 88 F.2d 399, 407 (8th Cir. 1937); Irwin v. Backus, 25 Cal. 214, 224 (1864); *In re* Est. of Holman, 250 N.W. 498, 499 (Iowa 1933); Nevitt v. Woodburn, 43 N.E. 385, 387 (Ill. 1895); Judge of Prob. v. Quimby, 36 A. 1049, 1050 (Me. 1897); Mitchell v. Columbia Cas. Co., 106 P.2d 344, 345 (Mont. 1940); Deobold v. Opperman, 19 N.E. 94 (N.Y. 1888); Boudinot v. Locust, 151 P. 579, 583 (Okla. 1915); Prob. Ct., Dist. of Lamoile v. Am. Fid. Co., 35 A.2d 495, 497 (Vt. 1944).
209. Hartford Fire Ins. Co. v. Est. of Sanders, 155 A.3d 915, 926–28 (Md. Ct. Spec. App. 2017) (noting that in the absence of a surety's receipt of prior notice and an opportunity to contest, a finding against a bond principal is prima facie but not conclusive evidence in subsequent litigation on a probate bond). *See also* C-E Bldg. Prods., Inc. v. Seal Rite Aluminum Prods., 316 A.2d 198, 199 (N.H. 1974); Cross v. Old Republic Sur. Co., 983 S.W.2d 771, 777 (Tex. App. 1998).
210. *In re* Geraerdts' Est., 231 N.Y.S.2d 692, 694 (Surr. Ct. 1962); Howze v. Sur. Corp. of Am., 584 S.W.2d 263, 265–66 (Tex. 1979); Goodwin v. Am. Sur. Co., 68 P.2d 619, 625 (Wash. 1937).
211. *Geraerdts' Est.*, 231 N.Y.S.2d at 694.

requiring the surety to be responsible for a judgment rendered against the principal, then the judgment may be conclusive against the surety even if the surety was not a party to the proceeding.[212]

Even where a surety is barred by res judicata or collateral estoppel principles from asserting its principal's defenses to a bond claim, the surety should not be precluded from asserting its own surety defenses, such as the scope of coverage afforded under the bond, which could not be asserted in prior proceedings where the surety was not a party.[213]

4. Whether a Probate Court's Approval of a Final Accounting Forecloses Further Claims Under a Probate Bond

In some cases, a claim is asserted against a probate bond surety after the bonded fiduciary's final accounting has been approved by the probate court, the appeal period has run, and the estate has been closed. These facts raise the question of whether the approval of the final accounting constitutes a bar against further claims under the probate bond.

Under the doctrine of res judicata, a final judgment bars further litigation against a party or those in privity with a party as to all matters that were litigated or could have been litigated in the prior proceeding.[214]

Applying res judicata principles, some courts have ruled that, in the absence of fraud or collusion, a probate court's approval of a final accounting constitutes a judicial finding that the fiduciary has properly performed and therefor bars further claims under a probate bond to the extent that the issues underlying the bond claim were or could have been litigated prior to the approval of the final accounting.[215] Since the surety is

---

212. *Id.*; *Howze*, 584 S.W.2d at 265–66; *Goodwin*, 68 P.2d at 625.
213. Higbee v. Am. Emps. Ins. Co., 278 N.W. 85, 87–88 (Mich. 1938).
214. Joe's Pizza, Inc. v. Aetna Life & Cas. Co., 675 A.2d 441, 446–47 (Conn. 1996); Desjardins v. Fontanella, No. CV135006229S, 2014 WL 4494414, at *3–4 (Conn. Super. Ct. July 30, 2014); First Nat'l Bank of Greenville v. U.S. Fid. & Guar. Co. 35 S.E.2d 47 (S.C. 1945).
215. Patterson v. Travelers Cas. & Sur. Co., 936 A.2d 241, 243 (Conn. App. Ct. 2007); *Desjardins*, 2014 WL 4494414, at *3–4; Gardner Heights Health Care Ctr. v. Korolyshun, No. CV064024480, 2008 WL 907511, at *3–4 (Conn. Super. Ct. Mar. 17, 2008); *In re* Wedge Tr., No. 271244, 2018 WL 2439904, at *2 (Mich. Ct. App. June 17, 2008). *See also* Winter v. Hope, 861 P.2d 1282, 1287 (Kan. 1993). *But see* Jewish Home for the Elderly v. Cantore, 901 A.2d 49 (Conn. App. Ct. 2006) (holding that a stipulated judgment in a collection action in favor of a nursing home and against the

in privity with the bond principal for purposes of claims on the bond, the applicability of res judicata as a defense should not depend on whether or not the surety was a party in the proceedings before the probate court.[216] However, res judicata may not be applicable as a defense to the extent that the facts underlying the bond claim could not reasonably have been subject to litigation prior to the approval of the final accounting or to the extent that the principal's fraud caused the probate court to approve the final accounting.[217]

Other courts have suggested that a probate court's approval of a final accounting may not be a bar to a claim subsequently asserted on a probate bond.[218]

5. Notice to the Surety

In the absence of statutory direction, notice to the surety is generally not a prerequisite to bringing suit on the bond or making application for recovery on the bond.[219] Some courts have held that a surety is presumptively aware of all orders entered in the settlement of the estate for which it has given a bond.[220]

6. Timing Issues Regarding the Claim: Statutes of Limitations and Laches

Not surprisingly, the limitations periods applicable to probate bond claims vary from jurisdiction to jurisdiction. Many jurisdictions have adopted specific statutes establishing a limitations period for probate

---

patient's conservator was not res judicata in the nursing home's action to recover on the conservator's probate bond; noting that although both actions sought to collect the debt owed by the conservator, the claims in each suit fundamentally differed as the collection action did not allege breach of fiduciary duty or breach of bond, and the surety was not in privity with conservator in the collection action).

216. *Id.* (all authorities in previous note). *See also* cases cited *supra* notes 168–175.

217. Alexandrou v. Alexander, 112 Cal. Rptr. 307, 314–15 (Cal. Ct. App. 1974).

218. Voss v. Budnik, 253 N.W. 270, 271 (Mich. 1934).

219. *See* Johnston v. Borders, 31 Ill. App. 426, 431–32 (1889).

220. *In re* Est. of Holman, 250 N.W. 498, 499 (Iowa 1933).

bond claims.[221] In other jurisdictions, the limitations period for probate bond claims is governed by a general statute applicable to certain classes of causes of action.[222] Jurisdictions vary greatly in the length of the limitations period applicable to claims or suits on surety bonds.[223] Another variable among the jurisdictions is the event that begins the running of the limitations period. In some states, the limitations period for bringing a suit on the probate bond begins to run when liability of the fiduciary is established by the appropriate judicial authority or the accrual of the cause of action on the bond.[224] In other states, the limitations period may begin to run upon the occurrence of other certain events set forth in the applicable statute, such as the date on which the principal is discharged, the date on which a court approves an interim accounting or the transactions performed by the bonded principal, or the date on which a court approves a final accounting for the estate.[225]

---

221. *See, e.g.*, CONN. GEN. STAT. ANN. § 52-579 (West 2021) (limitations period exclusively for probate bond claims); ME. REV. STAT. ANN. tit. 18-C, § 8-212 (West 2021); MASS. GEN. LAWS ANN. ch. 205, § 35 (West 2021); WIS. STAT. ANN. § 878.07 (West 2021); WYO. STAT. ANN. § 1-3-108 (West 2021).

222. *See* GA. CODE ANN. § 9-3-24 (West 2011) (general limitations statute for actions on a contract under seal); R.I. GEN. LAWS ANN. § 9-1-17 (West 2011) (limitations statute for contract under seal). *See also* Whelchel v. Haynes, 96 S.E. 568 (Ga. 1918).

223. *See, e.g.*, CONN. GEN. STAT. ANN. § 52-579 (West 2012) (six-year limitations period from the final settlement of account); MASS. GEN. LAWS ANN. ch. 205, § 35 (West 2012) (four-year limitations period from the date of discharge of the fiduciary, except if claimant is out of state, then within four years of claimant's return to state); 42 PA. CONS. STAT. § 5523 (West 2021) (one-year limitations period); TENN. CODE ANN. § 28-3-109(a)(2) (West 2021) (six-year limitations period beginning when cause of action accrues).

224. Warner v. First Nat'l Bank of Minneapolis, 236 F.2d 853, 860–61 (8th Cir. 1956); Lawton v. Bank of Am. Corp., No. 07-239S, 2007 WL 4480222, at *5 (D.R.I. Dec. 17, 2007); *In re* Est. of Bishop, No. 20102, 2004 WL 917693, at *4–5 (Ohio Ct. App. Apr. 30, 2004). *See* TENN. CODE ANN. § 28-3-109(a)(2) (West 2021) (six-year limitations period beginning when cause of action accrues).

225. CONN. GEN. STAT. ANN. § 52-579 (West 2021) (limitations period runs from the approval of a final accounting for the estate); MASS. GEN. LAWS ANN. ch. 205, § 35 (West 2021) (limitations period runs from date of discharge of guardian or conservator); MICH. COMP. LAWS ANN.

"Laches" is an equitable defense that may be properly asserted where there is an unreasonable and unexcused delay in the bringing of a bond claim, notwithstanding that the action is not barred by a statute of limitations, and the delay results in prejudice to the surety.[226] Prejudice will primarily take the form of the loss of evidence, and the unavailability of witnesses or even the principal himself or herself.

7. Equitable Defenses: Estoppel and Waiver

Like laches, estoppel and waiver are also equitable defenses that may be available to the probate bond surety in certain circumstances. A surety may be able to raise the defense of equitable estoppel claiming that, based upon the actions of the claimant, it would be unfair to hold the surety liable for damages. The elements of a successful equitable estoppel defense are that the surety reasonably relied upon statements or actions of the claimant and suffered a detriment as a result.[227] In some jurisdictions, the defense of equitable estoppel may not be allowed against a ward or a minor beneficiary.[228]

8. Surety's Standing to File Accounting

A principal may be unwilling or unable to submit a final accounting to the court for approval or otherwise document and prove to the probate court the legitimate uses of estate funds during his or her tenure. Some states will allow the surety to submit proof of the proper use of the estate assets

---

§ 700.3606(f) (West 2021) (limitations period for suit on bond expires same time as for action against principal); MISS. CODE ANN. § 15-1-27 (West 2021) (actions by ward on guardian's bond must be commenced within five years of ward reaching age of 21); WIS. STAT. ANN. § 878.07(3) (West 2021) (limitations period runs from the date of the fiduciary's discharge).

226. Wallace v. Swepston, 86 S.W. 398, 400 (Ark. 1905); Crumrine v. Dizdar, 140 P.2d 101, 106 (Cal. Ct. App. 1943); State v. Northrop, 106 A. 504, 507 (Conn. 1919); Sweet v. Lowry, 142 N.W. 882, 883 (Minn. 1913); *Est. of Bishop*, 2004 WL 917693, at *6; Lyerly v. Yeadon, 19 S.E.2d 648, 654 (S.C. 1942). *Cf.* Est. of Mason, 274 Cal. Rptr. 61, 65 (Cal. Ct. App. 1990).

227. State Tr. & Sav. Bank v. Otero, 252 P. 167, 169 (N.M. 1926).

228. *Matter of* Est. of O'Leary, 508 N.Y.S.2d 330, 331 (App. Div. 1986).

in order to minimize its exposure under the probate bond.[229] In other jurisdictions, only the principal has standing to file an accounting.[230] The question seems to remain open whether such a lack of standing would prevent the surety from being able to submit proof of the legitimacy of estate expenditures or the amount of estate's assets under the control of a successor administrator in order to reduce the amount due under the bond. A surety's inability to file a final accounting would be particularly unfair if there was a corresponding presumption that, absent a final accounting, any assets listed on the initial inventory not located or accounted for by the successor fiduciary would be a loss to the estate that could be charged to the surety.[231]

9. Setoffs

The remedy afforded by a probate bond is intended to place the claimant in the position it would have been in absent the principal's breach of duty.[232] Based on this proposition, a surety may be able to claim a right to set off against an alleged loss certain of its principal's claims against the estate.

To the extent that the principal is entitled to a distribution from the estate as a beneficiary or heir, a surety may have an argument for a setoff of the property interest of the principal against the losses incurred by the estate as a result of the principal's breaches of duty.[233] Where the surety pays the estate's losses, it is arguably subrogated to the estate's setoff rights against the principal and the estate is obligated to assert these

---

229. Fid. & Deposit Co. v. Schelper, 83 S.W. 871, 872–73 (Tex. Civ. App. 1904).
230. Ins. Co. of N. Am. v. Dragat, 332 A.2d 103, 105 (Conn. 1973).
231. *Cf.* Blakeman v. Sherwood, 32 Conn. 324, 330 (1865). *But see* State *ex rel.* Raskin v. Schachat, 180 A. 502, 505 (Conn. 1935) (noting that the magnitude of recovery under a probate bond should be limited to the amount necessary to put the estate and protected parties in the position that they would have been in but for the alleged breach of fiduciary duty); Edwards v. White, 12 Conn. 28, 37 (1837) (same).
232. *Raskin*, 180 A. at 505; *Edwards*, 12 Conn. at 37.
233. Am. Sur. Co. of N.Y. v. City of Akron, 95 F.2d 966, 969–70 (6th Cir. 1938).

setoff rights in order to mitigate the surety's losses.[234] However, some courts have determined that a surety's claimed setoff must fail for lack of mutuality of obligation; the action on the bond is brought on behalf of the estate, not on behalf of a particular beneficiary against whom the surety may have a claim.[235] A claim of setoff may be further complicated if the principal has sought bankruptcy protection, as the bankruptcy laws provide that any inheritance obtained within six months of the bankruptcy immediately vests in the bankruptcy trustee.[236]

If there are unpaid bond premiums owing to the surety, the surety should be entitled to a setoff for that amount to avoid a windfall to the estate.[237]

A principal, even one who has breached fiduciary obligations, may sometimes use his or her own assets to pay an estate's obligations as a matter of convenience or because the estate is experiencing temporary cash flow problems. Under these circumstances, the surety should be entitled to a credit for these contributions so that the estate is not afforded a windfall.[238]

There is a split among the jurisdictions as to whether the surety is entitled to a setoff equal to the administration fees that would have been owing to the principal for work but for his or her misconduct. In what seems to be the better reasoned view, some courts allow the surety and the principal to set off against the debt owed to the estate the fees to which the principal would have been entitled for services validly performed on behalf of the estate.[239] This view embraces the principle that the remedy under a probate bond is limited to putting the estate in the position it

---

234. *Id.* ("The surety can avail itself of whatever right the principal has, including that of set-off."). *See also generally* Transamerica Ins. Co. v. United States, 989 F.2d 1188 (Fed. Cir. 1993).

235. *Matter of* Guardianship of Middleton, No. 75 C. A. 47, 1976 WL 188516, at *2 (Ohio Ct. App. Feb. 4, 1976). *See also* Miller v. Bellamore Armored Car & Equip. Co., 86 A. 13, 13–14 (Conn. 1913); Yale New Haven Hosp. v. Orlins, No. CV6-10396, 1992 WL 110707, at *2 (Conn. Super. Ct. May 11, 1992).

236. *Middleton*, 1976 WL 188516, at *3. *But see In re* Booker's Est., 91 N.Y.S.2d 16, 17–18 (Surr. Ct. 1949) (allowing setoff where beneficiary who brought claim against surety also was indemnitor).

237. *Cf.* W. Sur. Co. v. Wilson, 484 S.W.2d 45, 48–49 (Tenn. Ct. App. 1972).

238. *See In re* Stewart's Est., 28 P.2d 642, 644 (Or. 1934).

239. *See In re* Est. of Bartlett, 680 P.2d 369, 378 (Okla. 1984); Lindseth v. Burkhart, 871 S.W.2d 693, 694–95 (Tenn. Ct. App. 1993).

would have been in absent a breach of duty. Other courts have held that a fiduciary who breaches duties is not entitled to any fees for services to the estate.[240] This outcome seems to result in a windfall to the estate, especially where the fiduciary actually performed his or her duties to the estate. Further, a judgment against the surety for this amount seems to impose a penalty on the surety and is therefore at odds with the concept that a surcharge on the bond is not intended to be punitive.[241]

E. Damages

1. Compensatory Damage Components

In general, a probate bond surety is liable to the estate for damages incurred as a result of the principal's negligence or breach of fiduciary duty, up to the penal sum of the bond.[242] In other words, the surety is obligated to put the estate or other proper claimant in the position it would have been in had the principal's breach not occurred.[243] The most straightforward example of damages are those that are equal to an amount of money misappropriated from the estate or improperly distributed. However, claims for damages to estates can be more complicated and may include lost interest or earnings when estate funds were not properly invested or diminution in value when real estate or business holdings are not sold at an appropriate and reasonable time and subsequently decline in value.[244]

---

240. Lowinger v. Herlihy, 472 N.E.2d 676, 679 (Mass. App. Ct. 1985).
241. *See* United Pac. Ins. Co. v. Berryhill, 620 So. 2d 1077, 1079 (Fla. Dist. Ct. App. 1993); Koch v. Merchants Mut. Bonding Co., 507 P.2d 189, 195 (Kan. 1973).
242. *See, e.g.*, Est. of Lindberg, 424 N.E.2d 1161, 1164 (Ill. App. Ct. 1981); Hamilton v. Mercantile Bank of Cedar Rapids, 621 N.W.2d 401, 406 (Iowa 2001); Est. of Wilde, 708 A.2d 273, 276 (Me. 1998); *In re* Testamentary Tr. of Hamm, 707 N.E.2d 524, 529 (Ohio Ct. App. 1997).
243. *See, e.g., Est. of Lindberg*, 424 N.E.2d at 1164; *Hamilton*, 621 N.W.2d at 406; *Est. of Wilde*, 708 A.2d at 276; *Testamentary Tr. of Hamm*, 707 N.E.2d at 529.
244. *See, e.g., In re* Dorson, 934 A.2d 545, 549–50 (N.H. 2007) (administrator liable for the appreciation that would have been earned if stolen funds had been properly invested); Sudnick v. Klein, No. 2001-G-2356, 2002 WL 31895117, at *5 (Ohio Ct. App. Dec. 31, 2002) (executor liable for decrease in value of business that should have been wound up and sold within one month of opening of estate); Appeal of Matthews, 57

Not all losses are the result of a breach by the fiduciary, and the surety should not be held liable for a loss that would have occurred even in the absence of wrongful conduct by the principal.[245] For example, a surety is not liable for losses to an estate to the extent those losses could have been caused by a different fiduciary, such as a successor fiduciary.[246] A surety is not liable for an unpaid debt of the fiduciary to the estate if the fiduciary was insolvent throughout the term of the estate.[247] A surety is not liable to a creditor for damages if there was no money legally available in the estate to pay that creditor until after the bond term expired.[248]

It is often true that the liability of the surety is coextensive with that of the principal for losses sustained by the estate up to the penal sum of the bond.[249] Sometimes the liability of the principal may exceed that of the surety.[250] For example, in a state that has a remedial statute that awards double damages for embezzlement from a decedent's or conserved person's estate, the surety is not liable for the punitive damages assessed against the principal.[251] A surety's liability may be less than that of its principal due to the scope of coverage afforded under the bond or the operative effect of various surety defenses.[252] A principal also may be liable for actions taken outside of his or her bonded capacity, such as actions taken in a unbonded prior fiduciary capacity or as a consequence of having the estate wrongfully assume control of non-estate property.[253]

A. 694, 697 (Conn. 1904) (administrator liable for losses on speculative investments that should have been settled at outset of estate).

245. *See, e.g.*, State *ex rel.* Raskin v. Schachat, 180 A. 502, 505 (Conn. 1935).
246. Laws. Sur. Corp. v. Whitehead, 719 So. 2d 833, 837 (Ala. 1998).
247. Md. Cas. Co. v. McCormack, 488 S.W.2d 347, 350 (Ky. 1972); *In re* Shaefitz Will, 160 N.Y.S.2d 698, 701 (Surr. Ct. 1957).
248. *See* King v. Jones, 971 S.W.2d 916, 922 (Mo. Ct. App. 1998).
249. *See* Lyerly v. Yeadon, 19 S.E.2d 648, 657 (S.C. 1942); Fid. & Deposit Co. of Md. v. Meldrum, 50 P.2d 570, 573 (Ariz. 1935).
250. Koch v. Merchants Mut. Bonding Co., 507 P.2d 189, 192 (Kan. 1973).
251. *Id.*
252. *See supra* text accompanying notes 89–194, 200–235.
253. *See supra* text accompanying notes 98–110, 134–135.

2. *Interest*

Most jurisdictions will allow for the recovery of interest on sums owed by the surety under the bond up to the penal sum.[254] There is a split among the jurisdictions regarding when interest begins to accrue on the surety's obligation to the estate. Some states adopt the "general rule" that interest begins to accrue against the surety on the entry of judgment against the principal.[255] Other jurisdictions compute interest beginning from the date the surety is notified of a breach or demand.[256] There is at least one jurisdiction that has held the surety liable for interest starting with the date of the breach, regardless of whether the surety had notice of the breach or potential claim.[257]

3. *Attorneys' Fees and Costs of Bond Recovery*

Investigating the actions of a fiduciary and pursuing a claim against a probate bond can be expensive. In some smaller estates, the legal costs associated with probate bond claims can eat up a significant portion of the estate itself. Successor fiduciaries will typically attempt to collect attorneys' fees in addition to the amount of any deficiency found in the estate.

Most jurisdictions follow the so-called "American rule" with respect to the recovery of attorneys' fees incurred in litigation. Under this rule, the prevailing party may collect attorneys' fees from the losing party only if the award of fees is specifically provided for in statute or contract.[258] Thus, if a bond or the statute requiring the bond authorizes the recovery

---

254. *See, e.g.*, *In re* Pacheco, 199 P.3d 676, 685 (Ariz. Ct. App. 2008); Est. of Tighe v. Prob. Appeal, No. CV-93-0130993-S, 1994 WL 131125 (Conn. Super. Ct. Apr. 5, 1994); Am. Fid. Co. v. Barnard, 181 A.2d 628, 633 (N.H. 1962); *In re* Davison, 642 P.2d 1259, 1261 (Wash. Ct. App. 1982). *See supra* text accompanying notes 138–139.
255. *Pacheco*, 199 P.3d at 685; Polk v. Am. Cas. Co. of Reading, Pa., 816 S.W.2d 178, 180 (Ky. 1991); *Barnard*, 181 A.2d at 633.
256. Burns v. Mass. Bonding & Ins. Co., 146 P.2d 29, 30 (Cal. Ct. App. 1944); McCauley v. Am. Sur. Co., 263 P. 90, 93 (Mont. 1927); *Davison*, 642 P.2d at 1262 (citing Ill. Sur. Co. v. John Davis Co., 244 U.S. 376 (1917)).
257. *In re* Huerta, 41 P.3d 814, 823 (Kan. 2002).
258. *See, e.g.*, ACMAT Corp. v. Greater N.Y. Mut. Ins. Co., 923 A.2d 697, 702 (Conn. 2007); Biomass One, L.P. v. S-P Constr., 799 P.2d 152, 156 (Or. Ct. App. 1990); McMullen v. Kutz, 985 A.2d 769, 775 (Pa. 2009);

of attorneys' fees by claimants on the bond, the surety will be liable for those attorneys' fees.[259]

In most jurisdictions, the American rule does not apply to the recovery of attorneys' fees incurred by the plaintiff in dealing with parties other than the defendant as a result of the defendant's conduct. Fees incurred for reasons other than litigating with the defendant are treated as an element of consequential damages and are more freely recoverable than fees incurred in litigating against the defendant.[260] For instance, attorneys' fees may be awarded as one element of consequential damages against a surety where a probate estate has incurred attorneys' fees in investigating whether the original fiduciary should be removed, removing the original representative, or compelling the original representative to perform neglected duties.[261] However, if the fees would have been incurred by the estate in the absence of the alleged breach of fiduciary duty by the principal, then, like other damages and losses that were not the result of the fiduciary's breach, the surety will not be liable for those attorneys' fees.[262]

4. Punitive, Statutory, and Treble Damages

Sometimes the fiduciary's actions make the fiduciary susceptible to punitive damages, such as double or treble damages for embezzlement or statutory theft. This may prompt some successor fiduciaries or probate courts to seek to recover these punitive damages from the surety. However, because the purpose of punitive damages imposed upon the fiduciary is not to compensate for actual losses, but to deter others from behaving in the same way, these damages generally are not recoverable from the surety. Recovery of punitive damages from the surety under such circumstances would be beyond the scope of the remedy afforded by the bond, which is for the estate's actual damages caused by the actions or

---

John Kohl & Co., P.C. v. Dearborn & Ewing, 977 S.W.2d 528, 534 (Tenn. 1998).

259. *See, e.g.*, Tex. Prob. Code Ann. § 245 (West 2010).

260. *See, e.g.*, Ranger Constr. Co. v. Prince William Cnty., 605 F.2d 1298 (4th Cir. 1979); Bagby v. Merrill, Lynch, Pierce, Fenner & Smith, Inc., 491 F.2d 192, 198 n.9 (8th Cir. 1974).

261. Est. of Kerns v. W. Sur. Co., 802 P.2d 1298, 1300 (Okla. Civ. App. 1990); Laws. Sur. Corp. v. Larson, 869 S.W.2d 649, 652 (Tex. App. 1994); Lee v. Lee, 47 S.W.3d 767, 796–97 (Tex. App. 2001).

262. *Larson*, 869 S.W.2d at 652.

inactions of the fiduciary.[263] Moreover, an assessment of punitive damages against the surety imposed for the actions of the fiduciary would not serve the deterrent function for which the penalties were designed. For these reasons, the innocent surety is not liable for exemplary damages arising from the conduct of its principal.[264]

In some jurisdictions, a surety may be assessed extra-contractual or punitive damages based on its own purported bad faith conduct in its handling of a claim on a probate bond. Where a court determines that a surety itself engaged in misconduct apart from the fiduciary's failure to faithfully manage the estate, damages or penalties may not be considered part of the penal sum of the bond and may be assessed against the surety in excess of the bond amount.[265]

---

263. RESTATEMENT (THIRD) OF SURETYSHIP AND GUARANTY § 73 (AM. L. INST. 1996); *see, e.g.*, United Pac. Ins. Co. v. Berryhill, 620 So. 2d 1077, 1079 (Fla. Dist. Ct. App. 1993); *In re* Est. of Gladstone, 814 S.E.2d 1 (Ga. 2018); Koch v. Merchants Mut. Bonding Co., 507 P.2d 189, 195 (Kan. 1973); U.S. Fid. & Guar. Co. v. State *ex rel.* Stringfellow, 182 So. 2d 919, 922 (Miss. 1966); Vicario v. Jenkins, 155 N.E.2d 488, 489 (Ohio Ct. App. 1958); Butler v. United Pac. Ins. Co., 509 P.2d 1184, 1185 (Or. 1973); Dawson v. Reliance Ins. Co., 482 S.W.2d 882, 882 (Tex. Civ. App. 1972); *see also* Arnold v. State *ex rel.* Burton, 245 S.W.2d 818, 819 (Ark. 1952) (holding that sheriff's bond did not cover punitive damages).

264. *Est. of Gladstone*, 814 S.E.2d at 3–4; *Koch*, 507 P.2d at 195. *See also* Mitchell v. McGuire, 12 So. 2d 180, 181 (Ala. 1943) ("[S]ureties upon official bonds are liable only for damages which one may sustain resulting from a breach of the bond and not damages or penalties that may be awarded by way of punishment of the principal."); Ames v. Comm'r of Motor Vehicles, 839 A.2d 1250, 1254 (Conn. 2004) (holding that punitive damages for actions of principal are not recoverable under motor vehicle dealers bond); C & I Steel, LLC v. Travelers Cas. & Sur. Co. of Am., 876 N.E.2d 442, 446–47 (Mass. App. Ct. 2007) (holding a surety not liable for punitive damages imposed for misdeeds of others); N.H. Ins. Co. v. Gruhn, 670 P.2d 941, 943 (Nev. 1983) (holding a surety on mortgage broker bond not liable for punitive damages against principal).

265. Nichols v. Preferred Nat'l Ins. Co., 704 So. 2d 1371, 1374 (Fla. 1998); *see also In re* Davison, 642 P.2d 1259, 1261 (Wash. Ct. App. 1982) (recognizing that a limitation on attorneys' fees beyond the penal sum could be varied by a showing of bad faith by the surety).

F. The Surety's Rights to Recovery of Claims Payments and Other Expenses

The surety fully expects the bonded fiduciary to properly perform the obligations associated with the estate. When a bond claim results in a payment by the surety, the surety's recovery rights in relation to the fiduciary are secured implicitly through the doctrine of equitable subrogation and, in some jurisdictions, state law relating to common law indemnification. Additionally, the fiduciary is often required to execute a separate contract of indemnity or a bond application embedded with less complex indemnity language in favor of the surety before the bond is issued.

1. Equitable Subrogation

The doctrine of equitable subrogation is premised on the concept that one who pays the obligation of another, for which the other is primarily liable, is entitled to all the rights held by the obligee against the principal obligor.[266] With respect to probate bonds, this means that when a surety pays a fiduciary's debt to the estate for breach of duty, the surety is entitled to any rights the estate had against the fiduciary; in short, the surety steps into the shoes of the creditor. The prerequisites to assert these rights are typically (1) payment made by the surety to protect its own interest; (2) the surety did not act as a volunteer; (3) the debt must be one for which the surety was not primarily liable; (4) the entire debt must be paid; and (5) exercising the right to subrogation must not work any injustice to the rights of others.[267] Consequently, the fiduciary's obligation to the estate must be completely satisfied before the surety is subrogated to all of the rights of the estate to the extent of its payment.[268] Some jurisdictions hold

---

266. Restatement (Third) of Suretyship and Guaranty §§ 27–28 (Am. L. Inst. 1996). *See, e.g.*, Union Bank v. Gradsky, 71 Cal. Rptr. 64, 68 (1968); *In re* Est. of Bishop, No. 20102, 2004 WL 917693, at *7 (Ohio Ct. App. Apr. 30, 2004).
267. *See, e.g.*, Caito v. United Cal. Bank, 576 P.2d 466 (Cal. 1978); Hill v. Wiley, 3 N.E.2d 1015, 1020 (Mass. 1936).
268. Restatement (Third) of Suretyship and Guaranty § 27 (Am. L. Inst. 1996). *Cf.* ACSTAR Ins. Co. v. Clean Harbors, Inc., 783 F. Supp. 2d 312, 317 (D. Conn. 2011) (discussing the "make whole doctrine" under which an insurer may not assert claims on behalf of insured until insured has been fully compensated for the loss).

that, for policy reasons, the surety may not be subrogated to the rights of a legal malpractice action.[269]

Potential recovery sources for the surety under the principles of subrogation may include the bonded fiduciary, those who improperly received estate funds,[270] and financial institutions or accountants whose negligent oversight of estate financial accounts may have contributed to the loss.[271] Locating estate assets may be challenging. A constructive trust may be an alternative when the fiduciary uses estate funds to purchase real estate for the fiduciary or a third party. The imposition of a constructive trust is an equitable remedy available when assets are used to acquire title in property in violation of a fiduciary relationship.[272] Under this remedy, the person who has wrongfully acquired title to property is under an equitable duty to convey it to another to avoid unjust enrichment.[273]

2. *Recovery Rights Derived Under State Law*

Most states impose a common law reimbursement obligation on principals to reimburse sureties for claims payments to the extent actually owed to the obligee or other claimant.[274]

State statutes in several jurisdictions address surety contracts and provide the surety with certain rights that may operate to reduce

---

269. Capitol Indem. Corp. v. Fleming, 58 P.3d 965, 969 (Ariz. Ct. App. 2002); W. Sur. Co. v. Peitrzkiewicz, No. FSTCV106007722S, 2011 WL 4447242 (Conn. Super. Ct. Sept. 6, 2011).
270. *See In re* Kapelsohn's Est., 182 N.Y.S.2d 472, 474 (Surr. Ct. 1958); *In re* Est. of McCoy, 418 N.Y.S.2d 863 (Surr. Ct. 1979).
271. *In re* Conservatorship of W.L., 552 N.W.2d 734, 736 (Minn. Ct. App. 1996) (allowing surety to recover against bank that permitted conservator to withdraw funds without inquiring as to his authority). *But see* Dolan Title & Guar. Corp. v. Hartford Accident & Indem. Co., 395 So. 2d 296, 299 (Fla. Dist. Ct. App. 1981) (holding conservator's misappropriation of funds not reasonably foreseeable so as to hold financial institution liable); W. Sur. Co. v. First Bank of S.D., N.A., 427 N.W.2d 840, 843 (S.D. 1988) (holding surety not subrogated to claims against bank absent showing of negligence or willful misconduct).
272. *See* Lesikar v. Rappeport, 33 S.W.3d 282, 304 (Tex. App. 2000).
273. *In re* Est. of Preston, 346 S.W.3d 137, 165 (Tex. App. 2011).
274. Smith v. Mitsubishi Motors Credit, 247 Conn. 342, 348–49 (1998); Johnson v. Mortenson, 110 Conn. 221, 229 (1929).

its loss. Generally, these laws encompass common law principles of reimbursement and indemnification. For example, in one jurisdiction the principal must reimburse the surety when it satisfies any part of the underlying obligation for the amount disbursed including necessary costs and expenses.[275] Similarly, in another jurisdiction all the creditors' rights to the judgment are assigned to the surety to the extent of its payment.[276] The surety may execute upon the judgment for the full amount of its payment together with costs and interest.[277] Some states have statutes that entitle the surety to seek contribution from cosureties for their proportionate share of the loss payment.[278]

3. Indemnity Agreements

Common law subrogation and reimbursement rights are often inadequate from the surety's perspective, and generally more costly to pursue. Consequently, it is often necessary for the fiduciary applicant to execute a separate indemnity agreement that provides the surety with broad protection. In this way, the surety's rights are not limited to general indemnity principles but are broadened by the express terms of the indemnity contract.[279] Typically the contract provisions require the principal/fiduciary to hold the surety harmless and procure its release from any claim. It also will require the principal/fiduciary to reimburse the surety for all loss, cost, expense, and attorneys' fees it may incur as a result of issuing the probate bond. Most indemnity agreements also give the surety the right to compromise any claim or suit in its sole discretion, along with the right to demand collateral. Such agreements are routinely enforced by the courts.[280]

---

275. CAL. CIV. CODE § 2847 (West 2021).
276. ARIZ. REV. STAT. ANN. § 12-1643 (2021).
277. *Id.*
278. *See, e.g.*, *id.* § 12-1644; CAL. CIV. PROC. CODE § 996.490 (West 2021); CAL. CIV. CODE § 2847 (West 2021); N.C. GEN. STAT. ANN. § 26-5 (West 2021).
279. *See, e.g.*, Fid. & Deposit Co. of Md. v. Bristol Steel & Iron Works, Inc., 722 F.2d 1160, 1163 (4th Cir. 1983).
280. *See, e.g.*, Seaboard Sur. Co. v. Niederhauser, No. Civ. 04-2814, 2006 WL 892705, at *3–4 (D.N.J. Apr. 6, 2006) (enforcing indemnity agreement to reimburse surety for claim paid on probate bond); Am. Contractors Indem. Co. v. Bryant, No. B283733, 2019 WL 2098833, at *5 (Cal. Ct. App. May 14, 2019) (same); Am. Sur. Co. of N.Y. v. Vinton, 112 N.E. 954

a. Demanding Collateral. As stated earlier, it is general practice to have the principal/fiduciary applicant(s) execute a contract of indemnity in exchange for a bond to be issued. Where an indemnity contract is executed, there generally are provisions that give the surety the express right to demand collateral. Issuing a collateral demand will protect the surety from a future loss, if it is placed in funds. Alternatively, a collateral demand can be used to get the principal/fiduciary's attention and cooperation with the defense of the claim. If an indemnity contract is not executed, the common law theory of *quia timet* may allow a collateral demand to still be issued by the surety.[281]

4. Principal's Defenses to Indemnity

It is often difficult for the principal to prevail in its defenses to the surety's recovery action due to the probate court's prior determination of the fiduciary's liability to the estate. A principal's defense may include assertions that the surety's recovery action is barred by the statute of limitations or that the provisions of the indemnity agreement are ambiguous and unenforceable.[282]

It is not uncommon for a fiduciary to seek bankruptcy protection after incurring a substantial surcharge. A principal has no duty to reimburse a surety to the extent that the bankruptcy laws have relieved the principal of the obligation.[283] However, the bankruptcy laws do not permit the discharge

---

(Mass. 1916) (same); McGeevy v. Bremers, 288 N.W.2d 490, 492 (Neb. 1980) (same); Old Republic Sur. Co. v. Palmer, 5 S.W.3d 357, 361 (Tex. App. 1999) (same). For the definitive discussion of a surety's contractual indemnity rights, see THE SURETY'S INDEMNITY AGREEMENT: LAW AND PRACTICE (Marilyn Klinger et al. eds., 2d ed. 2008).

281. RESTATEMENT (THIRD) OF SURETYSHIP AND GUARANTY § 25 (AM. L. INST. 1996). *See* Travelers Cas. & Sur. Co. v. Ockerland, No. 04C3963, 2004 WL 1794915, at *5–6 (N.D. Ill. Aug. 6, 2004) (holding that, under claims of *quia timet* and exoneration, a surety who had already paid claims against principals on a bond was entitled to a preliminary injunction requiring principals to deposit with court funds to protect it from future liability on the bond); Nw. Nat'l Ins. Co. v. Alberts, 741 F. Supp. 424 (S.D.N.Y. 1990) (same).

282. RESTATEMENT (THIRD) OF SURETYSHIP AND GUARANTY § 24 (AM. L. INST. 1996). *See, e.g.*, James v. Old Republic Sur., 674 So. 2d 615, 617 (Ala. Civ. App. 1996); *Palmer*, 5 S.W.3d at 361.

283. RESTATEMENT (THIRD) OF SURETYSHIP AND GUARANTY § 24 (AM. L. INST. 1996).

of an individual's debt that was incurred as a result of fraud, embezzlement, larceny, or defalcation while acting in a fiduciary capacity.[284] The burden is on the surety to prove to the bankruptcy court the elements of non-dischargeability by a preponderance of the evidence.[285]

Conclusion

The substantive coverage afforded by a probate bond should be defined by the bond's purpose—to provide a make-whole remedy for breaches of fiduciary duty perpetrated by administrators of probate estates. Wrongful conduct by the administrator does not fall within the bond coverage unless the wrongful conduct constitutes a breach of a fiduciary duty owed to the injured party. Assuming that a fiduciary duty is breached, the remedy provided by the bond should be limited to putting the injured party in the position that he or she would have been in but for the fiduciary breach.

The duration of the coverage afforded by a probate bond as well as the operative effect of the bond penal sum may vary greatly depending on the jurisdiction. In evaluating a probate bond claim where the bond was issued in the midst of the principal's performance as administrator, it may be important to determine whether the bond has retroactive effect or whether the surety continues to have exposure after the bond has been discharged. It may also be important to determine whether awards of attorneys' fees, interest, and punitive damages may be assessed against the surety in the forum state and, if so, to what extent such awards count against the penal sum.

Jurisdictions differ regarding the procedures used to adjudicate allegations against bond principals for purported breaches of fiduciary duty as well as regarding the procedures applied to adjudicate bond claims. In some jurisdictions, claims against the principal and the surety are adjudicated concurrently and in other jurisdictions they are adjudicated sequentially. Jurisdictions also may differ regarding to what extent the surety is bound by, or may claim as a defense rulings issued by, a probate court in advance of the initiation of a bond claim or without the surety's participation in such decision-making.

---

284. *Id. See* Bullock v. BankChampaign, N.A. (*In re* Bullock), 569 U.S. 267 (2013); *In re* Firer, 317 B.R. 457, 465 (Bankr. D. Conn. 2004). *See also* 11 U.S.C.A. § 523 (West 2021).

285. *Firer*, 317 B.R. at 465.

CHAPTER 5

BANKRUPTCY TRUSTEE/RECEIVER BONDS

Chad L. Schexnayder
Susan B. Jordan
Matthew H. Sloan

Introduction

This chapter discusses surety bonds written for individuals or entities who are appointed by the court to act as a bankruptcy trustee or a receiver. The role of the bankruptcy trustee and the receiver are closely related. In early England, the most common use of a receiver, aside from real estate matters, was to handle the dissolution and asset distribution of an insolvent entity. With the advent of a broadly applicable federal law of bankruptcy, this particular use of a receiver has largely disappeared in the United States.

Trustee or receiver surety bonds guarantee that the bankruptcy trustee or receiver will faithfully perform the fiduciary duties and responsibilities of their position. The court's appointment creates a position of trust and imposes upon the individual or entity elevated duties of good faith and honesty in discharging their obligations. Bankruptcy trustee bonds and receiver bonds are a type of "court fiduciary bond." For this reason, much of the law relating to bankruptcy trustee bonds and receivership bonds mirrors the law applicable to other types of fiduciary bonds.

I. Bankruptcy Trustee Bond

A. The Bond

The bankruptcy trustee plays a vital role in implementing the purposes and procedures of the Bankruptcy Code. Section 322 of the Bankruptcy Code governs the appointment of trustees.[1] A trustee does not qualify

---

1. 11 U.S.C. § 322. Section 322 provides:
   (a) Except as provided in subsection (b)(1), a person selected under section 701, 702, 703, 1104, 1163, 1183, 1202, or 1302 of this

for appointment until the trustee has filed with the court a bond in favor of the United States of America conditioned on the trustee's faithful performance of the trustee's official duties. The Office of the United States Trustee determines the amount and terms of the bond and the sufficiency of the surety on each bond.[2] The surety on any bond written in favor of the United States of America must be authorized by the secretary of the treasury.[3]

1. Types of Bonds

The following are the most common types of bonds available for bankruptcy trustees to meet the requirements of § 322.

a. Individual Case Bond. A single trustee is bonded for a single case for a scheduled amount. The face amount of the bond will typically include a cushion based upon a percentage of funds on deposit. The bond may be adjusted as the deposits significantly increase or decrease. This type of bond is often used for trustees in operating chapter 7 cases, trustees who are not on the active panel for receiving cases, and trustees who have a case in which the funds on hand exceed the per-case limit under a schedule bond.

b. Blanket or "Aggregate" Bond. This bond may cover multiple cases for one or more trustees, in an amount equal to the face amount of the

---

> title to serve as trustee in a case under this title qualifies if before seven days after such selection, and before beginning official duties, such person has filed with the court a bond in favor of the United States conditioned on the faithful performance of such official duties.
>
> (b) (1) The United States trustee qualifies wherever such trustee serves as trustee in a case under this title.
>
> (2) The United States trustee shall determine—
>
> (A) the amount of a bond required to be filed under subsection (a) of this section; and
>
> (B) the sufficiency of the surety on such bond.
>
> (c) A trustee is not liable personally or on such trustee's bond in favor of the United States for any penalty or forfeiture incurred by the debtor.
>
> (d) A proceeding on a trustee's bond may not be commenced after two years after the date on which such trustee was discharged.

2. *Id.* § 322(b)(2).
3. 31 U.S.C. §§ 9304, 9308.

bond.[4] There is no per-trustee limitation as might exist under a schedule bond.

c. Schedule Bond. This type of bond covers all trustees of a group, district, region, or other unit, based upon the discretion of the United States Trustee. Each trustee within the group is bonded for an individually scheduled amount. The scheduled amount would typically include a cushion based upon a percent of funds on deposit by trustee at the time the bond is issued or renewed. Scheduled amounts are only adjusted in the event of a dramatic fluctuation in the funds on deposit with a trustee. These bonds generally have a per-case cap, which means an individual case bond would ordinarily be used for bankruptcy estates containing funds over a designated amount.

2. *Bond Language*

Not every bankruptcy trustee bond reads the same, and the language of the bond may therefore have bearing on the coverage of the bond. A typical liability clause in a blanket bond might state:

> NOW THEREFORE, if the said Principals named or subsequently added as Trustee as aforesaid shall obey such orders as the United States Bankruptcy Court or the United States District Court or any of the Judges of such court may make in relation to the trust undertaken by said Trustee, and shall faithfully and truly account for all moneys, assets, and effects of the estate in each case in which he or she has been appointed or will be appointed, and shall in all respects faithfully perform all his or her official duties as Trustee, then this obligation to be void otherwise, to remain in full force and effect.

---

4. Federal Rule of Bankruptcy Procedure 2010, Qualification by Trustee, Proceeding on Bond, provides:
   (a) Blanket Bond. The United States trustee may authorize a blanket bond in favor of the United States conditioned on the faithful performance of official duties by the trustee or trustees to cover (1) a person who qualifies as trustee in a number of cases, and (2) a number of trustees each of whom qualifies in a different case.
   (b) Proceeding on Bond. A proceeding on the trustee's bond may be brought by any party in interest in the name of the United States for the use of the entity injured by the breach of the condition.

A bankruptcy trustee bond may contain additional provisions such as:

- A clause that there is no joint and several liability among trustees
- A reference to specific cases in which the trustee was appointed by the United States Trustee
- A clause that the trustee shall obey lawful orders of the bankruptcy judges and requirements of the United States Trustee
- A time frame for serving notice of cancellation on the United States Trustee (a 60-day notice is common)
- A clause that states the bonding company will seek indemnification from the trustees for any payments the bonding company is required to make to third parties

In addition, most bonds contain a clause stating that, regardless of the number of years the bond is in effect, the surety's liability is limited to the face amount of the bond. This term may be referred to as a non-aggregation clause. Thus, if a $10 million bond is renewed every year for five years, the surety is liable only for $10 million—not for $10 million each year for a total of $50 million.[5]

B. The Role of the Bankruptcy Trustee

The specific duties of the trustee, performance of which is the condition of the bond, are largely set out in three sections of the Bankruptcy Code. Section 704[6] focuses on a chapter 7 trustee's duties.

---

5. *See In re* Endeco, 718 F.2d 879 (8th Cir. 1983); *In re* Foodsource, Inc., 130 B.R. 549 (N.D. Cal. 1991).
6. 11 U.S.C. § 704(a). Section 704(a), Duties of Trustee, provides that the trustee shall:
   (1) collect and reduce to money the property of the estate for which such trustee serves, and close such estate as expeditiously as is compatible with the best interests of parties in interest;
   (2) be accountable for all property received;
   (3) ensure that the debtor shall perform his intention as specified in section 521(a)(2)(B) of this title;
   (4) investigate the financial affairs of the debtor;
   (5) if a purpose would be served, examine proofs of claims and object to the allowance of any claim that is improper;
   (6) if advisable, oppose the discharge of the debtor;

Section 1106(a)[7] defines these duties in a chapter 11 case.

---

(7) unless the court orders otherwise, furnish such information concerning the estate and the estate's administration as is requested by a party in interest;

(8) if the business of the debtor is authorized to be operated, file with the court, with the United States trustee, and with any governmental unit charged with responsibility for collection or determination of any tax arising out of such operation, periodic reports and summaries of the operation of such business, including a statement of receipts and disbursements, and such other information as the United States trustee or the court requires;

(9) make a final report and file a final account of the administration of the estate with the court and with the United States trustee;

(10) if with respect to the debtor there is a claim for a domestic support obligation, provide the applicable notice specified in subsection (c);

(11) if, at the time of the commencement of the case, the debtor (or any entity designated by the debtor) served as the administrator (as defined in section 3 of the Employee Retirement Income Security Act of 1974) of an employee benefit plan, continue to perform the obligations required of the administrator; and

(12) use all reasonable and best efforts to transfer patients from a health care business that is in the process of being closed to an appropriate health care business that—

(A) is in the vicinity of the health care business that is closing;

(B) provides the patient with services that are substantially similar to those provided by the health care business that is in the process of being closed; and

(C) maintains a reasonable quality of care.

7. *Id.* § 1106(a). Section 1106, Duties of Trustee and Examiner, provides that a trustee shall:

(1) perform the duties of the trustee, as specified in paragraphs (2), (5), (7), (8), (9), (10), (11), and (12) of section 704(a);

(2) if the debtor has not done so, file the list, schedule, and statement required under section 521(1) of this title;

(3) except to the extent that the court orders otherwise, investigate the acts, conduct, assets, liabilities, and financial condition of the debtor, the operation of the debtor's business and the desirability of the continuance of such business, and any other matter relevant to the case or to the formulation of a plan;

(4) as soon as practicable—

Section 1183(b)[8] describes the duties of a trustee in a chapter 11, subchapter V case, the newest form of small business bankruptcy

---

(A) file a statement of any investigation conducted under paragraph (3) of this subsection, including any fact ascertained pertaining to fraud, dishonesty, incompetence, misconduct, mismanagement, or irregularity in the management of the affairs of the debtor, or to a cause of action available to the estate; and

(B) transmit a copy or a summary of any such statement to any creditors' committee or equity security holders' committee, to any indenture trustee, and to such other entity as the court designates;

(5) as soon as practicable, file a plan under section 1121 of this title, file a report of why the trustee will not file a plan, or recommend conversion of the case to a case under chapter 7, 12, or 13 of this title or dismissal of the case;

(6) for any year for which the debtor has not filed a tax return required by law, furnish, without personal liability, such information as may be required by the governmental unit with which such tax return was to be filed, in light of the condition of the debtor's books and records and the availability of such information;

(7) after confirmation of a plan, file such reports as are necessary or as the court orders; and

(8) if with respect to the debtor there is a claim for a domestic support obligation, provide the applicable notice specified in subsection (c).

8. *Id.* § 1183(b). Section 1183, Trustee, provides in subsection (b), Duties, that the trustee shall:

(1) perform the duties specified in paragraphs (2), (5), (6), (7), and (9) of section 704(a) of this title;

(2) perform the duties specified in paragraphs (3), (4), and (7) of section 1106(a) of this title, if the court, for cause and on request of a party in interest, the trustee, or the United States trustee, so orders;

(3) appear and be heard at the status conference under section 1188 of this title and any hearing that concerns—

(A) the value of property subject to a lien;

(B) confirmation of a plan filed under this subchapter;

(C) modification of the plan after confirmation; or

(D) the sale of property of the estate;

(4) ensure that the debtor commences making timely payments required by a plan confirmed under this subchapter;

reorganization. The duties of chapter 12 and chapter 13 trustees are set out in § 1202(b)[9] and § 1302(b).[10] These sections principally define trustee duties by incorporating by reference subsections of §§ 704 and 1106.

---

(5) if the debtor ceases to be a debtor in possession, perform the duties specified in section 704(a)(8) and paragraphs (1), (2), and (6) of section 1106(a) of this title, including operating the business of the debtor;
(6) if there is a claim for a domestic support obligation with respect to the debtor, perform the duties specified in section 704(c) of this title; and
(7) facilitate the development of a consensual plan of reorganization.

9. *Id.* § 1202(b). Section 1202(b) provides that the trustee shall:
(1) perform the duties specified in sections 704(a)(2), 704(a)(3), 704(a)(5), 704(a)(6), 704(a)(7), 704(a)(9) of this title;
(2) perform the duties specified in section 1106(a)(3) and 1106(a)(4) of this title if the court, for cause and on request of a party in interest, the trustee, or the United States trustee, so orders;
(3) appear and be heard at any hearing that concerns—
(A) the value of property subject to a lien;
(B) confirmation of a plan;
(C) modification of the plan after confirmation; or
(D) the sale of property of the estate;
(4) ensure that the debtor commences making timely payments required by a confirmed plan;
(5) if the debtor ceases to be a debtor in possession, perform the duties specified in sections 704(a)(8), 1106(a)(1), 1106(a)(2), 1106(a)(6), 1106(a)(7), and 1203; and
(6) if with respect to the debtor there is a claim for a domestic support obligation, provide the applicable notice specified in subsection (c).

10. *Id.* § 1302(b). Section 1302(b) provides that the trustee shall:
(1) perform the duties specified in sections 704(a)(2), 704(a)(3), 704(a)(4), 704(a)(5), 704(a)(6), 704(a)(7), and 704(a)(9) of this title;
(2) appear and be heard at any hearing that concerns—
(A) the value of property subject to a lien;
(B) confirmation of a plan; or
(C)modification of the plan after confirmation;
(3) dispose of, under regulations issued by the Director of the Administrative Office of the United States Court, moneys received or to be received in a case number chapter XIII of the Bankruptcy Act;

Depending on the Bankruptcy Code chapter under which the trustee was appointed, and the particulars of an individual bankruptcy case, the trustee may function in very different roles. In a chapter 7 case, the bankruptcy trustee may examine the debtor, collect property of the bankruptcy estate, liquidate assets, prosecute claims against third parties or the debtor, and make distributions to creditors. In a chapter 11 case, a traditional trustee may manage the continuing operations of a business while it is being reorganized, or market and sell assets of the estate or even the entire going concern. He or she may refinance debt, hire or fire employees, or take other actions to restore the debtor to economic health. A chapter 11, subchapter V trustee may perform some of the duties under § 704(a) or § 1106(a), as well as facilitate the development of a consensual plan of reorganization. The chapter 11, subchapter V trustee may act as disbursing agent following plan confirmation. In a chapter 13 or chapter 12 case, trustees evaluate and advise the court regarding the debtor's proposed plan, and administer the periodic payments from a debtor, dividing up the payments for distribution to creditors in accordance with the terms of the plan that the court has approved.

C. Liability of the Bankruptcy Trustee and the Bond

Any "party in interest" may bring an action against the surety to recover under the trustee's bond, in the name of the United States.[11] With respect to a bankruptcy trustee bond, the surety is deemed to have submitted to the jurisdiction of the bankruptcy court, pursuant to Rule 9025 of the Federal Rules of Bankruptcy Procedure. A bankruptcy trustee is

---

(4) advise, other than on legal matters, and assist the debtor in performance under the plan;

(5) ensure that the debtor commences making timely payments under section 1326 of this title; and

(6) if with respect to the debtor there is a claim for a domestic support obligation, provide the applicable notice specified in subsection (d).

11. "Party in interest" is not a directly defined term under the Code. Section 1109 contains a nonexclusive listing that names the debtor, a creditor's committee, a creditor, an equity security holder, or an indenture trustee. "Party in interest" status is within the court's discretion, which is exercised on a case-by-case basis. *In re* Texaco, Inc. 81 B.R. 820 (Bankr. S.D.N.Y. 1988). *See* FED. R. BANKR. P. 2010(b) n.5.

the representative of the estate and has the capacity to sue or be sued.[12] As such, the trustee must be named as a party defendant in any action brought against or concerning the assets of the estate.[13]

Although several circuit courts have considered the question, there is no consensus among the circuits on the standard of conduct below which the trustee will be held personally liable.[14] The Second and First Circuits have held that mere negligence in the performance of the trustee's official duties will be enough.[15] Conversely, the Tenth and Sixth Circuits have held that only willful and deliberate breaches of duty will give rise to personal liability of the trustee.[16] Still other courts have adopted an intermediate

---

12. 11 U.S.C. § 323 (role and capacity of trustee). Section 323 provides:
    (a) The trustee in a case under this title is the representative of the estate.
    (b) The trustee in a case under this title has the capacity to sue and be sued.
13. Bellini Imps., Ltd. v. Mason & Dixon Lines, Inc., 944 F.2d 199, 202 (4th Cir. 1991).
14. A bankruptcy trustee can sue or be sued in his or her capacity as a representative of the bankruptcy estate. In such a case, the estate could be found liable for a claim, but that liability would not be imposed upon the trustee personally and, therefore, the surety bond is not implicated.
15. *In re* Cochise Coll. Park, Inc., 703 F.2d 1339, 1357 (9th Cir. 1983); *In re* Gorski, 766 F.2d 723 (2d Cir. 1985); *In re* Mailman Steam Carpet Cleaning Corp., 196 F.3d 1, 7 (1st Cir. 1999); *In re* Strum, 121 B.R. 443 (Bankr. D. Pa. 1990); *In re* Happy Hocker Pawn Shop, Inc., 212 Fed. App'x 811 (11th Cir. 2006).
16. Sherr v. Winkler, 552 F.2d 1367, 1375 (10th Cir. 1977); Ford Motor Credit Co. v. Weaver, 680 F.2d 451, 461 (6th Cir. 1982). *See also* United States v. Sapp, 641 F.2d 182, 184 (4th Cir. 1981) (dictum); *In re* Chi. Pac. Corp., 773 F.2d 909 (7th Cir. 1997); *In re* Ondova, No. 3:16-CV-00947-M, 2017 Bankr. LEXIS 325 (Bankr. N.D. Tex. Feb. 1, 2017) (in granting motion to dismiss gross negligence claim on trustee's bond, court noted that the surety's obligation arose only when trustee failed to obey the bankruptcy court's orders or failed to account faithfully for all assets of the estate, and that facts alleged failed to "articulate a failure to faithfully perform statutory and fiduciary duties on the part of the Bankruptcy Trustee"). *But see In re* Schooler, 725 F.3d 498 (5th Cir. 2013) (surety held liable on bankruptcy trustee bond where trustee breached her standard of care in failing to act in the face of obvious danger that debtors would misappropriate inherited assets belonging to bankruptcy estate).

level of misconduct standard, subjecting trustees to personal liability when the conduct was found to be grossly negligent.[17]

The bankruptcy trustee bond would cover a claim for a breach of fiduciary duty by the bankruptcy trustee, such as embezzlement of money or property. However, the surety on the bankruptcy trustee bond may be liable for more than just the property of the bankruptcy estate that is mishandled by the trustee, including property of third parties that is mishandled by the trustee.[18] The trustee, and the bond, may be held liable for the trustee's improper distribution of funds from the bankruptcy[19] or for the trustee's payment of professional fees without a court order.[20]

A trustee who embezzles or breaches his or her trust forfeits his or her fee. For this reason, the surety can be required to repay fees previously paid to the trustee, even if those fees had been approved by the court.[21] Courts have upheld awards against the trustee and the surety for the costs incurred to discover and investigate the trustee's defalcation.[22]

Courts frequently cite to decisions that appear to offer a measure of immunity to a trustee in matters requiring the exercise of discretion[23] or for actions taken in the performance of his or her duties.[24] Predictably,

---

17. *In re* Smyth, 207 F.3d 758 (5th Cir. 2000) (bankruptcy trustee has personal liability for errors that cause damage to the estate only if his conduct amounted to gross negligence); *In re* J.F.D. Enters., Inc., 223 B.R. 610, 627 (Bankr. D. Mass. 1998), *aff'd*, 236 B.R. 112 (D. Mass. 1999), *aff'd*, 215 F.3d 1312 (1st Cir. 2000).
18. At least one court has held that the bond may be liable for more than just the property of the bankruptcy estate that is mishandled by the trustee. *In re* Ferrante, 51 F.3d 1473, 1477 (9th Cir. 1995) (the fact that the funds mishandled may ultimately be paid to a secured creditor, as opposed to remaining a part of the bankruptcy estate, is not a defense to the surety).
19. *In re* Nash, 765 F.2d 1410 (9th Cir. 1985).
20. *In re* Baker, 15 B.C.D. 439 (Bankr. D. Or. 1986).
21. *Ferrante*, 51 F.3d at 1479.
22. *Id. Accord In re* Traffic Safety Co., Inc., 21 B.R. 669, 671 (Bankr. E.D. Pa. 1982).
23. *In re* Cochise Coll. Park, Inc., 703 F.2d 1339, 1357 (9th Cir. 1983) ("although a trustee is not liable in any manner for mistakes in judgment where discretion is allowed").
24. *In re* Mailman Steam Carpet Cleaning Corp., 196 F.3d 1, 8 (1st Cir. 1999); Lonneker Farms, Inc. v. Klobucher, 804 F.2d 1096 (9th Cir. 1986); Mullis v. Bankr. Ct., Dist. of Nev., 828 F.2d 1385 (9th Cir. 1987); Curry v. Castillo, 297 F.3d 940, 947 (9th Cir. 2002); Weissman v. Hasset, 12

the cases relating to the nature and extent of a bankruptcy trustee surety's liability are highly fact sensitive. As noted by the foregoing cases, courts appear to strain to protect trustees who have performed their duties in good faith from claims asserted against them. Conversely, the courts can be severe with dishonest or grossly indifferent trustees, with that liability often ultimately being visited upon the bankruptcy trustee bond surety.

D. Limitation Period for Claims on the Bond

Published decisions involving bankruptcy trustee bond sureties have grappled with conflicting views of the statute of limitations applicable to a claim against the bond. Section 322(d) of the Bankruptcy Code states that a proceeding on a trustee's bond may not be commenced more than two years after the date on which such trustee was discharged. However, some bankruptcy courts have held that an action for negligence against the trustee and the surety is subject to a shorter state law statute of limitations for negligence actions. These courts have held that § 332(d) represents an outside limit but does not preclude the application of shorter state law statutes of limitations.[25]

One such bankruptcy court decision adopting the shorter state law statute of limitations to protect the trustee and the surety[26] was reversed by the U.S. District Court for the Northern District of Texas.[27] The district court held that 11 U.S.C. § 332(d) preempted the Texas state law statute of limitations. Accordingly, because the trustee was still serving, the statute of limitations had not yet run on a negligence claim against the trustee and his surety. Some subsequent bankruptcy court decisions addressing this issue have followed the district court's preemption holding.[28]

The question of the correct statute of limitations applicable to a negligence action against a bankruptcy trustee and the surety remains an

---

B.C.D. 1355 (S.D.N.Y. 1985); *see also In re* XRX, Inc., 77 B.R. 797 (Bankr. D. Nev. 1987); Griffin v. Kelso, No. 2:10-cv-2525, 2011 WL 3583457, at *3 (E.D. Cal. Apr. 15, 2011).

25. *In re* Lewis Rosenberg Autoparts, Inc., 209 B.R. 668 (Bankr. W.D. Pa. 1997); *In re* Tri-State Hoists, Inc., No. 91-02125, 1991 WL 193733, at *6 (Bankr. E.D. Pa. Sept. 26, 1991); *In re* Smith, 426 B.R. 435, 443 (E.D.N.Y. 2010).

26. *In re* Oles Grain Co., 206 B.R. 126 (Bankr. N.D. Tex. 1997).

27. Oles Grain Co. v. Safeco Ins. Co. of Am., 221 B.R. 371 (N.D. Tex. 1998).

28. *In re* Armstrong, 245 B.R. 123 (Bankr. D. Neb. 1999); *In re* Schooler, 449 B.R. 502 (Bankr. Tex. 2010).

open one. None of the decisions to date appear to establish a definitive answer to the question. Because § 322 does not address whether a surety can be discharged by the running of the limitations period for an underlying cause of action against a trustee, courts may choose to turn to state law to fill in this gap in what might otherwise be perceived as a federal cause of action.[29] The general principles of surety law provide that the running of limitations for a claim against the bond principal will also prevent recovery from the surety.[30] Thus, it would be expected that the applicable limitations period for a negligence claim against a bankruptcy trustee should govern the surety's liability on a trustee bond, and the § 322 time frames would function as a statute of repose.

II. Receivership Bonds

A receivership bond is a type of court fiduciary bond. The bond guarantees that the court-appointed receiver, who is the principal on the bond, will faithfully perform fiduciary duties and responsibilities. An appointed receiver may take possession of, preserve, and dispose of disputed property under a court's jurisdiction. A receiver is "a disinterested person appointed by a court, or by a corporation or other person, for the protection or collection of property that is the subject of diverse claims"[31] and has also been defined as "a ministerial officer, agent, creature, hand or arm of, and a temporary occupant and caretaker of the property for, the court, and he represents the court appointing him, and he is the medium through which the court acts."[32]

There are many different circumstances under which a receiver may be appointed. Receivers may be appointed to oversee the dissolution of a corporation or partnership. Receivers may be appointed to manage insolvent insurance companies or banking entities. A receiver may be appointed to manage real property that is the subject of litigation between parties, or to collect rents and maintain property during the judicial foreclosure of a mortgage. Receivers may be appointed to temporarily manage a business while ownership is in dispute. A receiver may be appointed to manage property pending conclusion of

---

29. *Lewis Rosenberg Autoparts*, 209 B.R. 668.
30. Restatement (Third) of Suretyship and Guaranty § 34 (1996).
31. Black's Law Dictionary (11th ed. 2019).
32. Pac. Indem. Co. v. Workmen's Comp. Appeals Bd., 258 Cal. App. 2d 35 (1968) (citing 45 Am. Jur. 2d *Receivers* § 127 (1964)).

divorce proceedings. The list of possible uses of a receiver is limited, in many jurisdictions, only by the imagination of a judge. A receiver may be employed anywhere the concept of "safekeeping" will preserve or enhance the overall resolution of pending litigation.

Because a receiver is a judicial creation, the term is not properly used to refer to contractual or extra-judicial consensual appointment. Courts do not appoint a receiver as an end. Instead, a receiver is a remedy auxiliary to some other primary relief sought in litigation.

A. *State Court*

As a tool of the courts, receivership has a long history, dating back to English courts in the time of Queen Elizabeth I.[33] Because of the unique utility of the receiver, virtually every state, whether by court rule or law, has a procedure for court appointment of a receiver.[34] Some states impose a requirement that the receiver provide a bond. Other states merely allow for bonds, in the discretion of the court. Most state laws permit the receivership bond surety to be "surcharged." This means that the liability of the surety may be the subject of summary adjudication in the pending case that gave rise to the receiver's appointment. No new lawsuit naming the surety need be filed before the surety can be required to answer for the receiver's defalcation.

B. *Federal Court*

Under the federal court system, Rule 66 of the Federal Rules of Civil Procedure authorizes the appointment of a receiver in litigation before the U.S. district court.[35] Rule 66 does not apply to proceedings in the U.S. bankruptcy court. There is no federal law requirement that a receiver

---

33. Charles Alan Wright et al., *History and Purpose of Rule 66*, *in* 12 CHARLES ALAN WRIGHT & ARTHUR R. MILLER, FEDERAL PRACTICE AND PROCEDURE § 2981 (3d ed. 2021).
34. It is beyond the scope of this chapter to detail the differences of receivership law of the 50 states.
35. These rules govern an action in which the appointment of a receiver is sought, or a receiver sues or is sued. But the practice in administering an estate by a receiver or a similar court-appointed officer must accord with the historical practice in federal courts or with a local rule. An action in which a receiver has been appointed may be dismissed only by court order. FED. R. CIV. P. 66.

bond be posted whenever a receiver is appointed. Instead, the decision whether to require a bond is left to the discretion of the court.[36] This has resulted in district-by-district, and even judge-by-judge, variations in the frequency and amount of bond required. Prior to providing the bond, the surety typically will require that the receiver, the principal on the bond, sign an indemnity agreement.

Federal law describes the duties of a receiver.[37] Absent specific statutory language mandated in a bond, both state and federal courts restate the condition of the surety's liability in broad terms, an example of which would be "receiver will well and truly perform the duties of receiver and will duly account for all moneys and properties that may come into the receiver's hands, and that the receiver will abide by and perform all things that the receiver will be directed to do by this court."[38]

C. When and Where a Receiver Can Be Sued

While state rules and statutes, and the decisions interpreting them, will vary, general rules may be distilled regarding the circumstances pursuant to which the receiver, and therefore the surety, may be sued. Most suits naming a receiver are asserted against the receivership property and not against the receiver in his or her personal capacity. Where the receiver is operating a business, there are any number of potential claims that might be asserted against the "business" as a matter of commercial reality. The claims implicating the receivership bond surety are only those asserted against the receiver in his or her individual capacity, claiming that the receiver has acted outside the scope of the receiver's authority.[39]

---

36. Fed. Trade Comm'n v. Worldwide Factors, Ltd., 882 F.2d 344, 348 (9th Cir. 1989).
37. 28 U.S.C. § 959(b). Section 959(b) provides:

    Except as provided in section 1166 of title 11, a trustee, receiver or manager appointed in any cause pending in any court of the United States, including a debtor in possession, shall manage and operate the property in his possession as such trustee, receiver or manager, according to the requirements of the valid laws of the State in which such property is situated, in the same manner that the owner or possessor thereof would be bound to do if in possession thereof.
38. 11 BENDER'S FEDERAL PRACTICE FORMS form 66.12 (2021).
39. Capital Indem. Corp. v. Curiale, 871 F. Supp. 205, 209 (S.D.N.Y. 1994).

As a general rule, a receiver may not be sued in his or her individual capacity without the express permission of the appointing court.[40] This rule is jurisdictional in nature.[41] Ordinarily, a petitioner must clearly show the receiver acted outside the scope of his or her authority to permit such an action to be filed.[42] This concept is referred to as the "Barton Doctrine."[43] The Barton Doctrine has been recognized as a matter of federal common law.[44]

In the federal system, an exception is provided to the Barton Doctrine by 28 U.S.C. § 959(a), pursuant to which a receiver may be sued without leave of the court for acts "in carrying on business connected with the property of the estate."[45] Nonetheless, suits that are brought without leave of court against the receiver or trustee and its surety will be dismissed even if it is claimed that such suit relates to the receiver's business, if the claim also seeks to hold the receiver or trustee personally liable.[46]

The receiver, and the receiver's surety, will only be liable where the condition of the bond is violated (i.e., where property is mishandled or misappropriated, or where funds are misdirected or embezzled). In this

---

40. *See, e.g.*, Fed. Deposit Ins. Corp. v. J.D.L. Assocs., 866 F. Supp. 76, 78 (D. Conn. 1994).
41. Lawrence v. Goldberg, 573 F.3d 1265, 1269 (11th Cir. 2009) (holding court lacks jurisdiction to hear a case absent approval of the appointing court).
42. *Id.*
43. Barton v. Barbour, 104 U.S. 126 (1881).
44. Carter v. Rodgers, 220 F.3d 1249, 1252–53 (11th Cir. 2000); *In re* Linton, 136 F.3d 544, 546 (7th Cir. 1998); Lebovits v. Scheffel (*In re* Lehal Realty Assocs.), 101 F.3d 272 (2d Cir. 1996); *In re* DeLorean Motor Co., 991 F.2d 1236, 1240 (6th Cir. 1993); *In re* Kashani, 190 B.R. 875, 885 (9th Cir. B.A.P. 1995).
45. 28 U.S.C. § 959(a). Section 959(a) provides:

    > Trustee, receivers or managers of any property, including debtors in possession, may be sued, without leave of the court appointing them, with respect to any of their acts or transactions in carrying on business connected with such property. Such actions shall be subject to the general equity power of such court so far as the same may be necessary to the ends of justice, but this shall not deprive the litigant of his right to trial by jury.

46. Melvin v. Klein, 266 N.Y.S.2d 533 (1965); Maguire v. Puente, 466 N.Y.S.2d 934 (1983).

respect, the liability of the receivership bond surety is the same as with other fiduciary bonds.[47]

III. Special Rights of Subrogation Available to a Surety of a Fiduciary

When the surety on a bankruptcy trustee bond or a receiver bond has paid a claim, the ordinary rights of subrogation are available to the surety. In addition to subrogation, the surety likely has contractual indemnity rights or common law indemnity rights against the trustee or receiver. The surety may hold collateral or other security to which it may look for reimbursement.

If the surety has suffered its loss as a result of breach of fiduciary duty by the receiver or trustee, as distinguished from the mere negligence of the receiver or trustee, then the surety may be entitled to pursue its reimbursement claims, even after the trustee or receiver files a personal bankruptcy. Pursuant to the Bankruptcy Code, a debt incurred for fraud or defalcation while acting in a fiduciary capacity, embezzlement, or larceny may not be discharged.[48] The surety may assert by subrogation the claim of the entity to whom it has made payments. Subrogation allows the surety to stand in the defrauded party's shoes, and oppose the bankruptcy discharge of the surety's claim, thereby permitting the surety to continue collection efforts against the defalcating receiver or trustee, even after the conclusion of the bankruptcy case.[49]

By way of illustration, a court had appointed a trustee to oversee the sale of property, place the funds in a trust account, and subsequently distribute money to the beneficiaries.[50] The surety had posted two bonds on the trustee's behalf. The property was sold for $70,000. The trustee, without authorization, withdrew $46,000 from the trust account. As a result, the court ordered the trustee to reimburse the court for principal,

---

47. *See In re* Still, 963 F.2d 75, 77 (5th Cir. 1992) (receiver personally liable if he fails to perform duties with ordinary care and prudence).
48. 11 U.S.C. § 523(A)(4).
49. *See, e.g., In re* Barnes, 317 B.R. 187, 193–94 (Bankr. M.D. Ga. 2004) (citing cases); *In re* Eggleston, 243 B.R. 365, 371–72 (Bankr. W.D. Mo. 2000).
50. *In re* Richardson, 178 B.R. 19 (Bankr. D.C. 1995), *aff'd*, 193 B.R. 380 (D.D.C. 1995), *aff'd*, 107 F.3d 923 (D.C. Cir.), *cert. denied*, 118 S. Ct. 143 (1997).

interest, and attorneys' fees, totaling in excess of $58,000. After the trustee failed to make payment, judgment was entered against the trustee. The surety satisfied the judgment. The surety obtained a judgment against the trustee, who subsequently filed a chapter 7 petition.[51]

In the trustee's chapter 7 proceeding, the surety sought to subrogate to the claim of the beneficiaries under the original sale and distribution, and to pursue a non-dischargeable proceeding based upon the debtor's defalcation while acting in a fiduciary capacity. Among his arguments, the debtor contended that he had never acted as a fiduciary with regard to the surety and, thus, the surety was not entitled to bring the non-dischargeability action under § 523 of the Bankruptcy Code.[52] The court rejected the debtor's position, holding that "standing in the shoes of the trust beneficiaries, the surety would be entitled to all the rights and remedies against the debtor that the trust beneficiaries could have asserted."[53] The court therefore concluded that the surety was subrogated to the rights of the creditors in the case under § 509 of the Bankruptcy Code and could therefore assert the creditors' right to non-dischargeability under § 523.[54]

Conclusion

The bankruptcy trustee and the receiver have similar roles in the court system, the principal difference being that the former operates exclusively within the federal bankruptcy court. Court fiduciary bonds written by a surety are likely to have broad liability, particularly in the face of expansive language describing the official duties of the principal.

The courts that appoint and benefit from the services of these bond principals will offer a measure of protection from claims and liability asserted against court appointees, by typically requiring that the appointing court exclusively hear claims asserted against the bond principal. However, where the claim against the bond principal demonstrates any breach of trust, the surety can expect a summary adjudication of liability, and a broad view of the damages "resulting from" the defalcation.

---

51. *Id*. at 31.
52. *Id*. at 23.
53. *Id*.
54. *Id*.

CHAPTER 6

PUBLIC OFFICIAL BONDS

Patrick R. Kingsley
Gerald N. Carozza, Jr.
Joseph W. Catuzzi

Introduction

Public officials have been required to furnish surety bonds to cover the faithful performance of their duties since the inception of this country. As the Pennsylvania Supreme Court explained in 1802:

> Take a view of all the offices created by the legislature of Pennsylvania, as well before as since the revolution, and we must lay it down as a general rule, that where the officer . . . is necessarily entrusted with the money of individuals, or to perform a duty which he alone can perform . . . the wisdom and justice of the legislature have been manifested in prescribing that the officer shall give bond with sufficient sureties for the faithful payment of those monies, for the faithful performance of those duties . . . .[1]

There were few sources of domestic fidelity bonding until the Fidelity Insurance Company opened its doors on April 7, 1865, at 170 Broadway, New York City. The prospectus explained its reason for opening as follows:

> Persons of the highest character and qualifications frequently decline valuable appointments, either from an unwillingness to place themselves and their friends under so serious an obligation, or the difficulty of obtaining satisfactory sureties. . . . This company, for a small yearly payment, undertakes to make good to the Employer any loss by the fraud or dishonesty of the person Employed, according to the amount specified in the Bond, and

1. Yard v. Lea, 3 Yeates 335, 345 (Pa. 1802).

> therefore obviates the necessity for private sureties, as well as the evils arising therefrom . . . .[2]

The general purpose of public official bonds is to restore the government to the position it would have been in if the public official fulfilled its obligations.[3] Bureaucrats of all kinds and at every level of government must be bonded, including treasurers, comptrollers, tax collectors, assessors, agency heads, school officials, city officials, county clerks, court clerks, and sheriffs. These bonds may also cover defaults by subordinates.[4] The bond might cover either a single official or position, or multiple officials or positions as set forth in a schedule.[5]

The condition of the bond is usually that the official will faithfully perform the duties of his or her office. The bond also often guarantees that the official will account for all monies received in an official capacity. The public official bond may provide broader coverage than a fidelity bond conditioned on proof of dishonesty. In the case of a loss of public funds, the duty to account may be strict.

In addition to the traditional three-party surety bonds that officials in certain top positions are required to post, governmental units may also be required to obtain coverage in the form of two-party public official blanket bonds. These bonds are designed to protect against loss caused by public employees not personally obligated to furnish bonds, including lower-level officials and functionaries.[6] Unlike the traditional public official bond, which has few express terms beyond the basic condition of faithful performance, the public employee blanket bond may have

---

2. Willis D. Morgan, *The History and Economics of Suretyship*, 12 CORNELL L. REV. 487 (1927).
3. Centennial Sch. Dist. v. Kerins, 840 A.2d 377, 386 (Pa. Commw. Ct. 2003).
4. Federal officials, however, no longer must furnish bonds. Title 6 of the U.S. Code formerly required such bonding, Act July 30, 1947, ch. 390, § 1, 61 Stat. 646, but this was repealed by Act Sept. 13, 1982, Pub. L. No. 97-258, § 5(b), 96 Stat. 1085. Federal bankruptcy trustees and the like furnish bonds but these are considered court bonds, not public official bonds, although both types cover fiduciary duties.
5. *See* THOMAS W. RYNARD, INSURANCE RISK MANAGEMENT—STATE AND LOCAL GOVERNMENTS § 27.05 (2010).
6. *See, e.g.*, Erie Cnty. v. Am. States Ins. Co., 573 F. Supp. 479 (W.D. Pa. 1983); First Va. Bank-Colonial v. Baker, 301 S.E.2d 8 (Va. 1983).

numerous additional definitions, conditions, limitations, and exclusions, similar to a financial institution bond or a commercial crime policy.

I. Who Has Standing as an Obligee?

It depends.[7] The consensus view is that "the proper claimant on a statutory public official bond is the named obligee, unless the legislature has expressed in the statutory language its intent to allow others to sue directly on the bond."[8] Public official bonds typically name as obligee only the public entity that employs the official. It follows generally that a third party may not sue on the bond absent specific authority by the statute requiring the bond.[9] This includes public entities other than the intended obligee.[10] However, such authority is frequently provided.[11]

A. *The Narrow View*

Statutes of course may limit standing too. Illustrating this, in *Seider v. Hutchison*,[12] a candidate for sheriff lost an election and sued the state's coordinator of elections. The losing candidate also sued on a surety bond covering the coordinator. He argued that he had standing to sue on the bond because it was given under a statute requiring faithful performance in favor of anyone injured. The court disagreed. The bond was issued under another statute that required a bond covering all of the state's public employees but did not give anyone injured standing to sue. Only certain officers had to give (and execute as principal) official bonds covering faithful performance in favor of anyone injured, and this did not include the coordinator of elections.

Indeed, when the bond names only a specific obligee, and the statute does not require that it run in favor of anyone else, it will be enforced as written, and third parties will not be allowed to sue on it.[13] This is

---

7. Preliminarily, we note that the federal government maintains a prohibition against public official bonds for federal officials. 31 U.S.C. § 9302.
8. Bueker v. Madison Cnty., 72 N.E.3d 269, 272 (Ill. 2016).
9. Hicks v. Aetna Ins. Co., 423 N.E.2d 584 (Ill. App. Ct. 1981).
10. City of Manton v. Ryder, 417 N.W.2d 257 (Mich. Ct. App. 1987).
11. *Id.*
12. No. 3:06 CV 215, 2009 U.S. Dist. LEXIS 68410 (E.D. Tenn. Aug. 5, 2009).
13. *Ryder*, 417 N.W.2d 257 (holding that city could not sue on city treasurer's bond that named county as obligee and protected treasurer's duty to pay

especially true of public official blanket bonds. They are enforceable only by the named public entity, not by members of the public at large.[14] An International Organization for Standardization (ISO) Government Crime Policy Form, for example, limits the right to make claims to the public entity identified as the named insured. It does so by stating: "However, this policy is for your benefit only. It provides no rights or benefits to any other person or organization. Any claim for loss that is covered under this policy must be presented by you."[15]

In another instance, a Washington statute precludes anyone other than the named public obligee from suing on the bond of an official, except by leave of court.[16] And, in *Cortland v. Cowlitz County Clerk's Office*,[17] the court would not let a pro se plaintiff sue on a county clerk's bond because he did not first seek leave and had not prosecuted his underlying claims.

B. The Expansive View

On the other hand, under a Georgia statute, anyone injured by a public official will have standing to sue on the official's bond, as an intended third-party beneficiary.[18] Similarly, a Mississippi statute allows "any interested party to sue an official's bonding company for recovery of damages [provided that] those damages must be caused by the failure of that official to perform a mandatory duty."[19] And, in Alabama, a widow could sue a sheriff and his surety on the basis that her husband died as a result of the sheriff's failure to provide him with adequate medical treatment while in jail. As required, the bond provided it was "for the use and benefit of every person who is injured" by the principal's wrongful act

---

tax receipts to county); Boyle v. Bowman, 605 P.2d 1144 (Nev. 1980) (holding that a private person had no standing to sue on public official bond of clerk under statute referencing only losses to the county or city).

14. *Hicks*, 423 N.E.2d 584 (holding that members of public had no standing to sue on bond in favor of the Department of Agriculture); First Va. Bank-Colonial v. Baker, 301 S.E.2d 8 (Va. 1983) (bank had no standing to sue for loss from failure of deputy court clerk to properly index lien).
15. ISO Government Crime Policy (Loss Sustained Form), Form CR 0027 05 06, ¶ E.1.q.
16. WASH. REV. CODE § 42.08.030 (2012).
17. No. C06-5341, 2006 U.S. Dist. LEXIS 80285 (W.D. Wash. Oct. 24, 2006).
18. Cantrell v. Thurman, 499 S.E.2d 416 (Ga. Ct. App. 1998).
19. Short v. Williams, 303 So. 3d 87, 104 (Miss. Ct. App. 2020).

under color of office.[20] In Mississippi, the parents of school-age children in the township could sue on a school board's bond when the board had leased school property to a board member for an inadequate price.[21]

In *State ex rel. Mather v. Carnes*,[22] the co-owner of an airplane was allowed to proceed against a sheriff and his surety for the sheriff's failure to attach the plane in a partition action:

> At common law only the obligee named on the bond of a public official could maintain an action on that obligation. Our statutes have since enabled any person injured by the neglect of an official to proceed to suit in the name of the state to his own use. The law treats such a suit on an official bond as a private action which results in a private judgment and incurs private costs. The role of the state as obligee on the bond is only nominal in such proceedings.[23]

Just as standing is heavily reliant on the underlying statute, so too is the scope of a public official bond.

II. The Scope of Public Official Bond Coverage

A. *Faithful Performance*

The public official bond is usually conditioned on the official's faithful performance of his or her statutory duties (i.e., the duties imposed by statute for the office that is bonded).[24] The use of the word "faithful,"

---

20. Dixon v. Am. Liberty Ins. Co., 332 So. 2d 719 (Ala. 1976).
21. Holmes v. Jones, 318 So. 2d 865 (Miss. 1975).
22. 551 S.W.2d 272 (Mo. Ct. App. 1977).
23. *Id.* at 290–91 (citation omitted).
24. U.S. Fid. & Guar. Co. v. Conservatorship of Melson, 809 So. 2d 647, 655 (Miss. 2002) (recognizing that, in order for the surety to be held liable under its public official's bond, the official's act or omission must be within the scope or duties of his office); State *ex rel.* Avery Cnty. v. Braswell, 1 S.E.2d 864, 867 (N.C. 1939) ("A bond for the faithful performance of official duty is as binding on the principal and his sureties as if all the statutory duties of the officer were inserted in it."); Refugio Lumber Co. v. Bailey, 172 S.W.2d 133, 134 (Tex. Civ. App. 1943) ("the liability of public officials for negligently or fraudulently diverting and failing to account for public funds coming into their hands rests only upon

however, is somewhat of a misnomer as it suggests fidelity and good faith when, in practice, "*faithful*" performance typically ensures actual and proper performance of one's statutory and official duties. As explained by one court, "the purpose of public official bonds is to provide the Obligee (the State) with a measure of security in case the Principal (Byrd) absconds with public funds or otherwise causes the Obligee to suffer damages by failing to perform the duties of his office."[25]

The parameters of a public official's duties, however, vary from state to state and understanding the meaning of "faithful performance" will vary from state to state. Further, public official bonds may also cover duties traditionally appurtenant to or implied by the nature of the office.[26] The bond thus may cover a wide range of duties, including duties added after the bond is issued.[27] Liability may arise from the bonded official's

---

statutes"). *See generally* H. Bruce Shreves & Charles C. Coffee, *Faithful Performance under Fidelity, Public Official, and Statutory Bonds*, 3 FID. L.J. 97 (1997).

25. Seibert v. Travelers Cas. & Sur. Co. of Am., No. 1:14-CV-188-KS-MTP, 2018 WL 2770659, at *4 (S.D. Miss. Mar. 29, 2018).

26. *In re* Kappelman, 754 P.2d 449, 450–51 (Idaho 1988) ("The duties of a public officer include, not only those which lie within the direct definition of the statute, but also those which are necessary to the accomplishment of the purpose of his office, even though they may be an incident of his main duties, where they promote the execution of a mandate of law.") (quoting S. Pac. R.R. Co. v. Stibbens, 285 P. 374, 379 (Cal. Ct. App. 1930)); Miller v. Owsley, 422 S.W.2d 39, 41 (Mo. 1967) (holding that a bond given under statute to cover faithful discharge of sheriff's duties "would cover both duties prescribed by statute and common law duties").

27. *Kappelman*, 754 P.2d at 451 ("[S]ureties on an official bond are presumed to take notice of the fact that changes will be made concerning the duties of their principal, and where these changes are made in matters of minor importance, which, as a whole, do not substantially increase their responsibilities, the sureties will not be exonerated.") (quoting Spokane Cnty. v. Allen, 37 P. 428, 430 (Wash. 1894)). It has been suggested, however, that the imposition of duties on the principal beyond the scope of what the parties reasonably anticipated when the bond was issued could be a material alteration that would discharge the surety. City of Rice Lake v. Jensen, 255 N.W. 130 (Wis. 1934).

- negligent infliction of personal injuries;[28]
- civil rights violation;[29]
- self-dealing or conflict of interest;[30]
- failure to execute or enforce processes and court orders;[31]
- failure to advise a debtor of rights;[32]
- malicious prosecution;[33]
- breach of employment contract;[34]
- misappropriation of public funds or property;[35]
- failure to account for public funds;
- overpayment of salary; or
- failure to collect taxes, fees, or other public funds.

---

28. Smith v. Phillips, 451 S.E.2d 309 (N.C. Ct. App. 1994) (discussing sheriff's negligent failure to prevent inmate's suicide); *Miller*, 422 S.W.2d 39 (discussing sheriff's negligent failure to prevent prison beating).
29. Cameron v. Brock, 473 F.2d 608 (6th Cir. 1973) (discussing sheriff's deputy arrested and incarcerated election opponent who was distributing campaign pamphlets). *But see* Booth v. Firemen's Ins. Co., 477 S.E.2d 376 (Ga. Ct. App. 1996) (no liability for racial epithets by deputy sheriff).
30. Moore *ex rel.* City of Aberdeen v. Byars, 757 So. 2d 243 (Miss. 2000) (analyzing a situation when a city manager leased his house to dentist who received development loans from city); State *ex rel.* Pittman v. Ladner, 512 So. 2d 1271 (Miss. 1987) (holding that school board members awarded an emergency repair contract to a contractor who employed one of them).
31. Henry S. Miller Co. v. Evans, 425 S.W.2d 426 (Tex. 1970) (holding the surety liable for sheriff's refusal to levy execution).
32. Dancer v. Chenault, 527 S.W.2d 714 (Mo. Ct. App. 1975) (discussing the sheriff's failure to advise debtor of her right to a garnishment exemption).
33. State *ex rel.* Hailey v. Westmoreland, 267 F. Supp. 2d 497 (M.D.N.C. 2003) (allowing arrested driver to sue sheriff and surety for malicious prosecution).
34. Hill v. Medford, 582 S.E.2d 325 (N.C. Ct. App. 2003) (reasoning that a fired deputy could maintain breach of employment contract claim against sheriff and surety if termination was against public policy, even if deputy's employment was at will); Venable v. Vernon, 592 S.E.2d 256 (N.C. Ct. App. 2004) (dismissing deputy's claim against sheriff and surety for lack of evidence deputy had been terminated for not supporting sheriff's reelection).
35. Borough of Totowa v. Am. Sur. Co. of N.Y., 188 A.2d 586 (N.J. 1963); City of Milwaukee v. Hurless, 97 N.W.2d 399 (Wis. 1959).

The last three categories are considered further below, followed by a discussion of other duties generally.

B. Statutory Duties

The public official bond is statutory, which means it is required by a statute[36] and it must be consistent with the underlying statute.[37] It is essential to identify and consult the controlling statute, regulation, or ordinance. Indeed, some states may refer to what is known as the "read-in/read-out" rule when interpreting public official bonds. One court recently framed the importance of the underlying statute as follows:

> As a general rule, the liability of a surety on a bond which is plain and unambiguous is governed, like any other contract, by the intention of the parties as expressed in the instrument. However, in determining the legal effect of a statutory bond such as is here before the Court, certain rules of construction are to be considered. A statutory bond will be reviewed in the light of the statute creating the duty to give security. It will be generally held that the provisions of the statute and regulations will be read into the bond. *Maryland Casualty Co. v. United States*, 251 U.S. 342, 40 S. Ct. 155, 64 L. Ed. 297 (1919); *Whattoff v. United States*, C.A. 8, 1966, 355 F.2d 473; *Jones v. United States*, C.A. 8, 1951, 189 F.2d 601. So also, if a statutory bond contains provisions which do not comply with the requirements of law, they may be eliminated as surplusage and denied legal effect. *Fort Smith Structural Steel Co. v. Western Surety Co.*, W.D. Ark., 1965, 247 F. Supp. 674; 12 Am. Jur. 2d, Bonds § 26.[38]

---

36. *See, e.g.*, 5 Ill. Comp. Stat. 260/14.1 (2010); Cal. Gov't Code § 1450 *et seq.* (2010); Fla. Stat. Ann. § 113.07 (2010); N.Y. Pub. Off. Law §§ 20–28 (2010); Tenn. Code Ann. § 8-19-101 *et seq.* (2010).
37. We note that the law maintains a distinction between statutory and nonstatutory public official bonds. Generally speaking, the former will be read to conform to the underlying statute while the latter is often interpreted according to the bond's plain text.
38. W. Sur. Co. v. City of Nicholasville, 552 S.W.3d 101, 112 (Ky. Ct. App. 2018).

Generally speaking, omitted conditions will be read in; contrary ones read out.[39] "[P]ublic officials do not have the power to contract away the rights of the public for whose benefit the official bond is required. Therefore, provisions in official bonds which tend to limit or restrict the surety's liability are void."[40] For example, one court held a surety liable for the penal amount that the statute required when the bond on its face was for a lesser amount.[41] A bond not required by statute or in an amount greater than the statute requires may be enforceable against the surety as written if given for a lawful purpose.[42]

The liability of a surety on the public official bond is limited by the terms of the bond, but ambiguities will be resolved against the drafter.[43] Often, the form is drafted by the public entity. Sometimes the statute dictates the bond form; other times the agency in charge of the bond requirement publishes the nonnegotiable form. Other times, the bond is to be in a form acceptable to the solicitor for the obligee (planning board, zoning board, etc.). Construction should not be against the surety in such cases.

If the bond conforms to a statute, the doctrine of construing ambiguities against the drafter may not be necessary. Although the surety may still face a rule of statutory construction in favor of coverage, the surety should argue that what is really at stake is the liability of the principal, so a neutral construction or even a liberal one in favor of the principal (a public servant) and his or her surety is more appropriate.

On occasion bonds have been enforced as written in favor of the surety, even if they vary from what the statute may have contemplated. In *Washington v. Trust Co.*,[44] the term of the bonded office was six years but the bond recited it was given for only one year. The court enforced

---

39. City of Manton v. Ryder, 417 N.W.2d 257 (Mich. Ct. App. 1987); City of Oakland v. Snow, 78 P. 1060 (Cal. 1904); State *ex rel.* Switzer v. Overturff, 33 N.W.2d 405 (Iowa 1948) (construing bond as not requiring forfeiture of penal sum; surety was liable for actual damages only under controlling statutes despite arguably harsher wording of bond).
40. State v. Lidster, 467 N.E.2d 47 (Ind. Ct. App. 1984); Nat'l Sur. Corp. v. Morgan Cnty., 440 S.W.2d 791, 792 (Ky. Ct. App. 1969) (refusing to enforce clause terminating sheriff's bond on discovery of dishonesty; sheriff also was serving as *ex officio* tax collector).
41. State v. Moody, 198 So. 2d 586, 590–91 (Miss. 1967).
42. Pa. Tpk. Comm'n v. U.S. Fid. & Guar. Co., 194 A.2d 423, 428 (Pa. 1963).
43. Town of Scotland Neck v. W. Sur. Co., 271 S.E.2d 501 (N.C. 1980).
44. 171 S.E. 438 (N.C. 1933).

the bond as written, because the obligee had accepted the bond with knowledge of the contractual modification. In *Thornsberry v. Western Surety Co.*,[45] the court held that a police officer's bond naming only a city as obligee was a common law bond. Only the city could sue on it, not the public, unlike a statutory bond in favor of the state.

The bond statute may also dictate the standard of care or the level of culpability that must be proved. In *State ex rel. Pettis County R-XII v. Kahrs*,[46] a school district sued on the official statutory bonds of a county assessor and a county collector for failure to assess, levy, and collect taxes. The officials would be liable under the statute only if they refused or knowingly neglected to perform their duties. The court affirmed a summary judgment against the district on other grounds but spotted an issue for the future of whether officials "must know that they are evading the tax law when doing such."[47]

C. Specific Claims

1. Lost Public Funds

Most courts provide almost no excuse for the principal's inability to account for public funds. Due care is *not* enough. As explained in *Cecil v. Gila County*:

> [W]here a bond is conditioned for the payment over of public moneys, for the safekeeping of them, or the statute prescribes such, in substance, to be the duty of the officer, and the bond is conditioned for the faithful performance of the duties of the office, and no condition limiting that obligation is discoverable in the statute, the obligation thus imposed upon and assumed by the officer will be deemed absolute and the doctrine of strict liability applies, except perhaps for acts of God or public enemies. The plea that the money has been stolen or lost without his fault or negligence does not constitute a defense to an action for its recovery. There is no defense at law but a production of the funds, the contract being absolute in its terms. Loss by accident or otherwise is likewise not a defense in equity, as the allowance

---

45. 738 F. Supp. 209 (E.D. Ky. 1990).
46. 258 S.W.3d 85 (Mo. Ct. App. 2008).
47. *Id.* at 86 n.2.

of such a defense would be dangerous to the public interests and is forbidden by considerations of public policy.[48]

A surety may be liable to the extent the bonded official fails to account for or turn over public funds when required to do so. Usually this duty to account arises at the end of the official's term but it could ripen earlier if a shortage is discovered or an audit is conducted. The duty to account at the end of the term includes instances when the official succeeds himself or herself—begins a new term. It also extends to any holdover period beyond the expiration of the term.[49]

This concept of an absolute or strict liability can be traced to *United States v. Prescott.*[50] The U.S. Supreme Court held that anything less "would open the door to frauds."[51] The Court created a public enemy exception in *United States v. Thomas,*[52] which involved a Confederate seizure of funds from a customs agent in Tennessee. However, that was the only exception the Supreme Court ever recognized.[53] According to another court, not even a bank failure would relieve the surety: "Failure to pay over funds when required made him and his surety liable, and neither could successfully defend on the ground that a bank in which the funds were deposited had failed."[54]

The majority of state courts have followed *Prescott* in holding public officials and their sureties liable as insurers of public funds entrusted to them. That the money was stolen despite the official's due care is no defense.[55] Nor is the official excused if the money was lost by a subordinate.[56] For example:

---

48. 227 P.2d 217, 218 (Ariz. 1951).
49. Am. Sur. Co. v. Indep. Sch. Dist., 53 F.2d 178 (8th Cir. 1931).
50. 44 U.S. 578 (1845); *see* Lisa Weekley Coulter, Presentation at Surety Claims Institute Conference, Public Official Bonds: A Fresh Look at a Venerable Bond (June 23–24, 2000).
51. *Prescott*, 44 U.S. at 588.
52. 82 U.S. 337 (1872).
53. Coulter, *supra* note 50, at 1–3.
54. *Indep. Sch. Dist.*, 53 F.2d at 179.
55. Coulter, *supra* note 50, at 3–4 (citing Halbert v. Bd. of Comm'rs, 22 Ind. 125 (1864) (official who put money in safe as ordered by board was held liable on his bond when money was stolen from safe)).
56. Coulter, *supra* note 50, at 4 (citing City of Youngstown v. Hindman, 38 N.E.2d 319 (Ohio 1939)).

A bonded officer knows when he delegates to a subordinate the power to deal with public money that he is giving his appointee the power to ruin him by corrupt practices. . . . It is better that the bonded officer, rather than the public, bear the burden of scrutinizing the vouchers of subordinates and explaining those that need explanation.[57]

Thus, as already noted, cases began holding that even the consent of the public entity's board to a treasurer's decision to deposit funds in a bank that later failed was no defense.[58] This injustice has been mitigated by statute and deposit insurance. For example, in Nebraska, a statute provides that if the depository bank is approved and issues the bond itself, the treasurer of a public fund is not liable for loss sustained by reason of the failure of the bank.[59] However, this did not relieve a municipal treasurer and his surety from liability for loss as a result of a bank's failure when the treasurer was an officer, director, and stockholder of the bank and knew it was unsafe.[60]

2. *Unauthorized Spending*

Unauthorized spending of public funds by the official in excess of appropriations could leave the surety liable as well.[61] The surety has also been held liable for loss from misapplication of funds when the basis for payment was not properly documented.[62] In *Elsbury v. Stann & Associates*,[63] a state treasurer was found liable in the amount of her general bond to a workers' compensation claimant who had been unable to recover his award due to the insolvency of the employer, the workers' compensation trust, and the workers' compensation trust insolvency fund. As the ex officio custodian of the insolvency fund, the treasurer had to make good any shortfall, not merely safeguard any monies actually deposited.

The minority rule is that officials should be treated as bailees or trustees and therefore will not be liable on their bonds for a loss of

---

57. Sec'y of State v. Hanover Ins. Co., 441 P.2d 89, 92 (Or. 1966).
58. Bd. of Educ. of City of Detroit v. Brown, 105 N.W. 1118 (Mich. 1908).
59. NEB. REV. STAT. § 17-607 (2021); Vill. of Hampton v. Gausman, 286 N.W. 757 (Neb. 1939); City of S. Sioux City v. Mullins, 250 N.W. 549 (Neb. 1933).
60. City of Cozad v. Thompson, 252 N.W. 606 (Neb. 1934).
61. Fannin v. Davis, 385 S.W.2d 321 (Ky. 1967).
62. Leskinen v. Pucelj, 115 N.W.2d 346 (Minn. 1962).
63. 861 N.E.2d 1031 (Ill. App. Ct. 2006).

funds absent negligence.[64] States that have applied this approach include Alabama, California, Idaho, Iowa, Kentucky, Louisiana, Maine, Maryland, Montana, South Carolina, Tennessee, and Wyoming.[65]

Even in strict liability jurisdictions, a bond given under a statute requiring only an accounting for public funds does not cover nonfinancial duties of the official such as to keep a bridge in a safe condition.[66] Furthermore, the official must have had a duty to handle the funds at issue. He or she is not liable for funds that were never supposed to be in his or her custody.[67] There can be no liability absent actual loss of public funds. There must be a wrongful act and a loss resulting from that wrongful act; the wrongful act must be the act of the defendant, and the injury suffered by the plaintiff must be the natural and not merely a remote consequence of the defendant's act.[68]

3. *Overpayment of Salary*

There is authority that the public official bond does not cover the innocent or good faith overpayment of salary or other employee benefits to the principal/official. In *United States v. Boyd*,[69] the government had overcompensated one Sempronius Boyd, the United States consul in Bangkok, Siam. The Western District of Missouri held that his bond did not cover the loss:

> The matter of his salary, which was his individual perquisite, in its very nature could not have been the subjectmatter within the object and purview of the bond. It was not necessary that the government should exact of its consul a bond for money the government should pay him for his salary. Such money when paid by the government was not to be taken into an accounting between him and the government. It could not have been anticipated by, or within the contemplation of, the sureties that the treasury department in remitting salary to the consul general

64. Coulter, *supra* note 50, at 9.
65. *Id.*
66. Bynum v. W. Sur. Co. of Sioux Falls, 323 P.2d 972, 975 (Okla. 1958).
67. Hensley v. Holder, 307 S.W.2d 74 (Ark. 1957) (holding that the sheriff was not liable for state's overpayment of deputy).
68. Town of Thornton v. Winterhoff, 92 N.E.2d 163 (Ill. 1950) (analyzing a town treasurer's bond).
69. 118 F. 89 (W.D. Mo. 1902).

> would make a mistake and send him too much. The bond was not to cover the blunders of the disbursing officers of the government, but only the defalcations of the consul general as such in accounting, to the government for moneys coming to his office in the course of his official duties.[70]

But in *Maryland Casualty Co. v. Kansas City, Missouri*,[71] the Eighth Circuit took a different view: "Public officers claiming compensation for official duties performed must point out the statute authorizing such payment. Compensation paid to a public officer, when not authorized by law, or in excess of compensation authorized by law, may be recovered from the principal and his surety." Later cases have also allowed recourse against sureties for salary overpayments.[72]

4. Collection of Funds

Although a diligent good faith effort by the official ought to be a valid defense, there may be exposure to the surety when an official fails to collect taxes or other funds that could have been collected.[73] *Texas Department of Transportation v. Shaw*[74] is a harsh example. The state brought an action against a county tax collector and his surety, to recover license tag fees the official should have collected from Handy Andy, Inc. had it not gone bankrupt. The collector failed to remit the fees to the state every week as required and also failed to deputize the Handy Andy employees who were selling the tags and to require of Handy Andy a

---

70. *Id.* at 91.
71. 128 F.2d 998, 1001 (8th Cir. 1942).
72. Osborne v. State, 439 N.E.2d 677 (Ind. Ct. App. 1982) (holding trustee's surety liable for improper accumulation of annual and sick leave); State *ex rel.* Hardesty v. Stalnaker, 280 S.E.2d 697 (W. Va. 1981) (holding county employees' sureties liable for return of unauthorized salary increases); Busbee v. Reserve Ins. Co., 254 S.E.2d 324 (Ga. 1979) (holding prison director's surety liable for director's failure to return unauthorized salary increase).
73. Am. Cas. Co. v. Quitman Sch. Dist., 739 S.W.2d 144 (Ark. 1987) (discussing the failure to extend taxes at proper rates causing school district to lose revenue); Cnty. of Platte v. New Amsterdam Cas. Co., 6 F.R.D. 475 (D. Neb. 1946) (holding surety liable for county treasurer's failure to collect delinquent taxes).
74. 847 S.W.2d 618 (Tex. Ct. App. 1992).

contract and a fidelity bond. This was a lack of faithful performance even if it was not dishonest. The court rejected the surety's contention that Handy Andy's bankruptcy caused the loss. This case perhaps is better understood as the failure to account by Handy Andy as a subordinate of the principal.

Similarly, in *Centennial School District v. Kerins*, a tax collector collected but failed to timely remit its collection to a school district. Regardless of the tax collector's good or bad faith, the court framed the issue in simple terms as follows:

> In the instant case, [the tax collector] did not fulfill his statutory obligations. He maintained possession of funds after he was required to pay them and, by doing so, breached his fiduciary responsibility as to the proceeds. Under these circumstances, there is no reason why [the surety], having assured the District of the tax collector's faithful performance of his duties by issuing a bond on his behalf, should not be financially accountable for the collector's breach of these duties. That the funds may have, at some point, been paid over, does not alleviate the time-value lost by the delay. Accordingly, we find no error in the trial court's ruling that Fidelity could be held accountable for interest on the collected taxes.[75]

While the underlying statutory duties of an official must always be analyzed, *Kerins* reflects the often unforgiving nature of public official bonds.[76] This concept was recently played out in *Cordray v. International Preparatory School*,[77] when the court held "that an officer, employee, or duly authorized representative or agent of a community school is a public official and may be held strictly liable to the state for the loss of public funds."[78]

---

75. Centennial Sch. Dist. v. Kerins, 840 A.2d 377, 386 (Pa. Commw. Ct. 2003).
76. *Id.*
77. 941 N.E.2d 1170 (Ohio 2010).
78. *Id.* at 1171.

5. Other Unusual Claims

While there may be a strict duty on an official regarding the accounting, handling, and dispensing of public funds, a claimant may have to prove the principal's negligence or intentional wrongdoing to establish a failure to faithfully perform other duties,[79] or the liability may not be within the scope of the bond (despite the argument that if read literally the bond might cover all duties).[80] If the claim alleges a tort, the surety can argue that the liability is or could have been covered, if at all, by liability insurance. Depending on the nature of the office bonded, sureties should be prepared to deal with a variety of claims alleging breach of duties other than funds handling. For example, the surety could be liable for loss caused by an official's improper award of a public contract.[81] Many of these claims, however, may be frivolous or deficiently presented by pro se litigants.[82] A distinction can also be made between ministerial duties that the bond covers and discretionary duties that involve an exercise of judgment in governmental decision-making as a function of the office. The surety is not liable for loss resulting from the latter absent an abuse of discretion.[83]

---

79. Atlas Supply Co. v. U.S. Fid. & Guar. Co., 191 S.E.2d 103 (Ga. Ct. App. 1972) (holding that a court clerk's surety did not insure the solvency of a surety on a bond the clerk approved to discharge a lien, provided the clerk was not negligent).
80. Knight v. Newton Cnty., 806 F. Supp. 105 (S.D. Miss. 1992) (holding that the surety on sheriff's bond not liable to deputy for sheriff's administrative failure to compensate deputy).
81. Town of City of Peoria v. Rauschkolb, 78 N.E.2d 123 (Ill. App. Ct. 1948).
82. State *ex rel.* Timson v. Shoemaker, No. 02AP-1037, 2003 Ohio App. LEXIS 4216 (Ohio Ct. App. Sept. 4, 2003) (dismissing pro se claims against veterans service commissioners for failing to provide emergency assistance, meals-on-wheels, and bus passes to plaintiff, among other things).
83. Baker v. Seal, 694 S.W.2d 948, 952 (Tenn. Ct. App. 1984) ("When acting in a quasi-judicial or discretionary matter, a public officer or employee is usually given immunity from liability to persons who may be injured as the result of an erroneous or mistaken decision, however erroneous his judgment may be, provided the acts complained of are done within the scope of the officer's authority, the officer is acting in good faith, and without willfulness, malice, corruption, or oppression in office."). For further discussion of immunity, see *infra* Part III.E.

III. The Principal's Underlying Liability

A. *The Requirement That the Principal Be Independently Liable*

A fundamental precept of surety law is that a public official's surety is not liable unless its principal, the official, is liable.[84] The bond protects the public entity from loss caused by the principal but is not insurance for the principal.[85] If the principal makes the obligee or claimant whole, the surety is discharged.[86] The principal must have breached an underlying duty within the scope of the bond. In *Ledbetter v. Knox County*,[87] plaintiff alleged an illegal search by sheriff's deputies and included a claim against the sheriff and his surety. The court dismissed that count because "Tennessee law does not create a separate cause of liability based upon the sheriff's bond."[88] The principal must have an independent liability. Thus it is essential to develop an understanding of the claim against the official, including consultation of any statutes, regulations, ordinances, or case law bearing on the official's duties.

Gilmer v. Trowbridge[89] is a colorful illustration of a situation when a surety could not be held liable because its principal (a sheriff) was not independently liable. In that case, the plaintiff was shooting skeet near his fence line when a neighbor complained to the sheriff. When the sheriff's deputy attempted to talk to the plaintiff, he began beating on the squad car and yelling. The deputy arrested him for disorderly conduct. Plaintiff sued the sheriff and his surety alleging civil rights violations. The court held the sheriff was not liable and therefore his surety was not liable.

But it does not follow that the surety is liable whenever the principal is liable. For one thing, the surety must be joined as a party to the suit. In

---

84. Smith v. Sinclair, 424 F. Supp. 1108 (W.D. Okla. 1976); Spaniol Ford, Inc. v. Froggatt, 478 P.2d 598, 600 (Wyo. 1970); Thompson v. Dodge, D350 1986, No. 1:11-cv-479, 2011 U.S. Dist. LEXIS 63706 (W.D. Mich. June 14, 2011) (holding that, if the plaintiff fails to state a claim against the official, he cannot recover from the surety).

85. State *ex rel.* Mayle v. Aetna Cas. & Sur. Co., 166 S.E.2d 133, 136 (W. Va. 1969).

86. *Id.*

87. No. 3:05-CV-248, 2006 U.S. Dist. LEXIS 7908 (E.D. Tenn. Feb. 15, 2006).

88. *Id.*

89. No. 3:08 cv 36, 2009 U.S. Dist. LEXIS 18500 (S.D. Miss. Nov. 23, 2009).

Fowler v. Burns,[90] plaintiff sued a sheriff and his deputies for misconduct in the course of investigating a lawnmower theft. The plaintiff also sought to recover on the sheriff's bond but the court held that that the surety would have to be sued too. Plaintiff could not just sue the sheriff alone and allege he was liable on the bond nor name "Doe Insurance Company" as a party. The real surety had to be before the court before the action could proceed. Similarly, in *Simmons v. Surry County Sheriff Department*,[91] an inmate asserted a bond claim against a sheriff after the inmate was injured coming out of a van in shackles. The court dismissed the claim. While a statute waived the sheriff's sovereign immunity to the extent of his official bond, the inmate could not recover on the bond unless he joined the surety as a party and pleaded the waiver.

The surety must have notice and an opportunity to defend itself. In *Ohio Casualty Insurance Co. v. Kentucky Natural Resources & Environmental Protection Cabinet*,[92] a default judgment against a sheriff did not bind the sheriff's surety; the surety could raise any defenses the sheriff could have raised. Conversely, however, collateral estoppel applies in favor of a surety when an action against the principal is dismissed.[93] So does res judicata.[94] In deference to the surety's right to assert a defense of the principal, the surety will not be guilty of vexatious refusal to pay or bad faith if the defense is reasonable, even if it fails.[95]

Moreover, for the surety to be liable, the principal's liability must fall within the statutory purpose and scope of the bond, which may only cover acts or omissions under virtue of office.[96] An official bond should not cover duties for which liability insurance is separately required. In *Poole v. Brunt*,[97] the surety on a sheriff's faithful performance bond was not liable to a person injured by a deputy's negligent operation of a public vehicle. The bond was not intended to serve as automobile liability insurance, which the sheriff was separately required to provide for his deputies.

---

90. No. 2:08-CV-21, 2010 U.S. Dist. LEXIS 17015 (E.D. Tenn. Feb. 25, 2010), *reversed on other grounds*, 2011 U.S. App. LEXIS 16230 (6th Cir. Aug. 4, 2011).
91. No. 1:09 CV 94, 2010 U.S. Dist. LEXIS 32949 (M.D.N.C. Apr. 2, 2010).
92. 722 S.W.2d 290 (Ky. Ct. App. 1986).
93. Smith v. Sinclair, 424 F. Supp. 1108 (W.D. Okla. 1976).
94. Lawson v. Toney, 169 F. Supp. 2d 456 (M.D.N.C. 2001).
95. State *ex rel.* Pemiscot Cnty. v. W. Sur. Co., 51 F.3d 170 (8th Cir. 1995).
96. *See infra* Part III.B.
97. 338 So. 2d 991 (Miss. 1976).

B. Color of Office

The term "color of office" goes back to the reign of Henry VI, in the year 1444, when a statute was enacted to prohibit sheriffs from doing certain acts "by color of their office."[98] Color of office "signifies an act badly done under the countenance of an office."[99] Whether or not an act carries with it the "color of office," however, does not always turn on whether the act itself was officially authorized. For instance, in *Dive v. Maningham*,[100] a chief justice held that color of office could include legally unauthorized acts—the material issue was whether the sheriff did the act "as sheriff."

The inquiry is important because the liability of a surety on a faithful performance bond for the act or omission of a public official depends on whether the act or omission was at least committed under color of office.[101] Historically, courts attempted to distinguish between acts by virtue of office (surety liable) and acts under color of office (surety not liable). Acts by virtue of office are within the authority of the officer but performed improperly. Acts under color of office are outside or beyond the authority conferred by the office.[102] This distinction was never easy to make and some courts no longer regard it as important.[103] Even under a more simplified view though, the act must be "connected to the official's official activity."[104]

Generally, even an intentional or malicious act, such as a shooting, false imprisonment, or brutal assault, may be considered under color of office.[105] Yet a purely personal act is not. Thus, in *Kentucky Finance Co. v. Spradlin*,[106] when a county clerk's deputy forged the clerk's signature

---

98. 23 Hen. 6, c. 10, § 7.
99. 75 Eng. Rep. 96, 108 (Common Bench 1551); *see* Steven L. Winter, *The Meaning of "Under Color of" Law*, 91 MICH. L. REV. 323 (1992).
100. Antinerella v. Rioux, 690 A.2d 450, 454 (Conn. Super. Ct. 1995) (citing 75 Eng. Rep. 96, 109 (C.P. 1551)).
101. Jemison v. Crichlow, 531 N.Y.S.2d 919 (App. Div. 1988); Thompson v. Spikes, 663 F. Supp. 627, 641–42 (S.D. Ga. 1987).
102. Karr v. Dow, 507 P.2d 455 (N.M. Ct. App. 1973).
103. *Antinerella*, 690 A.2d at 454–55; *Karr*, 507 P.2d at 458 ("[T]he weight of authority . . . seems to be now that the sheriff is liable not only for acts virtute officii but also for acts colore officii. . . .").
104. *Spikes*, 663 F. Supp. at 641.
105. *Jemison*, 531 N.Y.S.2d at 923.
106. 717 S.W.2d 843, 846 (Ky. Ct. App. 1986).

on the release of a car lien and the finance company sued the clerk and his surety, the Kentucky Court of Appeals held that the bond did not cover the loss because the deputy's act was criminal, for private gain, and outside the scope of his duties. "[T]he bond is designed to protect the public against official misconduct as opposed to private misconduct."[107] The deputy was not hired to forge signatures or file false lien releases:

> The accepted rule is that without regard to the distinction between acts done by virtue of office and acts done under color of office, the liability upon an official bond arises only upon acts of the officer which pertain to some function or duty which the law imposes upon his office. The sureties to his official bond are not liable for his purely personal act, not done as a part of, or in connection with his official duties, and where he acts without the authority of his office, in doing such act, he is not to be considered an officer, but an individual wrongdoer for which his surety is not liable.[108]

Other courts have been more lenient about what meets this test. In *Monroe v. Darr*,[109] deputy sheriffs, without warning or warrant, broke into an apartment at dawn and held the residents in bed at gunpoint. On discovering they had invaded the wrong apartment, they left without explanation or apology. The residents sued the sheriff's surety, who argued that since the deputies were operating without a warrant, they were not acting under color of office. The court rejected that. The deputies were in uniform. Searching and arresting people was their job. The surety could escape liability only by proving the deputies "were on a private errand of their own, completely apart from the duties of a peace officer."[110]

In *Travelers Indemnity Co. v. State*,[111] McAllister "believed or pretended to believe he was a special deputy sheriff of Vigo County." He often helped Sheriff Brewster make traffic arrests. One day the two were on patrol when they spotted Howell racing a car. They chased Howell to Hack Brown's Tavern. Howell stopped his car and ran behind the tavern.

---

107. *Id.*
108. *Id.* (citing Commonwealth *ex rel.* Warren Cnty. v. Cox's Adm'r, 94 S.W.2d 632, 633 (Ky. 1936)).
109. 520 P.2d 1197 (Kan. 1974).
110. *Id.* at 1204.
111. 290 N.E.2d 456 (Ind. Ct. App. 1972).

Favre came out and began an altercation with Brewster. Brewster pulled his gun, Favre grabbed Brewster's arm, and as they struggled, Brewster told McAllister to "let him have it." McAllister shot and killed Favre. In the ensuing action on Brewster's faithful performance bond, the court held that Brewster was acting under color of office and it did not matter whether McAlister was legally a deputy; he was a citizen who could have been legally required to assist Brewster as sheriff.

However, in *Thomas v. Williford*,[112] a sheriff received surreptitious payments for unknown purposes from greyhound racers. His surety contended the payments were not public funds, but gifts. The Supreme Court of Arkansas agreed. The payments were not public funds and thus the sheriff and his surety had no duty to account for them even if the conduct was criminal. The dissent, citing *Yuma County v. Wisener*,[113] argued the payments were received by virtue of office, without the county's consent, and in violation of the state constitution. They were public trust funds, even if the sheriff had no right to receive them. Similarly, in *Lawyers Surety Co. v. Reina*,[114] a court clerk's surety was liable for the clerk's conversion of an insurer's deposit in a workers' compensation case. She accepted the deposit in trust and under color of her office as clerk even if the money was tendered without order of court.

If the old distinction between virtue of office and color of office can be maintained (or revived), then *Waters v. Bates*[115] is still of interest. The court understood a sheriff's surety is liable for a deputy's conduct only if the deputy is acting by virtue of office. Color of office was not enough. The surety before the court was not liable for the negligence of a deputy while driving a patrol car on routine law enforcement duty. That would convert the bond into a liability policy. "Nowhere yet have the Tennessee cases held that negligent driving of an automobile by a deputy while on routine patrol duty was an act by virtue of office."[116] By virtue of office did not mean merely an act in the scope of employment.[117]

---

112. 534 S.W.2d 2 (Ark. 1976).
113. 46 P.2d 115 (Ariz. 1935).
114. 483 S.W.2d 911 (Tex. Civ. App. 1972).
115. 227 F. Supp. 426, 465–66 (E.D. Tenn. 1964).
116. *Id.*
117. *Id.* (citing Ivy v. Osborne, 279 S.W. 384 (Tenn. 1925) (holding that, for the sheriff's surety to be liable, the act of the deputy must "be done in an attempt to serve or execute a process, or under a statute giving him the

In *Malone v. Howell*,[118] deputies located what appeared to be an illegal liquor still in the woods. Several of them went in at night and hid in the bushes. Malone and another man approached the still on a trail. When Malone stepped into the clearing, a deputy called to him and he tried to flee. The deputies shot him dead. They had no warrant to arrest him and he committed no crime in their presence though it developed later that he had come to inspect the mash. It was not unlawful to approach a still and for all the deputies knew Malone had nothing to do with it. Thus there was no evidence that could have authorized his arrest without a warrant. The Florida Supreme Court concluded the sheriff and surety were not liable because the deputies had no authority to make the arrest. What they did may have been "colore officii" but it was not "virtute officii."[119]

C. A Principal Holding Multiple Offices

Frequently the same public official is bonded in several different positions or capacities. For instance, in *Village of Arlington Heights v. Poder* and related litigation,[120] a village treasurer engaged in unauthorized derivatives trading. This man was also the treasurer of both the village's police pension fund and its firefighters; pension fund. It was important to ascertain whose money he was losing, for a bond given on behalf of an official in one capacity does not cover his performance in some other

---

right to arrest without a warrant, and if he acts otherwise he is doing so as an individual")).

118. 192 So. 224 (Fla. 1939).

119. *Id.* at 227. For more on the virtue of office/color of office distinction, see *Cleland v. U.S. Fidelity & Guaranty Co.*, 107 S.E.2d 904 (Ga. Ct. App. 1959) (holding that a surety was not liable where police officer procured arrest warrant for traffic violations not in his official capacity but as private citizen with personal grievance after plaintiff filed a suit against officer); *Walker v. U.S. Fidelity & Guaranty Co.*, 101 So. 2d 437 (Fla. Ct. App. 1958); and *Massey v. Standard Accident Insurance Co.*, 132 S.W.2d 530 (Ky. 1939).

120. No. 88 C 3892, 1989 WL 75189 (N.D. Ill. June 28, 1989); *see* Vill. of Arlington Heights Police Pension Fund v. Poder, 700 F. Supp. 405 (N.D. Ill. 1988) (earlier opinion); *see also* Vill. of Arlington Heights v. Poder, No. 88 C 3895, 1988 WL 89923 (N.D. Ill. Jan. 24, 1989); Bd. of Trs. of Fire Fighters' Pension Fund of Vill. of Arlington Heights v. Poder, No. 88 C 3848, 1988 WL 115288 (N.D. Ill. Oct. 26, 1988), *clarified*, 708 F. Supp. 1499 (N.D. Ill. 1989).

capacity. As *Baker v. Towle's Administratrix*[121] put it: "His sureties as sheriff are not responsible for his acts as collector. He gives a distinct bond."

In *Moore ex rel. City of Aberdeen v. Byars*,[122] a city manager was also serving as utilities manager. His bond from 1992 to 1995 listed him only as utilities manager. His 1995–1998 bond did not list any position. His misconduct occurred in the earlier bond period but did not relate to his role as utilities manager. The court refused to resolve the capacity issue as a matter of law, but did recognize that it created an issue of fact.

D. Vicarious Liability

Is a public official's surety responsible for the conduct of the official's subordinate employees? Do the doctrines of vicarious liability or respondeat superior apply against the surety?

In *Kentucky Finance Co. v. Spradlin*,[123] the court held that a county clerk's surety was not liable for his assistant's forgery of a lien release absent negligence by the clerk himself. Yet in *State ex rel. Benz v. Blackwell*,[124] *Monroe v. Darr*,[125] and *Smith v. Jordan*,[126] sheriffs and the sureties on their statutory bonds were found liable to the victims of wrongful conduct by the sheriffs' deputies. However, the *Smith* court also found that the surety was not liable for the deputy's misconduct under a separate nonstatutory blanket bond that ran only to the benefit of the county and that excluded coverage for "the deprivation or violation of the civil rights of any person" or "the tortious conduct of an Employee."[127]

Courts historically have been reluctant to impose vicarious liability on the bonded official for acts by subordinates beyond the official's control. The plaintiff in such a case is seeking to hold the official

---

121. Brown v. Edwards, 321 So. 2d 394 (La. Ct. App. 1974) (holding that bond for sheriff as ex officio tax collector did not cover his liability for a riot death where he also was bonded as sheriff) (citing 11 La. 432, 439 (1837)).
122. 757 So. 2d 243 (Miss. 2000).
123. 717 S.W.2d 843, 846 (Ky. Ct. App. 1986).
124. 716 S.W.2d 270 (Mo. Ct. App. 1986) (discussing deputy's false return of service).
125. 520 P.2d 1197 (Kan. 1974) (discussing deputies' decision to raid wrong apartment and assault innocent residents).
126. 527 F. Supp. 167 (S.D. Ohio 1981) (analyzing the deputy's strip search).
127. *Id.* at 173.

personally liable and even if the surety satisfied the liability, the surety would seek indemnity from the official. Courts do not wish to discourage public service. However, in *First Virginia Bank-Colonial v. Baker*,[128] the court concluded this was less of a concern, because an official today is likely to be covered by liability insurance and also because the public entity should have express coverage against unfaithful performance by subordinate officials in the form of public employee blanket bonds:

> Public service is a privilege and an honor. Yet, we recognize that a public official bears myriad heavy burdens. In the discharge of his public trust, he necessarily must delegate many of his official duties, discretionary and ministerial, to subordinates. It is virtually impossible for him to maintain constant surveillance and supervision over the manner in which those duties are performed. . . . [T]o hold a public official accountable for the misfeasance, nonfeasance, and malfeasance of those upon whom she is forced to rely is to impose an unfair burden on the purse of the individual or the public fisc.
>
> Once, this was a primary publicpolicy concern. Now, with the advent of comprehensive personal liability insurance and the growth of the practice of covering subordinate government employees as well as their superiors in the risk insured in performance bonds (a practice followed here), financial considerations have become a concern of secondary importance. As we have recently observed, government can function only through its servants, and certain of those servants must enjoy the same immunity in the performance of their discretionary duties as the government enjoys; but there is "no justification for treating a present day government employee as absolutely immune from tort liability, just as if he were an employee of an eighteenth century sovereign."
>
> While a clerk of court may be entitled to claim the protection of the doctrine of sovereign immunity for wrongs committed by him in the exercise of the discretionary duties of his office, we find no logic in a rule that exempts him from the doctrine of respondeat superior, whether the wrong committed by his deputy is discretionary or ministerial in character. We reject such a per se rule because we believe it would offend the general maxim,

128. 301 S.E.2d 8 (Va. 1983).

deeply rooted in public policy, that the interests of the public in the faithful performance of official duties outweigh the interests of those entrusted to perform them.[129]

A Tennessee statute gives more certain relief to sheriffs in that state at least by providing that neither the sheriff nor the surety on a sheriff's bond is liable for any act of a deputy whether acting by virtue of office, color of office, or otherwise.[130] This confers immunity from state law claims such as battery or false arrest by a deputy.[131] And, in effect, it confers immunity to certain federal claims such as claims under 42 U.S.C. § 1983, which preclude liability based on respondeat superior (i.e., vicarious) liability.[132]

E. Immunity

1. Immunity of the Principal

If the public official is immune from civil liability for his or her official act, then the official's surety is entitled to assert that immunity as a defense too.[133] "It would be an anomaly to hold the bonding company liable if its principal was not liable," thanks to an immunity.[134] In *Phelps v. Dawson*,[135] the Eighth Circuit offered a rationale:

> The immunity given the principals of these bonds is in no sense a personal privilege nor is it one arising from any legal incapacity in them. The sole basis of such immunity is a public policy resting entirely upon the public good to be brought about by having the official action of certain classes of public officials entirely uninfluenced by apprehension of personal civil liability. To allow recovery against the surety as to such official

---

129. *Id.* at 12.
130. Warner v. McMinn Cnty., No. 1:04-CV-399, 2005 U.S. Dist. LEXIS 28228 (E.D. Tenn. Nov. 10, 2005) (citing TENN. CODE ANN. § 8-8-301 (2005)).
131. Moore v. Buckles, 404 F. Supp. 1382 (E.D. Tenn. 1975).
132. Madewell v. Garmon, 484 F. Supp. 823 (E.D. Tenn. 1980).
133. Bd. of Educ. v. Hess, 488 N.E.2d 1358 (Ill. App. Ct. 1986); Wheeler v. Moe, 515 P.2d 679 (Mont. 1973).
134. Spaniol Ford, Inc. v. Froggatt, 478 P.2d 598, 600 (Wyo. 1970).
135. 97 F.2d 339 (8th Cir. 1938).

acts would (a) result in weakening (if not entirely destroying) the effectiveness of this public policy or (b) it would make it burdensome or impossible to secure official bonds.[136]

A recent Kentucky case emphasizes this point. In *St. Matthews Fire Protection District v. Aubrey*,[137] taxes for a fire protection district were levied on real property but not on tangible personal property. The district discovered the omission and sued the sheriff, county clerk, property valuation administrator, and their sureties. The court entered summary judgment in favor of the defendants. They were sued only in their official capacities so they were absolutely immune. The district argued a common law exception but the court held that a county is cloaked with sovereign immunity and this extends to officials of the county. The immunity applied both to tort and contract claims. The statutory requirement that bonds be posted was not a waiver of the immunity, "paradoxical as that might be."[138] Waiver occurs only by "the most express language or by such overwhelming implications from the text as [will] leave no room for any other reasonable construction."[139]

In *In re Hale*,[140] the Alabama Supreme Court held that a sheriff acting in the scope of his employment was entitled to assert immunity under the Alabama Constitution against inadequate medical care claims by the estate of a deceased inmate. The immunity extended to a claim against the sheriff in his individual capacity for breach of the sheriff's official bond. The court left the surety in the case because no one had addressed whether it should do so or revisit its holding against a surety in an earlier case.[141]

However, the rule in at least some states is that the public official bond is implicitly a waiver of immunity for a claim within its coverage.[142]

---

136. *Id.* at 342–43 (citations omitted).
137. 304 S.W.3d 56 (Ky. Ct. App. 2009).
138. *Id.*
139. *Id.* at 61 (citing Withers v. Univ. of Ky., 939 S.W.2d 340, 346 (Ky. 1997)).
140. 6 So. 3d 452 (Ala. 2008).
141. *Id.* at 457 n.4 (citing Dixon v. Am. Liberty Ins. Co., 332 So. 2d 719, 721 (Ala. 1976) (allowing suit against surety on bond of sheriff for failure to provide adequate medical treatment to inmate)).
142. Cantrell v. Thurman, 499 S.E.2d 416 (Ga. Ct. App. 1998); Duvall v. Tawney, 323 S.W.3d 804 (Mo. Ct. App. 2010) (analyzing a statute governing sheriff executing a writ of execution and calling for an official bond and holding that the statute precludes the sheriff from asserting the

One court suggested an official's immunity took effect only after his bond was exhausted.[143] A number of cases hold this in North Carolina.[144] For example, in *Frink v. Batten*,[145] the estate of an inmate sued the sheriff of Columbus County, the sheriff's surety, and other officials. The inmate had been transferred from Columbus County's overcrowded jail to Robeson County's jail. He began complaining that his mind was not right and tried to kill himself. Robeson County sent him back to Columbus County without medical records. Placed in the general population, he hanged himself. The court held that that the estate could sue both the sheriff and the surety. The sheriff's sovereign immunity was waived to the extent of the bond. The bond covered the negligence of the sheriff in the performance of his official duties.[146]

2. *Discretionary Acts Versus Ministerial Acts*

The king could do no wrong and even today a public official remains generally immune from liability for misdeeds within the scope of the

---

immunity at common law that would otherwise apply when the sheriff follows a judge's orders).

143. Bell v. Crump, 651 So. 2d 975 (La. Ct. App. 1995).

144. Smith v. Jackson Cnty. Bd. of Educ., 608 S.E.2d 399 (N.C. Ct. App. 2005) (holding that immunity of the official, if any, does not preclude a bond claim).

145. No. 08-696, 2009 N.C. App. LEXIS 1819 (N.C. Ct. App. May 19, 2009).

146. Greene v. Barrick, 680 S.E.2d 727 (N.C. Ct. App. 2009) (holding governmental immunity protected sheriff except to extent it was waived by official bond from claims by estate of deputy killed in a helicopter crash); Russ v. Causey, 732 F. Supp. 2d 589, 611 (E.D.N.C. 2010) (explaining sheriff's surety was liable because bond waived immunity but liability insurer was not liable, due to an immunity exclusion); Oliver v. Harper, No. 5:09-CT-3027, 2011 U.S. Dist. LEXIS 29499 (E.D.N.C. Mar. 22, 2011); Jones v. Houston, No. 4:08-CV-121, 2010 U.S. Dist. LEXIS 103800 (E.D.N.C. Sept. 28, 2010). Notably, in *Brooks v. Pennington*, a court determined that fact issues existed as to whether sheriff and surety were immune under the Mississippi Tort Claims Act from a suit by a convict. 995 So. 2d 733 (Miss. Ct. App. 2007). The convict alleged he was wrongfully jailed on surrender by a partially unpaid bondsman. *Id.* This occurred after the convict had appeared in court and served his time for the crime he had been charged with, such that his bail bond had already been discharged at the time of the surrender and only a civil debt to the bondsman remained. *Id.*

official's "discretionary" authority.[147] For instance, an investment decision is generally considered discretionary.[148] However, if the act is "ministerial," there is no immunity, and the official may be liable for mere negligence.[149] "A duty is ministerial when the law prescribes the mode and occasion of its performance with such certainty that nothing is left to judgment or discretion—a duty not involving official discretion."[150] The distinction is "nearly impossible to draw"[151] but generally upper-level employees (those who occupy managerial, legislative, or judicial or quasi-judicial positions) are immune,[152] while lower-level employees are not immune, for their jobs are said to involve little or no discretion.[153]

Ordinarily the activity of law enforcement officers, such as sheriffs, marshals, and police officers, is considered ministerial.[154] However, such officers (and their sureties) may be entitled to assert other immunities, such as the one against liability for failure to provide police protection.

---

147. Thompson v. Spikes, 663 F. Supp. 627, 643–44 (S.D. Ga. 1987); Scot Lad Foods, Inc. v. Sec'y of State, 418 N.E.2d 1368 (Ohio 1981) (holding that, absent bad faith or corrupt motive, a public official acting within the scope of his authority is not liable for failure to properly perform a duty involving judgment and discretion). For an in-depth study of public official immunity, see Steven L. Micas, *The Doctrinal Bases for Absolute and Qualified Public Official Immunities*, 29 URB. LAW. 47 (1997).
148. Integrated Res. Equity Corp. v. Fairbanks N. Star Borough, 799 P.2d 295 (Alaska 1990).
149. *Id.*; *Spikes*, 663 F. Supp. at 643–44.
150. Spaniol Ford, Inc. v. Froggatt, 478 P.2d 598, 599 (Wyo. 1970).
151. *Compare id.* (discussing the deputy clerk's issuance of certificate of title for stolen motor vehicle was not a ministerial act), *with* First Va. Bank-Colonial v. Baker, 301 S.E.2d 8 (Va. 1983) (holding that the failure of deputy court clerk to properly index lien was ministerial).
152. Hopkins v. INA Underwriters Ins. Co., 542 N.E.2d 679 (Ohio Ct. App. 1988) (probate judge immune from liability for failure to require a guardian to file an account and judge's surety could assert that immunity as a defense too; bond protected against default by judge in a ministerial or clerical capacity but not against errors by him in a judicial capacity).
153. *Spikes*, 663 F. Supp. at 641; Scot Lad Foods, Inc. v. Sec'y of State, 418 N.E.2d 1368, 1370 (Ohio 1981) (holding that the filing officer's failure to properly register a Uniform Commercial Code security interest was ministerial).
154. *Fairbanks N. Star Borough*, 799 P.2d at 297.

That immunity applies if there is no special relationship with the plaintiff or specific promise of protection.[155]

But for both lower- and higher-level officials, the analysis must be taken beyond the title of the office. On the one hand, discretionary authority may have been delegated even to a desk clerk; on the other, there is no immunity for a ministerial act by an upper-level employee, nor (at any level) for a willful, wanton, or malicious act, nor for an act outside the scope of the official's duties (though that last exception may be a defense to the official's surety).[156] In fact, when it comes to the duty to account for public funds, immunity is stripped. However exalted the official, there is no inquiry whether he or she was acting in a discretionary or ministerial capacity; as explained above, nothing generally will excuse a misappropriation or even an innocent failure to account for and turn over funds.[157]

IV. Damages

A. *Actual Damages*

A public official's surety is liable only to the extent of the actual damages; the penal sum of the bond is not forfeited unless the actual damages meet or exceed the penal sum.[158] Thus when a creditor could not prove the bonded sheriff's failure to levy caused him damage, the creditor could only recover nominal damages from the sheriff's surety.[159] The rule that liability is limited to actual damages means for example that liability on a sheriff's bond for failure to enforce a judgment by levying on property is measured not by the amount of the judgment but by what the property that could have been levied on would have actually yielded

---

155. Stafford v. Barker, 502 S.E.2d 1 (N.C. Ct. App. 1998) (holding sheriff's surety was not liable to widow for early release of inmate who killed husband during robbery).
156. *Spikes*, 663 F. Supp. at 641; *Scot Lad Foods, Inc.*, 418 N.E.2d at 1370.
157. *Fairbanks N. Star Borough*, 799 P.2d at 297; Spaniol Ford, Inc. v. Froggatt, 478 P.2d 598, 599 (Wyo. 1970).
158. Pa. Tpk. Comm'n v. U.S. Fid. & Guar. Co., 194 A.2d 423, 428 (Pa. 1963); Annotation, *Public Officers Bond as Subject to Forfeiture for Malfeasance in Office*, 4 A.L.R. 2D 1348 (1949).
159. Henry S. Miller Co. v. Evans, 425 S.W.2d 426 (Tex. 1970).

after satisfying prior liens.[160] Conversely, however, the penal sum does cap the surety's liability.[161]

In *Kinzer v. City of Chicago*,[162] the court held that loss under a blanket bond meant only actual loss; the surety was entitled to a setoff to the extent illegal expenditures had generated a profit: "the detriment to the public from the expenditure of unappropriated funds can be measured only by employing the following calculus: the totality of expenditures minus the benefit the public received therefrom. In other words, as a matter of civil law, no harm, no foul."[163] Otherwise an insured would be motivated to look the other way in the hope of a double recovery—first from the scheme and then from the bond.

Similarly, in *Town of Evans v. Catalino*,[164] a town sued its supervisor and his surety for an accounting of funds illegally transferred from capital reserve accounts to a general fund. The court held the town had to restore the transferred amount itself. The supervisor and his surety were liable for interest, but the town was not entitled to a windfall:

> [W]hile a fiduciary must be held strictly accountable for a diversion of funds in violation of statutory constraints and public trust, he should be permitted to set off any amounts used to pay valid obligations of the public entity. He then should remain liable for any amounts not so expended and for interest that would have accrued on all of the funds.[165]

B. The Penal Sum as a Cap on Damages

The bond's penal sum caps a surety's liability. Once the penal sum is exhausted by any one claim, the surety is discharged from any further liability to the same claimant or anyone else, not only as to that particular

---

160. U.M. & M. Credit Corp. v. Doss, 452 S.W.2d 45 (Tex. Civ. App. 1970) (holding sheriff and surety had burden of proving this though).
161. Pepka v. Schang, 704 A.2d 127 (Pa. Super. Ct. 1997).
162. 652 N.E.2d 20 (Ill. App. Ct. 1995).
163. *Id.* at 26–27; City of Springfield v. Brown, 289 S.W.2d 48 (Mo. 1956) (holding that the bond did not cover bribes paid to official); Town of Thornton v. Winterhoff, 92 N.E.2d 163 (Ill. 1950) (holding that the bond did not cover money improperly borrowed but repaid to a fund).
164. 425 N.Y.S.2d 918 (Sup. Ct. 1979).
165. *Id.* at 923.

claim, but also any related or unrelated claim.[166] "Under the great weight of authority, a surety's liability is limited by the penal sum named in the bond, even though different individuals assert claims based upon distinct wrongful acts of the principal."[167]

As the court explained in *Rolen v. Rauhuff*:

> In determining the amount of premium to charge on a bond the surety necessarily looks to the amount of the penalty. If the surety can be held in excess of the penalty, there would be no way to determine a proper amount to charge as a premium. The surety might receive the same premium for a $5000 penalty bond as a $100,000 or unlimited penalty bond, should it be held for a sum in excess of the penalty. Such a result would violate sound business principals and provide sureties no guidelines to determine property premium rates. This result was not the intent of the Legislature.[168]

Nevertheless, the surety should consider an interpleader if all known claimants will not agree to a pro-rata settlement.

In *Layman ex rel. Layman v. Alexander*,[169] a suspect fought with a deputy after arrest and was knocked out. He was not taken to the hospital and suffered brain damage. The suspect sued the sheriff and others, alleging civil rights violations and including a claim on the sheriff's bond, although he had already collected a judgment on that bond in state court, exhausting the penalty of same. The court entered summary judgment in favor of the surety.[170]

---

166. Rolen v. Rauhuff, 315 F. Supp. 935 (E.D. Tenn. 1970). The court found only one case to the contrary, *Paulsell v. Peters*, 115 P.2d 709 (Wash. 1941).
167. Md. Cas. Co. v. Alford, 111 F.2d 388, 390–91 (10th Cir. 1949).
168. *Rolen*, 315 F. Supp. at 939.
169. 343 F. Supp. 2d 483 (W.D.N.C. 2004).
170. Additional recent cases respecting the penal sum as a limit of liability include *Albercia v. Kingvision Pay-Per-View, Ltd.*, 217 S.W.3d 688 (Tex. Ct. App. 2007) (liability of surety on a constable's bond for failure to levy on assets of a judgment debtor was limited to the penal sum of the bond); *County of Hudson v. Janiszewski*, No. 06-319, 2007 WL 4554227 (D.N.J. Dec. 21, 2007) (holding the public official bond is not a forfeiture bond; the penal sum caps liability and actual damages would need to be proved); and

C. Interest

Cases on the surety's liability for interest have gone both ways. Some courts say the surety owes interest not from the principal's default forward but only from when demand is made on the surety.[171] The competing view is that the interest that the principal owes is compensatory, not penal, so the surety is liable for all such interest in order to make the obligee whole.[172] *Centennial School District v. Kerins*[173] held that a tax collector and his faithful performance bond surety were liable for interest on taxes the collector did not remit for several months. The collector and surety had an obligation to pay the interest at common law even if the collector had not been dishonest or even negligent.

D. Fines and Punitive Damages

The majority rule is that a surety is not liable for punitive damages assessed against the principal.[174] That said, sureties have on occasion been forced to pay fines or penalties imposed on an official even though his or her misconduct may not have caused the government to incur any actual loss. In *State ex rel. Summer v. Denton*,[175] an official's surety was held liable for a penalty assessed against the official for awarding gravel hauling contracts to his nephews in violation of a nepotism statute. In *McDaniel v. Carroll*,[176] the court affirmed judgment against a sheriff's surety for both compensatory and punitive damages awarded in a civil rights action. The sheriff's deputy had unjustifiably shot the plaintiff in the course of arresting him.

Hill v. Medford, 582 S.E.2d 325 (N.C. Ct. App. 2003) (fired deputy's tort claim against sheriff and surety was limited to amount of bond).

171. State v. Stockton, 270 S.W.2d 586 (Tenn. Ct. App. 1954).
172. Borough of Totowa v. Am. Sur. Co. of N.Y., 188 A.2d 586, 595 (N.J. 1963).
173. 840 A.2d 377 (Pa. Commw. Ct. 2003).
174. Vallindras v. Mass. Bonding & Ins. Co., 255 P.2d 457 (Cal. Ct. App. 1953).
175. 382 So. 2d 461 (Miss. 1980).
176. 457 F.2d 968 (6th Cir. 1972).

E. Attorney and Audit Fees

Whether a surety may be held liable for attorney and audit fees depends on the underlying statutes, state law governing indemnity, and liability imposed on the principal. In *Fidelity & Deposit Co. of Maryland v. Concerned Taxpayers of Lee County, Inc.*,[177] the plaintiffs recovered attorney fees from a surety for the trustees of a hospital district. The plaintiffs incurred the fees in securing an injunction and declaration that the district was unconstitutional. The surety argued the trustees had never even performed any official duties, but the court concluded they had met with each other in violation of the Open Meetings Act.

In *Travelers Casualty & Surety Co. of America v. Byrd*,[178] a surety was unable to recover attorneys' fees and costs incurred in defending a sheriff. A jury found that a detective in the sheriff's department acted in his personal/individual capacity—not in furtherance of his official duties. As a result, the conduct at issue was not covered by the public official bond. The surety subsequently sought to recover attorneys' fees and costs under an indemnity clause in the bond. The court, however, applied state law and found that the surety was estopped from recovering attorneys' fees because it consistently denied liability and repeatedly argued that "it had no liability to a third party for conduct outside of [the public official's] official duty as sheriff."[179] The Supreme Court of New Jersey held that "a surety is liable for the cost of a special audit of the records of the office in question and reconstruction of the records themselves, where the maintenance of those records is among the public officer's duties."[180] In *Alexander v. Maine Bonding & Casualty Co.*,[181] a 1971 decision from the Supreme Court of Maine, the court recognized that the cost of auditing the general affairs of a municipality are not entirely chargeable to the surety—only those caused by the bonded public official's defalcation. In other words, when the audit goes beyond the actions necessary to address the defaults of the principal and correct the public records, there must be an allocation between actions taken to correct the default and those not related to the default.

---

177. 829 S.W.2d 923 (Tex. Ct. App. 1992).
178. No. 1:20-CV-66-LG-RPM, 2020 WL 8298907, at *4 (S.D. Miss. Aug. 10, 2020).
179. *Id.* at *3.
180. Borough of Totowa v. Am. Sur. Co. of N.Y., 188 A.2d 586 (N.J. 1963).
181. 274 A.2d 439 (Minn. 1971).

It should also be noted that sureties may be able to recover their own attorneys' fees from a principal. For instance, in *Newton County v. State ex rel. Dukes*,[182] a court held that, even though a principal was found to have no liability to a plaintiff, the principal was not "relieved of his contractual liability to indemnify Union for its attorneys' fees and costs incurred in defending the lawsuit."[183] In reaching this conclusion the court explained that the principal's "bond application clearly contained a provision in which [the principal] agreed to indemnify [the surety] for loss or expense incurred by virtue of [the surety's] executing [the] bond."[184]

F. Stacking and the Cumulation of Liability

Bonded public officials tend to have yearly terms but often they will be reappointed to the same office year after year. There lurks in this a contentious issue, especially when the loss occurs over several bond periods. Either the surety's liability is limited to the amount of the one bond in force when the loss is discovered, or the claimant is entitled to additional coverage on the theory that there were earlier bonds (or bond periods) too, and the limits of those bonds (or periods) may be sought in addition to the limit of the current bond. In other words, the issue is whether the liability is cumulative.

As with the other issues described above, the answer may be found in the underlying statute. For instance, an Indiana law provides:

> In the case of a continuous [public official] bond, the maximum aggregate liability of the surety or insurer for the entire term that the bond is in effect is the penal sum of the bond for the current term of the bond and the penal sums of the bond for the five (5) immediately preceding years.[185]

However, statutes do not always address this issue.

Penn Township v. Aetna Casualty & Surety Co.[186] took on the question of how to proceed when the underlying statute is silent on stacking. A treasurer was bonded every year from 1985 to 1990. The township

---

182. 133 So. 3d 805 (Miss. 2014).
183. *Id.* at 807–08.
184. *Id.*
185. Ind. Code § 5-4-1-18 (2016).
186. 719 A.2d 749 (Pa. Super. Ct. 1998).

discovered an embezzlement and sought cumulative relief. The surety insisted it was liable only for a single bond limit. The court observed:

> The statute . . . neither requires nor prohibits a non-cumulative bond. Although some courts and commentators have questioned why a municipality would purchase a bond which limited its liability to a fixed sum over many years of operation, . . . we have not found this argument persuasive when the policy clearly provides for non-cumulative liability. . . . other factors, such as reduced premiums, elimination of the need to prove the precise date of a defalcation and a longer time period in which to bring a claim, can make a continuous, non-cumulative bond an attractive option.
>
> On the other hand, as this case shows, there is nothing inherently improbable in the proposition that a municipality would want to have the policy limit available to it every year. This is especially true if . . . it could have had such coverage at no extra cost merely by switching surety companies each year. Therefore a consensus has developed that a surety company may limit recovery to an aggregate sum over many years of coverage, but that the parties' intention to enter into a continuing bonding scheme must clearly appear.[187]

The court found the bond at issue ambiguous, but on the basis of parol evidence, it nonetheless held in favor of the surety. The bond was noncumulative; its limit could not be multiplied.

In *State ex rel. Guste v. Aetna Casualty & Surety Co.*,[188] a Louisiana court had this to say in construing a public employee blanket bond:

> No Louisiana case is precisely in point, but a careful review of the national jurisprudence reveals that where the terms of a fidelity bond, taken as a whole, indicate an intention that the original bond shall be continued for a new period or periods due to the payment of a consideration, the contract is a continuous one and the extent of liability is to be determined by the provisions of the original bond.
>
> * * *

---

187. *Id.* at 752.
188. 417 So. 2d 404 (La. Ct. App. 1982).

> The weight of authority is in favor of the surety companies, even where there has been no specific contract provision against cumulation of liability. It has generally been held that "where the bond is for an indefinite term, the date it begins to run being the only date given, the fact that the premiums were paid annually does not make the relation a series of separate yearly contracts."
> * * *
> Accordingly, even in the absence of a specific provision against cumulative liability, it has been held that the continuous term of the bond impliedly excluded liability in excess of the amount stated in the bond, in spite of the extent of actual losses over the years . . . . Where, as here, in addition to the continuous term of the bond, there was language in the bond or its attachments which militated against a finding of cumulative liability, the courts have consistently held liability to be limited, in the aggregate, to the amount stated in the bond (i.e., noncumulative).[189]

Town of Scotland Neck v. Western Surety Co.[190] involved a town clerk's bond. The Supreme Court of North Carolina observed:

> The extent of liability on a fidelity bond which is renewed from year to year is the subject of a distinct conflict of opinion. A large body of case law construes a fidelity bond accompanied by periodic premium payments as a single, continuous contract where the liability of the surety is limited to a specified amount stated in the bond which cannot be exceeded, although defaults by the principal occur at various times and exceed the stated liability figure in the bond. A large body of case law also construes a fidelity bond accompanied by periodic premium payments as separate and distinct contracts upon each of which the surety is liable for defaults by the principal occurring during the term each is in force to the maximum amount stated in the bond for each individual period. Case law in this State applies both rules. The reasoning most often applied is that a fidelity

---

189. *Id.* at 406–07 (quoting Columbia Hosp. for Women & LyingIn Asylum v. U.S. Fid. & Guar. Co., 188 F.2d 654, 657 (D.C. Cir. 1951)).
190. 271 S.E.2d 501 (N.C. 1980).

> bond is continuous and not cumulative, although this is a rule which has been criticized.
>
> In our view neither rule need be rejected and the other applied exclusively for all cases. Both are sound positions and can be appropriately applied depending on the facts and circumstances of each case and the bond in question. In fact, the two rules represent the final holdings of courts based on the facts and circumstances of the particular case. Thus, the question in this case is whether the facts and circumstances surrounding this bond and the words on the bond itself demonstrate an intent of the parties to contract for a continuous or a cumulative bond.[191]

The court went on to construe the bond before it as a single, noncumulative instrument. "No factual or statutory basis exists for construing the bond to provide $20,000 coverage each year or for each term of office."[192]

However, in *South Worcester County Regional Vocational School District v. Utica Mutual Insurance Co.*,[193] an employee embezzled $6.5 million over a number of years and the school district made a claim on its annual public employee bonds, each of which had a limit of $150,000. The court allowed the district to recover up to $150,000 a year. Each bond was a separate contract, not a continuation of a single contract. The district's own negligence was not a defense and limitations did not run until the insurer denied coverage so the suit was timely. The court later held the surety in bad faith.[194]

---

191. *Id.* at 503 (citations omitted).
192. *Id.* at 506. *But see* City of Middlesboro v. Am. Sur. Co., 211 S.W.2d 670, 673 (Ky. Ct. App. 1947) (discussing that liability of surety was not limited to amount of original bond when the surety renewed bond each time principal who embezzled funds was elected to successive one-year terms).
193. No. 06-40230, 2008 U.S. Dist. LEXIS 107280 (D. Mass. Sept. 16, 2008).
194. *Utica Mut. Ins. Co.*, No. 06-40230, 2010 U.S. Dist. LEXIS 83015 (D. Mass. Aug. 13, 2010).

V. Defenses

A. *Defaults Before and After the Bonded Term*

The surety on the public official bond is not liable for a default by the official before the execution of the bond unless the statute expressly so requires.[195] But a reappointed official has a duty to collect public funds from himself or herself in the prior term, and the surety may be liable for the official's failure to do so.[196] The surety ordinarily is not liable for a default occurring after the bonded term expires either,[197] but when an official remains in office beyond the term pending appointment of a successor, or reappointment, the official's surety has been held to remain on the hook.[198] But the surety is off the hook once the official is removed from the bonded position, except possibly for a default arising before or at the time of removal.[199]

In *Zsarmani v. Iredell County*,[200] a barber sued a sheriff and his surety for alleged civil rights violations after the sheriff on a search warrant found marijuana in the barber's shop. However, the barber sued the sheriff's current surety rather than the surety at the time of the alleged wrongs. The court held that the current surety was not liable for acts occurring before its bond period commenced.

In *County of Somerset v. George*,[201] a tax collector used a lapping scheme to conceal an embezzlement occurring over several years. The surety contended it was discharged from any liability for shortages in the earlier years by the fact that the shortages were not detected in annual audits. The court disagreed. The government's acquiescence was fraudulently induced. The bond claim was timely and the surety liable, even though the shortages were not discovered until after the surety's bond period. Irregularities such as difficulty in getting reports from the collector did not preclude coverage.

The effect of the obligee's knowledge of prior dishonesty was the issue in *Alcona County v. Michigan Municipal League Liability &*

---

195. Commonwealth v. Slack, 291 S.W.2d 553 (Ky. 1956).
196. Thurston Cnty. *ex rel.* Vesely v. Chmelka, 294 N.W. 857 (Neb. 1940).
197. Aetna Cas. & Sur. Co. v. Bd. of Supervisors, 168 S.E. 617 (Va. 1933).
198. *Id.*; Hartford Accident & Indem. Co. v. Tulare, 186 P.2d 121, 124 (Cal. 1947).
199. *Aetna Cas. & Sur. Co.*, 168 S.E. at 620.
200. No. 5:03-cv-00044, 2005 WL 2234605 (W.D.N.C. Sept. 13, 2005).
201. 587 A.2d 360 (Pa. Commw. Ct. 1991).

Property Pool.[202] A county treasurer was convicted in 1998 of forgery in his other job as a private certified public accountant. Although the county knew this, the treasurer continued to be reelected, the conviction was expunged, and it did not cause a loss to the county. In 2006 the treasurer embezzled $1.2 million of the county's funds by covertly squandering them on a "Nigerian Advance Fee Fraud Scam." The court held the county was not entitled to coverage on bonds covering the treasurer, nor on bonds covering him as finance director, because the bonds by their terms automatically terminated upon knowledge of a dishonest or fraudulent act (whether causing loss to the county or not) and the county had such knowledge before the loss it was claiming occurred.

B. Statutes of Limitations

The general rule is that the statute of limitations against a public official's surety does not begin to run until the close of the official's term.[203] In the event of a fraudulent concealment, the action may not accrue until the shortage is discovered.[204] In *Estate of Spiegel v. Western Surety Co.*,[205] a New Jersey judgment creditor sued some court clerks and their sureties after they failed to enroll the judgment in Mississippi. The Mississippi Court of Appeals held the action accrued when the plaintiff became aware of the clerks' error and thus was time barred both against the clerks and against their sureties.[206]

The bond statute itself may specify a limitations period but otherwise the courts will apply either the general period for an action created by statute (on the view that the bond is only collateral security) or the period for an action on a written contract.[207] Whatever the statutory period, the

---

202. No. 292155, 2011 Mich. App. LEXIS 473 (Mich. Ct. App. Mar. 10, 2011).
203. State *ex rel.* Grassie v. Masterson, 561 P.2d 796 (Kan. 1977); State *ex rel.* Obion Cnty. v. Cobb, 202 S.W.2d 819 (Tenn. 1947).
204. Vill. of Dolton v. Harms, 63 N.E.2d 785 (Ill. App. Ct. 1945).
205. 908 So. 2d 859 (Miss. Ct. App. 2005).
206. *See also* Alexander v. Taylor, 928 So. 2d 992 (Miss. Ct. App. 2006) (claim by purchasers of property at tax sale against county clerk and surety for refund of taxes paid after prior owner redeemed property was time barred).
207. Annotation, *What Period of Limitation Governs in an Action against a Public Officer and the Surety on His Official Bond*, 18 A.L.R. 2D 1176 (1951).

surety may not be permitted to contractually shorten it.[208] The limitation period governing the bond claim may be longer than the period governing the underlying claim and at least one court in such a case held the surety could not assert the lateness of the underlying claim as a defense to the bond claim.[209] Another court rejected a limitations defense by invoking the rule that statutes of limitations do not run against the state.[210]

C. Rescission

Most applications for public official bonds are made by the principal. In those cases, absent any documented inquiry to the obligee, rescission may be difficult. If a surety seeks to rescind the public official bond, then it will generally need to rely on the underlying state law governing contractual rescission.[211]

For example, in *Hanover Insurance Co. v. Treasurer & Receiver General*,[212] however, the court held that a blanket bond issued to a state treasurer's office could not be rescinded for misrepresentations in the application. The bond claim involved checks the treasurer issued but that the intended payees never deposited (about 2,500 out of eight or nine million checks a year). The office maintained an unclaimed check fund account and this is what the employees were stealing from. The insured had not reconciled the account or controlled it with a voucher system but the court held this was immaterial. The insured's representations that this had been done were accurate with respect to 99.9 percent of the checks it issued and that was good enough. A misrepresentation that there was an internal audit was also immaterial because the treasurer's office disclosed outside audits and state audits and the underwriter relied on that.

Likewise, in *Fidelity Federal Savings & Loan Association v. Felicetti*, the Eastern District of Pennsylvania refused to rescind the

---

208. State v. Lidster, 467 N.E.2d 47 (Ind. Ct. App. 1984).

209. Cnty. of Hudson v. Janiszewski, 520 F. Supp. 2d 631 (D.N.J. 2007), *aff'd*, 351 F. App'x 662 (3d Cir. 2009) (holding that Racketeer Influenced and Corrupt Organizations Act (RICO) claims against a county executive were barred by limitations but not a public official bond claim for the same conduct as that was subject to the longer period for breach of contract).

210. State *ex rel.* Pittman v. Ladner, 512 So. 2d 1271 (Miss. 1987).

211. Fid. Fed. Sav. & Loan Ass'n v. Felicetti, 813 F. Supp. 332, 335 (E.D. Pa. 1993) (applying Pennsylvania law to assess whether a fidelity bond was properly rescinded).

212. 910 N.E.2d 921 (Mass. Ct. App. 2009).

bond when the insurer failed to establish each contractual element of contractual recission under Pennsylvania law.[213] As in *Hanover Insurance*, the court stressed that the insurer failed to establish any *material* misrepresentations of fact that would have "caused the insurer to refuse to issue the policy altogether or to demand higher premiums."[214]

D. Traditional Suretyship Defenses

Courts adjudicating public official bond claims have not been as receptive to suretyship defenses (i.e., defenses arising from obligee conduct that prejudices the surety). The failure to advise the surety of problems with the principal before the surety issues its bond has been held no defense absent fraud.[215] Fraud by the principal is no defense unless the obligee participates in the fraud.[216] Obligee negligence before or after the bond issued is not a defense.[217] Courts have excused lack of due diligence to discover theft by the principal.[218] Failure to require periodic settlements has also been excused.[219] The obligee's failure to timely pursue the principal does not release the surety either.[220]

VI. Subrogation and Indemnity

On payment of a claim, a public official's surety is by operation of law subrogated to the obligee's rights against the principal.[221] This might not avail the surety if the obligee had no rights against the principal due to an immunity that did not also protect the surety. However, the surety could argue the principal is a party to the bond, so any immunity is waived.

Moreover, the surety has its own separate right of indemnity against the principal both at common law and possibly by agreement. In *American*

---

213. 813 F. Supp. at 335.
214. *Id.*
215. Nat'l Sur. Corp. v. Morgan Cnty., 440 S.W.2d 791 (Ky. Ct. App. 1969).
216. Commonwealth v. Edwards, 322 A.2d 416 (Pa. Commw. Ct. 1974).
217. Md. Cas. Co. v. Magoffin Cnty. Bd. of Educ., 358 S.W.2d 353, 358 (Ky. Ct. App. 1961).
218. City of Newburyport v. Davis, 95 N.E. 110 (Mass. 1911).
219. State v. Edwards, 71 S.E.2d 826 (S.C. 1911).
220. Brubaker v. Cnty. of Berks, 112 A.2d 620 (Pa. 1955).
221. State *ex rel.* Cnty. Comm'n of Jackson Cnty. v. McCoy, 291 S.E.2d 670 (W. Va. 1982).

Fire & Casualty Co. v. Johnson,[222] a bonded probate judge embezzled hearing fees paid to his court by the Department of Mental Health. The South Carolina Supreme Court reprimanded him, a grand jury indicted him, the governor removed him from office, and he pleaded no contest to the criminal charges. In light of these compelling facts, the principal was not in a position to credibly argue that the surety acted in "bad faith," which could preclude indemnification.

The surety may also be able to recover the loss from third parties. For instance, in *Ohio Casualty Insurance Co. v. Bank One*,[223] a township supervisor used two banks to embezzle public funds. He opened personal and business accounts, engaged in massive check-kiting, opened a secret township account without authority, and used that account to funnel funds to his personal account. This went on for 19 years. The supervisor's surety settled with the township and sued the banks. The court refused to dismiss a breach of contract count, provided the surety identify the contract it was suing upon. And, the surety could also pursue an unjust enrichment claim against the bank.

In *Fidelity & Deposit Co. of Maryland v. Dally*,[224] a city's fidelity insurer paid a loss resulting from an employee's deposit to her personal account of checks made payable to the city in various manners by its collection agency. The insurer sued the agency, under an indemnity agreement entered into between the collection agency and city, to recover the loss. The court, however, held the agency did not breach the indemnity contract and was not liable for not making the payments more secure or for failing to examine endorsements.

Conclusion

The public official bond shares much in common with other surety bonds, but it will still be terra incognita to the uninitiated. Just as anyone taking up a construction contract bond claim had better know something about construction, one will need to be a student of government when dealing with a public official bond. The responsibilities of the principal's office must be ascertained. But with that plus scrutiny of the bond statute, the bond itself, and the rules of law discussed above, the public official bond claim can be handled responsibly. That will be more important than ever in these times of fiscal distress.

---

222. 504 S.E.2d 356 (S.C. 1998).
223. No. 95-C-6613, 1996 WL 507292 (N.D. Ill. Sept. 5, 1996).
224. 201 P.3d 1040 (Wash. Ct. App. 2009).

CHAPTER 7

RECLAMATION BONDS

Walter Blaine Early, III
William T. Gorton III
Robert L. Scanlon
Laura M. Murphy

I. Introduction to Reclamation Bonds[1]

A. The Nature of the Industries

Reclamation bonds occupy a unique position in the universe of surety bonds. Like other bonds, they guarantee the principal's performance. But these bonds protect not only the obligee, they also safeguard environmental quality from the well-known adverse impacts of extracting earthen resources.[2] Performance is directly linked to compliance with complex laws intended to limit, and ultimately repair, the environmental impacts of extractive processes. The compliance framework may vary according to the resource (coal or other mineral), land ownership (federal, tribal, or private), jurisdiction (state, federal, or combined), and the requirements of a variety of local climatic, geophysical, and hydrologic settings. These variables challenge the surety from the inception of underwriting to monitoring the principal's performance to formulating practical responses in the event of a principal's default.

Reclamation bonds support American industrial and consumer uses of mineral resources that have been the foundation of much of the U.S. economy. Products from extraction of natural resources have led to a quality of life unknown in history. Coal continues to be an important

---

1. Selected portions of this chapter have been published in William T. Gorton et al., *Reclamation Bonds*, *in* THE LAW OF COMMERCIAL SURETY AND MISCELLANEOUS BONDS 261 (2d ed. 2012).
2. *See, e.g.*, Preston S. Chiaro & G. Frank Joklik, *The Extractive Industries*, *in* THE ECOLOGY OF INDUSTRY 13 (Deanna Richards & Greg Pearson eds., 1998) ("Extractive industries are commonly viewed as having unacceptable impacts on the environment.").

source of materials and energy for steelmaking and other industrial processes, heating, and generating electricity. A 2017 survey conducted by the U.S. Government Accountability Office (GAO) revealed that the regulatory authorities held approximately $10.2 billion in financial assurances to cover reclamation liabilities; $7.8 billion of that total (76 percent) were commercial surety bonds.[3] Although coal resources are found in 38 states, at this time only 23 states have active coal mining operations.[4] Regulatory oversight consists of a mixture of state, federal, and tribal programs.[5] In 2017, more than 4.1 million acres were covered by a coal mining permit issued by one of these regulatory authorities.[6]

Trends in electricity generation show a marked reduction in consumption of coal and increased reliance on natural gas and renewables. In recent decades coal as a source of electricity peaked in 2007 but steadily declined through 2020 in favor of other sources. During this 13-year period, electricity generation sourced from coal dropped from more than two trillion kilowatt hours (kWh) to 774 billion kWh, while electricity generation from natural gas rose from 897 billion kWh to 1.6 trillion kWh and renewables from 353 billion kWh to 792 billion kWh.[7] Tracking this decrease in coal-related electricity, coal production in the United States has declined from more than one billion tons in 2007 to about one-half billion tons in 2020.[8]

Forces causing these changes include economic and practical (market changes) and policy or philosophical (climate change and environmental impacts of coal mining). The 2016 bankruptcy of Peabody Energy Corporation and many of its subsidiaries reveals market forces driving

---

3. GAO, Coal Mine Reclamation: Federal and State Agencies Face Challenges in Managing Billions in Financial Assurances (2018) [hereinafter GAO Coal Mine Reclamation].
4. *Id.*
5. Office of Surface Mining Reclamation and Enforcement, U.S. Department of the Interior, 2017 Annual Report. *See also* 30 C.F.R. pt. 900 (2020).
6. Office of Surface Mining Reclamation and Enforcement, *supra* note 5, at 36.
7. *Electricity Explained: Electricity in the United States*, U.S. Energy Information Administration, https://www.eia.gov/energyexplained/electricity/electricity-in-the-us.php (last updated Mar. 18, 2021).
8. National Mining Association, http://www.nma.org (last visited Jan. 17, 2022) (citing data from the Energy Information Administration).

the decline in coal production and consumption.[9] Peabody, then the largest private-sector coal company by volume production, explained its poor financial performance due to "reduced demand and lower coal prices created by sluggish economic growth, an abundance of extremely low priced natural gas and increased regulatory hurdles."[10] The role of coal and other fossil fuels in causing climate change has been studied and debated, but the consensus that they do cause climate change has reached a critical inflection point.[11] The result is growing public sentiment that has caused businesses and communities across the country to reduce their use of coal and other fossil fuels and to adopt resolutions and other commitments to convert to "100% clean energy" by a date certain, sometimes as early as 2035.[12]

Although natural gas, like coal, is also a fossil fuel, it is thought to have a smaller impact on greenhouse gas emissions and related climate change. High-efficiency natural gas-fired generating units figured prominently in the now-abandoned Clean Power Plan adopted in 2015 under President Obama's administration.[13] The increased availability and low cost of natural gas as an alternative to coal is related to the increased production of oil and gas by the technique of hydraulic fracturing, or "fracking." Environmental concerns about this technique have spurred discussions of additional financial assurance to be supplied by the oil and

---

9. *In re* Peabody Energy Corp., No. 16-42529, (Bankr. E.D. Mo. Apr. 13, 2016).
10. Declaration of Amy B. Schwartz at 25, *In re* Peabody Energy Corp., No. 16-42529 (Bankr. E.D. Mo. Apr. 13, 2016), Doc. No. 7. *See also* Second Amended Disclosure Statement at 34, 44, and 131, *In re* Peabody Energy Corp., (Bankr. E.D. Mo. Jan. 17, 2017), Doc. No. 2231.
11. See, for example, the discussions throughout the INTERGOVERNMENTAL PANEL ON CLIMATE CHANGE, CLIMATE CHANGE 2021: THE PHYSICAL SCIENCE BASIS (Valérie Masson-Delmotte et al. eds., 2021), https://www.ipcc.ch/report/ar6/wg1/.
12. *See, e.g.*, *Ready for 100*, SIERRA CLUB, https://www.sierraclub.org/ready-for-100 (last visited Jan. 17, 2020) (documenting more than 180 cities across the country that have pledged to convert to using only "clean renewable energy").
13. Carbon Pollution Emission Guidelines for Existing Stationary Sources: Electric Utility Generating Units, 80 Fed. Reg. 64,661 (Oct. 23, 2015) (codified at 40 C.F.R. pt. 60).

gas industry.[14] Whether these new proposed requirements are adopted, current law requires bonds to secure obligations including compliance with lease terms and conditions and closure of the wells.[15]

Despite coal's decline, it continues to be an important part of the energy supply chain, and in 2020 coal-fired power plants provided more than 19 percent of U.S. electricity generation, which accounted for 91.5 percent of the coal used in 2020.[16] Industrial coke plants important in steelmaking and other industrial uses of coal other than heat combined for about 6.3 percent of the coal consumed.[17] Therefore, it appears that the need for coal reclamation bonds will continue.

The non-coal minerals industry includes the metal ore and nonmetallic mineral mining industries, which provide many of the raw materials used in modern life. It is estimated that every American consumer uses close to 40,000 pounds of newly mined minerals every year.[18] The Internal Revenue Service has projected that every person born in America will use 3.7 million pounds of minerals, metals, and fuels during their lifetime.[19] Many of today's high-technology devices such as phones and electric vehicle batteries require up to 40 different minerals for production, including aluminum, copper, gold, silver, iron, limestone, silica, boron, and rare-earth minerals. The construction industry accounts for more than half of U.S. copper demand.

---

14. *See, e.g.*, W. Blaine Early III, *Bond What You Know and Insure What You Don't: A Comment on a Market Approach to Regulating the Energy Revolution*, 45 ENV'T L. REP. 10756 (2015) (responding to David A. Dana & Hannah J. Wiseman, *A Market Approach to Regulating the Energy Revolution: Assurance Bonds, Insurance, and the Certain and Uncertain Risks of Hydraulic Fracturing*, 99 IOWA L. REV. 1523 (2014), and Thomas W. Merrill & David M. Schizer, *The Shale Oil and Gas Revolution, Hydraulic Fracturing, and Water Contamination: A Regulatory Strategy*, 98 MINN. L. REV. 145 (2013)).
15. *See, e.g.*, 30 C.F.R. § 556.900 (bonds for offshore, outer continental shelf wells); 43 C.F.R. § 3104.1 (onshore operations).
16. U.S. ENERGY INFORMATION ADMINISTRATION, ELECTRIC POWER MONTHLY (Feb. 2021).
17. *Id.*
18. NATIONAL MINING ASSOCIATION, *supra* note 8 (citing data from the U.S. Geological Survey, Energy Information Administration, and U.S. Census Bureau).
19. INTERNAL REVENUE SERVICE, U.S. DEPARTMENT OF THE TREASURY, OVERVIEW OF THE MINING INDUSTRY (2006).

Natural aggregates, including crushed stone, sand, and gravel, are abundant and a basic raw material used in construction, agriculture, and industries employing complex chemical and metallurgical processes.[20] More than 90 percent of asphalt pavements and 80 percent of concrete are aggregates. In 2020 the United States produced 1.46 billion tons of crushed stone from 3,440 quarries for a value of more than $17.8 billion.[21] Many of these operations are on privately owned lands. Production of non-coal, hardrock minerals on federal lands is significant, with 798 operations occupying more than 815,106 acres.[22] The use of fertilizers sufficient to support the United States' large agricultural industry requires production of more than 45 million tons of phosphorus and potash along with smaller amounts of other minerals each year.[23]

After many decades of merely abandoning mined lands following resource extraction in the United States, it is now public policy to minimize, mitigate, and remediate the adverse effects of mineral extraction and processing while obtaining the benefits of our natural resources. Mining in the United States is highly regulated at both the state and federal levels and has evolved to include the surety industry as the preferred guarantor that land and waters affected by mining and mineral processing operations will be restored.

Considered under the regulatory moniker of "financial assurances,"[24] state and federal laws and regulatory agencies with permitting and enforcement authority require mining companies to provide financial guarantees assuring that their operations will be conducted and closed according to technical criteria and affected lands and waters will be reclaimed according to mandatory environmental quality standards. Some states and federal regulatory agencies have a long history of

---

20. U.S. Geological Survey, Natural Aggregates—Foundation of America's Future (1997) (Fact Sheet No. 144-97), https://pubs.er.usgs.gov/publication/fs14497.
21. U.S. Geological Survey, Mineral Commodity Summaries (2021).
22. Letter from Anne-Marie Fennell, Director, GAO, to Representative Raul Grijalva, Chairman, House Committee on Natural Resources, Mining on Federal Lands: More Than 800 Operations Authorized to Mine and Total Mineral Production Is Unknown (May 28, 2020).
23. U.S. Geological Survey, Fertilizers—Sustaining Global Food Supplies (1999) (Fact Sheet No. 155-99), https://pubs.usgs.gov/fs/fs155-99/fs155-99.pdf.
24. The term "reclamation bond" is used commonly throughout the mining industry to cover *all* forms of reclamation financial guarantees.

requiring financial assurances for mine reclamation while to others the concept is relatively recent.[25] The maturity of those programs and the experience of the regulatory staff that administers them can also be important to a surety in working through complicated claims matters, as discussed below.

Although the mining regulatory programs allow various forms of financial assurances, in most cases they are in the form of surety bonds. In many instances throughout the United States the reclamation bond has come to be used for addressing issues other than "traditional reclamation"[26] through judicial interpretation[27] and what could be characterized as retroactive rulemaking.[28] Sureties with little experience in these specialized commercial bonds should be aware of the idiosyncrasies in this market niche.

This chapter addresses the nature of surety bonds in the context of the extractive industries including underwriting suggestions and the relevant legislative history associated with development of financial assurance programs. It also addresses how the corporate surety is a party to the administrative process surrounding the environmental laws under which the bonds were issued, and the procedures involved in obtaining bond releases and dealing with defaults.

---

25. Reclamation bonds were required in Pennsylvania under what evolved to become the Surface Mining Conservation and Reclamation Act, 52 Pennsylvania Statutes section 681.6, as early as 1947 under the Anthracite Strip Mining Law section 6, Act of June 27, 1947, Pub. L. No. 1095, amended, whereas U.S. Bureau of Land Management (BLM) regulations requiring the present form of financial assurances on federal land in the hardrock industry were promulgated in 2001, 30 C.F.R. § 3809.555, 66 Fed. Reg. 32,575 (June 15, 2001).
26. Traditional reclamation includes backfilling highwalls and pits, grading, topsoil replacement, revegetation, and drainage control removal. *See, e.g.*, 30 C.F.R. §§ 715.13–.20.
27. *See generally* W. Va. Highlands Conservancy v. Norton, 238 F. Supp. 2d 761 (S.D. W. Va. 2003) (discussing bond forfeiture funds for water treatment and traditional reclamation).
28. *See* discussion *infra* Part VIII; *see also* BLM discussion regarding the use of existing bonding for water treatment in relation to clarifying regulations. 66 Fed. Reg. 54,847 (Oct. 30, 2001).

B. Underwriting Reclamation Bonds

As statutory bonds, reclamation bonds are unique to the mineral industry and the regulatory programs requiring them, and an experienced underwriter should review more than a principal's balance sheet.[29] Since reclamation bonds are not cancelable for liabilities already incurred, they are long-term commitments.[30] Understanding the applicable regulatory procedures and the bonded obligations discussed below is important. Sureties successful in the reclamation bond segment of the market are represented by insurance agents or brokers and have underwriters that are familiar with mining operations and those sectors of the commodity markets. Important business considerations include whether a coal mine produces metallurgical-grade coal or a grade of coal more suitable for steam production at a power plant and whether the coal is being sold on the spot market or is committed to a long-term contract. Surety underwriters also review each mine to determine the remaining mine life—a mine life of at least ten to 15 years is typically viewed as more favorable—as well as the proven and probable reserves, average annual production, and location of each mine.

Related to mine locations are the site-specific characteristics of each operation in relation to local regulatory requirements; the physical location of each mine may bring its own set of underwriting concerns. It is helpful to involve claims staff who are aware of the particular pitfalls that may be common in a certain environmental setting or regulatory regime. For example, mines in Central Appalachia are more likely to have significant water contamination issues (discussed in more detail in Part VIII) than mines located in other areas, such as the Powder River Basin. Therefore, those mines that may be impacted by water quality or contamination issues must be underwritten with an understanding that water treatment may be long-term or perpetual and very costly. Underwriters will also consider how coal is transported. Mines that do not have cost-effective access to transportation (typically rail lines) may have higher transportation costs that reduce profitability.

---

29. *See infra* note 95 (regarding statutory bonds in Part III).
30. *See* 30 C.F.R. § 800.13(a)(1) ("[B]ond liability shall be for the duration of the surface coal mining and reclamation operation and for a period which is coincident with the period of extended responsibility for successful revegetation . . . ."); *see also id.* § 800.20(b) ("Surety bonds shall be noncancellable during their terms . . . .").

From a financial perspective, the surety underwriter will review the historical profitability of the mining concern, its current debt structure, maturities and covenant compliance, additional credit availability under established bank facilities, and capital expense budget needs. In addition, the underwriter will look for adequacy in establishing reclamation cost accruals, goodwill amortization, and the potential for asset impairment charges. The surety underwriter will also want to review future projections and business strategy with management. The underwriter may also consider whether any third parties, such as utility customers, guarantee the reclamation. If this is the case, a close review of any related documents (e.g., reclamation services agreements or trust documents) is required. Finally, the underwriter will review the sales of coal from each mine. Factors such as what percentage of the production is committed by contract to certain customers and whether the contracts are fixed-price or cost-plus are very important to assessing the potential profitability of the mine.

Factors that may escape the ordinary contract bond underwriting process but that provide useful insights to a commercial bond underwriter relate to the principal's operating history. A technical review of the principal's existing and prospective operations by a professional familiar with mining operations *and* the regulatory framework can provide relevant information regarding compliance and a company's overall commitment to timely reclamation. A review of whether the company's reclamation is contemporaneous with extraction is indicative of compliance. A mining company that has idled mines or mines in temporary cessation[31] should be reviewed closely. Typically, mining has ceased because it is unprofitable to continue operations. This could be an indication of financial distress and would pose a higher risk to the surety. For a financially distressed mining company, it is not unusual to lag behind in meeting reclamation obligations. A well-engineered mine may accomplish many of the activities associated with reclamation such as final overburden placement and grading, as part of its mining operation. A mine that leaves most of the reclamation activities until the resource is removed is a much higher surety risk because cash flow from the sale of the mineral has ceased.

A review of the principal's regulatory compliance history, along with that of its officers, directors, and senior management, should also be conducted.[32] Not addressed in this chapter but equally important to

---

31. *Id.* § 816.131.
32. *See infra* Part II.A.

the surety-principal relationship is the form of indemnity agreement and collateral requirements. There are peculiarities in the mining regulatory programs that can cause the traditional indemnity agreement to be inadequate for protecting the surety under certain circumstances. A common example is whether a permit transfer or change in ownership of a parent company should be a cause for reviewing whether the surety relationship should be revised. A transfer, assignment, or sale of a mining permit must first be approved by the regulatory agency.[33] If the agency views the transfer as a change in the actual permittee and not merely a change in the ownership and control structure, then the agency may require a complete transfer of the permit and a replacement of the existing surety bonds. If the transfer is not required, then the surety may find that it has now bonded a principal under the control of persons that it did not have the opportunity to evaluate. These and other issues known by practitioners familiar with both the surety industry and the mining industry can help to provide an underwriting protocol for mitigating surety risk in a critical industry.

II. Mining Program Financial Assurances Requirements

All mining operations throughout the United States, whether energy-related, metals, or nonmetals, are subject to significant state and federal law governing environmental performance and have financial assurance requirements. Notwithstanding any primary mining and reclamation statutes, all mines and processing facilities are also subject to the compliance requirements of the Clean Water Act (CWA)[34] related to water quality and wetlands protection, the Clean Air Act (CAA)[35] related to fugitive and process emissions, the Resource Conservation and Recovery Act (RCRA)[36] related to the management of non-mining/beneficiating wastes,[37] and other applicable environmental laws. Many of these other environmental protection statutes also require financial assurances for

---

33. *See, e.g.*, 30 C.F.R. § 774.17(a) ("No transfer, assignment, or sale of rights granted by a permit shall be made without the prior written approval of the regulatory authority.").
34. 33 U.S.C. §§ 1251–1387.
35. 42 U.S.C. §§ 7401–7671.
36. *Id.* §§ 6901–6992k.
37. RCRA does not regulate mineral extraction, beneficiation, and processing wastes under the "Bevill Amendment," which excludes them. *See* 42 U.S.C. § 6982(f); 40 C.F.R. § 261.4(b)(7).

some aspect of their performance standards.[38] It should be noted that in all of the regulatory programs requiring financial assurances, the amounts required are finite based on regulatory or statutory minimums or on an engineering cost analysis of specific, defined activities. The following discussions describe the primary mining statutes' requirements for financial assurances.

A. *Coal Industry: The Surface Mining Control and Reclamation Act*

The coal industry is regulated by the U.S. Department of Interior, Office of Surface Mining Reclamation and Enforcement (OSM) under the federal Surface Mining Control and Reclamation Act (SMCRA).[39] Purposes of SMCRA include to "protect society and the environment from the adverse effects of surface coal mining operations"[40] and to "assure that adequate procedures are undertaken to protect the environment."[41] Under SMCRA, each state may assume primary enforcement responsibility under the concept of "primacy."[42] SMCRA also authorizes Indian tribes to seek authorization to administer a mining program on reservation land.[43] With the exception of Tennessee,[44] Washington,[45] and Georgia,[46] which

38. Under RCRA, financial assurances for waste treatment, disposal, or storage area closure and post-closure must be provided. *See* 40 C.F.R. §§ 264–265; *id.* §§ 264.143, 264.145. Under the Outer Continental Shelf Lands Act, financial assurances to fund oil well closure and to address spills are required. See 30 C.F.R. §§ 256.52–.59 regarding well closure and *id.* § 253.14 regarding one-time catastrophic events. Under the CWA, financial assurances can be required to ensure that wetlands mitigation projects are completed. *See* 33 C.F.R. § 332.3(n)(1)–(6). Under the Safe Drinking Water Act, financial assurances are required for underground injection wells. *See* 40 C.F.R. §§ 144.28(d), 144.52(a)(7), 144.60–.70.
39. 30 U.S.C. § 1201 *et seq.*
40. *Id.* § 1202(a).
41. *Id.* § 1202(d).
42. *See id.* § 1235.
43. *Id.* § 1300(j).
44. 30 C.F.R. § 942.700.
45. *Id.* § 947.700.
46. *Id.* § 910.700.

have federal programs,[47] all other coal-producing states have primacy to enforce SMCRA[48] and have enacted their own state-law analogues to SMCRA. These statutes must meet and may exceed the federal regulatory requirements to control environmental impacts of coal mining activities.[49] A comparison of the regulatory programs in the coal and non-coal mineral industries illustrates that while SMCRA, adopted in 1977, is a relative newcomer, regulation of the coal industry is significantly more refined than that found in the non-coal arena, particularly with regard to individual responsibilities, reclamation, financial guarantees, and long-term pollution issues.

Consistent with the command-and-control nature of many environmental laws, a threshold aspect of SMCRA requires that surface coal mining be conducted only under authority of a permit issued by the applicable regulatory agency.[50] Surface coal mining activities have been interpreted to include almost all of the surface effects to land, facilities related to extraction and processing of coal resources, and the surface effects incidental to underground mining.[51] Permit applications require detailed background and baseline environmental information, geologic information, engineering design, operations plans, environmental performance standards, and reclamation plans consistent with an approved final land use.[52]

Prior to receiving its permit, the operator/permittee must post adequate financial assurance to provide funds necessary for the regulatory agency to complete final reclamation in compliance with the law and as detailed in the approved permit if the operator fails to do so.[53] SMCRA allows financial guarantees to be in the form of a corporate surety bond,[54] cash collateral bond (including letters of credit and securities),[55] or a self-bond.[56] Most coal companies use corporate surety bonds, but it

---

47. 30 U.S.C. § 1254.
48. *See generally* 30 C.F.R. pt. 900 (federal approval of individual coal-producing states' regulatory programs).
49. 30 U.S.C. § 1253.
50. *Id.* § 1256(a).
51. 30 C.F.R. § 700.5.
52. *Id.* §§ 779, 780.
53. 30 U.S.C. § 1259; 30 C.F.R. §§ 800.4, 800.12.
54. 30 C.F.R. §§ 800.12, 800.20.
55. *Id.* §§ 800.5(b), 800.21.
56. *Id.* § 800.23.

is not uncommon for a mining company to use a combination of financial assurance instruments.[57] Difficulties with the self-bonding programs are coming under intense scrutiny and self-bonding may soon cease to be an option.[58]

The amount of financial assurance is to be "sufficient to assure the completion of the reclamation plan if the work has to be performed by the regulatory agency in the event of forfeiture."[59] Reclamation obligations include, but are not limited to, backfilling open pits, grading, topsoil replacement, revegetation, removing drainage control facilities, highwall reduction, underground mine sealing, shaft and mine entry sealing, demolition of coal preparation and processing plants and related surface structures, reclamation of refuse and waste rock (spoil) disposal/storage areas, restoring the hydrologic regime, and, surprisingly to many sureties' underwriters, long-term water treatment.[60] Although under OSM's policies mining permits should *not* be approved "if the determination of probable hydrologic consequences or other reliable hydrologic analysis predicts the formation of post mining pollutional discharges that would require continuing long term treatment without a defined end point,"[61] it is not uncommon for a permitted coal mine to develop an unforeseen pollutional discharge based on site geochemical and hydrologic conditions.

Federal law provides that the bond amount is adjusted "from time to time as the area requiring bond coverage is increased or decreased or where the cost of future reclamation changes."[62] Some states calculate bond amounts annually, while others may wait years to determine changes. Whether the bond amounts truly reflect the cost of completing reclamation is an increasingly important question in light of concerns

---

57. Surety bonds constitute approximately 76 percent of the financial assurances held by state and federal regulators. *See* GAO COAL MINE RECLAMATION, *supra* note 3.
58. *Id.* at 20.
59. 30 C.F.R. § 800.14(b).
60. *Id.* §§ 715.10–.20.
61. *See* Bonding and Other Financial Assurance Mechanisms for Treatment of Long-Term Pollutional Discharges and Acid/Toxic Mine Drainage (AMD) Related Issues, 67 Fed. Reg. 35070 (May 17, 2002). *See also* OSM, U.S. DEPARTMENT OF THE INTERIOR, POLICY GOALS AND OBJECTIVES ON CORRECTING, PREVENTING, AND CONTROLLING ACID/TOXIC MINE DRAINAGE (1997), http://www.osmre.gov//lrg/docs/amdpolicy033197.pdf.
62. 30 C.F.R. § 800.15(a).

about the abilities of financially challenged mining companies to complete reclamation. A possible reason for the discrepancy is delay in enforcing SMCRA's requirement for contemporaneous reclamation.[63] If the permittee is not required to complete reclamation as mining progresses, then reclamation liability may accrue far above the predictions of an acceptable mining and reclamation plan. A study of mines in the Appalachian region found that the operations were under-bonded because their bonds available totaled $3.8 billion but estimated reclamation costs ranged from $7.5 to $9.8 billion.[64] Although this discrepancy does not subject the surety to additional liability beyond a bond penal sum, a site that is significantly under-bonded will limit the surety's options on principal default and bond forfeiture.

A final aspect of SMCRA important to the relationship of surety and principal is SMCRA's consideration of whether a particular person or entity is ineligible to be granted a permit or permit amendment because of outstanding violations of law.[65] An applicant for a mining permit must "file with his permit application a schedule listing any and all notices of violations of [SMCRA] . . . incurred by the applicant in connection with any surface coal mining operation."[66] If the agency determines that a "surface coal mining operation owned or controlled by the applicant is currently in violation of [SMCRA] . . . the permit shall not be issued until the applicant submits proof that such violation has been corrected or is in the process of being corrected."[67] OSM uses a computerized database known as the Applicant Violator System (AVS) to analyze ownership and control links among permit applicants and existing or former permittees. If an owner or controller is linked to certain violations and bond forfeitures, then the person is said to be "permit blocked."

---

63. *Id.* § 816.100.
64. Erin Savage, Appalachian Voices, Repairing the Damage: The Costs of Delaying Reclamation at Modern-Era Mines (2021), https://appvoices.org/resources/RepairingTheDamage_ReclamationAtModernMines.pdf.
65. The individual connection to, and vetting of, the leadership of the principal may play a role in evaluating the nature of the bond as a financial accommodation within the meaning of § 365 of the Bankruptcy Code. *See, e.g.*, Surety Aspects of Bankruptcy Law and Practice ch. V.F (Chad Schexnayder & Michael E. Collins eds., 2021).
66. 30 U.S.C. § 1260(c).
67. *Id.*

B. *Hardrock Industry (Federal Land): Federal Land Policy and Management Act*

Unlike their coal mine counterparts, non-coal mines on private property are not regulated by *federal* reclamation laws[68] though most do have analogous state reclamation and associated financial assurance requirements.[69] Under the General Mining Act of 1872 (Mining Act)[70] an individual or business entity can establish a claim to any hardrock mineral on public land upon recording the mining claim and paying a de minimis location fee and annual maintenance fee. The Mining Act was designed to encourage the settlement and development of the West, not to regulate the associated environmental effects of mining.[71] Until the passage of the Federal Land Policy and Management Act of 1976 (FLPMA),[72] development of hardrock minerals on public land remained largely unregulated.[73] Non-coal mines on federal land are therefore subject to regulation by *both* state and federal agencies under various laws. On federal land other than national forest lands, the U.S. Department of Interior, Bureau of Land Management (BLM)[74] administers performance and reclamation requirements known as the "3809 Regulations" based on their location in the *Code of Federal Regulations.* Under FLPMA, the secretary of interior is required to take any action required to prevent

---

68. State laws governing non-coal operations on private property have varying degrees of reclamation stringency; however, they are governed by *other* federal environmental laws including but not limited to the federal CWA, CAA, Endangered Species Act, and other applicable federal and state standards.
69. See, for example, surface effects of noncoal mining regulations implemented by the Kentucky Department of Natural Resources (405 Ky. Admin. Regs. ch. 5 (2022)) and the non-coal rules and regulations implemented by the Oklahoma Department of Mines (Okla. Admin. Code tit. 460, ch. 10 (2017)).
70. 30 U.S.C. §§ 22–47.
71. GAO, Hardrock Mining: BLM Needs to Better Manage Financial Assurances to Guarantee Coverage of Reclamation Costs 12 (2005).
72. 43 U.S.C. § 1701 *et seq.*
73. GAO, *supra* note 71, at 12.
74. *Id.* at 1 n.3, 8. BLM is responsible for managing 261 million acres of public land in 12 western states. Approximately 90 percent is open to the public for hardrock mining.

the "undue degradation of public land and its resources." BLM issued the initial 3809 Regulations effective in 1981 that require all operators to reclaim BLM land disturbed by their hardrock operations.[75] It was not until 2001, however, that BLM revised the rules requiring operators to include reclamation plans *and* cost estimates in their notices and plans of operations for BLM approval. The 2001 regulations require that financial assurances be provided to cover those estimated reclamation costs for notice- and plan-level hardrock operations.[76]

The revised bonding requirements for hardrock operations on federal lands expanded the acceptable types of financial assurances to include corporate surety bonds, cash, irrevocable letters of credit, certificates of deposit, government securities or bonds, investment-grade rated securities, or insurance.[77] The majority of mining operators throughout the United States choose to post corporate surety bonds as the preferred form of reclamation financial guarantee.

For non-coal operations on federal lands, FLPMA has reclamation requirements similar to SMCRA that require the plans approved by the agencies to be fulfilled. Reclamation standards include topsoil storage and placement, erosion and control measures, standards for "reshaping" the area disturbed (as opposed to SMCRA's requirement for "approximate original contour"), revegetation and habitat restoration, and other site-specific requirements contained in the approved plan of operations.[78] Unlike SMCRA, however, FLPMA's concept of "concurrent reclamation" is not generally applied and may allow the entire permitted mine footprint to be disturbed at one time[79] and actual major reclamation activities to be deferred until the mineral resource is depleted.

---

75. GAO, *supra* note 71, at 3.
76. *Id.*
77. 43 C.F.R. § 3809.555(e).
78. 30 U.S.C. § 1258(a)(13); 43 C.F.R. § 3809.420.
79. Compare SMCRA's requirements for contemporaneous reclamation, 30 C.F.R. § 816.100, and the regulations promulgated under FLPMA associated with concurrent reclamation, 43 C.F.R. § 3809.420(a)(5), (b)(3). While the concepts may be similar, due in part to the nature of hardrock mining practices, the enforcement is quite different (e.g., allowing a pit to remain open or allowing waste rock dumps to remain unreclaimed based on the potential for increases in the resources price that then may allow another cut at the pit or, arguably convert "waste rock" into a resource worth processing).

C. Other Lands

The U.S. Forest Service (USFS) within the U.S. Department of Agriculture manages approximately 193 million acres of public forest lands, some of which are sites of various mining operations: coal, hardrock, and other non-coal mining.[80] USFS, in balancing all public land stewardship obligations, has stated that "[it] recognizes that prospectors and miners have a statutory right, not a mere privilege under the Mining Law of 1872, the Surface Resources Act[81] and the Organic Administration Act of 1897,[82] to go upon certain National Forest System Lands for the purposes of locatable mineral exploration, development and production."[83] Statutes governing the use of public forest lands expressly allow use of those lands for mineral development,[84] but USFS is required to protect the lands from "depredations."[85] USFS regulations governing environmental protection and financial assurance (bonds) relating to mineral operations have remained relatively unchanged since 1974.[86]

In 2004, USFS adopted an augmented program to (1) analyze the potential for environmental impact of mining operations; and (2) impose requirements for financial assurance that would yield amounts adequate to do the necessary environmental remediation if the mine operators did not. USFS undertook this program "to capture the lessons learned by the Forest Service and other state and federal agencies, as a result of having to close a number of bankrupt and abandoned hard rock mines."[87] Based on these lessons, USFS has developed a procedure to estimate the tasks and costs of environmental reclamation to be covered by the financial assurance, yet recognizes that it needs to be updated.[88] In

---

80. *See, e.g.*, GAO, Hardrock Mining: Information on Abandoned Mines and Value and Coverage of Financial Assurance on BLM Land 6 (2008).
81. 30 U.S.C. §§ 611–615 (Multiple Use Mining Act of 1955).
82. 16 U.S.C. §§ 471–5466.
83. 73 Fed. Reg. 15,695 (Mar. 25, 2008). *See also* 39 Fed. Reg. 31,317 (Aug. 28, 1974).
84. 16 U.S.C. § 478.
85. *Id.* § 551.
86. 36 C.F.R. § 228.8; 39 Fed. Reg. 31,317 (Aug. 28, 1974).
87. USFS, Training Guide for Reclamation Bond Estimation and Administration 5 (2004).
88. *Id.* at 13 (identifying the following tasks: "Interim Operation and Maintenance; Hazardous Materials; Water Treatment; Demolition, Removal

2008, USFS recognized shortcomings in its regulatory framework and proposed revisions to address them,[89] but the proposed rules were not promulgated. In 2008, USFS attempted to reconcile its program with that of its sister agency, BLM, and the recommendations of the National Research Council following its publication *Hardrock Minerals on Federal Lands*. USFS proposed rules to, among other items, "provide additional detail with respect to the process the Forest Service uses to review and adjust reclamation bonds to ensure that those bonds cover the full cost of reclaiming National Forest Service lands."[90]

Mineral extraction on Indian lands presents unique requirements. At this time, no tribal nation has primacy under SMCRA, although some tribes have approved reclamation programs under the abandoned mine lands provisions of SMCRA.[91] Therefore, operations will proceed by authorization from the appropriate state or federal agency. If Indian lands are involved, the agency will generally consult with the affected tribe. In instances where the tribe owns surface and/or mineral interests, the operator must obtain a lease entered into with the U.S. Department of Interior, Bureau of Indian Affairs (BIA) as trustee for the tribe. Regulations under the Indian Mineral Development Act,[92] administered by the BIA governing coal mining on tribal lands, require a coal lessee to provide a bond in an amount sufficient enough to ensure compliance with all terms of the coal lease. These leases and the related bonds themselves often require compliance with all applicable laws. Therefore, the lease bond may become a supporting reclamation bond. In an action that raises the question of which regulatory agency or interested party is responsible for making permit- and bond-related decisions, in 2021 OSM issued notice to the state of Oklahoma that OSM was asserting jurisdiction over coal mining on Indian lands in Oklahoma based on the decision by the U.S. Supreme Court in *McGirt v. Oklahoma*.[93] Oklahoma has challenged

---

and Disposal of Uncontaminated Structures, Equipment and Materials; Earthwork; Revegetation; Mitigation; Long-term Operation, Maintenance and Monitoring").

89. 73 Fed. Reg. 15,694 (Mar. 25, 2008).
90. It appears that the USFS financial assurance program is the least mature of the federal mining agencies.
91. *See, e.g.*, 30 C.F.R. § 756.16.
92. 25 U.S.C. §§ 2101–2108.
93. 149 S. Ct. 2452 (2020).

OSM's actions, and the case is pending in federal court.[94] The impact of the *McGirt* decision and the reach of the definition of "Indian lands" remain to be determined.

III. Suretyship in an Environmental and Administrative Law Framework

General principles of surety law, which is contractual in nature, and the law regarding statutory bonds apply to reclamation bonds.[95] Therefore, the language of the bond establishes the parties' obligations, which the statutes involved further define. In practice, the form of the reclamation bond differs among jurisdictions. For example, the Wyoming bond form refers primarily to the principal's performance of permit obligations, while the Pennsylvania bond form incorporates several other environmental laws related to air, water, waste, and dam safety. These parameters establish the obligations in each jurisdiction.

On a fundamental question of surety law, however, it is common for mining and regulatory professionals, principals, and courts to confuse the concept of suretyship with insurance. Suretyship often is not considered until there is a default or, in the mining regulatory context, the mining company fails to perform its reclamation obligations and the agency is forced to forfeit the bond.[96] Another time that the nature of

---

94. Oklahoma v. U.S. Dep't of Interior, No. 21-cv-00719 (W.D. Okla. July 16, 2021).

95. A bond written in conformity with a statute must be read with the statute. The statute that provides for the giving of a bond becomes part of the bond. *See, e.g.*, Am. Cas. Co. of Reading v. Irvin, 426 F.2d 647, 650 (5th Cir. 1970) ("A statutory bond will be reviewed in the light of the statute creating the duty to give security."); United States v. De Visser, 10 F. 642, 648 (S.D.N.Y. 1882) ("The bond cannot in fact be understood or applied without reference to these laws."); Reliance Universal, Inc. v. Ernest Renda Contracting Co., 454 A.2d 39, 44–45 (Pa. Super. Ct. 1982); Am. Cas. Co. v. Dep't of Env't Res., 441 A.2d 1383, 1387 (Pa. Commw. Ct. 1982) ("[S]tatutory bonds are construed in the light of the statute creating the obligation secured and the purposes for which the bond is required, as expressed in the statute.").

96. Forfeiture of bonds or other financial assurances is an administrative action preceded by significant notice requirements and, as such, is also an appealable action. *See* William T. Gorton III, Understanding the Reclamation Surety Relationship before and after Operator

suretyship comes into focus is in the bankruptcy of a mining company when interested parties are asserting their priorities. It is critical in any legal context, especially in administrative and bankruptcy proceedings, that the parties (including the court) be educated on the nature of the surety relationships because, unlike the construction industry, there is a general unfamiliarity with the nature of suretyship.

A. *Suretyship Is a Three-Party Relationship*

The surety relationship involves three distinct parties, including the principal (permittee) who is the primary obligor, the obligee (regulatory agency), the party to whom the principal and surety owe a duty, and the surety (bonding company), the secondary obligor.[97] Understanding the roles of the parties is critical. Along with general surety rights, each party has distinct regulatory responsibilities and rights. Surprisingly to many who encounter the topic after there has been a reclamation bond forfeiture, a surety bond is not an insurance policy. It is black-letter law that suretyship is not insurance.[98] The surety relationship is a three-party relationship in which the surety can seek reimbursement from the principal once it has paid due to the principal's default. Insurance is a two-party relationship where an insurer makes an independent agreement (an insurance policy) with its insured to indemnify the insured against a particular risk. The insurer cannot seek to recover its own loss from the insured, unlike a surety. A surety bond is more like a credit transaction, and "surety bonds, issued by compensated sureties, are meant to function as credit accommodations in which the surety anticipates no loss."[99]

DEFAULT: MINE CLOSURE, FINANCIAL ASSURANCE, AND FINAL RECLAMATION 11-7 (Rocky Mountain Mineral Law Foundation, Paper No. 11, 2009). *See* discussions *infra* Parts V and VI.

97. EDWARD G. GALLAGHER, THE LAW OF SURETYSHIP § 1 (1993).

98. Pearlman v. Reliance Ins. Co., 371 U.S. 132, 139 n.19 (1962) ("Suretyship is not insurance."); Meyer v. Bldg. & Realty Serv. Co., 196 N.E. 250, 254 (Ind. 1935) ("We are clearly of the opinion that the contract here in question is a contract of suretyship and not an insurance policy."); Buck Run Baptist Church, Inc. v. Cumberland Sur. Ins. Co., Inc., 983 S.W.2d 501, 504 (Ky. 1998) ("A contract of suretyship is not a contract of insurance.").

99. Armen Shahinian, *The General Agreement of Indemnity*, *in* THE LAW OF SURETYSHIP 487 (Edward G. Gallagher ed., 2d ed. 2000).

B. Parties to the Relationship

The parties to a reclamation surety relationship are as follows:

1. **Permittee**. The mining company, as the permittee, is the principal and the party who has received the mining permit from the regulatory agency. The permittee has the primary obligation to conduct mining, reclamation, and environmental remediation activities according to the terms of its mining permit issued by the regulatory agency, which incorporates applicable operational, reclamation, and environmental performance standards. Often referred to as "contract miners," it is common industry practice for a permittee to engage a separate, unrelated mining company to actually operate the mining and/or reclamation activities. The permittee, however, remains primarily responsible for performance.
2. **Regulatory agency**. The regulatory agency is the obligee on a reclamation bond that has enforcement authority under SMCRA or FLPMA (or state laws if not on federal land) and its regulations. Where a state regulatory program is implemented on federal lands, both the state and the United States will be obligees.[100] The surety underwrites the risk assuming that the agency will enforce the reclamation regulations, and the agencies are responsible for inspecting the mines to assure reclamation performance and bond releases upon completion.[101] The regulatory agencies have significant authority and may issue notices of violation and cessation orders, and even suspend or revoke permits due to uncorrected violations.[102] They may also assess civil or criminal penalties to the permittee.[103]
3. **Bonding company**. The bonding company is the surety and is a secondary guarantor of performance of the permitted

---

100. 30 C.F.R. § 740.15(b). For example, a bond written for a gold mine on federal land in Nevada includes both the Nevada Department of Environmental Protection *and* BLM as obligees; a bond written for a coal mine on federal land in Wyoming includes the Wyoming Department of Environmental Quality *and* the OSM as obligees.
101. 30 C.F.R. § 840.
102. *Id.* §§ 840 (SMCRA state enforcement), 348 (SMCRA federal enforcement); 43 C.F.R. §§ 3809.600–.605.
103. 30 C.F.R. § 845; 43 C.F.R. § 3809.700.

reclamation obligations. The principal retains the primary duty to perform its obligations; it may not merely hand off that duty to the bonding company or rely on the reclamation bond.[104] The relationship between the permittee and the bonding company is a credit relationship under which the bonding company will ordinarily require collateral and, along with its common law indemnification rights against the principal, will also require a written indemnity agreement.[105] In order to adequately protect its rights, the bonding company should be familiar with the regulatory program under which it writes the bonds, other environmental regulatory requirements that may be interwoven in the concept of "reclamation" (e.g., hazardous waste disposal, water pollution treatment), and, just as importantly, the relevant regulatory administrative process since these are statutory bonds.

IV. Bond Releases

The procedures and performance standards for obtaining reclamation bond releases are controlled by statute and agency regulation. It is important to recognize that in dealing with state and federal agencies, each official agency decision is an administrative action and, as such, occurs under the additional legal umbrella of administrative law. Bond release is a good example of the administrative law concept of "procedural due process," requiring public notice, opportunity for comment by interested

---

104. *See, e.g.*, RESTATEMENT (THIRD) OF SURETYSHIP AND GUARANTY § 21(1) (1996) ("[T]he principal obligor has the duty to the secondary obligor [the surety] (a) to perform the underlying obligation . . . and (b) to refrain from conduct that impairs the expectation of the secondary obligor that the principal obligor will honor its duty of performance."); *id.* § 21 cmt a. ("As between the principal obligor and the secondary obligor, it is the principal obligor that should perform or bear the cost of performance. . . . The existence of the secondary obligation, typically having served as inducement to an action or forbearance by the *obligee*, is beneficial to the principal obligor . . . [T]he secondary obligor is entitled to the principal obligor's performance, not merely a cause of action for its failure to perform.").

105. A surety has certain very important and inherent rights in its relationship with the principal such as indemnity, subrogation, and equitable remedies that this chapter does not address but that a practitioner in this field should be aware of.

parties, and possibly an appeal.[106] A bond release request must be filed with the agency in a formal application. The site will be inspected to assure the standards are met and may be granted or denied.

A. *Release of Coal Mining Reclamation Bonds*

Although SMCRA allows release of the bond upon a determination that reclamation has been successfully completed, the bond is released in phases or stages: Phase I releases 60 percent of the bond amount when the operator completes basic reclamation tasks of backfilling, regrading, top soil replacement, and drainage control; Phase II usually releases about 25 percent, when successful revegetation has been established.[107] Final release of a reclamation bond may be applied for after full performance of the reclamation plan and a demonstration that the site is stabilized (usually five years in eastern states and ten years in western states, depending on success of the revegetation). Some statutes do allow for partial and incremental bond releases as reclamation progresses. However, unless the bond is written to accrue proportionally to the acreage affected (i.e., incrementally), a deficiency anywhere on the bonded area caused by mining is a basis for a bond release denial or forfeiture.[108]

B. *Release of Hardrock Mining Reclamation Bonds*

Bond release under FLPMA on hardrock mines may be obtained when the operator has completed all or any portion of the reclamation on its mine in accord with its approved plan of operations.[109] Like its coal regulatory counterparts, the federal regulations governing hardrock operations follow a percentage-release approach. For example, BLM may release up to 60 percent of the bond for a portion of the project area when successful completion of backfill, regrading, establishment of drainage control, and stabilization and detoxification of leaching solutions, heaps, tailings, and similar facilities.[110] Final bond release of the remaining amount for the same portion of the area may be sought following a demonstration of

---

106. This framework allows the landowners or other interested party to object to bond release if dissatisfied with the reclamation results.
107. 30 C.F.R. § 800.40(c)(1)–(3).
108. *See* James E. Martin & Am. Ins. Co. v. Pa. Dep't of Env't Res., 570 A.2d 122 (Pa. Commw. Ct. 1990).
109. 43 C.F.R. § 3809.590(a).
110. *Id.* § 3809.591(b).

successful revegetation and any effluent (water discharge) meets specific permitted water quality standards for one year without needing additional treatment.[111] In the event of a long-term pollutional discharge, the bond can only be released if the operator has established a long-term treatment funding mechanism such as a treatment trust.[112] Due to the nature of hardrock mineral mines, as distinguished from coal mines, it is common for the *entire* permitted mine and associated mineral processing areas to be affected until the minerals are depleted. Hence, the amount of bond exposure is often 100 percent until mine closure upon successful reclamation.

V. Principal Default: Bond Forfeiture

In both the coal and non-coal programs, there are several bases for the regulatory agency to forfeit reclamation bonds. The agency will initiate actions to forfeit the bond if

- an operator is unable to conduct reclamation of an unabated violation;
- the terms of the permit are not met; or
- the operator defaults on the condition under which the bond was accepted.[113]

Forfeiture is an administrative process and involves two procedural steps: (1) a notice to the permittee and the surety that the agency has determined forfeiture is appropriate and advising how the forfeiture may be avoided,[114] and (2) if no agreement is reached between the agency and the operator or surety, actual forfeiture of the bond.[115] Many states have made insolvency or bankruptcy grounds for bond forfeiture.[116] If there is no negotiated agreement with the surety to perform reclamation activities, the agency is to proceed to collect the bond amounts to complete the reclamation plan on the permit area to which the bond applies.[117] Unless

111. *Id.* § 3809.591(c)(1), (2).
112. *Id.* §§ 3809.591(c)(2), 3809.552(c).
113. 30 C.F.R. § 800.50(a); 43 C.F.R. § 3809.595.
114. 30 C.F.R. § 800.50(a)(1), (2); 43 C.F.R. § 3809.596.
115. 30 C.F.R. § 800.50(b); 43 C.F.R. § 3809.597.
116. *See, e.g.*, 25 PA. CODE § 86.181(a)(6) (2022).
117. 30 C.F.R. § 800.50(b)(2); 43 C.F.R. § 3809.597(d).

the surety continues to monitor its principal, the surety may first learn of the permittee's noncompliances when it receives the notice of the agency's intent to forfeit the bond. When the surety engages the agency, it is important for it to be familiar with the business background of its principal, the site conditions leading to forfeiture, the technical issues associated with the violations, and, very importantly, the regulatory framework under which the bonds were written. As discussed below, it may have to appeal the forfeiture to maintain the surety's right to perform in lieu of payment and develop a workout amidst a complicated legal process.[118]

Financial difficulties in the extractive industries challenge the reclamation surety. Myriad reasons may cause the principal's economic woes (making it important for the surety to continue to be vigilant in its underwriting).[119] By the time the principal's troubles are plainly evident it is probably too late to obtain additional collateral support by a place-in-funds provision common in many indemnity agreements; the principal and indemnitors either do not have the resources to comply or, if they do, receiving the additional collateral may be held to be a voidable preference in the likely soon-to-be-filed bankruptcy action.[120] In a bankruptcy case, the environmental compliance obligations covered by the reclamation bonds become claims along with the claims of other creditors. Ordinarily, debtors in bankruptcy must "manage and operate property . . . according to the requirements of the valid laws of the State in which such property is situated."[121] In an optimistic, theoretical scenario, therefore, a debtor in possession would be required to utilize its available resources to maintain compliance with environmental and reclamation laws. In reality that may not happen. In some cases, such as the Peabody bankruptcy case, the bankruptcy restructuring provided for continued operation of the mines. Difficult choices must be made when the available financial resources do not provide for compliance with law and a subsequent permittee cannot be found.

---

118. 43 C.F.R. §§ 3809.596, 3809.597; 30 C.F.R. § 800.50.

119. *See supra* Part I.B.

120. *See, e.g.*, SURETY ASPECTS OF BANKRUPTCY LAW AND PRACTICE, *supra* note 65, ch. VII.

121. 28 U.S.C. § 959(b). In the context of complying with environmental laws this statute does not allow a bankrupt estate to abandon property that exhibits ongoing environmental hazards. Midlantic Nat'l Bank v. N.J. Dep't of Env't Prot., 474 U.S. 494, 507 (1986).

The recent case *In re Blackjewel* is particularly troubling for reclamation sureties.[122] Mining company Blackjewel and its affiliates had acquired more than 300 coal mining permits and related assets in Kentucky, West Virginia, Virginia, and Wyoming. Many of these acquisitions came from the bankruptcy proceedings of other companies, and Blackjewel was the last one standing in this unfortunate game of mining musical chairs. A plan of liquidation proposed in late 2020 would have transferred some assets and a number of remaining mining permits and related real and personal property interests to a reclamation trust for the benefit of the affected sureties and the states that were home to the operations.[123] Objectors to the plan included affected sureties and the Kentucky regulatory agency with responsibility to implement SMCRA in Kentucky, the Energy and Environment Cabinet. That agency estimated the reclamation costs for the 32 mining permits to be abandoned in Kentucky exceeded the available bond amounts by $20 million.[124] By early 2021, the reclamation trust approach had failed, and the bankruptcy court confirmed a plan of liquidation that deleted all reference to the reclamation trust and left as many as 200 permits (and the associated bonds) with fates uncertain, but likely ending in bond forfeiture.[125]

In a recent case involving offshore oil operations, *Fieldwood Energy*,[126] the bankruptcy court overruled objections, based in part on *Midlantic*, made by various sureties to the debtor's abandonment of bonded oil and gas infrastructure. As a result, the court confirmed

---

122. No. 19-bk-30289 (Bankr. S.D. W. Va. July 1, 2019).

123. Notice of Plan Supplement, *In re* Blackjewel, LLC, No. 19-bk-30289 (Bankr. S.D. W. VA. Nov. 20, 2020), Doc. No. 2602.

124. Objection of the Commonwealth of Kentucky, Energy and Environment Cabinet, to Debtors' Joint Plan of Liquidation, *In re* Blackjewel, LLC, No. 19-bk-30289 (Bankr. S.D. W. Va. Dec. 10, 2020), Doc. No. 2642.

125. Findings of Fact, Conclusions of Law, and Order (I) Approving the First Amended Disclosure Statement for Joint Chapter 11 Plan of Liquidation for Blackjewel, LLC and Its Affiliated Debtors, and (II) Confirming the First Amended Joint Chapter 11 Plan of Liquidation for Blackjewel, LLC and Its Affiliated Debtors, *In re* Blackjewel, LLC, No. 19-bk-30289 (Bankr. S.D. W. Va. Mar. 22, 2021), Doc. No. 3147.

126. Findings of Fact, Conclusions of Law, and Order (I) Confirming Eighth Amended Joint Chapter 11 Plan of Fieldwood Energy LLC and Its Affiliated Debtors and (II) Granting Related Relief, *In re* Fieldwood Energy LLC, No. 20-33948 (Bankr. S.D. Tex. June 25, 2021), Docket No. 1751.

a plan that provided for abandonment of the infrastructure to prior responsible parties that the court found jointly and severally responsible for decommissioning. A provision of the regulation that governs bonds for offshore operations states that the bonds "must continue in full force and effect even though an event occurs that could diminish, terminate, or cancel a surety obligation under State surety law."[127] Because these statutory reclamation bonds are interpreted along with the laws and regulations that require them, the reclamation surety is cautioned to be aware of requirements that may dramatically alter the usual surety rights.

In another case involving bankruptcy of oil and gas development companies, *In re Falcon V, L.L.C.*,[128] the court held that the oil and gas bonds that secured payment and performance of lease obligations including plugging, abandoning, and decommissioning wells remained in place for the benefit of the reorganized debtors and the bond obliges.[129] But the bankrupt principals' obligations to the surety, including indemnity obligations, remained with the debtors with no meaningful chance of recovery.[130] The decision was based in part on the noncancelable character of these bonds and whether bonds and related indemnity agreements are executory contracts that can be assumed in bankruptcy.[131] As in the Fieldwood Energy matter, this is a harsh result for the sureties and urges caution in underwriting and in claims management in the time leading up to, and through, a bankruptcy proceeding.

VI. Appeals of Administrative Actions

Appeals of administrative decisions, including appeals of bond releases, bond forfeiture, and bond release denials, must be taken in the prescribed time frame and to the specific agency or tribunal that has jurisdiction to hear the appeal.[132] A party adversely affected by a bond-related decision—for instance a landowner who opposes a bond release, a permittee that disagrees with a denial of a bond release, or a surety subject to a bond forfeiture—may seek review of the decision but must

---

127. 30 C.F.R. § 556.902(d).
128. No. 19-10547 (Bankr. M.D. La. Sept. 22, 2020).
129. *See* Ruling and Order, Argonaut Ins. Co. v. Falcon V, L.L.C., No. 20-00702 (M.D. La. Sept. 29, 2021) (affirming the bankruptcy court's order).
130. *Id.*
131. *See supra* note 65.
132. 30 U.S.C. §§ 1275, 1276.

first exhaust its administrative remedies.[133] Many sureties have failed to recognize that the time frame for appealing a forfeiture is jurisdictional and process the actual forfeiture notice as they normally would a non-statutory contract bond claim. By failing to timely appeal the forfeiture, the surety loses significant bargaining power to mitigate its loss with the obligee regulatory agency. The standard of review of administrative action is whether the agency action was arbitrary, capricious, or otherwise inconsistent with law. Under SMCRA, the affected party has 30 days to appeal the action.[134] Under FLPMA, an adverse decision by BLM may be appealed within 30 days to the U.S. Department of Interior Office of Hearings and Appeals.[135] FLPMA also allows, on a discretionary basis, a less formal review of the issue with the state director prior to a formal appeal.[136]

VII. Surety Performance

SMCRA itself does not refer to a corporate surety's rights or accommodations made in the interest of the surety when the bond is forfeited. The federal regulations, however, do provide guidance on this murky area for the surety claims representative. Under the federal framework, the regulatory agency is required to send written notice of its determination to forfeit the bonds to both the permittee and the surety.[137] The notice advises the permittee and surety "of the conditions under which forfeiture may be avoided."[138] The regulations state:

> The regulatory authority may allow a surety to complete the reclamation plan, or a portion of the reclamation plan applicable to the bonded phase or increment if the surety can demonstrate an ability to complete the reclamation in accordance with the approved reclamation plan . . . . [N]o surety liability shall be

---

133. *See, e.g.*, S. Ohio Coal Co. v. Off. of Surface Mining, U.S. Dep't of Interior, 20 F.3d 1418 (6th Cir. 1994).
134. 30 U.S.C. § 1264; 30 C.F.R. § 775.1.
135. 43 C.F.R. § 3809.800(b).
136. *Id.* § 3809.801.
137. 30 C.F.R. § 800.50(a)(1).
138. *Id.* § 800.50(a)(2).

> released until successful completion of all reclamation under the terms of the permit . . . .[139]

In some states, this initial notice is referred to as the "notice of intent to forfeit."

Most states address surety reclamation in their regulations. Some programs, such as Ohio, have significant detail regarding surety reclamation.[140] Indiana encourages surety reclamation as a way to avoid forfeiture.[141] Kentucky addresses surety reclamation in both statutes and regulations,[142] whereas the Pennsylvania program has only one statutory provision, which states, "A corporate surety issuing bonds which are forfeited by the department shall have the option of reclaiming the forfeited site, in lieu of paying the bond amount to the department, upon consent and approval of the department."[143] This limited statement of law leaves a lot of discretion to the regulatory agency and puts a significant burden on counsel for the surety to propose, negotiate, and conduct a successful reclamation workout. Most states, like Colorado, allow a surety to avoid forfeiture if it can demonstrate the ability to complete the reclamation plan.[144]

Surety performance of defaulted reclamation obligations is supported in the federal non-coal program. As noted above, the surety will receive notice of an impending forfeiture prior to actual agency actions to collect the funds. The surety then may seek to investigate and, if advisable, enter into a written agreement with BLM for surety reclamation if it can demonstrate an ability to complete the reclamation in accordance with the permitted reclamation plan.[145]

Although the surety may have the right to perform, the decision to do so is carefully considered, and sureties typically proceed with caution. The surety must scrutinize many factors. These include an analysis of the cost of the remaining reclamation and the potential for any credit or reduction of the bond amounts. The surety also weighs whether the

---

139. *Id.* § 800.50(a)(2)(ii).
140. OHIO ADMIN. CODE § 1501:13-7-06(E) (2021).
141. IND. ADMIN. CODE tit. 312, r. 25-5-17, sec. 17(b) (2022).
142. KY. REV. STAT. ANN. § 350.130(1) (2022); 405 KY. ADMIN. REGS. 10:050 sec.1(2) (2022).
143. PA. STAT. ANN. tit. 52, § 1396.4(h) (2022).
144. COLO. CODE REGS. § 407-2:3.04.2(5) (2022).
145. 43 C.F.R. § 3809.596(d)(2).

mining company is capable or willing to continue the reclamation with financial support from the surety, which may be holding some collateral, or whether the surety must retain a third-party contractor to complete the work. If the surety decides to perform, it must draft specific reclamation agreements with the obligee detailing the performance and limitation of liability of the surety, and the conditions required for the phase reductions and eventual full release of the bond.

If the surety would not benefit by performing, the surety may make the decision to forfeit the bond. If the surety proceeds with forfeiture, an agreement regarding the release of the bond may be advised.

VIII. Unexpected Obligations

A. Water Quality

To the surety underwriter, reclamation bonds are intended to address traditional and quantifiable reclamation activities such as earthwork and revegetation. Until very recently, regulatory agencies did not set the amount of required financial assurance to account for the increased costs of pollution abatement. In recent years, though, concerns about hydrologic quality have caused reevaluation of the extent of reclamation bond liability. In the coal and non-coal programs, bonds will not be fully released if there is a long-term pollutional discharge unless other financial accommodations for perpetual treatment have been established.

Underwriters would not ordinarily provide a surety bond if it is known that a site will have long-term pollutional discharges since it is highly likely that the bond will not be released. Therefore, most water quality issues (including long-term pollutional treatment) relate to unanticipated pollutional discharges that were not part of any reclamation bond calculation. These conditions may be caused by acid mine or acid rock drainage or other forms of leachate seeps that were not predicted during the pre-mine planning and permitting process. The existing regulatory framework, while perhaps unfair to the corporate surety that did not envision pollutional problems, does allow an alternative mechanism for the regulatory agency to seek additional and appropriate financial assurances to address long-term pollution treatment or abatement if the permittee is financially able, although often it is not.

Water pollution associated with mining operations includes acid mine drainage, heavy metal contamination, and dissolved and suspended solids, and it has been a cause of concern throughout the country for many years. The primary concern in the eastern United States and through the Illinois Basin is acid mine drainage from coal mines, although the industry is receiving significant attention associated with heavy metals that have not historically been monitored. Heavy metals from non-coal mines have also presented a problem. Hardrock, mineral, and coal mining in the western United States has contaminated streams in the headwaters of more than 40 percent of the watersheds in the West.[146] Although the federal CWA is the primary federal statute for dealing with point source discharges from mine sites, SMCRA and FLPMA both address hydrologic quality as one of many criteria required to be addressed in a mine reclamation plan.

Under SMCRA, the mine plan must include "a detailed description of the measures to be taken during the mining and reclamation process" to assure the protections of "quality of service, both on and off site, from adverse effects of the mining and reclamation process."[147] The coal mine permit application must include a hydrologic reclamation plan that includes providing water treatment facilities if necessary.[148]

The operations plan requirements under FLPMA, as noted previously, describe how the permittee will address surface water and groundwater hydrologic conditions associated with or impacted by the mining operations. Other than dealing with processing facilities and heap leach operations, surface water and groundwater pollution associated with the mining operations are not anticipated and are not permitted. Historically, pollutional discharges from abandoned heap leach operations, process ponds, and unreclaimed waste rock facilities can be the source of surface water and groundwater pollution from non-coal hardrock or metal mines.

Long-term treatment trusts are an effective alternative to traditional reclamation surety bonds for the financial assurance for operations that exhibit these polluted discharges. Under SMCRA, the development of long-term treatment trusts to provide funds for treatment of acid mine drainage treatment developed first in Pennsylvania, a state with a long history of mining and acid mine drainage from abandoned and active mines. The federal OSM in Tennessee then modeled the Pennsylvania protocol for the federal program in Tennessee.[149] In order to address

---

146. U.S. Environmental Protection Agency, Liquid Assets 2000: America's Water Resources at a Turning Point 10 (2000).
147. 30 U.S.C. § 1258(a)(13).
148. 30 C.F.R. § 780.21.
149. Tennessee Federal Regulatory Program: Final Rule, 72 Fed. Reg. 9,616 (Mar. 2, 2007) (codified at 30 C.F.R. § 942.800(c) (Special consideration for sites with long-term postmining pollutional discharges).

long-term pollutional discharges specifically, the Pennsylvania analogue to SMCRA was amended to state:

> The department may establish alternative financial assurance mechanisms which shall achieve the objectives in purposes of the bonding program. These mechanisms may include, but are not limited to, the establishment of a site specific trust fund, funded by the operator for the treatment of post mining discharges of mine drainage.[150]

Under FLPMA, until the 2001 rulemaking, the costs of long-term water treatment were overlooked as part of the bonding requirements for mining operations. BLM noted that "the existing regulations are silent on the need to provide bonding for any necessary water treatment or site maintenance. BLM believes that it is necessary to specify this requirement to eliminate any argument about requiring such resource protection measures."[151] In the 2001 final rule calling for a trust, BLM imposed an additional yet distinct requirement for water treatment guarantees separated from reclamation financial guarantees: "When BLM identifies a need for it, you must establish a trust fund or other funding mechanism available to BLM to ensure the continuation of long-term treatment to achieve water quality standards and for other long term, post mining maintenance requirements."[152]

The main purpose of the trust fund is to generate sufficient income to cover the cost of treatment in perpetuity. The amount needed to fully fund a trust considers and models the quality and quantity of the discharge, treatment and capital costs, support facilities needed, treatment facility maintenance, chemicals required, renovation, maintenance and replacement, and factors necessary to ensure perpetual treatment. Those values are reduced to net present value to determine the trust corpus. The regulatory agency is the trust beneficiary. The trust is implemented through a negotiated agreement defining the applicable trust contribution amounts, the time frame for deposits, and a companion trust agreement with a third-party trustee. Once the trust is established and fully funded, the permittee may also be reimbursed from the trust for the yearly cost of treatment. In a bond forfeiture context where there is long-term pollution

---

150. PA. STAT. ANN. tit. 52, § 1396.4(d)(2) (2022).
151. 66 Fed. Reg. 54,847.
152. 43 C.F.R. § 3809.552(c).

at the bonded mine, the agencies may seek to use the bond as part of the trust corpus.[153]

Financial guarantees therefore are required for long-term water pollution treatment in both the coal and non-coal programs and the trust fund concept is gaining nationwide acceptance. The major problem for the surety is that if the regulatory agency does not require the permittee to establish and fund a trust for long-term pollution treatment, the bonds are at risk. In the case of default, however, contribution of a portion, or even all, of the bond penal sum to a long-term treatment trust can be an effective strategy to resolve the bond liability.

B. Other Potential Liabilities

Numerous articles in the surety literature about performing sureties draw attention to unanticipated liabilities under other environmental laws. Most of them caution sureties about environmental law-related risks, particularly those associated with hazardous materials. Because of the types of operations covered by reclamation bonds, it is reasonable for the surety to be cautious in deciding whether the proper action when the principal defaults is payment or performance. Under some sets of facts and circumstances, it might be possible for a performing surety to find itself considered an owner/operator/permittee of a discharge of pollutants to surface waters under the CWA,[154] an owner/operator or otherwise generator of hazardous waste under RCRA,[155] or a potentially responsible party for the release of hazardous substances under the Comprehensive Environmental Response, Compensation, and Liability Act (CERCLA).[156] It might even be possible for a performing surety to be so involved in the decision-making and control of coal mining operations of a coal company that the surety would be deemed an owner/controller and made subject to individual liabilities and alternative enforcement under SMCRA.[157] We have found, however, that proper due diligence about a site prior to making a decision on performance can avoid needless risk of involvement with long-term environmental liabilities. Once a decision

---

153. *See, e.g.*, Stipulation and Consent Order, *In re* Mon View Mining Co., No. 05-50219 (Bankr. W.D. Pa. Apr. 22, 2010), Docket No. 1119.

154. 33 U.S.C. §§ 1251–1387.

155. 42 U.S.C. §§ 6901–6992k.

156. 42 C.F.R. §§ 6901–6975 (CERCLA or "Superfund").

157. United States v. Dix Fork Coal Co., 692 F.2d 436, 440 (6th Cir. 1982).

is made to perform, careful planning and definition of the surety's role and authority in the conduct of reclamation operations can maintain the surety's role as a secondary obligor and financial creditor, and protect it from liability as permittee or operator of a troubled site.

Conclusion

Reclamation bonds are complex combinations of traditional surety law and environmental law intended to mitigate the harmful effects of extractive industries. The surety's obligations on these bonds are tied directly to the terms of the bond, of course, but also to the terms of the regulatory framework under which the bond is written. Effective underwriting and claims management require a thorough understanding of these laws, the characteristics of the principal, and the facts and circumstances related to each operation.

CHAPTER 8

COMMERCIAL BAIL BONDS

Jeffrey Clayton
Mark Holtschneider
James Portman
Leah Schoen

Introduction

Insurance companies, licensed by states or the U.S. Department of the Treasury to write surety bonds, act as guarantors on commercial bail appearance bonds in federal, state, and municipal trial courts across the country.[1] They also act as guarantors in federal immigration matters. A commercial bail appearance bond is a type of surety bond and is commonly referred to as a "bail bond." The execution and posting of a bail bond through our criminal justice system permits the release of an accused from custody pending trial, while ensuring his or her appearance at all required trial court proceedings. This chapter focuses on commercial bail: the release of a principal to the custody of a licensed bail bond producer[2] who posts an appearance bond in lieu of the principal being held in pretrial custody.

The inner workings of the commercial bail business can be confusing for several reasons. Bail wears two hats: criminal and civil. It is an integral part of a criminal case, yet any attempt to collect upon the bond following the principal's violation of bond conditions is strictly civil in

---

1. Commercial bail is authorized throughout the United States. The only exceptions are Illinois, Kentucky, Maine, Oregon, and Wisconsin. Two states, New Mexico and New Jersey, have substantially reduced the use of commercial bail bonds over the past decade by moving toward a model that closely mirrors the federal bail system, even though both states still legally allow the use of commercial bail bonds. In 2018, Massachusetts eliminated the use of commercial bail bonds. MASS. GEN. LAWS ch. 276, § 61(b) (2018).
2. Bail bond producers are also known as "bail bond agents" and "bondsmen." See Appendix A, Chapter Glossary, for more information.

nature.[3] In addition, statutory and regulatory variations currently exist between states with respect to bail forfeiture procedures, exoneration, remission, and fugitive recovery requirements. Significant variations can also exist intrastate between governmental subdivisions and state and federal criminal justice systems. Additional variations may exist at the local level via rules, procedures, standard practices, and even forms.

A persistent lack of uniformity also exists in bail bond producer licensing and regulation. Since commercial bail involves contracts of suretyship, most states regulate bail bond producers through departments or divisions of insurance. Each state has its own unique administrative requirements, forms, licensing standards, and regulatory expectations. The diversity of bail administrative and regulatory systems presents a monumental challenge to the surety companies that conduct business in multiple jurisdictions. As a result, the commercial bail industry routinely supports more comprehensive regulation, enhanced administrative clarity, and operational uniformity.

Perhaps the most confusing and misunderstood aspect of commercial bail arises from the multifaceted relationship(s) that exist between the bail bond producer that sells the bond, the surety company that underwrites and issues the bond, the governmental obligee, and third-party indemnitors. An accurate and functional understanding of the basics and resultant dynamics of these relationships is critical to the legal analysis and effective representation of a party in a commercial bail dispute.

Finally, this chapter will also address two topics in which much misunderstanding persists: the operation of the bail bond business itself and the process of retrieving and surrendering the absconding principal, or the "skip," back into custody. The activities of bail bond producers and fugitive recovery agents have been romanticized on various television programs, creating a largely distorted picture of everyday individuals

---

3. *See, e.g.*, United States v. Plechner, 577 F.2d 596, 597 (9th Cir. 1978) (enforcement of a bond forfeiture, although arising from a prior criminal proceeding, is nevertheless a civil action); United States v. Barger, 458 F.2d 396, 396–97 (9th Cir. 1972) (forfeiting bail compensates for damages and is deemed civil, not criminal in nature; hence it does not implicate the Double Jeopardy Clause when the defendant is also convicted of the crime of jumping bail); United States v. Garcia-Trevino, 843 F. Supp. 1134, 1134–35 (S.D. Tex. 1994) (entry of a civil forfeiture judgment serves a remedial purpose, is not punishment, and is not a bar to subsequent criminal prosecution for failure to appear based on the same conduct).

within the bail business who make important contributions to public safety and the administration of justice.

The purpose of this chapter is to make the reader more comfortable with commercial bail by addressing its basic legal principles in the context of its unique and frequently misunderstood operational details.

I. Background

Initially, bail bonds were posted with trial courts by individuals who pledged their own property as security, historically known as the personal surety system. Over time, individuals began to post personal surety bonds for a fee, prior to the regulation of bail bond producers beginning in the 20th century. In a landmark case in 1912, the U.S. Supreme Court held, contrary to the English Supreme Court, that allowing for compensated personal sureties does not run counter to public policy.[4] This decision ultimately paved the way for state regulation of compensated personal sureties, including the power to arrest and return the principal to trial court.

While most bail bonds are underwritten by bail bond producers appointed by licensed surety companies, another form of bondsman exists. Known as property bondsmen, these bondsmen pledge unencumbered real property with the court and not a surety company to secure the bond. A limited version of the property bondsmen model still exists in several jurisdictions, mostly southern states.[5] The property bond business model is unfavorable for two reasons. First, bail bond producers find it more advantageous to affiliate with a surety company to take full advantage of the surety company's financial stability and administrative capabilities. Second, trial courts and regulators are more comfortable relying ultimately on surety companies because of the financial assurance the surety provides by taking on the risk of the principal appearing before

---

4. Leary v. United States, 224 U.S. 567 (1912).
5. *See, e.g.*, GA. CODE § 17-6-15 (2020) & GA. R. PROB. CT. 15.1 (2021); MISS. CODE ANN. § 83-39-7 (2019); N.C. GEN. STAT. §§ 58-71-1, 58-71-145 (2020); S.C. CODE ANN. § 38-53-10 (2021); TENN. CODE ANN. § 40-11-122 (2021); TEX. CRIM. PROC. CODE ANN. arts. 17.01–.02 (2021); WASH. REV. CODE § 18.185.010 (2021). Colorado allows cash agents to write an unlimited amount of aggregate liability without a surety company based only upon the filing of a single $50,000 qualification bond with the insurance commissioner. *See* COLO. REV. STAT. § 10-23-105 (2017).

the trial court and because surety companies must comply with stringent state-imposed requirements to obtain a certificate of authority. This also includes various strict enforcement mechanisms for payment of forfeiture judgments, where trial courts or regulators can entirely suspend the right of all appointed bail bond producers of the surety company to issue bail bonds to force payment on a single forfeiture judgment under a particular bail bond.

A. Bail's Purpose

The primary objective of a bail bond is to assure the principal's appearance at trial and all trial court proceedings when required.[6] Historically, the right to freedom before trial is intertwined with the Anglo-Saxon doctrine that an accused is innocent until proven guilty.[7] The principal's freedom before trial "permits unhampered preparation of a defense and serves to prevent the infliction of punishment prior to conviction."[8] Accordingly, the right to bail is a fundamental underpinning of our criminal justice system[9] and is an essential safeguard to the presumption of innocence.[10] Bail should never be used as a means of punishing a principal before conviction[11] or as a mechanism for public funding. When enforcing a bail forfeiture or considering a request for remission, it is improper for a court

---

6. United States v. Toro, 981 F.2d 1045, 1049 (9th Cir. 1992); Cohen v. United States, 82 S. Ct. 526, 528 (1962) ("The purpose of a bail bond is to ensure the accused will reappear at a given time by requiring another to assume personal responsibility for him, on penalty of forfeiture of property."); United States v. Bass, 573 F.2d 258, 260 (5th Cir. 1978) ("The purpose of a bail bond is not punitive; it is to secure the presence of the defendant."); *see also* United States v. Nebbia, 357 F.2d 303, 304 (2d Cir. 1966) ("It 'is not the sum of bail bond that society asks for, but rather the presence of the defendant.'").
7. *See generally* Ray v. State, 679 N.E.2d 1364 (Ind. Ct. App. 1997).
8. Stack v. Boyle, 342 U.S. 1, 4 (1951) (citing Hudson v. Parker, 156 U.S. 277, 285 (1895)).
9. Sistrunk v. Lyons, 646 F.2d 64, 70 (3d Cir. 1981).
10. *Stack*, 342 U.S. at 4.
11. *See, e.g.*, People v. Benmore, 299 N.W. 773, 775 (Mich. 1941); Lucero v. Dist. Ct., 532 P.2d 955, 957 (Colo. 1975); McConathy v. State, 528 S.W.2d 594, 596 (Tex. Ct. App. 1975) (a bail forfeiture cannot be used as a means of imposing a fine).

to weigh the impact of its decision upon the public treasury.[12] However, while assuring the appearance of the accused at all judicial proceedings is the primary reason bail is set, it is not every court's sole consideration.[13] Essential public interests such as the protection of witnesses and public safety are also often taken into serious consideration.[14]

B. How Bail Works

Upon the showing of probable cause that a criminal offense has been committed, an individual is arrested by law enforcement and incarcerated in a local detention facility. Bail is then set, meaning that conditions are established upon which, if met, the principal may be released from custody. These conditions can include a monetary bail penal sum and nonmonetary conditions that are set by either a pre-arranged bail schedule or by a judicial officer at a hearing. A local bail bond producer is then contacted by the principal, or someone acting on the principal's behalf. Arrangements are made by way of a signed bonding contract for the bail bond producer to post the bail bond in exchange for payment of a premium, typically in the range of 10 to 15 percent of the penal sum value of the bond, recognizing that nearly all states allow for bail bond producers to enter into an interest-free installment agreement. After the requisite paperwork is completed, the bail bond producer procures the bond and a power of attorney that shows the bail bond producer is duly authorized by a qualified surety company to post bonds. The bail bond producer then posts the bond and the power of attorney with the trial court or detention facility to secure the release of the principal from custody.

---

12. United States v. Velez, 693 F.2d 1081, 1084 (11th Cir. 1982) ("Enrichment of the government is not the relevant purpose of a bail bond."); *In re* Forfeiture of Bail Bond, 531 N.W.2d 806, 808 (Mich. Ct. App. 1995) ("It is well settled that the purpose of a bond is to assure the appearance of a defendant and not to collect revenue."); People v. Wilcox Ins. Co., 349 P.2d 522, 525 (Cal. 1960) ("In matters [relating to bail bonds] there should be no element of revenue to the state nor punishment of the surety.").
13. There are a handful of states, however, including Delaware and New York, that only permit judges to consider appearance of the principal for purposes of setting bail and not public safety.
14. United States v. Salerno, 481 U.S. 739, 752 (1987); Bell v. Wolfish, 441 U.S. 520, 538 (1979) ("This Court has recognized a distinction between punitive measure that may not constitutionally be imposed prior to a determination of guilt and regulatory restraints that may.").

If the principal fails to appear in trial court as ordered, the bail bond is declared forfeited and a warrant is issued for the principal's arrest. In the event of a forfeiture, a bail bond producer then has a remission period, which varies based on state statute or trial court rule, wherein they either produce the principal in trial court or the surety must pay the full penal sum of the bond.

II. Agreements Critical to the Process

A. *The Bail Bond*

A bail bond is a three-party contract between the obligee, the principal, and the surety company. The obligee is the state holding the principal in custody. The surety company is typically a property and casualty insurance company, regulated and licensed by state insurance departments, which initially bears the risk if the principal fails to appear before the trial court for all judicial proceedings by issuing the bail bond.[15] Bail bonds are conditioned primarily upon the principal's agreement to make all required trial court appearances and to pay the entire penal sum value of the bond if he or she fails to appear. If the principal fails to pay, the surety company pays the penal sum value of the bond to the obligee.

B. *The Power of Attorney*

A specialized, limited power of attorney ("power") is attached to and becomes a permanent part of the bail bond. This power of attorney is essential to the commercial bail industry. It establishes that the bail bond producer executing the bail bond does so as an attorney-in-fact for, and with the authority of, the surety company. The bail bond producer signs the bail bond on behalf of the named surety company, binding the surety to the penal sum of the bond. The surety company issues prenumbered powers of attorney to its appointed bail bond producers. Each power indicates a set maximum penal sum value of bail that can

---

15. State v. Weissenburger, 459 A.2d 693, 696 (N.J. Super. Ct. App. Div. 1983) ("It is well settled that a bail bond constitutes a surety agreement in which the defendant is the principal, and the creditor is the State. Consequently, the legal principle applicable to the construction and consequences of surety agreements are equally applicable to bail bonds."); Weigand v. State, 768 A.2d 43, 49 (Md. 2001); State v. Two Jinn, Inc., 228 P.3d 1019, 1023 (Idaho 2010).

be written with the power and generally sets an expiration date. The bail bond producer cannot write a bond that exceeds the penal sum value stated on the power and cannot cumulate (or "stack") powers to reach a particular bond penal sum value. Each power has a unique number that allows the surety company to track the power of attorney inventory of the bail bond producer. This important feature creates the foundation for commercial bail's business management systems to prevent the issuance of unauthorized bonds.

Powers do not contain the preprinted names of specific bail bond producers authorized as attorneys-in-fact. A power can be used to post a bail bond by any licensed bail bond producer holding an appointment from the issuing surety company. Powers are supplied to bail bond producers in a tightly controlled process. Bail bond producers are contractually obligated to report (and pay bond costs) to the surety company for all bonds executed on the surety company's powers of attorney.[16] They must also account for unexecuted powers of attorney.

C. General Qualifying Power of Attorney

General qualifying powers of attorney are usually filed on an annual basis with the clerk of the county in which the bail bond producer will post bonds. This type of power of attorney "qualifies" that the bail bond producer is authorized to write bail for the surety company and sets the maximum per bond penal liability the bail bond producer can execute for that surety company. This qualifying document also states that the surety company has no liability for any bond unless a duly executed power of attorney is attached to the bail bond itself.

D. The Bail Bond Application

This document incorporates a variety of risk control features that form the basis for underwriting the bail bond. Executed by the principal and/or third-party indemnitors, the application captures essential personal background and contact information. Bail applications typically require the principal and/or third-party indemnitors to verify the accuracy of all

---

16. "Bond costs" refer to the premium paid by the bail bond producer to the surety company for bonds executed under the authority granted by the surety company's powers of attorney.

information supplied and authorize the surety company to obtain further information from additional sources, as needed.

E. The Indemnity Agreement

An indemnity agreement (also known as a "bail bond agreement") is always executed in conjunction with the issuance of a bail bond. This agreement governs the relationship between the surety/bail bond producer and the principal/third-party indemnitors. The primary obligation flowing to the surety company/bail bond producer is for the principal/third-party indemnitor to indemnify and hold harmless the surety company/bail bond producer for any losses under the bond, including losses caused by the principal's failure to appear in trial court, fugitive recovery expenses, and any forfeiture of the bond for the full penal sum. The indemnity agreement is commercial bail's most fundamental and significant risk control device.

Practically speaking, third parties such as family and friends typically sign the agreement and constitute the "backbone" of the indemnity obligations. These indemnitors are, in essence, vouching for the principal; that is, that the principal will appear in trial court as ordered and, if not, that they will reimburse the surety company for the full penal sum of the paid loss. The relationships between the principal and the family and friends who serve as indemnitors provide incentive for the principal to appear in trial court, lest the risk of causing financial losses to his or her family members or friends. The indemnitors who are seeking the principal's release, or who agree to assist the principal, are likely to be the very people the principal least wishes to disappoint or harm. Individuals with significant, long-term relationships with the principal give the principal an incentive to appear at all trial court dates that would not exist otherwise. In the event the principal fails to appear, the same disappointed indemnitors, now facing imminent financial loss, also tend to become the surety company's best and most reliable source of information, thereby aiding in the principal's apprehension.

F. The Surety and Bail Bond Producer Agreement

This agreement between the bail bond producer and surety company defines the rights, duties, and authority of each party. It establishes, among other things, (1) the bail bond producer is firmly bound to indemnify and hold the surety company harmless from loss, costs, or damages connected with any issued bonds; (2) the bail bond producer is a true independent contractor; (3) the customers and risks undertaken are selected by the bail bond producer; and (4) the surety company will allow the bail bond producer to use the surety's financial standing and authority to write bail, subject to full compliance with a variety of regulatory administrative requirements.

This agreement also establishes the amount of premium the bail bond producer pays to the surety company. Out of the premium paid by the customer, the bail bond producer receives a significantly larger portion as commission than the portion of premium paid to the surety company because the bail bond producer indemnifies the surety from all losses arising out of the issuance of any bail bonds under the agreement. The bail bond producer has effectively assumed the primary risk of loss in the event of a forfeiture. The fact that the bail bond producer has thus assumed primary liability for any forfeiture loss, however, is not a defense to the surety company's liability in a forfeiture enforcement proceeding initiated by the bond obligee.

III. The Regulatory Framework

Commercial bail is regulated in most states as a form of insurance.[17] The surety company must qualify for admission in each state under the same standards that apply to any other insurance company and make the required statutory deposits. Bail bond producers are generally licensed and regulated in the same manner as insurance producers for other standard lines of insurance. Prelicensure and continuing education requirements for bail bond producers are also common.[18]

Bail regulations can differ significantly from state to state. For example, bail bond producers in California are licensed and regulated by the California Department of Insurance, whereas in Texas, bail bond

---

17. A regulatory body does not exist in eight states: three states regulate by the supreme court of the state (Massachusetts, Rhode Island, and the District of Columbia); two states regulate by the state licensing board (Arkansas and Washington); New Hampshire regulates through its secretary of state; Virginia regulates through its State Corporation Commission; and Connecticut regulates through its commissioner of public safety.

18. *See, e.g.*, Wash. Rev. Code § 18.185.060 (2021); Colo. Rev. Stat. § 10-2-415.5 (2019) (Colorado requires only prelicensure education). Florida, Nevada, and Tennessee require continuing education. *See also* Fla. Stat. § 648.385 (2020); Nev. Rev. Stat. § 697.230(1)(a) (2021); Tenn. Code Ann. § 40-11-401 (2019).

producers are licensed and regulated by county bail bond boards.[19] Many surety companies conduct background checks prior to contracting with a bail bond producer. Many states also require that surety companies submit appointments for each bail bond producer or agency with the state regulator of insurance.[20] Some jurisdictions go one step further and require that a certified and current "qualified power of attorney" be filed with every trial court or county where the bail bond producer seeks to do business.[21] Qualified powers of attorney are provided by the surety company and certify the bail bond producer has authority to execute bonds up to a specified penal sum for the surety company. These powers must be resubmitted annually to each trial court or county. In lieu of a qualifying power of attorney, Arizona, California, and Nevada require bail bond producers to provide a "bond of bail agent," in a specified penal sum, naming the state as obligee, which is conditioned upon the bail bond producer's compliance with state statutory obligations.[22] A separate system applies to bail bonds posted in federal courts.[23]

States use a variety of means and methods to ensure that bail bond forfeitures are paid. Forfeiture enforcement may be the responsibility of a state's department of insurance, its court system, or an independent regulatory entity. A bail bond producer who fails to pay a forfeiture judgment risks license revocation, along with significant fines and penalties.[24] Trial courts and detention facilities in jurisdictions may refuse to accept bail bonds from any bail bond producer who fails to

---

19. CAL. INS. CODE § 1802 (2021); TEX. OCC. CODE ANN. § 1704-051 (2021).
20. *See, e.g.*, CAL. INS. CODE § 1802 (2021). *See* FLA. STAT. § 648.382(1) (2021).
21. *See, e.g.*, IND. CODE § 27-10-3-17 (2021); NEV. REV. STAT. § 697.270 (2019); N.C. GEN. STAT. § 58-71-140 (2020).
22. Arizona requires a $10,000 bond. *See* ARIZ. REV. STAT. § 20-340.02 (2021). California requires a $1,000 bond. *See* CAL. INS. CODE § 1802 (2021).
23. In the federal system, a judicial officer must determine the bail bond was executed by a solvent surety. *See* 18 U.S.C. § 3142(c)(xii) (2011). Typically, federal courts will require the surety issuing bail bonds be listed on the Bureau of the Fiscal Service, U.S. Department of the Treasury, Companies Holding Certificates of Authority as Acceptable Sureties on Federal Bonds and as Acceptable Reinsuring Companies (Dept. Circular 570, 2021 rev.).
24. *See, e.g.*, CAL. PENAL CODE § 1308 (2021); MO. REV. STAT. § 374.763(1) (2021); N.C. GEN. STAT. § 58-71-80 (2021).

timely satisfy a forfeiture judgment.[25] A defaulting bail bond producer may be placed "on the board," a regularly updated list of bail bond producers with unsatisfied forfeiture judgments, which is available in the trial courts or detention facilities in that jurisdiction.[26]

In North Carolina, the surety company may also find itself "on the board" if a judgment against its bail bond producer remains unsatisfied. A surety company that is "on the board" will be precluded from issuing any more bail bonds and the powers of attorney for that surety company will not be accepted until the forfeiture is satisfied. This means that all bail bond producers appointed by that surety company will be adversely affected, even those bail bond producers who have no outstanding forfeitures. Like bail bond producers, surety companies will remain precluded from issuing any new bail bonds until all forfeiture judgments are satisfied, exonerated, or otherwise resolved.

States also use a variety of means to regulate bail transactions and to ensure those transactions comply with state statutes and regulations. Many states set premium rates by statute or require each surety company to submit a rate filing for approval. In addition to the filing of rates, many states require surety companies to file bail bond forms for review and approval before they are distributed to bail bond producers. In a select few states, regulators of insurance conduct compliance audits or require the surety company to conduct audits of their appointed bail bond producers on an annual or semiannual basis.[27]

A. *The Nuts and Bolts*

1. Setting Bail

The Eighth Amendment's excessive bail provision is integral to our concept of ordered liberty and is binding upon the states under the 14th Amendment.[28] Excessive bail or denial of bail violates the Equal

---

25. *See, e.g.*, FLA. STAT. § 648.45 (2021); NEB. REV. STAT. § 11-124 (2021).
26. Both the bail bond producer and the surety can be placed "on the board" in Colorado if forfeiture judgments are not paid when due. *See* COLO. REV. STAT. § 16-4-114 (2021). While on the board, the bail bond producer is prohibited from writing bonds anywhere in the state. *See id.* § 18-13-130(g).
27. *See, e.g.*, CONN. GEN. STAT. § 38a-660(b) (2018); Minn. Consent Order (2015).
28. Meechaicum v. Fountain, 696 F.2d 790, 791 (10th Cir. 1983).

Protection Clause.[29] Because the practical effect of excessive bail is the denial of bail, logic compels the conclusion that the harm the Eighth Amendment seeks to prevent is the unnecessary deprivation of pretrial liberty.[30]

State constitutions and statutes guarantee the right to bail in virtually all criminal cases except for capital offenses and cases that involve repeat or extremely violent offenders. Trial courts consider numerous statutory and constitutional factors when setting the bail penal sum and the conditions of release that will reasonably assure both the appearance of the principal and the safety of the victim and the community. The Supreme Court held in *Stack v. Boyle* that "bail set before trial at a figure higher than an amount reasonably calculated to fulfill the purpose of assuring the presence of the defendant is 'excessive' under the Eighth Amendment."[31] The Supreme Court further held: "The right to release before trial is conditioned upon the accused's giving adequate assurance that he will stand trial and submit to sentence if found guilty."[32] Other statutory factors typically include (1) the nature and seriousness of the charges; (2) the weight of the evidence; (3) the principal's character; (4) family and community ties; (5) flight risk; (6) mental and physical condition; (7) criminal history; (8) drug and alcohol involvement; and (9) the danger posed to witnesses and the community.[33] These same factors are considered for nonmonetary conditions of release as well, such as wearing a GPS monitor or various other conditions of conduct. Most state and local bail rules and statutes involve the setting of standard bail conditions, such as not committing any new crimes or leaving the jurisdiction of the trial court without permission.

It is worth noting over the past six years there has been significant litigation involving the post-review procedures used by courts when using a system of preset bail schedules in the form of equal protection and due

---

29. Pugh v. Rainwater, 572 F.2d 1053, 1057 (5th Cir. 1983).
30. *See, e.g.*, Sistrunk v. Lyons, 646 F.2d 64, 70 n.23 (3d Cir. 1981); United States *ex rel.* Goodman v. Kehl, 456 F.2d 863, 868 (2d Cir. 1972).
31. 342 U.S. 1, 5 (1951).
32. *Id.*
33. *See, e.g.*, United States v. Orena, 986 F.2d 628, 631 (2d Cir. 1993) (danger to the community as a basis for refusing to grant bail); United States v. Gebro, 948 F.2d 1118, 1121 (9th Cir. 1991) (discussing "flight risk"); Ray v. State, 679 N.E.2d 1364, 1367 (Ind. Ct. App. 1997) ("both insuring a defendant's presence at trial and community safety may be considered in setting bail for defendants"); *see also* 18 U.S.C. § 3142(g) (2011).

process lawsuits alleging poverty-based discrimination. The result has been to affirm the use of such schedules but also require meaningful, prompt review of the bail and consideration of the principal's ability to pay. This began when former U.S. Attorney General Eric Holder filed a statement of interest in the case of *Varden v. City of Clanton*.[34]

The U.S. Court of Appeals in both the Fifth Circuit[35] and 11th Circuit[36] recently approved the use of a preset bond schedule if the principal appears before a judge within 48 hours of being booked to have a meaningful opportunity to be heard relative to the principal's financial ability to post bond. Only two U.S. district courts have held that the use of a preset bond schedule is unconstitutional. However, in one case the U.S. district court did not defend the bail schedule,[37] while the other case is still pending before the U.S. Court of Appeals for the 11th Circuit.[38]

The *Varden* case and many others including suits against towns and cities such as Moss Point in Mississippi, Ascension Parish in Louisiana, and Dodge City in Kansas, for example, allow the continued use of a preset bond schedule, but require all principals have a meaningful opportunity to be heard relative to their financial ability to post bond within a short time frame, usually 24–48 hours.

Various commentators have suggested there is a right to affordable bail under federal and state case law, and, thus, if the principal cannot afford bail the principal must be released. Commentators for a generation have termed this *sub rosa* detention.[39] Trial courts that have confronted this issue have said there is indeed equal protection discrimination when a person cannot get meaningful and prompt review in front of a judicial officer due to his or her poverty. However, once a judge has considered all the facts, and finds public safety and appearance issues are paramount

---

34. No. 2:15-cv-00034-MHT-WC, 2015 WL 5387219 (M.D. Ala. Sept. 14, 2015).
35. O'Donnell v. Harris County, Texas, 892 F.3d 147 (5th Cir. 2018).
36. Walker v. City of Calhoun, Georgia, 901 F.3d 1245 (11th Cir. 2018).
37. Buffin v. City & Cnty. of San Francisco, No. 15-cv-04959-YGR (N.D. Cal. 2015).
38. Hester v. Gentry, No. 5:17-cv-270-MHH (N.D. Ala.), *appeal filed*, No. 18-13894 (11th Cir.) (2020).
39. *Sub rosa* detention is "the detention of allegedly dangerous defendants secured through the setting of extremely high bail under the pretense of concern about flight risk." JIM CLEARY ET AL., NATIONAL CRIMINAL JUSTICE REFERENCE SERVICE, HISTORY, ISSUES, AND ANALYSIS OF PRETRIAL RELEASE AND DETENTION: A POLICY ANALYSIS (1995).

and rules the bond is not excessive pursuant to the Eighth Amendment of the U.S. Constitution, the principal may be held in jail pending trial. The Fifth Circuit said relative to the right to an affordable bail, "no such right is in view."[40]

2. *Preventative Detention*

In 1987, the U.S. Supreme Court ruled in the case of *United States v. Salerno* that a principal can only be held for trial under preventative detention if, after a hearing, the judicial officer finds no condition or combination of conditions will reasonably assure the appearance of the principal as required and the safety of others within the community.[41]

The *Salerno* case remained the standard, until case law emerged in two states that applied heightened due process requirements if a principal is to be held in preventative detention in the federal system. In *Valdez-Jimenez v. Eighth Judicial District Court*,[42] the Nevada Supreme Court held that if bond is set in an amount the principal cannot afford, the prosecutor must prove by clear and convincing evidence that the principal is a flight risk or danger to the community and therefore shall remain in custody. The California Supreme Court followed suit in the case of *People v. Kenneth Humphrey*,[43] when the court did not decide the constitutionality of California's preset bond schedules, but held that a prosecutor, within days after arrest, must provide clear and convincing evidence of a flight risk or danger to the community to retain a principal in custody. These cases are emerging but stand for the proposition that long-term or lengthy pretrial detention may require stronger evidence of a flight risk or a risk to public safety. Significantly, a principal can assert rights to a heightened due process burden that must be proven by the prosecutor within a matter of hours or no more than a few days from the date of arrest.

Statistics show that financial release, including commercial bail, is not a major method of release for felony principals when released pending trial. This is likely a result of the cost incurred by the court if or when a principal fails to appear for their scheduled hearing. A 2013 study of the Dallas, Texas, bail system revealed that every time a principal

---

40. *O'Donnell*, 892 F.3d at 163.
41. 481 U.S. 739, 742 (1987).
42. 163 Nev. Adv. Op. 20 (2020).
43. No. S247278, 2021 WL 1134487 (Cal. Mar. 25, 2021).

fails to appear in trial court, it costs the local jurisdiction $1,775.[44] The numbers on misdemeanors are not available, as judges typically impose lower and fewer financial conditions of release since misdemeanors involve lower penalties and less risk of nonappearance. This is further propelled by a movement that has arisen over the past decade, dubbed the "Third Generation of Bail Reform," which aims to reduce the use of monetary bail in lower-level misdemeanors, petty offenses, and even in some felony cases. This decade-long movement has contributed to the overall reduction in the volume of bonds executed by bail bond producers across the United States.

Financially secured release by posting a commercial surety bond is only one method of pretrial release. The other forms of pretrial release include (1) partially secured release or "deposit bail"; (2) own recognizance release; and (3) unsecured release or unsecured recognizance bonds. Partially secured release or "deposit bail" does not require a surety company, as 10 percent of the bail amount is paid directly to the trial court by the principal or often friends and family of the principal. If the principal makes all court appearances a percentage of the deposit is returned. Own recognizance release, also known as personal recognizance bonds, does not require a surety company and the principal is released upon a mere promise to appear. An unsecured release or unsecured recognizance bond is issued when a principal promises to pay a certain sum of money if he or she fails to appear for court without having to secure that promise with any assets or other security.

Comprehensive studies for a generation have demonstrated that the most effective method of getting principals to trial court for disposition of their case is the posting of a commercial surety bond.[45] One such study issued by the U.S. Department of Justice analyzed 55,000 state felony cases in the nation's 75 most populous counties over an eight-year span. One finding was: "Compared to release on recognizance, principals on financial release were more likely to make all scheduled trial court

---

44. Robert G. Morris, University of Texas at Dallas, Pretrial Release Mechanisms in Dallas County, Texas 5 (2013).

45. *See, e.g.*, Bureau of Justice Statistics, U.S. Department of Justice, Pretrial Release of Felony Defendants, 1992, at 10 (1994) (NCJ-148818). This study demonstrates the superior performance of commercial bonding, as compared to all other pretrial release methods, in getting persons back to court.

appearances.'"[46] From a public safety perspective, it is also significant that these studies demonstrate misconduct is higher when a financially secured commercial bail release is not used. Other peer-reviewed research on this topic found principals without bail bonds who failed to appear were 50 percent more likely to be on the loose after one year than those principals who did post a bail bond. As such, the fugitive recovery agents hired by bail bond producers to return the absconding principals were the "true long-arms of the law."[47]

3. *Underwriting*

Operating through their appointed local bail bond producers, surety companies have long had an effective system to achieve financial security and profitability despite their engagement in what would appear to the unfamiliar to be a particularly risky business. The system they employ, however, has worked very well through the years, and several surety companies have maintained active and profitable books of bail bond business for many decades.

The goal of bail bond underwriting is the prevention of loss arising from a bail bond forfeiture. To underwriters in more customary lines of insurance, assessment of the risk of a bail forfeiture may seem unscientific in nature. Indeed, bail bond underwriting has always been more of an art than a science. Nevertheless, bail bond underwriting centers on the same principles as those of more traditional lines of suretyship: risk analysis and risk control.

a. Risk Analysis. In determining the risk underlying a bail bond, the bail bond producer considers the risk of the principal missing a trial court date, the likelihood the principal will return in time if trial court is missed, and the likelihood that liquidation of collateral and payment from indemnitors will cover any surety bond loss. Complete information relative to several important issues is essential, such as the penal sum of the bond, the nature of the charges, principal information, indemnitor information, available collateral, and the principal's attorney.

---

46. Bureau of Justice Statistics, U.S. Department of Justice, Special Report: Pretrial Release of Felony Defendants in State Courts (2007) (NCJ-214994).

47. Eric Helland & Alexander Tabarrok, *The Fugitive: Evidence on the Public versus Private Law Enforcement from Bail Jumping*, 47 J.L. & Econ. 93, 118 (2004).

The penal sum of the bond is often set as one amount but in certain jurisdictions the principal may be required to post several bonds. It is important for the bail bond producer and surety to know the total bond exposure for any one principal.

The nature of the criminal charges against the principal is critical. The incentive to avoid appearance at trial is always increased by the severity of punishment and the principal's assessment of the potential outcome of the case. Similarly, charges that give rise to a limited chance of future incarceration result in a greater likelihood of appearance.

It is imperative the bail bond producer collect detailed contact and personal information about the principal, all the way down to tattoos, hobbies, favorite pastimes, prior criminal history, and even best friends. This information will become essential to the bail bond producer in apprehending the principal after a failure to appear. Extensive commercial bail bond application forms are aimed at capturing this critical information. Thoroughness also creates a favorable mindset on the part of the principal; the more the principal thinks the bail bond producer knows about the principal, the less inclined the principal is to abscond.

There are several good reasons for having persons close to the principal guarantee the risk and indemnify the surety company for any loss or expense associated with the principal's failure to appear. Besides the obvious benefit of having indemnitors pay for any bond loss, there are two additional benefits. First, indemnitors serve as a deterrent to missed trial court dates because the principal understands that family and friends will bear financial loss if he or she absconds. Second, indemnitors can be a valuable source of information regarding the principal's whereabouts.

Collateral encourages appearance and offsets the surety company's loss in the event of a forfeiture. Typically, the larger the bail bond, the greater the need for collateral. On larger or riskier bail bonds, the bail bond producer may insist upon speaking with the principal's defense counsel to obtain non-privileged information about the theory of the defense and the potential outcomes of the trial. The better the chance of a good outcome, the less fear the trial process holds for the principal. Most capable defense attorneys are happy to visit with the bail bond producer. In addition, principals who are current in paying their attorney will normally be around for trial.

b. Risk Control. Once a bail bond is posted, the bail bond producer can take several actions to ensure that the principal makes all trial court appearances and thus exonerates the bond. A responsible bail bond producer will often stay in communication with the principal via text, phone, or email. Many understand that a forfeiture is most likely when a risk is improperly managed and that losing touch with the principal is begging for trouble. Bail bond producers will require the principal to make regular "check-ins," as casual or periodic contact with the principal is sometimes insufficient. For larger or riskier bonds, the principal is often required to appear personally at the bail bond producer's office on a weekly basis. These meetings verify that the principal is still in the area and allow the bail bond producer to confirm the principal (1) is still at the same address; (2) has the same phone numbers; (3) knows the next trial court date; (4) is employed; (5) is paying his or her attorney; and (6) is fully complying with trial court-imposed conditions of release, such as participation in drug rehabilitation. Bail bond producers often provide text, email, and phone reminders to principals of upcoming trial court dates. These reminders are also given to indemnitors to reduce the chance of the principal missing trial court.

4. Forfeiture

The principal's failure to appear in trial court violates the primary condition of a bail bond. This breach triggers a series of events, including the issuance of a warrant for the principal's arrest and a declaration that the bail bond has been forfeited.[48] In most jurisdictions, the principal will also face a separate criminal offense and additional charges.[49] While the prompt issuance of an arrest warrant is common to all jurisdictions, bond forfeiture procedures vary widely depending on the timing of the entry of judgment, rules concerning stays of execution, and time limits for satisfaction of the forfeiture judgment. In deference to the primary purpose of the bail bond, which is to assure the principal's appearance as opposed to enriching the state treasury,[50] a bail bond producer is generally allowed a reasonable period to apprehend and surrender the principal before a judgment on the forfeiture must be paid. California,

---

48. *See, e.g.*, CAL. PENAL CODE § 1305 (2021); FLA. STAT. § 903.26(2)(b) (2021); United States v. Nolan, 564 F.2d 376 (10th Cir. 1977); *see* FED. R. CRIM. P. 46(e)(1). For further discussion on this issue, see also Nancy M. King, Annotation, *Forfeiture of Bail for Breach of Conditions of Release Other Than That of Appearance*, 68 A.L.R. 4TH 1082 (1989).
49. *See, e.g.*, People v. Aleman, 823 N.E.2d 1136, 1140 (Ill. App. Ct. 2005); People v. Allen, 28 Cal. Rptr. 2d 669 (Cal. Ct. App. 1994); COLO. REV. STAT. § 18-8-212 (2021).
50. United States v. Velez, 693 F.2d 1081, 1084 (11th Cir. 1982).

Idaho, Nevada, and Utah allow the surety company up to six months to surrender the principal before payment of the forfeiture is required.[51]

The trial court must give the surety company notice of the forfeiture, of any show cause hearing date, and of any entry of judgment. The notice period ranges from seven days,[52] to 15 days,[53] to 30 days.[54] The time allotted for payment of a bail forfeiture judgment varies by jurisdiction. Some jurisdictions enter judgment promptly upon the declaration of a forfeiture while others provide a bail bond producer with as long as one year.[55] Other jurisdictions leave forfeiture procedures to the discretion of the trial court.[56] Typically, a show cause hearing is set to allow the bail bond producer an opportunity to explain why judgment should not be entered, or why a stay of execution should be granted or not expire.

Trial courts understand forfeiture issues involve far more than the financial interests of the bail bond producer and the surety company. Collateral tendered by the principal's family, sometimes including the family residence, is held by the surety company. As a result, family and friends of the principal face significant liability for the bond forfeiture loss as well as the bail bond producer's investigation and apprehension expenses. Thus, it is in the best interest of an indemnitor for the principal to be located and safely surrendered into custody. Indemnitors frequently

---

51. CAL. PENAL CODE § 1305(c)(1) (2021); IDAHO CODE § 19-2918 (2021); NEV. REV. STAT. § 178.514 (2021); UTAH CODE ANN. § 77-20b-102 (2021).
52. *See, e.g.*, MICH. COMP. LAWS § 765.28 (2021); *In re* Bail Bond Forfeiture, 852 N.W. 2d 747 (Mich. 2014).
53. *See, e.g.*, OHIO REV. CODE § 2937.36(c) (2021); State v. Dye, 122 N.E.3d 678 (Ohio Ct. App. 2019).
54. *See, e.g.*, CAL. PENAL CODE § 1305(b) (2021).
55. Indiana allows the bonding agent 120 days to return a fugitive to custody without penalty; late surrender fees are assessed over the next 245 days, with the full amount due if the fugitive is not surrendered by the 365th day. *See* IND. CODE ANN. § 27-10-2-12 (2021). Hawaii allows 30 days. *See* HAW. REV. STAT. § 804-51 (2021). Alabama, Mississippi, and Oklahoma allow 90 days. *See* ALA. CODE § 15-13-136 (2021); MISS. CODE ANN. § 99-5-25 (2018); OKLA. STAT. tit. 59, § 1332 (2021). Other states allow 180 days. *See, e.g.*, CAL. PENAL CODE § 1305 (2021); NEV. REV. STAT. § 178.508 (2021). Louisiana allows 180 days. LA. REV. STAT. ANN. § 15:85 (2021). In Idaho the defendant can appear up to 180 days of the court's order of forfeiture. *See* IDAHO CODE § 19-2922 (2021).
56. *See, e.g.*, ARIZ. R. CRIM. PROC. 7.6(c) (2021).

provide meaningful assistance to bail bond producers. When trial courts are shown that material progress locating the principal is being made, they tend to allow recovery efforts to proceed before compelling the forfeiture judgment to be paid.

Forfeiture judgments create civil liability that is typically enforced against bail bond producers and surety companies through regulatory proceedings. In some states, bail bond producers are precluded from filing any further bail bonds until past due forfeiture judgments are paid.[57] These preclusion systems provide a strong incentive and have been highly successful because noncompliant bail bond producers and surety companies are placed at immediate risk. As such, there is rarely need for the state to pursue payment of a judgment through civil collection proceedings.

In the real world, the failure of the principal to appear does not necessarily mean the principal has fled. In many cases, the principal will soon appear and voice a time-honored excuse such as a misunderstanding of the time or place of the hearing, or problems with traffic. Once a forfeiture has been ordered, however, the bail bond cannot be reinstated without the consent of the surety company.[58]

Trial courts have wide discretion to set aside a forfeiture judgment.[59] If the principal is promptly surrendered or if the trial court is satisfied that the appearance and surrender of the principal are impossible and without fault, the forfeiture is likely to be set aside. A trial court may evaluate several factors when considering whether an injustice has been committed by the forfeiture, including (1) the willfulness of the breach of the bond conditions; (2) the cost, inconvenience, and prejudice suffered by the government as a result of the breach; (3) explanatory or mitigating factors; (4) the appropriateness of the penal sum of the bond; and (5) the nature and extent of participation by the surety company in apprehending and surrendering the principal back into custody.[60]

---

57. *See, e.g.*, FLA. STAT. § 903.27 (2021); MD. CODE ANN., INS. § 21-103 (2021); TEX. OCC. CODE § 1704.212 (2021).
58. People v. Maldonado, 268 N.Y.S. 2d 271 (1966), *aff'd*, 295 N.Y.S.2d 597 (App. Div. 1968).
59. United States v. Amwest Sur. Ins. Co., 54 F.3d 601, 602 (9th Cir. 1995); *see* United States v. Nguyen, 279 F.3d 1112 (9th Cir. 2002); *see* also FED. R. CRIM. P. 46(f)(3) & (4) (2021).
60. *See, e.g.*, State v. Perez, 216 Ohio 848 (Ohio Ct. App. 2016).

5. Revocation

The term "revocation" is sometimes used to refer to the right of the bail bond producer to return the principal to custody, with or without cause, to be relieved of further liability before a forfeiture occurs.[61] A trial court can order the arrest of the principal and the revocation of a bail bond for a variety of reasons. Prior to forfeiture, revocation can be ordered when the accused violates any condition of the release.[62] For example, when a trial court imposes conditions of release such as drug testing and home detention, a breach of a bond condition routinely results in bond revocation. Bail is also likely to be revoked if the principal is charged with another criminal offense while released on bail.[63] Other reasons for revocation may arise when a trial court finds a reasonable probability that the principal intends to not appear or that he or she presents a public safety risk.[64] If a bail bond producer becomes aware of an increased risk of flight by the principal, it may become necessary to return the principal to custody so the bond can be exonerated.

The principal's indemnitors are typically the first to know that trouble is on the horizon. They are frequently the triggering mechanism of bond revocation when they seek to extinguish their own liability. For example, indemnitors may believe that the risk of flight has become too great if they receive information that the principal is violating bond conditions or

---

61. The sole exception to this rule is violation of the primary condition of the bond, namely failure to appear. In that event, the bond will be forfeited, not revoked.
62. *See, e.g.*, VA. CODE ANN. § 19.2.135 (2021) ("A court may, in its discretion, in the event of a violation of any condition of a recognizance taken pursuant to this section, remand the principal to jail until the case is finally disposed of, and if the principal is remanded to jail, the surety is discharged from liability.").
63. *See, e.g.*, MICH. COMP. LAWS § 765.26 (2021); United States v. Maack, 25 F. Supp. 2d 586, 586 (E.D. Penn. 1998) (upholding revocation of defendant's bail because there was probable cause he would pose danger to the community); United States v. McNeal, 960 F. Supp. 245, 246–47 (D. Kan. 1997) (discussing the types of factors a judicial official may consider before revoking a principal's pretrial release, including the issue of whether defendant poses a danger to the community).
64. *See, e.g.*, Johnson v. Cnty. of Kittitas, 11 P.3d 862, 864 (Wash. Ct. App. 2000); Kiperman v. Klenshetyn, 35 Cal. Rptr. 3d 178, 180 (Cal. Ct. App. 2005).

that the principal faces new charges. Indemnitors are typically the first to learn when the principal has lost a job or become embroiled in domestic disputes that jeopardize his or her ties to the community and increase the risk of failure to appear.[65] In addition, increased risk of flight is normally present when the principal fails to check in with the bail bond producer. Although some jurisdictions require the return of bail premium upon surrender of the principal to custody, trial courts do not require the bail bond producer to involuntarily remain on a risk.[66]

6. Exoneration and Discharge

The surety company is exonerated and relieved of further bond liability when the terms and conditions of the bond are met. The ability of the bail bond producer to properly document an exoneration is essential to the normal course of commercial bail business operations. Collateral securing bail bond liability cannot be released or returned to the bond principal or third-party indemnitors until the surety's risk of loss has been fully extinguished.

Furthermore, bail bond producers must show their appointing surety company that existing liability written by the bail bond producer has been fully resolved. The agreement between surety companies and their indemnifying bail bond producers uniformly requires producers to regularly report the status of previously issued powers of attorney before new powers of attorney will be entrusted to the bail bond producer. Prudent business practices mandate all surety companies implement effective administrative controls to prevent their appointed bail bond producers from writing an amount of bail bond liability that exceeds the producer's financial capacity to indemnify the surety company.

Due to the bail bond producer's underwriting and pretrial monitoring, most criminal proceedings do not result in a bond forfeiture. The principal appears at all trial court proceedings, the bail bond is fully discharged, and the surety company is exonerated when the principal is convicted, acquitted, pleads guilty or nolo contendere, or the charges are

---

65. *See, e.g.*, Knauf v. Cont'l Bail Bonds, Inc., 549 So. 2d 905 (La. Ct. App. 1989); Jordan v. Knight, 35 So. 2d 178, 179–81 (Ala. 1948); CAL. CODE REGS. tit. 10, § 2090 (2021).

66. *See* Johnson v. Hicks, 702 S.W.2d 797, 798 (Ark. 1986) (concluding the agent had probable cause to believe the defendant committed a felony while released on his bond).

dropped.[67] When a disposition of the case has been reached, a bail bond is exonerated automatically in some states by statute.[68] In other states, the bond is not deemed discharged or exonerated absent the issuance of a trial court order.[69] When a bail bond has forfeited and the judgment has been paid, but the principal has since been returned to custody, the surety company may have to file a motion to set aside the forfeiture and request a refund of the forfeiture payment.[70] Generally, if the bond is to be continued until sentencing, the surety must consent.[71]

The principal's compliance with the terms and conditions of a bail bond is not the only grounds for exoneration. Bail will be discharged or exonerated when performance of the condition is rendered impossible by an act of God, an act of the obligee, or the law.[72] If the principal dies prior to the date of the scheduled appearance, the bond is exonerated.[73] The surety company is entitled to exoneration of the bond upon payment

---

67. *See, e.g.*, People v. Henry, 308 N.Y.S.2d 245 (App. Div. 1970) (reversing lower court's order to reinstate released bail bond where the surety had performed all necessary contractual obligations and was exonerated from liability even though the judgment of conviction was reversed). *Cf.* Commonwealth v. Hill, 119 A.2d 572, 573 (Pa. Super. Ct. 1956) (reversing the lower court's decision to release the surety because the defendant appeared as required and "[u]nder the terms of the recognizance the condition had therefore been fulfilled and the subsequent forfeiture was unwarranted").
68. *See, e.g.*, N.M. Stat. Ann. § 31-3-10 (2021) (automatically exonerating all bail bonds and declaring them null, void, and terminated upon a finding of guilt); State v. Valles, 143 P.3d 496 (N.M. 2004); State v. French, 945 P.2d 752, 761 (Wis. Ct. App. 1997).
69. When the conditions of a bail bond have been satisfied, the court may be required to discharge or exonerate a bond. *See, e.g.*, Nev. Rev. Stat. § 178.522 (2021).
70. People v Am. Banker Ins. Co., 284 Cal. Rptr. 617 (Cal. Ct. App. 1991).
71. Rodriguez v. People, 554 P.2d 291, 292 (Colo. 1976) (holding that the consent of the surety is required after a guilty plea because the risk of the surety has materially increased). Events that materially increase the risk of the surety have the effect of terminating the obligation. *See* Restatement (Second) of Security § 128(b) (1941).
72. Taylor v. Taintor, 83 U.S. (16 Wall.) 366, 370 (1872). *See* United States v. Stephens, 1 F. Supp. 33, 34 (S.D. Fla. 1932).
73. *Taintor*, 83 U.S. at 370 (1872);*see also* J.P. Ludington, Annotation, *Death of a Principal as Exoneration, Defense, or Ground for Relief, of Sureties on Bail or Appearance Bond*, 63 A.L.R. 2d 830, § 7[a] (1956).

of the forfeiture judgment.[74] The surety company may also be entitled to exoneration if the bond is void because it was improperly taken by the trial court—for example, if the power of attorney used for the underlying bond is invalid.[75] Exoneration may also result from the obligee's failure to give the surety company proper notice of the principal's failure to appear and the court's issuance of a bond forfeiture.[76] Finally, exoneration in some states is automatic after the expiration of a certain time period, such as in Florida, where bonds expire three years after they are written.[77]

Exoneration becomes significantly more complex after a forfeiture has occurred.[78] The rules and procedures relating to exoneration vary widely between jurisdictions. They are greatly affected by the stage of the proceeding at which exoneration is sought. For example, a bail bond producer will find it much easier to get a bond exonerated if the principal is promptly apprehended and surrendered before the trial court enters judgment on the forfeiture.

7. Remission

Upon payment of a forfeiture judgment, the surety company may be able to qualify for return or "remission" of all or part of the payment by returning the principal to custody or by showing that the forfeiture judgment should not have been entered. Whether the surety company qualifies for remission depends entirely upon the local statutes and rules. In Maryland, remission is allowed under limited circumstances for up to ten years after the bond was posted.[79] Shorter time periods are far more common. In West Virginia, for example, the limit is two years and in Mississippi the remission period expires 18 months after

---

74. *See, e.g.*, COLO. REV. STAT. § 16-4-110 (2021).
75. *See* Francis M. Dougherty, Annotation, *Liability of Surety on Bail Bond Taken without Authority*, 27 A.L.R. 4TH 246, § 3 (1984).
76. People v. Ranger Ins. Co., 46 Cal. Rptr. 3d 448 (Cal. Ct. App. 2006).
77. FLA. STAT. § 903.3(1) (2021); Forman v. Tay, 180 So. 3d 1221 (Fla. Dist. Ct. App. 2015); GA. CODE ANN. § 17-6-31(e) (2021); First Choice Bonding Co. v. State, 679 S.E. 2d 830 (Ga. Ct. App. 2009); N.J. REV. STAT. § 2A:14-1 (2021).
78. *See, e.g.*, People v. Lexington Nat'l Ins. Co., 69 Cal. Rptr. 3d 738, 741 (Cal. Ct. App. 2007).
79. Maryland Rule 4-217(j)(1)(A) (2021) allows for remission if the surety produces evidence the defendant is incarcerated in a foreign jurisdiction and the state will not issue a detainer or extradite.

bond forfeiture.[80] Ordering remission is left entirely to the discretion of the trial court in many states, including Arizona, North Carolina, Ohio, Tennessee, and Texas.[81] Other states, like California, do not allow any remission after a judgment is paid.[82] Other preconditions may also apply. For example, in Florida, Maryland, and Pennsylvania, the surety's entitlement to remission is preserved only if the bail penal sum is paid before judgment is entered.[83] Entitlement to remission may also require direct involvement by the surety company in the apprehension and surrender of the principal.[84] A principal's failure to appear will result in a bond default and a forfeiture will often occur if the principal is incarcerated on other charges when his or her trial court appearance date arrives. If the principal is incarcerated by the bailing state, the forfeiture should be set aside because the state is in a position to produce the principal in trial court, while the bail bond producer cannot.[85] The law is not as uniform when the principal is incarcerated in a state other than the bailing state.[86] Although some states refuse to grant relief, the majority of states will grant the surety company relief from the forfeiture. This will often depend on various factors, such as the voluntary nature of the circumstances of the principal's departure from the bailing state, the nature of the charges pending against the principal, and whether the bailing state has sought extradition.[87]

---

80. MISS. CODE ANN. § 99-5-25(3) (2021); W. VA. CODE § 62-16-12 (2021).
81. *See* ARIZ. REV. STAT. ANN. § 13-4309 (2021); N.C. GEN. STAT. § 15A-544.8(c)(4) (2021); OHIO REV. CODE § 2937.39 (2021); TENN. CODE ANN. § 40-11-204(a) (2021); TEX. CRIM. PROC. CODE § 22.16 (2021).
82. CAL. PENAL CODE § 1305 (2021).
83. FLA. STAT. § 903.28 (2021); MD. CODE ANN., CRIM. PROC. § 5-208 (2021); PA. CONS. STAT. § 5747.1 (2021).
84. *See, e.g.*, ALA. CODE § 15-13-139 (2021); FLA. STAT. § 903.28(2) (2021). *See also, e.g.*, People v. Johnson, 395 P.2d 19, 23 (Colo. 1964).
85. *See* Lee R. Russ, Annotation, *Bail: Effect on Surety's Liability under Bail Bond of Principal's Subsequent Incarceration in Same Jurisdiction*, 35 A.L.R. 4TH 1192 (1981); MISS. CODE § 99-5-25 (2021); VA. CODE ANN. § 19-2-143 (2021). *See, e.g.*, State v. Yount, 175 Ohio App. 3d 733 (Ohio Ct. App. 2008).
86. *See, e.g.*, State v. Fields, 347 A.2d 810, 811 (N.J. Super. Ct. App. Div. 1975).
87. *See generally* Russ, *supra* note 85; State v. Dye, 122 N.E.3d 678 (Ohio Ct. App. 2019).

Entitlement to remission may also be affected by the Uniform Criminal Extradition Act (UCEA), which has been enacted by a majority of states.[88] The UCEA establishes a mandatory series of trial court proceedings a foreign bail bond producer must follow to obtain an arrest warrant and remove a fugitive from another jurisdiction.[89] In Hawaii, for example, the court of appeals found that a bail bond producer did not show sufficient good cause to set aside a forfeiture judgment when the bail bond producer failed to exercise any of the options available under American Samoa's UCEA to secure the principal's arrest as a fugitive.[90]

8. Recovery

A bail bond producer has the right and authority to take the principal into custody for the purpose of exonerating the surety's liability under the bail bond. This authority is founded upon common law, contract, and statute.

The common law basis for the surety's authority was first enunciated by the U.S. Supreme Court in *Taylor v. Taintor*:

---

88. 11 Unif. Crim. Extradition Act 36 (1936 & Supp. 1993); *see* Cuyler v. Adams, 449 U.S. 433, 435 (1981).
89. Under the terms of the UCEA, as enacted in New Jersey, a fugitive in an asylum state may not be delivered to the demanding state unless he or she is first taken before a court and advised of the extradition demand, the crime charged, and asked if he or she desires to contest extradition. N.J. REV. STAT. § 2A:160-1 *et seq.* (2013). Only four issues are "open for consideration before the fugitive is delivered up: (a) whether the extradition documents on their face are in order; (b) whether the petitioner has been charged with a crime in the demanding state; (c) whether the petitioner is the person named in the request for extradition; and (d) whether the petitioner is a fugitive." McGeachy v. Doe, No. 10-3342, 2011 U.S. Dist. LEXIS 59686, at *10 (D.N.J. June 2, 2011); *see* State v. Lopez, 734 P.2d 778, 782 (N.M. Ct. App. 1986), *cert. denied*, 499 U.S. 1092 (1987) (addressing the New Mexico version of the UCEA found at N.M. STAT. ANN. §§ 31-4-1 to 31-4-30) (2021)).
90. *See* State v. Flores, 962 P.2d 1008, 1015–17 (Haw. Ct. App. 1998). Under the UCEA the bail agent could have petitioned a judge or magistrate for an arrest warrant of a person alleged to have violated the terms of bail and upon meeting the UCEA's procedural requirements a warrantless arrest could have been made by the bail surety and the defendant promptly taken before a judge or magistrate to be held pursuant to the UCEA.

> When bail is given, the principal is regarded as delivered to the custody of his sureties. Their dominion is a continuance of the original imprisonment. Whenever they choose to do so, they may seize him and deliver him up in their discharge; and if that cannot be done at once, they may imprison him until it can be done. They may exercise their rights in person or by retailer. They may pursue him into another State; may arrest him on the Sabbath; and, if necessary, may break and enter his house for that purpose. The seizure is not made by virtue of new process. None is needed. It is likened to the rearrest by the sheriff of an escaping prisoner.[91]

The extensive common law authority of the bail bond producer recognized in *Taintor* is supplemented by the contractual relationship that exists between the surety company and the principal.[92] An indemnity agreement executed by the principal during the underwriting process provides that, in consideration of the surety company posting the bond, the principal agrees the surety company can retake him or her at any time, even before forfeiture of the bond.[93] By entering into this agreement, not only does the principal voluntarily consent to the custody of the surety company but, under common law, the principal also implicitly agrees that the bail bond producer may use reasonable force in their apprehension.[94] The indemnity agreement underscores the private nature of the surety's right of recapture and is the basis for the expectation the government will not interfere.[95] Thus, this common law right of recapture establishes that

---

91. Taylor v. Taintor, 83 U.S. (16 Wall.) 366, 373 (1872).
92. Ouzts v. Md. Nat'l Ins. Co., 505 F.2d 547, 553 (9th Cir. 1974) (holding that California's version of the UCEA abrogated a foreign bonding agent's common law right to pursue, apprehend, and remove his principal from California without resort to process); State v. Mathis, 509 S.E.2d 155 (1998); State v. Tapia, 468 N.W.2d 342, 344 (Minn. Ct. App. 1991).
93. Fitzpatrick v. Williams, 46 F.2d 40, 42 (5th Cir. 1931) (holding that the surety's right to arrest is "an original right that arises from the relationship between the principal and his bail, and not one derived through the State"); State v. Nugent, 508 A.2d 728, 731 (Conn. 1986); Livingston v. Browder, 285 So. 2d 923, 925 (Ala. Civ. App. 1973).
94. Reese v. United States, 76 U.S. (13 Wall.) 22, 25 (1869).
95. In Colorado, a bail bond producer has statutory authority to seize and surrender a defendant. COLO. REV. STAT. § 16-4-108(1)(c) (2021). The bonding agent's common law privilege does not exist. Oram v. People,

the seizure of the principal by the surety is not technically an "arrest" and may be accomplished without process of law. Since the bail bond producer is contractually obligated to satisfy any forfeiture judgment entered against the surety company, the contractual rights of the surety company also flow to the bail bond producer. State[96] and federal[97] statutes have modified and supplemented traditional common law rights of the surety to apprehend and return the principal to custody. The synergistic relationship between private-sector fugitive recovery and the criminal justice system results in tens of thousands of apprehensions per year at virtually no public expense.[98]

A bail bond producer may use reasonable means to ensure the principal appears in trial court.[99] If the principal is apprehended in the state where the bail bond was posted, and there are no statutes to the contrary, the principal can be apprehended without any judicial or administrative process.[100] In many states, a bail bond producer must, however, follow specific procedures to apprehend a fugitive principal. For example, in Connecticut, a bail bond producer or fugitive recovery agent (i.e., bounty hunter) must notify local authorities of their intent to arrest a fugitive principal.[101] The bail bond producer surrendering the

---

255 P.3d 1032 (Colo. 2011) (holding that bail agents knew their entry into a residence was unlawful); *see, e.g.*, ALA. CODE § 15-13-162 (2020); *Livingston*, 285 So. 2d at 926.

96. In Colorado, a bail bond producer has statutory authority to seize and surrender a defendant. COLO. REV. STAT. § 16-4-108(1)(c) (2021). The bonding agent's common law privilege does not exist. *Oram*, 255 P.3d 1032 (holding that bail agents knew their entry into a residence was unlawful); *see, e.g.*, ALA. CODE § 15-13-162 (2020); N.C. GEN. STAT. § 58-71-30 (2020); *see Livingston*, 285 So. 2d at 926.

97. 18 U.S.C. § 3149 (2021).

98. *See, e.g.*, Adam M. Royval, United States v. Poe: *A Missed Opportunity to Reevaluate Bounty Hunters' Symbiotic Role in the Criminal Justice System*, 87 DENV. U. L. REV. 789 (2010); Alexander Tabarrok, *The Bounty Hunter's Pursuit of Justice*, 35 WILSON Q. 56 (2010); Helland & Tabarrok, *supra* note 47, at 118 ("These finding indicate that bond dealers and bail enforcement agents (bounty hunters) are effective at discouraging flight and at recapturing defendants. Bounty hunters, not public police, appear to be the true long arms of the law").

99. *See generally* State v. Nugent, 508 A.2d 728, 732 (Conn. 1986).

100. Kear v. Hilton, 699 F.2d 181, 182 (4th Cir. 1983).

101. CONN. GEN. STAT. § 29-152k (2021).

principal may be required to supply to the sheriff a certified copy of the bail bond.[102] A statute may also require an apprehended principal be brought before a trial court within a specific period of time.[103] Failure to follow statutory procedures of the state where the arrest is made can expose the arresting bail bond producer or fugitive recovery agent to civil[104] and criminal[105] liability.

It is not necessary for a bail bond producer to use the extradition process.[106] Although a state cannot arrest a fugitive in another state without using formal extradition proceedings,[107] a bail bond producer has the right to cross state lines to apprehend principals with proper licensing. Under the UCEA, however, a foreign bail bond producer must seek a trial court warrant. If the fugitive is arrested without a warrant, the bail bond producer must produce the fugitive principal in trial court in the state of the arrest so that proceedings can be initiated to determine if the arrestee is the wanted person and whether the charges are extraditable.[108] The few cases that have directly addressed the impact of the UCEA in the context of bail fugitive recovery have diluted the common law and contractual

---

102. N.Y. CRIM. PROC. LAW § 530.80(1)(A) (2021) (surety may surrender the defendant to the court in which his case is pending or to the sheriff to whose custody he was committed at the time of giving bail, in the following manner: "(a) A certified copy of the bail bond must be delivered to the sheriff, who must detain the defendant in his custody thereon, as upon a commitment. The sheriff must acknowledge the surrender by a certificate in writing, and must forthwith notify the court in which the case is pending that such surrender has been made.").
103. *See* CAL. PENAL CODE § 1301 (2021) (stating the defendant is required to be delivered to the court without undue delay, within 48 hours).
104. *See generally* O.K. Bonding Co. Inc. v. Milton, 579 So. 2d 602 (Ala. 1991).
105. *See, e.g.*, Oram v. People, 255 P.3d 1032 (Colo. 2011); Collins v. Commonwealth, 702 S.E.2d 267 (Va. Ct. App. 2010).
106. *See* Lopez v. McCotter, 875 F.2d 273, 277 (10th Cir. 1989); Ouzts v. Md. Nat'l Ins. Co., 505 F.2d 547, 554 (9th Cir. 1974); United States v. Goodwin, 440 F.2d 1152, 1156 (3d Cir. 1971).
107. *See, e.g.*, California v. Superior Ct., 482 U.S. 400, 407 (1987). The extradition process is also required in federal cases pursuant to 18 U.S.C. § 3182 (1994).
108. *See generally* State v. Epps, 585 P.2d 425, 428 (Or. 1978).

recovery rights of the bail bond producer.[109] The extent to which an express waiver executed by the principal during the underwriting process will be enforced remains to be decided.[110]

Freelance bounty hunters frequently locate and retrieve principals on forfeited bonds.[111] They accept unilateral offers or negotiate with the bail bond producer to surrender the fugitive principal back into custody for an agreed price, which is typically a percentage of the bail bond. In this recovery activity the bounty hunters are viewed as acting with the authority of the executing bail bond producer and with the same rights to pursue and arrest principals.[112] The activities of fugitive recovery agents, however, are subject to a variety of specific state requirements

---

109. *See, e.g.*, Landry v. A-Able Bonding, Inc., 75 F.3d 200, 206 (5th Cir. 1996) (holding that the Texas UCEA required the surrender of a Louisiana fugitive to Texas court); *McCotter*, 875 F.2d at 277 (holding that a commercial surety could not reasonably anticipate that the common law rights of a bail agent were proscribed and was thus deprived of due process); *Ouzts*, 505 F.2d at 552–53 (holding that a California UCEA abrogates common law rights of bail surety); Commonwealth v. Wilkinson, 613 N.E.2d 914, 917 (Mass. 1993) (common law rights of bail surety abrogated by UCEA in Massachusetts); *Epps*, 585 P.2d at 429 (recognizing that Oregon abrogates a foreign bonding agent's common law right to pursue, apprehend, and remove principal from state without resort to due process); State v. Lopez, 734 P.2d 778, 782 (N.M. Ct. App. 1986), *cert denied*, 499 U.S. 1092 (1987) (holding that the UCEA must be followed in the absence of the consent of bond principal).

110. *See Lopez*, 734 P.2d at 782 (holding that the UCEA must be followed in the absence of the consent of bond principal). *But see Epps*, 585 P.2d at 427 (holding that the use of force obviates "consent" as the term is used in the UCEA).

111. Florida and South Carolina prohibit freelance bounty hunting. FLA. STAT. § 648.30(2)(3) (2020) (it is unlawful to hold oneself out as a "bounty hunter" or "bail recovery agent"); S.C. CODE ANN. §§ 15-17-740, 38-53-50, 38-53-60 (2020). In North Carolina, bounty hunters must work for only one bonding company and cannot act on a freelance basis. N.C. GEN. STAT. § 58-71-65 (2019).

112. Jonathan Drimmer, *When Man Hunts Man: The Rights and Duties of Bounty Hunters in the American Criminal Justice System*, 33 HOUS. L. REV. 731, 761 (1996).

and limitations over and above the requirements applicable to bail bond producers.[113]

IV. The Administration of Justice and Economic Benefits of Commercial Bail

Commercial bail is an effective, functional, and significant tool in our system of criminal justice. It also gives rise to several important economic advantages that are frequently overlooked. These concepts deserve additional attention.

A. *The Impact of Secured Release on the Administration of Justice*

The administration of justice is impossible if principals do not appear for trial. Pretrial release secured by commercial bail provides the most effective mechanism to achieve this goal. To understand this important concept requires a brief explanation of the many layers of financial commitments that are unique to commercial bail transactions when the

---

113. For example, bail enforcement licenses are required in Arizona, Connecticut, Georgia, Indiana, Iowa, Louisiana, Mississippi, Nevada, South Dakota, Utah, and West Virginia. *See* ARIZ. REV. STAT. § 20-340.02 (2011); CAL. PENAL CODE § 1299.06 (2011); CONN. GEN. STAT. § 29-152f (2011); GA. CODE ANN. §§ 16-11-129, 17-6-56 to 17-6-58 (2011); IND. CODE § 27-10-3-6 (2021); IOWA CODE § 80A.3 (2021); LA. ADMIN. CODE tit. 49, §§ 4905–4907 (2011); MISS. CODE ANN. § 83-39-3 (2018); NEV. REV. STAT. § 178.526 (2014); S.D. CODIFIED LAWS § 23A-43-29 (2011); UTAH CODE ANN. § 53-11-122 (2011); W. VA. CODE §§ 51-10A, 56-3-34 (2021). In Arkansas, only a licensed private investigator, the bail agent, or a person under the bail agent's direct supervision can arrest the fugitive. ARK. CODE ANN. § 16-84-114 (2020). A recovery agent cannot be employed in Colorado without a background investigation. COLO. REV. STAT. § 12-7-105.5 (2011). When a bail enforcement agent is used in Arizona, the Department of Insurance must be promptly notified. Annual reports are also required. *See* ARIZ. REV. STAT. § 13-3885C, D (2018). In Florida, it is unlawful to represent oneself as a "bounty hunter" or "bail enforcement agent." No one other than a certified law enforcement officer is authorized to apprehend, detain, or arrest a principal on a bond in Florida, unless that person is qualified, licensed, and appointed as a bail bond agent in Florida, or by the state where the bond was written. FLA. STAT. § 648.30(2), (3) (2021).

surety company is not the only party assuming a financial risk if the principal absconds.

Typically, there are at least three categories of commitments in each commercial bail transaction: (1) the surety company obligates itself as surety; (2) the bail bond producer agrees to indemnify the loss; and (3) third-party indemnitors obligate themselves by signing a bail agreement that protects the surety from all losses on the bond. The bail bond producer agrees to indemnify loss in their producer agreement with the surety company. Through this commitment, the surety company is, in effect, guaranteed reimbursement of any loss. The surety company may also hold security in the form of a build-up fund, also known as a "BUF" account, consisting of funds collected from the bail bond producer that secures their indemnity obligations per the producer agreement. This risk of loss significantly motivates the bail bond producer to take all necessary steps to assure principal compliance.

The term "secured release" in the context of a commercial bail bond refers to more than the surety's commitment. It means all commitments and risk control factors operating in concert. The practical result is that in this "circle of responsibility" several parties have a financial stake in the principal's appearance, unlike an unsecured release where the principal's failure to appear has no consequences to friends and family. It is these layers of financial commitment that make commercial bail the most effective form of pretrial release.

B. Positive Economic Impact

Commercial bail results in many economic benefits to state and county governments, including (1) insurance premium taxes; (2) forfeiture payments; (3) savings from higher appearance rates; and (4) the "uncalculated cost" of recidivism.

Just as with the sale of any other insurance product, each bail bond posted results in payment of the attendant premium tax. If the surety company is unable to produce the principal as promised, a forfeiture is paid to the trial court. While the percentage of cases in which this occurs is small, the aggregate losses paid can be substantial. Counties anticipate this revenue source, with some even building forfeiture payments into their fiscal planning, allocating the anticipated funds to their road and bridge funds, school administration, and the like. Every failure to appear costs the jurisdiction money in terms of judicial resources, thus higher appearance rates result in savings.

Just as commercial bail has a lower failure to appear rate than unsecured release, it also has a lower misbehavior rate of its principals pending trial. A federal Bureau of Justice Statistics study found that the misconduct rate of principals released before trial on an unsecured basis was more than twice as high as that of principals whose release was secured.[114] The same report showed the percentage of principals still a fugitive after one year from release date being almost twice as high for unsecured as opposed to secured release. The effectiveness of commercial bail, coupled with its indisputable economic benefits, supports the proposition that commercial bail is a greater boon to public safety than unsecured release.

Conclusion

Bail is the least understood and most underappreciated form of suretyship. The fact that this method of release dramatically outperforms all others in reappearance rates and has the lowest recidivism among its charges results in it being seen with increasing favor among judicial officers. Another significant benefit of commercial bail is it is "user funded." The same financial incentives that drive the commercial bail industry also keep the responsibility for recovering fugitives within the private sector, placing no additional burden on taxpayers. In addition, commercial bail is an effective means of reducing jail overcrowding at no expense to local government. A more comprehensive understanding of commercial bail will facilitate the enactment of reasonable and more uniform laws that will enhance the efficiency of the industry and augment its long record of accomplishment.

---

114. BUREAU OF JUSTICE STATISTICS, *supra* note 46.

APPENDIX A

CHAPTER GLOSSARY

Attorney-in-Fact
Attorneys-in-fact have the authority to execute a bail bond on behalf of a qualified surety company. In the commercial bail industry, a licensed bail bond producer holding an authentic power of attorney from a surety company by whom that bail bond producer has been appointed may rely on the power of attorney to write a bail bond in the name of that surety company.

Bail Bond
A tripartite agreement conditioned upon a principal's appearance and that names the government as the bond obligee, the principal is the defendant in the criminal case, and an insurance company licensed to issue surety bonds is the surety.

Bail Bond Producer
A bail bond producer is a retailer, also known as a bail bonding agent, who sells bail bonds to the public. The bail bond producer selects the individual to bond (the principal), what requirements must be met as a condition of issuing the bond, and monitors the principal for court appearances. The bail bond producer, as attorney-in-fact, executes the bond. Typically, bail bond producers operate as independent contractors and hold their appointing surety company harmless from all loss and adjustment expense.

Bond Conditions
The primary condition of a bail bond is that the bond principal must appear in court as ordered. Breach of a bond condition can result in forfeiture of the bail bond or revocation of bail. Typical supplemental bond conditions include orders mandating forbearance from further criminal activity, forbearance from communications with victims and witnesses, drug testing, and other forms of monitoring.

Consent of Surety
If the conditions of a bail bond have been met, or if the bail bond is forfeited, a surety company cannot be compelled to remain liable on the bail bond while the principal is free. Reinstatement of a bond after

forfeiture always requires surety consent. Further, after conviction or a guilty plea, principals must ask for a consent of surety if the bail bond is to remain in effect and allow the principal to be released from custody until sentencing.

Discharge and Exoneration

A surety company is discharged when the primary condition of a bond is fulfilled, the bond penalty paid, or the bond is otherwise terminated by court order or by operation of law. Discharge of the bond is typically a condition precedent to the return of collateral and replenishment of the stock of powers the bail agent will require to write new liability.

Forfeiture

A declaration by the court, upon the principal's failure to appear as directed, that the government, as the bond obligee, may now pursue a claim under the bond.

Forfeiture Judgment

A formal order of the court following the declaration of a forfeiture, entering judgment against the principal and surety company in the penal amount of the bail bond.

Indemnitor

A third-party indemnitor of the surety's liability. Typically, indemnitors are friends or relatives of the bond principal who seek release of the principal from custody and sign an agreement to indemnify the surety company from loss if the principal fails to appear.

Power of Attorney

A power of attorney, also known in the commercial bail industry as a "power," is a serially numbered and stringently controlled instrument that is issued by surety companies to a licensed, qualified, and duly appointed bail bond producer. These powers of attorney authorize the bail bond producer to bind the surety company as the surety on a single bail bond in the amount of a specific penal sum.

Recognizance

Recognizance is the promise of the bond principal to appear, or pay, in the event of the principal's unexcused failure to appear.

Recovery Agent

A recovery agent is an independent contractor hired to return a fugitive to custody. Terms may vary, but compensation typically includes a percentage of remission paid when the fugitive is returned to custody. A "bounty hunter" is another term for a recovery agent, referring primarily to those working on a freelance basis.

Remission/Remittitur

A court order directing that all or part of the monies paid by the surety company on a forfeiture judgment be returned to the surety company. Remission is typically ordered when an absconding principal is surrendered because of the surety company's actions.

Revocation

When a principal violates a bond condition the court can order return of the principal to custody. A surety company also has the right to revoke the bond and return the principal to custody, with or without probable cause, before a forfeiture occurs.

Set-Aside

A ruling by the court at a hearing prior to the entry of a forfeiture judgment, that the principal's failure to appear was excusable and the forfeiture is not to be enforced.

CHAPTER 9

LICENSE AND PERMIT BONDS

Patrick Q. Hustead
Connor L. Cantrell
Patricia Framke

I. Dispensaries, Motor Vehicle Dealers, Slaughterhouses, and Shooting Gallery Operators

License and permit bonds are nonglamorous workhorses within the surety realm. As their names suggest, license and permit bonds are bonds statutorily required to procure licenses or permits for various occupations and professions. As a result, license and permit bonds evolve along with the ever-changing regulatory schemes and interpretative case law related to the occupations and professions themselves.

The language and structure of license and permit bonds have historically developed from state statutes, local ordinances, or other regulations. Thus, examination of license and permit bonds and their concomitant obligations requires a thorough analysis of the pertinent regulation, statute, or ordinance from which the bond originates, a review of the bond form itself, and relevant case law within the jurisdiction. Generally, license and permit bonds set forth that the surety shall indemnify the obligee(s) against all losses, costs, expenses, damages, and so on the obligee suffers as a result of the principal's noncompliance with or breach of pertinent laws, statutes, ordinances, or regulations applicable to the particular license or permit issued to the principal.

As one would expect from their regulatory/statutory origins, license and permit bonds come in a myriad of shapes and sizes. The most common license and permit bonds are those required of businesses particularly prone to dishonest conduct and those that protect citizens against loss of property entrusted to the principal. Examples of these most common types of license and permit bonds include motor vehicle dealer bonds and real estate broker bonds.

A more recent trend involves statutorily required bonds for marijuana dispensaries and grow operators.[1] In Florida, for example, as a condition to obtain a license, medical marijuana operators are required to post a $5 million bond that guarantees, inter alia, the costs incurred by the Department of Health related to the revocation of a license, costs incurred by patients that are attributable to obtaining alternative sources of medical marijuana in the event a license is revoked, and costs incurred by other medical marijuana treatment centers related to adjusting cultivation, processing, or dispensing operations to ensure access to patients affected by the revocation of an operator's license.[2]

Other examples of common license and permit bonds involve those whose work impacts public health and safety, such as bonds issued to public works contractors. For example, in California, anyone performing construction work that totals $500 or more in labor and materials must be licensed by the California Contractors State License Board.[3] These bonds serve to protect homeowners contracting for home improvements, anyone damaged by intentional violations of the contractor's bond statutes (e.g., abandoning work, diverting funds, violating safety codes, etc.), and employees damaged by the contractor's failure to pay wages or benefits.[4]

Yet other license and permit bonds include those that assure payment of taxes collected by the principal. Such tax-related license and permit bonds are commonly issued in the form of sales tax and fuel-tax bonds, which guarantee payment of taxes, penalties, and interest owed to the state government by fuel sellers.[5]

If the contemplated license or permit is not actually issued to the principal for some reason, the surety's obligation under the bond will

---

1. *See, e.g.*, Michael Herranen, *How Surety Bonds Are Covering California's Cannabis Industry*, INS. J., WEST W8 (2018).
2. FLA. STAT. § 381.986(8)(b)(7)(a) (2021) ("[u]pon approval, the applicant must post a $5 million performance bond issued by an authorized surety insurance company rated in one of the three highest rating categories by a nationally recognized rating service. However, a medical marijuana treatment center serving at least 1,000 qualified patients is only required to maintain a $2 million performance bond").
3. CAL. BUS. & PROF. CODE §§ 7048, 7071.5 (2021).
4. *Id.* § 7071.5.
5. See for example Washington Revised Code section 82.38.110 (2021), which requires fuel distributors to secure a surety bond to guarantee fuel tax payments, penalties, and interest in order to be eligible for a license.

typically not arise.[6] If the license or permit is issued and the bond takes effect, the license or permit bond will usually run concurrently with the license or permit period and any renewals of such periods.[7] Either new bonds or continuation certificates relating to the original bond are required for the renewals of the license or permit. If a principal's license or permit is revoked or suspended for any reason, the bond will be considered ineffective as of the end of the license or permit period.

The range of these bonds is far-reaching, from contractors, motor vehicle dealers, and real estate brokers, to dispensaries, slaughterhouses, and shooting gallery operators. Regardless, given their regulatory/statutory origins, license and permit bonds are sometimes viewed as noncomplex, innocuous instruments. As discussed in greater detail below, however, license and permit bonds can surprise, occasionally engendering thorny legal issues and unanticipated exposures.

II. Bond Coverage

License and permit bonds, like all surety bonds, are to be interpreted according to the standards that govern the construction of contracts in general.[8] Unlike other surety bonds, however, license and permit bonds also have a close connection to statutes, regulations, or ordinances that must also be considered when interpreting such bonds.[9] Thus, when asked to determine the scope of a license or permit bond, a court will consider the language and purpose of the bond in conjunction with the terms of the statute, regulation, or ordinance upon which the bond is based.[10] In many cases, it will be key for a court to consider not only the

---

6. *See* Watson v. Welton, 563 P.2d 331 (Ariz. Ct. App. 1977).
7. *See* United States v. Smith, 75 U.S. (8 Wall.) 587 (1869); *cf.* City of Detroit v. Blue Ribbon Auto Drivers Ass'n, Inc., 237 N.W. 61 (Mich. 1931) (holding that surety remained liable on the bond after the license expired where the ordinance did not, by its express terms, limit the bond to the period of the license nor was such a limitation found in the bond itself). *But see* Karton v. Ari Design & Constr., Inc., 276 Cal. Rptr. 3d 46 (Cal. Ct. App. 2021) (where the surety was liable on the license bond despite the fact that the principal was unlicensed).
8. *See* Edmonds v. W. Sur. Co., 962 P.2d 323 (Colo. Ct. App. 1998); W. Sur. Co. v. Smith, 914 P.2d 451 (Colo. Ct. App. 1995); RESTATEMENT (THIRD) OF SURETYSHIP AND GUARANTY § 14(b) (: 1996).
9. *See Smith*, 914 P.2d 451.
10. *See id.*

plain language of the statute, regulation, or ordinance, but also the intent of the enacting body.[11]

The scope of coverage of license and permit bonds will generally be interpreted consistently with the intent of the regulation, statute, or ordinance upon which the particular bond is based.[12] Thus, the provisions of the statute are generally controlling and bond language that attempts to lessen a surety's liability will be disregarded.[13] Of course, a surety may choose to assume greater liability than required by regulation, statute, or ordinance, and such an undertaking by a surety will usually be enforced, as long as the surety voluntarily assumes the increased exposure.[14]

III. Not as Simple as They Seem

As discussed above, given their regulatory/statutory origins, license and permit bonds are often given little consideration in the surety world. Seen as simple and usually involving smaller bond penalties, license and permit bonds have historically received comparatively little attention from courts, commentators, and sureties compared to more mainstream contract or even commercial bonds.

The remainder of this chapter will focus on several interesting cases dealing with license and permit bonds. As these cases show, the simple, harmless license and permit bond has created some surprisingly large, complicated problems for sureties expecting such problems to arise only in conjunction with larger bonds.

A. The Extent of Recovery on a Bond

The amount recoverable under a bond required by licensing legislation depends not only on the terms of the bond, but also on the purpose behind the legislation.[15] In general, most statutes provide that a surety's liability under a license bond is aggregate, meaning that all claims by claimants cannot exceed the penal sum of the bond for each coverage

11. *See id.*; *see also* Gen. Elec. Credit Corp. v. Wolverine Ins. Co., 362 N.W.2d 595 (Mich. 1984).
12. *See* U.S. Fid. & Guar. Co. v. Bross, 578 P.2d 1028 (Ariz. Ct. App. 1978).
13. *See* State v. Easley, 299 N.W.2d 439 (Neb. 1980); Aetna Cas. & Sur. Co. v. Woods, 565 S.W.2d 861 (Tenn. 1978).
14. *See* Dennis Dillon Oldsmobile, GMC, Inc. v. Zdunich, 668 P.2d 557 (Utah 1983).
15. *See, e.g.*, Cont'l Cas. Co. v. Grabe Brick Co., 401 P.2d 168 (Ariz. 1965).

period.[16] The penal sum of the California contractor's bonds noted earlier, for example, is $15,000, and the aggregate liability of a surety on such a bond shall not exceed $7,500 unless the claims involve claims by a homeowner contracting for home improvement on his or her personal family residence.[17]

Unfortunately, the basic principle that a surety's liability is capped at the penal sum of the bond is not always embraced by the courts. Colorado requires motor vehicle dealers to post a $50,000 motor vehicle dealer bond (or a cash equivalent).[18] The $50,000 bond (or cash equivalent) is intended to serve as a reserve fund for reimbursement "for any loss or damage suffered by any retail consumer caused by violation of [this statute] by a motor vehicle dealer."[19] One can thus easily imagine the surety's surprise when it faced liability of $1.5 million on a simple, run-of-the-mill $30,000[20] motor vehicle dealer bond it issued to a Colorado dealer.

In *Western Surety Co. v. Smith*,[21] the surety challenged the trial court's ruling against the surety on summary judgment, which found that the language of the motor vehicle dealer bond at issue was more expansive than the provisions of Colorado's motor vehicle dealer bond statute. Interpreting the bond's "to indemnify any and all persons . . . for any loss suffered . . . in the penal sum of $30,000" language, the trial court concluded that Western Surety Company was liable to pay up to the face amount of the bond ($30,000) to each of the approximately 50 claimants who had made a claim against the bond—an aggregate liability of up to $1.5 million on a $30,000 face value motor vehicle dealer bond.[22]

The Colorado Court of Appeals reversed, however, finding that, notwithstanding the bond's arguably more expansive language, the bond's language tracked the statutory language close enough that it should be interpreted consistently with the intent of its originating statute that, in this case, intended a surety's obligation to be limited to the face amount of the bond—regardless of the number of claimants.[23] Thus, the surety's

16. *See, e.g.*, N. River Ins. Co. v. Claar, 382 S.E.2d 8 (S.C. Ct. App. 1989).
17. CAL. BUS. & PROF. CODE § 7071.6 (2021).
18. *See* COLO. REV. STAT. § 44-20-112 (2020).
19. *See id.*
20. *Id.* § 12-6-111 (repealed 2018) (formerly required a $30,000 bond).
21. W. Sur. Co. v. Smith, 914 P.2d 451 (Colo. Ct. App. 1995).
22. *See id.*
23. *See id.*

liability was limited to the face amount of the bond and the specter of a potential $1.5 million liability was thankfully avoided.

One might view the *Smith* case as an anomaly given the general rule that a surety's liability is generally limited to the penal sum of the bond.[24] At least one state supreme court, however, has made the *Smith* scenario a reality for a surety. In *Dennis Dillon Oldsmobile, GMC, Inc. v. Zdunich*,[25] the Utah Supreme Court interpreted similarly broad bond language and found it to be broader than that required by statute. Consequently, the *Zdunich* court upheld the lower court's holding that there was no aggregate limitation on the surety's liability on the bond, resulting in a potential liability of the full face value of the bond ($20,000) per claim.[26]

The Tenth Circuit has since tempered the *Zdunich* ruling somewhat. In *Strebel v. Milton Wagstaff Motor Co., Inc.*,[27] the plaintiff, Strebel, brought claims against a motor vehicle dealer and its surety for odometer fraud under the Motor Vehicle Information and Cost Savings Act of 1972, the Utah Motor Vehicle Act, and the Utah Consumer Sales Practices Act. After the trial court found for Strebel and against the dealer and its surety on the fraudulent transaction claim, the Tenth Circuit was asked to determine whether, under Utah law and *Zdunich*, the surety was liable for the full amount of the judgment against the dealer, including exemplary damages, attorneys' fees, and costs.

In order to do so, the court was asked to construe bond language binding the principal and surety to indemnify the plaintiff "for loss suffered," along with language in the same bond obligating the surety to "pay judgments and costs adjudged against said principal."[28] Notwithstanding the obvious discrepancy in terms and *Zdunich*'s rule that "the contract of a surety for hire, is to be strictly construed against the surety," the court held that the surety's liability extends only to those

---

24. *See, e.g.*, Leggitt v. Humphreys, 50 U.S. 297 (1850); Bill Curphy Co. v. Elliott, 207 F.2d 103 (5th Cir. 1953); Md. Cas. Co. v. Alford, 111 F.2d 388 (10th Cir. 1940); Rolen v. Ravnuff, 315 F. Supp. 935 (E.D. Tenn. 1970).
25. 668 P.2d 557 (Utah 1983).
26. *See id.* The *Zdunich* opinion has been cited in two lower Utah appellate court decisions. *See* W. Sur. Co. v. Murphy, 754 P.2d 1237 (Utah Ct. App. 1988); Shelter Am. Corp. v. Ohio Cas. & Ins. Co., 745 P.2d 843 (Utah Ct. App. 1987).
27. 46 F.3d 1152 (10th Cir. 1995).
28. *Id.*

actual damages sustained as a result of the principal's actions, not any exemplary damages or attorneys' fees.[29]

The court reasoned that the reference to the payment of judgments should be read together with the repeated references to "for loss suffered," and that the most reasonable interpretation is that the surety is only obligated to pay actual damages and not exemplary damages or attorneys' fees, at least where the claimant has not made a showing that he or she lost "a great deal more than the initial damages by spending extra money and time" such that an award of treble damages would be seen as compensatory rather than exemplary or punitive.[30]

The lessons of *Smith*, *Zdunich*, and *Strebel* are instructive. When drafting bond language for license and permit bonds, it is crucial to track precisely the language of the originating regulation, statute, or ordinance and to maintain consistency throughout. Likewise, unless some valid consideration is given, the surety should not undertake to assume more exposure than required by state laws. Tracking statutory language is the only sure way to constrict a surety's obligation to that contemplated by the statute. Thus, the statute itself should always be incorporated into the bond by specific reference, and it may be advisable to include a proviso that, to the extent there is a conflict between the terms of the bond and the statute, the statute should apply. To fail to do so can mean increasing potential maximum liability into the stratosphere, should a court interpret bond language, and consequently the surety's obligation, as broader than that dictated by statute.

A related consideration highlighted by these cases is the importance of the surety's use of an interpleader action to resolve all claims in one action, if possible, in order to obtain a discharge from further liability. Although a surety is not a trustee for all claimants and is under no general affirmative duty to discover all possible claimants to guarantee that a pro rata distribution is made, it could be held liable to remaining claimants even though it has already paid the full penalty of the bond if it is aware that other claims exist.[31] As a result, a surety should always consider the option of an interpleader action, ensuring, of course, that it gives proper

---

29. *Id.*
30. *Id.* (citing Tomlinson v. Camel City Motors, Inc., 408 S.E.2d 853 (N.C. 1991)).
31. *See* Transamerica v. C.B. Concrete Co., 669 P.2d 246 (Nev. 1983); *see also* Fid. & Deposit Co. v. Stephenson, 79 P.2d 115 (Cal. Ct. App. 1938).

notice to claimants of the pending action, to resolve all known claims and obtain an express discharge from liability.

B. *Liability Periods: Cumulative Versus Continuous*

As mentioned previously, license bonds provide recourse for parties who are damaged by a licensee's noncompliance with the statutes and regulations that govern the licensee's operations. License bonds are typically coterminous with the licenses they guarantee.[32] The liability period on the bond may be limited, however, by the statute requiring the bond, by a more general statute of limitations on contract claims, by the life span of the underlying license, or by the express terms of the bond itself.

Many license bonds secure licenses that have a one-year term. Often, these bonds must be renewed annually per statute. Such frequently renewed bonds may be "cumulative" or "continuous." If a bond is continuous, the surety's liability is limited to the amount of the bond for a single year, regardless of how many years the bond was in effect. If the bond is cumulative, on the other hand, the surety may be liable for the penal sum of the bond in each of the years it was renewed, and a plaintiff suffers losses. A surety bond that is to exist for an indefinite period of time will generally be construed to impose continuous liability.[33]

There is no uniform rule that governs whether a license bond is cumulative or continuous. Rather, courts have looked to several different factors to make this determination, and their conclusions vary.[34] Two

---

32. Brown Wholesale Elec. Co. v. Merchants Mut. Bonding Co., 713 P.2d 291 (Ariz. Ct. App. 1984) (holding that surety bond is coterminous with the license). *See also* U.S. Fid. & Guar. Co. v. Bross, 578 P.2d 1028 (Ariz. Ct. App. 1978); Watson v. Welton, 563 P.2d 331 (Ariz. Ct. App. 1977) (contractor's license bond cannot exist without an accompanying contractor's license).
33. *See* United States v. Md. Cas. Co., 129 F. Supp. 45 (D. Md. 1955).
34. *See, e.g.*, A.B.S. Clothing v. Home Ins. Co., 41 Cal. Rptr. 2d 166 (Cal. Ct. App. 1995) (finding a private bond to be cumulative where policy provisions did not support a finding that the bond was continuous); Columbia Hosp. for Women & Lying-In Asylum v. U.S. Fid. & Guar. Co., 188 F.2d 654 (D.C. Cir. 1951) (finding a private bond to be continuous due to express language against cumulation in bond); Giese v. Engelhardt, 175 N.W.2d 578 (N.D. 1970) (finding a statutory bond to be cumulative where legislative intent was for cumulative liability).

factors that weigh heavily in this uncertain analysis are the language of the bond itself and the language of the statute that requires the bond.[35]

The issue of cumulative versus continuous liability was the central question in *Giese v. Engelhardt*.[36] There, the plaintiffs purchased stock from a securities dealer whose dealings were guaranteed by an annual license bond. The buyers brought action against the securities dealer for fraud in the sale of stock certificates and against the surety on a license bond guaranteeing that the securities dealer would comply with relevant securities regulations.

The buyers claimed that they had been defrauded in transactions over the course of five annual license periods. The license bond at issue had been renewed in each of those years in the penal sum of $5,000. The buyers took the position that the surety was liable for the penal sum of the bond in each of the five annual periods for a total of $25,000. Conversely, the surety argued that it was liable for the penal sum of the bond only once for the entire period.

The bond itself did not specify whether it was continuous or cumulative, providing only that the surety's liability on the bond "shall continue for each successive year until canceled by the surety or the North Dakota Securities Commissioner."[37] The securities licensing statute (North Dakota Century Code section 10-04-10 (1970)) required securities dealers to either furnish a new bond or renew an existing bond annually.

The trial court treated the bond as continuous and held that the total bond penalty on all claims was the face value of the penal sum of the bond (i.e., $5,000). The Supreme Court of North Dakota reversed, treating the bond as cumulative and finding that the surety was liable for the penal sum of the bond in each of the five years for which it renewed the bond (i.e., $25,000). The court held:

---

35. Speir v. United States, 31 App. D.C. 476, 483 (D.C. Cir. 1908) (holding that statutory conditions "must be considered as read into and made a part of the bond"); *cf.* Royal Indem. Co. of N.Y. v. Bus. Factors, Inc., 393 P.2d 261, 262 (Ariz. 1964) ("In the case of a bond required by statute, however, the obligation of a bonding company is determined by the statute, and not by the wording of the bond.").
36. 175 N.W.2d 578.
37. *Id.* at 584.

> [W]here the state sets up an annual licensing system and requires a bond for the protection of the public, the bonds must be construed as giving protection for their full face amount for each year that they are in force, and any provision in the bond attempting to limit this liability is a nullity.[38]

The court reasoned that, had the securities dealer posted separate bonds from different sureties for each of the five years, each bond would be subject to its individual penal sum. The court explained that the fact that the securities dealer "chose to continue to do business with its original bonding company does not decrease the protection to the public for each year."[39]

The result in *Giese* is not universal. It should be noted that courts may afford significance to limiting language in a bond when the bond clearly states that the obligation is continuous, rather than cumulative.[40] Regardless, practitioners should not presume a bond to be continuous and should consider the language of the bond and the statute requiring it when evaluating exposure.

C. The "Loss Suffered" May Know No Bounds

The issue of what exactly constitutes "loss suffered" by a claimant on a motor vehicle dealer bond arose in *Edmonds v. Western Surety Co.*[41] In *Edmonds*, the surety faced a claimant who had failed to collect $10,400 from the principal. Although the surety conceded liability on the $10,400 claim, the claimant sought to recover the entire amount of its judgment against the principal, which included treble damages pursuant to Colorado deceptive trade practices law, as well as attorneys' fees and prejudgment interest—the total of which exceeded the $30,000 bond limit.[42]

Interpreting the bond language and that of its originating statute, the Colorado Court of Appeals held that the obligation imposed upon the surety by the bond and the statute was one of indemnification.[43]

---

38. *Id.* at 586.
39. *Id.*
40. *See* Nat'l Grange v. Prioleau, 236 S.E.2d 808 (S.C. 1977) (finding a statutory bond to be continuous where the bond explicitly stated as much and the legislature intended it to be continuous).
41. 962 P.2d 323 (Colo. Ct. App. 1998).
42. *See id.*
43. *See id.*

Consequently, the *Edmonds* court, like the *Strebel* court applying Utah law, held that the award of treble damages represented a penalty in excess of loss actually suffered by the claimant and was therefore not recoverable under the bond against the surety.[44]

On the other hand, however, the *Edmonds* court found that attorneys' fees were properly recoverable under the bond against the surety. Attorneys' fees, while not ordinarily recoverable in a contract action pursuant to the American rule,[45] were characterized as losses suffered by the claimant in light of specific statutory authorization of recovery of such fees in the instant case. The *Edmonds* court was careful to restrict its basis for its award of attorneys' fees to those cases in which a claimant recovers a judgment under a statute that expressly provides for such a recovery, but the case nevertheless demonstrates the potential pitfalls of what "loss suffered" really means.[46]

The *Edmonds* court also awarded the claimant prejudgment interest, noting that such interest was also a creature of statute and Colorado law, which expressly provides for recovery of interest on claims made against motor vehicle dealer bonds. Interestingly, the *Edmonds* court hinted that a possible defense to a claim of interest might be made by a surety who could provide proof that it had "stood ready" to pay an amount the surety considered the claimant's "actual loss."[47]

As the *Edmonds* decision reveals, the originating regulation, statute, or ordinance must be examined to determine what fees, costs, and so on a claimant may be able to recover. In addition, if a statutory recovery is the source of the claimant's "loss," attorneys' fees may be recoverable as well. Finally, sureties may ultimately face challenges based upon claimants seeking to recover excess damages—and a claimant may eventually win such a claim to the extent such excess damages can be characterized as "loss" as opposed to "penalty."[48]

---

44. *See id.*; *see also* Darr v. Long, 313 N.W.2d 215 (Neb. 1981) (minimum statutory recovery represented a reward for bringing a successful action and not actual damages and was therefore not recoverable).
45. *See* Globe & Republic Ins. Co. of Am. v. Indep. Trucking Co., 387 P.2d 644 (Okla. 1963).
46. *See Edmonds*, 962 P.2d 323; *see also* Md. Cas. Co. v. Cunningham, 173 So. 506 (Ala. 1937); State Sur. Co. v. Lamb Constr. Co., 625 P.2d 184 (Wyo. 1981).
47. *Edmonds*, 962 P.2d 323.
48. *See* Geters v. Eagle Ins. Co., 834 S.W.2d 49 (Tex. 1992) (holding surety liable for damages awarded pursuant to a Deceptive Trade Practices Act).

Shortly after *Edmonds* was decided, a similar issue arose in Connecticut. In *Western Surety Co. v. State of Connecticut Department of Motor Vehicles*,[49] Caswell, a customer of the Department of Motor Vehicle's principal Pete's Auto Repair, obtained a judgment against the surety in the amount of $4,439. The surety appealed to the extent that the lower court required it to pay $1,000 in punitive damages, $875 in attorneys' fees, and $244 in costs.

The bond language at issue was nearly identical to that in *Edmonds*, requiring "indemni[fication] for any loss sustained."[50] The dispositive issue before the court was, therefore, whether "any loss" includes the award of punitive damages, attorneys' fees, and costs.

Here, the only specific provision, providing for an award of attorneys' fees, was the Connecticut Unfair Trade Practices Act (CUTPA).[51] The court, however, refused to apply the CUTPA and instead focused solely on the language of the motor vehicle dealer bond statute itself. As the bond language in question did not explicitly provide for the recovery of attorneys' fees, the court held that the fees should not have been included in the final award.

In Florida, sureties face a separate statutory construction issue. Consider *Snow v. Jim Rathman Chevrolet, Inc.*,[52] a Florida Court of Appeals decision in which successful claimants on a motor vehicle dealer bond sought attorneys' fees pursuant to Florida Insurance Code section 627.428, which authorizes an award of attorneys' fees to an insured or beneficiary who obtains a judgment against an insurer.[53] The trial court denied the claimants' request for fees and the claimants appealed.

---

49. No. CV 990494408S, 1999 WL 1289053 (Conn. Super. Ct. Dec. 5, 1999).
50. *Id.* at *1 (quoting CONN. GEN. STAT. § 14-52(b)(4) (1999)).
51. CONN. GEN. STAT. § 42-110(b) (2021).
52. 39 So. 3d 368 (Fla. Dist. Ct. App. 2010).
53. Florida Statutes section 627.428(1) provides:

> Upon the rendition of a judgment or decree by any of the courts of this state against an insurer and in favor of any named or omnibus insured or the named beneficiary under a policy or contract executed by the insurer, the trial court or, in the event of an appeal in which the insured or beneficiary prevails, the appellate court shall adjudge or decree against the insurer and in favor of the insured or beneficiary a reasonable sum as fees or compensation for the insured's or beneficiary's attorney prosecuting the suit in which recovery is had.

The issue, as postulated by the *Snow* court, was whether a surety fits within the definition of an insurer and, thus, is subject to the same regulations as insurers even though there is no specific attorney fee provision in the statute requiring car dealers to obtain dealer bonds.[54]

The *Snow* court held that Florida Insurance Code section 627.428 trumped the motor vehicle dealer bond statute and, therefore, held that the surety is obligated to pay reasonable attorneys' fees.[55] The court cited previous decisions conflating suretyship with insurance and reasoned that Florida Insurance Code section 627.428 mandates an award of reasonable attorneys' fees if an insured or beneficiary recovers a judgment against a surety.[56] The court reversed the trial court and remanded the case.

The court did not, however, address whether the penal sum was a limit on the recovery including the fee award.[57] Given the *Snow* court's misguided reliance on section 627.428 to the exclusion of the motor vehicle dealer bond language at issue, it seems to reason that the $25,000 penal sum[58] may not cap a claimant's losses.

Given that litigation creates the possibility of loss in excess of the penal sum of a license bond, practitioners are wise to investigate the legitimacy of any claim against the principal, evaluate its exposure, and consider how to best minimize the costs of the bond dispute. The surety should consider the probability and potential magnitude of loss at trial (including attorneys' fees where authorized by statute) in comparison with the prospects of settlement or the option of interpleading the bonded funds. Sureties should beware that the costs of litigation may greatly exceed the sum of the bond, and gambling with litigation can result in unnecessary loss.

This is precisely what occurred in *Karton v. Ari Design & Construction, Inc.*[59] In *Karton*, the surety issued a contractor's license bond in the amount of $12,500 on behalf of a construction contractor for a residential construction project. When the homeowners discovered the contractor was unlicensed, they sued for the sum of their payments to the contractor ($92,651) under a California statute that voids an unlicensed

---

54. FLA. STAT. § 320.27(10) (2021).
55. *See Snow*, 39 So. 3d at 370.
56. *See id.* at 371.
57. *See id.* at 368.
58. FLA. STAT. § 320.27(10) (2021).
59. 276 Cal. Rptr. 3d 46 (Cal. Ct. App. 2021).

contractor's right to any payments.[60] The homeowners also included a count against the bond. The contractor took the position that it performed $79,651 of work on the home and had only been overpaid by $13,000 (and therefore only owed $13,000 to the homeowners).

With minimal investigation, the surety opted to tender its defense to the contractor, rather than interplead the bond funds or negotiate and pay a settlement, and the case proceeded to trial. The trial court entered judgment for the homeowners and against the contractor for all payments, and against the surety for the penal sum of the bond, plus interest. The trial court also awarded the homeowners $90,000 in attorneys' fees but exempted the surety from liability for those attorneys' fees.[61]

On appeal, the appellate court considered whether the contractor's liability for $90,000 in attorneys' fees extended to the surety. The court of appeal reversed, rejecting the surety's assertion that its liability was limited to the penal sum of its bond and holding that the surety's liability was commensurate with its principal's. The appellate court reasoned, "When a surety decides to fight a lawsuit, it can make itself liable for the costs of that litigation in excess of the face value of its bond."[62]

While proceeding to trial may provide an opportunity to avoid liability altogether on the merits, it is a risky wager that can result in substantial losses. In situations like *Karton* where the principal owes more than the value of the bond under any theory, litigation is unlikely to minimize the costs to the surety. A more thorough investigation of the principal's liability may have helped the surety in *Karton* avoid an enlarged loss.

D. *Extraterritorial Application of License and Permit Bonds*

One might assume that, given the regulatory/statutory origin of license and permit bonds, their reach would not extend beyond state lines (i.e., a particular motor vehicle dealer bond would have no extraterritorial effect beyond the state in which it was issued). As the cases discussed next show, such an assumption will not always hold true.

---

60. CAL. BUS. & PROF. CODE § 7031(b) (2021).
61. In California, attorneys' fees are recoverable as costs in cases against unlicensed professionals. CAL. CIV. PROC. CODE § 1029.8(a).
62. *Karton*, 276 Cal. Rptr. 3d at 60.

In *Mawyer v. Lumbermens Mutual Casualty Co.*,[63] the surety issued a motor vehicle dealer bond pursuant to the North Carolina Motor Vehicle Dealers and Manufacturers Licensing Law. A representative of the principal was subsequently sued in federal court for fraud for tampering with the odometer of a car that was sold to a wholesaler and ultimately to the plaintiff, a purchaser in Virginia. The plaintiff obtained a judgment of $5,767.50, which he in turn attempted to collect from the surety.[64]

The trial court granted summary judgment in favor of the surety, holding that the bond, issued under North Carolina's motor vehicle dealer bond statute, had no extraterritorial effect and thus could not be a source of relief for plaintiff, a resident of Virginia. The Supreme Court of Virginia, however, reversed the trial court's finding.[65]

Noting a split of authority on the issue, the *Mawyer* court held that there was no language in either the North Carolina motor vehicle dealer bond statute or the surety's bond explicitly limiting the bond's application to North Carolina's borders. Admitting that neither the North Carolina statute nor the bond language expressly gave the bond extraterritorial effect, the court nonetheless gave the bond a broad interpretation "in favor of protecting the consumer and strictly against the fraudulent dealer and his surety."[66]

Other courts have agreed with the *Mawyer* court's analysis, holding that, absent statutory or bond language explicitly limiting a bond's application to intrastate transactions, a bond will be given extraterritorial effect.[67] Evidencing the split to which the *Mawyer* court refers, however, some courts have held that, when a regulation, statute, or ordinance conditions issuance of a license or permit upon the execution of a surety bond, a presumption exists that the bond's application does not extend beyond the borders of the issuing state.[68]

---

63. 377 S.E.2d 401 (Va. 1989).
64. *See id.*
65. *See id.*
66. *Id.* at 402.
67. *See, e.g.*, U.S. Fid. & Guar. Co. v. Colonial Baking Co., 247 S.W.2d 997 (Ark. 1952); S. Seattle Auto Auction, Inc. v. W. Cas. & Sur. Co., 598 P.2d 1269 (Or. Ct. App. 1979).
68. *See, e.g.*, Peerless Ins. v. Clark, 487 P.2d 574 (Colo. Ct. App. 1971); Ore-Ida Potato Prods., Inc. v. United Pac. Ins. Co., 392 P.2d 191 (Idaho 1964); State Sur. Co. v. Lensing, 249 N.W.2d 608 (Iowa 1977).

Another approach to this problem was taken by the Alabama Supreme Court in *Ex Parte Old Republic Surety Co.*[69] In *Old Republic Surety*, Old Republic issued a used-motor-vehicle-dealer bond to the principal, an Alabama used car dealer. During the effective term of the bond, the principal traveled to Illinois and purchased from Auction Way, a wholesale automobile dealer, eight automobiles worth $47,000. After the principal's checks and drafts were returned because of insufficient funds, Auction Way filed an indemnity action to recover the amount of the bond. Old Republic contended that because the Alabama statute did not specifically permit extraterritorial application, it should not be required to indemnify Auction Way for a sale that occurred in Illinois.[70]

The Alabama Supreme Court held that Old Republic's argument was misplaced. The court held that Old Republic was a corporation licensed to do business in Alabama and was, thus, subject to the laws of Alabama. The court reasoned that this was not a situation where the enforcement of the statute would impose a burden on a non-citizen of Alabama or would impose upon a party a burden based upon a right or claim that did not vest while the party was in Alabama. The court concluded that, because the statute only operates on an in-state dealer bond, the fact that the principal was outside of the state when the transaction took place did not present a question of the extraterritorial application of the statute.[71]

Following the *Old Republic* logic, the Kansas Court of Appeals held that a garnishee could garnish Missouri automobile dealer bonds to satisfy Kansas judgments against Missouri dealers once the judgments were filed in Missouri court, regardless of whether Missouri's dealer bonds contemplated extraterritorial application.[72] In *Carlson Auction Services, Inc. v. Lopez*, Carlson Auction Services brought an action in Kansas alleging that the defendants purchased vehicles in Kansas with bad checks. After obtaining a judgment against the defendants and their surety, Carlson registered the judgments in Missouri, where the dealers were licensed.

Carlson also sent the Missouri Department of Revenue a letter seeking revocation of the defendants' license and making a claim under the surety's bonds. Carlson then sought to garnish the defendants and the surety in Missouri. The surety objected to the trial court in Kansas,

---

69. 733 So. 2d 881 (Ala. 1999).
70. *Id.*
71. *Id.*
72. Carlson Auction Servs., Inc. v. Lopez, 61 P.3d 117 (Kan. Ct. App. 2003).

arguing that its bonds did not apply to activities outside Missouri, and, thus, the surety's bonds could not be garnished. The trial court agreed, citing *Mawyer*.[73]

On appeal, after noting the split of authority and explaining both sides, the *Lopez* court adopted *Old Republic* and held that, because the surety knowingly issued dealer bonds to Missouri dealers in accordance with Missouri law, once the judgments were registered in Missouri court, the claimant's right to be indemnified arose under the Missouri motor vehicle statute, regardless of where the underlying activity took place. The *Lopez* court, therefore, reversed the trial court and entered an order of garnishment.

Thus, there remains a split of authority on whether license and permit bonds have extraterritorial effect. Consult the Idaho Supreme Court's reasoning in *Ore-Ida Potato Products, Inc. v. United Pacific Insurance Co.*[74] for a persuasive argument that the evolving general rule should be one of no extraterritorial application. The important lesson for a surety, however, is to study the law of the states in which license and permit bonds are being written to determine the likely extent of its obligation on those bonds.

Conclusion

Given the variation in statutory language, legislative histories, the purpose and intent of the bonds, and the language of the bonds themselves, it is difficult to generalize about license and permit bonds. Suffice it to say that license and permit bonds are capable of deceptive complications due to either their language, their origins, or a court's skewed interpretation of either or both. While certain issues unique to license and permit bonds have been examined herein, one should remember that license and permit bonds also face a number of other issues, common to bonds of all types, which are discussed throughout this book.

---

73. *Id.* at 118.
74. 392 P.2d 191 (Idaho 1964).

CHAPTER 10

MECHANIC'S LIEN DISCHARGE BONDS

Jonathan J. Dunn
Derek Popeil[1]

Introduction

This chapter analyzes the law applicable to mechanic's lien discharge bonds. Necessary background to any discussion on this topic is a general understanding of mechanic's lien laws. A lien is "[a] charge or security or encumbrance upon property."[2] Mechanics, those who work with their hands, have historically enjoyed liens upon the personal property they crafted or improved.[3] However, no such lien was available at common law against real property.[4] Thus, the now-familiar construction mechanic's lien against real property came into being purely as a creature of statute.[5] In order to encourage development in what is now Washington, D.C., Thomas Jefferson and James Madison oversaw enactment of the first mechanic's lien statute by the state of Maryland in 1791.[6] Through mechanic's lien statutes, certain persons not paid for their work in constructing improvements on real property are granted

---

1. The authors wish to thank Ross Steinbach, a 2021 George Washington University Law School graduate and summer associate in SMTD Law LLP's Irvine office, for his valuable research assistance.

2. BLACK'S LAW DICTIONARY 832 (5th ed. 1979).

3. "At common law the only lien available in favor of artisans, tradespeople, mechanics or laborers was on personal property and was limited to payment for work performed on that specific item of property. It was a possessory lien which was lost when the property was surrendered to the owner." STEVEN STEIN, CONSTRUCTION LAW ¶ 9.01 (2021).

4. *See, e.g.*, Tubridy v. Wright, 39 N.E. 640 (N.Y. 1895); Frederick Contractors, Inc. v. Beltre Med. Ctr., Inc., 334 A.2d 526, 530 (Md. 1975); Indep. Tr. Corp. v. Stan Miller, Inc., 796 P.2d 248 n.8 (Colo. 1990). *See also* LAWRENCE M. FRIEDMAN, A HISTORY OF AMERICAN LAW 214–15 (1973).

5. *See* LAWRENCE M. FRIEDMAN, A HISTORY OF AMERICAN LAW 214–15 (1973).

6. *Id.*; 1791 Md. Laws ch. 45, § 10.

the right to perfect a security interest in the real property and structures they improve. Once perfected, mechanic's lien claimants have a right to foreclose their security interest in the property or improvement in derogation of the property owner's rights.

This chapter, from a broad perspective, is about protecting the property owner from a mechanic's lien foreclosure. Specifically, by recording a mechanic's lien discharge bond on title for the property in the pertinent land records, a property owner may remove a mechanic's lien from his or her property, thereby avoiding the risk of the lien claimant's foreclosure of the lien on the property. This chapter considers the law applicable to mechanic's lien discharge bonds,[7] including the nature and purpose of lien discharge bonds, the scope of the surety's liability, the surety's defenses, and the surety's subrogation and contribution rights related to lien discharge bonds.[8]

I. Nature and Purpose of Mechanic's Lien Discharge Bonds

Mechanic's lien statutes are often part of a broad remedial scheme[9] intended to protect certain persons[10] improving real property and

---

7. Some states also include liens upon money due to a general contractor from the owner or to the owner from a construction lender, as well as bonds releasing such claims. *E.g.*, CAL. CIV. CODE §§ 8510, 9364 (Deering 2012). This chapter does not address such "stop notice" release bonds, though many of the principles discussed in this chapter may be applicable.

8. Because each state may differ in its protections, and due to the subject's breadth, this chapter does not attempt to define those who have standing to bring mechanic's lien claims in each state, nor much of the law applicable to enforcement of mechanic's liens. An excellent work on that subject already exists. 1 FIFTY STATE CONSTRUCTION LIEN AND BOND LAW (Laurence Schor ed., 2021 ed.); 2 FIFTY STATE CONSTRUCTION LIEN AND BOND LAW (Laurence Schor ed., 2021 ed.).

9. Most states provide those improving property or structures with remedies on both public and private construction projects. *See* 1 FIFTY STATE CONSTRUCTION LIEN AND BOND LAW, *supra* note 8; 2 FIFTY STATE CONSTRUCTION LIEN AND BOND LAW, *supra* note 8. See also, for example, California Civil Code division 4, part 6, Works of Improvement (commencing with sections 8000–9568), which provides public works payment bond and stop notice remedies, and private works mechanic's lien, payment bond, and stop notice remedies.

10. The persons and entities that qualify for mechanic's lien rights are often known, and will be referred to in this chapter, as "lien claimants."

structures affixed to real property. All 50 states have enacted mechanic's lien statutes.[11] Conversely, most states also provide a property owner with

---

Mechanic's lien statutes vary from state to state and rights under such statutes are a topic beyond this chapter. Typically, however, the lien statutes give standing to assert a claim to general contractors, subcontractors, laborers, and certain tier material suppliers, with more limited rights for those without a direct contractual relationship to the general contractor. *See* 1 FIFTY STATE CONSTRUCTION LIEN AND BOND LAW, *supra* note 8; 2 FIFTY STATE CONSTRUCTION LIEN AND BOND LAW, *supra* note 8.

11. *See* ALA. CODE § 35-11-210 *et seq.* (Michie 1996); ALASKA STAT. §§ 34.35.050–.120 (Lexis-Nexis 1978); ARIZ. REV. STAT. § 33-981 *et seq.* (Lexis-Nexis 1998); ARK. CODE ANN. § 18-44-101 *et seq.* (Lexis-Nexis 1995); CAL. CIV. CODE § 8160 *et seq.* (Deering 2012); COLO. REV. STAT. § 38-22-101 *et seq.* (Lexis-Nexis 2000); CONN. GEN. STAT. § 49-33 *et seq.* (as amended in CT LEGIS 99-153 (1999) (Lexis-Nexis 1953)); DEL. CODE ANN. tit. 25, § 2701 *et seq.* (Lexis-Nexis 1953); FLA. STAT. ch. 713.001 *et seq.* (Lexis-Nexis 2007); GA. CODE ANN. § 44-14-360 *et seq.* (2021); HAW. REV. STAT. § 507-41 *et seq.* (Michie 1984); IDAHO CODE § 45-501 *et seq.* (Lexis-Nexis 2001); 770 ILL. COMP. STAT. 60/0.01 *et seq.* (2018); IND. CODE § 32-28-3-0.2 *et seq.* (Burns 1999); IOWA CODE § 572.1 *et seq.* (Lexis-Nexis 2012); KAN. STAT. ANN. § 60-1101 *et seq.* (Lexis-Nexis 2005); KY. REV. STAT. ANN. § 376.010 *et seq.* (Michie 2002); LA. REV. STAT. § 9:4801 *et seq.* (Lexis-Nexis 2020); ME. REV. STAT. tit. 10, § 3251 *et seq.* (Lexis-Nexis 2015); MD. CODE ANN., REAL PROP. § 9-101 *et seq.* (Michie 1983); MASS. GEN. LAWS ch. 254, § 1 *et seq.* (1996); MICH. COMP. LAWS ANN. § 570.1101 *et seq.* (1982); MINN. STAT. § 514.01 *et seq.* (Lexis-Nexis 1986); MISS. CODE ANN. § 85-7-401 *et seq.* (2014); MO. REV. STAT. § 429.010 *et seq.* (Lexis-Nexis 2013); MONT. CODE ANN. § 71-3-521 *et seq.* (Lexis-Nexis 1987); NEB. REV. STAT. § 52-125 *et seq.* (1981); NEV. REV. STAT. § 108.221 *et seq.* (2005); N.H. REV. STAT. ANN. § 447:2 *et seq.* (Lexis 2012); N.J. STAT. ANN. § 2A:44A-1 *et seq.* (Lexis-Nexis 1995); N.M. STAT. ANN. § 48-2-1 *et seq.* (Michie 1953); N.Y. LIEN LAW § 1 *et seq.* (N.Y. Consol. 1929); N.C. GEN. STAT. § 44A-7 *et seq.* (1996); N.D. CENT. CODE § 35-27-01 *et seq.* (N1993); OHIO REV. CODE ANN. § 1311.01 *et seq.* (Page 2007); OKLA. STAT. ANN. tit. 42, §§ 141–154, 171–180 (Lexis-Nexis 2013); OR. REV. STAT. § 87.010 *et seq.* (Lexis-Nexis 1981); 49 PA. CONS. STAT. § 1101 *et seq.*; R.I. GEN. LAWS § 34-28-1 *et seq.* (1991); S.C. CODE ANN. § 29-5-10 *et seq.* (Lexis-Nexis 2003); S.D. CODIFIED LAWS § 44-9-1 *et seq.* (Lexis-Nexis 1939); TENN. CODE ANN. § 66-11-101 *et seq.* (2013); TEXAS PROP. CODE § 53.001 *et seq.* (Lexis-Nexis 2022); UTAH CODE ANN. § 38-1-1 *et seq.* (2021); VT. STAT. ANN. tit. 9, § 1921 *et seq.* (2003); VA. CODE ANN.

the right to challenge a mechanic's lien and also one or more methods of avoiding mechanic's lien foreclosures.[12] For instance, an owner may be able to limit his or her liability for mechanic's lien claims to the amount of the owner's contract with the general contractor.[13] Statutes affording the owner with such limited liability usually apply only to lower tier lien claimants and often require the owner to record the general contract in the real property records at the commencement of the project as a prerequisite.[14] To be entitled to such limited liability in some states, the

---

§ 43-1 *et seq.* (2010); WASH. REV. CODE § 60.04.021 *et seq.* (1991); W. VA. CODE § 38-2-1 *et seq.* (Michie 1991); WIS. STAT. § 779.01 *et seq.* (Lexis-Nexis 2005); WYO. STAT. § 29-1-201 *et seq.* (2012).

12. For example, Kansas allows the owner to obtain a payment bond at any time to avoid mechanic's lien liability. Kansas Statutes Annotated section 60-1110 (Lexis-Nexis 2005) provides:

> The contractor or owner may execute a bond to the state of Kansas for the use of all persons in whose favor liens might accrue by virtue of this act, conditioned for the payment of all claims which might be the basis of liens in a sum not less than the contract price . . . with good and sufficient sureties, to be approved by a judge of the district court and filed with the clerk of the district court. When bond is approved and filed, no lien . . . shall attach under this act, and if when such bond is filed liens have already been filed, such liens are discharged. Suit may be brought on such bond by any person interested . . . .

Surprisingly, a few states do not afford the property owner any method of removing perfected mechanic's liens other than by payment or the claimant's waiver or release. See, for example, *Enviro-Fab, Inc. v. Blandin Paper Co.*, 349 N.W.2d 842, 848–49 (Minn. Ct. App. 1984) (citation omitted), wherein the court stated: "Some states have provisions in their statutes allowing for the release of a mechanic's lien on the filing of an approved bond. Our Minnesota statute has no such provision. Appellant could not cite any Minnesota case law allowing the posting of a bond to release a mechanic's lien."

13. *See, e.g.*, ALA. CODE § 35-11-210 (Michie 1996); Crane Co. v. Sheraton Apartments, 58 So. 2d 614 (Ala. 1952) (interpreting prior version of statute).

14. *See, e.g.*, COLO. REV. STAT. §§ 38-22-101(2), (3), 38-22-102 (Lexis-Nexis 2000).

property owner must also cause a payment bond to be posted or recorded for the protection of potential mechanic's lien claimants.[15]

In addition or as an alternative to such owner remedies, most states also allow an owner or other interested person to remove a mechanic's lien from real property by providing a lien discharge bond in favor of the lien claimant.[16] Because lien discharge bonds typically arise from

---

15. See, for example, California Civil Code section 8600 (Deering 2012), which provides, in pertinent part:

> (a) This section applies if, before the commencement of work, the owner in good faith files a direct contract with the county recorder, and records a payment bond . . . (b) . . . the court shall, where equitable to do so, restrict the lien enforcement under this title to the aggregate amount due from the owner to the direct contractor . . . .

16. ALA. CODE § 35-11-233(b) (Michie 1980); ALASKA STAT. § 34.35.072 (1978); ARIZ. REV. STAT. § 33-1004 (Lexis-Nexis 2020); ARK. CODE ANN. § 18-44-118 (2009); CAL. CIV. CODE § 8424 *et seq.* (Deering 2011); COLO. REV. STAT. §§ 38-22-131, 38-22-133 (2022); CONN. GEN. STAT. § 49-37 (Lexis-Nexis 1955); DEL. CODE ANN. tit. 25, § 2729 (1990); FLA. STAT. ch. 713.24 (Lexis-Nexis 2019); GA. CODE ANN. § 44-14-364 (2012); HAW. REV. STAT. § 507-45 (Michie 1998); IND. CODE § 32-28-3-11 (Burn 2002); IOWA CODE § 572.15 (Lexis-Nexis 2013); KY. REV. STAT. ANN. § 376.212 (Michie 2011); LA. REV. STAT. § 9:4835 (Lexis-Nexis 2020); ME. REV. STAT. tit. 10, § 3263 (Lexis-Nexis 2020); MASS. GEN. LAWS ANN. ch. 254, § 14 (2003); MICH. COMP. LAWS § 570.1116 (1982); MONT. CODE ANN. §§ 71-3-551, 71-3-552 (Lexis-Nexis 2007); NEB. REV. STAT. § 52-142 (1981); NEV. REV. STAT. § 108.2413–.2425 (2003); N.H. REV. STAT. §§ 511:37–511:49 (Lexis 2020); N.J. STAT. ANN. § 2A:44A-31 *et seq.* (Lexis-Nexis 2011); N.M. STAT. § 48-2-9 (Michie 2007); N.Y. LIEN LAW §§ 19, 37 (N.Y. Consol. Laws Serv. 2011); N.C. GEN. STAT. § 44A-16(6) (2013); OHIO REV. CODE §§ 1311.11 (private projects), 1311.311 (public projects) (Page 1991); OKLA. STAT. tit. 42, § 147.1 (Lexis-Nexis 2019); OR. REV. STAT. § 87.076 (Lexis-Nexis 2009); 49 PA. STAT. § 1101 (Lexis-Nexis 1963); R.I. GEN. LAWS § 34-28-17 (2008); S.C. CODE ANN. § 29-5-110 (Lexis-Nexis 1976); S.D. CODIFIED LAWS § 44-4-1 *et seq.* (Lexis-Nexis 1966); TENN. CODE ANN. § 66-11-142 (2020); TEX. PROP. CODE § 53.171 (Lexis-Nexis 1997); VA. CODE § 43-70 (1992); WASH. REV. CODE § 60.04.161 (1991); WIS. STAT. § 779.08 (Lexis-Nexis 2005); WYO. STAT. § 29-1-501 (2010).

statutes,[17] they are likely to be deemed statutory bonds such that the courts will often construe them accordingly.[18] Statutory bonds are usually interpreted as though the terms of the controlling statutes are express terms of the bond.[19] Where the bond's terms differ from the statute, the statute normally controls.[20] If the bond's or statute's language

---

17. *See supra* note 16. Indeed, where no statute can be cited to allow a lien discharge bond, a property owner is not entitled to post a bond as substitute security to remove the lien. *See Enviro-Fab*, 349 N.W.2d at 848–49. A few states allow a mechanic's lien discharge bond by application to the court through what is akin to the court bond process. *See, e.g.*, ME. REV. STAT. tit. 10, § 3263; MD. R. P. 12-307. *But see* Massasoit-Pocasset Nat'l Bank v. Borden, 117 N.E. 911 (Mass. 1917) (bond not complying with statute deemed common law bond, despite intention of parties).
18. *See, e.g.*, Frank Curren Lumber Co. v. Eleven Co., 271 Cal. App. 2d 175, (Cal. Ct. App. 1969).
19. *See id.* at 182 ("Where a surety bond is given pursuant to the requirements of a particular statute, the statutory provisions are incorporated into the bond and become a part of it."). *See also, e.g.*, Northquip Rental Corp. v. Sky Steel Erectors, Inc., 854 P.2d 1185 (Ariz. Ct. App. 1993); Town Radio & Television, Inc. v. Kilpatrick, 275 A.2d 627 (Conn. Cir. Ct. 1970); North v. Waffle House, Inc., 338 S.E.2d 750 (Ga. Ct. App. 1985); DeFrancis Marble & Tile Co. v. Coxe, 148 So. 2d 83 (La. Ct. App. 1962); Dutchess Quarry & Supply Co., Inc. v. Firemen's Ins. Co. of Newark, N.J., 596 N.Y.S.2d 898 (App. Div. 1993); Hard Hat Workforce Sols., LLC v. Mech. HVAC Servs., 750 S.E.2d 921 (S.C. 2013); Baxter Constr. Co., Inc. v. Hou-Tex Prods., Inc., 718 S.W.2d 355 (Tex. App. 1986); Com. Constr. Specialties, Inc. v. ACM Constr. Mgmt. Corp., 405 S.E.2d 852 (Va. 1991); *cf.* Scaccia Concrete Corp. v. Hartford Fire Ins. Co., 628 N.Y.S.2d 746 (App. Div. 1995) (bond providing coverage broader than statutory requirements deemed common law bond and not constricted to statutory coverage).
20. See, for example, *River Dock & Pile, Inc. v. Insurance Co. of North America*, 747 A.2d 1060 (Conn. App. Ct. 2000) (citations omitted), where the lien claimant argued that the bond was a common law bond because it was not given pursuant to a court order, as required under the statute, but was provided voluntarily. In rejecting the argument, the Connecticut Appellate Court stated:

    > The bond voluntarily furnished by the defendant must be treated the same as if the bond had been furnished pursuant to a court order in accordance with § 49-37(a). "A contrary rule would give the lienor greater rights than those prescribed by the statute, and would deny the right of a principal or surety to challenge the validity of

is vague or ambiguous, the bond will be construed in accordance with the legislature's intent in enacting the statute.[21]

A. Bond Serves as Substitute Security for Property

The purpose of the lien discharge bond is usually twofold. First, the lien discharge bond protects the property owner by removing the lien from the real property, eliminating the owner's risk that the claimant may foreclose and providing the owner with clear and otherwise marketable title to the property.[22] Second, the bond protects the lien claimant by taking the place of the property and serving as substitute security for payment should the lien claimant ultimately prevail.[23] The California Supreme Court summarized these dual purposes in the case of *Hutnick v. U.S. Fidelity & Guaranty Co.*, as follows:

> The purpose of the release bond procedure is to provide a means by which, before a final determination of the lien claimant's rights and without prejudice to those rights, the property may be freed of the lien, so that it may be sold, developed, or used

---

> the underlying lien as authorized by the statute . . . It . . . would discourage the substitution of bonds by agreement because of a fear of waiving defenses . . . [and] lead to public mischief by compelling judicial intervention when not needed nor desired."

Six Carpenters, Inc. v. Beach Carpenters Corp., 172 Conn. 1, 7 (1976). *Accord DeFrancis Marble & Tile Co.*, 148 So. 2d 83. *But see Borden*, 117 N.E. 911 (bond not complying with statute deemed common law bond, despite intention of parties); *Scaccia Concrete Corp.*, 628 N.Y.S.2d 746 (bond providing coverage broader than statutory requirements deemed common law bond and not constricted to statutory coverage).

21. *See, e.g.*, Henry F. Raab Conn., Inc. v. J.W. Fisher Co., 438 A.2d 834 (Conn. 1981); Weber v. Pac. Indem. Co., 22 Cal. Rptr. 366 (Cal. Ct. App. 1962) (performance bond).

22. *See generally* 53 AM. JUR. 2D *Mechanics' Liens* § 313 (1996). *See also Henry F. Raab*, 438 A.2d 834; Beacon Constr. Co., Inc. v. Matco Elec. Co., Inc., 521 F.2d 392 (2d Cir. 1975) (superseded by statute on other grounds as stated in *In Re* LoPriore, 115 B.R. 462 (Bankr. S.D.N.Y. 1990); J.R. Christ Constr. Co. v. Willete Assocs., 221 A.2d 538 (N.J. 1966) (interpreting repealed mechanic's lien law); George v. Hartford Accident & Indem. Co., 412 S.E.2d 43 (N.C. 1992); Hutnick v. U.S. Fid. & Guar. Co., 763 P.2d 1362 (Cal. 1988).

23. *Hutnick*, 763 P.2d 1326.

> as security for a loan . . . [California's statute] provides that a mechanic's lien release bond "shall be conditioned for the payment of any sum which the claimant may recover on the claim together with his costs of suit in the action, if he recovers therein." The "claim" for which the principal and surety assume liability in the bond is the "claim of lien." . . . The release bond procedure thus protects the lien claimant by providing an alternate source of recovery on the claim of lien. The release bond procedure "does not deprive the [lien claimant] of its constitutional right to a lien" but "[o]n the contrary, it provides for the speedy and efficient enforcement of such lien . . . ." The recording of the release bond does not extinguish the lien; rather, the bond is substituted for the land as the object to which the lien attaches.[24]

Accordingly, the rights and liabilities of the lien discharge bond surety, as substitute security for the property at issue, should mirror the rights and liabilities of a property owner subject to mechanic's lien litigation.[25]

B. Any Interested Person May Provide the Lien Discharge Bond

Although the bond is intended to protect the property owner, most lien discharge bond statutes allow any interested person to serve as principal on and to provide the lien discharge bond.[26] At least one case defined an

---

24. *Id.* at 1330 (citation omitted). *See also* Royster Constr. Co. v. Urb. W. Communities, 47 Cal. Rptr. 2d 684 (Cal. App. Dep't Super. Ct. 1995).
25. The case of *York Federal Savings & Loan Association v. William Hazel, Inc.*, 506 S.E.2d 315 (Va. 1998), is illustrative. In *York*, a mortgage lending company provided a mechanic's lien discharge bond. York, the mortgage lending company, conceded that the lien claimant met all the requirements of the lien and was owed money, but argued that property was void of any equity beyond the deed of trust securing York's loan. The Virginia Supreme Court ruled that the lien discharge bond substitutes as security for the property and held that, to recover on the bond, the lien claimant must prove the property would have held enough equity to satisfy the lien, or the lien had priority over York's deed of trust. *See also* Regal Wood Prods., Inc. v. First Wis. Nat'l Bank, 347 So. 2d 643 (Fla. Dist. Ct. App. 1977).
26. ALA. CODE § 35-11-233(b) (Michie 1980); ALASKA STAT. § 34.35.072 (1978); ARIZ. REV. STAT. § 33-1004 (Lexis-Nexis 2020); ARK. CODE

"interested" person as any person with an interest in the property or an interest in defeating the lien claim.[27] Allowing any interested person, not just the property owner, to provide the bond makes sense, as the person most invested in contesting the lien claim may be a subcontractor, the general contractor, a mortgage holder, or the property owner's successor in interest.[28]

C. Unless Owner Is Principal on Bond or Privity Exists, Owner Is to Be Dismissed

In the absence of contractual privity, the right to enforce a mechanic's lien claim does not typically give rise to the property owner's personal

---

ANN. § 18-44-118 (2009); CAL. CIV. CODE § 8424 (Deering 2012); CONN. GEN. STAT. § 49-37 (Lexis-Nexis 1955); DEL. CODE ANN. tit. 25, § 2729 (1990); FLA. STAT. ch. 713.24 (Lexis-Nexis 2019); HAW. REV. STAT. § 507-45 (Michie 1998); KY. REV. STAT. ANN. § 376.212 (Michie 2011); LA. REV. STAT. § 9:4835 (Lexis-Nexis 2020); MD. R. P. 12-307 (State & Fed. Ct. Rules 1976); MASS. GEN. LAWS ANN. ch. 254, § 14 (2003); MICH. COMP. LAWS § 570.1116 (1982); NEB. REV. STAT. § 52-142 (1981); NEV. REV. STAT. § 108.2415 (2003); N.J. STAT. ANN. § 2A:44A-31 (Lexis-Nexis 2011); N.C. GEN. STAT. § 44A-16(6) (2013); OHIO REV. CODE § 1311.11(C) (Page 1991); OKLA. STAT. tit. 42, § 147.1 (Lexis-Nexis 2019); OR. REV. STAT. § 87.076 (Lexis-Nexis 2009); 49 PA. STAT. § 1101 (Lexis-Nexis 1963); S.C. CODE ANN. § 29-5-110 (Lexis-Nexis 1976); S.D. CODIFIED LAWS § 44-4-2 (Lexis-Nexis 1966); TENN. CODE ANN. § 66-11-142 (2020); TEX. PROP. CODE § 53.171 (Lexis-Nexis 1997); VA. CODE § 43-70 (1992); WASH. REV. CODE § 60.04.161 (1992); WIS. STAT. § 779.08 (Lexis-Nexis 2005); WYO. STAT. § 29-1-501 (2010); *cf.* COLO. REV. STAT. § 38-22-131 (2011) (owner of any legal or beneficial interest in property); GA. CODE ANN. § 44-14-364 (2012) (owner or contractor employed to improve the property); KAN. STAT. ANN. § 60-1110 (Lexis-Nexis 2005) (payment bond by owner or contractor); ME. REV. STAT. tit. 10, § 3263 (Lexis-Nexis 2005); MONT. CODE ANN. § 71.3.551 (Lexis-Nexis 2007) (contracting owner of any interest in such property); N.H. REV. STAT. § 511:37 (Lexis); N.M. STAT. § 48-2-7 (Michie 1953); N.Y. LIEN LAW § 19 (N.Y. Consol. Laws Serv. 2011) (owner or contractor); R.I. GEN. LAWS § 34-28-17 (2008).

27. *Henry F. Raab*, 438 A.2d 834.

28. *See, e.g.*, Deltona Corp. v. Indian Palms, Inc., 323 So. 2d 282 (Fla. Dist. Ct. App. 1975) (owner's successor in interest may contest lien claim).

liability.[29] Once the lien discharge bond is provided to remove the property from being subject to the lien, the lien claim should proceed against the principal and surety on the bond.[30] Accordingly, a property owner, in his capacity as such, may not be a necessary or proper party to litigation on a lien discharge bond.[31] On the other hand, the claimant may maintain actions against the owner if the owner is the principal on the bond or if the owner is in privity with the lien claimant.[32] If no privity exists and the owner is not the bond principal, the property owner is usually entitled to be dismissed from the action due to the posting of the lien discharge bond.[33] The lien claimant's failure or refusal to dismiss the owner or release the property after a lien discharge bond is filed may subject it to statutory damages, sanctions, or penalties.[34]

D. Effect of Posting Bond Prior to or Post Litigation

In some jurisdictions, the lien discharge bond is not valid unless it is filed and served before the lien claimant commences a foreclosure action.[35] In most jurisdictions, however, the lien discharge bond is effective in removing the lien claim from the property when executed and delivered or recorded, whether before or after the lien claimant commences a

---

29. *See, e.g.*, R.D. Reeder Lathing Co. v. Allen, 425 P.2d 785 (Cal. 1967). *But see* Soundwall Constr. Corp. v. Moncarol Constr. Corp., 290 N.Y.S.2d 363 (Sup. Ct. 1968).
30. *See, e.g.*, Winick v. Cnty. Sanitation Dist. 2, 230 Cal. Rptr. 289 (Cal. Ct. App. 1986); *see also* Servewell Plumbing, LLC v. Summit Contractors, Inc., 210 S.W.3d 101 (Ark. 2005).
31. *See, e.g.*, Mesch v. Berry, 528 So. 2d 1250 (Fla. Dist. Ct. App. 1988); Williams, Hatfield & Stoner, Inc. v. A&E Design, Inc., 538 So. 2d 505 (Fla. Dist. Ct. App. 1989); George W. Kane, Inc. v. Nuscope, Inc., 416 S.E.2d 701 (Va. 1992). *But see* Martirano Constr. Corp. v. Briar Contracting Corp., 481 N.Y.S.2d 105 (App. Div. 1984), *and compare with* Maverick Constr. Servs., LLC v. Desford Partners, LLC, 971 N.Y.S.2d 72, 72 (Sup. Ct. 2013).
32. *See, e.g.*, Hutnick v. U.S. Fid. & Guar. Co., 763 P.2d 1362 (Cal. 1988).
33. *See, e.g.*, Frank Curren Lumber Co. v. Eleven Co, 271 Cal. App. 2d 175 (Cal. Ct. App. 1969).
34. *See* Hatch Cos. Contracting, Inc. v. Arizona Bank, 826 P.2d 1179 (Ariz. Ct. App. 1992); *Winick*, 230 Cal. Rptr. 289.
35. *See* James Talcott Constr. v. P&D Land Enters., 862 P.2d 395 (Mont. 1993).

foreclosure action.[36] On the other hand, whether the lien release bond is executed before or after a foreclosure action is commenced may affect the rights and defenses of the parties. For example, some courts find the lien claimant's further compliance with notice and other procedural obligations are waived if the bond was posted before the lien claimant commenced an action to enforce the lien.[37] Where the bond is filed and served post litigation, the lien claimant may be able to reach the bond by amending his or her pleadings or by motion.[38]

E. Scope of the Surety's Liability

Consistent with the bond's purpose, the scope of the surety's liability under lien discharge bonds is usually commensurate with a property owner's liability under mechanic's lien statutes.[39] Where the mechanic's lien is invalid for any reason, the bond may be held to secure nothing.[40] Thus, lien discharge bonds usually cover only claims from persons entitled to be claimants under the applicable mechanic's lien statutes.[41] Further, except where courts find them waived, the claimant must follow all notice requirements and other technical or procedural requirements

---

36. See, for example, California Civil Code section 8424(c), which provides: "The bond may be recorded either before or after commencement of an action to enforce the lien. On recordation of the bond, the real property is released from the claim of lien and from any action to enforce it."
37. *See, e.g.*, Burgess v. Travelers Indem. Co., 363 S.E.2d 308 (Ga. Ct. App. 1988).
38. *See* Ohio Plate Glass Co. v. Paskin, 4 Ohio Misc. 136 (Ohio Ct. Com. Pl. 1965); Grade-Way Constr. Co. v. Golden Eagle Ins. Co., 16 Cal. Rptr. 2d 649 (Cal. Ct. App. 1993).
39. *See, e.g.*, Royster Constr. Co. v. Urb. W. Communities, 47 Cal. Rptr. 2d 684 (Cal. App. Dep't Super. Ct. 1995); Camputaro v. Stuart Hardwood Corp., 429 A.2d 796, 798 (Conn. 1980) ("rights on the bond can rise no higher than those acquired under the underlying mechanic's lien for which the bond is merely a substitute"); Jungbert v. Marret, 231 S.W.2d 84 (Ky. 1950); J.L. Hart Lumber Co. v. Reid, 220 N.W. 717 (Mich. 1928); Sexauer & Lemke v. Luke A. Burke & Sons Co., 127 N.E. 329 (N.Y. 1920).
40. *See, e.g.*, Hartlin v. Cody, 134 A.2d 245 (Conn. 1957), *superseded by statute on other grounds*, New England Sav. Bank v. Meadow Lakes Realty Co., 706 A.2d 465 (Conn. 1998); Bell & Zajicek, Inc. v. Heyward-Robinson Co., 182 A.2d 339 (Conn. Super. Ct. 1962); *Jungbert*, 231 S.W.2d 84.
41. *See infra* discussion in Part II.A.1, on defenses.

under the mechanic's lien statutes to properly perfect a claim against a lien discharge bond.[42] Once the claimant establishes a right to claim under the mechanic's lien statute, the lien discharge bond generally covers no greater damages than those recoverable under the mechanic's lien statutes and no claims other than mechanic's lien claims.[43]

II. The Surety's Defenses

A number of defenses are available to sureties on lien discharge bonds. The surety's defenses can be categorized as (1) defenses arising from the mechanic's lien statutes due to defects in the lien claim; (2) substantive defenses to the claim; (3) the statute of limitations; (4) the lien claimants' waiver or release of the lien claim; and (5) certain suretyship defenses.

A. *Defects in Lien Claim*

Mechanic's lien statutes are subject to certain rules of judicial construction. Some courts strictly construe the mechanic's lien statutes in recognition of the fact that mechanic's liens are in derogation of common law.[44] Many courts, however, require only reasonable compliance with standing and

---

42. *See infra* discussion in Part II.A.2, on defenses.
43. *See, e.g.*, *Royster Constr. Co.*, 47 Cal. Rptr. 2d 684; Richter Plumbing & Heating, Inc. v. Rademacher 729 P.2d 1009, 1012 (Colo. Ct. App.) (1986); Indep. Tr. Corp. v. Stan Miller, Inc., 796 P.2d 483, 490 (Colo. 1990) (contractual late charges denied); Royal Ins. Co. of Am. v. Citizens Devs. of Oneonta, Inc., 606 N.Y.S.2d 428 (App. Div. 1994) (judgment based upon stipulation—not on lien claim—is not a proper basis for recovery on lien discharge bond).
44. *See, e.g.*, Hartford Accident & Indem. Co. v. Am. Country Clubs, Inc., 353 So. 2d 1147 (Ala. 1977); First Colored Cumberland Presbyterian Church v. W.D. Wood Lumber Co., 88 So. 433 (Ala. 1921); Egan-Ryan Mech. Co. v. Cardon Meadows Dev. Corp., 818 P.2d 146 (Ariz. Ct. App. 1991); *Richter Plumbing & Heating, Inc.*, 729 P.2d at 1012; Mullen Lumber Co. v. Lore, 537 N.E.2d 123 (Mass. 1989) (lien statutes given strict construction). *But see* S.K. Drywall, Inc. v. Devs. Fin. Corp., 819 P.2d 931 (Ariz. 1991); *New England Sav. Bank*, 706 A.2d 465 (lien statutes create rights in derogation of common law, but are liberally construed in order to meet the legislature's remedial purpose). *See generally* 1 FIFTY STATE CONSTRUCTION LIEN AND BOND LAW, *supra* note 8; 2 FIFTY STATE CONSTRUCTION LIEN AND BOND LAW, *supra* note 8.

notice requirements in mechanic's lien statutes.[45] Once a lien claimant establishes a right to the lien, courts typically construe the lien claimant's rights liberally to accomplish the remedial purpose of mechanic's lien statutes.[46] Functionally, these rules of construction provide defenses to the lien discharge bond surety based upon defects in the lien claim, including the lien claimant's failure (1) to meet the standing requirements of the lien statute; (2) to meet the notice requirements of the lien statute; and (3) to perfect the lien claim. The surety may also defend the lien claim, when applicable, due to the claimant's failure to maintain licensing requirements.

1. Failure to Meet Standing Requirements of Lien Statute

Mechanic's lien statutes protect only those persons included within the statute for the type of work or services described in the statute.[47]

---

45. *See* 2 FIFTY STATE CONSTRUCTION LIEN AND BOND LAW, *supra* note 8. Also, one court in Arizona harmonized that jurisdiction's rules as follows:

> Arizona case law has frequently repeated the principle that the statutory requirements for mechanic's and materialmen's liens must be strictly followed to perfect a lien. A parallel line of Arizona cases has enunciated the complementary principle that, because the purpose of the mechanic's and materialmen's lien statutes is to protect laborers and materialmen who enhance the value of other persons' property, the statutes are remedial and must be liberally construed. This court has harmonized these two principles as follows: "[T]he steps required by A.R.S. § 33-993 to impose the lien must be followed but in determining what these steps are the court will give the words a meaning which is reasonable, consistent with all the language used, and conducive to the purpose to be accomplished by the enactment of the statute. Thus, substantial compliance not inconsistent with the legislative purpose is sufficient."

MLM Constr. Co., Inc. v. Pace Corp., 836 P.2d 439, 442 (Ariz. Ct. App. 1992) (citations omitted).

46. *See* 2 FIFTY STATE CONSTRUCTION LIEN AND BOND LAW, *supra* note 8; Bell & Zajicek, Inc. v. Heyward-Robinson Co., 182 A.2d 339 (Conn. Super. Ct. 1962).

47. Typically, mechanic's lien statutes protect only those persons directly improving property. *See, e.g.*, Primo-Team, Inc. v. Blake Constr. Co., 4 Cal. Rptr. 2d 701 (Cal. Ct. App. 1992). In *Primo-Team*, the court considered a standing argument against a payment bond, which referred to the mechanic's lien statute, by a claimant who helped a subcontractor

By extension, those failing to meet the standing requirements under mechanic's lien statutes are typically not entitled to recover from mechanic's lien discharge bonds.[48] For example, if no mechanic's lien lies for a grader whose work was never incorporated into the raising, removal, or repair of any building, then neither the principal nor surety on the lien discharge bond is liable for the grader's claim.[49] Similarly, if the claimant provided items that were deemed personal property and the statute only allows claims for items that become fixtures on the property, the lien discharge bond is not liable for the claim.[50] Even where

---

assemble a work force. The claimant argued that its services were "necessary" for the project, giving it standing under the lien statute. Rejecting the argument, the court reasoned as follows:

> It is readily apparent that Primo's labor did not directly "improve property of another and increase its value." Primo's labor instead only facilitated and enabled another party (R.J.) to perform such work. While Primo's contributions were beneficial to R.J. and its workers, enabling them to work toward enhancement of the property's value, Primo appears no different from any other entity or person whose "necessary" services provide support solely to the work force and/or the employer rather than the work of improvement itself. Thus, for example, even though providing food to a work force is undoubtedly "necessary" for the workers to labor on the work of improvement, the cook may not claim a mechanic's lien for his services.

Id. at 707 (citations omitted).

48. *See, e.g.*, Camputaro v. Stuart Hardwood Corp., 429 A.2d 796 (Conn. 1980); Resnick Devs., Inc. v. Clerici, Inc., 340 So. 2d 1194 (Fla. Dist. Ct. App. 1976) (where lower tier claimant lacked standing to assert mechanic's lien, owner's placement of lien discharge bond did not create right to assert lien against the bond); Sexauer & Lemke v. Luke A. Burke & Sons Co., 127 N.E. 329 (N.Y. 1920) (where no right to lien exists, there is no liability on lien discharge bond).

49. *See, e.g.*, *Camputaro*, 429 A.2d at 798.

50. *See, e.g.*, Hartlin v. Cody, 134 A.2d 245 (Conn. 1957), *superseded by statute on other grounds*, New England Sav. Bank v. Meadow Lakes Realty Co., 706 A.2d 465 (Conn. 1998).

the person otherwise qualifies for protection under the lien statute, the lien discharge bond will not cover claims other than the mechanic's lien claim.[51]

2. Failure to Meet Notice Requirements of Lien Statute

Mechanic's lien statutes often include notice requirements as preconditions to enforcement of the lien claim.[52] Notice requirements vary under the mechanic's lien statutes for each state. However, some form of written notice must usually be provided to the property owner and a written statement of the lien claim must generally be recorded against the real property.[53] The lien claimant's failure to comply with the notice requirements of the lien law is a defense to the mechanic's lien claim.[54] By extension, failure to comply with the notice provisions also constitutes a defense available to the lien discharge bond surety.[55] For example, where a lien claimant failed to provide the requisite sworn oath concerning the validity of the lien claim in the notice provided to the property owner,

---

51. *See, e.g.*, Royal Ins. Co. of Am. v. Citizens Devs. of Oneonta, Inc., 606 N.Y.S.2d 428 (App. Div. 1994).
52. *See generally* 1 Fifty State Construction Lien and Bond Law, *supra* note 8; 2 Fifty State Construction Lien and Bond Law, *supra* note 8.
53. *See generally* 1 Fifty State Construction Lien and Bond Law, *supra* note 8; 2 Fifty State Construction Lien and Bond Law, *supra* note 8.
54. *See generally* 1 Fifty State Construction Lien and Bond Law, *supra* note 8; 2 Fifty State Construction Lien and Bond Law, *supra* note 8.
55. *See, e.g.*, Bell & Zajicek, Inc. v. Heyward-Robinson Co., 182 A.2d 339 (Conn. Super. Ct. 1962); Valentine Lumber & Supply Co. v. Thibeault, 146 N.E.2d 349 (Mass. 1957) (technical lien requirements apply notwithstanding posting of lien discharge bond), *but see* City Elec. Supply Co. v. Arch Ins. Co., 119 N.E.3d 735, 743 (Mass. 2019); *Matter of* Listle/Shreeves Corp., 20 B.R. 421 (Bankr. M.D. Fla. 1982); Des Lauriers Metal Prods. Co. v. Rhodes, 217 N.W. 922 (Mich. 1928). *But see* Burgess v.

the claim fails against the lien discharge bond.[56] Additionally, where the lien notice contains defects in the description of the property or services related to the lien, courts have declined to allow the claim against the lien discharge bond.[57] Even in jurisdictions where substantial compliance suffices,[58] lien claimants who have not substantially complied with notice requirements are not entitled to enforce a lien claim against the lien discharge bond.[59]

Travelers Indemnity Co., 363 S.E.2d 308 (Ga. Ct. App. 1988), where the court waived the notice requirements after the lien discharge bond was posted, reasoning:

> In this case, construing OCGA § 44-14-361.1(a)(3) to mean that the notice designed to protect persons interested in the real estate against which the lien was claimed is a necessary precondition to a suit on a bond, where the real estate can no longer be affected, is not only "wholly unreasonable," but "futile and useless" as well, and we decline to so interpret the statute. . . . [¶] We hold that, under the circumstances presented here, appellant's failure to file the notice required under [the mechanic's lien statute] was not a bar to a recovery in a suit against appellee on the bond . . . .

Id. at 309.

56. *See, e.g.*, *Bell & Zajicek, Inc.*, 182 A.2d 339; *Valentine Lumber & Supply Co.*, 146 N.E.2d 349 (*questioned in City Elec. Supply Co.*, 119 N.E.3d 735, 743). *But see* Bob Eldridge Constr. Co., Inc. v. Pioneer Materials, Inc., 684 P.2d 355 (Kan. 1984) (interpreting Kansas's payment bond/lien discharge bond statute, holding lien claimant need not satisfy lien statute requirements once bond is received, provided lien claimant can prove that it could have done so).
57. *See, e.g.*, New England Sav. Bank v. Meadow Lakes Realty Co., 706 A.2d 465 (Conn. 1998).
58. *See, e.g.*, Egan-Ryan Mech. Co. v. Cardon Meadows Dev. Corp., 818 P.2d 146 (Ariz. Ct. App. 1991); MLM Constr. Co., Inc. v. Pace Corp., 836 P.2d 439 (Ariz. Ct. App. 1992). *See also* 1 FIFTY STATE CONSTRUCTION LIEN AND BOND LAW, *supra* note 8; 2 FIFTY STATE CONSTRUCTION LIEN AND BOND LAW, *supra* note 8.
59. *See, e.g.*, *MLM Constr. Co.*, 836 P.2d 439.

3. Failure to Perfect the Lien Claim[60]

Mechanic's lien statutes require claimants to perfect their lien claims by filing a foreclosure suit within stated time periods.[61] Generally, where the lien discharge bond is filed after the claimant commences a lien foreclosure action, the lien claimant must have filed its action to foreclose the lien within the time provided by statute and its failure to do so is a defense available to the surety.[62] However, if the bond is posted before the mechanic's lien claimant files suit on the lien claim and the lien claimant is, thereby, precluded from suing to foreclose the lien on the property, the surety may be precluded from defending the claim on the grounds that the claimant did not commence a timely foreclosure suit against the property.[63] On the other hand, the surety may have a defense based upon

---

60. In some states, the time to foreclose the lien and the time to sue on a lien discharge bond are the same. *See, e.g.*, ALA. CODE § 35.-11-233; ARK. CODE ANN. § 18-44.-119 (2005); FLA. STAT. ch. 713.24. Where the time to foreclose and the time to sue on the bond are not the same, however, a distinction should be made between a surety's defense based upon the claimant's failure to perfect the lien claim and one based upon the statute of limitations. The statute of limitations defense on the lien discharge bond claim applies when the lien claimant fails to sue the surety within the applicable period, and is discussed below in this section.
61. *See, e.g.*, CAL. CIV. CODE § 8460 (Deering 2012); Koudmani v. Ogle Enters., 55 Cal. Rptr. 2d 330 (Cal. Ct. App. 1996) (timely commencement of action to foreclose mechanic's lien is substantive provision of law and must be established to enforce lien claim); Automatic Sprinkler Corp. v. S. Cal. Edison Co., 266 Cal. Rptr. 662 (Cal. Ct. App. 1989).
62. *See, e.g.*, Corry Constr. Co., Inc. v. Hector Constr. Cos., Inc., 363 So. 2d 1125 (Fla. Dist. Ct. App. 1978); Hensel v. Metro. Cas. Ins. Co. of N.Y., 262 N.Y.S. 675 (App. Div. 1933).
63. *See, e.g.*, Norden Elec. v. Ideal Elec. Supply, 546 N.Y.S.2d 409 (App. Div. 1989) (construing Connecticut law). *Compare Hensel*, 262 N.Y.S. 675 (New York maintains the fiction of lien discharge bond action as being against the property. In this case, after the general contractor filed a lien discharge bond, the subcontractor filed an action on "contract" against the general contractor and the lien discharge bond. In the interim, the limitations period for filing an action to foreclose the lien expired. The court held that the subcontractor failed to foreclose the lien against the owner and the lien discharge bond's filing did not obviate its obligation to do so. Therefore, the claim was untimely.); *see, e.g.*, New Age Gen.

the statute of limitations if the claimant fails to file a timely suit against the surety bond.[64]

4. Failure to Maintain Licensing Requirements

Whenever a contractor, subcontractor, or other person is required to be licensed by statute for a particular business or profession,[65] most licensing statutes, or courts interpreting the statutes, also prohibit unlicensed persons from maintaining actions to collect money for those services.[66] The licensing statutes sometimes require persons subject to

---

Contracting v. 1882 Third LLC, 2016 NY Slip Op. 30888(U) ¶ 3 (Sup. Ct. 2016).

64. *See infra* Part II.B.1, discussing statutes of limitations; Stonepecker, Inc. v. Shepherd Constr. Co., Inc., 373 S.E.2d 295 (Ga. Ct. App. 1988).

65. *See, e.g.*, ALA. CODE §§ 34-8-1 to 34-8-28 (Michie 2009); ALASKA STAT. § 08.18.011 *et seq.* (2003); ARIZ. REV. STAT. § 32-1121 *et seq.*; ARK. CODE ANN. § 17-25-301 *et seq.* (2019); CAL. BUS. & PROF. CODE §§ 7000–7199 (Deering 2021); CONN. GEN. STAT. § 20-341 (Lexis-Nexis 2014); DEL. CODE ANN. tit. 30, §§ 2501–2503; FLA. STAT. ch. 489.101 *et seq.* (Lexis-Nexis 2021); GA. CODE ANN. §§ 43-41-1 to 43-41-17 (2004); HAW. REV. STAT. § 441-1 *et seq.* (Michie 1985); IDAHO CODE § 54-5201 *et seq.* (2005); IOWA CODE § 105.10 (Lexis-Nexis 2021); LA. REV. STAT. ANN. § 37:2150 *et seq.* (Lexis-Nexis 1989); MD. CODE ANN., BUS. REG. § 17-602 (Michie 1993); MICH. COMP. LAWS §§ 339.2401–.2412 (2020); MINN. STAT. § 326B.805 (Lexis-Nexis 2010); MISS. CODE ANN. § 31-3-15 *et seq.* (1972); NEV. REV. STAT. § 624.700 *et seq.* (1999); N.M. STAT. ANN. §§ 60-13-12, 60-13-30 *et seq.* (Michie 1989); N.C. GEN. STAT. § 87-1 *et seq.* (2011); N.D. CENT. CODE § 43-07-01 *et seq.* (2019); OR. REV. STAT. § 701.026 *et seq.* (Lexis-Nexis 2021); R.I. GEN. LAWS § 5-65-1 *et seq.* (2019); S.C. CODE ANN. § 40-11-10 *et seq.* (Lexis-Nexis 2005); TENN. CODE ANN. § 62-6-101 *et seq.* (1994); UTAH CODE ANN. § 58-55-301 *et seq.* (2017); VA. CODE ANN. § 54.1-1100 *et seq.* (2019); WASH. REV. CODE § 18.27.010 *et seq.* (2015); W. VA. CODE § 21-11-1 *et seq.* (Michie 2021).

66. *See, e.g.*, ALASKA STAT. § 08.18.151 (2003); ARIZ. REV. STAT. § 33-981(C), (G) (Lexis-Nexis 1998); CAL. BUS. & PROF. CODE § 7031 (Deering 2021); FLA. STAT. ch. 713.02(7) (Lexis-Nexis 2007); GA. CODE ANN. § 43-41-17(b) (2008); HAW. REV. STAT. § 444-22 (Michie 1969); Butler v. Obayashi, 785 P.2d 1324 (Haw. 1990). *Cf.* U.S. Pipelining Ltd. Liab. Co. v. Johnson Controls, Inc., No. 16-00132 HG-RLP, 2016 U.S. Dist. LEXIS 150767, at *23 (D. Haw. Oct. 31, 2016); IDAHO CODE

the licensing requirements to affirmatively plead, and prove if disputed, maintenance of the license to support their claim.[67] Where applicable, failure to maintain a license often constitutes a defense to the lien claim.[68] Likewise, the surety on a lien discharge bond is usually entitled to defend the claim on the basis of the lien claimant's failure to maintain its licensing requirements.[69]

B. Substantive Defenses

The lien discharge bond surety is generally entitled to present its principal's defenses in any action on the bond.[70] In addition, the principal and surety on the bond may usually assert any and all substantive defenses available to the owner, general contractor, and lower tier contractors.[71] Substantive defenses may include, inter alia, payment, claimant-caused delay damages, or defective materials or workmanship.[72]

---

§ 54-5208 (2005); NEV. REV. STAT. ANN. § 108.222(2) (2005); N.M. STAT. ANN. § 60-13-30 (Michie 1977). *See also*, *generally*, THE LAW OF PAYMENT BONDS 279–82 (Kevin H. Lybeck & H. Bruce Shreves eds., 1998).

67. *See, e.g.*, CAL. BUS. & PROF. CODE § 7031(a); *see generally* THE LAW OF PAYMENT BONDS (Wayne Lambert et al. eds., 2d ed. 2011); 1 FIFTY STATE CONSTRUCTION LIEN AND BOND LAW, *supra* note 8; 2 FIFTY STATE CONSTRUCTION LIEN AND BOND LAW, *supra* note 8.
68. *See, e.g.*, Fillmore v. Irvine, 194 Cal. Rptr. 319 (Cal. Ct. App. 1983); *see generally* THE LAW OF PAYMENT BONDS, *supra* note 67; 1 FIFTY STATE CONSTRUCTION LIEN AND BOND LAW, *supra* note 8; 2 FIFTY STATE CONSTRUCTION LIEN AND BOND LAW, *supra* note 8.
69. *See, e.g.*, Blake Elec. Contracting Co., Inc. v. Paschall, 635 N.Y.S.2d 205 (App. Div. 1995).
70. *See, e.g.*, Apex Supply Co. v. Com. Union Ins. Co., 237 S.E.2d 649 (Ga. Ct. App. 1977); Des Lauriers Metal Prods. Co. v. Rhodes, 217 N.W. 922 (Mich. 1928).
71. *See, e.g.*, M. Shapiro & Son, Inc. v. Yates Constr. Co., 231 S.E.2d 497 (Ga. Ct. App. 1976) (replacement contractor, as principal, and surety on lien discharge bond may defend subcontractor's lien claim based upon defaulted general contractor and owner's defenses even where defaulted general contractor gave consent judgment to claimant).
72. For examples under California law, see generally *California Mechanics Liens and Related Construction Remedies* (4th ed. 2020).

1. Statute of Limitations

Claimants and defendants have heavily litigated statute of limitations defenses on lien discharge bonds and courts have not been consistent in the results. Consider the case where the lien claimant provides all notices prior to recording the lien, records the lien against the property, and is provided with a lien discharge bond days before it must file suit to perfect the lien. Must the claimant file suit against the principal and surety on the bond within the days remaining on the statute of limitations for the lien, or may it file suit against the bond within the longer limitations period applicable to contracts, instruments, or bonds? Alternatively, what if the lien is properly perfected (i.e., suit was timely filed) and the bond is then provided (other than within the action)? Must the claimant amend the pleadings to add the claim against the bond and, if so, what statute of limitations period applies to the added cause of action or parties, if any?

Courts have struggled with these questions and there does not appear to be a general rule of law that governs. Unlike other surety bond claims where, unless the bond or a specific statute provides otherwise, an action against a surety must generally be commenced within the time applicable to the bonded obligation (i.e., measured from when the cause of action accrues against the principal),[73] courts apparently do not apply this rule to lien discharge bonds. While some statutes provide a specific limitations period,[74] the California Supreme Court distinguished the application of California's statute of limitations for lien discharge bonds when the bond was provided post litigation.[75] As explained in the following section, in

---

73. *See, e.g.*, CAL. CIV. CODE § 2807; Winick Corp. v. Gen. Ins. Co., 231 Cal. Rptr. 606 (Cal. Ct. App. 1986) (analyzing accrual of an action against a stop notice release bond); Bernard v. Ohio Cas., 339 S.E.2d 20 (N.C. Ct. App. 1986) (analyzing accrual of action on motor vehicle bond).

74. See, for example, California Civil Code section 8424(d) (Deering 2012), which provides:

> A person that obtains and records a release bond shall give notice to the claimant. . . . Failure to give the notice required by this section does not affect the validity of the bond, but the statute of limitations for an action on the bond is tolled until notice is given.

See also River Dock & Pile, Inc. v. Ins. Co. of N. Am., 747 A.2d 1060 (Conn. App. Ct. 2000).

75. *See* Hutnick v. U.S. Fid. & Guar. Co., 763 P.2d 1362 (Cal. 1988) (holding that CAL. CIV. CODE § 3144.5 (repealed July 1, 2012; replaced with

general, courts vary in applying different rules depending on whether the bond was posted before or after the date of the lien foreclosure action.

2. Bond Provided Prior to Suit

If the lien discharge bond was posted and served upon the claimant prior to litigation, the claimant's limitations period for filing suit on the bond may be controlled under the statute for enforcing a mechanic's lien[76] or the specific statute relating to the lien discharge bond. If the mechanic's lien statutes do not clearly control the lien discharge bond action, however, some courts have extended the limitations period to the longer time for other claims against a bond.[77]

3. Bond Provided After Suit Commenced

Where the bond is posted after the foreclosure action is filed, courts have found creative ways to allow the claimant to reach the bond. For instance, courts have calculated the limitations period starting at the date of the claimant's judgment.[78] Courts have also held that, since the bond

---

CAL. CIV. CODE § 8424), quoted above, is not applicable if the bond was provided after the lien foreclosure action is commenced).

76. *See, e.g.*, Gen. Guar. Ins. Co. v. Sunrise Nursing Homes, Inc., 326 So. 2d 446 (Fla. Dist. Ct. App. 1976); Stonepecker, Inc. v. Shepherd Constr. Co., Inc., 373 S.E.2d 295 (Ga. Ct. App. 1988); Brunet v. Justice, 264 So. 2d 743 (La. Ct. App. 1972) (private works lien discharge bond); D & J Constr. Co., Inc. v. Mid-Continent Stone Co., Inc., 571 So. 2d 762 (La. Ct. App. 1990) (public works lien discharge bond).

77. *See, e.g.*, CAL. CIV. CODE § 8424 (Deering 2012) (applying only when claimant has yet to file suit on lien claim); *Hutnick*, 763 P.2d 1362; *River Dock & Pile, Inc.* 747 A.2d 1060. *See, e.g.*, Bob Eldridge Constr. Co., Inc. v. Pioneer Materials, Inc., 684 P.2d 355 (Kan. 1984) (claimant has five years under Kansas statute relating to actions against bonds to file lawsuit against lien discharge bond given before claimant commenced suit); *Winick Corp.*, 231 Cal. Rptr. 606 (analyzing accrual of an action against a stop notice release bond and providing the claimant with three years under the statute relating to obligations created by statute).

78. *See, e.g.*, George v. Hartford Accident & Indem. Co., 412 S.E.2d 43 (N.C. 1992); *Hutnick*, 763 P.2d 1362 (limitations period relating to lien discharge bond does not apply when the bond was executed after the claimant commenced a timely lien foreclosure action and lien claimant may obtain recovery against the surety without having to plead a new

substitutes for the real property, the claimant need not bring a further action against the bond to recover from it, but may do so procedurally by motion upon obtaining a final judgment.[79] Finally, some courts have held that no statute of limitations applies at all to the lien discharge bond if a lien foreclosure suit was timely filed, reasoning that the lien statutes' requirements are fully met if an action on the lien is timely commenced.[80]

4. Waiver or Release of Lien Claim

In many states, a lien claimant's advance waiver of lien rights is invalid by statute or case law.[81] Further, some states only allow mechanic's lien claims to be waived if the parties use statutory forms or specific statutory language.[82] Courts interpret lien waivers and releases liberally in favor of the lien claimant.[83] Nonetheless, some courts recognize the

---

cause of action or comply with any additional suit limitations period); Grawer Bear Constr. Corp. v. Bellino Constr. Co., Inc., 600 N.Y.S.2d 254 (App. Div. 1993) (holding that claimant may await judgment on lien claim before pursuing surety on lien discharge bond and indirectly implying that limitations period on claim against surety commences then).

79. *See, e.g.*, Standard Accident Ins. Co. v. Lloyd, 157 A. 657 (N.J. 1931) (interpreting version of repealed mechanic's lien law); Grade-Way Constr. Co. v. Golden Eagle Ins. Co., 16 Cal. Rptr. 2d 649 (Cal. Ct. App. 1993).

80. Dennis Elec., Inc. v. U.S. Fid. & Guar. Co., 269 Cal. Rptr. 26 (Cal. Ct. App. 1990) (surety on lien discharge bond is successor to owner on lien foreclosure action and claimant not subject to statute of limitations on lien discharge bond where bond was procured after lien claimant filed a timely lien foreclosure action).

81. *See, e.g.*, Ariz. Rev. Stat. § 33-1008; Cal. Civ. Code §§ 8122, 8124, 8126, 8128, 8130, 8132, 8134, 8136, 8138 (Deering 2012); Am. Cas. Co. v. Coastal Drill Co., 542 So. 2d 957 (Fla. 1989); Ga. Code Ann. § 44-14-366 (2021); Md. Code Ann., Real Prop. § 9-113(a) (Michie 1995); Minn. Stat. § 337.10 (Lexis-Nexis 2019); N.J. Stat. Ann. § 2A:44A-38 (Lexis-Nexis 1993) (*see also* Thomas Grp., Inc. v. Wharton Senior Citizen Hous., Inc., 750 A.2d 743 (N.J. 2000)).

82. *See, e.g.*, Ariz. Rev. Stat. § 33-1008; Cal. Civ. Code §§ 8122, 8124, 8126, 8128, 8130, 8132, 8134, 8136, 8138 (Deering 2012); Ga. Code Ann. § 44-14-366 (2021).

83. *See, e.g.*, United Metro Materials, Inc. v. Pena Blanca Props., LLC, 4 P.3d 1022 (Ariz. Ct. App. 2000); Twin Island Dev. Corp. v. Winchester, 512 A.2d 319, 323 (Me. 1986); Giles & Ransome, Inc. v. First Nat'l Realty Corp., 238 Md. 203 (1965).

lien claimant's waiver or release of the lien claim as a defense available to the lien discharge bond surety,[84] but the defense may be limited to the extent the person seeking to enforce the lien waiver or release relied upon the waiver or release to its detriment.[85] Even where advance waivers of lien rights are not allowed, a creditor may be able to have a claimant subordinate a lien claim to a lender under a subordination agreement,[86] all of which may implicate the interests of the surety issuing the lien release bond.

C. Suretyship Defenses

Due to their position as secondary or conditional obligors, sureties often enjoy certain special "suretyship" defenses. Suretyship defenses include the obligee's alteration of the bonded obligation, the obligee's impairment of security or collateral, the obligee's release or discharge of the principal, and the obligee's concealment or misrepresentation in procuring the bond.[87] Because the lien discharge bond is given to secure against a potential judgment in the context of a disputed claim, many of the suretyship defenses may not often apply. For instance, the surety may not generally assert an impairment of collateral defense when the lien discharge bond claimant accepts its bond even though the acceptance of the bond removes the lien from the real property at issue.[88] Although that

---

84. *See, e.g.*, Santa Clara Land Title Co. v. Nowack & Assoc., 277 Cal. Rptr. 497 (Cal. Ct. App. 1991) (*cf.* Solit v. Tokai Bank, Ltd., 81 Cal. Rptr. 2d 243 (Cal. Ct. App. 1999)); Beacon Constr. Co., Inc. v. Matco Elec. Co., Inc., 521 F.2d 392 (2d Cir. 1975).
85. *See, e.g.*, AMFAC Distrib. Corp. v. J.B. Contractors, Inc., 703 P.2d 566 (Ariz. Ct. App. 1985); Mid-West Eng'g & Constr. Co. v. Campagna, 397 S.W.2d 616 (Mo. 1965); George M. Morris Constr. Co. v. Four Seasons Motor Inn, Inc., 567 P.2d 965 (N.M. 1977).
86. *See, e.g.*, Moorefield Constr., Inc. v. Invervest-Mortgage Inv. Co., 178 Cal. Rptr. 3d 709 (Cal. Ct. App. 2014). N.B., subordination agreements can be complex in their impact on lien rights. *See, e.g.*, APCO Constr. v. Eighth Jud. Dist. Court (*In re* Manhattan W. Mechanic's Lien Litig.), 359 P.3d 125 (Nev. 2015).
87. *See generally* THE LAW OF PERFORMANCE BONDS (Lawrence R. Moelmann et al. eds., 3d ed. 2019).
88. *See, e.g.*, Union Indem. Co. of New Orleans v. Worthingstun, 123 So. 759 (Fla. 1929); *see also* S. Sur. Co. v. Hudsen, 160 P. 209 (Kan. 1916); Lindberger v. Zweifel, 262 P. 538 (Kan. 1928).

lien would otherwise be the claimant's "security" to which the surety would be subrogated, the surety's argument is contrary to the bond's purpose of freeing the property from the lien. Accordingly, as one might expect, little case law exists on suretyship defenses in the context of lien discharge bonds. Of note, however, there are a few cases holding that the surety is discharged if the lien claimant releases the bond principal, as distinguished from the claimant's release of the lien claim against the surety.[89]

1. Penal Sum as Limit of Surety's Liability

Consistent with the rule of law applicable to other surety bonds,[90] the surety's liability under a lien discharge bond is limited to the amount stated in the bond,[91] also known as the bond penalty or penal sum.[92] Therefore, a portion of the lien claimant's judgment may be unsecured if the judgment on the lien claim exceeds the penal sum of the lien discharge bond.[93] However, in some states the surety may be liable for costs in an action beyond the penal sum based upon its status as a party-litigant.[94]

---

89. *See, e.g.*, R.P. Richards, Inc. v. Chartered Constr. Corp., 99 Cal. Rptr. 2d 425 (Cal. Ct. App. 2000) (stop notice release bond); Brooks-Wright, Inc. v. Md. Cas. Co., 39 A.2d 446 (N.J. 1944); John N. Price & Sons v. Md. Cas. Co., 146 F.2d 807 (3rd Cir. 1945).
90. *See* 74 AM. JUR. 2D *Suretyship* § 165 (1974); *see also*, *e.g.*, Hartford Accident & Indem. Co. v. Indus. Accident Comm'n, 13 P.2d 699 (Cal. 1932) (employer's worker's compensation insurance bond); Lawrence Tractor Co. v. Carlisle Ins. Co., 249 Cal. Rptr. 150 (Cal. Ct. App. 1998) (common law bond securing obligation under subordination agreement).
91. *See, e.g.*, Aetna Cas. & Sur. Co. of Am. v. Buck, 594 So. 2d 280 (Fla. 1992); Williams, Hatfield & Stoner, Inc. v. A&E Design, Inc., 538 So. 2d 505 (Fla. Dist. Ct. App. 1989).
92. For a discussion wherein a court rejected a claimant's creative arguments for damages in excess of the penal sum see *In re Technology for Energy Corp.*, 140 B.R. 214 (Bankr. E.D. Tenn. 1992).
93. *See, e.g.*, *Buck*, 594 So. 2d at 283; Coppenbarger Homes, Inc. v. Williamson, 611 So. 2d 33 (Fla. Dist. Ct. App. 1993).
94. *See, e.g.*, Harris v. Nw. Nat'l Ins. Co., 8 Cal. Rptr. 2d 234 (Cal. Ct. App. 1992) (liability for court costs stems from status as party-litigant, and such costs may be awarded in excess of the penal sum of the bond).

2. Amended and Successive Liens

Significant mischief can occur when the lien discharge bond involves a lien claimant who records more than one lien on the same claim or amends the lien claim and the bond does not expressly or clearly refer to the operable and proper lien claim asserted in the pleadings.[95] Only a few statutes expressly allow for a lien to be amended.[96] Some amendments may only be made with leave of court,[97] for limited purposes,[98] or where the amendment does not increase the lien amount.[99] Although the statutes are silent as to amending a lien claim, some case law has addressed and allowed or rejected amended liens in certain circumstances, tending to allow the amendment as long as no prejudice results.[100] However, where the statutes are silent as to the ability of a claimant to amend a lien, some

---

95. *See, e.g.*, Cordeck Sales, Inc. v. Constr. Sys., Inc., 887 N.E.2d 474 (Ill. App. Ct. 2008) (in litigation with lender, court disallowed lien due to amendment, noting statute only allowed amended liens in claims against the owner); Romspen Mortg. Ltd. P'ship v. SB Winnetka, LLC, Case No. 19 C 5610, 2021 U.S. Dist. LEXIS 47318 (N.D. Ill. Mar. 13, 2021) (lien claimant recorded a lien, released it, then recorded a second lien causing litigation of its validity).
96. *See* COLO. REV. STAT. § 38-22-109(3); FLA. STAT. ch. 713.22(1); GA. CODE ANN. § 44-14-361.1(a)(3); IOWA CODE § 572.26; KAN. STAT. ANN. § 60-1105(b); MISS. CODE ANN. § 85-7-405(1)(e); NEV. REV. STAT. § 108.229; N.Y. LIEN LAW § 12-a(1).
97. *See, e.g.*, IOWA CODE § 572.26 (allowed only with leave of court); KAN. STAT. ANN. § 60-1105(b).
98. *See, e.g.*, GA. CODE ANN. § 44-14-361.1(a)(3) (to add the required oath in the notice).
99. *See, e.g.*, IOWA CODE § 572.26 (amendment with leave except as to the amount).
100. *See, e.g.*, Atl. Mill & Lumber Realty Co. v. Keefer, 20 A.2d 178 (Md. 1941) (amended lien found invalid because recorded after deadline for recording liens and without leave of court); *cf.* Real Estate & Improvement Co. v. Phillips, 45 A. 174 (Md. 1900) (finding a court order allowing a lien to be amended after the deadline to record liens to properly identify the owner as allowed, because the statute allows for amendments so long as the amount is not increased). *See also* MacQuesten Gen. Contracting, Inc. v. HCE, Inc., 296 F. Supp. 2d 437 (S.D.N.Y. 2003).

courts treat the amended lien the same as a new lien, requiring the lien claimant to meet all the rigors of filing an original lien.[101]

III. Subrogation, Contribution, Subsuretyship, and the Competing Obligations of Lien Discharge and Payment Bond Sureties

In addition to the surety's indemnity and reimbursement rights against its principal,[102] subrogation, contribution, and subsuretyship doctrines may provide the lien discharge bond surety with recovery rights or theories of shifting primary liability to other parties or sureties.

A. Subrogation

Generally, subrogation is a principle of equity entitling a surety who pays or performs under a bond to assert all of the principal's and all of the creditors' rights relating to the obligation.[103] Therefore, the owner's lien discharge bond surety, if it pays the lien claim, should arguably be subrogated to all the rights of its principal and the lien claimant, including a lower tier lien claimant's rights against, inter alia, the general contractor and its payment bond surety.[104] Conversely, a general contractor's payment bond surety that pays a lien claimant should arguably be subrogated to the lien claimant's rights to enforce a mechanic's lien claim against the owner's property or against the owner and, presumably, the surety on a lien discharge bond.[105] Because the purpose of the lien discharge bond is

---

101. *See, e.g.*, Big-D Constr. Corp. v. Simplot Phosphates, LLC, Case No. 2:16-CV-0242-SWS. 2017 U.S. Dist. LEXIS 155735 (Wyo. Dist. Ct. Feb. 16, 2017).

102. *See generally* The Law of Performance Bonds, *supra* note 87; The Law of Payment Bonds, *supra* note 67; Restatement (Third) of Suretyship and Guaranty 455–525 (E. Gallagher ed., 2d ed. 2000).

103. Restatement (Third) of Suretyship and Guaranty, *supra* note 102, at 419–53.

104. *See, e.g.*, Lackawanna Steel Constr. Co. v. Longacre Eng'g & Constr. Co., 270 N.Y.S. 864 (Sup. Ct. 1934) (allowing subrogation to funds in public owner's hands); *cf.* Alamar v. Dunbar Constr. Co., 270 N.Y.S. 773 (Sup. Ct. 1931).

105. *See, e.g.*, Golden Eagle Ins. Co. v. First Nationwide Fin. Corp., 31 Cal. Rptr. 2d 815 (Cal. Ct. App. 1994) (payment bond surety entitled to foreclose lien claimant's mechanic's liens against owner because owner had not fully paid surety's principal or surety on construction contract).

to free the property from the lien claim, however, the lien discharge bond surety may not generally assert a subrogation right to foreclose the lien claim against the property.[106]

B. Contribution and Subsuretyship

Contribution is the right of one cosurety to recover a share of its loss from another cosurety, so as to equalize the suretyship burden.[107] Contribution is the applicable equitable principle only when the same person serves as bond principal for two surety bonds that cover the same claim or loss.[108] Even then, it is not clear whether one or the other surety may be entitled to subsuretyship status.[109] In subsuretyship, one surety is deemed the "primary surety," and primarily liable for the claim, due to its relationship to the lien claimant or due to its principal's relationship to the other surety's principal.[110] For instance, on a lower tier supplier's claim, the subcontractor's payment bond is usually deemed primary to the general contractor's payment bond because, as between the general

---

106. *See, e.g.*, Union Indem. Co. of New Orleans v. Worthingstun, 123 So. 759 (Fla. 1929); *see also* S. Sur. Co. v. Hudsen, 160 P. 209 (Kan. 1916); Lindberger v. Zweifel, 262 P. 538 (Kan. 1928).
107. *See generally* Restatement (Third) of Suretyship and Guaranty §§ 55, 57 (1995); 74 Am. Jur. 2d *Suretyship* §§ 4, 5 (1974).
108. *See generally* 74 Am. Jur. 2d *Suretyship* §§ 4, 5 (1974); *accord* S. Sur. Co. v. Tessum, 228 N.W. 326 (Minn. 1929); Ind. Ins. Co. of N. Am. v. Am. Sur. Co., 268 N.Y.S. 203 (App. Div. 1933); *In re* Gen. Indem. Corp. of Am., 289 N.Y.S. 1046 (Sup. Ct. 1936); Fid. & Cas. Co. of N.Y. v. Am. Sur. Co. of N.Y., 169 A. 226 (Pa. 1933); Assets Realization Co. v. Am. Bonding Co., 102 N.E. 719 (Ohio 1913).
109. Consider the confusing and potentially conflicting scenarios possible under the Restatement (Third) of Suretyship and Guaranty section 53. Section 53(4)(a)(iii) holds one surety a subsurety where it reasonably believes that another's previously executed bond covers the claim. However, section 53(4)(c) would find the more specific bond provides primary coverage for the claim. *See, e.g.*, Sullivan v. Goodwin, 51 N.Y.S. 1000 (App. Div. 1898) (finding subsequently placed appeal bond acted as suretyship for previously placed lien discharge bond, which was primarily liable for the lien claimant's judgment).
110. 74 Am. Jur. 2d *Suretyship* § 4 (2022); Restatement (Third) of Suretyship and Guaranty §§ 5961 (1996).

contractor and the subcontractor, the subcontractor is primarily obligated to pay its sub-subcontractors and suppliers' claims.[111]

C. Lien Discharge Bond Versus Payment Bond

The equitable principles of subrogation, contribution, and subsuretyship may collide when a lien discharge bond and a payment bond cover the same lien claim.[112] Because principles of equity govern, the result in the cases often depends on the facts of the case, including the conduct of the sureties and the conduct of the principals, plus the exact nature of their competing obligations.[113]

For instance, consider the case of *Bear v. Standard Accident Insurance Co.*[114] In *Standard Accident*, the project was completed by the general contractor and final payment was pending. The prime contract

---

111. *See, e.g.*, A & P Sheet Metal Co., Inc. v. Edward Hanson, Inc., 357 A.2d 37 (N.J. Super. Ct. App. Div. 1976) (and cases cited therein); Lowe v. Albertazzie, 516 S.E.2d 258 (W. Va. 1999); Am. Cas. Co. of Reading v. Brezina, 295 F.2d 603 (8th Cir. 1961); Cont'l Cas. Co. v. Hartford Accident & Indem. Co., 52 Cal. Rptr. 533 (Cal. Ct. App. 1966); Mai Steel Serv., Inc. v. Blake Constr. Co., 981 F.2d 414 (9th Cir. 1992); Fin. Indem. Co. v. Steele & Sons, Inc., 403 So. 2d 600 (Fla. Dist. Ct. App. 1981); Argonaut Ins. Co. v. Com. Standard Ins. Co., 380 So. 2d 1066 (Fla. Dist. Ct. App. 1980); St. Paul Fire & Marine Ins. Co. v. Cent. Nat'l Ins. Co. of Omaha, 480 N.W.2d 681 (Minn. Ct. App. 1992); Menorah Nursing Home, Inc. v. Zukov, 548 N.Y.S.2d 702 (App. Div. 1989). However, equity may compel a contrary result. *See* Glens Falls Indem. Co. v. United States, 229 F.2d 370 (9th Cir. 1956) (subcontractor's supplier given judgment against prime contractor and prime's payment bond surety, prime contractor and prime's surety given judgment of indemnity against subcontractor and subcontractor's surety for supplier's claim, and subcontractor and subcontractor's surety given judgment back against prime contractor and prime's payment bond surety for nonpayment on subcontract, subject to prime contractor and prime's surety's right to offset amount paid to supplier).

112. Consider the cases of *Glens Falls Indem. Co.*, 229 F.2d 370; Standard Accident Ins. Co. v. Bear, 184 So. 97 (Fla. 1938) (including prior decisions on the case, cited at 168 So. 18, 26 So. 792, 126 So. 645, 150 So. 614); Golden Eagle Ins. Co. v. First Nationwide Fin. Corp., 31 Cal. Rptr. 2d 815 (Cal. Ct. App. 1994).

113. *Golden Eagle Ins. Co.*, 31 Cal. Rptr. 2d 815.

114. 184 So. 97.

allowed the owner to require lower tier lien waivers from the general contractor as a condition to payment. One lien claimant, Duval Lumber, filed a notice of lien claim before the owner's final payment. The owner paid the prime contractor without offset or joint check to account for Duval Lumber's claim. Duval Lumber filed suit to foreclose the lien and against the prime contractor and its payment bond surety, Standard Accident. The owner, with Bear as its surety, posted a lien discharge bond in Duval Lumber's favor and asserted that the prime contractor and Standard Accident are primarily liable for the lien claim.

Payment bond surety (Standard Accident) eventually paid Duval Lumber's judgment and sought to enforce the lien claim, by subrogation or assignment, against Bear's (surety's) lien discharge bond. Initially, the trial court held that Standard Accident was entitled to recover from the lien discharge bond. The Supreme Court of Florida, however, decided that the owner and its surety (Bear) were entitled to a determination of their rights against Standard Accident on the payment bond.[115] On remand, the trial court entered judgment for the owner and its lien discharge surety, Bear, against Standard Accident as the payment bond surety. On appeal by Standard Accident (in its fifth and final trip to the Florida Supreme Court), the Florida Supreme Court held that the owner had prejudiced Standard Accident's rights by paying the principal while Duval Lumber's claim was pending, such that Standard Accident's obligation on the prime contractor's bonds were discharged and it was entitled to recover the lien claim against the owner and the lien discharge bond surety, Bear.[116]

Notwithstanding the *Standard Accident* cases, the principle of subsuretyship, providing equity does not demand a contrary result, leads courts to hold the lower tier principal's surety is primarily responsible for the lien claim.[117] Thus, where the equities are otherwise equal, the general contractor's payment bond should be primary to the lien discharge bond that the owner, as principal, provided on a lower tier lien claim.[118]

---

115. Bear v. Standard Accident Ins. Co., 168 So. 18 (1936).
116. *Standard Accident Ins. Co.*, 184 So. 97.
117. No reported cases were found on point. By analogy, however, the rule laid out in *A & P Sheet Metal Co., Inc., v. Edward Hanson, Inc.*, 357 A.2d 37 (N.J. Super. Ct. App. Div. 1976), regarding lower tier primacy, should apply.
118. *See, e.g.*, Aetna Cas. & Sur. Co. v. U.S. Gypsum Co., 39 S.W.2d 234 (Ky. 1931) (subsuretyship was not discussed, but court found that the owner's procurement of a lien discharge bond did not render the prime

Similarly, the subcontractor's payment bond should be primary and thus liable before the lien discharge bond of either the general contractor or owner on a lien claim arising under the subcontractor. Conversely, with respect to liability, the lien discharge bond of the subcontractor should be primary to the payment bond of the general contractor, or the lien discharge bond of the general contractor or owner, where the lien claimant supplies its labor or materials under the subcontractor.

In the few cases deciding between the lien discharge and payment bonds, the courts are inconsistent in their reasoning or results.[119] Where the applicable mechanic's lien statutes shield the owner from all liability for lien claims if the general contractor or owner (which some states allow to post a bond) provides a payment bond, the payment bond may be considered primarily liable for the lien claim.[120] The reason, of course, is the lien discharge bond is superfluous because the property is exempt from lien claims due to the existence of the payment bond.[121] On the other hand, the facts and circumstances of the case may allow the lower tier payment bond surety to assert subrogation claims or otherwise recover from the owner or general contractor and, presumably, its surety on a lien discharge bond.[122]

---

contractor's payment bond secondarily liable, nor constitute an alteration of the obligation such that it would discharge the payment bond surety).

119. *Compare Bear*, 168 So. 18 (including prior decisions on the case, cited at 126 So. 792, 126 So. 643, 150 So. 614); Golden Eagle Ins. Co. v. First Nationwide Fin. Corp., 31 Cal. Rptr. 2d 815 (Cal. Ct. App. 1994) (lien rights only); *U.S. Gypsum Co.*, 39 S.W.2d 234; Bankers & Shippers Ins. Co. v. AIA Insulation Indus., Inc., 390 So. 2d 734 (Fla. Dist. Ct. App. 1980); Alpha Elec. Supply, Inc. v. F. Fenster, Inc., 358 So. 2d 892 (Fla. Dist. Ct. App. 1978) (existence of payment bond is complete defense to claim on subsequently filed lien discharge bond); Edward L. Nezelek, Inc. v. Concreform Co., 351 So. 2d 1046 (Fla. Dist. Ct. App. 1977).

120. *See, e.g.*, *Bankers & Shippers Ins. Co*, 390 So. 2d 734; *Alpha Elec. Supply, Inc.*, 358 So. 2d 892 (existence of payment bond is complete defense to claim on subsequently filed lien discharge bond); *Edward L. Nezelek, Inc.*, 351 So. 2d 1046.

121. *See, e.g.*, *Bankers & Shippers Ins. Co.*, 390 So. 2d 734.

122. *See, e.g.*, *Bear*, 168 So. 18 (including prior decisions on the case, cited at 126 So. 792, 126 So. 643, 150 So. 614); *Golden Eagle Ins. Co.*, 31 Cal. Rptr. 2d 815.

Conclusion

The law applicable to lien discharge bonds is often peculiar to the bond's purpose: to serve as a substitute security for the lien claim. Because lien discharge bonds are most often part of a comprehensive statutory scheme for allowing and enforcing mechanic's lien claims, each jurisdiction's laws should be thoroughly researched to determine the respective rights and liabilities of the surety issuing the lien discharge bond. Hopefully, this chapter will provide the reader some guidance in analyzing this obscure, yet interesting, area of the law.

CHAPTER 11

FRINGE BENEFIT BONDS

David C. Olson
James D. Houston
Ellen M. Cavallaro

Introduction

This chapter examines issues arising from the issuance of fringe benefit surety bonds, beginning with a general overview of the instrument. The chapter covers both statutory and private common law bonds, as well as the issue of a surety's liability under a general payment bond for unpaid fringe benefit contributions. Finally, the chapter explores the Employee Retirement Income Security Act (ERISA) preemption jurisprudence in this area.

I. Fringe Benefit Bonds—Generally

A fringe benefit bond guarantees the payment of contributions to trust funds to support benefits for workers such as pensions, health and welfare, and job training. Fringe benefits do not include employer contributions or payments required by other federal, state, or local law, such as Federal Insurance Contributions Act (FICA) taxes, workers' compensation, or unemployment compensation. Ordinarily, an employer is required to make such contributions for each hour a unionized or covered employee works, usually on construction projects.

A. *Overview*

When a fringe benefit bond is issued directly to a trust fund that manages the provision of the benefits, the obligation to post the bond usually arises from a collective bargaining agreement between the principal as employer and the labor union that represents the principal's employees.

Such an arrangement fits the classic suretyship model.[1] The employer is the primary obligor with respect to the underlying obligation, which is the employer's duty to make specific employee fringe benefit contributions under the terms of collective bargaining agreements. The fringe benefit bond creates a secondary obligation that provides the obligee (the union or the trust fund) with recourse against a secondary obligor (the surety) with respect to the performance of the underlying obligation.[2] Thus, the union and its members are direct beneficiaries of the bond between the employer and the surety with the right to demand performance through payment of the benefits either directly or through a representative.

Usually the bond principal/employer is required to report monthly to the fringe benefit trust fund the hours worked by its employees and to remit payment for the fringe benefits. The fund will audit the principal to verify the self-reporting, and if there is a perceived underpayment, the fund will make demand on the principal and the surety.

Union contractors normally send to the fund a monthly remittance report that reflects all hours worked, regardless of the identity of the project. Certified payroll reports are provided weekly and are project specific. It may be necessary to compare the certified payroll reports to any claim based on an audit of the monthly remittance reports, to confirm the accuracy of a claim against a particular bonded project, if the bond does not cover all projects. Union benefit trust funds frequently compute their claims based on the aggregate amount unpaid, rather than on a project-by-project basis. The term of a fringe benefit bond is typically coterminous with the collective bargaining agreement that requires it to be provided. Such a bond covers not just one project but all projects in which the principal employs workers covered by the collective bargaining agreement. To limit the surety's risk and liability in this context, fringe benefit bonds typically have relatively modest, and fixed, penal sums of no more than a few tens of thousands of dollars. The bond penal sum can

---

1. *See* RESTATEMENT (THIRD) OF SURETYSHIP AND GUARANTY § 1(1)(a) (1996) ("[P]ursuant to contract (the 'secondary obligation'), an obligee has recourse against a person (the 'secondary obligor') or that person's property with respect to the obligation (the 'underlying obligation') of another person (the 'principal obligor') to that obligee.").
2. *See id.* § 2(d) ("The secondary obligation may be created by contract between the secondary obligor and the principal obligor whereby the secondary obligor agrees to be a secondary obligor with respect to an underlying obligation of the principal obligor, if the obligee is an intended beneficiary of that contract.").

be adjusted through the issuance of a rider as an employer increases its workforce in the field.

The terms of the underlying collective bargaining agreement may further define the surety's liability under a particular fringe benefit bond. Experienced surety counsel review the bonded contract when a claim is first presented to assist in risk assessment. A claimant seeking coverage arising from work performed outside the scope of the agreement that imposed the payment obligation ought not to have recourse against the surety bond whose coverage is limited to that agreement. In addition, the surety ordinarily is entitled to assert any defense available to the principal against the claims of the unions or the trustees of the benefit fund. However, the surety is not protected from liability by the discharge of the principal's obligation in bankruptcy.[3]

Fringe benefit bond liability can also arise under the provisions of the Davis-Bacon Act[4] and related laws, which impose duties upon contractors and subcontractors performing on federally funded or assisted contracts. Davis-Bacon contractors and subcontractors must pay their laborers and mechanics employed under the contract no less than the locally prevailing wages and fringe benefits for corresponding work on similar projects in the area. Davis-Bacon applies to about 60 statutes under which federal agencies assist construction projects through grants, loans, loan guarantees, and insurance (hereinafter related acts). For example, federal highway funds are typically used on highway projects performed through the departments of transportation for the individual states. Recipients of funds under the related acts must comply with Davis-Bacon and commit to remit the fringe benefit payments.[5]

"Flow-down" obligations are commonly found on public works projects using federal funding that imposes the obligations to satisfy the elements of Davis-Bacon on the general contractor and its subcontractors. A contractor may agree to a contract with a party who has entered into a federal contract. The federal contract requires that certain federal grant provisions be made a part of any subsequent contracts related to

---

3. *See id.* § 34(1).
4. 40 U.S.C. §§ 3141–3148.
5. Form FHWA-1273 (rev. May 1, 2012), which defines the obligations incorporated by reference into contracts for road projects that are constructed after the state entity received federal funds for the work. That form states the enabling statutes and cites to the various federal programs that apply to work performed under 23 U.S.C. § 101 *et seq.* regarding federal highway funds.

furthering the performance or deliverables required under the federal contract. The contractor agrees to flow down the applicable clauses to its lower-tier subcontractors.

A general contractor may be liable for the payment of Davis-Bacon obligations of its subcontractors, and the surety for the general contractor may have exposure for these fringe benefits. Contract payments may be withheld in sufficient amounts to satisfy liabilities for underpayment of wages and fringe benefits and for liquidated damages for overtime violations under the Contract Work Hours and Safety Standards Act.[6] In addition, violations of Davis-Bacon contract clauses may be grounds for contract termination, contractor liability for any resulting costs to the government, and debarment from future contracts for a period up to three years.[7] The contractor may also face criminal liability if it is determined the Davis-Bacon violations were willful.[8]

Twenty-six states and the District of Columbia have state prevailing wage laws similar to Davis-Bacon.

B. Typical Provisions

Sometimes a collective bargaining agreement requires that an employer furnish a bond—often called a "wage and welfare bond" or a "collective bargaining bond"—that covers not only the fringe benefit payments but also the wages due to be paid under the agreement. The operative language in such a bond is generally very similar to that in a purely fringe benefit bond. Terms like the following are typical.

Bond by Contractors to Secure Payment
of Wages and Fringe Benefits

Know All Men by These Presents:

THAT ____ , as Principal, hereinafter called Principal, and ____, as Surety, hereinafter called Surety, are held and firmly bound unto [local union], as Obligee, for the use and benefit

---

6. 40 U.S.C. § 3701 *et seq.*; Form FHWA-1273, *supra* note 5, outlines the powers delegated to the state entity receiving the funds, including the right to withhold all payments due to non-compliance with the provisions of Davis-Bacon.
7. 29 C.F.R. § 5.12 (rev. July 1, 2011).
8. *Id.* § 5.10.

of claimants as hereinafter defined, in the amount of ______ Dollars ($______), to the payment of which said sum of money said Principal binds himself, or itself, his or its executors, administrators, successors, and assigns; and the Surety binds itself, its successors, and assigns, jointly and severally by these presents;

WHEREAS: The principal is a Party to a Collective Bargaining Agreement with the Union that provides for the payment of wages, check off Union dues, deductions from wages and payment of the same to or for the Union's [various specifically enumerated benefit and welfare plans], and for the Employer contributions to [various specifically enumerated benefit and welfare plans], said Collective Bargaining Agreement being made a part hereof as fully and to all intents and purposes as if set forth in full herein;

NOW THEREFORE: The condition of this obligation is such that if the Principal shall promptly make payments and contributions to all claimants as hereinafter defined and in accordance with the terms and conditions of said Collective Bargaining Agreement, then this obligation shall be void; otherwise it shall remain in full force and effect, subject however, to the following conditions: . . .

The above named Principal and Surety hereby jointly agree with the [named local union] that every claimant as herein defined who has not been paid in full at the completion of each week's work, or at the completion of any labor done and performed for the Principal, or for deductions due [various specifically enumerated benefit and welfare plans], may sue on this bond for the use and benefit of said claimant in the name of [named local union] or the Trustees of the aforesaid Funds, or any other claimant on behalf of all claimants, and prosecute the suit to final judgment for such sum or sums as may be justly due to any claimant under said Collective Bargaining Agreement or Agreements and Declarations of Trust establishing said funds and have execution thereon.

II. Payment Bonds as Fringe Benefit Bonds

The absence of a fringe benefit bond does not necessarily absolve the surety of potential liability for the payment of the fringe benefits in the event that an employer fails to make agreed-upon fringe benefit contributions. The surety under a general payment bond covering a specific project may also be liable for unpaid fringe benefits when a contractor or subcontractor defaults in the performance of such obligations. Unlike wages, union employers typically agree to pay fringe benefits and dues directly to the unions.[9] Laborers assign, usually expressly, the portion of their wages intended to cover fringe benefits to the benefit trust fund. The collective bargaining agreement will generally require that employers make lump-sum remittances to the union benefit trust fund. Courts usually reason that, because a general payment bond covers labor that workers provide to a project and because the cost of labor includes not just wages but also the payment of benefits where a bonded agreement requires such contributions, a general payment bond surety is liable for unpaid fringe benefit contributions. The existence and scope of such liability, however, depends in part on whether the project covered by the payment bond is an undertaking of the federal government, a state or local government, or private developers.

A. Federal Public Works Projects—Miller Act Payment Bonds

The Miller Act requires that a contractor furnish payment and performance bonds for any contract of more than $100,000 for "the construction, alteration, or repair of any public building or public work of the Federal Government."[10] The Miller Act "is highly remedial in nature . . . and is entitled to a liberal construction and application in order properly to effectuate the Congressional intent to protect those whose labor and materials go into public projects."[11] The penal amount of a Miller Act payment bond usually must be the full value of the bonded contract.[12] Among those who are eligible to bring an action on a Miller Act payment bond is "[e]very person that has furnished labor or material in carrying out work provided for in a contract" covered by the bond and "that has not been paid in full."[13] Importantly, unions and fringe benefit funds are subject to the same defenses as any other Miller Act claimant.

---

9. Nat'l Elec. Indus. Fund v. Bethlehem Steel Corp., 463 A.2d 858, 862 (Md. 1983).
10. 40 U.S.C. § 3131(b) (2006).
11. United States *ex rel.* Olson v. W.H. Cates Constr. Co., 972 F.2d 987, 990 (8th Cir. 1992).
12. 40 U.S.C. § 3131(b)(2).
13. *Id.* § 3133(b).

More than 60 years ago in *United States ex rel. Sherman v. Carter*,[14] the U.S. Supreme Court held that the surety on a Miller Act payment bond was liable to the trustees of a union health and welfare fund for the payment of per-hour fringe benefit contributions that an employer had promised but failed to pay. The Court found that the Miller Act "does not limit recovery on the statutory bond to 'wages,'" and concluded that workers had not been "paid in full" within the meaning of the statute until such contributions were made.[15] Moreover, although the trustees had not directly "furnished labor," the Court found that "the trustees' relationship to the employees, as established by the master labor agreements and the trust agreement, [was] closely analogous to that of an assignment."[16] Because prior decisions under the similar predecessor statute, the Heard Act,[17] established that "assignees of the claims of persons furnishing labor or material came within the protection of the statutory bond,"[18] the trustees were valid claimants.

Although the parties in *Sherman* "stipulated that contributions to the fund were part of the consideration [the principal] agreed to pay for the services of laborers,"[19] courts have not viewed such an explicit stipulation or finding as an essential element in that decision.[20] In general, a contractual obligation on the part of a principal contractor or subcontractor to make such contributions is sufficient under the Miller Act to render a payment bond surety liable in the event that the employer fails to make the payments.

A Miller Act payment bond claim is limited to "those with a contractual relationship with the prime contractor or with a

---

14. 353 U.S. 210, 218–19 (1957).
15. *Id.* at 217–18.
16. *Id.* at 220.
17. Ch. 280, 28 Stat. 278 (1894), *as amended*, ch. 778, 33 Stat. 811 (1905), *as amended*, ch. 231, § 291, 36 Stat. 1167 (1911), *repealed by* ch. 642, § 5, 49 Stat. 793–94 (1935).
18. *Sherman*, 353 U.S. at 219.
19. *Id.* at 217.
20. *See, e.g.*, J.W. Bateson Co. v. United States *ex rel.* Bd. of Trs. of Nat'l Automatic Sprinkler Indus. Pension Fund, 434 U.S. 586, 588 n.1 (1978) (citing *Sherman* for the proposition that "amounts which the employer agreed to contribute to union trust funds could be recovered by the employees or their representatives under the [Miller Act] payment bond").

subcontractor."[21] Thus, employees of a sub-subcontractor fall outside the scope of the statute's protection,[22] as do employees of materialmen.[23] Only laborers of a first-tier subcontractor may assert a claim against a Miller Act payment bond. The Supreme Court held that employees of a sub-subcontractor were not entitled to recover under the prime contractor's Miller Act payment bond for failure of the sub-subcontractor to turn over fringe benefit funds and union dues that had been withheld from the union employees, since those employees did not have a contractual relationship with the prime contractor or a subcontractor.[24]

B. State Public Works Projects—"Little Miller Act" Payment Bonds

Many states have "Little Miller Acts," which are statutes that require contractors on state public works projects to furnish surety bonds that would include payment bonds. Some states actually set forth the terms of these statutory bonds in the statute itself.[25] Courts in many of those states have applied the Supreme Court's reasoning in *Sherman* to hold a surety liable under such a bond for unpaid fringe benefit contributions. Because of the requirement that a payment bond surety satisfy claims from laborers for wages, the majority of the courts have held that the surety is generally obligated to pay claims for union fringe benefits and that the authorized representative, usually a trustee, of the fringe benefit funds is entitled to assert such claims on behalf of the union employees.[26]

---

21. United States *ex rel.* Polied Env't Servs., Inc., 238 F. Supp. 2d 456, 459 (D. Conn. 2002).
22. *Id.* at 589 ("persons who lack a 'contractual relationship express or implied with the [prime] contractor' [must] show a 'direct contractual relationship with a subcontractor' in order to recover on the bond").
23. *See* Clifford F. MacEvoy Co. v. United States *ex rel.* Calvin Tomkins Co., 322 U.S. 102, 110–11 (1944).
24. *J.W. Bateson Co.*, 434 U.S. at 588 n.1.
25. *See, e.g.*, Ohio Rev. Code § 5525.16 (2020) (bond terms are specified for highway projects); *id.* §§ 153.57, 153.571 (specify bond language for other public work).
26. *See* United States *ex rel.* Sherman v. Carter, 353 U.S. 210 (1957) (holding that fringe fund trustees stood in the shoes of employees and thus were entitled to recover the sums withheld from their wages as union benefits); Forsberg v. Bovis Lend Lease, Inc., 184 P.3d 610 (Utah Ct. App. 2008)

In some jurisdictions, the state's Little Miller Act or other statutory requirement may specifically require payment of union dues and fringe benefits under the payment bond. For example, the New York Little Miller Act includes all sums due for benefits pursuant to labor law, contract, or a collective bargaining agreement.[27] New York's Little Miller Act expressly provides that a trustee authorized to collect benefits is permitted to proceed to collect benefits on behalf of the workers. A defense that might be raised, but appears not to have been litigated, is whether the worker has provided actual authorization to the union benefit trust funds to collect benefits. Proof of authorization should be provided by the claimant, as the statute does not provide that the authority is automatic.[28]

(allowing recovery under a payment bond for unpaid fringe benefits owed to union-related trusts as constituting payment for "labor" under the applicable payment bond statute); Hartford Fire Ins. Co. v. Trs. of Constr. Indus., 208 P.3d 884 (Nev. 2009) (allowing recovery of unpaid fringe benefits because the trust "stood in the shoes" of the workers); Fid. & Deposit Co. of Md. v. Sheet Metal Workers' Int'l Ass'n Loc. Union No. 20, 7 N.E.3d 1024 (Ind. Ct. App. 2014) (surety liable for unpaid union fringe benefits owed to employees of a second-tier subcontractor); United States *ex rel.* Vealey v. Suffolk Constr. Co., No. 95 Civ. 9363, 1998 WL 241628, at *3 (S.D.N.Y. May 12, 1998) (union benefit fund was a proper party to sue on a payment bond to recover benefits owing to the subcontractor's union laborers); Operating Eng'rs Health & Welfare Tr. Fund v. JWJ Contracting Co., 135 F.3d 671 (9th Cir. 1998) (union was a proper claimant against the payment bond for unpaid benefits); Alibrandi Bldg. Sys., Inc. v. Wm. C. Pahl Constr. Co., Inc., 590 N.Y.S.2d 370 (N.Y. App. Div. 1992) (union had a claim under the State Finance Law for union dues plus interest against a payment bond); Trs., Fla. W. Coast Trowel Trades Pension Fund v. Quality Concrete Co., Inc., 385 So. 2d 1163 (Fla. Dist. Ct. App. 1980); Ind. Carpenters Cent. & W. Ind. Pension Fund v. Seaboard Sur. Co., 601 N.E.2d 352 (Ind. Ct. App. 1992); Dobbs v. Knudson, Inc., 292 N.W.2d 692 (Iowa 1980); 3 PHILIP LANE BRUNER & PATRICK J. O'CONNOR, BRUNER & O'CONNOR ON CONSTRUCTION LAW § 8:165 (West 2002); 11A STEVEN PLITT ET AL., COUCH ON INSURANCE 3D § 165:20 (rev. 2004) .

27. N.Y. STATE FIN. LAW § 137(5)(b) (McKinney 2021).

28. *Id.* New York Labor Law section 220-g similarly provides that an unpaid laborer may permit an employee organization to commence an action on his or her behalf.

The Arizona Supreme Court held in 1982 that a union trust fund could bring a claim against the general contractor and its surety on a statutory public works payment bond, notwithstanding that the claim arose from a subcontractor's unpaid fringe benefit contributions.[29] The court cited *Sherman*, noting that the state statute was "taken from the federal Miller Act" and that the principal and surety admitted that *Sherman* was controlling.[30]

Similarly, in 1979 the Colorado Supreme Court concluded that both a local union and the trustees of the union health and welfare fund could pursue claims against the principal general contractor and its surety for fringe benefit contributions that a subcontractor failed to make on a public works project.[31] In interpreting the state's Little Miller Act, the court found that such contributions were "amounts lawfully due to . . . persons supplying or furnishing (a contractor) or his subcontractors with labor," even though the contributions were actually payable to the union fund, and not directly to the workers who supplied the labor.[32] In addition, the court held that the union and the trustees were valid claimants under the statute because they had legal interests in the disputed contract and brought suit on behalf of the workers.[33]

The Supreme Court of Washington has ruled in a similar manner.[34] State courts of appeals in Florida, Indiana, and California have added to the weight of precedent that effectively applies *Sherman* not only to the

---

29. Ariz. Laborers, Teamsters & Cement Masons Loc. 395 Health & Welfare Tr. Fund v. New Pueblo Constructors, Inc., 640 P.2d 209 (Ariz. Ct. App. 1982).
30. *Id.* at 210. The concession by the principal and surety is curious, given that the Supreme Court's decision in *Sherman* clearly did *not* constitute binding precedent for a state court interpreting a state statute. *See* also Trs. of Iowa Laborers Dist. Council Health & Welfare Tr. v. Ankeny Cmty. Sch. Dist., 860 N.W.2d 923 (Iowa Ct. App. 2014) (claimants could submit a claim even though they did not themselves perform labor because the benefit fund payments were owed for labor furnished by the subcontractor's workers).
31. Trs. of Colo. Carpenters & Millwrights Health Benefit Tr. Fund v. Pinkard Constr. Co., 604 P.2d 683 (Colo. 1979).
32. *Id.* at 684–85.
33. *Id.* at 686.
34. Crabtree v. Lewis, 544 P.2d 10 (Wash. 1975).

federal Miller Act but also to Little Miller Act public works statutes in the various states.[35]

Although most courts have followed *Sherman* to find that trustees are valid public bond claimants, the existence of a statutory public works bond does not always result in liability being imposed on the surety. In 2009, the Nevada Supreme Court characterized *Sherman* as persuasive in finding that fund trustees were similar to assignees of covered workers and, therefore, generally had standing to bring claims on public works project bonds required by state statute.[36] However, the trustees in the case were denied actual recovery from the surety because the trustees had not complied with the statutory requirement that a party with a claim against a subcontractor must provide notice to the contractor before bringing an action on the contractor's bond.[37] This failure did not preclude recovery against the principal, but merely against the surety. The notice requirements in the statute governed the bond, which was the source of any liability on the surety's part.[38] But the principal's liability arose directly from its contractual obligations to its employees, and so the statutory notice requirements did not limit those obligations.[39]

---

35. *See, e.g.*, Trs., Fla. W. Coast Trowel Trades Pension Fund v. Quality Concrete Co., 385 So. 2d 1163 (Fla. Dist. Ct. App. 1980); Ind. Carpenters Cent. & W. Ind. Pension Fund v. Seaboard Sur. Co., 601 N.E.2d 352 (Ind. Ct. App. 1992); Bernard v. Indem. Ins. Co. of N. Am., 329 P.2d 57 (Cal. Dist. Ct. App. 1958).
36. Hartford Fire Ins. Co. v. Trs. of Constr. Indus., 208 P.3d 884, 890 (Nev. 2009), *enforced*, 578 F.3d 1126 (9th Cir. 2009).
37. *Id.* at 894–95.
38. *Id.* at 886. The court reasoned that "notice is required to proceed with claims against the bond. Because the employees would be required to provide notice of their claims to the general contractor before recovering on the payment bond under NRS [Nevada Revised Statutes] 339.035's clear terms, the trustees, standing in their shoes, likewise are required to do so."
39. *Id.* where the court reasoned:

    > [T]he trustees are not required to provide notice to proceed with NRS 608.150 claims against the contractor. NRS 608.150 is in a statutory chapter completely separate from NRS 339.035, and NRS 608.150 plainly does not require that the trustees provide the contractor with notice of their claims before seeking to recover from the contractor under that statute.

A surety also avoided liability under a statutory labor and material bond for a public works project under somewhat unusual facts in a 1998 Tenth Circuit decision.[40] In *Lenon v. St. Paul Mercury Insurance Co.*, a contractor performed work on an airport and was required by state statute to furnish a payment bond for the project.[41] The contractor was party to a collective bargaining agreement that required the use of union labor on such projects, as well as the payment of fringe benefit contributions, but the contractor neither used union labor nor made the required contributions.[42] The trustees of the union trust funds won a judgment against the contractor in federal district court for breach of the collective bargaining agreement, and the court awarded the trustees, as damages for the breach of the contract, the amounts that the contractor should have paid in contributions for the union workers it should have hired, but did not actually hire.[43] The Tenth Circuit reversed the lower court and held that the surety was not liable for these damages. The court found that the breach-of-contract damages were not based on the claims of "persons supplying or furnishing labor" within the meaning of the state statute. Since the contractor's obligation was to pay fringe benefits for the work actually performed and the work was never performed, there was no breach of the terms of the bond. The court adhered to the general rule that breach of contract damages unrelated to the actual work performed were "not recoverable under public works bond statutes."[44]

A minority of courts have held that a surety is not liable under its payment bond for such benefit claims. The trustees of fringe benefit trust funds asserted a claim against a payment bond in a federal court in Michigan. The surety argued for a strict construction of the Michigan Little Miller Act, namely that the trustees (1) did not have standing because they were not "claimants," as defined by the statute, and (2) could not obtain the relief sought because fringe benefits are not included within the provisions of the statute. The court held that it was required to strictly construe the Little Miller Act and that the trustees of the employee benefit funds were not claimants within the meaning of the statute and

---

40. Lenon v. St. Paul Mercury Ins. Co., 136 F.3d 1365 (10th Cir. 1998).
41. *Id.* at 1368.
42. *Id.*
43. *Id.*
44. *Id.* at 1374.

lacked standing to sue the surety.[45] A Massachusetts court held that the provisions of the payment bond extended bond coverage only to those providers of labor or material who qualify as defined claimants. The bond expressly defined a "claimant" as "one having a direct contract with the principal for labor, material, or both," and permitted only "Claimant[s] as herein defined" to sue on the bond. Based on the language of the bond, the court held that the trustees had no rights under the bond or standing to sue on it.[46] In a New Jersey case, the trial court found that under New Jersey's Public Works Bond Act,[47] the union benefit trust funds were not "within the class of intended beneficiaries of the bond."[48]

C. Private Payment Bonds

Payment bonds are not ordinarily required by statute in nonpublic projects, but the parties may still require the use of a performance and a payment bond on a private project. Consequently, the law governing interpretation of private payment bonds is generally the law of private agreements, which is to say a state's common law for the formation and enforcement of contracts and the principles of suretyship. In the freedom-to-contract analysis, the language of the bond itself, basic contract construction principles, and perhaps the language of agreements requiring the bond will control the parties' specific rights and obligations under the bond. Those documents would govern whether, and to what extent, the bond covers unpaid fringe benefit contributions for the work performed.

Three New York cases illustrate how differences in language and facts can drive the outcome of disputes in the private bond context.

In a 1958 decision, a New York appellate court held that, where a common law payment bond required the principal and surety to pay claims for "wages and compensation for labor performed and services rendered," the sureties were liable for unpaid fringe benefit contributions.[49] The court found the language in the bond to reflect the parties' intent that

---

45. Operating Eng'rs Loc. 324 Health Care Plan v. Sentry Ins., 654 F. Supp. 191 (E.D. Mich. 1985).
46. Trs. of Sheet Metal Workers' Loc. Union No. 17 v. U.S. Fire Ins. Co., 899 N.E.2d 919 (Mass. App. Ct. 2009).
47. N.J. Rev. Stat. Ann. § 2A:44-143 (2015).
48. Laborers Loc. Union No. 779 Pension, Welfare & Annuity Funds v. Am. Cas. Co. of Reading, Pa., 771 A.2d 712 (N.J. Super. Ct. Law Div. 2000).
49. Martin v. William Casey & Sons, Inc., 170 N.Y.S.2d 228, 230 (N.Y. App. Div. 1958).

the entire economic benefit due to the workers should be covered by the bond.[50] Also significant in the analysis was the fact that the collective bargaining agreement between the parties obligated the employer to pay both wages and fringe benefit contributions.[51] Thus, the court considered the terms of an agreement outside the four corners of the bond as it determined the breadth of the language found in the bond itself.

By contrast, in a 1997 decision applying New York law, a state trial court found that a union could not recover unpaid fringe benefit contributions where the bond provided that the principal's obligation extended only to "payment for all labor and materials" because the plain meaning of "payment for all labor" did not include fringe benefits.[52]

Finally, in a 2000 decision, a federal district court in New York compared the two previous decisions and concluded that a payment bond did cover fringe benefit contributions where the bond language guaranteed "sums that may be justly due claimant" for labor in performance of the project contract.[53] Among the reasons the court gave for preferring the approach of the 1958 appeals court decision to that of the later trial court decision (*Chamberlain*) was that *Chamberlain* was inconsistent with the U.S. Supreme Court's decision in *Sherman* that interpreted the Miller Act.[54] Although *Sherman* was not binding precedent, the court found it persuasive. But the court's primary reason for interpreting the bond's language flexibly and finding against the surety was the distinction between private sureties and compensated corporate sureties.[55] The court acknowledged the "well-settled common law doctrine that a private surety is a favored actor in the law and its obligations are construed narrowly in its favor," but found it to be superseded by the rule that "a compensated, corporate surety is not a favorite of the law and its contract of suretyship will be construed in a manner most favorable to a claimant."[56]

---

50. *Id.* at 231–32.
51. *Id.* at 231.
52. Iron Workers Dist. Council of W. N.Y. v. D. R. Chamberlain Corp., 673 N.Y.S.2d 797, 800 (N.Y. Sup. Ct. 1997).
53. Mountbatten Sur. Co. v. Kips Bay Cinemas, Inc., No. 00 Civ. 0430, 2000 U.S. Dist. LEXIS 17176, at *6 (S.D.N.Y. Nov. 29, 2000).
54. *Id.* at *31 (citing United States *ex rel.* Sherman v. Carter, 353 U.S. 210 (1957), which the court in *Mountbatten* refers to by its alternate short-form designation, *Carter*, instead of *Sherman*).
55. *Id.* at *28.
56. *Id.* at *28–29.

Maryland, Virginia, California, the District of Columbia, and New York have enacted laws that impose joint liability on general contractors for a subcontractor's failure to pay timely and proper wages to their employees and lower-tier subcontractors.

In California, general contractors on private construction projects "assume, and [are] liable for any debt" of a subcontractor of any tier for unpaid wages, fringe benefits, or other employee contributions. The legislation does not provide for a private right of action to the unpaid employees but instead permits the commissioner of labor to file suit on behalf of an unpaid employee(s) and also allows labor unions to sue for unpaid wages or benefits.[57]

The state of Maryland passed a similar law called the General Contractor Liability for Unpaid Wages Act.[58] The Maryland act applies only to private construction projects and makes prime contractors financially responsible for the unpaid wages of subcontractor employees of any tier. If an employee is not paid within two weeks of the payment due date, the employee has a private right of action against the prime contractor.

The D.C. Wage Payment and Collection Law (WPCL)[59] requires employers to pay timely wages to their employees; and if they fail, the employer is liable, as liquidated damages, for 10 percent of the unpaid wages for each working day that the failure persists, or an amount equal to treble the unpaid wages, whichever is smaller. The WPCL goes on to provide that the subcontractor and general contractor are jointly and severally liable for these violations.

In Virginia, general contractors on construction projects over $500,000 are liable for any wages its subcontractors of any tier fail to pay.[60] Further, general contractors are deemed to be the employer of the subcontractor's employees for the purposes of Virginia Code section 40.1-29, which imposes civil and criminal penalties on employers in the case of unpaid wages. The criminal penalties range from misdemeanors to felonies, depending upon the amount of unpaid wages.

In New York, any contractor entering into a construction contract will assume liability for any wages or debt owed to a worker "incurred by a subcontractor at any tier acting under, by, or for the contractor or

---

57. CAL. LAB. CODE § 218.7 (2020).
58. MD. CODE ANN., LAB. & EMPL. § 3-507 (2020).
59. D.C. CODE § 32-1301 (2020).
60. VA. CODE § 11-4.6 (2021).

its subcontractors for the [worker's] performance of labor." Where an action is filed against a subcontractor, the upstream contractor will be "considered jointly and severally liable for any unpaid wages, benefits, wage supplements, and any other remedies" provided under the law. Upstream contractors may be liable not only for the unpaid wages, but also for the claimant's attorneys' fees, interest, and liquidated damages.[61]

The statutes at issue do not contain any language extending the surety's liability for such wages beyond the four corners of the bond. The surety's liability will be determined by the particular bond's language and the facts.

III. Issues Affecting the Surety's Liability

The surety's liability under a fringe benefit bond or under a payment bond frequently depends on issues of standing, scope of coverage, cancellation and expiration, and notice. A recent court opinion has introduced the issue of traceability as well.

A. The Bond Claimant's Standing

A surety sometimes can avoid liability under a bond by showing that the claimant lacks standing to bring the claim under the plain language of the bond, under the controlling statute, or at common law.

In *Laborers Local Union No. 779 Pension, Welfare & Annuity Funds v. American Casualty Co.*,[62] a New Jersey court held in 2000 that unions could not bring bond claims against a surety under that state's Little Miller Act. The statute required that the bond promise payment for "all labor performed" on a public works project, much like the statute in *Hartford Fire Insurance Co.* But the statute also listed a number of different activities that a beneficiary might have performed and that would potentially give rise to a bond claim.[63] The court found that the class of beneficiaries the statute identified was precise and did not extend to the union pension and benefit funds.[64]

More often, courts find that unions or plan trustees have standing to bring claims for unpaid fringe benefit contributions based on the finding

---

61. N.Y. LAB. LAW § 198(1-a) (2021).
62. 771 A.2d 712 (N.J. Super. Ct. Law Div. 2000).
63. *Id.* at 718.
64. *Id.* at 719.

that the trustees or union stands in the shoes of the workers for purposes of bringing a claim. For example, in 2008 a Utah appellate court held that benefit trust funds had standing to assert claims under the state's mechanic's lien and bond statutes because the trust agreements gave the trust funds the authority to take legal action on behalf of the laborers.[65] This reasoning is similar to that of the Supreme Court in *Sherman*,[66] where the Court found that "the trustees' relationship to the employees, as established by the master labor agreements and the trust agreement, [was] closely analogous to that of an assignment."[67] Of course, timely assignment to the union or trustees of the claims of the individual workers will generally take the issue of standing off the table altogether.[68] And courts sometimes find that a bond's language excludes rather than encompasses certain plaintiffs.[69]

On other occasions, the standing of trustees or union representatives turns on interpretation of a statute. In *Connecticut Carpenters Benefit Funds v. Burkhard Hotel Partners II*,[70] the court held that an employee benefits fund had standing under the state's mechanic's lien law to bring an action on behalf and for the benefit of the employees who performed the work. The statute provided:

> If any person has a claim for more than ten dollars for . . . services rendered in the construction . . . of any building . . . and the claim is by virtue of an agreement with . . . some person having

---

65. Forsberg v. Bovis Lend Lease, Inc., 184 P.3d 610 (Utah Ct. App. 2008).
66. United States *ex rel.* Sherman v. Carter, 353 U.S. 210 (1957).
67. *Id.* at 220.
68. *See, e.g.*, Sprinkler Fitters Loc. Union No. 692 v. First Indem. Ins. Co., 840 F. Supp. 38, 39 n.4, 41 (E.D. Pa. 1993) (where unions obtained timely assignment of individual workers' claims, which led the surety to argue that the unions were not proper claimants because the collective bargaining agreements were not "direct" agreements within the meaning of the bonds' language; the court found this argument without merit and the supporting interpretation unreasonable).
69. *See, e.g.*, State *ex rel.* Lawrence v. Am. Ins. Co., 559 A.2d 1247, 1249 (Del. 1989) (finding that trustees for a subcontractor's employees could not bring a claim under the contractor's bond because the contractor was not "liable" to pay benefit contributions for those employees within the meaning of the bond, where the contractor was not in privity with those employees).
70. 849 A.2d 922 (Conn. App. Ct. 2004).

> authority from or rightfully acting for the owner in procuring the labor . . . , the building, with the land on which it stands . . . is subject to the payment of the claim.[71]

The court addressed the question of "whether a benefit fund acting on behalf of those who have performed services" constituted "any person who has a claim" within the meaning of the statute.[72]

Once again, the Supreme Court's decision in *Sherman* proved so compelling that a court was persuaded to adopt it in a context where it did not strictly apply.[73] Unlike *Sherman*, which "was decided under the [federal] Miller Act and involved a claim under a payment bond,"[74] the governing statute in *Burkhard* was a state mechanic's lien law, and plaintiffs brought their claim against the owner under that statute. The court found the language and purpose of the Miller Act and the mechanic's lien statute to be similar and found the facts in *Burkhard* similar to those in *Sherman*.[75] Thus, the state court concluded that the statute's language ought to be construed liberally, giving the benefit trust fund standing to sue on the employees' behalf.[76]

Similarly, in *Hartford Fire Insurance Co.*, fund trustees in 2009 sued a surety under Nevada's Little Miller Act, which allowed "any claimant who has performed labor or furnished material" for a bonded, public works project to bring a claim.[77] The court concluded that the trustees had standing under the statute, but rejected the workers' claim because the trustees had failed to comply with the statute's notice requirements.[78] Absent noncompliance with applicable notice requirements, however, plaintiffs will generally be able to maintain their claims when they have standing to do so.[79]

---

71. *Id.* at 925–26 (quoting CONN. GEN. STAT. § 49-33(a) (2002)).
72. *Id.* at 926.
73. *Id.* ("[W]e find [*Sherman*'s] legal and factual underpinnings sufficiently analogous to apply its rationale to our analysis of [the state statute]").
74. *Id.* at 927.
75. *Id.*
76. *Id.* at 928.
77. Hartford Fire Ins. Co. v. Trs. of Constr. Indus., 208 P.3d 884 (Nev. 2009).
78. *Id.* at 893.
79. *See, e.g.*, Cement & Concrete Workers Dist. Council Welfare Fund v. Frascone, 68 F. Supp. 2d 166, 175 (E.D.N.Y. 1999) (finding that, where the payment bond "was issued pursuant to and in compliance with the mandate of" a state statute, so that "for the purposes of contractual

Language in the bond that precisely identifies who can bring claims can serve either to permit or to exclude certain parties, but does not always guarantee the expected outcome. In *Trustees of Plumbers & Steamfitters Local 21 Annuity Fund v. Hartford Fire Insurance Co.*,[80] a New York trial court in 2005 found that the union trustees were "claimants" under the bond, notwithstanding language that restricted such status to "[a]n individual or entity having a direct contract with the contractor or with a subcontractor."[81] Potential claimants seeking to eliminate uncertainty as to their status may choose to negotiate language similar to the following:

> A Claimant is defined as any employee of a Principal to whom or with respect to whom the Principal is required to pay wages or to make contributions pursuant to the terms and conditions of the aforesaid Collective Bargaining Agreement.
>
> [Specific union local name] is also defined as a claimant for checked off dues, payments to [various specifically enumerated benefit and welfare plans]. Also defined as claimants are [specific union benefit and welfare funds and plans].

Coverage has been found against a performance bond, based on the Illinois Little Miller Act. A school district sued the subcontractor's surety on behalf of a union fund to recover amounts that the subcontractor had not paid to the union fund.[82] The surety had furnished a performance bond and payment bond. The payment bond contained a one-year limitations period, and the performance bond contained a two-year limitations period. Both parties moved for summary judgment.

---

construction . . . the Bond may be deemed to be governed by the provisions of" the statute, the bond gave plaintiff trust funds standing to sue contractor's surety for contributions that subcontractor failed to pay); *but see* State *ex rel.* Lawrence v. Am. Ins. Co., 559 A.2d 1247, 1250 (Del. 1989) (trustees for subcontractor's employees lacked standing under state public works statute to sue contractor's surety; because employees lacked privity with the contractor, they did not perform labor "under the contract for which the successful bidder is liable" within the meaning of the statute).

80. No. 842/05, 2005 N.Y. Misc. LEXIS 2800 (N.Y. Sup. Ct. Nov. 15, 2005).

81. *Id.* at *3–4.

82. Valley View Sch. Dist. 365-U *ex rel.* IBEW Loc. 176 Health, Welfare, Pension, Vacation & Training Tr. Fund Trs. v. Hartford Fire Ins. Co., 2018 Ill. App. 3d 150477-U (Ill. App. Ct. 2018).

The surety argued that the action was time barred by the one-year limitations period under the payment bond and that the school district lacked standing to bring an action on behalf of the union fund under the performance bond. The trial court granted summary judgment in favor of the school district and against the surety, and the surety appealed. The court of appeals stated that under a recent Illinois Supreme Court decision, *Lake County Grading Co., LLC v. Village of Antioch*,[83] bonds for public construction in Illinois are deemed to include the Bond Act's provisions for performance and payment. Further, the Prevailing Wage Act mandated that public entities require contractor and subcontractor bonds to include provisions that will secure the faithful performance of prevailing wage clauses. The court concluded that making contributions to the union fund was part of the subcontractor's obligation to perform under the subcontract. Therefore, it held that the one-year limitation period in the payment bond and the Bond Act for payment claims was not applicable. It held that the two-year limitation period for performance claims was applicable and the action was timely.

The surety argued that even if the action was timely under the performance bond, the only claimants under the performance bond were the general contractor and the school district (as obligees on the performance bonds). The surety argued that the union fund did not have standing and therefore the school district could not bring a claim on behalf of the fund. The court rejected this argument. It stated that the school district was a named obligee on the bond. Further, it held that "[o]nce we accept that payment to the Fund by Grace [the subcontractor] was a performance obligation owed to Valley View . . . any argument that Valley View has no standing to enforce Grace's performance on the bond must fail."[84]

B. *Scope of Bond Coverage*

The liability of a principal or surety under a fringe benefit bond or payment bond may in some cases extend beyond unpaid contributions to include attorneys' fees, litigation costs, and other types of damages. In *Sherman*,[85] the Supreme Court held that the trustees' claim against the surety for liquidated damages, attorneys' fees, court costs, and other

---

83. 19 N.E.3d 615 (Ill. 2014).
84. *Valley View Sch. Dist. 365-U*, 2018 Ill. App. 3d 150477-U, at *6.
85. United States *ex rel.* Sherman v. Carter, 353 U.S. 210 (1957).

related expenses of litigation was valid because the contractor was obligated to pay those costs under the trust agreement, which had been negotiated by the parties to the master labor agreements. If employees were to be "paid in full" the "sums justly due" to them, as the Miller Act required, the Supreme Court held that these items must be included.[86] Where the agreement between the parties provides for the recovery of such damages, courts generally award them.[87]

However, in its 1995 decision *Ragan v. Tri-County Excavating*,[88] the Third Circuit held that the award of attorneys' fees and liquidated damages was improper, even though the trust agreement between the union and the employer provided for such damages. Because state law limited the surety's obligations to those detailed in the bond itself, attorneys' fees and liquidated damages were not "sums justly due" under the bond.[89] Thus, not only the agreement between the parties, but also relevant state laws, must be taken into account when determining the extent of the surety's liability.

Central Laborers' Pension Fund v. Fidelity & Deposit Co. of Maryland[90] involved a general contractor and its subcontractor, which contracted with union labor to complete a school construction project. The parties settled all claims except for attorneys' fees. Plaintiffs alleged that the general contractor and the surety owed fees under the terms of the bond and the statute. The court held that it need not reach those issues because plaintiffs expressly released defendants from all underlying claims.[91]

Nonetheless, an agreement between the parties exerts substantial influence. In a Miller Act case in 2003, a federal district court in Massachusetts disallowed an electrical subcontractor's state law claims that would have permitted recovery of attorneys' fees because the Miller Act preempted those claims and "the Miller Act makes no provision for enhanced damages or attorneys' fees for failure to pay Miller Act

---

86. *Id.* at 220.
87. *See, e.g.*, Pa. Dep't of Transp. v. Manor Mines, Inc., 544 A.2d 538, 543–44 (Pa. Commw. Ct. 1988); Granite Constr. Co. v. Am. Motorists Ins. Co., 34 Cal. Rptr. 2d 835 (Cal. Ct. App. 1994).
88. 62 F.3d 501, 512–13 (3d Cir. 1995).
89. *Id.* at 513–14.
90. 2019 Ill. App. 2d 170781-U (Ill. App. Ct. 2019).
91. *Id.* at *51.

claims."[92] The subcontract did not contain any provision for attorneys' fees in the event of litigation between the contractor and subcontractor.[93] The subcontractor's state law claims were for failure to pay "without conducting a reasonable investigation" or to settle "when liability had become reasonably clear."[94] The court noted that "exceptions to the general federal rule that attorneys' fees are not recoverable . . . occur [only] when the underlying contract contains a provision providing for fees in the event of litigation or when a party has 'acted in bad faith, vexatiously, wantonly, or for oppressive reasons.'"[95] However, the subcontractor did recover overhead costs and profit on the work it had already performed.[96] Thus, the absence of provision for litigation costs in an agreement or statute usually precludes recovery of such costs, but claimants will be entitled to the full benefit of their bargain in most respects.

State public works bond statutes may also play a role in determining the scope of liability for the surety. In 2002, a federal district court in Indiana found that, under state law, a surety on a Little Miller Act payment bond was not liable for consequential damages, lost profits, loss of bonding capacity, or unjust enrichment that might be assessed against a contractor under a breach of contract claim,[97] notwithstanding a liquidated damages provision in the subcontract.[98] The court found that "extensive authority" supported the position that lost profits were not recoverable against the surety in an action for payment against a bond issued under state public works payment bond statutes.[99] Cases interpreting the Miller Act were relevant, the court found, when interpreting state statutory payment bonds, and the majority held that lost profits were not recoverable from a

---

92. United States *ex rel.* Metric Elec., Inc. v. Enviroserve, Inc., 301 F. Supp. 2d 56, 74 (D. Mass. 2003).
93. *Id.* at 60.
94. *Id.* at 75.
95. *Id.* at 73 n.8 (quoting F.D. Rich Co. v. United States *ex rel.* Indus. Lumber Co., 417 U.S. 116, 129 (1974)).
96. *Id.* at 69.
97. Murdock & Sons Constr., Inc. v. Goheen Gen. Constr., Inc., No. IP 99-1723-C-T/F, 2002 U.S. Dist. LEXIS 2690, at *37–38 (S.D. Ind. Jan. 14, 2002), *reconsideration granted by, vacated by in part, summary judgment denied by* 2003 U.S. Dist. LEXIS 22212 (S.D. Ind. Sept. 15, 2003).
98. *Id.* at *6–7.
99. *Id.* at *31.

surety in an action on a Miller Act payment bond.[100] Because the "Miller Act was not meant to replace subcontractors' state law contract remedies, which allow for recovery of lost profits . . . [but, rather, was meant to give] subcontractors an additional remedy to recover costs expended in furnishing labor . . . [a] claim for profit . . . falls outside both the letter and the spirit of the Miller Act" because it does not involve actual cash outlay.[101]

The federal ERISA permits the recovery of interest, liquidated damages, and attorneys' fees in claims to recover unpaid contributions.[102] Thus, unions and trustees that are able to bring their claims under ERISA can generally expect to recover such damages if successful.[103] Sureties may not be liable for unpaid contributions under ERISA because many courts have ruled that a surety does not meet the statutory definition of an "employer."[104]

C. Cancellation and Expiration of the Bond

In general, a surety's liability terminates with the expiration or cancellation of the bond.[105] Many bonds also contain provisions specifying a period of time after which even claims that arose within the term of the bond are barred, and courts generally enforce such provisions.[106]

---

100. *Id.* at *32, *34–35.
101. *Id.* at *35–36 (citing Consol. Elec. & Mechs., Inc. v. Biggs Gen. Contracting, Inc., 167 F.3d 432, 435–36 (8th Cir. 1999)).
102. 29 U.S.C. § 1132(g)(2) (2006).
103. *See* Trs. of Iron Workers Loc. 25 Pension Fund v. Crawford Door Sales, Inc., No. 09-CV-12370-DT, 2010 WL 3488963 (E.D. Mich. Sept. 3, 2010) (awarding attorneys' fees, interest, and liquidated damages in addition to unpaid contributions); Operating Eng'rs Loc. No. 101 Pension Fund v. Christiansen-Foust Steel, LLC, No. 07-2068-KHV, 2007 WL 1455889 (D. Kan. May 15, 2007) (awarding plaintiff attorneys' fees and costs despite no award for unpaid contributions).
104. *See* 29 U.S.C. § 1002(5) (2006).
105. *See, e.g.*, United States *ex rel.* Modern Elec., Inc. v. Ideal Elec. Sec. Co., 868 F. Supp. 10, 15 (D.D.C. 1994) (surety not liable where claims related solely to work performed after the date on which payment bond expired).
106. *See, e.g.*, Camelot Excavating Co. v. St. Paul Fire & Marine Ins. Co., 280 N.W.2d 491 (Mich. Ct. App. 1979) (court enforced provision precluding subcontractor from bringing action for payment under bond more than one year after contractor ceased work on project); Quality Glass &

For example, in a 2010 case[107] the surety was absolved of liability because the bond had been properly cancelled prior to the claim arising. Resolution of the case turned on the following cancellation provision:

> This bond is continuous in nature and may be cancelled by the serving of sixty (60) days written notice on the part of the Principal or Surety . . . . This bond shall remain in effect unless and until written notice of cancellation is received by the Administrator as aforesaid.

The surety served proper notice dated October 21, 2009, that, in accordance with the cancellation provision, it was electing to terminate its liability under the bond:

> NOW, THEREFORE, be it known that [surety] shall at the expiration of this bond on December 31, 2009, be released from all liability by reason of any default committed thereafter by the said Principal.

The plaintiff, a union pension fund, was left with no alternative but to stipulate to dismissal with prejudice of its claims against the surety.[108]

But even a clearly stated expiration date does not always effectively limit a surety's liability. In *Leary v. McDowell County National Bank*,[109] West Virginia's highest court held in 2001 that a surety was liable on a statutory bond where the surety received the notice of claims more than eight months after the bond's express expiration date. The surety, a bank, issued an irrevocable letter of credit that the court held to be valid and enforceable as a wage payment bond under a state statute that required such a bond for employers who had been active in the state for less than

---

Mirror, Inc. v. Ritch, 373 So. 2d 723 (Fla. Dist. Ct. App. 1979) (statutory one-year limitation period applied to bond); *but see* United States *ex rel.* Atlas Erection Co. v. Cont'l Cas. Co., 357 F. Supp. 795 (E.D. La. 1973) (where cause of subcontractor's delay in filing claim on bond was fault of surety, surety was estopped from asserting one-year period of limitations as defense).

107. Sheet Metal Workers Loc. 98 Pension Fund v. Aero-Fab, Inc., No. 10-CV-00683 (S.D. Ohio filed July 30, 2010).
108. *Id.* (stipulation entered May 23, 2011).
109. 552 S.E.2d 420 (W. Va. 2001).

five years.[110] The irrevocable letter of credit specified an expiration date of June 30, 1992.[111] On March 12, 1993, the state labor commissioner notified the surety that former employees of the principal had claims for unpaid wages and fringe benefits.[112] The surety refused to pay the remainder of the bond, claiming that the letter of credit had expired.[113] The parties did not dispute that the former employees had valid claims for unpaid wages and fringe benefits.[114] The surety argued that, under the state's Uniform Commercial Code, the letter of credit was irrevocable only during its stated duration, not for an indefinite period of time.[115] However, the relevant statute provided that an irrevocable letter of credit cannot be modified or revoked without the consent of the customer or beneficiary.[116] The court considered, but rejected, the argument that the expiration date set forth in the letter of credit constituted an agreement by the commissioner that the bond would be revoked on that date.[117] Instead, the court ruled that the state labor commissioner was the beneficiary of the letter of credit and that the letter of credit could be terminated only with the commissioner's approval.[118] Thus, the surety was liable for the unpaid wages and fringe benefits, despite the bond's expiration date having passed.[119]

D. Notice to the Surety

Statutory notice provisions often limit the claims that may be brought under a surety bond. Claimants under a Miller Act payment bond may include sub-subcontractors who have no privity of contract with the contractor who furnished the payment bond, provided they give timely written notice to the contractor.[120]

---

110. *Id.* at 422, 425.
111. *Id.* at 422 n.3.
112. *Id.* at 422–23.
113. *Id.* at 423.
114. *Id.* at 423–24.
115. *Id.* at 426.
116. *Id.* at 427.
117. *Id.*
118. *Id.*
119. *Id.* at 428. This case appears to be limited to its unusual facts.
120. 40 U.S.C. § 3133(b) (2006); *see also* United States *ex rel.* Sherman v. Carter, 353 U.S. 210, 217 n.4 (1957).

The sufficiency of the written notice may be disputed. A union entity owed benefits by a subcontractor on a Miller Act project sued the prime contractor and its Miller Act surety. The surety moved for summary judgment on the Miller Act claim for failure to provide the required 90-day notice. The court found that a series of timely (i.e., within the 90-day period) emails between the claimant and the prime contractor were sufficient to meet the Miller Act notice requirement.[121]

The notice must state with substantial accuracy the amount claimed. In *Trustees of the Heating, Piping & Refrigeration Pension Fund v. Milestone Construction Services, Inc.*, the trustees of a series of union benefit plans sued the prime contractor and payment bond surety claiming benefits not paid by a bankrupt subcontractor.[122] The subcontractor worked for the prime contractor on three federal construction projects, and the union benefit plans claimed that the prime contractor and surety owed the unpaid benefits pursuant to the Miller Act payment bonds on the projects.

The subcontractor abandoned the projects and the claimants sent "notices of claim" to the prime contractor and surety. The letters identified the projects but did not quantify the claims. More than 90 days after the claims accrued, the claimants quantified the claims. The prime contractor and surety moved for summary judgment based on the claimants' failure to satisfy the 90-day notice provision of the Miller Act, and the court granted their motion.[123]

Similar notice requirements in a state statute provided the surety with a viable defense against at least some of a subcontractor's claims in a 1999 New York case.[124] In another New York case, a laborer's union made a claim under a payment bond asserting that its members were not

---

121. Trs. of the Bricklayers & Allied Craftworkers, Loc. 5 N.Y. Ret., Welfare, Lab. Mgmt. Coal. v. Preferred Masonry Restoration, Inc., No. 17-CV-3662 (KMK), 2019 U.S. Dist. LEXIS 164526 (S.D.N.Y. Sept. 25, 2019).
122. 991 F. Supp. 2d 713 (D. Md. 2014).
123. *Id.* at 721.
124. Cement & Concrete Workers Dist. Council Welfare Fund v. Frascone, 68 F. Supp. 2d 166, 176 (E.D.N.Y. 1999) (finding that plaintiff union trust funds forfeited their right of action on claims arising under the first of two agreements with subcontractor where plaintiffs failed to provide timely notice of those claims to the general contractor's surety, as required by the statute pursuant to which the bond was issued).

paid by the bond principal.[125] The union moved for summary judgment. In opposition, the surety argued that the bulk of the laborers' claims were time-barred. The surety argued that the limitations period was measured on a per-employee basis, and several employees had last performed work more than a year prior to the commencement of the action. The court rejected this argument and held that when an "employee organization" sues, the last date on the project for the trade organization as a whole controlled for the purposes of statute of limitations. The court concluded that the action was timely. The court granted summary judgment in favor of the union and ordered an inquest to determine the amount owed.[126]

Notice may even be required prior to a claim arising, if that is what the relevant statute provides. In a 2000 New Jersey case, a subcontractor's claim against the general contractor's surety failed, in part because the subcontractor had not provided notice of its status as beneficiary under the bond, prior to commencing work, as required by the state's public works statute.[127]

Because statutory notice requirements pertain only to the bonds issued pursuant to those statutes, a claimant's failure to comply with such requirements impairs its claims only as to the surety on the bond. The plaintiff's claims against the principal or other parties will generally be unaffected to the extent that they arise from an agreement other than the bond. For example, in a 2009 decision discussed earlier in Part II.B, the Nevada Supreme Court concluded that benefit trust funds for the employees of a subcontractor could not bring claims against the general contractor's surety because the funds had failed to comply with statutory notice requirements.[128] However, the plaintiffs were not required to provide notice to proceed with their claims against the general contractor because the statute that permitted those claims did not require such notice.[129]

---

125. Trs. of the N.Y. Council of Carpenters Pension Fund v. Arch Ins. Co., 2018 N.Y. Slip Op. 30578, 2018 N.Y. Misc. LEXIS 1129 (N.Y. Sup. Ct. Apr. 2, 2018).
126. *Id.* at *1132–1133.
127. Laborers Loc. Union No. 779 Pension, Welfare & Annuity Funds v. Am. Cas. Co. of Reading, Pa., 771 A.2d 712, 715–16 (N.J. Super. Ct. Law Div. 2000).
128. Hartford Fire Ins. Co. v. Trs. of Constr. Indus., 208 P.3d 884, 886 (Nev. 2009).
129. *Id.*

In a federal case construing Pennsylvania law, the bonds required the fund to notify the surety of a claim within one year of "actual knowledge of default" by either of two related principals.[130] However, the bonds also provided that the point in time when default occurred was within the obligee's "sole and exclusive discretion."[131] In the case, the obligee sued the delinquent principals in 2008, and settled with them by a payment plan and consent judgments in 2009. The obligee did not notify the surety of the delinquencies, the demands for payment, the suits, or the settlements. After the principals failed to make the payments promised in the settlements and failed to pay additional contributions, the obligees submitted claims on the bonds in 2010. The surety argued that the claims were untimely because the fund had knowledge of the default no later than August 2008 when the fund filed suit against the principals.[132]

The court found that a trustee's decision to file suit over delinquencies did not constitute an admission, as a matter of law, that the delinquencies cannot ever be resolved. The court agreed that, by the plain language of the surety bonds, the parties left the determination of default to the "sole and exclusive" discretion of the fund. The fund determined that default occurred in January 2010 and notified the surety of the companies' default in June 2010. Therefore, the June 2010 notices of default were timely.[133]

E. Traceability Requirement

In *McDonald v. Fidelity & Deposit Co. of Maryland*,[134] Idaho Iron, Inc. was a subcontractor on a public works project for the Southern Utah University (SUU). Fidelity and Deposit Company of Maryland (F&D) provided surety credit under a payment bond provided to Idaho Iron under the state law in effect in 2010, which was amended in 2013. Idaho Iron was a subcontractor working on a public project and had a workforce consisting of union and nonunion employees.[135] Idaho Iron failed to pay pension and welfare benefits for the eight employees working on the

---

130. Bd. of Trs., Roofers Loc. No. 30 Combined Welfare Fund v. Int'l Fid. Ins. Co., 644 F. App'x 133, 135 (3d Cir. 2016).
131. *Id.*
132. *Id.* at 136.
133. *Id.*
134. 462 P.3d 343 (Utah 2020).
135. *Id.* at 345.

SUU project. It then filed for bankruptcy, and the debt remained unpaid. The fringe benefit trustees then pursued the surety claim under the Utah public works bond.[136]

Under the payment bond required by the statute, a claimant had a "right of action on a payment bond" for "any unpaid amount due" the claimant.[137] The pension and welfare trusts argued that they stood in the shoes of the employees such that they had standing.[138] As noted, Idaho Iron had failed to make any contributions to the various trust funds for the employees working on the public project.

The district court granted the motion for summary judgment filed by the pension and welfare trust fund and denied the cross-motion by F&D. The surety advanced an appeal.[139] F&D argued that the bond covered only sums that are "due *to* an employee."[140] The pension and welfare trust, on the other hand, asked the court to interpret the statute to cover all "claims for any amount due *for* an employee or on the employees' behalf."[141]

The Supreme Court of Utah adopted what it deemed "a middle position," holding that, in order to present a valid payment bond claim, there must be a means to trace the amount due to an individual employee: "The statutory right of action is a right to sue for amounts 'due' a person—meaning any amounts specifically traceable to that person."[142] The court then reviewed the various accounts into which contributions would have been moved if proper payments had been made to the pension and welfare trusts. In doing so, the court rejected the argument advanced by the trust funds that they "get it all." At the same time, the court noted that there were elements of the trust funds that could conceivably be "traceable" to an employee and thus recoverable.

> We thus read the statute to encompass any and all traceable amounts that are ultimately "due" an individual employee. This will clearly encompass wages or other payments made directly

---

136. *Id.*
137. *Id.*
138. *Id.*
139. *Id.* at 346.
140. *Id.*
141. *Id.*
142. *Id.* at 347–48.

> to an employee. But it would also extend to employment benefits that are "due" an employee in a less immediate or direct sense.[143]

The court gave some examples of benefits available under the pension and welfare trusts that fell into the "traceable" and "non-traceable" buckets. For example, the pension and welfare funds may provide "general financial support" to keep the funds solvent. The elements of that cost are traceable to an individual employee.

> The record includes references to funds that "provide for a variety of benefits to ironworks' industry, union, signatory employees, and workers in general," but that "do not provide benefit directly to individual ironworkers." This suggests a lack of traceability, and thus a lack of a right of action on the payment bond. The same could conceivably hold for the claims for prejudgment interest, liquidated damages, audit fees, and court costs. If these amounts benefit employees only by increasing the trusts' financial well-being generally, and not by providing any benefit that is traceable to individual employees, then these amounts would also be unavailable in an action on the payment bond.[144]

The notion that these items fall outside of the "traceable" elements may well eliminate several pieces of the potential claim. The court also described some benefits that are far more "traceable," such as a vacation fund or a tax fund.[145]

IV. When Both a Fringe Benefit Bond and a General Payment Bond May Provide Coverage

Where both a fringe benefit bond and a general payment bond exist, determining the respective liabilities of the sureties requires ascertaining the relative priority of the two bonds and then apportioning coverage between them. The doctrines of cosuretyship and subsuretyship can be helpful to this analysis. However, few if any decisions provide definitive

---

143. *Id.* at 348.
144. *Id.* at 349.
145. *Id.*

answers on the issue of determining liability as between two different sureties.[146]

A. Cosuretyship

Cosuretyship is somewhat analogous to joint and several liability among sureties, although the liability of each is limited to the penal amount of its bond. The proportionate liability of each surety is also generally defined by the penal sums of the bonds,[147] and each cosurety has a right of contribution against the others if it pays more than its proper share.[148]

For example, two sureties might be liable as cosureties on a principal's primary obligation where surety A issued a fringe benefit bond with a $50,000 penal limit and surety B issued a general payment bond with a $200,000 penal limit. If a union brought a valid claim for $100,000

---

146. Only a handful of cases even present the relevant fact pattern. *See, e.g.*, I.B.E.W. Loc. 99 v. United Pac. Ins., 573 A.2d 270 (R.I. 1990) (both fringe benefit bond surety and general payment bond surety had potential liability for union's unpaid benefits claims, but fringe benefit bond surety settled before trial); United States *ex rel.* Trs. of Elec. Workers Loc. Pension Fund v. D Bar D Enters., Inc., 772 F. Supp. 1167 (D. Nev. 1991) (both sureties settled, and dispute involved one surety's indemnity rights); Merchants Bonding Co. v. Utica Cmty. Sch., No. 0160194, 2003 U.S. Dist. LEXIS 9105 (E.D. Mich. May 2, 2003) (one surety issued both a fringe benefit bond and general payment and performance bonds for the same project, and paid claims on both bonds, although the decision did not attribute specific amounts to each bond); Liberty Mut. Ins. Co. v. Consol. Elec. & Tech. Assocs. Corp., No. 06-CV-10217-DT, 2007 WL 118938 (E.D. Mich. Jan. 10, 2007) (where a fringe benefit bond surety paid claims and sought to recover from a party who had purportedly indemnified the principal, the surety was unable to recover because the purported indemnitor successfully asserted a statute-of-frauds defense). However, in none of these four cases did the pertinent issue of allocating liability among sureties arise.

147. RESTATEMENT (THIRD) OF SURETYSHIP AND GUARANTY § 57 (1996); *see also* U.S. Fid. & Guar. Co. v. Naylor, 237 F. 314, 315 (8th Cir. 1916); Humphrey v. Am. Sur. Co., 197 S.E. 137, 139 (N.C. 1938); Fid. & Deposit Co. of Md. v. Phillips, 84 A. 432, 434–35 (Pa. 1912); Cont'l Ins. Co. v. Morgan, Olmstead, Kennedy & Gardner, Inc., 148 Cal. Rptr. 57 (Cal. Ct. App. 1978); Gray v. Am. Sur. Co., 175 N.E. 686, 688 (Ind. Ct. App. 1931).

148. RESTATEMENT (THIRD) OF SURETYSHIP AND GUARANTY § 55(2) (1996).

for unpaid fringe benefit contributions, A would pay 20 percent of the claim and B would pay 80 percent. This is because A is responsible for 20 percent of the combined penal sum limit of $250,000, whereas B is responsible for 80 percent of that combined limit. If, for some reason, A instead paid $50,000 (50 percent) of the claim, A would then have a right of contribution against B in the amount of $30,000.[149]

This relationship is defined precisely in the Restatement of Security: "Cosuretyship is the relation between two or more sureties who are bound to answer for the same duty of the principal, and who as between themselves should share the loss caused by the default of the principal."[150] Where there are multiple secondary obligors for the same underlying obligation, the default rule is that they are presumed to be cosureties, unless a different relationship among them is shown.[151] The obligations of the cosureties may arise out of separate transactions, out of different contracts, at different times, and with or without the knowledge of the other cosureties.[152]

Sheet Metal Workers' Local Union v. Western Surety[153] presents an interesting discussion regarding cosuretyship. In that case, Western Surety issued a fringe benefit bond on behalf of a sheet metal subcontractor, United Sheet Metal Inc., which failed to pay the benefit funds. Western Surety argued that it had been released from liability under the fringe benefit bond because the union benefit funds breached their duty to pursue or exhaust any project-specific contract bonds that may have been available to them upon United's default. According to Western Surety, because certain construction projects on which union members worked

---

149. Both A and B would have the right to recover from the principal whatever *amount* each paid on the primary obligation. *See id.* § 22.

150. Restatement (First) of Security § 144 (1941).

151. Restatement (Third) of Suretyship and Guaranty § 53(3) cmt. f (1996); *see also, e.g.*, Elson v. Nickles, 36 N.W.2d 343, 346–47 (Iowa 1949).

152. *See* Schoenfeld v. Neher, 453 F.2d 896, 897 (10th Cir. 1972); U.S. Fid. & Guar. Co. v. Yeilding Bros. Co., 143 So. 176, 182–83 (Ala. 1932); *see also* Restatement (First) of Security § 144 cmt. a (1941); Harrison v. Lane, 32 Va. (5 Leigh) 414 (1834) ("If the sureties in the second bond were bound for the same thing for which the sureties in the first bond were bound, they would be liable to contribution, although their engagement was made at a subsequent time, by a different instrument, and even without the knowledge of the first bond.").

153. 187 F. Supp. 3d 569 (2016).

during the relevant time period were covered by payment bonds relevant to those particular projects, the union benefit funds had an obligation to pursue recovery under those project-specific bonds before seeking recovery from Western Surety. However, the court found that the fund had no obligation to first make claim on the payment bonds. The only benefit that might be obtained by Western Surety would be to allow it to seek contribution from those cosureties in the event it paid more than its proportionate share of the liability to the funds. Accordingly, the existence of other bonds covering specific construction contracts does not impact Western Surety's liability on the bond at issue in this case.[154]

B. Subsuretyship

Where multiple sureties on the same obligation are neither equally liable for that obligation, nor liable proportionately to the amounts of their bonds, a relationship of subsuretyship may exist among them. That is, if one surety is principally liable for a given obligation, and another surety is only secondarily liable for that obligation relative to the first surety, then the two are in a subsuretyship relationship with respect to one another. As defined in the Restatement of Security, "[s]ubsuretyship is the relation between two or more sureties who are bound to answer for the same duty of the principal where one, the principal surety, in respect of the other, the subsurety, has the whole duty of performance."[155]

If a subsuretyship relationship exists, then the outcome of the example discussed above would be very different. Recall that, in that example, surety A issued a fringe benefit bond with a $50,000 penal limit, surety B issued a general payment bond with a $200,000 penal limit, and a union brought a valid claim for $100,000 for unpaid fringe benefit contributions. If A was deemed to be the principal surety and B was deemed to be the subsurety, then A would be liable for the entire claim, up to the penal amount of A's bond, $50,000. B's liability would begin, if at all, only where A's ended, and so B would only be liable for the remaining amount of the claim, up to the penal amount of B's bond. In this example, the remaining amount of the claim would be $50,000, which would be well below the penal amount of B's bond, $200,000, and so B would be liable for the entire $50,000 balance. If B instead paid the entire $100,000 claim, B would have a right of reimbursement against A

---

154. *Id.* at 579–80.
155. Restatement (First) of Security § 145 (1941).

in the amount of $50,000.[156] By contrast, where the relationship between the sureties was one of cosuretyship rather than subsuretyship, A was liable for only $20,000 of the $100,000 claim.

C. *Which Doctrine (Cosuretyship or Subsuretyship) Applies to the Coexisting Fringe Benefit Bond-Payment Bond Situation?*

Where more than one surety is liable on the same underlying obligation, a cosuretyship relationship exists unless either the sureties together agree to a subsuretyship relationship or other circumstances demonstrate that a subsuretyship relationship exists.[157] The restatements synthesize much of the common law concerning the circumstances sufficient for a court to find that a subsuretyship relationship exists.

The general test is found in section 53(3) of the Restatement (Third) of Suretyship and Guaranty: subsuretyship exists if circumstances "demonstrate that, as between themselves, one secondary obligor (the 'principal surety') rather than the other (the 'subsurety') should perform or bear the cost of performance."[158] The next subsection provides a non-exhaustive list of three sets of circumstances that satisfy the general test.[159]

First, a subsuretyship relationship exists if surety B assumes its obligation after surety A does, and if at least one of three things is also true when B takes on its obligation:[160] (1) B reasonably believes that

---

156. Restatement (Third) of Suretyship and Guaranty § 59 cmt. c. (1996).

157. *Id.* § 53.

158. Lowe v. Albertazzie, 516 S.E.2d 258, 264 (W. Va. 1999) (adopting the doctrine of subsuretyship and holding that courts may invoke it as an equitable remedy (1) in the absence of an agreement between the secondary obligors; (2) when the agreement is ambiguous; or (3) when a plaintiff "claims fraud, mistake, or material misrepresentations in the execution of such agreement").

159. Restatement (Third) of Suretyship and Guaranty § 53(4) (1996); *see also* Cooke & Moses, LLC v. QSS-Engineered Sys. Grp., LLC, No. 1:06-CV-147, 2007 U.S. Dist. LEXIS 63650 (N.D. W. Va. Aug. 28, 2007) (holding that plaintiffs could claim fraud, supported by extrinsic evidence, to prove the circumstances that demonstrated that one of the sureties was the principal subsurety on the note).

160. Restatement (Third) of Suretyship and Guaranty § 53(4)(a) (1996).

A is a principal obligor;[161] (2) B manifests an intent to be bound only as a subsurety and is not duty-bound otherwise;[162] or (3) B otherwise reasonably believes that A has a duty to perform or bear the cost of performance.[163] It is not sufficient that A is bound before B is bound, or that B becomes bound at A's request. Few cases discuss this issue, but one case involving individual sureties addressed the problem. In *Kurzman v. Steir*,[164] surety B sued surety A, alleging that A had been unjustly enriched at B's expense when a bank exercised its rights with respect to the shares of stock that both parties had pledged as security for the bank's loan to a person who subsequently defaulted.[165] B argued that A was already a surety when A asked B to pledge his stock; therefore, B was a subsurety who would be liable only if A's stock was not sufficient to cover the defaulted loan.[166] The court disagreed, finding that the correct test considered the totality of the circumstances and the equity of the outcome.[167] The court found that both sureties shared a common goal to enhance the collateral supporting the loan and that both stood to benefit from this enhancement.[168] The court also rejected B's contention that he was misled into believing that A's stock would be exhausted first.[169] Without more, and absent a finding of inequity,[170] the court could not conclude that B was a subsurety.

Second, a subsuretyship relationship may exist if both principal X and principal Y owe the same performance to an obligee,[171] and surety A secures X's performance while surety B secures Y's.[172] If, as between X and Y, X ought to perform or bear the cost of performing the obligation

---

161. *Id.* § 53(4)(a)(i).
162. *Id.* § 53(4)(a)(ii).
163. *Id.* § 53(4)(a)(iii).
164. 426 N.E.2d 165 (Mass. Ct. App. 1981).
165. *Id.* at 166.
166. *Id.*
167. *Id.* at 167.
168. *Id.* at 168.
169. *Id.* (citing Snelling v. State St. Bank & Tr. Co., 265 N.E.2d 350, 355 (Mass. 1970) (an "optimistic prediction" does not constitute an agreement of subsuretyship)).
170. *Id.* at 168–69.
171. Restatement (Third) of Suretyship and Guaranty § 53(4)(b)(i) (1996).
172. *Id.* § 53(4)(b)(iii).

to the obligee,[173] then A is the principal surety and B is the subsurety.[174] Similarly, under the same facts, if X defaults, thus imposing liability also on Y, then X's surety, A, is the principal surety and Y's surety, B, is the subsurety.[175]

An example of the latter scenario occurred in *A & P Sheet Metal Co. v. Edward Hansen, Inc.*[176] Surety B, securing performance of the general contractor, moved for summary judgment, alleging that it was not responsible for an equal share of a sub-subcontractor's claims made against a bankrupt contractor because surety B was merely a subsurety for the subcontractor's surety, A.[177] The court held that B was indeed a subsurety of A because the bankrupt contractor caused the loss and the bond was written for the purpose of protecting the owner from such a loss.[178]

Third, if A and B both secure X's performance of an obligation, and A's obligation "is specific and limited to that performance," while B's obligation "is broader in scope," then A is the principal surety and B is the subsurety, unless circumstances reveal a contrary intention.[179] Courts have generally adhered to this as a rule of thumb. For example, in *United States v. Horvath Brothers, Inc.*,[180] a federal district court in Wisconsin held that the surety on a bond covering a specific agreement was the principal surety and the surety on a statutory license bond was the subsurety when a claim arose under the agreement. And the Minnesota Supreme Court found in an earlier case that where there was a failure properly to account for the proceeds of a real estate sale, the surety on the bond covering the specific sale was the principal surety and the surety on a general administrator's bond was the subsurety.[181]

Because the analysis is at its core about achieving equity under all the circumstances, general rules of thumb need not always be followed. For example, a court might conclude on equitable grounds that the surety

---

173. *Id.* § 53(4)(b)(ii).
174. *Id.* § 53(4)(b)(iii).
175. RESTATEMENT (FIRST) OF SECURITY § 147(3) (1946).
176. 357 A.2d 37 (N.J. Super. Ct. Law Div. 1976).
177. *Id.* at 38.
178. *Id.* at 44.
179. RESTATEMENT (THIRD) OF SURETYSHIP AND GUARANTY § 53(4)(c) (1996); RESTATEMENT (FIRST) OF SECURITY § 146(b) cmt. b (1946).
180. 278 F. Supp. 159 (E.D. Wis. 1967).
181. Hartford Accident & Indem. Co. v. Anderson, 256 N.W. 185 (Minn. 1934).

on a project payment bond is the principal surety for a claim on behalf of laborers on that project for unpaid fringe benefit contributions, and that the surety on a fringe benefit bond is the subsurety because the latter covers the principal's fringe benefit obligations generally for the period of the collective bargaining agreement. Under one interpretation, this might seem to violate the principle that the surety with respect to the more specific obligation is the principal surety. Such interpretation views the fringe benefit bond as more specific to the type of dispute at issue (i.e., the failure to pay fringe benefit contributions). However, under another interpretation, the payment bond actually *is* the more specific obligation because it covers the specific *project* in which the dispute arises. Thus, a thorough analysis of the facts and circumstances in each given case is necessary to predict how a court might rule.[182]

V. The ERISA Preemption Defense

The federal ERISA[183] has in some cases preempted state law actions against employers and sureties by unions or fund trustees seeking to recover unpaid fringe benefit contributions. ERISA contains a broad preemption clause, which provides that the statute "shall supersede any and all State laws insofar as they may now or hereafter relate to any employee benefit plan [that is subject to ERISA]."[184] Where ERISA

---

182. Cook v. Crabtree, 733 S.W.2d 67 (Tenn. 1987) (finding that where assignees and their wives all signed a suretyship agreement, the assignees were principal sureties and a wife was a subsurety because the wife had no interest in the business; she was not a stockholder, officer, director, or employee; she assumed her obligation at the request of another surety who was already bound; she was not a party to the underlying agreement; and the bank had required her and the other wives to sign the suretyship agreement).
183. 29 U.S.C. § 1001 *et seq.* (2006).
184. *Id.* § 1144(a). The U.S. Supreme Court has characterized this provision as "conspicuous for its breadth." IngersollRand Co. v. McClendon, 498 U.S. 133, 138 (1990). The Supreme Court consistently interpreted ERISA's preemption provision broadly until 1995. *See* Shaw v. Delta Air Lines, 463 U.S. 85, 96–97 (1983) (a "law relates to an employee benefit plan if it has a connection with or reference to such a plan"). *See also* Pilot Life Ins. Co. v. Dedeaux, 481 U.S. 41 (1987); Mackey v. Lanier Collection Agency & Serv., 486 U.S. 825, 829–30 (1988); FMC Corp. v. Holliday, 498 U.S. 52 (1990).

preempts state law claims, it limits the claimant to pursuing only those causes of action provided by ERISA itself. Not only are fund trustees thus precluded from availing themselves of state statutory and common law remedies, but they may be left with no recourse whatsoever against sureties, whom the relevant provisions of ERISA may not reach.

ERISA mandates:

> Every employer who is obligated to make contributions to a multiemployer plan under the terms of the plan or under the terms of a collectively bargained agreement shall, to the extent not inconsistent with law, make such contributions in accordance with the terms and conditions of such plan or such agreement.[185]

The statute grants a right to bring a civil action to any "participant, beneficiary, or fiduciary" with respect to "any act or practice which violates any provision of this title."[186] But ERISA limits who is an "employer" within the meaning of the statute to "any person acting directly as an employer, or indirectly in the interest of an employer, in relation to an employee benefit plan."[187]

A number of courts have found that a surety cannot be an "employer who is obligated to make contributions" under ERISA's definition.[188] Some of these courts have found significant the fact that sureties are not signatories to the employment or collective bargaining agreements that give rise to the obligation to make fringe benefit contributions.[189] Because the obligation to make contributions arises under those agreements, sureties are precluded from being obligors as to those obligations. Some courts have also found that sureties do not act "in the interest of an

---

185. 29 U.S.C. § 1145 (2006).
186. *Id.* § 1132(a)(3).
187. *Id.* § 1002(5).
188. Xaros v. U.S. Fid. & Guar. Co., 820 F.2d 1176, 1179–80 (11th Cir. 1987); Carpenters S. Cal. Admin. Corp. v. D & L Camp Constr. Co., 738 F.2d 999, 1000 (9th Cir. 1984); Ragan v. Tri-County Excavating, 62 F.3d 501, 512–13 (3d Cir. 1995); Bleiler v. Cristwood Constr., 72 F.3d 13, 15–16 (2d Cir. 1995).
189. Examples include Greenblatt v. Delta Plumbing & Heating Corp., 68 F.3d 561, 575–76 (2d Cir. 1995); Laborers Loc. 938 Joint Health & Welfare Tr. Fund v. B.R. Starnes Co. of Fla., 827 F.2d 1454, 1456–57 (11th Cir. 1987); Trs. of the Screen Actors Guild-Producers Pension & Health Plans v. NYCA, Inc., 572 F.3d 771 (9th Cir. 2009).

employer," but rather for the benefit of employees or others.[190] For similar reasons, some courts have found that even general contractors do not qualify as "employers" under ERISA's provisions, at least with respect to employees directly hired by subcontractors.[191] Another line of cases employs similar reasoning to conclude that an individual owner or officer of an employer corporation is not an "employer" within the meaning of ERISA, perhaps laying the foundation in those jurisdictions for similar future decisions with regard to sureties and general contractors.[192]

Thus, a great deal often is at stake in determining whether ERISA preempts a state action to recover unpaid fringe benefit contributions. A claimant that would otherwise be able to recover under state law may be unable to recover under ERISA if no defendant—or at least no solvent defendant—qualifies as an "employer who is obligated to make contributions" under the federal statute.[193]

Beginning in 1995, the Supreme Court adjusted course in its ERISA preemption jurisprudence, pulling back from its earlier expansiveness, but without overruling any of its prior decisions. In 1995, the Supreme Court held in *New York State Conference of Blue Cross & Blue Shield Plans v. Travelers Insurance Co.* that state laws did not "relate to" employee benefit plans within the meaning of 29 U.S.C. § 1144(a) where those state laws had "only a tenuous, remote, or peripheral connection with covered

---

190. Giardiello v. Balboa Ins. Co., 837 F.2d 1566 (11th Cir. 1988); *Ragan*, 62 F.3d at 512–13.

191. Carpenters Health & Welfare Tr. Fund v. Tri Capital Corp., 25 F.3d 849 (9th Cir. 1994), *cert. denied*, 513 U.S. 1018 (1994); *B.R. Starnes Co. of Fla.*, 827 F.2d at 1456–57; *Bleiler*, 72 F.3d at 15–16. By the same reasoning, a subcontractor is not an "employer" with respect to the employees of a contractor. *See Xaros*, 820 F.2d 1176.

192. *See* Int'l Bhd. of Painters & Allied Trades Union v. George A. Kracher, Inc., 856 F.2d 1546, 1548 (D.C. Cir. 1988); Rockney v. Blohorn, 877 F.2d 637, 643 (8th Cir. 1989); Scarbrough v. Perez, 870 F.2d 1079, 1082–84 (6th Cir. 1989). A branch of this line of cases finds that such individuals can be "employers" under ERISA's definition, but may not be "obligated to make contributions" within the meaning of the statute. *See* Mass. Laborers' Health & Welfare Fund v. Starrett Paving, 845 F.2d 23 (1st Cir. 1988); Sullivan v. Cox, 78 F.3d 322 (7th Cir. 1996).

193. *But see Ragan*, 62 F.3d at 512–13 (finding that, because the surety was not an "employer" under ERISA's definition, the surety was unable to invoke ERISA preemption as a defense).

plans, as is the case with many laws of general applicability."[194] The Court reaffirmed that in the ERISA context, as in others, it would address "claims of pre-emption with the starting presumption that Congress does not intend to supplant state law."[195] In determining whether a given state law has a "connection with" ERISA plans,[196] the Court announced that it would look to "the objectives of the ERISA statute as a guide to the scope of the state law that Congress understood would survive."[197] Congress's core purpose in giving ERISA express preemptive effect was, the Court concluded, "to avoid a multiplicity of regulation in order to permit the nationally uniform administration of employee benefit plans."[198]

Two years later, the Court in *California Division of Labor Standards Enforcement v. Dillingham Construction, N.A., Inc.* took a second step in the same direction, clarifying the applicable tests for the two-part ERISA preemption inquiry: "A law relates to a covered employee benefit plan for purposes of § 514(a) [29 U.S.C. § 1144(a)] if it (1) has a connection with or (2) reference to such a plan."[199] Under the test for the second part of the inquiry, a state law "refers to" employee benefit plans with preemptive effect where it "acts immediately and exclusively upon ERISA plans . . . or where the existence of ERISA plans is essential to the law's operation."[200] To determine whether a state law "has a 'connection with' ERISA plans" under the first part of the inquiry, the Supreme Court pointed to "the objectives of the ERISA statute as a guide to the scope of the state law that Congress understood would survive, as well as to the nature of the effect of the state law on ERISA plans," and directed that the inquiry adopt the "assumption that the historic police powers of the States were not to be superseded by the Federal Act unless that was the clear and manifest purpose of Congress."[201] The Supreme Court thus drew boundary lines around the open-ended language of the statute and its own earlier decisions.

---

194. 514 U.S. 645, 661 (1995) (quoting District of Columbia v. Greater Wash. Bd. of Trade, 506 U.S. 125, 130 n.1 (1992)).
195. *Id.* at 654.
196. *Id.* at 656 (quoting Shaw v. Delta Air Lines, 463 U.S. 85, 97 (1983)).
197. *Id.*
198. *Id.* at 657.
199. 519 U.S. 316, 324 (1997) (internal quotes and edits omitted).
200. *Id.* at 325.
201. *Id.*

In another 1997 decision, the Supreme Court held that ERISA did not preempt a state tax on gross receipts for patient services at diagnostic and treatment centers, even where those treatment centers were operated directly by ERISA funds.[202] Repeating some of the formulations it had announced in earlier decisions, the Supreme Court found that the state tax operated in "a field that has been traditionally occupied by the States"[203] and was "one of myriad state laws of general applicability that impose some burdens on the administration of ERISA plans but nevertheless do not 'relate to' them within the meaning of the governing statute."[204] The Supreme Court rejected the appeals court's attempt to distinguish the case from *Travelers* on the basis that the impact on affected ERISA plans that operated their own treatment centers was direct, whereas the impact of the state law at issue in *Travelers* had been indirect, finding that the substantive effect was the same in either case.[205]

But the ERISA preemption decisions since *Travelers* and *Dillingham* have not been uniformly deferential to state law. Two years after *Dillingham* and *De Buono*, the Supreme Court held that ERISA preempted a state supreme court decision that conflicted with an express provision in a disability insurance policy.[206] A covered employee who became disabled had given notice of his disability to his employer, the group policyholder, and administrator, rather than directly to the insurer within a specified period as the policy required.[207] A state supreme court decision in a different case had established the rule that "the employer is the agent of the insurer in performing the duties of administering group insurance policies."[208] But the Supreme Court found that the state law "related to" ERISA plans because the law

> would have a marked effect on plan administration: It would force the employer, as plan administrator, to assume a role, with attendant legal duties and consequences, that it has not undertaken voluntarily . . . [and] would affect not merely the plan's

---

202. De Buono v. NYSA-ILA Med. & Clinical Servs. Fund, 520 U.S. 806 (1997).
203. *Id.* at 814.
204. *Id.* at 815.
205. *Id.* at 816.
206. UNUM Life Ins. Co. of Am. v. Ward, 526 U.S. 358 (1999).
207. *Id.* at 365.
208. *Id.* at 378.

> bookkeeping obligations regarding to whom benefits checks must be sent, but would also regulate the basic services that a plan may or must provide to its participants and beneficiaries.[209]

Therefore, the Supreme Court held that ERISA preempted the state court's decision.[210]

Two years later, the Supreme Court held that ERISA preempted a state statute that provided for the automatic revocation upon divorce of the designation of a spouse as the beneficiary of a life insurance policy or employee benefit plan.[211] The Supreme Court found that the state law had a "connection with" ERISA plans (and, therefore, "related to" such plans) because the statute "directly conflict[ed] with ERISA's requirements that plans be administered, and benefits be paid, in accordance with plan documents,"[212] and because the statute "govern[ed] the payment of benefits, a central matter of plan administration."[213] The Court's analysis was as follows:

> The statute binds ERISA plan administrators to a particular choice of rules for determining beneficiary status. The administrators must pay benefits to the beneficiaries chosen by state law, rather than to those identified in the plan documents. The statute thus implicates an area of core ERISA concern. In particular, it runs counter to ERISA's commands that a plan shall "specify the basis on which payments are made to and from the plan," § 1102(b)(4), and that the fiduciary shall administer the plan "in accordance with the documents and instruments governing the plan," § 1104(a)(1)(D), making payments to a "beneficiary" who is "designated by a participant, or by the terms of [the] plan." § 1002(8).[214]

Finally, the decision rested on the finding that the state statute "interfere[d] with nationally uniform plan administration," undermining "[o]ne of the

---

209. *Id.* at 379.
210. The plaintiff employee in *Ward* brought his claim under ERISA, so he did not seek to escape the reach of the statute entirely, but merely sought the benefit of a favorable state law rule.
211. Egelhoff v. Egelhoff, 532 U.S. 141, 143 (2001).
212. *Id.* at 150.
213. *Id.* at 148.
214. *Id.* at 147.

principal goals of ERISA," which "is to enable employers to establish a uniform administrative scheme [providing] a set of standard procedures to guide processing of claims and disbursement of benefits" instead of permitting "plans [to be] subject to different legal obligations in different States."[215]

Since the Supreme Court's 1995 decision in *Travelers*, only five federal appellate courts have ruled expressly on the issue of whether ERISA preempts a bond claim against a surety for unpaid fringe benefits. All five have found the claims not to be preempted. In *Greenblatt v. Delta Plumbing & Heating Corp.*, the Second Circuit held that ERISA did not preempt state surety law with respect to a union fund's claim under a bond for unpaid fringe benefit contributions.[216] The court found the state surety law (1) made no explicit reference to ERISA plans; (2) did not bind the hands of ERISA trustees or regulate them in any fashion; (3) did not threaten a multiplicity of regulations that would interfere with the nationally uniform administration of employee benefit plans; (4) did not conflict with any enforcement mechanism or cause of action specified in ERISA; and (5) did not touch upon any rights or duties incident to the ERISA plan itself; but (6) was merely a run-of-the-mill state law claim.[217] Therefore, the court concluded, ERISA did not preempt state surety law, and, because the district court lacked any other source of subject matter jurisdiction, the appeals court dismissed the complaint.[218]

In *Ragan v. Tri-County Excavating*, the Third Circuit held that ERISA did not preempt a union's common-law third-party beneficiary action on a surety bond.[219] The court held that the state law was generally applicable and made no reference to, functioned irrespective of, and was not predicated on, the existence of an ERISA plan.[220] The court contrasted *Tri-County*, in which the court needed only to determine the surety's obligations under the bond, with the Supreme Court's 1990 decision in *Ingersoll-Rand*, which stated that "in order to prevail in the cause of action, a plaintiff must plead, and the court must find, that an

---

215. *Id.* at 148.
216. 68 F.3d 561 (2d Cir. 1995).
217. *Id.* at 574–75.
218. *Id.* at 576–77.
219. 62 F.3d 501 (3d Cir. 1995). The court found ERISA was not preemptive under either the statute's own preemption provision or ordinary conflict preemption principles. *Id.* at 512.
220. *Id.* at 511.

ERISA plan exists and the employer had a pension-defeating motive in terminating the employment."[221]

In a thinly supported decision, the Sixth Circuit held that ERISA did not preempt a state's Little Miller Act because the state law was a statute of general applicability.[222] The Ninth Circuit also held that ERISA did not preempt a state's Little Miller Act, finding no evidence that Congress intended for ERISA "to pre-empt either the area of state statutory payment bonds or their guarantee by third-party sureties," and concluding that the state law regulated "an area that Congress has traditionally left to the states: enforcing rights and obligations arising by contract, pursuant to state law, for the protection of the public."[223] Like the Ninth Circuit, the First Circuit reversed its own previous decisions to hold that ERISA did not preempt a state's Little Miller Act, on grounds that the public works bond statute did not impermissibly supply an alternative enforcement mechanism for ERISA plan benefits, but rather "regulated an area of the law traditionally thought to be the states' preserve: enforcing contracts under state law for the citizenry's protection."[224]

There is currently no split among the circuits that have expressly decided the issue of whether ERISA preempts a bond claim against a surety for unpaid fringe benefits, and the general ERISA preemption jurisprudence of the other circuits provides no reason to believe that such a split might occur in the future.[225] In recent decisions, several of the other circuits have found that ERISA preempts state law only in narrow circumstances.[226] The Supreme Court's failure to expressly overrule

---

221. *Id.*

222. Trs. for Mich. Laborers' Health Care Fund v. Seaboard Sur. Co., 137 F.3d 427, 429 (6th Cir. 1998).

223. Operating Eng'rs Health & Welfare Tr. Fund v. JWJ Contracting Co., 135 F.3d 671, 678 (9th Cir. 1998).

224. Carpenter's Loc. Union No. 26 v. U.S. Fid. & Guar. Co., 215 F.3d 136, 141 (1st Cir. 2000).

225. *See, e.g.*, Sharp Elecs. Corp. v. Metro. Life Ins. Co., 578 F.3d 505, 514 (7th Cir. 2009) (ERISA did not preempt claims where the ERISA plan was the subject of the contract under which the claims arose, but nothing in the contract depended on the particular content of the plan); Trs. of AFTRA Health Fund v. Biondi, 303 F.3d 765, 774 (7th Cir. 2002) (ERISA did not preempt state common law fraud claim).

226. *See, e.g.*, Griggs v. E.I. Dupont de Nemours & Co., 237 F.3d 371 (4th Cir. 2001) (ERISA preempted state negligent misrepresentation claim where the false representations concerned the existence or extent of benefits

any of its early decisions establishing the broad scope of the ERISA preemption has effectively left the doctrine available in the legal toolbox. However, the federal appellate courts seem disinclined to find a use for it in the fringe benefit surety bond context.

Conclusion

The context in which a fringe benefit bond or payment bond is issued plays a significant role in determining the liability of the bond's surety with respect to a given claim. The surety's liability may vary depending on whether the bond is required by statute or is a common law bond provided pursuant to a private agreement between the parties. If the bond is statutory, its interpretation will be influenced by the language of the statute that requires it. By contrast, a common law bond is generally interpreted primarily in light of the terms of the agreement between the parties and principles of state contract law.

Where both a fringe benefit bond and a general payment bond exist, liability is generally allocated according to principles of cosuretyship and subsuretyship, although there remains little case law to guide the application of these doctrines.

---

under an employee benefit plan); Jackson v. Wal-Mart Stores, Inc., No. 01-1232, 24 F. App'x 132 (4th Cir. Dec. 4, 2001) (ERISA preempted state statute where statutory claim entailed an inquiry into the terms and administration of the employee benefits plan to determine whether the employer deducted unauthorized amounts from the employee's wages); Bullock v. Equitable Life Assurance Soc'y of U.S., 259 F.3d 395 (5th Cir. 2001) (ERISA preempted state law claims for breach of contract, unjust enrichment, and promissory estoppel where the claims addressed "areas of exclusive federal concern, such as the right to receive benefits under the terms of an ERISA plan" and "directly affect[ed] the relationship among traditional ERISA entities—i.e., the employer, plan administrators, fiduciaries, participants, and beneficiaries"); Menchaca v. CNA Grp. Life Assurance Co., No. 08-20658, 331 F. App'x 298 (5th Cir. Aug. 18, 2009) (ERISA preempted state law claims because they related to a claim for benefits under an ERISA disability plan); Dobbs v. Anthem Blue Cross & Blue Shield, 600 F.3d 1275, 1286 (10th Cir. 2010) (ERISA would preempt state law claims where the improper conduct for which plaintiffs sought relief was not insurer's misrepresentation of insurance plan terms, but insurer's failure to abide by those terms).

Although Supreme Court precedent defining a robust ERISA preemption defense remains good law, the recent trend has been toward abandoning that defense in the context of bond claims against a surety for unpaid fringe benefits.

CHAPTER 12

CUSTOMS BONDS, CLAIMS, AND LITIGATION

T. Randolph Ferguson
Laura Maurer

Introduction

In the second decade of the 21st Century, international internet commerce has greatly expanded.[1] On January 20, 2015, the electronic bond (E-bond) went into effect allowing for the electronic filing of most customs bonds directly with U.S. Customs and Border Protection (CBP). As a result, CBP has increased the electronic transfer of information back to the surety on a monthly, weekly, and daily basis. These data feeds provide the surety with updates on bonds filed, entries cleared, and claims made under its bonds. Accordingly, for a surety to become a significant player in the customs bond market, the surety needs to create an electronic system to store and manipulate the data received from CBP in order to process claims and analyze risk on the bonds that it undertakes.

I. Customs Bonds

The Secretary of the Treasury authorizes CBP to require such bonds or other security as the Secretary, or CBP, may deem necessary for the protection of the revenue or to assure compliance with any provision of law, regulation, or instruction that the Secretary of the Treasury or CBP may be authorized to enforce.[2] In addition to customs bonds, 19 U.S.C. § 1623(e) authorizes the Secretary of the Treasury to accept money or obligations of the United States in lieu of a surety bond. The latter alternative of depositing money or obligations of the United States may seem an attractive option to purchasing a surety bond and having to

1. The authors thank James A. Carpenter, T. Scott Leo, and Ann T. Hester for their work on the prior version of this chapter in THE LAW OF COMMERCIAL SURETY AND MISCELLANEOUS BONDS (Bruce Charles King et al. eds., 2d ed. 2012). This chapter updates, supplements, and expands upon their work.
2. 19 U.S.C. § 1623(a); 19 C.F.R. § 113.0 *et seq.* (2015).

deposit collateral with the surety, but CBP is not known to cancel surety bonds as a matter of course and obtaining the return of security from the United States may prove to be far more difficult than negotiating the return of collateral from a surety company.

The basic CBP importation and entry bond secures the release of imported merchandise from the custody of CBP pending determinations by CBP or other federal agencies as to the product's admissibility into the commerce of the United States and CBP's final determination as to the principal's (the importer's) liability for duties under the Harmonized Tariff Schedule of the United States. It is a cornerstone of our nation's successful global supply chain, allowing goods to enter commerce immediately—prior to the days, weeks, and years necessary for the government to make final decisions on the quantity, duty rates, appraised value, and admissibility of the goods. The standard bond form is Customs Form (CF) 301.

The U.S. customs bond[3] secures two elements of the customs entry transaction: (1) the obligation of the importer to pay duties and (2) the obligation of the importer to perform all obligations necessary to ensure the admissibility of the entered merchandise into the commerce of the United States.[4] The liability of the principal and the surety under the terms of a customs bond are joint and several. A demand may be

---

3. Custom Form (CF) 301. CF 301 sets out 17 "activities" that can be undertaken under the bond, each one with the corresponding reference to the bond obligations set out in the CBP regulations that apply to that activity (e.g., Activity Code 1 covers the activities of importers and brokers with reference to the bond obligations set out in 19 C.F.R. § 113.62, which govern the obligations of importers and customhouse brokers).
4. The obligations secured by the customs bond are set out at 19 C.F.R. § 113.62 and incorporated by reference into the customs bond form CF 301. The basic importation and entry bond contains the following 13 conditions that are set out in 19 C.F.R. § 113.62:
    (a) Agreement to Pay Duties, Taxes, and Charges.
    (b) Agreement to Make or Complete Entry.
    (c) Agreement to Produce Documents and Evidence.
    (d) Agreement to Redeliver Merchandise [found inadmissible].
    (e) Agreement to Rectify Any Non-Compliance with Provisions of Admission.
    (f) Agreement for Examination of Merchandise.
    (g) Reimbursement and Exoneration of the United States.
    (h) Agreement on Duty-Free Entries or Withdrawals.

made against either the principal or the surety when the principal has breached an obligation incurred by the principal under the terms of the bond. As will be discussed hereinbelow, the liabilities of the surety and the importer under the bond are different. The liability of the surety for duties and liquidated damages is limited to the penal value of the bond. On the other hand, while the liability of the importer for liquidated damages is also limited to the face value of the bond, the importer's liability for duties is not. Moreover, while the liability of the surety for liquidated duties is limited by a six-year statute of limitations; there is no statute of limitations that protects the importer from the collection of claims for duties.

There are two types of customs bonds: the single transaction bond (STB) and the continuous transaction bond (CTB). The penal value of a bond is calculated differently depending on whether the bond is an STB or a CTB. An STB is used for only one entry transaction. The penal value of an STB is calculated at the value of the merchandise covered by the entry plus the total of all duties, taxes, and fees. If an STB is covering merchandise regulated by a partner government agency (PGA),[5] the penal value of the bond may require calculation at three times the value of the merchandise.[6]

On the other hand, the CTB allows an importer to clear multiple entries at one or more ports over the course of a one-year period. The penal value of a CTB is calculated at a minimum of $50,000 or on the basis of 10 percent of the total duties, taxes, and fees paid by the principal during the prior year rounded up to the next $10,000 (where annual duty, tax, and fee payments are $1,000,000 or less) or to the next $100,000 (where annual duty, tax, and fee payments are more than $1,000,000).

(i) Agreement to Comply with CBP Regulations Applicable to Customs Security Areas at Airports.
(j) Agreement to Comply with Importer Security Filings.
(k) Agreement to Comply with Electronic Entry and/or Advance Cargo Information Filing Requirements.
(l) Agreement to Comply with Air Cargo Advance Screening (ACAS) Requirements
(m) Agreement to Ensure and Establish Issuance of Softwood Lumber Export Permit and Collection of Export Fees.
(n) Consequence of Default.

5. *See infra* note 16.
6. 19 C.F.R. § 141.113(i) (1973).

The "Monetary Guidelines for Setting Bond Amounts"[7] may be found on the CBP website.

A CTB remains in effect for one-year periods and is automatically renewed unless otherwise terminated by CBP, the principal, or the surety. So, unless the CTB has been terminated earlier, a $50,000 bond filed on January 1, 2021, will remain in effect with a $50,000 liability cap for 12 months until December 31, 2021. On January 1, 2022, the $50,000 bond will automatically renew at $50,000, and the additional $50,000 liability will be "stacked" on top of the original $50,000 liability creating a new aggregate liability of $100,000. The "stacking" will also occur each time CBP requires the importer to increase its bond amount whether prior to or at the renewal date. CBP may require additional security at any point during an annual period of the bond, in which case the bond (e.g., a $50,000 CTB) is terminated and replaced by a new bond (e.g., a $100,000 CTB) containing the addition security. In that case, the importer's CTB bond liability is "stacked" (e.g., to $150,000) to account for the increased security.[8]

A surety on a customs bond stands in the shoes of the importer[9] and has all the rights to administratively and judicially challenge demands made by CBP upon the surety under its bond. However, it is not a "performance bond" so if the bond is charged because the importer failed to file an entry or redeliver goods, the surety can eliminate the liability by filing the entry or redelivering the goods.

The demands made by CBP upon the importer and surety that we will focus on in this chapter are (1) the demands for payment of liquidated damages incurred for the failure of an importer to meet one or more of the obligations set out in the bond;[10] and (2) the demands for payment of duties.

II. Liquidated Damages Claims

As a general rule, the first demands that are encountered by the surety against its bond occur early in the life of an entry transaction made under the bond.

---

7. Customs Directive No. 3510-004 (July 23, 1991).
8. However, note each bond secures only the transactions made during its effective time period as discussed in Part IX of this chapter.
9. *See infra* note 29.
10. 19 C.F.R. § 113.62(n) (1984). *See supra* note 4.

A. *Failure to File Entry Documents or Deposit Estimated Duties*

If the importer principal fails to file the documents necessary to complete the entry process including the deposit of estimated duties, CBP will assess liquidated damages on a CF 5955A. If the entry was made under an STB, the claim will be made for the full penal value of the bond.[11] If the entry was made under a CTB, the claim for liquidated damages will be made based on the same calculation used to determine the penal value of an STB bond (value of the entered merchandise plus duty plus taxes and fees).

The importer has ten working days to file the required entry documents[12] and pay estimated duties[13] following release of its imported merchandise from CBP custody. However, an importer may apply for permission to pay its estimated duty, taxes, and fees on a consolidated periodic monthly statement (PMS).[14] A failure to pay the duties or file the documents in a timely manner will result in CBP's issuing a claim for liquidated damages for breach of either one or both bond obligations. A description of the liquidated damages claims for a failure to timely file entry documents or deposit estimated duties is fully set out in the Informed Compliance Publication *Mitigation Guidelines: Fines, Penalties, Forfeitures, and Liquidated Damages* (FP&F Handbook).[15]

Over the past few years, CBP has changed its liquidated damages collection procedure for some non-file duty deposit claims at various ports. Previously, after receipt of the 5955A demand for liquidated damages for a failure to deposit estimated duties, an importer or surety had to deposit the unpaid estimated duties before CBP would consider mitigation by transforming the claim from a "non-file" for full liquidated

---

11. As noted above, the penal value of an STB bond is calculated at the value of the merchandise covered by the entry, plus duties and taxes. If the merchandise is restricted or prohibited merchandise, the bond calculation will be supplemented by a factor of three times the value of the merchandise. *Id.* § 141.113.
12. *Id.* § 113.62(b).
13. *Id.* § 113.62(a)(1)(i).
14. The PMS can be found at *Periodic Monthly Statement*, CBP, https://www.cbp.gov/document/guidance/periodic-monthly-statement (last modified Dec. 16, 2020).
15. CBP, What Every Member of the Trade Community Should Know: Mitigation Guidelines: Fines, Penalties, Forfeitures, and Liquidated Damages 195 (2004).

damages to a "late file," allowing for mitigation of the full liquidated damages originally assessed. In such cases, the importer or surety would deposit the non-filed amount with the Port Fines, Penalties, and Forfeitures (Port FP&F) Office and the Port FP&F Office would reissue the claim as a "late file," allowing for an Option 1 mitigation calculation of 0.1 percent per calendar day that the payment was late.

Lately, however, when the importer's broker has filed the entry summary without the duty deposit, CBP may liquidate the entry immediately and issue a bill for liquidated duties from CBP's Revenue Division at the CBP National Finance Center (NFC) before the liquidated damages claim is resolved at the port. In such a case, since the liquidated duty billing incurs interest from the date of liquidation, the surety is advised to pay the liquidated duty bill through the NFC and provide the Port FP&F Office with evidence of payment to the NFC. To coordinate the processing and remission or mitigation of the liquidated damages bill, the surety should reference (1) the liquidated duty bill number; (2) the entry number; and (3) the Port FP&F case number on the check by which the increased duties are paid. Thereafter, the surety's cover correspondence to the Port FP&F Office should reference in this order (1) the liquidated damages case number; (2) the entry number; and (3) the increased duty bill number. In the cover letter, it is recommended that the surety advise the port that the payment to the NFC included the payment of post-liquidation interest under 19 U.S.C. § 1505 and request remission or mitigation based on the interest already paid. A copy of the check by which the liquidated duties were paid to the NFC should be provided under cover of the letter to the Port FP&F Office.

B. Failure to Evidence Admissibility of Merchandise or Failure to Comply with Notice to Redeliver

The admissibility of merchandise is determined by CBP or by one or more of its PGAs.[16] CBP determines admissibility with regard to compliance

---

16. CBP's PGAs are the U.S. Department of Agriculture, the U.S. Department of Health and Human Services, the U.S. Department of Commerce, the U.S. Department of Transportation, the U.S. Department of Justice, the U.S. Department of the Interior, and the U.S. Department of the Treasury. The PGAs and each of their subagencies are set out on the CBP website at *Partner Government Agencies Import Guides*, CBP, https://www

with the United States country of origin marking statutes,[17] and the textile marking requirements.[18] The other PGAs determine compliance with the statutes and regulations for which each agency is responsible. CBP acts as the enforcement arm for each of the PGAs with the power to order redelivery for exportation or destruction of any merchandise previously released under bond that is subsequently determined by a PGA to be inadmissible into the commerce of the United States.

If CBP, or one of its PGAs, requests a sample of merchandise from the entry to test it for admissibility under the statutes or regulations administered by CBP or the PGA and the importer fails to provide the sample, CBP will issue a notice to redeliver, CF 4647, or its electronic equivalent ordering the principal to redeliver the merchandise within 60 days or some other specified time period to CBP custody to show evidence of compliance or exportation or destruction under CBP supervision.[19] If the importer fails to redeliver the merchandise within 60 days from the notice to redeliver with evidence of compliance or evidence of exportation or destruction under CBP supervision, CBP will issue a demand for liquidated damages against the importer (with a copy to the surety) on CF 5955A.[20] The liquidated damages will be calculated in the same manner as described above.

Likewise, if CBP, or its PGA, examines the merchandise and finds it fails to be in compliance with the laws and regulations administered by CBP or its PGA, CBP upon its finding, or at the request of the PGA, will issue a notice to redeliver, CF 4647, ordering the principal to redeliver the merchandise within the specified time appearing on the CF 4647 to CBP custody to show evidence of compliance or for exportation or destruction under CBP supervision.[21] If the importer fails to redeliver the merchandise within the specified time from the notice to redeliver with evidence of compliance or evidence of exportation or destruction under CBP supervision, CBP will issue a demand for liquidated damages against the principal (with a copy to the surety) on a CF 5955A. Once again, the amount of liquidated damages assessed will be governed by

---

.cbp.gov/trade/basic-import-export/e-commerce/partner-government-agencies-import-guides (last modified Sept. 24, 2021).

17. 19 U.S.C. § 1304; 19 C.F.R. § 134 *et seq.* (1984).

18. 19 C.F.R. § 11.12b (2016).

19. *See id.* § 141.113 and discussion *infra* Part V.

20. 19 C.F.R. § 113.62(c), (d), (e), (f) (1984).

21. *See id.* § 141.113.

the penal value of an STB or if the bond is a CTB by whatever amount would have been calculated had the bond been an STB.

The CF 5955A will show the liquidated damages case number; the name of the principal, its importer number (federal tax identification number, social security number, or CBP-assigned importer number), and its address; the name of the surety and CBP-assigned surety number; the amount of the bond and its effective date; and the details of the specific violation and reference to the bond obligation breached. CBP issues a "courtesy copy" to the surety of the 5955A issued to the importer. The importer has 60 days to respond to the 5955A demand. Best practices would lead the surety to contact the importer and its broker upon receipt of the courtesy 5955A. An early entrance into the process with the importer and broker can lead to a claim being resolved without the surety having to become more involved if the importer takes no action during the first 60 days and demand is thereafter made upon the surety.

III. Increased Duty Claims

A. Liquidation of Entries

After release of merchandise from CBP's custody, CBP is tasked with liquidating the entry. That is, making the final determination as to the admissibility, appraisement (the valuation), and classification (the correct tariff rate) to be used in the calculation of duties, fees, and taxes to be assessed against the merchandise. Liquidation, then, is the "final reckoning" of the entry.[22]

1. Regular Duties

Regular duties are calculated by multiplying the tariff rate against the value or quantity of the merchandise. In addition to regular duties,

---

22. United States v. Utex Int'l, Inc., 857 F.2d 1408, 1409 (Fed. Cir. 1988). On liquidation of the entry, CBP may determine that the valuation declared at the time of entry was too low or that the classification and rate declared at the time of entry was too low and issue a bill to the importer for any underpayment of the duties at the time of entry. On the other hand, CBP may determine that the importer overpaid duties and, in that case, CBP will issue a refund. Finally, CBP may determine that the agency agrees with the importer's deposit of estimated duties at the time of entry and will designate the entry as a "no change" liquidation.

CBP may assess additional duties; for example, marking duties[23] and antidumping duties (ADDs) and/or countervailing duties (CVDs).[24]

2. Additional Duties

ADDs and CVDs are additional duties determined by the U.S. Department of Commerce, International Trade Administration (DOC/ITA) in addition to regular duties assessed by CBP on imported merchandise to remediate unfair trade practices employed by foreign sellers or governments to the detriment of the manufacturers and sellers of U.S. domestic merchandise.

B. Entries Deemed Liquidated by Operation of Law

Any entry not suspended or extended beyond its first anniversary date will be deemed liquidated at the rate of duty, value, quantity, and amount of duties asserted by the importer of record at the time of entry.[25] Any entry that has been extended before its first anniversary but not liquidated before its fourth anniversary shall, on its fourth anniversary, also be liquidated by operation of law at the rate of duty, value, quantity, and amount of duties asserted by the importer of record.[26]

1. Regular Duties

Liquidation of an entry that is not subject to an ADD or CVD investigation may occur on or before the first anniversary of the date of entry,[27] but if extended,[28] no later than the fourth anniversary.

---

23. Marking duties are additional duties in the amount of 10 percent assessed on merchandise that CBP has determined not to have been properly marked with the correct country of origin or other marking requirement at the time of entry and release. 19 U.S.C. § 1304; 19 C.F.R. pt. 134 (1994). See 19 C.F.R. § 141.113 for other marking requirements.
24. ADDs and CVDs are additional duties determined by the U.S. Department of Commerce, International Trade Administration.
25. 19 U.S.C. § 1504(a).
26. *Id.*
27. *Id.* Typically, if the liquidation is not suspended or extended, the entry liquidates within 314 days following the date of entry. Such liquidations apply the rate, value, and quantity used by the principal/importer in calculating the estimated duty at the time of entry. The liquidations are posted in the Automated Commercial Environment (ACE) system.
28. *Id.* § 1504(b).

2. Additional Duties

Entries subject to ADD or CVD investigations and orders are suspended by operation of law and, if the ADD or CVD order is challenged in the Court of International Trade, liquidation of the entry may be further suspended by court order until the reviewing court's determination has become final. As discussed above, while the liquidation of entries not subject to ADD or CVD investigations and orders may not be extended beyond the fourth anniversary of the date of entry, the liquidation of entries subject to an ADD and/or CVD order may be suspended indefinitely if the underlying order or annual review of the order is judicially challenged until such time as the suspension of liquidation is released by the court.

Any entry suspended by court order or operation of law shall be deemed liquidated at the rate of duty, value, quantity, and amount of duties asserted by the importer if not liquidated within 180 days of DOC/ITA's publication of the notice of removal of suspension in the *Federal Register.*[29] Notice of removal of suspension of liquidation occurs when the DOC/ITA publishes in the *Federal Register* the final ADD or CVD order, or the final results of an annual administrative review of a final ADD or CVD order. Notice of removal of suspension of liquidation also occurs when the DOC/ITA publishes in the *Federal Register* the recission of an investigation or administrative annual review of an ADD or CVD order. Finally, a DOC/ITA publication in the *Federal Register* of notice of a "Court Decision Not in Harmony with . . ." a final order or the final results of an annual administrative review of a final order also acts as notice of removal of suspension of liquidation setting the clock for DOC and CBP to liquidate the entry within 120 days of such publication before the entry is automatically deemed liquidated. While 19 U.S.C.

---

29. When suspension occurs by statute, the notice of removal of suspension generally occurs when DOC publishes the final order or the final results of administrative review in the *Federal Register*. Int'l Trading Co. v. United States, 281 F.3d 1268, 1271 (Fed. Cir. 2002). When suspension occurs by court order, the notice of removal of suspension only occurs when the court renders its "final decision" in the matter, and the time to appeal that decision has expired. Fujitsu Gen. Am. Inc. v. United States, 283 F.3d 1364, 1378–79 (Fed. Cir. 2002). Specific liquidation instructions from DOC via email or mailed notice and publishing notice of a decision in the *Federal Register* are adequate (but not exclusive) forms of notice under 19 U.S.C. § 1504(d). Travelers Indem. Co. v. United States, 31 Ct. Int'l Trade 1057, 1061 (2008).

§ 1504 calls for deemed liquidation to be calculated at the rate and value asserted by the importer at the date of entry, deemed liquidation of ADDs calls for a calculation at the rate and value required by CBP to be asserted at the time of entry.[30]

IV. Collection of Lost Revenue Resulting from an Importer's Negligence or Fraud in Making the Entry

CBP has the authority, under the provisions of 19 U.S.C. § 1592(d), to recover lost revenue (duties, taxes, or fees) on liquidated entries from both the importer and the surety that arise from the importer's negligence or fraud in making entry of its imported merchandise. The surety can be held liable for the lost revenue whether or not a penalty claim is asserted under 19 U.S.C. § 1592(a) against the importer.[31] CBP may initiate an investigation under 19 U.S.C. § 1592 based upon its own inquiry and review of an entry prior to liquidation, or as the result of a "tip" by a third party, be it a competitor or disgruntled employee, or through a voluntary disclosure by the principal attempting to minimize its exposure to liability for penalty under 19 U.S.C. § 1592(c)(4). If the error is systemic and occurred for a period preceding discovery, CBP may reach back five years to cover all entries made during the five-year period prior to discovery or disclosure of the error. As discussed later in Part IX.B, the statute of limitations for collection of duties under 19 U.S.C. § 1592(d) is limited to five years from the date of the violation for losses based upon the importer's negligence or gross negligence; and to five years from the date of "discovery" for losses based upon fraud.

V. Surety Remedies and Defenses

"The surety stands in the shoes of the importer."[32] Both surety and importer have the right to defend against a claim for liquidated damages

---

30. American Permac, Inc. v. United States, 642 F. Supp. 1187, 1195 n.12 (Ct. Int'l Trade 1986); Detroit Zoological Soc'y v. United States, 630 F. Supp. 1350, 1356 n.9 (Ct. Int'l Trade 1986).
31. United States v. Aegis Sec. Ins. Co., 398 F. Supp. 2d 1354, 1356 (Ct. Int'l Trade 2005) (citing United States v. Blum, 858 F.2d 1566, 1569–70 (Fed. Cir. 1988)).
32. United States v. Lincoln Gen. Ins. Co., 341 F. Supp. 2d 1265, 1269 (Ct. Int'l Trade 2004).

and challenge a claim for increased duties. The demand for liquidated damages is defended through the petition process.[33] The demand for increased duties is challenged through the protest process.[34]

A. *Petition to Remit or Mitigate the Assessment of Liquidated Damages Claimed on CF 5955A*

"Proof that the importer has complied with the conditions of the bond has traditionally been and still remains a complete defense to a collection suit brought on a bond."[35] Demand claims for liquidated damages are not protestable.[36]

A most useful tool for any practitioner dealing with a CBP demand for liquidated damages is the FP&F Handbook.[37] The FP&F Handbook will aid the practitioner in dealing with the "how to" of handling and responding to any claim for liquidated damages for any breach of the bond obligations set out in 19 C.F.R. § 113.62.

In addition to the FP&F Handbook, there are several elements of defense that are not addressed in the handbook. These defenses arise when (1) there are multiple violations under a single CTB; or (2) CBP or its PGA fails to act in a timely manner in ordering the redelivery of merchandise found inadmissible for entry into the commerce of the United States.

1. *Exhaustion of the Bond*

The face value of the bond limits the liquidated damages that CBP may demand under the bond. If you are dealing with a demand made under a CTB, make sure to determine whether any other claim for liquidated damages has been issued for entries made under the same bond during the same period. If multiple claims for liquidated damages and duties have been incurred during a single bond period, the aggregate claims cannot be collected from the surety and the importer in an amount that exceeds the penal value of the bond.[38]

---

33. 19 C.F.R. pt. 172 (2000).
34. 19 U.S.C. § 1514; 19 C.F.R. pt. 174 (2022).
35. United States v. Toshoku Am., Inc., 879 F.2d 815, 818 (Fed. Cir. 1989).
36. *Id.*
37. *See* CBP, *supra* note 15.
38. While duties paid by the surety for entries made during the bond period can be used in the exhaustion of the bond defense, the assessment and

For example, the principal filed three entries under its $50,000 CTB in one annual period. The three entries each valued at $30,000 were refused admission and the importer failed to redeliver any of the merchandise after receiving a proper and timely CF 4647 notice to redeliver. Three actions for liquidated damages were initiated and issued to the importer and surety on three separate CF 5559A forms. In this case, notwithstanding the fact the three claims aggregate $90,000, the importer and the surety together are not liable for more than the $50,000 in liquidated damages under the penal sum of the bond. If either one pays the $50,000, the bond is exonerated as to the other party on the aggregate claims. If one party pays $30,000 on the first claim, the liquidated damages liability will be reduced on the other two demands to a maximum of $20,000 under the bond.

2. *Expiration of the Conditional Release Period*

19 C.F.R. § 141.113 limits the amount of time CBP and its PGAs have to act in determining the admissibility of imported merchandise. Section 141.113 of the CBP regulations sets out the "conditional release periods" for the government to request samples, make determinations of admissibility, and order such merchandise for redelivery to CBP with evidence of compliance, destruction, or exportation. The conditional release period is typically limited to 30 days but is extendable under certain circumstances described in the regulations.[39] A failure on the part of CBP or a PGA to act within the period guidelines is a defense to any claim for liquidated damages assessed under the principal's import bond. CBP does not always monitor its or its PGA's compliance with the conditional release periods and will often proceed with liquidated damages claims without checking. For that reason, it is up to the practitioner to review the entry history through the principal's or its broker's hard or electronic documentation to find and raise the defense.

---

payment of duties by the principal does not count toward the "exhaustion" calculation. This is because the liability of the principal (importer) for the payment of duties is separate and independent from the bond.

39. See, for example, § 141.113(c)(1) regarding U.S. Food and Drug Administration-regulated imports.

A corollary to a defense based upon the expiration of a conditional release period is the rule that any notice to redeliver merchandise must be issued prior to liquidation of the entry.[40]

B. Protest to Challenge the Assessment of Increased Duties

The surety receives notice of an increased duty bill via a computer-generated report known as the "612 Report," which is titled "Formal Demand on Surety for Payment of Delinquent Amounts Due." The 612 Report breaks down its demands by importer number and principal's name. The 612 Report identifies the entry number, date of entry and date of liquidation, the amount of the bill assessed on each entry, and the interest accrued on each bill.

One of the major problems a surety confronts upon receiving a bill from CBP is that the bill does not come with an explanation. Accordingly, the surety must undertake an investigation to determine the nature of the merchandise, its country of origin, any classification or valuation issues underlying the increased duty bill, or whether the bill is the result of ADDs or CVDs being assessed against the merchandise.

A first clue as to whether the bill is for regular duties or ADDs or CVDs is found in examining the 612 Report to determine the length of time between the date of entry and the date of liquidation. If fewer than four years, chances are the duties assessed are regular duties. If the length of time exceeds four years, the entries were liquidated with ADDs or CVDs. Beyond that quick test, there is little more to learn from the 612 Report other than what might be revealed by the principal's name and the first three digits of the entry numbers, which reveal the filer code for the principal's customhouse broker. Armed with that little bit of information, the surety may commence its investigation into the liquidation decision made by CBP.

The filer code that appears as the first three digits of each entry number on the 612 Report may be matched up with the CBP online portal to determine the contact information for the broker on the entry. The broker codes are accessed by querying "CBP Broker Codes" on the

---

40. United States v. Utex Int'l, Inc., 857 F.2d 1408, 1409 (Fed. Cir. 1988). A notice to redeliver must be issued prior to liquidation of the entry covering the merchandise. Nothing in the refusal of admission creates liability under the customs bond; CBP must issue a notice to redeliver prior to liquidation.

CBP website. Once the broker has been identified, it may be contacted directly by the surety, and the broker should be able to provide the entry details to the surety[41] if the five-year broker record-keeping requirement has not expired.[42] Of particular interest to the surety in understanding the liquidation decision will be any request for information (CF 28) or notice of action (CF 29) issued on the entry by CBP to the importer and its broker. Those documents will be found in the broker's entry file and will give a good idea as to what CBP was interested in leading up to its assessment of the increased duties.

If the importer's customhouse broker does not have the records, the surety may file directly with CBP a request for documents under the Freedom of Information Act (FOIA).[43] The request should provide the FOIA officer with the name and surety code of the requesting surety; the name and importer number of the importer of record; and the entry number(s) and date(s) of entry. The request should list the following documents requested: the CF 7501 entry summary; the invoice and packing list accompanying the entry; the bill of lading; any CF 28 or CF 29 issued in connection with the entry; and any liquidation instructions issued by DOC to CBP.

Upon receipt and analysis of the documents from the broker or from CBP through the FOIA, a surety should have sufficient information to determine whether a protestable issue exists and whether to file a protest.

A surety has a legal right, independent of its principal, to protest any increased duty bill or exaction demanded of it by CBP under the terms of its bond. The surety's right to protest extends beyond the limited time available for the principal to file a protest. The right of the principal to protest runs 180 days from the date of liquidation. The right of the surety runs 180 days from the date of *mailing* the first demand on the surety, and first demand is made approximately 60 days after liquidation. Recognizing the surety's right to protest should not become a vehicle to revive expired importer protest rights; the statute, 19 U.S.C. § 1514(c), prohibits a surety from filing a "collusive protest" (i.e., a protest filed at the request of the principal who has allowed its protest period to expire

---

41. 19 C.F.R. § 111.24 authorizes, but does not require, brokers to share information, data, and documents with the surety.
42. 19 C.F.R. § 111.23 (2012).
43. See *Freedom of Information Act*, CBP, https://www.cbp.gov/site-policy-notices/foia (last modified June 18, 2020), to submit an FOIA request to CBP for the entry information.

without itself filing its own timely protest).[44] That does not mean that a surety is precluded from protecting itself through the process of filing an administrative protest if the principal or its broker has not already filed a protest on its own behalf. So long as the surety is protecting its own interest and filing for its own benefit, the surety may execute the necessary certification that it is not collusively filing the protest for the benefit of another who has missed its protest deadline. If there exists a real threat of loss to the surety and a basis exists to avoid that loss through the filing of the protest, such filing would not be considered collusive.

A surety must file its protest "within 180 days from the date of mailing of notice of demand for payment under its bond."[45] The "notice of demand for payment" of liquidated duties and other exactions is the 612 formal demand on surety. The easiest date to use in calculating the 180-day protest period is the "run date" appearing on the first 612 formal demand that lists the entry and the bill.[46] However, the source of the most accurate date for triggering the protest statute is the mailing date on the envelope containing a copy of the 612 Report that CBP prints out on paper and mails to the surety in order to comply with the statute that requires a "mailed" notice but does not authorize a "transmitted" notice.

If all of the information necessary to protest the liquidation has not been received by the surety by the 180th day following the first demand, the protest period may be tolled during the pendency of the FOIA procedures.[47] In *Alyeska Pipeline*,[48] the court held that in circumstances

---

44. 19 U.S.C. § 1514(c)(3) provides:

> A protest by a surety which has an unsatisfied legal claim under its bond may be filed within 180 days from the date of mailing of notice of demand for payment against its bond. If another party has not filed a timely protest, the surety's protest shall certify that it is not being filed collusively to extend another authorized person's time to protest as specified in this subsection.

45. 19 U.S.C. § 1514(c). However, if the date entry was before December 18, 2004, the protest period is 90 days as a result of the 2004 amendment to 19 U.S.C. § 1514, Pub. L. No. 108-429, §§ 2103, 2108, 118 Stat. 2598 (2004).

46. Unless the surety keeps and records an image of the postmarked package in which the 612 Report was mailed, the "run date" is an accurate date to use for calculating the protest period.

47. *See* Alyeska Pipeline v. United States, 643 F. Supp. 1128, 1129–30 (Ct. Int'l Trade 1986).

48. *Id.*

in which documents underlying a changed liquidation are unavailable for review by the importer the protest period is tolled until such time as the entry documents are made available. However, if the practitioner is going to cite the *Alyeska Pipeline* holding to toll the protest period pending a response to an FOIA request, be sure that the FOIA request was made in a timely manner (e.g., within a reasonable time after receipt of the CF 612 formal demand) and not at the last minute before the protest is due.

The procedures for filing a protest are found in part 174 of the CBP regulations.[49] A useful tool for challenging a valuation decision is the *U.S. Customs and Border Protection Valuation Encyclopedia*, which may be accessed on the CBP website.[50] When initiating a classification review, the surety practitioner will find helpful the CBP Informed Compliance Publication *What Every Member of the Trade Community Should Know About: Tariff Classification* also on the CBP website.[51] Another excellent resource for the surety in evaluating the protest potential of a CBP liquidation decision is the CROSS (Customs Ruling Online Search System) database, which is also found on the CBP website.[52] A search of the CROSS database using the information received from CBP in response to the surety's FOIA request, or from the broker, will allow the surety to examine whether CBP has previously ruled on the classification, valuation, or other issue manifest in the liquidated entry documents.

If the broker or FOIA documents indicate that the billing is a result of the assessment of ADDs or CVDs, the surety practitioner will find the DOC/ITA portal found on the CBP website[53] an excellent starting point for researching any ADD or CVD issues.

---

49. 19 C.F.R. § 174.0 *et seq.* (1993).
50. CBP, U.S. CUSTOMS AND BORDER PROTECTION VALUATION ENCYCLOPEDIA (1980–2015) (2016), https://www.cbp.gov/sites/default/files/assets/documents/2020-Feb/ICP-Valuation-Encyclopedia-2015-Final.pdf.
51. CBP, WHAT EVERY MEMBER OF THE TRADE COMMUNITY SHOULD KNOW ABOUT: TARIFF CLASSIFICATION (2004), https://www.cbp.gov/sites/default/files/documents/icp017r2_3.pdf.
52. *Customs Rulings Online Search System (CROSS)*, CBP, https://rulings.cbp.gov/home (last visited Jan. 17, 2022).
53. *Information on AD/CVD Orders*, ITA, https://www.trade.gov/information-adcvd-orders (last visited Jan. 17, 2022).

The ADD or CVD case number appearing on the CF 7501 entry summary or referred to in a CF 29 notice of action is a key element necessary to initiate an inquiry on the CBP website.[54]

Issues of classification, appraisement, admissibility, and ADD and CVD assessments must be protested within 180 days of the first mailed demand to achieve relief either administratively through the protest process or judicially in the event that the protest is denied. Liquidation decisions not protested after 180 days become final as to all parties including the government.

In ADD and CVD cases, the timeliness of the liquidation may be protested. If the research turns up evidence CBP used an ADD or CVD rate that is not supported by the order or the final results of administrative review, the surety may protest the incorrect rate. However, a note of caution is in order here. The practitioner must look beyond the "timeliness" issue to be assured that the entered deposit rate is not higher than the rate used by CBP on liquidation of the entry.[55] In such case, a protest can result in a higher bill at the end of the day.

It is also important to note that when an entry has been "deemed liquidated" an importer or the surety may protest the deemed liquidation. For example, this is particularly important in those cases in which CBP has rejected an entry and demanded that estimated duties be redeposited at a certain amount based upon a classification, valuation, or under an ADD or CVD order with which the importer disagrees or that is not supported by evidence known to the surety.[56]

Neither the surety nor the principal may raise issues that could have been protested as defenses in a collection action against the bond.[57] The surety, however, may raise certain defenses in a collection action against the bond[58] that are matters of contract and the law of suretyship that are not available to the importer and do not need to be protested.

---

54. In addition to the ADD or CVD case number, the merchandise description with country of origin (e.g., "Silicon photovoltaic cells from the People's Republic of China") will also suffice to open a search in the ADD/CVD portal.
55. *See* Rheem Metalurgica S/A v. United States, 951 F. Supp. 241 (Ct. Int'l Trade 1996).
56. *See* discussion, Part 5.B, *supra.*
57. United States v. Am. Home Assurance Co., 857 F.3d 1329, 1336 (Fed. Cir. 2017).
58. 28 U.S.C. § 1582(2); *see* United States v. Cherry Hill Textiles, Inc., 112 F.3d 1550 (Fed. Cir. 1997).

C. Subrogation

After a surety pays a claim for increased duties or liquidated damages to CBP, the surety subrogates to all rights and remedies that CBP had against the importer.[59] Unfortunately, the importer is rarely around at that time. It is most often out of business, has disappeared, is insolvent, or is in bankruptcy.

If the importer is in bankruptcy, the surety does have the right to subrogate to CBP's claim against the estate under 11 U.S.C. § 507 for recovery of the debt paid. However, that right to subrogate does not extend to allow the surety to acquire the government's priority in the bankruptcy proceeding.[60] Although CBP has attempted to grant sureties its priority status by regulation, via 19 C.F.R. § 141.1(c), the bankruptcy court cases have held the CBP regulation does not trump the bankruptcy code.

VI. Delinquent Sureties: Billing, Show Cause, and Sanctions

When the surety fails to respond to a CBP demand for liquidated damages or duties by payment or by petition or protest as appropriate, CBP will seek collection enforced by its ultimate authority to "sanction" a delinquent surety.[61] Sanction will be considered if the delinquency is without just cause, and is significant either in the number of outstanding bills or dollar amounts thereof. "Sanction" is the authority of CBP to reject bonds from the delinquent surety. Sanction may be issued for a short period (e.g., a minimum of five days) allowing the surety to pay the demand and seek removal from the sanction list or the sanction may be permanent until the delinquent demand is paid. A permanent sanction is the removal of a surety from the Treasury Department Circular 570 (the "Treasury List of Certified Companies").

Before sanctions will issue against a surety for a delinquent debt, CBP will send the surety a series of bills followed by a pre-show cause letter, which, if not responded to, a show cause letter.

---

59. *See* Restatement (Third) of Suretyship and Guaranty § 28.
60. *In re* Brickel Assocs., Inc., 170 B.R. 140 (Bankr. W.D. Wis. 1994) (inability of surety (or any party other than the government) to succeed to CBP priority in bankruptcy proceedings where surety or other party pays duty to CBP on behalf of bankrupt importer).
61. 19 C.F.R. § 113.38(c)(1) (2015).

A. Billing Delinquent Debts

1. Billing Delinquent Liquidated Damages Debts

Prior to issuing show cause letters and sanctioning a surety on a delinquent liquidated damages debt, CBP will bill the surety on a CF 6084 if the full claim has not been petitioned or paid without just cause within 60 days after a CF 5955A has been sent to the surety. If the liquidated damages claim was petitioned by the surety and the petition denied or the claim mitigated, and not timely paid, the mitigation benefit will be cancelled, and the CF 6084 billing will commence 60 days after the time specified in the mitigation decision or denial of the surety's petition. CBP will issue three bills addressed to the surety's home office on the CF 6084.[62] The first bill will issue 65 to 75 days after CBP has made its formal demand on the surety. The second bill will issue approximately 14 days thereafter, and the third bill approximately 14 days after the second bill. With issuance of the first CF 6084, the liquidated damages case is in the "billing stage."

Once a liquidated damages case has reached the billing stage, the surety has three options: (1) pay or induce the importer to pay the full amount of liquidated damages; (2) file an untimely petition for mitigation or cancellation with a submission of documentation that evidences that the violation never occurred or is worthy of mitigation; or (3) make an offer in compromise.[63] As previously noted, a protest is not an option, because mitigation decisions in a liquidated damages case cannot be protested.[64]

A late petition can be accepted by CBP during the billing stage but not after CBP has issued a show cause letter to the surety. CBP can mitigate the claim on the basis of an untimely petition but will not mitigate to an amount less than would have been assessed had the petition been timely filed.

The surety can make an offer in compromise, but CBP cannot suggest the amount of an offer in compromise that it would accept. However, the surety can determine an amount that CBP would likely consider. CBP will consider an offer in compromise if the FP&F Handbook allows for

---

62. *See Bill Form 6084*, CBP, https://www.cbp.gov/trade/priority-issues/revenue/bill-form-6084 (last modified Sept. 19, 2016).

63. *See* 19 C.F.R. § 172.31 (2002).

64. *Id.* § 172.22(a).

mitigation and the surety adds a meaningful increase over and above an authorized mitigation amount.

If the offer in compromise is rejected or if any mitigated sum is not paid and the surety takes no further steps to pay or mitigate the claim, CBP will turn the matter over to the U.S. Department of Justice for collection. If the Department of Justice is successful in its collection litigation, the surety will be liable for prejudgment interest calculated from the date of CBP's first CF 5955A demand upon surety for liquidated damages. The surety practitioner must note that CBP turning the matter over to the Department of Justice does not prevent CBP from moving forward on a track to sanction a recalcitrant surety.

2. *Billing Delinquent Increased Duty Debts*

As noted previously, CBP demands for delinquent increased duty assessments are first made on CF 612, "Formal Demand on Surety for Payment of Delinquent Amounts Due." If either the surety or its principal (or both) files a protest, the bill will still be considered delinquent during the pendency of the protest(s) and interest will accrue,[65] but CBP will not take further action to collect on the bills until the protest(s) has been decided.

If both the principal and the surety file protests, the first filed protest will be identified on the 612 Reports until the protest has been decided. Thereafter, disposition of the protest will appear on subsequent 612 Reports as either "approved" or "denied." If a protest is approved, the bill will usually fall off the next 612 Report. However, the surety practitioner must be careful here; just because a protest has been approved it does not mean that the cancelled bill cannot or will not be followed up by a lesser bill on the same entry. If the surety is holding collateral, as discussed below, the surety will want to hold collateral for at least 120 days to be sure that a new bill does not reappear on the 612 Report for the same entry as the result of a reliquidation arising out of the approved protest. Also, if the first filed protest is denied and the second filed protest is still pending, the second filed protest number will replace the first on the 612 Report until the second protest is decided.

If the importer and the surety do not file a protest and have not paid the increased duty claim within 180 days, CBP's Revenue Division at NFC in Indianapolis, Indiana, will issue to the surety a "formal demand"

---

65. 19 U.S.C. § 1505(d).

in a letter format to pay the claim within 30 days or provide substantial justification for nonpayment. If no payment or substantial justification is received, the claim will be turned over to the Office of Assistant Chief Counsel for collection through the Department of Justice in the Court of International Trade. Once again, notwithstanding referral of the claim to the Department of Justice for collection, both the surety and the importer remain subject to sanction by CBP.

B. Show Cause Letters

1. Pre-Show Cause Letter

If the surety fails to adequately respond to the CF 6084 billing or formal demand, the case will move into the "sanction eligible" status and CBP will issue a pre-show cause letter to the surety. After a thorough review of the file, the pre-show cause letter is prepared and issued by the national seizure and penalty officer (NSPO) for liquidated damages delinquencies or by the director of the Revenue Division for delinquent duty claims. The pre-show cause letter is a warning to the surety that a show cause letter will issue within 30 business days if the claims are not resolved.

2. Show Cause Letter

A show cause letter will demand payment of the delinquent claims within 15 business days of the date of the letter. The thresholds for sanction vary between surety and circumstances; the thresholds may include all open claims for liquidated damages or delinquent duties in addition to the one or more cases that initiated the original show cause letter. CBP will review its sanction eligible demands on a case-by-case basis. The show cause letter will describe the sanction to be taken and allow the surety 15 additional days to pay the claims or demonstrate substantial legal issues to justify withholding payment of the claim(s). The surety practitioner should keep in mind that CBP is prohibited from compromising delinquent duty claims and, at that point, CBP is no longer required to negotiate the liquidated damages claims. While offers in compromise may be submitted, all the way up to and until the expiration of the 15-day payment period under the show cause demand, even payment and acceptance of such compromise may not stop progress of the sanction action at that point. Once the show cause letter has issued, only full payment or substantive justification for nonpayment in writing can stop the sanction process if CBP decides to continue to move forward.

C. Sanctions

The failure of the surety to respond to the show cause letter will result first in CBP's temporary rejection of the surety's bonds at one or all of the CBP ports of entry for a minimum period of five days. That means the surety is taken out of the customs bond business for a minimum of five days. Even a five-day prohibition could have catastrophic implications for the surety in the marketplace for customs bonds. A failure to remedy the delinquencies within the first five days will result in a more permanent sanction until the delinquent debts are paid. Of course, the surety has the right to challenge the sanction and seek an injunction in the Court of International Trade. That tactic, however, is a tough road to travel.[66]

VII. Waiver of the Statute of Limitations

Occasionally, either CBP or the importer (on its own or at the request of CBP) will ask or "invite" the surety to waive the statute of limitations. At the outset, it must be understood that a surety is under no obligation to waive the statute of limitations for any purpose or for any party. It is equally important for the surety to note that there is no statute of limitations or bond cap on the importer's obligation to pay duty. Therefore, a waiver of the statute of limitations only increases the risk already undertaken by the surety under its bond. A waiver allows the government additional time to make its case against the principal and, moreover, allows the principal additional time to deplete its assets, cease doing business, or otherwise place the surety in a position of greater jeopardy. Incurring additional risk through a waiver should and can be justified by the surety's demand and acceptance of collateral from the importer.

Without collateral, a waiver of the statute of limitations has little benefit to the surety. The waiver only serves to take the pressure off of CBP to pursue its claim against the importer and off of the importer to make its defense against CBP's claim. In most cases, the importer will have waived the statute of limitations before the surety is invited to do so. That fact should not influence the surety's decision as to whether it should waive the statute or not.

Requests for waiver of the statute of limitations are quite often made in the context of claims for increased duties during a protracted protest

---

66. *See* Intercargo Ins. Co. v. United States, 20 Ct. Int'l Trade 951 (1996).

period, for liquidated damages against which the importer wants to raise a defense in the Court of International Trade, and for lost revenue under the 19 U.S.C. § 1592 "fraud/negligence statute." The requests for a waiver are based on the chance that the importer and surety will fare better in the administration of the claim by CBP than either would if scrutinized by the Department of Justice and the Court of International Trade. That chance is more hope than reality. In that regard, the surety must request a copy of the claim and, more importantly, an outline of the proposed defense from the importer or its counsel. Playing into the surety's determination will be the quality and track record of the importer's counsel mounting the defense as well as the financial status of the importer.

In making its decision on a proposed waiver, the surety must also be mindful that, if the claim cannot be resolved administratively by CBP and the claim proceeds into the Court of International Trade for collection, the surety will also be liable for any interest accrued on the debt calculated from the date of first demand on the surety. Therefore, any collateral required by the surety should be measured with a healthy projected calculation of interest.

In any case in which the surety declines waiver of the statute of limitations, CBP may proceed against the surety in the Court of International Trade at any time, subject only to the relevant statutes of limitation.[67] As will be discussed later in Part VIII.C, when the government does sue the surety, it is advisable the surety answer the complaint and immediately file its third-party claim against the importer for indemnity and reimbursement. Thereafter, CBP will focus its discovery and litigation activity against the importer while the indemnity and reimbursement rights of the surety are preserved in a court of the most competent jurisdiction to handle surety issues for reimbursement and indemnity in the context of the customs laws.

VIII. The Court of International Trade

The U.S. Court of International Trade has exclusive jurisdiction to hear all CBP matters.[68] For purposes of this discussion, there are two types of actions in the court that are of interest to the surety: (1) the recovery of duties paid by the surety under protest, and (2) enforcement actions against the surety to collect money under the bond.

---

67. *See* 28 U.S.C. § 1581; 19 U.S.C. § 1621.
68. 28 U.S.C. § 1581.

A. Denied Protests

In order to recover monies paid to CBP, a party must first exhaust the administrative procedures for challenging a CBP decision and that requires the filing of an administrative protest.[69] In order to invoke the jurisdiction of the Court of International Trade to review a denied protest filed by the principal or the surety, there are two preconditions to jurisdiction that must be met: (1) the principal must pay all of the duties plus accrued interest before it files a summons,[70] and (2) the summons must be filed within 180 days after mailing notice of the denial of the protest.[71] However, if the summons is filed by the surety, the first precondition, payment of duty plus interest, is limited to the penal value of the surety's bond.

The Court of International Trade has the power to receive new evidence and to review and reverse or uphold all decisions of CBP regarding the appraisement (valuation), classification (tariff rate of duty assessed), admissibility, exclusion of merchandise, and all other decisions or actions set out at 19 U.S.C. § 1514(a). The court determines these issues de novo (i.e., it is not limited to any administrative record and can substitute its own judgment as the correct decision rather than affirming a federal agency decision as reasonable, not contrary to law, and not arbitrary or capricious). In simplest terms, there are very few activities undertaken by CBP that are not subject to the protest and judicial remedies. In fact, jurisdiction of the Court of International Trade is most often declined if the importer or the surety has not exhausted its protest remedy prior to seeking relief in the Court of International Trade.

On the other hand, for those issues that are strictly contract issues and personal to the surety under the terms of its bond, such issues may be raised in an enforcement action initiated by CBP to collect monies under the terms of the bond.[72]

---

69. *Id.* § 4647(a); Hartford Fire Ins. Co. v. United States, 544 F.3d 1289 (Fed. Cir. 2008).
70. 28 U.S.C. § 2637.
71. *Id.* § 2636.
72. St. Paul Fire Marine & Ins. Co. v. United States, 959 F.2d 960, 964 (Fed. Cir. 1992); United States v. Am. Home Assurance Co., 151 F. Supp. 3d 1328, 1347 (Ct. Int'l Trade 2015) ("As to defenses related to its contractual obligations under a bond . . . a surety is not precluded from raising them in a collection action brought by the Government. This is the case even if

B. Enforcement Actions

In an enforcement action, the surety may raise the statute of limitations as an affirmative defense. As noted above, the surety may also raise any contract or equitable remedy, such as impairment of suretyship, in those fact scenarios wherein CBP failed in performance of a statutory or regulatory obligation such as giving the surety notice of the suspension of liquidation of an entry.[73]

Both the Court of International Trade and the Court of Appeals for the Federal Circuit have refused to grant relief to the surety in contract or in equity in the absence of evidence of actual prejudice suffered by the surety. In the absence of prejudice, the Court of International Trade has held that the rights of the surety were not impaired by CBP accepting bonds with facial defects.[74] In the *Hartford* case, CBP accepted bonds that were unsigned by the principal, or unsealed by the corporate surety or otherwise prepared and submitted "technically incomplete" and out of compliance with the CBP regulations. The court noted that the subsections of part 113 of the CBP regulations cited by the surety were promulgated to protect the government and not the surety.[75]

As also noted in *Great American Insurance Co. of New York*, the court would "be most reluctant to conclude that every failure of an agency to observe a procedural requirement voids subsequent agency action, especially when important public rights are at stake."[76] Accordingly, in the absence of facts that the surety has suffered substantial prejudice as a result of an action taken by CBP or its failure to act, the courts have refrained from releasing the surety's liability under a bond.

C. Third-Party Claims for Indemnity and Reimbursement

While the Court of International Trade shares jurisdiction with state and other federal district courts to hear third-party claims, as between the

---

the defenses replicate the claims it made, or could have made, in a protest brought to determine an importer's liability on liquidation.").

73. United States v. Great Am. Ins. Co. of N.Y., 35 Ct. Int'l Trade 1130 (2011).

74. Hartford Fire Ins. Co. v. United States, 254 F. Supp. 3d 1333 (Ct. Int'l Trade 2017).

75. *Id.* at 1348 (citing United States v. Great Am. Ins. Co., 738 F.3d 1320, 1334 (Fed. Cir. 2013)).

76. United States v. Great Am. Ins. Co., 738 F.3d 1320, 1330 (Fed. Cir. 2013).

surety and its principal in a collection action[77], there is no better court than the Court of International Trade to understand the nuances of the role of the surety in the tripartite transactions between surety, principal, and CBP when the enforcement of a customs bond is involved. Filing the third-party claim along with the answer to the government's complaint draws the importer into the litigation and allows for the principal to immediately defend the action through discovery and fact-based affirmative defenses while maintaining the necessary jurisdiction over the principal to assure indemnification and reimbursement of the surety. The surety's third-party claims can be litigated at the beginning or at the end of the government's underlying litigation against the surety.

IX. Indemnity, Collateral, and Collateral Return

The deposit of collateral by importers, in addition to the payment of premium, is routinely required by customs sureties. While it is easy to measure the immediate financial burden imposed on the principal by the deposit of collateral, it is more difficult to calculate the long-term burdens imposed: how long will the collateral be held; will the demand for collateral be increased; when will the collateral be released; and under what circumstances will it be released. The purpose of this section is to provide the tools necessary to seek the return of collateral. The goal is to address the basic considerations undertaken by the surety in performing its due diligence risk analysis necessary for the surety to require, hold, reduce, and release collateral.

The right of the surety to demand collateral and the obligation of the importer to provide collateral are generally covered under the terms of a general indemnity agreement entered into between the principal and the surety. A surety will require that a principal execute a general indemnity agreement either as a condition precedent to the surety issuing a surety bond in the first instance or later, as a condition to either renew the surety bond or increase the penal sum as may be demanded by CBP.

As important as the indemnity agreement is to the surety, a written statement from the surety covering the surety's collateral release policy is equally important to the principal. The principal should have, in writing from the surety, some basic understanding of what will be required of the principal for the release of the collateral by the surety in the future. The basic general indemnity agreement allows the surety sole discretion in its

---

77. 28 U.S.C. § 1582 and Rule 14 of the U.S. Court of International Trade.

right to both require and release collateral. That discretion is based solely on the surety's perceived risk.

At one time, the return of collateral was a fairly easy and predictable task for sureties. The surety could reliably determine that its ongoing risk had been eliminated or substantially diminished by checking the current status of entries and open claims (i.e., dates filed, opened, liquidated, petitioned, protested, or decided) and then applying the two relevant statutes of limitations governing surety exposure. The two statutes of limitations are the six-year statute of limitations for the collection of liquidated damages and duties incurred under the bond,[78] and the five-year statute of limitations for collection of lost revenue incurred as the result of negligence, gross negligence, or fraud in connection with the filing of an entry under the bond.[79]

One uncertainty existed that sometimes compelled sureties to prolong the holding of collateral; that was the analysis of *future risk* based upon the "discovery rule" (i.e., for the collection of lost revenue resulting from fraud on the part of the importer or its agent in the entry of merchandise under bond).[80] Under the "discovery rule," the five-year statute of limitations is tolled until such time as CBP first learns of the act or omission that caused the loss of revenue or at least had knowledge of facts that would have led a reasonable person to investigate whether a loss of revenue had occurred.[81] A surety's risk analysis could be managed by an examination of the principal's prior history of compliance and its relationship with CBP to determine the chance of CBP "discovering" fraud long after the bond had terminated and all other claims under the

---

78. 28 U.S.C. § 2415(a).

79. 19 U.S.C. § 1621.

80. The first clause of 19 U.S.C. § 1621 (2000) sets out the "discovery rule":

> No suit or action to recover any duty under section 1592(d), 1593a(d) of this title, or any pecuniary penalty or forfeiture of property accruing under the customs laws shall be instituted unless such suit or action is commenced within five years after the time when the alleged offense was discovered . . .; except that—(1) in the case of an alleged violation of section 1592 or 1593(a) of this title, no suit or action (including a suit or action for restoration of lawful duties under subsection (d) of such sections) may be instituted unless commenced within 5 years after the date of the alleged violation or, if such violation arises out of fraud, within 5 years after the discovery of fraud . . . .

81. United States v. Spanish Foods, Inc., 24 Ct. Int'l Trade 1052, 1056 (2000).

bond had been extinguished or failed to materialize in the ordinary course by the time that the return of collateral was requested by the principal or its successor.

However, in September 2020, CBP dramatically changed the landscape of the surety's risk analysis and the continued retention of collateral for the near future. Heretofore, the U.S. customs surety industry relied upon the six-year statute of limitations for collection of duties as commencing on or within 30 days of the date of liquidation of the entry.[82] On September 16, 2020, and September 30, 2020, CBP initiated two separate duty collection actions against two different surety companies, American Home Assurance Company[83] and Aegis Security Insurance Company,[84] claiming in each action that the six-year statute of limitations under 28 U.S.C. § 2415(a) is not initiated by the liquidation of an entry but only on the failure of the importer to pay the liquidated duties within 30 days of CBP's *billing* thereof. The surety can easily calculate and assume the risk of a 30-day period for billing but has no reliable way to calculate or assume the risk if the government can postpone billing indefinitely (i.e., for more than eight years in the two cases now in court).

If CBP's new theory concerning the initiation of the statute of limitations is upheld, there will be no statutory or regulatory limitation on when CBP may issue a bill for duties determined on liquidation of

---

82. United States v. Am. Home Assurance Co., 151 F. Supp. 3d 1328, 1342–43 (Ct. Int'l Trade 2016), *as amended* (Mar. 14, 2016), *aff'd sub nom.* Am. Home Assurance Co. v. Hartford Fire Ins. Co., No. 18-1960 (Fed. Cir. Sept. 6, 2019), ECF No. 66 (per curiam). *See also* United States v. Int'l Fid. Ins. Co., 273 F. Supp. 3d 1170, 1177 (Ct. Int'l Trade 2017) ("When liquidation occurs by operation of law, the six-year statute of limitations commences on the date of the deemed liquidation"); United States v. Great Am. Ins. Co. of N.Y., 35 Ct. Int'l Trade 1130, 1161 (2011) ("The Government's cause of action accrued six months after the publication of the Notice of Rescission when the [importer's] Entries [were] deemed liquidated [by operation of law] and the Government's right to collect additional duties attached."); United States v. Ataka Am., Inc., 17 Ct. Int'l Trade 598, 607 (1993) ("The right to collect immediately on liquidation carries with it the responsibility to act within six years of liquidation to collect on the contract obligation of the surety.").
83. United States v. Am. Home Assurance Co., No. 20-00175 (Ct. Int'l Trade Sept. 16, 2020).
84. United States v. Aegis Sec. Ins. Co., No. 20-03628 (Ct. Int'l Trade Sept. 30, 2020).

an entry. In both cases, CBP's interpretation of its right to collect duties stems from the agency's unilateral assumption of authority to extend the statute of limitations to be measured from its date of billing. CBP has rationalized its authority on a 1993 amendment to 19 U.S.C. § 1505(b),[85] which moved the date on which duties are "delinquent" from 15 days after liquidation or reliquidation to 30 days after billing. In both of the current cases, the billings occurred more than six years after the entries were deemed liquidated by operation of law. However, in both cases, the surety argues there is no legislative history to 19 U.S.C. § 1505(b) to support CBP's position. The sureties argue the statute was amended solely for the purpose of establishing a date to begin the accrual of post-liquidation interest. The sureties assert there is no support for CBP's argument that Congress intended to extend the finality of liquidation. In fact, the amendment to the statute relied upon by CBP specifically provides that interest begins to accrue on a delinquent debt as of the date of liquidation not on a date 30 days following billing.

The customs bond surety industry had no previsibility of this unilateral assumption of authority and the effect it would have on its calculus of future risk. Entries that were made but unliquidated at the termination of the bond could be reviewed and a calculation of future risk made. Until September 2021, such calculation would be made on the basis of the nature of the imported merchandise and whether the merchandise was subject to ADDs or CVDs; or, if subject to neither, whether the statute of limitations for collection of regular duties had expired, generally seven to ten years following date of entry (e.g., one to four years to liquidate plus the six-year statute of limitations) for entries reported as unliquidated after termination of the bond.

The surety practitioner must remember, however, a surety on a bond is only liable for claims made on entries filed during each separate annual bond period or the period that the bond was in effect notwithstanding how many periods the bond has been in effect or how many times the

---

85. In 1993, the language of 19 U.S.C. § 1505 was amended. The pre-amendment statute provided that duties determined to be due upon liquidation or reliquidation were due "15 days after . . . liquidation or reliquidation." 19 U.S.C. § 1505(b) (1990). The 1993 amendment provides that duties are due "30 days after issuance of the bill for such payment." *Id.*; North American Free Trade Agreement Implementation Act, Pub. L. No. 103-182, § 642, 107 Stat. 2205 (1993).

bond has been "stacked."[86] This is true even if the entries are liquidated and duty claims or liquidated damages claims are assessed far in excess of the $50,000 penal sum of the bond.[87] It is also true where the bond is terminated and replaced during the annual period of the bond (i.e., if a bond, filed on January 1, 2021, in the amount of $50,000 is replaced on April 1, 2022, with a new bond in the amount of $100,000), the surety remains obligated up to $50,000 for entries filed from January 1 to March 31, 2021, and for $100,000 for entries filed from April 1, 2022, to March 31, 2023.

As a consequence of stacking, a surety may require, under the terms of its indemnity agreements,[88] the deposit of collateral at any time after the bond is in effect even if no collateral was originally required for the first bond period or any bond renewal thereafter.

Increasing collateral requirements resulting from stacking may become sufficiently onerous on the principal that the viability of its business is threatened. In such cases, it is not uncommon for principals and surety companies to undertake the analysis discussed in this chapter to repurpose collateral held for earlier bond periods and apply them to current or future bond periods or to release some part of the stacked collateral back to the principal upon a determination by the surety that its future risk for a particular bond period is minimal. In such cases, the surety may be inclined to substitute the cash collateral for an updated general indemnity agreement with the principal.

To protect its interests, the surety will hold collateral at least until CBP liquidates all entries covered by the bond and the liquidation(s) become final. As noted above, a liquidation will become final as to all parties including the government, if the government has not voluntarily

---

86. This is not true for the principal. As noted above in Part I, the importer has a separate personal liability for all liquidated duties imposed upon its imported merchandise. Meredith v. United States, 28 U.S. 486, 493 (1839). That liability is not limited by the penal value of any bond undertaken to secure the release of the merchandise at the time of entry, nor is the importer's liability for duties subject to any statute of limitations. *Ataka Am., Inc.*, 826 F. Supp. 495, 497–98.

87. It is important to note that if either the principal or the surety pays a liquidated damages claim up to the $50,000 penal value limitation of the bond, the bond is exonerated for any and all claims in excess of the penal sum incurred in the same bond year.

88. Or, as consideration for the annual renewal of a bond not previously supported by an indemnity agreement.

reliquidated the entry for any reason within 90 days of the original liquidation[89] and if the importer or its agent or surety has not protested the liquidation within 180 days of its billing.[90] Where a liquidation is timely protested, it becomes final 180 days after denial of the protest. If the protest is approved or partially approved, a new liquidation may occur, and the finality cycle begins anew.

Let us stop for a moment at this point and recap: if the entry under an STB has not been liquidated or if CTB has not been terminated, it is premature to consider the return of collateral. Likewise, if any entry under a CTB is unliquidated regardless of whether the CTB has been terminated, it is premature to consider the return of collateral. This is and will remain particularly true until the current judicial controversy concerning whether the liquidation of an entry or the billing of the liquidated duties is the act that initiates the running of the six-year statute of limitations for collection of duties.[91]

At this point, it is also important to review the options of the principal and surety on a CTB that has been in effect for a number of years but under which entries made during earlier bond periods may have already liquidated and there are no outstanding claims for duties or liquidated damages for entries made during the early bond period(s).

Returning to the elements of a surety's risk analysis, and assuming the entry under an STB has liquidated and all of the entries under the CTB have liquidated, the surety is in a position to further analyze its risk in releasing the collateral. The release of collateral requires an examination of current exposure and risk:

1. Is the bond an STB or a CTB?
2. If the bond is a CTB, what is its current status: ongoing or terminated? If the CTB is terminated, what is the date of termination?
3. What is the status of all the entries filed under the CTB throughout its life? Are the entries liquidated or are some yet unliquidated?
4. Did the CTB have a predecessor? And what is the status of the entries under the predecessor bond? Liquidated or unliquidated?

---

89. 19 U.S.C. § 1501.
90. *Id.* § 1514(b).
91. The Court of International Trade heard oral argument on dispositive motions in the *American Home* and the *Aegis* cases on July 15 and July 16, 2021 (*see supra* notes 83 and 84).

5. Identify the bond(s) (both CTBs and any STBs) under consideration by the surety's bond number, the CBP assigned bond number, and the penal value of the bond.
6. Identify the bond's (both CTBs and any STBs) effective dates: "The Bond was in effect approximately ___months between ____and ____."
7. Identify the collateral securing the bond: "The Bond is secured by a cash deposit or an irrevocable letter of credit in the amount of _______."
8. Specify the termination date of the bond: "The bond was terminated on _____."
9. Verify the source of information concerning the liquidation status of the entries covered by the bond.
10. Have the entries made during the bond period all liquidated according to CBP's official liquidation reports that CBP maintains on the entry activities of each importer of record?[92] These records are the *masterfile extract* (MFX) and the *liquidation extract* (LSX) maintained by CBP.[93]
11. Verify that all liquidations occurred more than 180 days prior to the date of the initiation of the surety's collateral return analysis: "The last liquidation occurred __________."
12. Verify that there are no open claims on any of the entries covered by the bond; or, if there are open claims for duties or liquidated damages, that protests have been filed (against the duty claims) and petitions filed (against the liquidated damages claims) and that collateral will be retained to secure payment of any open claims (including interest on the unpaid duty that will accrue up to the penal sum of the bond on the duty claims[94]).
13. Verify that there are no open investigations or claims for "lost revenue" under 19 U.S.C. § 1592(d)[95] against the principal on

---

92. By the importer of record's importer of record number or employer identification number (EIN).
93. The surety has no access to an importer's MFX or LSX. These reports must be obtained by the importer requesting each one directly from CBP and then forwarding the reports to the surety. The importer of record may obtain the reports by sending an email request to EXTRACTREPORTS@CBP.DHS.GOV.
94. 19 U.S.C. § 1505(d).
95. *Id.* § 1592.

the bond as charged by CBP or as the result of a "voluntarily disclosure" by the principal.

14. Determine whether the principal is, or has been, a "trusted importer" and currently an active participant in the CBP Customs Trade Partnership against Terrorism (CTPAT) and Importer Self-Assessment (ISA) programs.

There is a common misconception that a customs bond has a *six-year tail*. That is not true. There is no "tail" to a customs bond. Liability under the bond can extend far beyond six years, depending on when the six-year statute of limitations for the collection of liquidated duties is determined by the courts to be triggered.[96] The life of a customs bond runs from its "effective date" to the date of its "termination" (the "bond period") or its exhaustion (payment of full bond amount). The concept of a "tail" applies only to a "claim" or "claim(s)" arising under the bond on an entry filed by the principal during the bond period. Therefore, it is simply not correct to say that a bond has a tail liability of six years. Liability under a bond can be significantly greater or significantly less than six years. It all depends on if and when liability for a claim is incurred. The "six years" only has meaning in the context of an outstanding claim arising out of a breach of a bond obligation at some point within the life of an entry secured by the bond. If no breach occurred in connection with an entry secured by the bond, then no liability under the bond is incurred.

If all entries have been liquidated for more than 90 days without a bill[97] or all liquidated duties have been paid either before or after the termination of the bond, the surety may consider return of collateral if no claims for liquidated damages remain outstanding at termination of the bond. As discussed earlier in Parts II.A, II.B, and V.A.2, liquidated damages are generally incurred within six months of the date of entry due to the administrative "conditional release periods" and their respective six-month or less statutes of limitations created by 19 C.F.R. § 141.118.[98]

As discussed earlier, if there is an open claim or the potential for an open claim on an entry covered by the bond when the bond is terminated, we must once again turn to the relevant statutes of limitations to determine whether the surety is at risk; these two statutes of limitations are (1) *a*

96. *See supra* notes 83 and 84.

97. CBP has 90 days following a liquidation or a reliquidation to voluntarily reliquidate the entry for any reason under authority of 19 U.S.C. § 1501.

98. *See supra* note 40.

six-year statute of limitations[99] for the collection of duty and liquidated damages claims arising during the bond period; and (2) *a five-year statute of limitations*[100] for the collection of a claim for "lost revenue" under 19 U.S.C. § 1592(d) that has arisen as the result of an error made by the importer in its declaration of the value or the rate of duty due on the merchandise, its country of origin, or its admissibility at the time of entry. The five-year statute of limitations begins to run on the date of entry in cases in which the claim is based on an allegation of simple negligence or gross negligence; or five years from the date of discovery by CBP when based upon an allegation of fraud.

A. The Six-Year Statute of Limitations: Duty and Liquidated Damages

1. Claims for Duties

The six-year statute of limitations for the collection of duties under a bond[101] depends entirely on what claims, if any, are created on any entry during the life of the bond. Simply stated, if, upon termination of a bond, there are no open claims for the collection of duties or liquidated damages on any entry covered during the life of a bond, then the six-year statute of limitations has nothing to attach to, and for all intents and purposes, the relevance of the statute of limitations as a "tail" simply evaporates as to the bond in question.

In that case, the surety bears no continued liability for the payment of any duty claims. The bond is terminated; there are no open claims for duties, all entries filed under the bond have liquidated,[102] and the liquidations are now final.[103] In the absence of any fraud or gross or simple

99. 28 U.S.C. § 2415(a).
100. 19 U.S.C. § 1621.
101. 28 U.S.C. § 2415(a).
102. Liquidation in customs is the finalization of the CBP entry process and constitutes settlement of duties due the United States and finalizes liability of importers, and such action is final and conclusive upon all parties unless protest is filed against valid liquidation or action of CBP, pursuant to 19 U.S.C. § 1514. A.N. Deringer, Inc. v. United States, 80 Cust. Ct. 17 (1978), *vacated*, 593 F.2d 1015 (C.C.P.A. 1979).
103. It is well established that all decisions by CBP relating to an entry merge into the liquidation, which, in turn, becomes final and conclusive unless challenged in accordance with § 1514. *See* Volkswagen of Am., Inc. v.

negligence during the bond period, the surety in these circumstances has no further liability under the bond for duty because CBP has no legal authority to make a new or additional claim for duty under the bond.

2. *Claims for Liquidated Damages*

Liquidated damages can only be incurred before an entry liquidates.[104] That does not mean that liquidated damages cannot be claimed after liquidation. They can, but the statute for collection of liquidated damages limits the right to collect to the six-year period following the date of the breach of the bond obligation, not the date of assessment and not the date of liquidation. As discussed earlier, there are 12 bond obligations, the breach of which can give rise to a "timely" claim for liquidated damages but only if CBP invokes the obligation with proper and timely notice to the importer. If timely notice is not given to the principal, the principal has no obligation to perform. The 12 bond obligations for the type of bond we are reviewing, the basic importation and entry bond, are found at 19 C.F.R. § 113.62.[105] The time periods during which performance under the 12 bond obligations must be demanded by CBP and performed by the importer are short-lived and limited under 19 C.F.R. § 141.113 with a minimum of 30 days to a maximum of 210 days after the date of entry. Since liquidated damages cannot be assessed for breaches occurring after liquidation, in all but the most unusual case, a claim for liquidated damages will appear well before the date of liquidation.

Therefore, in a case in which there are no open claims for liquidated damages on an entry, and liquidation has become final as to all of the entries covered by the bond, CBP has no claim to which it can attach the six-year statute of limitations under 28 U.S.C. § 2415(a) for collection. Consequently, the surety is not at risk for liability on a future claim for liquidated damages under the subject bond once the entry has liquidated

---

United States, 532 F.3d 1365, 1370 (Fed. Cir. 2008) (citations omitted). The finality of those decisions applies to both importer duty recovery suits and to government enforcement actions. *See* United States v. Cherry Hill Textiles, Inc., 112 F.3d 1550 (Fed. Cir. 1997).

104. Liquidated damages can only be incurred prior to liquidation of an entry. A notice to redeliver must be issued before liquidation. United States v. Utex Int'l, Inc., 857 F.2d 1408 (Fed. Cir. 1988); *see also* CBP Ruling 221017 (Nov. 19, 1990).

105. *See supra* note 4.

and there have been no open claims for liquidated damages asserted within 180 days following the liquidation.[106]

B. The Five-Year Statute of Limitations: Claims for "Lost Revenue"

As also discussed earlier in Part V, the five-year statute of limitations under 19 U.S.C. § 1621, to collect on a claim for lost revenue under 19 U.S.C. § 1592(d), expires five years after the date of entry in the case of negligence or gross negligence or five years after the date of "discovery" by CBP of the transgression if the allegation is based on fraud. At the outset, the surety practitioner must distinguish between claims for liquidated duties under 19 U.S.C. §§ 1504 and 1505 from claims for lost revenue under 19 U.S.C. § 1592(d). While the importer is not protected by the six-year statute of limitations set forth at 28 U.S.C. § 2415(a) for collection of liquidated duties under 19 U.S.C. §§ 1504 and 1505, the importer is protected by the five-year statute of limitations under 19 U.S.C. § 1621 for collection of lost revenue.

Claims for "lost revenue" issuing after a bond has terminated are rare under the circumstances of a case in which the bond has been terminated, all entries under the bond have been liquidated, with all liquidations final, with no outstanding claims for liquidated duties, and no open claims for liquidated damages against entries made under the bond. To evaluate the risk of any future liability from claims for "lost revenue" "discovered" after a bond has terminated, the surety will need to evaluate its principal's history and current standing with CBP.

One important question is whether the principal or its predecessor is or had been subject to a chapter 11 bankruptcy proceeding.[107] In cases in which the principal or its predecessor successfully emerge as successor to the chapter 11 debtor in possession and the principal and/or its predecessor survived the crucible of CBP scrutiny of its past

---

106. This would be highly unusual, but it could occur.

107. 11 U.S.C. § 362. The government is not hindered by the automatic stay under 19 U.S.C. § 362(a) from following up on penalty claims against an importer so long as the proceedings do not seek to enforce a money judgment. 19 U.S.C. § 362(b) exempts penalty actions from the automatic stay when the penalty action only constitutes an action for entry of judgment rather than the enforcement of a money judgment. United States v. Rupari Food Servs. Inc., 254 F. Supp. 3d 1367 (Ct. Int'l Trade 2017).

activities during that proceeding, the future risk to the surety diminishes. If CBP never raised a question about the integrity of the principal's CBP compliance, although certainly not dispositive, that may be considered a plus in favor of release of collateral.

Of equal importance is whether the principal or its predecessor has undertaken and been accepted into a formal compliance program monitored by CBP; for example, CBP's CTPAT or ISA program. The CTPAT and ISA programs are strict importer partnerships with CBP opening up the importer's supply chain details to CBP's scrutiny. Under the ISA program, the importer is required to prepare and submit detailed periodic self-assessment reports on its customs compliance activities. If CBP has found the principal and its predecessor to be compliant under the program based upon the principal's periodic self-assessment filing(s), the surety may add an additional plus in favor of the release of collateral.[108]

In further assessing the possibility or risk of the surety having to respond to a future CBP claim for "lost revenue" under the subject bond, it is equally important to note the principal's and any predecessor's compliance history with CBP. The future risk of a loss of revenue claim is minimized when, to the best of the principal's knowledge, there is no record that any circumstance has ever arisen that would have necessitated the principal or its predecessor to file a voluntary disclosure under 19 U.S.C. § 1592(c)(4) concerning an import transaction that would give rise to a claim for lost revenue. So also, when the principal's compliance history indicates the principal and its predecessor were active in their compliance responsibilities by successfully identifying prior errors, disclosing them to CBP under 19 U.S.C. § 1592(c)(4), and tendering any loss of revenue, it is illustrative of an importer's effort to be compliant. Based upon that type of compliance history with the CBP statutes and regulations, the chances of CBP opening a loss of revenue claim in the future may be downgraded to marginal or nonexistent or upgraded to a high level of risk.

On the basis of the foregoing analysis, the termination of the bond, with no current claims thereunder, and with all entries being liquidated and the liquidations all having become final, a rational determination may be made that there is minimal risk of loss to the surety for future

---

108. Surety companies treat this risk element differently. For example, where the surety is concerned about the financial stability of a company and its ability to meet future exposure, the compliance status of the importer will take a backseat to the financial stability consideration.

claims. Based upon the principal's and its predecessor's history and current strong relationship with CBP, a rational determination may also be made that there is little or no reason to anticipate a claim for lost revenue arising in the future from CBP for any prior activities of the principal.

Conclusion

During the past decade of the 21st century, CBP ramped up enforcement of the customs laws and regulations to plug the holes created during the first decade by the Continued Dumping and Subsidy Offset Act of 2000. CBP used its bond program as a major tool for enforcing importer obligations and thereby protecting its revenue from unscrupulous importers undertaking circumvention activities to avoid duties and retaliatory tariffs. Today, more than ever before, CBP regularly reviews the sufficiency of the bond penal sum and based thereon demands increases to the penal value of bonds already on file. At the same time, the bonds are being called as a result of business failures resulting from the global pandemic and its disruption of supply chains. In response, the customs surety bond community regularly requires collateral to mitigate its risk. The effect of the foregoing upon the practitioner is the necessity to jump into claims for liquidated damages and increased duties earlier and to petition or protest, as appropriate, because there is no guarantee the principal will survive the administrative review of claims by CBP. It is equally important for practitioners to stay aware of, and monitor, the collateral requirements of both CBP in demanding increased bonding and the principals in seeking the return of the collateral previously demanded by the surety in response to CBP's demands.

CHAPTER 13

FEDERAL EXCISE BONDS PAST, PRESENT, AND FUTURE IN A POST-PANDEMIC WORLD

Jane A. Horne
Frank J. Tanzola

"Look, when Britain taxed our tea, we got frisky. Imagine what gon' happen when you try to tax our whisky."[1]

Introduction

In the present-day era of small craft breweries, micropubs, and even the more recent burgeoning of online alcohol consumption, the landscape of how alcohol is produced and consumed has certainly changed. This is especially the case as we begin to emerge from a post-COVID-19 pandemic world where certain businesses have, among other things, started to offer alcohol in different ways, such as "to-go" consumption. Indeed, in a post-pandemic world, the way we consume alcohol is changing rapidly. As such, the way that alcohol is taxed has likewise started to change and will likely continue to change in ways that are still to be determined.

To understand where we are at the present, however, we must take a look at the past. Internal revenue excise bonds, also known as ATF (Bureau of Alcohol, Tobacco, and Firearms) or TTB (Alcohol and Tobacco Tax and Trade Bureau) bonds, have a long history, dating back to the 1791 whiskey tax championed by Treasury Secretary Alexander Hamilton.[2] Distillers in the towns were taxed on the gallons they produced.[3] Larger operations could either pay the taxes quarterly or post

---

1. LIN-MANUEL MIRANDA, HAMILTON: AN AMERICAN MUSICAL (2015) (quote from Thomas Jefferson to Alexander Hamilton during Cabinet Battle #1).
2. Excise Act of 1791, ch. 15, 1 Stat. 199.
3. WILLIAM HOGELAND, THE WHISKEY REBELLION: GEORGE WASHINGTON, ALEXANDER HAMILTON, AND THE FRONTIER REBELS WHO CHALLENGED AMERICA'S NEWFOUND SOVEREIGNTY 70 (2006).

bonds periodically to cover their tax obligations.[4] The smaller distilleries found it more difficult to meet their tax obligations and often resorted to punitive bonds, which had the effect of increasing the amount of tax they had to pay per gallon.[5]

Despite their long history, excise tax bonds remain with us today. Even Prohibition did not sweep them away: alcoholic beverages may have been illegal, but they were still taxed.[6] Excise tax payment bonds helped secure the government's ability to collect on these taxes if, for example, alcohol for industrial uses (generally not taxable) was diverted for use in alcoholic beverages.[7] After the repeal of Prohibition, the federal government still took an active hand in regulating the production of alcoholic beverages, pursuing criminal charges against distilleries for, among other violations, failing to post the appropriate excise tax bonds.[8]

In more recent years, excise bonds have settled into a more stable role: safeguarding the federal government's ability to collect revenue on alcohol or tobacco taxes.[9] Modern tax obligations for alcohol and tobacco are, without question, complex. The variability of tax obligations based on such factors as the use and destination of the commodity, which themselves may shift during the life of the commodity, inject some uncertainty into excise tax obligations. For example, distilled spirits intended for non-beverage use may be untaxed at one time, but taxable at another if later diverted to use in beverages. The various bonds required by the government help ensure that at the end of the day, the Internal Revenue Service will be able to collect the taxes owed, either from the principal or the surety.

I. TTB Bonds—General Overview

A TTB bond is essentially a guarantee by a brewer, vintner, or distiller that it will pay the excise taxes owed to the federal government. The bond itself is a legal document that covers the business's federal excise tax liability of whatever it is producing, be it spirits, beer, or wine. The

---

4. *Id.*
5. *Id.*
6. United States v. Glidden Co., 119 F.3d 235, 243 (6th Cir. 1941).
7. *Id.*
8. United States v. Bacon, 7 F. Supp. 590, 590–91 (W.D. Tex. 1934); United States v. Braverman, 125 F.2d 283, 284 (6th Cir. 1942).
9. *Glidden*, 119 F.3d at 243.

bond guarantees the federal government that whatever excise taxes are owed to it will be paid, whether by the business or by a third party (e.g., an insurance company). Federal surety bonds are required by the TTB for businesses that sell, manufacture, or distribute alcohol products, and surety bond amounts vary.

A bond is one of the many pieces of documentation required in order for a business to obtain a permit. The *Code of Federal Regulations* requires, for example, every person or entity "intending to commence the business of a brewer" to file a bond.[10] The business may not begin to operate until first receiving notice that a TTB officer has approved the bond. However, pressure from the increasing number of smaller operations, such as microbreweries, that produce relatively small amounts of alcohol, prompted a more recent change in the federal rules. This is discussed further below.

Sometimes, bonds are guaranteed by a third party, such as a surety company. A surety company is similar to an insurance company, in that the distillery, brewery, or winery pays the surety a yearly fee (generally a small amount of the actual tax liability owed) and, in exchange, the surety guarantees the federal government that it will cover excise taxes for the business's products should the business default in paying the tax. A surety bond is a legal contract between three entities: (1) the principal (in the case of alcohol bonds, the business or individual producing beer, wine, or distilled spirits); (2) the obligee (the U.S. Department of the Treasury, TTB); and (3) the surety (the insurance company that guarantees the bond).

Some might say that in this newer landscape, bond requirements have actually become friendlier for the small craft brewers, distillers, wineries, and the like. One more recent example is discussed below in Part I.A. A kindlier approach may bode well for businesses as the way in which alcohol is produced and consumed continues to change.

A. *New Federal Bond Exemptions for Breweries, Distilleries, and Wineries*

On November 7, 2016, the TTB announced that, beginning on January 1, 2017, breweries, distilleries, and wineries that owed $50,000 or less in federal excise taxes in the previous calendar year of operations and expect to owe $50,000 or less in federal excise taxes in the current

---

10. 27 C.F.R. § 25.91 (2017).

calendar year of operations are exempt from carrying a federal bond to ensure the payment of such taxes. Although the Internal Revenue Code has been amended to exempt a large number of brewers, wineries, and the like, it is important to note that most individual states still require alcohol tax surety bonds.

1. The PATH Act

On December 18, 2015, the Consolidated Appropriations Act, 2016[11] was signed into law. Division Q of the act, the "Protecting Americans from Tax Hikes Act of 2015" (PATH Act), amends the Internal Revenue Code (IRC) to change tax return due dates and remove bond requirements for certain eligible taxpayers beginning January 1, 2017. These PATH Act amendments apply to certain taxpayers who expect to be liable for not more than $50,000 in taxes imposed with respect to distilled spirits, wines, and beer for the calendar year and who were not liable for more than $50,000 in such taxes in the preceding calendar year. Regarding tax return dates, section 332 amends section 5061(d) of the IRC to authorize a new annual return period for the deferred payment of taxes. "Deferred payment" refers to payment of taxes by the proprietor of a distilled spirits plant, wine premises, or brewery after the alcohol product is removed from the facility, rather than payment immediately before or at the time the alcoholic product is removed from the facility. To be eligible to use the new annual deferred payment period, the taxpayer must expect to be liable for not more than $1,000 in excise taxes imposed with respect to distilled spirits, wines, and beer for the calendar year (and not more than $1,000 in such taxes in the preceding year). To be eligible to use quarterly deferred payment periods, the taxpayer must also expect to be liable for not more than $50,000 in such taxes imposed for the calendar year (and not liable for more than $50,000 in such taxes in the preceding year).

Section 332 of the PATH Act also amended several provisions of the IRC to remove bond requirements for certain eligible taxpayers. To be exempt, taxpayers must be eligible to use quarterly or annual return periods and must pay such taxes on a deferred basis. Even if taxpayers choose to pay taxes semi-monthly, they still qualify for the bond exemption if they meet the criteria to pay taxes quarterly or annually. Taxpayers are also exempt from the bond requirements with respect to distilled spirits and wine to the extent that the products are for nonindustrial use.

---

11. Pub. L. No. 114-113, 129 Stat. 2242 (2015).

These new bond exemptions relieve qualifying existing breweries, distilleries, and wineries form the administrative burden of carrying, amending, and updating their federal bonds with the TTB until they increase their current production to significantly higher levels. It is believed that most craft breweries, distilleries, and wineries will qualify for the new bond exemption and continue to qualify.

To put this into perspective, consider U.S. wineries, for example. As of 2017 there were more than 8,000 wineries in the United States. Nearly 80 percent of these wineries produce fewer than 5,000 cases of wine per year. This means that they will likely qualify to cancel their TTB wine bond(s).

2. 2020 Final Adoption

Effective June 2, 2020, the TTB adopted as final the temporary regulations relating to excise taxes imposed on distilled spirits, wines, and beer that were published in the *Federal Register* on January 4, 2017.[12] These regulatory amendments implemented certain changes made to the IRC by the PATH Act, which amended the IRC to remove bond requirements and change tax return due dates for certain eligible excise taxpayers.

B. Taxable Goods and Types of Excise Bonds

Alcohol- and tobacco-related products are subject to federal taxes. Beer, wine, and distilled spirits for use in beverages are usually taxed. These commodities may on occasion escape taxation depending on their use (e.g., alcohol for industrial use) or destination (e.g., to a bonded storehouse), but these commodities may eventually be directed to taxable locations and uses.[13] In such instances, the excise tax bonds act as a "safeguard for the protection of revenue and to reimburse the government for the expense of investigation."[14] A given commodity or alcohol or tobacco enterprise may be covered by several different bonds. The two main bonds are as follows:

---

12. Changes to Certain Alcohol-Related Regulations Governing Bond Requirements and Tax Return Filing Periods, 82 Fed. Reg. 1,108 (Jan. 4, 2017).
13. *Glidden*, 119 F.3d at 242–43.
14. *Id.* at 243.

1. **Operational**. Operational bonds guarantee payment of tax obligations relating to the operation of facilities such as distilled spirit plants, breweries, wine cellars, tobacco manufacturers, and tobacco export warehouses.[15] None of these facilities can be operated without an operations bond.[16]
2. **Withdrawal or tax deferral**. Withdrawal or tax deferral bonds guarantee the payment of taxes due on the withdrawal of alcohol from a bonded premises (that is, a location covered by an operations bond) after taxes are determined, but before the taxes are paid.[17] The withdrawal bond is in addition to the operations bond. If the alcohol is withdrawn under the withdrawal bond, the operations bond will no longer cover liability for payment of taxes on the withdrawn alcohol.

Any action or activity that may even potentially implicate a tax obligation is covered by an excise tax bond. For example, if alcohol has been removed from a bonded premises for transportation to another bonded location, the transfer will be covered by a bond.[18] Bonds even cover entities that have already paid their taxes: a proprietor that has paid taxes on distilled spirits that are used for non-beverage purposes, and thus not taxable, may claim a "drawback" on the taxes paid.[19] A chart of products and activities requiring excise tax bonds is located at Appendix A.

---

15. Distilled spirits Plants, 27 C.F.R. § 19.152(1) (2011); Wine, *id.* §§ 24.100–.101; Manufacture of Tobacco Products and Cigarette Tubes and Papers, *id.* § 40.66; Exportation of Tobacco Products and Cigarette Papers and Tubes, without Tax, or with Drawback of Tax, *id.* § 44.86.
16. Bonded Wine Cellar, 26 U.S.C. § 5351 (2011); Qualifying Documents, *id.* 5401; 27 C.F.R. § 24.100 (2017).
17. 27 C.F.R. § 19.152(2) (2011); *id.* § 24.146(b); Removal of Tobacco Products and Cigarette Papers and Tubes, without Payment of Tax, for Use of the United States, *id.* § 45.32 (2011).
18. Transfer of Distilled Spirits between Bonded Premises, 26 U.S.C. § 5212 (2011).
19. Drawback of Taxpaid Distilled Spirits Used in Manufacturing of Non-Beverage Products, 27 C.F.R. § 17.101 (2011).

C. Features of Internal Revenue Excise Bonds

Although the features of the excise bonds for the various covered commodities and taxable activities are not uniform, they tend to have similar requirements.

1. Bond Provisions

Bond terms typically include provisions that the proprietor will comply with the law and pay all taxes and any penalties or fines.[20] For each bond, there is a form required by the TTB. These forms are available on the TTB website[21] and are listed at Appendix A.

2. Who Can Issue and Approve Bonds

Bonds are issued by a company called a "corporate surety." The bonds must be obtained by a corporate surety approved by the secretary of the treasury.[22] As noted above, bonds require approval by the TTB.[23]

3. Satisfaction of Bond Requirement by Deposit of Securities

As an alternative to a corporate surety bond, a person can file a bond that guarantees payment of the tax liability by pledging negotiable securities or in some instances cash with a face amount equal to or greater than the penal sum required under the bond. Only certain securities for which principal and interest are guaranteed by the United States, such as treasury notes and treasury bills, are acceptable.[24] Pledged securities or

---

20. Distilled Spirits Plants, *id.* § 19.152(a); Wine, *id.* § 24.146; Beer, *id.* § 25.91.
21. The forms may be found at *TTB Bond Forms*, TTB, https://www.ttb.gov/forms/bond-forms (last updated Mar. 3, 2021).
22. 27 C.F.R. § 17.103 (2022); *id.* § 19.153; *id.* § 24.149; *id.* § 25.98; Manufacture of Tobacco Products and Cigarette Tubes and Papers, *id.* § 40.131 (2011).
23. *Id.* § 24.145.
24. *Id.* § 17.104; Distilled Spirits Plants, *id.* § 19.154; Wine, *id.* § 24.151; Beer, *id.* § 25.98(e), (f) (2017); Manufacture of Tobacco Products and Cigarette Tubes and Papers, *id.* § 40.132 (2011).

cash deposited as collateral in lieu of a corporate surety bond will not be released until the bond for which they are pledged is terminated.[25]

4. Changes to the Surety Bond Terms

The terms of a bond cannot be changed unless the principal and the surety both consent.[26] The bond forms themselves, however, are established by the TTB, and courts will construe the completed bond forms so that they are consistent with applicable statutes and regulations.[27] The government cannot expand a surety's liability beyond that set forth in the bond form by implication.[28] It should be noted that courts are generally not forgiving of mistakes made in the completion of the bond form. For example, in *United States v. Fidelity & Deposit Co.*, the surety claimed that it had intended to issue two separate bonds (with separate limits) for operations and withdrawal on the same bond form, but because it also checked the box indicating a unit bond, the Fifth Circuit held that it was subject to a combined, aggregate limit for both operations and withdrawal liabilities.[29]

Because an action by the government to enforce the terms of a bond is contractual in nature, the statutes of limitation that might pertain to the underlying tax obligation are inapplicable.[30]

5. Single Bonds for Multiple Premises or Tax Liabilities

In some circumstances, a single bond may cover multiple premises that would otherwise require multiple operations bonds. For example, a proprietor who operates a bonded wine cellar that is adjacent to the proprietor's distilled spirits plant may file a single operations bond to cover both premises.[31] A proprietor may also secure a "unit bond" that

---

25. *Id.* § 17.114; *id.* § 19.173.
26. *Id.* § 17.106; Distilled Spirit Plants, *id.* § 19.155; Wine, *id.* § 24.152; Beer, *id.* § 25.92; Liquors and Articles from Puerto Rico and Virgin Islands, *id.* § 26.64; Exportation of Alcohol, *id.* § 28.54.
27. United States v. Fid. & Deposit Co., 10 F.3d 1150, 1153 (5th Cir. 1994); United States v. Fulton Distillery, 571 F.2d 923, 924–25 (5th Cir. 1978).
28. United States v. Mass. Bonding & Ins. Co., 51 F. Supp. 574, 576–77 (D.N.J. 1943).
29. 10 F.3d at 1152–53.
30. United States v. Van Schaack Bros. Chem. Works, 33 F. Supp. 822, 830 (N.D. Ill. 1940).
31. Distilled Spirits Plants, 27 C.F.R. §§ 19.152(b), 19.162 (2011).

provides a single aggregate limit for both operational and withdrawal tax liabilities.[32]

6. Increase in Bond Coverage

If tax liabilities increase such that they exceed the penal sum of the applicable bond, the proprietor must increase the amount of the bond to cover the increased liability by replacing the existing bond with a new, larger bond or by supplementing the existing bond with a separate strengthening bond. The strengthening bond must be with the same surety as the original bond and must state both its execution date and effective date. The strengthening bond will be rejected by the TTB if it can be construed as releasing or limiting the liability of the original bond.[33]

7. Superseding Bond

In some circumstances, the proprietor must replace the existing bond with a superseding bond. These circumstances include (1) if the original surety becomes insolvent or is removed from the list of approved corporate sureties; (2) if there is a change of control in the business of the principal (unless there is consent by the surety); or (3) if the surety terminates the bond.[34] If a superseding bond is not furnished to the TTB, the proprietor may not continue operations (in the case of an operations bond) or withdraw alcohol (in the case of a withdrawal bond).[35]

8. Surety's Relief from Bond Liability

A surety on a bond may, at any time, notify the appropriate TTB officer that it wishes to be relieved of liability under the bond. The surety

---

32. *Fid. & Deposit Co.*, 10 F.3d at 1152–53; 27 C.F.R. § 19.152 (b)(3) (2011).
33. Drawback of Taxpaid Distilled Spirits Used in Manufacturing of Non-Beverage Products, 27 C.F.R. § 17.107 (2011); Manufacture of Tobacco Products, Cigarette Papers and Tubes, and Processed Tobacco, *id.* § 40.135; *id.* § 19.167; Wine, *id.* § 24.153; Beer, *id.* § 25.94.
34. Distilled Spirit Plants, *id.* § 19.168; Wine, *id.* § 24.154; Beer, *id.* § 25.95(a); *id.* § 25.96; Manufacture of Tobacco Products, Cigarette Papers and Tubes, and Processed Tobacco, *id.* § 40.136.
35. Distilled Spirits Plants, *id.* § 19.169; Manufacture of Tobacco Products and Cigarette Tubes and Papers, *id.* § 40.136.

must notify the principal of its intent to terminate the bond and provide evidence of such notice to the TTB.[36] The amount of notice required varies from ten days to 90 days, depending upon the specific type of bond. The surety is not required to have reasonable cause for the termination.[37] Notably, however, the government's laxness or errors in pursuing the underlying tax obligation will not excuse a surety from its obligations under a bond, even if the government's missteps arguably increased the surety's exposure.[38]

9. Termination of Bonds

Liability under a bond may be terminated (1) on application of the surety; (2) by replacement of the bond; (3) by discontinuing withdrawals (for a withdrawal bond); or (4) discontinuing the operations bond.[39] In certain cases, the liability may also be terminated where the principal becomes exempt from bond requirements, as, for instance, in the example noted towards the beginning of this chapter addressing the PATH Act.[40]

10. Subrogation

When the government secures payment on a bond from the surety, the surety may be subrogated to the government's right of recovery against the principal, and traditional subrogation rules will apply.[41] The surety

---

36. Drawback on Tax Paid Distilled Spirits Used in Manufacturing Non-Beverage Products, *id.* § 17.112; Distilled Spirit Plants, *id.* § 19.171; Wine, *id.* §§ 24.157, 24.159; Beer, *id.* § 25.103.
37. United States v. Sherwood Distilling Co., 235 F. Supp. 776, 783–84 (D. Md. 1964).
38. United States v. Fid. & Deposit Co., 10 F.3d 1150, 1154–55 (5th Cir. 1994) (citing Hart v. United States, 95 U.S. 316 (1877), and United States v. Fulton Distillery, 571 F.2d 923 (5th Cir. 1978)).
39. 27 C.F.R. § 17.111 (2006); *id.* § 19.170; *id.* § 24.156; *id.* § 25.102; *id.* § 40.139.
40. Distilled Spirit Plants, *id.* § 19.151(d); Wine, *id.* § 24.160(d); Beer, *id.* § 25.104(a)(4).
41. *In re* Beverages Int'l Ltd., 96 B.R. 407, 412 (Bankr. D. Mass. 1989), *aff'd sub nom.* Creditor's Comm. v. Mass. Dep't of Revenue, 105 B.R. 145 (D. Mass. 1989).

will not, however, assume a taxing authority's priority of payment in bankruptcy proceedings.[42]

Conclusion

As the manner and ways in which we manufacture, market, and consume alcohol are constantly changing—particularly in a post-pandemic world—it is all but a certainty that the ways in which alcohol is taxed will continue to evolve and change. Although continued changes are likely, the bonds themselves are unlikely to leave this landscape anytime soon. Excise tax bonds have been with us for hundreds of years, and will continue to remain a part of the way alcohol is taxed, both by the federal government and the states. Thus, it is important to understand the requirements and adhere to the compliance obligations.

---

42. *Id.*

APPENDIX A

INTERNAL REVENUE EXCISE BONDS

Title	Relevant Statutes	Bond-Specific Regulations	Bond Forms
Drawback on Taxpaid Distilled Spirits Used in Manufacturing Non-Beverage Products	26 U.S.C. § 5131	27 C.F.R. §§ 17.101–.114	TTB F 5154.3 (Bond for Drawback under 26 U.S.C. § 5111)
Distilled Spirits Plants	26 U.S.C. §§ 5173, 5176	27 C.F.R. §§ 19.56, 19.58, 19.151–.173, 19.231	TTB F 5100.12 (Specific Exportation Bond-Distilled Spirits or Wine Withdrawn for Transportation to Manufacturing Bonded Warehouse—Class Six) TTB F 5110.56 (Distilled Spirits Bond) TTB F 5110.67 (Continuing Bond—Distilled Spirits and Wines Withdrawn for Transportation to Manufacturing Bonded Warehouse)

Title	Relevant Statutes	Bond-Specific Regulations	Bond Forms
Wine	26 U.S.C. §§ 5351–5392	27 C.F.R. §§ 24.65–.66, 24.101–.109, 24.145–.159	TTB F 5120.36 (Wine Bond) TTB F 5120.36 (Instructions) TTB F 5120.36 (Worksheet) TTB F 5100.12 (Specific Exportation Bond—Distilled Spirits or Wine Withdrawn for Transportation to Manufacturing Bonded Warehouse—Class Six) TTB F 5110.67 (Continuing Bond—Distilled Spirits and Wines Withdrawn for Transportation to Manufacturing Bonded Warehouse) TTB F 5120.32 (Tax Referral Bond—Wine)

Title	Relevant Statutes	Bond-Specific Regulations	Bond Forms
Beer	26 U.S.C. § 5401	27 C.F.R. §§ 25.91–.105	TTB F 5130.25 (Brewer's Collateral Bond) TTB F 5130.27 (Brewer's Collateral Bond Continuation Certificate) TTB F 5130.16 (Tax Deferral Bond—Beer) TTB F 5130.22 (Brewer's Bond) TTB F 5130.23 (Brewer's Bond Continuation Certificate)
Liquors and Articles from Puerto Rico and the Virgin Islands		27 C.F.R. §§ 26.61–.75	TTB F 5110.50 (Tax Deferral Bond—Distilled Spirits—Puerto Rico)
Exportation of Liquors	26 U.S.C. §§ 5175, 5214(a)	27 C.F.R. §§ 28.25–.28, 28.51–.80, 28.331–.335	TTB F 5100.12 (Specific Exportation Bond—Distilled Spirits or Wine Withdrawn for Transportation to Manufacturing Bonded Warehouse—Class Six)

Title	Relevant Statutes	Bond-Specific Regulations	Bond Forms
Manufacture of Tobacco Products and Cigarette Papers and Tubes	26 U.S.C. §§ 5706, 5711	27 C.F.R. §§ 40.66–.68, 270.131–.140	TTB F 5200.17 (Bond Drawback of Tax on Tobacco Products, Cigarette Papers, or Tubes) TTB F 5200.25 (Tobacco Bond—Collateral) TTB F 5200.26 (Tobacco Bond—Surety) TTB F 5210.12 (Deferral Bond—Tobacco Products)
Importation of Tobacco Products and Cigarette Papers and Tubes	26 U.S.C. § 7652(a)	27 C.F.R. §§ 41.109–.110, 41.119–.129	TTB F 5210.12 (Deferral Bond—Tobacco Products)
Exportation of Tobacco Products and Cigarette Papers and Tubes, without Payment of Tax, or with Drawback of Tax	26 U.S.C. § 5711	27 C.F.R. §§ 44.86–.88, 44.121–.129	TTB F 5200.17 (Bond Drawback of Tax on Tobacco Products, Cigarette Papers, or Tubes) TTB F 5200.26 (Tobacco Bond—Surety)

CHAPTER 14

WORKERS' COMPENSATION BONDS

CharCretia V. Di Bartolo
*Gary Case**

Introduction

Workers' compensation laws are designed to ensure that employees who are injured or disabled on the job are provided with fixed benefits, eliminating the need for litigation. All states have a system of statutes, rules, and administrative procedures providing for a more expeditious remedy to employees for work-related injuries than resorting to the court system.

Every employer subject to the workers' compensation laws of a state is liable for workers' compensation benefits for personal injury or death of its employees caused by accidents or occupational diseases arising out of and in the course of the employee's employment. The employer must bear the cost for workers' compensation benefits. Generally, there are three ways in which the employer may cover this risk. While not all states or jurisdictions allow all three methods, most allow a combination of the following: (1) commercial insurance; (2) insurance enabled by statute or contribution to a state fund; or (3) self-funding or self-insurance. This chapter focuses on workers' compensation bonds provided to cover an employer's self-funding or self-insurance obligation.

I. Self-Insurance Generally

Most states allow employers, after meeting rigid financial and loss control standards, to self-insure their workers' compensation liabilities. Self-insurance is permitted in 48 states and the District of Columbia.[1] In

---

* The authors thank Lawrence Lerner of Levy and Craig, P.C. and Sean P. Hamer of Scharnhorst Ast Kennard Griffin P.C. for their work on the prior version of this chapter. The current chapter is based on and updates their work.

1. North Dakota and Wyoming do not provide for a self-insurance option and require employers to obtain insurance through a state-administered

each of these jurisdictions, there are statutes enabling the rules governing the respective self-insured programs. Appendix A provides relevant statutory references for each state and territory in the United States.

Although the requirements vary from state to state, each state requires an employer seeking to self-insure its workers' compensation liability to undergo an application process to determine whether the employer qualifies as a self-insurer. Typically, the application is submitted to a state Division of Workers' Compensation or other such regulatory body. The scope of the application review is generally directed at the financial capability of the employer to meet all current and long-term obligations for workers' compensation benefits. Factors frequently considered in determining whether an employer is financially capable of meeting those obligations include (1) profitability, efficiency, solvency, and liquidity ratios; (2) profit and loss history; (3) organizational structure and management background; (4) workers' compensation loss history; (5) source and reliability of financial information; (6) number of employees; (7) excess insurance coverage; (8) guarantee by parent company; (9) surety bond and other securities; (10) claims administration; and (11) safety program.[2] States typically place emphasis, however, on the number of employees a company has, the period of time in which it has been in existence, its profit history, and its debt-to-equity ratio.

If an employer is approved to self-insure its workers' compensation liability, the employer is required to provide security in a form and amount required by the state. This security is required to cover future liabilities for payment of workers' compensation benefits to its employees and serves to protect the employees in the event the employer fails to make the benefit payments. The standards and different types of security vary widely from state to state. In fact, many states allow a combination of

---

fund. Puerto Rico has similar restrictions. *See infra* Appendix A to this chapter.

2. *See, e.g.*, CONN. GEN. STAT. § 38a-1003(b)(2) (2021) (to obtain approval of a self-insurance group, statute requires combined net worth of all members of group of private employers of at least $5,000,000 and minimum working capital of $250,000 and security in the amount of $500,000 in the form of a surety bond, security deposit, or financial security endorsement or combination thereof); HAW. REV. STAT. § 386-194(b)(2) (2021) (a workers' compensation self-insurance group complies with the statutory requirements by establishing a combined net worth of $1,000,000 and posting security in the form of a surety bond, security deposit, financial security endorsement, or any combination thereof).

various forms of security. Accepted forms of security typically consist of letters of credit, securities, funds deposited in escrow, and surety bonds.[3]

II. Self-Insurance Surety Bonds

A workers' compensation self-insurance surety bond is one method of security permitted by states for qualified self-insured employers. The unmistakable and primary purpose of the surety bond is to assure, to the fullest extent possible, that there will be a financial source available from which workers' compensation obligations of a defaulting employer may be satisfied.

It is important to keep in mind in reviewing a claim on a workers' compensation self-insurance bond that typically such bonds are mandated by a specific statute or regulation. Accordingly, the scope and potential liability of a surety on such bond, as well as the mechanisms available to the surety for cancellation and termination of liability, cannot be ascertained without first reviewing both the bond and the applicable statute or regulation. (See Appendix A to this chapter, State Workers' Compensation Statutes (Employer Self-Insurance/Financial Responsibility Obligations).) Although each state has different bond requirements and prescribed bond forms and procedures, there are common elements among workers' compensation self-insurance bonds.

A. Parties

1. Obligee

The obligee named in the bond is typically the state "for the use and benefit" of the employees of the principal (i.e., the employer) named in the bond.

---

3. *See, e.g.*, CAL. LAB. CODE § 3701(e) (West 2021) (only cash, securities, surety bonds, or irrevocable letters of credit in any combination the director deems adequate may be used as security for a self-insured obligation); COLO. REV. STAT. ANN. § 8-44-201 (2021) (alternatives for self-insurance security requirements include trust funds, surety bonds, excess insurance, or other security acceptable to the executive director).

2. Principal—Subsidiaries or Affiliate Companies

Although it is obvious the principal is the employer named in the bond, the issue frequently arises whether subsidiaries or affiliate companies are covered by the same bond.[4] Generally, although each corporation or separate legal entity desiring to self-insure must submit a separate application, a subsidiary corporation or other subsidiary legal entity may be covered by the same bond. Some states require, however, that the subsidiary corporation or other subsidiary legal entity have the parent corporation guarantee its liability for workers' compensation benefits.[5]

3. Claimant

The party entitled to make a claim under the bond is largely determined from the language of the bond and its accompanying statute or regulation. Statutory bond forms may designate the obligee as the state requiring the bond. In addition to being for the benefit of the named obligee (i.e., the state), the bond may provide that it is also "for the use of" or "on behalf of" the employees of the principal and the dependents of such employees. In other instances, the bond may designate the obligee as the employees of the principal. The issue of who may make a claim under the bond is focused on the general purpose of the self-insurance bond: to secure payment of benefits to employees.[6] In some states the right to

---

4. In limited circumstances, the surety may actually be considered to be the "employer." *See, e.g.*, Holben v. Interstate Motor Freight Co., 509 N.E.2d 938 (Ohio 1987) (surety for an insolvent self-insured employer, who bears the financial responsibility for benefit payments from the statutory surplus fund, is included within the definition of "employer" in Ohio Revised Code Annotated section 4123.01(B) for the limited purpose of participating in the workers' compensation benefit determination proceedings, and therefore may appeal a decision of the Industrial Commission or a regional board of review to the court of common pleas).
5. *See, e.g.*, Mo. Code Regs. Ann. tit. 8, § 50-3.010(3)(B)(2) (2021).
6. *See, e.g.*, Jensen v. N. River Ins. Co., No. 15-083, 2015 WL 8041998 (D.R.I. Dec. 4, 2015) (court held that Rhode Island's workers' compensation laws, General Laws of Rhode Island sections 28–33, did not require surety to pay remaining penal sum to Rhode Island Department of Labor and Training without a corresponding identified and approved claim where department sought simply to maintain fund for potential future claims); Helmsman Mgmt. Servs., Inc. v. Colo. Dep't of Lab. & Emp., 31

make a claim under the bond is given only to the state; in other states the right extends to the individual employee seeking workers' compensation benefits. The procedure for asserting a claim also varies by jurisdiction and will depend upon the provisions of the bond, statute, and applicable regulation. For example, some states require the state regulatory agency governing self-insured employers to declare a default against the employer first. Upon such a declaration and a failure of the principal to cure it, the state agency then may draw down the proceeds of the bond for the purpose of paying any outstanding claims for workers' compensation benefits.[7]

B. Penal Sum of the Bond

The penal sum of the bond is generally determined based on an estimated future liability for workers' compensation benefits for an employer. Typical statutory language regarding the minimum security amount and, consequently, the minimum penal sum of the bond is as follows:

> An applicant for a permit shall provide security in the amount and in a manner prescribed by the Executive Director to insure payment of all workers' compensation claims required by the Act. The minimum amount of such security shall be $300,000.[8]

State regulatory bodies examining applications for self-insurance are given broad discretion in setting the amount of the penal sum of a bond. It has been held that the surety is not liable for any compensation benefits in excess of the penal sum of the bond even if the bond subsequently is proven to be inadequate to fully cover workers' compensation benefits of

---

P.3d 895, 898 (Colo. App. 2000) (claims administrator for bankrupt self-insured employer could not seek reimbursement from surety for amounts paid by claims administrator because it was not a third-party beneficiary of the bond; claims paid by administrator prior to principal's default not eligible for reimbursement by surety).

7. *See, e.g.*, MO. CODE REGS. ANN. tit. 8, § 50-3.010(3)(B)(1) (2021).

8. *See, e.g.*, State of Colorado Division of Workers Compensation Rules Governing the Issuance of Self Insurance Permits under the Workers Compensation Act, 7 COLO. CODE REGS. § 1101-4, Part III(A)(4)(d) found at https://codwc.app.box.com/v/self-insurance-rules; CAL. LAB. CODE § 3701(a) (2021).

a defaulting employer.[9] In some states the bond language may expressly provide that any legal fees and adjusting expenses incurred by the surety in administering its obligations under the bond are not counted against the surety's penal sum.[10] Thus, in these states the surety's total exposure for a default may in fact exceed the penal sum of the bond when the surety incurs legal fees and claim adjustment costs.

C. Tail Exposure Under the Bond

A significant issue with the surety bond forms prescribed by several states is the potential long-tail exposure.[11] Claimants may allege the surety should be liable for long-tail claims and payment of benefits beyond the expiration or termination of its bond and for incidents that occurred prior to the issuance of the bond. This argument for such exposure stems from two forms of bonds. The first is essentially a traditional bond form in an "occurrence" bond format. The typical "occurrence" bond form language states:

> [The] surety shall be liable to the full extent of the penal sum herein stipulated for the default of the Principal in fully discharging any liability on his part accruing during the life of this obligation. . . . [T]ermination shall not relieve the Surety of its continual liability under this bond for obligations that occurred prior to the effective date of such termination.[12]

Under this language, the surety is liable for the payment of the principal's workers' compensation obligations occurring during the time the bond is in force. When the bond is cancelled, the surety continues to have liability for all workers' compensation claims incurred between the effective date of the bond and the cancellation or termination date of the bond, but not for claims for injuries occurring after the effective date of cancellation or termination.

---

9. *See* Whitehead v. Davis, 692 S.W.2d 801, 803 (Ky. 1985).
10. *See, e.g.*, N.C. GEN. STAT. § 97-185(c) (2021); N.M. STAT. ANN. § 52-1-4 (2021); S.D. CODIFIED LAWS § 62-5-5 (2021); TEX. LAB. CODE ANN. § 407.064 (West 2021); UTAH CODE ANN. § 34A-2-201.5 (2021).
11. For a discussion of the potential for stacking or cumulative liability under the bond see Part II.I of this chapter.
12. Extracted from State of New Hampshire Workers' Compensation Bond.

The second form of bond used is described generally as a "last surety on" bond form. The typical "last surety on" bond form language states:

> The surety agrees that the obligation of this bond shall cover and extend to all past, present, existing and potential liability of said Principal, incurred as a self-insurer, to the extent of the penal sum of the bond without regard to specific injuries, date or dates of injuries, happenings or events.[13]

Under the "last surety on" bond form, the surety assumes all past, present, and future liability to pay the principal's self-insured workers' compensation obligations. A surety issuing this type of bond must consider whether, and how, it can secure its eventual release from liability. States using this type of form will typically grant the surety a complete release of all liability only if the principal later posts an acceptable replacement surety or alternate form of security that is approved by the state. Without acceptable replacement security, the surety may be exposed to liability on an open-ended basis.

In some states the principal and the surety are provided with the right to request a reduction to (and eventual release of) the bond based on the diminished risk of future claims and losses.[14] Presenting such a request may require actuarial evidence and expert opinion. Regardless of this language, at least one court has held that fairness requires the surety in force at the time of the accident or injury to pay the resulting claim.[15]

---

13. Extracted from State of Washington Department of Labor & Industries Self-Insurers Bond.
14. *See, e.g.*, S.C. CODE ANN. § 42-5-20 (2021); MISS. CODE ANN. § 71-3-75 (2021).
15. Lee v. E. Freightways, Inc., 431 N.Y.S.2d 204, 206 (N.Y. App. Div. 1980); *see infra* Part II.F for discussion of effect of multiple sureties; *see also In re* Kemper, 819 N.E.2d 485 (Ind. Ct. App. 2004) (surety liable for all principal's workers' compensation liability dating back to 1979 even though bond not issued until 2000 due to "last on" bond form, which means that surety covers all past, present, and future liability until bond terminated; purpose of bond to provide injured workers with expeditious and adequate remedy).

D. Claims Administration Under the Bond

One of the obligations imposed on self-insured employers is to put in place a claims administration process either internally or with a third-party adjusting company. Some states require that, to the extent claims are payable under the bond, the surety is responsible for adjusting its own claims. These states incorporate adjusting obligations in their mandatory bond forms[16] For example, the state of Kansas Department of Human Resources' Self-Insurance Aggregate Surety Bond Form provides:

> The Surety subject to approval by the Division of Workers' Compensation, shall discharge their obligations under this Surety Bond by adjusting its own claims or contracting with an adjusting company, risk management company, insurance company or other company that has expertise and capabilities in adjusting and paying workers' compensation claims. The company designated to handle claims shall be subject to approval of the Division of Workers' Compensation. . . . If an adjusting company other than the Surety is designated to handle claims, the costs of such adjusting company shall be borne by the Surety and not deducted from the penal amount of this Bond.[17]

This type of provision arguably increases the surety's exposure on any bond to include loss adjustment expenses for all claims for compensation for which the employers are otherwise responsible. In some states these loss adjustment expenses are not counted against the penal sum. In the event of a default the surety must carefully consider its options and the risks associated with each option. For example, a surety seeking to administer claims itself may risk extracontractual liability arising out of its adjustment and claim-paying decisions. Further, the surety may lack the expertise and the state-specific knowledge needed to adequately administer workers' compensation claims. Given the specialized nature of workers' compensation claims and rules, the authors recommend a surety should always give serious consideration to a claims adjustment firm or consultant with expertise in workers' compensation. While this

---

16. *See, e.g.*, MD. CODE ANN., LAB. & EMPL. § 9-405(d) (West 2021); S.D. CODIFIED LAWS § 62-5-5 (2021).
17. Extracted from State of Kansas Department of Human Resources Self-Insurance Aggregate Surety Bond.

may result in additional upfront costs, it will likely minimize the surety's ultimate exposure.

If the surety becomes responsible for claims administration, it is imperative that the surety become familiar with the rights and defenses of an employer under the applicable workers' compensation law or delegate the claims process to a third-party administrator with experience in administering workers' compensation claims in the applicable jurisdiction. Although the defenses to a claim for compensation are beyond the scope of this chapter, the general categories of claim defenses to be considered include, but are not limited to, the following:

1. Conduct-related defenses such as the employee's knowing self-infliction of injury, intoxication, *knowing* failure to use a safety appliance, or *knowing* failure to obey a *reasonable written or printed* safety rule that has been posted in a conspicuous position in the place of work
2. Defenses related to the employer-employee relationship when the injury occurred (i.e., was there an employment relationship between the claimant and the principal under the bond within the meaning of the workers' compensation law?)
3. Procedural defenses such as the claimant's failure to provide proper notice of the accident or failure to timely file a claim with the Division of Workers' Compensation pursuant to the law of the applicable jurisdiction
4. Defenses related to whether the claimed injury occurred during the course and scope of the employee's employment with the bond principal[18]
5. Defenses related to whether the injury was caused by a work-related incident or some other cause

---

18. With the increase in remote work, this defense may arise more frequently. *See, e.g.*, Verizon Pa. v. W.C.A.B (Alston), 900 A.2d 440 (Pa. 2016) (upholding decision of workers' compensation judge in favor of remote employee; evidence supported finding that workers' compensation claimant, who suffered a head and neck injury when she fell down steps inside her home after getting a glass of juice, sustained her injuries within the course and scope of her employment; claimant suffered her injury during her normal working hours at her "at-home" worksite, which was approved by employer, and the injury occurred while talking on the telephone with her supervisor and returning to her computer to attend to a business matter that the supervisor called to discuss).

E. Discharge or Termination of Liability Under the Bond

Generally, most states have a mandatory procedure for cancelling or terminating the bond. The procedure will be set forth in the bond itself. A written notice of cancellation or termination generally must be given within a specified period in advance of the effective date of the cancellation or termination. Generally, the cancellation or termination does not relieve the surety of liability for claims based on accidents or injuries that occur before the effective date of cancellation or termination. In many states the surety can only be completely released (that is, released for all past, present, and future liability) if the principal obtains a replacement surety or other form of security that has been approved by the state.[19] If no replacement security is filed, the surety remains liable for claims based on injuries and accidents occurring before the effective date of cancellation or termination, and there are generally no time limits for claims in the bond. As such, the surety's potential liability in this scenario can be indefinite and open-ended. Some states provide a process for the surety or the principal to request a reduction or release of the bond based upon the diminished risk of claims.

Further, some states provide that the bond terminates upon the revocation of the employer's self-insured status except with respect to all past, present, and existing workers' compensation liabilities.[20]

Changes in corporate form, such as mergers and acquisitions, can complicate a surety's obligations to employees of the new or subsumed companies. In *In re Chateaugay Corp.*, for example, a surety argued, in the context of its principal's bankruptcy proceeding, that bonds issued to certain predecessor companies were terminated by operation of law or by agreement. The court ultimately agreed, after wading through significant extrinsic evidence submitted by the parties as to the intention of the surety when providing the substituted bonds. In the end, the court

---

19. *See, e.g.*, Mo. Code Regs. Ann. tit. 8, § 50-3.010(3)(B)(1)(A) (2021); *see, e.g.*, Or. Rev. Stat. § 656.407 (2021); S.D. Codified Laws § 62-5-5 (2021); Tex. Lab. Code Ann. § 407.064 (West 2021); Wash. Rev. Code § 34A.2.201.5 (2021).

20. *See, e.g.*, Nev. Rev. Stat. § 616B.300 (2021); N.J. Stat. Ann. § 34:15-77 (West 2021).

determined the surety was liable with respect to its principal's default on only one (the last bond issued) of five bonds.[21]

F. Effect of Multiple Sureties

In the case of multiple sureties securing the same underlying obligation, it is a general rule that as between cosureties, each surety is responsible for its contributive share of the underlying obligation.[22] This general principle is modified somewhat in the context of workers' compensation bonds. As set forth above, the statutes, regulations, and language of the bonds of a particular state govern the nature and extent of the surety's liability for past, present, and future workers' compensation claims under the bond. In most states mandating "last surety on" bond forms, regardless of previous bonds covering the same claim for compensation, the last surety is responsible for all such claims whether they are past, present, or contingent liabilities.[23] However, even in a "last surety on" state where multiple sureties cover the same claim, fairness may require that the surety in current force at the time of the accident or injury pay the resulting claim.[24]

In *Lee v. Eastern Freightways*, the court was faced with overlapping liability by several sureties on workers'' compensation obligations of a defaulting employer. The sureties had filed various bonds that made each surety liable for any workers' compensation obligations that arose out of an accident or injury that occurred before the effective date of the bond as well as for similar obligations arising during the term of each of their bonds. By reason of the continuing responsibility provisions in the bonds, several claims for compensation were subject to protection from at least two or more bonds. The court upheld the following ruling of the New York Workers' Compensation Board:

---

21. *In re* Chateaugay Corp., 116 B.R. 887, 911–12 (Bankr. S.D.N.Y. 1990). *See also* Hanover Ins. Co. v. Sharpe, 250 S.E. 2d 815, 818 (Ga. Ct. App. 1978) (when self-insured employer A merged with employer B, the surety for employer A was released from its bond upon the effective date of the merger).
22. Restatement (Third) of Suretyship and Guaranty § 55 (2021).
23. *See* Mont. Code Ann. § 39-71-2106(1)(a) (2021); Okla. Stat. tit. 85A, § 38 (2021); S.D. Codified Laws § 62-5-5 (2021).
24. Lee v. E. Freightways, Inc., 431 N.Y.S.2d 204, 206 (N.Y. App. Div. 1980).

> [F]or each of the aforementioned claims, compensation payments were to be made by the surety whose bond was executed and not yet terminated at the time the particular accident took place and that in situations of this nature, where multiple sureties cover the same claim, fairness requires that the sureties in current force at the time of the accident or injury pay the resulting claim.[25]

Regardless of this holding in *Lee v. E. Freightways*, careful attention should be paid to the specific language of the bond, the statutes, and the regulations under which the bond is issued and, to the extent that the bond has been interpreted, any case law interpreting the bond obligations.

G. Effect of Other Forms of Replacement Security

The circumstance of a workers' compensation bond and another form of security potentially covering the same loss is similar to the instance of multiple sureties covering the same loss. In states where there is a continuing obligation under the bond, when the bond is issued after or is replaced by another form of security such as a letter of credit or treasury bond, the question arises whether a claim for compensation is first payable under the workers' compensation bond or under the other form of security.[26] Resolution of this issue will depend upon the state's statutory language or the bond language. Although the general rule is the surety is relieved of all liability under the bond where subsequent replacement security is issued and accepted, some states release a surety from liability only if the replacement security is in the form of another surety bond.[27] Likewise, it has been held that payments for compensation benefits as between a surety and a subsequent letter of credit are shared as cosureties.[28]

---

25. *Id.*
26. *See generally In re* Janocha's Case, 100 N.E.3d 740 (Mass. App. Ct. 2018) (self-insured employer's reinsurer required to pay where surety bond otherwise exhausted; the self-insured trust fund was not liable because the injury at issue did not occur during the period of no insurance (or self-insurance)).
27. Theodore G. Martinez, *Workers Compensation Self-Insurance Bonds*, *in* THE LAW OF SURETYSHIP 271 (Edward Gallagher ed., 2d ed. 2000).
28. Am. Ins. Co. v. Bureau of Workers' Comp., 616 N.E. 2d 979, 982 (Ohio Ct. App. 1992).

H. Liability for Multiple Claims That Exceed the Penal Sum of the Bond

Because of the nature of workers' compensation self-insurance bonds, a surety is frequently exposed to multiple claims that exceed the penal sum of the bond. Some states address this situation by requiring that upon the insolvency or default of the principal, the full penal sum of the bond be paid to the Division of Workers' Compensation or other regulatory body for the distribution and payment of existing, future, and potential liabilities for workers' compensation benefits.[29] In this situation, the surety's payment of the full penal sum is deemed to release the surety from any remaining liability, and if the state does not eventually pay out the full penal sum, the surety at some future date may be entitled to a refund for the amounts not paid under the bond. In cases where the surety is faced with multiple claims exceeding the penal sum, it has been held that claimants under the bond are entitled to a pro-rata share of the penal sum of the bond based on the amount due to each prospective claimant.[30] Any surety faced with claims exceeding the penal sum must review the law of the particular state and the terms of the bond to ascertain the best course of action so it does not inadvertently expose itself to liability in excess of the penal sum.

I. Potential Cumulative or Stacking Liability

Workers' compensation self-insurance bonds are often automatically renewed from year to year or are required to remain in full force and effect until the surety is released or the bond is successfully cancelled or terminated. Consequently, the issue may arise whether all the bonds and the accompanying bond penalties are cumulative and may be stacked year to year providing a recovery substantially greater than any single bond penalty.[31]

---

29. *See, e.g.*, Mo. Code Regs. Ann. tit. 8, § 50-3.0101(3)(B)(1)(A) (2021).
30. Hartford Accident & Indem. Co. v. Indus. Accident Comm'n, 13 P.2d 699, 702 (Cal. 1932).
31. *See, e.g.*, State *ex rel.* Pope v. U.S. Fire Ins. Co., 145 S.W.3d 529 (Tenn. 2004) (holding that bond provided continuous rather than cumulative coverage; despite lack of adequate security for all claimants, which was not the fault of the surety, surety's liability limited to penal sum/face amount of bond).

Some states have anti-stacking provisions in their mandated bond forms. For example, the Kansas statutory bond form states: "This bond shall be an aggregate bond continuous in form and shall remain in full force and effect until the Surety is released as set out in this Agreement."

In other states, particularly in states where the surety bond is an annual term obligation, the issue of stacking may be more problematic for the surety. However, the surety may argue that because self-insurance bonds are frequently provided in lieu of some other form of liquid security such as a cash deposit or a fixed-sum irrevocable letter of credit, the surety's liability should be limited to the single penal sum. In other words, because the other forms of security remain constant from year to year and do not accumulate or cannot be stacked, the surety's liability should similarly be limited to a single penal sum. Again, careful attention should be paid to the applicable bond language, state statutes, and regulations on this issue.

J. Potential Liability for Attorneys' Fees

In some jurisdictions, the surety may be liable for attorneys' fees exceeding the penal sum of the bond. A typical bond provision imposing liability for attorneys' fees provides as follows:

> The undersigned are held and firmly bound for the payment of all legal costs, including reasonable attorney's fees and costs incurred or expended in order to force payment of this bond, separate from, and additional to, the penal sum of the bond.[32]

Absent a similar express statutorily mandated provision in the bond, courts have held that even when the bond stipulates damages shall include attorneys' fees, a surety on such bond is not liable for attorneys' fees beyond the penal sum set forth in the bond.[33]

K. The Surety's Subrogation Rights

It is a generally recognized principle that a surety that pays the debt of another is entitled to all the rights and defenses of the person it paid to

---

32. Extracted from Missouri Department of Labor and Industrial Relations Bond of Employer Carrying His Own Risk.
33. *Hartford Accident & Indem. Co.*, 13 P.2d at 703.

enforce its right to be reimbursed.[34] This principle has been recognized with respect to the rights of sureties on workers' compensation self-insurance bonds.

In *American Insurance Co. v. Ohio Bureau of Workers' Compensation*,[35] for example, the court held that, under the doctrine of equitable subrogation, the surety could step into the shoes of its principal, the employer, and acquire its rights and remedies to exercise its right to indemnification under an excess insurance policy. The court held:

> [W]here the surety is called to answer for the principal's default, the surety is subrogated to the principal's rights against others who by their negligence, breach of contract or breach of warranty contributed to that default . . . . We think the proper rule is that, when equitable, a surety is subrogated not only to the rights of the obligee, but also to the rights and remedies of the principal against third parties, where those rights arise from or are closely related to the debt the surety is called to pay under the suretyship agreement.[36]

The nature and extent of the surety's right of subrogation to the rights of an injured employee against third parties that cause or contribute to the injury of the employee depends on the workers' compensation law of the state. Many states grant an employer paying workers' compensation benefits to an employee (and, consequently, the surety on a workers' compensation self-insurance bond) a statutory right of subrogation to the rights of the employee or the dependents of the employee against third parties.[37] The right to be exercised by the surety is not one merely for indemnity or reimbursement of the compensation it paid or is obligated to pay pursuant to workers' compensation law, but generally encompasses the claimant's entire cause of action against the third party. A claimant may be deemed to act in a fiduciary capacity with respect to any recovery

---

34. Pearlman v. Reliance Ins. Co., 371 U.S. 132, 136–41 (1962).
35. 577 N.E.2d 756 (Ohio Ct. App. 1991). *Compare* Tri-City Constr. Council, Inc. v. Westfall, 112 P.3d 558 (Wash. Ct. App. 2005) (sponsor for retrospective rating plan that allowed employers to join together to lower premiums could equitably subrogate against contractor).
36. *American Ins. Co.*, 577 N.E.2d at 759.
37. *See, e.g.*, MO. REV. STAT. § 287.150.1 (2021); MINN. STAT. § 176.061 (2021); OKLA. STAT. tit. 85, § 44 (2021).

from the third party holding any amounts recovered from the third party for the benefit of the surety.[38]

L. Bankruptcy Issues

In some jurisdictions, a bankruptcy or receivership filing by the employer/principal constitutes a default, justifying a demand on the bond.[39] In others, the state obligee may demand payment of the full penal sum regardless of the actual exposure when the principal files for bankruptcy.[40] Thus, although a comprehensive discussion of bankruptcy and receivership is beyond the scope of this chapter, certain issues arise with sufficient regularity or are specific to workers' compensation bonds to merit discussion here.

The surety's obligations under a workers' compensation bond are often secured by collateral, whether it is the principal's real or personal property (including cash and cash equivalents) or by a letter of credit from an issuing bank.[41] The surety's collateral held in the form of the principal's real or personal property is property of the principal's bankruptcy estate but subject to the surety's rights pursuant to its bond, indemnity agreement, collateral agreement, and any other agreements between the surety and its principal. As respects collateral held in the form of letters of credit, the proceeds of such instruments are not property of the estate unless or until they become "excess proceeds"—that is,

---

38. State *ex rel.* Royal-McBee Corp. v. Luten, 390 S.W.2d 931 (Mo. Ct. App. 1965).

39. *See, e.g.*, N.M. STAT. ANN. § 52-1-4 (2021) (upon failure of the principal to pay a claim, bankruptcy, or deterioration of the principal's financial condition, the state may demand and the surety must pay the entire penal sum of the bond for the state's use in administering and paying claims, with any excess unused funds returned to the surety).

40. The Missouri self-insurance scheme, for example, provides that upon insolvency, "the proceeds of the surety bond shall be transferred to Missouri Private Sector Individual Self-Insurers Guaranty Corporation, if applicable, in anticipation of payment for compensation obligations which the employer has not paid . . . ." MO. CODE REGS. ANN. tit. 8, § 50-3.010(3)(B)(1)(A) (2021).

41. For a discussion of the commercial surety's collateral in the principal's bankruptcy case, see Chapter 20, The Commercial Surety's Collateral in the Principal's Bankruptcy Case.

proceeds that exceed amounts the surety needs to secure and protect itself from exposure and loss pursuant to the underlying agreements.[42]

Depending on the principal's business and the types and status of claims received pre-bankruptcy, the surety's exposure may not be fully realized at the time of its principal's bankruptcy filing. Similarly, as discussed in previous sections, the surety's exposure may continue beyond the principal's bankruptcy discharge or reorganization, due to, for example, long-tail claims or unknown claims caused by toxic exposures at the workplace. Therefore, the surety must be careful not to jeopardize its collateral by conceding the extent of its potential exposure or its rights to collateral held to secure its bond obligations.[43]

To the extent the surety handles claim administration, that process may also be impacted by the bankruptcy filing, requiring supervision or approval of payment of claims by the bankruptcy court and potentially necessitating relief from the automatic stay before the surety remits payments if such payments impact the surety's rights to use its collateral, either to pay the claims directly or to reimburse the surety for its payments. To the extent there is a cancellation option provided for by the bond or the relevant state statute, the surety may need to obtain relief from the automatic stay to proceed with that process.[44]

---

42. *Id. See also In re* Irving Tanning Co., No. 10-11757-LHK, 2012 WL 3744954 (Bankr. D. Me. Aug. 28, 2012) (debtor's reorganization plan denied where debtor sought to rely on use of excess self-insurance funds from collateral held to secure two workers' compensation bonds; court held that debtors held only a chose in action as to those excess funds and therefore could not use those funds as a basis for its reorganization plan).
43. *See, e.g.*, Sugarman v. Fed. Ins. Co., 265 Cal. App. 2d 563 (1968) (trial court decision declaring that surety might retain its collateral "until such time as all its liability and all its potential liability as surety on and under said bond . . . shall have been discharged, satisfied, and exonerated" upheld by court; creditors sought release of collateral held by surety, which argued that its exposure to long-tail claims for silicosis merited retention of the collateral). See Chapter 20, The Commercial Surety's Collateral in the Principal's Bankruptcy Case, regarding the surety's rights to retain its collateral pursuant to its underlying agreements with the principal, now the debtor in bankruptcy.
44. For a discussion of how these issues may be dealt with generally in the principal's bankruptcy case, see Chapter 20, The Commercial Surety's Collateral in the Principal's Bankruptcy Case.

The surety also should consider its rights to recovery from the bankruptcy estate through its rights of indemnity under its indemnity agreement and its rights of equitable subrogation. Creditors may not understand that the surety acts not as an insurer but as a guarantor and that it may enforce these rights for recovery from the principal's assets to the extent the surety incurs a loss.[45]

Conclusion

Each state allowing self-insurance has statutes and regulations that govern workers' compensation self-insurance bonds as one option for an employer to secure these obligations. These bonds are intended to provide a financial source from which workers' compensation obligations otherwise owed by a defaulting self-insured principal may be satisfied. In reviewing claims under self-insurance bonds, it is important to bear in mind that because the bonds are governed by a variety of statutes and regulations, it is possible that different jurisdictions may have entirely different requirements for self-insurance bonds. Therefore, the requirements of the state statutes and regulations as well as applicable case law in the relevant jurisdiction must be closely scrutinized to become familiar with how each relevant state addresses claims made against statutory workers' compensation self-insurance bonds.

45. *See, e.g.*, *In re* Farley, 236 F.3d 359, 362 (7th Cir. 2000) (recognizing that surety is different from insurer, court allowed state-funded surety company to seek recovery from bankrupt's assets pursuant to rights of equitable subrogation). For more information regarding a surety's rights to recovery from a bankruptcy estate, see Chapter 20, The Commercial Surety's Collateral in the Principal's Bankruptcy Case.

APPENDIX A

STATE WORKERS' COMPENSATION STATUTES (EMPLOYER SELF-INSURANCE/FINANCIAL RESPONSIBILITY OBLIGATIONS)

State	Statutory References	Comments
Alabama	ALA. CODE §25-5-8(b) (2021)	Provides option to employer to operate as self-insurer. No specific reference to surety or bond but an employer subject to this chapter who elects not to insure his or her liability under the statute shall furnish satisfactory proof to the secretary of his or her financial ability to directly pay compensation in the amount and manner and when due as provided by this chapter. The secretary may prescribe other reasonable rules and regulations for the purpose of protecting the injured employee or the employee's dependents and set reasonable fees to accompany self-insurance applications.
Alaska	ALASKA STAT. ANN. § 23.30.045(A); ALASKA ADMIN. CODE tit. 8, § 46.010 (2021)	An employer meets the self-insurance obligations by providing satisfactory proof that it has the ability to meet current and future obligations, has available claims-adjusting facilities and agrees to post required security deposits.

State	Statutory References	Comments
Arizona	ARIZ. REV. STAT. ANN. § 23-961A(2) (2021)	Employer may satisfy self-insurance obligations by furnishing proof that employer is a member of an approved workers' compensation pool. The commission may require a deposit or other security in an amount not less than $100,000 for workers' compensation liabilities.
Arkansas	ARK. CODE ANN. § 11-9-404(2)(B) (2021)	The commission may authorize an employer to self-insure by securing its financial ability to pay with an indemnity bond, irrevocable letter of credit, or securities of a kind and in an amount determined by the commission.
California	CAL. LAB. CODE § 3701(e) (West 2021)	Only security, cash, securities, surety bonds, or irrevocable letters of credit in any combination the director deems adequate may be used as security for a self-insured obligation under the statute.
Colorado	COLO. REV. STAT. ANN. § 8-44-201 (2021); 7 COLO. CODE REGS. § 1101-4 Part III (A)(4)(d) (2021)	Alternatives for self-insurance security requirements include trust funds, surety bonds, irrevocable letter of credit, excess insurance, or other security acceptable to the executive director.

State	Statutory References	Comments
Connecticut	CONN. GEN. STAT. § 38a-1003(b)(2) (2021)	To obtain approval of a self-insurance group, statute requires combined net worth of all members of group of private employers of at least $5,000,000 and minimum working capital of $250,000 and security in the amount of $500,000 in the form of a surety bond, security deposit, or financial security endorsement or combination thereof.
Delaware	DEL. CODE ANN. tit. 19, § 2372(b) (2021)	Department may require deposit of an acceptable security, indemnity, or bond to secure the payment of compensation liabilities as they are incurred. All bonds of insurance carriers or self-insurers deposited to secure their obligations under this chapter shall be deposited with the state insurance commissioner.
District of Columbia	D.C. CODE § 32-1534 (2021)	Employer may secure obligation by furnishing satisfactory proof of financial ability to pay and receiving authorization from mayor.
Florida	FLA. STAT. § 440.38(4)(a) (2021)	Department may require an employer to deposit with the association a qualifying security deposit, which can be in the form of a surety bond or letter of credit; in the event of an individual self-insurer's insolvency, such qualifying security deposits and reinsurance policies are payable to the Florida Self-Insurers Guaranty Association, Inc., created in section 440.385.

State	Statutory References	Comments
Georgia	GA. CODE ANN. § 34-9-121(a), (d) (2021)	Board may, in its discretion, require the deposit of acceptable security, indemnity, or bond to secure the payment of compensation liabilities as they are incurred for a self-insuring employer. Bond may be released upon filing of a certificate certifying to the existence of an insurance contract to take over outstanding liability resulting from any presently pending claim or any future unrepresented claims.
Hawaii	HAW. REV. STAT. § 386-194(b)(2) (2021)	A workers' compensation self-insurance group complies with the statutory requirements by establishing a combined net worth of $1,000,000 and posting security in the form of a surety bond, security deposit, financial security endorsement, or any combination thereof. If a surety bond is used to meet the security requirement, it shall be issued by a corporate surety company authorized to transact business in this state. The bond, security deposit, or financial security endorsement shall be for the benefit of the state solely to pay claims and associated expenses and payable upon the failure of the group to pay workers' compensation benefits it is legally obligated to pay.

State	Statutory References	Comments
Idaho	IDAHO CODE § 72-301(1)(b) (2021)	An employer may become self-insured by obtaining the approval of the Industrial Commission, and by depositing and maintaining in a custodial account with the state treasurer money or acceptable security instruments satisfactory to the commission securing the payment by said employer of compensation according to the terms of this law. Such acceptable security instruments are bonds, treasury bills, interest-bearing notes, or other obligations of the United States for which the full faith and credit of the United States is pledged for the payment of principal and interest. In lieu of such money or security instruments, the commission may allow or require such employer to file or maintain with the state treasurer a surety bond with any company authorized to transact surety insurance in Idaho.

State	Statutory References	Comments
Illinois	820 ILL. COMP. STAT. ANN. 305/4(a)(2) (2021)	One option for an employer to be approved as a self-insurer is to furnish security, indemnity, or a bond guaranteeing the payment by the employer of the compensation provided for in this act, provided that any such employer whose application and financial statement shall not have satisfied the commission of his or her financial ability and who shall have secured his or her liability in part by excess liability insurance shall be required to furnish to the commission security, indemnity, or bond guaranteeing his or her payment up to the effective limits of the excess coverage.
Indiana	IND. CODE § 22-3-2-5-1(a), (b) (2021)	Board may require the deposit of an acceptable security, indemnity, or bond to secure the payment of compensation liabilities as they are incurred to approve employer as self-insurer.

State	Statutory References	Comments
Iowa	Iowa Code § 87.11 (2021)	Security furnished to secure workers' compensation obligation is held in trust for the sole purpose of paying compensation and benefits and is not subject to attachment, levy, execution, garnishment, liens, or any other form of encumbrance. However, the insurance commissioner shall be reimbursed from the security for all costs and fees incurred by the insurance commissioner in resolving disputes involving the security. If approved self-insured employer discontinues status or enters bankruptcy, employer or successor in interest may petition for release of security, which shall be released if employer has not been self-insured for at least four years, ten years have elapsed from the last open claim, and acceptable replacement security is provided.

State	Statutory References	Comments
Kansas	KAN. STAT. ANN. § 44-532 (2021); KAN. ADMIN. REGS. § 51-14-4 (2021)	Applicant to become a self-insurer shall furnish to the Division of Workers' Compensation a bond written by a surety company admitted to the state and authorized by the Kansas Insurance Department to write surety bonds as required by the division. The bond shall be in an amount to adequately ensure that if the employer should become insolvent, payments on all claims will be guaranteed to the injured workers.
Kentucky	KY. REV. STAT. ANN. § 304.50-045, § 342.340 (West 2021); 803 KY. ADMIN. REGS. 25:021 (2021) (for specific requirements for individual self-insurers)	Commissioner shall require the deposit of an acceptable security, indemnity, or bond to secure, to the extent the commissioner directs, the payment of compensation liabilities as they are incurred.
Louisiana	LA. STAT. ANN. § 23:1168 (2021); LA. ADMIN. CODE tit. 40, § 1709 (2021) (for acceptable securities or surety requirements)	One of several ways that a self-insurer may secure workers' compensation obligation is to deposit with the assistant secretary securities or a surety bond in an amount determined by the assistant secretary that would be at least an average of the yearly claims for the past three years.

State	Statutory References	Comments
Maine	ME. STAT. tit. 39-a, § 403(3) (2021)	Treasurer of state to be listed as beneficiary of the bond or the irrevocable standby letter of credit, both of which forms for security shall be conditional upon the faithful performance of this act relating to the payment of compensation. In case of cash or securities being deposited, or drawn on a surety bond or letter of credit, the cash or securities must be placed in an account bearing interest by the treasurer of state, and the accumulation of interest on the cash or securities so deposited must be credited to the account and may not be paid to the employer to the extent that the interest is required to secure the employer's self-insurance obligations, including the amount needed to support any present value discounting in the determination of the amount of the deposit. Any security deposit must be held by the treasurer of state in trust for the benefit of the self-insurer's employees for the purposes of making payments under this act.

State	Statutory References	Comments
		The superintendent of insurance shall prescribe the form of the surety bond. The bond must be continuous, be subject to nonrenewal only upon at least 60 days' notice to the superintendent, cover payment of all present and future liabilities incurred under this act while the bond is in force, and cover payments that become due while the bond is in force that are attributable to injuries incurred in prior periods and otherwise unsecured by cash, irrevocable standby letters of credit, or acceptable securities. A bond must be held until all payments secured by the bond have been made or until the bond has been replaced by other eligible security approved by the superintendent that covers all outstanding liabilities. Payments under the bond are due within 30 days after notice has been given to the surety by the board that the principal has failed to make a payment required under the terms of an award, agreement, or governing law. A trust established to satisfy the requirements of this section may not be funded by a surety bond.

State	Statutory References	Comments
Maryland	MD. CODE ANN., LAB. & EMPL. § 9-405 (West 2021)	Security provided to secure self-insured workers' compensation obligation may be released if the employer secures compensation through an insurer, has not been liable on a claim during the five years immediately following the date on which it became insured and, if required, submits an indemnity bond.
Massachusetts	MASS. GEN. LAWS ch. 152, § 25A(2)(a)–(c) (2021)	Bond runs to the commonwealth by a surety authorized to transact business in the commonwealth as surety, in form approved by the department, and in amount not less than $20,000; bond shall provide that if the license of the principal shall be revoked or if the principal shall cease to transact business in the commonwealth or if the department shall refuse to renew the license or if the principal shall insure with an insurer, the principal shall upon demand deposit with the state treasurer an amount of securities equal to the penal sum of the bond.

State	Statutory References	Comments
Michigan	MICH. COMP. LAWS § 418.611.(1)(a) (2021)	Self-insurance may be granted by the director upon a reasonable showing by the employer of the employer's solvency and financial ability to meet its obligations to pay compensation and benefits to the employees directly as they become due. If the director determines it to be necessary, the director shall require the furnishing of security in a reasonable form and amount, which may be in the form of specific excess insurance, aggregate excess insurance coverage through a carrier authorized to write in this state in an amount acceptable to the director, a surety bond, an irrevocable letter of credit in a format acceptable to the agency, and claims payment guarantees.
Minnesota	MINN. STAT. § 79A.04(3a) (2021); see MINN. STAT. § 79A.15 (2021) (Surety Bond Form)	May secure obligation in multiple ways, including by furnishing a surety bond in amounts and in a form approved by the commissioner.

State	Statutory References	Comments
Mississippi	MISS. CODE ANN. § 71-3-75 (2021); 20 Miss. Gov't Reg. pt. 1, R. 1.7(4) (LexisNexis Oct. 2020) (specific requirements for indemnity bond)	Bond held by the commission for the benefit of, as applicable, the Mississippi Workers' Compensation Commission, the Mississippi Workers' Compensation Individual Self-Insurer Guaranty Association, or the Mississippi Workers' Compensation Group Self-Insurer Guaranty Association, as security for the payment of the self-insurer's or group self-insurer's covered claims and other obligations under the law; includes expenses incurred by either association in evaluating, adjusting, defending, or settling the self-insurer's covered claims; and for any assessment made against the self-insurer pursuant to the Guaranty Association Act, Mississippi Code Annotated sections 71-3-151 through 71-3-181. Bond held by the commission shall also be for the benefit of the commission to the extent of any assessment made against the self-insurer pursuant to the applicable provisions of the act. Bond not to be returned to a self-insurer or released any earlier than at least one year after the last known claim against such self-insurer has been closed. Prior to releasing or reducing or increasing by 30 percent or more any security or bond held in whole or part for the benefit of the individual association or the group association, the commission will notify the individual or group association of the commission's intent to release, reduce, or increase the security or bond.

State	Statutory References	Comments
Missouri	Mo. Code Regs. Ann. tit. 8, § 50-3.010 (2021)	This rule sets forth requirements and standards for authority to self-insure an employer's liability under the Workers' Compensation Law, including for provision of a bond as security for self-insurance. Surety must be a company admitted by the Missouri Department of Insurance, Financial Institutions, and Professional Registration to transact such business in the state and an AM Best rated A– or better or have reserves acceptable to the department for a new and unrated company. Form of bond prescribed by the Division of Workers' Compensation and included in statute (Bond of Employer Carrying His Own Risk, WC-82 Bond). Bond is perpetual and not released by the division unless additional replacement security approved by the division is provided. In the case of solvency, the proceeds of the surety bond shall be transferred to Missouri Private Sector Individual Self-Insurers Guaranty Corporation, if applicable, in anticipation of payment for compensation obligations that the employer has not paid; but no funds shall be used to make payments of compensation until the division has given the employer and surety company 30 days' written notice.

State	Statutory References	Comments
Montana	MONT. CODE ANN. § 39-71-2106(1)(a) (2021)	Per mandated bond form, award against employer is binding on surety; bond covers all injuries and claims without regard to date of occurrence except injuries occurring after termination of the bond; surety payment required within 20 days of demand; bond may be cancelled on 60 days' written notice to the state.
Nebraska	NEB. REV. STAT. § 48-145 (2021)	Surety bond can be used as security as required by the Nebraska Workers' Compensation Court.
Nevada	NEV. REV. STAT. § 616B.300 (2021)	Bond payable to the state only; bond may be terminated on 90 days' written notice; after termination surety remains liable for liabilities incurred before the termination; upon termination of self-insurance status the bond must remain in place for at least 36 months.
New Hampshire	N.H. REV. STAT. ANN. § 281-A:5-a (2021)	Bond payable to the state only; bond may be terminated on 90 days' written notice; surety remains liable for obligations occurring prior to termination.
New Jersey	N.J. STAT. ANN. § 34:15-77 (West 2021)	Upon termination of self-insurance, surety bond shall remain for a period of at least 26 months.

State	Statutory References	Comments
New Mexico	N.M. STAT. ANN. § 52-1-4 (2021); N.M. CODE R. § 11.4.8, § 11.4.9 (2016)	Per the required bond form, upon failure of the principal to pay a claim, bankruptcy, or deterioration of the principal's financial condition, the state may demand and the surety must pay the entire penal sum of the bond for the state's use in administering and paying claims, with any excess unused funds returned to surety; surety can terminate its liability with 30 days' written notice, provided that a notice of termination does not relieve surety of liability for compensable accidents occurring before termination unless the principal has provided a replacement bond acceptable to the state; payment by surety required within ten days of demand; surety is liable under the bond form for legal fees incurred in actions to enforce the bond, at the maximum amount of 20 percent of the penal sum (suggesting that surety's total exposure is the penal sum plus 20 percent).
New York	N.Y. WORKERS' COMP. LAW § 50 (Consol. 2021)	Bond payable to the people of the state of New York; upon termination of self-insurance status the bond must remain in place for such time as the state deems proper and warranted under the circumstances.

State	Statutory References	Comments
North Carolina	N.C. GEN. STAT. § 97-185(c) (2021)	Surety's liability under bond includes reimbursement for costs incurred, including attorneys' fees, in securing amounts due under the bond, up to 15 percent of the penal sum, with the statute expressly providing that the liability for attorneys' fees is deemed in addition to (and not inclusive of) the bond's stated penal sum.
North Dakota		No self-insurance option. Employers must obtain insurance through state-administered fund.
Ohio	OHIO REV. CODE ANN. § 4123.35(D), §4123.351(C) (West 2021)	Bond for self-insuring employers required in an amount no less than that paid or furnished out of the state insurance fund in similar cases to injured employees or to dependents of killed employees; self-insurance allowed by employers must contribute to state-administered self-insurance fund.

State	Statutory References	Comments
Oklahoma	OKLA. STAT. tit. 85A, § 38 (2021)	Bond covers all past and present liabilities regardless of date of injury; bond may be terminated on 30 days' written notice, but termination does not release the surety from existing and potential liabilities incurred prior to termination; surety can be released in full if the principal posts a replacement bond that is acceptable to the state; upon principal's bankruptcy or failure to pay claims, surety must pay full amount of the bond to the state; or, alternatively with the agreement of the state the surety may pay claims directly to claimants, with those payments deducted from the penal sum of the bond; the surety's administrative and legal costs are not deducted from the penal sum.
Oregon	OR. REV. STAT. § 656.407 (2021)	Per bond form, surety's obligation to pay arises after ten days following principal's failure to pay; bond may be cancelled on 30 days' notice, but cancellation does not release the surety from liabilities accrued prior to termination; the surety may be released in full if a substitute bond is submitted and accepted by the obligee and if the obligee issues a written release of the bond.
Pennsylvania	77 PA. CONS. STAT. § 501 (2021)	If approved for self-insurance, applicant is given a one-year license for self-insurance.

State	Statutory References	Comments
Puerto Rico		No self-insurance option. Employers must obtain insurance through state-administered fund.
Rhode Island	R.I. GEN. LAWS § 28-36-1 (2021)	Per required bond form, the surety is directly liable to employees and can be sued directly by employees; bond may be cancelled after 12 months; cancellation does not release surety from liabilities accrued before termination; surety can be fully released only if a satisfactory replacement bond is provided, and the state signs a release.
South Carolina	S.C. CODE ANN. § 42-5-20 (2021)	Per South Carolina Annotated Code of State Regulations section 67-1505, bond may be cancelled as to future liabilities on 60 days' notice; the state Workers' Compensation Commission has the authority to determine whether to release the bond following cancellation or termination of self-insurance, and a written request for a release of the bond may be submitted to the commission; the commission's decision to release (or not) is subject to review under the administrative procedural rules.

State	Statutory References	Comments
South Dakota	S.D. CODIFIED LAWS § 62-5-5 (2021)	Per bond form, bond applies to all past, present, and future obligations; surety can be released fully if a new surety bond is provided to replace existing bond; subject to state approval, the surety can either adjust and pay claims itself or retain adjusting or risk management company; surety's costs in adjusting claims and legal fees in defending claims are not deducted from the bond's penal sum; surety may pay claimants directly.
Tennessee	TENN. CODE ANN. § 50-6-405 (2021)	Action on bond shall be commenced by the state (not employee); bond (or other security) must be in place for at least ten years following end of self-insurance status.
Texas	TEX. LAB. CODE ANN. § 407.064 (West 2021)	Texas Labor Code section 407.066 vests with the commissioner of labor the jurisdiction to resolve disputes involving the bond and the surety; per mandated bond form, bond applies to all workers' compensation liabilities regardless of date of injury; surety can be released only by paying penal sum or with provision of replacement security satisfactory to the commissioner; surety is liable for all legal fees incurred by the state in enforcing the bond obligations, and this liability is in excess of the penal sum; the state is given the authority to demand the entire penal sum upon impairment of the principal.

State	Statutory References	Comments
Utah	UTAH CODE ANN. § 34A-2-201.5 (West 2021)	Bond covers all liability without regard to date of accident until released; surety can be released in the entirety if a new bond is supplied that will supersede the bond in place; if no new bond is provided, surety remains for claims arising out of injuries or accidents taking place before the bond is released; surety may adjust its own claims or hire an adjusting/risk management company with the approval of the department; administrative, adjusting, and legal fees incurred by surety do not count against the penal sum.
Vermont	VT. STAT. ANN. tit. 21, § 687 (2021)	Bond may be cancelled by surety on 90 days' written notice; cancellation does not release surety from injuries occurring before the cancellation.
Virginia	VA. CODE ANN. § 65.2-801 (2021)	Bond may be cancelled on 30 days' notice; upon cancellation surety remains liable for precancellation injuries and deaths.
Washington	WASH. REV. CODE § 51.14.020 (2021)	Bond may be cancelled on 30 days' notice; surety to remain liable for injuries occurring before termination; surety may be released in the entirety if a replacement bond is filed.

State	Statutory References	Comments
West Virginia	W. VA. CODE § 23-2-9 (2021)	Upon default of the employer, the "Insurance Commissioner shall, in an appropriate case, determine the full accrued value based upon generally accepted actuarial and accounting principles of the employer's liability, including the costs of all awarded claims and of all incurred but not reported claims. The amount determined may, in an appropriate case, be assessed against the employer. The Insurance Commissioner may demand and collect the present value of the defaulted liability."
Wisconsin	WIS. STAT. § 102.28 (2021)	Liabilities under the bond "enforceable against sureties in the same manner as an award [against the employer] may be enforced."
Wyoming		No self-insurance option.

CHAPTER 15

JUDICIAL BONDS

Gina D. Lockwood
Scott Williams

Introduction

Judicial bonds are among the myriad of bonds issued by commercial sureties. Briefly, the judicial bond is intended "to indemnify an adverse party in a lawsuit against loss occasioned by delay or deprivation of property resulting from the lawsuit."[1] Judicial bonds are typically issued upon the disposition of the underlying litigation or issue, and their purpose is to ensure that the appellant will satisfy obligations arising from such disposition of the litigation or issue.[2] Judicial bonds ordinarily[3] involve three parties: (1) the principal for whom the bond is issued and "whose debt or default is the subject matter of the transaction"; (2) the obligee to whom the principal's obligation runs; and (3) the surety who agrees that the principal's debt or obligation to the obligee will be performed.[4]

Whether a judicial bond is required, as well as the form and substance of the judicial bond, is usually determined by the applicable jurisdiction's rules or statutory law. This chapter introduces the pertinent federal civil and appellate rules, federal statutes, and interpretive decisional law applicable to judicial bonds. This chapter does not address judicial bonds on a state-by-state basis. Thus, although some states' rules and statutes may be similar to the federal statutes and rules discussed in this chapter, practitioners should carefully review and analyze state law, as well as

---

1. *Judicial Bond*, BLACK'S LAW DICTIONARY (11th ed. 2019).
2. Fred C. Statum III et al., *Judicial Bonds*, *in* THE LAW OF COMMERCIAL SURETY AND MISCELLANEOUS BONDS 461 (Samuel J. Arena, Jr. et al. eds., 2d ed. 2013).
3. The exception arises in circumstances "where there is statutory authority for the filing of an undertaking, which is a two party instrument—the surety and the obligee." Norris G. Nordahl, *Judicial Bonds*, 34 MARQ. L. REV. 183, 183 (1951).
4. *Id.* at 183–84.

applicable case law and local rules in the appropriate jurisdiction when faced with an issue or question regarding judicial bonds.

I. Types of Judicial Bonds and the Federal Rules That Govern Them

A. *Appeal Bonds*

When the court awards a "money judgment and there are grounds for appeal," the party against whom judgment was entered (i.e., the judgment debtor or appellant) is forced to decide between two primary options: (1) it can tender the amount of the judgment to the party to whom the judgment debtor is now obligated (i.e., the judgment creditor or appellee) in exchange for an acknowledgment and satisfaction to file with the court; or (2) the judgment debtor can appeal the decision granting judgment to the appropriate appellate court.[5] In the former instance, the judgment debtor's satisfaction of the judgment concludes the litigation. In the latter instance, the litigation moves to the appellate phase. But, what happens to the judgment pending appeal? What are the respective rights of the judgment debtor and judgment creditor pending appeal? To answer these questions, the parties must check the applicable rules and statutes to determine whether it must post one or more appeal bonds to stay the judgment creditor's enforcement of the judgment pending appeal.

Appeal bonds typically fall into two categories—supersedeas bonds and cost bonds. Each bond serves a specific purpose. To understand the purposes of each, consider that the judgment debtor's appeal of a judgment does not operate to stay enforcement of the underlying judgment. So, to protect the judgment debtor against enforcement and, additionally, to assure that the judgment creditor's right to immediate collection is not prejudiced, local rules and statutes may require that the judgment debtor deposit sufficient security. This security typically is in the form of a supersedeas bond.

"A supersedeas bond is a contract by which a surety obligates itself to pay a final judgment rendered against its principal under the conditions stated in the bond."[6] Thus, the supersedeas bond "ensures that the

---

5. Dan Huckabay, *Staying Judgment with Appeal Bonds*, A.B.A. (Sept. 6, 2019), https://www.americanbar.org/groups/judicial/publications/appellate_issues/2019/summer/staying-judgment-with-appeal-bonds/.
6. Rand-Whitney Containerboard Ltd. P'ship v. Town of Montville, 245 F.R.D. 65, 67 (D. Conn. 2007) (quoting Amwest Sur. Ins. Co. v. Graham, 949 S.W.2d 724, 726 (Tex. App. 1997)).

judgment creditor will be able to enforce its judgment if the appellate court affirms the trial court's decision."[7] In addition to the supersedeas bond, local rules and statutes may require that the judgment debtor post a cost bond to ensure the payment of the judgment creditor's costs in the event that the judgment debtor's appeal is unsuccessful and the judgment is affirmed. For comparison, a supersedeas bond is retrospective, covering sums already awarded on the merits and for which a stay of execution has been granted.[8] In contrast, a cost bond is prospective, covering costs arising in connection with the go-forward appeal.[9]

1. Cost Bond

Federal Rule of Appellate Procedure 7 provides district courts with authority to require a cost bond to ensure the payment of costs on appeal.[10] Specifically, Rule 7 provides that, "[i]n a civil case, the district court may require an appellant to file a bond or provide other security in any form and amount necessary to ensure payment of costs on appeal."[11] The cost bond covers only appellate costs, not costs incurred in the district court.[12] So, when the appellant files a notice of appeal, the district court retains jurisdiction to issue orders in aid of the judgment, including orders regarding bonds.[13] The district court is afforded discretion to require a cost bond and to set the amount of the cost bond.[14]

---

7. Statum et al., *supra* note 2.
8. *See, e.g.*, Adsani v. Miller, 139 F.3d 67, 70 n.2 (2d Cir. 1998).
9. *Id.*
10. Fed. R. App. P. 7.
11. *Id.*
12. *In re* Meabon, No. 3:15-cv-00398, 2017 WL 374921, at *3 (W.D.N.C. Jan. 25, 2017); United States *ex rel.* Terry Inv. Co. v. United Funding & Invs., Inc., 800 F. Supp. 879, 882 (E.D. Cal. 1992); Cent. Mfg. Co. v. B-M-K Corp., 160 F. Supp. 318, 318 (D. Del. 1958).
13. Tennille v. W. Union Co., 774 F.3d 1249, 1253 (10th Cir. 2014) (recognizing that the district court's order requiring appeal bond is reviewable as part of merits appeals); *see also* McCammon v. United States, 588 F. Supp. 2d 43, 45 n.2 (D.D.C. 2008); Sec. Indus. Ass'n v. Bd. of Governors of Fed. Rsrv. Sys., 628 F. Supp. 1438, 1440 n.1 (D.D.C. 1986).
14. Young v. New Process Steel, LP, 419 F.3d 1201, 1208 (11th Cir. 2005); Fed. Prescription Serv., Inc. v. Am. Pharm. Ass'n, 636 F.2d 755, 756 (D.C. Cir. 1980); Lundy v. Union Carbide Corp., 598 F. Supp. 451 (D. Or. 1984).

Unless a rule enumerating specific factors applies, district courts generally weigh the following factors to determine whether to require a bond: "(1) the [judgment debtor's] financial ability to post a bond, (2) the risk that the [judgment debtor] would not pay [judgment creditor's] costs if the [judgment debtor] loses, (3) the merits of the appeal, and (4) whether the [judgment debtor] has shown any bad faith or vexatious conduct."[15] The party protected by the cost bond bears the burden of proving that a cost bond is necessary and justifying the amount of the bond.[16]

As stated above, the appeal cost bond is prospective in nature, and assures that the appellant whose appeal is unsuccessful will be able to pay the appellee's appeal costs (not the costs incurred in the district court).[17] The district court considers anticipated "costs on appeal" in setting the bond amount.[18] Rule 7 does not define the term "costs on appeal"; however, the advisory committee's notes under Rule 7 suggest that the bond amount should bear a relationship to "actual costs."[19] Further, considering the purpose of the cost bond is to cover anticipated costs on appeal, the amount of the judgment should not be a factor in setting the bond amount.[20]

The advisory notes to Rule 7 provide little to no guidance on the meaning of "costs on appeal." Generally, courts have interpreted "costs

---

15. *See, e.g.*, *In re* Countrywide Fin. Corp. Customer Data Sec. Breach Litig., No. 3:08-MD-01998, 2010 WL 5147222, at *2 (W.D. Ky. Dec. 13, 2010) (quoting Chiaverini, Inc. v. Frenchie's Fine Jewelry, Coins & Stamps, Inc., No. 04-CV-74891, 2008 WL 2415340, at *1 (E.D. Mich. June 12, 2018)).
16. *Id.*
17. *Meabon*, 2017 WL 374921, at *3; *Terry Inv. Co.*, 800 F. Supp. at 882; *Cent. Mfg. Co.*, 160 F. Supp. at 318.
18. Fed. R. App. P. 7.
19. Fed. R. App. P. 7 advisory committee's note to 1979 amendment ("The amendment would eliminate the provision of the present rule that requires the appellant to file a $250 bond for costs on appeal at the time of filing his notice of appeal. The $250 provision was carried forward in [the current rules] from former Rule 73(c) . . . , and the $250 figure has remained unchanged since the adoption of that rule in 1937. Today it bears no relationship to actual costs.").
20. *See In re* Am. Invs. Life Ins. Co. Annuity Mktg. & Sales Pracs. Litig., 695 F. Supp. 2d 157, 164 (E.D. Pa. 2010); *see also In re* Am. President Lines, Inc., 779 F.2d 714, 717 (D.C. Cir. 1985).

on appeal" to mean "costs that a successful appellant litigant can recover pursuant to a specific rule or statute."[21] Some courts have interpreted the phrase to mean that costs on appeal are "strictly limited to the costs of filing and proceeding with a case in the court of appeals."[22] Those courts interpret Rule 7 in conjunction with Federal Rule of Civil Procedure 39, which specifically references the "costs on appeal . . . taxable in the district court for the benefit of the party entitled to costs."[23] Rule 39 states:

> The following costs on appeal are taxable in the district court . . . under this rule:
> (1) the preparation and transmission of the record;
> (2) the reporter's transcript, if needed to determine the appeal;
> (3) premiums paid for a supersedeas bond or other bond to preserve rights pending appeal; and
> (4) the fee for filing the notice of appeal.[24]

The advisory committee's notes to the rule further clarify that "[t]he costs described in this subdivision are costs of the appeal and, as such, are within the undertaking of the [Rule 7] bond."[25] While the phrase "costs on appeal" in Rule 7 can be explained with reference to Rule 39(e), Rule 39 does not state or imply that the Rule 39(e) costs are the only types of "costs on appeal" that may be considered.[26] Thus, some circuit courts allow district courts to consider additional costs while setting the amount of a Rule 7 bond.[27]

---

21. *See* Tennille v. W. Union Co., 774 F.3d 1249, 1254 (10th Cir. 2014).
22. *Terry Inv. Co.*, 800 F. Supp. at 882.
23. FED. R. APP. P. 39(e); *see Am. President Lines, Inc.*, 779 F.2d at 716–17 ("The costs referred to [in Rule 7] are simply those that may be taxed against an unsuccessful litigant under Federal Appellate Rule 39 . . . ."); *see also* Sky Cable, LLC v. Coley, No. 5:11-cv-48, 2016 WL 8138819, at *3 (W.D. Va. Dec. 5, 2016).
24. FED. R. APP. P. 39.
25. FED. R. APP. P. 39 advisory committee's note to 1967 amendment.
26. *See generally* FED. R. APP. P. 39.
27. *See, e.g.*, Horowitz v. 148 S. Emerson Assocs. LLC, 888 F.3d 13, 25–26 (2d Cir. 2018) ("[T]he term 'costs' in Rule 54(d) of the Federal Rules of Civil Procedure is written such that it includes attorneys' fees . . . , [but] Rule 7 of the Federal Rules of Appellate Procedure [reference to] 'costs' includes attorneys' fees . . . where the cause of action under which the suit

In a few instances, district courts have considered the attorneys' fees for the appeal in setting the amount of a Rule 7 bond;[28] however, the issue is far from settled.[29] Recognizing that the "American rule" requires each party pay its own attorneys' fees, some circuit courts limit the district courts' ability to factor in costs other than those listed in Rule 39(e).[30] Conversely, the First, Second, Sixth, and Eleventh Circuits have adopted the opposite view.[31]

As explained in an unpublished opinion of the Western District of Virginia, these circuits reason that the "'costs on appeal' under Rule 7 are not limited solely to the costs taxable on appeal under Fed. R. Civ. P. 39, but include all expenses defined as 'costs' by the underlying statute in each case, including attorneys' fees if applicable."[32] In *International*

---

at issue is brought so allows . . . ." (citing Marek v. Chesny, 473 U.S. 1, 9 (1985); Adsani v. Miller, 139 F.3d 67, 79 (2d Cir. 1998))).

28. *See Sky Cable, LLC*, 2016 WL 8138819, at *3 ("The First, Second, Sixth, Ninth and Eleventh Circuits have found that 'costs on appeal' under Rule 7 are not limited solely to the costs taxable on appeal under Fed. R. Civ. P. 39, but include all expenses defined as 'costs' by the underlying statute in each case, including attorneys' fees if applicable."); *see also* Pedraza v. United Guar. Corp., 313 F.3d 1323, 1333 (11th Cir. 2002).

29. *Compare* Rossi v. Proctor & Gamble Co., No. 11-7238, 2014 WL 1050658, at *2 (D.N.J. Mar. 17, 2014) ("[T]he Court sees no reason to deviate from the Third Circuit's practice of excluding attorneys' fees from Rule 7 appeal bonds."), *with* Tennille v. W. Union Co., 774 F.3d 1249, 1256 (10th Cir. 2014) (recognizing that, absent "any rule or statute that allows" the recovery of attorneys' fees or administrative costs on appeal, the district court must set the amount of a Rule 7 bond sufficient only to cover those costs listed in Rule 39(e)), *and Pedraza*, 313 F.3d at 1323, 1328–29 ("[T]he meaning of 'costs,' as used in Rule 7, should be derived from the definition of costs contained in the statutory fee shifting provision that attends the plaintiff's underlying cause of action.").

30. *See, e.g.*, Hirschensohn v. Laws. Title Ins. Corp., No. 96-7312, 1997 WL 307777, at *1 (3d Cir. June 10, 1997).

31. Hines v. City of Albany, 862 F.3d 215, 220 (2d Cir. 2017); Int'l Floor Crafts, Inc. v. Dziemit, 420 F. App'x 6, 16 (1st Cir. 2011); Young v. New Process Steel, LP, 419 F.3d 1201, 1207–08 (11th Cir. 2005); *In re* Cardizem CD Antitrust Litig., 391 F.3d 812, 817–18 (6th Cir. 2004).

32. *Sky Cable, LLC*, 2016 WL 8138819, at *3 (citing Azizian v. Federated Dep't Stores, Inc., 499 F.3d 950, 958 (9th Cir. 2007)).

Floor Crafts, Inc. v. Dziemit,[33] the First Circuit elaborated on the reasoning behind this view as follows:

> Although the American rule establishes that each party to a litigation is responsible for paying its own attorneys' fees, several statutes enacted prior to both the 1968 adoption of the Federal Rules of Appellate Procedure and the 1979 amendment to Rule 7 contain exceptions to the American Rule and define costs recoverable to include fees. Courts understand these fee-shifting statutes to account for appellate fees as well . . . . It is presumed that the Rule drafters were aware of these statutes and understood "costs" under Rule 7 to provide for these fees when applicable.[34]

Finding support in the U.S. Supreme Court's decision in *Marek v. Chesny,*[35] the First Circuit resolved that, if Federal Rule of Civil Procedure 68 permits the recovery of attorneys' fees, district courts could consider attorneys' fees in determining the amount of the cost bond "when the relevant statute underlying the litigation defined awardable costs as both costs and fees."[36] The First Circuit distinguished the contrary view on the basis that the governing statute, the Racketeer Influenced and Corrupt Organizations Act, contained a fee-shifting provision,[37] while prominent opinions to the contrary did not derive from statutes that contained such

---

33. 420 F. App'x 6.
34. *Id.* at 16.
35. 473 U.S. 1 (1985). In *Marek v. Chesny*, the U.S. Supreme Court determined that, "absent congressional expressions to the contrary, where the underlying statute defines 'costs' to include attorney's fees, we are satisfied such fees are to be included as costs for purposes of Rule 68." *Id.* at 8 (citing Delta Air Lines, Inc. v. August, 450 U.S. 346, 362–63 (1981) (Powell, J., concurring); Fulps v. Springfield, 715 F.2d 1088, 1091–95 (6th Cir. 1983); Waters v. Heublein, Inc., 485 F. Supp. 110, 113–17 (N.D. Cal. 1979); Scheriff v. Beck, 452 F. Supp. 1254, 1259–60 (Colo. 1978)).
36. *Int'l Floor Crafts, Inc.*, 420 F. App'x at 17 n.10.
37. *Id.*; *see* 18 U.S.C. § 1964(c) (1995) ("Any person injured in his business or property by reason of a violation of section 1962 [may pursue the actor] and shall recover threefold the damages he sustains and the cost of the suit, including a reasonable attorney's fee . . . ."). *But see, e.g.*, Hirschensohn v. Laws. Title Ins. Corp., No. 96-7312, 1997 WL 307777, at *3 (3d Cir. June 10, 1997).

a provision.[38] This reasoning has been applied to permit consideration of attorneys' fees in setting the amount of cost bonds when the underlying litigation arose under the Copyright Act[39] and the Clayton Act.[40]

A second controversy exists concerning whether Federal Rule of Appellate Procedure 38 may be a factor for the district court to consider when setting the amount of the Rule 7 bond.[41] Rule 38 grants district courts discretion to award damages resulting from a determination "that an appeal is frivolous."[42] In *Hill v. State Street Corp.*,[43] "the district court used Federal Rule of Appellate Procedure 7 to bar objectors from appealing unless they posted a bond [sufficient to] ensure there would be funds available to pay plaintiffs' attorneys' fees for defending the frivolous appeal."[44] The First Circuit recognized that a preliminary review of the appeal's merits by the appellate court "is crucial in protecting against the possibility that a district court could effectively immunize its decisions from review by declaring any appeal frivolous."[45] After conducting its own preliminary review of the appeal's merits, the First Circuit was "less comfortable with any prejudgment that the appeal would be frivolous" and stayed the district court's order to post a bond.[46] Although the First Circuit disagreed with the district court's assessment in this instance,[47]

---

38. *See, e.g.*, *Hirschensohn*, 1997 WL 307777, at *1 n.1.
39. Adsani v. Miller, 139 F.3d 67, 78 (2d Cir. 1998).
40. Azizian v. Federated Dep't Stores, Inc., 499 F.3d 950, 955–59 (9th Cir. 2007).
41. *Compare* Sckolnick v. Harlow, 820 F.2d 13 (1st Cir. 1987), *with Azizian*, 499 F.3d 950.
42. FED. R. APP. P. 38.
43. 794 F.3d 227 (1st Cir. 2015).
44. *Id.* at 229.
45. *Id.* at 229–30 (citing *Azizian*, 499 F.3d at 961 ("Allowing district court to impose high Rule 7 bonds on where the appeals might be found frivolous risks 'impermissibly encumber[ing]' appellants' right to appeal and 'effectively preempt[ing] this court's prerogative' to make its own frivolousness determination." (quoting *In re* Am. President Lines, Inc., 779 F.2d 714, 717 (D.C. Cir. 1985)))).
46. *Id.* at 230.
47. *Id.* at 229, 231 ("[A]lthough we easily conclude . . . that [the] arguments with respect to the notice and fee rulings lack merit, we decline to impose a sanction against objectors' counsel for filing a frivolous appeal." (citations omitted)).

consistent with its prior decision in *Sckolnick v. Harlow*,[48] it accepted the district court's consideration of Rule 38 in setting the amount of the cost bond.[49] The opposite view was reflected by the Ninth Circuit in *Azizian v. Federated Department Stores, Inc.*[50] In *Azizian*, the court rejected the First Circuit's stance that Rule 38 was a consideration in setting the amount of the bond, reasoning that "a Rule 7 bond including the potentially large and indeterminate amounts awardable under Rule 38 is more likely to chill an appeal than a bond covering the other smaller, and more predictable, costs on appeal."[51] The Ninth Circuit supported its reasoning by highlighting that an "[a]ward of appellate attorney's fees for frivolousness under Rule 38 is highly exceptional, making it difficult to gauge prospectively, and without the benefit of a fully developed appellate record, whether such an award is likely."[52] Whether or not the applicable jurisdiction considers attorneys' fees as costs on appeal or evaluates the possibility of an award under Rule 38, the Rule 7 bond must not be burdensome as to deprive the appellant of due process and equal protection of the law.[53]

The differing approaches necessitate a close examination of the prevailing opinions from the applicable jurisdiction. Regardless, the party requesting the cost bond must justify the amount of the cost bond requested and provide an estimate of the anticipated costs.[54]

2. Supersedeas Bond

"The purpose of requiring a supersedeas bond pending appeal 'is to secure the judgment throughout the appeal process against the possibility

---

48. 820 F.2d 13, 15 (1st Cir. 1987).
49. *Hill*, 794 F.3d at 229–30.
50. 499 F.3d 950.
51. *Id.* at 960.
52. *Id.*
53. Tennille v. W. Union Co., 774 F.3d 1249, 1257 (10th Cir. 2014) ("[C]ourts have acknowledged the possibility that an appeal bond might so burden a party's pursuit of an appeal that it violates due process and equal protection."); Adsani v. Miller, 139 F.3d 67, 78 (2d Cir. 1998) (recognizing that the cost requirement, valid on its face, may still "be unconstitutional as applied to a particular case").
54. *Tennille*, 774 F.3d at 1257 (finding that the appellees failed to justify their estimate of costs on appeal, thus reducing the Rule 7 bond to $5,000 "to cover printing, copying, and record preparation costs").

of the judgment debtor's insolvency.'"[55] Cost bonds can be distinguished from supersedeas bonds in that cost bonds ensure the appellant's ability to pay the prevailing party's costs during an appeal, while supersedeas bonds "protect the prevailing plaintiff from the risk of a later uncollectible judgment and compensate[] him for delay in the entry of the final judgment."[56]

After a judgment has been entered, the non-prevailing party may decide to pursue its appeal; however, the prevailing party may seek execution of the judgment before the appeal is resolved. To alleviate these concerns, Federal Rule of Civil Procedure 62 offers the non-prevailing party protection in the form of a 30-day automatic stay of "execution on a judgment and proceedings to enforce it . . . , unless the court orders otherwise."[57] Rule 62(b) allows the non-prevailing party to extend the stay through the pendency of the appeal should the non-prevailing party post "a bond or other security."[58] Though Rule 62(b) states that "a party *may* obtain a stay by providing a bond or other security,"[59] this provision is interpreted to mean that a party taking an appeal from a judgment is *entitled* to a stay of execution if he or she posts "a bond acceptable to the court."[60] Rule 62 provides that the stay is available to parties

---

55. Olcott v. Del. Flood Co., 76 F.3d 1538, 1559–60 (10th Cir. 1996) (quoting Grubb v. Fed. Deposit Ins. Corp., 833 F.2d 222, 226 (10th Cir. 1987)).
56. Cotton *ex rel.* McClure v. City of Eureka, Cal., 860 F. Supp. 2d 999, 1025 (N.D. Cal. 2012) (quoting NLRB v. Westphal, 859 F.2d 818, 819 (9th Cir. 1988)).
57. FED. R. CIV. P. 62(a). The advisory committee's note to the 2018 amendments clarify that a court may "dissolve the automatic stay or supersede it by a court-ordered stay." FED. R. CIV. P. 62(a) advisory committee's note to 2018 amendments. A court may elect to dissolve the automatic stay or supersede it due to "a risk that the judgment debtor's assets will be dissipated" or because "it may be important to allow immediate enforcement of a judgment that does not involve the payment of money." *Id.*
58. FED. R. CIV. P. 62(a)–(b).
59. *Id.* 62(b) (emphasis added).
60. Jordan v. Wonderful Citrus Packing LLC, No. 1:18-CV-00401, 2020 WL 7360585, at *1 (E.D. Cal. Dec. 15, 2020) ("Where a party has posted a bond acceptable to the court, the party is entitled to a stay 'as a matter of right' under Rule 62." (quoting *In re* Combined Metals Reduction Co., 557 F.2d 179, 193 (9th Cir. 1977))); *see also* United States v. Wylie, 730 F.2d 1401, 1402 n.2 (11th Cir. 1984) (recognizing that Rule 62(d) allows

seeking relief from final and interlocutory judgments,[61] unless one of the following limitations applies:

> (c) Stay of an Injunction, Receivership, or Patent Accounting Order. Unless the court orders otherwise, the following are not stayed after being entered, even if an appeal is taken:
> (1) an interlocutory or final judgment in an action for an injunction or receivership; or
> (2) a judgment or order that directs an accounting in an action for patent infringement;
>
> (d) Injunction Pending an Appeal. While an appeal is pending from an interlocutory order or final judgment that grants, continues, modifies, dissolves, or refuses to dissolve or modify an injunction, the court may suspend, modify, restore, or grant an injunction on terms for bond or other terms that secure the opposing party's rights. If the judgment appealed from is rendered by a statutory three-judge district court, the order must be made either:
> (1) by that court sitting in open session; or
> (2) by the assent of all its judges, as evidenced by their signatures.[62]

---

for a stay pending appeal as "a matter of right" if the appellant posts a supersedeas bond or provides sufficient security).

61. Fed. R. Civ. P. 62(a) advisory committee's note to 1937 adoption.

62. Fed. R. Civ. P. 62(c)–(d). While "[t]he provisions for staying an injunction, receivership, or order for a patent accounting" were reorganized by the 2018 amendment, "[t]here is no change in meaning." Fed. R. Civ. P. 62(c)–(d) advisory committee's note to 2018 amendment. Subsections (a), (b), (c), and (d) were revised to include the language of "28 U.S.C. § 1292(a)(1) to describe the right to appeal from interlocutory actions with respect to an injunction, but subdivisions (c) and (d) apply both to interlocutory injunction orders and to final judgments that grant, refuse, or otherwise deal with an injunction." *Id.*; *see* 28 U.S.C. § 1292(a)(1) ("Interlocutory orders of the district courts of the United States, the United States District Court for the District of the Canal Zone, the District Court of Guam, and the District Court of the Virgin Islands, or of the judges thereof, granting, continuing, modifying, refusing or dissolving injunctions, or refusing to dissolve or modify injunctions, except where a direct review may be had in the Supreme Court.").

Recent amendments to Rule 62 carry forward the supersedeas bond provisions of the former Rule 62 and reaffirm that the "stay takes effect when the court approves the bond . . . and remains in effect for the time specified in the bond."[63] The amendments, however, modified former Rule 62 to allow parties to benefit from the stay by posting "other security" in place of the usual supersedeas bond.[64] Again, the stay is limited in duration, so it is critical that an appellant who desires to stay the execution of a money judgment against it act within the 30-day stay period. The appellant should procure a sufficient supersedeas bond or other security and take any necessary steps to have it approved by the court or, at a minimum, attempt to reach an agreement with the opposition to extend the automatic stay period pending court approval of the bond. The appellant's failure to act promptly could create a window for the judgment creditor to begin executing on the money judgment before the court's approval of the bond. As the Southern District of California recognized in an unpublished opinion, the supersedeas bond "does not have retroactive effect, so any enforcement action had on the judgment before the stay becomes effective is not automatically set aside or rendered void after the stay is imposed."[65] Consequently, at least one court has held that if the appellant fails to post a supersedeas bond and the appellee obtains a levy pursuant to a writ of execution, the levy will not be vacated by a subsequently filed supersedeas bond.[66]

An appellant who is unable or unwilling to post a supersedeas bond will not be deprived of the right to appeal, even if the judgment

---

63. FED. R. CIV. P. 62(b) advisory committee's note to 2018 amendment. *Compare* FED. R. CIV. P. 62(d) (2017) (dictating that the stay takes effect at the time the court approves the bond), *with* FED. R. CIV. P. 62(b) (2018) (recognizing that the stay "takes effect when the court approves the bond . . . and remains in effect for the time specified in the bond").

64. FED. R. CIV. P. 62(b) (2018); *see* Athridge v. Iglesias, 464 F. Supp. 2d 19, 23–24 (D.D.C. 2006) (recognizing that appellants usually post security in the form of a supersedeas bond).

65. Carlock v. Collins Motors, Inc., No. 04-CV-0370-J, 2008 WL 11508484, at *2 (S.D. Cal. Dec. 12, 2008) (citing Moses v. K-Mart Corp., 922 F. Supp. 600, 604 (S.D. Fla. 1996); Imperial Commodities Corp. v. S.S. Maria Auxiliadora, 115 F.R.D. 305, 307–08 (S.D.N.Y. 1987)).

66. *Imperial Commodities Corp.*, 115 F.R.D. 305; *see also Moses*, 922 F. Supp. 600 ("[A]pproval of a supersedeas bond and granting of stay pending appeal did not serve to vitiate any execution of judgment taken prior to approval of bond.").

is executed.[67] Although Federal Rule of Civil Procedure 62(b) "makes explicit the opportunity to post security in a form other than a bond,"[68] case law recognizes that a federal court does not possess the power to require a party to post a supersedeas bond.[69] State civil and appellate procedural rules generally follow the federal rule's approach to supersedeas bonds.[70] However, state rules may differ as to the duration of the automatic stay and may also provide different factors to consider in setting the amount of the supersedeas bond.[71]

A stay pending appeal deprives the appellee of the right to execute on the judgment for the duration of the supersedeas bond, so most courts require that the supersedeas bond be sufficient to cover the full amount of the principal judgment.[72] Local rules for certain district courts expressly require the amount of the supersedeas bond be sufficient to cover the full amount of the judgment.[73] For example, Local Rule 67.1(d) of the U.S. District Court for the Northern District of New York provides:

---

67. Strong v. Laubach, 433 F.3d 1297 (10th Cir. 2006), *overruled on other grounds*, Metzler v. Fed. Home Loan Bank, 464 F.3d, 1171 n.2 (10th Cir. 2006).
68. Fed. R. Civ. P. 62(b) advisory committee's note to 2018 amendment.
69. *Id.*
70. *See* Tenn. R. Civ. P. 62.01 (providing a 30-day automatic stay provision); *see also* Colo. R. Civ. P. 62(a) (providing a 14-day automatic stay provision).
71. Tenn. R. Civ. P. 62.01; Colo. R. Civ. P. 62(a).
72. *See, e.g.*, RLI Ins. Co. v. Nexus Servs., Inc., No. 5:18-CV-66, 2020 WL 7407466, at *1 (W.D. Va. Dec. 17, 2020) (recognizing that, under former Rule 62(d), stay is available as a matter of right "by posting a supersedeas bond in the full amount of the judgment, but . . . '[d]efendants are not entitled to a stay [when they] have not posted a supersedeas bond in the full amount of the judgment.'" (quoting Schmidt v. FCI Enters. LLC, No. 118-CV-1472, 2020 WL 2748499, at *4 (E.D. Va. Feb. 3, 2020)) (citing E.I. DuPont de Nemours & Co. v. Kolon Indus., Inc., No. 3:09-CV-58, 2012 WL 1202485, at *2 (E.D. Va. Apr. 10, 2012)); *see also* Rachel v. Banana Republic Inc., 831 F.2d 1503, 1505 n.1 (9th Cir. 1987) ("[A] full supersedeas bond should . . . be required."); Poplar Grove Planting & Refin. Co. v. Bache Halsey Stuart, Inc., 600 F.2d 1189 (5th Cir. 1979); Sec. & Exch. Comm'n v. O'Hagan, 901 F. Supp. 1476 (D. Minn. 1995) (stating that, generally, the amount of a supersedeas bond should include principal amount of judgment plus costs); Fed. Prescription Serv., Inc. v. Am. Pharm. Ass'n, 636 F.2d 755 (D.C. Cir. 1980).
73. *See, e.g.*, N.D.N.Y. Civ. R. 67.1.

> 67.1 Deposits in Court
>
> (d) A supersedeas bond, where the judgment is for a sum of money only, shall be in the amount of the judgment plus 11% to cover interest and any damage for delay as may be awarded, plus $250 to cover costs.
>
> When a stay shall be effected solely by the giving of the supersedeas bond, but the judgment or order is not solely for a sum of money, the Court, on notice, shall fix the amount of the bond. In all other cases, the Court shall, on notice, grant a stay on the terms it deems proper.[74]

Likewise, Local Rule 62.1 for the District of New Hampshire provides:

> 62.1 Bonds or Other Security Staying Execution of Money Judgment
>
> A supersedeas bond staying execution of a money judgment shall be in the amount of the judgment, plus interest at a rate consistent with 28 U.S.C. § 1961(a), plus an amount to be set by the court to cover costs and any award of damages for delay. The parties may waive the supersedeas bond by stipulation without order of the court.[75]

A court may further increase the amount of a supersedeas bond to encompass prejudgment interest and anticipated postjudgment interest,[76] and the court may account for obligations potentially accruing during the appeal.[77] Courts disagree as to whether supersedeas bonds should account for punitive damages in addition to compensatory damages.[78]

---

74. *Id.* (emphasis added).
75. D.N.H. Civ. R. 62.1 (emphasis added).
76. Lexington Ins. Co. v. Scott Homes Multifam. Inc., No. CV-12-02119, 2015 WL 6956091, at *2 (D. Ariz. Nov. 10, 2015) (setting bond at the full amount of the judgment plus prejudgment and postjudgment interest).
77. *See, e.g.*, Ariz. Rev. Stat. Ann. § 12-1179(D) (2004) (requiring unsuccessful state law litigants to file a supersedeas bond in an amount sufficient to cover "rent accruing from the date of the judgment until the next periodic rental date, together with costs and attorneys fees, if any").
78. *Compare* Cotton *ex rel.* McClure v. City of Eureka, Cal., 860 F. Supp. 2d 999, 1029 (N.D. Cal. 2012) (requiring a supersedeas bond sufficient to cover compensatory and punitive damages, plus interest), *with In re*

Courts declining to require a supersedeas bond in an amount sufficient to cover punitive damages reason that the appellee's "merely incidental interest in punitive damages should not be protected automatically by bonding."[79]

As mentioned above, Federal Rule of Civil Procedure 62 does not require an appellant to post a supersedeas bond to stay execution on the judgment.[80] "District courts have inherent discretionary authority in setting the amount of the supersedeas bonds."[81] Normally, "a full bond should be required."[82] In *Olympia Equipment Leasing Co. v. Western Union Telegraph Co.*,[83] the Seventh Circuit Court of Appeals explained:

Arb. of Sarofim v. Tr. Co. of the W., No. H-04-4114, 2005 WL 8177562, at *5 (S.D. Tex. May 9, 2005) (declining to require a supersedeas bond encompassing a punitive damages award and instructing the appellant to obtain a lien under state law "should she have concerns about the security of the punitive damages award"). *See generally* Olympia Equip. Leasing Co. v. W. Union Tel. Co., 786 F.2d 794, 797 (7th Cir. 1986) (declining to require security to cover the punitive damages award); Umbrella Bank, FSB v. Jamison, 341 B.R. 835 (W.D. Tex. 2006) (finding that appellant had to post supersedeas bond only in amount of compensatory damages awarded plus interest, and costs, without including any additional amount for usury penalties assessed by court); Timothy S. Bishop & Jeffrey W. Sarles, *Supersedeas Bonds: A Crushing Burden*, NAT'L L.J., Nov. 1, 1995, at C25.

79. Bishop & Sarles, *supra* note 78.

80. *See* Kirby v. Gen. Elec. Co., 210 F.R.D. 180, 195 (W.D.N.C. 2000) (recognizing that former "Rule 62(d) does not preclude the issuance of a stay on the basis of some lesser bond, or no bond at all" (citing Alexander v. Chesapeake, Potomac & Tidewater Books, Inc., 190 F.R.D. 190, 192 (E.D. Va. 1999))); Wunschel & Small, Inc. v. United States, 554 F. Supp. 444, 445 (Cl. Ct. 1983) (recognizing that former Rule 62(d) "does not . . . preclude the court from issuing a stay without a bond, upon the posting of a partial bond, upon the posting of alternative security, or upon such conditions as the court deems appropriate" (citing Fed. Prescription Serv., Inc. v. Am. Pharm. Ass'n, 636 F.2d 755, 758 (D.C. Cir. 1980))).

81. Goldgroup Res., Inc. v. DynaResource De Mexico, S.A., De C.V., No. 16-cv-02547, 2020 WL 1452246, at *3 (D. Colo. Mar. 25, 2020) (citing Miami Int'l Realty Co. v. Paynter, 807 F.2d 871, 873 (10th Cir. 1986); Strong v. Laubach, 443 F.3d 1297, 1299 (10th Cir. 2006)).

82. *Id.*

83. 786 F.2d 794.

> [A]n inflexible requirement of a bond would be inappropriate in two sorts of cases: where the defendant's ability to pay the judgment is so plain that the cost of the bond would be a waste of money; and the opposite case, one of increasing importance in an age of titanic damage judgments—where the requirement would put the defendant's other creditors in undue jeopardy.[84]

Stated differently, when an appellant objectively demonstrates its financial ability to satisfy a judgment or that its posting of a supersedeas bond would jeopardize the appellant's ability to satisfy other debts, the court may elect to require some form of guaranty in place of the usual supersedeas bond. Nonetheless, the court may require that the appellant offer a secure plan for maintaining its solvency throughout the appeal. In circumstances when an appellant is unable to obtain a full supersedeas bond without enduring further financial burden, a court may decide to stay execution on the judgment in exchange for a limit on the appellant's financial freedom.[85] As the Southern District of New York recognized in an unpublished opinion:

> In spite of the general requirement that a judgment debtor post a supersedeas bond in the full amount of the judgment . . . , the district court, in its discretion, may use equitable principles to grant such a stay without a full bond if the filing of a supersedeas bond would irreparably harm the judgment debtor and, at the same time, such a stay would "not unduly endanger the judgment creditor's interest in ultimate recovery."[86]

In efforts to "protect judgment creditors as fully as possible without irreparably injuring judgment debtors,"[87] district courts have exercised

---

84. *Id.* at 796.
85. Poplar Grove Planting & Refin. Co. v. Bache Halsey Stuart, Inc., 600 F.2d 1189 (5th Cir. 1979).
86. Teachers Ins. & Annuity Ass'n, v. Ormesa Geothermal, No. 87 Civ. 1259, 1991 WL 254573, at *3 (S.D.N.Y. Nov. 21, 1991) (quoting Texaco Inc. v. Pennzoil Co., 784 F.2d 1133, 1155 (2d Cir. 1986)) (citing Liberty Mut. Ins. Co. v. Bankers Tr. Co., 769 F. Supp. 130, 131 (S.D.N.Y. 1991)).
87. *Texaco, Inc.*, 784 F.2d at 1154–55 (citing Fed. Prescription Serv., Inc. v. Am. Pharm. Ass'n, 636 F.2d 755, 760 (D.C. Cir. 1980); *Poplar Grove Planting & Refin. Co.*, 600 F.2d at 1191; United States v. Kurtz, 528 F. Supp. 1113, 1115 (E.D. Pa. 1981); C. Albert Sauter Co. v. Richard S.

the discretion afforded by Federal Rule of Civil Procedure 62 to stay execution on judgments in exchange for alternate security in various forms, including real estate holdings,[88] letters of credit,[89] accounts receivable, stocks, and cash.[90] Without regard to the security's form, "the burden is on the moving party to demonstrate the reasons for 'depart[ing] from the usual requirement of a full security supersedeas bond.'"[91] Thus, the appellant generally bears the burden of justifying its request.[92] Further, the appellee need not provide contrary proof.[93] This is due to the supersedeas bond generally being viewed as a "privilege" extended to the appellant as a price of interdicting the validity of a judgment.[94]

B. *Injunction Bond*

Unlike monetary judgments, injunctions demand or restrict a party's action and are viewed as "drastic remedies."[95] "The injunction 'is not a

---

Sauter, Co., 368 F. Supp. 501, 520 (E.D. Pa. 1973); Trans World Airlines, Inc. v. Hughes, 314 F. Supp. 94 (S.D.N.Y. 1970)).

88. Athridge v. Iglesias, 464 F. Supp. 2d 19, 22 (D.D.C. 2006).

89. Gaus v. Conair Corp., No. 94 Civ. 5693, 2003 WL 542652, at *2 (S.D.N.Y. Feb. 14, 2003) (staying "enforcement of the judgment for a period of ten days, during which time [the judgment debtor could] post either a supersedeas bond or an irrevocable letter of credit in the amount of $28,500,000").

90. *Albert Sauter Co.*, 368 F. Supp. at 520–21.

91. Est. of Casillas v. City of Fresno, 471 F. Supp. 3d 1035, 1037 (E.D. Cal. 2020) (quoting *Poplar Grove Planting & Refin. Co.*, 600 F.2d at 1190). In *Estate of Casillas*, the Eastern District of California recognized that the economic impact of the COVID-19 pandemic was too speculative to rebut the City of Fresno's "convincing showing that its resources are more than sufficient to make good on the judgment in this case." *Id.* at 1038. Further, the court reasoned that requiring the City post a supersedeas bond "would be a waste of public resources." *Id.* (citing Safeco Ins. Co. of Am. v. City of San Bernardino, No. EDCV 05-194-VAP, 2007 WL 9719254, at *2–3 (C.D. Cal. July 27, 2007)). Accordingly, the court authorized an unsecured stay. *Id.*

92. *Poplar Grove Planting & Refin. Co.*, 600 F.2d at 1190.

93. *Id.*

94. *Id.*

95. Left Field Media LLC v. City of Chicago, 137 F. Supp. 3d 1127, 1133 (N.D. Ill. 2015) (citing Goodman v. Ill. Dep't of Fin. & Pro. Regul., 430 F.3d 432, 437 (7th Cir. 2005)).

remedy which issues as a matter of course.'"[96] An injunction involves an exercise of the court's equitable authority.[97] Accordingly, "[a]n injunction should issue only where the intervention of a court of equity 'is essential in order effectually to protect property rights against injuries otherwise irremediable.'"[98] "[T]aking into account all of the circumstances that bear on the need for prospective relief," a court may elect to award injunctive relief.[99]

A permanent injunction may be awarded only after a full hearing on the merits; although, an interlocutory injunction may temporarily maintain the status quo between the parties until the court issues its definitive order on the merits. Interlocutory injunctions are further classified as preliminary injunctions or temporary restraining orders, depending on the immediacy of the relief and the relief's duration. A temporary restraining order is valid for a maximum of 14 days and is fairly viewed as a makeshift measure to preserve the status quo until the court ultimately rules on the request for a preliminary injunction, which acts to preserve the status quo until trial.[100]

The limited availability of an injunction derives from the remedy's drastic nature and potential implications when an injunction is improvidently granted.[101] To alleviate these concerns, injunction bonds "provide a wrongfully enjoined party a source from which it may readily collect damages without further litigation."[102] Thus, the injunction bond

---

96. Musselman v. Blue Cross & Blue Shield of Ala., 684 F. App'x 824, 830 (11th Cir. 2017) (Tjoflat, J., concurring) (quoting Harrisonville v. W.S. Dickey Clay Mfg. Co., 289 U.S. 334, 337–38 (1933)).
97. Sarazar v. Buono, 599 U.S. 700, 714 (2010) (citing Weinberger v. Romero-Carcelo, 456 U.S. 305, 312 (1982); Hecht Co. v. Bowles, 321 U.S. 321, 329 (1944); United States v. Swift & Co., 286 U.S. 106, 114 (1932); 11A CHARLES ALAN WRIGHT & ARTHUR R. MILLER, FEDERAL PRACTICE AND PROCEDURE § 2942 (3d ed. 1995)).
98. *Weinberger*, 456 U.S. at 312 (quoting Cavanaugh v. Looney, 248 U.S. 453, 456 (1919)).
99. *Sarazar*, 599 U.S. at 714 (citations omitted).
100. FED. R. CIV. P. 65(b)(2).
101. Continuum Co. v. Incepts, Inc., 873 F.2d 801, 803 (5th Cir. 1989), *on reconsideration sub nom.* Continuum Co. v. Incepts, Inc., 901 F.2d 1111 (5th Cir. 1990).
102. OTR Wheel Eng'g, Inc. v. W. Worldwide Servs., Inc., No. 2:14-CV-00085, 2019 WL 8503837, at *1 (E.D. Wash. Nov. 12, 2019) (citing Nintendo of Am., Inc. v. Lewis Galoob Toys, Inc., 16 F.3d 1032, 1037 (9th Cir. 1994)).

ensures that the enjoined party will be able to collect damages if the party was wrongfully enjoined, and some courts limit the potential damages to the amount of the injunction bond, assuming the party had a good faith basis to petition for the injunction.[103]

Federal Rule of Civil Procedure 65 governs the availability of injunctive relief in federal court. Rule 65(c) affords district courts the discretion to "issue a preliminary injunction or a temporary restraining order *only if* the movant gives security in an amount that the court considers proper to pay the costs and damages sustained by any party found to have been wrongfully enjoined or restrained."[104] Case law confirms that Rule 65(c), at a minimum, obligates a court to consider and expressly rule on a request that security be given.[105] Courts reason that security is a prerequisite to the injunctive relief according to the plain language of Rule 65(c).[106] While adhering to the plain language of Rule 65(c) in most circumstances, the Third Circuit has recognized that Rule 65(c)'s language is "almost mandatory" but "instances in which a bond may not be required are . . . rare."[107] Acknowledging that "the language of Rule 65(c) appears to be mandatory, and that many circuits have so interpreted it," the Sixth Circuit also recognizes that security may not be required in certain circumstances.[108] The First,[109] Second,[110] Fifth,[111]

---

103. Murray v. Fid. & Deposit Co. of Md., No. 1:10CV1367, 2014 WL 4458895, at *2 (N.D. Ohio Sept. 10, 2014).
104. FED. R. CIV. P. 65(c) (emphasis added).
105. Life After Hate, Inc. v. Free Radicals Project, Inc., 410 F. Supp. 3d 891, 912 (N.D. Ill. 2019) ("'Absent extraordinary circumstances, the court errs in not granting' a defendant's request for a bond." (quoting Reinders Bros., Inc. v. Rain Bird E. Sales Corp., 627 F.2d 44, 53 (7th Cir. 1980)).
106. *See, e.g.*, Zambelli Fireworks Mfg. Co. v. Wood, 592 F.3d 412, 426 (3d Cir. 2010) ("Rule 65(c) constraints a district court's authority to enter a preliminary injunction, making it contingent upon the posting of a bond.").
107. Frank's GMC Truck Ctr. v. Gen. Motors Corp., 847 F.2d 100, 103 (3d Cir. 1988).
108. Moltan Co. v. Eagle-Picher Indus., Inc., 55 F.3d 1171, 1176 (6th Cir. 1995).
109. Int'l Ass'n of Machinists & Aerospace Workers v. E. Airlines, Inc., 925 F.2d 6, 9 (1st Cir. 1991).
110. Doctor's Assocs., Inc. v. Stuart, 85 F.3d 975, 985 (2d Cir. 1996).
111. Corrigan Dispatch Co. v. Casa Guzman, S.A., 569 F.2d 300, 302 (5th Cir. 1978).

Sixth,[112] Ninth,[113] and Tenth[114] Circuits have found the language of Rule 65(c) to be permissive. As explained by the Second Circuit, district courts in these circuits reason:

> Rule 65(c) gives the district court wide discretion to set the amount of a bond, and even to dispense with the bond requirement "where there has been no proof of likelihood of harm, or where the injunctive order was issued to aid and preserve the court's jurisdiction over the subject matter involved."[115]

In addition, some courts find exceptions when a party's financial condition is such that requiring security would effectively deny that party access to judicial review[116] or when "a plaintiff alleges the infringement of a fundamental constitutional right."[117]

"The amount of [an injunction] bond is committed to the discretion of the district court."[118] A few general principles guide the court's analysis in making this determination. First, courts have advised that "'district courts should err on the high side' when setting the amount of the bond."[119] This recommendation derives from the fact that an "injunction

---

112. *Moltan Co.*, 55 F.3d at 1176.
113. Jorgensen v. Cassiday, 320 F.3d 906, 919 (9th Cir. 2003).
114. Cont'l Oil Co. v. Frontier Refin. Co., 338 F.2d 780, 781–82 (10th Cir. 1964).
115. Doctor's Assocs., Inc. v. Distajo, 107 F.3d 126, 136 (2d Cir. 1997) (quoting *Stuart*, 85 F.3d at 985).
116. *See, e.g.*, Jeffreys v. My Friend's Place, Inc., 719 F. Supp. 639, 649 (M.D. Tenn. 1989).
117. *See, e.g.*, Complete Angler, LLC v. City of Clearwater, Fla., 607 F. Supp. 2d 1326, 1335 (M.D. Fla. 2009); Westfield High Sch. L.I.F.E. Club v. City of Westfield, 249 F. Supp. 2d 98, 129 (D. Mass. 2003); Smith v. Bd. of Election Comm'rs for City of Chicago, 591 F. Supp. 70, 72 (N.D. Ill. 1984).
118. Groupe SEB USA, Inc v. Euro-Pro Operating LLC, No. 14-137, 2014 WL 2002126, at *13 (W.D. Pa. May 15, 2014) (citing Zambelli Fireworks Mfg. v. Wood, 592 F.3d 412, 426 (3d Cir. 2010)).
119. Steves & Sons, Inc. v. JELD-WEN, Inc., No. 3:20-cv-98, 2020 WL 2312030, at *2 (E.D. Va. May 8, 2020) (quoting Mead Johnson & Co. v. Abbott Labs., 201 F.3d 883, 888 (7th Cir. 2000)).

bond is intended to secure against possible as well as certain" risks.[120] As the Eastern District of Wisconsin explains:

> [A] district court cannot simply set the bond at whatever high number it thinks appropriate; instead, reasons must support the number chosen so that a reviewing court can determine whether such number "was within the range of options from which one could expect a reasonable trial judge to select."[121]

Both parties should justify the amount of the bond requested.[122] If neither party presents a basis for the amount of the bond, the court should require that the parties do so, and the court may require an injunction bond in a nominal amount until a proper determination as to the amount is made.[123]

"The general rule is that damages are recoverable only if they 'arise from the operation of the injunction itself and not from damages occasioned . . . . independently of the injunction.'"[124] Generally, "[a]ttorneys' fees and legal expenses . . . are not . . . items to be included in the determination of the amount of the bond."[125] Additionally, costs and expenses incurred in connection with the injunction proceeding should not be a factor in determining the bond amount.[126] However,

---

120. Habitat Educ. Ctr. v. U.S. Forest Serv., 607 F.3d 453, 459 (7th Cir. 2010).
121. Manpower Inc. v. Mason, 405 F. Supp. 2d 959, 976 (E.D. Wis. 2005) (citing Gateway E. Ry. Co. v. Terminal R.R. Ass'n of St. Louis, 35 F.3d 1134, 1141–42 (7th Cir. 1994)).
122. *See* Builder's World, Inc. v. Marvin Lumber & Cedar, Inc., 482 F. Supp. 2d 1065, 1078 (E.D. Wis. 2007) (citing *Gateway E. Ry. Co.*, 35 F.3d at 1141–42).
123. *See id.*
124. Cappaert Enters. v. Citizens & S. Int'l Bank of New Orleans, 564 F. Supp. 214, 225 (E.D. La. 1983) (quoting Lever Bros. Co. v. Int'l Chem. Workers Union, Local 217, 554 F.2d 115, 120 (4th Cir. 1976)); *see* Pargas, Inc. v. Empire Gas Corp., 423 F. Supp. 199, 244 (D. Md. 1976) (recognizing that injunction bonds cover "'costs and damages' directly sustained as the result of an improvident issuance of the restraining order or preliminary injunction").
125. Powelton Civic Home Owners Ass'n v. Dep't of Hous. & Urb. Dev., 284 F. Supp. 809, 840 (E.D. Pa. 1968) (citations omitted).
126. *Cappaert Enters.*, 564 F. Supp. at 255 (rejecting a request for expert witness's fees incurred in the injunction proceeding).

in *International Association of Machinists & Aerospace Workers v. Eastern Airlines, Inc.*,[127] the First Circuit authorized the recovery of attorneys' fees when the governing statute required security for and allowed recovery of attorneys' fees incurred in litigation leading up to a wrongfully issued injunction.[128] The First Circuit concluded that attorneys' fees were recoverable because Federal Rule of Civil Procedure 65(e) does not modify "any federal statute relating to . . . preliminary injunctions in actions affecting employer and employee."[129] Thus, the court reasoned that provisions of the governing statute requiring a bond were not changed by Rule 65(c).[130]

The time value of the principal amount of a monetary judgment, however, may be considered if the injunction delays the receipt of money.[131] Otherwise, "a court is not required to order security in respect of . . . damages that are no more than speculative[, and] the party seeking security [bears the burden of] establish[ing] a rational basis for the amount of the proposed bond."[132] For this reason, a court should require that parties requesting security to ensure lost profits and sales, for example, represent a basis for the amount.[133] The court should find that such parties have not carried their burden when an amount is represented to the court without justification.[134] In other words, numbers alone are not a "coherent basis for fixing security."[135]

The district court is afforded a significant amount of discretion in determining the amount of the bond, and the court's decision will not be

---

127. 925 F.2d 6 (1st Cir. 1991).
128. *Id.* at 9–10.
129. FED. R. CIV. P. 65(e).
130. *E. Airlines, Inc.*, 925 F.2d at 9–10.
131. *Id.*
132. Int'l Equity Invs., Inc. v. Opportunity Equity Partners Ltd., 441 F. Supp. 2d 552, 566 (S.D.N.Y. 2006) (citing Interlink Int'l Fin. Serv., Inc. v. Block, 145 F. Supp. 2d 312, 315 (S.D.N.Y. 2001); Interflight Newspapers, Inc. v. Magazines In-Flight, LLC, 990 F. Supp. 119, 140 (E.D.N.Y. 1997); Bass v. Richardson, 338 F. Supp. 478, 491 (S.D.N.Y. 1971)); *see also* AB Electrolux v. Bermil Indus. Corp., 481 F. Supp. 2d 325, 337 (S.D.N.Y. 2007).
133. *Int'l Equity Invs., Inc.*, 441 F. Supp. 2d 552, 566.
134. *AB Electrolux*, 481 F. Supp. 2d at 337.
135. *Id.*

disturbed absent an abuse of discretion.[136] In making this determination, the district court should produce "definite findings with regard to the amount of the bond."[137] When the court fails to do so, a reviewing court may remand for clarification.[138]

C. Bonds for Remedies Provided by Federal Rule of Civil Procedure 64

Federal Rule of Civil Procedure 64 governs the availability of remedies relating to seizure of a person or property. Rule 64(b) delineates the available remedies as follows:

> The remedies available under this rule include the following—however designated and regardless of whether state procedure requires an independent action:
> - arrest;
> - attachment;
> - garnishment;
> - replevin;
> - sequestration; and
> - other corresponding or equivalent remedies.[139]

Rule 64(a) clarifies that these remedies are ordinarily governed by state law:

> At the commencement of and throughout an action, every remedy is available that, under the law of the state where the court is located, provides for seizing a person or property to

---

136. Stockslager v. Carroll Elec. Coop. Corp., 528 F.2d 949, 951 (8th Cir. 1976).
137. Gateway E. Ry. Co. v. Terminal R.R. Ass'n of St. Louis, 35 F.3d 1134, 1142 (7th Cir. 1994).
138. *Id.* (remanding to obtain a definite statement for the reviewing court to evaluate whether or not the amount of the bond "was 'within the range of options from which one could expect a reasonable trial judge to select'" (quoting United States v. Koen, 982 F.2d 1101, 1114 (7th Cir. 1992))).
139. FED. R. CIV. P. 64(b).

> secure satisfaction of the potential judgment. But a federal statute governs to the extent it applies.[140]

Thus, Rule 64 makes remedies provided for by state law available to federal court litigants.

1. Attachment

While a plaintiff's aspirations when filing a lawsuit are endless, a judgment against a defendant with no assets could prove worthless. Although, a plaintiff may curb its fears that the defendant's assets may be lost or dissipated by attempting to attach the defendant's property before the claims are litigated and judgment is entered. Attachment is a legal remedy enabling a plaintiff to "acquire a lien upon property or effects of the defendant for satisfaction of a judgment which the plaintiff may obtain."[141] Attachment is an "ancillary remedy" because it cannot be awarded in the absence of an underlying action.[142] Consequently, "it is legally and factually impossible to obtain a pre-commencement order of attachment in federal court."[143]

Attachment is considered a harsh and extraordinary remedy,[144] "amount[ing] to the voluntary dispossession of the owner prior to any adjudication to determine the rights of the parties."[145] Attachment is a "creature of statute,"[146] and no general independent federal right to attachment exists.[147] Thus, the availability of attachment is ordinarily governed by state law, and standards used by the courts to determine

---

140. *Id.* 64(a).
141. 8 LONNIE E. GRIFFITH, JR., FEDERAL PROCEDURES § 21:17 (2d ed. 2021) (citations omitted).
142. Mitsubishi Int'l Corp. v. Cardinal Textile Sales, Inc., 14 F.3d 1507, 1521 (11th Cir. 1994).
143. New England Merchs. Nat'l Bank v. Iran Power Generation & Transmission Co., 495 F. Supp. 73, 76 (S.D.N.Y. 1980) (citations omitted).
144. Bank of China, N.Y. Branch v. NBM L.L.C., 192 F. Supp. 2d 183, 186 (S.D.N.Y. 2002).
145. Siegel v. N. Boulevard & 80th St. Corp., 295 N.Y.S.2d 804, 806 (N.Y. App. Div. 1968) (citing Penoyar v. Kelsey, 44 N.E. 788, 789 (N.Y. 1896)).
146. *Id.*
147. Sullivan v. Rivera Holdings Corp., No. 2:14-cv-00165, 2015 WL 13678961, at *2 n.2 (D. Nev. May 4, 2015) (citing *In re* Pro-Fit Holdings Ltd., 391 B.R. 850, 856 n.8 (Bankr. C.D. Cal. 2008)).

whether attachment is warranted in a particular case will vary by jurisdiction.

In federal court, the remedy of attachment is only available to the extent it is made available by an applicable federal statute or state law. A plaintiff may attempt to attach the defendant's property in the underlying lawsuit by filing a motion requesting that the court issue a writ of attachment. If granted, the motion results in an order of attachment. Despite the remedy's harsh and extraordinary nature,[148] Federal Rule of Civil Procedure 64 does not necessarily require that a party seeking attachment in federal court obtain an attachment bond. Rather, the federal statute or state law authorizing attachment will dictate whether an attachment bond is required in federal court.

2. *Replevin*

Unlike the attachment remedy, replevin is a remedy deeply rooted in the common law.[149] However, the availability of replevin may be governed by statute, depending on the jurisdiction.[150] Replevin is a separate cause of action "to regain possession of goods and chattels."[151] Replevin merely deals with the right to possession rather than the right to the property.[152] Replevin actions are often decided by weighing the possessory interests of the plaintiff and defendant.[153] In addition to the remedy of attachment, Federal Rule of Civil Procedure 64 also specifically addresses replevin actions. Thus, replevin actions are generally governed by state law, and state law will dictate whether a replevin bond is required.

When required, the "manifest object of the [replevin] bond is to secure the prosecution of the replevin suit in which it is to give effect and without delay and make return of the property to the defendant if the return of the property is awarded; the bond is intended to assist the

---

148. *Bank of China, N.Y. Branch*, 192 F. Supp. 2d at 186.
149. Peruto v. Roc Nation, 386 F. Supp. 3d 471, 475 (E.D. Pa. 2019) (citing Fuentes v. Shevin, 407 U.S. 67, 78 (1972)).
150. 66 AM. JUR. 2D *Replevin* § 1 (2011).
151. *Peruto*, 386 F. Supp. 3d at 475.
152. 66 AM. JUR. 2D *Replevin* § 1 (2011).
153. *Id.*; *see* Dubied Mach. Co. v. Vt. Knitting Co., Inc., 739 F. Supp. 867, 872 (S.D.N.Y. 1990) (indicating that a defendant in a replevin action may present any defense to support the contention that it has superior possessory rights).

parties in obtaining justice."[154] Thus, much like an injunction bond, the replevin bond offers security for the defendant if the plaintiff does not prevail in its replevin action.

3. *State Law Most Often Governs Attachment and Replevin Bonds Requirements*

As mentioned above, the availability of attachment and replevin remedies, bond requirements, and, if required, the factors to consider in determining the amount of such a bond are generally governed by state law.[155] A survey of state attachment bond cases reveals that when an attachment bond is required, it should generally be in an amount sufficient to secure all damages arising from the attachment.[156] Of the jurisdictions that require a bond, certain jurisdictions refer to the value of the property to be attached to determine the amount of the bond. By way of example, the District of Columbia's statute governing attachment provides the following:

> Before a writ of attachment and garnishment is issued, the plaintiff shall first file in the clerk's office a bond, executed by himself or his agent, with security to be approved by the clerk, in twice the amount of his claim, conditioned to make good to the defendant all costs and damages which he may sustain by reason of the wrongful suing out of the attachment; except that in any case in which the plaintiff states in his affidavit that the value of specified property to be levied upon is less than the amount of his claim, the court may set the amount of such bond in an amount twice the value of the property being attached.[157]

---

154. Azar v. Statewide Ins. Co., 681 N.E.2d 84, 87 (Ill. App. Ct. 1997) (citing Magerstadt *ex rel.* T.A. Shaw & Co. v. Field, 160 Ill. App. 23, 29–30 (Ill. App. Ct. 1911); 735 ILL. COMP. STAT. 5/19-122 (West 1994)).
155. Morozov v. ICOBOX Hub Inc., No. 18 Civ. 3421, 2020 WL 5665639, at *10 (S.D.N.Y. May 5, 2020) ("Federal Rule of Civil Procedure 64 permits federal courts to grant certain provisional remedies in accordance with state law . . . ."); *see* FED. R. CIV. P. 64.
156. *E.g.*, Estate of Hevia v. Portrio Corp., 497 F. Supp. 2d 312, 314 (D.P.R. 2007).
157. D.C. CODE § 16-501 (1998).

Thus, practitioners are encouraged to refer to state law in the appropriate jurisdiction to determine whether an attachment or replevin bond is required in a particular case and the amount of the bond when required.

II. Enforcement of Judicial Bonds

In federal court, there are rules governing proceedings against the surety having issued a judicial bond. Specifically, Federal Rule of Civil Procedure 65.1 states as follows:

> Whenever these rules (including the Supplemental Rules for Admiralty or Maritime Claims and Asset Forfeiture Actions) require or allow a party to give security, and security is given with one or more security providers, each provider submits to the court's jurisdiction and irrevocably appoints the court clerk as its agent for receiving service of any papers that affect its liability on the security. The security provider's liability may be enforced on motion without an independent action. The motion and any notice that the court orders may be served on the court clerk, who must promptly send a copy of each to every security provider whose address is known.[158]

Federal Rule of Appellate Procedure 8(b) mirrors Federal Rule of Civil Procedure 65.1 and affords the same enforcement procedure for bonds issued in appellate courts.[159] The rules clarify that the surety's issuance of a bond subjects the surety to the district court's personal jurisdiction and that bond obligees may enforce the bond against the surety in the underlying proceeding.[160] Though the rules do not foreclose the possibility of the bond obligee bringing an independent action against

---

158. Fed. R. Civ. P. 65.1.

159. Fed. R. App. P. 8 advisory committee's note to 1967 amendment.

160. Fed. R. App. P. 8(b); Fed. R. Civ. P. 65.1; *see* PPC Broadband, Inc. v. Corning Optical Commc'ns RF, LLC, No. 5:11-CV-0761, 2018 WL 3432741, at *2–3 (N.D.N.Y. June 18, 2018) ("A prevailing party may enforce a surety's liability on a supersedeas bond using the summary procedure provided under Rule 65.1 or through an independent action in a state or federal court.").

the surety, the rules do not provide a basis for subject matter jurisdiction in such action.[161]

The Eleventh Circuit's holding in *Milan Express, Inc. v. Averitt Express, Inc.* dealt with the precise issue concerning a district court's subject matter jurisdiction in an independent action by a bond obligee to enforce a judicial bond.[162] The Eleventh Circuit considered whether the underlying district court had subject matter jurisdiction to award damages against a surety and bond principal on an injunction bond resulting from a wrongfully issued preliminary injunction.[163] A Federal Rule of Civil Procedure 65.1 motion to enforce the bond was filed in the original action, but the district court judge elected to reserve the motion in an independent action.[164] The obligee on the bond argued that Rule 65.1 provided the basis for the court's jurisdiction over the independent action.[165] The Eleventh Circuit plainly rejected this argument, abruptly stating, "[a] federal rule cannot be the basis of original jurisdiction . . . , [thus,] Rule 65.1 is not a basis for jurisdiction."[166] While subject matter jurisdiction for the independent action may be established by relying on statutes, the simplest mechanism to enforce a judicial bond against the surety is a motion in the underlying proceeding, as contemplated by the rules.[167]

Venue over enforcement of a judicial bond by a Federal Rule of Civil Procedure 65.1 or Federal Rule of Appellate Procedure 8(b) motion is proper in the court hearing the underlying action.[168] When a party brings an independent action to enforce a bond, venue is governed by 31 U.S.C. § 9307. Under § 9307, venue over an action against a surety is proper in either "the judicial district in which the surety bond was provided [or] the district in which the principal office of the [surety] is located."[169] The statute provides that a surety bond is provided in any of the following: (1) the judicial district "in which the principal office of the [surety] is

---

161. Milan Express, Inc. v. Averitt Express, Inc., 208 F.3d 975, 979 (11th Cir. 2000); *PPC Broadband, Inc.*, 2018 WL 3432741, at *2–3.
162. *Milan Express, Inc.*, 208 F.3d 975.
163. *Id.* at 978.
164. *Id.* at 979.
165. *Id.*
166. *Id.* (concluding that "28 U.S.C. § 1352 provide[d] a basis for jurisdiction over [the] injunction bond claim").
167. *See, e.g.*, FED. R. CIV. P. 65.1 ("The security provider's liability may be enforced on motion without an independent action.").
168. *See* FED. R. APP. P. 8(b); FED. R. CIV. P. 65.1.
169. 31 U.S.C. § 9307(a) (1982).

located"; (2) the judicial district "to which the surety bond is returnable"; (3) the judicial district "in which the surety bond is filed"; and (4) the judicial district "in which a person required to provide a surety bond resided" at the time the bond was provided.[170]

A. *Enforcement by Motion in the Underlying Proceeding*

The simplest mechanism by which to enforce a judicial bond is by motion in the underlying proceeding pursuant to Federal Rule of Civil Procedure 65.1 or Federal Rule of Appellate Procedure 8(b).[171] Under the rule, the motion and any other required filings, such as notice of the motion and a proposed order granting relief, should be served on the clerk of the district court.[172] Upon service of the motion and required filings, the clerk of the court must forward a copy of the documents to the surety.[173] At least one court has held that the failure to offer such notice to the surety could undermine a subsequent judgment against the surety.[174]

Once the motion for judgment against the surety on the bond is filed, the surety will file a response to the motion. After the response is filed or the window in which a response may be filed closes, the court will hold a hearing and enter judgment on the motion. If the court rules against the surety, the surety's obligation arises upon the entry of the court's order, and the surety generally will deliver payment directly to the judgment creditor.[175]

B. *Enforcement by an Independent Action*

When the party seeking recovery under a judicial bond elects to bring an independent action against the surety, the action is initiated just as

---

170. *Id.* § 9307(b).

171. *See* U.S. D.I.D. Corp. v. Windstream Commc'ns, Inc., 755 F.3d 128, 135 (2d Cir. 2014) ("[T]he defendant's recovery on the Rule 65(c) security [c]ould . . . be sought by motion and adjudicated in a summary proceeding."); *see also* PPC Broadband, Inc. v. Corning Optical Commc'ns RF, LLC, No. 5:11-CV-0761, 2018 WL 3432741, at *2–3 (N.D.N.Y. June 18, 2018).

172. Fed. R. App. P. 8(b); Fed. R. Civ. P. 65.1.

173. Fed. R. App. P. 8(b); Fed. R. Civ. P. 65.1.

174. Astoria v. Slayne, 1 F.R.D. 742, 743 (E.D.N.Y. 1941).

175. The exception to the general rule arises in situations when the surety's obligation is created in a probate court case. There, the surety will remit payment to the court.

any proceeding is commenced—by filing a complaint and serving a summons and the complaint in accordance with the Federal Rules of Civil Procedure.[176] As with any lawsuit, the court must have personal jurisdiction and subject matter jurisdiction, and venue must be proper.

III. Scope of Liability

A. *Terms of the Bond*

One of the most fundamental and elementary rules of suretyship is that "a surety cannot be bound beyond the scope of his engagement."[177] However, this principle "does not imply that a strained construction is to be put on the words of the bond in favor of the surety, or that it may have one force and meaning when the principal is defendant, and a different force and meaning when the surety is defendant."[178] The terms of the bond will be interpreted through the lens of contract principles, and the court will endeavor to reflect the mutual intention of the parties in its interpretation.[179] Therefore, even unnamed parties may recover against a judicial bond if the bond can be reasonably interpreted as running to the party.[180]

Of particular importance to practitioners is the language prescribing the trigger of the bond or the "condition" of the surety's liability under the bond. The surety becomes obligated to fulfill its obligations only when

---

176. While "a surety's liability may be enforced under either Rule 65.1's summary procedure or through an independent action," Rule 65.1 "was intended to provide a uniform rule for summary proceedings against sureties on bonds required or permitted under original Rules 65 and 73." Bass v. First Pac. Networks, Inc., 219 F.3d 1052, 1054 (9th Cir. 2000) (citing 28 U.S.C. § 1352 (providing for federal court jurisdiction to enforce the bonds); FED. R. CIV. P. 65 advisory committee's note to 1966 amendment; 11A CHARLES ALAN WRIGHT & ARTHUR R. MILLER, FEDERAL PRACTICE AND PROCEDURE § 2971 (3d ed. 1995)).
177. Miller v. Stewart, 22 U.S. 680, 704 (1824).
178. C.V.V., Annotation, *Amount Named in Appeal or Supersedeas Bond as the Maximum Limit of Sureties' Liability or as a Limitation of the Amount Which They Undertake Shall Be Paid on the Judgment Appealed From*, 87 A.L.R. 257 (originally published in 1933).
179. White v. Indem. Ins. Co. of N. Am., 54 Cal. Rptr. 630, 632 (Cal. Ct. App. 1966).
180. *Id.*

the condition of the bond has been met. For this reason, sureties should ensure that the language of the bond accurately reflects the condition with sufficient specificity.

Additionally, close attention to local rules, statutes, and the court's order requiring security is imperative for the parties, as any of these may address the time frames surrounding a surety's liability under a judicial bond. Courts have held that the right to sue on an attachment bond may accrue in several different circumstances. The cause of action may arise immediately after the defending party prevails in the action for which a writ of attachment was issued.[181] As recognized by the Supreme Court of Indiana, the cause of action on an attachment bond could be triggered by abandonment of an attachment or on the court's dismissal of the underlying action on procedural grounds, despite the court's failure to address the merits of the claims.[182] With regard to injunction bonds, courts have found that when a party who has obtained an injunction bond elects to voluntarily dismiss its action without prejudice, the termination entitles the opposing party to recover on the bond as it is the equivalent of adjudication on the merits.[183] These cases demonstrate that a surety's liability may be triggered upon the court's disposition of the case on any one of several different grounds. Therefore, sureties would be well-advised to incorporate bond language that specifically states the type of disposition that will trigger liability on the bond.

B. Damages

As previously mentioned, courts consistently recognize that, "except in limited circumstances, a surety's liability cannot extend beyond the penal sum announced in the bond."[184] The exceptions are limited but

---

181. Bookasta v. Hartford Accident & Indem. Co., 120 Cal. Rptr. 229, 231–32 (Cal. Ct. App. 1975).
182. Ashland Oil, Inc. v. Arnett, 507 N.E.2d 561, 564 (Ind. 1987); Audit Servs., Inc. v. Haugen, 591 P.2d 1105, 1110 (Mont. 1979) (dissolving the attachment and determining that the order dissolving the attachment was equivalent to a "judgment made, entered and filed," where the requirements were statutorily prescribed).
183. *See, e.g.*, Rogers v. Stanec, 971 S.W.2d 340, 353 (Mo. Ct. App. 1998).
184. Morrison Knudsen Corp. v. Ground Improvement Techs., 532 F.3d 1063, 1072 (10th Cir. 2008) (citing Md. Cas. Co. v. Alford, 111 F.2d 388, 390 (10th Cir. 1940); Houston Fire & Cas. Ins. Co. v. E.E. Cloer Gen. Contractor, Inc., 217 F.2d 906, 912 (5th Cir. 1954) ("The surety's

arise in situations when, for example, a bond is required by local rule or statute, which requires that any bond issued in furtherance of the law is deemed to include the statutorily mandated terms. In these exceptional circumstances, the surety's liability may exceed the penal sum of the bond to the extent that the local rule or statute requires.[185] Outside of these narrow circumstances, the surety's liability cannot exceed the penal sum of the bond. Conversely, the principal's liability is not limited by the penal sum.

1. Cost Bond

As stated in the discussion concerning the amount of a cost bond, the types of damages enumerated in Rule 39(e) are recoverable under a cost bond. Additionally, it appears to be the majority rule that, when the appeal is from an action in which the cause of action arose from a statute with a fee-shifting provision for attorneys' fees, appellate attorneys' fees will be recoverable under the cost bond.[186] In the majority of cases, when a cost bond is posted to secure the costs on appeal, the damages that will be recoverable are those provided for in Federal Rule of Appellate Procedure 39.

2. Supersedeas Bond

A supersedeas bond provides compensation for damages suffered as a "natural and proximate result of the stay."[187] Thus, the damages recoverable under a supersedeas bond are "those damages arising from the delay occasioned by (the stay pending appeal) which are properly

---

obligation is of course limited to the penal sum named in the bond."); Mass. Bonding & Ins. Co. v. United States, 97 F.2d 879, 881 (9th Cir. 1938) ("It is fundamental in the law of suretyship that a bondsman cannot be held for any default of his principal in an amount greater than the penal sum of the bond.")).

185. RESTATEMENT (THIRD) OF SURETYSHIP AND GUARANTY § 71(2) (1996).

186. *See* Azizian v. Federated Dep't Stores, Inc., 499 F.3d 950, 958 (9th Cir. 2007) ("We agree with the Second, Sixth, and Eleventh Circuits and hold that the term 'costs on appeal' in Rule 7 includes all expenses defined as 'costs' by an applicable fee-shifting statute, including attorney's fees.").

187. Weiner v. 222 E. Chestnut Corp., 303 F.2d 630, 634 (7th Cir. 1962).

a legal damage to the party delayed"[188] and should be "reasonably foreseeable consequences of the stay pending appeal."[189]

Specifically, courts have held that interest resulting from the delay,[190] capital gains tax benefits lost as a result of a stay,[191] and damages resulting from construction delays[192] were recoverable under supersedeas bonds. When the stay relates to real property, the U.S. Supreme Court advised that damages recoverable under a supersedeas bond may include:

> (1) the depreciation of the property in market value pending the appeal; or (2) its deterioration by waste, or want of repair, or the accumulation of taxes or other burdens; or (3) the use and detention of the property pending the appeal—that is, the rents and profits; or (4) the nonpayment of the costs of the appeal . . . ."[193]

However, attenuated damages are not recoverable under the supersedeas bond. By way of example, one court has recognized that "moving costs" associated with intolerable living conditions resulting from the court's order forcing the sale of real property were not recoverable under the supersedeas bond.[194]

The determination of the damages that parties may recover under the bond often turns on the language of the bond. For example, in *Tornatore v. Cohen*,[195] the appellate court analyzed the terms of a supersedeas bond to determine whether the liability of an insurer, acting as surety, could exceed the amount referenced in the bond.[196] Specifically, the bond

---

188. Kountze v. Omaha Hotel Co., 107 U.S. 378, 394 (1883).
189. Moore v. Townsend, 577 F.2d 424, 428 (7th Cir. 1978); *222 E. Chestnut St. Corp.*, 303 F.2d at 637.
190. *Townsend*, 577 F.2d at 427.
191. *Id.* at 428.
192. 222 *E. Chestnut St. Corp.*, 303 F.2d at 637.
193. *Kountze*, 107 U.S. at 392.
194. *Id.*
195. 185 A.D.3d 1394, 1395 (N.Y. App. Div. 2020). In *Tornatore*, "the defendant's malpractice insurer[] issued a supersedeas bond in the amount of $1,217,474.20." Delaney L. Beier & Ryan B. DeLaune, Fidelity Law and Commercial Surety Law Update 2021: March 1, 2020, through April 1, 2021, Presentation at Surety Claims Institute Annual Meaning 20 (June 23–25, 2021); *see Tornatore*, 185 A.D.3d at 1395.
196. *Tornatore*, 185 A.D.3d at 1395.

bound the insurer "in the amount of $1,217,474.20 and does pursuant to the statute in such cases, undertake that if the judgment or order . . . or any part thereof, is affirmed, or the appeal is dismissed, [the judgment debtor] will pay the sum directed to be paid by the judgment or order."[197] When the appellate court affirmed the judgment and remanded to the trial court, the trial court ordered the insurer to satisfy the amount of the judgment, plus "unpaid prejudgment and postjudgment interest."[198] The insurer appealed, "contend[ing] that the language of the [supersedeas] bond unambiguously limits its liability as a surety to the present value of $1,217,474.20 and does not obligate it to pay any additional monies such as prejudgment and postjudgment interest."[199] The Appellate Division of the Supreme Court of New York disagreed, holding:

> Pursuant to the plain language of the appeal bond, [the insurer] gave an undertaking in the amount of $1,217,474.20 for the purpose of securing a stay of the judgment on behalf of defendant and—in the conjunctive—undertook to "pay the sum directed to be paid by the judgment" if the judgment was affirmed.[200]

Stated differently, the court held that the latter clause "does not in express language limit the amount [to be paid on the judgment] to any fixed sum."[201] Thus, the trial court's order was affirmed, and the insurer was obligated to pay "the full amount of the judgment inclusive of prejudgment and post judgment interest."[202] Language purporting to make "any and all damages" recoverable prompts a broad interpretation of recoverable damages. Thus, the damages recoverable under supersedeas bonds invokes a highly factual inquiry that will heavily depend on the language of the bond and the nature of the damages.

---

197. *Id.*
198. *Id.* at 1396.
199. *Id.*
200. *Id.*
201. *Id.* (quoting Hotop v. Md. Cas. Co., 274 N.Y. 327, 329–30 (1937)) (citing Shapiro v. Equitable Cas. & Sur. Co., 256 N.Y. 341, 345 (1931)).
202. Beier & DeLaune, *supra* note 195, at 20; *see Tornatore*, 185 A.D.3d at 1397.

3. Injunction Bond

The "injunction bond rule" states that liability resulting from an improvidently granted injunction is limited to the amount of the bond.[203] Stated differently, "[t]he bond can thus be viewed as a contract in which the court and plaintiff 'agree' to the bond amount as the 'price' of a wrongful injunction."[204] Damages recoverable under an injunction bond generally "arise from the operation of the injunction itself and not from damages occasioned by the suit independently of the injunction."[205] An injunction bond covers the consequential damages resulting from a wrongfully issued injunction.[206] Thus, the economic impacts leading to a loss of profits due to an improvidently granted preliminary injunction have been included in the potential damages available under Federal Rule of Civil Procedure 65(c).[207] As another example, the Southern District of California has reasoned that loss in stock value that is not too speculative could be recoverable when the price of the stock dropped during the time the wrongfully issued injunction was in place.[208] As discussed in detail above, courts have found that, when the statute providing the injunctive remedy contains a fee-shifting provision, the wrongfully enjoined party may recover attorneys' fees incurred in the party's efforts to fight the injunction; however, this carve-out is limited to situations in which the statute contains a fee-shifting provision, and the general rule that attorneys' fees and expenses incurred by a wrongfully enjoined party

---

203. Int'l Ass'n of Machinists & Aerospace Workers v. E. Airlines, Inc., 925 F.2d 6, 10 (1st Cir. 1991).
204. Morrison Knudsen Corp. v. Ground Improvement Techs., 532 F.3d 1063 (10th Cir. 2008).
205. Lever Bros. Co. v. Int'l Chem. Workers Union, Local 217, 554 F.2d 115, 120 (4th Cir. 1976); *see also* CVI/Beta Ventures, Inc. v. Custom Optical Frames, Inc., 893 F. Supp. 508 (D. Md. 1995); Flag Fables, Inc. v. Jean Ann's Country Flags & Crafts, Inc., 753 F. Supp. 1007 (D. Mass. 1990); *In re* Rest. Servs., Inc., 26 B.R. 215 (W.D. Ky. 1982).
206. Silvers v. TTC Indus., Inc., 484 F.2d 194, 199 (6th Cir. 1973).
207. Atomic Oil Co. of Okla. v. Bardahl Oil Co., 419 F.2d 1097, 1103 (10th Cir. 1969); Pro Edge L.P. v. Gue, 451 F. Supp. 2d 1026, 1035–36 (N.D. Iowa 2006).
208. Sionix Corp. v. Moorehead, 299 F. Supp. 2d 1082, 1089 (S.D. Cal. 2003).

while resisting or appealing an injunction are not recoverable under an injunction bond remains true in a majority of cases.[209]

4. Attachment Bonds and Replevin Bonds

As state law dictates the availability of attachment and replevin remedies, state statutes or rules may prescribe the types of damages recoverable against an attachment bond or replevin bond. When no statute or rule addresses the types of damages recoverable under the bond, practitioners are encouraged to refer to case law in determining the potential scope of recoverable damages. One court has reasoned:

> To be awarded money from a bond posted in return for an Attachment before Judgment, [] two requirements must be met: money from the bond must be to reimburse costs or remedy damages only, and the costs or damages must have been caused by the attachment itself.[210]

The latter notion—that damages must result from the attachment or replevin itself—can be interpreted to mean that the party seeking to recover on the bond must prove that the losses sustained were proximately caused by the attachment or replevin.[211] The Second Circuit has determined that this proximate cause exists when a plaintiff attached funds in a defendant's bank account and the defendant paid interest charges on resulting overdrafts, finding that the interest charges "were a direct consequence of the withdrawal from and the depletion of its account by reason of the attachment."[212] "Proper travel expenses" have also been recovered under an attachment bond.[213] The language of the bond may contemplate or explicitly provide for the recovery of damages

---

209. Fireman's Fund Ins. Co. v. S.E.K. Constr. Co., 436 F.2d 1345, 1352 (10th Cir. 1971); Wells Fargo Nw. Bank, Nat'l Ass'n v. Varig-S.A., No. 02 Civ. 6078, 2003 WL 21508339, at *1 (S.D.N.Y. 2003); Powelton Civic Home Owners Ass'n v. Dep't of Hous. & Urb. Dev., 284 F. Supp. 809, 840 (E.D. Pa. 1968); Monolith Portland Midwest Co. v. R.F.C., 128 F. Supp. 824, 878 (S.D. Cal. 1955).
210. MLT Enters., Inc. v. Miller, 694 A.2d 497, 502 (Md. Ct. Spec. App. 1997).
211. *See, e.g.*, *id.* at 504.
212. Aerotrade, Inc. v. Republic of Haiti, 552 F.2d 60, 61 (2d Cir. 1977).
213. Maglificio Italiano Di Zironi Incerti Valintina v. Fid. & Deposit Co. of Md., 312 N.Y.S.2d 113, 113 (N.Y. App. Div. 1970).

not directly resulting from the issuance of the writ of attachment or replevin.[214] Thus, when the bond's terms sought to encompass "all legal costs and damages," such costs and damages were recoverable from the surety.[215]

Numerous jurisdictions allow parties to recover their attorneys' fees in actions on an attachment or replevin bond.[216] Cases decided in these jurisdictions suggest that a central issue is whether the attorneys' fees were incurred in defending the action or during the party's attempt to extinguish the writ of attachment or replevin.[217]

IV. Discharge of Judicial Bonds

A. *Injunction, Attachment, and Replevin Bonds*

Typically, judicial bonds are discharged upon the court rendering judgment in favor of the party seeking relief. Generally, this occurs when the court grants a reversal in favor of an appellant, the court determines that an injunction was justifiably issued, or the court concludes that a writ of attachment or replevin was rightfully issued. In the latter two scenarios, the time at which the surety is entitled to discharge is fairly straight forward. However, with regard to the supersedeas bond, determining the point at which the surety should be discharged from liability is slightly more complicated.

B. *Supersedeas Bonds*

When ascertaining the extent of the surety's liability under a supersedeas bond, there is no federal statute or rule of civil procedure outlining when the surety's obligations are discharged, and the bond released. Therefore, the surety's liability will be governed solely by the bond and the specific language contained therein. After an appellate decision is issued, the surety's liability will often depend on whether the appellant

---

214. *Id.*
215. *Id.*
216. *See, e.g.*, White v. Indem. Ins. Co. of N. Am., 54 Cal. Rptr. 630, 632 (Cal. Ct. App. 1966); Baird v. Liepelt, 210 N.E.2d 1, 3 (Ill. App. Ct. 1965); Siegel v. N. Blvd. & 80th St. Corp., 295 N.Y.S.2d 804, 811 (N.Y. App. Div. 1968).
217. *White*, 54 Cal. Rptr. at 632.

has prosecuted the appeal "to effect" as that phrase, or similar phrase, is defined in the bond.

As explained by the U.S. Supreme Court in 1879, "[i]f, on the final disposition of a writ of error on appeal, the judgment or decree . . . is not substantially reversed . . . [the] appeal has not been prosecuted with effect."[218] When the court completely vacates the judgment, thereby discharging the bond, or affirms the judgment as to liability and damages, thereby triggering coverage under the bond, the supersedeas bond surety can easily determine the scope of its bonded obligation. In situations when the appeal is unsuccessful and the judgment is paid, the surety may simply file a motion to release or discharge the bond, relying on the terms of the bond. As recognized by the Southern District of Texas in *WesternGeco L.L.C. v. Ion Geophysical Corp.*,[219] when the appeal is unsuccessful and the judgment is paid, the court will grant the motion and release the surety or discharge the bond as "no further damages [can] be awarded."[220] However, if the court affirms in part and reverses in part or affirms liability and vacates the damage award, the surety's liability may be less clear.

1. When Judgment Is Vacated, and the Appellee Must Again Prove Entitlement to Damages

Federal courts have previously discharged a surety's obligations under a supersedeas bond when the appellate court affirms the judgment as it relates to the defendant's liability but remands the matter on the issue of damages.[221] Therefore, when the only issue remaining is the plaintiff's damages on remand, the surety's supersedeas bond obligations are discharged. In *Aetna Casualty & Surety Co. v. LaSalle Pump & Supply Co.*,[222] the Fifth Circuit specifically held that the reversal of a judgment on appeal, based on inadequate proof of damages, discharged the appeal

---

218. Gay v. Parpart, 101 U.S. 391, 391 (1879); *see also* Crane v. Buckley, 203 U.S. 441, 447 (1906) (explaining "prosecuting to effect" means "prosecuting his appeal with success; to make substantial and prevailing his attempt to reverse the decree or judgment awarded against him").
219. No. 4:09-cv-01827 (S.D. Tex. May 15, 2017).
220. *Id.*
221. *See, e.g.*, Neeley v. Bankers Tr. Co. of Tex., 848 F.2d 658, 659–60 (5th Cir. 1988) (holding appellant prosecuted appeal to effect when court of appeals ordered retrial because plaintiff failed to prove damages).
222. 804 F.2d 315, 318 (5th Cir. 1986).

bond such that the bond did not cover the portion of the judgment awarding damages on remand after taking of additional evidence on damages.[223] The court explained that unlike the situation when a case is remanded "merely for the addition of expenses whose final amount could not earlier have been determined," when a party fails to prove its entitlement to a specific damage award and the judgment in its favor is accordingly reversed, the bond does not remain in effect.[224]

By way of further example, in *Neeley v. Bankers Trust Co. of Texas*,[225] the judgment creditors were awarded a jury verdict of $1.5 million for fraud.[226] One of the judgment debtors appealed and filed a supersedeas bond in an amount exceeding $1.8 million.[227] The Fifth Circuit affirmed liability for the fraud, but vacated the award for damages and the case was remanded for a new trial on the issue of damages only.[228] The court explained that if a judgment is merely reduced and rendered on appeal, then the surety remains liable for that amount.[229] However, recognizing that the entire award of damages was vacated, the court affirmed the surety's discharge from liability on the supersedeas bond. The Fifth Circuit reasoned that "[t]he retrial on damages results in an entirely new judgment."[230] Stated differently, "[t]he bond is limited to any decree of the court of appeals; it does not include an entirely new judgment of the district court."[231]

2. *When Appellee Has Proven That Some Damages Are Due, and Remand Is to Determine Proper Quantum of Injury*

A minority of jurisdictions have concluded that a supersedeas bond is not discharged when the court affirms a portion of the damages on appeal and remands the matter for the sole purpose of modifying the damage award. In a majority of these cases, the court is not reconsidering whether the damages are appropriate but, instead, issuing a "recalculation of

223. *Id.*
224. *Id.* at 317–18.
225. 848 F.2d 658.
226. *Id.* at 658–59.
227. *Id.*
228. *Id.* at 660.
229. *Id.*
230. *Id.*
231. *Id.*

damages" as more of an administrative function. For example, in *Beatrice Foods v. New England Printing*, the Federal Circuit explained:

> [W]hen an appellee has proven that damages are due, and the remand is merely to determine the proper quantum of injury, then it is not unreasonable that the bond remain effective during this recalculation period. Put another way, when an appellant has merely succeeded in having the case remanded for recomputation of damages, it would be a stretch to say that the appeal was "substantially" successful, or that the judgment was "substantially" reversed.[232]

The court added:

> [T]he surety remains liable when the question on remand is not whether a party will receive damages, but merely how the damages will be calculated . . . . If, after an appeal, there remains a question of whether *any* compensable harm was done, then the bond may be allowed to lapse. When the plaintiff has yet to prove any damages, it is unnecessary and unfair to ask the defendant to continue to provide a bond to ensure that money will be available should damages be proven. An appeal has been prosecuted to effect, then, when appellee must still prove on remand that he suffered a compensable harm.[233]

Similarly, in an unpublished opinion, the Western District of Louisiana evaluated whether a reduction—a recalculation—of damages should result in a discharge of the supersedeas bond.[234] Relying on two cases from the Fifth Circuit,[235] the court reasoned, "when a damages award is completely reversed by the appellate court, the bond should be discharged and the surety released but when the appellate court remands

---

232. Beatrice Foods Co. v. New England Printing & Lithographing Co., 930 F.2d 1572, 1576 (Fed. Cir. 1991); *see also* Franklinville Realty Co. v. Arnold Constr. Co., 132 F.2d 828, 829 (5th Cir. 1943) (continuing to hold the surety liable when remand was to determine whether the judgment "should be for the same or a less sum").

233. *Beatrice Foods*, 930 F.2d at 1576.

234. PHI, Inc. v. Apical Indus., Inc., No. 6:13-CV-00015, 2020 WL 1303965, at *1 (W.D. La. Mar. 17, 2020).

235. *Franklinville Realty Co.*, 132 F.2d at 829; *Neeley*, 848 F.2d at 660.

for a recalculation of damages, the bond should remain in place and the surety should not be released."[236]

Sureties may argue that the appeal was successful because the bonded judgment was no longer enforceable after the appeal; however, courts have generally held that if both liability *and* damages are certain, the sureties should not be discharged from their obligations under the bond.

3. Hybrid Situation

Occasionally, courts are faced with situations that fall in between the two examples listed prior. For example, in *Morrison Knudsen Corp. v. Ground Improvement Techniques*,[237] the supersedeas bond surety was appealing the trial court's decision to deny the surety's motion for discharge. Despite the fact that the Tenth Circuit had previously vacated the judgment in the underlying case with respect to damages, the trial court denied the surety's motion for discharge, characterizing the court's decision to remand as a remand "for a quantification of amounts due to [the judgment creditor]."[238] The Tenth Circuit concluded that the appellee was entitled to some form of damages; however, the court was prevented from affirming those portions of the judgment based solely on the fact that the district court failed to use a special verdict form.[239] The Tenth Circuit concluded:

> This case lies somewhere between a remand for mere recalculation of damages, i.e., *Beatrice Foods*, 930 F.2d at 1576, and one in which no sum of damages was properly proved and the entire judgment was vacated, i.e., *Neeley*, 848 F.2d at 660. Because [the judgment creditor] proved entitlement to some damages in the first trial, this case is more like *Beatrice Foods* and less like *Neeley*.[240]

---

236. *PHI, Inc.*, 2020 WL 1303965, at *1.
237. 532 F.3d 1063, 1067 (10th Cir. 2008).
238. *Id.* at 1069; *see* Morrison Knudsen Corp. v. Fireman's Fund Ins. Co., 175 F.3d 1221, 1261 (10th Cir. 1999).
239. *Morrison Knudsen Corp.*, 532 F.3d at 1071.
240. *Id.* (citing Beatrice Foods Co. v. New England Printing & Lithographing Co., 930 F.2d 1572, 1576 (Fed. Cir. 1991) (explaining that the surety is released only when an issue concerning the existence of any compensable harm remains)).

The court held that the bond principal had failed to prosecute its appeal "to effect," and observed that "although the judgment with respect to damages was vacated . . . this alone is not the touchstone of prosecuting an appeal 'to effect.'"[241] Therefore, the supersedeas bond remained enforceable.[242] However, even though the court determined that the surety was not discharged, the surety was able to persuade the court to stay execution against the supersedeas bond pending the surety's appeal and did not require the surety to post an additional supersedeas bond.[243]

As stated previously, any analysis regarding the discharge of a supersedeas bond upon an appellate court's decision should begin with the bond's specific language. In *Werbungs Und Commerz Union Austalt v. Collectors' Guild, Ltd.*,[244] the trial court was to determine whether the supersedeas bond had been discharged after the Second Circuit affirmed the original judgment as to liability, but vacated the damages award and remanded the issue for retrial.[245] The supersedeas bond provided as follows:

> [The surety] . . . does hereby undertake in the sum of three hundred thousand and no/100 ($300,000) that if [the judgment debtor] shall satisfy the judgment herein in full together with cost, interest and damages for delay, if for any reason the appeal is dismissed or if the judgment is affirmed, and shall satisfy in full such modification of the judgment and such costs, interest, and damages as the Appellate Court may adjudge and award, then this obligation shall be void, otherwise the same shall be and remain in full force and virtue.[246]

The court focused on the specific language of the bond, and concluded that the bond therefore remained in effect "unless one of two conditions is met: (1) the appellant satisfies the judgment after the appeal is either dismissed or the judgment is affirmed; or (2) the appellant satisfies any

---

241. *Id.* at 1071 n.5 (citing *Beatrice Foods*, 930 F.2d at 1576).
242. *Id.*
243. *Id.* at 1081–82.
244. 782 F. Supp. 870 (S.D.N.Y. 1991).
245. *Id.*; *see* Werbungs Und Commerz Union Austalt v. Collectors' Guild, Ltd., 930 F.2d 1021, 1028 (2d Cir. 1991).
246. Werbungs Und Commerz Union Austalt, 782 F. Supp. at 875.

modification of the judgment as the appellate court awards."[247] The parties ended up settling the case instead of retrying the damages portion on remand; however, because neither of the conditions for discharge of the bond had occurred, the court concluded that the surety's obligation remained in effect.[248]

V. Quick Reference Practice Tips

A. *Judicial Bonds' Relevance in Practice*

Judicial bonds arise in several circumstances. To name a few, judgment debtors may post a supersedeas or cost bond to stay enforcement of a judgment pending appeal, or a court may require the party seeking an injunction post an injunction bond to cover any damages arising from an unwarranted injunction. Regardless of how the supersedeas or cost bond arises, it is imperative to understand the mechanics of judicial bonds in practice.

1. Supersedeas and Cost Bonds

Generally, supersedeas or cost bonds may be required when the defendant (i.e., the judgment debtor) appeals a trial court's adverse decision.[249] Once judgment is entered, the judgment debtor becomes legally liable to the plaintiff (i.e., the judgment creditor) for the amount awarded.[250] Should the judgment debtor elect to appeal the trial court's decision, a judgment creditor may pursue the judgment debtor for the amount awarded during the appeal, unless the judgment debtor posts sufficient security to ensure payment of the judgment.[251]

Federal Rule of Civil Procedure 62 automatically stays execution on a judgment for 30 days. A judgment debtor may stay execution on a judgment beyond the 30-day period by providing security in a form and amount sufficient to protect the judgment creditor's interests.[252] Trial

---

247. *Id.*
248. *Id.*
249. *See* discussion *supra* Section I.A.
250. *Id.*
251. *Id.*
252. FED. R. CIV. P. 62(b); *see* discussion *supra* Section I.A.1.

courts have discretion to determine the form of security, but courts often require security in the form of a supersedeas bond.[253]

A supersedeas bond ensures that the judgment debtor can pay the amount of the judgment, including postjudgment interest and obligations potentially accruing during the appeal.[254] Although supersedeas bonds are more commonly posted by judgment debtors in an effort to benefit from the stay, supersedeas bonds can arise in a multitude of other situations. For example, third parties may be contractually obligated to post a supersedeas bond. This situation arises when an insurer or surety posts a supersedeas bond on behalf of its insured (i.e., the principal) to stay enforcement of a judgment against the principal. When the bond or policy, as the case may be, is potentially implicated, the surety or insurer may post a supersedeas bond to pursue the appeal. Alternatively, the insurer or surety could be required to post a supersedeas bond by the terms of the policy or bond.[255] No matter the party posting the bond, supersedeas bonds ensure that the judgment debtor can pay the amount of

---

253. *See* discussion *supra* Section I.A.1.

254. Beatrice Foods Co. v. New England Printing & Lithographing Co., 930 F.2d 1572, 1574 (Fed. Cir. 1991); *see supra* notes 40–46 and accompanying text.

255. Certain insurance policies and bonds require that the insurer/surety furnish bonds. Diana Shafter Gliedman, *Will Your Insurance Company Put up the Supersedeas Bond Required for Your Appeal?*, ANDERSON KILL POLICYHOLDER ADVISOR (Apr. 4, 2017), https://www.andersonkill.com/Publications/Will-your-insurance-company-put-up-the-supersedeas-bond-required-for-your-appeal; Kevin Risley, *Defending an Insured during the Appeal of an Adverse Judgment*, 8 J. TEX. INS. L. 18, 24–25 (2007) ("When part or all of the judgment against an insured is a covered loss . . . , the insurer may be subjecting itself to the risk of bad faith liability if it does not assist the insured in obtaining a bond for at least the covered portion of a loss."). Even when the policy language does not require that the insurer/surety furnish a supersedeas bond, some courts have held that the bond could constitute a necessary cost of the defense. *Id.* (citing Wiegert-Stathes v. Am. Fam. Mut. Ins. Co., No. A-08-1041, 2009 WL 3381578, at *7 (Neb. Ct. App. Oct. 20, 2009) ("We can envision that posting a supersedeas bond, by either posting cash or paying for a surety to post a bond, could be required as a 'cost of defense' in certain situations. The obvious example would be where the appealed judgment is less than the policy limits and the insured justifiably expects to be protected from levy while the adverse judgment is on appeal.")).

the judgment if the appeal fails while offering a benefit to the judgment debtor in the form of a stay on execution of the judgment.[256]

While cost bonds protect the judgment creditor's rights on appeal, the difference between the two is that the cost bond ensures payment of the judgment creditor's costs in the event the reviewing court affirms the trial court's decision.[257] Federal Rule of Appellate Procedure 7 grants the district court discretion to "require an appellant to file a bond or provide other security in any form and amount necessary to ensure payment of costs on appeal."[258] While Rule 7 does not define "costs on appeal," the trial court will consider the anticipated costs on appeal.[259] In the absence of a rule specifying the factors the court should consider when determining whether a cost bond is required, the trial court considers the following factors: "(1) the [judgment debtor's] financial ability to post a bond, (2) the risk that the [judgment debtor] would not pay the [judgment creditor's] costs if the appeal [fails], (3) the merits of the appeal, and (4) whether the [judgment debtor] has shown any bad faith or vexatious conduct."[260]

In short, supersedeas and cost bonds are similar in the sense that both bonds serve to protect the judgment creditor's rights on appeal. The difference between the two is that a supersedeas bond ensures payment of the judgment when the reviewing court affirms the trial court's decision, and a cost bond ensures payment of the judgment creditor's costs on appeal.

2. *Injunction, Attachment, and Replevin Bonds*

An injunction bond may be required to safeguard against damages suffered as a result of an incautiously granted injunction or temporary restraining order.[261] Similarly, attachment and replevin bonds secure damages resulting from a court's mistaken decision to award remedies

---

256. *See* discussion *supra* Section II.A.2.
257. *See supra* notes 3–6 and accompanying text.
258. *Id.*; FED. R. APP. P. 7.
259. *See supra* notes 9–29 and accompanying text.
260. *In re* Countrywide Fin. Corp. Customer Data Sec. Breach Litig., No. 3:08-MD-01998, 2010 WL 5147222, at *2 (W.D. Ky. Dec. 13, 2010) (quoting Chiaverini, Inc. v. Frenchie's Fine Jewelry, Coins & Stamps, Inc., No. 04-CV-74891, 2008 WL 2415340, at *1 (E.D. Mich. June 12, 2018)); *see supra* notes 7–8 and accompanying text.
261. *See* discussion *supra* Section I.B.

in the form of attachment or replevin.[262] Under Federal Rule of Civil Procedure 64(b), state law governs the availability and procedures relating to attachment and replevin, including whether an attachment or replevin bond is required.[263] However, due to the drastic nature of an injunction, Federal Rule of Civil Procedure 65(c) addresses injunction bonds differently.[264] Federal Rule of Civil Procedure 65(c) dictates that a preliminary injunction or temporary restraining order may be granted "only if the movant gives security in an amount that the court considers proper."[265] While this language seems more mandatory than permissive, a split of authority exists regarding whether Rule 65(c) requires that an injunction or temporary restraining order be accompanied with an injunction bond.[266]

Federal courts differ in their interpretation of Rule 65(c), and attachment and replevin bonds are governed by state law, so it is imperative that parties seeking relief determine whether an injunction, attachment, or replevin bond is a prerequisite to obtain the requested relief in the jurisdiction where the lawsuit is pending.[267]

B. Enforcement of Judicial Bonds in Practice

Parties may pursue the surety on a judicial bond when an appeal ensured by a supersedeas or cost bond is affirmed, or an injunction, attachment, or replevin bond secures the court's improvidently awarded remedies. To recover from the surety, a party will follow the procedures set forth in Federal Rule of Civil Procedure 65.1.[268]

Rule 65.1 authorizes the enforcement of judicial bonds in the underlying proceeding or in an independent action.[269] In practice, the judgment creditor will likely elect to enforce the judicial bond by filing a Rule 65.1 motion in the underlying proceeding to avoid the necessity of filing an independent action.[270] After the Rule 65.1 motion is filed, if the

---

262. *See* discussion *supra* Sections I.C.1, I.C.2.
263. *See* discussion *supra* Section I.C.
264. *See* discussion *supra* Section I.B.
265. FED. R. CIV. P. 65(c); *see supra* notes 76–84 and accompanying text.
266. *See supra* notes 82–94 and accompanying text.
267. *Id.*
268. FED. R. CIV. P. 65(c); *see* discussion *supra* Section II.
269. FED. R. CIV. P. 65(c).
270. *Id.*

surety opposes the motion, it may file a response, and the court will hold a hearing before issuing an order granting or denying the motion.

It is important to note that, until the court issues an order granting the Rule 65.1 motion and instructs the surety to deliver payment to the judgment creditor,[271] the principal may satisfy the obligation or make arrangements to satisfy the obligation. After payment is delivered to the judgment creditor, the judgment creditor will file a notice of satisfaction of the judgment with the court.

Conclusion

The central aim of a judicial bond is to provide security for parties that are deprived of their immediate right to execute on a judgment, have relinquished their right to act in a certain manner, or have surrendered their right to property pursuant to a specific rule or statutory provision. Understanding and appreciating the nuances of judicial bonds should assist the surety in ensuring proper procedure is followed by parties seeking to enforce its bond and could also potentially aid the surety in tailoring the bond conditions appropriately to ensure that its liability is triggered on the happening of the relevant event and limited to the penal sum of the judicial bond. The Federal Rules of Civil Procedure and Federal Rules of Appellate Procedure create a starting point in analyzing whether the court will require a particular judicial bond, the factors it will consider in determining the amount of judicial bonds, and the judgment creditors' rights with regard to enforcement of the bonds. Absent a specific rule or statutory provision addressing the judicial bond requirement, courts are typically afforded wide discretion to determine whether a judicial bond is required. Thus, meticulous attention to the form and language of the judicial bond, applicable rules, statutory provisions, and case law is essential.

---

271. Generally, payment is remitted directly to the judgment creditor. The exception arises when the underlying action was initiated in probate court.

CHAPTER 16

SEAS, SHIPS, AND SURETYSHIP

Maura Z. Pelleteri
Robert G. Lavitt

Introduction

Suretyship has a historical and, in fact, ancient connection with maritime endeavors. Surety lawyers' typical experience is with land-based activity and disputes and only infrequently with maritime matters and disputes. Despite this fact, suretyship in the context of admiralty law is important and integral in securing the rights afforded to those who are at risk or otherwise involved in a maritime activity. Suretyship and other forms of security peculiar to admiralty law and procedure ensure that maritime commerce continues unimpeded by freeing up cargo movement and the use of vessels while securing the rights of those impacted by maritime torts or contracts.

In addition to traditional maritime endeavors involving navigable waters and vessels, suretyship plays a critical role in near admiralty activity, such as vessel construction. While vessel repair is, with few exceptions, a maritime contract subject to admiralty jurisdiction, vessel construction is a land-based activity not considered a maritime contract. Whether a bond will be deemed a maritime contract subject to admiralty jurisdiction turns on the bond's underlying obligation and an evolving set of criteria as to the degree of maritime activity involved in that obligation.

This chapter provides a basic overview of admiralty jurisdiction, law, and procedure. It explains how suretyship is used in providing security to ensure that maritime commerce is unimpeded while protecting the rights of those involved in maritime contracts, torts, and other maritime endeavors.

I. Admiralty Jurisdiction

Admiralty jurisdiction in the United States has its roots in England, where admiralty courts tried maritime cases separately from the common law courts.[1] In enacting the Judiciary Act of 1789, Congress recognized the national importance of vesting federal courts with exclusive original jurisdiction over civil cases in admiralty. Federal courts' admiralty jurisdiction has long been deemed necessary because maritime suits affect commerce and international relations. In *Exxon Corp. v. Central Gulf Lines, Inc.*, the U.S. Supreme Court acknowledged that the "protection of maritime commerce" is what gives rise to federal courts' maritime jurisdiction.[2]

Article III, Section 2 of the U.S. Constitution grants federal district courts original subject matter jurisdiction over cases and controversies arising in admiralty. The codification of admiralty jurisdiction is found in 28 U.S.C. § 1333. That statute provides that federal district courts have original jurisdiction, exclusive of state courts of "[a]ny civil case of admiralty or maritime jurisdiction, saving to suitors in all cases all other remedies to which they are otherwise entitled."[3] Further, the Federal Rules of Civil Procedure apply to federal court cases of admiralty and maritime jurisdiction in conjunction with Supplemental Rules for Certain Admiralty and Maritime Claims A through G.[4]

The savings-to-suitors clause, found in 28 U.S.C. § 133(1), provides state courts with jurisdiction for in personam claims and bars removal to federal court absent a separate basis for federal jurisdiction. State courts have concurrent jurisdiction with federal courts over most maritime subject matters that do not involve in rem actions or determining vessel title. Federal courts have exclusive jurisdiction over in rem actions in admiralty.[5] State courts cannot have procedures with respect to in

---

1. Grant Gilmore & Charles L. Black, Jr., The Law of Admiralty 8–11 (2d ed. 1975).
2. 500 U.S. 603, 608 (1991).
3. 28 U.S.C. § 1333.
4. Until 1966, federal courts had separate dockets for admiralty cases where separate terminology and procedure were utilized. For instance, a complaint was called the "libel"; the plaintiff called the "libellant"; the defendant called the "respondent"; and admiralty lawyers called "proctors." In 1966, federal courts merged their civil and admiralty dockets. From then on, they used the Federal Rules of Civil Procedure combined with enacted Supplemental Rules for Certain Admiralty and Maritime Claims A through G for handling admiralty suits.
5. Madruga v. Superior Ct., 346 U.S. 556, 560 (1954).

rem actions involving maritime liens on vessels.[6] Federal admiralty jurisdiction does not provide the right to a jury trial regarding actions in rem. However, claimants bringing in personam cases under the savings-to-suitors clause are entitled to a jury trial. Should there be a separate basis for federal jurisdiction, such as removal under 28 U.S.C. § 1331, and the matter is removed, the claimant does not lose the right to a jury trial.

A. *Vessels and Navigable Waters*

A necessary element for any matter arising in admiralty is that a vessel must be involved. In admiralty law, a vessel includes "every description of watercraft or other artificial contrivance used or capable of being used, as a means of transportation on water."[7] The Supreme Court has defined "vessels" as "all navigable structures intended for transportation."[8] Whether an object is a vessel is best determined by answering in the affirmative the question of whether it is a floating structure capable of transporting something over water.[9]

Admiralty jurisdiction in the United States covers all maritime activity occurring on navigable waters—that is, all waters used or capable of being used in interstate or foreign commerce. For instance, navigable waters under admiralty jurisdiction includes a lake on the border of two states,[10] but not a manmade canal on which artificial obstructions prevent commercial waterborne activities.[11] The U.S. Coast Guard regulations define "navigable waters" as "waters that are subject to the ebb and flow of the tide and/or are presently used, or have been used in the past or may be susceptible for use to transport interstate or foreign commerce."[12] Further, once a determination of navigability is made, it "applies laterally over the entire surface of the waterbody, and is not extinguished by later actions or events which impede or destroy navigable capacity."[13] The Admiralty Extension Act extends admiralty and maritime jurisdiction to all cases of injury or damage to person or property caused by a

---

6. Coast Engine & Equip. Corp. v. Sea Harvester, Inc., 461 F. Supp. 1053, 1055 (W.D. Wash. 1978), *aff'd*, 641 F.2d 723 (9th Cir. 1981).
7. 1 U.S.C. § 3.
8. Cope v. Vallette Dry-Dock Co., 119 U.S. 625, 629 (1887).
9. GILMORE & BLACK, *supra* note 1, at 33.
10. Wilburn Boat Co. v. Fireman's Fund Ins. Co., 348 U.S. 310 (1955).
11. Tundidor v. Miami-Dade Cnty., 831 F.3d 1328, 1332 (11th Cir. 2016).
12. 33 C.F.R. § 329.4 (1986).
13. *Id.*

vessel on navigable waters, even though the injury or damage is done or consummated on land.[14]

B. Maritime Contracts and Torts

Admiralty jurisdiction extends over maritime contracts and torts. Only those contracts for maritime services support admiralty jurisdiction. Whether a contract is maritime is a question of law[15] and generally involves a case-by-case analysis.[16] Conceptually, the test involves an examination of the nature and character of the contract, and whether the contract has reference to maritime service or maritime transactions.[17] In determining whether a dispute involves a maritime contract, the decisive factor is not whether a vessel was involved or where the contract was formed or performed, but rather whether "the principal objective of a contract is maritime commerce."[18]

Whether a contract is maritime can have serious implications, especially in the offshore oil and gas industry and in mixed services contracts, when it comes to risk allocation, the governing law, and the enforceability of contractual indemnity provisions. Following the U.S. Supreme Court's 2004 decision in *Norfolk Southern Railway Co. v. Kirby*, courts have used various factors to try to make more predictable the determination of whether a maritime contract is involved in a dispute, often with inconsistent results. In 2018, the Fifth Circuit, sitting en banc, sought to harmonize itself with *Kirby* by abandoning its previous six-part test for determining whether a contract was maritime[19] and adopting

---

14. 46 U.S.C. § 30101(a).
15. Barrios v. Centaur, L.L.C., 942 F.3d 670, 680 (5th Cir. 2019).
16. Kossick v. United Fruit Co., 365 U.S. 731, 735, *reh'g denied*, 366 U.S. 941 (1961).
17. Norfolk S. Ry. Co. v. Kirby, 543 U.S. 14, 24 (2004).
18. *Id.* at 25–26.
19. *See* Davis & Sons, Inc. v. Gulf Oil Corp., 919 F.2d 313 (5th Cir. 1990) (test for maritime contract determination involved answers to the following questions: "1) what does the specific work order in effect at the time of injury provide? 2) what work did the crew assigned under the work order actually do? 3) was the crew assigned to work aboard a vessel in navigable waters? 4) to what extent did the work being done relate to the mission of that vessel? 5) what was the principal work of the injured worker? and 6) what work was the injured worker actually doing at the time of injury?").

a two-part test.[20] The Fifth Circuit's new two-prong maritime contract inquiry required that a contract must (1) be for services to facilitate activity on navigable waters and (2) provide, or the parties must expect, that a vessel will play a substantial role in the completion of the contract.[21] *Doiron* involved a work order for "flowback"[22] services on an oil well in navigable waters. Although there was no expectation that a vessel would be used to perform the work order, after it was determined that some heavy equipment was needed to complete the job, a crane barge was used. Unfortunately, a worker was injured when he was struck by the crane, whose owner asserted admiralty jurisdiction in the resulting lawsuit. The Fifth Circuit ruled that the work order was non-maritime because it found that the use of the vessel, while important, was an insubstantial part of the job and not work the parties expected to be performed.[23]

A year later, the Fifth Circuit extended its ruling in *Doiron* to a "mixed services contract" in *Barrios v. Centaur, L.L.C.*[24] In *Barrios*, an employee of a barge lessor was injured while offloading a generator from a crew boat to the barge after the crew boat separated from the barge.[25] The injured worker sued the crew boat owner and the lessor of the barge. In turn, the crew boat owner sued the barge lessor for contractual indemnity pursuant to a dock contract between the barge lessor and the dock owners.[26] The lessor argued that the state's anti-indemnity statute applicable to land-based construction contracts[27] rendered the dock contract's indemnity provision unenforceable. The Fifth Circuit disagreed, finding that both

---

20. *In re* Larry Doiron, Inc., 879 F.3d 568, 575–76 (5th Cir.) (en banc), *cert. denied*, 138 S. Ct. 2033 (2018).
21. *Id.* at 576.
22. Flowback in the oil and gas industry refers to process fluids collected at the surface after fracturing operations are completed.
23. *Id.* at 577.
24. 942 F.3d 670, 680 (5th Cir. 2019), *cert. denied sub nom.* Centaur, L.L.C. v. River Ventures, L.L.C., 140 S. Ct. 2675 (2020); *see also Larry Doiron, Inc.*, 879 F.3d at 576 n.3 (while *Doiron* dealt with determining the maritime or non-maritime nature of contracts involving oil and gas exploration, drilling, and production, the standard enunciated in *Doiron* would help in determining whether a non-oil-and-gas contract is maritime if the activity involves maritime commerce and work from a vessel).
25. *Barrios*, 942 F.3d at 674.
26. *Id.*
27. Louisiana Revised Statutes section 9:2780.1(B) is a Louisiana statute that renders null, void, and unenforceable any provision in, or collateral

prongs of *Doiron* were satisfied.[28] The court ruled that the dock contract was a maritime contract because the services to be performed facilitated the loading, offloading, and transportation of coal and petroleum via vessels on navigable water and the contracting parties had an expectation that a vessel would play a significant role in the completion of the work.[29] Accordingly, because maritime law does not prohibit indemnity obligations, the indemnity provision was enforceable.[30]

Traditionally, admiralty jurisdiction over tort actions was largely determined by application of a locality test—that is, whether the tort occurred on navigable waters. The enactment of the Extension of Admiralty Jurisdiction Act extended admiralty jurisdiction to include "cases of injury or damage to person or property, caused by a vessel on navigable waters, even though the injury or damage is done or consummated on land."[31] A series of Supreme Court decisions[32] have refined admiralty jurisdiction to extend to torts occurring on navigable waters when the incident bears a significant relationship to traditional maritime activity and arises in a manner having a potentially disruptive effect on maritime commerce.[33] For instance, admiralty jurisdiction was found in a case in which a pleasure vessel passenger was injured while diving off the vessel into shallow but navigable waters, because there was a potential for maritime commerce to be affected.[34]

Admiralty jurisdiction also extends to certain actions based on federal statutes, including the Jones Act,[35] the Longshore and Harbor

---

to, a construction contract that purports to indemnify or hold harmless a person from liability for its own negligence, or has the effect of doing so.

28. *Barrios*, 942 F.3d at 680.

29. *Id.* at 680–81.

30. *Id.* at 682. *See also* Couvillion Grp., LLC v. Quality First Constr., LLC, No. 19-676, 2021 WL 860241 (E.D. La. Mar. 8, 2021) (ruling that a contract for the relocation of a hydraulic flood control gate on the Mississippi River was a maritime contract, applying the two-prong test, and permitting parole evidence as to contracting parties' intent).

31. 46 U.S.C. § 30101(a).

32. *See* Jerome B. Grubart, Inc. v. Great Lakes Dredge & Dock Co., 513 U.S. 527 (1995); Foremost Ins. Co. v. Richardson, 457 U.S. 668 (1982); Exec. Jet Aviation, Inc. v. Cleveland, 409 U.S. 249 (1972).

33. *In re* Germain, 824 F.3d 258, 273–74 (2d Cir. 2016) (discussing extensively the jurisprudential history of the nexus test in its ruling).

34. *Id.* at 273.

35. 46 U.S.C. §§ 30104–30105.

Workers' Compensation Act,[36] the Death on the High Seas Act, the Suits in Admiralty Act,[37] and the Oil Pollution Act of 1990.[38]

1. Vessel Repair and Construction

A shipbuilding contract is "a contract made on land, to be performed on land,"[39] and therefore maritime jurisdiction does not extend to vessels under construction. But once a vessel is launched and put into service, repair contracts are maritime contracts subject to admiralty jurisdiction and attachment of maritime liens. If a vessel has been taken out of navigation for major reconstruction, that contract is not within admiralty jurisdiction.[40] Furthermore, admiralty jurisdiction will not apply if a ship loses its status as a vessel. This can occur when the work performed on it alters its character or takes it out of navigation by removing it from maritime commerce for prolonged periods of time.[41]

Under the federal Commercial Instruments and Maritime Liens Act,[42] repair work on existing vessels, including modification, conversion, refurbishment, refitting, and routine equipment repair, is subsumed under the statute's furnishing of "necessaries."[43] The term "necessaries" has been interpreted broadly to include any item reasonably needed for the venture in which the vessel in engaged. For instance, fuel used to operate a vessel is a necessary and suppliers have a maritime lien on the vessel for which it supplied fuel. However, fuel delivered by a supply vessel

---

36. 33 U.S.C. §§ 901–950.
37. 46 U.S.C. §§ 30901–30918.
38. *Id.* §§ 2701–2720.
39. People's Ferry Co. of Bos. v. Beers, 61 U.S. 393, 402 (1857).
40. Robert E. Blake Inc. v. Excel Env't, 104 F.3d 1158, 1160–61 (9th Cir. 1997) (ruling that a contract to activate a vessel from reserve fleet was not maritime because the ship was removed from navigation until the activation was complete).
41. *See* Evansville & Bowling Green Packet Co. v. Chero Cola Bottling Co., 271 U.S. 19, 22 (1926) (wharf boat lost vessel status when no longer used as a means of transportation, did not carry freight from one place to another, and evidenced a permanent location by being connected to the city's water, electricity, and telephone system).
42. 46 U.S.C. § 31310 *et seq.* (formerly the Ship Mortgage Act of 1920).
43. *Id.* § 31301(4).

for use to operate another vessel is not considered a necessary and no maritime lien attaches.[44]

While vessel repair contracts are not required to be bonded, as a practical matter, vessel owners often will obtain bonds securing the performance and payment obligations attendant to large-dollar vessel repair. Because there is no statutory requirement for bonding of private vessel repair contracts, such bonds are conventional bonds. Sureties that bond vessel repair contracts subject themselves to maritime liens when there is a breach as well as the possibility of an in rem action against the vessel.

Shipbuilding is considered preliminary to a vessel's primary function; as long as a ship is under construction it is not in navigation and, therefore, not subject to maritime contracts. Conversely, once a vessel is complete and has been put into service, it becomes an instrument of maritime commerce and subject to admiralty jurisdiction. Maritime contracts must have a direct connection with maritime commercial transaction or navigation, and "such a connection is lacking in a contract to create a new ship, or if not lacking entirely, it is remote and contingent, so that it is not perceptible at the time that the contract goes into effect."[45] In that regard, a breach of a shipbuilding contract is not subject to admiralty jurisdiction. Accordingly, bonding a shipbuilding contract is not considered a maritime contract but one governed by state law and the terms of the bond. Further, a contract to supply materials for the construction of a vessel is a non-maritime contract.

C. Maritime Liens

A valid maritime lien is a prerequisite for any action in admiralty in rem. A maritime lien and a proceeding in rem are correlative; "where one exists, the other can be taken, and not otherwise."[46] "A maritime lien is a nonpossessory security device that is created by operation of law."[47] In the United States, maritime liens are based on the fiction of a "personified" vessel.[48] This fiction holds that is the vessel itself that is held liable for its

---

44. Martin Energy Servs., L.L.C. v. Bourbon Petrel M/V, 962 F.3d 827, 832 (5th Cir. 2020).
45. The Manhattan, 46 F. 797, 799–800 (D. Wash. 1891).
46. The Rock Island Bridge, 73 U.S. 213, 215 (1867).
47. 2 ROBERT FORCE ET AL., ADMIRALTY AND MARITIME LAW 2-1 (2012).
48. ROBERT FORCE, ADMIRALTY AND MARITIME LAW 173 (2d ed. 2013).

torts and for contractual obligations undertaken on its behalf to facilitate the accomplishment of its mission.[49] "The basic purpose of the maritime lien is to provide security for a claim while permitting the ship to proceed on her way in order to earn the freight or hire necessary to pay off the claim."[50] "As a corollary to this doctrine, an action based on a maritime lien may only be brought *in rem* against the vessel itself."[51]

Thus, any action pursuant to Supplemental Rule C ("In Rem Actions") must be premised on the existence of a valid maritime lien at the time that the action was filed.[52] Courts will uphold the assertion of a lien as long as the lien arose at the time the structure was still a vessel.[53] In a majority of cases the same facts that sustain in rem liability of a vessel also provide a basis for in personam liability of the vessel owner.[54]

A maritime lien is different from a general common-law lien in several respects.[55] A common-law lien is a charge on property for the payment of a debt, whereas a maritime lien is a special property right in a vessel given to a creditor by law as security for a debt or claim arising from some service rendered to the ship to facilitate her use in navigation or from an injury caused by the vessel in navigable waters. Every maritime lien involves the assertion of a lien against a vessel in navigation. Conceptually, a maritime lien is best understood as a lien arising out of maritime contracts or torts that:

1. Cannot be created by stipulation of the parties;
2. Can only be executed by an admiralty court exercising in rem jurisdiction;
3. Is generally, but not necessarily, "secret" in that recordation is not a prerequisite; and

---

49. *Id.*
50. *Id.*
51. *Id.*
52. *See* Belcher Co. of Ala., Inc. v. M/V Maratha Mariner, 724 F.2d 1161, 1163 (5th Cir. 1984); Amstar Corp. v. S/S Alexandros T., 664 F.2d 904, 908 (4th Cir. 1981); Rainbow Line, Inc. v. M/V Tequila, 480 F.2d 1024, 1028 (2d Cir. 1973) (in rem jurisdiction in the admiralty exists only to enforce a maritime lien).
53. Vlavianos v. The Cypress, 171 F.2d 435 (4th Cir. 1948), *cert. denied*, 337 U.S. 924 (1949).
54. FORCE, *supra* note 48, at 174.
55. GILMORE & BLACK, *supra* note 1, at 587–89.

4. Is "indelible" in the sense that it stands "against the world" until validly and fully extinguished through payment of the underlying claim or adjudicated by an admiralty court sitting in rem.[56]

D. Enforcing Maritime Liens—In Rem Actions

A maritime lien can only be enforced by an admiralty court sitting in rem. The in rem action is one of the strongest weapons in prosecuting a maritime lien claim because it allows claimants to arrest an offending vessel pursuant to the Supplemental Rules for Certain Admiralty and Maritime Claims. The federal court's jurisdiction over maritime liens is exclusive of state courts. To enforce the lien, the plaintiff is required to file a verified complaint in federal court naming the vessel as a party and requesting the court to order the vessel's arrest. Rule C of the Supplemental Rules permits a plaintiff to arrest a vessel by having a warrant of arrest issued and served on the vessel. A U.S. marshal then physically takes the vessel into custody. The arrest of a vessel serves several important purposes, including obtaining jurisdiction over the vessel and prejudgment security for the plaintiff's claims against the vessel itself. In the event that a vessel's owner fails to adequately compensate a plaintiff for his or her damages or post adequate security with the court for the plaintiff's claims to secure the vessel's release from the arrest, the plaintiff is entitled to have the court sell the vessel at a U.S. marshal's sale and use the proceeds of the sale to satisfy the plaintiff's in rem claim against the vessel. The sale of a vessel in an action in rem is not a typical judicial sale of property, as it divests all existing liens and mortgages of any kind.

If it is determined that it is not in the client's best interest to arrest a vessel, then another option available to preserve the plaintiff's maritime tort lien is to file a notice of the lien with the U.S. Coast Guard National Vessel Documentation Center.[57] Filing this notice of lien, which can be

---

56. *Id.* However, certain maritime liens are recorded, such as a preferred ship mortgage, discussed *infra* Section I.D, and those whose liens relate to documented vessels under 46 U.S.C. § 31343.

57. The National Vessel Documentation Center located in Falling Waters, West Virginia, is the only entity authorized to issue Certificates of Documentation, which are "required for vessels engaged in commercial trade and is optional for vessels five net tons and over engaged in recreational" use and activities. To file a notice lien claim with the National Vessel Documentation Center, the lien claim must include

accomplished with minimum effort and cost, puts the world on notice of the lien and places a cloud on the vessel's title. Most vessel owners will eventually satisfy the lien, because having a lien may violate the terms and conditions of the vessel owner's preferred ship mortgage or deter potential buyers from purchasing the vessel.

E. Quasi In Rem Attachment

Quasi in rem jurisdiction provides a method for a court to obtain limited jurisdiction over a person not physically present in its jurisdiction nor subject to its long-arm jurisdiction, but who has property in the jurisdiction such as a vessel, bank account funds, a receivable account, or cargo. Quasi in rem attachment actions are based on the property rights of a person absent from the jurisdiction. While the court may lack personal jurisdiction over the defendant, the court has jurisdiction over the defendant's tangible and intangible property. The property subject to the attachment need not be related to the cause of action and is attached in a process similar to arrest. The case against the defendant can thereafter be litigated and a judgment entered up to the value of their interest in the attached property.

Procedurally, Supplemental Rule B requires the filing of a verified complaint seeking attachment of defendant's property that is in a garnishee's possession up to the amount sued for.[58] The complaint must be filed with an affidavit from the plaintiff or plaintiff's attorney stating that to the affiant's knowledge, information, and belief the defendant cannot be found within the district.[59] The court then reviews the complaint and affidavit and, if justified, authorizes the process of attachment and garnishment. The garnishee serves an answer and answers to interrogatories within 21 days of service. Further, defendants must file an answer within 30 days of process being executed.

---

specific information and notices (e.g., vessel name and official number; claimant's name and address; date of lien established; total amount of liens claims; whether signed, dated, acknowledged, or notarized; and notice sent to vessel owner, etc.); *see* 46 U.S.C. § 31343 and *Coast Guard Deputy Commandant for Operations (CG-DCO)*, U.S. COAST GUARD, https://www.dco.uscg.mil (last visited Jan. 17, 2022).

58. FED. R. CIV. P. SUPP. R. B(1)(a).

59. *Id.*; *id.* B(1)(b).

Issues regarding the degree of ownership of the attached property under Supplemental Rule B have been the subject of several cases. In *Shipping Corp. of India Ltd. v. Jaldhi Overseas Pte Ltd.*, the Second Circuit noted that for "maritime attachments under Rule B . . . the question of ownership is critical."[60] In *Jaldhi,* the Second Circuit dealt with the attachment of electronic funds held by an intermediary bank and whether the defendant had an undefined property interest in the electronic funds at issue.[61] Because under New York law electronic fund transfers in the temporary possession of an intermediary bank were neither property of the originator nor of the beneficiary, they could not be the subject of a Rule B attachment.[62]

F. Amount of Security

The amount of security required in litigation involving a vessel in rem is prescribed by 28 U.S.C. § 2464, which provides:

> Except in cases for forfeiture under any law of the United States, whenever a warrant of arrest or other process *in rem* is issued in any admiralty case, the United States marshal shall stay the execution of such process, or discharge the property arrested if the process has been levied, on receiving from the respondent or claimant of the property a bond or stipulation in double the amount claimed by the libelant, with sufficient surety, to be approved by the judge of the district court where the case is pending, or, in his absence, by the collector of the port, conditioned to answer the decree of the court in such case.[63]

This statute, in conjunction with Supplemental Rule E(5), specifies the requirements for posting security with respect to special bonds and general bonds to obtain the release of property. With respect to special bonds, Supplemental Rule E(5) provides that the amount and nature of a special bond shall be set by the court, the clerk, or by stipulation of the

---

60. 585 F.3d 58, 69 (2d Cir. 2009).
61. *Id.* at 68–69, 71.
62. *Id.* at 71.
63. 28 U.S.C. § 2464(a). 31 U.S.C. §§ 9301–9309 establish the standards of acceptable surety security or substituted surety security and the qualifications for a surety corporation to furnish a surety bond in cases allowed by federal law.

parties in cases of actual or imminent arrest or attachment of property. Should the court be called upon to act, it must set:

> [T]he principal sum of the bond or stipulation at an amount sufficient to cover the amount of plaintiff's claim fairly stated with accrued interest and costs, but the principal sum shall in no event exceed (i) twice the amount of the plaintiff's claim or (ii) the value of the property on due appraisement, whichever is smaller. The bond or stipulation shall be conditioned for the payment of the principal sum and interest thereon at 6 percent per annum.[64]

Supplemental Rule E provides that in the case of a general bond or stipulation, the bond must be filed with a sufficient surety and guarantee that it will respond to any judgment of the court in any actions that have been or may be brought in the court in which the vessel was attached or arrested. As long as the amount secured by the general bond or stipulation is at least double the aggregate amount claimed by plaintiffs in all the actions, execution of process against the vessel is stayed. Judgments are satisfied against the bond or stipulation as if a special bond or stipulation had been filed with respect to each of the actions filed.[65]

G. Priority of Maritime Liens

A single vessel may be subject to numerous parties' maritime liens against it. If an attached vessel is sold for less than the amount of all the liens, a court must determine the distribution of the sale proceeds among the various lienholders. While not treated as a lien per se, the expenses incurred by the U.S. marshal in arresting and keeping the vessel have top priority. Then, in descending order of priority, are:

1. liens for seamen's wages and maintenance and cure;
2. salvage and general average liens;
3. tort liens including property damage from collision, personal injury, and death;
4. pre-mortgage liens for necessaries;

---

64. FED. R. CIV. P. SUPP. R. E(5)(a).
65. *Id.* E(5)(b).

5. preferred ship mortgage liens;[66]
6. liens for necessaries;
7. state-created liens of a maritime nature;
8. liens for penalties and forfeitures under federal law;
9. preferred non-maritime liens including tax liens;
10. attachment liens; and
11. maritime liens in bankruptcy.[67]

In addition to the rules for ranking maritime liens by type, admiralty law ranks maritime liens by timing. Unlike in common-law liens, such as real estate liens, the more recent maritime lien has priority over an earlier maritime lien. This theory is known as the "last in time, first in right" rule and one of the purported reasons for this rule is that those that provided goods or services to keep the vessel in service do so for the benefit of earlier-in-time lien holders.[68]

*1. **Preferred Ship Mortgage***

Historically, an agreement to finance a vessel was not considered a maritime contract. In order to encourage lenders to finance vessels, Congress enacted the Ship Mortgage Act of 1920, which created the preferred ship mortgage. The Ship Mortgage Act set forth the requirements for recording preferred ship mortgages,[69] provided that only maritime liens would have priority over ship mortgages, and established the means for enforcing preferred mortgage liens in admiralty.[70]

---

66. See 46 U.S.C. § 31326(b)(1), which provides that upon foreclosure, the preferred mortgage lien has priority over all claims against the vessel except claims for expenses and fees allowed by the court, costs imposed by the court, and preferred maritime liens.
67. Marilyn Raia, *Maritime Liens for Necessaries 101*, PAC. MAR. MAG. (July 8, 2010), http://www.bullivant.com/maritime-liens-for-necessaries-101.
68. *See also* Kristen van de Biezenbos, *A Sea Change in Creditor Priorities*, 48 U. MICH. J.L. REFORM 595 (2015) (discussing the tension between admiralty and bankruptcy courts' differing prioritization of unsecured maritime lienholders and secured ship creditors with emphasis on maritime tort victims).
69. To be eligible, the vessel owner must be a U.S. citizen and the vessel must be constructed in the United States.
70. Dietrich v. Key Bank, N.A., 72 F.3d 1509, 1513 (11th Cir. 1996).

The creation of a preferred ship mortgage gives the mortgage higher priority than many competing claims to a vessel that may arise. Lenders routinely secure their financing with a preferred ship mortgage. Without it, at default, a lender will rank near the bottom of the maritime creditors. Once a vessel is completed and satisfies the size, citizenship, and documentation requirements of the federal Commercial Instruments and Maritime Liens Act[71] and the preferred ship mortgage is filed with the National Vessel Documentation Center, it is the recognized and enforceable encumbrance against the vessel and its rank and priority attaches.[72] The act requires substantial compliance with the formal prerequisites for filing. The preferred ship mortgage's rights are enforceable in admiralty actions in rem and actions on the mortgage indebtedness can be brought in personam in admiralty or in state court.[73]

II. Suretyship in Admiralty

It is axiomatic that the obligations the surety undertakes are governed by the underlying commitment. If the surety guarantees the performance of any part of the underling maritime contract, the bond itself is a maritime contract.[74] Sureties that bind themselves to perform a contract determined to be a maritime contract subject themselves to admiralty jurisdiction. The surety that guarantees to compensate for a breach of a maritime contract, however, is not subject to admiralty jurisdiction.[75] Actions against sureties on a performance bond can be brought in admiralty if "the surety's obligation under the bond is the same as that of the original promisor, but not if the surety is obligated only to pay a sum of money and the duties of the original promisor were otherwise."[76]

---

71. 46 U.S.C. § 31301 *et seq.*
72. *Id.* § 31322.
73. *Id.* § 31325.
74. Aqua-Marine Constructors, Inc. v. Banks, 110 F.3d 663, 671–72 (9th Cir.), *cert. denied sub nom.* Polaris Ins. Co. v. Aqua Marine Constructors, Inc., 522 U.S. 933 (1997).
75. Pac. Sur. Co. v. Leatham & Smith Towing & Wrecking Co., 151 F. 440, 443–44 (7th Cir. 1907).
76. *Aqua-Marine*, 110 F.3d at 672.

A. *Special Admiralty Procedures*

The former "Admiralty Rules" were rescinded in 1966 by the adoption of the Federal Rules of Civil Procedure for admiralty procedure along with the Supplemental Rules for Certain Admiralty and Maritime Claims. Since their promulgation, Supplemental Rules A through G have preserved the special procedures of arrest and attachment that are unique to admiralty law. The Supplemental Rules apply to procedures in admiralty and maritime claims within the meaning of Federal Rule of Civil Procedure 9(h) with respect to the remedies of maritime attachment and garnishment, actions in rem, possessory, petitory and partition actions, and actions for exoneration from or limitation of liability.[77] Practitioners should be mindful of all applicable local admiralty rules as well.[78]

The Supplemental Rules directly implicate and acknowledge the use, requirements, and importance of commercial surety bonds as a favored form of maritime security.

1. Special Bonds

The release of arrested property for a specific in rem action can be obtained following the issuance of a "special bond" as provided for in Supplemental Rule E(5)(a). Special bonds permit the release of a maritime attachment or the stay of garnishment or process in rem once security conditioned on responding to any judgment with respect to that action is issued. Special bonds guarantee payment of the judgment that may be obtained against the vessel but are limited only to that action. In this way, owners can continue to use property that was attached while

---

77. FED. R. CIV. P. SUPP. R. A.

78. *E.g.*, Local Admiralty Rule 65.1 of the U.S. District Court for the Eastern District of Louisiana provides:

> In all cases where the surety on a bond or stipulation for the release of a vessel or other property under seizure is not a corporate surety holding a certificate of authority from the Secretary of the Treasury, and the bond or stipulation is not approved as to amount and nature by the party at whose instance the vessel or other property is detained, or by his or her attorney, the vessel or property shall not be released without an order of a judge approving the surety, or in the absence of a judge, the clerk, after reasonable notice and opportunity to be heard.

providing assurance to the claimant that they are secured in any judgment obtained against the vessel. The parties can by stipulation set the amount of special bonds or letters of undertaking or, if they are unable or refuse to do so, the court will set the amount of the bond.[79] Special bonds can be obtained commercially, usually through agencies that specialize in maritime and admiralty bonds.

Special bonds do not foreclose the attachment of the property with respect to other lienholders, but only as to the lien made the subject of the underlying in rem action. If a special bond is not obtained to secure the release of an arrested vessel, and the vessel is sold to meet the resulting judgment, the proceeds of the sale are deposited in the registry of the court. Third persons who claim an interest in the proceeds may then intervene.[80] Those who did not participate in the proceeding but who have claims against the vessel that were obliterated by the sale are then permitted to assert their claims against the fund into which the vessel has been converted. The proceeds remaining after the libel has been satisfied represent the vessel. The surety bond provides no such residual fund for other claimants. It is posted to assure the payment of a single claim, not to stand in place of the vessel for all claims that might be asserted against her.[81]

2. Letters of Undertaking

A letter of undertaking is commonly obtained and is a form of a stipulation for value provided for under Supplemental Rule E(5)(c). A traditional letter of undertaking serves the same function as a special bond in that the owner may agree to appear and defend as if the vessel had been arrested and agrees to pay any judgment that may be entered against the vessel, even if the vessel is subsequently lost.[82] A letter of undertaking has the same legal effect as a formal release of vessels through a bond or stipulation. However, at least some courts hold that a plaintiff cannot be compelled to accept a letter of undertaking as opposed to a bond issued

---

79. Fed. R. Civ. P. Supp. R. E(5)(a).
80. *See id.* E(9)(c) (proceeds of sale to be paid into registry and disposed of according to law).
81. Overstreet v. Water Vessel Norkong, 706 F.2d 641, 643–44 (5th Cir. 1983).
82. Panaconti Shipping Co. v. M/V Ypapanti, 865 F.2d 705, 707–08 (5th Cir. 1989).

by a surety approved by the state insurance commissioner.[83] Moreover, by accepting a letter of undertaking, the plaintiff does not waive his or her in rem rights against the vessel; rather, the letter of undertaking perfects in rem jurisdiction in the absence of an arrest of the vessel.[84]

3. General Bonds

If a vessel is attached or arrested, a vessel owner may file a general bond or stipulation, with sufficient surety and with court approval, to stand in answer to any judgment of such court to any or all actions that may be brought in that court.[85] Posting a general bond releases a vessel and applies to all actions that may be brought for the vessel's arrest or attachment of property of the vessel. Supplemental Rule E(5)(b) requires that the bond amount must be double the sum of all asserted and pending claims against the vessel.[86] Further, any judgments rendered or remedies ordered may be made against the general bond as if a special bond had been filed with respect to each of the pending actions. However, if a special bond or stipulation is given with respect to a particular case, the liability of the general bond (or stipulation) ceases as to that case.[87] The expense associated with posting a general bond is obviously greater than that of a special bond.

4. Security for Costs and Countersecurity

Supplemental Rule E(2)(b), in conjunction with Rule 54 of the Federal Rules of Civil Procedure, sets forth the procedure for obtaining security for costs and expenses in an admiralty action.[88] Under the rule, at the filing of the complaint, the appearance of the defendant or any other party, or at any later time, the court may require the plaintiff, defendant, or any other party to give security for costs and expenses that may be awarded against that party by "any interlocutory order or by final

---

83. *See, e.g.*, Thyssen Inc. v. M/V Sena Deniz, No. 00-3455, 2000 WL 1772652, at *1 (E.D. La. Nov. 30, 2000).
84. Cont'l Grain Co. v. Fed. Barge Lines, Inc., 268 F.2d 240, 243 (5th Cir. 1959).
85. FED. R. CIV. P. SUPP. R. E(5)(b).
86. *Id.*
87. *Id.*
88. *Id.* E(2)(b).

judgment, or on appeal by any appellate court."[89] Security for costs and expenses are subject to Rule 54 of the Federal Rules of Civil Procedure and other relevant statutes.[90] Although a court has broad discretion in setting the amount of security, an attaching plaintiff can only be required to post security under this rule for a limited range of costs.[91]

Security for a counterclaim in an admiralty action is governed by Supplemental Rule E(7) of the Supplemental Rules. The rule provides that if a person who has given security for damages in the original complaint asserts a counterclaim arising out of the same transaction or occurrence at issue in the original complaint, the plaintiff shall give security for the counterclaim unless the district court, for cause shown, directs otherwise.[92] The original proceeding is stayed until security is given unless the court rules otherwise.[93] The district court has broad discretion in determining whether and in what amount countersecurity should be ordered.[94] The purpose of the rule is to place the parties on equal footing with regard to security.[95] While a court has broad discretion in determining the security, notions of fairness and equity should guide the court.[96]

A court may reject security for counterclaims deemed totally frivolous although countersecurity is required for a colorable counterclaim.[97] Defendants must consider the costs and expenses they would incur, including the cost of the premium for bonds obtained to release an

---

89. *Id.*
90. *Id.*
91. Result Shipping Co., Ltd. v. Ferruzzi Trading USA Inc., 56 F.3d 394, 401–02 (2d Cir. 1995) (security for costs limited and would not include attorneys' fees defendant incurred for defending against the attachment); Canaveral Port Auth. v. Tug Penobscot, No. 17-1079, 2017 WL 11017605, at *4 (M.D. Fla. June 15, 2017) ("Rule E(2)(b) gives the court power to require security for costs and expenses to be posted by the party initiating the in rem seizure to protect parties affected by the seizure."
92. FED. R. CIV. P. SUPP. R. E(7).
93. *Id.*
94. *Result Shipping*, 56 F.3d at 399–400; Afram Lines Int'l, Inc. v. M/V Cap Yiannis, 905 F.2d 347, 349 (11th Cir. 1990).
95. *Result Shipping*, 56 F.3d at 399; Washington-Southern Navigation Co. v. Balt. & Phila. Steamboat Co., 263 U.S. 629, 638 (1924).
96. *Result Shipping*, 56 F.3d at 399.
97. Ocean Line Holdings Ltd. v. China Nat'l Chartering Corp., 578 F. Supp. 2d 621, 627–28 (S.D.N.Y. 2008).

attachment, as the basis for the amount required rests upon expenses that the court decides would be "taxable as costs" in favor of the prevailing party.[98]

5. Arbitration Security

A person bound by an arbitration agreement may nevertheless bring an action in admiralty including in rem and quasi in rem actions, subject to a stay of the admiralty action. The Federal Arbitration Act's provisions for a stay of judicial proceedings do not deprive an admiralty court of jurisdiction pending the conclusion of the arbitration proceeding.[99] If the subject matter of the controversy is within admiralty jurisdiction, the claimant may begin the proceeding by arresting the vessel or attaching other property. The court has jurisdiction to direct the parties to proceed with arbitration while retaining jurisdiction over the property and thereafter to enter its decree upon the arbitration award.[100] Section 8 of the Federal Arbitration Act[101] provides that the maritime prejudgment remedies of attachment and arrest are available for claims subject to arbitration.[102] An arrest or attachment action can be brought even if the arbitration has already begun,[103] or even if the forum designated for arbitration is outside the United States.[104] "Usually, a party will secure *in rem* jurisdiction over a vessel, within the limitations period, before seeking arbitration, so as to secure a possible *in personam* award."[105]

---

98. *Id.* at 627 (citing *Result Shipping*, 56 F.3d at 401–02).
99. 9 U.S.C. § 3.
100. *Id.* § 8; *see also* The Anaconda v. Am. Sugar Refin. Co., 322 U.S. 42, 45 (1944).
101. 9 U.S.C. §§ 1, 8.
102. Greenwich Marine, Inc. v. S.S. Alexandra, 339 F.2d 901, 904 (2d Cir. 1965).
103. Unitramp, Ltd. v. Mediterranean Brokerage & Agents, S.A.S., No. 93-2831, 1993 WL 386298, at *1 (E.D. La. Sept. 20, 1993) (quoting Reefer Express Lines Pty, Ltd. v. Petmovar S.A., 420 F. Supp. 16 (S.D.N.Y. 1976)).
104. Paramount Carriers Corp. v. Cook Indus., Inc., 465 F. Supp. 599, 600, 602 (S.D.N.Y. 1979).
105. Petroleos Mexicanos Refinacion v. M/T King A, 554 F.3d 99, 109 (3d Cir. 2009). *Cf.* ProShipLine Inc. v. Aspen Infrastructures, Ltd., 609 F.3d 960 (9th Cir. 2010).

6. Limitations of Liability

The Limitation of Liability Act[106] was enacted by Congress to "encourage shipbuilding and to induce capitalists to invest money in this branch of industry."[107] The act provides a type of action "peculiar to the admiralty and maritime context"[108] by allowing a vessel owner to limit his or her liability for negligence claims to the value of the vessel.[109] Owners and/or charterers facing claims arising from any "embezzlement, loss, or destruction of any property, goods, or merchandise shipped or put on board the vessel, any loss, damage, or injury by collision, or any act, matter, or thing, loss, damage, or forfeiture, done, occasioned, or incurred, without the privity or knowledge of the owner" or charterers can be exonerated or have their liability limited to the value of the vessel and pending freight.[110]

In a limitation action, the first task will be to establish that the incident occurred on "navigable waters" subject to the jurisdiction of a federal court. If the incident occurred on navigable waters, a court must then (1) determine what acts of negligence or conditions of unseaworthiness caused the accident; and (2) determine whether the ship owner had knowledge or privity of those acts or conditions.[111] An owner or charterer can only be exonerated if the collision, cargo damage, or personal injury occurred without the privity and knowledge of the owner.[112] Where the owner, or the owner's employees or independent contractors, have daily contact with the vessel, it will be difficult, if not impossible, to prove that the owner did not have knowledge or some level of involvement, oversight, or responsibility in the operation of the vessel or the circumstances of the accident.

Procedurally, the owner of a vessel files a petition in federal court seeking total exoneration from or limitation of liability of damages caused by the negligence of the vessel's captain or crew.[113] If the amount of the vessel owner's liability is determined to be insufficient to pay all losses

---

106. Limitation of Liability Act of 1851, 46 U.S.C. §§ 30501–30512.
107. Lewis v. Lewis & Clark Marine, Inc., 531 U.S. 438, 446 (2001).
108. Tandon v. Captain's Cove Marina of Bridgeport, Inc., 752 F.3d 239, 243 (2d Cir. 2014).
109. Am. Car & Foundry Co. v. Brassert, 289 U.S. 261, 264 n.1 (1933).
110. 46 U.S.C. § 30505.
111. Farrell Lines, Inc. v. Jones, 530 F.2d 7, 10 (5th Cir. 1976).
112. 46 U.S.C. § 30505.
113. *Id.* § 30511(a); FED. R. CIV. P. SUPP. R. F.

in full, and the portion available to pay claims for personal injury is less than $420 times the tonnage of the vessel, that portion will be increased to $420 times the tonnage of the vessel.[114] That portion may be used only to pay claims for personal injury or death. The vessel owner may bring a civil action in a federal district court for limitation of liability within six months after a claimant gives the owner written notice of a claim.[115] When such an action is brought, the owner has the option of depositing with the court for the benefit of claimants "the amount equal to the value of the owner's interest in the vessel and pending freight, or approved security."[116]

In a limitation action, the court issues a stay of all pending proceedings and brings all claims arising from the underlying casualty into a federal court concursus proceeding. Once a limitation action is filed and security is deposited, the district court enjoins the further prosecution of claims brought against the ship owner arising from the subject casualty.[117] The court will also set a time period during which all claimants must file their respective claims in the limitation action. A concursus of claims allows all actions rising out of a marine casualty to be adjudicated in a single proceeding. It also provides a great benefit to the ship owner by making all potential litigants bring their claims in a single federal forum rather than suing piecemeal in multiple jurisdictions.

Courts have held the Limitation of Liability Act applicable to both commercial[118] and recreational vessels, including jet skis,[119] a floating boarding house,[120] a 15-foot powerboat,[121] a barge,[122] and a 16-foot

---

114. 46 U.S.C. § 30506(b).
115. *Id.* § 30511.
116. *Id.* § 30511(b).
117. Fed. R. Civ. P. Supp. R. F(3). *See also In re* Complaint of Paradise Holdings, Inc., 619 F. Supp. 21, 27 (D. Haw. 1984), *aff'd*, 795 F.2d 756 (9th Cir. 1986).
118. *In re* Germain, 824 F.3d 258, 273–74 (2d Cir. 2016) (limitation of liability applied and admiralty jurisdiction applied in a matter when a pleasure boat passenger was injured while diving into shallow but navigable waters).
119. Keys Jet Ski, Inc. v. Kays, 893 F.2d 1225 (11th Cir. 1990).
120. *In re* Kan. City Bridge Co., 19 F. Supp. 419 (W.D. Mo. 1937).
121. Feige v. Hurley, 89 F.2d 575 (6th Cir. 1937).
122. *In re* P. Sanford Ross, 1968 F. 921 (E.D.N.Y. 1912).

catamaran.[123] Oil rigs and fixed towers,[124] however, are not considered vessels subject to limitations actions. In addition, a vessel dismantled for scrap metal is no longer a vessel and the owners are not protected by the act for any claim arising from the dismantling process.[125]

The most cited example of a limitation action was filed in the United States by the parent company of the White Star Line involving the April 15, 1912, sinking of the *Titanic*. The value of the *Titanic* was appraised at the sum of $97,772.12. The value of a sunken or damaged vessel was based on the salvage, which in 1912 consisted largely of the *Titanic*'s life boats.

III. Conventional Performance Guarantees in Maritime Setting

As noted previously, "[a] performance bond which compensates an obligee for loss in the event of nonperformance by the principal obligor is not a maritime contract."[126] Nevertheless, contractual performance guarantees constitute an important area of suretyship in a maritime setting. Whether the surety's rights are within admiralty jurisdiction is subject to an analysis of whether the underlying obligation to which the surety guarantees performance is a maritime contract. As has been discussed, a mere payment guarantee is not a maritime contract. Whether it be through a performance bond or through a letter of undertaking, performance guarantees are often employed in maritime chartering and affreightment contexts. A prime example of this (albeit in a statutory setting) is 46 U.S.C. § 57518, which requires the charterer of a government vessel to furnish acceptable performance security.

A. *Statutory Passenger-Related Protections*

Federal law mandates that the owner or charterer of vessels, whether American or foreign, provide proof of financial responsibility by a combination of insurance, bonds, qualified self-insurance, or other evidence of financial responsibility to stand available for the payment

---

123. *In re* Boca Grande Club, Inc., 715 F. Supp. 341 (M.D. Fla. 1989).
124. *In re* U.S. Air Force Tex. Tower No. 4, 203 F. Supp. 215 (S.D.N.Y. 1962).
125. *In re* Wepfer Marine, Inc., 344 F. Supp. 2d 1120, 1124–26 (W.D. Tenn. 2004).
126. Aqua-Marine Constructors, Inc. v. Banks, 110 F.3d 663, 671 (9th Cir. 1997).

of any judgment for damages for death or injury of persons on voyages to or from U.S. ports.[127] The requirement is limited to vessels that have accommodations for 50 or more passengers.[128] If a bond is used it must be issued by a bonding company authorized to do business in the United States.[129] The security's amount is determined by the number of passenger accommodations on the biggest vessel of the given owner's or charterer's fleet.[130]

Likewise, federal law mandates that a person in the United States may not arrange, offer, advertise, or provide transportation on a vessel with accommodations for 50 or more passengers and that embark passengers from U.S. ports unless the person has filed with the Federal Maritime Commission evidence of financial responsibility to indemnify passengers for nonperformance of the transportation.[131] In the event a bond is used to establish proof of financial responsibility, it must be issued by a bonding company authorized to do business in the United States.[132] This mandatory financial security has been applied to reimburse passengers when a booked cruise was cancelled.[133] At present, the obligee on such bonds is the Federal Maritime Commission. The commission is currently considering a number of changes that the Surety & Fidelity Association of America has resisted, including creating a direct right of action by individual passengers against the bond. Given the literally thousands of passengers on many cruise ships, handling such claims would be burdensome.

B. Security for Maritime Safety and Environmental Disasters

Several federal statutes provide for the filing of a bond or other security satisfactory to the secretary to foster the availability of deemed statutory compliance under exceptional circumstances. These statutes include

---

127. 46 U.S.C. § 44103.
128. *Id.* § 44101(1).
129. *Id.* § 44103(d)(2).
130. *Id.* § 44103(b)(1), (b)(2).
131. *Id.* § 44102.
132. *Id.* § 44102(c).
133. Effjohn Int'l Cruise Holdings, Inc. v. A&L Sales, 346 F.3d 552, 567–68 (2003) (holding that the statute does not grant maritime liens to passengers whose fares for a canceled voyage were unrefunded).

programs for safety of ports and waterways,[134] inland navigation rules,[135] actions for violation of vessels' clean hulls,[136] management of vessels,[137] and the carriage of dangerous cargo.[138] In addition to these statutes, maritime endeavors are often subject to international laws and treaties not mentioned in this chapter.

In the event of an environmental disaster, federal statutes mandate proof of financial responsibility be provided by maritime operators. These statutes include the Clean Water Act,[139] the Oil Pollution Act of 1990,[140] the Federal Water Pollution Control Act,[141] the Vessel Financial Responsibility Act,[142] and the Outer Continental Shelf Lands Act.[143] Proof of financial responsibility can consist of bonds or other security devices authorized by the regulatory authorities. The Oil Pollution Act provides that financial responsibility be part of the Oil Spill Liability Trust Fund and the Outer Continental Shelf Lands Act provides for an Offshore Oil Spill Pollution Fund.

Conclusion

Suretyship in admiralty law is an established and practical method for providing security for those at risk or otherwise involved in a maritime endeavor while ensuring that maritime commerce continues unimpeded. Suretyship also provides valuable protections for maritime activity not

---

134. 33 U.S.C. § 1232 (title 33, chapter 25, Ports and Waterways Safety Program).
135. *Id.* § 2072 (title 33, chapter 34, Inland Navigation Rules).
136. *Id.* § 3854 (title 33, chapter 51, Clean Hulls: Action on Violation, Penalties, and Referrals).
137. 46 U.S.C. § 3205 (from title 46, subtitle II, part B, chapter 32, Management of Vessels).
138. *Id.* § 3718 (title 46, subtitle II, part B, chapter 37, Carriage of Liquid Bulk Dangerous Cargoes).
139. 33 U.S.C. § 1321 *et seq.*
140. *Id.* § 2701 *et seq.* (the Oil Spill Liability Trust Fund is addressed at 33 C.F.R. pt. 136 (2010)).
141. As amended (33 U.S.C. § 1251 *et seq.*; 33 C.F.R. § 153.413 (2010)).
142. Vessel financial responsibility (including evidence of financial responsibility through suretyship) is dealt with at 33 C.F.R. pt. 136 (2010)), and, particularly, 33 U.S.C. § 2716.
143. Title III (Offshore Oil Spill Pollution Fund), 43 U.S.C. § 1811 *et seq.*; 33 C.F.R. pt. 135 (2010) (particularly §§ 135.205, 135.209–.211, 135.223).

necessarily subject to admiralty jurisdiction, such as vessel construction. This chapter has explained some fundamentals of admiralty jurisdiction, law, and procedure as well as discussed certain federal statutes governing maritime undertakings. The reader now hopefully understands the important role suretyship plays in the context of admiralty law and maritime activities.

CHAPTER 17

LOST INSTRUMENT BONDS

David C. Veis
Laura P. Nash
Meeghan H. Tirtasaputra
Jonathan Schneider

Introduction

Lost instrument bonds fall under the classification of indemnity bonds. If any valuable written instrument is lost, stolen, or destroyed, securing a lost instrument bond may allow the owner of the lost instrument to obtain a duplicate of that instrument.

The lost instrument bond ensures that the issuer of the instrument does not incur additional liability should the original instrument reemerge and be negotiated.[1] The bond requires the owner of the lost instrument to indemnify the issuer from a third-party claim on the instrument, and the surety that issued the bond acts as a secondary guarantor of the owner's indemnity obligation.

For example, a bank writes Mr. X a certified check for $100,000, but Mr. X loses the check before he cashes it. The bank may condition the issuance of a replacement check on Mr. X obtaining a lost instrument bond to ensure that it will only pay the $100,000 once. If, after Mr. X cashes the replacement check, a third party cashes the original check, Mr. X, pursuant to the bond, will be required to indemnify the bank for the additional $100,000 it was required to pay. If Mr. X does not or cannot do so, the surety that issued the bond will indemnify the bank and will then look to Mr. X to indemnify it.

Instruments that may require a lost instrument bond include, but are not limited to:

---

1. *See* Miles v. Wells Fargo Bank, No. 09-CV-02973-CMA, 2010 WL 3894048, at *2 (D. Colo. Sept. 30, 2010).

- Stock certificates[2]
- Promissory notes[3]
- Deeds of trust[4]
- Traveler's checks[5]
- Veteran benefits certificates[6]

See Appendix A and Appendix B at the end of this chapter for two examples of lost instrument bonds.

I. The Relationships Formed upon the Issuance of a Lost Instrument Bond

Typically, a lost instrument bond is an agreement between three parties: (1) the principal, the owner of the lost instrument; (2) the obligee, the person or institution that issued the instrument; and (3) the surety, the issuer of the lost instrument bond.[7] The principal and the surety both promise to indemnify the obligee from additional liability that may arise upon the reemergence of the original instrument. This constitutes the traditional tripartite relationship under which the surety's obligation is secondary to that of the principal. Under general tenets of suretyship, the surety is entitled to be indemnified by the principal for any loss.[8] Notwithstanding the foregoing tenet, the surety will likely require the principal to enter into a separate agreement that specifically gives the surety broad indemnity rights (discussed further in Section V.A.).

Not all lost instrument bonds follow the traditional tripartite relationship. Institutions dealing with large volumes of original instruments sometimes adopt policies requiring that a lost instrument

---

2. *See* First Sw. Corp. v. Lampton, 724 So. 2d 988, 994 (Miss. Ct. App. 1998).
3. *See* Tropicana Shipping v. Empresa Nacional Elcano, 366 F.2d 729, 734 (5th Cir. 1966).
4. *See* Evans v. U.S. Fid. & Guar. Co., 127 A.2d 842, 845 (D.C. 1956).
5. *See* Fid. & Cas. Co. of N.Y. v. Harrison, 274 S.W. 1002 (Tex. Ct. App. 1925).
6. *See* United States v. Cont'l Cas. Co., 139 F.2d 770 (4th Cir. 1944).
7. *See Lampton*, 724 So. 2d at 994 (for reissuance of lost stock certificate pursuant to Uniform Commercial Code section 8-405(2), the bond "should be executed by the owner of the stock, as principal, and by a recognized surety or indemnity company, as surety").
8. *Harrison*, 274 S.W. at 1004.

bond be obtained by in-house document custodians whenever the originals cannot be located.[9] In this scenario, there is typically no principal requesting the reissuance of the instrument, and the bond is written with only two parties in mind, the surety and the obligee.

This type of a direct indemnity bond is more akin to an insurance policy than a traditional surety bond. Under this type of lost instrument bond, the surety's liability is not secondary but direct, and the surety cannot expect to recover a potential bond loss as it does under a traditional tripartite bond. On the other hand, the surety's potential risk of receiving a claim in this type of scenario is probably less than when dealing with individual owners of lost instruments. Dealing with a large-volume institutional client has other undeniable advantages in underwriting and risk assessment. Institutional clients typically have established internal controls to minimize the risk of loss in connection with their instruments. Additionally, the surety is typically dealing with a limited bond form providing a cap on liability.

II. The Bond Penalty Amount—Fixed Versus Open Penalty

There are two types of lost instrument bonds: fixed penalty bonds and open penalty bonds.

A. Fixed Penalty Bonds

Fixed penalty bonds apply to instruments that have a fixed dollar amount assigned to them, such as certified checks, certificates of deposit, or any items with a fixed or determinable value.

While calculations of fixed penalties will differ depending on the type of lost instrument and other circumstances, the fixed penalty is generally "not more than twice principal and accrued interest of the security on the date of delivery of the bond."[10] Institutional issuers will

---

9. *See* GOVERNMENT NATIONAL MORTGAGE ASSOCIATION, GINNIE MAE MORTGAGE-BACKED SECURITIES PROGRAM DOCUMENT CUSTODIAN MANUAL app. V-01, at 3-7, 3-8 (2016) [hereinafter GINNIE MAE DOCUMENT CUSTODIAN MANUAL], https://www.ginniemae.gov/issuers/issuer_tools/Documents/2016_document_custody_manual.pdf.

10. *Lampton*, 724 So. 2d at 993 (quoting EGON GUTTMAN, MODERN SECURITIES TRANSFERS ¶ 18.02[8][a] (3d ed. 1987)); *see also* THE LAW OF MISCELLANEOUS AND COMMERCIAL SURETY BONDS 247 (Todd C. Kazlow & Bruce C. King eds., 2001).

typically have their own formulas fixing the amount of the bond, as well as their own prescribed bond form. For instance, Ginnie Mae requires a bond penalty in the amount that is the remaining principal balance on the note plus 20 percent, or, for certain mortgage types, in the amount of a formula-based "Maximum Claim Amount" of the loan.[11]

B. Open Penalty Bonds

Open penalty bonds apply to instruments with changing values, such as stock certificates, which may appreciate or depreciate.

The open penalty bond gives additional security to the obligee by ensuring that the bond will provide adequate coverage even if the value of the underlying security rises dramatically before a claim is made. To the surety, however, an open penalty bond presents an unlimited and unpredictable risk, which will cause the surety to apply greater scrutiny on the bond principal's indemnity and/or collateral pledged.

Fixing the bond penalty for instruments with fluctuating values is not an easy endeavor. Limited guidance is found in the Uniform Commercial Code provisions governing investment securities. Uniform Commercial Code section 8-405 provides that a lost instrument bond must be "sufficient." What is considered "sufficient" may vary depending on the instrument and may ultimately have to be determined by a court.[12] As one court grappling with the question of whether a lost instrument bond penalty was sufficient noted, "[D]ifficult questions arise as to the meaning of a 'sufficient indemnity bond.' No precise rule has been stated because of the different kinds of securities that may be involved, with the

---

11. GINNIE MAE DOCUMENT CUSTODIAN MANUAL, *supra* note 9, app. V-I.
12. *See* Kircher v. Superior Ct., No. A125577, 2009 WL 3349339, at *2–3 (Cal. Ct. App. Oct. 19, 2009) (where the court remanded the case to the trial court, instructing it that it needs to determine whether or not the bond is sufficient in order to further determine whether money seized should be returned to the petitioner); *see also In re* Max Sugarman Funeral Home, Inc., 94 B.R. 16, 17 (Bankr. D.R.I. 1988) ("[T]he form, the amount, and the sufficiency of the bond generally, are matters within the discretion of and for determination by the bankruptcy court."); *see also* Cent. States, Se. & Sw. Areas Pension Fund v. Sloan, No. 89 C 5073, 1990 WL 103594, at *1 (N.D. Ill. June 29, 1990) ("Objections to the form of the bond or to the sufficiency of the surety shall be determined by the court.").

consequence that there is a variety of losses that might be sustained by the issuer."[13]

Courts that have dealt with the issue of the bond penalty generally interpret the Uniform Commercial Code's sufficiency requirement favorably to the obligee and with an eye toward providing the obligee full indemnity and protection from liability, holding that the bond penalty should be in the amount encompassing "any liability or expense, including attorney fees, to which [the obligee] may be subjected by reason of the reappearance of the original securities."[14] For this reason, including expenses, attorneys' fees, and costs as part of the bond penalty is also viewed as reasonable, because it is consistent with the purpose behind Uniform Commercial Code section 8-405: protecting the issuer from liability that may arise where the original certificate is transferred to a bona fide purchaser.[15]

On the other hand, "[w]here a nonconvertible debt security is involved, the problem of sufficiency is relatively simple" since the issuer's maximum exposure is "limited by the sum of principal, accrued interest, and concomitant expenses," thus fixing the penalty.[16] The penalty is generally not more than twice principal and accrued interest of the security on the date of delivery of the bond.[17] Nonconvertible, nonparticipating preferred shares, particularly if callable, may be treated similarly.[18]

One bright-line rule with respect to the bond penalty is that its reasonableness and sufficiency must be determined as of the time when the bond is requested and based upon the circumstances and the value of the instrument existing at the time,[19] not in hindsight or at the time a claim was made.

---

13. *Lampton*, 724 So. 2d at 993 (quoting RONALD A. ANDERSON, UNIFORM COMMERCIAL CODE § 8-405:14 (3d ed. 1996)).
14. *Id.* (under the specific facts of the case, the bond penalty in the amount of 110 percent of the principal and 125 percent of interest on the underlying lost debentures was upheld as reasonable).
15. THE LAW OF MISCELLANEOUS AND COMMERCIAL SURETY BONDS, *supra* note 10, at 247.
16. EGON GUTTMAN, MODERN SECURITIES TRANSFERS ¶ 19.14 (4th ed. 2018).
17. *Id.*
18. *Id.*
19. *Lampton*, 724 So. 2d at 993–94.

III. The Scope of the Surety's Liability in the Event of a Claim on a Lost Instrument Bond

Due to the circumstances necessitating the issuance of lost instrument bonds, courts tend to interpret the scope of the risk covered by the bond broadly and, arguably, with a bias toward imposing liability on the surety.

A. Third-Party Forgery or Fraud Does Not Relieve the Surety of Liability

One of the general principles of suretyship is that "fraud by a creditor (*i.e.*, someone claiming a benefit under the bond) touching the surety contract annuls it."[20] Because the only rightful claimant under the lost instrument bond is the obligee, the foregoing principle has little application in the context of lost instrument bonds, so long as the obligee was not involved in the fraud and did not act in bad faith. As exemplified in *Fidelity & Casualty Co. of New York v. Harrison*,[21] forgery or fraud by third parties does not negate coverage under the bond.

Harrison involved a bond relating to lost American Express traveler's checks. The principal purchased a large amount of traveler's checks at the American Express office in Paris, France, before traveling to New York.[22] Upon arrival in New York, he reported the traveler's checks lost or stolen.[23] American Express agreed to pay him the value of the lost checks without surrendering the originals but required the principal to post a lost instrument bond.[24] Subsequently, all of the traveler's checks resurfaced and were presented for payment to American Express by third parties. After paying them out, American Express made a claim against the lost instrument bond, and the surety satisfied it.[25]

In the surety's indemnity action against the principal, the principal defended the action on the basis that his signatures on the checks were forged.[26] The principal cross-complained against American Express, arguing that due to the forgeries, its payment of the forged checks was

---

20. Rosenberg v. Bank of N.Y., 186 A.D. 2d 496, 496 (N.Y. 1992).
21. 274 S.W. 1002 (Tex. Ct. App. 1925).
22. *Id.*
23. *Id.* at 1002–03.
24. *Id.* at 1003.
25. *Id.*
26. *Id.*

unauthorized and improper.[27] The principal additionally argued that the loss was not covered under the bond because American Express was under no legal obligation to honor the forged checks and that it therefore had no right to demand payment from the surety.[28]

The court rejected the principal's arguments, finding that the surety's payment to American Express was proper and that the forgery of the checks by third parties did not excuse the surety from liability on the bond, or the principal's indemnity obligation to the surety.[29] The court found that the risk of forgery on the lost traveler's checks was one of the risks covered under the bond:

> Since the checks by their terms were payable upon presentation and surrender, it is clear that it was within the contemplation of the parties that they might thereafter be presented by persons claiming the right to collect them, and with the name of the defendant countersigned thereon . . . by third parties.[30]

The court further observed that banks and other commercial institutions lack the expertise to determine whether the resurfaced instrument is genuine, which is one of the factors necessitating the posting of a lost instrument bond.[31] The surety, however, does not bear this risk alone, because in conjunction with issuing the bond, it obtains an unconditional indemnity promise from the principal.[32]

B. *The Obligee's Mistake or Neglect May Not Release the Surety of Liability*

With respect to other common types of bonds, such as construction payment and performance bonds, the surety may be entitled to certain

---

27. *Id.*
28. *Id.*
29. *Id.* at 1005–06; *cf.* Schlitz v. Thomas, 61 Cal. App. 635 (1923) (holding that in order to entitle surety to reimbursement, it must appear that the surety's payment was made under compulsion, that is, under legal obligation, and not as a "volunteer").
30. *Harrison*, 274 S.W. at 1005.
31. *Id.*
32. *Id.* at 1004, 1005.

defenses if the obligee's conduct contributes to or exacerbates the loss.[33] In contrast, the lost instrument bond surety may be held liable even where the obligee's loss was caused entirely by the obligee's own mistake or neglect. The difference in treatment stems from courts' views that the risk of such mistake is one of the risks covered under the bond. *United States v. Continental Casualty Co.*[34] demonstrates that the obligee can "mistakenly" issue the replacement instrument in the wrong amount or misidentify the instrument and the instrument's owner, and still be held liable for the full amount of the lost instrument bond.

Continental Casualty involved two bond claims brought by the U.S. Veterans Administration (VA) relating to the reissuance of lost veteran benefit certificates (a form of negotiable instrument). Pursuant to a federal statute then in effect,[35] the VA was authorized to require that a lost instrument bond be posted as a condition for the reissuance of veteran benefit certificates (similar to the current requirements under the Uniform Commercial Code relating to the reissuance of lost securities).[36]

In the first bond claim, the VA failed to reduce the face value of the replacement certificate despite the veteran-principal specifically informing the VA that he had previously cashed out half of the certificate's value. Although the principal asked the VA to issue the replacement certificate only on the balance that the VA verified he could still collect, the VA issued the replacement certificate in the original full amount.[37] After the veteran cashed out the reissued certificate, the VA realized its overpayment and made a bond claim.[38] The surety defended the claim on the ground that the VA's loss was not covered under the bond because the loss was caused by the VA's own mistake in calculating the outstanding value of the certificate, failing to account for its own prior payments.[39] The appellate court disagreed, holding that, under the terms of the lost instrument bond, the surety promised to indemnify and save harmless

---

33. *See, e.g.*, Dragon Constr., Inc. v. Parkway Bank & Tr., 678 N.E.2d 55 (Ill. Ct. App. 1997) (obligee's action prejudicing the surety's interests exonerates the bond (construction performance bond)); *see also* Sch. Bd. of Escambia Cnty., Fla. v. TIG Premier Ins. Co., 110 F. Supp. 2d 1351 (N.D. Fla. 2000).
34. 139 F.2d 770 (4th Cir. 1944).
35. World War Adjusted Compensation Act, 38 U.S.C. § 642 (1926).
36. *Continental Cas.*, 139 F.2d at 771.
37. *Id.*
38. *Id.*
39. *Id.*

the VA from any damage "in consequence of the granting of relief on account of said adjusted service certificate."[40] The court reasoned that the VA would not have sustained the loss but for the reissuance of the certificate and, therefore, the loss was covered under the literal terms of the bond.[41] Although the foregoing holding was sufficient to impose liability on the surety, the court took it a step further and held that imposing liability on the surety was consistent not only with the literal terms of the bond but also with its "true meaning,"[42] which was to serve the veteran-principal while protecting the government from "*any* loss."[43] The fact that the loss was caused by the obligee's mistake, its issuance of the replacement certificate in the wrong amount, did not provide the surety with a defense to the claim.

In the second bond claim, the obligee made a mistake regarding the identity of the instrument owner. When the veteran-principal applied for reissuance of a service certificate by the VA, the VA issued a replacement for twice the claimed amount, mistakenly relying on service records of a different person with the same name but residing in a different city.[44] Subsequently, both the principal and his namesake cashed out their certificates, resulting in overpayment by the VA and prompting the VA's claim against the lost instrument bond.[45] In granting relief to the VA, the appellate court held that the "carelessness" of the VA did not constitute a valid defense to the bond claim.[46] The court rejected the surety's evidence of fraud and collusion between the two veterans as irrelevant, finding that it was immaterial whether the reissuance of the lost certificate was a result of fraud or mere mistake, because the terms of the bond impose liability on the surety without this distinction.[47] As in the first claim, the fact that the loss was caused by the obligee's mistake, its issuance of the replacement certificate to the wrong person, did not provide the surety with a defense to the claim.

As an alternative defense to the second claim, the surety sought rescission of the lost instrument bond on the theory of mutual mistake,

---

40. *Id.*
41. *Id.* at 772.
42. *Id.*
43. *Id.* (emphasis added).
44. *Id.*
45. *Id.*
46. *Id.* at 772–73.
47. *Id.*

arguing that the bond and the replacement certificate were both issued with the wrong person in mind.[48] The court held the defense of mutual mistake inapplicable, explaining:

> [The bond was given to] aid in a situation caused by *someone's* mistake or neglect and also to safeguard the United States against loss if the issuance of the duplicate certificate should prove to have been mistaken. Under these circumstances, the rule has no relevance that the parties who contract upon the assumption that a certain state of facts or fact exists should be relieved from their bargain if the assumption is erroneous.[49]

Thus, the lost instrument bond surety may be held liable where the *issuance* of the replacement instrument is the result of the obligee's mistake, and where the bond was *written* based on mistaken information. *Continental Casualty* further held that the traditional doctrine of mutual mistake, which generally supports a claim for rescission of contract, is inapplicable to lost instrument bonds.[50]

Decided in the midst of World War II, *Continental Casualty* is in many respects a product of its time and political climate. With the nation at war and the VA charged with the weighty task of taking care of the returning war heroes and numerous benefit claims, it was easier for the court to allocate the risk of "someone's mistake or neglect" to the surety. Also of note is that the bond form at issue in the case was based upon the World War Adjusted Compensation Act, a wartime statute that is no longer in effect.[51] Nevertheless, no published decisions have attempted to distinguish or limit the holdings of *Continental Casualty.* Considering the dearth of case law dealing with the issue of the obligee's mistake or neglect, *Continental Casualty* and its expansive interpretation of the scope of risks covered by lost instrument bonds remains good law and presents a significant hurdle to the surety contemplating denial of coverage based on the obligee's conduct.

---

48. *Id.* at 773.
49. *Id.* (emphasis added).
50. *Id.*
51. 38 U.S.C. § 642 (1926).

C. The Surety Is Not Liable to Third Parties

A lost instrument bond exists solely to protect the obligee. Thus, the issuing surety is only liable to the obligee and not to third-party claimants.

If there *is* a bright-line rule with respect to lost instrument bonds, it is that a lost instrument bond surety is not liable to any claimant other than the obligee and cannot be subject to liability for bad faith resulting from the surety's handling of a bond claim presented by third parties.[52]

The leading case on point is *Broadwater v. Old Republic Surety.*[53] In that case, the plaintiff, LeAnne Broadwater, purchased a stock certificate in Check Rite International from an investment company, which, in turn, had purchased it from the putative original owner, Fletcher.[54] At the time of Broadwater's purchase, the certificate was still registered to Fletcher.[55] After the transfer of the certificate to Broadwater, Fletcher reported the certificate as lost and stolen and requested its reissuance from Check Rite's transfer agent, Atlas.[56] As a condition for the reissuance of the stock certificate, Fletcher, as the principal, posted a lost instrument bond written by Old Republic Surety's predecessor in interest, Northwestern Surety (collectively, Old Republic Surety), as surety, and naming Check Rite and Atlas as the obligees.[57]

Several years later, after the value of the stock had risen significantly, Broadwater attempted to negotiate her certificate, only to be told that the certificate had been reported as lost or stolen and was the subject of a "stop transfer" notice.[58] When Broadwater contacted Atlas, the transfer agent, she was referred to Old Republic Surety.[59]

---

52. *See* Beardmore v. Am. Summit Fin. Holdings, LLC, No. CIV.01-9948(DWF/SRN), 2002 WL 523899, at *6 (D. Minn. Apr. 5, 2002) ("The purpose of such a bond is to protect the interests of the issuer, not third-parties. While third-party interests may be ultimately protected in the event that the issuer may become liable for injury to a third-party bona fide purchaser, the bond is an instrument the issuer may choose to use to protect against that risk.").
53. 854 P.2d 527 (Utah 1993).
54. *Id.* at 529.
55. *Id.*
56. *Id.*
57. *Id.*
58. *Id.*
59. *Id.*

The surety's claims counsel contacted Broadwater, requesting that she provide proof of ownership and, in the same communications, offering to settle the claim for the amount Broadwater originally paid for the stock, $0.31 per share.[60] Broadwater refused, demanding that the surety instead provide her replacement stock certificate so that she could sell it at the appreciated value.[61] In the meantime, during the several months the surety investigated Broadwater's claim, the value of Check Rite's stock fluctuated wildly, rising well above $1 per share, then drastically dropping.[62] In the end, the surety denied Broadwater's claim, advising her that she should be dealing directly with the corporate issuer, Check Rite, and Atlas, its transfer agent.[63]

Broadwater sued Check Rite and Atlas for wrongful refusal to transfer her stock, conversion, and breach of the implied covenant of good faith and fair dealing.[64] She prevailed against both defendants.[65] The only issue on appeal as to these defendants was the correct measure of damages, which came down to the valuation of stock in light of the market fluctuation.[66]

Broadwater also sued Old Republic Surety for breach of an implied covenant of good faith and fair dealing, breach of an implied third-party beneficiary contract, and bad faith refusal to settle a claim.[67] The appellate court affirmed the trial court's dismissal of all of her claims.[68]

In dismissing the contractual claims, the appellate court recited the settled rule that, to have an enforceable right as a third-party beneficiary to a contract, "the contracting parties must have clearly intended to confer a separate and distinct benefit upon the third party."[69] A third party who benefits only incidentally from the performance of a contract has no right to recover under that contract.[70] With respect to the lost instrument bond issued by Old Republic Surety at Fletcher's request, the court found that nothing in the bond indicated that the principal or the surety intended to

---

60. *Id.*
61. *Id.*
62. *Id.*
63. *Id.*
64. *Id.*
65. *Id.*
66. *Id.* at 531–33.
67. *Id.* at 530.
68. *Id.* at 536.
69. *Id.*
70. *Id.* at 537.

confer a right to enforce payment on anyone but the obligee.[71] While a lost instrument bond is intended to safeguard against the presentation of the lost certificate, the bond is only intended to protect and indemnify the obligee from that risk.[72] The bond is not intended to protect third parties who purchase an instrument that is reported lost or stolen.[73]

The court also quashed Broadwater's hopes of recovering from the surety on a bad faith claim.[74] While bad faith refusal to settle a claim is a tort, this type of claim is predicated on the existence of contractual privity between the insurer and the injured party, such as an insurance policy.[75] Since Broadwater was not a party to the lost instrument bond, Old Republic Surety owed her no duty of investigating or settling the claim in good faith.[76]

Broadwater's holdings deserve a word of caution for those handling claims against lost instrument bonds. *Broadwater* merely held that the surety is not directly liable to third-party claimants for bad faith refusal to settle a claim. However, the court said nothing about the surety's potential liability *to the obligee* under the bond for bad faith. This issue was not before the court.

Notably, although a lost instrument bond surety is not liable to third parties, its conduct could indirectly impact its loss exposure. In defending against Broadwater's claim, one of the arguments presented by Check Rite and Atlas was that she failed to mitigate her damages because she unreasonably delayed presenting her demand to them until the stock prices fell. Broadwater argued, and the appellate court agreed, that any delay was "reasonable" while her bond claim was pending with the surety. The court found that the surety's request for documentation, investigation, and the early offer of settlement only perpetuated Broadwater's assumption that the bond would cover her loss. To the extent that the obligee seeks to

---

71. *Id.*
72. *Id.*
73. *Id.*
74. *Id.*
75. *Id.*
76. Broadwater further argued that the surety was equitably estopped from denying the existence of a contract because the surety had initially offered to settle her claim and based on the surety's communications and investigation of the claim. The court avoided deciding this issue, stating that, even assuming that the elements of equitable estoppel were met, Broadwater failed to allege sufficient facts to support equitable estoppel against the surety. *Id.* at 536.

recoup its payments to a third-party claimant from the surety under the lost instrument bond, the surety's conduct in investigating a third-party claim may indirectly impact the surety's exposure under the bond.

IV. Courts' Strict Enforcement of the Bond Requirements Imposed by the Uniform Commercial Code and Comparable State Statutes

The most common use of lost instrument bonds is for lost stock certificates, which is governed by the Uniform Commercial Code and its state counterparts. The Uniform Commercial Code requires the corporate issuer to issue a replacement certificate in the event the original was lost, destroyed, or stolen, but only if the owner of the lost certificate is able to post an appropriate lost instrument bond. To that effect, Uniform Commercial Code section 8-405 provides:

> (a) If an owner of a certificated security, whether in registered or bearer form, claims that the certificate has been lost, destroyed, or wrongfully taken, the issuer shall issue a new certificate if the owner:
> (1) so requests before the issuer has notice that the certificate has been acquired by a protected purchaser;
> (2) files with the issuer a sufficient indemnity bond; and
> (3) satisfies other reasonable requirements imposed by the issuer.
>
> (b) If, after the issue of a new security certificate, a protected purchaser of the original certificate presents it for registration of transfer, the issuer shall register the transfer unless an overissue would result. In that case, the issuer's liability is governed by section 8-210. In addition to any rights on the indemnity bond, an issuer may recover the new certificate from a person to whom it was issued or any person taking under that person, except a protected purchaser.[77]

The Editor's Notes on section 8-405 further provide "[w]here an 'original' security certificate has reached the hands of a protected purchaser, the registered owner . . . is now deprived of the new security

---

77. *See* U.C.C. § 8-405 (Unif. L. Comm'n 1994).

certificate issued as a replacement."[78] This is in contrast to pre-Uniform Commercial Code law under which the original certificate would be rendered ineffective after a replacement was issued.[79] In the event that both the original certificate and the replacement certificate end up in the possession of protected purchasers, the issuer must honor both unless an overissue would result and the security is not reasonably available for purchase.[80] In the latter case alone, the protected purchaser of the original certificate is relegated to an action for damages.[81] In either case, the issuer itself may recover on the indemnity bond.[82]

A number of states have adopted provisions modeled after section 8-405 or have statutes with substantially similar provisions.[83]

---

78. See *Smouha v. MTA & J.P. Morgan Chase*, 797 N.Y.S.2d 278, 283 (Sup. Ct. 2005), which stated:

> Pursuant to [Uniform Commercial Code] § 8-405, if an issuer has replaced a purportedly lost or wrongfully taken [stock] certificate and the original certificate is then produced by a "protected purchaser," the issuer must register the transfer of ownership to the "protected purchaser" even if such transfer will result in duplication of the shares. The issuer will then have recourse under the indemnity bond provided by the owner which requested the replacement . . . and may proceed to recover the replacement certificate from the person to whom it was improperly issued "except a protected purchaser."

But see *In re* Hawaii Corp., 829 F.2d 813, 816 (9th Cir. 1987), where the court stated:

> [I]f the registered owner sells his stock to a bona fide purchaser and then presents a claim to the issuer that the stock is lost, the issuer is protected in issuing a new security to the registered owner *only* if the issuer does not have notice of the certificates' acquisition by the bona fide purchaser. Further, even if the issuer proceeds to issue a new security without notice of the bona fide purchaser, the issuer must register the old certificates when a bona fide purchaser presents them. The issuer is then left to recover his loss from the original registrant. In short, the risk of loss is put on the issuer.

79. Keller v. Eureka Brick Mach. Mfg. Co., 43 Mo. App. 84 (1890).
80. *See* U.C.C. § 8-210 (Unif. L. Comm'n 1994).
81. *Id.* § 8-405.
82. *Id.*
83. See generally Cornell University Law School Legal Information Institute's correlation chart indicating status of adoption of Uniform Commercial Code chapter 8 by the 50 states as of March 2004, at https://www.law.cornell.edu/wex/table_ucc (last visited Jan. 17, 2022).

Courts strictly enforce the requirements of Uniform Commercial Code section 8-405 and their state equivalents. An issuer cannot be compelled to issue the replacement unless each of the requirements has been met.[84] The requirement that a lost instrument bond be actually posted is strictly construed, and substitutes, such as depositing into court certain stocks in lieu of a bond, are not permitted.[85]

Compliance with section 8-405 requirements is routinely required in corporate bankruptcy proceedings, when the trustee or the court requires creditors claiming an interest under notes, stock certificates, or other negotiable instruments to either surrender the original instruments to the trustee or post a lost instrument bond prior to receipt of any distributions on the account of such instruments.[86]

Numerous other statutes and regulations require a lost instrument bond to be posted as a condition to certain claims. For instance, posting of a lost instrument bond may be required when a person claims an interest in certain types of unclaimed property[87] or as a condition for maintaining a litigation claim or defense premised upon a lost or destroyed instrument.[88]

V. Notable Aspects of Lost Instrument Bond Underwriting

In underwriting a lost instrument bond, so as to minimize exposure to loss and maximize the likelihood of recoupment in the event of a loss, the surety's evaluation of the risk should address the issues discussed below.

A. The Principal's Integrity and Financial Responsibility

The surety must conduct a thorough investigation of the principal's financial background, business practices, past bonding history, and litigation to determine how likely the principal is to reimburse the surety should it suffer a loss.

---

84. *See* Glaser v. Texon Energy Corp., 702 F.2d 569, 570–71 (5th Cir. 1983); First Sw. Corp. v. Lampton, 724 So. 2d 988, 992 (Miss. Ct. App. 1998).

85. *See Lampton*, 724 So. 2d at 992 (interpreting MISS. CODE ANN. § 75-8-405 (rev. 1981)).

86. *See, e.g.*, *In re* EnviroSolutions of N.Y., LLC, No. 10-11236 (SMB), 2010 Bankr. LEXIS 2840, at *37 (Bankr. S.D.N.Y. July 22, 2010).

87. *See* OR. REV. STAT. § 98.392 (2011); THE LAW OF MISCELLANEOUS AND COMMERCIAL SURETY BONDS, *supra* note 10, at 247.

88. LA. REV. STAT. ANN. § 13:3741 (Acts 1986, No. 172, § 1).

Having satisfied itself of the principal's financial position, it is equally important that the indemnity agreement executed by the principal secures the surety's indemnity rights to the fullest extent. A critical right that should be included is the surety's right to investigate and settle a bond claim in the surety's sole discretion. The indemnity agreement should further provide that evidence of the surety's payment to the obligee is sufficient evidence of the principal's indemnity obligation to the surety. Following is an example of language to the foregoing effect.

> In the event of any payment by the Surety, the Principal and Indemnitors further agree that in any accounting between the Surety and Principal, or between the Surety and the Indemnitors, or either or both of them, the Surety shall be entitled to charge for any and all disbursements, made by it in good faith in and about the matters herein contemplated by this Agreement under the belief that it is or was liable for the sums and amounts so disbursed, or that it was necessary or expedient to make such disbursements, whether or not such liability, necessity or expediency existed; and that the vouchers or other evidence of any such payments made by the Surety shall be prima facie evidence of the fact and amount of the liability to the Surety.[89]

The enforceability of these types of provisions in indemnity agreements has been widely upheld by courts, with respect to bonds in general[90] and with respect to lost instrument bonds specifically.[91] In the words of one appellate court:

> There is nothing wrong or unreasonable, or against public policy, in this stipulation . . . . The expense, delay, trouble, and risk of loss to the guarantee company is a sufficient safeguard against

89. Adapted from a standard general indemnity agreement used by Zurich North America.
90. *See* Fid. & Deposit Co. v. Whitson, 187 Cal. App. 2d 751 (1960); Gen. Ins. Co. of Am. v. Singleton, 40 Cal. App. 3d 439, 443–44 (1974) ("Provisions in indemnity agreements granting the indemnitor the right to compromise and settle claims, and providing that vouchers and other evidence of payment shall be *prima facie* evidence of the propriety thereof, have been upheld as not against public policy and enforced by the courts.").
91. Fid. & Cas. Co. of N.Y. v. Harrison, 274 S.W. 1002, 1004–05 (Tex. Ct. App. 1925) (citing Guar. Co. of N. Am. v. Pitts, 30 So. 758, 759 (1901)).

> unwarranted payment; and, without such a stipulation . . . guarantee companies could not safely do business anything like as cheaply as they do, and to the evident advantage of the parties and the general public.[92]

B. The Nature and Negotiability of the Instrument

To the extent available, the surety should request a copy of the lost instrument and should generally be familiar with its terms. Some of the obvious factors in determining the risk of a claim relating to the issuance of the duplicate instrument are whether the lost instrument is in bearer form and whether it has been assigned, endorsed, or executed under a power of attorney, all of which should prompt the surety to proceed with caution.

C. The Circumstances Surrounding the Lost Instrument

The surety underwriter must obtain sworn declaration of the facts and circumstances surrounding the need for a duplicate instrument (i.e., destruction, wrongful taking, or loss). In the case of wrongful taking, a police report may provide significant information.

D. The Duration of the Surety's Exposure Under the Bond

In addition to the statutes of limitations applicable to bond claims in general, the surety must consider any statutory or contractual limitations on the enforceability of the underlying lost instrument. The general statutes of limitations for claims arising under a written contract, ranging from two to ten years depending upon the state, will determine how soon the obligee must make a claim after receiving notice of claim on the underlying lost instrument or after suffering a loss. That period arguably may be tacked onto the statute of limitations or the enforceability period of the underlying lost instrument, and these will vary widely depending on the type of the instrument and the laws of the jurisdiction that govern the instrument.

For securities and negotiable instruments governed by the Uniform Commercial Code, the enforceability periods vary depending on the specific type of instrument, as follows:

---

92. *Id.* at 1004 (citing federal and state cases from multiple jurisdictions).

- On an action to enforce the obligation to pay a note payable at a definite time, six years after the due date or the accelerated due date[93]
- On an action to enforce the obligation to pay a note payable on demand, six years after the demand[94]
- On an action to enforce the obligation under an unaccepted draft, within three years after dishonor of the draft or ten years after the date of the draft, whichever period expires first[95]
- On an action to enforce the obligation of the acceptor of a certified check or the issuer of a teller's check, cashier's check, or traveler's check, three years after demand for payment is made to the acceptor or issuer[96]
- On an action to enforce the obligation of a party to a certificate of deposit, within six years after demand for payment or from the due date[97]
- On an action to enforce the obligation of a party to pay an accepted draft, other than a certified check, six years after the due date or acceptance[98]

As a catch-all provision, Uniform Commercial Code section 3-118 sets forth a general three-year limitation on actions relating to negotiable instruments not governed by other law regarding claims for indemnity or contribution.[99]

Based on the foregoing, the enforceability periods vary depending on the specific type of instrument, requiring an evaluation of the particular lost instrument for which the lost instrument bond is requested.

---

93. U.C.C. § 3-118, subdiv. (a) (UNIF. L. COMM'N 1994).
94. *Id.* subdiv. (b).
95. *Id.* subdiv. (c).
96. *Id.* subdiv. (d).
97. *Id.* subdiv. (e).
98. *Id.* subdiv. (f).
99. *Id.* subdiv. (g).

Conclusion

Lost instrument bonds have come a long way since the early days, when "their conditionless form and unlimited term"[100] put surety underwriters in "awe."[101] For the more common types of lost instrument bonds, such as the bonds required for reissuance of corporate stock certificates, the Uniform Commercial Code and its state counterparts now provide some guidance, with further guidance to be gleaned from the modest body of case law that has developed with respect to lost instrument bonds. For underwriters, claims adjusters, and counsel dealing with lost instrument bonds, the statutory provisions and the case law do not provide all the answers. Perhaps more than any other kind of bonds, lost instrument bonds are designed to allocate the risks of human error, making the underwriting, liability analysis, and recovery subject to endless and unpredictable variations.

---

100. EDWARD C. LUNT, SURETY BONDS: NATURE, FUNCTIONS, UNDERWRITING REQUIREMENTS 309 (1922).

101. *Id.*

APPENDIX A

LOST INSTRUMENT BOND WITH LIMITED LIABILITY[102]

WHEREAS, [*issuer*] is a contract servicer of mortgages collateralizing Ginnie Mae-guaranteed mortgage-backed securities in pool number [*number*] and mortgagee of record for the mortgage securing the note identified as

Issuer Loan Number: ______________________________
FHA/VA/RHS Number: ___________________________
Mortgagor: _____________________________________
Address of Property: _____________________________
Mortgage Recording Information: ___________________
Amount of Bond: _________________________________

which note has been lost, mislaid, destroyed or stolen and cannot be found or produced.

WHEREAS, Ginnie Mae is the equitable owner of said note and desires assurance that no adverse claims shall be made as to its ownership rights by reason of said note being lost, mislaid, destroyed or stolen.

[*Name of surety*] as obligor, its heirs, legal representatives, successors and assigns of the Obligor shall indemnify and save harmless the Government National Mortgage Association, the contract servicer of mortgages collateralizing Ginnie Mae guaranteed mortgage-backed securities or their successors or assigns (hereinafter called Obligee), from and against any and all losses, claims, actions, suits, damages, charges or expenses of any nature and character by reason of said lost, mislaid, destroyed or stolen instrument(s) being presented by a holder other than the Obligee, for partial or complete payment.

This Bond may be immediately enforced by the Obligee upon presentation of the original and/or duplicate note(s) for partial or complete payment by the mortgagor by a holder other than the Obligee.

This Bond shall be void only if the instrument(s) so lost, mislaid, destroyed or stolen be found or come into the hands of the Obligee.

Date this ___ day of ____, _____ ______________________
Obligor

---

102. GINNIE MAE DOCUMENT CUSTODIAN MANUAL, *supra* note 9, app. I, at 1-1 (Lost Instrument Bond with Limited Liability).

APPENDIX B

BOND OF INDEMNITY[103]

KNOW ALL MEN BY THESE PRESENTS:

That we, [*principal*] (hereinafter called the "Principal") and [*surety*] duly authorized to transact the business of indemnity and suretyship in [*state(s)*], as Surety, are held and firmly bound unto [*name of gas and electric company*] and [*name of trust and savings bank*], Transfer Agent and Registrar and their successors and assigns, jointly and severally, as their interest may appear (hereinafter collectively referred to as "Obligees"), in the full sum of $[*dollar amount*] lawful money of the United States, said sum to be paid to the Obligees or their legal representatives; for which payment, well and truly to be made, the said Principal and Surety bind themselves, their heirs, executors, administrators, successors and assigns, jointly and severally, firmly by these presents.

SIGNED, SEALED, DELIVERED, AND DATED this _____ day of ________, _______.

WHEREAS, the aforesaid Principals represent that they are the registered owners of one hundred (100) shares of common stock of [*name of gas and electric company*], represented by Certificate No. [*certificate number*], and that the said certificate has been lost, mislaid, stolen or destroyed so that the same cannot be found or produced;

AND WHEREAS, the said Principals have requested the Obligees to issue a new certificate in place of the one lost, mislaid, stolen or destroyed;

AND WHEREAS, the Obligees have agreed to issue a new certificate for one hundred (100) shares of common stock in the names of [*names of joint tenants*], as joint tenants with right of survivorship and not as tenants in common. Upon the undertaking on the part of the Principals hereto to indemnify and save them harmless and to deliver up the said certificate which it is alleged has been lost, mislaid, stolen or destroyed, if the same should ever be recovered.

NOW THEREFORE, THE CONDITIONS OF THIS OBLIGATION ARE SUCH, that if the Principal, the heirs, legal representatives, successors or assigns of the Principal or any of them shall in case the lost, mislaid, stolen, or destroyed original certificate be found or come

---

103. RICHARD GILLMAN, WEST'S LEGAL FORMS § 18:11 (2020).

into the hands or power of any of them or to the hands, custody, or power of any person or corporation, deliver or cause the same to be delivered unto the Obligees in order for them to be canceled, and shall at all times indemnify and save harmless the Obligees from and against any and all claims, actions and suits whether groundless or otherwise, and from and against any and all liabilities, losses, damages, costs, charges, counsel fees, and other expenses of every nature and character based upon or arising from or by reason of such loss, mislaying, theft, or destruction or based upon or arising from or by reason of the said lost, mislaid, stolen or destroyed original certificate, and/or the issuance of new certificate in lieu thereof or the making of the transfer, exchange, or delivery called for by the original certificate with or without the surrender thereof, and whether or not based upon or arising out of the honoring or refusing to honor the original certificate when presented by any one or based upon or arising from inadvertence, accident, oversight, or neglect on the part of the Obligees or their respective officers, agents, clerks, and employees and/or omission or failure to inquire into, contest or litigate the right of any applicant to receive transfer, exchange or delivery in respect of the original certificate and/or the new certificate issued in lieu thereof, and/or based upon or arising out of any determination which the Obligees may in fact make as to the merits of any such claim, right or title, and/or based upon or arising out of any other matter or thing whatsoever, then this obligation shall be void; otherwise shall remain in full force and effect.

The Surety agrees that its liability hereunder shall be absolute and unconditional regardless of any liability of the Principal hereunder, whether by reason of any irregular or unauthorized execution of, or failure to execute, this bond, or any absence of interest of the Principal in the subject matter hereof, or otherwise, and that its liability hereunder shall accrue and become enforceable without prior demand or any other precedent action or proceeding against the Principal.

CHAPTER 18

NOTARY BONDS

Michael Safris
*Douglass F. Wynne, Jr.**

I. What Is a Notary Bond?

Notary bonds are surety bonds posted with jurisdictions that appoint notaries public. Because a notary is a public officer, the bond is posted to protect the interest of the public in the jurisdiction in which the notarial commission has been issued.[1] The surety generally binds itself to the jurisdiction in the amount of the penal sum of the notary bond for the notary to faithfully perform any notarial act for which a bond is given under the laws of the state where the bond is issued.[2] When a notary is liable for breach of an official duty to anyone injured thereby, the surety on the notary bond is generally liable, along with the notary, up to the amount of the penal sum of the bond.[3]

II. What Bond Is Required?

Each state has its own statutes that provide for the appointment of notaries. These statutes generally set forth the requirements to achieve and retain a notarial commission in the jurisdiction, fix application fees, specify whether notarial seals and stamps must be used, and establish state record-keeping duties and bonding requirements.

---

* Joshua D. Ecuyer of Simon, Peragine, Smith & Redfearn, L.L.P., contributed to the research and drafting of this chapter.

1. Villanueva v. Brown, 103 F.3d 1128 (3d Cir. 1997) (applying New Jersey law).
2. *See, e.g.*, Davis v. Adoption Auto, Inc., 731 F. Supp. 1475 (D. Kan. 1990).
3. Ohio Cas. Ins. Co. v. Cox, No. 5:11-CV-334-HRW-REW, 2015 WL 5626374 (E.D. Ky. June 5, 2015); Vancura v. Katris, 939 N.E.2d 328, 339 (Ill. 2010); Aladdin Oil Co. v. Marque, 157 So. 2d 368 (La. Ct. App. 1963), *writ refused*, 158 So. 2d 613 (La. 1963).

The website for the National Notary Association (NNA) provides helpful summaries of state requirements and links to each state's department responsible for notarial commissions.[4] According to the NNA website, notaries are not required to post a bond in 20 states.[5] However, for policy reasons, the majority of states require notaries to post a bond with the jurisdiction issuing the notarial commission. Current bond amount requirements, as stated by the NNA, are:

NNA Notary Bond Amount Requirements	
Amount	**State**
$25,000	Alabama, Indiana, Montana
$15,000	California, Nebraska
$10,000	Idaho, Louisiana,[6] Michigan, Missouri, Nevada, New Mexico, Pennsylvania, Tennessee, Texas, Washington
$7,500	Arkansas, Florida, Kansas, North Dakota
$5,000	Arizona, Illinois, Mississippi, South Dakota, Utah
$2,000	District of Columbia
$1,000	Alaska, Hawaii, Kentucky, Oklahoma
$500	Wisconsin,[7] Wyoming

The reader is advised to check the current statutes in the relevant jurisdiction.

III. How Are the Notary's Powers and Duties Known?

"The powers of a notary, which is a very ancient office, are largely founded on customary law . . . [i]t is true that perhaps in every state the

4. NNA, https://www.nationalnotary.org/ (last visited Jan. 17, 2022).
5. The states identified by the NNA as not requiring notaries to post bonds are Colorado, Connecticut, Delaware, Georgia, Iowa, Maine, Maryland, Massachusetts, Minnesota, New Hampshire, New Jersey, New York, North Carolina, Ohio, Oregon, Rhode Island, South Carolina, Vermont, Virginia, and West Virginia. *Id.*
6. Only non-attorney notaries are required to post a bond. *Id.*
7. Only non-attorney notaries are required to post a bond. *Id.*

powers of notaries . . . have been regulated by statutes, which, however, are largely declaratory in their nature."[8]

Many jurisdictions have enacted statutes specifying the powers and the method of appointment of notaries public. Multiple states have adopted the Uniform Law on Notarial Acts.[9] In 2010, the Uniform Law Commission adopted the Revised Uniform Law on Notarial Acts. To date, 17 states have adopted the Revised Uniform Law on Notarial Acts.[10] That number will grow, as at least three other states introduced legislation in 2021 to adopt the Revised Uniform Law.[11] The Revised Uniform Law on Notarial Acts defines a "Notarial Act" as any act that a notary is authorized to perform, whether by the Revised Uniform Law on Notarial Acts or the state that adopts it, specifically including:

- Taking an acknowledgment
- Administering an oath or affirmation
- Taking a verification upon oath or affirmation
- Witnessing or attesting a signature
- Certifying or attesting a copy
- Noting a protest of a negotiable instrument[12]

---

8. Wood v. St. Paul City Ry. Co., 44 N.W. 308, 308–09 (Minn. 1890).
9. *See, e.g.*, Del. Code Ann. tit. 29, § 4301 *et seq.* (West 2021); Okla. Stat. tit. 49, § 111 *et seq.* (West 2021); Or. Rev. Stat. Ann. § 194.205 *et seq.* (West 2021); Wis. Stat. Ann. § 140.01 *et seq.* (West 2021); D.C. Code Ann. § 1-1231.01 *et seq.* (West 2021); Iowa Code Ann. § 9B.1 *et seq.* (West 2021); Nev. Rev. Stat. Ann. § 240.001 *et seq.* (West 2017); N.M. Stat. Ann. § 14-14-1 *et seq.* (West 2021).
10. These states are Arizona, Hawaii, Idaho, Iowa, Kansas, Kentucky, Maryland, Minnesota, Montana, New Hampshire, New Mexico, North Dakota, Oregon, Pennsylvania, South Dakota, Washington, and Wisconsin. *See Law of Notarial Acts, Revised (2018)*, Uniform Law Commission, https://www.uniformlaws.org/committees/community-home?CommunityKey=8acec8a5-123b-4724-b131-e5ca8cc6323e (last visited Jan. 17, 2022).
11. *Id.*
12. National Conference of Commissioners on Uniform State Laws, Revised Uniform Law on Notarial Acts 6 (2021), https://www.uniformlaws.org/HigherLogic/System/DownloadDocumentFile.ashx?DocumentFileKey=ff9047d6-bd84-a1d3-d3ba-03ad1f3daacf&forceDialog=0.

Other states' statutes expand the notary public's powers to include additional functions. For example, Ohio notaries "have the power that is by law vested in judges of county courts to compel the attendance of witnesses and punish them for refusing to testify."[13] In addition, notaries in Florida, Maine, and South Carolina have the authority to perform marriages.[14]

When a statute provides for the appointment of notaries, but notarial powers and duties are not statutorily defined, courts historically have looked to the common law to ascertain the powers and duties of the notary.[15]

IV. What Is the Liability of the Notary and Surety?

A notary bond is an official bond on which the liability of the surety is no greater than that of the notary.[16] Thus, when the primary obligation is barred or in any way extinguished, the surety is relieved of liability. Dismissal against the principal precludes the right of recovery against the surety.[17]

To recover from the notary or the notary's surety for the act or default of a notary in the performance of notarial duties, a plaintiff has the burden of showing:

- That the notary did not faithfully perform the duties of the office
- That the plaintiff was damaged as a result of such failure
- That such failure was a proximate cause of the loss and injury sustained by the plaintiff[18]

---

13. *See* Gall v. St. Elizabeth Med. Ctr., 130 F.R.D. 85 (S.D. Ohio 1990).
14. *See* FLA. STAT. ANN. § 117.01 *et seq.* (West 2020); ME. REV. STAT. tit. 19-A, § 655 (2012); S.C. CODE ANN. § 26-1-5 *et seq.* (2014).
15. Kirksey v. Bates, 7 Port. 529, 18, 38 WL 1337 (Ala. 1838).
16. *See* Westchester Fire Ins. Co. v. JWS Energy, LLC, No. 11-CV-35-J, 2012 WL 12551248 (D. Wyo. Jan. 24, 2012); Kekona v. Abastillas, 140 P.3d 436 (Haw. Ct. App.), *vacated in part*, 150 P.3d 823 (Haw. 2006); Breckenridge v. Mason, 64 Cal. Rptr. 201 (Cal. Ct. App. 1967).
17. *Breckenridge*, 64 Cal. Rptr. 201.
18. *See* Talmer Bank & Tr. v. Minton Firm, P.C., 660 F. App'x 439, 448 (6th Cir. 2016) (unpublished); RLI Ins. Co. v. Athan Contracting Corp., 667 F. Supp. 2d 229, 236 (E.D.N.Y. 2009); State *ex rel.* Koste v. Md. Cas. Co. of Balt., 344 S.W.2d 55 (Mo. 1961).

In the words of the Third Circuit: "[I]t is not enough that a notary's negligence be shown in order for a plaintiff to recover against a notary. A causal relationship between the notary's negligence and [plaintiff's] loss must be shown."[19] For example, in *Kirk Corp. v. First American Title Co.*, the court held that the notary could not be held liable to the borrower because they suffered no damages that were caused by the notary's failure to comply with her duties, despite the fact that her actions could be grounds for the revocation or suspension of her notary commission.[20] Further, because neither the notary nor its surety is a guarantor or an insurer of the truth of the contents of an instrument, liability can generally be found only if the notary were negligent, malicious, or corrupt.[21]

V. Negligent Misconduct

Notaries public, like all public officers, must act with the care and diligence that a reasonably prudent and cautious person would exercise under like circumstances in performing the duties of their office. In addressing the duty of care owed by a notary, the Third Circuit, applying New Jersey law, has observed that because the notary is a public officer, this duty of diligence is owed to any member of the public who might rely on the notary's certification.[22] Similarly, the Washington Supreme Court, applying Washington law, has noted: "The notary, as a public officer, has a duty to take reasonable precautions to assure that his seal will not be the vehicle by which a fraudulent transaction is consummated."[23]

Where the notary's failure to perform the duties of office faithfully was only negligent, the injured party generally must have relied on the notary's false certificate in order to recover any damages from the notary and the surety. Courts have often found that the proximate cause element of proof is not satisfied unless reliance on the negligent act is shown. For example, in *Davis v. Adoption Auto, Inc.*, the plaintiffs, who did

---

19. Villanueva v. Brown, 103 F.3d 1128, 1137 (3d Cir. 1997); *see also* Gulledge v. Shaw, 880 So. 2d 288 (Miss. 2004).
20. 270 Cal. Rptr. 24 (Cal. Ct. App. 1990); *see also* Yerkes v. Asberry, 938 S.W.2d 307 (Mo. Ct. App. 1997).
21. NationsBank of N.C., N.A. v. Parker, 535 S.E.2d 597, 599 (N.C. Ct. App. 2000); Werner v. Werner, 84 Wash. 2d 360 (Wash. 1974); *Villanueva*, 103 F.3d 1128.
22. *Villanueva*, 103 F.3d 1128; *see also* Biakanja v. Irving, 49 Cal. 2d 647, 650–51 (Cal. 1958).
23. *Werner*, 84 Wash. 2d at 367.

not know until months after their automobile purchase that a document was allegedly notarized negligently, could not recover purchase-related damages from the notary or surety.[24] The proximate cause element was not present because the plaintiffs did not rely on the negligently notarized document to make the automobile purchase in question.[25]

A notary public has a duty not to negligently certify, and the notary and the notary's surety generally will be liable for any damages resulting from such a negligent act.[26] In *Bernd v. Eu*, in addition to certifying a signature not made in her presence, the notary negligently certified a signature on a subscribing witness form rather than on a personal acknowledgment form, as the notary had intended. The court rejected the notary's attempt to blame the mistake on a secretarial error, concluding that the notary "was grossly negligent in processing the certification when the notary did not bother to read its contents."[27]

A notary has a duty to exercise reasonable care in establishing the identity of the person for whom notarial services are being provided.[28] The notarization of an instrument signed by a person with whom the notary did not have a sufficient degree of acquaintanceship, and who is actually an imposter, can subject the notary and the notary's surety to liability.[29]

---

24. 731 F. Supp. 1475, 1476 (D. Kan. 1990).
25. *Id.* at 1478; *see also* Quicken Loans, Inc. v. Downing, No. 1:10-CV-1565-TWP-DKL, 2012 WL 4762411 (S.D. Ind. Oct. 5, 2012) (notary found liable for negligent misrepresentation after it was determined that third party had relied on the representation and suffered damages as a result).
26. *See* Bernd v. Eu, 100 Cal. App. 3d 511 (Cal. Ct. App. 1979) (an appeal from a lower court decision that approved an administrative suspension of a notary public's commission).
27. *Id.* at 517.
28. *See, e.g.*, Wiggins v. Ellis, No. 2:12-CV-02705-SGC, 2021 WL 535536, at *6 (N.D. Ala. Feb. 12, 2021); Simmons v. Bellco Credit Union, No. 18-CV-00348-MEH, 2019 WL 1745209, at *9 (D. Colo. Apr. 18, 2019); Peltz v. Peltz, No. M199902299COAR3CV, 2000 WL 1532996 (Tenn. Ct. App. Oct. 18, 2000); Lowe v. Wright, 292 S.W.2d 413 (Tenn. Ct. App. 1956).
29. Knighton v. Hayes, No. W2003-00837-COA-R3CV, 2004 WL 250903, at *6 (Tenn. Ct. App. Feb. 10, 2004); Villanueva v. Brown, 103 F.3d 1128, 1137 (3d Cir. 1997); Transamerica Title Ins. Co. v. Green, 89 Cal. Rptr. 915 (Cal. Ct. App. 1970).

However, if the notary has reasonable grounds to believe in the alleged identity of the person who seeks notarial services and has no reason to suspect any wrongdoing, there is no negligence.[30] For example, in *Brown v. Rives*, a notary had never met the person seeking notarial services, but relied on the person's introduction from a trusted acquaintance.[31] The acquaintance had done business with the person, who had always used an assumed name. The court held that the notary correctly certified the document that was signed under the assumed name in the notary's presence.

The case of *Howcott v. Talen* also involved the introduction of an imposter to the notary by someone known to the notary.[32] The court opined:

> [I]t can hardly be expected that [the notary] will ordinarily require more than the reasonable identification of persons who come before him merely to acknowledge their signatures to instruments of any kind. He most assuredly is not obliged to examine the titles of the property which the instruments purport to affect or to verify the truth of the affidavits which the parties propose to sign. In fact, so long as he exercises the precaution of an ordinarily prudent businessman in certifying to the identity of the persons who appear before him, it may be doubted whether he has any other function to discharge; and we are of the opinion that such precaution was exercised by [the notary] in the matters here complained of.[33]

Where a notary negligently makes a defective or an untrue certification, both the notary and the notary's surety are generally liable for any damages proximately or legally caused by the negligent act. For example, in *Keck v. Keck*, where an Ohio statute required the notary public to receive "satisfactory evidence" of the identification of a person executing an instrument, a court held that a notary who fails to obtain such

---

30. Tevrow v. Arowolo, No. A-3173-13T4, 2015 WL 9694315, at *9 (N.J. Super. Ct. App. Div. Aug. 27, 2015); Brown v. Rives, 184 P. 32 (Cal. Ct. App. 1919); Howcott v. Talen, 63 So. 376 (La. 1913).
31. 184 P. 32.
32. 63 So. at 379.
33. *Id.*

evidence under circumstances that would have made a reasonable person suspicious is negligent and is thus liable for the plaintiff's damages.[34]

The notary in *Keck* took the uncorroborated word of a stranger about the identity of a person seeking to transfer title to a vehicle. The court held that the notary was liable for damages resulting from the forged signature of the plaintiff, the husband of the woman who had sought the notary's services, stating:

> A reasonable person in the position of the notary public should have at least been suspicious when a stranger tried to sign her husband's name on the representation that she wanted to do so because her husband was ill. The obvious inference was that he was too ill to accompany her. When she thereafter, upon the notary's refusal to take her signature for his, immediately produced a man whom she represented to be her husband the notary public in the exercise of ordinary care should have taken or required some satisfactory evidence of his identity. Moreover, he is required to do so by positive mandate of R.C. [Ohio Revised Code] 147.53. We hold as a matter of law that the failure of the notary public to get some evidence independent of a stranger's representation that the man was her husband was negligent as a matter of law.[35]

Where the injured party can establish that an acknowledged signature is forged or that a notary's certificate is false, the burden of proof can shift to the notary to show that the proper standard of care was exercised.[36] This shift of the burden of proof evidences the strong public policy of ensuring the accuracy of notarial certifications and is justified by the "probability that the notary was negligent in ascertaining the identity of the forger."[37]

---

34. 375 N.E.2d 1256 (Ohio Ct. App. 1977).
35. *Id.* at 1258.
36. Wash. Mut. Sav. Bank v. Thurmond, 91 Wash. App. 1009 (Wash. Ct. App. 1998) (citing Werner v. Werner, 84 Wash. 2d 360 (Wash. 1974)); *see also* Farm Bureau Fin. Co., Inc. v. Carney, 605 P.2d 509, 515 (Idaho 1980); *see also* Sroka-Calvert v. Watkins, 971 S.W.2d 823 (Ky. Ct. App. 1998) (where a mistake on the part of a notary is alleged then a notary's testimony is no longer conclusive on the issue of the authenticity of a signature).
37. Meyers v. Meyers, 503 P.2d 59, 62 (Wash. 1972).

In some states, statutes impose liability on notaries for "misconduct" or neglect of duty.[38] Where a statute provides for liability to injured parties as a result of the "misconduct" of a notary public in the performance of any powers, such misconduct may include negligent acts as well as intentional, fraudulent, or willful acts.[39]

Other specific acts of negligence for which the surety or notary may be found liable include the following:

- Notary fails to take the required care to properly ascertain the identity of a forger[40]
- Notary fails to obtain signer's thumbprint[41]
- Notary fails to read a certificate of acknowledgment and thereby certifies, on the wrong document, the signature of a person who never appeared before the notary[42]
- Notary fails to complete a certificate before signing it[43]
- Notary fails to describe vendee's marital status accurately in immovable property transfer, as required by statute[44]
- Notary acknowledges his own signature[45]
- Notary breaches a statutory duty to record outstanding liens in an act of sale[46]

---

38. *See, e.g.*, Hatchett v. W2X, Inc., 993 N.E.2d 944 (Ill. App. Ct. 2013); Torrealba v. Kesmetis, 178 P.3d 716, 721 (Nev. 2008); Joost v. Craig, 63 P. 840 (Cal. 1901); Hous. Auth. of Lafayette v. Fid. & Deposit Co. of Md., Inc., 309 So. 2d 920 (La. Ct. App. 1975), *cert. denied*, 313 So. 2d 826 (La. 1975).
39. Indep. Leasing Corp. v. Aquino, 133 Misc. 2d 564 (N.Y. Cnty. Ct. 1986).
40. *Hatchett*, 993 N.E.2d 944; *Keck*, 375 N.E.2d 1256; *Werner*, 84 Wash. 2d 360.
41. Buck v. Buck, No. G053279, 2017 WL 3404678, at *20 (Cal. Ct. App. Aug. 9, 2017).
42. Smith v. Walker, 91 So. 3d 77, 84 (Ala. Civ. App. 2012); Bernd v. Eu, 100 Cal. App. 3d 511 (Cal. Ct. App. 1979).
43. *Bernd*, 100 Cal. App. 3d 511.
44. Succession of La Salle v. Clark, 503 So. 2d 694 (La. Ct. App. 1987), *cert. denied*, 505 So. 2d 1146 (La. 1987).
45. Bank of Am. Nat'l Tr. & Sav. Ass'n v. Dowdy, 9 Cal. Rptr. 779 (Cal. Ct. App. 1960).
46. Roth v. B&L Enters., 420 So. 2d 1094 (La. 1982).

- Notary fails to record an act of sale[47]
- Notary fails to fulfill statutory requirement to obtain necessary tax certificates to prove that all taxes on a property being conveyed or transferred are paid[48]
- Notary affixes stamp and seal, without "subscribed and sworn" notation, to an affidavit signed by a forger bearing an alleged power of attorney for the intended affiant[49]
- Notary falsely seals and certifies a release of lien affidavit where an affiant did not appear before the notary[50]

However, even if negligent, a notary public, and thus his or her surety, will not be held liable for a loss when the direct cause of the loss was the intervening negligence of a third person.[51]

VI. Willful Misconduct

The Alabama Supreme Court has succinctly described the notary's liability for willful and wanton misconduct as follows:

> Where an officer, by wanton misconduct, starts on its way in the commercial world a false certificate upon which the public has the right to rely, he ought to be held responsible for all proximate consequences, not only to the person who takes immediately

---

47. Anderson v. Hinrichs, 457 So. 2d 225 (La. Ct. App. 1984), *cert. denied*, 462 So. 2d 192 (La. 1984).
48. Jackson Title Corp. v. Swayne, 411 So. 2d 690 (La. Ct. App. 1982).
49. Commonwealth Ins. Sys., Inc. v. Kersten, 115 Cal. Rptr. 653 (Cal. Ct. App. 1974).
50. Commonwealth *ex rel.* Smolovitz v. Am. Sur. Co. of N.Y., 149 A.2d 515 (Pa. Super. Ct. 1959).
51. *See, e.g.*, May v. Nationstar Mortg. LLC, No. 3:12cv43, 2012 U.S. Dist. LEXIS 102956, at *16 (N.D.W. Va. July 25, 2012) (finding that the plaintiff had no possible claim of unconscionable conduct against a notary public when she admitted that she signed the subject loan documents); Davis v. EQT Prod. Co., No. 5:12CV51, 2012 WL 6111694, at *3 (N.D. W. Va. Dec. 10, 2012) (similar holding); Burck v. Buchen, 116 P.2d 958 (Cal. Ct. App. 1941); Joost v. Craig, 63 P. 840 (Cal. 1901); Halton v. Holmes, 31 P. 1131 (Cal. 1893); *see also* Couch v. Babb, 423 S.W.2d 464 (Tex. Civ. App. 1968).

> and directly under the instrument bearing the certificate, but to everyone damaged as the proximate result of it.[52]

The Missouri Supreme Court analogized the doctrine of willful misconduct by a notary to the doctrine of coconspirator liability:

> When a man acts in his official capacity as a notary to do one of the wrongful things necessary to carry a fraudulent scheme to fruition, and in his individual capacity does other fraudulent acts necessary to the perfection of the fraudulent scheme, he is liable as an official for the damage resulting from the perpetration of the fraud and for all of the acts which constitute a part of the criminal scheme. The doctrine is analogous to the doctrine that every coconspirator is liable for all of the acts done in furtherance of the conspiracy.[53]

The high court found that the notary's false certification of an affidavit combined with his fraudulent individual conduct as a used car dealer to produce the realtor's loss. Accordingly, the notary bond surety was held liable on the bond for the notary's breach of his official duty.

Courts in several states have held that persons injured by the false certificates of notaries are entitled to recover from the notary and the notary's surety even though the injured persons had not relied on the certificates. In *Aetna Casualty & Surety Co. v. Commonwealth*, the grantor of an alleged deed was permitted to recover on the notary's bond because the notary's false certification of acknowledgment had resulted in a loss to the grantor when the property was conveyed to an innocent purchaser.[54] A similar result was reached by the Mississippi Supreme Court in *U.S. Fidelity & Guaranty Co. v. State ex rel. Ward* where the court found that a notary, who certified as true that which she knew to be false, was the proximate cause of injury to a purchaser of property who discovered his property was purchased under a fraudulent deed.[55] While

---

52. Butler v. Olshan, 191 So. 2d 7, 16 (Ala. 1966) (quoting Am. Sur. Co. of N.Y. v. Boden, 50 S.W.2d 10, 13 (Ky. 1932)).
53. State *ex rel.* Koste v. Md. Cas. Co. of Balt., 344 S.W.2d 55, 58 (Mo. 1961) (quoting State *ex rel.* Park Nat'l Bank v. Globe Indem. Co., 29 S.W.2d 743 (Mo. Ct. App. 1930)).
54. 25 S.W.2d 51 (Ky. 1930).
55. 211 Miss. 864, 879 (1951).

the court recognized the principle that a surety usually has no liability when the injured party did not rely on the false certificates, the court observed that the rule should not be applied to cases of egregious fraud committed by the notary.[56] In allowing recovery, the court observed that "appellees should not be deprived of a recovery because at the time of the fraud they did not see or know of the false acknowledgments in their chain of title."[57]

In a Missouri case, a notary falsely certified that the plaintiff, a husband seeking a divorce, had subscribed and sworn to the divorce petition. After the husband obtained the divorce by default, the wife sued the notary's surety, alleging that she had been deprived of spousal support and had suffered other damages as a result of the notary's false certification. Even though the wife herself did not rely on the notary's certificate, she was permitted to recover because the fraudulent act of the notary was the proximate cause of the damages.[58]

A surety on a notary bond has also been held liable to those damaged by the following specific acts:

- False certification on a fictitious firm-name document[59]
- Wrongfully permitting use of notary's signature and seal on instruments[60]
- Forgery of signatures and fraudulent acknowledgment of signatures on a mortgage[61]
- Inducement by the notary of illiterate persons to sign a deed they thought was a mortgage[62]

---

56. *Id.* at 878–79.
57. *Id.* at 879.
58. State *ex rel.* Sappington v. Am. Sur. Co. of N.Y., 41 S.W.2d 966 (Mo. Ct. App. 1931); *see also* Means v. Clardy, 791 S.W.2d 433, 436 (Mo. Ct. App. 1990).
59. Bank of Am. Nat'l Tr. & Sav. Ass'n v. Dowdy, 9 Cal. Rptr. 779 (Cal. Ct. App. 1960).
60. Lewis v. Agric. Ins. Co., 82 Cal. Rptr. 509 (Cal. Ct. App. 1969).
61. Fogleman v. Nat'l Sur. Co., 132 So. 317 (Ala. 1931).
62. Olson v. Goetz, 15 Pa. D. & C. 261 (1930).

VII. What Are the Surety's Defenses?

The surety's defenses will depend on the facts and circumstances of each claim, the statutory duties of the notary, and the language of the notary bond itself, which may be specified by statute. The reader is cautioned to review these factors very carefully. What follows is a discussion of defenses that may be available to the notary bond surety for consideration by surety claims professionals and outside counsel when analyzing notary bond claims.

In some instances, a surety's liability for the acts of a notary public depended upon whether the acts complained of were "authorized by law," "under color of the office of Notary Public," or "within the official duties of the notary," terms that are generally interchangeable.[63]

Some courts have held that the notary bond surety is not responsible for the acts of a notary who does a thing that the law does not authorize the notary to do, even though the notary does the unlawful thing in the capacity of notary public.[64] In *Schmidt v. Drouet*, the court held that the notary's false inscription was not a notarial activity authorized by law and, therefore, the surety had no liability.[65] In reaching its decision, the court explained:

> Although it is manifest that the notary in this case has committed wrongful and criminal acts for which he could have been prosecuted and punished had he lived, it does not follow that his surety can be held pecuniarily responsible . . . because his principal, the notary, has done acts which the law did not authorize him or compel him to perform, and which were therefore not incumbent upon him.[66]

In some cases, the notary bond surety was not accountable for a notary's false representation, forgery, and embezzlement because the

---

63. Mason v. Crabtree, 71 Ala. 479 (1882); Aetna Cas. & Sur. Co. v. Commonwealth, 25 S.W.2d 51 (Ky. 1930).
64. *See, e.g.*, Schmidt v. Drouet, 8 So. 396 (La. 1890) (notary falsely wrote on a promissory note that a nonexistent act prolonging payment of the debt had been passed before the notary).
65. *Id.*
66. *Id.* at 397.

acts were not part of the notary's duties.[67] In Hallenbeck v. Lillico, the cause of action against the surety was based upon the wrongful action of a notary public in making an allegedly false certificate.[68] However, the actual proximate causes of the plaintiff's losses were the notary's misrepresentations, embezzlement of funds, and forgery of a mortgage office clerk's endorsement, not the notarial duties performed by the notary. Accordingly, the surety was not held liable for the false acknowledgment. The court reasoned that, had the notarial duties been performed by another notary, the plaintiff's losses still would have occurred as a result of the notary's non-notarial actions.

A notary is not a depositary or custodian of funds and receives funds only as a trusted individual and not in an official capacity.[69] In Roth v. B&L Enterprises, the notary bond surety was not liable for the plaintiff's damages that resulted when the notary absconded with funds left with the notary to complete a sale.[70] The court held that when the notary accepted the funds, it was not in his official capacity as a notary. Therefore, the surety was not liable for damages related solely to the notary's handling of the funds. As the Roth court noted, "[f]urthermore, the bond required of notaries is only for the minimal sum . . . not a sufficient amount to protect innocent parties who entrust their funds to a notary . . . ."[71]

However, where the official misconduct of the notary is a proximate cause joined with other, non-notarial causes to produce damage, the surety may be liable.[72] In one California case, a notary, who also was a real estate broker, was alleged to have falsely acknowledged trust deeds, making the trust deeds appear valid, and to have induced the plaintiffs to purchase the deeds.[73] The court held that because the plaintiffs pled that the defendant's conduct as a notary was a proximate cause of their losses, the plaintiffs stated a cause of action against the notary bond surety.

Where a notary's alleged alteration of a deed, or the notary's alleged permission to alter a deed, occurred after the deed was lawfully acknowledged and properly certified, the alteration has been held to have

---

67. People *ex rel.* Young v. Nederlander, 143 N.W. 753 (Mich. 1913) (by implication); Hallenbeck v. Lillico, 266 P. 730 (Wash. 1928).
68. 266 P. 730.
69. Roth v. B&L Enters., 420 So. 2d 1094 (La. 1982).
70. *Id.*
71. *Id.* at 1096.
72. Tutelman v. Agric. Ins. Co., 102 Cal. Rptr. 296 (Cal. Ct. App. 1972).
73. *Id.*

occurred after the notary's official duties had ceased. Therefore, the surety was not liable for the alteration.[74]

Similarly, when an instrument was forcibly taken from a notary before the notarial act was complete, the notary's actions were held not to be the proximate cause of the plaintiff's damages, and the surety was not liable.[75] The taking of the documents was held to be an intervening, superseding proximate cause. Therefore, the surety was not liable for any negligence by the notary in performing her duties.[76]

The notary's certificate is not deemed to certify or guarantee the facts stated in the instrument. Accordingly, the surety on the notary bond is not liable for all misstatements contained in the notarized instrument.[77] "A notary may take all due precautions and fully comply with the statute and still be deceived. In that scenario, the notary will not be held liable."[78] The surety, entitled to assert its principal's defenses, also would not be held liable. Therefore, if it can be shown that a reasonably careful notary had no knowledge of the falseness of the statements in an instrument acknowledged before the notary, the surety has no liability for damages resulting from an instrument containing false statements by the person signing the instrument.

As with any surety bond, the surety is entitled to assert the principal's defenses. When the primary obligation is barred or in any way extinguished, the surety is relieved of liability. Dismissal against the principal with prejudice precludes recovery against the surety.[79] Thus, a plaintiff is not entitled to recover from the notary or surety where the suit against the notary had already been dismissed with prejudice.[80]

---

74. Sitton v. Am. Ins. Co., 390 S.W.2d 34 (Tex. Civ. App. 1965).
75. Couch v. Babb, 423 S.W.2d 464 (Tex. Civ. App. 1968).
76. *Id.*
77. Atlas Sec. Co. v. O'Donnell, 232 N.W. 121 (Iowa 1930); State *ex rel.* Koste v. Md. Cas. Co. of Balt., 344 S.W.2d 55 (Mo. 1961); *see also* Anthony v. Am. Gen. Fin. Serv., Inc., 697 S.E.2d 166, 176 (Ga. 2010), *answer to certified question confirmed to* 626 F.3d 1318 (11 Cir. 2010) (citing GA. CODE ANN. § 45-8(f) (West 2020)).
78. Joost v. Craig, 63 P. 840 (Cal. 1901).
79. Breckenridge v. Mason, 64 Cal. Rptr. 201 (Cal. Ct. App. 1967).
80. *Id.*

VIII. What Damages Are Recoverable?

Proof of actual damages is essential to any recovery against the notary bond surety. Accordingly, where no damages resulted from a notary's failure to perform a statutory duty, such as keeping a record of official acts, at least one court has found that there was no liability on the notary bond.[81] In that case, the court firmly rejected the argument that the statute that required the keeping of records was a penal statute imposing liability even without resulting damages.[82]

The measure of damages in an action on a notary bond is compensation for injuries suffered by the plaintiff. The plaintiff bears the burden of showing the extent of the alleged injury.[83]

In *Independence Leasing Corp. v Aquino*, a New York court permitted the victim of a forged, notarized document to recover litigation expenses, including attorneys' fees, from the notary and his employer under a theory of implied indemnity.[84] The victim, the father of the forger, had been sued by a third party to enforce a lease that the forger had signed in the presence of the notary public. The notary public negligently signed and affixed his stamp to the forged lease. The court observed that, without the "grossly negligent" conduct of the notary and his employer that resulted in the forgery of the victim's name on the lease, the victim would not have been sued by the plaintiff under the lease. Thus, the court held that the victim "established his right to recover his litigation expenses against [the notary and his employer] under a theory of implied indemnity."[85]

The notary bond surety, like other sureties, is generally liable only up to the penal sum of the bond. However, in one case, where the notary was found negligent for certifying a forged signature, a surety was found liable for litigation costs incurred by the bond claimant in addition to the penal sum of the bond.[86] The court in that case held that the risk

---

81. Mortensen v. Pac. Indem. Co., 479 P.2d 288 (Colo. App. 1970); *see also* Fid. Nat'l Title Ins. Co. v. W. Sur. Co., 277 So. 3d 40, 45 (Ala. Civ. App. 2018).
82. *Mortensen*, 479 P.2d at 288–89.
83. Thomas v. State for Use of Thorp Fin. Corp., 171 So. 2d 303 (Miss. 1965).
84. 133 Misc. 2d 564 (N.Y. Cnty. Ct. 1986).
85. *Id.* at 573.
86. Harris v. Nw. Nat'l Ins. Co., 8 Cal. Rptr. 2d 234 (Cal. Ct. App. 1992); *see also* Great Am. Ins. Co. v. N. Austin Mun. Util. Dist. No. 1, 908 S.W.2d 415 (Tex. 1995).

of having to pay for the litigation costs was assumed by the notary and surety, who were represented by the same attorney, when they declined to settle the dispute prior to trial.[87] The surety's liability for the litigation costs, under a separate statute that imposed the obligation to pay costs on the losing party, was not limited to the penal sum of the notary bond.[88]

IX. The Rise of Online Notarization

As a result of the ever-increasing reliance on the internet and technology, many states have begun to allow for online notarization. Once unheard of, remote online notarization (RON) is now authorized in at least 29 states, all of which have adopted some form of permanent legislation on its use.[89] The push for more widespread use of RON became more pronounced during the COVID-19 pandemic. Federal legislation, respectively Senate Bill 3533 and House Bill 6364, were both introduced in 2020. While this federal legislation has not yet been adopted, if passed in its current form it would authorize every notary in the United States to perform RONs when handling interstate transactions. In the interim, several federal agencies, including the Internal Revenue Service (IRS), have allowed limited use of remote notarization for certain transactions.[90]

The use of RON, while advantageous in terms of both its efficiency and its relative convenience, may create some interesting issues in terms of the duties and potential risks incurred by the participating notary and, therefore, the notary's surety. For example, online notarization creates significantly greater data privacy issues than traditional notarization. Electronic privacy breaches could expose sensitive information of both the signatories and the notaries. For instance, some RON statutes require the notary to keep and maintain the audio-video recordings of each

---

87. *Harris*, 8 Cal. Rptr. 2d 234.
88. *Id.*
89. The 29 states (as of April 26, 2021) that have adopted some permanent legislation allowing for online notarization are Alaska, Arizona, Colorado, Florida, Hawaii, Idaho, Indiana, Iowa, Kentucky, Louisiana, Maryland, Michigan, Minnesota, Missouri, Montana, Nebraska, Nevada, North Dakota, Ohio, Oklahoma, Pennsylvania, Tennessee, Texas, Utah, Vermont, Virginia, Washington, Wisconsin, and Wyoming.
90. *IRS Extends Relief on Remote Notarization*, NAPA (Dec. 23, 2020), https://www.napa-net.org/news-info/daily-news/irs-extends-relief-remote-notarization.

remote notarization for at least ten years after the date of the notarial act.[91] If those recordings are maintained in an electronic database, then there is a risk that a data breach could occur or that the information could be lost.

In addition, notaries performing an online notarization will still have to take reasonable steps to confirm the signer's identity. In lieu of in-person identification, the notary will have to confirm identity via remote presentation, which essentially consists of reviewing the signer's identifications via a webcam. While the use of a webcam has become increasingly commonplace in the past several years in terms of its utilization in conducting business and even court proceedings, it remains less secure than an in-person meeting.

For instance, it is often the case that the notary or witnesses must attest that he or she believes that the signer appears to be of sound mind and not under or subject to duress, fraud, or undue influence. Obviously, it is much more difficult for a remote witness or notary to ascertain who is in the signer's presence and to confirm that no one is unduly influencing the signer than it is when the notarization is done in person.[92] This is a practical risk that may not be able to be fully mitigated by RON procedures.

Another serious concern with RON is the proper validation of the signer's identity. To address that concern, many states' RON legislation requires knowledge-based authentication (KBA) and credential analysis to ensure that the signer is who they claim to be.[93] KBA requires the signer to answer a set of computer-generated questions related to their life and financial history. An obvious problem with KBA is that it is ineffective at verifying the identities of minors or young adults because they likely lack financial history. It is also ineffective at verifying the identity of non-American citizens or non-resident aliens because they do not have a Social Security number. Credential analysis simply involves using RON software to scan the signer's identification to confirm that it is genuine.

---

91. *See, e.g.*, FLA. STAT. ANN. § 117.245(2) (West 2021).
92. Danielle Halachoff Frye & Richard E. Davis, *Changing with The Times: Remote Signings and Pandemic Notarization*, PROB. L.J. OHIO, July/Aug. 2020, at 30.
93. *See, e.g.*, 2020 La. Acts 254.

Some states have even more safeguards. For instance, South Dakota requires that the notary have "personal knowledge" of the remote signer's identity before the transaction can go forward.[94] Other states require that both the signer and the property affected by the notarization be located in-state.[95] Virginia is a notable exception to this rule, and allows its RON notaries to perform remote notarizations even if neither the signer nor the relevant property is situated in Virginia.[96] As a result, many companies providing RON services elect to operate out of Virginia to take advantage of that law.[97]

Given the relative newness of RON and its associated legislation, both notaries and sureties should carefully review those state statutes to ensure that they are complying with all applicable regulations and are minimizing any potential risk.

Conclusion

Notaries perform a vital public service to the communities that they serve. While the way in which those services are performed continues to change and evolve over time, the duties and obligations of the notary remain the same. Notary bonds continue to provide a degree of protection both to the notary and to the public. However, as highlighted throughout this chapter, the shield provided by the notary bond is not absolute—certain actions by the notary can and will operate to relieve the surety of its obligations under the bond.

Although willful misconduct by the notary often will absolve the surety, whether negligence will lead to the same result will depend heavily on the specific facts and the governing law. Further, notaries and sureties have numerous defenses that may allow them to avoid liability entirely, even when the notary is at fault. Notaries, notary bond sureties, and attorneys who practice in this area of surety law, are advised to educate

94. N.D. CENT. CODE ANN. § 44-06.1-13.1 (West 2021).
95. Brett J. Natarelli et al., *Notarization and Property Recording Requirements in the Age of Social Distancing*, 76 BUS. LAW. 607, 613 (2021).
96. *Id.*
97. *Id.*

themselves on these issues to avoid unnecessary risk and to provide the best possible service to their clients, and to the public.[98]

98. This discussion of notary bonds and our citation to case authority is necessarily condensed due to page limitations. Additional case citations are available in two annotations by John D. Perevich, J.D. *See* John D. Perevich, Annotation, *Liability of Notary Public or His Bond for Negligence in Performance of Duties*, 44 A.L.R. 3d 555 (originally published in 1972); John D. Perevich, Annotation, *Liability of Notary Public or His Bond for Wilful or Deliberate Misconduct in Performance of Duties*, 44 A.L.R. 3d 555 (1972) (*superseded by Plaintiff's Diligence as Affecting His Right to Have Defendant Estopped from Pleading the Statute of Limitations*, 44 A.L.R. 3d 760). For a more detailed discussion regarding the measure of damages for a false or incomplete certificate by a notary public, see D.E. Ytreberg, *Measure of Damages for False or Incomplete Certificate by Notary Public*, 13 A.L.R. 3d 1039 (originally published in 1967).

CHAPTER 19

WAREHOUSE AND CUSTOMS BONDS

Elliot Scharfenberg
Chris Simmelink

Introduction

Contracts of deposit, much like suretyship, have their roots in antiquity.[1] Also like suretyship, these ancient contracts of deposit have evolved to serve the needs of modern commerce. In the modern world, warehouse bonds play an integral role in establishing trust between the producers of agricultural goods and the end-users of those goods or those who extend credit on the basis of those goods. Warehouse bonds give commercial value to warehouse receipts by conditionally guaranteeing the warehouse operator's obligations to faithfully perform its duties as bailee.

Although it is tempting to spend a substantial portion of this chapter on the evolution of contracts of deposit and how those contracts play a critical role in our modern financial infrastructure, this chapter has a more narrow focus. This chapter is intended to be more practical and geared toward businesspeople and their lawyers as they encounter and litigate disputes concerning warehouse bonds. Customs bonds, though similar in some ways, will be addressed separately.

To that end, this chapter provides an overview of the federal and state statutory and regulatory schemes that apply to bonded warehouse

---

1. Roman law, as reported by Justinian, included only four nominate contracts involving personal property: a loan for use (*commodatum*), a loan for consumption (*mutuum*), a pledge (*pignus*), and a *depositum* contract (*depositum*). ANDREW BURKOWSKI & PAUL J. DU PLESSIS, TEXTBOOK ON ROMAN LAW (4th ed. 2010). With regard to *depositum*, the person accepting the deposit could not benefit financially, and the contract could only involve the deposit of corporeal movables—tangible personal property. Additionally, the standard of care of the person accepting the deposit was *culpa lata*, similar to a gross negligence standard. The vestiges of the Roman law can be found even today in the Louisiana codification of the contract of deposit. *See* LA. CIV. CODE ANN. art. 2926 *et seq.* (2008).

operators and their sureties, with a heavy focus on the surety's rights and obligations under warehouse bonds. Generally speaking, the surety's obligations under a warehouse bond are similar to other bonds that require the "faithful performance" of certain duties. Warehouse bonds, in particular, are typically conditioned upon the faithful performance of the warehouse operator's obligations to store and to deliver the goods upon demand. The general principles of suretyship apply to warehouse bonds, and the surety's obligations are typically determined by the applicable statutes and regulations, as well as the express terms of the bond.

Warehouse bonds are required by certain federal and state statutes and regulations. Warehouse operators in the business of storing agricultural products who choose to be licensed under the United States Warehouse Act do not have to comply with state statutes because the United States Warehouse Act preempts state law.[2] In those circumstances, federal law governs the liability of the principal as well as the surety. Additionally, certain states require a public warehouse operator in the business of storing certain goods or merchandise to be bonded. To the extent that provisions of the Uniform Commercial Code (U.C.C.) are consistent with the state statutes governing warehouse bonds, its terms and definitions regarding warehouse receipts, liens, and bonds apply to state-bonded warehouses.

Other bonds, such as U.S. customs bonds or intoxicating liquors warehouse bonds, can be limited to only certain obligations of a bailee, such as the payment of duties, taxes, and penalties when dutiable goods enter U.S. commerce or leave the warehouse. These bonds will be addressed in a separate section.

I. United States Warehouse Act

The United States Warehouse Act, 7 U.S.C. §§ 241–256, "provides a national system of warehouse bonding for the protection of depositors, sets up a national system of inspection and grading of grain, and established warehouse receipts as a secure and readily negotiable form of property."[3] Section 869.1 of title 7 of the *Code of Federal Regulations* provides regulations under which the secretary of agriculture, through

---

2. 7 C.F.R. § 869.1(c) (2021).
3. Farmers Elevator Mut. Ins. Co. v. Jewett, 394 F.2d 896, 902 & n.4 (10th Cir. 1968) (citing House report appearing at 53 CONG. REC. 7063–64; Senate debates at 53 CONG. REC. 10772–78; Rice v. Santa Fe Elevator

the Agricultural Marketing Service (AMS), administers the Warehouse Act.[4] The AMS administers all provisions and activities regulated under the Warehouse Act under the discretion and supervision of the AMS's director, Warehouse and Commodity Management Division.[5]

The United States Warehouse Act only governs warehouses in the business of storing agricultural products. To be licensed under the Warehouse Act, a warehouse operator is required to "execute and file with the Secretary [of Agriculture] a bond, or provide such other financial assurance as the Secretary determines appropriate, to secure the [warehouse operator's] performance of the activities so licensed or approved."[6]

A. *Bond Requirements Under the United States Warehouse Act*

As a condition to receiving a license or authorization under the Warehouse Act, pursuant to 7 C.F.R. § 869.14, the warehouse operator is required to provide a warehouse operator's bond. Section 869.14 provides as follows:

> As a condition of receiving a license or authorization under the [Warehouse] Act, the person applying for the license or authorization must execute and file with AMS a bond or provide such other financial assurance as AMS determines appropriate to secure the person's compliance with the [Warehouse] Act;
>
> . . . .
>
> Such bond or assurance must be for a period of not less than one year and in such amount as required by AMS.[7]

The AMS determines the required amount of the bond.[8] If the AMS determines that a previously accepted bond is insufficient, the AMS may immediately suspend or revoke the license or authorization covered by the bond if the person who filed the bond does not provide an additional bond that the AMS determines is appropriate.[9] The warehouse operator is required to provide, or renew, a bond each year, and failure to do so

---

Corp., 331 U.S. 218, 235 n.13 (1947); Greater Baton Rouge Port Comm'n v. United States, 287 F.2d. 86, 90 n.4 (5th Cir. 1961)).

4. 7 C.F.R. § 869.1(a) (2021).
5. *Id.* § 869.2(a).
6. 7 U.S.C. § 245 (2021).
7. 7 C.F.R. § 869.14(a), (b) (2021).
8. *Id.* § 869.14(a), (d).
9. *Id.* § 869.14(d).

will result in immediate and automatic revocation of the warehouse operator's license.[10]

B. Obligations of the Federally Licensed Warehouse Operator

The secretary of agriculture prescribes the duties of a warehouse operator with respect to the care of and responsibility for agricultural products stored or handled by a warehouse operator.[11] The warehouse bond is conditioned upon the warehouse operator's faithful performance of all obligations of a licensed warehouse operator under the terms of the Warehouse Act and the federal regulations promulgated thereunder. The Warehouse Act and the federal regulations impose the following obligations on the warehouse operator and expose the surety to liability under the bond for any breach of those obligations.

1. Inspecting, Grading, and Weighing the Agricultural Product

Pursuant to the warehouse regulations, before the warehouse operator may issue a warehouse receipt, the quality, condition, and weight of the agricultural product must be ascertained by a licensed inspector and weigher.[12]

2. Issuing Warehouse Receipts

The warehouse operator must issue warehouse receipts that comply with the format and regulations prescribed by 7 C.F.R. § 869.300. Paper warehouse receipts must be issued per the requirements set forth in 7 C.F.R. § 869.302. Electronic warehouse receipts must be issued per the requirements set forth in 7 C.F.R. § 869.303. A receipt may not be issued for an agricultural product unless the agricultural product is actually stored in the warehouse at the time of the issuance of the receipt.[13]

3. Commingling of Agricultural Products

The warehouse operator is permitted to commingle a depositor's agricultural products in a manner approved by the secretary of

---

10. *Id.* § 869.14(c).
11. 7 U.S.C. § 242(g) (2021).
12. 7 C.F.R. § 869.300(b)(3) (2021); Staple Cotton Coop. Ass'n v. D.G. & G., Inc., 503 F. Supp. 2d 1217, 1224–25 (E.D. Mo. 2007).
13. 7 U.S.C. § 250(b) (2021).

agriculture.[14] However, the warehouse operator is severally liable to each depositor for the care and redelivery of the share of the depositor's commingled agricultural product to the same extent and under the same circumstances as if the agricultural product had been stored separately.[15]

4. *Transferring of Agricultural Products*

Pursuant to 7 C.F.R. § 869.106(b), "a warehouse operator who desires to transfer stored agricultural products to another warehouse may do so either by physical movement, by other methods as may be provided in the applicable licensing agreement, or as authorized by AMS."[16] Thus, the warehouse operator is permitted to transfer a stored agricultural product from one warehouse to another warehouse for continued storage.[17] However, the warehouse operator from which agricultural products have been transferred has a duty to deliver to the rightful owner of such products, at the request of the original warehouse, such products in the "quantity and of the kind, quality, and grade called for by the receipt or other evidence of storage of the owner."[18]

5. *Providing Insurance*

Each warehouse operator must comply fully with the terms of insurance policies or contracts covering their licensed warehouse and all products stored therein, and must not commit any acts, nor permit others to do anything, that might impair or invalidate such insurance.[19]

6. *Requesting Reasonable Charges and Tariffs*

The warehouse operator may not make unreasonable or exorbitant charges for services rendered.[20]

7. *Promptly Delivering Agricultural Products*

Pursuant to 7 C.F.R. § 869.110(a), the warehouse operator,

---

14. *Id.* § 248(a).
15. *Id.* § 248(b).
16. 7 C.F.R. § 869.106(b) (2021).
17. 7 U.S.C. § 249(a) (2021); 7 C.F.R. § 869.106 (2021).
18. 7 U.S.C. § 249(b) (2021).
19. 7 C.F.R. § 869.104 (2021).
20. *Id.* § 869.107(a).

> in the absence of a lawful excuse, will, without unnecessary delay, deliver the agricultural product stored or handled in the warehouse on a demand made by: (1) The holder of the warehouse receipt of the agricultural product; or (2) The person that deposited the agricultural product, if no warehouse receipt has been issued.[21]

8. Exercising Reasonable Care

At all times, including any period of suspension of the warehouse operator's license, each warehouse operator is required to "exercise such care in regard to stored and non-storage agricultural products in their custody as required in the applicable licensing agreement."[22] Furthermore, the warehouse operator shall deal in a fair and reasonable manner with persons storing or seeking to store an agricultural product in the warehouse if the agricultural product (1) is of the kind, type, and quality customarily stored or handled in the area in which the warehouse is located; (2) is tendered to the warehouse operator in a suitable condition for warehousing; and (3) is tendered in a manner that is consistent with the ordinary and usual course of business.[23] However, there is some question as to whether an injured third party has a private cause of action against the *warehouse operator*, as opposed to only a cause of action "on the bond," for the warehouse operator's breach of such fair treatment obligations.[24]

C. Federal Question Jurisdiction and Preemption

Section 245 of title 7 of the U.S. Code provides:

> Any person injured by the breach of any obligation arising under this chapter for which a bond or other financial assurance has been obtained as required by this section may sue with respect to the bond or other financial assurance in a district court of the

---

21. *Id.* § 869.110(a); *see also* 7 U.S.C. § 251(a) (2021) (using slightly different language).
22. 7 C.F.R. § 869.105 (2021).
23. 7 U.S.C. § 247(a) (2021).
24. Syngenta Seeds, Inc. v. Bunge N. Am., Inc., 773 F.3d 58, 63 (8th Cir. 2014) ("The text of section 247(a) does not implicitly authorize a private cause of action for violations of a warehouse operator's fair treatment obligations.").

> United States to recover the damages that the person sustained as a result of the breach.[25]

Thus, bonds issued under the United States Warehouse Act are governed by federal law and raise federal question jurisdiction.[26]

The Warehouse Act also preempts state warehousing laws. "Under the Supremacy Clause, U.S. Const. Art. VI, cl. 2, the United States Constitution and federal laws and treaties are 'the supreme Law of the Land.' Thus, Congress, by passing certain legislation, may act to preempt state law."[27] Pursuant to 7 U.S.C. § 242(a):

> The Secretary [of Agriculture] shall have exclusive power, jurisdiction, and authority, to the extent that this chapter applies, with respect to—(1) each warehouse operator licensed under this chapter; (2) each person that has obtained an approval to engage in an activity under this chapter; and (3) each person claiming an interest in an agricultural product by means of a document or receipt subject to this chapter.[28]

As recognized by the Eighth Circuit, in *Rice v. Santa Fe Elevator Corp.*,[29] the U.S. Supreme Court determined:

> "[T]he special and peculiar history" of the United States Warehouse Act . . . precludes limiting preemption to circumstances where a state's actions "in fact dilute[] or diminish[] the federal program . . . ." That is, state grain warehouse laws can be preempted even when they do not collide with a specific federal law; no direct conflict is required.[30]

"The test [regarding preemption], therefore, is whether the matter on which the State asserts a right to act is *in any way* regulated by the Federal

---

25. 7 U.S.C. § 245(d) (2021).
26. Heart of Am. Grain Inspection Serv., Inc. v. Mo. Dep't of Agric., 123 F.3d 1098 (8th Cir. 1997) (quoting Rice v. Santa Fe Elevator Corp., 331 U.S. 218 (1947)); *see also* Syngenta Seeds, Inc. v. Bunge N. Am., Inc., 820 F. Supp. 2d 953, 972 (N.D. Iowa 2011); Staple Cotton Coop. Ass'n v. D.G. & G., Inc., 503 F. Supp. 2d 1217, 1222 (E.D. Mo. 2007).
27. *Heart of Am. Grain Inspection Serv.*, 123 F.3d at 1103.
28. 7 U.S.C. § 242(a) (2021).
29. 331 U.S. at 222.
30. *Heart of Am. Grain Inspection Serv.*, 123 F.3d at 1103–04.

Act."[31] Under *Rice*, a warehouse operator that chooses to be licensed under the Warehouse Act is "authorized to operate without regard to State acts and [is] solely responsible to the Federal Act."[32] The Court found that a warehouse operator cannot be required by the state to do anything more than what is required by the federal act notwithstanding the fact that the state regulations do not directly conflict with the federal Warehouse Act.[33] Likewise, in *Heart of America Grain Inspection Service*,[34] the Eighth Circuit held that "Missouri's attempt not only to regulate the certification of grain weights in federally licensed warehouses, but to usurp that function entirely, is an unconstitutional exercise of state power, notwithstanding that the [United States Warehouse Act] does not explicitly regulate Class II certified weights or the persons who provide them."[35]

Courts still rely on the U.S. Supreme Court's decision in *Rice* when addressing the issue of whether the Warehouse Act preempts state regulations of warehouse operators. For example, in *Allenberg Cotton Co. v. Staple Cotton Cooperative Ass'n*,[36] a buyer of cotton alleged that the negotiable warehouse receipts that were issued by a federally licensed cotton warehouse failed to disclose defects in the cotton, despite the fact that the cotton was clearly contaminated.[37] The buyer asserted state law claims for negligent misrepresentation and breach of statutory duties against the warehouse and also brought federal causes of action under the Warehouse Act.[38] Relying on the holding in *Rice*, the court granted summary judgment in favor of the warehouse and found that the Warehouse Act addressed the issue of the standard of care required by warehouse operators in the operation of federally licensed warehouses and, therefore, state regulation of the matter was preempted.[39] Additionally, the court held that there was no genuine issue

---

31. *Rice*, 331 U.S. at 236 (emphasis added).
32. *Id.* at 233–34 (quoting S. REP. NO. 1775, at 2 (1929)).
33. *Id.* at 237–38.
34. *Heart of Am. Grain Inspection Serv.*, 123 F.3d 1098.
35. *Id.* at 1104–05 (citing Campbell v. Hussey, 368 U.S. 297, 302 (1961) ("We have then a case where the federal law excludes local regulation, even though the latter does no more than supplement the former.")).
36. No. 4:07-CV-123-SA-DAS, 2009 WL 1619950, at *1 (N.D. Miss. June 9, 2009).
37. *Id.*
38. *Id.* at *2.
39. *Id.* at *5.

of disputed fact as to whether the warehouse violated the Warehouse Act by not disclosing the defect in the cotton because the Warehouse Act imposed no duty on the warehouse operator to inspect the quality of the agricultural goods stored at the warehouse.[40]

Similarly, in *Staple Cotton Cooperative Association v. D.G. & G., Inc.*,[41] the court held that the Warehouse Act preempted claims that the operator of a federally licensed cotton warehouse had violated state statutory and common law when it issued "clean" warehouse receipts, which failed to identify any defects in baled cotton.[42] The Warehouse Act and its regulations preempted claims that the operator violated a state-mandated standard of care by "using block stacking to store cotton bales with excess moisture and providing polyethylene bags to wrap the cotton."[43] The court acknowledged that the federal scheme prevails regardless of whether it is a "more modest, less pervasive regulatory plan than that of the State."[44]

D. The Liability of the Warehouse Bond Surety

The surety's liability under bonds issued pursuant to the Warehouse Act is much like its liability under other "faithful performance" type bonds. General principles of the law of suretyship are equally applicable to warehouse bond sureties. The surety's liability is governed by the statute and terms of the bond consistent therewith, as well as any "further obligations" of the warehouse operator existing at or during the one-year period of the bond. The following are some examples of the surety's potential liability under a warehouse bond.

1. Failure to Issue Warehouse Receipts

The surety can be liable for the principal's failure to properly issue warehouse receipts in compliance with the Warehouse Act. In *Farmers Elevator Mutual Insurance Co. v. Jewett*,[45] the Tenth Circuit affirmed summary judgment holding a surety liable on a federal warehouse

---

40. *Id.* at *7.
41. 503 F. Supp. 2d 1217 (E.D. Mo. 2007).
42. *Id.* at 1223.
43. *Id.* at 1225.
44. *Id.* at 1223 (citing Rice v. Santa Fe Elevator Corp., 331 U.S. 218, 236 (1947)).
45. 394 F.2d 896 (10th Cir. 1968).

bond for the warehouse operator's failure to issue warehouse receipts upon acceptance of grain for storage. The warehouse operator issued scale tickets only to the depositor and then issued separate warehouse receipts to others for the grain deposited with the warehouse. Because the Warehouse Act required the issuance of a warehouse receipt upon delivery of the grain, and the principal violated its duty to provide the warehouse receipt, the depositor was entitled to recover against the surety to the extent that the depositor was damaged.[46]

2. Conversion and Breach of Quality and Quantity Obligations

In *Appley Brothers v. United States*,[47] the court granted summary judgment in favor of the United States and against the surety on three consecutive warehouse bonds issued to a grain elevator whose employee converted the grain during each of three bonding periods and failed to redeliver the goods upon demand and surrender of warehouse receipts.[48] "A warehouseman who coverts to his own use the property deposited with him, or the proceeds thereof, is liable on his bond for such conversion.'"[49] The *Appley Brothers* court held that "[w]hen a warehouseman violates the conditions of his bond during each of three bonding periods, the surety on the bond is liable on all of the bonds for the loss caused by the warehouseman's violations, even if the loss was not discovered during the bonding periods."[50] The surety was held liable on all three bonds for the conversion.[51]

The bonds at issue in *Appley Brothers* contained the language required by the federal regulations.[52] The surety argued that the bond language was ambiguous and, thus, should be construed against the

---

46. *Id.* at 899–900.
47. 924 F. Supp. 935 (D.S.D. 1996).
48. *Id.* at 940.
49. *Id.* (quoting APPLEMAN, INSURANCE LAW AND PRACTICE § 5725, at 549 (1981); Fid. & Deposit Co. of Md. v. State of Montana, 92 F.2d 693, 695–97 (9th Cir. 1937)).
50. *Id.* at 940–41 (citing St. Paul Ins. Cos. v. Fireman's Fund Am. Ins. Cos., 245 N.W.2d 209, 215 (Minn. 1976) (applying state law, but reasoning is instructive); Giese v. Engelhardt, 175 N.W.2d 578, 587 (N.D. 1970) (same); Gen. Ins. Co. of Am. v. Commodity Credit Corp., 430 F.2d 916, 917 (10th Cir. 1970) (holding that the claimant could collect under prior year bond when the shortage began in one bond year and continued into next bond year)).
51. *Id.* at 944.
52. *Id.* at 937.

government.[53] The *Appley Brothers* court disagreed because each uniform grain storage agreement (UGSA) states that "[t]he terms of this Agreement . . . , shall prevail over the written or printed words of the warehouse receipts representing the grain . . . ."[54] The surety conceded that the bonds secured "further obligations" of the warehouse operator, which necessarily included the obligations imposed by the UGSA.[55] As it was undisputed that the warehouse operator breached its quality and quantity obligations and its obligation to load out grain upon surrender of warehouse receipts, in violation of the Warehouse Act and the UGSA, the *Appley Brothers* court held the surety liable under all three bonds on this additional ground.[56]

In defense, the surety argued that it should not be held liable under its bonds because the warehouse operator's grain deficiency was known or should have been known by proper inspections and that the warehouse operator's license should have been suspended before the surety issued the third bond.[57] "The Restatement [of Security section 124] clearly allows a defense to bond liability only if the surety can establish that the creditor knew certain facts that materially increased the surety's risk and yet the creditor did not share those facts with the surety."[58] Moreover, "there is no burden on the creditor to investigate for the surety's benefit."[59] In *Appley Brothers*, the court held the surety liable for the full penal sum of the three bonds and awarded prejudgment interest in excess of the penal sum "to compensate the creditor for the loss of the penal sum of the bond on its due date."[60] As neither the bonds nor the government cited an applicable interest provision, prejudgment interest was assessed consistent with state law.[61]

---

53. *Id.* at 941.
54. *Id.* at 942 (quoting 1986–1987 UGSA § 19(a); 1988 UGSA § 1.D.1).
55. *Id.*
56. *Id.*
57. *Id.*
58. *Id.* (citing United States v. Ohio Cas. Ins. Co., 399 F.2d 387, 388–89 (6th Cir. 1968) (holding that the claimant had no duty to disclose to surety when the government had no actual knowledge of grain shortages)).
59. *Id.* (citing Restatement of Security § 124 cmt. (b)).
60. *Id.* at 943 (citing Ins. Co. of N. Am. v. United States, 951 F.2d 1244, 1246 (Fed. Cir. 1991) (citing United States v. U.S. Fid. & Guar. Co., 236 U.S. 512, 530–31 (1915)); *see* United States v. Emp. Mut. Cas. Co., 226 F.2d 895, 900 (8th Cir. 1955) (holding that surety on warehouse bond could be liable for prejudgment interest from date of warehouseman's default).
61. *Appley Bros.*, 924 F. Supp. 935 (D.S.D. 1996).

3. *Failure to Deliver*

The surety may also be responsible under its warehouse bond for the principal's failure to deliver the goods in accordance with the Warehouse Act. In *Schilling v. Book*,[62] the issue presented was whether a proper and sufficient demand for delivery of the grain was made to the warehouse operator.[63] The appellate court affirmed the trial court's holding that there was a conflict between the statutory provisions of the Warehouse Act and the regulations promulgated thereunder as to the warehouse operator's obligation to make delivery upon a negotiable receipt.[64] The appellate court cited the pre-2000 version of the act, which provided:

> That a warehouseman conducting a warehouse licensed under this Act, in the absence of some lawful excuse, shall, without unnecessary delay, deliver the agricultural products stored therein upon a demand made either by the holder of a receipt for such agricultural products or by the depositor thereof if such demand be accompanied with (a) an offer to satisfy the warehouseman's lien; (b) an offer to surrender the receipt, if negotiable, with such endorsements as would be necessary for the negotiation of the receipts; and (c) a readiness and willingness to sign, when the products are delivered, an acknowledgement that they have been delivered if such signature is requested by the warehouseman.[65]

In contrast, the administrative regulations promulgated by the secretary of agriculture under the pre-2000 Warehouse Act provided in pertinent part:

> Except as permitted by law or by the regulations in this part a warehouseman shall not deliver grain for which he has issued a negotiable receipt until the receipt has been returned to him and cancelled . . . .[66]

---

62. 405 N.E.2d 824 (Ill. App. Ct. 1980).
63. *Id.* at 825.
64. *Id.*
65. *Id.* at 826 (quoting 7 U.S.C. § 262).
66. *Id.* (quoting Regulations for Grain Warehouses, section 10224, Fed. Reg. 15,730, as amended, 30 Fed. Reg. 8,089, 8,093 (June 24, 1965)).

The warehouse receipt at issue in *Schilling* contained the language of the regulation requiring return and cancellation of the receipt.[67] In *Schilling*, the appellate court agreed with the trial court's determination that the statute governed and the regulation was invalid because the "regulation, requiring surrender [and cancellation] of the receipt prior to delivery, was in conflict with the statute, requiring only an offer to surrender prior to delivery."[68] However, the *Schilling* court reversed the directed verdict and remanded the case for a new trial to determine whether a proper offer was made to surrender the warehouse receipt.[69] The *Schilling* court wrote:

> [I]f, upon [remand] and retrial, [the warehouse operator] is found liable for conversion of the grain, [its surety] is also liable for damages to plaintiff on its surety bond .... If it is determined that [the warehouse operator] breached his obligations under the Act by his refusal to deliver in the face of sufficient demand, then he would not have faithfully performed his duties and obligations under the Act and the regulations. The surety, under the terms of the bond, is liable for the insured's lack of faithful performance.[70]

The warehouse operator's good faith reliance on the regulations did not operate to negate the surety's liability under the bond.[71]

II. State Warehouse Statutes

Most states[72] have adopted statutes that require bonds for warehouses that are in the business of storing agricultural products, alcohol (intoxicating liquors), cotton, oil, personal property, and tobacco. If a warehouse operator is not licensed under the United States Warehouse Act (which only governs agricultural products), then the surety's liability under its

---

67. *Id.*
68. *Id.*
69. *Id.* at 829.
70. *Id.*
71. *Id.*
72. States and territories that do not appear to have warehouse bond statutes include Arizona, Delaware, District of Columbia, Guam, Hawaii, Maine, Maryland, Nevada, Northern Mariana Islands, Rhode Island, Vermont, and West Virginia.

bond will typically be governed by the applicable state warehousing statutes and the administrative regulations promulgated thereunder, as well as the U.C.C. provisions to the extent adopted by the particular state. The definitions, exemptions, obligations of the warehouse operator, and the liability of the surety vary from state to state. The reader is encouraged to consult the laws and regulations of a particular state to determine the warehouse bond surety's liability under the applicable state's laws and regulations. Unlike the federal Warehouse Act, several states limit the surety's aggregate liability to the penal sum of the bond, regardless of how many renewal periods are implicated.[73]

Article 7 of the U.C.C., which has been adopted by all 50 states, generally governs warehouse receipts and the warehouse operator's liens to the extent not inconsistent with the operative warehouse statute. Due to the breadth of these statutes, this chapter provides only a general overview of warehouse bonds issued pursuant to state law.

A. *State-by-State Bonding Requirements*

1. Agricultural Products

At least 28 states or territories require bonds for warehouse operators in the business of storing agricultural products. These states and territories include Alabama,[74] Arkansas,[75] Colorado,[76] Georgia,[77] Idaho,[78] Indiana,[79]

---

73. *See, e.g.*, Mo. Rev. Stat. § 411.276 (2021) ("In no event shall the liability of the surety on any bond required by section 411.275 accumulate for each successive license period during which the bond is in force. The liability of the surety shall be limited in the aggregate to the face amount of the bond.").
74. Ala. Code § 8-15-7 (2021) (requiring bond for public warehouseman in the amount of no more than $5,000 plus all expenses if state prevails for storing agricultural commodities "conditioned upon the faithful performance of his or its duties as public warehouseman").
75. Ark. Stat. Ann. § 2-17-209 (2021). However, alternative security may be posted in lieu of a bond. *Id.*
76. Colo. Rev. Stat. Ann. § 35-36-103 (2021).
77. Ga. Code Ann. § 10-4-12 (2021).
78. Idaho Code § 69-208 (2021).
79. Ind. Code § 26-3-7-9 (2021).

Iowa,[80] Kansas,[81] Kentucky,[82] Michigan,[83] Minnesota,[84] Mississippi,[85] Missouri,[86] Montana,[87] Nebraska,[88] New Mexico,[89] North Dakota,[90] Ohio,[91] Oklahoma,[92] Oregon,[93] Puerto Rico,[94] South Carolina,[95]

---

80. IOWA CODE § 203C.6 (2021); *id.* § 203C.14 (provides right of action by injured party in certain circumstances); IOWA ADMIN. CODE r. 2190.9(203C) (2021) (prescribing forms for bonds, procedures for termination of security, and giving the warehouse operator the option to post an irrevocable letter of credit in lieu of a surety bond).
81. KAN. STAT. ANN. § 82-165 (2021) (stating that the bond shall be in the penal sum of not less than $5,000 and not more than $50,000).
82. KY. REV. STAT. ANN. §§ 251.365, 251.440 (2021).
83. MICH. COMP. LAWS ANN. § 285.63 (2021). Additionally, section 285.88 provides that a separate bond in the amount of $100,000 must be provided by a grain merchandiser or farm produce trucker.
84. MINN. STAT. §§ 232.21, 232.22(4) (2021).
85. MISS. CODE ANN. §§ 75-44-29 (establishing bonding requirements and giving option to post security in lieu of bond), 75-44-31 (2021) (requiring bonds ranging from $15,000 to $1,000,000). Under Mississippi law, a surety is subject to liability for court costs and attorneys' fees if the evidence reveals that the surety "has willfully and without just cause refused to pay the loss upon demand." *Id.* § 75-44-35. Mississippi has a separate statute requiring a "farm warehouseman" to post a bond. *Id.* § 75-43-31.
86. MO. REV. STAT. § 411.275 (2021).
87. MONT. CODE ANN. §§ 80-4-405, 80-4-505 (2021).
88. NEB. REV. STAT. § 88-530 (2021).
89. N.M. REV. STAT. § 56-6-3 (2021) (bond required in the penal sum of $5,000).
90. N.D. CENT. CODE § 60-02-09 (2021) (providing that the penal sum of the bond shall not be less than $100,000 for any one warehouse, and providing conditions under which the bond is written); *id.* § 60-02-09.1 (providing conditions under which the bond is terminated and the period of liability ends).
91. OHIO REV. CODE ANN. § 926.06 (2021) (requiring a bond or irrevocable letter of credit to be posted if the warehouse operator does not satisfy financial net worth requirements).
92. OKLA. STAT. ANN. tit. 2, §§ 9–22 (2021).
93. OR. REV. STAT. §§ 586. 270, 586.300, 586.529 (2021); OR. ADMIN. R. 603-032-0505 (2021) (bond requirements).
94. P.R. LAWS ANN. tit. 10, §§ 347, 349 (2021).
95. S.C. CODE ANN. §§ 39-22-10, 39-22-20 (2021) (requiring a $25,000 bond for each warehouse and providing that a prevailing claimant is entitled to recover "all damages, costs, and expenses resulting from the default").

South Dakota,[96] Tennessee,[97] Texas,[98] Washington,[99] Wisconsin,[100] and Wyoming.[101] Because the United States Warehouse Act preempts state law for warehousing of agricultural products in interstate commerce, some state statutes have express exemption provisions.[102]

2. *Alcohol (Intoxicating Liquor)*

To secure payment of excise taxes applicable to distilled spirits to the Internal Revenue Service, warehousemen of distilled spirits are required to post bonds.[103] The federal government requires that "[e]xcept as otherwise provided by law, operations as a distiller, warehouseman, or processor may be conducted only on the bonded premises of a distilled spirits plant by a person who is qualified under this subchapter."[104] A person in the business of distilling spirits or warehousing such spirits is required to post a bond:

> [C]onditioned that the person furnishing the bond . . . will faithfully comply with all provisions of law and regulations relating to the activities covered by such bond, and . . . will pay . . . all taxes imposed by this chapter, and . . . all penalties incurred by, or fines imposed on, such person for violation of any such provision.[105]

---

96. S.D. Codified Laws Ann. §§ 49-43-4.3, 49-43-5.3, 49-43-5.7 (2021).
97. Tenn. Code Ann. §§ 43-32-105, 43-32-106 (2021).
98. Tex. Agric. Code §§ 14.031 (requiring bonds in amounts between $35,000 and $500,000, specifying conditions of the bond, and allowing for alternate security to be posted in lieu of surety bond), 14.032, 14.033 (2021) (liability of surety does not accumulate for each successive license period during which the bond is in force).
99. Wash. Rev. Code §§ 22.09.030, 22.09.060, 22.09.090, 22.09.100 (2021). Washington also requires the warehouse operator to post a bond not to exceed $5,000 to cover any loss resulting from the misuse of warehouse receipts. *Id.* § 22.09.300.
100. Wis. Stat. § 99.03 (2021).
101. Wyo. Stat. § 11-11-105 (2021).
102. *E.g.*, Ga. Code Ann. § 10-4-4 (2021); Wash. Rev. Code § 22.09.030 (2021).
103. 26 U.S.C. §§ 5173, 5175 (2021).
104. *Id.* § 5171(a).
105. *Id.* § 5173(e); United States v. Smith, 456 F. App'x 200, 202 (4th Cir. 2011).

The regulations also require an export bond to be posted before distilled spirits may be withdrawn from bonded premises for exportation or transfer to a customs bonded warehouse.[106]

In addition to the federal bonding requirements discussed above, at least eight states require warehouse operators in the business of storing intoxicating liquor to post surety bonds to secure payment of applicable taxes, namely Florida,[107] Georgia,[108] Kansas,[109] New York,[110] Oregon,[111] South Dakota,[112] Tennessee,[113] and Utah.[114] These bonds generally have low penal sums and the obligations under the bond are often strictly limited to the payment of taxes.

---

106. 26 U.S.C. § 5175 (2021).

107. FLA. STAT. § 562.25 (2021) (requiring that state licensed warehouse operators storing alcoholic beverages subject to tax under the Beverage Law file a "bond payable to the division, conditioned upon the full compliance by such operator"). Under Florida's law, the penal sum of the bond ranges from a minimum of $1,000 to a maximum of $5,000. *Id.*

108. GA. CODE ANN. § 10-4-2 (2021).

109. KAN. STAT. ANN. § 41-401 (2021).

110. Under New York Consolidated Laws Service on Alcoholic Beverage Control section 81.1 *et seq.*, the penal sum of the bond is based on the type of license obtained, ranging from $1,000 to $25,000. The condition of the bond is that the warehouse operator "will not suffer or permit any violation of the provisions of the Alcoholic Beverage Control Law or the rules of the State Liquor Authority." N.Y. ALCO. BEV. CONT. § 81.1 (Consol. 2021). In addition to the penal sum of the bond, the bond must provide for recovery of costs up to $1,000. *Id.*

111. OR. REV. STAT. §§ 471.155, 471.242 (2021). As of 2021, there is pending legislation that could require bonding for cannabis warehousing as well.

112. S.D. CODIFIED LAWS ANN. §§ 35-5-7, 35-5-7.1 (2021) (requiring bonding or alternate security in an amount not to exceed $50,000 and providing conditions under which the period of liability terminates).

113. TENN. CODE ANN. § 57-5-110 (2021) (requiring a bond in the minimum amount of $20,000 payable to the commissioner of revenue to secure the payment of taxes levied).

114. UTAH CODE ANN. § 32B-12-206 (2021) (requiring liquor warehousing licensees to post a bond "in the penal sum of $10,000 payable to the department . . . conditioned upon the liquor warehouser licensee's faithful compliance with [the Alcoholic Beverage Control Act] and the rules of the commission").

3. Cotton

At least four states, including Alabama,[115] North Carolina,[116] Texas,[117] and Virginia,[118] require bonds for the warehousing of cotton.[119]

4. Personal Property

A bond may be issued for the storage of personal property by a public warehouse operator in the following 11 states: Alabama,[120] Illinois,[121] Kansas,[122] Louisiana,[123] Massachusetts,[124] Minnesota,[125]

---

115. ALA. CODE § 8-15-7 (2021).
116. N.C. GEN. STAT. §§ 66-35, 66-36 (2021).
117. TEX. AGRIC. CODE § 14A.001 (2021) (defining "public warehouse operator" as "a person who stores cotton, wheat, rye, oats, grapes, or rice, or any kind of produce"). The bond must be in the amount of $5,000. *Id.* § 14A.004.
118. VA. CODE ANN. § 3.2-4764 (2021) (defining "cotton warehouse" as "any enclosure in which producer-owned cotton is stored or held for longer than forty-eight hours"). The cotton handler/warehouse operator is required to post a bond in the amount of $500,000 conditioned upon compliance with the provisions of the code and upon prompt and accurate settlement with the consignor. *Id.* §§ 3.2-4765(E), 3.2-4767.
119. In some states, cotton is defined as an agricultural commodity, and, therefore, cotton warehouses do not have separate statutes or bond requirements. In these states, cotton is included in the state statute that requires a bond for the warehousing of agricultural products.
120. ALA. CODE §§ 8-15-1, 8-15-7 (2021) (requiring bond for warehouses storing most types of personal property).
121. 240 ILL. COMP. STAT. ANN. 10/1, 10/2, 10/6 (2021).
122. KAN. STAT. ANN. §§ 82-162, 82-164 (2021) (setting forth an optional licensing and bonding regime).
123. LA. REV. STAT. ANN. §§ 54:111 (defining "warehouseman" as "a person lawfully engaged in the business of storing goods for profit," whereas "goods" are defined as "movable [personal] property of every description"), 54:114 (2021) (recognizing that the surety's liability is limited to the period in which bond existed; bond period is two years).
124. MASS. ANN. LAWS ch. 105, § 1 *et seq.* (2021).
125. MINN. STAT. § 231.01 (2021) (defining "household goods" as "personal effects and property used or to be used in a dwelling"); *Id.* § 231.17.

Missouri,[126] New Hampshire,[127] North Carolina,[128] South Carolina,[129] and Wyoming.[130]

5. Tobacco

Warehouse operators in the business of storing tobacco and certain employees at those warehouses in Georgia,[131] Kentucky,[132] and Tennessee[133] are required to post bonds to secure payment of applicable taxes.

B. Damage or Loss During Bond Period and Failure to Deliver

Although the laws of each state vary slightly, there are a few general principles that run through the various state statutes. Among those principles is that a surety is liable for damages or losses during the bond period and for the failure to deliver the goods upon proper demand.

In *Planters & Citizens Bank v. Home Insurance Co.*,[134] for example, a warehouse operator's secured lender filed suit against a warehouse bond surety who issued a performance bond to a warehouse operator in the business of storing pecans pursuant to Georgia law.[135] The bond clearly stated that the surety would not be liable for any default by the warehouse operator unless the default occurred during the term of the bond.[136] The

---

126. MO. REV. STAT. § 415.030 (2021) (requiring a $25,000 bond each year).
127. N.H. REV. STAT. ANN. § 348:1 *et seq.* (2021).
128. N.C. GEN. STAT. §§ 66-35, 66-36 (2021) (requiring bond for, among other things, "goods, wares, and other merchandise").
129. S.C. CODE ANN. § 39-19-20 (2021).
130. WYO. STAT. ANN. §§ 33-31-101, 33-31-102 (2021) (setting forth an optional licensing and bonding regime; penal sum of bond cannot be less than $2,000).
131. GA. CODE ANN. § 10-4-144 (2021) (requiring bond in the amount of $10,000).
132. KY. REV. STAT. ANN. § 248.410 (2021) ("Warehouses shall submit to the department a list of the names of all weighmen employed. Each weighmen so listed shall furnish a bond in the amount of five hundred dollars ($500) to the department for the faithful performance of his duty.").
133. TENN. CODE ANN. §§ 43-19-103, 43-19-105 (2021) (requiring a $5,000 bond conditioned upon keeping the warehouse in good condition and repair, so as effectually to protect the tobacco stored therein).
134. 786 F. Supp. 977 (S.D. Ga. 1992).
135. *Id.* at 978.
136. *Id.* at 979.

secured lender moved for summary judgment against the surety on the basis that at least 500,000 pounds of pecans were destroyed prior to the date that the bond expired.[137] It submitted evidence establishing that the warehouse operator had insufficient inventory to meet the obligations of the warehouse receipts, which was required in order to recover for a breach of the bond.[138] The surety filed a cross-motion for summary judgment against the secured lender and argued that the loss did not occur during its period of coverage.[139] The evidence established that the warehouse operator was in default during the bond period and failed to maintain and secure sufficient pecan inventory as collateral.[140] The surety, however, presented some evidence that raised questions of whether the loss resulted in depletion of the inventory below that covered by the warehouse receipts.[141] Therefore, the court denied both motions for summary judgment and left the issue for the finder of fact to decide.[142]

The surety in *Planters* also argued in its motion for summary judgment that the secured lender was barred from recovering under the warehouse bond because it did not make a demand for delivery of the pecans during the period the bond was in force.[143] Under Georgia's warehouse statute, a warehouse operator's obligation to deliver the product does not arise until the holder of the warehouse receipt makes a proper demand.[144] The court held that although a demand might be necessary to establish conversion, demand was not necessary if the warehouse operator, regardless of knowledge of the receipt holder, had violated state law and its obligations during the bond period.[145] The court found that there was strong evidence to support that the warehouse operator was in violation of state law during the bond period and, consequently, that the surety was liable to the secured lender under the bond.[146] The evidence established that the receipt holders would have been unable to redeem the warehouse receipts during the period of the bond and, therefore, demand

---

137. *Id.*
138. *Id.* at 988 (citing Hartford Accident & Indem. Co. v. State of Kansas, 247 F.2d 315 (10th Cir. 1957)).
139. *Id.* at 981–82.
140. *Id.* at 988.
141. *Id.* at 988–89.
142. *Id.* at 984–85.
143. *Id.* at 989.
144. *Id.* (citing GA. CODE ANN. § 10-4-21 (1982)).
145. *Id.* at 990.
146. *Id.*

would have been futile.[147] Therefore, the court denied the surety's cross-motion for summary judgment as to its demand argument and stated that if the finder of fact found that the warehouse operator breached its obligations as a public warehouse operator during the bond period, and that demand would have been futile, then this breach would obviate the need for demand.[148]

C. Faithful Performance of the Principal's Obligations

It is also a general rule that the surety guarantees only the principal's faithful performance of its duties. In *North Dakota Public Service Commission v. Jamestown Farmers Elevator Inc.*,[149] for example, the warehouse operator held a substantial quantity of grain in good condition in storage, for which it issued warehouse receipts, when it filed for bankruptcy.[150] After the bankruptcy proceeding was filed, the grain deteriorated in quality due to heat, moisture, and insect damage.[151] The claimant held warehouse receipts that were pledged as collateral for loans received by farmers.[152] After the value of the grain decreased due to the deteriorated quality, the trustee sold it to the claimant.[153] The claimant filed a claim against the bond for the difference in value.[154] In its defense, the warehouse bond surety argued that it only "insured the acts of the warehouseman which, after the filing of the bankruptcy petition, had neither the legal authority nor the capacity to care for the grain."[155] Applying North Dakota law under which the bond was issued, the court in *Jamestown Farmers* determined that the surety:

> was required to insure only [the warehouseman's] faithful performance of its duties [under North Dakota's statutes] as a public warehouseman. The [North Dakota] statutes did not require that [the surety's] bond insure the faithful performance of the bankruptcy trustee's duties. [The surety] is, therefore,

---

147. *Id.* at 989.
148. *Id.* at 990.
149. 422 N.W.2d 405 (N.D. 1988).
150. *Id.* at 406–07.
151. *Id.* at 406.
152. *Id.*
153. *Id.*
154. *Id.*
155. *Id.* at 410.

> not liable for any loss suffered by [the claimant] as a result of deterioration in the quality of the grain while it was in the custody and control of the bankruptcy trustee.[156]

Because the deterioration in the quality of the grain occurred well after the warehouse operator had responsibility, the court reversed the judgment against the surety.[157]

By contrast, in *North Dakota Public Service Commission v. Woods Farmers Cooperative Elevator Co.*,[158] the trial court required a surety on a grain warehouse operator's bond to pay the North Dakota Public Service Commission the sum of $780,000 for claims made by grain receipt holders after the bonded warehouse filed for bankruptcy.[159] Relying on *Jamestown Farmers*, the surety appealed and argued that it should not be liable under the warehouse operator's bond because "the acts which precipitated the claims against the bond were those which took place subsequent to bankruptcy petition and over which the warehouseman could not have placed any control or influence."[160] The Supreme Court of North Dakota disagreed and found the surety's reliance on *Jamestown Farmers* misplaced:

> [In *Jamestown Farmers* w]e held that the bonding company was not liable for losses caused by deterioration in the quality of the grain resulting from the bankruptcy trustee's egregious neglect of the grain while it was in his custody and control. In this case, there has been no assertion of any neglect on the part of the bankruptcy trustee . . . .[161]

The Supreme Court of North Dakota found that under the state statutes governing grain warehouses, receipt holders are entitled to be made whole, if possible, when a warehouse operator becomes insolvent:

> A warehouseman is required to furnish a bond to provide that protection to producers who deliver grain for sale or storage. The receipt holders in this case have not been made whole. [The

156. *Id.* at 414.
157. *Id.*
158. 488 N.W.2d 860 (N.D. 1992).
159. *Id.* at 865.
160. *Id.*
161. *Id.*

> surety] is, therefore, liable under its bond to the extent necessary to make the receipt holders whole . . . .[162]

Therefore, the Supreme Court of North Dakota affirmed the trial court's holding and found the surety liable for the penal sum of its bond.

III. U.S. Customs Bonded Warehouses

Section 1555 of title 19 of the U.S. Code authorizes the establishment of U.S. customs bonded storage warehouses. Dutiable goods, with certain exceptions, may be entered for warehousing and be deposited in a U.S. customs bonded warehouse without payment of duty.[163] The merchandise may remain in a bonded warehouse for a maximum period of five years from the date of importation without payment of customs duties.[164] Generally speaking, duties will be owed only if the goods are withdrawn from the warehouse and used for domestic consumption or are stored beyond the five-year period. U.S. customs warehouse bonds are a mechanism to ensure that duties are properly paid by the customs bonded warehouse.

In *Xerox Corp. v. County of Harris*, the U.S. Supreme Court gave an excellent explanation of the U.S. customs system:

> Pursuant to its powers under the Commerce Clause, Congress established a comprehensive customs system which includes provisions for Government-supervised bonded warehouses where imports may be stored duty-free for prescribed periods. At any time during that period the goods may be withdrawn and re-exported without payment of duty. Only if the goods are withdrawn for domestic sale or stored beyond the prescribed period does any duty become due.[165]

One of the purposes of the customs bonded warehouse is to ensure that the federal government will collect its federal customs duties.[166]

---

162. *Id.*
163. 19 U.S.C. § 1557 (2021).
164. *Id.*; R.J. Reynolds Tobacco Co. v. Durham Cnty., 479 U.S. 130, 134 n.3 (1986).
165. Xerox Corp. v. Cnty. of Harris, 459 U.S. 145, 150 (1982).
166. *See R.J. Reynolds*, 479 U.S. at 148.

Essentially, the United States has a lien upon imported goods for the payment of any duties due but permits the lien to be replaced by surety bond.[167] Duty is due and payable when the goods are removed—that is exported, withdrawn for supplies to a vessel or aircraft in international traffic, destroyed under U.S. Customs and Border Protection (CBP) supervision, or withdrawn for consumption within the United States. Jurisdiction lies with the Court of International Trade, which is appealable to the Federal Circuit.

The U.S. Supreme Court has specifically recognized that the federal regulatory scheme governing customs bonded warehouses preempts most state taxes on goods stored in such warehouses and destined for exportation.[168] In *Ammex, Inc. v. Department of Treasury*, the court relied on the legal analysis used by the U.S. Supreme Court and found that the comprehensive federal scheme regulating customs bonded warehouses preempted the imposition of Michigan's motor fuel tax and sales tax on gasoline and diesel fuel stored in a customs bonded warehouse and sold as duty-free.[169] The court held that the "imposition of these particular taxes is an obstacle to the accomplishment and execution of the full objectives of Congress."[170] The regulatory scheme for customs bonded warehouses evinces a congressional intent to benefit American industry by remitting duties otherwise due on certain goods.[171]

A. *Classes of Customs Bonded Warehouses*

Pursuant to 19 C.F.R. § 19.1, the following are the different types or classes of customs bonded warehouses, each with its own set of regulations and bonding requirements:

> (1) **Class 1.** Premises that may be owned or leased by the Government . . . and used for the storage of merchandise undergoing inspection by the Customs, under seizure, or pending final release from Customs custody . . . .

---

167. 10A John Alan Appleman & Jean Appleman, Insurance Law and Practice § 6168 (1980) (citing United States v. St. Paul Mercury Indem. Co., 96 F. Supp. 870 (E.D. Pa. 1951), *aff'd*, 194 F.2d 68 (3d Cir. 1952)).
168. *See Xerox Corp.*, 459 U.S. 145; McGoldrick v. Gulf Oil Corp., 309 U.S. 414 (1940).
169. 726 N.W.2d 755 (Mich. Ct. App. 2006).
170. *Id.* at 770.
171. *Id.* at 767.

(2) **Class 2**. Importers' private bonded warehouses used exclusively for the storage of merchandise belonging or consigned to the proprietor thereof . . . .
(3) **Class 3**. Public bonded warehouses used exclusively for the storage of imported merchandise.
(4) **Class 4**. Bonded yards or sheds for the storage of heavy and bulky imported merchandise; stables, feeding pens, corrals, or other similar buildings or limited enclosures for the storage of imported animals; and tanks for the storage of imported liquid merchandise in bulk . . . .
(5) **Class 5**. Bonded bins or parts of buildings or of elevators to be used for the storage of grain. The bonded portions shall be effectively separated from the rest of the building.
(6) **Class 6**. Warehouses for the manufacture in bond, solely for exportation, of articles made in whole or in part of imported materials or of materials subject to internal-revenue tax; and for the manufacture for home consumption or exportation of cigars in whole of tobacco imported from one country.
(7) **Class 7**. Warehouses bonded for smelting and refining[172] imported metal-bearing materials for exportation or domestic consumption.
(8) **Class 8**. Bonded warehouses established for the purpose of cleaning, sorting, repacking, or otherwise changing in condition, but not manufacturing, imported merchandise, under Customs supervision and at the expense of the proprietor.[173]
(9) **Class 9**. Bonded warehouse, known as "duty-free stores," used for selling, for use outside the Customs territory, conditionally duty-free merchandise owned or sold by the proprietor and delivered from the Class 9 warehouse to an airport or other exit point for exportation by, or on behalf of, individuals departing from the Customs territory for destinations other than foreign trade zones. . . .

. . .

---

172. 19 U.S.C. §§ 1311, 1312 (2021).

173. Pursuant to 19 C.F.R. § 19.1(b) (2021), "the whole or part of any warehouse of class 1, 2, 3, 4, 5, 6, 7, or 11 may be designated a constructive manipulation (class 8) warehouse when exigencies of the service so require."

> (11) **Class 11**. Bonded warehouses, known as "general order warehouses," established for the storage and disposition exclusively of general order merchandise. . . .[174]

B. Bond Requirements for Customs Bonded Warehouses

Section 113 of title 19 of the *Code of Federal Regulations* governs customs bonds. The liability of the surety and the principal remains for obligations incurred during the period in which the bond is in force.[175] Sections 113.61 through 113.75 provide the requisite conditions of the customs bonds. Section 113.61 provides:

> Each section of this subpart identifies specific coverage for a particular customs activity. When an individual or organization files a bond with CBP the activity in which they plan on engaging will be identified on the bond. The bond conditions listed in this subpart which correspond to that activity will be incorporated by reference into the bond.[176]

There are conditions for the following types of bonded customs activities: bond for basic importation and entry;[177] basic custodial bond;[178] bond for international carriers;[179] bond for repayment of erroneous drawback;[180] bond for control of containers and instruments of international traffic;[181] commercial gauger's bond and commercial laboratory's bond;[182] bond to comply with the Wool and Products Labeling Act, Fur Products Labeling Act, and Textile Fiber Products Identification Act;[183] bond to produce a bill of lading;[184] bond to indemnify the

---

174. Class 10 is currently reserved. 19 C.F.R. § 19.1(a)(10) (2021).
175. *See id.* § 113.3 ("The surety, as well as the principal, remains liable on a terminated bond for obligations incurred prior to termination.").
176. *Id.* § 113.61.
177. *Id.* § 113.62.
178. *Id.* § 113.63.
179. *Id.* § 113.64.
180. *Id.* § 113.65.
181. *Id.* § 113.66.
182. *Id.* § 113.67.
183. *Id.* § 113.68.
184. *Id.* § 113.69.

United States for detention of copyrighted material;[185] bond to observe neutrality;[186] bond to pay court costs (condemned goods);[187] bond of a foreign trade zone operator;[188] bond to indemnify a complainant under section 337 of the Tariff Act of 1930, as amended;[189] and bond for deferral of entry completion and duty deposit pursuant to 19 U.S.C. § 148b for a dutiable large yacht imported for sale at a U.S. boat show.[190]

The bond conditions for basic importation and entry require the principal and surety to agree, jointly and severally, to pay duties, taxes, and charges at the time the merchandise is released.[191] "Proof that the importer has complied with the conditions of the bond has traditionally been and still remains a complete defense to a collection suit brought on the bond."[192] Upon default, the principal and surety also are liable for liquidated damages in an amount equal to the value of the merchandise involved in the default or three times the value of the merchandise involved in the default if the merchandise is restricted or alcoholic beverages, or such other amount as may be authorized by law or regulation.[193] If no merchandise is involved in the default, the principal and surety are liable for liquidated damages in the amount of $1,000.[194] The principal's and surety's liability upon default of the conditions of a basic custodial bond is substantially the same.[195] The sureties on such bonds shall also be

---

185. *Id.* § 113.70.
186. *Id.* § 113.71.
187. *Id.* § 113.72.
188. *Id.* § 113.73.
189. *Id.* § 113.74.
190. *Id.* § 113.75.
191. *Id.* § 144.2 ("Under the conditions of the bond, the sureties on the bond shall be held liable for the payment of duties and Customs charges not paid by the principal on the bond, whether such duties and charges are finally ascertained before the merchandise is withdrawn from Customs custody or thereafter.").
192. United States v. Toshoku Am., Inc., 879 F.2d 815, 818 (Fed. Cir. 1989) (citing United States v. Utex Int'l, Inc., 857 F.2d 1408, 1413–14 (Fed. Cir. 1988); 1 PETER FELLER, U.S. CUSTOMS AND INTERNATIONAL TRADE GUIDE §§ 13.06, 13–31 (1988)).
193. 19 C.F.R. § 113.62 (2021).
194. *Id.*
195. *Id.* § 113.63.

advised in writing, at the same time as the principal, of the liability for liquidated damages.[196] However:

> The Commissioner of CBP may authorize the cancellation of any [customs] bond . . . or any charge that may have been made against the bond, in the event of a breach of any condition of the bond, upon payment of a lesser amount or penalty or upon such other terms and conditions as may be deemed sufficient.[197]

C. The Liability of the Customs Bond Surety

The general principles of suretyship law apply to the government seeking to recover duties and taxes under customs bonds as to individuals seeking recovery under other bonds.[198] In *St. Paul Mercury Indemnity*, the court acknowledged that "[i]t is fundamental that a surety's obligation is limited to the terms of his contract, for that is the extent of his risk."[199] The *St. Paul Mercury Indemnity* court held that the government's failure to comply with the requirement that it liquidate the entry within three years from the date of the original importation effectively prolonged the surety's risk without its consent and, thus, the court held that the surety's liability under the bond was discharged.[200]

In *United States v. Cocoa Berkau, Inc.*,[201] the issue on appeal was whether "the default of redelivery by the bond principal or the default of non-payment of liquidated damages by the bond surety, constituted the breach of the bond which fixed liability for purposes of triggering the statute of limitations."[202] The court looked to the terms of the bond and determined that "the government's action for liquidated damages arose from an alleged breach of paragraph 4 of the entry bond."[203] The *Cocoa Berkau* court determined that "[t]he bond was breached, and thus the government's right of action accrued when the principal failed to redeliver upon proper demand, not when the surety failed to pay liquidated

---

196. *Id.* § 172.1.
197. *Id.* § 113.51.
198. United States v. St. Paul Mercury Indem. Co., 96 F. Supp. 870, 872 (D.C. Pa. 1951), *aff'd*, 194 F.2d 68 (3d Cir. 1952).
199. *Id.*
200. *Id.* at 873.
201. 990 F.2d 610 (Fed. Cir. 1993).
202. *Id.* at 613.
203. *Id.*

damages."[204] Unless the parties have agreed otherwise, the surety incurs "derivative liability" when the principal breaches the bond.[205]

In *United States v. Utex International Inc.*,[206] the Federal Circuit reversed an award of liquidated damages against the surety and in favor of the government on an entry bond.[207] The government sought liquidated damages on a surety bond following importation of contaminated frozen shrimp.[208] In *Utex International*, CBP improperly liquidated 115 cartons of frozen shrimp in violation of regulations regarding foodstuffs.[209] "The various statutes and regulations make clear that Customs is the enforcement arm of the process wherein admissibility is determined by the FDA [U.S. Food and Drug Administration]."[210] The court also stated:

> It is the Customs Service that is responsible for . . . liquidation pending determination of admissibility by the FDA . . . . In this suit against a surety on its entry bond, the surety's liability arises under and is in terms of the customs law . . . . [B]oth the legality and correctness of a liquidation are determined, at least initially, through the protest procedure, and "any challenge to the propriety of a liquidation [not specifically excepted] must be through this statute."[211]

Although the Federal Circuit found the liquidation improper, it determined that it was final as to all aspects of the entry.[212] The Federal Circuit held

204. *Id.*; United States v. Reul, 959 F.2d 1572, 1576 (Fed. Cir. 1992) (interpreting the same bond provision and determining that "the default of redelivery by the bond principal constituted breach of the bond, at which point a suit for the consequences of such default accrued for purposes of 28 U.S.C. § 2415(a)").
205. United States v. Hanover Ins. Co., No. 92-11-00733, 1993 WL 273662, at *2 (Ct. Int'l Trade July 9, 1993).
206. 857 F.2d 1408 (Fed. Cir. 1988).
207. *Id.* at 1412.
208. *Id.* at 1409.
209. *Id.* at 1410 (citing 19 C.F.R. § 159.55(a), which provides in pertinent part: "The liquidation . . . shall be suspended until it is determined whether admission of the merchandise into the United States is permitted under the law.").
210. *Id.* at 1411.
211. *Id.* at 1410 (citations omitted).
212. *Id.* at 1414.

that the liquidation discharged the surety's liability on the bond.[213] The government, however, continued to argue that the surety was liable under paragraph 7 of the entry bond, the part that addresses requisite action after goods are deemed inadmissible.[214] The Federal Circuit rejected the government's argument that the statutory and contractual notice requirements did not apply to paragraph 7 because "the bond cannot be interpreted contrary to law and regulations."[215]

In *United States v. Toshoku America, Inc.*,[216] the government filed suit against the entry bond to recover liquidated damages assessed for failure to export adulterated tuna.[217] The Federal Circuit reversed the Court of International Trade's summary judgment in favor of the government holding that there was inadequate evidence to support CBP's demand for liquidated damages under the entry bond.[218] Paragraph 4 of the entry bond "protects the government in the event that the importer fails to redeliver inadmissible foodstuffs to Customs' custody upon demand by the district director. Default in that obligation results in the liability for liquidated damages for the importer, 19 C.F.R. § 141.113(g), and upon the importer's surety under the bond, 19 C.F.R. § 172.1(a)."[219] The Federal Circuit concluded that no liability existed under the bond because the importer had the options of exporting the adulterated tuna, redelivering the adulterated tuna to CBP, or destroying the adulterated tuna under paragraph 7 of the entry bond.[220] Exportation was optional, not mandatory. Thus, the bond conditions in paragraphs 4 and 7 were not breached.[221]

---

213. *Id.* at 1413–14.
214. *Id.* at 1412.
215. *Id.* at 1413 (citing United States v. DeVisser, 10 F. 642 (S.D.N.Y. 1882) (customs bond must be interpreted in reference to applicable statutes and regulations), *cited with approval in* Old Republic Ins. Co. v. United States, 645 F. Supp. 943, 953 (Ct. Int'l Trade 1986)).
216. 879 F.2d 815 (Fed. Cir. 1989).
217. *Id.* at 818.
218. *Id.* at 819–20.
219. *Id.* at 819.
220. *Id.* at 819–20.
221. *Id.*

CHAPTER 20

THE COMMERCIAL SURETY'S COLLATERAL IN THE PRINCIPAL'S BANKRUPTCY CASE

George J. Bachrach
Michael A. Stover
Nina M. Durante

Introduction

There is an enormous market in the United States for commercial surety bonds of all types covering a wide variety of obligations.[1] Those commercial surety bonds include judicial bonds, fiduciary/probate bonds, license and permit bonds, utility bonds, various statutory bonds (customs bonds, tax bonds, workers' compensation bonds, notary bonds, etc.), mechanic's lien release and discharge bonds, commercial surety performance-type bonds such as subdivision bonds, reclamation bonds, and the like, non-statutory guaranty and/or faithful performance bonds, public official bonds, and others.[2] Because of the nature of the commercial surety bond obligations, the surety may require that it receive collateral in some form from the principal in order to secure the surety for its obligations under the commercial surety bonds. The surety may

---

1. For the purposes of this chapter, the commercial bond surety is referred to as the "surety"; the surety's principal is referred to as the "principal" at all times, whether before the principal files its bankruptcy case or after the principal files its bankruptcy case and becomes a debtor; however, the term "debtor" may be used in generally describing a debtor under the Bankruptcy Code who is not a surety's principal in a bankruptcy case; and commercial surety bonds of all types covering many obligations are referred to collectively as "commercial surety bonds" unless a specific type of commercial surety bond is described.
2. For a brief listing of many different kinds of commercial surety bonds, see Bruce C. King et al., *Commercial Surety Indemnity Agreement Issues*, *in* THE SURETY'S INDEMNITY AGREEMENT: LAW AND PRACTICE 448–58 (Marilyn Klinger et al. eds., 2d ed. 2008) [hereinafter SURETY'S INDEMNITY AGREEMENT]. *See also* the Table of Contents of this book for some specific types of commercial surety bonds.

acquire the principal's collateral either at the inception of the suretyship relationship and the execution and issuance of the commercial surety bonds, or later when the surety demands to be "placed in funds." The surety's intent is to use the collateral to exonerate the surety prior to the surety making a payment and incurring a loss and/or to indemnify and reimburse the surety in the event it may or does suffer a loss under the commercial surety bonds.

However, the surety's ability to use the collateral, and even maintain its rights in the collateral that it has obtained pre-petition, or prior to the principal's filing of a bankruptcy case, may change when the principal files a bankruptcy case.[3] This chapter will examine the surety's ability to obtain, maintain, and use the collateral it receives pre-petition from the principal in order to secure the surety for its obligations under the commercial surety bonds in the event the principal subsequently files a bankruptcy case.[4]

I. Underwriting the Principal and Obtaining the Collateral

There is an ancient saying that a bird in the hand is worth two in the bush.[5] Thus, while the surety may have a strongly worded indemnity agreement requiring the principal to exonerate and/or indemnify and reimburse the surety for any and all losses in exchange for the surety's issuance of commercial surety bonds, ancient wisdom suggests that it is better for the surety to have collateral in hand rather than just the principal's promise to pay later in the future.

---

3. For the purposes of this chapter, it is assumed that the principal's bankruptcy case is a chapter 11 reorganization under the U.S. Bankruptcy Code, 11 U.S.C. § 101 *et seq*. However, many of the discussions in this chapter would be applicable to a principal becoming a debtor pursuant to a chapter 7 liquidation under the Bankruptcy Code. For a brief overview of chapter 11 business reorganizations, see *Overview of the Bankruptcy Code*, *in* SURETY ASPECTS OF BANKRUPTCY LAW AND PRACTICE 40–42 (Michael E. Collins & Chad L. Schexnayder eds., 2021) [hereinafter SURETY ASPECTS OF BANKRUPTCY]. For an in-depth review of chapter 11 reorganizations, see *Chapter 11 Reorganizations*, *in* SURETY ASPECTS OF BANKRUPTCY, *supra*, at 415–68.
4. See *infra* note 35 concerning a surety's receipt of collateral from its principal *after* the principal files its bankruptcy case.
5. The Proverbs of the Aramean Ahikar (c. 700 B.C.E.), No. 49.

In the commercial surety bond context, sureties generally address collateral and require the principal to provide collateral to the surety in several situations. First, the surety may require some form of collateral from the principal prior to or contemporaneously with the surety's issuing the commercial surety bonds. In those instances, the surety may determine, because of the principal's financial condition and/or the nature and risk of the commercial surety bond obligations, that some form of collateral is necessary to exonerate the surety prior to its payment of any loss under the commercial surety bonds and/or to indemnify and reimburse the surety for its subsequent payments resulting from the surety's execution of the commercial surety bonds. This may be especially true when the commercial surety bond obligation may arise instantaneously due to the actions of a third party that are outside of the principal's control[6] or when the principal (and the surety) may have little or no defense to the particular commercial surety bond claim.[7]

Second, if the surety does not require the principal to provide collateral at the outset of the surety's issuance of the commercial surety bonds, subsequent events and/or financial circumstances, including a change in the principal's financial condition, may cause the surety to require collateral from the principal after the issuance of the commercial surety bonds. This may occur as a condition for the surety's providing new commercial surety bonding for the principal in the future (and to induce the surety's forbearance from cancelling existing commercial surety bonds) and/or the surety's "collateral demand" or request to be "placed in funds" either for the surety's forbearance from exercising its rights to cancel the existing commercial surety bonds or to protect the surety from actual or potential claims against the commercial surety bonds. In these situations, as discussed next, it is important for the surety

---

6. For example, with certain judicial bonds such as supersedeas bonds or appeal bonds, the appellate court's decision that may be adverse to the principal's position may result in the surety having to pay immediately on the judicial bond after the expiration of the applicable time periods for any final appeals.
7. For example, there may be little or no defense to the pre-petition utility charges claimed against a utility bond that the principal may not pay post-petition due to either or both the automatic stay under the Bankruptcy Code, 11 U.S.C. § 362, or the avoidance of certain post-petition transfers under the Bankruptcy Code, 11 U.S.C. § 549.

to have strong indemnity agreement provisions regarding a "collateral demand" or a "place in funds demand" to obtain the collateral.

A. *The Surety's Indemnity Agreement with the Principal*

Prior to executing commercial surety bonds for the principal, sureties generally require the principal (and possibly some indemnitors)[8] to execute some form of an indemnity agreement. The indemnity agreement may be a short-form indemnity agreement based upon an application for the commercial surety bond or may be an indemnity agreement that covers numerous commercial surety bonds.[9] There are several indemnity agreement provisions regarding collateral that may be relevant, especially in the event that the principal subsequently files a bankruptcy case.

First, the indemnity agreement may allow the surety to either make a "collateral demand" or a "place in funds demand" at any time after the execution of the commercial surety bonds.[10] Such provisions are

---

8. While many surety indemnity agreements require the principal, and certain indemnitors, to execute an indemnity agreement that provides for the principal's and the indemnitors' joint and several liability to the surety for any surety losses as may be defined in the indemnity agreement, this chapter will only address the effect of a filing of a bankruptcy case on the obligations of a principal to the surety under the indemnity agreement and will not address the issues that may arise with respect to any indemnitors. Many of the issues are the same, but it is a less complex presentation to limit this chapter to a discussion of the collateral provided by the principal only rather than also addressing the surety's rights against the indemnitors and any collateral provided by the indemnitors.
9. *See* King et al., *supra* note 2, at 447–70.
10. For the surety's right to demand collateral from the principal under the indemnity agreement, see Shannon J. Briglia et al., *The Surety's Enforcement of Its Rights to Collateral from the Principal and the Indemnitors*, *in* SURETY'S INDEMNITY AGREEMENT, *supra* note 2, at 284–90. Such provisions frequently are enforced and upheld by the courts. *See* Fid. & Deposit Co. of Md. v. Bristol Steel & Iron Works, Inc., 722 F.2d 1160, 1163 (4th Cir. 1983); Com. Ins. Co. of Newark v. Pacific-Peru Constr., 558 F.2d 948, 953 (9th Cir. 1977); Transamerica Ins. Co. v. Bloomfield, 401 F.2d 357, 362–63 (6th Cir. 1968); Engbrock v. Fed. Ins. Co., 370 F.2d 784, 786 (5th Cir. 1967); Am. Sur. Co. of N.Y. v. Inmon, 187 F.2d 784, 786 (5th Cir. 1951); U.S. Fid. & Guar. Co. v. Jones, 87 F.2d 346, 348 (5th Cir. 1937); Carroll v. Nat'l Sur. Co., 24 F.2d 268, 270–71 (D.C. Cir. 1928); Cincinnati Ins. Co. v. Am. Glass Indus., No. 1:07cv1133

standard in many indemnity agreement forms, but are rarely contained in the short-form indemnity agreement provisions in commercial surety bond applications. "Collateral demand" and/or "place in funds demand" provisions may address some of the following issues:

- **Type of collateral**. The surety may demand any type of collateral at its sole discretion, including but not limited to letters of credit or the principal's real and/or personal property, including cash and cash equivalents.
- **Amount of collateral**. The amount of the collateral demand may be at the surety's sole discretion, and may or may not be tied to or limited by the amount of any reserves for any loss exposure that the surety may establish.
- **Collateral coverage**. The amount of the collateral demand may cover all of the commercial surety bonds—current, past, and future—and not just one or several of the commercial surety bonds, as well as any surety losses that are incurred under the indemnity agreement.
- **Use of collateral**. The collateral would normally be available to pay any surety losses, be held as a reserve against future

---

(JCC), 2008 WL 4642228, at * 4 (E.D. Va. Oct. 15, 2008); Nat'l Sur. Corp. v. Peoples Milling Co., 57 F. Supp. 281, 282–83 (W.D. Ky. 1944); Martin v. Lyons, 558 P.2d 1063, 1066 (Idaho 1977); Mass. Bonding & Ins. Co. v. Gautieri, 30 A.2d 848, 850 (R.I. 1943); Cent. Sur. & Ins. Corp. v. Martin, 224 S.W.2d 773, 779 (Tex. Civ. App. 1949). The surety may exercise its rights under the indemnity agreement "collateral demand" and "place in funds" provisions at any time prior to the principal filing its bankruptcy case. However, the surety's demand after the principal files its bankruptcy case may be a violation of the automatic stay. Even if the principal complies with the surety's demand post-petition, any such payments may be voidable as a post-petition transaction under § 549 of the Bankruptcy Code and other possible Bankruptcy Code provisions. The surety may obtain collateral post-petition under § 364 of the Bankruptcy Code if it extends new surety credit to the principal pursuant to a bankruptcy court order. *See infra* note 35. Finally, unless the surety negotiates for additional collateral under the plan of reorganization and the confirmation order, or at least preserves its rights to obtain collateral post-confirmation, the surety may not be able to obtain collateral after the entry of the confirmation order for its bond exposure (pre-petition or post-petition). *See In re* Falcon, 620 B.R. 256 (Bankr. M.D. La. 2020).

claims, pay premiums, pay costs for the investigation of claims by consultants, attorneys, accountants, and others, and exonerate and/or indemnify and reimburse the surety for any surety losses that are incurred under the indemnity agreement.

- **Conditions of holding the collateral**. The provision may discuss whether the collateral is to be insured, protected, invested, or who is entitled to any interest accrued while the collateral is held.
- **Return of collateral**. The provision may state the terms under which the surety may release the collateral and return the balance of the collateral to the principal (i.e., any excess collateral held by the surety after all potential risk of exposure for the surety has expired and the commercial surety bonds are released and discharged).

Second, the indemnity agreement may state that it constitutes a security agreement and financing statement for purposes of the Uniform Commercial Code (U.C.C.) with respect to the surety's ability to obtain a lien against the principal's personal property, and/or authorize the surety to obtain or execute a lien (mortgage, deed of trust, or other such lien) against the principal's real property. This may allow the surety to obtain secured creditor status with respect to certain types of the principal's collateral, and may provide the surety with a priority and/or secured position in any future principal bankruptcy case if the appropriate perfection steps are taken sufficiently in advance of the principal's filing its bankruptcy case.

Third, the indemnity agreement may have a "power of attorney" or "attorney in fact" provision that may allow the surety to execute documents on behalf of the principal such as agreements, checks, title documents, transfer documents, and so on. This type of provision may allow the surety to take any necessary steps with respect to its collateral to secure, protect, and preserve the surety's interest in the collateral and enforce the surety's rights under the indemnity agreement.

Finally, there are no standard form indemnity agreements in the commercial surety bond industry, as each surety drafts and requires its own form of indemnity agreement. While there may be many similarities in concepts and language in these various indemnity agreements, the surety may require an indemnity agreement from the principal that also contains other provisions that may assist the surety with respect to the collateral in the event that the principal files a bankruptcy case. Such indemnity agreement provisions may address certain of the principal's rights in bankruptcy (the automatic stay, the use of the surety's collateral, executory contracts, and financial accommodations, and other issues) and provide the surety with additional procedural and substantive rights upon the principal's filing of a bankruptcy case.

If the surety does not have a "collateral demand" or "place in funds demand" provision in its indemnity agreement, the surety, prior to the filing of the principal's bankruptcy case, may still be able to compel the principal to provide collateral to the surety in a number of ways. The first is a common law or equitable action to enforce the surety's exoneration rights, quia timet rights, or other legal process in the appropriate court to compel the principal to pay the obligations for which the surety may be secondarily liable or to indemnify and reimburse the surety. The second is through the principal's pure economic necessity. For example, if the principal requires continuing commercial surety bonds to operate its business, it may have little choice but to provide the surety with sufficient collateral in exchange for the surety's agreement to continue to issue the commercial surety bonds and/or to forebear from cancelling the existing commercial surety bonds.

Notwithstanding the surety's rights to obtain collateral from the principal through the provisions of the indemnity agreement or as part of the underwriting process, the surety must next take the appropriate steps to enforce such provisions. The surety must acquire the collateral and perfect the surety's rights, liens, and/or security interests in that collateral so that the surety may secure, preserve, protect, and use the collateral as necessary, whether or not the principal subsequently files a bankruptcy case.

B. Acquiring the Collateral and the Collateral Agreement

The collateral that the surety obtains from the principal may take a number of forms, and the surety must take certain steps in acquiring the collateral to ensure that it has good, valid, and perfected rights and lien rights in the collateral.[11] Frequently, the surety obtaining the collateral from the principal may require the principal to execute a "collateral agreement" in addition to providing the surety with its more general rights under the indemnity agreement. The collateral agreement normally will describe the type and the amount of the collateral that the principal provides to

---

11. *See* J. Michael Franks et al., *Documents and Agreements Related to the Indemnity Agreement*, *in* SURETY'S INDEMNITY AGREEMENT, *supra* note 2, at 130–56.

the surety, define the surety's rights to use the collateral (including the surety's rights to pay losses, to reimburse the surety for any losses the surety pays as described in the collateral agreement and/or the indemnity agreement, to pay surety premiums, to pay the surety's attorneys' fees and expenses, etc.), and may define the period of time in which the surety may retain the collateral and when the surety may be required to release all or a portion of the collateral and return the balance of the collateral to the principal (or the entity entitled to the return of the balance of the collateral).

The advantages of the collateral agreement over the more general terms of the indemnity agreement are that the collateral agreement may be more specific and detailed and may be tailored to the particular type of collateral involved or address any unique issues regarding specific forms of collateral and the surety's use of the collateral or its return to the principal. Indemnity agreements, on the other hand, rarely focus on what happens to the collateral once it is obtained by the surety, whether at the inception of the commercial surety bond relationship, pursuant to a "collateral demand," or pursuant to a "place in funds demand."

The following are various types of collateral that the surety may obtain from its principal either before the commercial surety bonds are executed or after, and the general methods for perfecting the surety's rights in the collateral.

1. Letters of Credit as Collateral[12]

The surety may receive a letter of credit from the principal as collateral for the commercial surety bonds. The U.C.C.[13] defines a letter of credit as follows:

> [A]n engagement by a bank or other person made at the request of a customer and of a kind within the scope of this Article . . . that the issuer will honor drafts or other demands for payment upon compliance with the conditions specified in the credit. A

---

12. *See id.* at 130–32.
13. For the purposes of this chapter, the authors are using the standard provisions of the U.C.C. as adopted by the National Conference of Commissioners on Uniform State Laws. It should be noted that each state may amend and change the provisions of the standard terms, and the appropriate state version of the U.C.C. should be reviewed in each case.

> credit may be either revocable or irrevocable. The engagement may be either an agreement to honor or a statement that the bank or other person is authorized to honor.[14]

As discussed later in this chapter, in the bankruptcy context there are many advantages for the surety obtaining a letter of credit as the principal's collateral instead of the principal's real or personal property as collateral. In addition to the favorable treatment under the Bankruptcy Code and the relevant bankruptcy case law, letters of credit are a preferable form of collateral for other reasons as well. Letters of credit are considered to be "liquid collateral." Sureties prefer liquid collateral in the form of the proceeds of a letter of credit as opposed to collateral that must be liquidated over time by a sale or transfer of the property. In addition to liquidity, letters of credit also have the advantage of not requiring any fees, expenses, or transaction costs to the surety to make demand on the letter of credit, such as would be required with other collateral such as real or personal property. Finally, letters of credit are in fixed and known amounts, whereas other forms of real or personal property collateral may be subject to prior liens affecting the remaining equity or value of the collateral, and may have estimated values that may vary widely from the actual liquidated value upon sale and may fluctuate over time with economic and market conditions while the collateral is being held by the surety.

Letters of credit are generally issued with expiration dates.[15] However, many letters of credit are known as "evergreen," which means that the

---

14. *See* U.C.C. § 5-103 (1995). In addition to Article 5 of the U.C.C., one should review the Uniform Customs and Practice for Documentary Credits, Publication 600 (commonly referred to as the UCP 600), which is published by the International Chamber of Commerce Commission on Banking Technique and Practice. The UCP 600 is frequently incorporated by reference into letters of credit and addresses certain aspects and issues related to presentment, honor, and the banking standards for dealing with letters of credit. With regard to the UCP 600, *see* Ala. Textile Co. v. Chase Manhattan Bank, N.A., 982 F.2d 813, 816 (2d Cir. 1992); MSF Holding Ltd. v. Fiduciary Tr. Co. Int'l, 435 F. Supp. 2d 285, 293–94 (S.D.N.Y. 2006); W. Int'l Forest Prods., Inc. v. Shinhan Bank, 860 F. Supp. 151, 153 (S.D.N.Y. 1994).
15. The U.C.C. provides that "[i]f there is no stated expiration date or other provision that determines its duration, a letter of credit expires one year after its stated date of issuance or, if none is stated, after the date on

terms of the letter of credit permit its automatic renewal on a periodic basis.[16] Evergreen letters of credit generally permit the issuer (the bank) to notify the beneficiary (the surety) that the letter of credit will not renew for an additional period. If the letter of credit is not evergreen and is set to expire by its terms, or in the event that the issuer of the letter of credit provides notice to the surety as the beneficiary that the letter of credit will not be renewed, the surety may need to draw on the letter of credit and obtain the letter of credit proceeds rather than allow its collateral to disappear. The ability to draw on a letter of credit prior to its expiration solely to preserve the collateral emphasizes the critical nature of having a letter of credit with no conditions on the surety's ability to make a draw on the letter of credit.

Ideally, the surety wants to have its letter of credit state as follows, or with similar wording: "[t]his irrevocable letter of credit is not subject to any condition, qualification or contingency." If the letter of credit is conditioned on the existence of valid claims against the commercial surety bonds or losses paid by the surety or other such terms before the issuing bank has to honor the letter of credit and make payment of the proceeds to the surety, the surety may not be able to protect the collateral if the surety receives notice that the letter of credit is about to expire prior

---

which it is issued." U.C.C. § 5-106(c). The U.C.C. further provides that "[a] letter of credit that states that it is perpetual expires five years after its stated date of issuance, or if none is stated, after the date on which it is issued." *Id.* § 5-106(d).

16. JOHN F. DOLAN, THE LAW OF LETTERS OF CREDIT ¶ 5.03[3][b] n.232 (4th ed. 2007); Golden W. Refin. Co. v. SunTrust Bank, 538 F.3d 1233, 1240 (9th Cir. 2008). In *Molter Corp. v. Amwest Surety Insurance Co.*, 642 N.E.2d 919 (Ill. App. Ct. 1994), the court describes and defines the elements of an "evergreen" letter of credit and the fact that an evergreen letter of credit automatically renews on an annual basis unless the issuer (the bank) provides notice to the beneficiary (the surety) of the issuer's intent to terminate the letter of credit as of the expiration date stated in the letter of credit. Furthermore, the extension of the expiration date in the letter of credit to a new date does not convert the letter of credit to a one-year letter of credit that expires by its terms on the new expiration date because the letter of credit, as an evergreen letter of credit, still provides that notice given to the beneficiary is the only manner in which the issuer may terminate the letter of credit.

to the surety's contractual right to draw on the letter of credit and obtain the proceeds.[17]

The surety "perfects" its security interest in the letter of credit by "control" of the letter of credit.[18] The U.C.C. defines "control" for purposes of letters of credit as follows:

---

17. A brief example illustrates this issue. As part of the underwriting for the issuance of commercial surety bonds for its principal, the surety demands collateral in the form of an "evergreen" letter of credit. The letter of credit provides that it expires after a period of one year, but that it will automatically be extended for successive one-year periods unless, at least 30 days prior to any expiration date, the bank notifies the surety that the bank elects not to renew the letter of credit. The letter of credit also stipulates that the surety may make demand on the letter of credit conditioned/contingent upon presentment of a valid proof of claim from a claimant of the principal under one or more commercial surety bonds or presentment of the surety's cancelled check(s) evidencing payment of one or more claims arising from the commercial surety bonds. The letter of credit renews automatically for several years with no problem. Then the issuing bank, through its confidential financial dealings with the principal, learns that the principal is heading into financial trouble. At this point, the principal has been able to convince its suppliers and creditors to continue to deal with it and to work out new short-term arrangements so there have not been any commercial surety bond claims, but the principal has a looming cash flow crisis coming. The issuing bank, realizing that the principal is in trouble, decides not to renew the letter of credit and notifies the surety that the letter of credit will not be renewed. In this scenario, 30 days after the bank's issuance of the notice, the letter of credit will expire and the surety, with no commercial surety bond claims or payments made, will have no collateral. Assuming that the surety receives the notice of nonrenewal from the issuing bank and recognizes its importance, by the time the surety goes back to the principal, it may be too late for the surety to obtain any replacement collateral from the principal. The letter of credit expires because the surety is unable to satisfy the conditions of making a demand (i.e., it has not received any claims or made any payments), leaving the surety with no collateral. It is at this point that the commercial surety bond claims will start arriving. If the letter of credit had no conditions or contingencies, the surety may have timely drawn down the entire amount of the letter of credit proceeds and placed the proceeds in a surety controlled account to serve as cash collateral for the payment of any future claims.
18. *See* U.C.C. § 9-314, Perfection by control.

> A secured party has control of a letter-of-credit right to the extent of any right to payment or performance by the issuer or any nominated person if the issuer or nominated person has consented to an assignment of proceeds of the letter of credit under Section 5-114(c) or otherwise applicable law or practice.[19]

In other words, for purposes of control under the U.C.C., the surety must be the party to whom the letter of credit is issued or payable or have a valid assignment of such payment rights. Letters of credit are not like instruments. The mere fact that a person may actually hold or have possession of the letter of credit does not mean that the person, as the holder, has any right to make demand for or receive payment under the letter of credit.[20]

2. Cash, Deposit Accounts, and/or Certificates of Deposit as Collateral[21]

Cash, deposit accounts, and/or certificates of deposit provided by the principal to the surety as collateral are considered to be the principal's property even though they have been pledged to the surety as collateral.[22] While cash is definitely liquid, deposit accounts, including certificates of deposit, with various lenders, unless otherwise agreed with the surety, may be subject to the lender's set-off rights in the event the principal is indebted to the lender. Furthermore, certificates of deposit may have penalties for early withdrawal.

To perfect a security interest in cash or money, the surety must be in *possession* of the money.[23] Perfection by possession, as is the case with perfection by control, does not require the filing of a U.C.C.-1 financing statement or any formal filing.[24] While the U.C.C. does not

---

19. *See id.* § 9-107, Control of letter-of-credit right.
20. *In re* United Energy Coal, Inc., No. 06–453, 2008 WL 496142, at *6–7 (Bankr. W. Va. Feb. 21, 2008).
21. *See* Franks et al., *supra* note 11, at 132.
22. *See, e.g.*, Int'l Fin. Corp. v. Kaiser Grp. Int'l (*In re* Kaiser Grp. Int'l), 399 F.3d 558, 566 (3d Cir. 2005); *In re* S-Tran Holdings, Inc., 414 B.R. 28, 32 (Bankr. D. Del. 2009); *see In re* Oakley, 397 B.R. 36, 50 (Bankr. S.D. Ohio 2008); *In re* MJK Clearing, Inc., 286 B.R. 862, 874 (Bankr. D. Minn. 2002); *In re* Julien Co., 117 B.R. 910, 919 (Bankr. W.D. Tenn. 1990); 11 U.S.C. § 541(c).
23. *See* U.C.C. §§ 9-312(b)(3), 9-313.
24. *See id.* § 9-313 cmt. 2.

expressly define "possession," the term has been held to mean exactly what it implies, namely that the secured party must have actual, physical possession of the cash or money in order to have a perfected security interest in that form of collateral.[25]

The U.C.C. defines "deposit account" as a "demand, time, savings, passbook, or similar account maintained with a bank. The term does not include investment property or accounts evidenced by an instrument."[26] To perfect a security interest in deposit accounts, the surety must "control" the account.[27] The U.C.C. defines "control" over a deposit account in relevant part as follows:

> (a) Requirements for control. A secured party has control of a deposit account if: . . . .
>
> (2) the debtor, secured party, and bank have agreed in an authenticated record that the bank will comply with instructions originated by the secured party directing disposition of the funds in the deposit account without further consent by the debtor; or
>
> (3) the secured party becomes the bank's customer with respect to the deposit account.[28]

With respect to certificates of deposit, the question of perfection is fairly complicated and depends on the nature of the certificate of deposit (i.e., whether it is transferrable, negotiable, or nonnegotiable) and whether the particular jurisdiction will treat the certificate of deposit as a "deposit account" or an "instrument." In addition, the question of whether the certificate of deposit is "certificated" or "uncertificated" also impacts the analysis. The definition of a "deposit account" as noted above states that such accounts evidenced by Article 9 "instruments" are excluded from the definition. Thus, the definition of "deposit account" was intended to clarify the proper treatment of nonnegotiable or uncertificated certificates of deposit. The Official Comments of the U.C.C. state:

---

25. *See In re* Wright Grp., Inc., 443 B.R. 795, 804 (Bankr. N.D. Ind. 2011).
26. *See* U.C.C. § 9-102(29).
27. *See id.* § 9-312(b)(1).
28. *See id.* § 9-104. Section (1) of this provision is unrelated as it addresses a bank's exercise of control over a customer's account.

> Under the definition [of deposit account], an uncertificated certificate of deposit would be a deposit account (assuming there is no writing evidencing the bank's obligation to pay) whereas a nonnegotiable certificate of deposit would be a deposit account only if it is not an "instrument" as defined in this section (a question that turns on whether the nonnegotiable certificate of deposit is "of a type that in ordinary course of business is transferred by delivery with any necessary indorsement or assignment.").[29]

A certificate of deposit evidenced by an instrument is subject to the rules applicable to perfection of instruments. U.C.C. section 9-312(a) requires filing of a financing statement for the perfection of a security interest in instruments. To avoid any concerns regarding perfection of a security interest in a certificate of deposit, the surety should consider perfecting by exercising control as required for deposit accounts *and* by filing as required for instruments.

3. Other Collateral (Real and Personal Property)[30]

In the event that the principal does not have liquid collateral in the form of a letter of credit, cash, deposit accounts, or certificates of deposit, the surety may obtain collateral in the form of real or personal property.[31] With respect to the principal's real property, state law will determine how the surety obtains a mortgage, deed of trust, or other recording to secure its lien on the real property.[32] With respect to the principal's personal property (which could include equipment, inventory and materials, stocks and bonds and other financial investments, general intangibles, intellectual property, life insurance, and other personal property), the surety must perfect its interest in the personal property as collateral in accordance with state law, normally the U.C.C.[33]

Neither real property nor personal property is considered liquid. Some judicial or administrative action may be necessary prior to the surety's exercising its rights to the principal's real or personal property.

---

29. *See id.* § 9-102, Official Comment 12 (clarification added).
30. *See* Franks et al., *supra* note 11, at 134–38.
31. *Id.* at 139–47.
32. *Id.* at 139–41.
33. *Id.* at 141–47, 307–22.

The surety may be required to sell the real and/or personal property (whether at auction or foreclosure or even a private sale, each of which have the attendant costs of sale) prior to obtaining the net funds necessary (assuming there is sufficient equity or value) to either pay a claim on a commercial surety bond or reimburse the surety for any payments the surety makes.[34] Furthermore, the real and/or personal property collateral may have prior liens on the collateral that reduce the equity (the net funds) available for the surety in the event it seeks reimbursement for any losses. In addition, as noted above, the value of the collateral is generally only an estimate that cannot be actually determined until after a sale of the property and such value may fluctuate over time with economic and other market conditions. Finally, there are typically transaction costs associated with maintaining, selling, or transferring most forms of real and personal property such as taxes, insurance, fees, and expenses.

II. The Effect of the Principal's Bankruptcy Case on the Surety's Collateral

When the principal files its bankruptcy case and becomes a debtor in possession under chapter 11 of the Bankruptcy Code, the surety's rights in the collateral obtained from the principal prior to the principal's filing of its bankruptcy case[35] may be subject to various provisions of the Bankruptcy Code.

---

34. *Id.* at 151–55.
35. This chapter will not address the surety's ability and/or right to obtain collateral from the principal, now the debtor, *after* the principal's filing of its bankruptcy case. The principal/debtor may request that the surety execute new post-petition commercial surety bonds after the principal files its bankruptcy case. The surety's execution of post-petition commercial surety bonds is the equivalent of the surety's providing new credit to the principal/debtor and requires bankruptcy court approval under the Bankruptcy Code pursuant to 11 U.S.C. § 364. As part of its agreement to execute new post-petition commercial surety bonds, the surety may require post-petition collateral from the principal/debtor. The surety's rights to obtain and use the post-petition collateral would be provided in any agreements between the surety and the principal/debtor as authorized by the applicable bankruptcy court order. *See Case Administration*, *in* SURETY ASPECTS OF BANKRUPTCY, *supra* note 3, at 160–74; Chad L. Schexnayder et al., *The Indemnity Agreement in Bankruptcy*, *in* SURETY'S INDEMNITY AGREEMENT, *supra* note 2, at 517–19.

A. *The Property of the Principal's (the Debtor's) Estate (11 U.S.C. § 541)*

Section 541 of the Bankruptcy Code provides that the commencement of the debtor's bankruptcy case under the Bankruptcy Code creates an estate.[36] The debtor's estate comprises certain broadly defined property, "wherever located and by whomever held."[37] Specifically, the property of the debtor's bankruptcy estate (or the "property of the estate") includes all of the debtor's legal or equitable interests in property as of the commencement of the bankruptcy case and also includes proceeds or profits of or from the property of the estate.[38] "The intent of this provision [§ 541(a)(1) of the Bankruptcy Code] is to include all property rights of the Debtor, even if the property right is contingent."[39] Thus, the "conditional, future, speculative, or equitable nature" of an interest does not prevent it from becoming property of the estate.[40]

The legislative history of the Bankruptcy Code reveals that the concept of "property of the estate" is to be interpreted broadly.[41] The U.S. Supreme Court has affirmed that the scope of § 541(a) of the Bankruptcy Code is broad, covering all kinds of property, including tangible or intangible property, causes of action, and all other forms of property.[42] Notwithstanding the broad interpretation, however, the debtor's interests in an asset or its rights against others are not expanded by the filing of a bankruptcy case.[43] "To the extent that the legal or equitable interest of the

---

36. 11 U.S.C. § 541(a). *See Case Administration*, *supra* note 35, at 103–13; *Bankruptcy Estate*, *in* SURETY ASPECTS OF BANKRUPTCY, *supra* note 3, at 309–14.
37. 11 U.S.C. § 541(a).
38. *Id.* § 541(a)(1), (6).
39. *In re* Palmer, 167 B.R. 579, 585 (Bankr. D. Ariz. 1994) (citing Neuton v. Danning, 922 F.2d 1379, 1382–83 (9th Cir. 1990)) (clarification added).
40. *In re* Anders, 151 B.R. 543, 545 (Bankr. D. Nev. 1993); *In re* Anderson, 128 B.R. 850 (D.R.I. 1991).
41. *See* H.R. REP. NO. 595, at 367–68 (1977), *reprinted in* U.S.C.C.A.N. 5787, 5963, 6323–24.
42. United States v. Whiting Pools, Inc., 462 U.S. 198, 204–05 & n.9 (1983).
43. *Matter of* Sanders, 969 F.2d 591 (7th Cir. 1992); *Matter of* Vill. Rathskeller, Inc., 147 B.R. 665 (Bankr. S.D.N.Y. 1992); *In re* Squyres, 172 B.R. 592, 594 (Bankr. C.D. Ill. 1994).

debtor in property is limited in the debtor's hands, it is equally limited as property of the estate."[44]

Bankruptcy law defines what property is included in the estate, but state law generally determines whether a debtor has a legal or equitable interest in property for purposes of § 541 of the Bankruptcy Code and the extent of such interest.[45] The debtor's cash, deposit accounts, certificates of deposit, real property, and personal property will most likely be deemed property of the estate and be subject to the remaining provisions of the Bankruptcy Code, such as the automatic stay as described below.[46] However, also as described below, a letter of credit and the proceeds of the letter of credit are generally not considered to be property of the estate.

B. The Automatic Stay (11 U.S.C. § 362)

Section 362 of the Bankruptcy Code provides that the filing of a petition and the commencement of the bankruptcy case operates as a stay of virtually all actions against the debtor and the property of the estate, and is applicable to all entities, including the surety.[47] Upon

---

44. *Squyres*, 172 B.R. at 594 (citing *In re* Balay, 113 B.R. 429 (Bankr. N.D. Ill. 1990)).
45. *See* Butner v. United States, 440 U.S. 48 (1979); *In re* Thomas, 883 F.2d 991, 995 (11th Cir. 1989); *In re* Moore, 448 B.R. 93, 99–100 (Bankr. N.D. Ga. 2011); *In re* Bell, 279 B.R. 890, 895 (Bankr. N.D. Ga. 2002).
46. *Whiting Pools, Inc.*, 462 U.S. at 204–05; *Moore*, 448 B.R. at 100.
47. 11 U.S.C. § 362(a) provides that the automatic stay prohibits creditors from taking the following actions against a debtor or its property:
(1) the commencement or continuation, including the issuance or employment of process, of a judicial, administrative, or other action or proceeding against the debtor that was or could have been commenced before the commencement of the case under this title, or to recover a claim against the debtor that arose before the commencement of the case under this title;
(2) the enforcement, against the debtor or against property of the estate, of a judgment obtained before the commencement of the case under this title;
(3) any act to obtain possession of property of the estate or of property from the estate or to exercise control over property of the estate;
(4) any act to create, perfect, or enforce any lien against property of the estate;

the commencement of the principal's bankruptcy case, the surety may not enforce its rights against the principal's property without risking a violation of the automatic stay. The automatic stay remains in effect until the principal's property is no longer the property of the estate.[48] A violation of the automatic stay may result in sanctions, assessment of damages, attorneys' fees, and even punitive damages.[49] Moreover, any action taken in violation of the automatic stay is void and without effect.[50] As one court stated:

> A "willful" violation of the stay does not require a specific intent to violate the automatic stay. Rather, the statute provides for damages upon a finding that the defendant knew of the automatic stay and that the defendant's actions which violated the stay were intentional. Whether the party believes in good faith that it had a right to the property is not relevant to whether the act was "willful" or whether compensation must be awarded.[51]

---

(5) any act to create, perfect, or enforce against property of the debtor any lien to the extent that such lien secures a claim that arose before the commencement of the case under this title;
(6) any act to collect, assess, or recover a claim against the debtor that arose before the commencement of the case under this title;
(7) the setoff of any debt owing to the debtor that arose before the commencement of the case under this title against any claim against the debtor; and
(8) the commencement or continuation of a proceeding before the United States Tax Court concerning the debtor.
See Case Administration, *supra* note 35, at 113–24.

48. 11 U.S.C. § 362(c).
49. *Id.* § 362(h).
50. Kalb v. Feuerstein, 308 U.S. 433, 438 (1940); Franklin Sav. Ass'n v. Off. of Thrift Supervision, 31 F.3d 1020, 1022 (10th Cir. 1994) (citing Ellis v. Consol. Diesel Elec. Corp., 894 F.2d 371, 372–73 (10th Cir. 1990)); *In re* Advent Corp., 24 B.R. 612, 614 (B.A.P. 1st Cir. 1982); *In re* Young, 14 B.R. 809, 811 (Bankr. N.D. Ill. 1981). Acts done in violation of the stay are void ab initio regardless of lack of knowledge of the filing of the petition. *In re* Wariner, 16 B.R. 216, 218 (Bankr. N.D. Tex. 1981); *In re* Miller, 10 B.R. 778, 780 (Bankr. D. Md. 1981).
51. Pinkstaff v. United States (*In re* Pinkstaff), 974 F.2d 113, 115 (9th Cir. 1992) (quoting Goichman v. Bloom (*In re* Bloom), 875 F.2d 224, 227 (9th Cir. 1989)).

The surety may seek relief from the automatic stay in order to enforce its rights against the principal's property of the estate that serves as the surety's collateral. After notice and a hearing, the bankruptcy court may provide relief, such as by terminating, annulling, modifying, or conditioning the automatic stay, for the following reasons:

- For cause, including the principal's lack of adequate protection of the surety's interest in the principal's property[52]
- With respect to a stay of any act against the property of the principal's estate, if the principal does not have any equity in the principal's property that serves as the surety's collateral and the surety's collateral is not necessary to an effective reorganization[53]

It is the surety's burden of proof on the issues of cause and/or whether the principal has any equity in the principal's property that serves as the surety's collateral, while it is the party opposing the surety's requested relief (usually the principal) that has the burden of proof on all other issues.[54]

C. The Surety's Secured Claim (11 U.S.C. § 506)

To the extent that the surety has a valid and perfected lien or security interest in the principal's property and the surety's collateral that is deemed to be property of the estate under § 541 of the Bankruptcy Code, the surety has a secured claim under § 506 of the Bankruptcy Code.[55] Section 506(a)(1) provides:

> An allowed claim of a creditor secured by a lien on property in which the estate has an interest, or that is subject to setoff under section 553 of this title, is a secured claim to the extent of the value of such creditor's interest in the estate's interest in such property, or to the extent of the amount subject to setoff, as the case may be, and is an unsecured claim to the extent that the

---

52. 11 U.S.C. § 362(d)(1).
53. *Id.* § 362(d)(2).
54. *Id.* § 362(g)(1), (2).
55. *See Surety Claims in Bankruptcy*, *in* SURETY ASPECTS OF BANKRUPTCY, *supra* note 3, at 253–65.

> value of such creditor's interest or the amount so subject to setoff is less than the amount of such allowed claim. Such value shall be determined in light of the purpose of the valuation and of the proposed disposition or use of such property, and in conjunction with any hearing on such disposition or use or on a plan affecting such creditor's interest.[56]

Therefore, the surety has a secured claim against the surety's collateral to the extent that the collateral, as property of the estate, has value or equity. If the surety's collateral has no value or equity to the surety because prior liens on the surety's collateral exceed the value of the surety's collateral, then the surety's claim is an unsecured claim and not a secured claim.

In the event that the surety's collateral, as property of the principal's estate, does have equity, § 506(b) of the Bankruptcy Code allows the surety's secured claim to be paid interest and other reasonable fees, costs, and claims under any agreements between the principal and the surety such as the indemnity agreement or the collateral agreement.[57]

Section 506(c) of the Bankruptcy Code allows the debtor/trustee to "recover from property securing an allowed secured claim the reasonable, necessary costs and expenses of preserving, or disposing of, such property to the extent of any benefit to the holder of such claim."[58] The surety may be the holder of such a secured claim against such property.

Section 506(d) of the Bankruptcy Code provides that "[t]o the extent that a lien secures a claim against the debtor that is not an allowed secured claim, such lien is void, unless," among other reasons, the claim is disallowed under certain sections of the Bankruptcy Code, including § 502(e). Section 502(e) of the Bankruptcy Code is important to the surety because it deals with the disallowance of the surety's contingent claim for reimbursement, which may occur at a time when the surety has

---

56. 11 U.S.C. § 506(a)(1).
57. 11 U.S.C. § 506(b) provides:

    To the extent that an allowed secured claim is secured by property the value of which, after any recovery under subsection (c) of this section, is greater than the amount of such claim, there shall be allowed to the holder of such claim, interest on such claim, and any reasonable fees, costs, or charges provided for under the agreement or State statute under which such claim arose.
58. *Id.* § 506(c).

a secured claim in the principal's collateral (property), but the surety's claim is still contingent because there are outstanding and unresolved claims against the surety's bonds. The surety wants to maintain its liens and secured claim until all of its commercial surety bond liability and exposure is resolved, and the surety may assert its rights to the collateral. This issue is discussed more fully later in this chapter.[59]

D. The Principal's (the Debtor's) Use of the Collateral (11 U.S.C. § 363)

Notwithstanding the surety's lien or security interest in the surety's collateral that is property of the estate, the principal may have a right to use the surety's collateral during the principal's bankruptcy case pursuant to § 363 of the Bankruptcy Code,[60] which distinguishes the principal's right to use different kinds of property that may serve as the surety's collateral. The principal may use property of the estate in the ordinary course of business without court approval,[61] and may use property of the estate other than in the ordinary course of business after a notice and hearing and bankruptcy court approval.[62] Therefore, to the extent that the surety's collateral constitutes property of the estate (the principal's real property, personal property such as motor vehicles, equipment, inventory, etc.), the principal may use the surety's collateral in the ordinary course of business without a bankruptcy court order, but may not sell, use, or lease the surety's collateral other than in the ordinary course of the principal's business without bankruptcy court approval.

The principal's property that is defined as "cash collateral"[63] has more restrictions. Section 363(c)(2) of the Bankruptcy Code provides:

---

59. *See infra* Section V.C.1.

60. *See Case Administration*, *supra* note 35, at 124–60.

61. Pursuant to 11 U.S.C. § 363(c)(1):

> If the business of the debtor is authorized to be operated under section 721, 1108, 1203, 1204, or 1304 of this title and unless the court orders otherwise, the trustee may enter into transactions, including the sale or lease of property of the estate, in the ordinary course of business, without notice or a hearing, and may use property of the estate in the ordinary course of business without notice or a hearing.

62. *Id.* § 363(b)(1).

63. 11 U.S.C. § 363(a) provides in part: "In this section, 'cash collateral' means cash, negotiable instruments, documents of title, securities, deposit

(2) The trustee may not use, sell, or lease cash collateral under paragraph (1) of this subsection unless—

(A) each entity that has an interest in such cash collateral consents; or

(B) the court, after notice and a hearing, authorizes such use, sale, or lease in accordance with the provisions of this section.[64]

Therefore, before the principal may use the surety's collateral that is deemed to be "cash collateral" (cash, deposit accounts, or certificates of deposit), the surety must either consent to the principal's use of the cash collateral or the bankruptcy court, after a notice and a hearing, must authorize such use.[65]

If the surety does not consent to the principal's use of the surety's collateral deemed to be "cash collateral," the surety may either object to the principal's motion to use the surety's "cash collateral" or the surety may request that the bankruptcy court prohibit the principal's use of the surety's "cash collateral"[66] unless the surety is provided with adequate protection of its interest in the surety's "cash collateral."[67]

---

accounts, or other cash equivalents whenever acquired in which the estate and an entity other than the estate have an interest . . . ."

64. *Id.* § 363(c)(2).

65. Pursuant to 11 U.S.C. § 363(c)(4): "Except as provided in paragraph (2) of this subsection, the trustee shall segregate and account for any cash collateral in the trustee's possession, custody, or control."

66. Pursuant to 11 U.S.C. § 363(e):
Notwithstanding any other provision of this section, at any time, on request of any entity that has an interest in property used, sold, or leased, or proposed to be used, sold, or leased, by the trustee, the court, with or without a hearing, shall prohibit or condition such use, sale, or lease as is necessary to provide adequate protection of such interest.

67. Pursuant to 11 U.S.C. § 361:
When adequate protection is required under section 362, 363, or 364 of this title of an interest of an entity in property, such adequate protection may be provided by—
(1) requiring the trustee to make a cash payment or periodic cash payments to such entity, to the extent that the stay under section 362 of this title, use, sale, or lease under section 363 of this title, or any grant of a lien under section 364 of this title results in a decrease in the value of such entity's interest in such property.

Section 363 of the Bankruptcy Code is very relevant in the contract surety bond situation (performance and payment bonds) because bonded contract funds, subject to the provisions of the Bankruptcy Code, may be both property of the estate and "cash collateral." But the "cash collateral" issue may also arise in commercial surety bond situations. Not only may the surety be holding property of the principal's estate as the surety's collateral that the principal/debtor may want to use pursuant to § 363 of the Bankruptcy Code, but the surety may also be holding the principal's property as the surety's collateral that is deemed to be "cash collateral," such as cash, deposit accounts, and/or certificates of deposit.[68] The principal/debtor may not use the surety's collateral that is deemed to be "cash collateral" without complying with the provisions of § 363 of the Bankruptcy Code.

Section 363(f) and other subsections of the Bankruptcy Code authorize the debtor or trustee to sell property of the estate subject to liens held by secured creditors free and clear of those liens, with the liens attaching to the net proceeds of sale in the amounts of such liens and in the order of priority of such liens. Therefore, the surety's collateral may be sold and liquidated at some point, with the surety's lien as a secured creditor attaching, as appropriate, to the net proceeds of sale.

E. The Principal's (the Debtor's) Plan of Reorganization

1. Generally

Under chapter 11 of the Bankruptcy Code, the principal, now the debtor, is authorized to continue to operate its business, remain in possession of

---

(2) providing to such entity an additional or replacement lien to the extent that such stay, use, sale, lease, or grant results in a decrease in the value of such entity's interest in such property; or

(3) granting such other relief, other than entitling such entity to compensation allowable under section 503(b)(1) of this title as an administrative expense, as will result in the realization by such entity of the indubitable equivalent of such entity's interest in such property.

68. Although the letter of credit proceeds drawn by a surety from the issuer of the letter of credit may be in the form of "cash," that "cash" held by the surety is not property of the estate that may be used by the principal/debtor under § 363 of the Bankruptcy Code, and may not be "cash collateral" unless such letter of credit proceeds are later deemed to be "excess proceeds." *See infra* Section III.A.2.

its property, and reorganize its financial affairs as an on-going business concern rather than shut the business down and conduct a liquidation under chapter 7 of the Bankruptcy Code. The provisions of the Bankruptcy Code discussed above (property of the estate; the automatic stay; the principal's use, sale, or lease of its property; as well as the principal's ability to obtain new credit; assume, assume and assign, or reject various executory contracts; and others) help facilitate the principal's continuing business operations that may lead to the principal's proposing a plan of reorganization to its creditors.[69]

The plan of reorganization process normally entails negotiations between a debtor and a majority of its creditors—secured, unsecured, and equity holders, among others—in order to reach a consensual agreement concerning the debtor's business and financial plans going forward into the future that offer some realistic chance of success.[70]

The Bankruptcy Code is very specific about what needs to be contained in a plan of reorganization,[71] including the classification of the various creditor claims against the debtor,[72] which classes of claims are not impaired and which classes of claims are impaired[73] under the

---

69. *See Chapter 11 Reorganization*, *in* SURETY ASPECTS OF BANKRUPTCY, *supra* note 3, at 415–68.

70. 11 U.S.C. § 1121, Who May File a Plan, addresses the issues of who may file a plan of reorganization (the debtor and then other parties in interest) and the timing (including the debtor's exclusive period for filing a plan of reorganization and certain extensions of time). *See Chapter 11 Reorganization*, *supra* note 69, at 430–32 (exclusivity period).

71. 11 U.S.C. § 1123, Contents of Plan. Pursuant to § 1123, a plan of reorganization must:
(a) Classify claims and interests;
(b) Specify any classes of claims or interests that are not impaired under the plan of reorganization;
(c) Specify the treatment of impaired classes and interests;
(d) Provide the same treatment for each member of a class unless a holder of a particular claim agrees to less favorable treatment;
(e) Provide adequate means of implementing the plan of reorganization; and
(f) Other provisions.
See Chapter 11 Reorganization, *supra* note 69, at 437–60.

72. 11 U.S.C. § 1122, Classification of Claims or Interests. *See Chapter 11 Reorganization*, *supra* note 69, at 437–54 (including a discussion of impairment of claims under § 1124 of the Bankruptcy Code).

73. 11 U.S.C. § 1124, Impairment of Claims or Interests.

plan of reorganization, and the treatment of those classes of claims that are impaired under the plan of reorganization. The Bankruptcy Code then addresses the debtor's disclosure of information necessary for the acceptance or rejection of the plan of reorganization (the disclosure statement, which must contain adequate information to enable those entitled to vote on the plan of reorganization to make an informed decision) and the solicitation of acceptance of the plan of reorganization,[74] the requirements for the acceptance of the plan of reorganization,[75] the hearing on the confirmation of the plan of reorganization,[76] and what is necessary for any confirmation of the plan of reorganization.[77]

2. *The Plan of Reorganization's Treatment of Secured Claims and the Surety's Collateral*

The surety may have collateral from the principal that is property of the estate, such as the principal's real and/or personal property. As a result, as provided under § 506 of the Bankruptcy Code described above,[78] the surety may have a secured claim. If so, the plan of reorganization and the subsequent confirmation order must be reviewed concerning their effect on the surety's secured claim.[79] The surety may be treated either like all other creditors with secured claims, or separately, in its own classification,

---

74. *Id.* § 1125, Postpetition Disclosure and Solicitation. *See Chapter 11 Reorganization, supra* note 69, at 432–36.
75. 11 U.S.C. § 1126, Acceptance of Plan. *See Chapter 11 Reorganization, supra* note 69, at 436–37.
76. 11 U.S.C. § 1128, Confirmation Hearing.
77. *Id.* § 1129, Confirmation of Plan. The requirements under § 1129 include:
(a) That the plan of reorganization be proposed in good faith;
(b) That each creditor or equity interest holder have accepted the plan of reorganization or be entitled to receive at least what it or they would receive in a chapter 7 liquidation of the debtor; and
(c) That each class has either accepted the plan of reorganization or is not impaired under the plan of reorganization.
See Chapter 11 Reorganization, supra note 69, at 455–60.
78. *See supra* Section II.C.
79. A surety may file an objection to the disclosure statement and/or an objection in opposition to the confirmation of a plan of reorganization, and may vote either in favor of or against the confirmation of the plan of reorganization. Therefore, a surety may have several opportunities to affirm or oppose what the principal plans to do with the surety's secured claim and collateral under the plan of reorganization and the confirmation order.

as provided in the plan of reorganization, so long as the treatment of the surety's secured claim is "fair and equitable."[80] Therefore, to the extent that the surety has a secured claim with respect to the surety's collateral that is property of the principal's estate, § 1129(b)(2) of the Bankruptcy Code provides as follows:

> (2) For the purpose of this subsection, the condition that a plan be fair and equitable with respect to a class includes the following requirements:
>
> (A) With respect to a class of secured claims, the plan provides—
>
> (i)(I) that the holders of such claims retain the liens securing such claims, whether the property subject to such liens is retained by the debtor or transferred to another entity, to the extent of the allowed amount of such claims; and
>
> (II) that each holder of a claim of such class receive on account of such claim deferred cash payments totaling at least the allowed amount of such claim, of a value, as of the effective date of the plan, of at least the value of such holder's interest in the estate's interest in such property;
>
> (ii) for the sale, subject to section 363(k) of this title, of any property that is subject to the liens securing such claims, free and clear of such liens, with such liens to attach to the proceeds of such sale, and the treatment of such liens on proceeds under clause (i) or (iii) of this subparagraph; or
>
> (iii) for the realization by such holders of the indubitable equivalent of such claims.[81]

---

80. To the extent that a surety has a secured claim against the principal's property of the estate, the surety's secured claim should not be treated any differently than the secured claims of any other secured creditor under the plan of reorganization or the confirmation order.

81. *See* 11 U.S.C. § 1129(b)(2).

Even if the surety's secured claim is disallowed under § 502(e) of the Bankruptcy Code because it is a contingent claim for reimbursement, the surety's lien on the surety's collateral remains in effect.[82]

If the surety's collateral is a letter of credit, which is not property of the estate,[83] then the plan of reorganization may not directly address the surety's claim—it is not a secured claim because the letter of credit and its proceeds are not property of the estate. However, if the surety has drawn on the letter of credit prior to the entry of a confirmation order concerning the plan of reorganization and the surety is now holding the proceeds of the letter of credit (namely, cash), the principal, or its trustee, may subsequently claim that the surety is holding "excess proceeds" from the letter of credit that they assert may later become property of the estate.[84] Furthermore, if the surety has not drawn on the letter of credit prior to the entry of a confirmation order concerning the plan of reorganization, the release and injunction provisions that may be found in the plan of reorganization may affect the surety's ability to draw on the letter of credit after the confirmation of the plan of reorganization.[85]

3. *The Plan of Reorganization's Confirmation Order*

There are many document filings in a typical chapter 11 bankruptcy case—first day motions; various requests for the debtor to use, sell, or lease its property; post-petition financing of the debtor; the debtor's assumption, assumption and assignment, and/or rejection of executory contracts and leases; and so on.[86] However, most of them lead up to the debtor's filing of its plan of reorganization and disclosure statement soliciting acceptance of the plan of reorganization. But the filing of the plan of reorganization is not the end product. Frequently, after further negotiations, amended plans of reorganization may be filed along with plan supplements that address different issues (such as executory contracts to be assumed, assumed and assigned, or rejected; the terms of post-confirmation financing of the reorganized debtor; the organizational chart for the reorganized debtor; etc.). But, ultimately, upon the acceptance of a plan of reorganization

---

82. *See infra* Section V.C.1.
83. *See infra* Section III.A.2.
84. *See infra* Section V.C.2.
85. *See infra* Section V.C.3.b.
86. *See Commencement of Case*, *in* SURETY ASPECTS OF BANKRUPTCY, *supra* note 3, at 87–101; *Case Administration*, *supra* note 35, at 103–242.

by the affirmative votes necessary as required by the Bankruptcy Code and the entry of a confirmation order for a plan of reorganization, it is the confirmation order that controls the final arrangement between the debtor and its creditors.[87]

Most confirmation orders contain or provide for:

- The restatement of the Bankruptcy Code requirements for confirmation of the plan of reorganization
- The jurisdiction and factual prerequisites for confirmation of the plan of reorganization
- The repetition of the provisions of the plan of reorganization, and the final version of the plan of reorganization will then be attached to the confirmation order
- Very importantly, the statements that address any final amendments or changes to the plan of reorganization as a result of negotiations prior to or at the confirmation hearing, or the inclusion of separate provisions negotiated by the debtor and specific creditors addressing their rights that do not fit squarely within a particular provision of the plan of reorganization concerning a particular creditor or group of creditors[88]

While a draft of the confirmation order is usually circulated just prior to the confirmation hearing, it is an ongoing project right up to the time that it is submitted to the bankruptcy court and entered as an order after the hearing on confirmation. If the surety requires some separate treatment of its rights that may not be adequately addressed in the provisions of the plan of reorganization, but are critical for the surety to maintain its collateral rights, then the surety must be vigilant in making sure that the confirmation order contains any language agreed to with the debtor to protect the surety's rights in its collateral, whether it is property of the estate, a letter of credit, or the proceeds of a letter of credit, upon the bankruptcy court's entry of the confirmation order approving the plan of reorganization.

---

87. *See* 11 U.S.C. § 1141, Effect of Confirmation.

88. See Section V.C.3.b for an example concerning the plan of reorganization release and injunction provisions.

III. The Surety's Right and Ability to Use the Surety's Collateral After the Principal Files for Bankruptcy

Because of the effect of the Bankruptcy Code's provisions on the surety's collateral, the surety must analyze the surety's collateral to determine the surety's right and ability to use the collateral after the principal files its bankruptcy case. The issue of whether the surety's collateral is deemed to be property of the principal's estate, and therefore subject to the automatic stay and the other Bankruptcy Code provisions described above, is critical. This is highlighted by the different ways that the Bankruptcy Code and the bankruptcy case law decisions treat letters of credit and their proceeds as the surety's collateral as opposed to the surety's other collateral (the principal's real and personal property, including "cash" and other cash equivalents), which may be deemed to be property of the estate.

A. *Letters of Credit as the Surety's Collateral in Bankruptcy*

Letters of credit and their proceeds are not deemed to be property of the estate under § 541 of the Bankruptcy Code. Therefore, the automatic stay under § 362 of the Bankruptcy Code is not in effect with respect to the surety's rights to draw against the letter of credit and obtain and use the letter of credit proceeds, nor may the principal use the letter of credit proceeds under § 363 of the Bankruptcy Code. The following is a more detailed discussion of letters of credit and their proceeds as the surety's collateral in the principal's bankruptcy case.

1. Nature and Purpose of Letters of Credit

A letter of credit typically is defined as "an engagement by an issuer, usually a bank, made at the request of a customer for a fee, to honor a beneficiary's drafts or other demands for payment upon satisfaction of the conditions set forth in the letter of credit."[89] Historically, a letter of credit was a common payment mechanism in international trade that permitted the buyer in a transaction to substitute the financial integrity of a stable credit source, the bank that issues the letter of credit, for its

---

89. Tudor Dev. Grp., Inc. v. U.S. Fid. & Guar. Co., 968 F.2d 357, 360 (3d Cir. 1992). *See supra* Section I.B.1.

own.[90] Recently, the letter of credit has been used more as a form of payment guarantee than as an actual form of payment. This more recent letter of credit form is typically referred to as a "standby" letter of credit and it is the form that the surety frequently requires as collateral from the principal. The standby letter of credit is used in a non-sales transaction as a guarantee against the principal's default on its contractual obligations.[91] If the principal satisfies the underlying contractual obligation, the letter of credit will not be drawn upon.

A letter of credit arises from a transaction involving three separate contracts.[92] The first contract generally arises between a buyer and a seller. In the surety context, the principal (as the buyer), by offering its contractual indemnity to the surety under the indemnity agreement, requests that the surety (as the seller) issue commercial surety bonds to various of the principal's creditors/obligees to allow the principal to pursue its business operations and goals. The surety may accept the principal's offer of its contractual indemnity under the indemnity agreement by issuing the commercial surety bonds. The second contract arises between the account party or customer (the principal) and the issuer of the letter of credit to the surety (typically a bank). Finally, the third contract arises between the issuer of the letter of credit (the bank) and the beneficiary of the letter of credit (the surety) pursuant to the terms of the letter of credit.

In discussing the unique nature of letters of credit, one commentator observed:

> The linchpin of the letter of credit transaction is the unique legal relationship between the bank and the beneficiary. Unlike a guarantor, the bank is primarily liable whenever the beneficiary presents a draft and documents that conform to the letter. Unlike its counterpart in a third-party beneficiary contract, the bank

---

90. Bouzo v. Citibank, N.A., 96 F.3d 51, 56 (2d Cir. 1996) (quoting Ala. Textile Co. v. Chase Manhattan Bank, N.A., 982 F.2d 813, 815 (2d Cir. 1992)); *accord* All Serv. Exportacao, Importacao Comercio, S.A. v. Banco Bamerindus Do Brazil, S.A., N.Y. Branch, 921 F.2d 32, 34 (2d Cir. 1990).

91. Demczyk v. Mut. Life Ins. Co. (*In re* Graham Square, Inc.), 126 F.3d 823, 827–28 (6th Cir. 1997) (quoting Gerald T. McLaughlin, *Standby Letters of Credit and Penalty Clauses: An Unexpected Synergy*, 43 OHIO ST. L.J. 1, 6 (1982)).

92. *Id.* at 827.

> may not invoke the defenses its customer might have on the underlying contract. Moreover, the status of a beneficiary of a letter of credit is radically different from that of a payee of a check, who has no right to compel payment from the drawee bank. In the letter of credit transaction, the beneficiary does have the right to compel payment, and once the letter of credit is issued, the customer is powerless to stop payment in the absence of fraud. This difference exists because a letter of credit, unlike a negotiable instrument such as a check, is a binding and irrevocable obligation of the bank itself, not of the customer who procured it. The legal relationship between bank and beneficiary is governed by special principles which, like the law merchant in an earlier era, are nearly uniform throughout the world.[93]

The letter of credit basically serves the purpose of shifting risk. The risk that the principal will not be able to exonerate and/or reimburse the surety for losses under the commercial surety bonds and the indemnity agreement is shifted from the surety to the issuing bank by means of the letter of credit.[94]

2. *Independence Principle: Letters of Credit and Their Proceeds Are Not Property of the Estate Under 11 U.S.C. § 541*

The independent nature of each of the three contracts involved in a letter of credit transaction is known as the "independence principle."[95] This principle seeks to preserve the viability of letters of credit, whose commercial purpose is to allow the beneficiary to draw on the money before obtaining a judgment. Indeed, it has been observed that "[t]he salient feature of a letter of credit and the principal reason for its use

---

93. Douglas G. Baird, *Standby Letters of Credit in Bankruptcy* 49 UNIV. CHI. L. REV. 130, 134–35 (1982) (citations omitted).

94. Kellogg v. Blue Quail Energy, Inc. (*In re* Compton Corp.), 831 F.2d 586, 590 (5th Cir. 1987); *In re* N. Shore & Cent. Ill. Freight Co., 30 B.R. 377, 378 (Bankr. N.D. Ill. 1983).

95. "The relationship between each pair of parties involved in a letter of credit transaction is entirely independent, although each relationship is necessary to support a letter of credit, somewhat like the three legs of a tripod." P.A. Bergner & Co. v. Bank One, N.A. (*In re* P.A. Bergner & Co.), 140 F.3d 1111, 1114 (7th Cir. 1998), *cert. denied*, 525 U.S. 964 (1998).

in commercial transactions is the 'independence principle,'"[96] and strict adherence to this principle "is necessary to protect the integrity of letters of credit as a valuable commercial tool."[97]

The independence principle has been codified in the U.C.C. Section 5-103 of the U.C.C. provides:

> (d) Rights and obligations of an issuer to a beneficiary or a nominated person under a letter of credit are independent of the existence, performance, or nonperformance of a contract or arrangement out of which the letter of credit arises or which underlies it, including contracts or arrangements between the issuer and the applicant and between the applicant and the beneficiary.[98]

The independence principle insulates the letter of credit from disputes over performance of any separate agreements between the issuer of the letter of credit and the principal (the applicant) or between the principal (the applicant) and the surety (the beneficiary), and allows the letter of credit to function as a swift and certain payment mechanism.[99]

As a result of the independence principle, letters of credit and their proceeds are not property of the estate because the bank issuing the letter of credit to the surety distributes *the bank's own assets* to the surety upon the surety's demand on the letter of credit and *not* the assets of the principal/applicant who caused the letter of credit to be issued.[100] Thus, the proceeds of the letter of credit, which come into the possession of

---

96. Tudor Dev. Grp., Inc. v. U.S. Fid. & Guar. Co., 968 F.2d 357, 360 (3d Cir. 1992).
97. *In re* War Eagle Constr. Co., 283 B.R. 193 (S.D. W. Va. 2002); *In re* Prime Motor Inns, Inc., 130 B.R. 610, 613 (S.D. Fla. 1991).
98. *See* U.C.C. § 5-103(d).
99. *In re* Graham Square, 126 F.3d 823, 827 (6th Cir. 1997); *Compton*, 831 F.2d at 589; *In re* W.L. Mead, Inc., 42 B.R. 57 (Bankr. N.D. Ohio 1984); *In re* M.J. Sales & Distrib. Co., 25 B.R. 608 (Bankr. S.D.N.Y. 1982).
100. *See In re* Spring Ford Indus., 338 B.R. 255 (Bankr. E.D. Pa. 2006); *In re* Metro Commc'ns, Inc., 115 B.R. 849, 854 (Bankr. W.D. Pa. 1990); *In re* Leisure Dynamics, Inc., 33 B.R. 171 (Bankr. Minn. 1983); *M.J. Sales*, 25 B.R. 608. See also *Colonial Courts Apartment Co. v. Proc Associates, Inc.*, 57 F.3d 119, 123 (1st Cir. 1995), which states:

    > [C]ourts have considered the letter of credit to be a separate agreement between the issuer and the beneficiary, wholly distinct

the surety upon the surety's demand and the issuing bank's payment, are assets of the bank, and as such are not the principal's assets or property. It is because of the independence principle that the majority of courts recognize and hold that the proceeds from a letter of credit do not constitute property of the estate under § 541 of the Bankruptcy Code.[101]

Because of the independence principle, the sole duty of the issuer of a letter of credit is ministerial. Namely, the issuer has to determine if the beneficiary has properly complied with the conditions in the letter of credit. Once the beneficiary fulfills the requirements of the letter of credit and draws on it, the issuer of the letter of credit cannot then direct

---

> from the underlying contract between the customer and the beneficiary.

The authors White and Summers have observed:

> The most unique and mysterious part of this [letter-of-credit] arrangement is the so-called "independence principle." The principle states that the bank's obligation to the beneficiary is independent of the beneficiary's performance on the underlying contract . . . . [T]he obligation of the issuer to pay the beneficiary is also independent of any obligation of the customer to its issuer.

If, for example, the applicant goes into bankruptcy after the letter has been issued, but before it has been drawn upon, the issuer must pay despite the fact that the applicant will not be able to pay the issuer.

3 James J. White & Robert S. Summers, Uniform Commercial Code § 26-2 (5th ed. 2009) (clarification added).

101. *See In re* Stonebridge Techs., 430 F.3d 260 (5th Cir. 2005); Willis v. Celotex, 978 F.2d 146, 148 n.3 (4th Cir. 1992); *In re* Air Conditioning, Inc. of Stuart, 845 F.2d 293 (11th Cir. 1988); *Compton*, 831 F.2d at 589; *In re* Oakwood Homes Corp., 342 B.R. 59 (Bankr. D. Del. 2006); *In re* Kmart Corp., 297 B.R. 525 (N.D. Ill. 2003); *Spring Ford Indus.*, 338 B.R. 255; *War Eagle Constr. Co.*, 283 B.R. 193; *In re* Hechinger Inv. Co. of Del., 282 B.R. 149 (Bankr. D. Del. 2002); *In re* Farm Fresh Supermarkets of Md., 257 B.R. 770 (Bankr. D. Md. 2001); *In re* Baja Boats, 203 B.R. 71 (Bankr. N.D. Ohio. 1996); *In re* Milford Grp., 197 B.R. 31 (Bankr. M.D. Pa. 1996); *In re* Duplitronics, 183 B.R. 1010 (Bankr. N.D. Ill. 1995); *In re* Zenith Labs., 104 B.R. 667 (Bankr. D.N.J. 1989); *In re* San Jacinto Glass Indus., 93 B.R. 934 (Bankr. S.D. Tex. 1988); *W.L. Mead, Inc.*, 42 B.R. 57; *In re* Elegant Merch., 41 B.R. 398 (Bankr. S.D.N.Y. 1984); *In re* Pine Tree Elec., 34 B.R. 199 (Bankr. D. Me. 1983); *In re* Leisure Dynamics, Inc., 33 B.R. 171 (Bankr. Minn. 1983); *In re* N. Shore & Cent. Ill. Freight Co., 30 B.R. 377 (Bankr. N.D. Ill. 1983); *Matter of* Planes, Inc., 29 B.R. 370 (Bankr. N.D. Ga. 1983); *M.J. Sales*, 25 B.R. 608.

how the beneficiary uses the proceeds.[102] After the issuing bank pays the funds to the beneficiary, the letter of credit is a fully executed contract, and the issuing bank must look to its customer for repayment just as would any other creditor.[103]

3. Letters of Credit and the Automatic Stay (11 U.S.C. § 362)

Because the letter of credit and its proceeds are not considered to be property of the debtor's estate, the automatic stay as provided by § 362 of the Bankruptcy Code does not apply to a beneficiary's draw request on the letter of credit or the issuing bank's obligation for the payment of the beneficiary's request.[104]

The case of *In re North Shore & Central Illinois Freight Co.*[105] is illustrative of the unique nature of letters of credit and the inapplicability of the automatic stay. The debtor arranged for a $50,000.00 letter of credit with a bank.[106] The beneficiary of the letter of credit was a surety, Protective Insurance Company. The letter of credit was issued to provide Protective with adequate security against any liability it might incur while serving as surety for the debtor. Subsequently, the debtor filed a voluntary petition for relief under chapter 11 of the Bankruptcy Code. Thereafter, Protective sought to draw the $50,000.00 from the bank as permitted under the terms of the letter of credit. The debtor then filed an adversary proceeding in the bankruptcy court against Protective and the issuing bank seeking to prevent the bank from disbursing the letter of credit proceeds to Protective. Protective moved to dismiss the debtor's adversary proceeding. Thus, the issue before the bankruptcy court was "whether the debtor's bankruptcy affects the right of Protective to draw upon the letter of credit."[107]

The debtor argued that the automatic stay of § 362 of the Bankruptcy Code prevented Protective from drawing upon the letter of credit. Implicit in the debtor's argument was the proposition that the letter of credit was

---

102. *See In re* E. Freight Ways, Inc., 9 B.R. 653, 662 (Bankr. S.D.N.Y. 1981).
103. *Id.*; *In re* Lancaster Steel, 284 B.R. 152, 160 (Bankr. S.D. Fla. 2002).
104. *In re* Ill.-Cal. Express, Inc., 50 B.R. 232, 235 (Bankr. Colo. 1985) (citing *Elegant Merch.*, 41 B.R. at 399); *In re* Clothes, 35 B.R. 487 (Bankr. D.N.D. 1983): *Planes*, 29 B.R. 370; *M.J. Sales*, 25 B.R. 608; *In re* Page, 18 B.R. 713 (Bankr. D.D.C. 1982).
105. 30 B.R. 377.
106. *Id.*
107. *Id.* at 378.

property of the debtor's estate. The bankruptcy court noted that the automatic stay was inapplicable to property that was not property of the debtor's estate pursuant to § 541 of the Bankruptcy Code.[108] In analyzing the issue, the bankruptcy court recognized the important function that letters of credit play in the commercial marketplace and that the bank issuing the letter of credit is the party obligated to the beneficiary, not the debtor.[109] The bankruptcy court observed:

> The transaction involved in this controversy resembles a standby letter of credit arrangement. Under a standby letter of credit arrangement, the bank becomes primarily liable to the beneficiary upon the default of the bank's customer. In return the bank charges the customer a fee based upon the customer's probability of insolvency. It is argued that this arrangement spreads the allocation of risk to the parties who are best able to ascertain the risk.[110]

Accordingly, the bankruptcy court held that the letter of credit was not property of the debtor's estate and the automatic stay did not bar the surety's drawdown of the letter of credit.[111]

The U.S. Bankruptcy Court for the Eastern District of Virginia has also recognized that letters of credit are not property of the debtor's estate and are not subject to the automatic stay.[112] In *In re Printing Department*,[113] the debtor moved for an order showing cause why the beneficiary of a letter of credit should not be found in contempt based on an alleged violation of the automatic stay to prevent the beneficiary from drawing down on a letter of credit, and to seek recovery of any monies paid under the letter of credit.

The bankruptcy court observed that a "letter of credit" is "an engagement by a bank or other person made at the request of a customer . . . that the issuer will honor drafts or other demands for

---

108. *Id.* (citing Globe Constr. Co. v. Okla. City Hous., 571 F.2d 1140, 1143 (10th Cir. 1978), *cert. denied*, 439 U.S. 835 (1979)).

109. *Id.*

110. *Id.*

111. *Id.* at 379. *See also In re* M.J. Sales & Distrib. Co., 25 B.R. 608 (Bankr. S.D.N.Y. 1982).

112. *In re* Valley Vue Joint Venture, 123 B.R. 199 (Bankr. E.D. Va. 1991); *In re* Printing Dep't, 20 B.R. 677 (Bankr. E.D. Va. 1981).

113. 20 B.R. 677.

payment upon compliance with the conditions specified in the credit."[114] Further, the bankruptcy court noted that under the U.C.C., the issuer of a letter of credit "must honor a demand for payment which complies with the terms of a letter of credit regardless of compliance with the underlying contract,"[115] and concluded that "the issuer of the letter of credit, therefore, assumes an original primary obligation wholly apart from the underlying contract which exists between the beneficiary and the customer."[116] Thus, the bankruptcy court held that when the creditor submitted its draft to the issuing bank, it was not asserting a claim against the debtor or against any of the property of the debtor's estate; rather, it was enforcing a contract that existed between the creditor and the bank that issued the letter of credit, which was independent of any relationship between the debtor and the issuing bank.[117] In that regard, the bankruptcy court stated:

> [T]he issuer of a letter of credit "acts as the principal, not as agent for its customer, and engages its own credit." . . . That obligation is fully independent of any underlying agreement. This independence from any underlying agreement allows banks to negotiate letters of credit freely without facing the risks which could arise on an ordinary contract.[118]

The bankruptcy court also held that letters of credit are not property of the debtor's estate and as such the automatic stay does not apply, and the debtor's claimed relief was denied.[119]

---

114. *Id.* at 679.
115. *Id.* at 680.
116. *Id.* at 681.
117. *Id.*
118. *Id.* (citing Dullen Steel Prods. v. Bankers Tr., 189 F. Supp. 922, 927 (S.D.N.Y. 1960), *aff'd*, 298 F.2d 836 (2d Cir. 1962)); Paul R. Verkuil, *Bank Solvency and Guaranty Letters of Credit*, 25 Stan. L. Rev. 716, 720 (1973).
119. *See* Norton Annual Survey of Bankruptcy Law (1983); Michael Stern, *The Independence Rule in Standby Letters of Credit*, 52 Univ. Chi. L. Rev. 218 (1985); Baird, *supra* note 93.

B. The Principal's Property as the Surety's Collateral in Bankruptcy

As stated previously, the surety may obtain the principal's real or personal property as collateral for the execution and issuance of the commercial surety bonds, including cash, deposit accounts, and certificates of deposit, whether contemporaneously with the execution and issuance of the commercial surety bonds or pursuant to a "place in funds" demand under the indemnity agreement. However, once the principal files its bankruptcy case and becomes a debtor, the automatic stay of § 362 of the Bankruptcy Code prevents the surety from exercising its rights against such collateral (the principal's real or personal property) in order to pay any claims, indemnify and reimburse the surety for any payments that it has made and/or may make to the commercial surety bond claimants, or otherwise reimburse the surety for any of its losses under the indemnity agreement.[120]

Assuming that the surety has a valid, perfected, and non-avoidable (under the Bankruptcy Code) lien and/or security interest in the collateral from the principal that is property of the estate, the surety may eventually be able to use that collateral to reimburse its loss.[121] This eventuality may occur (1) when the surety obtains relief from the automatic stay pursuant to § 362(d) of the Bankruptcy Code;[122] (2) the principal, as debtor, consents to the surety's use of the collateral to pay any claims or reimburse the surety for any losses in a separate order; or (3) the principal's plan of reorganization in some way authorizes the surety to exercise its rights against the surety's collateral that is property of the estate (or the principal itself under its plan of reorganization satisfies

---

120. *See supra* Section II.B.

121. Even if the surety's secured claim is disallowed under § 502(e) of the Bankruptcy Code because it is a contingent claim for reimbursement, the surety's lien securing its claim against the debtor and the property of the estate is not void as provided in § 506(d) of the Bankruptcy Code. *See infra* Section V.C.1. Furthermore, under § 502(e)(2) of the Bankruptcy Code, if the surety's claim for reimbursement becomes fixed after the commencement of the bankruptcy case, it may be allowed as a secured claim against the property of the estate as if it had become fixed before the date of the debtor's filing of the petition.

122. Under § 362(c)(1) of the Bankruptcy Code, the stay of any surety action against the surety's collateral continues until such property serving as the surety's collateral is no longer property of the estate.

the commercial surety bond obligations and, therefore, the surety's liquidation of the surety's collateral is unnecessary in order for the surety to avoid loss under the commercial surety bonds).

C. The Surety's Use of the Surety's Collateral

The surety does not need relief from the automatic stay to exercise its rights against a letter of credit or the proceeds of a letter of credit. Assuming that the surety has obtained the ability to exercise its rights against the surety's collateral that is property of the estate after seeking relief from the automatic stay under § 362 of the Bankruptcy Code, the next question is how the surety may use the surety's collateral to protect the surety from loss.

The surety only needs to use the surety's collateral in the event that the surety either anticipates a loss and expects to make a payment or the surety incurs a loss under the commercial surety bonds and seeks to enforce its indemnity and reimbursement rights. Whether the surety has obtained the proceeds from a letter of credit or is able to liquidate the surety's collateral that is property of the estate and has received the net funds from the liquidation, the surety will either want to use the proceeds or the funds to pay any loss prior to the surety's use of its own funds to pay the loss (exoneration and/or quia timet) or use the proceeds or the funds to indemnify and reimburse the surety for any losses that it pays or incurs. Those losses include any commercial surety bond claims that the surety must pay, and any costs and expenses that the surety incurs, such as attorneys' fees, accounting fees, investigative fees and expenses, and so on, in enforcing the surety's indemnity agreement rights and in handling and resolving the commercial surety bond claims. The surety may also seek payment and/or reimbursement for premiums, interest, and the surety's attorneys' fees and expenses in taking action in the principal's bankruptcy case.

1. The Surety's Rights Under the Indemnity Agreement

Pursuant to the surety's indemnity agreement, the surety has indemnity and reimbursement rights for various losses that the surety has incurred as a result of its issuing commercial surety bonds to the principal, including any losses paid and incurred by the surety, any costs and expenses, including attorneys' fees, consulting fees, investigative fees, and so on, and possibly interest on any of the surety's payments.[123] However, while the indemnity agreement may provide that the principal will pay premiums for the commercial surety bonds, the indemnity agreement may not have a provision that both compels the payment and deems the principal's failure to pay the premiums as a loss for which the surety may seek reimbursement.

2. *The Surety's Rights Under the Collateral Agreement*

Because the surety's collateral agreement focuses on the collateral the principal provides to the surety, the collateral agreement may be more detailed with respect to the surety's rights to use the surety's collateral. Many collateral agreements mimic the surety's indemnity agreement with respect to the payment or reimbursement of the surety's losses, costs, and expenses, but the collateral agreement may also provide that the surety's collateral may be used to pay the surety's premiums for the commercial surety bonds, interest, and any other costs and expenses. Furthermore, many collateral agreements may provide that the surety may use the surety's collateral until the collateral is either exhausted or the surety is satisfied that it has no future liability under (and/or the surety has been released and discharged from) all of the commercial surety bond obligations.

3. *What Happens If the Agreement Is Silent?*

If there is no indemnity agreement and/or no collateral agreement provision regarding how the surety may use the collateral, the surety has several options. First, the surety may negotiate with the principal and attempt to reach an understanding or agreement as to how the collateral will be used. Second, the surety may petition the bankruptcy court and seek an order authorizing the use of the collateral in the manner proposed by the surety. Third, the surety may simply make such use of

---

123. *See* Lawrence R. Moelmann et al., *Liability of the Principal and Indemnitors to Indemnify and Reimburse the Surety*, *in* SURETY'S INDEMNITY AGREEMENT, *supra* note 2, at 179–224.

the collateral as it deems appropriate under the typical broad general rights provided in the indemnity agreement and/or the surety's common law rights.

IV. Obligee and Third-Party Claims Against Commercial Surety Bonds as They Affect the Surety's Use of the Collateral

There are an enormous number of types and kinds of commercial surety bonds and each has one or more possible claimants. If a surety makes no payments and incurs no losses under the commercial surety bonds, it may not need to exercise its rights against the surety's collateral.[124] However, because of the automatic stay and the principal's legal (and possible financial and practical) inability to pay its pre-petition obligations during its bankruptcy case, the surety is frequently faced with claims from various claimants against the commercial surety bonds. This section of the chapter will discuss the nature and types of claims that may be made against the commercial surety bonds, the surety's mechanics and procedures for handling claims against the commercial surety bonds, and the possible attempt that may be made by the principal in the bankruptcy case to establish a commercial surety bond claim bar date (the Surety Claims Bar Date for claims against the commercial surety bonds. The principal's goal in establishing a Surety Claims Bar Date is to obtain the surety's release and discharge from the commercial surety bonds and the surety's liabilities to the obligees and other claimants, therefore resulting in the release and return of the surety's "excess collateral" to the principal for the benefit of the bankruptcy estate.[125]

---

124. A surety may have claims for attorneys' fees and other expenses under the indemnity agreement for which it may seek indemnity and reimbursement from the surety's collateral even if the surety does not incur losses under the commercial surety bonds.

125. The concepts of "excess collateral" (the principal's real and personal property, which is already property of the estate while subject to the surety's liens) and "excess proceeds" of a letter of credit (which, if there are any "excess proceeds," may become property of the estate pursuant to the provisions of the underlying agreements between the surety and the principal) may result in a return of all or a portion of the surety's collateral to the bankruptcy estate, and are discussed later in this chapter. *See infra* Section V.C.2.

A. The Nature of the Claimants and the Types of Bonds

Because of the large number of different kinds and types of commercial surety bonds, they have different goals, terms, and conditions and pose a variety of different exposures and risks to the surety in varying amounts. These exposures and risks are affected by statutes, codes, regulations, case law, and other contracts and agreements, either described or not described in the commercial surety bonds, all of which may affect the surety's ultimate risk of loss. Furthermore, the identity and nature of the claimants—the commercial surety bond obligees and other named or possible claimants—who may make claims against the commercial surety bonds vary greatly.[126]

For some commercial surety bonds, for example utility bonds (bonds that provide the surety's financial protection to those entities that supply electric, gas, water, and other services to the principal (both pre-petition and post-petition)), there is one named private single-party obligee under the bond (the utility), which is the only entity and the sole claimant as the obligee under the commercial surety bond. The surety's liability under such a commercial surety bond would be released and discharged in the event it pays a penal sum loss under the commercial surety bond and obtains a full release from the obligee. Or, the obligee may release and discharge the surety from its obligations under the commercial surety bond for the payment of a portion of the penal sum because the obligee has been paid in full for any and all claims that the obligee may have against the principal and the surety under the commercial surety bond. Or, the obligee may agree that it has no claims and may voluntarily release and discharge the commercial surety bond. Once the commercial surety bond is released and discharged, the surety has no further obligations under the commercial surety bond. If the surety has incurred a loss, the surety will seek reimbursement from the surety's collateral to the extent of its loss. To the extent the surety receives a release and discharge on the commercial surety bond and obtains full reimbursement for any loss, the remaining amount of the surety's collateral may be available to reimburse the surety for losses on other commercial surety bonds, or may become "excess collateral" that the surety may no longer need to maintain.

---

126. While the identity and nature of the claimants may vary, for the vast majority, if not all, of the commercial surety bonds, the liability and obligations of the principal and the surety are joint and several to the claimants.

Many commercial surety bonds are required by state or local jurisdictions in order for the principal to operate and continue to perform its business and have a statutory obligee (the various state or local governments). Such commercial surety bonds include many forms of license bonds, tax bonds, permit bonds, and so on. There are also such types of commercial surety bonds required by the federal government, such as customs/importer bonds (to cover certain duties, taxes, and other financial charges imposed during the principal's importation of goods and merchandise from foreign countries). To the extent that the statutory bonds have only one obligee, and no other persons or entities may claim under the statutory bond, the surety's obligations to "claimants" under such commercial surety bonds are limited to the federal, state, and/or local government entities and are similar to the private single-party obligees under those bonds (such as utility bonds).

However, many statutory commercial surety bonds name as the obligee the state or local government, but also provide rights to third-party claimants who may make claims against the statutory commercial surety bonds either through the government obligee or independent of the government obligee. These commercial surety bonds may include statutory-required, self-insured workers' compensation bonds (which are difficult to secure a release and discharge and more difficult to determine their duration and how long the surety's exposure will continue), contractor license bonds, mortgage broker bonds, automobile and mobile home dealer bonds, warranty bonds, games of chance bonds, and other business-related commercial surety bonds that allow third-party claimants other than the government obligee to make a claim. It may be impossible for the surety to receive a release and discharge of such a commercial surety bond when the obligee and other third-party claimants may have claims unless the surety has paid out the full penal sum of the commercial surety bond and received a release and discharge as a result. Otherwise, the surety may have no knowledge of what other claimants may exist and how to identify those potential claimants.

In addition to the above shared and different characteristics, the commercial surety bonds have different cancellation provisions and abilities as well as different statutes of limitations for the accrual and/or filing of claims against the respective commercial surety bonds that affect the surety's risk and exposure to loss.

The cancellation provisions may be contained as provisions in the commercial surety bonds themselves, or in accordance with any statutes, codes, and/or regulations that govern the commercial surety bonds. Furthermore, cancellations usually require both a notice of cancellation being sent to the obligee and a period of time before the date that the cancellation is effective to stop any further liability of the surety under the commercial surety bonds. The surety is normally liable up to the effective date of the cancellation for any valid claims arising against the commercial surety bonds, up to the penal sum of the commercial surety bonds. Finally, not all commercial surety bonds may be cancelled, and the surety may be liable until the later of expiration date of the respective commercial surety bonds or the applicable statute of limitations.

Regardless of the surety's ability to cancel the commercial surety bonds, the surety's exposure to risk and liability is further extended until the expiration of the applicable statute of limitations for the accrual and/or filing of an action against the commercial surety bonds. Such statutes of limitation may be the jurisdiction's normal statute of limitations on contracts, may be a special statute of limitations on bonds, or may be contained in the statutory and/or regulatory framework that requires the particular commercial surety bonds. Because the surety's exposure to risk under the commercial surety bonds remains until obligees and claimants no longer have rights of action against the surety and the commercial surety bonds, the earliest that the surety may believe that its exposure and risk of loss and its required retention of the surety's collateral to cover that exposure and risk of loss, is after the expiration of the many applicable statutes of limitation related to the commercial surety bonds.

B. The Surety's Claims Handling

The surety may receive numerous claims fairly quickly after the principal files its bankruptcy case. Because the automatic stay prevents the principal's creditors from collecting their pre-petition debts from the principal, those claimants may quickly look to the jointly and severally liable surety under the commercial surety bonds to pay those pre-petition obligations. Occasionally, as the principal's bankruptcy case proceeds, claimants may make claims against the commercial surety bonds for the principal's obligations incurred both pre-petition *and* post-petition, after the date of the filing of the principal's bankruptcy case.[127] While

127. The Bankruptcy Code has a specific provision with respect to utility services and the debtor's obligations to the utility after it files its bankruptcy case. 11 U.S.C. § 366. In fact, 11 U.S.C. § 366(a) specifically provides that "a utility may not alter, refuse, or discontinue service to, or discriminate against, the trustee or debtor solely on the basis of the

such post-petition obligations are treated differently from pre-petition obligations, mainly because post-petition obligations are administrative expenses of the principal in its bankruptcy case, the commercial surety bonds may still be exposed to pay both pre-petition and post-petition obligations. The following is a brief discussion of the surety's claims handling mechanics and procedures when it receives claims against the commercial surety bonds after the principal files its bankruptcy case.

1. Investigation, Including Notice to the Principal and the Principal's Input on the Claim

Each time that the surety receives a claim against a commercial surety bond, it is advisable to notify the principal and the principal's counsel and obtain the principal's input on the claim. Frequently, the principal in a large commercial surety bankruptcy case has good records concerning what it owes and what it may dispute, and many of the claims against the commercial surety bonds may be valid claims. If the principal disputes the claim, the surety may obtain additional information from the claimant and the principal in an attempt to determine whether or not the claim is a valid claim against the commercial surety bond that should or should not be paid.

---

commencement of a case under this title or that a debt owed by the debtor to such utility for service rendered before the order for relief was not paid when due." The utility may want to refuse to provide or to discontinue service unless it receives adequate assurance of the payment of post-petition utility services bills. The bankruptcy court may order the debtor to provide a deposit or other security necessary in order to give the utility adequate assurance of post-petition payment. The term "adequate assurance of payment" includes cash, a letter of credit, certificate of deposit, surety bond, and other forms of security. *Id.* § 366(c)(1)(A). When the principal/debtor provides "assurance of payment" to a utility that already has a pre-petition utility bond from the surety, the surety may have rights in the security and/or may compel the utility to assert its claims against the post-petition security before it may make a claim against the utility bond for a post-petition obligation (an event that may require the surety to use the surety's collateral). See *Commencement of Case*, *supra* note 86, at 97–98, concerning utility first day motions. There are other first day motions that may be filed on many other issues. *See Chapter 11 Reorganization*, *supra* note 69, at 424–26.

2. The Surety's Right to Settle the Claim

Under many indemnity agreements, the surety has the right to settle claims against the commercial surety bond.[128] The question of whether the surety may settle a claim against a commercial surety bond without violating the automatic stay has not been definitively addressed by the bankruptcy courts.[129]

The risk to the surety in settling a claim under the indemnity agreement is less that there is a violation of the automatic stay (because the surety is jointly and severally liable to the claimant with the principal that is now in bankruptcy), and more that the principal, who disputes the claims, may later dispute and object to the propriety and/or the amount of the surety's payments to resolve the commercial surety bond claims, and then the surety's right to use its collateral to reimburse the surety for its loss payments as discussed below.

3. The Effect on the Surety's Right to Use the Collateral upon Settlement of the Claim

While the surety may not be violating the automatic stay by exercising its indemnity agreement rights to settle a claim against a commercial surety bond, if the principal has disputed the surety's settlement of the claim,

---

128. *See* M. Michael Egan, Jr. et al., *The Indemnity Agreement and the Handling of Surety Claims*, *in* SURETY'S INDEMNITY AGREEMENT, *supra* note 2, at 333–59; Schexnayder et al., *supra* note 35, at 484–85 (discussing the surety's substantive contractual rights, including those under the indemnity agreement, and their validity in a bankruptcy case).

129. *See, e.g.*, *In re* Levitz Elec., Inc., 100 B.R. 602 (Bankr. S.D. Fla. 1989). Generally, the automatic stay is not violated when the surety makes a payment for a debtor's obligations under a bond because it is the surety's obligation to pay regardless of the fact of the debtor's bankruptcy case. The authors have not found any cases directly addressing the issue of the surety's right to settle a claim against the bond. In the absence of clear authority supporting the surety's indemnity agreement rights to make such settlements of claims against the commercial surety bonds and in light of the potential penalties the surety may face for violating the automatic stay, one course of action for the surety is to negotiate a settlement of claims order with the principal that includes relief from the automatic stay and agreed upon terms for handling and settling claims. Such an order may be put in place early in the principal's bankruptcy case and cover all future claims.

that dispute may lead to a subsequent claim objection and have an effect on the surety's rights to use its collateral to either pay the settlement of the claim or to reimburse the surety for its payment of the settlement of the claim. If the surety uses the proceeds from the letter of credit to settle the claim despite the principal's disputes, the surety would argue that it has the right to use the letter of credit proceeds because they are not property of the principal's estate, and, therefore, it is not costing the principal anything. If the surety attempts to use the surety's collateral that is property of the principal's estate, assuming that it has the right to use such collateral (the surety has obtained relief from the automatic stay), the principal may have greater rights to dispute the surety's actions in settling the claim and may subsequently assert a clam objection to the surety's right and ability to either exonerate the surety or obtain reimbursement of the surety from the surety's collateral for its payment of the settlement of the claim.

C. The Principal's Attempts to Set a Surety Claims Bar Date Against the Commercial Surety's Bonds to Obtain a Release and Return of the Collateral

If the surety is retaining rights and holding onto collateral that is property of the principal's estate, the principal may eventually want the collateral back in order for the principal to use that property to partially fund the principal's plan of reorganization and/or to pay other debts and expenses. The principal may contend that the surety is either more than fully collateralized for any potential loss under its remaining commercial surety bonds or that the surety's risk of exposure to loss is minimal because of the nature of the risk of the commercial surety bonds and/or the passage of time.

The surety's risk of exposure under a commercial surety bond is eliminated after the surety has paid out the penal sum of the commercial surety bond in full and received a release and discharge of the commercial surety bond, and may be eliminated if the surety has made a partial payment or no payment under the commercial surety bond and still has received a voluntary release and discharge from the obligee.[130] However, this may not occur when there are third-party claimants, in addition to

130. *See* Franks et al., *supra* note 11, at 155–56. *See also* Pittston Warehouse Corp. v. Am. Motorists Ins. Co., 715 F. Supp. 1221 (S.D.N.Y. 1989).

the named obligee, who may have a claim against the commercial surety bond.

More importantly, the surety's obligations under commercial surety bonds may or may not expire upon the passage of the applicable statutes of limitations for the commercial surety bonds regardless of who the claimants may be.[131] The statute of limitations issue exists whether or not the surety has been able to successfully cancel the commercial surety bonds either prior to or after the date of the principal's bankruptcy case.[132]

Because the surety's liabilities under the commercial surety bonds may extend out for many years, the principal in its bankruptcy case may attempt to set a "Surety Claims Bar Date" against all possible claimants under the commercial surety bonds in order to cut off the claimants' rights and initiate and/or require the surety's release and return of the surety's collateral to the principal.

While the concept of setting a Surety Claims Bar Date sounds initially enticing for the surety (to accelerate the identification, evaluation, and possible elimination of and injunction against any possible future claims against the commercial surety bonds) and the principal (to get its property serving as the surety's collateral back into the bankruptcy estate), the reality is that the bankruptcy court may not have the authority to issue such relief. If the bankruptcy court issues an order that sets a Surety Claims Bar Date for the case and the surety is then required to release the surety's collateral and return that collateral to the principal's estate after the Surety Claims Bar Date, the surety may still be exposed to claimants who could argue that they are not bound by the Surety Claims Bar Date bankruptcy court order after the surety surrenders the collateral.

In the context of setting a Surety Claims Bar Date, it must be recognized that the surety is a non-debtor third party to the bankruptcy case and the potential claimants under the commercial surety bonds are also non-debtor third parties to the bankruptcy case. There is a split among the federal circuit courts regarding whether and under what conditions a bankruptcy court may impose a bar on or release of third-party claims against a third party. Bankruptcy courts have only limited authority to

---

131. The expiration of the applicable statute of limitations only makes the obligation or debt unenforceable, it does not eliminate the obligation/debt or prevent the reaffirmation of the obligation/debt after the expiration of the applicable statute of limitations. *See infra* Section V.D.4.b.

132. The surety's cancellation of the commercial surety bonds is discussed briefly in this chapter. *See infra* Section V.A.2.

address the claims of one third party (bond claimants) against another third party (the surety). There is no provision in the Bankruptcy Code that expressly gives the bankruptcy court authority to enter an order that releases the surety's liability, as a non-debtor third party, to other non-debtor third-party claimants under the commercial surety bonds or enjoins third-party claims against a non-debtor third party such as the surety. In that regard, the Bankruptcy Code provides:

> The court may issue any order, process, or judgment that is necessary or appropriate to carry out the provisions of this title. No provision of this title providing for the raising of an issue by a party in interest shall be construed to preclude the court from, sua sponte, taking any action or making any determination necessary or appropriate to enforce or implement court orders or rules, or to prevent an abuse of process.[133]

While § 105(a) of the Bankruptcy Code appears to provide broad power to the bankruptcy courts, the question is whether it is intended merely to supplement a bankruptcy court's enumerated powers under the Bankruptcy Code or to provide a basis to broaden its powers. The Third Circuit Court of Appeals in *United States v. Pepperman*[134] stated that § 105(a) does not "create substantive rights that would otherwise be unavailable under the Bankruptcy Code."[135] Similarly, the Ninth Circuit Court of Appeals has recognized that "[b]ankruptcy judges have no more power than any others to ignore the plain language of a statute in order to reach a result more in keeping with their notions of equity."[136]

Moreover, some courts point to § 524 of the Bankruptcy Code, which specifically provides that the bankruptcy discharge of a debtor under a confirmed plan of reorganization does not relieve non-debtor third parties of their liabilities.[137] Thus, the bankruptcy discharge of

---

133. 11 U.S.C. § 105(a).
134. 976 F.2d 123, 131 (3d Cir. 1992).
135. *Id.* (quoting *In re* Morristown & Erie R.R. Co., 885 F.2d 98, 100 (3d Cir. 1989)); *see also* Norwest Bank Worthington v. Ahlers, 485 U.S. 197, 206 (1988) (noting that the bankruptcy court's equitable powers can only be exercised within the confines of the Bankruptcy Code).
136. *In re* Kelly, 841 F.2d 908, 913 n.4 (9th Cir. 1988).
137. 11 U.S.C. § 524(e) provides: "Except as provided in subsection (a)(3) of this section, discharge of a debt of the debtor does not affect the liability of any other entity on, or the property of any other entity for, such debt."

the principal would ordinarily not relieve the surety of its joint and several obligations and liabilities to commercial surety bond obligees and claimants.[138] Other courts, including the Fifth, Ninth, and Tenth Circuit Courts of Appeal, have concluded that § 524(e) precludes them from authorizing releases of and/or injunctions against the claims of third parties against non-debtors, finding these to be the equivalent of a non-debtor discharge.[139] Courts in other jurisdictions, including the Second, Fourth, Sixth, Seventh, and 11th, have taken a contrary view and have held that § 105(a) modifies § 524(e).[140] For example, the Fourth Circuit appellate court exercised authority over non-debtor liability in the context of a chapter 11 reorganization plan approval in *Menard-Sanford*

---

138. Restatement (Third) of Suretyship and Guaranty § 34(1)(a) (1996). Comment b to section 34(1)(a) highlights the situation when the principal is financially unable to perform the underlying contractual obligation and the obligee, who required the surety's bond to protect the obligee from such an event, looks to the surety for performance. The value of the surety's performance obligation under the bond would be "seriously diminished" if the surety was able to assert, as a defense to the obligee's claim, the principal's discharge in bankruptcy from the underlying contractual obligation.

139. *See, e.g.*, Feld v. Zale Corp. (*In re* Zale Corp.), 62 F.3d 746 (5th Cir. 1995); Resorts Int'l v. Lowenschuss (*In re* Lowenschuss), 67 F.3d 1394, 1401–02 (9th Cir. 1995), *cert. denied*, 517 U.S. 1243 (1996); Landsing Diversified Props.-II v. First Nat'l Bank & Tr. Co. of Tulsa (*In re* W. Real Estate Fund, Inc.), 922 F.2d 592, 601 (10th Cir. 1990), *modified by* Abel v. West, 932 F.2d 898 (10th Cir. 1991); *In re* Future Energy Corp., 83 B.R. 470, 486 (Bankr. S.D. Ohio 1988) ("The clear weight of decisional authority supports the proposition that Chapter 11 plans which call for the release of nonparties (such as guarantors) from liability upon obligations of the debtor are violative of § 524(e)."); *see also* Richard L. Epling, *Third-Party Releases in Bankruptcy Cases: Should There Be Statutory Reform?*, 75 Bus. Law. 1747 (2020).

140. *See* Airadigm Commc'ns, Inc. v. Fed. Commc'ns Comm'n (In re Airadigm Commc'ns, Inc.), 519 F.3d 640 (7th Cir. 2008); Deutsche Bank AG v. Metromedia Fiber Network, Inc. (In re Metromedia Fiber Network, Inc.), 416 F.3d 136 (2d Cir. 2005); Class Five Nev. Claimants v. Dow Corning Corp. (In re Dow Corning Corp.), 280 F.3d 648 (6th Cir. 2002); Gillman v. Cont'l Airlines (In re Cont'l Airlines), 203 F.3d 203 (3d Cir. 2000); Munford v. Munford, Inc. (In re Munford, Inc.), 97 F.3d 449 (11th Cir. 1996); Menard-Sanford v. Mabey (In re A.H. Robins Co.), 880 F.2d 694 (4th Cir. 1989), cert. denied, 493 U.S. 959 (1989).

v. Mabey (In re A.H. Robins Co.).[141] In *A.H. Robins*, the maker of the Dalkon Shield was forced into bankruptcy by overwhelming liability exposure arising from product liability litigation. In that context, the Fourth Circuit approved a reorganization plan that provided releases of third-party claims against other third parties to the bankruptcy such as the debtor's directors, insurers, and their attorneys (some of whom had indemnity rights against the debtor). The Fourth Circuit held that such assertion of authority was necessary for a successful reorganization. However, it should also be noted that the Fourth Circuit required that consideration be given to the third-party claimants for the releases, including consideration given by some of the parties receiving releases.[142] Thus, in exchange for the debtor's insurers creating a pool of funds to be distributed to the third-party claimants, the Fourth Circuit released the insurers from any further liability.

The Second Circuit in *Deutsche Bank AG v. Metromedia Fiber Network, Inc. (In re Metromedia Fiber Network, Inc.)*[143] enumerated the following factors to consider in releasing third-party claims, whether (1) the estate received substantial consideration for the release; (2) the enjoined claims were channeled to a settlement fund rather than extinguished; (3) the enjoined claims would indirectly impact the debtor's reorganization, such as claims for contribution or indemnity; and (4) the plan otherwise provided for the full payment of the enjoined claims.[144] Aside from the mass tort context, there is little legal authority to support the extraordinary relief of barring third-party claims against a non-debtor third party.[145]

Given the split of authority, the surety must be cognizant of the limits of the bankruptcy court's authority when the surety's collateral is at stake because if the bankruptcy court acts beyond the scope of its authority, a future claimant may be able to raise that as a defense and preserve its claim

---

141. 880 F.2d at 701–02.
142. See also Sec. & Exch. Comm'n v. Drexel Burnham Lambert Grp., Inc. (In re Drexel Burnham Lambert Grp., Inc.), 960 F.2d 285, 293 (2d Cir. 1992); MacArthur Co. v. Johns-Manville Corp. (In re Johns-Manville Corp.), 837 F.2d 89, 94 (2d Cir. 1988), cert. denied, 488 U.S. 868 (1988).
143. 416 F.3d 136.
144. *Id.* at 142; Behrmann v. Nat'l Heritage Found., 663 F.3d 704 (4th Cir. 2011) (factors).
145. See 11 U.S.C. § 524(g), which provides explicit authorization for non-debtor releases in a plan relating to asbestos bankruptcies under certain circumstances.

against the surety (which may no longer be holding its collateral that was released and returned pursuant to the Surety Claims Bar Date order).[146]

In summary, although the surety would like the bankruptcy court to establish an *effective* Surety Claims Bar Date that would cut off the surety's responsibilities and joint and several obligations under the commercial surety bonds as of a certain date, such a Surety Claims Bar Date may not eliminate the surety's exposure under the commercial surety bonds. And, if the surety has collateral to reduce or eliminate such exposure, it must maintain and hold onto the surety's collateral in the event that future claims arise against the commercial surety bonds.

V. Maintaining and Preserving the Surety's Collateral for Future Claims

The next question to address is how does the surety maintain and preserve the surety's collateral for future claims that may arise against the commercial surety bonds. Initially, while the surety may

---

146. Of equal concern to the surety is whether the commercial surety bond obligees and/or third-party claimants even received the notice of the establishment of the Surety Claims Bar Date and knew, or had reason to know, that their claims may be released and/or discharged if they did not file their claims against the commercial surety bonds by the Surety Claims Bar Date. As far as the obligees and claimants are concerned, they are only worried about whether they assert their claims prior to the expiration of the applicable statute of limitations, which is inevitably a much longer time frame to assert such claims. Furthermore, it is one thing to hope that the principal/debtor provides adequate notice to an obligee under the commercial surety bond of the Surety Claims Bar Date (such as to the sole obligee under a utility bond). It is another and more difficult task and effort to provide notice to unknown third-party claimants who may have rights under the commercial surety bonds. If the surety is compelled to release its collateral prematurely due to the establishment of a Surety Claims Bar Date, the surety may face future claims having to assert and having the burden to prove the following defenses: (1) that the obligee or claimants received the notice of the Surety Claims Bar Date (and that such a Surety Claims Bar Date would be effective and binding upon the obligees and claimants); and (2) that the surety was prejudiced by the failure of the obligees and claimants to assert their claims against the commercial surety bonds prior to the expiration of the Surety Claims Bar Date, which prejudice resulted in the bankruptcy court's ordered and required release of the surety's collateral to the bankruptcy estate.

have paid certain claims of obligees and third-party claimants under the commercial surety bonds, the surety may still retain some of the remaining surety collateral. Whether or not some or all of the commercial surety bonds have been validly cancelled, and assuming that no Surety Claims Bar Date has been established (either because the principal has not attempted to set such a Surety Claims Bar Date or the principal's attempt has been denied by the bankruptcy court), the surety may continue to have contingent joint and several liabilities to the obligees and any third-party claimants up to the penal sums under the remaining commercial surety bonds. The surety's goal at this juncture is to maintain and preserve the surety's collateral for the payment of such future contingent liabilities and claims, and to hold onto the surety's collateral until the surety is completely released and discharged from all of its possible commercial surety bond obligations.

As much as the surety wishes to maintain and preserve the surety's collateral, the principal, or its succeeding trustee, may assert rights to the remaining portion of the unused surety collateral and demand that the collateral be returned to the principal's estate in order to distribute those funds to various creditors, including administrative expense claims, priority claims, and unsecured claims. Essentially, the principal and/or the trustee will see a "pot of money" represented by the surety's collateral that the surety is holding due to the potential but contingent claims remaining under the commercial surety bonds.

There are three issues to address. First, what actions may the surety take to avoid future claims against the commercial surety bonds and/or to preserve the surety's rights against the surety's collateral? Second, what actions may the principal and/or its trustee take against the surety under the Bankruptcy Code in order to obtain a release and return of the surety's collateral to the principal's estate? Third, what else may happen to the surety's collateral in the principal's bankruptcy case? With respect to this third issue, there are several concepts addressed as well as litigation issues to consider and plan of reorganization and confirmation order issues to consider.

A. *The Surety's Actions to Avoid Future Claims and/or to Preserve the Surety's Rights Against the Surety's Collateral*

The surety may take the following actions in order to avoid future claims and/or to maintain and preserve the surety's right against the surety's collateral.

1. The Surety's Proof of Claim[147]

The surety should file a proof of claim in the principal's bankruptcy case.[148] The surety's proof of claim will assert a secured claim for the surety's collateral that is property of the principal's estate (real and personal property). In the event that the principal's "security" serving as the surety's collateral is a letter of credit or its proceeds, the surety's proof of claim will assert the surety's rights in the letter of credit and the proceeds while stating that the letter of credit and the proceeds are not property of the principal's estate.

The surety's proof of claim may be contingent because it is based, in part, upon the amount of the unpaid penal sums of the commercial surety bonds and there are potential future claims, presently contingent, against the commercial surety bonds. The principal may object and seek to disallow the surety's secured proof of claim based upon the contingent nature of all or a portion of the surety's secured claim pursuant to

---

147. There have been a number of publications and papers concerning the surety's proof of claim. These include *Surety Claims in Bankruptcy*, *supra* note 55, at 243–308, George J. Bachrach & Jacqueline T. Lewis, The Surety's Claim in Bankruptcy—Obtaining Reimbursement for the Surety's Loss (Sept. 10, 2009) (unpublished paper submitted at the Pearlman Conference), and George J. Bachrach & Frank M. Lanak, The Surety's Proof of Claim: Obtaining Reimbursement for the Loss (Sept. 18, 2008) (unpublished paper submitted at the 19th Annual Northeast Surety and Fidelity Claims Conference).

148. It must be noted that by filing a proof of claim, a creditor consents to the jurisdiction of the bankruptcy court to adjudicate the creditor's claims and any debtor/trustee counterclaims related to the creditor's claims. Langenkamp v. Culp, 498 U.S. 42, 44 (1990); Gardner v. State of New Jersey, 329 U.S. 565, 573 (1947) ("he who invokes the aid of the bankruptcy court by offering a proof of claim and demanding its allowance must abide the consequences of that procedure"). *See also* United Student Aid Funds, Inc. v. Espinosa, 559 U.S. 260, 275 (2010) ("[Creditor] filed a proof of claim regarding [Debtor's] student loan debt, thereby submitting itself to the Bankruptcy Court's jurisdiction with respect to that claim"). Further, in the surety context, it is doubtful that a surety will be able to avoid bankruptcy court jurisdiction to resolve any claims involving the debtor/trustee and the surety with respect to the surety's collateral.

§ 502(e) of the Bankruptcy Code.[149] The surety's right to retain its lien against the surety's collateral that is property of the principal's estate even if the surety's secured claim is disallowed as a contingent claim for reimbursement under § 502(e) of the Bankruptcy Code is addressed in § 506(d) of the Bankruptcy Code.[150]

2. *The Surety's Cancellation of the Commercial Surety Bonds*

Assuming that the surety has taken the appropriate steps, including obtaining relief from the automatic stay,[151] the surety may cancel those commercial surety bonds that may be cancelled.[152] While the surety's cancellation of any commercial surety bonds may cut off the surety's exposure for any claims that may arise *after* the commercial surety bonds' respective cancellation effective dates, the surety will remain contingently liable for up to the amounts of the penal sums of the remaining commercial surety bonds until, at least, the dates that the applicable statutes of limitations for each of the commercial surety bonds have expired.

Care must be taken in the process of cancelling the commercial surety bonds as the requirements of cancellation must be followed precisely to avoid a later claim that the commercial surety bond was not properly cancelled and is therefore still open and in effect. Cancellation provisions may exist in the terms of the commercial surety bond itself or may be contained in the provisions of an applicable statute or regulation, or both. Furthermore, there may be conflicting provisions among the

---

149. 11 U.S.C. § 502(e)(1) provides:

> [T]he court shall disallow any claim for reimbursement or contribution of an entity that is liable with the debtor on or has secured the claim of a creditor, to the extent that—(B) such claim for reimbursement or contribution is contingent as of the time of allowance or disallowance of such claim for reimbursement or contribution.

150. *See infra* Section V.C.1.

151. Cancelling a commercial surety bond without bankruptcy court approval for relief from the § 362 automatic stay of the Bankruptcy Code has been held to be a violation of the automatic stay. *See In re* Advent Corp., 24 B.R. 612, 614 (B.A.P. 1st Cir. 1982) (the cancellation is ineffective); *In re* Wegner Farms Co., 49 B.R. 440, 442 (Bankr. Iowa 1985); *In re* R.O.A.M., Inc., 15 B.R. 616, 617 (Bankr. Nev. 1981).

152. *See Case Administration*, *supra* note 35, at 117–19; Schexnayder et al., *supra* note 35, at 520–22.

commercial surety bond, the statute, and/or the regulation. Moreover, persons or locations identified for providing notice may no longer be in existence due to the passage of time or the business circumstances of the obligee. The surety must also check for any riders or amendments to the commercial surety bonds to see if any changes were made to the cancellation provisions. Finally, the specific manner of cancelling the commercial surety bonds must be followed, such as sending the notice by certified or registered mail, sending copies to certain persons, and other similar provisions regarding the logistics of the cancellation.

As part of the cancellation process, the surety may consider sending all cancellation notices out by certified mail, return receipt requested so that the surety may track and have a record of the dates of the obligees' receipt of the notices. While there may be some cost to this approach, documenting the obligees' receipt of the notices as of a firm and known date may be critical to obtaining an effective cancellation. Moreover, the surety may want to include an acknowledgment form with the cancellation notice for each commercial surety bond that would request the relevant obligee to acknowledge that it has no precancellation claims against the commercial surety bond and/or that the obligee consents to a release of the commercial surety bond in full.

3. The Surety Claims Bar Date

As discussed previously in this chapter,[153] if a Surety Claims Bar Date is tied together with a bankruptcy court-ordered requirement for the surety's release and return of the surety's collateral, the surety should have real concern with a principal's attempts to establish such a Surety Claims Bar Date in the bankruptcy case. On the other hand, the establishment of a Surety Claims Bar Date may be helpful to the surety as long as it is not tied to a required release and return of the surety's collateral. In cases when the potential bond claimants (obligees) are known and have received notice of the Surety Claims Bar Date, and such claimants have also asserted claims in the bankruptcy case against the principal, it may be effectively argued that such claimants are indeed subject to and bound by the Surety Claims Bar Date and the surety may seek to use the Surety Claims Bar Date as a defense against claims from such claimants

---

153. *See supra* Section IV.C.

(claim preclusion).[154] If there is no release of the surety's collateral and the Surety Claims Bar Date is ultimately deemed to be ineffective for some reason, the surety may still be protected by its collateral.

The surety may want to seek a middle ground when a Surety Claims Bar Date is proposed and the surety agrees to release some of its collateral in exchange for an agreement with the principal/debtor that the surety may retain the remainder of its collateral for an extended period of time until all potential liability is extinguished. Under this approach, the surety may need to engage consultants and experts to evaluate the surety's potential future liability under the commercial surety bonds issued so that the surety may determine what amount of collateral it must safely retain. There may be other arrangements that may be made with the principal as it emerges from bankruptcy in the form of new collateral that could also protect the surety from future claims, such as the issuance of a new or replacement letter of credit, preferred stock, or bonds to the surety in the reorganized principal.

B. The Principal's/Trustee's Actions Under the Bankruptcy Code to Obtain a Release and Return of the Surety's Collateral to the Bankruptcy Estate

Notwithstanding the surety's attempts to maintain and preserve its rights to the surety's collateral, the principal, or its successor trustee (collectively, the principal/trustee), has certain actions that it may take under the Bankruptcy Code to require the surety to release and/or return the surety's collateral to the principal's estate. Those actions may differ depending upon whether the surety's collateral is in the form of a letter of credit and its proceeds or whether the surety's collateral is deemed to be property of the principal's estate under § 541 of the Bankruptcy Code. Regardless, the concept is the same—whether the surety's collateral is property of the estate (the principal's real and/or personal property, including cash and other cash equivalents) or a letter of credit or the proceeds of a letter of credit and not property of the estate. The surety's rights to retain and maintain the surety's collateral is dependent upon the underlying agreements between the principal and the surety, whether

---

154. The issue of claim preclusion due to the commercial surety bond claimant's claims against the joint and severally liable principal under the commercial surety bonds is discussed in this chapter. *See infra* Section V.D.4.c.

the indemnity agreement, the collateral agreement, both, or any other agreement that determines the disposition of the surety's collateral and the rights in that collateral for both the principal and the surety.

When the surety's collateral is property of the principal's estate, the surety's collateral is not treated any differently than any other secured creditor's rights and/or obligations with respect to their collateral that is property of the estate. Numerous sections of the Bankruptcy Code address the debtor and/or trustee rights to gather property of the estate from wherever and whomever it is being held, even if the property of the estate is held as collateral.

With respect to a letter of credit and the proceeds of a letter of credit, which are not property of the estate, there is an initial hurdle for the principal/trustee to jump over. Namely, the letter of credit and its proceeds do not become property of the estate to which the principal/trustee's rights attach until they become excess to what the surety requires to be secured for the principal's obligations under the underlying agreements—the commercial surety bonds, the indemnity agreement, the collateral agreement, and/or any other agreement. It is for that reason that this chapter will *only* discuss the possible principal/trustee actions that may be taken against the surety's collateral in the context of when the surety's collateral is a letter of credit or its proceeds, and not when the surety's collateral is already property of the estate.

1. Letters of Credit and Turnover Powers Under 11 U.S.C. § 542

Section 542 of the Bankruptcy Code[155] provides in relevant part:

> (a) [A]n entity, . . . in possession, custody, or control, during the case, of property that the trustee may use, sell, or lease under section 363 of this title, or that the debtor may exempt under section 522 of this title, shall deliver to the trustee, and account for, such property or the value of such property, unless such property is of inconsequential value or benefit to the estate.
>
> (b) [A]n entity that owes a debt that is property of the estate and that is matured, payable on demand, or payable on order, shall pay such debt to, or on the order of, the trustee, except to the

155. *See Bankruptcy Estate*, *supra* note 36, at 368–75.

> extent that such debt may be offset under section 553 of this title against a claim against the debtor.[156]

Implicit in the bankruptcy concept of turnover is the idea that the property being sought is clearly the property of the debtor's estate, but the property is not in the debtor's possession.[157] Turnover under § 542 of the Bankruptcy Code is a remedy available to trustees and debtors to obtain what is acknowledged to be property of the estate.[158] It is not a remedy available to recover claimed debts that remain unliquidated and/or in dispute.[159] Thus, it has been held under the Bankruptcy Code

---

156. 11 U.S.C. § 542. The proper procedural method for initiating a turnover action is to file a complaint in an adversary proceeding, and not by motion. Federal Rule of Bankruptcy Procedure 7001 states that "[t]he following are adversary proceedings: (1) a proceeding to recover money or property . . ." *See also In re* Perkins, 902 F.2d 1254, 1258 (7th Cir. 1990) ("a turnover action is an adversary proceeding which must be commenced by a properly filed and served complaint"); Roffman v. Butler (*In re* ROPT Ltd. P'ship), 209 B.R. 144, 151 (B.A.P. 1st Cir. 1997); *In re* Donato, No. 11-34418, 2011 Bankr. LEXIS 4763, at *3 (Bankr. N.D. Ohio Dec. 6, 2011) ("Rule 7001 required Debtor to file his request for turnover as an adversary proceeding, subject to the procedural rules governing such proceedings, including rules governing service of the summons and complaint in Bankruptcy Rule 7004"); *In re* World Wide Fin. Servs., Inc., No. 05-75180, 2008 Bankr. LEXIS 391, at *4 (Bankr. E.D. Mich. Jan. 23, 2008) ("Bankruptcy Rule 7001(1) clearly requires an adversary proceeding to be filed to obtain the relief requested by the Trustee's corrected motion [seeking relief under § 542]"); *In re* Interpictures, Inc., 86 B.R. 24, 29 (Bankr. E.D.N.Y. 1988); *In re* Gold Leaf Corp., 73 B.R. 146, 147 (Bankr. N.D. Fla. 1987); *In re* Ace Indus., Inc., 65 B.R. 199, 200 (Bankr. W.D. Mich. 1986); *In re* Riding, 44 B.R. 846, 858 (Bankr. D. Utah 1984).
157. *See* FLR Co. v. United States (*In re* FLR Co.), 58 B.R. 632, 634 (Bankr. W.D. Pa. 1985).
158. *See In re* Hechinger Inv. Co. of Del., 282 B.R. 149, 160–62 (Bankr. D. Del. 2002) (citing *In re* Asousa P'ship, 264 B.R. 376, 384 (Bankr. E.D. Pa. 2001)); *In re* Rosenzweig, 245 B.R. 836, 839–40 (Bankr. N.D. Ill. 2000). *See* 5 COLLIER ON BANKRUPTCY ¶ 542.01 *et seq.* (Alan N. Resnick & Henry J. Sommer eds., 16th ed. 2011).
159. *See In re* Oakwood Homes Corp., 342 B.R. 59, 67–69 (Bankr. D. Del. 2006). In *Smith v. McLeskey* (*In re Bay Vista of Virginia, Inc.*), No. 08-7046-SCS, 2009 Bankr. LEXIS 916, at *30 (Bankr. E.D. Va. Feb. 2,

that a bankruptcy court may generally order a third party to turn over property of the debtor's estate in its possession if the following three primary requirements are met:

> First, such property must be "property of the estate." Second, at the moment the debtor filed a petition, the debtor must have had the right to use, sell, or lease the property. Finally, upon request, the court must ensure that the third party's interest in the property is adequately protected.[160]

Because a letter of credit and its proceeds are generally not considered to be property of the estate, many of the rights and powers of the trustee or debtor do not apply to the letter of credit or its proceeds. The trustee/debtor right of "turnover" under § 542 of the Bankruptcy Code is not applicable to the proceeds of a letter of credit because such proceeds are not property of the estate.[161] While there may be a subsequent determination that the letter of credit proceeds are "excess proceeds,"[162] the filing of a turnover action is not the proper procedure for making the determination that the letter of credit proceeds are "excess proceeds."

2009) (report and recommendation adopted, No. 2:09cv46, 2009 U.S. Dist. LEXIS 87154 (E.D. Va. June 2, 2009), the district court held that turnover under the Bankruptcy Code is a remedy available to obtain what is acknowledged to be property of the bankruptcy estate. It is not a remedy available to recover claimed debts that remain unliquidated and/or in dispute (citing United States v. Inslaw, Inc., 932 F.2d 1467, 1472 (D.C. Cir. 1991)). *See also In re* Charter Co., 913 F.2d 1575, 1579 (11th Cir. 1990); Weiner's, Inc. v. T.G. & Y. Stores Co., 191 B.R. 30, 32 (S.D.N.Y. 1996); *Asousa P'ship*, 264 B.R. at 384 (turnover under § 542 cannot be used to determine the rights of parties in legitimate contract disputes); *In re* N. Parent, Inc., 221 B.R. 609, 626 (Bankr. D. Mass. 1998).

160. *In re* Lewis, 137 F.3d 1280, 1282 (11th Cir. 1998).

161. *Hechinger*, 282 B.R. at 161–62 ("Turnover under 11 U.S.C. § 542 is a remedy available to debtors to obtain what is acknowledged to be property of the bankruptcy estate. It is not a remedy available to recover claimed debts which remain unliquidated and/or in dispute." The debtor may not use a turnover action to "circumvent" its contract claims and "recover that to which [it] has not yet established an undisputed, liquidated claim.") (citations omitted).

162. *See infra* Section V.C.2.

In *In re Hechinger*,[163] the debtor arranged for the issuance of a letter of credit to its pre-bankruptcy lender as part of a post-bankruptcy agreement with its pre-bankruptcy lender to allow a pre-petition deposit account to remain open. After being notified that the letter of credit would not be renewed, the pre-bankruptcy lender, as the beneficiary of the letter of credit, drew down the entire amount of the letter of credit. The debtor brought an adversary proceeding against the beneficiary of the letter of credit (the defendant) alleging that the draw on the letter of credit was improper and asserting that the letter of credit proceeds in the possession of the defendant were property of the estate to which the debtor was entitled to turnover pursuant to § 542 of the Bankruptcy Code.

The defendant moved to dismiss the turnover count of the adversary proceeding asserting that the proceeds of the letter of credit did not constitute property of the debtor's estate as the funds issued from the letter of credit belonged to the issuing bank and not to the debtor who caused the letter of credit to be issued. The debtor countered that the letter of credit proceeds constituted property of the estate in the possession of the defendant because the debtor had an alleged equitable interest in its claim to the return of the funds as funds improperly debited from its account and because the debtor had an alleged equitable interest in the issuing bank's claim for breach of contract against the defendant arising out of the defendant's allegedly inaccurate certification under the letter of credit.

The bankruptcy court observed that "it is well settled that the proceeds from a letter of credit do not constitute property of the estate under section 541 of the Bankruptcy Code. Therefore, such proceeds . . . are not subject to turnover under section 542 as property that the Debtor 'may use . . . under section 363.'"[164] The bankruptcy court further noted that "[t]he fact that Debtor may have equitable interests in certain breach of contract claims which seek to recover the . . . [letter of credit proceeds], which interests constitute property of the estate, does not alter the result."[165] Accordingly, the bankruptcy court granted the defendant's motion to dismiss the turnover count.

---

163. 282 B.R. 149.

164. *Id.* at 161.

165. *Id.*

2. Letters of Credit and Preference Avoidance Powers Under 11 U.S.C. § 547

a. The Surety's Collateral (Generally). Any time that the surety receives collateral from the principal, and the principal then files a bankruptcy case within 90 days (the preference period), the surety may face the principal's attempt to avoid the principal's transfer of its property as collateral to the surety as a preference under § 547 of the Bankruptcy Code.[166] Section 547 of the Bankruptcy Code requires that in order for a transfer to be subject to avoidance as a preference (1) there must be a transfer of an interest of the debtor in property; (2) on account of an antecedent debt; (3) to or for the benefit of a creditor; (4) made while the debtor was insolvent; (5) made within 90 days prior to the commencement of the bankruptcy case; and (6) that left the creditor better off than it would have been if the transfer had not been made and the creditor had asserted its claim in a chapter 7 bankruptcy liquidation.[167]

As the foregoing elements demonstrate, for a transfer to be avoided under § 547, "it is essential that the debtor have an interest in the property transferred so that the estate is thereby diminished."[168] The purpose of the trustee/debtor preference avoidance powers is to discourage creditors from "racing to the courthouse to dismember the debtor during his slide into bankruptcy," and to "facilitate the prime bankruptcy policy of equality of distribution among creditors of the debtor."[169] The preference powers under the Bankruptcy Code are subject to certain defenses as set forth in the Bankruptcy Code. Chief among those defenses are transfers that are made for new value or in the ordinary course of business.[170]

To the extent that the surety receives the principal's collateral (the principal's real and/or personal property) that is part of the property of the estate within the preference period, and the surety does not have any of the statutory defenses under § 547(c) of the Bankruptcy Code, the

---

166. 11 U.S.C. § 547. *See Bankruptcy Estate*, *supra* note 36, at 330–65. *See* 5 Collier on Bankruptcy *supra* note 158, ¶ 547.01 *et seq.*

167. *See In re* Interior Wood Prods. Co., 986 F.2d 228, 230 (8th Cir. 1993); *In re* Jet Fla. Sys., Inc., 861 F.2d 1555, 1558 n.2 (11th Cir. 1988); Brown v. First Nat'l Bank, 748 F.2d 490, 491 (8th Cir. 1984) (citing DeAngio v. DeAngio, 554 F.2d 863, 864 (8th Cir. 1977)).

168. Coral Petroleum, Inc. v. Banque Paribas-London, 797 F.2d 1351, 1355–56, *reh'g denied*, 801 F.2d 398 (5th Cir. 1986); *In re* Grabill Corp., 135 B.R. 101, 107 (Bankr. N.D. Ill. 1991).

169. *In re* Issac Leaseco, Inc., 389 F.3d 1205, 1209 (11th Cir. 2004).

170. 11 U.S.C.A. § 547(c) *et seq.*

surety may lose its collateral in a preference action. What makes the loss of the surety's collateral even more disturbing is the fact that the loss of the collateral may not occur until two years or more after the bankruptcy case was filed. Pursuant to the Bankruptcy Code, the principal, as debtor, and/or a trustee have up to two years from the "entry of the order for relief," which is the date of the filing of the bankruptcy petition, to initiate preference actions.[171]

b. The Surety's Collateral (Letter of Credit and Its Proceeds). The trustee/debtor preference avoidance powers as provided by § 547 of the Bankruptcy Code do not apply to the letter of credit or its proceeds because they are not considered to be property of the principal's/debtor's estate.

In *Wooten v. United States through Department of Interior*,[172] the bankruptcy court held that because letters of credit are not property of the debtor's estate, the trustee's preference avoidance powers under § 547 of the Bankruptcy Code do not apply. The debtor was an oil refining company that entered into a contract for the purchase of crude oil from the U.S. Department of the Interior.[173] The contract was secured by letters of credit issued by a bank in favor of the Department. The contract was terminated by the Department because the debtor failed to pay for oil deliveries. The Department then drew down on the letters of credit both before and after the debtor had filed its bankruptcy case. Among other assertions, the trustee alleged that the drawdowns on the letters of credit constituted preferences under § 547 of the Bankruptcy Code.[174]

The Department sought dismissal of the trustee's preference claims on the grounds that letters of credit are neither property of the debtor nor property of the estate. The bankruptcy court noted that a letter of credit and its proceeds are property of the issuing bank, not the debtor.[175] The bankruptcy court explained as follows:

> In issuing the letter of credit the Bank entered into an independent contractual obligation to pay [the beneficiary of the letter of credit] out of its own assets. Although cashing the letter will immediately give rise to a claim by the Bank against the debtors

---

171. 11 U.S.C. § 546(a).
172. 56 B.R. 227 (W.D. La. 1985).
173. *Id.* at 228.
174. *Id.*
175. *Id.* at 231–32.

> pursuant to the latter's indemnification obligations, that claim will not divest the debtors of any property since any attempt to enforce that claim would be subject to an automatic stay.[176]

The bankruptcy court held that "[n]o avoidable transfer occurred because the assets of [the bank], rather than those of [the debtor], were depleted. Thus, the trustee's claim pursuant to 11 U.S.C. § 547 is dismissed for failure to state a cause of action."[177]

Similarly, in *In re Illinois-California Express, Inc.*,[178] the bankruptcy court held that the preference avoidance powers of the trustee do not apply to letters of credit. In *Illinois-California Express*, the principal entered into a loan credit agreement with various banks under which the banks agreed to issue letters of credit, secured by the property of the principal, for the benefit of the surety.[179] Under the terms of the letters of credit, the surety would draw on the letters of credit as necessary in order to pay loss and damage claims filed against the debtors by third parties.[180] The letters of credit were all issued prior to the filing of the bankruptcy case. The surety made several draws against the letters of credit both before and after the bankruptcy case was filed. The trustee filed an adversary proceeding against the banks and the surety alleging among other claims that the draws on the letters of credit were voidable preferences. The banks and the surety moved to dismiss the adversary proceeding.[181]

In addressing the motion to dismiss the preference claims, the bankruptcy court noted that the "overwhelming authority" of the law indicates that money advanced under a letter of credit is not property of the debtor's estate.[182] The bankruptcy court observed that a letter of credit creates a separate and distinct obligation between the issuer and the beneficiary in which the issuer obligates itself to honor all drafts of the beneficiary that are presented in compliance with the letter of credit and that when the issuer honors a proper draft, it does so from its own assets

---

176. *Id.* at 232 (citing *In re* Page, 18 B.R. 713, 715–16 (Bankr. D.D.C. 1982)).
177. *Id.* (clarification added).
178. 50 B.R. 232 (Bankr. Colo. 1985).
179. *Id.* at 233.
180. *Id.*
181. *Id.*
182. *Id.* at 239.

and not from the assets of the customer.[183] The bankruptcy court stated that "[t]he Bankruptcy Court's jurisdiction does not extend to control property in which the debtor has no property interest."[184] Accordingly, the bankruptcy court granted the motion to dismiss and held that because the letters of credit are not property of the estate nor property of the principal, now the debtor, the trustee had no legal claims.

c. Property Pledged by the Principal as Collateral to Secure the Issuing Bank for the Issuance of the Letter of Credit. While letters of credit and their proceeds are not property of the estate, the principal's property that is pledged to the issuing bank as collateral to secure the bank's issuance of the letter of credit to the surety as collateral may be held to be property of the estate.[185] Several courts, including the Fifth, Ninth, and 11th Circuit Courts of Appeal, have held that the principal's property provided to the issuer (bank) to secure the issuance of a letter of credit is property of the estate.[186] The Third Circuit Court of Appeals has stated that "where the claim centers around the *collateral* pledged to the bank and *not* the distribution of the proceeds themselves, 'the fact that letters of credit themselves are not property of the estate is a red herring.'"[187] Similarly, in *In re Compton Corp.*, the Fifth Circuit Court of Appeals expressly held: "Overall, the letter of credit itself and the payments thereunder may not be property of [the] debtor, but the collateral pledged as a security interest for the letter of credit is."[188]

d. When Letters of Credit and Their Proceeds May Be Avoidable Preferences to the Surety under 11 U.S.C. § 547. As discussed above, with respect to collateral in the form of letters of credit, because of the independence principle and the fact that letters of credit are not property of the debtor's estate, many courts hold that the trustee/debtor preference

---

183. *Id.* at 240.

184. *Id.* (citing Jordan v. Randolph Mills, Inc., 29 B.R. 398 (Bankr. M.D.N.C. 1983)); *In re* Dr. C. Huff Co., 44 B.R. 129 (Bankr. W.D. Ky. 1984).

185. *In re* Kaiser Grp. Int'l, 399 F.3d 558 (3d Cir. 2005); *In re* S-Tran Holdings, Inc., 414 B.R. 28, 32–33 (Bankr. D. Del. 2009); *In re* Oakwood Homes Corp., 342 B.R. 59, 67 (Bankr. D. Del. 2006).

186. *In re* Compton Corp., 831 F.2d 586, 590–91 (5th Cir. 1987); *In re* Mayan Network, 306 B.R. 295, 299 (B.A.P. 9th Cir. 2004); *In re* Air Conditioning, Inc. of Stuart, 845 F.2d 293, 296 (11th Cir. 1988); *In re* Metro Commc'ns, Inc., 115 B.R. 849, 854 (Bankr. W.D. Pa. 1990).

187. *Kaiser Grp.*, 399 F.3d at 566 (quoting *Mayan Networks*, 306 B.R. at 299); *S-Tran Holdings*, 414 B.R. at 33–34.

188. *Compton*, 831 F.2d at 590–91.

avoidance powers do not apply to letters of credit or their proceeds.[189] However, under certain circumstances, even though a letter of credit and its proceeds are not property of the estate, courts have held that the surety's receipt of a letter of credit may constitute a preferential payment to the surety.[190]

In *In re Compton Corp.*,[191] the Fifth Circuit Court of Appeals held that the issuance of the letter of credit constituted an indirect preference to a creditor that could be avoided under § 547 of the Bankruptcy Code. In *Compton*, a supplier delivered a shipment of oil to a buyer. The buyer was unable to pay for the oil, but it was able to get its bank to issue an irrevocable standby letter of credit in favor of the supplier. Under the terms of the letter of credit, the issuing bank was obligated to pay up to the full amount owed for the shipment of oil if the buyer failed to pay the supplier by a certain date. To obtain the letter of credit, the buyer paid the issuing bank a small fee and gave a promissory note payable on demand for the full amount of the letter of credit. The issuing bank was also covered by a prior perfected security agreement with the buyer that included the issuance of the letter of credit under the "future advances" clause. The letter of credit on its face noted that it was for an *antecedent debt* due to the supplier. The day after the letter of credit was issued, several of the buyer's creditors filed an involuntary bankruptcy petition against the buyer. The buyer failed to make payment to the supplier for the oil and the issuing bank paid the full amount of the letter of credit to the supplier.

In the ensuing bankruptcy case, the issuing bank was ultimately paid in full for its secured losses, including the payment made under the letter of credit, from the proceeds of the liquidation of the buyer. The trustee filed an adversary proceeding against the *supplier* seeking to avoid the payment under the letter of credit to the supplier as a preference. The trustee claimed that the direct transfer to the issuing bank of the increased security interest also constituted an indirect transfer to the supplier, which occurred one day prior to the filing of the involuntary bankruptcy petition and was therefore voidable as a preference under § 547 of the Bankruptcy Code.

The appellate court acknowledged that letters of credit are not property of the estate and that the payment under the letter of credit was

---

189. *See supra* Section V.B.2.b.

190. *Air Conditioning, Inc.*, 845 F.2d 293(citing *Compton*, 831 F.2d at 594–95).

191. 831 F.2d 586.

made from the assets of the issuing bank.[192] However, the appellate court observed that it was "important" to note that the irrevocable standby letter of credit in the case was not arranged in connection with the supplier's initial decision to sell the oil to the buyer on credit.[193] Rather, the buyer arranged for the letter of credit after the supplier had shipped the oil and after the buyer had defaulted in payment. The appellate court stated:

> The letter of credit in this case did not serve its usual function of backing up a contemporaneous credit decision, but instead served as a backup payment guarantee on an extension of credit already in jeopardy. The letter of credit was issued to pay off an antecedent unsecured debt. This fact was clearly noted on the face of the letter of credit. [The supplier], the beneficiary of the letter of credit, did not give new value for the issuance of the letter of credit by [the issuing bank] . . . , or for the resulting increased security interest held by the [issuing bank].[194]

Under the appellate court's analysis, when a debtor pledges its assets to secure a letter of credit, a transfer of the debtor's property has occurred under the provisions of § 547 of the Bankruptcy Code.[195] Specifically, by the debtor subjecting its assets to the issuing bank's reimbursement claim in the event the letter of credit was paid, the debtor makes a transfer of its property. The appellate court noted that the broad definition of "transfer" under § 101(50) of the Bankruptcy Code is clearly designed to cover such action. Thus, the appellate court stated, "Overall, the letter of credit itself and the payments thereunder may not be property of debtor, but the collateral pledged as a security interest for the letter of credit is."[196]

Essentially, the *Compton* court believed that an unsecured creditor was being "substituted" for a secured creditor to the detriment of the estate. If there had been no letter of credit, the buyer would have defaulted on the payment for the oil shipment and the supplier would have been an unsecured creditor in the bankruptcy case. But, because of the letter of credit arrangement, the buyer entered into a secured transaction with the issuing bank in the amount of the letter of credit, the supplier was paid

192. *Id.* at 589.
193. *Id.* at 590.
194. *Id.* (clarification added).
195. *Id.*
196. *Id.* at 590–91.

in full by the issuing bank, and the supplier's obligation was in effect transferred to the issuing bank as a secured claim. Thus, both the issuing bank and the supplier were paid in full and the unsecured creditors of the debtor's estate received less. If the buyer had attempted to make a payment to the supplier directly for the antecedent debt, it would have been a preference. Therefore, the appellate court held:

> To constitute a preference, it is not necessary that the transfer be made directly to the creditor. If the bankrupt has made a transfer of his property, the *effect* of which is to enable one of his creditors to obtain a greater percentage of his debt than another creditor of the same class, circuity of arrangement will not avail to save it.[197]

The *Compton* case turned on the specific facts of the case when the letter of credit was issued after the fact for an antecedent debt. The *Compton* court acknowledged that had the letter of credit been issued as part of the original transaction for the purchase and sale of the oil, there would not have been a preference because the letter of credit would have been part of the new value consideration. The appellate court stated:

> In the letter of credit cases . . . the letters of credit were issued contemporaneously with the initial extension of credit by the beneficiaries of the letters. In those cases, the letters of credit effectively served as security devices for the benefit of the creditor beneficiaries and took the place of formal security interests. The courts in those cases properly found there had been no voidable transfers, direct or indirect, in the letter of credit transactions involved. New value was given contemporaneously with the issuance of the letters of credit in the form of the extensions of credit by the beneficiaries of the letters. As a result, the 11 U.S.C. § 547(c)(1) preference exception was applicable.[198]

In the surety context, if the surety receives the letter of credit prior to or contemporaneously with the execution of the indemnity agreement and then the commercial surety bonds, the surety has provided new value

---

197. *Id.* at 591 (citing Nat'l Bank of Newport v. Nat'l Herkimer Cnty. Bank, 225 U.S. 178, 184 (1912)).

198. *Id.* at 594.

under § 547(c)(1) of the Bankruptcy Code and may be able to successfully assert that defense. But if the surety has already issued the commercial surety bonds on behalf of the principal and then, pursuant to a "place in funds demand," obtains the letter of credit, and the principal files its bankruptcy case within 90 days of that transfer of the letter of credit to the surety while providing its property as security to the issuing bank, the surety may not be able to assert the new value defense.[199]

3. *Letters of Credit and Post-Petition Transfer Powers Under 11 U.S.C. § 549*

Section 549 of the Bankruptcy Code provides that the trustee may avoid an unauthorized post-petition transfer of property of the debtor's estate, stating as follows:

> (a) Except as provided in subsection (b) or (c) of this section, the trustee may avoid a transfer of property of the estate—
>
> (1) that occurs after the commencement of the case; and
>
> (2)(A) that is authorized only under section 303(f) or 542(c) of this title; or
>
> (B) that is not authorized under this title or by the court.[200]

Accordingly, to avoid a transfer under § 549, it must be demonstrated that (1) a transfer occurred; (2) of property of the estate; (3) which occurred post-petition; and (4) was not authorized by the Bankruptcy Code or the bankruptcy court.[201] Unlike other avoidance powers, the question of "diminution of estate" is not relevant. Although the primary purpose of § 549 of the Bankruptcy Code is to allow the avoidance of post-petition transfers of property that deplete the debtor's estate, the inability to demonstrate a measurable depletion of the property of the estate is not enough to allow a transfer to stand when it is otherwise

---

199. The surety may be able to assert other defenses under § 547(c) of the Bankruptcy Code.

200. 11 U.S.C. § 549. The Bankruptcy Code provides only two exceptions to a trustee's § 549 avoiding power, which are not typically relevant in the surety collateral context. First, subsection (b), which involves only involuntary bankruptcy cases, and second, subsection (c), which protects good faith purchasers of real property.

201. *See* Manuel v. Allen, 217 B.R. 952, 955 (Bankr. M.D. Fla. 1998).

avoidable under § 549 of the Bankruptcy Code.[202] Once a court finds a transfer avoidable, § 550(a) of the Bankruptcy Code allows the trustee to recover the property transferred.[203]

In *In re M.J. Sales & Distributing Co.*,[204] Aetna Casualty and Surety Company issued an "open default" bond on behalf of the principal in favor of a claimant as a condition for a state court vacating an earlier entered order of default against the principal. The bond assured payment of any future judgment for the claimant against the principal. With the posting of the bond, the state court action between the principal and the claimant proceeded as a contested action.

As a condition of issuing the bond, Aetna required that its principal obtain a letter of credit as collateral. The letter of credit was issued by a bank and the principal provided a treasury bond to the bank as security for the bank's issuance of the letter of credit. Subsequently, the principal filed its bankruptcy case. The claimant obtained relief from the automatic stay to allow the state court action to proceed; however, the principal's counsel withdrew and the principal was in danger of being in default again. Accordingly, Aetna made demand on the bank to draw on the letter of credit. Ultimately, a default judgment was entered against the principal and the claimant filed suit against Aetna to collect on the bond. The trustee sought to enjoin the bank and Aetna from drawing on the letter of credit asserting among other things that § 549 of the Bankruptcy Code barred such action.

The bankruptcy court noted that a bank honors a letter of credit and pays the beneficiary with its own funds, and not with assets belonging to the debtor.[205] The bankruptcy court stated, "It is clear that the funds from which [the bank] must honor the letter of credit do not constitute property of the estate. Hence, there are no provisions under the Bankruptcy Code that would prevent payment to Aetna pursuant to the letter of credit."[206]

---

202. *In re* Straightline Invs., 525 F.3d 870, 878–79 (9th Cir. 2008) (citing 5 COLLIER ON BANKRUPTCY, *supra* note 158, ¶ 549.02 *et seq.*).

203. *See In re* Delco Oil, 599 F.3d 1255, 1258–59 (11th Cir. 2010); 11 U.S.C. § 550(a) ("[T]o the extent that a transfer is avoided under section . . . 549 . . . the trustee may recover, for the benefit of the estate, the property transferred, or if the court so orders, the value of such property, from—(1) the initial transferee of such transfer . . . ."). *See* 5 COLLIER ON BANKRUPTCY, *supra* note 158, ¶ 550.01 *et seq.*

204. 25 B.R. 608 (Bankr. S.D.N.Y. 1982).

205. *Id.* at 614.

206. *Id.* at 615 (clarification added) (citation omitted).

4. Post-Petition Effect of the Surety's Security Interest in Property Under 11 U.S.C. § 552

Unrelated to letters of credit and their proceeds as the surety's collateral, the surety may have a perfected security interest in property that is deemed to be property of the principal's estate under § 541 of the Bankruptcy Code. Section 552 of the Bankruptcy Code provides that unless covered by a security agreement entered into between the surety and the principal before the commencement of the bankruptcy case, "property acquired by the estate or by the debtor after the commencement of the case is not subject to any lien resulting from any security agreement entered into by the debtor before the commencement of the case."[207]

The exception in § 552(b) of the Bankruptcy Code is that if the security agreement is entered into by the surety and the principal before the commencement of the bankruptcy case, and if the security interest created extends to the "proceeds, products, offspring or profits" of the property subject to the security interest created before the commencement of the bankruptcy case, then the security interest extends to the same "proceeds, products, offspring or profits" acquired by the estate after the commencement of the principal's bankruptcy case.[208] This would include the proceeds from any contract rights that are subject to the surety's security interest and to the proceeds of sale of any of the surety's collateral after the filing of the principal's bankruptcy case.

---

207. 11 U.S.C. § 552(a).

208. Pursuant to 11 U.S.C. § 552(b)(1):

> Except as provided in sections 363, 506(c), 522, 544, 545, 547, and 548 of this title, if the debtor and an entity entered into a security agreement before the commencement of the case and if the security interest created by such security agreement extends to property of the debtor acquired before the commencement of the case and to proceeds, products, offspring, or profits of such property, then such security interest extends to such proceeds, products, offspring, or profits acquired by the estate after the commencement of the case to the extent provided by such security agreement and by applicable non-bankruptcy law, except to any extent that the court, after notice and a hearing and based on the equities of the case, orders otherwise.

See 5 COLLIER ON BANKRUPTCY, *supra* note 158, ¶ 552.01 *et seq.*

C. What Else May Happen to the Surety's Collateral in the Principal's Bankruptcy Case?

Whether the surety's collateral is a letter of credit and its proceeds or property of the principal's estate, the next question is, what else may happen to the surety's collateral in the principal's bankruptcy case? The surety's position should start from the premise that the surety may maintain its rights to the surety's collateral, whether it is a letter of credit and its proceeds or property of the principal's estate, until both (1) the surety's contingent liability under the commercial surety bonds is extinguished, discharged, and/or released; and (2) the surety has been fully indemnified and reimbursed for all of its loss payments and expenses pursuant to the underlying rights and agreements between the principal and the surety (the indemnity agreement, the collateral agreement, and/or any other principal and surety agreements or common law rights).

1. The Surety's Collateral Is Protected Under 11 U.S.C. § 506(d) to the Extent of the Surety's Lien Even If the Surety's Claim Is Disallowed as a Contingent Claim for Reimbursement Under 11 U.S.C. § 502(e)

Section 506(d) of the Bankruptcy Code may allow a surety to retain its liens on property in which the debtor has an interest, including real or personal property of the principal's estate, until the surety is fully released and discharged from all of its contingent liabilities under the commercial surety bonds and the surety has been fully indemnified and reimbursed for all of its loss payments and expenses pursuant to the underlying agreements between the principal and the surety (the indemnity agreement, the collateral agreement, any other principal and surety agreements, and/or the surety's common law rights).

Section 506(d) of the Bankruptcy Code provides in relevant part:

> To the extent that a *lien* secures a *claim* against the debtor that is not an allowed secured claim, such lien is void, unless—
>
> (1) such claim was disallowed only under section 502(b)(5)[209] or 502(e) of this title; or . . . .[210]

209. Section 502(b)(5) is not applicable to this discussion.

210. 11 U.S.C. § 506(d) (emphasis added). The legislative history for § 506(d) of the Bankruptcy Code is sparse and a comparable section did not exist under the prior Bankruptcy Act before the enactment and adoption of the Bankruptcy Code on October 1, 1978. However, the legislative history

Section 101(37) of the Bankruptcy Code defines "lien" as a "charge against or interest in property to secure payment of a debt or performance of an obligation."[211] As noted earlier, "property of the estate" is defined in § 541 of the Bankruptcy Code.[212] Section 101(5) of the Bankruptcy Code defines "claim" broadly as a:

> (A) right to payment, whether or not such right is reduced to judgment, liquidated, unliquidated, fixed, contingent, matured, unmatured, disputed, undisputed, legal, equitable, secured, or unsecured; or
>
> (B) right to an equitable remedy for breach of performance if such breach gives rise to a right to payment, whether or not such right to an equitable remedy is reduced to judgment, fixed, contingent, matured, unmatured, disputed, undisputed, secured, or unsecured.[213]

Thus, in order to have a secured claim in bankruptcy the surety must have a lien against the debtor's interest in property to secure payment of an obligation or debt. Liens can be judicial, statutory, or consensual and include liens created by properly perfected U.C.C. security interests and judgments.

As described above with respect to the surety's proof of claim, the surety must file a proof of claim and assert its secured claim in the surety's collateral even if the surety's claim is a contingent claim based upon the remaining penal sums of all of the outstanding commercial surety bonds, and even if the surety believes that it holds sufficient collateral to cover its commercial surety bond exposure.

The principal may file an objection to the surety's proof of claim.[214] With respect to the surety's contingent claims, § 502(e) of the Bankruptcy Code provides in relevant part:

---

available reveals that § 506(d) of the Bankruptcy Code is intended to permit certain liens to pass through the bankruptcy case unaffected. H.R. REP. NO. 595, at 357 (1977), *reprinted in* U.S.C.C.A.N. 1978, 5787, 6313.

211. 11 U.S.C. § 101(37).

212. *See supra* Section II.A.

213. 11 U.S.C. § 101(5).

214. *See id.* § 502(a); FED. R. BANKR. P. 3007.

> (e)(1) Notwithstanding subsections (a), (b), and (c) of this section and paragraph (2) of this subsection, *the court shall disallow any claim for reimbursement* or contribution of an entity that is liable with the debtor on or has secured the claim of a creditor, to the extent that—
>
> (A) such creditor's claim against the estate is disallowed;
> (B) *such claim for reimbursement* or contribution *is contingent as of the time of allowance or disallowance of such claim for reimbursement* or contribution; or
> (C) such entity asserts a right of subrogation to the rights of such creditor under section 509 of this title.[215]

Notwithstanding any such possible future disallowance that may occur with respect to the surety's secured contingent claim for reimbursement under § 502(e), pursuant to § 506(d), to the extent that the surety has and maintains its liens securing its claims against the surety collateral that is property of the principal's estate, the surety should retain its rights and its lien on such collateral.[216]

With respect to collateral in the form of letters of credit, the analysis may be different. The authors of the treatise *Collier on Bankruptcy* state:

---

215. *See* 11 U.S.C. § 502(e) (emphasis added).
216. Section 551 of the Bankruptcy Code (11 U.S.C. § 551) provides that "any lien void under section 506(d) of this title . . . is preserved for the benefit of the estate but only with respect to property of the estate." With respect to a letter of credit and its proceeds, they are not property of the principal's estate unless they become property of the estate because they are "excess proceeds" under the terms of any underlying agreements between the principal and the surety. Even in the event that such "excess proceeds" become property of the estate, they may be subject to the lien rights of another entity (such as the issuing bank or another assignee with a perfected interest in the "excess proceeds") that are better than the rights of the trustee/debtor. *See infra* Section II.C and Section V.C.1. With respect to any other surety collateral for its contingent claims that may be property of the principal's estate, under § 506(d) the surety's lien is not void if the surety's secured claim was disallowed as a contingent claim for reimbursement under § 502(e) of the Bankruptcy Code. *See* 5 COLLIER ON BANKRUPTCY, *supra* note 158, ¶ 506.01 *et seq.*

> [T]he beneficiary of a letter of credit issued by a bank to assure payment of the beneficiary's prepetition claim against the debtor does not have a secured claim against the estate under section 506(a) by virtue of the letter of credit. The letter of credit is not a lien on property in which the estate has an interest. Instead, the letter of credit is a conditional claim against the issuing bank.[217]

As noted previously in our discussion of the independence principle and the unique nature of letters of credit, such collateral is not property of the estate and as such does not meet the definition of a "lien" under the Bankruptcy Code.

The court in *New England Dairies, Inc. v. Dairy Mart Convenience Stores, Inc.* (*In re Dairy Mart Convenience Stores, Inc.*)[218] expressed this same view in response to a creditor's claim for adequate assurance. In *Dairy Mart*, the creditor held a $2.75 million letter of credit that was about to expire during the debtor's bankruptcy. The terms of the letter of credit conditioned the creditor's right to draw down on the letter to circumstances when a final judgment had been entered against the debtor. The creditor petitioned the court under § 361 of the Bankruptcy Code for an order directing the debtor to renew the letter of credit. The bankruptcy court denied the request. The appellate court, in affirming the bankruptcy court on different grounds, noted that § 361 protects only secured creditors and provides that a party is entitled to adequate protection of its security interest when the automatic stay endangers "an interest of an entity in property" of the estate. The appellate court stated that the creditor was ineligible to receive adequate protection because it was not a secured creditor as defined by the Bankruptcy Code.[219] The appellate court referred to § 506(a) of the Bankruptcy Code defining a "secured claim" as a claim of a creditor secured by a "*lien on the property in which the estate has an interest.*"[220] The *Dairy Mart* court ruled that the creditor's only interest was in the letter of credit and that it had no direct interest in any of the property of the debtor. "The letter of credit creates a conditional claim on the assets of the bank; it does not

---

217. 4 COLLIER ON BANKRUPTCY ¶ 506.03[5][a] (Alan N. Resnick & Henry J. Sommer eds., 16th ed. 2015).
218. 351 F.3d 86 (2d Cir. 2003).
219. *Id.* at 90.
220. *Id.* at 91.

create a security interest in the assets of [the debtor]."[221] Accordingly, the appellate court held that as an unsecured creditor, it was not eligible to receive adequate protection.

Therefore, if the surety still has contingent liability under the commercial surety bonds, and the surety's contingent claim for reimbursement is disallowed under § 502(e), that does not affect the surety's rights to retain the letter of credit and the proceeds of the letter of credit that have not yet been determined to be "excess proceeds" pursuant to the underlying agreements as discussed later in this chapter. Until the letter of credit proceeds are determined to be "excess proceeds," they are not yet "property of the estate" and the surety has a possessory "lien" on such letter of credit proceeds under the U.C.C. Once the surety's liability and exposure under the commercial surety bonds has been eliminated and the surety agrees to relinquish its rights to the letter of credit proceeds pursuant to the underlying agreements and the proceeds become "excess proceeds," the surety no longer needs its possessory "lien" and has no need to continue to hold the "excess proceeds" as collateral.

2. *Excess Surety Collateral/Excess Proceeds from a Letter of Credit*

a. Defined. As discussed above, the surety at some point may determine that it is holding either surety collateral (the principal's real and/or personal property) and/or letter of credit proceeds whose value is or are in excess of the amount necessary for the surety to hold to eliminate any future loss or to reimburse the surety's total current and anticipated future loss payments and expenses. The surety's determination may be based upon the provisions of the underlying agreements between the surety and the principal, namely the indemnity agreement, the collateral agreement, any other agreements between the parties, and/or the surety's common law rights.

With respect to the surety's collateral that is property of the principal's estate, the surety's rights to the collateral pursuant to the underlying agreements will be determined according to the same law and cases that govern the rights of any secured creditor holding collateral that is deemed to be property of the debtor's estate.

The proceeds of a letter of credit are not property of the estate when the surety draws on the letter of credit, whether before or after the filing

---

221. *Id.*

of the principal's bankruptcy case.[222] However, it is recognized that letter of credit proceeds may become property of the debtor's estate *if* such proceeds have become "excess proceeds." The term "excess proceeds" has been defined as "an amount in excess of that which the beneficiary of the letter of credit is legally entitled to receive."[223] This means that there are really three questions to answer. First, *when* are such letter of credit proceeds determined to become "excess proceeds"? Namely, when do such letter of credit proceeds become excess to the amount that the surety needs to retain to protect itself from losses? Second, if there is a determination that the letter of credit proceeds have become "excess proceeds," *who* has rights to the "excess proceeds"? Third, *how* are these other two issues resolved—when is the determination made and to whom are the "excess proceeds" delivered—either by agreement or by litigation?

b. When the Surety's Letter of Credit Proceeds Become "Excess Proceeds": The Underlying Agreements. In the event that the surety has drawn on a letter of credit and is now holding the letter of credit proceeds as the surety's collateral, the surety may not be able to hold all of the letter of credit proceeds indefinitely and use the independence principle as a shield. Despite the fact that the vast majority of courts uphold the view that letters of credit and their proceeds are not property of the debtor's estate, several courts have reasoned and held that excess letter of credit proceeds are property of the debtor's estate.[224]

---

222. *See supra* Section III.A.2.

223. *In re* S-Tran Holdings, Inc., 414 B.R. 28, 35 (Bankr. D. Del. 2009) (quoting Litzler v. Chamblee & Ryan, P.C. (*In re* TIC United Corp.), No. 00–37234–BJH–7/No. 06–3261, 2008 WL 2437868, at *6 (Bankr. N.D. Tex. June 17, 2008)); Phar-Mor, Inc. v. Fla. Self-Insurers Guar. Ass'n, 344 B.R. 852, 856 (Bankr. N.D. Ohio 2005) (excess proceeds from a letter of credit are those "in excess of the amount needed to satisfy Debtor's obligation").

224. *See Phar-Mor, Inc.*, 344 B.R. at 856; *In re* Lancaster Steel, 284 B.R. 152 (Bankr. S.D. Fla. 2002); *In re* Onecast Media, 439 F.3d 558 (9th Cir. 2006); Two Trees v. Builders Transp., Inc. (*In re* Builders Transp., Inc.), 471 F.3d 1178 (11th Cir. 2006). *See also Litzler*, 2008 WL 243868, at *6 ("Once the beneficiary has received the proceeds, it can retain them only if the funds rightfully belong to the beneficiary under its underlying agreement or contract with the purchaser of the letter of credit."). "State law determines the rights as between the purchaser/debtor and the

In *Two Trees v. Builders Transport, Inc.* (*In re Builders Transport, Inc.*),[225] the 11th Circuit Court of Appeals decided that the doctrine of independence does not apply once the letter of credit proceeds are paid to the beneficiary and, therefore, permitted the debtor to bring a turnover adversary proceeding against the beneficiary to recover any excess letter of credit proceeds pursuant to the terms of the underlying agreements between the debtor and the beneficiary. The appellate court stated:

> Once the proceeds of a letter of credit have been drawn down, the underlying contracts become pertinent in determining which parties have a right to those proceeds. In other words, an irrevocable standby letter of credit *does not nullify the obligations set forth in the underlying contracts*. Rather the letter of credit serves, among other things, to shift the burden of litigation . . . [The] beneficiary of the letter of credit holds the stake during the litigation.[226]

The appellate court considered which party had the right to the letter of credit proceeds by examining the relevant contract under the applicable state law. The appellate court decided that the letter of credit beneficiary had a duty to return to the debtor any excess proceeds drawn down from the letter of credit that were not used to secure the debtor's obligations.[227] The appellate court noted, "The doctrine of independence protects only the *distribution* of the proceeds of the letter of credit."[228]

Similarly, in *In re Onecast Media, Inc.*,[229] the Ninth Circuit Court of Appeals addressed a dispute between a landlord and the trustee of the debtor tenant over the excess letter of credit proceeds that the landlord had drawn down and held as a security deposit. The appellate court held that the trustee's interest in those funds is property of the estate.[230] Citing to other decisions, the appellate court noted that "[i]t is one thing to attempt to prevent the distribution of the proceeds of a letter of credit,

---

beneficiary under their "underlying agreement or contract." *See, e.g.*, *Builders Transp., Inc.*, 471 F.3d at 1187–88.

225. 471 F.3d 1178.
226. *Id.* at 1186 (citation omitted).
227. *Id.* at 1187.
228. *Id.* (citing *In re* Graham Square, 126 F.3d 823, 827 (6th Cir. 1997)).
229. 439 F.3d 558.
230. *Id. In re* Kaiser Grp. Int'l, 399 F.3d 558, 566 (3d Cir. 2005); *Graham Square*, 126 F.3d at 828.

an attempt the doctrine of independence is designed to prevent; but it is quite another to bring an action on the underlying contract that created the letter of credit."[231] The appellate court further noted, "The fact that Debtor seeks the return of funds that are proceeds of a letter of credit does not negate the breach of contract claim on the underlying obligation."[232]

As discussed previously in this chapter, there may be numerous agreements between the principal and the surety that induced the surety's execution of the commercial surety bonds on behalf of the principal, including the indemnity agreement, the collateral agreement, possible other agreements, as well as the surety's state law common law and equitable rights and the agreements providing the collateral to the surety, whether a mortgage or deed of trust on the principal's real property, a security agreement and financing statement on the principal's personal property, and/or the letter of credit, among others. These documents constitute the "underlying agreements" or contracts between the principal and the surety that must be reviewed as they will determine whether the surety's collateral—whether it is property of the estate or proceeds of a letter of credit—becomes "excess" to the surety, namely more than the surety needs to be made whole with no further exposure under the commercial surety bonds and full reimbursement of the surety's loss.

c. Who May Have Rights to the "Excess Proceeds"? Since the letter of credit proceeds the surety holds as collateral do not become "excess proceeds" until the surety no longer has any rights in the letter of credit proceeds pursuant to the underlying agreements, the surety is not a party who may have continuing rights in the "excess proceeds." There are really three other parties who may have a claim to the "excess proceeds"—the debtor or its trustee, the issuer of the letter of credit, or an assignee (secured creditor) of the debtor who has taken a perfected security interest in the letter of credit and its proceeds.

If the letter of credit proceeds become "excess proceeds" and property of the estate, then the debtor or its trustee has rights to the "excess proceeds." Much of the litigation addressed in the case law arises from the debtor/trustee asserting rights to the "excess proceeds."[233]

---

231. *In re Kaiser Grp. Int'l*, 399 F.3d 558; *Graham Square*, 126 F.3d at 828.

232. *Id.* (citing In re Papio Keno Club Inc., 247 B.R. 453, 460 (B.A.P. 8th Cir. 2000)).

233. The trustee or debtor has prevailed in many cases, including *In re Spring Ford Industries*, 338 B.R. 255 (Bankr. E.D. Pa. 2006) (the beneficiary of the letter of credit admitted that the proceeds had become "excess proceeds"),

Occasionally, the issuer of the letter of credit conditions the letter of credit on the return of any "excess proceeds" by the letter of credit beneficiary to the issuer. If the principal obtains such a letter of credit, both the principal and the beneficiary may be bound by the terms and must return any "excess proceeds" to the issuer.[234] The agreement between the principal and the issuer may also stipulate what must happen to any "excess proceeds."

Finally, there may be an assignee who has a perfected security interest in any "excess proceeds." That assignee could be the issuer of the letter of credit, the post-petition debtor-in-possession financing lender, or even the lender to the reorganized debtor. The assignee may also be some other party that obtained a security agreement and perfected its security interest in any "excess proceeds" prior to the filing of the principal's bankruptcy case.[235]

---

and *Phar-Mor, Inc. v. Florida Self-Insurers Guaranty Association*, 344 B.R. 852, 855 (Bankr. N.D. Ohio 2005). *But see In re* TIC United Corp., No. 00–37234–BJH–7/No. 06–3261, 2008 WL 243868, at *6 (Bankr. N.D. Tex. June 17, 2008). When the bankruptcy court was not persuaded that the trustee was entitled to any excess proceeds (in several cases cited by the trustee), the bankruptcy court found that "the court examined the underlying agreement between the debtor and the beneficiary of the letter of credit to determine whether there were any proceeds of the letter of credit that the beneficiary held improperly—*i.e.*, in breach of the agreement between the debtor and the beneficiary." *Id.* at *7.

234. *See Spring Ford Indus.*, 338 B.R. 255 (the issuing bank did not reserve its rights in the letter of credit to a refund of any "excess proceeds" from the beneficiary, and the debtor was entitled to receive the "excess proceeds" based upon its reversionary rights). When the issuing bank has been repaid in full, it has no interest in any "excess proceeds." *Phar-Mor, Inc.*, 344 B.R. at 855.

235. *See* Hunter v. Allied Clearings (*In re* Challenge-Cook Bros.), No. 97-3259, 1998 WL 34000001 (Bankr. N.D. Ohio June 1, 1998) (the bankruptcy court found that the "excess proceeds" paid by the beneficiary to the trustee were clearly a pre-petition asset and property of the estate that was subject to the pre-petition secured creditor's security interest, which prevailed over the rights of the trustee). One question that always needs to be addressed is the rights of the issuer of the letter of credit (the bank), which may be a pre-petition lender to the principal, a post-petition lender to the principal/debtor, or a lender to the reorganized debtor, and whether it has been paid in full for its secured losses, including for its payment made to the beneficiary under the letter of credit. If the answer is "yes"

Once it is determined, whether by agreement or litigation, that the surety is holding "excess proceeds" from a letter of credit in which the surety no longer has an interest, the surety must then determine who is the correct party to receive the "excess proceeds."[236] While it may be obvious or agreed to by all of the interested parties, the surety may need to protect itself by paying the "excess proceeds" into the bankruptcy court in an interpleader action in order to allow any interested parties to make their claims to such proceeds.

d. How Are the Issues of When and to Whom Resolved: Agreement or Litigation? The surety, as the beneficiary and recipient of the letter of credit proceeds, may reach a point in time when it agrees with the trustee or the principal/debtor that the remaining letter of credit proceeds in the surety's possession are "excess proceeds" no longer needed by the surety to reduce its exposure to loss or reimburse the surety for its prior losses. At that time, the surety and the trustee/debtor may enter into a settlement agreement concerning the payment of the "excess proceeds" to the trustee/debtor (assuming that there are no other interested parties asserting rights to the "excess proceeds"). Any such settlement agreement should be the subject of a motion for compromise and settlement in the

---

and the issuer has been paid in full, then the bank, as the issuer of the letter of credit, may no longer have rights in the "excess proceeds" either. *See In re* Compton Corp., 831 F.2d 586 (5th Cir. 1987).

236. Whether the surety's unused collateral is in the form of excess proceeds drawn from a letter of credit that are not used to secure the principal's obligations to the surety or is other surety collateral that is property of the principal's estate, the surety may be faced with claims asserted by third parties to those letter of credit proceeds or any excess collateral that is property of the principal's estate. Those third-party claims may be based upon a notice of a security interest, a garnishment or other judicial process obtained prior to the date of the filing of the principal's bankruptcy case, or other asserted lien rights in the excess surety collateral, such as lien rights asserted by the principal's post-petition lender under a financing order pursuant to § 364 of the Bankruptcy Code, any post-confirmation order lender, or any other assignee or entity claiming a right to such "excess proceeds" or "excess collateral." In that event, the surety, which no longer needs the collateral, may have to interplead the excess surety collateral into the bankruptcy court in order to allow the various claimants to the excess surety collateral to assert their rights and priorities.

principal's bankruptcy case, notice and a hearing, and a bankruptcy court order.[237]

If there is a dispute between the surety and the trustee/debtor as to whether some or all of the letter of credit proceeds have become "excess proceeds," the dispute may be resolved in litigation. The kind of litigation (the causes of action), the jurisdictional and procedural aspects of the litigation, and the substantive issues that may be involved in the litigation are briefly discussed later this chapter.[238]

3. *The Plan of Reorganization and Plan Confirmation Order*

a. The Plan of Reorganization and the Surety's Secured Claim in the Debtor's Property. The surety's secured claim is discussed earlier in this chapter.[239] The plan of reorganization's treatment of secured claims, including the surety's secured claim, is also discussed earlier in this chapter.[240] The surety's rights in the surety's collateral (the principal's real and personal property that is property of the estate) will be affected by the provisions of the plan of reorganization, which must be reviewed by the surety to determine the treatment of the surety's secured claim and collateral and help determine whether the surety should object to the plan of reorganization's treatment of the surety's secured claim and collateral.

Because letters of credit and letter of credit proceeds are not property of the estate, the surety's collateral rights to and under the letter of credit and the letter of credit proceeds should not be affected by the treatment of the claims of secured creditors under the plan of reorganization. Whether there is a separate class and classification of creditors holding letters of credit and letter of credit proceeds, or some other provision addressing

---

237. The terms of the settlement agreement must be carefully drafted because of the mutual release provisions normally found in such settlement agreements, among other provisions. See *California Self-Insurers Security Fund v. Siegel, Trustee of Circuit City Stores*, No. 3:18cv619, 2019 WL 4740234 (E.D. Va. Sept. 27, 2019), for an example of a settlement agreement with a detailed mutual release provision that went far beyond what the beneficiary of the letter of credit proceeds thought it would, and resulted in a bad surprise for the beneficiary and a benefit not only to the trustee, but also to a surety that was not even involved in the litigation or the settlement agreement.

238. *See infra* Sections V.D.1–4.

239. *See supra* Section II.C.

240. *See supra* Section II.E.2.

the rights of the holders of letters of credit and their proceeds in a plan of reorganization, may only be determined by a review of the plan of reorganization.[241] But, that does not mean that other provisions of the plan of reorganization may not affect the surety's rights to draw on the letter of credit and obtain the proceeds.

b. The Plan Release and Injunction Provisions and Their Effect on the Surety's Letter of Credit and Letter of Credit Proceeds. Most plans of reorganization in large commercial bankruptcy cases contain release and injunction provisions that are very broad in scope and complexity. Such provisions seek to both (1) release certain parties in the bankruptcy case, including the debtor (or debtors in bankruptcy cases involving multiple debtors, whether the bankruptcy cases of the multiple debtors are administratively and/or substantively consolidated, as well as releasing their officers, directors, and others) and other non-debtor third parties active on behalf of or in conjunction with the debtors (lenders, attorneys, accountants, consultants, insurers, and many others) or related to the debtors (other debtor or non-debtor affiliates and subsidiaries), from any defined claims and causes of action; and (2) enjoin certain parties from taking certain actions against any such released parties.

Typical release language in a plan of reorganization may be as simple as the following, with each of the underlined terms being defined in the plan of reorganization or using the § 101 definitions provision of the Bankruptcy Code: "As of the <u>Effective Date</u> of the <u>Confirmed Plan</u>, each <u>Releasing Party</u> releases and discharges each <u>Released Party</u> from any and all <u>Claims</u> and <u>Causes of Action</u>." Frequently, however, the language in the release provision may be a page or two long in the plan of reorganization and cover every conceivable action undertaken or contemplated by the "Released Parties" throughout the duration of the bankruptcy case, every conceivable document filed in the bankruptcy case, every agreement (including contracts, instruments, or other documents) attached to every filing in the bankruptcy case, including those subject to a bankruptcy court order, and every ruling made in

---

241. Because neither the letter of credit nor its proceeds are property of the bankruptcy estate, it is doubtful that there would be a separate creditor class for those creditors holding letters of credit and their proceeds as collateral.

the bankruptcy case by the bankruptcy court, as well as supplements, exhibits, and addenda to the plan of reorganization.[242]

Regardless, when the prior definitions are reviewed, the surety may be deemed to be a "Releasing Party"; the issuer of the letter of credit may be deemed to be a "Released Party"; the surety's "Claims" against the issuer of the letter of credit for the payment of the proceeds of the letter of credit may be a "Claim" to be released; and the surety's "Causes of Action" against the issuer of the letter of credit to enforce the surety's rights to draw on the letter of credit may be released (and, as shown below, enjoined from being asserted).

Typical injunction language in a plan of reorganization may be as simple as the following, with each of the underlined terms being defined in the plan of reorganization provisions: "A Releasing Party is enjoined from enforcing its Claims and Causes of Action against a Released Party." Just like the preceding discussion, if the surety is a "Releasing Party" and the issuer of the letter of credit is a "Released Party," then the surety may be enjoined from both drawing the proceeds from the letter of credit (a "Claim") and filing suit against the issuer (a "Cause of Action") to enforce the surety's rights to draw on the letter of credit.

The first question is whether such broad plan of reorganization release (and injunction) provisions are legal, whether generally or specifically with respect to claims by third parties against other third parties. As noted in the earlier discussion regarding Surety Claims Bar Dates, there is a split among the circuits on the issue of whether bankruptcy courts can release

---

242. While this chapter addresses the effect of the principal's bankruptcy case on the surety's collateral, the plan of reorganization release and injunction provisions may adversely affect the surety in other ways, such as the surety's attempt to enforce its indemnity agreement and common law rights of indemnity and reimbursement. The case of *In re Kimball Hill, Inc.*, 565 B.R. 878 (Bankr. N.D. Ill. 2017), *vacated and remanded by Fidelity & Deposit Co. of Maryland v. TRG Venture Two, LLC*, No. 19 C 389, 2019 WL 5208853 (N.D. Ill. Oct. 16, 2019), provides a chilling and cautionary tale. In *In re Falcon*, 620 B.R. 256 (Bankr. M.D. La. 2020), the court found that the surety's post-confirmation demand for collateral as provided in the indemnity agreement violated the confirmed plan of reorganization injunction provision notwithstanding the debtor's first day motion that approved the debtor's surety bond program as a "necessary cost of preserving the estate" (a debtor admission effectively saying that the surety bond program was a post-petition administrative expense obligation of the debtor's estate).

third parties from claims held by other third parties in connection with a debtor's reorganization plan. Some circuits, such as the Fifth, Ninth, and Tenth Circuits, have held that third-party releases are beyond the power of a bankruptcy court.[243] Other circuits, such as the Second, Fourth, Sixth, and 11th Circuits, have held that such plan releases are permissible under certain circumstances, typically recognizing that such provisions are only proper in unusual, extraordinary, or rare circumstances.[244] The Third Circuit has indicated that it *may be willing to allow for such*

---

243. *See* Bank of N.Y. Tr. v. Official Unsecured Creditors' Comm. (*In re* Pac. Lumber), 584 F.3d 229, 251–53 (5th Cir. 2009); *In re* Zale Corp., 62 F.3d 746, 760 (5th Cir. 1995) ("we must overturn a § 105 injunction if it effectively discharges a nondebtor"); *In re* Lowenschuss, 67 F.3d 1394, 1401 (9th Cir. 1995), *cert. denied*, 517 U.S. 1243 (1996); *In re* W. Real Estate Fund, Inc., 922 F.2d 592, 601–02 (10th Cir. 1990), *modified sub nom.* Abel v. West, 932 F.2d 898 (10th Cir. 1991) ("while a temporary stay prohibiting a creditor's suit against a nondebtor . . . during the bankruptcy proceeding may be permissible to facilitate the reorganization process . . . the stay may not be extended post-confirmation in the form of a permanent injunction that effectively relieves the nondebtor from its own liability to the creditor").

244. *See* SE Prop. Holdings, LLC v. Seaside Eng'g & Surveying (*In re* Seaside Eng'g & Surveying, Inc.), 780 F.3d 1070, 1078 (11th Cir. 2015) (holding that releases and bar orders are permitted but "ought not to be issued lightly, and should be reserved for those unusual cases in which such an order is necessary for the success of the reorganization, and only in situations in which such an order is fair and equitable under all the facts and circumstances"); Behrmann v. Nat'l Heritage Found., 663 F.3d 704, 712 (4th Cir. 2011); *In re* Airadigm Commc'ns, Inc., 519 F.3d 640 (7th Cir. 2008) (approving non-debtor release when release was necessary for the reorganization and appropriately tailored affected only claims arising out of or in connection with the reorganization itself, not blanket immunity); *In re* Metromedia Fiber Network, Inc., 416 F.3d 136 (2d Cir. 2005) (warning that "a nondebtor release is a device that lends itself to abuse" and "[n]o case has tolerated nondebtor releases absent the finding of circumstances that may be characterized as unique," and holding that the bankruptcy court finding that the non-debtor seeking the release made a material contribution to the reorganization was not independently sufficient to justify such a release); Stuart, LLC v. First Mount Vernon Indus. Loan Ass'n (*In re* Peramco Int'l, Inc.), 3 F. App'x 38, 42 (4th Cir. 2001); *In re* Drexel Burnham Lambert Grp., Inc., 960 F.2d 285 (2d Cir. 1992); *In re* A.H. Robins Co., 880 F.2d 694 (4th Cir. 1989).

releases.[245] But the court expressly declined to "establish [its] own rule regarding the conditions under which non-debtor releases and permanent injunctions are appropriate or permissible."[246] Thus, the split among the circuits occupies the spectrum between "impossible" and "very rare."[247]

The leading decision on this subject permitting the release of third-party claims against non-debtors is the Sixth Circuit's opinion in *Class Five Nevada Claimants v. Dow Corning Corp.* (*In re Dow Corning Corp.*).[248] In that case, the appellate court held that while such releases were not categorically prohibited by the Bankruptcy Code, such provisions remain an exception, not the rule. The appellate court stated such measures are dramatic and should be used cautiously and that "enjoining a non-consenting creditor's claim is only appropriate in unusual circumstances."[249]

When the surety's collateral is property of the estate (the principal's real and/or personal property), and the surety has an allowed secured claim in the surety's collateral, then the plan of reorganization provisions addressing the treatment of the surety's secured claim will control, and the surety will have the rights as provided in those plan of reorganization provisions.

However, when the surety's collateral is in the form of a letter of credit, and the surety has not drawn down either any or the full amount of the proceeds of the letter of credit, the plan of reorganization release and injunction provisions may impede the surety's ability to draw on the letter of credit proceeds after the confirmation of the plan of reorganization. Reading thousands and thousands of pages filed in the bankruptcy case to determine, if it is even possible or clearly described or not, whether the plan of reorganization's release and injunction provisions alter the surety's rights against the letter of credit and its proceeds is expensive and is, essentially, looking for a needle in a haystack.

In summary, in the way they are worded, after the entry of the confirmation order, the plan of reorganization release and injunction

---

245. *In re* Cont'l Airlines, 203 F.3d 203 (3d Cir. 2000).
246. *Id.* at 214.
247. *In re* FirstEnergy Sols. Corp., 606 B.R. 720, 733 (Bankr. N.D. Ohio 2019).
248. 280 F.3d 648, 658 (6th Cir. 2002).
249. *Id.* (citing *Drexel Burnham Lambert*, 960 F.2d at 293; *A.H. Robins*, 880 F.2d at 702; *In re* Johns-Manville Corp., 837 F.2d 89, 93–94 (2d Cir. 1988), *cert. denied*, 488 U.S. 868 (1988)).

provisions may release the issuer of the surety's letter of credit from having to honor the letter of credit and pay the letter of credit proceeds to the surety upon demand (the surety's claim), and then enjoin the surety from taking legal action (the surety's cause of action) to enforce the surety's rights to draw on the letter of credit and obtain the proceeds.

Therefore, the surety's alternatives are to either (1) jump ahead of the release and injunction provisions in the plan of reorganization by drawing down on the letter of credit proceeds prior to the entry of the confirmation order for the plan of reorganization,[250] and then maintaining those proceeds as the surety's collateral; or (2) fix the problem with appropriate language in the plan of reorganization's confirmation order.

c. The Importance of the Plan Confirmation Order.[251] The surety's ability to make meaningful changes to the provisions of a plan of reorganization in a principal's commercial bankruptcy case may be limited. Many of these types of cases are large commercial entities with many banks and other large creditors involved who are familiar with seeing certain provisions in plans of reorganization, especially broad release and injunction provisions, among others. As a result, when faced with the prospect of overcoming the resistance not only of the debtors, but many of the debtor's largest creditors, the surety has to consider its two alternatives. First, draw down on the letter of credit and obtain the full amount of the letter of credit proceeds prior to the entry of the confirmation order. Second, determine if a provision can be negotiated in the confirmation order to get around the plan of reorganization release and injunction provisions.

There is no language that will fit every case. But the following issues and concepts must be considered and negotiated with the debtor, and, as discussed below, placed in the language of the confirmation order and not the plan of reorganization itself to preserve the surety's rights in the letter of credit and its proceeds.

First, notwithstanding anything contained in the plan of reorganization, the surety must retain and must not waive any and/or all of its claims, rights, abilities, and protections under the letter of credit

---

250. The surety's ability to draw down at any time on the letter of credit proceeds depends upon whether the letter of credit has conditions or contingencies that must be met first. *See supra* Section I.B.1.

251. For more discussion about the confirmation of a plan of reorganization, see *Chapter 11 Reorganization*, *supra* note 69, at 455–60.

and its proceeds, or those claims and rights against the issuing bank (the "surety's rights") in the confirmation order.

Second, none of the surety's rights should be released, changed, modified, or amended under any provision of the plan of reorganization, any plan supplement, or the confirmation order. Namely, some loose language that may appear in some other document or bankruptcy court filing cannot be allowed to affect the surety's rights as set forth in the agreed language in the confirmation order.

Third, there should be a description of the "paper trail" concerning the "issuer" of the letter of credit. Assuming that the letter of credit was issued by the pre-petition lender for the debtor, there must be language that describes whether the debtor-in-possession lender (the DIP lender) during the debtor's chapter 11 bankruptcy case has assumed the pre-petition lender's obligations under the letter of credit and whether the pre-petition lender has been "released" of those obligations under the DIP financing order. Namely, have the surety's rights and the lender's pre-petition lender's obligations under the pre-petition letter of credit become the obligations of a different lender, the DIP lender? Then, continuing up the chain, will the DIP lender's obligations be assumed by the post-confirmation lender to the reorganized debtor after the confirmation of the plan of reorganization? Furthermore, will that assumption release the DIP lender and make the post-confirmation lender to the reorganized debtor liable for and subject to the surety's rights under the letter of credit? The appropriate language must "connect the dots" to make certain that the surety's rights either continue through the full chain of lenders or be the liability of the lender (pre-petition, post-petition DIP lender, or post-confirmation lender) that eventually gets "stuck" with the obligations to pay the surety under the letter of credit. This "stuck lender" is going to be most certainly within the definition of a "Released Party," and, without appropriate language in the confirmation order, could assert that plan release provision as a defense to a later claim by the surety on the letter of credit when the surety attempts to draw down the letter of credit proceeds.

Fourth, the reorganized debtor may want to replace the original letter of credit with a new letter of credit after the effective date of the entry of the confirmation order. The surety should require the specific terms and the necessity of the surety's consent for any such post-confirmation replacement of the surety's original letter of credit.

While the plan of reorganization sets forth the debtor's contractual obligations to its creditors, the language in the confirmation order governs and controls over the language in the plan of reorganization if there are conflicts, inconsistencies, or ambiguities. Therefore, the language protecting the surety's rights must be in the confirmation order and not in the plan of reorganization. *More importantly*, the language should state that "notwithstanding any other provisions of the plan of reorganization or any other provisions contained in the confirmation order," they shall not change or modify the letter of credit language and provisions agreed upon by the surety and the debtor and contained in the confirmation order.[252] This is necessary in the confirmation order to override any conflicting language that may be contained in the plan of reorganization or the hundreds of other documents related to the debtor's bankruptcy case.

When you go back over the simple examples and the full text of the plan of reorganization release and injunction provisions, which are essentially long run-on sentences that include the proverbial "kitchen sink" of "Releasing Parties" (including the surety), "Released Parties" (including the issuer of the surety's letter of credit), and the released claims, causes of action, transactions, events, and so on (everything done before and during the debtor's bankruptcy case up to the date of the confirmation order), it becomes clear that a surety does not want to be in the position of later having to argue, after the confirmation of the plan of reorganization, whether the surety can draw on a letter of credit if it incurs losses under the commercial surety bonds and the indemnity agreement. There are too many documents to review and too many angles and arguments that can be raised to contend that the surety has no ability to assert its rights to draw under the letter of credit after the entry of the confirmation order for the plan of reorganization.

Therefore, there are really only two options for the surety:

- Fully draw on the letter of credit prior to the entry of a confirmation order that could prevent the surety from a later draw on the letter of credit as a result of the confirmed plan of reorganization release and injunction provisions.
- Negotiate language to be placed in the confirmation order clarifying and protecting the surety's rights in the letter of

252. Procedurally, if the surety's letter of credit is going to be assumed after the effective date of the confirmation order by a post-petition lender to the reorganized debtor, the debtor should give notice to the surety of that fact in either or both the notice of the entry of the confirmation order and the notice of the effective date of the confirmed plan of reorganization.

credit and the surety's ability to draw on the letter of credit proceeds after the entry of the confirmation order for the plan of reorganization notwithstanding the plan of reorganization release and injunction provisions or other such provisions.

D. Litigation Issues to Consider

1. Causes of Action

There are some creative causes of action that may be filed by the debtor/trustee in their attempt to have a bankruptcy court determine when the surety is holding excess collateral (the principal's real and/or personal property) or "excess proceeds" of a letter of credit (which proceeds of a letter of credit are not property of the estate until it is determined that the proceeds are no longer necessary for the surety and become "excess proceeds" available to the debtor/trustee). As discussed previously in this chapter, neither the surety's collateral that is property of the estate nor the proceeds of a letter of credit that are not property of the estate become excess collateral or "excess proceeds" until the surety no longer has rights to the surety's collateral pursuant to the underlying agreements.[253] The question is: how is that "excess collateral/proceeds issue" determined either in litigation or in a resolution/settlement agreement?

Also as discussed previously in this chapter, the debtor's/trustee's turnover adversary proceeding is not a cause of action that can be used to make a determination that the surety's collateral is excess collateral or "excess proceeds" of a letter of credit.[254] Other causes of action, such as a claim for an accounting of the surety's collateral, either under state law or pursuant to § 542(a) of the Bankruptcy Code, or a claim that the surety is unjustly enriched because the debtor/trustee contends that the surety is holding excess collateral, may or may not be susceptible to a motion to dismiss for a failure to state a claim for relief that resolves the issues.

In order to raise the issues in a manner that they may be resolved, one way may be the debtor's/trustee's filing of a declaratory judgment-type of action that brings in the necessary parties and succinctly states the issues to be resolved to determine whether the surety's underlying agreements dictate that the surety no longer has a need for the surety's collateral, either in whole or in part. That leads to two issues.

---

253. *See supra* Section V.C.2.
254. *See supra* Section V.B.1.

First, procedurally, who are the necessary parties to such a declaratory judgment action that are required parties to the litigation to make this determination? The debtor/trustee and the surety are clearly necessary parties. The debtor/trustee wants a return of the surety's "alleged" excess collateral to the estate. The surety wants to hold onto the surety's collateral until all potential claims against the surety under the commercial surety bonds are eliminated—released and discharged—by the bond obligees and other claimants, or the bond obligees and other claimants no longer have the right to make a claim against the commercial surety bonds due to some defense to the potential claims. As a result, the surety would contend that all of the bond obligees and other claimants for whom the surety still has exposure under the commercial surety bonds are necessary parties to the declaratory judgment action. The reasons include the fact that the bankruptcy court would be attempting to make a determination that the bond obligees and other claimants no longer have claims against the commercial surety bonds that are enforceable, thereby finding that the surety's rights to the surety's collateral pursuant to the underlying agreements are no longer valid. There may also be other necessary parties who claim rights to the "excess collateral/proceeds" with priority over the rights of the debtor/trustee such as the issuer of the letter of credit or an assignee/secured creditor who has better rights than the debtor's rights in the "excess collateral/proceeds."

Second, substantively, what factual and legal determinations must be made either by the debtor/trustee and the surety in an agreement or by the bankruptcy court in an adversary proceeding to find that the surety's collateral is, in whole or in part, "excess collateral or excess letter of credit proceeds"? While each bankruptcy case is different, the factual and legal findings may include, among others, (1) that the surety may have been released and discharged from some or all of the commercial surety bonds; (2) that the expiration of the applicable statutes of limitation may extinguish the surety's liability to the bond obligees and other claimants under the commercial surety bonds; and/or (3) that certain claim preclusion issues may arise because of actions taken in the bankruptcy case that may extinguish the surety's liability under the commercial surety bonds. A resolution of these same issues, by agreement among the parties or in litigation among the parties, may also lead to a settlement agreement between the debtor/trustee and the surety that results in an agreement that the surety is holding some excess collateral or excess letter of credit proceeds that may be returned to the debtor's bankruptcy estate.

However, before these litigation issues and causes of action may be addressed, it is first necessary to determine the bankruptcy court's jurisdiction—subject matter, core, and non-core jurisdiction—to make the factual and legal findings concerning the issues of the surety's collateral and whether some or all of the surety's collateral is excess to what the surety needs to retain pursuant to its underlying agreements with the principal, now the debtor.

2. *Jurisdiction Issues in the Bankruptcy Court: Subject Matter, Core, and Non-Core Issues*

a. Subject Matter Jurisdiction of the Bankruptcy Courts Generally. In Northern Pipeline v. Marathon Pipe Line Co.,[255] the Supreme Court held unconstitutional the broad congressional grant of jurisdiction to the non-Article III bankruptcy courts to decide "private rights" matters, such as state breach of contract claims.[256] Congress responded to the Marathon decision by enacting the Bankruptcy Amendments and Federal Judgeship Act of 1984,[257] restructuring the jurisdiction of the bankruptcy courts. The act created a distinction between "core" and "non-core" proceedings. Pursuant to the act, bankruptcy courts have jurisdiction to adjudicate and render final orders and judgments in matters constituting "core" proceedings[258] pursuant to 28 U.S.C. § 157(b)(1).[259] In proceedings involving core matters, a district court reviews the bankruptcy court's

255. 458 U.S. 50 (1982).
256. *Marathon* involved the adjudication in a bankruptcy court of a state breach of pre-petition contract claim brought by a debtor against a defendant who had not filed a claim with the bankruptcy court. As explained in a later decision, *Marathon* held "that Congress may not vest in a non-Article III court the power to adjudicate, render final judgment, and issue binding orders in a traditional contract action arising under state law, without consent of the litigants, and subject only to ordinary appellate review." Thomas v. Union Carbide Agric. Prod. Co., 473 U.S. 568, 584 (1985).
257. 28 U.S.C. § 151.
258. *Id.*
259. Although the statute does not define the term "core," § 157(b)(2) sets forth a nonexclusive list of matters that constitute core proceedings.

findings of facts under a "clearly erroneous" standard and its conclusions of law de novo.[260]

Bankruptcy courts may hear matters that are "non-core" but are otherwise related to the bankruptcy case.[261] In these non-core-related matters, which are also left undefined by the statute, bankruptcy courts may issue findings of fact and conclusions of law, but are not empowered to issue *final* orders. The district court reviews both the factual findings and legal conclusions of the bankruptcy court in these matters de novo.[262]

b. The Bankruptcy Court's Core and Non-Core Subject Matter Jurisdiction.[263] To determine whether a bankruptcy court has authority to hear a matter and issue a final decision, the bankruptcy court must make a determination, in the first instance, whether a proceeding is a core proceeding.[264] A "core proceeding" is generally defined as "a proceeding that invokes a substantive right provided by the Bankruptcy Code or is a proceeding that by its nature could only arise in the context of a bankruptcy case."[265] Core proceedings represent those disputes so

---

260. *See* Brunner v. N.Y. State Higher Educ. Serv., 831 F.2d 395, 396 (2d Cir. 1987).

261. *See* 28 U.S.C. § 157(c)(1).

262. *See id.*; FED. R. BANKR. P. 9033(d); IAM v. E. Air Lines, 121 B.R. 428, 432 n.5 (S.D.N.Y. 1990), *aff'd*, 923 F.2d 26 (2d Cir. 1991).

263. *See Jurisdictional Issues*, *in* SURETY ASPECTS OF BANKRUPTCY, *supra* note 3, at 45–57.

264. The burden of proof is on the debtor to establish jurisdiction. *In re* Berks Behavioral Health, LLC, 464 B.R. 684, 686–91 (Bankr. E.D. Pa. 2012). Once challenged, the party asserting subject matter jurisdiction has the burden of proving its existence. *Id.* (citing 2 MOORE'S FEDERAL PRACTICE § 12.30[5] (3d ed. 1997)); Robinson v. Overseas Mil. Sales Corp., 21 F.3d 502, 507 (2d Cir. 1994) (burden of proving jurisdiction is on party asserting it).

265. *In re* Desmond, 334 B.R. 78, 88–89 (Bankr. D.N.H. 2005) (quoting Halper v. Halper, 164 F.3d 830, 836 (3d Cir. 1999) (citations omitted)); *In re* Wood, 825 F.2d 90, 97 (5th Cir. 1987). The bankruptcy court in *In re Desmond*, in ruling that the claims before it were non-core, noted that the claims exclusively relied upon state laws, the claims existed prior to the filing of the bankruptcy case, and the claims were not directly affected by the plaintiff's bankruptcy. 334 B.R. at 88–89. *See also* Arnold Print Works, Inc. v. Apkin (*In re* Arnold Print Works, Inc.), 815 F.2d 165, 167 (1st Cir. 1987) (state law claims arising prior to bankruptcy filing are typically "non-core" proceedings that a bankruptcy court can hear only with the parties' consent); Comco Assocs. v. Faraldi Food Indus., Ltd., 170 B.R.

intertwined with the bankruptcy process "that Congress has the power under Article I of the Constitution to direct a non-tenured judicial officer (*i.e.*, bankruptcy judge) to render a final determination of their merits."[266] In contrast, non-core proceedings include "the broader universe of all proceedings that are not core proceedings, but are nevertheless related to a bankruptcy case."[267]

Bankruptcy courts do not categorize claims as core or non-core by means of the debtor's characterization of its claims or the debtor's words used to describe its claims.[268] Accordingly, the bankruptcy court must look beyond the labels to the substance of the action in order to discover whether it can be fairly said to arise under the Bankruptcy Code and fall within the bankruptcy court's core jurisdiction.[269]

c. Bankruptcy Court Jurisdiction to Determine the Rights of Third Parties in the Commercial Surety Bonds. Previously, this chapter addressed the issue of whether the bankruptcy court has the power and authority under the Bankruptcy Code and bankruptcy case law to establish a Surety Claims Bar Date with respect to the claims of non-debtor third parties (such as bond obligees and other bond claimants) against a non-debtor third party such as the surety.[270] However, there is a second issue—whether the bankruptcy court has the *jurisdiction* to determine the rights of non-debtor third parties against a non-debtor third

---

765, 772 (E.D.N.Y. 1994) (holding that a "non-core proceeding" is one concerned only with state law issues that did not arise in core bankruptcy function of adjusting debtor-creditor rights).

266. *See Berks Behavioral Health*, 464 B.R. at 686–91.

267. *Id. See also* Sec. Farms v. Int'l Bhd. of Teamsters, Chauffers, Warehouseman & Helpers, 124 F.3d 999, 1008 (9th Cir. 1997) ("Actions that do not depend on bankruptcy laws for their existence and that could proceed in another court are considered 'non-core.'"); *In re* Gardner, 913 F.2d 1515, 1518 (10th Cir. 1990) (same).

268. The Second Circuit Court of Appeals has stated that "[t]he relevant analysis is whether the nature of [the] adversary proceeding, rather than the state or federal basis for the claim, falls within the core of federal bankruptcy power." *In re* Manville Forest Prods. Corp., 896 F.2d 1384, 1389 (2d Cir. 1990).

269. *In re* CIS Corp., 172 B.R. 748, 754–57 (S.D.N.Y. 1994); *In re* Treadway, 117 B.R. 76, 81 (Bankr. D. Vt. 1990) (mere characterization of claims within the terms of the Bankruptcy Code is not dispositive of core/non-core determination).

270. *See supra* Section IV.C.

party such as the surety. Whether the debtor's or the trustee's attempt to obtain a return of the surety's collateral to the debtor's estate is in the form of a motion to establish a Surety Claims Bar Date or the filing of a complaint under a cause of action such as a declaratory judgment, the bankruptcy court must first determine whether it has the jurisdiction to resolve the issues under either approach.

Regardless of the manner or the form of the cause of action asserted by the debtor or the trustee for a bankruptcy court determination as to whether the surety's collateral—whether it is property of the estate, a letter of credit, or the proceeds of a letter of credit—is excess to what the surety requires, and therefore the collateral should be brought into the estate as property of the estate, the debtor or the trustee must request that the bankruptcy court judicially determine that the surety's exposure under the commercial surety bonds has been terminated by ruling that the obligees and other claimants under the commercial surety bonds can no longer make any claims under the commercial surety bonds. Substantively, the debtor's/trustee's arguments are that the surety's liability and obligations under the commercial surety bonds have been released and/or discharged, whether by a release agreement with the applicable obligees and other claimants, by the passage of the applicable statute of limitations, or because of certain preclusive effects, such as from prior bankruptcy court rulings on claims or the passage of any established Surety Claims Bar Date. Therefore, the linchpin of the debtor's/trustee's claims in their causes of action is the determination of third parties' rights—the rights of the obligees, other bond claimants, and the surety—in the commercial surety bonds.

The jurisdictional problem with this approach is that the obligees and other claimants under the commercial surety bonds are not parties to the bankruptcy case and the commercial surety bonds are not property of the debtor's bankruptcy estate. The bankruptcy court may not have jurisdiction to determine the rights of third parties against the surety, who is also a third party, in commercial surety bonds that are not property of the debtor's bankruptcy estate.

Pursuant to the U.S. Code,[271] the district court in which a bankruptcy case under title 11 is commenced or is pending has jurisdiction over all of the property, wherever located, of the debtor as of the commencement of the bankruptcy case, and of property of the estate. Thus, a bankruptcy court's jurisdiction does not extend to property that is not property of

---

271. 28 U.S.C. § 1334(e)(1).

a debtor's estate.[272] Federal courts, including bankruptcy courts, are courts of limited jurisdiction,[273] and their jurisdiction is lacking until it is proved.[274] Indeed, the Supreme Court has observed that "[i]t is to be presumed that a cause lies outside this limited jurisdiction, and the burden of establishing the contrary rests upon the party asserting jurisdiction."[275] Thus, courts "must be alert to avoid overstepping their limited grants of jurisdiction."[276] Furthermore, it is a fundamental jurisdictional principle that a court cannot "write its own jurisdictional ticket."[277] Therefore, neither the court nor the parties can confer subject matter jurisdiction on the court when the court does not have jurisdiction in the first place.[278]

It is generally recognized in the bankruptcy court and elsewhere that "jurisdiction over non-bankruptcy controversies with third parties who are otherwise strangers to the civil proceeding and to the parent bankruptcy does not exist."[279] "[T]he mere fact that there may be common issues of fact between a civil proceeding and a controversy involving the bankruptcy estate does not bring the matter within the scope of section 1471(b). Judicial economy itself does not justify federal jurisdiction."[280]

---

272. Rutherford Hosp., Inc. v. RNH P'ship, 168 F.3d 693, 699 (4th Cir. 1999); *accord* Black v. U.S. Postal Serv. (*In re* Heath), 115 F.3d 521, 524 (7th Cir. 1997); Torkelsen v. Maggio (*In re* Guild & Gallery Plus, Inc.), 72 F.3d 1171, 1181 (3d Cir. 1996) (when action does not involve property of the estate, it is beyond the bankruptcy court's jurisdiction).
273. *See* Celotex v. Edwards, 514 U.S. 300, 307 (1995); Bender v. Williamsport Area Sch. Dist., 475 U.S. 534, 541 (1986); Canal Corp. v. Finnman (*In re* Johnson), 960 F.2d 396, 399 (4th Cir. 1992).
274. Fairfax Countywide Citizens v. Fairfax Cnty., 571 F.2d 1299 (4th Cir. 1978), *cert. denied*, 439 U.S. 1047 (1978).
275. Kokkonen v. Guardian Life Ins. Co., 511 U.S. 375 (1994); McNutt v. Gen. Motors Acceptance Corp., 298 U.S. 178, 182–83 (1936); Goldsmith v. Mayor & City Council of Balt., 845 F.2d 61 (4th Cir. 1988).
276. McCorkle v. First Pa. Banking & Tr. Co., 459 F.2d 243, 244 n.1 (4th Cir. 1972).
277. *In re* Poplar Run Five Ltd. P'ship, 192 B.R. 848, 859 (Bankr. E.D. Va. 1995) (quoting Zerand-Bernal Grp., Inc. v. Cox, 23 F.3d 159, 164 (7th Cir. 1994)).
278. *Id.*
279. *In re* McConaghy, 15 B.R. 480, 481 (Bankr. E.D. Va. 1981); Transamerica Fin. Life Ins. v. Merrill Lynch & Co., 302 B.R. 620, 625 (N.D. Iowa 2003) (citing *In re* Haug, 19 B.R. 223, 224–25 (Bankr. D. Or. 1982)).
280. *See* Aldinger v. Howard, 427 U.S. 1, 15 (1976); Pacor, Inc. v. Higgins (*In re* Pacor), 743 F.2d 984, 994 (3d Cir. 1984).

The authority is clear that a bond issued by the surety to secure the obligations of a debtor does not constitute property of the debtor's estate, and that a bankruptcy court lacks jurisdiction to enjoin proceedings to collect on the bond.[281] Accordingly, when faced with the prospect of litigation, the surety must consider whether the proposed actions are within the jurisdiction of the bankruptcy court in the first instance.

3. *Procedural Issue: Necessary Parties to the Litigation*

Assuming that the debtor/trustee has filed a declaratory judgment action (or some other cause of action) to have the bankruptcy court make a determination concerning whether the surety is holding excess collateral or "excess proceeds" from a letter of credit that should become property of the estate (litigation), and the bankruptcy court has found sufficient jurisdiction to adjudicate the litigation, there is a procedural issue concerning the necessary parties to the litigation.

The debtor or trustee may file the litigation to have the bankruptcy court determine whether a surety's exposure under the commercial surety bonds is terminated. In that litigation, a ruling may be sought that the obligees and the other claimants under the commercial surety bonds can no longer make any claims under the commercial surety bonds because of certain grounds such as the prior release and discharge of the surety under the commercial surety bonds, the passage of the applicable statute of limitations, or because of certain preclusive effects. The problem arises when the obligees and the other claimants under the commercial surety bonds are not parties to the debtor's bankruptcy case and the commercial surety bonds are not property of the debtor's estate. Assuming for the purposes of argument that the bankruptcy court has subject matter jurisdiction[282] to issue a ruling in the litigation that is binding on the obligees and the other claimants under the commercial surety bonds, the obligees and the other claimants must be included as parties to the litigation. The question is whether the debtor's/trustee's failure to add the

---

281. *See In re* Mansfield Tire & Rubber, 660 F.2d 1108 (6th Cir. 1981); Globe Constr. Co. v. Okla. City Hous. Auth., 571 F.2d 1140 (10th Cir. 1978); *In re* Buna Painting & Drywall, 503 F.2d 618 (9th Cir. 1974); *In re* McLean Trucking, 74 B.R. 820, 828 (Bankr. W.D.N.C. 1987); *In re* M.J. Sales & Distrib. Co., 25 B.R. 608 (Bankr. S.D.N.Y. 1982); *In re* Hathaway's Liquidation & Appraisers, 1 B.R. 189 (Bankr. N.D. Ga. 1979); *In re* Goldsby, 51 F. Supp. 849 (S.D. Fla. 1943).

282. *See supra* Section V.D.2.a.

obligees and, possibly, the other claimants as parties to the litigation may lead to its dismissal for failure to join necessary parties.

The Federal Rules of Bankruptcy Procedure, incorporating Federal Rule of Civil Procedure 12(b)(7), provide for dismissal of an action when the plaintiff fails to join a necessary party.[283] The issue in the litigation is the surety's right to hold onto the surety's collateral, whether it is property of the debtor's estate or the proceeds of a letter of credit. As discussed in this chapter,[284] the surety's rights to retain and use the collateral are dependent upon the underlying agreements. Pursuant to most if not all indemnity agreements (and most if not all collateral agreements), the surety's exposure under the commercial surety bonds is the key element to the determination of the issue of whether and when the surety's collateral becomes "excess collateral/proceeds."

In any litigation brought by the debtor/trustee to obtain the surety's collateral that has allegedly become "excess collateral/proceeds," the obligees and the other claimants under the commercial surety bonds are necessary parties in the litigation. The obligees and the other claimants have an interest in and claim rights under the commercial surety bonds (the obligees are the named beneficiaries under the commercial surety bonds and the other claimants are third-party beneficiaries under the commercial surety bonds). Their interests are to receive the protection up to the penal sums of the commercial surety bonds for any losses incurred as a result of the debtor's failures to perform its obligations. If the obligees and the other claimants are not parties to the litigation, as a practical matter their ability to protect their own interests in the commercial surety bonds will be impaired and/or impeded.[285] Furthermore, the surety, which is jointly and severally liable under the commercial surety bonds to the obligees and other claimants, will face a substantial risk of incurring double, multiple, or otherwise inconsistent obligations to the obligees and other claimants under the commercial surety bonds if their interests are not addressed or determined in the litigation.[286]

Another necessary party may be the issuer of the letter of credit, normally a bank, which, under the "independence principle," paid out the letter of credit proceeds to the surety with the issuing bank's own funds.

---

283. Federal Rule of Civil Procedure 12(b)(7) is applicable in adversary proceedings by Federal Rule of Bankruptcy Procedure 7012(b).
284. *See supra* Section V.C.2.
285. *See* FED. R. CIV. P. 19(a)(1)(B)(i).
286. *See id.* 19(a)(1)(B)(ii).

Unless the issuing bank has been fully reimbursed by the debtor for its payout of the letter of credit proceeds to the surety, the issuing bank may have a superior interest in any return of the "excess proceeds" from the letter of credit that has priority over and is ahead of the rights of the debtor/trustee.[287] Furthermore, the same situation may arise with respect to a prior secured creditor with a claim against the "excess collateral/proceeds."[288] Complete relief cannot be accorded among the parties without joinder under Rule 19(a)(1)(A) of any interested party asserting an interest in the "excess collateral/proceeds." Any absent party with an interest in either the commercial surety bonds or the "excess collateral/proceeds" will not, as a practical matter, be able to protect its own interest in the "excess collateral/proceeds" under Rule 19(a)(1)(B)(i), and the surety may face the substantial risk of incurring double, multiple, or otherwise inconsistent obligations if the surety is forced to return the "excess collateral/proceeds" to the debtor/trustee and is later forced to face exposure to and/or pay a second time to one of the interested parties.

In cases challenging the enforceability or validity of a contract, joinder of all parties to that contract will typically be required.[289] This is true primarily because the absent contract party has a legally protected interest in the outcome of the litigation.[290] In addition, nonjoinder of a contract party would undermine the court's ability to render complete relief among existing parties since the absent party would not be bound by the court's judgment on the challenged contract.[291]

---

287. Those issuing bank rights may include provisions in the letter of credit itself that require the return of any letter of credit "excess proceeds" to the bank or the bank's perfected security interest in any "excess proceeds." *See supra* Section V.C.2.c.
288. *See In re* Challenge-Cook Bros., No. 97-3259, 1998 WL 34000001 (Bankr. N.D. Ohio June 1, 1998). *See supra* Section V.C.2.c.
289. *See* Raimbeault v. Accurate Mach. & Tool, 302 F.R.D. 675, 684 (S.D. Fla. 2014) (citing Dawavendewa v. Salt River Project Agric. Improvement & Power Dist., 276 F.3d 1150, 1156–57 (9th Cir. 2002)).
290. *Id.*
291. *Id.* (citing Fireman v. Travelers Cas. & Sur. Co. of Am., No. 10-81564, 2011 U.S. Dist. LEXIS 18426, at *12–13 (S.D. Fla. Feb. 24, 2011)); Mazzio v. Kane, No. 14-CV-616 (ARR) (MDG), 2014 U.S. Dist. LEXIS 86033, at *18 (E.D.N.Y. June 24, 2014); Hardy v. IGT, Inc., No. 2:10-CV-901-WKW [WO], 2011 U.S. Dist. LEXIS 90852, at *16 (M.D. Ala. Aug. 15, 2011); NFC Acquisition, LLC v. Comerica Bank, 640 F. Supp. 2d 964, 973 (N.D. Ohio 2009) ("invalidation of one of the intertwining contracts

In summary, the obligees and the other claimants under the commercial surety bonds are parties to the commercial surety bonds and/or are direct beneficiaries of the bonds, and have a financial claim and interest to protect in those bonds, especially because of the debtor's filing of its bankruptcy case. They are necessary parties to any adversary proceeding that may determine their rights in conjunction with the surety's liability and exposure under the commercial surety bonds resulting from the debtor's/trustee's litigation to determine whether the surety's liability to the obligees and other claimants has been released and discharged and, therefore, as a result, the surety's continuing and subsequent rights to the "excess collateral/proceeds." If the debtor/trustee fails to add these necessary parties to the adversary proceeding, the adversary proceeding may be dismissed.

4. Substantive Issues

There are at least three substantive issues and/or defenses that may be explored when the surety is faced with the debtor's or trustee's claim in any litigation that the surety's collateral has become "excess collateral" or "excess proceeds" of a letter of credit and that the collateral is now property of the estate that may be used by the debtor/trustee. If the surety's future exposure to loss is eliminated and the surety has been fully reimbursed for its loss from its collateral under the indemnity agreement and/or the collateral agreement, then the surety does not need to retain the "excess collateral/proceeds" to avoid a risk and exposure to loss. Those three substantive issues are (1) whether the surety has been released and discharged from its obligations under the commercial surety bonds; (2) whether the surety's exposure under the commercial surety bonds has been extinguished by the expiration of the applicable statute of limitations; and/or (3) the potential results of any bankruptcy court rulings concerning the preclusive effect on the claims of the commercial surety bond obligees and/or other third-party claimants, and/or the passage of an effective Surety Claims Bar Date. These substantive issues will be addressed next.

---

could create inconsistent obligations for the parties"); KnowledgePlex, Inc. v. Placebase, Inc., No. C 08-4267 JF (RS), 2008 U.S. Dist. LEXIS 103915, at *13–14 (N.D. Cal. Dec. 17, 2008); Ryan v. Volpone Stamp Co., 107 F. Supp. 2d 369, 387 (S.D.N.Y. 2000).

a. The Surety's Release and Discharge from the Commercial Surety Bonds. If the surety is released and discharged from all of its obligations under the commercial surety bonds, the surety's risk and exposure (other than any reimbursement rights under the indemnity agreement and/or the collateral agreement) comes to an end. When the surety has no further risk and exposure to loss pursuant to the underlying agreements, any surety collateral that the surety is retaining may become "excess collateral/proceeds."

In *Pittston Warehouse Corp. v. American Motorists Insurance Co.*,[292] the principal obtained two letters from the obligee with respect to the surety's future liability under the commercial surety bond in question (a customs bond). The court found that the obligee's first letter stating that there was no likelihood of a claim was ambiguous language because the obligee might subsequently pursue a claim against the surety. However, the obligee's second letter released the surety from any future liability after a specific date. Furthermore, the principal obtained a new customs bond from a different surety that covered the prior obligations of the first surety under its customs bond. The court found that "[the principal] cannot establish [the surety's] lack of liability merely by showing that there was no likelihood of a claim; instead, they must show that there is no future liability" for the surety.[293] The surety was obligated to return the surety's collateral to the principal when it had no future liability and was fully protected from incurring any loss.

b. Does the Expiration of the Applicable Statute of Limitations Extinguish the Surety's Liability under the Commercial Surety Bonds? The question addressed in this section is whether the expiration of the applicable statute of limitations extinguishes the surety's liabilities under the commercial surety bonds. The debtor/trustee may contend in the litigation that the expiration of the applicable statute of limitations for the commercial surety bonds results in a release of the surety's exposure under the commercial surety bonds and that the surety's collateral for those commercial surety bonds then becomes "excess collateral/proceeds."

However, the expiration of the applicable statute of limitations does not always equate to a release and discharge of the surety's risk and exposure under the commercial surety bonds. Rather, the expiration of the applicable statute of limitations terminates an obligee's or other

---

292. 715 F. Supp. 1221 (S.D.N.Y. 1989).
293. *Id.* at 1226.

claimant's ability to enforce its rights against the surety under the commercial surety bonds. But, the expiration of the applicable statute of limitations for a claim against a bond does not extinguish the obligee's or claimant's cause of action entirely for the claim or debt. Only the obligee's or claimant's procedural ability to enforce the cause of action for its claim or debt is barred.[294]

In *School Board of City of Norfolk v. U.S. Gypsum Co.*, the Virginia Supreme Court observed that "[a]n ordinary statute of limitations is a procedural statute, one which creates a temporal bar to the maintenance of a legal remedy arising out of an accrued cause of action."[295] Other courts have also observed that a statute of limitations extinguishes the right to prosecute an accrued cause of action after a period of time—it cuts off the remedy—while a statute of repose abolishes the cause of action after the passage of time.[296]

Because of the unique nature of sureties, the surety could still have exposure to obligees under the bonds if the surety issued other bonds to those same obligees for other principals. For example, if the surety issued a tax revenue bond to a state as obligee and the surety also issued other bonds to that state (whether for the same principal or another) and it is later determined that claims against the tax revenue bond are barred by the applicable statute of limitations, the state could still set off the amount of its claims on the tax revenue bond against any funds that might otherwise be due to the surety under its other bonds.[297] In *Smith*

---

294. McDonald v. Nat'l Enters. Inc., 547 S.E.2d 204, 207 (Va. 2001); Fid. & Cas. Co. of N.Y. v. Lackland, 8 S.E.2d 306, 309 (Va. 1940); State *ex rel.* Battle v. Demkovich, 136 S.E.2d 895, 898 (W. Va. 1964); Cook v. E. Gas & Fuel Assocs., 39 S.E.2d 321, 325 (W. Va. 1946).

295. 360 S.E.2d 325, 327 (Va. 1987); *see also* Prasad v. Holder, 776 F.3d 222, 226 (4th Cir. 2015).

296. Burlington N. & Santa Fe Ry. Co. v. Poole Chem. Co., 419 F.3d 355, 363 (5th Cir. 2005); Servicios-Expoarma, C.A. v. Indus. Mar. Carriers, 135 F.3d 984, 989 (5th Cir. 1998) (quoting Harding v. K.C. Wall Prods., 831 P.2d 958, 967 (Kan. 1992)).

297. *See, e.g.*, Chambers v. Cooney, 537 F. Supp. 2d 1248, 1251 (S.D. Ala. 2008) ("all compulsory counterclaims, whether offensive or defensive, are not subject to the statute-of-limitations defense"); Sallaz v. Rice, 384 P.3d 987, 992–93 (Idaho 2016), *reh'g denied*, Dec. 14, 2016; *In re* Meyer, 563 B.R. 708, 714 (Bankr. N.D. Iowa 2017); Prochelo v. Prochelo, 346 N.W.2d 527, 530 (Iowa 1984); Johnson v. Dist. VII, 536, 204 P.3d 714, 719 (Mont. 2009); Collard v. Nagle Constr., Inc., 57 P.3d 603, 608–09

v. Idaho State University Federal Credit Union, the court observed, "However, the running of the statute of limitations does not extinguish the debt. 'Statutes of limitations are limitations on a party's right to bring an action. A statute of limitations does not apply (1) to defenses where no affirmative relief is sought, or (2) to self-help set-offs and pledges.'"[298]

Thus, despite the common misperception that the expiration of the statute of limitations extinguishes the surety's liability, in certain circumstances the surety may still be exposed to the set-off rights of the time-barred obligee claims on subsequent bonds, even for other principals. This exposure exists because the statute of limitations bars only the assertion of the claim, but does not discharge or release the claim or debt itself. The claim still exists as a debt or obligation.[299]

c. Claim Preclusion: May Actions Taken in the Bankruptcy Case Extinguish the Surety's Liability under the Commercial Surety Bonds? The question addressed in this section is whether the debtor/trustee may contend in the litigation that there may be a preclusive effect imposed on the claims of the obligees and/or other claimants against the commercial surety bonds resulting from the claims process in the bankruptcy case (the disallowance of scheduled claims, the disallowance of creditor-filed proofs of claims, and/or the passage of the general claims bar date against the debtor) that may become applicable to the surety's joint and several obligations to those obligees and claimants under the commercial surety bonds.

Specifically, the debtor/trustee must allege sufficient facts to support their claim preclusion theory. However, the surety may contend (1) that any preclusive effect on the obligees' and the claimants' rights against the commercial surety bonds will only apply if the bankruptcy court's ruling was on the merits of the disallowed or allegedly barred claim; (2) that the claims that were ruled upon were claims that could have been asserted against one of the commercial surety bonds; and (3) that there is no preclusive effect simply by virtue of the passage of the general claims bar date because the obligees and the claimants are third parties that

---

(Utah Ct. App. 2002) ("Under this doctrine, a defendant may even 'utilize a counterclaim, normally barred by the statute of limitations, to offset a plaintiff's claim.'"); Coulon v. Coulon, 915 P.2d 1069, 1072 (Utah Ct. App. 1996).

298. 760 P.2d 19, 22 (Idaho 1988) (citations omitted).

299. This is yet another reason why the obligees under the commercial surety bonds are necessary parties to the litigation.

have separate claims against the surety, another third party, under the commercial surety bonds (almost all of the bonds provide the surety with "several liability") and the commercial surety bonds are not property of the estate.

The debtor/trustee may argue that the surety must return all or a portion of the surety's collateral (1) because of a court order disallowing a filed or scheduled claim; and/or (2) because no claims were filed with respect to certain of the commercial surety bonds by the date specified in the general bar date order. The argument would be, therefore, that no claims can be maintained against the debtor or the surety by the obligees or other claimants under the commercial surety bonds. Accordingly, the debtor's/trustee's argument would be that the surety would face no potential exposure under applicable commercial surety bonds due to a purported res judicata effect of the previous bankruptcy claim proceedings and/or bankruptcy court rulings.

Such an argument is mistaken because a surety only enjoys the benefit of res judicata protection when the underlying claim against the principal/debtor was disallowed (or released or discharged) for reasons going to the merits of the claim or debt rather than a mere procedural bar. Furthermore, the debtor/trustee must allege sufficient facts regarding the bankruptcy court orders that purportedly disallowed the claims to provide evidence that there is an available res judicata defense to a claim or debt against the surety's commercial surety bonds.

For most commercial surety bonds, the principal and the surety are jointly and severally liable to the obligees and other claimants. When the surety and the principal have joint and several liability under a bond, the obligee or claimant may bring a claim on the bond against only the surety, only the principal, or both concurrently.[300] The obligee's or claimant's right to maintain an action against the principal on a bond is independent of its rights to maintain an action against the surety on a

300. *See, e.g.*, Georgetown Coll. v. Madden, 505 F. Supp. 557 (D. Md. 1980) ("Where the surety's bond binds him *jointly and severally* for the faithful performance of the obligation of the principal, the obligee may sue the surety separately without joining the principal as a party defendant . . . or he may sue the principal without joining any or all of the sureties. On the other hand, the obligee may, if he wishes, sue the principal and the sureties in the same action and recover a judgment against all of them.") (quoting 12 AM. JUR. 2D *Bonds* § 29, at 497 (1964)).

bond.[301] Therefore, an obligee's or claimant's claim against the surety may only be barred by the principle of res judicata if a previous proceeding involving the principal can be said to have preclusive effect.

There are two doctrines under which preclusive effect can be created: issue preclusion and claim preclusion. For example, Virginia law provides that the doctrine of issue preclusion (sometimes referred to as "collateral estoppel") can only apply if an issue of fact "actually was litigated and was essential to the final judgment in the first proceedings."[302] On the other hand, the doctrine of claim preclusion bars relitigation of a cause of action that *could have* been litigated in a prior case between the same parties and their privies, but "a party asserting the bar of a previous judgment must still show that the previous judgment was a valid, final judgment on the merits."[303] Every jurisdiction has similar cases defining the doctrines of issue preclusion and claim preclusion.

The passage of the bankruptcy court's general claims bar date does not render the commercial surety bonds immune from future claims that may be brought against the surety under those bonds. The running of a deadline to file claims against the principal in a principal's bankruptcy case does not require the "actual litigation" of an issue of fact, and it is not a "final judgment on the merits." It is a procedural cutoff meant to facilitate the principal's purposes in filing a bankruptcy case. While it prevents any further claim being brought against the principal, the expiration of the claims bar date deadline does not provide the surety, which is severally liable under a commercial surety bond, a defense under the doctrines of issue preclusion or claim preclusion.[304]

---

301. *See, e.g.*, *id.* at 597; *see also* Lynch v. Johns-Manville Sales Corp., 710 F.2d 1194, 1196 (6th Cir. 1983) (automatic stay created by principal's bankruptcy does not prevent obligee from maintaining claim against surety).

302. Martin-Bangura v. Commonwealth Dep't of Mental Health, 640 F. Supp. 2d 729, 736 (E.D. Va. 2009) (quoting Whitley v. Commonwealth, 538 S.E.2d 296, 299 (Va. 2000)).

303. *Id.* at 738 (citing Smith v. Ware, 421 S.E.2d 444, 445 (Va. 1992)); State Water Control Bd. v. Smithfield Foods, Inc., 542 S.E.2d 766, 769 (Va. 2001).

304. RESTATEMENT (THIRD) OF SURETYSHIP AND GUARANTY § 34(1)(a) (1996). Comment b to section 34(1)(a) highlights the situation when the principal is financially unable to perform the underlying contractual obligation and the obligee, who required the surety's bond to protect the obligee from such an event, looks to the surety for performance. The

Conversely, the disallowance of a claim submitted by an obligee or other claimant in the bankruptcy case *may* have preclusive effect depending on the reason for the disallowance. A disallowance predicated on procedural grounds (i.e., non-provable) does not have preclusive effect on a concurrent or subsequent suit by the obligee or claimant against the surety under a commercial surety bond.[305] On the other hand, when a claim is disallowed based on a decision on the merits (i.e., no debt is found to exist), the surety may rely on the preclusive effect of the disallowance against the obligee's or claimant's later claim against the bond.[306] Without such a decision on the merits, the surety cannot rely on the disallowance of the claim in a bankruptcy case as a "conclusive adjudication that the principal has not violated any of the conditions of the bond," and there can be no preclusive effect.[307]

In a case involving a personal guaranty on a commercial lease, the U.S. District Court for the District of Utah elaborated on the distinction between non-provable and nonexistent debts:

> As for the question of whether an order of disallowance can furnish the basis for claim preclusion, the analysis turns on the reasons underlying the decision. As the Second Circuit notes, while the disallowance of a claim "should be given like effect as any other judgment of a competent court" in subsequent proceedings, "the distinction must be noted between disallowance of a claim because the creditor had a nonprovable debt and disallowance because he had no debt at all. Disallowance on the former ground decides nothing as to the merits of the claim." Thus, if a claim is disallowed for reasons that do not touch on the actual validity of the debt, the decision can have no preclusive effect.[308]

Whether a future claim may be brought by an obligee or claimant against the surety on the commercial surety bonds is therefore

---

value of the surety's performance obligation under the bond would be "seriously diminished" if the surety was able to assert, as a defense to the obligee's claim, the principal's discharge in bankruptcy from the underlying contractual obligation. *Id.*

305. United States v. Am. Sur. Co., 56 F.2d 734, 736 (2d Cir. 1932).

306. *Id.*

307. *Id.*

308. AFP W. LLC v. Cox, 528 B.R. 446, 450 (D. Utah 2015).

dependent on whether the corresponding filed or scheduled claims were disallowed because they were non-provable or because there was no debt. Furthermore, the disallowance of a claim because no response is filed to the debtor's objection to that claim is not a decision on the merits and does not require the actual litigation of the claim, meaning that the obligee or the claimant would not be precluded from pursuing a claim against the surety under a commercial surety bond for which the surety is severally liable.

In summary, there are many issues, both substantive and procedural, that must be considered when it comes to litigation over whether the surety's collateral is excess. These issues must be thoroughly researched under the laws of the applicable jurisdiction to safeguard as much as possible the surety's continued rights to retain the surety's collateral.

5. Litigation Settlement Agreements and the Possible Effect of Broad Release Provisions

Whenever there is litigation over the surety's rights to collateral that may be property of the estate, the prospects of a settlement are always available. The bases for the settlement—both the decisions made concerning the surety's continuing rights in its collateral and the amount of any "excess collateral/proceeds" to be released to the debtor/trustee—are dependent upon the facts and circumstances of the case as well as the applicable law. Settlement agreements may take a myriad number of forms and substantive terms. However, whatever the settlement terms and provisions may be, the settlement agreement eventually contains various terms and provisions that include a release of any other obligations and liabilities between and among the settling parties.

Such releases and their terms must be drafted and reviewed carefully to avoid a surety releasing more rights than expected or anticipated.[309]

---

309. *See* Cal. Self-Insurers Sec. Fund v. Siegel, Tr. of Circuit City Stores, No. 3:18cv619, 2019 WL 4740234 (E.D. Va. Sept. 27, 2019) (settlement agreement with a detailed mutual release provision that went far beyond what the beneficiary of the letter of credit proceeds thought it would, resulted in a bad surprise for the beneficiary and a benefit not only to the trustee, but also to a surety that was not even involved in the litigation or the settlement agreement).

Conclusion

The principal's bankruptcy case may have far-reaching impacts on the surety and the surety's collateral received from the principal prior to the filing of the principal's bankruptcy case. Initially, the surety must undertake its best efforts to acquire and secure the surety's collateral with the understanding that the principal's bankruptcy may occur in the future. The surety requires the essential and necessary provisions in the indemnity agreement and/or the collateral agreement and then obtains the appropriate liens on the principal's property or rights in any letter of credit that will assist in the surety's planning and protect the surety's collateral in the event of a subsequent principal bankruptcy case.

Once the principal has filed its bankruptcy case, the surety must understand the principal's/debtor's and the surety's rights and obligations with respect to the surety's collateral and the possible Bankruptcy Code effect on those rights and obligations. Whether the surety's collateral is considered to be property of the estate or not and whether the principal/debtor may compel the return of the surety's collateral to the estate are issues that must be understood based on the type of the surety's collateral, the timing and manner in which the surety obtained the surety's collateral, and the status of any claims, contingent or liquidated, against the commercial surety bonds.

Whether the automatic stay and other Bankruptcy Code provisions may apply to the surety's use of the collateral or the surety's resolution of any claims against the commercial surety bonds are issues that will impact the surety's claims handling process and ability to obtain reimbursement from the surety's collateral for any surety payments made and losses incurred. Furthermore, the bankruptcy court's power, authority, and ability to affect the claims against the commercial surety bonds is not unlimited. The bankruptcy court may not have the power to limit, cancel, or restrict the rights of third-party claimants against a commercial surety bond, especially if those claimants are not provided notice and an opportunity to be heard on the merits of their claims.

Ultimately, the surety must resist the principal's/debtor's efforts to obtain the return of the surety's collateral to the bankruptcy estate in order to protect the surety's rights to the surety's collateral to cover all of the potential future (and contingent) claims against the commercial surety bonds and to reimburse the surety's payments and losses as provided under the indemnity agreement and/or the collateral agreement.